Comprehensive School Health Education

2nd Edition

Totally Awesome Strategies for Teaching Health™

Linda Meeks • Philip Heit • Randy Page

The Ohio State University   The Ohio State University   University of Idaho

Everyday Learning Corporation
Editorial, Sales, and Customer Service Office
P.O. Box 812960
Chicago, IL 60681

Director of Editorial: Julie DeVillers
Editorial Associates:Ann G. Turpie, Mary Baker
Director of Art and Design: Jim Brower
Illustrator: Jennifer King
Director of Marketing: David Willcox

Printed in the United States of America.

8 9 10 EB 04 03 02 01

ISBN 1-886693-09-9

Comprehensive School Health Education:
Totally Awesome Strategies for Teaching Health™

CONSULTANTS AND REVIEWERS

MEDICAL CONSULTANT

Robert T. Brown, M.D.
Professor of Clinical Pediatrics
College of Medicine
The Ohio State University
Director of Adolescent Medicine
Children's Hospital
Columbus, Ohio

ADVISORY BOARD MEMBERS

W. P. Buckner, Jr., HSD, C.H.E.S.
Professor and Health Coordinator
Department of Health and Human Performance
University of Houston
President, Association for the Advancement
  of Health Education
American Alliance for Health,
  Physical Education,
  Recreation, and Dance

Reba Bullock, M.Ed.
Health Education Curriculum Specialist
Baltimore City Public Schools
Baltimore, Maryland

Russell Henke, M.Ed.
Coordinator of Health
Montgomery County Public Schools
Rockville, Maryland

Wanda Jubb, Ed.D., C.H.E.S.
Coordinator
Comprehensive Health Education
Centers for Disease Control and Prevention
Atlanta, Georgia

David Lohrmann, Ph.D., C.H.E.S.
Evaluation Project Director
Academy for Educational Development, Inc.
Washington, D.C.

Alex McNeill, Ph.D.
Dean of The School of Education
University of Alaska–Anchorage
Anchorage, Alaska

Deborah A. Miller, Ph.D., C.H.E.S.
Associate Professor and Health Coordinator
College/University of Charleston
Charleston, South Carolina

Jo Anne Owens-Nauslar, Ed.D.
Director of Health and Physical Education
Director of HIV/AIDS
President-Elect
The National Association of Sport
  and Physical Education
Nebraska Department of Education
Lincoln, Nebraska

John B. Ray, M.S.
Coordinator
Health and Physical Education
Office of Health Schools
West Virginia Department of Education
Charleston, West Virginia

Spencer Sartorius, M.S.
Administrator, Health Enhancement Division
Administrator, Drug-Free Schools
  and Communities Program
Office of Public Instruction
Helena, Montana

Sherman K. Sowby, Ph.D., C.H.E.S.
Professor
Health Science
California State University–Fresno
Fresno, California

Bambi Sumpter, Dr. PH
Education Associate
South Carolina Department of Education
Columbia, South Carolina

Mike Tenoschok, Ed.D.
Supervisor of Health
  and Physical Education
Cobb County Public Schools
Marietta, Georgia

Suzanne Ulmer, M.Ed.
Bureau Director
Office of Innovative Support
Mississippi Department of Education
Jackson, Mississippi

Robert Wandberg, Ph.D.
Program Specialist
Minnesota Department of Education
St. Paul, Minnesota

Consultants and Reviewers

Mae Waters, Ph.D., C.H.E.S.
Project Director
NaSHEC University Preservice/Inservice Project
Center for the Study of Teaching and Learning
Florida State University
Tallahassee, Florida

Linda Wright, M.A.
Health Education Consultant
Teacher Trainer
Washington, D.C.

REVIEWERS

Donna Breitenstein, Ed.D.
Coordinator and Professor of Health Education
College of Education
Appalachian State University
Boone, North Carolina

Galen Cole, Ph.D., M.P.H.
Division of Adolescent and School Health
National Center for Chronic Disease Prevention
 and Health Promotion
Centers for Disease Control and Prevention
Atlanta, Georgia

Patricia M. Dashiell, M.S.
Children's Literature Consultant
Columbus, Ohio

Betsy Gallun, M.Ed.
Supervisor of Drug Programs
Prince George's County Public Schools
Upper Marlboro, Maryland

Dawn Graff-Haight, Ph.D., C.H.E.S.
Assistant Professor
Department of Health Studies
Portland State University
Portland, Oregon

Shelia Harbet, Ph.D., H.S.D.
Professor
Health Education
Department of Health Science
California State University–Northridge
Northridge, California

Chris T. Hasegawa, Ph.D.
Associate Professor of Teacher Education
College of Education
California State University–Sacramento
Sacramento, California

Fred Hebert, M.S.
Senior Lecturer
University of Wisconsin–Stevens Point
Stevens Point, Wisconsin

Janet Henke, B.S.
Middle School Team Leader
Old Court Middle School
Baltimore County Public Schools
Baltimore, Maryland

Peggy Holstedt, M.S.
Oregon Department of Education
Health Promotion Specialist
Salem, Oregon

Linda Johnson, M.Ed.
Health Coordinator
North Dakota Department of Public Instruction
Bismarck, North Dakota

J. Leslie Oganowski, Ph.D.
Associate Professor of Health Education
University of Wisconsin–LaCrosse
LaCrosse, Wisconsin

Michael Pejsach, Ed.D.
State Coordinator of Comprehensive
 School Health
Louisiana State Department of Education
Baton Rouge, Louisiana

Fred Peterson, Ph.D.
Associate Professor of Adolescent
 and School Health
Department of Kinesiology and Health Education
The University of Texas
Austin, Texas

LaNaya Ritson, M.S., C.H.E.S.
Department of Health Education
Western Oregon State College
Monmouth, Oregon

Michael Schaffer, M.A.
Supervisor of Health Education, K–12
Prince George's County Public Schools
Upper Marlboro, Maryland

Bridget Susi, M.S.
Health Education Consultant
Georgia Department of Education
Atlanta, Georgia

Edith Thompson
Assistant Professor of Health
 and Physical Education
Department of Health and Physical Education
College of Professional Studies
Rowan College of New Jersey
Glassboro, New Jersey

Deitra Wengert, Ph.D., C.H.E.S.
Associate Professor
Department of Health Science
Towson State University
Towson, Maryland

Preface

Tell me, I forget.
Show me, I remember.
Involve me, I understand.

We were pleased that the first edition of **Comprehensive School Health Education: Totally Awesome Strategies for Teaching Health**™ became the leading teacher resource book used to prepare future and current elementary, middle, and secondary teachers to teach health. The first edition also has been the most widely used teacher resource book selected by state departments of education, school districts, and departments of health for inservice and train-the-trainers programs. Our ongoing commitment to improve the quality of life of children and adolescents prompted us to produce a second edition that is even more practical, comprehensive, and on the cutting edge of educational reform. We surveyed and interviewed key professionals—professionals at Centers for Disease Control and Prevention, professionals affiliated with professional associations, college professors, directors of state departments of education, educators at health departments, curriculum coordinators, elementary teachers, middle school teachers, high school teachers, and undergraduate and graduate students for their suggestions. We also visited elementary, middle, and secondary schools to observe and evaluate the use of our *Totally Awesome Teaching Strategies*™.

Then we began the "awesome" task of producing a complete revision which includes EVERYTHING teachers need to have the background and skills to teach health. We revised every chapter, added a chapter on Safe and Healthful School Environment, included instructional technology, added over 200 pages of up-to-date health content, designed new *Totally Awesome Teaching Strategies*™ which include The National Health Education Standards and performance indicators, and added a state-of-the art Curriculum Guide. We even three-hole punched this practical teacher resource book so that you can place it in a three-ring binder!

What are the key components in this teacher resource book that make it the most widely used for comprehensive school health education?

Section 1. Comprehensive School Health Education includes five chapters and is designed to provide you with a framework for comprehensive school health education. In Chapter 1, you will learn about the six categories of risk behaviors that affect today's students, the national initiatives that support the need for comprehensive school health programs, and the eight components of the comprehensive school health program. You also will become acquainted with the framework for comprehensive school health education. Chapter 2 prepares you for your role in school health services. This chapter includes *An Encyclopedia of Health Concerns of School-Age Youth...from A to Z*. Chapter 3 describes a safe and healthful school environment. You will learn how to provide a healthful school environment, including ways you can create a positive emotional climate. You will learn how to provide a safe school environment. Special concerns in today's school environment such as what to do about violence, sexual harassment, drug use, environmental tobacco smoke, and exposure to bloodborne pathogens will be highlighted. Also included are suggestions for planning and implementing health promotion programs for staff. Chapter 4 will acquaint you with the comprehensive school health education curriculum. You will learn about educational reform and how to design a comprehensive school health education curriculum that promotes health literacy and the mastery of the performance indicators identified for the National Health Education Standards. Also included in this chapter are innovative ways to teach life skills, as well as evaluation techniques. Chapter 5 identifies instructional strategies and technologies that help students gain health knowledge and develop and practice life skills.

Section 2. Health Content includes over 200 pages of health content so that you are well-informed with up-to-date health knowledge in ten areas of health. Health knowledge pertaining to the six categories of risk behaviors is included in one or more of the ten health content areas. The health knowledge for each health content area is organized by life skills. Life skills pertaining to the six categories of risk behaviors are included in one or more of the ten health content areas. The following chapters are included:
- Chapter 6.   Mental and Emotional Health
- Chapter 7.   Family Living
- Chapter 8.   Growth and Development
- Chapter 9.   Nutrition
- Chapter 10. Personal Health
- Chapter 11. Alcohol, Tobacco, and Other Drugs
- Chapter 12. Communicable and Chronic Diseases
- Chapter 13. Injury Prevention and Safety
- Chapter 14. Consumer and Community Health
- Chapter 15. Environmental Health

Section 3. *Totally Awesome Teaching Strategies*™ explains how to design your classroom as a laboratory in which students develop and practice life skills for health. You will learn how to use *Totally Awesome Teaching Strategies*™. Then you are provided with *Totally Awesome Teaching Strategies*™ for each grade level K–12 for each of the ten health content areas. These *Totally Awesome Teaching Strategies*™ also cover the six categories of risk behaviors identified by the Centers for Disease Control and Prevention. All of the materials needed to implement the *Totally Awesome Teaching Strategies*™ are readily available. Each of the *Totally Awesome Teaching Strategies*™ is designed to help students develop and practice life skills for health and be able to master the performance indicators for The National Health Education Standards. Teaching masters, student masters, family health newsletters, and health behavior contracts have been added to enhance the *Totally Awesome Teaching Strategies*™.

Section 4. *The Health Resource Guide* includes *The Health Resource Guide* which provides the names, addresses, and telephone numbers of agencies and organizations involved in promoting health in each of the ten health content areas in the curriculum. Within each major heading of the health content areas are subheadings of specialized areas. Whenever possible, toll-free numbers are listed for your convenience.

Section 5. The Curriculum Guide describes the ways you can use *The Comprehensive School Health Education Curriculum Guide*. This new state-of-the-art guide includes (1) a statement of philosophy and *The Wellness Scale*; (2) *The Responsible Decision-Making Model*; (3) *The Model for Using Resistance Skills*; (4) A *Scope and Sequence Chart* that includes the components of health literacy, The National Health Education Standards, the performance indicators, the content areas and life skills, and the health topics; (5) *Totally Awesome Teaching Strategies*™ infused into several curriculum areas other than health, designed to promote health literacy, and with designated: health education standards, performance indicators, life skills, motivation, evaluation, suggestions for multicultural infusion, and suggestions for inclusion of students with special needs; (6) suggestions for including parents and involving the community.

The **Appendix** contains a copy of *The Opportunity-to-Learn Standards* for local agencies, community agencies, state agencies, teacher preparation institutions, and national health agencies. The **Glossary** includes vocabulary words and definitions. The **Index** provides a listing of page numbers that will help you quickly locate topics.

We created ***Comprehensive School Health Education: Totally Awesome Strategies for Teaching Health***™ especially for you. We want you to use it as you engage in a most important task—educating today's youth about health!

Linda Meeks
Philip Heit
Randy Page

TABLE OF CONTENTS

Table of Contents

Table of Contents

Table of Contents

XI

Table of Contents

Chapter 7
FAMILY LIVING 167

Chapter 8
GROWTH AND DEVELOPMENT 187

Table of Contents

Table of Contents

Table of Contents

Table of Contents

Chapter 14
CONSUMER AND COMMUNITY HEALTH

Table of Contents

Table of Contents

Table of Contents

Table of Contents

Section 1

COMPREHENSIVE SCHOOL HEALTH EDUCATION

Figure 1-1

A Nation at Risk

Today, many students have added agendas that influence their ability to learn. Many of today's students are at risk.

Chapter 1

A NATION AT RISK:
The Need for Comprehensive School Health Education

Perhaps no profession is more vital to the future of this nation than that of the teaching profession. Every teacher has the potential for affecting the lives of many students. Today, many students have added agendas that influence their ability to learn (Figure 1-1). Some students are not adequately nourished, lack sleep, lack immunizations, and are not properly clothed. Others are being reared in families in which there is domestic violence, chemical dependency, or some form of abuse. Still others are managing health conditions such as asthma, anorexia nervosa, or depression.

To be an effective teacher, a teacher must be aware of the health status of the students. A teacher must be committed to working with students to maintain and improve their health status. A teacher must be a positive role model for healthful living. And, of course, a teacher must be motivated to create a dynamic and challenging classroom where students can learn and practice life skills for health. In other words, today's teacher must be *totally awesome*™. A ***totally awesome teacher***™ is a teacher who is committed to promoting health literacy, improving health, preventing disease, and reducing health-related risk behaviors in students, and to creating a dynamic and challenging classroom where students learn and practice life skills for health. Although this task demands training and effort, it has many rewards . . . the future of this nation depends upon the life skills that our students are learning and practicing in school today.

This *Totally Awesome*™ teacher resource book on Comprehensive School Health Education was written by teachers who want to make a difference for teachers who want to make a difference. The style of this resource is very "teacher friendly" and "interactive." This is not a resource to gather dust on your bookshelf; it is a resource you can use. Let's discuss how you will be able to use the information in this first chapter. The chapter begins with a review of the six categories of risk behaviors identified by The Centers for Disease Control and Prevention. You will learn more about the risk behaviors that compromise the health status of today's students. The next discussion examines *Healthy People 2000, The National Education Goals for the Year 2000*, and The Safe Schools Act. You will learn why comprehensive school health programs are being implemented in school districts throughout this country in response to these national initiatives. Then the discussion will focus on a key component of the comprehensive school health program—comprehensive school health education. You will learn what you can do to help your students become health literate, maintain health, prevent disease, and reduce health-related risk behaviors. And finally, you will learn how you can use the wealth of material in this resource to be a *totally awesome*™ health teacher.

3

Six Categories of Risk Behaviors in Today's Students

Risk behaviors are voluntary actions that threaten self-esteem, harm health, and increase the likelihood of illness, injury, and premature death. Risk behaviors usually:
- are established during youth;
- persist into adulthood;
- are interrelated;
- contribute simultaneously to poor health, education, and social outcomes;
- are preventable (CDC, 1992).

The Centers for Disease Control and Prevention has identified six categories of risk behaviors in today's students:
1. Behaviors that result in unintentional and intentional injuries
2. Tobacco use
3. Alcohol and other drug use
4. Sexual behaviors that result in HIV infection, other STDs, and unintended pregnancy
5. Dietary patterns that contribute to disease
6. Insufficient physical activity

The following information acquaints you with the prevalence of each of these six categories of risk behaviors. You will learn what students are doing in their daily lives. You will learn why being involved in these risk behaviors places the students in our nation at risk. Later, this information will help you understand the importance of the comprehensive school health education program.

Unintentional and Intentional Injuries

The first category of risk behaviors is unintentional and intentional injuries. **Unintentional injuries** are injuries that are accidental. **Intentional injuries** are injuries resulting from interpersonal violence, including homicide, and self-directed violence, including suicide. Unintentional and intentional injuries are the leading cause of death and disability in today's students.

First, let's focus on unintentional injuries. Approximately 40 percent of the deaths in children under age four and 70 percent of the deaths in older children are due to injuries that could have been prevented (Office of Technology Assessment, 1991). Leading causes of unintentional injuries include those that are the result of being struck by a motor vehicle or being in a motor vehicle crash, those that result from being in fires, and those that result because safety rules around water are not being followed.

Motor Vehicle Related Injuries There are two ways young people sustain motor vehicle related injuries. They might be struck by a motor vehicle or they might be in a motor vehicle crash. Being struck by a motor vehicle is the number one cause of injury and death in children ages five to nine. Unfortunately, children under the age of nine are unable to perceive the distance and speed at which oncoming cars are traveling. Teaching them how to cross the street safely is imperative if this risk is to be reduced.

Injuries from being in a motor vehicle crash are the leading cause of death among one- to twenty-four-year-olds. Most motor vehicle crashes in which someone dies involve a driver who had been drinking alcohol and/or involve young people who were not using safety belts (Waxweiler, Harel, and O'Carroll, 1993). Thirty percent of fatal crashes involving drivers between the ages of fifteen and twenty are alcohol-related. Adolescents have the highest proportion of safety belt nonuse of any age group involved in motor vehicle crashes (National Highway Safety Administration, 1992). A prevention program must focus on teaching about the dangers of riding in a car with someone who has been drinking and the dangers of failing to use safety belts.

Fires Another leading cause of unintentional injuries in today's students is being in a fire. Many of these injuries could be prevented by teaching children how dangerous it is to play with matches and lighters. Playing with cigarette lighters and matches is a major cause of fatal fires (Division of Injury Control, 1992). A further means of preventing these injuries involves informing parents of the importance of having smoke detectors installed in the home and checking their batteries regularly. Smoke detectors have been installed in 80 percent of American households, however in one-third of these households the smoke detectors are not functioning because the batteries are missing or not working. Children who live in homes without smoke detectors and those that live in below-standard housing are especially vulnerable to fire-related injuries.

Drownings Drowning is the second leading cause of unintentional injury in today's students. There are two ways to prevent most drownings: properly supervise children around water and encourage young people of all ages to adhere to safety rules when they are around water. Drowning as a cause of death is highest among children five and under and among males ages fifteen to twenty-four. Young children need to be observed closely when they are near swimming pools. Nearly one-half of the children who drown in swimming pools were out of sight for only five or fewer minutes (Division of Injury Control, 1992). Adults also can improve safety and reduce the risk of childhood drownings by using child-proof enclosures to prevent entry into home swimming pools and whirlpools. As children reach adolescence, they need to be educated as to the danger of drinking alcohol and participating in boating and water activities. The increased risk of drowning for males ages fifteen to twenty-four has been attributed to the increased incidence of drinking alcohol and participating in boating and water activities (*Healthy Children 2000*, 1991).

Now let's focus on intentional injuries. Intentional injuries involving interpersonal violence and self-directed violence exact a disproportionately high toll among today's students and this risk is worsening (*Healthy People 2000*, 1991). **Violence** is defined as the use of physical force with the intent to harm oneself or another person. An increasing number of today's students are not only becoming victims of violence but also are routinely witnessing violence in their communities and committing violent acts (Fitzpatrick, 1993). The National School Boards Association has declared youth violence an "epidemic."

Interpersonal Violence Unfortunately, many students are at risk for violence in their own homes. **Domestic violence** is violence that occurs within the family or within other relationships in which people live together. Students may witness spouse abuse in which one spouse harms another. They may experience violent actions from brothers or sisters. They may be victims of child abuse. **Child abuse** is the harmful treatment of a person under the age of eighteen and includes physical abuse, emotional abuse, sexual abuse, and neglect. More than 2.5 million students under the age of eighteen are abused or neglected each year (Meeks, Heit, and Page, 1995). And, 1,100 young people die from abuse each year. A family member is the person who is the abuser 85 to 90 percent of the time. Young people who are abused often are abusive when they are older and become parents. Over 80 percent of people in prison report they were abused during their childhood.

Other forms of interpersonal violence occur between students. Today's students are more likely to bully one another and to get into fights. **Bullying** is an attempt by a person to hurt or frighten people who are perceived to be smaller or weaker. Most students report that they have been bullied. In fact, 75 percent of students in middle school and high school say they have been bullied. More than 10 percent of students in high school say they have been bullied in an extreme way (CDC, 1993). Bullying often leads to fighting. **Fighting** is taking part in a physical struggle. The first experience children have with fighting is often a fistfight. By the time students reach high school, 40 percent say they have been in a fight within the last year. Eight percent report that they have been in a fight in the last thirty days in which someone needed medical treatment for injury.

Today many students carry guns or have easy access to guns. It is estimated that over 66 million handguns and 200 million other kinds of guns are in circulation in this country (Larson, 1994). In about one-half of all households, someone owns a gun. In one-quarter of all households, someone owns a handgun. It is possible for students to obtain a gun from their homes without their parents or guardians

5

knowing. Unfortunately, students can buy guns on the street, from drug dealers, and from pawnshops. In fact, more than half of students in grades six through twelve said they could "get a handgun if they wanted one" (*Newsweek*, 1993). One in twenty high school students has reported carrying a gun. A gun is used in more than 60 percent of homicides (CDC, 1993). **Homicide** is the accidental or purposeful killing of another person. Homicide is the tenth leading cause of death in the United States. It is the second leading cause of death in people ages fifteen to thirty-four. It is the leading cause of death in African-American males of this age group. Knowing these statistics should help convince you of the importance of teaching students to resolve problems without fighting and to avoid carrying guns.

Suicide **Suicide** is the intentional taking of one's own life. Each year, almost one-half million students attempt suicide. The majority who attempt suicide do not receive medical or mental health care (Smith and Crawford, 1986). This places them at risk for making another attempt. Approximately 5,000 students ages fifteen to twenty-four commit suicide each year (National Center for Health Statistics, 1993). The number is probably even higher because many suicides go unreported. Many suicide attempts are classified as being parasuicide. **Parasuicide** is a suicide attempt in which a person does not intend to die. The person is making a plea for help and wants others to know of his/her pain. Parasuicide should always be taken seriously.

Tobacco Use

The second category of risk behaviors involves tobacco use. **Tobacco use** includes the use of cigarettes, pipes, cigars, and smokeless tobacco. Tobacco use contributes to four of the five leading causes of death in the United States: cardiovascular disease, cancer, cerebrovascular disease, and chronic obstructive pulmonary disease. Smoking declined in the late 1970s and early 1980s, but has since leveled off, particularly

among older adolescents. This suggests the generation of current adolescent smokers is more resistant to the "no use" message than were their peers a decade ago (Western Regional Center, 1994). By their senior year of high school, slightly more than two-thirds have tried smoking and nearly one-third reported having smoked a cigarette in the past month (Western Regional Center, 1994). This news is alarming given what we now know about patterns of behavior. Most adults who smoke cigarettes began smoking during childhood or early adolescence. The earlier they began to smoke cigarettes, the less likely they will ever quit. People who begin smoking at younger ages are at increased risk of becoming heavy smokers and becoming ill or dying from smoking-attributable causes. Smoking cigarettes is a risk behavior about which we need to be greatly concerned. Further concern must focus on the number of students who are experimenting with smokeless tobacco. Between 1970 and 1986, smokeless tobacco use increased fifteen-fold (Marcus et al., 1993). Most new users of smokeless tobacco are adolescent males. If we are going to change this risk behavior, we need to influence students in the primary grades never to begin to use tobacco.

Alcohol and Other Drug Use

The third category of risk behaviors focuses on alcohol and other drug use. Despite reports that alcohol and other drug use is declining, the United States continues to have one of the highest rates of alcohol and other drug use among young people (Johnson, O'Malley, and Bachman, 1991). Let's examine the use of alcohol, marijuana, cocaine, steroids, and inhalants by today's students.

Alcohol **Alcohol** is a psychoactive drug that depresses the central nervous system, dulls the mind, impairs thinking and judgment, lessens coordination, and interferes with the ability to respond quickly to dangerous situations. The effects of alcohol are influenced by blood alcohol level. This has especially dangerous implications for young people—the smaller their body, the more quickly their judgment and motor coordination will be affected. This is alarming knowing that the

6

average age that students take their first drink of alcohol is between twelve and thirteen. And the drinking of alcohol continues to be a risk. Nearly nine of ten high school students reported that they had been drinking alcohol. In fact, six of ten high school students reported drinking alcohol at least once within the past thirty days. Over 1.1 billion beers are consumed each year by students age eighteen and under. Students age eighteen and under drink 35 percent of all wine coolers sold (Meeks, Heit, and Page, 1994).

Marijuana Marijuana is a drug containing THC that impairs short term memory and changes mood. THC (tetrahydrocannabinol) is the main active ingredient in marijuana. In the past, marijuana usually had about 1 to 5 percent THC in it. Today, it may have as much as 8 to 15 percent THC in it. This is why use of marijuana has become more dangerous. It increases heartbeat rate and damages the lungs. Use of this drug blocks short-term memory and causes restlessness and mood swings. Students who use marijuana may have hallucinations. They may become extremely worried and feel threatened.

Despite the risks associated with marijuana use, marijuana is the most widely used illegal drug among students. The average age at which marijuana is first used is thirteen (Johnson, O'Malley, and Bachman, 1993). Over 40 percent of high school seniors reported trying marijuana. Over 25 percent of high school seniors reported they had used marijuana in the past year, and 14 percent reported they had used marijuana in the past month. Marijuana is used on a daily basis by approximately one in forty-five high school seniors.

Cocaine Cocaine is a drug that stimulates the central nervous system and whose use frequently results in dependence. **Dependence** is a condition in which people have to have a drug or they experience withdrawal. Cocaine is snorted through the nose, smoked, or injected into a vein. The effects occur quickly. Heart rate and blood pressure increase. The heart may work so hard that the heartbeat becomes irregular. There may be personality changes. Students who use cocaine may become very hostile toward others. They may become very depressed. Cocaine use is often linked to harming others or suicide. Almost 6 percent of high school seniors have used cocaine at least once (Kane, 1993).

Anabolic Steroids Anabolic steroids are powerful derivatives of male hormones that produce muscle growth and can change health and behavior. People who use anabolic steroids can experience "roid rages." Roid rages are outbursts of very angry behavior. During roid rages, the person using steroids may harm others. After using these powerful drugs for some time, depression may occur. Steroid users are at risk for suicide. Steroid use among adolescents appears to be on the increase. Three percent of high school students reported using steroids and 5 percent of all males reported having tried steroids at least once.

Inhalants Inhalants are drugs that are gases or emit gases at room temperature and cause feelings of "drunkenness," exhilaration, disorientation, and sedation. They increase feelings of invincibility and omnipotence and may produce hallucinations and time and space distortions. Inhalants are often the first type of drug to be abused. Inhalant use has been reported in children as young as four years old. Eighteen percent of high school seniors reported using inhalants at least once (ASHA, 1988). Unfortunately, students who use inhalants increase their likelihood of injury because they lose their ability to perceive time and space correctly. They also gain a false sense of invincibility and may be involved in actions that they do not believe to be risky.

Every teacher, principal, administrator, and parent must work together to prevent the use of drugs by students. This risk behavior is having a devastating effect on our students.

Sexual Behaviors That Result in HIV Infection, Other STDs, and Unintended Pregnancy

The fourth category of risk behaviors focuses on sexual behaviors that result in HIV infection, infection with other sexually transmitted diseases, and unintended pregnancies. The sexual behavior of today's students is alarming. By age fifteen, 25 percent of students have had sexual intercourse at least once. By age seventeen, 75 percent of both male and female students have had sexual intercourse at least once. More than one-third of high school students reported having had more than two sexual partners. Let's examine the possible consequences students might experience if they are sexually active, especially if they have had more than one partner.

HIV Infection The **human immunodeficiency virus** (**HIV**) is the pathogen that destroys the body's immune system allowing the development of AIDS. Currently, there is no cure for AIDS, and the disease is fatal. Unprotected sexual intercourse (sexual intercourse without a latex condom with nonoxynol-9) is a risk behavior for HIV infection, yet many students engage in unprotected sexual intercourse. The number of twelve- to twenty-one-year-olds in the United States who have become infected with HIV has increased by 77 percent since 1991. A significant proportion of young adults who currently have AIDS were infected with HIV during their adolescent years as a result of risk behaviors they practiced (Kolbe, 1992).

Infection with Other Sexually Transmitted Diseases **Sexually transmitted diseases** are diseases caused by pathogens that are transmitted from an infected person to an uninfected person during intimate sexual contact. Common sexually transmitted diseases reported in students include chlamydia, gonorrhea, syphilis, chancroid, genital herpes, and genital warts. One in six adolescents develops one or more of these sexually transmitted diseases each year. This means that more than three million adolescents are infected each year with one or more STDs (American Medical News, 1992). Some of these sexually transmitted diseases may result in sterility. Some sexually transmitted diseases, such as genital herpes, are recurring. Once a person is infected with genital herpes that person will always be infected.

Unintended Pregnancies Students who choose to be sexually active often must face the consequence of unintended pregnancy. It is now estimated that three out of ten adolescent females will become pregnant before age twenty; many will become pregnant more than once. Of those who become pregnant before age fifteen, 60 percent will have three

children by age nineteen (Attico, 1992). Suicide rates for adolescent mothers are ten times that of the general population (Attico, 1992). Rates of child abuse and neglect are disproportionately high among adolescent parents, about twofold higher than expected, demonstrating the lack of parenting skills in adolescent parents (Attico, 1992). Babies born to adolescents are more likely to have low birthweight, increasing the likelihood that their health status will be impaired.

Clearly, the sexual behavior of students is risky and may result in serious consequences. There is no doubt that much effort must be directed at encouraging students to choose abstinence and to delay the onset of sexual intercourse.

Dietary Patterns That Contribute to Disease

The fifth category of risk behaviors focuses on dietary patterns that contribute to disease. There is a saying, "You are what you eat." Unfortunately, today's students are not making healthful diet choices. Obesity continues to be a problem for elementary school children. Obesity usually results from poor diet choices and inactivity. The trend toward making poor diet choices continues from elementary school to middle school to high school. Approximately 87 percent of high school students reported that they did not eat the recommended daily allowance of five or more servings of fruits and vegetables the previous day. Over 25 percent of high school students reported eating more than two servings of foods high in fat content (Kann, 1993). Two-thirds of adolescents do not eat breakfast. The diet choices of today's students will affect their health status in the years to come. Seven out of ten of the leading causes of death are related to nutritional and diet choices.

Insufficient Physical Activity

The sixth category of risk behaviors focuses on insufficient physical activity. **Physical activity** is any bodily movement produced by skeletal muscles that results in energy expenditure. When students are physically active, they are more likely to be energetic, maintain their desirable weight, and cope with stress. They are less likely to have chronic diseases. Unfortunately, one-third of today's students do not get enough physical activity. Recent reports indicate that the physical fitness of today's students has declined. Only 36 percent of students in grades one through twelve are enrolled in daily physical education. Only one-half of students are enrolled in physical education through high school. There has been a significant decline in the percentage of adolescents who can satisfactorily perform a series of physical fitness tests when compared to adolescents of previous generations.

The Sum Total of Risk Behaviors

Each of the six categories of risk behaviors about which you have just learned threatens the health of our nation's students. Now consider the alarming fact that many of today's students engage in several of these risk behaviors at the same time. The bad news is as follows: The sum total of risk behaviors in today's students is overwhelming and has serious consequences. Yet, the good news still remains: Risk behaviors are "voluntary actions" that can be prevented.

The National Initiatives That Support The Comprehensive School Health Program

There have been several national initiatives directed at reducing risk behaviors in today's students. In 1987, a consortium facilitated by the Institute of Medicine of the National Academy of Sciences in conjunction with the United States Public Health Service developed goals and objectives designed to help improve the health and well-being of people in the United States. The efforts of the consortium culminated in the development of a document titled *Healthy People 2000: National Health Promotion and Disease Prevention Objectives* (*Healthy People 2000*, 1991). Although this document focused on Americans of all ages, many of the goals and objectives identified were targeted at reducing the previously discussed risk behaviors prevalent in today's students. A few years later, in 1991, President George Bush and the nation's governors challenged the nation to rebuild its education system to be among the best in the world. This effort resulted in *The National Education Goals for The Year 2000*. This important effort was followed by the Safe Schools Act in 1994. The following discussion will focus on *Healthy People 2000*, *The National Education Goals for The Year 2000*, and the Safe Schools Act. You will learn how these national initiatives support the current emphasis placed on comprehensive school health programs in today's schools.

Healthy People 2000

The document titled *Healthy People 2000* identifies ways the quality and quantity of life can be enhanced by setting goals and objectives for all Americans to be attained by the year 2000. The three principal goals that are identified are:
1. to increase the span of healthy life of Americans;
2. to reduce the health disparities among Americans;
3. to achieve access to preventative services for all Americans.

To help meet these goals, 298 specific objectives are identified in 22 separate priority areas such as physical fitness, alcohol and other drugs, unintentional injuries, mental health and mental disorders, and education and community-based programs. The objectives describe the changes desired by the year 2000.

To promote the achievement of the objectives that focused on age and population groups at special risk, the United States Public Health Service funded different organizations to work with particular high risk populations in specific settings. The American Medical Association (AMA) received funding to focus on the adolescent population through its "Healthier Youth by the Year 2000 Project." The AMA assembled a special volume called *Healthy Children 2000* that includes the objectives from *Healthy People 2000* which pertain to people ages ten to twenty-four (*Healthy People 2000*, 1991).

The objectives are identified as belonging to one of three categories:
1. Health status: objectives to reduce death, disease and disability.
2. Risk reduction: objectives to reduce the prevalence of risks to health or to increase behaviors known to reduce such risks.

3. Services and protection: objectives to increase comprehensiveness, accessibility, and/or the quality of preventative services and preventative interventions.

These objectives are statements of the changes that are desired in young people by the year 2000. It is important for you to be familiar with these objectives. Table 1-2 identifies the *Year 2000 Objectives for Youth*. You also will want to be familiar with the objectives that identify the changes that are expected in our schools by the year 2000. Table 1-3 identifies *Year 2000 Objectives for Schools*.

Table 1-2

Year 2000 Objectives for Youth

Physical Activity and Fitness

Risk Reduction	Increase to at least 20 percent the proportion of people aged 18 and older and to at least 75 percent the proportion of children and adolescents aged 6 through 17 who engage in vigorous physical activity that promotes the development and maintenance of cardiorespiratory fitness 3 or more days per week for 20 or more minutes per occasion. *Objective #1.4*	(Baseline: 12 percent for people aged 18 and older in 1985; 66 percent for youth aged 10 through 17 in 1984)
Services and Protection	Increase to at least 50 percent the proportion of children and adolescents in 1st through 12th grade who participate in daily school physical education. *Objective #1.8*	(Baseline: 36 percent in 1984-86)
Services and Protection	Increase to at least 50 percent the proportion of school physical education class time that students are being physically active, preferably engaged in lifetime physical activities. *Objective #1.9*	(Baseline: Students spent an estimated 27 percent of class time being physically active in 1984)

Related Objectives

Risk Reduction	Increase to at least 30 percent the proportion of people aged 6 and older who engage regularly, preferably daily, in light to moderate physical activity for at least 30 minutes per day. *Objective #1.3, 15.11, 17.3*	(Baseline: 22 percent of people aged 18 and older were active for at least 30 minutes 5 or more times per week and 12 percent were active 7 or more times per week in 1985)
Risk Reduction	Reduce to no more than 15 percent the proportion of people aged 6 and older who engage in no leisure-time physical activity. *Objective #1.5*	(Baseline: 24 percent for people aged 18 and older in 1985)
Risk Reduction	Increase to at least 40 percent the proportion of people aged 6 and older who regularly perform physical activities that enhance and maintain muscular strength, muscular endurance, and flexibility. *Objective #1.6*	(Baseline data available in 1991)
Risk Reduction	Increase to at least 50 percent the proportion of overweight people aged 12 and older who have adopted sound dietary practices combined with regular physical activity to attain an appropriate body weight. *Objective #1.7, 2.7*	(Baseline: 30 percent of overweight women and 25 percent of overweight men for people aged 18 and older in 1985)

Nutrition

Health Status	Reduce overweight to a prevalence of no more than 20 percent among people aged 20 and older and no more than 15 percent among adolescents aged 12 through 19. *Objective #1.2, 2.3, 15.10, 17.11*	(Baseline: 26 percent for people aged 20 through 744 in 1976-80, 24 percent for men and 27 percent for women; 15 percent for adolescents aged 12 through 19 in 1976-80)
Risk Reduction	Increase calcium intake so at least 50 percent of youth aged 12 through 24 consume three or more servings daily of foods rich in calcium. *Objective #2.8*	(Baseline: 7 percent of women and 14 percent of men aged 19 through 24 consumed three or more servings in 1985-86)

============================== **Related Objectives** ==============================

| Risk Reduction | Reduce iron deficiency to less than 3 percent among children aged 1 through 4 and among women of childbearing age.

Objective #2.10 | (Baseline: 5 percent for women aged 20 through 44 in 1976-80) |

| Risk Reduction | Increase to at least 85 percent the proportion of people aged 18 and older who use food labels to make nutritious food selections.

Objective #2.13 | (Baseline: 74 percent used labels to make food selections in 1988) |

Tobacco

| Risk Reduction | Reduce the initiation of cigarette smoking by children and youth so that no more than 15 percent have become regular cigarette smokers by age 20.

Objective #3.5 | (Baseline: 30 percent of youth had become regular cigarette smokers by ages 20 through 24 in 1987) |

| Risk Reduction | Reduce smokeless tobacco use by males aged 12 through 24 to a prevalence of no more than 4 percent.

Objective #3.9 | (Baseline: 6.6 percent among males aged 12 through 17 in 1988; 8.9 percent among males aged 18 through 24 in 1987) |

============================== **Related Objectives** ==============================

| Risk Reduction | Increase to at least 50 percent the proportion of cigarette smokers aged 18 and older who stopped smoking cigarettes for at least one day during the preceding year.

Objective #3.6 | (Baseline: In 1986, 34 percent of people who smoked in the preceding year stopped for at least one day during that year) |

| Risk Reduction | Increase smoking cessation during pregnancy so that at least 60 percent of women who are cigarette smokers at the time they become pregnant quit smoking early in pregnancy and maintain abstinence for the remainder of their pregnancy.

Objective #3.7 | (Baseline: 39 percent of white women aged 20 through 44 quit at any time during pregnancy in 1985) |

Alcohol and Other Drugs

| Risk Reduction | Reduce deaths among people aged 15 through 24 caused by alcohol-related motor vehicle crashes to no more than 18 per 100,000.

Objective #4.1b | (Baseline: 21.5 per 100,000 in 1987) |

| Risk Reduction | Increase by at least 1 year the average age of first use of cigarettes, alcohol, and marijuana by adolescents aged 12 through 17.

Objective #4.5 | (Baseline: Age 11.6 for cigarettes, age 13.1 for alcohol, and age 13.4 for marijuana in 1988) |

Risk Reduction — Reduce the proportion of young people who have used alcohol, marijuana, and cocaine in the past month, as follows:

Substance age	Baseline 1988	Target 2000
Alcohol/aged 12-17	25.2%	12.6%
Alcohol/aged 18-20	57.9%	29.0%
Marijuana/aged 12-17	6.4%	3.2%
Marijuana/aged 18-25	15.5%	7.8%
Cocaine/aged 12-17	1.1%	.6%
Cocaine/aged 18-25	4.5%	2.3%

Objective #4.6

| Risk Reduction | Reduce the proportion of high school seniors and college students engaging in recent occasions of heavy drinking of alcoholic beverages to no more than 28 percent of high school seniors and 32 percent of college students. *Objective #4.7* | (Baseline: 33 percent of high school seniors and 41.7 percent of college students in 1989) |

| Risk Reduction | Reduce alcohol consumption by people aged 14 and older to an annual average of no more than 2 gallons of ethanol per person. *Objective #4.8* | (Baseline: 2.54 gallons of ethanol in 1987) |

Risk Reduction

Increase the proportion of high school seniors who perceive SOCIAL DISAPPROVAL associated with the heavy use of alcohol, occasional use of marijuana, and experimentation with cocaine, as follows:

Behavior	Baseline 1989	Target 2000
Heavy use of alcohol	56.4%	70%
Occasional use of marijuana	71.1%	85%
Trying cocaine once or twice	88.9%	95%

Objective #4.9

Risk Reduction

Increase the proportion of high school seniors who associate RISK OF PHYSICAL OR PSYCHOLOGICAL HARM with the heavy use of alcohol, regular use of marijuana, and experimentation with cocaine, as follows:

Behavior	Baseline 1989	Target 2000
Heavy use of alcohol	44%	70%
Occasional use of marijuana	77.5%	90%
Trying cocaine once or twice	54.9%	80%

Objective #4.9

| Risk Reduction | Reduce to no more than 3 percent the proportion of male high school seniors who use anabolic steroids. *Objective #4.11* | |

Related Objectives

| Risk Reduction | Reduce drug-related deaths to no more than 3 per 100,000 people. *Objective #4.3* | |

Family Planning

Health Status

Reduce pregnancies among girls aged 17 and younger to no more than 50 per 1,000 adolescents. (Baseline: 71.1 pregnancies per 1,000 girls aged 15 through 17 in 1985)

Special Population Targets

Pregnancies per 1,000	1985 Baseline	2000 Target
Black adolescents 15-19	186	120
Hispanic adolescents 15-19	158	105

Objective #5.1

| Risk Reduction | Reduce the proportion of adolescents who have engaged in sexual intercourse to no more than 15 percent by age 15 and no more than 40 percent by age 17. *Objective #5.4, 18.3, 19.9* | (Baseline: 27 percent of girls and 33 percent of boys by age 15, 50 percent of girls and 66 percent of boys by age 17; reported in 1988) |

| Risk Reduction | Increase to at least 90 percent the proportion of sexually active, unmarried people aged 19 and younger who use contraception, especially combined method contraception that both effectively prevents pregnancy and provides barrier protection against disease. *Objective #5.6* | (Baseline: 78 percent at most recent intercourse and 63 percent at first intercourse; 2 percent used oral contraceptives and the condom at most recent intercourse; among young women aged 15 through 19 reporting in 1988) |

Services and Protection	Increase to at least 85 percent the proportion of and people aged 10 through 18 who have discussed human sexuality, including values surrounding sexuality, with their parents and/or have received information through another parentally endorsed source, such as youth, school, or religious programs. *Objective #5.8*	(Baseline: 66 percent of people aged 13 through 18 have discussed sexuality with their parents; reported in 1986)
Services and Protection	Increase to at least 60 percent the proportion of primary care providers who provide age-appropriate preconception care and counseling. *Objective #5.10, 14.12*	(Baseline data available in 1992)

Related Objectives

Health Status	Reduce to no more than 30 percent the proportion of pregnancies that are unintended.	(Baseline: In 1988, 56% of pregnancies in the previous five years were unintended, either unwanted or earlier than desired)

Special Population Target

Unintended pregnancies	1988 Baseline	2000 Target
Black women	78%	40%

Objective #5.2

Mental Health and Mental Disorders

Health Status	Reduce suicides among youth aged 15 through 19 to no more than 8.2 per 100,000 people. *Objective #6.1a, and 7.2a*	(Age adjusted baseline: 10.3 per 100,000 in 1987)
Health Status	Reduce suicides among men aged 20-34 to no more than 21.4 per 100,000 people. *Objective #6.1b and 7.2b*	(Age adjusted baseline 25.2 per 100,000 people in 1986)
Health Status	Reduce by 15 percent the incidence of injurious suicide attempts among adolescents aged 14 through 17. *Objective #6.2 and 7.8*	(Baseline: An estimated 12 percent among youth younger than age 18 in 1989)
Health Status	Reduce to less than 10 percent the prevalence of mental disorders among children and adolescents. *Objective #6.3*	(Baseline: An estimated 12 percent among youth younger than age 18 in 1989))

Related Objectives

Health Status	Reduce to less than 35 percent the proportion of people aged 18 and older who experienced adverse health effects from stress within the past year.	(Baseline: 42.6 percent in 1985)

Special Population

	Target 1985 Baseline	2000 Target
People with disabilities	53.5%	40%

Objective #6.5

Risk Reduction	Increase to at least 20 percent the proportion of people aged 18 and older who seek help in coping with personal and emotional problems.	(Baseline: 11.1 percent in 1985)

Special Population

	1985 Baseline	2000 Target
People with disabilities	14.7%	30%

Objective #6.8

Risk Reduction	Decrease to no more than 5 percent the proportion of people aged 18 and older who report experiencing significant levels of stress who do not take steps to reduce or control their stress.	(Baseline: 21 percent in 1985)

Violent and Abusive Behavior

Health Status

Reduce homicides to no more than 7.2 per 100,000 people.

Special Population Targets

Homicide Rate per 100,000	1987 Baseline	2000 Target
Black men aged 1--34	90.5	72.4
Hispanic men aged 15-34	53.1	42.5
Black women aged 15-34	20.0	16.0

Objective #7.1

(Baseline: 21 percent in 1985)

Health Status

Reduce weapon-related deaths to no more than 12.6 per 100,000 people from major causes.

Objective #7.3

(Age adjusted baseline: 12.9 per 100,000 firearms; 1.9 per 100,000 by knives in 1987)

Health Status

Reverse to less than 25.5 per 1,000 children the rising incidence of maltreatment of children younger than age 18.

Type Specific Targets

Type of per 1,000	1986 Baseline	2000 Target
Physical abuse	5.7	<5.7
Sexual abuse	2.5	<2.5
Emotional abuse	3.4	<3.4
Neglect	15.9	<15.9

Objective #7.4

(Baseline: 25.2 per 1,000 in 1986)

Health Status

Reduce rape and attempted rape of women aged 12 through 34 to no more than 225 per 100,000.

Objective #7.7a

(Baseline: 250 per 100,000 in 1986)

Risk Reduction

Reduce by 20 percent the incidence of physical fighting among adolescents aged 14 through 17.

Objective #7.9

(Baseline: data available in 1991)

Risk Reduction

Reduce by 20 percent the incidence of weapon-carrying by adolescents aged 14 through 17.

Objective #7.10

(Baseline: data available in 1991)

Related Objectives

Health Status

Reduce assault injuries among people aged 12 and older to no more than 10 per 1,000 people.

Objective #7.6

(Baseline: 11.1 per 1,000 in 1986)

Educational and Community-Based Programs

Risk Reduction

Increase the high school graduation rate to at least 90 percent, thereby reducing risks for multiple problem behaviors and poor mental and physical health.

Objective #8.2

(Baseline: 79 percent of people aged 20 through 21 had graduated from high school with a regular diploma in 1989)

Service and Protection

Establish community health promotion programs that separately or together address at least three of the Healthy People 2000 priorities and reach at least 40 percent of each state's population.

Objective #8.10

(Baseline: data available in 1992)

Related Objectives

Services and Protection

Increase to at least 75 percent the proportion of people aged 10 and older who have discussed issues related to nutrition, physical activity, sexual behavior, tobacco, alcohol, other drugs, or safety with family members on at least one occasion during the preceding month.

Objective #8.9

(Baseline: data available in 1991)

The Need for CSHE

Unintentional Injuries

Health Status	Reduce deaths among youth aged 15 through 24 caused by motor vehicle crashes to no more than 33 per 100,000 people. *Objective #9.3b*	(Baseline: 36.9 per 100,000 people in 1987)

Health Status	Reduce drowning deaths to no more than 1.3 per 100,000 people.	(Age-adjusted baseline: 2.1 per 100,000 in 1987)

Special Population Targets

Drowning deaths per 100,000	1987 Baseline	2000 Target
Men aged 15-34	4.5	2.5
Black males	6.6	3.6

Objective #9.5

Health Status	Reduce nonfatal spinal cord injuries so that hospitalizations for this condition are no more than 5.0 per 100,000 people. *Objective #9.10*	(Baseline: 5.9 per 100,000 in 1988)

Risk Reduction	Increase use of helmets to at least 80 percent of motorcyclists and at least 50 percent of bicyclists. *Objective #9.13*	(Baseline: 60 percent of motorcyclists in 1988 and an estimated 8 percent of bicyclists in 1984)

Environmental Health

Health Status	Reduce asthma morbidity, as measured by a reduction in asthma hospitalizations, to no more than 160 per 100,000 people.	(Baseline: 188 per 100,000 in 1987)

Special Population Targets

Hospitalizations per 100,000	1987 Baseline	2000 Target
Blacks and other nonwhites	334	265
Children (aged 14 and younger)	284	225

Objective #11.1

Oral Health

Health Status	Reduce dental caries (cavities) so that the proportion of children with one or more caries... is no more than 60 percent among adolescents aged 15.	(Baseline: 75 percent of adolescents aged 15 in 1986-7)

Special Population Targets

Prevalence of caries 1983-4	Baseline	2000 Target
American Indian/Alaskan Native aged 15	93%	70%

Objective #13.1

Health Status	Reduce untreated dental caries so that the proportion of children with untreated caries is no more than... 15 percent among adolescents aged 15.	(Baseline: 11 percent of children aged 8 and 8 percent of adolescents aged 14 in 1986-7)

Special Population Targets

Untreated dental caries	1986-7 Baseline	2000 Target
Adolescents aged 15 whose parents have less than a high school education	41%	25%
American Indian/Alaskan Native adolescents aged 15	84%*	40%
Black adolescents aged 15	38%	20%
Hispanic adolescents aged 15	31-47%**	25%

*1983-84 baseline
**1982-84 baseline

Objective #13.2

| Risk Reduction | Increase to at least 50 percent the proportion of children who have received protective sealants on the occlusal (chewing) surfaces of permanent molar teeth.

Objective #13.8 | (Baseline: 11 percent of children aged 8 and 8 percent of adolescents aged 14 in 1986-7) |

Maternal and Infant Health

Related Objectives

| Health Status | Reduce the maternal morality rate to no more than 3.3 per 100,000 live births. | (Baseline: 6.6 per 100,000 in 1987) |

Special Population Targets

Maternal Mortality	1987 Baseline	2000 Target
Blacks	14.2*	5*

*per 100,000 live births

Objective #14.3

| Health Status | Reduce the incidence of fetal alcohol syndrome to no more than 0.12 per 1,000 live births. | (Baseline: 0.22 per 1,000 live births in 1987) |

Special Population Targets

Incidence per 1,000 births	1987 Baseline	2000 Target
American Indians and Alaskan Natives	4	2
Blacks	0.8	0.4

Objective #14.4

| Risk Reduction | Reduce low birthweight to an incidence of no more than 5 percent of live births and very low birthweight to no more than 1 percent of live births. | (Baseline: 6.9 and 1.2 percent, respectively, in 1987) |

Special Population Targets

Incidence	1987 Baseline	2000 Target
Low Birthweight Blacks	12.7%	9%
Very Low Birthweight Blacks	2.7%	2%

Objective #14.5

| Risk Reduction | Increase to at least 85 percent the proportion of women who achieve the minimum recommended weight gain during their pregnancies.

Objective #14.6 | (Baseline: 67 percent of married women in 1980) |

| Risk Reduction | Reduce severe complications of pregnancy to no more than 15 per 100 deliveries.

Objective #14.7 | (Baseline: 22 hospitalizations prior to delivery per 100 deliveries in 1987) |

| Risk Reduction | Increase abstinence from tobacco use by pregnant women to at least 90 percent and increase abstinence from alcohol, cocaine, and marijuana by pregnant women by at least 20 percent.

Objective #14.10 | (Baseline: 75 percent of pregnant women abstained from tobacco use in 1985) |

| Services and Protection | Increase to at least 90 percent the proportion of all pregnant women who receive prenatal care in the first trimester of pregnancy. | (Baseline: 26 percent of sexually active, unmarried, young women reported that their partners used a condom at last sexual intercourse in 1988) |

Special Population Targets

Proportion of Pregnant Women Receiving Early Prenatal Care	1987 Baseline	2000 Target
Black Women	61.1*	90*
American Indian/ Alaska Native	60.2*	90*
Hispanic Women	61.0*	90*

*Percent of live births

Objective #14.11

17

The Need for CSHE

| Services and Protection | Increase to at least 90 percent the proportion of pregnant women and infants who receive risk-appropriate care.

 Objective #14.14 | (Baseline: data available in 1991) |

HIV Infection

| Risk Reduction | Increase to at least 60 percent the proportion of sexually active, unmarried young women aged 15 through 19 whose partners have used a condom at last sexual intercourse.

 Objective #18.4a and 19.10a | (Baseline: 26 percent of sexually active, unmarried, young women reported that their partners used a condom at last sexual intercourse in 1988) |
| Risk Reduction | Increase to at least 60 percent the proportion of sexually active, unmarried young men aged 15 through 19 who used a condom at last intercourse.

 Objective #18.4b and 19.10b | (Baseline: 57 percent of sexually active, unmarried young men reported that they used a condom at last sexual intercourse in 1988) |

Related Objectives

| Health Status | Increase to at least 50 percent the proportion of all intravenous drug abusers who are in drug abuse treatment programs.

 Objective #18.5 | (Baseline: an estimated 11 percent of opiate abusers were in treatment in 1989) |
| Health Status | Increase to at least 50 percent the estimated proportion of intravenous drug abusers not in treatment who use only uncontaminated drug paraphernalia ("works").

 Objective #18.6 | (Baseline: 25 to 35 percent of opiate abusers in 1989) |

Sexually Transmitted Diseases

| Health Status | Reduce gonorrhea among adolescents 15-19 to no more than 750 cases per 100,000.

 Objective #19.1b | (Baseline: 1,123 per 100,000 in 1989) |

Immunization and Infectious Diseases

Health Status

Reduce indigenous cases of vaccine-preventable diseases as follows:

Special Population Targets

Disease:	1988 Baseline per 100,000	2000 Target per 100,000
Diptheria among those 25 and younger	1	0
Tetanus among those 25 and younger	3	0
Polio (wild type virus)		
Measles	3,058	0
Rubella	225	0
Congenital Rubella Syndrome	6	0
Mumps	4,866	500
Pertussis	3,450	1,000

Objective #20.1

Clinical Preventive Services

| Risk Reduction | Increase to at least 50 percent the proportion of adolescents aged 13 through 18 who have received, as a minimum within the appropriate interval, all of the screening and immunization services and at least on of the counseling services appropriate for their age and gender as recommended by the U.S. Preventive Services Task Force.

 Objective #21.2c | (Baseline: data available in 1991) |

18

Table 1-3

Year 2000 Objectives for Schools

Physical Activity and Fitness

Services and Protection	Increase to at least 90 percent the proportion of school lunch and breakfast services and child care food services with menus that are consistent with the nutrition principles in the Dietary Guidelines for Americans. *Objective #2.17*	(Baseline: data available in 1993)
Services and Protection	Increase to at least 75 percent the proportion of the nation's schools that provide nutrition education from preschool through 12th grade, preferably as part of quality school health education. *Objective #2.19*	(Baseline: data available in 1991)
Services and Protection	Establish tobacco-free environments and include tobacco use prevention in the curricula of all elementary, middle, and secondary schools, preferably as part of quality school health education. *Objective #3.10*	(Baseline: 17 percent of school districts totally banned smoking on school premises or at school functions in 1988: anti-smoking education was provided by 78 percent of school districts at the high school level, 81 percent at the middle school level, and 75 percent at the elementary school level in 1988)
Services and Protection	Provide to children in all school districts and private and secondary school educational programs on alcohol and other drugs, preferably as a part of quality school health education. *Objective #4.13*	(Baseline: 63 percent provided some instruction, 39 percent provided counseling, and 23 percent referred students for clinical assessments in 1987)
Services and Protection	Increase to at least 50 percent the proportion of elementary and secondary schools that teach nonviolent protection conflict resolution skills, preferably as a part of quality school health education. *Objective #7.16*	(Baseline: data available in 1991)
Services and Protection	Increase to at least 75 percent the proportion of the nation's elementary and secondary schools that provide planned and sequential kindergarten through 12th grade quality school health education. *Objective #8.4*	(Baseline: data available in 1991)
Services and Protection	Increase to at least 50 percent the proportion of post-secondary institutions with institution wide health promotion programs for students, faculty, and staff. *Objective #8.5*	(Baseline: at least 20 percent of higher education institutions offered health promotion activities for students in 1989-90)
Services and Protection	Provide academic instruction on injury prevention and control, preferably as part of quality school health education, in at least 50 percent of public school systems (grades K through 12). *Objective #9.18*	(Baseline: data available in 1992)

Services and Protection	Extend requirement of the use of effective head, face, eye, and mouth protection to all organizations, agencies, and institutions sponsoring sporting and recreation events that pose risks of injury. *Objective #9, 19, 13, 16*	(Baseline: only National Collegiate Athletic Association football, hockey, and lacrosse; high school football; amateur boxing; and amateur ice hockey in 1988)
Services and Protection	Increase to at least 95 percent the proportion of schools that have age-appropriate HIV education curricula for students in 4th through 12th grade, preferably as part of quality school health education. *Objective #18.10*	(Baseline: 66 percent of school districts required HIV education but only 5 percent required HIV education in each year for 7th through 12th grade in 1989)
	Note: Strategies to achieve this objective must be undertaken sensitively to avoid indirectly encouraging or condoning sexual activity among teens who are not yet sexually active.	
Services and Protection	Provide HIV education for students and staff in at least 90 percent of colleges and universities. *Objective #18.11*	(Baseline: data available in 1995)
Services and Protection	Include instruction in sexually transmitted disease transmission prevention in the curricula of all middle and secondary schools, preferably as part of quality school health education. *Objective #19.12*	(Baseline: 95 percent of schools reported offering at least one class on sexually transmitted diseases as part of their standard curricula in 1988)
	Note: Strategies to achieve this objective must be undertaken sensitively to avoid indirectly encouraging or condoning sexual activity among teens who are not yet sexually active.	

The National Education Goals for The Year 2000

Table 1-4 identifies *The National Education Goals for The Year 2000*. Two of these goals, Goal One and Goal Six, amplify the importance of reducing risk behaviors in today's students in order that they might better be able to learn.

Goal One of *The National Education Goals for the Year 2000* focuses on School Readiness and states that by the year 2000, all children in America will start school ready to learn. The objectives related to the achievement of Goal One state that:

- All children will have access to high-quality and developmentally appropriate preschool programs that help prepare children for school;
- Every parent in the United States will be a child's first teacher and devote time each day to helping such parent's preschool child learn, and parents will have access to the training and support parents need;
- Children will receive the nutrition, physical activity experiences, and health care needed to arrive at school with healthy minds and bodies; and the number of low birthweight babies will be significantly reduced through enhanced health systems.

Goal Six focuses on Safe, Disciplined, and Alcohol- and Drug-Free Schools and states that by the year 2000, every school in America will be free of drugs, violence, and the unauthorized presence of firearms and alcohol and will offer a disciplined environment conducive to learning. The objectives related to the achievement of Goal Six state that:

- Every school will implement a firm and fair policy on use, possession, and distribution of drugs including alcohol;
- Parents, businesses, government and community organizations will work together to ensure the rights of students to study in a safe and secure environment that is free of drugs and crime, and that schools provide a healthy environment and are a safe haven for all children;
- Every local educational agency will develop and implement a policy to ensure that all schools are free of violence and the unauthorized presence of weapons;

Table 1-4

THE NATIONAL EDUCATION GOALS FOR THE YEAR 2000

By the Year 2000 —

1. ALL CHILDREN in America will start school ready to learn.

2. THE HIGH SCHOOL graduation rate will increase to at least 90 percent.

3. ALL STUDENTS will leave grades 4, 8, and 12 having demonstrated competency over challenging subject matter including civics and government, economics, the arts, history, and geography, and every school in America will ensure that all students learn to use their minds well, so they may be prepared for responsible citizenship, further learning, and productive employment in our nation's modern economy.

4. UNITED STATES students will be first in the world in mathematics and science achievement.

5. EVERY ADULT American will be literate and will possess the knowledge and skills necessary to compete in a global economy and exercise the rights and responsibilities of citizenship.

6. EVERY SCHOOL in the United States will be free of drugs, violence, and the unauthorized presence of firearms and alcohol and will offer a disciplined environment conducive to learning.

7. THE NATION'S teaching force will have access to programs for the continued improvement of their professional skills and the opportunity to acquire the knowledge and skills needed to instruct and prepare all American students for the next century.

8. EVERY SCHOOL will promote partnerships that will increase parental involvement and participation in promoting the social, emotional, and academic growth of children.

The Need for CSHE

- Every local educational agency will develop a sequential, comprehensive kindergarten through twelfth-grade drug and alcohol prevention education program;
- Drug and alcohol curricula should be taught as an integral part of sequential, comprehensive health education;
- Community-based teams should be organized to provide students and teachers with needed support;
- Every school should work to eliminate sexual harassment.

The Safe Schools Act

Signed into law on March 23, 1994 as part of Goals 2000 legislation, the Safe Schools Act authorizes competitive grants to local education agencies to enable them to carry out projects of up to two years designed to achieve Goal Six of *The National Education Goals for the Year 2000* by helping to ensure that all schools are safe and free of violence. This goal recognizes that violence prevention is a key to the success of educational reform.

Grants are used to support a variety of activities, which include identifying school violence, addressing discipline problems, conducting school safety audits, planning comprehensive violence prevention programs, training school personnel, acquiring metal detectors, hiring security guards, and other prevention/protection measures. The Safe Schools Act also authorizes the Secretary of Education to conduct a variety of national activities, which include research, program development and evaluation, data collection, and training and technical assistance to school districts and local education agencies.

The Comprehensive School Health Program

A review of each of these national initiatives targets the need for comprehensive school health programs designed specifically to meet the needs of today's students. Currently, there is emphasis being placed on implementing a comprehensive school health program in every school district. A **comprehensive school health program** is an organized set of policies, procedures and activities designed to protect and promote the health, safety, and well-being of students and staff. The eight components of the comprehensive school health program are: (1) health education,

(2) school health services, (3) safe and healthful school environment, (4) physical education, (5) nutrition services, (6) counseling, psychological and social services, (7) health promotion for staff, and (8) parent and community involvement (Figure 1-5). The following discussion describes each of these components and provides definitions adapted from The Division of Adolescent and School Health at The Centers for Disease Control (Allensworth, 1992).

Health Education

Health education is a planned sequential K-12 curriculum that addresses the physical, mental, emotional and social dimensions of health. The curriculum is designed to motivate and assist students to maintain and improve their health, prevent disease, and reduce health-related risk behaviors. It helps students develop and demonstrate increasingly sophisticated health-related knowledge, attitudes, skills, and practices. The curriculum is comprehensive and includes a variety of topics: (1) mental and emotional health, (2) family living, (3) growth and development, (4) nutrition, (5) personal health, (6) alcohol, tobacco, and other drugs, (7) communicable and chronic diseases, (8) injury prevention and safety, (9) consumer and community health, and (10) environmental health. Health education is taught by qualified teachers who have been well trained in content as well as in the process of teaching life skills.

School Health Services

School health services are services designed to appraise, protect, and promote the health of students. Health services are designed to: (1) insure access and/or referral to primary health care services, (2) foster appropriate use of primary health care services, (3) prevent and control communicable diseases and other health conditions, (4) manage chronic diseases, (5) provide emergency care for illness or injury, (6) promote and provide optimum sanitary conditions for a safe school facility and school environment, and (7) provide education and counseling opportunities for the promotion and maintenance of individual, family, and community health. School health services are provided by qualified professionals such as physicians, nurses, dentists, and other allied health personnel.

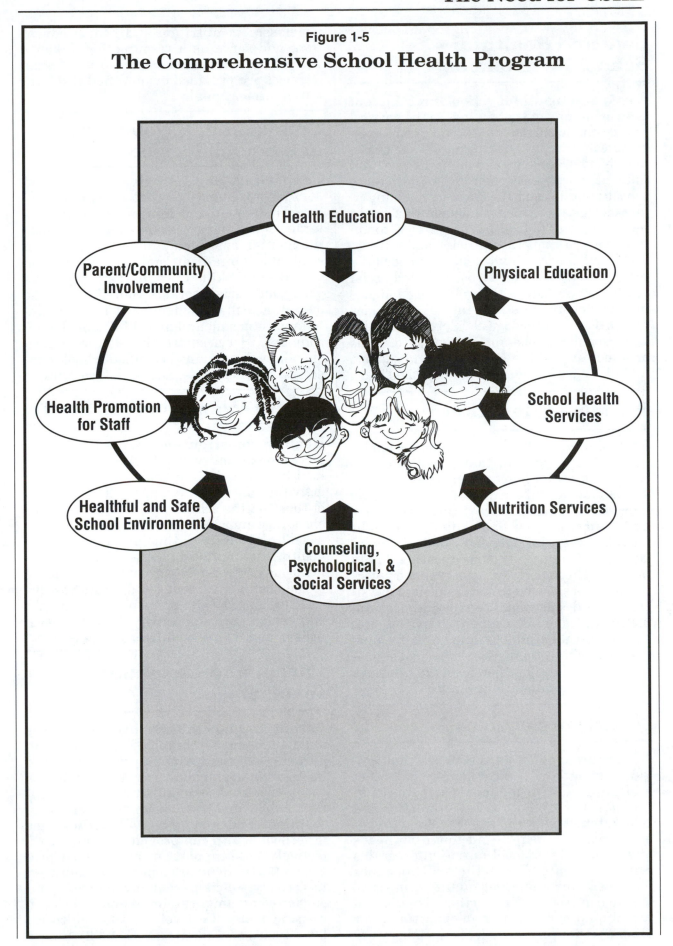

Figure 1-5

The Comprehensive School Health Program

Safe and Healthful School Environment

A **safe and healthful school environment** is an environment that attends to the physical and aesthetic surroundings, and psychosocial climate and culture that maximizes the health and safety of students and staff. Factors that influence the physical environment include the school building and the area surrounding it, any biological or chemical agents that might be detrimental to health, and physical conditions such as temperature, noise, and lighting. The psychological environment includes the interrelated physical, emotional, and social conditions that affect the well-being and productivity of students and staff. This includes physical and psychological safety, positive interpersonal relationships, recognition of needs and successes of the individual, and support for building self-esteem in students and staff.

Physical Education

Physical education is a planned, sequential K–12 curriculum that provides cognitive content and learning experiences in a variety of activity areas including basic movement skills; physical fitness, rhythms, and dance; games; team, dual, and individual sports; tumbling and gymnastics; and aquatics. Quality physical education should promote, through a variety of planned physical activities, each student's optimal physical, mental, emotional, and social development, and should promote activities and sports that all students enjoy and can pursue throughout their lives. Physical education is taught by qualified teachers who have been trained to teach the subject.

Nutrition Services

Nutrition services are services that provide students with nutritionally balanced, appealing, and varied meals and snacks in settings that promote social interaction and relaxation. Meals and snacks take into consideration the health and nutrition needs of all students. School nutrition programs reflect the United States Dietary Guidelines for Americans and other quality criteria to achieve nutrition integrity. The school nutrition programs offer an opportunity for students to experience a learning laboratory for classroom nutrition and health education, and serve as a resource for linkages with nutrition-related community services. Services are provided by qualified child nutrition professionals.

Counseling, Psychological, and Social Services

Counseling, psychological, and social services are services that provide broad-based individual and group assessments, interventions, and referrals which attend to the mental, emotional, and social health of students. Organizational assessment and consultation skills of counselors, psychologists, and social workers contribute to the overall health of students and to the maintenance of a safe and healthful school environment. Services are provided by professionals such as trained/certified school counselors, psychologists, and social workers.

Health Promotion for Staff

Health promotion for staff is health promotion programs such as health assessments, health education, and health-related fitness activities that protect and promote the health of those on the school staff. Such programs encourage and motivate school staff to pursue a healthful lifestyle, thus promoting better health, and improved morale. This commitment may transfer into greater commitment to the health of students, and create positive role modeling. Health promotion programs for staff can improve productivity, decrease absenteeism, and reduce health insurance costs.

Parent and Community Involvement

Parent and community involvement is a dynamic partnership in which the school, parents, agencies, community groups, and businesses work collaboratively to address the health needs of children and their families. School health advisory board councils, coalitions, and broadly-based constituencies for school health can provide a means to effectively build support for school health program efforts. Schools should be encouraged to actively solicit parent involvement and engage community resources and services to respond more effectively to the health-related needs of students (CDC, 1992).

Comprehensive School Health Education

This teacher resource has been designed to focus on one component of the comprehensive school health program—comprehensive school health education. **Comprehensive school health education** is an organized, sequential K–12 plan for teaching students information and helping them develop life skills that promote health literacy and maintain and improve health, prevent disease, and reduce health-related risk behaviors. The following discussion will help you examine *The Umbrella of Comprehensive School Health Education* (Figure 1-6). Then you will learn how you can use this *Totally Awesome™* teacher resource book to implement comprehensive school health education in your school district, school, and classroom.

The Umbrella of Comprehensive School Health Education

The Umbrella of Comprehensive School Health Education (Figure 1-6) illustrates concepts which describe the purpose of comprehensive school health education. *The Umbrella of Comprehensive School Health Education* protects the young people from the six categories of risk behaviors identified by The Centers for Disease Control and Prevention:
1. Behaviors that result in unintentional and intentional injuries
2. Tobacco use
3. Alcohol and other drug use
4. Sexual behaviors that result in HIV infection, other STDs, and unintended pregnancy
5. Dietary patterns that contribute to disease
6. Insufficient physical activity

At the top of the umbrella are three stripes, each of which illustrates an important component from which the comprehensive school health education curriculum is derived: Health Literacy, The National Health Education Standards, and The Performance Indicators. These might be defined as follows (The Joint Committee on Health Education Standards, 1995):

* **Health Literacy** is competence in critical thinking and problem solving, responsible and productive citizenship, self-directed learning, and effective communication. When young people are health literate, they possess skills that protect them from the six categories of risk behaviors.

* **The National Health Education Standards** are standards that specify what students should know and be able to do. There are seven health education standards. The young people in Figure 1-6 are protected from the six categories of risk behaviors because they can achieve the seven health education standards:
1. comprehend concepts related to health promotion and disease prevention;
2. demonstrate the ability to access valid health information and health-promoting products and services;
3. demonstrate the ability to practice health-enhancing behaviors and reduce health risks;
4. analyze the influence of culture, media, technology, and other factors on health;
5. demonstrate the ability to use effective interpersonal communication skills to enhance health;
6. demonstrate the ability to use goal-setting and decision-making skills that enhance health;
7. demonstrate the ability to advocate for personal, family, and community health.

* **The Performance Indicators** are a series of specific concepts and skills students should know and be able to do in order to achieve each of the broader National Health Education Standards. For each of the health education standards, there are several performance indicators. The performance indicators designate what students should know and be able to do after grades four, eight, and eleven. The young people protected by the umbrella of comprehensive school health education attend a school that helps them master these performance indicators at age-appropriate intervals.

The umbrella that protects the young people in Figure 1-6 is divided into ten sections. These ten sections represent areas of health content about which these young people gain health knowledge and skills. **Health knowledge** consists of information that is needed

Figure 1-6

The Umbrella of Comprehensive School Health Education

The comprehensive school health education curriculum is an organized, sequential K-12 plan for teaching students the information and skills they need to become health literate, maintain and improve health, prevent disease, and reduce health-related risk behaviors.

to develop health literacy, maintain and improve health, prevent disease, and reduce health-related risk behaviors. Health knowledge in these content areas contributes to the achievement of the performance indicators identified for each of The National Health Education Standards. Each of the six categories of risk behaviors is included within one or more of these ten content areas, therefore, health knowledge will be obtained for each of the six categories of risk behaviors. Students are not adequately protected with health knowledge alone, however. They need to develop and practice life skills. **Life skills** are actions that promote health literacy, maintain and improve health, prevent disease, and reduce health-related risk behaviors. The ten content areas for which students learn health knowledge and life skills are:

1. **Mental and Emotional Health** is the area of health that focuses on gaining health knowledge and practicing life skills; making responsible decisions; using resistance skills when appropriate; choosing behaviors to promote a healthy mind; developing positive self-esteem; communicating with others in healthful ways; expressing feelings; and coping with stress in healthful ways.

2. **Family Living** is the area of health that focuses on developing relationship skills; avoiding discrimination; practicing conflict resolution skills; striving for healthful family relationships; making healthful adjustments to family changes; forming healthful and responsible friendships; recognizing harmful relationships; identifying resources to improve relationships; developing skills to prepare for future family life; and practicing life skills to support abstinence.

3. **Growth and Development** is the area of health that focuses on caring for the body systems; recognizing changes during growth periods; accepting maleness/femaleness; accepting physical appearance; accepting one's learning style; achieving appropriate developmental tasks; learning about the beginning of new life; recognizing the needs of people of different ages, preparing for aging; and sharing feelings about dying and death.

4. **Nutrition** is the area of health that focuses on planning a healthful diet and includes choosing foods from The Food Guide Pyramid; adhering to dietary guidelines; reading food labels; making healthful food selections to reduce the risk of disease; making healthful selections when dining out; considering food safety; maintaining desirable weight; eating for healthful reasons; and recognizing eating disorders.

5. **Personal Health** is the area of health that focuses on making a personal health management plan that includes being well-groomed; caring for the body; having regular checkups; following a dental health plan; obtaining adequate rest and sleep; and achieving a desirable level of physical fitness.

6. **Alcohol, Tobacco, and Other Drugs** is the area of health that focuses on kinds of drugs and their safe use; understanding the risk factors and protective factors associated with drug misuse and abuse; preventing the misuse and/or abuse of alcohol, tobacco, and controlled substances; recognizing how drug use increases the likelihood of HIV infection; seeking help for personal or family drug misuse or abuse; being aware of school and community intervention and treatment resources; choosing to be safe and drug-free, and using resistance skills when pressured to use drugs.

7. **Communicable and Chronic Diseases** is the area of health that focuses on recognizing communicable and noncommunicable diseases; keeping the immune system healthy; preventing the spread of pathogens; reducing the risk of infection with common communicable diseases, STDs, and HIV; obtaining a family history for diseases; reducing the risk of cardiovascular diseases and cancer; and recognizing ways to manage chronic diseases.

8. **Injury Prevention and Safety** is the area of health that focuses on following safety rules in the home, school, and community; following safety guidelines for different weather conditions and natural disasters; being able to get help for emergency situations; being skilled in basic first aid procedures; reducing the risk of violence; protecting oneself from those who are dangerous; and staying safe while riding in a car and when enjoying exercise.

9. **Consumer and Community Health** is the area of health that focuses on choosing sources of health-related information, products and services; analyzing advertising; recognizing and reporting quackery; spending money and time wisely; using school nurse and school health services when appropriate; using health care providers and health care facilities; cooperating with people in the community who protect health and safety; and volunteering in school clubs and community organizations and agencies that promote health.

10. **Environmental Health** is the area of health that focuses on showing concern about environmental issues; keeping the air clean; keeping the water clean; keeping the indoor environment free of pollution; keeping noise at a healthful level; protecting oneself from radiation; disposing of solid wastes properly; recycling; being aware of the effects of overcrowding; and cooperating with environmental protection agencies.

Notice that the students under the umbrella are enthusiastic, radiant, and energetic. They are confident because they have health knowledge and life skills that give them a firm foundation for healthful living. These students:

1. *Have health knowledge.* **Health knowledge** consists of information that is needed to develop health literacy, maintain and improve health, prevent disease, and reduce health-related risk behaviors.

2. *Choose wellness behaviors.* **Wellness behaviors** are actions that promote health, prevent illness, injury, and premature death, and improve the quality of the environment.

3. *Choose to be in healthful situations.* **Healthful situations** are circumstances that promote health, prevent illness, injury, and premature death, and improve the quality of the environment.

4. *Choose to have healthful relationships.* **Healthful relationships** are relationships that promote self-esteem and productivity, encourage health-enhancing behavior, and are free of violence and drug misuse and abuse.

5. *Make responsible decisions.* **Responsible decisions** are decisions that promote health, protect safety, protect laws, show respect for self and others, follow guidelines set by responsible adults such as parents and guardians, and demonstrate good character.

6. *Use resistance skills when appropriate.* **Resistance skills** are skills that are used when a person wants to say NO to an action and/or leave a situation that threatens health, threatens safety, breaks laws, results in lack of respect for self and others, disobeys guidelines set by responsible adults, or detracts from character.

7. *Possess protective factors.* **Protective factors** are ways that a person might behave and characteristics of the environment in which a person lives that promote health, safety, and well-being. Key protective factors found in these students include (1) having a caring and supportive relationship with at least one person, (2) having received, clear, consistent, and high expectations, and (3) having ample opportunities to participate in and contribute meaningfully to their social environment (Benard, 1992).

8. *Are resilient.* **Resiliency** is the ability to prevent or to recover, bounce back, and learn from misfortune, change, or pressure. The protective factors previously mentioned helped these students develop resiliency.

9. *Are health literate.* **Health literacy** is competency in critical thinking and problem solving, responsible and productive citizenship, self-directed learning, and effective communication. (Joint Health Education Standards Committee, 1995).

These students always have the option of participating in the six categories of risk behaviors. However, these students AVOID these health-related risk behaviors. Why? These students have health knowledge and life skills that help them know the difference between wellness behaviors and these health-related risk behaviors. They know the difference between healthful situations and situations that are risky. They know the difference between healthful relationships and destructive relationships. They have responsible decision-making skills and can evaluate options before deciding what to do. They have resistance skills and know how to say NO when pressured to participate in health-related risk behaviors. They possess several protective factors. They are resilient and are not tempted by health-related risk behaviors when they experience misfortune, change, or pressure. And, they are health literate. They feel empowered and describe themselves as critical thinkers, problem solvers, responsible citizens, self-directed learners, and effective communicators. These students have an umbrella of protection because they attend a school where they have *totally awesome teachers*™ who are committed to teaching comprehensive school health education.

Using This Valuable Teacher Resource

You can make a difference in the lives of students. You can be a *totally awesome teacher*™ who is committed to teaching comprehensive school health education so that your students have an umbrella of protection from the health-related risk behaviors that place our nation at risk. Consider the commitment of the old man in the following story, "The Starfish":

> There was a young man walking down a deserted beach just before dawn. In the distance, he saw a frail old man. As he approached the old man, he saw him picking up stranded starfish and throwing them back into the sea. The young man gazed in wonder as the old man again and again threw the small starfish from the sand into the water. He asked, "Old man, why do you spend so much energy doing what seems to be a waste of time?"

> The old man explained that the stranded starfish would die if left in the morning sun. "But, there must be thousands of beaches and millions of starfish!" exclaimed the young man. "How can you make any difference?" The old man looked at the small starfish in his hand and as he threw it to the safety of the sea, he said, "I make a difference to this one."

The old man knew that he made a difference, even if he never had contact with the millions of other starfish on the thousands of beaches in the world. He knew he could give life back to the starfish whose lives he did touch.

Your role is much the same. As a teacher, you will have contact with many students who are lacking skills needed for optimal living. They are like the starfish stranded on the beach—they are alone, untouched, and lacking life skills needed to have a healthful and vibrant life. They need someone to touch their lives, to give them hope, and to help them learn important life skills. They need a teacher who wants to make a difference. You can be a *totally awesome teacher*™. You can touch the lives of your students and give them hope and the life skills they need for a healthful and vibrant life. Our nation is presently at risk. Health-related risk behaviors have compromised the health status of today's students. But, if teachers like you join together and make a commitment to providing comprehensive school health education, we can build a nation in which our students are healthy and safe.

This teacher resource is designed to help you with this important task. It provides you with valuable information and "teacher-friendly" materials that can be used in your classroom. This teacher resource is divided into the following sections:

Section 1: Comprehensive School Health Education
Section 2: Health Content
Section 3: *Totally Awesome Teaching Strategies*™
Section 4: *The Health Resource Guide*
Section 5: The Curriculum Guide

Section 1. Comprehensive School Health Education Section 1 includes five chapters and is designed to help you have a framework for comprehensive school health education. In Chapter 1, you learned about the six categories of risk behaviors that affect today's students, the national initiatives that support the need for comprehensive school health programs, the components of the comprehensive school health program, and the umbrella of comprehensive school health education. Chapter 2 discusses school health services. This chapter includes *An Encyclopedia of Health Concerns...from A to Z*. Chapter 3 describes a safe and healthful school environment. You will learn how to provide a healthful school environment, including ways you can create a positive emotional climate. You will learn how to provide a safe school environment. Special concerns in today's school environment such as what to do about violence, sexual harassment, drug

The Need for CSHE

use, environmental tobacco smoke, and spillage of bloodborne pathogens will be highlighted. Also included are suggestions for planning and implementing health promotion programs for staff. Chapter 4 will acquaint you with the comprehensive school health education curriculum. You will learn about educational reform. You will learn how to design a comprehensive school health education curriculum that promotes health literacy and the mastery of the performance indicators identified for the National Health Education Standards. Also included in this chapter are innovative ways to teach life skills and evaluation techniques. Chapter 5 identifies instructional strategies that help students gain health knowledge and develop and practice life skills. You also will learn about instructional technologies including multimedia and telecommunications.

Section 2. Health Content Section 2 includes health content so that you are well-informed with up-to-date health knowledge in ten health content areas. Health knowledge pertaining to the six categories of risk behaviors is included in one or more of the ten health content areas. The health knowledge for each health content area is organized by life skills. Life skills pertaining to the six categories of risk behaviors are included in one or more of the ten health content areas. The following chapters are included:

- Chapter 6. Mental and Emotional Health
- Chapter 7. Family Living
- Chapter 8. Growth and Development
- Chapter 9. Nutrition
- Chapter 10. Personal Health
- Chapter 11. Alcohol, Tobacco, and Other Drugs
- Chapter 12. Communicable and Chronic Diseases
- Chapter 13. Injury Prevention and Safety
- Chapter 14. Consumer and Community Health
- Chapter 15. Environmental Health

Section 3. *Totally Awesome Teaching Strategies*™ Chapter 16 explains how to design your classroom as a laboratory in which students develop and practice life skills for health. You will learn how to use *Totally Awesome Teaching Strategies*™. Then you are provided with *Totally Awesome Teaching Strategies*™ for each of the ten health content areas in the comprehensive school health education curriculum. These *Totally Awesome Teaching Strategies*™ also cover the six categories of risk behaviors identified by the Centers for Disease Control and Prevention. All of the materials needed to implement the *Totally Awesome Teaching Strategies*™ are readily available. Each of the *Totally Awesome Teaching Strategies*™ is designed to help students develop and practice life skills for health and be able to master the performance indicators for The National Health Education Standards. Teaching masters, student masters, parent letters, and health behavior contracts have been added to enhance the *Totally Awesome Teaching Strategies*™.

Section 4. The Health Resource Guide. Chapter 17 describes ways you can use *The Health Resource Guide*. *The Health Resource Guide* provides the names, addresses, and telephone numbers of agencies and organizations involved in promoting health in each of the ten health content areas in the curriculum. Within each major heading of the health content areas are subheadings of specialized areas. Whenever possible, toll-free telephone numbers are listed for your convenience.

Section 5. The Curriculum Guide Chapter 18 describes ways you can use The Curriculum Guide. *The Comprehensive School Health Education Curriculum Guide* includes (1) a statement of philosophy and *The Wellness Scale*; (2) *The Responsible Decision-Making Model*; (3) *The Model for Using Resistance Skills*; (4) *A Scope and Sequence Chart* that includes the components of health literacy, The National Health Education Standards, the performance indicators, the content areas and life skills, and the health topics; (5) *Totally Awesome Teaching Strategies*™ infused into several curriculum areas other than health, designed to promote health literacy, and with designated: health education standards, performance indicators, life skills, motivation, evaluation, suggestions for multicultural infusion, and suggestions for inclusion of students with special needs; (6) suggestions for including parents and involving the community. Section 5 also includes an *Appendix* of other materials that will be helpful to you.

Bibliography

Allensworth, Diane. *Research Base for Innovative Practices in School Health Education.* In: Centers for Disease Control. (1993) *Comprehensive School Health Education Programs: Innovative Practices and Issues in Setting Standards.* Atlanta, GA: Centers for Disease Control and Prevention.

American Medical Association Healthier Youth by the Year 2000 Project. (1991) *Healthy Youth 2000: National Health Promotion and Disease Prevention Objectives for Adolescents.* Chicago, IL: American Medical Association.

American School Health Association, Association for the Advancement of Health Education, and Society for Public Health Education. (1988) National Adolescent Health Survey: Highlights of the survey. *Health Education, August/September, 4–8.*

Attico, N. B; Hartner, J. (1992) "Teenage Pregnancy: Identifying the scope of the problem." *Family Practice Recertification,* Volume 14, No. 6.

Austin, Gregory. (1994) "Prevention Research Update No.13 Fall, 1994: Cigarette Smoking Among Adolescents: Recent Research Findings and Prevention Recommendations." *Western Center News,* Portland, OR: Northwest Regional Educational Laboratory.

Baker, S.P., O'Neill, B, Ginsburg, MJ, and Guohua, L. (1992) The injury fact book. Oxford University Press, NY.

Benard, B. (1991) Fostering Resiliency in Kids: *Protective Factors in the Family, School, and Community.* Portland, OR: Northwest Regional Educational Laboratory.

—— (June 1992) How schools convey high expectations for kids. *Western Center News,* 5 (3). Portland, OR: Northwest Drug-Free Schools and Communities.

—— (1994) "The health realization approach to resiliency." *Western Center News.* Corner on Research. Portland, OR: Northwest Regional Educational Laboratory.

Centers for Disease Control. (1993) *Comprehensive School Health Education Programs: Innovative Practices and issues in Setting Standards.* Atlanta, GA: Centers for Disease Control and Prevention.

Centers for Disease Control. (1992) *Suicide Surveillance Summary Report 1980-1990.* Atlanta, GA: Centers for Disease Control and Prevention.

Centers for Disease Control. (1993) *Fact Sheet: Firearm Injuries and Fatalities.* Atlanta, GA: Centers for Disease Control and Prevention.

Johnston, L.D; O'Malley; and Bachman (1991) *Drug Use Among American High School Seniors, College Students, and Young Adults, 1975-1990. Volume I: High School Seniors.* DHHS Publication No. (ADM) 91-1813. Rockville, MD: National Institute on Drug Abuse.

The Joint Committee on Health Education Standards. (1995) *The National Health Education Standards: Achieving Health Literacy.* Questions about *The National Health Education Standards* might be directed to The American Cancer Society; The American School Health Association; The Association for The Advancement of Health Education; The School Health Education and Services Section, American Public Health Association; and The Society of State Directors of Health, Physical Education, Recreation, and Dance. For copies of *The National Health Education Standards,* call or write The American Cancer Society, 1599 Clifton Road NE, Atlanta, Georgia 30329 (1-800-ACS-2345).

Kann, L., Warren, W., Collins, J., Ross, J., Collins, B., & Kolbe, L.J. (1993) Results from the national school-based 1991 youth risk behavior survey and progress toward achieving related health objectives for the nation. *Public Health Reports,* 108 (Supplement 1), 47-67.

Kolbe, L.J. (1992) Statement. In select Committee on Children, Youth, and Family, U.S. House of Representatives, *The risky business of adolescence: How to help teens stay safe - Part I. Hearing Before the Select Committee on Children, Youth, and Families, 22-23.* Washington, D.C.: U.S. Government Printing Office.

Meeks, L; Heit, P; and Page, R. (1995) *Drugs, Alcohol, and Tobacco: Totally Awesome™ Teaching Strategies.* Meeks Heit Publishing Company, Columbus, OH.

Bibliography

Meeks, L; Heit, P; and Page, R. (1995) *Violence Prevention: Totally Awesome™ Teaching Strategies for Safe and Drug-Free Schools*. Meeks Heit Publishing Company, Columbus, OH.

National Centers for Health Statistics. (1993) Annual Summary of births, marriages, divorces, and deaths: United States, 1992. *Monthly Vital Statistics Report* 41(13). Hyattsville, MD: US Public Health Service.

National Highway Safety Administration: Fatal Accident reporting system, 1990. (1992) Department of Transportation, Washington, DC.

U.S. Department of Health and Human Service, U.S. Government Office. (1991) *Healthy People 2000: National Health Promotion and Disease Prevention Objectives*. Washington, DC.

Waxweiler, R.; Harel, Y.; O'Carroll, P. (1993) Measuring adolescent behaviors related to unintentional injury. *Public Health Reports*, Washington, DC.

Figure 2-1

School Health Services

School health services are delivered through the cooperative efforts and activities of teachers, nurses, physicians, allied health personnel, social workers, and others to appraise, protect, and promote the health of students as well as personnel.

Chapter 2

SCHOOL HEALTH SERVICES:
Promoting and Protecting Student Health

The *totally awesome teacher™* is the person with the greatest potential for having a positive impact on the student in the school environment. Of primary importance is the integral role that the *totally awesome teacher™* plays in promoting and protecting student health. This is made possible by the teacher's access to certain health services and health professionals available through the school. These health resources can prevent and control communicable disease, provide emergency care for injury or illness, and provide learning opportunities conducive to the maintenance and promotion of individual and community health. This chapter examines the school's role in providing school health services, the teacher and school health services, and the school nurse and school health services. Specific information for dealing with the special health concerns of children and adolescents also is provided.

The School's Role in Providing School Health Services

Promoting and protecting the health of the 48 million students who attend our nation's schools requires the provision of a wide range of health services. **School health services** are services designed to appraise, protect, and promote the health of students. These health services are delivered through the cooperative efforts and activities of teachers, nurses, physicians, allied health personnel, social workers, and others to appraise, protect, and promote the health of students as well as school personnel (Figure 2-1). Students often are first introduced to school health services through routine health checks and health appraisals such as hearing tests, vision testing, and scoliosis screening. When physical or emotional problems are suspected or detected through observation or health appraisal, students and their families can be directed to appropriate health resources for further evaluation and help by appropriate school personnel (teachers, school nurses, school physicians, counselors, etc.) or by other appropriate health professionals through referrals.

A system for referral of students and families to agencies and health professionals with careful follow-up is often necessary and is a key component of school health services. Consultation and coordination among teachers, school health personnel, parents, and administrators about the specific health needs of students are essential. Follow-up services are necessary to make sure that intended health service activities are carried out and properly recorded on each student's health record.

Most schools do not have the money or personnel to offer all of the services that could be included in a comprehensive school health services program. Recognizing this fact, schools are increasingly relying upon community support and linkages. This interaction enhances schools' ability to offer the range of services that should be provided to meet the escalating health needs of today's youth. This section of the chapter focuses on community partnerships, school-based health clinics, and youth services centers.

Community Partnerships

By working in partnership with families, community organizations, businesses, and health care professionals, schools can increase their capacity to offer a comprehensive array of services to meet health needs. The degree to which health services should be provided by schools depends on the needs of the students, the extent to which health service needs are met elsewhere in the community, and the resources of the school district. At a minimum, all schools should provide routine first aid and emergency care, care for students with chronic and episodic illnesses, operate vision and hearing screenings, maintain immunization and current health assessment records, and make appropriate referrals for further care and attention.

Must all schools provide an extensive range of health services?

> No. Many communities already have high-quality, affordable health care resources that meet the needs of children. Schools can take the lead in coordinating health services so that they are easily accessible to school-aged children and their parents. Schools also can encourage children to use community health resources.

> Where these resources do not exist in the community, where they are not readily accessible to students, or where it is clear that students are not using them, schools should consider providing needed health services in or near the school building. This may mean building new partnerships with community health care agencies or tapping nontraditional funding sources such as private foundations or state and federal health programs (Council of Chief State School Officers, 1991).

Today, the difficult health problems of children and adolescents cannot be solved by the schools alone:

> ...schools cannot do it alone, school nurses cannot heal all the wounds, school guidance counselors cannot deal with the rapidly rising incidence of depression and stress, school social workers cannot patch up dysfunctional families, and there are not enough other school personnel to cope with the "new morbidities." Schools need all the help they can get to prevent the negative consequences of early initiation to drugs, sex, aggressive behavior, and other forms of "acting out." The American educational system was not conceived or organized to address the 21st-century issues of homelessness and AIDS (Dryfoos, 1991).

School-Based Health Clinics

Many schools have the capacity and resources to go beyond the minimum to provide a range of health-related services through school-based health clinics. **School-based health clinics** are clinics that offer a wide range of services including physical examinations and screenings, immunizations, treatment of minor injuries and illness, family life education, counseling for substance abuse and mental health, and referral services. Adolescents often provide input into the planning and management of these health clinics. Many adolescents who use school-based health clinic services have no other source of health care. However, these clinics are often opposed because of the controversial nature of some of the programs that they sometimes offer and because of the added budgetary pressures that they place on already financially burdened school districts. In addition, there is limited evidence available to confirm the effectiveness of school-based health clinics in reducing the incidence of such problems as teenage pregnancy, sexually transmitted diseases, and substance abuse.

Youth Services Centers

Young people face financial, legal, family, and cultural barriers to getting adequate health care (Dougherty et al., 1992). One of every seven 10- to 18-year-olds has no health insurance coverage at all and one-third of poor 10- to 18-year-olds have no access to Medicaid. Those young people who do have coverage through private health insurance are likely to have limitations in obtaining routine physical exams, immunizations, dental care, vision services, preventive screenings, prenatal care, substance abuse treatment, mental health services, and access to extended care facilities (Office of Technology Assessment, 1991).

One promising approach to reducing these barriers and assisting young people with obtaining adequate health care and related services is youth services centers. **Youth services centers** are school-linked, community-based centers that aspire to provide comprehensive services for the many problems young people face (Dougherty et al., 1992; Office of Technology Assessment, 1991). Although similar to school-based health clinics, youth services centers offer a broader range of medical, educational, and social services. Staffed by knowledgeable and committed professionals, youth services centers aspire to offer care at no charge to young people, keep evening and weekend hours, and protect clients' confidentiality. Most operating youth services centers are funded through foundations, and some centers have received limited state and federal funding. However, because funding is meager, the number of centers providing comprehensive services is small (Office of Technology Assessment, 1991).

The range of services provided by youth services centers may extend to the following:
- care for acute physical illnesses;
- general medical examinations, particularly for involvement in athletics;
- mental health counseling;
- laboratory tests;
- reproductive health care;
- counseling for family members;
- prescriptions;
- advocacy;
- coordination of care;
- educational services;
- vocational services;
- legal assistance;
- recreation opportunities;
- child care services;
- parenting education for adolescent parents.

The Teacher and School Health Services

Teachers play a central role in educating about and helping students and their families gain access to school health services. Because of ongoing contact with students in the school environment, the teacher is in a position to observe students as they function in daily situations. In this way, teachers are able to observe when students are functioning in healthful ways and to recognize when students are functioning in unhealthful ways. The teacher will thus be able to suspect and detect needs and be in a position to refer students to the appropriate person or agency when necessary. The teacher's role does not involve diagnosing diseases, illnesses, or injuries. It involves being supportive in appropriate ways and includes getting prompt help in emergency situations.

Teachers are often in a position to observe when a student's appearance, behavior, and emotional expression seem unusual. The teacher is responsible for intervening on behalf of the student. The principal, guidance counselor, or school nurse needs to be notified of any unusual observations. But referring a student for evaluation or for help does not mean that a teacher's responsibility has been fulfilled, nor does it mean that a major problem exists. Once a student has been referred, it is important to follow through on what interventions, if any, have been recommended and are being implemented. For the majority of the student health problems that arise in school, perhaps no two people play a greater role than that of the teacher and school nurse.

The School Nurse and School Health Services

The school nurse plays many different roles in the school system. Traditionally, the school nurse's responsibilities have been to:
1. maintain individual health records and histories;
2. interpret the results of health appraisals;
3. provide information to school personnel about community health resources;
4. perform health screening in such areas as scoliosis, head lice, vision, and hearing;
5. help students seek help for personal health problems;
6. provide emergency care for injuries and illnesses;
7. counsel parents, students, and teachers about special health concerns;
8. assist in the identification of students who need special health-related attention.

School Health Services

Recently, the role of the school nurse has expanded to include involvement in the health education program. Many college preparation programs provide nurses with the skills they need to teach health education. In many school districts, the school nurse also is a health educator, serves on curriculum and textbook committees, implements faculty/ staff wellness programs, and offers health education inservice programs for faculty.

Unfortunately, the standards for school nurses in the United States are not uniform and, in many school systems, school nurses are the first staff members to be terminated when there are budget cuts. Ideally, there should be a school nurse in every school. However, in many school districts there are too few school nurses. And if a school district is small, there may be only one nurse assigned to the entire school district. Some school districts employ health aides to assist the school nurse. Health aides may perform tasks such as handling clerical responsibilities, answering telephones, and arranging screening examinations. Health aides can be extremely helpful to the school nurse.

Student Health Concerns

As a teacher, you will be called on to handle an increasing number of health situations, some of which were nonexistent only a few years ago. And an increasing number of students are coming to school with health-related concerns. In order to respond effectively to these situations and concerns, a teacher needs to know the nature of these situations and concerns, his/her limitations, when it is appropriate to request medical assistance, and where and how to obtain it. *The Encyclopedia of Health Concerns of School-Age Youth from A to Z* addresses the major issues and concerns of students of which you will need to be well-informed.

The Encyclopedia of Health Concerns of School-Age Youth...from A to Z

Acne

Acne is a skin disorder characterized by inflammation of skin glands and hair follicles and the eruption of pimples. Pimples and blackheads (comedones) are usually scattered over the face, neck, shoulders, upper arms, and trunk. Increased hormone production, which is characteristic of adolescence, and the presence of bacteria on the skin play important roles in the development of acne. Most adolescents suffer from some degree of acne, which is the most common ailment of the skin during the adolescent years. Males are more frequently afflicted with acne than females and are more likely to experience serious cases.

Acne is one of the easiest skin conditions for teachers and school nurses to detect. Students with severe cases of acne should be advised to seek medical care from dermatologists. Treatments may include dietary changes, antibiotics, benzoyl peroxide, and topical medications such as antibiotics. Teachers should instruct students to avoid vigorously scrubbing areas affected by acne when washing. However, they should realize that the primary cause of acne is the flow of the hormones associated with puberty. In addition, they should be advised not to squeeze or rub pimples because this may lead to secondary infections or scarring. Many students have misconceptions about the role of diet in acne formation and believe that foods such as chocolate, sweets, milk, and fatty foods can cause acne. However, none of these foods has been shown to cause acne.

Young people with acne may suffer from impaired self-concept and poor body image. Proper treatment often can reduce the severity of acne and help improve self-concept and body image. Sometimes psychological counseling is needed, particularly in instances where severe cases of acne result in permanent scarring.

Adolescent Pregnancy

Adolescent pregnancy is pregnancy in the years between puberty and the end of the teen years. Each year, one million adolescent females in the United States become pregnant. The United States has one of the highest rates of adolescent pregnancy in the developed world. Many pregnant adolescents do not seek early prenatal care. As a result, they have more problem pregnancies than adult females who seek prenatal care. Adolescents are at a much higher risk than adult females of suffering from serious medical complications of pregnancy, including anemia, pregnancy-induced hypertension, toxemia, cervical trauma, and premature delivery. They are also at increased risk of giving birth to premature and low birthweight infants. Even normal birthweight infants of adolescent mothers have a higher rate of rehospitalization than infants of adult mothers.

Females who are pregnant and their partners have unique needs. Pregnant females need to understand what is happening to their bodies and what to expect during their pregnancy. They also need support. Fathers need this information too as well as support in their own way. Adolescent fathers and mothers need counseling to help them handle the needs of the baby as well as to help them with their relationship. They also need information on planning for the future. For example, they need to make financial plans for supporting the baby. Most states now require the male to make child-support payments when no marriage occurs.

Through education, schools can play a significant role in the prevention of adolescent pregnancy. What to teach is an issue that is determined by each school district. The United States government promotes the teaching of abstinence in schools. Students need to be taught how to use resistance skills to say NO to being sexually active. In Chapter 4, *The Model for Using Resistance Skills*, is presented.

In health education classes, it is important for students to be given the opportunity to learn about the healthful expression of sexuality including why choosing to practice abstinence is a responsible choice during adolescence, and to learn about the consequences of adolescent pregnancy.

Airway Obstruction

Airway obstruction is a condition in which breathing is partly or completely prevented by a blockage in the part of the air passages known as the larynx. Choking on a piece of food or an object is a common and potentially dangerous occurrence in the school setting. In almost all cases, the object will become dislodged by itself. But on occasion, a student may choke on something and not be able to dislodge it by himself/herself. The student may cough or attempt to cough and may show the universal distress signal. The **universal distress signal** is a warning demonstrated by a person clutching at the throat with one or two hands.

A student may have a partial airway obstruction or a complete airway obstruction. A student who has a partial airway obstruction may be able to inhale and exhale but will gasp for air. If the airway is completely obstructed, the student will not be able to speak, breathe, or cough. The student also may have cyanosis. **Cyanosis** is a condition that results from the lack of oxygen to body tissues, and manifests itself as bluishness around the lips and mouth.

The **Heimlich Maneuver** is a technique that makes use of abdominal thrusts to dislodge an object in the air passage of a conscious person who is choking. Before using the Heimlich Maneuver, ask the student if (s)he is choking. If the student can speak or cough easily, do not do anything. If the student cannot speak, breathe, or cough, stand behind him/her and wrap your hands around his/her waist. Make a fist with one hand and place the thumb side of the fist into the student's abdomen above the navel and below the rib cage. Grab your fist with the other hand and give quick upward thrusts into the abdominal area. Repeat these thrusts until the object is dislodged. Each thrust should be separate and distinct.

If the object is not dislodged, the student may become unconscious. Call an emergency medical service immediately. Open the student's airway by grasping the lower jaw and tongue. Lift the jaw. Using what is called a finger sweep, attempt to dislodge and remove the object by sweeping it out with your finger. Use a hooking action with your finger. If nothing happens, while tilting the student's head and lifting the chin and, with appropriate mouth protection, give the student two full breaths. If air does not get into the lungs, the airway is still blocked. Give six to ten abdominal thrusts. To give abdominal thrusts, straddle the student's thighs. Place the heel of one hand on the student's abdomen just above the navel but below the tip of the breastbone. Place your other hand on top of the fist. Make sure the fingers of your hands point toward the student's head. Give quick, upward thrusts. If nothing happens after six to ten thrusts, do another finger sweep. Then give two full breaths. If you cannot get breaths into the student, repeat the same procedures—thrusts, finger sweeps, and two breaths. Do this sequence until emergency medical personnel arrive.

Alcohol-Related Problems

Alcohol is a psychoactive drug that depresses the central nervous system, dulls the mind, impairs thinking and judgment, lessens coordination, and interferes with the ability to respond quickly to dangerous situations. **Alcohol-related problems** include abuse of alcohol by the student as well as a student's exposure to alcohol problems through alcohol abuse by a family member. Alcohol is one of most commonly abused drugs of school-age youth. Young people who abuse alcohol may exhibit one or more of the following signs and symptoms:
- drinking secretively;
- lying about drinking;
- drinking during times of stress and worry;
- gulping drinks;
- trying to find parties where alcoholic beverages will be served;
- preoccupation with drinking;
- declining grades;
- decrease in muscular coordination;
- not following through on class projects;
- becoming irritable too easily.

Many students are affected by the drinking behavior of family members. One of every four families is affected by a family member who drinks. Under these circumstances, students may come to school tense and often are not well-fed. These students may withdraw so that they do not call attention to drinking problems at home. They may not want to invite friends back to their home for fear of being embarrassed by a parent who is drunk. They often have low self-esteem. Because of behavior they observe at home, these students are more likely to begin drinking themselves.

Alcohol-related problems involving youth require immediate intervention. The first step in helping young people with alcohol-related problems is identification and recognition of the problem. By being aware of the signs and symptoms of alcohol-related problems, teachers are often in a position to identify alcohol-dependent and/or alcohol-abusing youth or youths who are at risk as a result of alcohol problems in the home. Once recognition is made, school professionals should intervene by linking students to available treatment services. This requires a team approach with parents, administrators, counselors, school nurses, and community treatment providers working with students. Some schools are able to offer school-based treatment and/or counseling services to students suffering from alcohol and other drug abuse, and to students who are exposed to alcohol-related problems in the home. Other schools rely on school-linked treatment options with community programs or must make referrals to community-based programs. Follow-up and tracking of students throughout treatment are fundamental aspects of a responsible and effective intervention policy.

One approach used by many schools for dealing with alcoholism and problems of children of parents with alcoholism is the Student Assistance Program. A **Student Assistance Program** is a school-based approach to the prevention and treatment of alcohol abuse. This type of program is modeled after Employee Assistance Programs in business and industry. Teachers and school personnel are trained to recognize alcohol and other drug involvement or related problems that interfere with a student's ability to function at school and then to use a referral process for getting appropriate help for the student. Students also can refer themselves to program services. The goals of Student Assistance Programs include:

- identifying early drug involvement or other problems;
- referring students to designated "helpers" within the school;
- providing in-school support and/or counseling services and groups;
- referring students to outside mental health, drug-treatment, and family-services organizations and professionals.

The key component in successful Student Assistance Programs is the endorsement, support, and involvement of school officials and administrators, community leaders and organizations, parents, and students.

Additional related information is included under **Drug Abuse.**

Allergies

Allergies are hypersensitive reactions by the immune system to a foreign antigen (protein). An **allergen** is a substance that stimulates the production of antibodies and subsequently results in allergic reactions. Many young people experience food allergies. Common food allergens are milk, strawberries, wheat, eggs, corn, nuts, citrus fruits, and shellfish. Airborne allergens include pollen, dust, and molds. Medications such as antibiotics and aspirin also can be allergens for some people. Allergic reactions can develop at any stage during the life cycle. While many allergic reactions are mild and localized, some people may experience a severe anaphylactic reaction. An **anaphylactic reaction** is a sudden systemic reaction that can be life-threatening. Symptoms include dizziness, nausea, itching, hives, sudden weakness, drop in blood pressure and constriction of bronchial tubes. A severe anaphylactic reaction requires immediate medical emergency care. Children and adolescents prone to these reactions should have quick access to kits that contain oral antihistamines and epinephrine-filled syringes to counteract the anaphylactic reactions. School professionals should be trained and prepared to assist and/or administer these medications according to school policies for administering medications.

Allergies should be listed on each student's health record, and teachers should be aware of each student's allergies. Teachers should be trained to recognize signs and symptoms of anaphylactic reactions and should be skilled in proper procedures for activating proper emergency care. Reducing children's exposure to allergens is a preferred mode of allergy control, and action should be taken to remove any identified allergens from the school environment whenever such action is feasible and practical.

Anabolic Steroid Use

Anabolic steroids are powerful derivatives from the male hormones that produce muscle growth and can change health and behavior. Steroids have been used by athletes, both male and female, to build muscles and thus to improve performance. However, they are now illegal and have been banned from use in sporting events.

The continued use of anabolic steroids poses serious health consequences for both males and females. Males may experience testicular shrinkage and reduced sperm production. Females may experience breast reduction and sterility. Both males and females may experience liver tumors, kidney damage, and heart disease. Behavioral changes including aggression and violence accompany steroid use. Even when the use of steroids is discontinued, the effects of steroids often cannot be reversed.

It is essential that schools include education about steroids in the drug education curriculum. Students and educators alike need to recognize that the hazards and risks associated with steroid use are serious and real. Steroid education efforts should assist students in learning to evaluate present motivations regarding steroid use with long-term consequences. Education should not be limited to students only; coaches, athletic trainers, nurses, administrators, parents, and others should be familiar with the hazards that steroids pose, the reasons young people use steroids, and how to recognize steroid abuse.

Anorexia Nervosa

Anorexia nervosa is an eating disorder in which a person is preoccupied with being excessively thin. This disorder is also known as anorexia. Approximately 95 percent of all people with anorexia nervosa are female. Approximately one in 100 families has a member who has anorexia nervosa. A large number of people who have anorexia nervosa are between the ages of twelve and eighteen. Symptoms of anorexia include an intense fear of gaining weight, a distorted body image, and, in females, three consecutive missed menstrual cycles.

School-age females who have anorexia are often perfectionists. They have good grades, but show little enjoyment from success. These females are usually very obedient, intelligent, and thoughtful. They are preoccupied with weight loss and may be sad and lonely. Females with anorexia nervosa will not want to dress for physical education classes or change clothes in front of other people. Teachers who notice these signs and symptoms should report them to the school nurse, who can keep a record of weight.

Students who have anorexia need to receive medical treatment. Treatment may require a hospital stay or may be done on an outpatient basis. Psychological treatment is emphasized and goals such as gaining specific amounts of weight are set.

Additional related information is included under **Eating Disorders** and **Bulimia**.

Asthma

Asthma is an allergic disease of the lungs manifested by constrictions of the small air passages called bronchioles. An asthma attack causes a person to have difficulty breathing. Most cases of asthma are moderate, although a number of young children have severe asthma. Children may be treated with injections or medications taken orally. If treatment is needed during the school day, the parent can make arrangements with the school nurse. The school nurse has directions to follow if a child has an attack. Many children use an inhaler to get medicine that helps them to breathe easier. If a child is using an inhaler, it is important that it be used correctly.

Additional related information is included under **Chronic Health Conditions**.

Attention Deficit Hyperactivity Disorder (ADHD)

Attention **Deficit Hyperactivity Disorder (ADHD)** is a developmental disorder characterized by inattention, and frequently, impulsiveness, hyperactivity, and inability to follow rules. It usually begins before age seven and is believed to persist throughout the lifespan. The prevalence of ADHD is very hard to determine; studies involving strict diagnostic criteria by mental health professionals report 3 to 5 percent of the students in the school-age population have ADHD. When teachers report prevalence of ADHD, rates range between 10 to 20 percent and rates are often even higher when parents report the incidence. ADHD is believed to be much more prevalent in males. However, some experts contend that prevalence among females may be greater than thought, and that ADHD manifests itself differently and more subtly than in males. For example, females with ADHD may act out less than males with ADHD.

Students who have ADHD may have special needs in the classroom, where ADHD symptoms often manifest themselves. Students with ADHD are likely to display the following behavioral symptoms: difficulty concentrating on school work or other tasks requiring sustained attention; difficulty sticking to play activities; being distracted; often failing to finish things they start; acting before thinking; shifting from one activity to another; requiring a lot of supervision; frequently calling out in class; difficulty waiting in turn in games or group situations; difficulty sitting still or staying seated; fidgeting excessively; and frequently engaging in random or aimless activity.

ADHD may also be associated with temper tantrums, low frustration tolerance, low self-esteem, difficulties with friendships and other interpersonal relationships, and poor academic achievement. Young people with ADHD often are very immature and have difficulty with their peers. As a result of their immaturity, they often associate with people younger than they are. Because of their impulsiveness, young people with ADHD often have difficulty in school.

Educators should assist children with ADHD by providing structure and routine in order to alleviate distraction. Allowing enough time for these young people to process information is important. Using positive rewards instead of punishments helps bolster self-esteem. Providing opportunities for positive peer interaction both in and outside the classroom is especially important. Being certain to assign specific tasks to these young people is a necessity.

Bleeding

Bleeding is a condition in which blood escapes from the vessels that naturally contain it. **External bleeding** is bleeding that takes place through a break in the skin. The simplest way to control external bleeding is by applying direct pressure. **Direct pressure** is the placement of pressure over the wound to restrict blood flow and promote normal clotting. Universal precautions should be followed.

If a student suffers a wound and (s)he is bleeding externally, seek emergency help and take the following steps:
1. Place direct pressure over the wound using a sterile gauze or a clean washcloth to keep germs from entering the wound.
2. Place firm pressure over the wound.
3. Elevate the injured area above the level of the heart.
4. If blood soaks through the bandage, do not remove the bandage but add more bandages.

If the student continues to bleed, a pressure point may need to be compressed. A **pressure point** is a location where an artery that is supplying blood to the area that is bleeding can be compressed. The two main pressure points are the brachial artery in the arm and the femoral artery in the groin area. It is important to be skilled in first aid before using pressure points.

Internal bleeding is bleeding within the body in which lost blood escapes into some internal cavity or into surrounding tissue. Internal bleeding can be a very serious injury. Internal bleeding is more difficult to detect and to stop than external bleeding. When extensive internal bleeding is suspected, emergency care should be sought immediately. Until help arrives, the following steps should be taken:

1. Keep the student lying down to help the heart beat with as little force as possible and to keep the blood pressure as low as possible.
2. Avoid excitement.
3. Keep the student warm.
4. Avoid stimulants.
5. If internal bleeding is suspected in the chest or abdominal region, ice bags or cold compresses can be applied to these areas until help arrives.

Most wounds teachers will see in the school setting are minor. All wounds must be kept clean. Use a sterile gauze or clean cloth that is saturated with soap and water to clean a wound. Any foreign matter such as dirt or gravel that is in the wound should be removed to reduce the risk of infection. Cover the wound with sterile gauze. Do not keep the dressing airtight. An airtight bandage traps moisture from the skin and encourages bacterial growth.

When dealing with blood, take precautions against possible transmission of viruses such as HIV and hepatitis B. These precautions are outlined in Chapter 3.

Bone Injuries

Bone injuries are damage to bones that result from physical trauma. One type of bone injury suffered by many students is a fracture. A **fracture** is a break in a bone. A bone that is fractured may be chipped, broken partially, or completely broken.

If a bone is broken, there will be any number of signs and symptoms. Pain and tenderness will be present. In some cases, there will be deformity in the area of the break. Swelling and discoloration in the area may be present and the student may not be able to use the injured body part. If a student appears to have suffered a fracture, treat the student for shock. Be sure not to move the injured area, as the pieces of the broken bone might shift and cause further injury to the underlying tissue in the surrounding area. Call for emergency medical personnel immediately.

Another common bone injury is dislocation. A **dislocation** is the separation of a bone from its joint. Dislocations will often result in the same kinds of signs and symptoms as a broken bone. There may be deformity, dislocation, severe pain, swelling, and an inability to move the area. First aid for a dislocation includes not moving the joint and applying ice.

Additional related information is included under **Shock, Sprains** and **Strains.**

Bulimia

Bulimia is an eating disorder in which a person has uncontrollable urges to eat excessively and then engages in self-induced vomiting, and/or the excessive use of laxatives or diuretics. This disorder also is known as the binge-purge syndrome. Binge eating usually occurs in solitude. The person will stop binge eating if observed by someone else. Unlike the person who has anorexia nervosa, the person who has bulimia often is near normal weight. Yet a person who has bulimia may eat 10,000 calories or more per binge.

A person who has bulimia may develop feelings of depression and hopelessness, and, in some cases, may even consider suicide. Psychological and medical interventions are prescribed for a person who has bulimia.

Additional related information is included under **Anorexia Nervosa** and **Eating Disorders.**

Cardiac Arrest

Cardiac arrest is a condition in which a person's heart has stopped beating. **Cardiopulmonary resuscitation (CPR)** is an emergency procedure that is used to revive a person whose heart has stopped beating. CPR should be used only by a person trained to administer this procedure. All teachers should be properly trained in how to administer CPR.

The American Red Cross suggests the following procedure be administered when a person's heart has stopped beating. Send someone to obtain emergency medical attention immediately. If the person is not breathing, pinch his/her nose shut, use appropriate protection and seal your lips tightly around the person's mouth, and give two full breaths that last about one to one and one-half seconds. Watch to see that the chest rises, indicating the breaths have entered the lungs. Feel the pulse for five to ten seconds. If a pulse is present, check for severe bleeding and recheck breathing. CPR begins if a person does not have a pulse.

To perform CPR, these steps should be followed.

1. Locate the notch of the lower end of the sternum with the index and middle fingers. Place the heel of the hand on the sternum next to the fingers. Remove the hand from the notch and put it on top of the other hand. Keep the fingers on the chest.
2. Position your shoulders over your hands and compress the sternum one and one-half to two inches. Do fifteen compressions in about ten seconds. Compress up and down smoothly.
3. Open the airway with a head-tilt/chin lift, pinch the nose shut, and, using appropriate protection, seal your lips tightly around the person's mouth. Give two full breaths that last one to one and one-half seconds. Watch the chest to see if it rises.
4. Repeat the compression/breathing cycles three times.
5. Recheck the pulse for five seconds. If the person has a pulse and is breathing, keep the airway open, monitor breathing, and await the arrival of emergency medical personnel. If a person has a pulse but is still not breathing, do rescue breathing until emergency medical personnel arrive. If no pulse or breathing is present, continue CPR.
6. Give two full breaths, each lasting one to one and one-half seconds making sure the chest rises.
7. Continue the compression/breathing cycles. Locate the correct hand position, continue cycles of fifteen compressions and two breaths, and recheck the pulse every few minutes.

Child Abuse

Child abuse is maltreatment of a person under the age of eighteen. There are four kinds of abuse: physical abuse, emotional abuse, neglect, and sexual abuse. Teachers are in a position to recognize cases of child abuse. By law, any teacher or health professional must report suspected cases of abuse. Most school districts have specific policies about the reporting of abuse. A teacher who reports a case of suspected abuse has immunity from civil and criminal liability. When an abuse case is filed, the identity of the person reporting the abuse remains confidential. Reports of child abuse are often made to child welfare agencies or the police. Most reported cases of child abuse will be investigated rapidly. If an investigation indicates that a child is in danger, that child will likely be placed in protective custody or in a foster home.

Child abuse occurs in all sectors of society. Child abuse occurs in families with high incomes as well as in those with low incomes. In 85 to 90 percent of cases, the person who is abusing a child is a family member.

How would a teacher know if a student was being or has been abused? The student might confide that (s)he is being abused. If this happens, it is extremely important to report the abuse to the principal and/or follow procedures established in your school district. While this information may be shared with you in strictest confidence by the student, you have an obligation to report it promptly in order to protect the student and to abide by the law.

In most cases of abuse, the student who has been abused tells no one. Help is provided only when an adult recognizes the signs and symptoms, and obtains help for the student. Teachers need to be aware of these signs and symptoms and of the other characteristics that will help them assist students who are abused.

Additional related information is included under **Emotional Abuse, Neglect, Physical Abuse,** and **Sexual Abuse.**

Childhood Infectious Diseases

Childhood infectious diseases are communicable diseases, usually in young persons, that are caused by microorganisms and viruses that are readily transmitted from one person to another. Children and adolescents are susceptible to a variety of infectious diseases. Children have greater susceptibility to many illnesses than adults. Children's immune systems lack the degree of immunity that adults have because they lack previous exposure to many viruses and bacteria. Lack of exposure means that there are fewer antibodies available to the immune system to fight the disease agents to which children are exposed. Susceptibility to communicable diseases also is heightened when children attend school because they are exposed to many germs.

Certain childhood infectious diseases are preventable through immunization. School professionals should require that students have immunizations before entering school. In addition, school professionals should advocate that children younger than school age receive recommended immunizations as a part of school readiness efforts. Immunizations are available for the following childhood infectious diseases: diphtheria, pertussis (whooping cough), tetanus, measles, mumps, rubella, polio, and Hemophilus influenza type B (HIB). Hepatitis B was a leading cause of bacterial meningitis.

In addition to promoting childhood immunizations, the role of schools in infectious disease control includes: identification of infectious illness in students; enforcing policies for excluding students capable of infecting other children from school and determining when readmission is safe; and educating parents, staff, and students about procedures to reduce/prevent spread of infectious disease. The threat of infectuous diseases spreading in schools has caused school professionals to make infection control procedures and policies in schools a priority. Most schools have well-defined policies and procedures for dealing with infectious diseases.

Additional related information is included under **HIV/AIDS**.

Chronic Health Conditions

Chronic health conditions are recurring or persistent health conditions. It is estimated that 5 to 15 percent of students have chronic health conditions. More than three-quarters of teachers report teaching students with chronic health conditions during their career. However, many teachers feel that their professional preparation was inadequate in terms of knowing how to deal with chronic health conditions in the classroom. The chronic health conditions most commonly seen in students are asthma, diabetes, epilepsy, cerebral palsy, heart disease, cancer, and spina bifida (Johnson, Lubker, and Fowler, 1988). The fastest growing chronic health condition in children is HIV/AIDS.

Children with chronic health conditions require carefully planned school programs that are determined by each child's condition. Some of the considerations that need to be included in school programs are:
- balancing academic needs with health care needs;
- making provisions for students who require technology (specialized electrical outlets, private areas for catheterization, etc.) and/or trained personnel to provide daily or emergency care;
- scheduling adjustments to accommodate the need for rest periods and to take care of personal needs;
- arranging for students to make up school work;
- developing individual education plans (IEPs);
- employing specialized learning techniques;
- having procedures to control and prevent infectious disease;
- having teachers or other school personnel make home or hospital visits;
- planning for emergency care;
- training needs of school personnel and students.

The Council for Exceptional Children (1989) advocates the following for teachers of chronically ill children:

Interruptions for suctioning, medication, or other medical interventions should be nondisruptive to the classroom and learning atmosphere. Focus should be on maximizing opportunities for educational success and social interaction, not only limitations and isolation. For example, class parties can include food treats that meet a student's dietary restrictions, or medical intervention can be completed during individual work times rather than during group learning activity periods.

Educational curricula are always chosen to meet individual student needs. Modifications for students with specialized health care needs may be similar to those adopted for students with physical disabilities. For example, adaptive response modes, adjusted timing requirements, or adjustment for limited hand use or mobility may facilitate learning success.

Additional related information is included under **Asthma**, **Diabetes**, and **Epilepsy**.

Cold-Temperature-Related Emergencies

Cold-temperature-related emergencies are physical conditions that result from exposure to low temperatures, either below or above freezing. The most common types of cold-temperature-related emergencies are frostbite and hypothermia. **Frostbite** is the freezing of body tissues, most likely those tissues of the extremities. Most cases of frostbite occur to the fingers, toes, ears, and nose. A person who is exposed to subfreezing temperatures or snow is at risk for developing frostbite. Signs of frostbite include numbness in the affected area, waxy appearance of skin, skin that is cold to touch, and discolored skin.

Treatment for frostbite includes handling the affected area gently. The area should be warmed by soaking the affected part in water that has a temperature between 100 degrees Fahrenheit and 105 degrees Fahrenheit. To determine if the water is too warm, a person's hand that has not been exposed to the cold should be soaked in it. If the water feels too warm to the hand, it is too warm for the person who needs treatment. Keep the affected body part in water until it appears red and feels warm. Do not rub the affected part.

Hypothermia is a reduction in the body temperature so that it is lower than normal. Hypothermia results from exposure to a cool environment. The temperature can be as high as 50 degrees Fahrenheit and a person can suffer from hypothermia. A combination of cool temperatures and exposure to moisture and wind can cause a person to have hypothermia. Most cases of hypothermia are mild. A person will shiver and feel cold. As body temperature drops, the pulse rate may slow down and become irregular. Eventually, a person can become unconscious and, if the hypothermia remains untreated, death can result.

The best treatment for hypothermia is to place the person in a warm environment, remove any wet clothing, and replace it with dry clothing. The best approach for cold-temperature-related illness is prevention. Wearing the proper clothing and avoiding exposure to harmful conditions will reduce the risks of cold-temperature-related emergencies.

Conjunctivitis

Conjunctivitis is an inflammation of the membrane lining the eyelids and covering the eyeball (conjunctiva). Commonly known as "pinkeye," conjunctivitis is a highly contagious condition. It is most often caused by bacterial or viral infection. However, it also can be caused by allergies, certain drugs, or from irritation from foreign objects. Conjunctivitis is rarely serious unless infection progresses to the deeper tissues of the eye, which may result in vision being affected. Recognition of this condition is most often through observation of redness and swelling of the eyes and significant tearing. A discharge may also be present. Students with conjunctivitis may complain of a "gritty" feeling in the eyes and of their eyelids sticking together upon waking from sleep.

A student who has conjunctivitis should be isolated and should not attend school. Parents should also be advised to seek medical consultation for their child. In most cases, conjunctivitis is treated effectively with antibacterial eyedrops or ointments. Conjunctivitis cannot effectively be treated with over-the-counter eye medications. It is imperative that family members understand that conjunctivitis can easily be spread from person to person through sharing the same towels and bedding. Careful handwashing is also helpful in preventing spread of infection. Students who have received treatment can usually return to school within a few days without risk of spreading infection.

Death

Death is the permanent cessation of brain, heart, and lung function. At some time, a teacher will be faced with a student in class who has experienced the death of a loved one. A student's grandparent or parent may have died, or a pet may have been hit by a car or died of old age. At times, students may even be faced with the death of another student.

A student who suffers a loss will experience any number of reactions. The death of a parent is the most stressful life event for a school-age student. The kind of reaction that a student has will often depend on the situation. For example, when a family member had a prolonged illness prior to death, a student may have already begun the grieving process. The family influences how a student adjusts to the death. A student whose family discusses death in an open and honest manner will be able to grieve openly and share feelings more easily than a student whose family does not share feelings and information about death. The age of a student also helps determine how (s)he reacts to death. The young student believes that death is temporary and like being asleep. Between the ages of five and nine, a student begins to understand the finality of death and that death can be caused by an environmental force. Once a student reaches the age of nine, death is understood as a part of the life cycle and is viewed as being able to happen to anyone.

Elisabeth Kübler-Ross identified five stages in the grieving process that accompanies dying and death (Kübler-Ross, 1975). These stages are denial, anger, bargaining, depression, and acceptance. At first, students experience denial. They do not believe that someone they know or to whom they have been close has died. When they realize the person will not return, they are angry. Then they bargain, believing that the person can come back. They focus on it not being fair to have this loss. This stage is followed by depression and sadness. Guilt may accompany depression. Much support is needed. Young people also can be vulnerable to thoughts of their own death. Finally, acceptance is reached. But, it is important to remember that in young people the grieving process is not short.

There are ways that a teacher can help a students who have experienced the death of someone to whom they were close.

1. Do not shield students from or mislead them about death. Students need to know that death is not temporary and that it is not like sleeping.
2. When questions are raised, give simple, direct answers. For example, a student might ask, "Why did my grandma die?" An appropriate answer is "Grandma was very ill for a long time, and her heart finally stopped beating." If the student is given a discourse that is extremely complex and long, confusion may result.
3. Answer questions as they arise. If you do not have an answer to a question, say so. But you can tell the student you will try to find an answer.
4. Recognize that students need to grieve. Remember the five stages. Help students understand the grieving process. For example, if a student acts out in angry ways, you might say, "You are very angry that your father died. I can understand you feel it is unfair." This helps the student understand his/her feelings.
5. Watch for signs of severe depression. Remember students are especially vulnerable to depression if a parent dies, and they need extra support and understanding.

Dental Problems

Dental problems are nontraumatic tooth-related conditions that exist as a result of structure, infection, or diet. The dental problems that may occur in school-age students are cavities, tooth abscesses, need for extraction, gingivitis, and malocclusion. Dental caries, or cavities, are the most common health disorder in children and adolescents. A **cavity** is an area of decay in a tooth. Cavities that are detected and treated by a dentist usually do not represent a significant threat to health. However, not attending to a cavity may lead to an abscess and destruction of the tooth, requiring the need for tooth extraction by a dentist. An **abscess** is localized collection of pus. **Extraction** is surgical removal of a tooth. Tooth abscesses and extraction may be painful. When more than one tooth is involved, a student's nutritional status may be compromised because eating may be difficult. Poor dental hygiene also can lead to gingivitis. **Gingivitis** is inflammation of the gums. Severe gingivitis often results in ulceration and bleeding of the gums. Another dental problem frequently found in students is malocclusion. **Malocclusion** is the improper alignment of teeth; a condition that can lead to oral tissue destruction if not corrected.

Some schools provide dental inspections. Whether a school district offers inspections or not, teachers and other professionals are often in a position to observe dental problems. Signs and symptoms of dental problems are crooked teeth, bleeding gums, offensive breath, reports of toothache or other oral pain, poor hygiene, soreness or pain in the mouth upon eating, and visual caries on teeth. Universal precautions should be followed when teachers observe bleeding from the mouth or gums. Students with signs or symptoms of dental problems should be referred to the school nurse, and parents should be notified.

Diabetes Mellitus

Diabetes mellitus is a condition characterized by an excess of glucose in the blood, resulting when the pancreas produces too little or no insulin. Diabetes mellitus is often called "sugar diabetes" or just diabetes. **Insulin** is a pancreatic hormone that regulates the sugar in the blood. There are two types of diabetes. Type I diabetes is called juvenile onset diabetes or insulin-dependent diabetes mellitus (IDDM). Type II diabetes is called adult-onset diabetes or noninsulin-dependent diabetes mellitus (NIDDM). Type I diabetes can occur at any age during childhood. It is very rare that a student will develop Type II diabetes. Type I diabetes will be discussed because it is the type that most often occurs in students.

The symptoms of Type I diabetes include frequent urination, thirst, and loss of weight and appetite. There may also be blurred vision, itching, and infections of the skin. These symptoms can progress rapidly. If diabetes is suspected, a school nurse may be able to have a student take a urine test. School nurses have urine test paper strips that can be used to detect diabetes.

Students who have Type I diabetes need to take insulin on a regular basis. In most cases, they will receive doses of insulin at home—in the morning before school and in the early evening after coming home from school. It is important that a student who has Type I diabetes follows a strict diet. Meals are to be eaten at specific times during the day.

As a teacher, it is important to understand that a student who has diabetes can suffer from fluctuations in blood sugar levels. Therefore, any unusual behavior of a student who has diabetes can be indicative of an imbalance of blood sugar. Teachers need to be aware of complications that may occur. The most common complication is hypoglycemia. **Hypoglycemia** is a condition in which the blood sugar is low as a result of excess insulin in the body. The signs and symptoms of hypoglycemia include pale skin, blurred vision, trembling, sweating, and rapid pulse. If symptoms occur, the student should be given a glass of milk or orange juice. This will cause the sugar in the blood to rise. If the student is not treated, (s)he may exhibit symptoms such as confusion, disorientation, and possible unconsciousness.

Another complication of diabetes is diabetic acidosis. **Diabetic acidosis** is a condition in which there is a production of two abnormal acids or a lowering of the alkali in the blood as a result of faulty metabolism. Symptoms include thirst, loss of appetite, increased urination, nausea, and vomiting. Diabetic acidosis is treated with insulin and fluids.

Additional related information is included under **Chronic Health Conditions**.

Drug Abuse

Drug abuse is the use of drugs that results in impairment of a user's ability to function normally or that is harmful to the user or others. One of the most pressing health problems among school-age youth is the abuse of drugs. Drugs most often abused include stimulants, depressants, hallucinogens, marijuana, alcohol, tobacco, and anabolic steroids.

In the classroom, teachers are in a unique position to identify students who have problems that could signal drug use. Through proper inservicing, teachers and other school professionals should be thoroughly trained in how to intervene when they suspect that a student is using drugs. Proper action on the part of teachers or others who suspect drug use is reinforced if a school has enacted clear policies regarding the use and possession of drugs. School staff members should be adequately trained in how to recognize drug use. Signs and symptoms that indicate a student might be abusing drugs are:

- neglect of personal hygiene and appearance;
- depression, irritability, and mood swings;
- decline in academic performance;
- changes in friendships to those who are suspected of using drugs;
- inability to remain alert;
- fascination with drug-related music and drawings;
- stealing;
- possessing drug paraphernalia.

Information for establishing comprehensive school-based drug prevention programs is detailed in **Drugs, Alcohol, and Tobacco: *Totally Awesome*™ Teaching Strategies** by Linda Meeks, Philip Heit, and Randy Page (1995). This book provides training in setting school standards that reinforce the nonuse of drugs; assessing drug-use problems in schools; establishing effective school policies; positive peer programs; resistance training; drug-free activities; student assistance programs; early-childhood programs; working with high-risk students; and inservice programs. A model drug education curriculum also is provided which includes: goals and philosophy; life skills for inner wellbeing; protective factors that promote resiliency; a scope and sequence chart with objectives for grades pre-K through 12; *A Responsible Decision-Making Model; a Model For Using Resistance Skills*; and *totally awesome teaching strategies*™. The drug education curriculum is organized into a sequential spiral of learning in which life skills for inner wellbeing are learned, practiced, evaluated, and reinforced at every grade level. For each objective, there is a specific *Totally Awesome Teaching Strategy*™ in **Drugs, Alcohol, and Tobacco: *Totally Awesome*™ Teaching Strategies**. The table, *Objectives from the Meeks Heit Drug Education Curriculum Guide* (Table 2-2), contains a scope and sequence chart of objectives at every grade level.

Additional related information is included under **Alcohol-Related Problems**.

Table 2-2

Objectives from the Meeks Heit Drug Education Curriculum Guide

Objectives: Pre-K–2

Students will:

1. describe how they are special;
2. identify features that make them unique;
3. identify different feelings they experience;
4. tell how to share feelings in healthful ways;
5. tell ways to cope with stress;
6. practice making choices that promote health;
7. practice ways to say NO to harmful choices;
8. describe ways in which families and friends influence decisions;
9. describe ways to be a good friend;
10. describe ways medicines can be healthful and harmful;
11. describe the harmful effects of tobacco;
12. describe the harmful effects of alcohol;
13. name illegal drugs and their harmful effects;
14. name responsible adults who protect health, safety, school rules, and laws;
15. tell the difference between loving feelings and loving actions.

Objectives: Grades 3–5

Students will:

1. practice ways to improve self-esteem;
2. practice healthful ways to share feelings;
3. select healthful ways to manage stress;
4. practice making responsible decisions;
5. practice using resistance skills;
6. differentiate between healthful and harmful relationships;
7. differentiate between the healthful and harmful use of over-the-counter drugs;
8. describe ways alcohol harms physical, mental, and social health;
9. describe ways tobacco harms physical, mental, and social health;
10. identify illegal drugs and ways they harm physical, mental, and social health;
11. describe how the use of alcohol, tobacco, and illegal drugs interferes with reaching goals;
12. follow school rules and laws related to the use of drugs;
13. identify support groups that assist people and families who need help with alcoholism, smoking cessation, and other drug treatment;
14. interpret messages in the media about drug use;
15. explain why drug use promotes violent behavior.

(Continued)

Source: Meeks, L., Heit, P., and Page, R. (1995) **Drugs, Alcohol, and Tobacco:** *Totally Awesome*™ **Teaching Strategies.** Blacklick, OH: Meeks Heit Publishing Company.

Objectives: Grades 6–8

Students will:

1. develop skills that improve self-esteem;
2. develop ways to manage stress;
3. develop skills needed for healthful and responsible relationships;
4. practice responsible decision-making skills;
5. practice resistance skills when pressured to use or abuse drugs;
6. examine the responsible use of prescription and over-the-counter drugs;
7. evaluate the holistic effects of alcohol on health and well-being;
8. evaluate the holistic effects of tobacco on health and well-being;
9. evaluate the harmful consequences that result from using anabolic steroids;
10. evaluate the effects of illegal drugs on well-being;
11. analyze the ways in which the use of alcohol, tobacco, and other drugs interferes with achieving goals;
12. evaluate the benefits of being drug free;
13. describe the relationship between using intravenous drugs and the transmission of HIV;
14. discuss how the use of drugs interferes with making responsible decisions about sexuality;
15. identify school and community resources involved in the prevention and treatment of drugs, alcohol, and tobacco;
16. describe the relationship between heredity and drug dependency;
17. examine the impact of drug dependency on the behavior of family members and friends;
18. analyze the impact of television, movies, videos, and advertising on the use and abuse of drugs;
19. evaluate the impact of drug use on the incidence of violence;
20. examine ways to support law enforcement to eradicate drug trafficking.

Objectives: Grades 9–12

Students will:

1. engage in activities that promote positive self-esteem and high level wellness;
2. practice stress management skills;
3. select healthful and responsible relationships;
4. differentiate between loving, functional families and dysfunctional families;
5. utilize responsible decision-making skills to remain drug free;
6. practice resistance skills when pressured to use harmful drugs and/or belong to gangs;
7. describe the short-term and long-term effects of harmful drugs on physical, mental, and social health;
8. outline choices that promote the responsible use of over-the-counter and prescription drugs;
9. examine ways in which laws pertaining to the use of alcohol, tobacco, and other harmful drugs help protect personal and community health;
10. examine ways in which the use of alcohol interferes with health and well-being and achieving goals;
11. examine ways in which the use of tobacco interferes with health and well-being and achieving goals;
12. examine ways in which the use of anabolic steroids interferes with health and well-being and achieving goals;
13. examine ways in which the use of illegal drugs interferes with health and well-being and achieving goals;
14. discuss how drug dependency affects family relationships;
15. identify risk factors and protective factors associated with the use of alcohol, tobacco, and illegal drugs;
16. identify risk factors and protective factors associated with violence;
17. describe how to use school and community interventions for the treatment of problems associated with the use of alcohol, tobacco, and illegal drugs;
18. discuss the role citizens can play in eradicating drug sales and trafficking in the community;
19. describe ways in which drug use increases the likelihood of HIV infection;
20. evaluate the effects of using drugs on healthful and responsible sexuality.

© Meeks Heit Publishing Company

Eating Disorders

Eating disorders are food-related dysfunctions in which a person changes eating habits in a way that is harmful to the mind or body. Two eating disorders are anorexia nervosa and bulimia.

Additional related information is included under **Anorexia Nervosa** and **Bulimia**.

Emotional Abuse

Emotional abuse is maltreatment that involves assault in a nonphysical way. For example, excessive verbal assaults may take the form of threatening, yelling, belittling, and blaming. Ignoring a child and not communicating in any way is also a form of emotional abuse. Signs that may indicate that a student is being emotionally abused include:
- The student is depressed and/or apathetic.
- The student exhibits behavioral difficulties.
- The student withdraws from peers.
- The student verbally indicates that (s)he is being emotionally abused.

Just as physical abuse is dangerous, so is emotional abuse. The student may have low self-esteem. The student may believe that (s)he cannot succeed at anything. Students who are emotionally abused are more likely to attempt suicide. Unfortunately, determining emotional abuse may be difficult. Unlike other kinds of abuse, determining emotional abuse is more subjective. If a teacher suspects emotional abuse, the school psychologist or another responsible individual in the school should be notified. A teacher should be aware of his/her school's standard policy for reporting cases of suspected emotional abuse. Counseling may be recommended to assist the family in handling this situation.

Epilepsy

Epilepsy is a condition in which there is a disturbance of impulses in the brain leading to seizures. A **seizure** is an episode during which a person experiences neurological disturbances. A **grand mal seizure** is a major convulsive seizure during which a person drops to the ground, exhibits jerking motions, and stops breathing temporarily. A student may know when a seizure is about to occur because an aura precedes the seizure. An **aura** is a dreamlike state in which there are unusual bodily sensations such as numbness, tingling, or odors. A **petit mal seizure** is a minor seizure during which a person experiences a brief loss of consciousness. (S)he may drop whatever (s)he is holding or, more often, exhibit a very small change such as staring into space, rolling the eyes, or losing the place in a sentence when reading. This type of seizure is also called absence spells. A teacher may view this lapse in a student as inattention rather than epilepsy. In psychomotor epilepsy, a student may experience a jerking of the mouth or face. Consciousness is rarely lost. This type of seizure can last from one to ten minutes.

Witnessing a seizure can be frightening if a person does not know what to do. During a seizure, a student should be protected from injury. Nothing should be placed in the mouth between the teeth. The American Red Cross states that a person rarely bites the tongue.

Additional related information is included under **Chronic Health Conditions**.

Eye Injuries

Eye injuries are irritations to the eye and damage to the eyeball. Sometimes foreign bodies such as dirt and sand get on the eyeball. If a piece of dirt or sand gets on the eyeball, have the student blink several times. If the foreign body is still there, have the student flush the eye with water. Never rub the eye. If the object remains, the student needs to obtain prompt medical attention.

Fainting

Fainting is the partial or complete loss of consciousness that occurs when there has been reduced blood flow to the brain. Fainting is one of the most common sudden emergencies that occurs in the classroom. First aid for a student who has fainted begins with laying the student on the ground. Elevate the legs eight to twelve inches. Loosen any clothing that is restrictive such as a collar or a belt. Do not give the student anything to eat or drink and do not splash water on the face.

Usually the student will recover rather quickly and there will be no lasting effects. However, the student should seek medical care if there are any suspicions about underlying health problems.

Head Injuries

Head injuries are traumatic physical events that involve the head. Most injuries to the head are not serious. But on occasion, a student will suffer a blow to the skull. The student may fall to the ground and hit his/her head. If the student is conscious, keep him/her still. If there is blood flowing from the ear, do not block its flow. Blocking the flow will cause undue pressure to build up on the brain. Keep the student lying flat. Do not move the student in case there is a neck injury. Do not elevate the legs as this will cause increased blood flow to the brain. Do not give the student anything to eat or drink. If the student is unconscious, check the airway to be sure breathing is unobstructed. Get emergency medical assistance immediately.

Additional related information is included under **Eye Injuries**, **Knocked-Out Teeth**, and **Nosebleeds.**

Hearing Loss

Hearing loss is the reduced ability to detect sound. Hearing loss ranges from mild to profound deafness. There are many causes of hearing loss. Causes include prenatal exposure to drugs or infection, premature birth, respiratory distress upon birth, birth defects, certain viral diseases early in life, middle ear infection, high fevers, and accidents. Recurring exposure to loud music, particularly through headphones and walkabout radios and tape players, also can lead to hearing loss.

Mild or moderate hearing impairment may be detected in the school setting by observation as well as through hearing tests. School professionals should be aware that the following may indicate hearing impairment in children: inattentiveness, turning the head to hear, talking loudly or in monotone, failure to respond to questions, and reports of dizziness, ringing in ears, or earache.

Audiometry is the most frequently used hearing test used in schools. The **audiometer machine** is a machine used to assess the range of sounds that student can hear at various frequencies and intensities.

Hearing loss may be classified as either conductive or sensorineural. **Conductive hearing loss** is hearing loss that occurs when sound waves are prevented from reaching the inner ear. Causes can be excessive earwax buildup, damage or malformation of ear structures, or middle ear infection. Hearing aids are most often used to remedy conductive hearing loss, and surgery is often necessary to alleviate situations where damaged or malformed ear structures result in conductive hearing loss. **Sensorineural hearing loss** is hearing loss that results when sound waves are effectively carried to the inner ear but are not conveyed to the brain. In some cases, sound impulses are carried to the brain but the brain fails to interpret the sound impulses. This type of hearing loss is also known as perception deafness. Frequently, little can be done to correct this type of hearing loss. However, recent advances have been made in the development of electrical implants (e.g., cochlear implants) that may allow some people to hear certain sounds.

Heat Emergencies

Heat emergencies are physical conditions that result when a person is exposed to higher than normal temperatures for varying periods of time. Heat cramps, heat exhaustion, and heat stroke are the most common heat-related emergencies. **Heat cramps** are painful muscle spasms that occur most often in the legs and arms due to excessive fluid loss through sweating. A student with heat cramps should rest comfortably in a cool, shaded place and be given cool water to drink. The affected muscle should be stretched lightly and massaged. The student can resume activity when the spasms or cramps subside.

Heat exhaustion is extreme tiredness due to the inability of the body temperature to be regulated. Signals of heat exhaustion include body temperature that is below normal; skin that is cool, moist, pale, or red; nausea; headache; dizziness; and weakness. As soon as a student feels these signals during activities, (s)he should rest in a cool place and drink cool water. If heat exhaustion is not treated, it can progress to heat stroke.

Heat stroke is a sudden attack of illness from exposure to high temperatures. It is the beginning of stoppage of the body functions due to cessation of functioning of normal body temperature. Sweating ceases so that the body cannot regulate its temperature. Body temperature increases. Pulse and breathing rates increase and the skin becomes hot, wet, and dry. The student may feel weak, dizzy, and have a headache. A student who suffers from heat stroke should be placed in a cool environment. If possible, the student should be wrapped in cool, wet towels. A student who suffers heat stroke should receive immediate medical care.

School professionals should be aware that both humidity and temperature contribute to the risk of heat-related emergencies. Students participating in physical activities should rest and drink at least eight ounces of water every twenty minutes.

Hemophilia

Hemophilia is a hereditary disorder characterized by the impaired ability of the blood to clot. As a result, people with hemophilia have an increased tendency to bleed following external or internal injury. Hemophilia is much more likely to occur in males than females. School health services for people with hemophilia include prevention of injury and early identification and care for episodes of bleeding. External bleeding is easy to recognize but internal bleeding is more difficult. Pain in a joint, restricted movement of an extremity, or a limp could indicate internal bleeding.

School professionals should encourage people with hemophilia to realize that they can pursue special interests, participate in a variety of interesting activities, and have fulfilling lives, while still observing their special needs. Classroom teachers, physical education teachers, school nurses, guidance counselors, and other school personnel should be notified of people who have hemophilia. Universal precautions should be followed if bleeding

occurs. During the 1980s, some people with hemophilia became infected with HIV, the virus that causes AIDS, from HIV-contaminated blood transfusions and/or clotting factor. Today, however, due to blood screening procedures implemented in 1985, the risk of HIV infection in the United States through blood transfusions is extremely low.

Additional related information is included under **HIV/AIDS**.

HIV/AIDS

HIV (human immunodeficiency virus) is the pathogen that destroys the body's immune system allowing the development of AIDS. **AIDS** is the acquired immunodeficiency syndrome, the final stage of HIV infection during which there is a significant decrease in the disease-fighting cells inside the body. During this stage the immune system cannot defend the body, leaving the body vulnerable to opportunistic infections. AIDS is one of the most compelling health issues in recent times. Many people use the term AIDS when they mean infected with HIV. When HIV enters the body, a person is said to be infected with HIV. Being infected with HIV does not mean that a person has AIDS. A person has AIDS when the immune system fails and opportunistic infections are present. The following are signs and symptoms that indicate potential HIV infection:

- rapid weight loss for no apparent reason;
- recurring fever or night sweats;
- swollen lymph glands;
- diarrhea that lasts for more than one week;
- white spots or unusual blemishes on the tongue, in the mouth, or in the throat;
- memory loss, depression, and other neurological disorders;
- persistent dry cough or shortness of breath;
- recent appearance of pink or purple blotches under the skin or inside the mouth, nose, or eyelids;
- recurring infections.

HIV is transmitted in different ways. The major methods of transmission in adults include sexual contact with an infected partner and sharing an infected needle to inject intravenous drugs. The most common way

HIV is transmitted sexually is by male-to-male sexual contact. However, the rate of heterosexual transmission is rapidly increasing. Intravenous drug use is the second most common method of transmission. A third mode of transmission involves transmission of HIV from a female who is infected to her baby. This may involve transmission through the placenta to the developing fetus (perinatal), at the time of labor and delivery, and through breast-feeding. A fourth method of transmission involves a person receiving HIV-infected blood through a blood transfusion. This is no longer a common method of transmission because in the United States and industrialized countries, all blood is screened before it is used in a transfusion.

Teachers often have questions pertaining to HIV/AIDS. Should teachers teach about HIV/AIDS in school? Should students who are HIV-infected or have AIDS be permitted to attend school? Can other students in school become infected from the student who has tested positive for HIV or has AIDS? To best understand AIDS-related issues, the teacher needs basic information about this condition.

The federal government and most states have guidelines for school districts to follow regarding HIV/AIDS. Students who are infected with HIV should be allowed to attend school. Students who are infected with HIV and who bite other children, vomit, or cannot control their bowel or bladder should not attend school. School personnel should follow guidelines to protect against infection. Surfaces where bodily fluids are spilled should be wiped immediately with a solution made up one part bleach and one part water. If there is an outbreak of communicable diseases such as flu, students with HIV should not attend school since these students have a weakened immune system. Becoming infected with a communicable disease can be serious for a person infected with HIV. If a student must be excluded from school, that student should receive an alternative education.

To date, education is considered the best way to prevent HIV infection as there is no vaccine currently available. Information for developing and implementing human sexuality curricula is detailed in **Education for Sexuality and HIV/AIDS: Curriculum and Teaching Strategies** by Linda Meeks, Philip Heit, and John Burt (1993). The human sexuality curriculum is organized into a sequential spiral of learning in which life skills for inner well-being are learned, practiced, evaluated, and reinforced at every grade level. For each objective, there is a specific *Totally Awesome Teaching Strategy*™ in **Education for Sexuality and HIV/AIDS: Curriculum and Teaching Strategies**. The table, *Objectives from the Meeks Heit Human Sexuality Curriculum Guide* (Table 2-3), identifies important objectives for covering HIV/AIDS education that were excerpted from the *Meeks Heit Human Sexuality Curriculum Guide* (Meeks, Heit, and Burt, 1993).

Table 2-3

Objectives from the Meeks Heit Human Sexuality Curriculum Guide

Kindergarten
The student will:

- explain what germs are;
- identify ways germs are spread;
- identify ways the body fights germs;
- explain why it is important to have vaccines to stay healthy;
- explain that AIDS is caused by a germ;
- tell that a person with AIDS is very sick;
- identify ways (s)he cannot become infected with HIV;
- explain how to help a friend or family member who has AIDS.

Grade 1
The student will:

- define what a germ is;
- identify a virus as a type of germ;
- discuss that there are different kinds of viruses;
- describe ways that viruses may be spread;
- explain how cells in the body fight germs;
- explain how vaccines help the body to fight germs;
- tell that AIDS is caused by a virus;
- tell that the virus that causes AIDS may be spread through blood;
- tell ways the virus that causes AIDS is not spread.

Grade 2
The student will:

- describe how germs are spread;
- identify ways the body protects itself from germs;
- describe ways the virus that causes AIDS is spread;
- describe ways the virus that causes AIDS is not spread;
- explain why the virus that causes AIDS is dangerous.

Grade 3
The student will:

- describe ways germs are spread;
- explain how T-cells and antibodies help protect a person from illness;
- tell how the virus that causes AIDS is not spread;
- describe how the virus that causes AIDS diminishes the ability of the body to protect itself from other germs.

Grade 4
The student will:

- describe the role of the immune system in protecting the body against disease;
- explain how HIV destroys the immune system;
- identify sexual contact as a means of HIV transmission;
- identify sharing an infected needle to use illegal intravenous drugs, to tattoo, and to pierce ears as a means of HIV transmission;
- recognize ways that HIV transmission is not believed to occur;
- describe the signs and symptoms of AIDS.

Grade 5
The student will:

- explain how HIV is transmitted through sexual intercourse and sharing a needle to inject illegal intravenous drugs, to design tattoos, and to pierce ears;
- describe the impact of HIV infection on the immune system and the ability of the body to protect itself from disease;
- discuss the progression of AIDS;
- discuss ways that HIV infection is not believed to occur;
- discuss ways to show compassion for people with AIDS.

(Continued)

Grade 6
The student will:

- explain how the immune system protects the body against disease;
- explain how infection with HIV diminishes the ability of the immune system to fight infection;
- discuss the transmission of HIV through sexual intercourse and sharing a needle to inject illegal intravenous drugs, to design a tattoo, or to pierce ears;
- explain how a pregnant female who is infected with HIV may infect her baby with HIV prior to or during the birth process;
- discuss ways HIV infection is not believed to occur;
- describe the progression of HIV;
- explain how a diagnosis of AIDS is made;
- explain the impact of the AIDS epidemic on society.

Grades 7-8
The student will:

- describe how HIV destroys the immune system;
- describe risk behaviors and risk situations for HIV infection;
- explain that the latex condom with nonoxynol-9 reduces but does not eliminate the risk of HIV transmission;
- identify ways that HIV infection does not occur;
- explain why a person infected with HIV is susceptible to opportunistic infections;
- describe treatment available to a person infected with HIV;
- identify life skills a person infected with HIV may practice to help keep his/her immune system healthy.

Grades 9-12
The student will:

- differentiate between the terms HIV and AIDS;
- explain how the immune system helps to protect the body from pathogens;
- describe how HIV destroys the human immune system;
- discuss the epidemiology of HIV infection in the United States and the world;
- describe risk behaviors and risk situations for HIV infection;
- identify the diagnostic tests for HIV infection;
- identify opportunistic infections commonly associated with AIDS;
- discuss treatment for a person infected with HIV;
- identify life skills a person infected with HIV may practice to help keep his/her immune system healthy.

Source: Meeks, L., Heit, P., and Burt, J. (1993) **Education for Sexuality and HIV/AIDS: Curriculum and Teaching Strategies**. Blacklick, OH: Meeks Heit Publishing Company.

Impetigo

Impetigo is a highly contagious bacterial infection of the skin. Impetigo lesions are characterized by sores containing clear or yellow-colored fluid that eventually rupture and form a crust. Infection may be spread through person-to-person contact as well as contact with contaminated clothing or bedding. With prompt medical treatment which usually consists of antibiotic therapy, infected persons rarely suffer serious complications. Because of the highly contagious nature of impetigo, students should not attend school until they have taken antibiotics for at least twenty-four hours. School nurses should instruct family members of infected students in ways to reduce transmission of infection and ways to care for impetigo lesions.

Insect Stings and Bites

Insect stings and bites are wounds from bees, spiders, wasps, and other insects. They are often painful, but pain and discomfort are usually the most serious effects. If a student is stung by an insect, the stinger needs to be removed from the skin. Scrape the stinger away from the skin with your fingernail or a thin and sturdy object such as a plastic credit card. Do not remove the stinger with tweezers because there is usually a sac with venom attached to the stinger. The squeeze of the tweezers against the sac can force venom into the body.

After the stinger is removed, wash the affected area with soap and water. Cover the area and keep it clean. You can apply an ice pack to the area to help reduce pain and swelling.

Some students will suffer from allergic reactions when stung by an insect. Every student who is stung by an insect should be observed for thirty minutes for reactions. Many students who are allergic to stings carry special medication, or the school nurse has made arrangements with a student's family for treatment procedures. Immediate treatment is needed if there is an allergic reaction.

In most parts of the country, there are spiders that are extremely dangerous. Two kinds of spider bites that can be fatal are bites from the black widow spider and the brown recluse spider. The black widow spider is black with a reddish hourglass shape underneath its body. The brown recluse spider is light brown and has a darker brown violin-shaped mark on top of its body. If a student thinks (s)he has been bitten by either of these insects, immediate medical care is needed.

Recently, there has been great concern about diseases spread by ticks. Ticks can cause a number of diseases. Two such diseases are Lyme disease and Rocky Mountain spotted fever. **Lyme disease** is a bacterial disease transmitted through a tick. Cases of Lyme disease have been reported in over forty-two states.

The ticks that carry the Lyme disease are commonly carried by field mice and deer. The ticks are very small, as small as a poppy seed. The bacteria that cause Lyme disease can be transmitted through the bite of an infected tick. Usually a rash starts and spreads to be about seven inches across. The center of the rash is light red and the outer ridges are darker red and raised. A student may have fever, headaches, and weakness. When these symptoms appear, prompt medical attention is needed. The sooner medical help is obtained, the better the chances for recovery.

If a tick is found on the body, it should be removed. Grasp the tick with tweezers. Pull it slowly away from the skin. Once the tick is removed, wash the area with soap and water. Observe the site for the development of a rash that resembles a bull's-eye. If symptoms of Lyme disease follow, a physician should be seen. Antibiotics are an effective cure.

Rocky Mountain spotted fever is a potentially life-threatening disease carried by a tick. Although the disease was first discovered in the Rocky Mountain region, cases have been reported throughout the United States. Symptoms include high fever, weakness, rash, leg pains, and coma. If these symptoms appear, immediate medical attention is needed. Effective treatment includes use of tetracycline and other antibiotics.

59

Knocked-Out Teeth

Knocked-out teeth are teeth that have been knocked out of their socket. There are various recommendations on how to respond to this situation. The following recommendation is from the American Red Cross and is to be used for children. Follow universal precautions. Place the tooth in a cup of milk or in water if milk is not available. The student should see a dentist immediately because the sooner the tooth is placed back inside the socket, the better the chance it can be saved. With proper treatment, most knocked-out teeth can be saved.

Learning Disabilities

Learning disabilities are physical or psychological disorders that interfere with learning. A person with a learning disability has difficulty learning basic scholastic skills due to a disorder that interferes with the learning process. Young people who have learning disabilities have special learning needs. Many schools offer individual education plans (IEPs) to meet the special needs of these students. Teachers and counselors work closely with the students' parents, stepparents, and/or guardians. These young people also need to learn coping strategies because their frustration level is frequently high.

Students with learning disabilities often compare themselves unfavorably to peers who do not experience difficulty learning. They may also experience added pressures because they become overly concerned with their futures. It is important for educators to understand the needs of young people with learning disabilities, and to give them the support and encouragement necessary to enhance their self-image. This can be accomplished by providing them with a variety of opportunities to be integrated into school activities and to interact with their peers in positive ways.

Neglect

Neglect is maltreatment that involves lack of proper care and guidance. A parent, stepparent, or guardian may not follow practices that protect a child from injury.

Those who are responsible for caring for them may not provide adequate food, shelter, clothing, or medical care. Neglect may involve not arranging for adequate supervision when adults are away from home. Adults who do not arrange for adequate supervision in their absence leave their children vulnerable to suffer from injury and violence. A student who is neglected may:

• be hungry and appear sleepy;
• wear dirty, smelly, and/or tattered clothing;
• need medical attention.

Conditions in the home in which a neglected student lives may be unsatisfactory: food is lacking or not nutritious, water and electricity are not present, and the living areas are untidy. Some of these conditions exist in many homes, but extreme cases indicate neglect.

For the most part, school districts have specific policies about the reporting of neglect. Most reported cases of neglect will be investigated rapidly. If an investigation indicates that a student is in danger, that student will likely be placed in protective custody or in a foster home.

Additional related information is included under **Child Abuse**.

Nosebleeds

Nosebleeds are loss of blood from the mucous membranes that line the nose. Many students suffer from nosebleeds. Most nosebleeds are caused by a blow to the nose or cracked mucous membranes in the nose. Nosebleeds are usually easy to control. Remember to follow universal precautions for bleeding. Have the student sit with his/her head slightly forward and pinch the nostrils firmly together. Sitting slightly forward enables the blood to flow toward the external opening of the nose instead of backward down the throat. The nostrils should be pinched for about five minutes before releasing. The student should breathe through the mouth. An ice pack may be applied to the bridge of the nose. If the bleeding does not stop, repeat this pressure for another ten minutes. If bleeding persists or serious injury is suspected, obtain medical care immediately.

Pediculosis Pubis

Pediculosis Pubis is infestation with lice. **Lice** are insects that pierce the skin and secrete a noxious salivary secretion that results in itching and swelling. The head louse, which is common in outbreaks among students, attaches itself to the hair of the head, the hairy parts of the body, or clothing. Transmission is by direct contact with a louse-infected person or by indirect contact with an infected person's belongings such as hats or clothing.

Control of head lice requires treatment with lindane lotion or permathrin hair rinse, as well as proper hygiene and thorough laundering of clothing. Lice infestation can be detected by close and thorough inspection by school nurses and teachers. A thorough examination includes observing for lice eggs (nits) that attach themselves to hair shafts. It is critical that students and families who experience lice infestation understand that lice can affect students of all socioeconomic levels and lice infestation is not necessarily a matter of hygiene. Rather, lice infestation is a matter of being exposed through direct or indirect contact.

Physical Abuse

Physical abuse is maltreatment that harms the body. A student who is unusually bruised may be suffering from physical abuse. Bruises may appear on the back, genitals, face, eyes, and/or buttocks. Sometimes the outline of a hand or implement used to cause the bruise is evident. For example, a student may have an imprint of a stick or electrical cord where the contact was made. The bruises may be red or reddish-blue in color. The bruises may be yellow or pale green indicating that the healing process has begun. Sometimes heavy implements are used to inflict pain. A student may have been hit with a baseball bat or a heavy rubber tube. In these cases, bruises may not be evident, yet internal injury to the muscles and internal organs may be evident on an X-ray.

Burn marks are another indication of physical abuse. Burns may result from being forcibly held in hot water. This may be evidenced by burns around the buttocks and genitals when the student has been held in a jackknife position in hot water in a bath tub. Cigarette burns are also common indicators of physical abuse. They are often found on the palms of the hand, soles of the feet, and the back.

Biting is another form of inflicting physical abuse. Any part of the body can be bitten. Usually, bite marks are evident. In many cases, tooth impressions are used as evidence in abuse cases. Other signs that a student has been physically abused include internal injuries, fractures (especially of the long bones), and abrasions on different body parts.

By law, any teacher or health professional must report suspected cases of abuse. For the most part, school districts have specific policies about the reporting of abuse. A teacher who reports a case of suspected abuse has immunity from civil and criminal liability. When an abuse case is filed, the identity of the person doing the reporting remains confidential. Reports of child abuse are often made to child welfare agencies or the police. Most reported cases of child abuse will be investigated rapidly. If an investigation indicates that a student is in danger, that student will likely be placed in protective custody or in a foster home.

Additional related information is included under **Child Abuse**.

Plant Poisoning

Plant poisoning is poisoning that results when a person either comes in contact with or eats certain plants or plant parts. One of the more common types of poisoning that affects school-age males and females is that from contact with poisonous plants that may be growing on or near school grounds. The most common types of plant poisoning result from contact with poison ivy, poison oak, and poison sumac. If a student comes in contact with a poisonous plant, immediately wash the affected area thoroughly with soap and water. If a rash begins to develop, apply wet compresses. Calamine lotion or zinc oxide may help soothe the affected area. If the condition worsens, medical care by a physician will be needed.

Internal plant poisoning in children is most often the result of eating colorful berries. Symptoms of internal plant poisoning may include abdominal pain, vomiting, and breathing difficulties. Medical help should be sought immediately.

Reye's Syndrome

Reye's syndrome is a serious condition, which may follow influenza and chicken pox in children and adolescents, that is characterized by swelling of the brain and damage to liver tissue. Reye's syndrome can lead to permanent brain damage and death. Children and adolescents who are given aspirin to treat their influenza or chicken pox are at increased risk for developing Reye's syndrome. School professionals should counsel parents about Reye's syndrome and the increased risk posed by administering aspirin to a child. Reye's syndrome generally occurs during recovery from an acute viral illness. Symptoms include severe vomiting, lethargy, and coma. If a student exhibits these symptoms, prompt medical attention is needed.

Scabies

Scabies is an infectious skin disease caused by small parasitic mites than burrow themselves under the skin. Scabies infection is found most often in children. Itching is the most common symptom. Frequent locations for scabies infestation are the waist, the armpit, pubic area, face, scalp, arms, and between the fingers. Scabies is transmitted through skin-to-skin contact and through contact with contaminated clothing and other personal articles. Students infected with scabies should not attend school until successfully treated.

Scoliosis

Scoliosis is a deformity of the spine in which the spine shows either a lateral or S-shaped curvature. Scoliosis is found in approximately one in every 50 people. Scoliosis is more common in females than males, and becomes most apparent in young people ages ten to sixteen. Untreated scoliosis can lead to permanent disfigurement. Detection of scoliosis in preadolescence and appropriate referral and treatment often prevent the need for surgery. The most accurate method of determining the presence and severity of scoliosis is an X-ray examination. However, because few children and adolescents visit physicians on a regular basis for physical examinations, and have X-ray examinations when they visit physicians, many schools screen students for scoliosis. The screening technique that is usually used is called the bending test and screening is usually done in physical education classes. This simple test requires an examiner to observe the bare back of a student as (s)he stands erect with his/her feet together and arms hanging naturally to the side (females may wear brassieres). The observer checks to see if the left and right shoulders and shoulder blades are at an even height and to what degree the spine appears to be aligned. Next, the student is instructed to bend forward with the head and arms hanging in a relaxed position. This allows the observer to check for back symmetry and for unevenness on the surface of the back. Students with irregularities should be referred to a physician.

Sexual Abuse

Sexual abuse is maltreatment that involves inappropriate sexual behavior between an adult and a child. Sexual abuse can take many different forms. It can consist of a single incident of sexual contact or prolonged sexual contact between an adult and a child. Kinds of sexual abuse include rape, incest, lewd acts upon a child, oral or genital intercourse, penetration of any object into the genitalia or anus, or any form of sexual molestation. Exploitation can consist of promoting minors to engage in sex acts, using minors to produce pornography, or encouraging and promoting prostitution.

Teachers should be aware of behaviors that indicate a student may have been abused. If a student has only one of the behaviors or signs, sexual abuse may have occurred. If a student has more than one behavior or sign, the likelihood of sexual abuse is increased. The behaviors and signs include:
- the presence of a sexually transmitted diseases;
- pregnancy;
- itching or scratching in the genital or anal area;

- a strong knowledge of sexual terms and behaviors;
- inappropriate sexual acting out with friends and younger children;
- a strong curiosity about sexual matters;
- indirect questions about sexual abuse. For example, during a classroom discussion, a student says, "What could I do if I think a friend of mine is being abused sexually?" Often, students make statements in the third person when, in effect, they are telling you about personal abuse.
- problems with schoolwork;
- poor relationships with peers;
- crying and depression in school;
- attempted suicide;
- fear of using public showers or restrooms;
- difficulty walking or sitting due to pain in the genital area or anus;
- discharge or infection in the genital area.

Incest is sexual abuse in which the abuser is a close relative of the child. Incest is the most common form of sexual abuse. Most often, heterosexual contact takes place between a father, stepfather, or mother's boyfriend and a young female. The second most common type of incest is homosexual contact involving male family members and a younger male. Incest involving a female adult and a child or adolescent is less common.

A student who is sexually abused may have difficulty sharing information about this abuse. The student may fear that his/her parent will be penalized by law enforcement authorities. The student may worry that the family will break up. As a result, the student is reluctant to report the abuse. A student also may feel unjustly ashamed and guilty. However, television programs, articles in newspapers and magazines, and school-based educational programs on sexual assault prompt students to tell someone they have been sexually abused.

By law, any teacher or health professional must report suspected cases of abuse. For the most part, school districts have specific policies about the reporting of abuse. A teacher who reports a case of suspected abuse has immunity from civil and criminal liability. When an abuse case is filed, the identity of the person doing the reporting remains confidential. Reports of child abuse are of-ten made to child welfare agencies or the police. Most reported cases of child abuse will be investigated rapidly. If an investigation indicates that a student is in danger, that student will be placed in protective custody or in a foster home.

Sexually Transmitted Diseases (STDs)

Sexually transmitted diseases (STDs) are diseases caused by pathogens that are transmitted from an infected person during intimate sexual contact. Many adolescents are engaging in behaviors that promote the spread of sexually transmitted diseases (STDs). This has implications for teachers and health professionals.

There are a number of different kinds of STDs that are known to infect adolescents. The major types of STDs, their signs and symptoms, diagnosis, and treatment are reviewed in Chapter 12.

Shock

Shock is a condition in which the blood cannot be circulated to all parts of the body. Any person who suffers an injury should be evaluated for shock. Shock can be caused by any kind of sudden illness or injury. Signals of shock are rapid and weak pulse, rapid breathing, pale or bluish color skin, cool moist skin, nausea, vomiting, drowsiness, or loss of consciousness.

If a student goes into shock, help him/her retain normal body temperature. Place blankets around the student. If no other injury exists, elevate the legs and feet keeping them locked. The legs and feet should be elevated eight to twelve inches while the student lies on his/her back. Do not lie a student on the back if there is head injury or if breathing difficulties or chest injuries exist. Obtain prompt medical attention.

Soft Tissue Injuries

Soft tissue injuries are injuries to the layers of skin, fat, and muscles. The most common injuries among students are injuries to the soft tissues. The most common type of wound is an abrasion. An **abrasion**, or scrape, is an injury in which the skin is rubbed away. Abrasions occur most often at the knees and elbows. The most important concern is infection, because bleeding will usually be minimal. Universal precautions should be followed when treating abrasions. Abrasions should be cleansed with soap and water. Most kinds of soap will be effective in removing harmful bacteria. Other wounds such as lacerations, avulsions (the skin and other soft tissues are torn away), and punctures may need medical attention. Of particular concern is tetanus. **Tetanus** is a bacteria that grows in the body and produces a strong poison that affects the nervous system and muscles. Tetanus may result in lockjaw.

Be aware of signs of infection in any type of wound. The early signs of infection are redness and swelling around the wound. The area around the wound may feel warm and there may be a throbbing sensation present. If the infection is not treated, other signs may be present such as fever and a feeling of illness. Any initial signs of infection should be treated. The wound must be kept clean, a warm compress applied, and an antibiotic ointment applied daily. The coverings over the wound should be changed daily.

Sprains and Strains

Sprains are stretching or partial or complete tearing of ligaments at a joint. Many sprains occur to twisted ankles and knees. The most common symptom of a sprain is pain. Treatment consists of the RICE method. The "R" means rest. Do not move the injured area. The "I" stands for ice. Apply ice to the injured area to help reduce swelling. The "C" stands for compression. Press the ice over the wound. "E" indicates elevation. The injured body part should be elevated above the level of the heart. Some people become confused between a sprain and a strain. A **strain** is a stretching or tearing of muscles, usually due to overexertion. A strain should be treated the same way as a sprain.

Additional related information is included under **Bone Injuries**.

Suicide

Suicide is the intentional taking of one's own life. It is a leading cause of death among children and adolescents. Suicide attempts have been reported in children as young as five years old. Suicide attempts among preteens are increasing. There are a number of reasons why children and adolescents attempt suicide. They may be abused, have difficulty at school, lack love from families, experience separation or divorce of parents, experience the death of a parent, or have poor peer relationships.

Adolescents' reasons for attempting suicide commonly include:
- fights with parents;
- high parental expectations;
- feelings of inferiority;
- difficulty making positive social adjustments;
- friction with peers;
- difficulty at school;
- breakup of a romantic relationship;
- depression;
- academic failure;
- changes in the family;
- death of a parent or a family breakup.

Children and adolescents who are thinking about a suicide attempt will usually give indications. Some of these indications may be through conversations. They may mention they are thinking about suicide. They may mention they are thinking about attempting suicide. They may make statements such as, "I sometimes wish I were dead." or "I'm not important to anyone so why not take my life. No one will miss me." Some students indicate they are considering a suicide attempt by exhibiting certain behaviors. A student who has made a previous attempt is at risk for making another attempt. Students who are contemplating a suicide attempt may plan for their death. They may do things such as give away their valuable possessions to peers or siblings. Other behavioral indicators include extreme changes in mood, feelings of guilt, truancy, involvement with drugs, promiscuity, quitting teams and after school clubs and activities, and aggressive behavior.

A student may share with a teacher his/her intention of making a suicide attempt. If a student confides in you, procedures outlined by the school should be followed. Usually this involves notifying the school counselor who notifies the family. When a crisis is imminent, the student should not be left alone. Most of the time, a student is seeking help and telling a teacher is one way of asking for help. If a student indicates (s)he is thinking of suicide, do not panic. Tell the student you are really concerned about him or her and that you would like to offer your help. In addition to school personnel, there are many different community health agencies such as community mental health agencies that have trained personnel to help the student. The family, school personnel, and mental health professionals work together to support the student and teach the student additional coping strategies.

Visual Disorders

Visual disorders are conditions that adversely affect a person's sight. There are several disorders that affect school-age children and can affect school performance if not corrected. Through vision screenings, school professionals can detect the visual disorders that are discussed in this section. Teachers also are instrumental in detecting visual disorders from observing students who may squint or frequently exhibit postural signs of not being able to see clearly. Poor academic progress, inattentiveness, headaches, reports of double vision, and itching and burning eyes also may be signs and symptoms of visual disorders.

Visual acuity is the clearness of sight. A standard of visual acuity for distance that is frequently used is 20/20 vision. A student with 20/20 vision can read what the average student is able to read at twenty feet. Visual acuity for distance can be measured by standard vision charts such as the Snellen chart. The **Snellen chart** is a chart used for testing visual acuity for distance, in which letters, symbols, or numbers are organized in decreasing size from the top to the bottom of the chart. Visions charts are helpful in detecting myopia.

Myopia is a refractive error of the eye, usually due to an elongated-shaped eyeball, that causes nearsightedness (e.g. a student cannot read numbers on a blackboard). **Refractive errors** are defects in the shape of eye structures that result in the inability of images to focus on the retina. Myopia typically appears in student after age eight and visual acuity can be achieved through the use of corrective lenses such as glasses or contact lenses. Another refractive error that reduces visual acuity for distance is astigmatism. **Astigmatism** is an irregular curvature of the cornea that results in blurred vision. Corrective lenses are used to correct for astigmatism. Another refractive error affecting visual acuity is hyperopia. **Hyperopia** is a refractive error that results in farsightedness (e.g., a student has difficulty reading a book). Corrective lenses also can be used for correcting the acuity of hyperopic student. Visual acuity tests for distance do not effectively detect hyperopia.

Vision testing is recommended for preschoolers because undetected and untreated strabismus and amblyopia can lead to vision loss before age six. **Strabismus** is misalignment of the eyes and commonly referred to as "crossed-eyes." Misalignment is usually due to imbalanced muscles and leads to either a turning in or turning out of an eye. When detected early in life, medical treatment (usually surgery) can correct imbalances in eye muscles. If left untreated blindness in an eye can occur. Another important cause of blindness in student before age six is amblyopia. **Amblyopia** is a condition characterized by dimness of vision in one eye. These visual disturbances cause an amblyopic or misaligned eye to fail to develop and stop functioning. The functioning eye may overcompensate, causing the student to become blind in one eye. Amblyopia is often treated by placing a patch over the functioning eye, which forces the nonfunctioning eye to develop. Corrective lenses and eye exercises are also treatments for amblyopia. The outlook for students who develop amblyopia and strabismus is very positive if detected early and treated promptly.

Bibliography

American Red Cross. (1991) *First Aid: Responding to Emergencies.* St Louis: Mosby Year Book.

Council for Exceptional Children. (1989) Students with specialized health care needs. *ERIC Digest,* Digest #458 (ERIC Document Reproduction Service No. ED 309 590).

Council of Chief State School Officers. (1991) *Beyond the Health Room.* Washington, DC: Council of Chief State School Officers.

Dougherty, D., Eden, J., Kemp, K.B., Metcalf, K., Rowe, K., Ruby, G., Strobel, P., and Solarz, A. (1992) Adolescent health: A report to the U.S. Congress. *Journal of School Health,* 62:167–174.

Dryfoos, J. (1991) School-based social and health services for at-risk students. *Urban Education,* 26: 118–137.

Johnson, M.P., Lubker, B.B., and Fowler, M.G. (1988) Teacher needs assessment for the educational management of children with chronic illness. *Journal of School Health,* 58: 232–235.

Kauffman, J.M. (1993) *Characteristics of Emotional and Behavioral Disorders of Children and Youth.* New York: Macmillan.

Meeks, L., Heit, P., and Page, R. (1993) *Education for Sexuality and HIV/AIDS: Curriculum and Teaching Strategies.* Blacklick, OH: Meeks Heit Publishing Company.

——. (1995) Drugs, Alcohol, and Tobacco: *Totally Awesome*™ Teaching Strategies. Blacklick, OH: Meeks Heit Publishing Company.

Office of Technology Assessment, U.S. Congress. (1991) *Adolescent Health: Volume III—Crosscutting Issues in the Delivery of Health and Related Services* (OTA-H-467). Washington, DC: U.S. Government Printing Office.

Public Health Service. (1991) *Healthy People 2000: National Health Promotion and Disease Prevention Objectives.* DHHS Publication No. (PHS) 91-50213. Washington, DC: U.S. Government Printing Office.

——. (1992) *Healthy Children 2000 National Health Promotion and Disease Prevention Objectives Related to Mothers, Infants, Children, Adolescents, and Youth.* DHHS Publication No. HRSA-M-CH 91-2. Washington, DC: U.S. Government Printing Office.

Thomas, C.F., English, J.L., and Bickel, A.S. (1993) *Moving Toward Integrated Services: A Literature Review for Prevention Specialists.* Portland, OR: Northwest Regional Education Laboratory.

Figure 3-1

A Safe and Healthful School Environment

Schools are responsible for providing an environment that protects the health and safety of students.

Chapter 3

SAFE AND HEALTHFUL SCHOOL ENVIRONMENT:
Protecting the Health and Safety of Students, Faculty, and Staff

Schools are responsible for providing a safe and healthful school environment that optimizes opportunities for learning and growth (Figure 3-1). A **safe and healthful school environment** is an environment that attends to the physical and aesthetic surroundings, and psychosocial climate and culture that maximizes the health and safety of students and staff. In a safe and healthful school environment, potential hazards have been identified and actions have been taken to reduce the potential for illness or injury. Effective action to correct and/or maintain a safe and healthful school environment requires cooperation from all members of the school staff—teachers, administrators, food service personnel, custodians, teacher aides, clerical workers, school nurses—as well as students and parents. A safe and healthful school environment also includes efforts that enhance emotional well-being in staff and students as well as those that eliminate hazards in the physical environment. This chapter discusses providing a healthful school environment, providing a safe school environment, special environmental concerns in today's school environment, and health promotion for staff.

Providing a Healthful School Environment

Environment is the multitude of dynamic conditions that are external to a person. Environment consists of the physical, socio-cultural, familial, emotional, and political conditions and circumstances under which a student lives. All students respond to their environment. Favorable environmental conditions stimulate healthful growth and development; unfavorable conditions impede well-being. Being raised in a loving, functional family is an example of a favorable environmental condition. This circumstance is known to increase a student's potential for remaining violence-free. On the other hand, being raised in a dysfunctional family places a student at risk for being involved in violent behavior because (s)he may not learn the skills necessary to protect herself/himself against pressures to be involved in situations that may become violent.

The environmental conditions at school exert considerable influence upon the well-being of students. Environmental conditions at the schoolsite can be either supportive or nonsupportive. **Supportive environmental conditions** are those circumstances and situations that facilitate healthful choices and/or protect a student's well-being. For example, the serving of healthful foods as part of the school food services program reinforces what students learn in health class about healthful eating. The implementation of procedures that ensure safe transportation to and from school is another example of a supportive environmental condition because it helps protect students from injury.

Figure 3-2

The Physical Conditions
Necessary for Optimal Learning

The following factors maximize the potential for students to learn:

1. School size
2. Lighting
3. Temperature and ventilation
4. Noise control
5. Sanitation and cleanliness
6. Accessibility

Nonsupportive environmental conditions are circumstances and situations that detract from commitments for healthful behavior and could lead to injury, illness, or distress. The availability of junk food in vending machines at a school does not support student efforts to eat healthful foods. Unsafe equipment on a playground is another example of a nonsupportive environmental condition.

This section of the chapter will include a discussion of the physical conditions necessary for optimal learning, positive emotional school environment, the teacher's role in healthful school environment, student involvement, and parent and community involvement.

Physical Conditions Necessary for Optimal Learning

The physical conditions of the school environment play an important role in promoting optimal student well-being. The physical environment increases or decreases the possibility of injuries, the spread of infectious disease, feelings of anxiety and stress, and the potential for learning. School professionals should give serious attention to the following factors in order to maximize the potential of students to learn (Figure 3-2).

School Size School and classroom size are important environmental conditions. However, these are usually conditions over which teachers and other school professionals have little control. Student distraction is more likely to occur in large classes compared to small classes. It is more difficult for teachers to give individualized attention to students when a class is large.

According to recent studies, school size appears to be negatively associated with student well-being. In a study of high school students, those attending large schools reported using illicit drugs, drinking alcohol, and using tobacco more frequently than students from smaller schools (Page, 1991).

Lighting Proper lighting is necessary for reading and other academic work. Electrical lighting is necessary in most classrooms, especially during cloudy days. School professionals should consult with their local health department or power company to determine if lighting is adequate. Illumination is measured in footcandles. A **footcandle** is the amount of illumination from a standard candle on a surface at one foot of distance. General classroom illumination requires 50 to 100 footcandles of illumination and play areas require 30 to 50 footcandles of illumination. Besides the necessity of lighting in order for students and staff to participate effectively in academic work, adequate lighting is useful because it discourages unsanitary conditions and encourages high morale.

Glare is another important consideration in the classroom environment because it detracts from learning and can cause eyestrain that leads to fatigue and tension. A common source of glare in the classroom is the reflection of light off chalkboards or other objects. Inadequately shaded windows is another source of glare. Still another important source of glare is the light from computer screens. Glare problems can often be remedied by simple measures such as rearranging desks or computer stations, not standing in front of open windows when instructing students, avoiding the use of teaching materials with glossy finishes, closing window shades during times of the day when outside light intensity is high, and not placing posters and charts between windows. Other practical guidelines for helping students avoid eyestrain and/or glare in the classroom are:

alternating periods of close eye work with learning activities that rely less on visually demanding tasks; avoiding the use of textbooks and other reading materials with small type; avoiding use of duplicated materials with poor reading quality; writing large numbers and letters on chalkboards; using high-quality chalk for chalkboard writing; maintaining clean chalkboards; and replacing burned out light bulbs or light filaments.

Careful consideration should be given to selecting wall paint that helps create a cheerful, pleasant classroom mood or tone. Certain colors and textures of paint can brighten up a room and, at the same time, maintain a peaceful atmosphere. The use of light colors also is important because it enhances the illumination of the lighting system.

Temperature and Ventilation It is difficult for students to learn in a classroom environment that is too warm, too stuffy, or too cool. Temperatures that are too high deplete energy from students, making the students listless and sluggish. Temperatures that are too low can cause students to be restless and inattentive. Teachers should monitor the temperature of the classroom and frequently ask students if they are comfortable. It is preferable for each classroom to have a thermometer and a thermostat with which a teacher can control the room temperature. Teachers should report temperature and ventilation problems that they cannot control to building principals and/or custodians.

Optimal classroom temperature varies from regions of the country and with the seasons of the year. During the winter, in schools that must be heated, a temperature range of approximately 65 to 70 degrees Fahrenheit is desirable. Because vigorous physical activity causes students to generate more heat, adjustments in room temperature are necessary when students are very active. In gymnasiums, the temperature of 65 degrees Fahrenheit or a few degrees cooler may be optimal. Elementary school students have higher metabolic rates and are more active than older students and adults. As a result, they may be comfortable at a lower temperature than adults. To compensate for this difference, it is often necessary for adults to wear heavier clothing or a sweater in the classroom.

High temperatures and high humidity can make classrooms uncomfortable during the beginning and end of the traditional school year, particularly in southern states. Air temperature, ventilation, humidity, and air freshness are best controlled through central air conditioning systems. Central air conditioning is the ideal, but its high expense makes it prohibitive for many school buildings. Room-type air conditioners provide an option for cooling. However, room-type air conditioners are often noisy, and the noise can make it difficult to carry out classroom activities. In buildings not equipped with air conditioning, teachers should use fans and open windows and doors for cooling. Teachers should make sure that students drink plenty of water to avoid dehydration and should be alert for any signs of heat exhaustion in students.

In addition to temperature control, classrooms and other areas in the school need adequate ventilation or air circulation to provide comfort, remove body odors, and remove indoor air pollutants. Air movement should be only barely felt; stronger air movement can chill or distract students. In areas of the school where arts and crafts are conducted, extra care may be needed to ensure adequate ventilation. Exhaust hood systems or other devices may be needed in areas where there are toxic fumes.

Noise Control Noise control is important in a healthful school environment. Noise can be annoying and distracting, making it difficult for learning to take place. Prolonged noise is stressful for both educators and students and often leads to feelings of anxiety, irritation, frustration, or fatigue.

Classroom noise can be controlled by dampening noise with carpeting, acoustic tile, and other noise-absorbing materials as well as by keeping the noise level of students to a minimum. Other school noise control measures include: building new schools in vicinities with little noise exposure and away from traffic noise; insulating schools from outside noise; locating noisy activity areas (e.g., gymnasiums, shop classes, the lunch room), away from other classroom areas; teaching students to avoid shouting in halls and in school buses; and planting shrubs between the school buildings and traffic areas.

Students need to be taught that exposure to loud noise can lead to hearing loss. They should be required to wear ear plugs when using equipment that emits high noise levels. And school professionals need to alert students to the dangers of listening to very loud noise through portable stereos with headphones. These devices are commonly operated at levels that exceed safety limits and can contribute to hearing loss.

Sanitation and Cleanliness A healthful school is a sanitary and clean school. Sanitation and cleanliness require not only well-trained maintenance staff but also the cooperation of teachers, administrators, and students. **Sanitation** is the protection of health and prevention of disease by means of freeing the environment from filth and infectious material. Sanitation requires cleaning and washing, disinfecting, sewage disposal, waste removal, safe water supply, handwashing, proper food handling and food preservation, and pest control. Personal sanitation procedures such as handwashing should also be stressed for all students and personnel in the school environment. Schools are required by law to maintain a sanitary environment, and, in most states, are regularly inspected by public health sanitarians. Sanitation procedures for dealing with body fluids are provided later in this chapter.

Accessibility Healthful schools are accepting of students with a wide range of physical abilities and make appropriate accommodations in the physical environment whenever possible. Students with physical disabilities often require modifications in the school environment in order to gain access to the classroom, lunchroom, restroom, playground, and other facilities. This access often requires the installation of special equipment or modification of existing physical facilities such as ramps, wider doorways, and elevators. Adjustments in time schedules may also be necessary.

Inspections and Needs Assessment Regularly scheduled school inspections are helpful to detect and assess physical conditions that pose hazards to the health of students and staff. Most schools will receive regular sanitation inspections from the local public health department. In addition to these inspections, it is recommended that schools also

Figure 3-3

The Emotional Environment Contributes to School Health

The **emotional environment** is the set of expectations, interpersonal relationships, and experiences that contribute to the development of the student by way of feeling and sensibilities.

implement a comprehensive environmental inspection that assesses needs and hazards in relation to:
- lighting;
- heating, cooling, and ventilation;
- noise control;
- school food services;
- nutritional standards in the food service program;
- accessibility;
- student and parent involvement in healthful school environment;
- traffic and school bus safety;
- playground safety;
- safety and accident reporting procedures;
- disaster and emergency preparedness;
- liability protection;
- supervision procedures and activities;
- security and violence prevention;
- sexual harassment;
- system for dealing with death of a student or staff member;
- alcohol and other drug policies and enforcement;
- environmental tobacco smoke control;
- procedures for handling blood and other body fluids;
- disaster/emergency preparedness;
- employee health promotion activities.

Inspections and needs assessment activities are helpful only when there is a commitment to correct identified areas of need. Teachers must be advocates for improvements in healthful school environment.

Positive Emotional Environment

The emotional environment of the school setting deserves special attention. The **emotional environment** is the set of expectations, interpersonal relationships, and experiences that contribute to the development of the student by way of feelings and sensibilities (Figure 3-3). The emotional environment is as fundamental to healthful development as is the physical environment.

School Environment

Emotionally warm and nonthreatening learning environments promote health and learning. Threatening school environmental conditions take a toll on students as well as school professionals. School professionals who become stressed or burned out find it difficult to be effective teachers and to be supportive of their students.

The teacher's personality and behavior are important determinants of emotional climate. Teachers should consider the following suggestions as ways to enhance the emotional environment of the classroom:
* have high expectations for student achievement and behavior;
* be an effective listener and observer of students;
* show respect for each student;
* deal with each student as a unique and valuable person;
* model respect, concern, and caring for people of all backgrounds;
* become familiar with the talents and interests of students;
* use firmness, fairness, and friendliness as guiding principles in disciplining students;
* enforce classroom rules;
* give immediate attention to behavioral and disciplinary problems and do not allow pressures to mount;
* give genuine praise and recognition for student achievement;
* provide for more successes than failures in student work;
* have a good sense of humor;
* be optimistic and enthusiastic;
* do not allow students to put down one another;
* promote student involvement in planning individual learning goals;
* make learning fun, relevant, and challenging;
* avoid speaking to students in a harsh or scolding tone;
* give appropriate praise and avoid giving "empty" praise;
* utilize student involvement in instructional planning and classroom management;
* maintain a clean, neat, and orderly classroom;
* allow students to express feelings and attitudes;
* accept your limitations and the limitations of students;
* avoid overly encouraging competitiveness in learning activities and evaluation practices;
* be sure that the demands placed upon students are realistic, meaningful, and appropriate;
* be alert to any behaviors that may indicate emotional problems.

Emotional Security The potential for learning is optimized when students feel secure. Feeling secure means more than physical security but also extends to emotional security. **Emotional security** is a feeling of freedom from anxiety in which individuals feel that they can present and express themselves without fear of ridicule, threat, or belittling. Overt, belittling putdowns are all too common verbal exchanges between students (e.g., "Get a life!" "Hey stupid!"). In childhood, putdowns are overt and direct. As students grow older, putdowns usually take a more subtle form but can just as surely injure one's emotional security.

Putdowns of any form should not be tolerated in the school setting. Without dismissing or ignoring negative behavior, school professionals should systematically look for and praise the good that they see in students and colleagues. This is a very simple concept, yet is often difficult to implement. Many people are more likely to tear others down rather than build others up. The power of being a positive builder of other people is immense. Supportive and affirmative behaviors can be taught and then passed on to others by example. If students and fellow staff members feel caring, compassion, and consideration from another person, they often begin to respond to others within their environment in the same positive manner. Sadly, some students have never had anyone who really cared for them. Feeling cared for is a necessary prerequisite to emotional security. This is an important key to developing supportive, affirming relationships in the classroom and the broader school environment.

The modeling of empathetic behavior by school professionals is an important way to build healthful school environments. Schools need to set high levels of expectation regarding supportive and affirmative behaviors and low tolerance for putdowns. Teaching and modeling these behaviors increases the emotional security through the building of positive, affirming relationships. Positive,

74

affirming relationships form the backbone of a healthful school climate.

Sensitivity to Differences Today's schools are becoming increasingly diverse—composed of students and staff of various skin colors, religious and ethnic backgrounds, and physical, mental, and emotional capabilities. Every student is unique; different from everyone else in some way. Healthful schools promote attitudes of respect, understanding, and sensitivity to these differences. These attitudes are supported when school professionals model respect, concern, and caring for people of all backgrounds. Schools can also foster sensitivity to differences by incorporating opportunities for multicultural understanding into the curriculum. School environments characterized by an openness to differences support students and staff in working through any fears that they may have developed about people who are different from themselves.

Effective Classroom Management Healthful classrooms are characterized by effective classroom management. **Effective classroom management** is the use of managerial skills by teachers to decrease disruptive behavior in the classroom and improve on-task behavior. Effective classroom management is essential because it is associated with student achievement and development of self-control. The ability to organize the classroom and manage student behavior is an important factor in classroom effectiveness and job satisfaction among teachers. Poor classroom management skills are a major cause of teachers' feelings of failure.

An important part of effective classroom management is having clearly defined classroom rules. Clearly defined rules give students a sense of security and help diminish discipline problems. Student involvement in setting classroom rules encourages feelings of control and ownership. A helpful tool in defining rules is a contingency contract that clearly explains classroom policies and procedures. Students commit to adherence to policies and procedures by signing the contract. Penalties and rewards for adherence to rules are clearly stated on the contract along with the consequences. To be effective, rewards must be given out only after the desirable behavior is performed. Rewards must be privileges that are desirable to students. In addition, rewards must be things that cannot be obtained except

by adhering to the established rules and policies.

Discipline is an important part of effective classroom management. **Discipline** is training that corrects and improves student behavior. The goal of discipline is much more than the elimination of disruptive behavior. The goal is the development of self-control. Positive reinforcement is one approach that fosters self-control. **Positive reinforcement** is a training approach in which people are given positive reinforcers immediately following a desired behavior. There are a variety of reinforcers that can be used in classroom settings and can be categorized as social, time, privilege, and tangible reinforcers:

> Social reinforcers would include praise, a smile, a nod of agreement, or a gesture of approval. Time reinforcers might include extra free time, or time spent with the teacher, a classroom aide, or principal. A privilege reinforcer might be an opportunity to be a team captain, to choose the game, to help with equipment, or to be the first in line. Tangible reinforcers include behavior awards, complimentary notes, or stars (Thomas et al., 1988).

Positive Nutritional Environment

Just as important to healthful development as physical environment and emotional environment is the nutritional environment. The **nutritional environment** is the set of conditions that include the school setting, facilities, food services, and attitudes toward healthful food habits that together contribute to the healthful development of the student by way of providing nourishment for growing and developing bodies and minds. For example, it has been shown that eating a healthful breakfast improves academic performance (National Dairy Council, 1993). And some school professionals claim that beginning the day with a healthful breakfast leads to positive behavior changes including less tardiness and absenteeism (Van Leer and Thomson, 1993).

School food services should reinforce healthful eating behaviors by serving meals and snacks that reflect the *Dietary Guidelines for Americans* (see Chapter 9), The Food

Guide Pyramid (see Chapter 9), and provide a variety of healthful food choices (Figure 3-4). To achieve this, school districts need to offer routine nutrition education for food service personnel. In turn, school food service personnel can also work with classroom teachers in providing nutrition education to students. Students should have the opportunity to choose healthful meals and snacks at school—such as salads, fresh fruit, and low-fat offerings. School health service personnel need to work closely with food service personnel in meeting the nutritional needs of students with special nutritional requirements. Many schools now offer healthful foods in vending machines as alternatives to junk food and point-of-choice nutritional information in the school food program.

Nearly 25 million students participate in the National School Lunch Program and 51 percent of school lunch participants receive lunches at no cost or at a substantially reduced price (National Dairy Council, 1992). In addition to lunch, many schools now offer breakfast at school. The School Breakfast Program, which like the National School Lunch Program also is administered by the U.S. Department of Agriculture, serves daily breakfasts to nearly 5 million students in 46,000 schools. Currently, less than half of the nation's schools participate in this program, which offers free and low-cost breakfasts to students from needy families (National Dairy Council, 1992).

The Teacher's Role in Healthful School Environment

Throughout this chapter we discuss many actions that teachers can take to develop supportive environmental conditions within the classroom and school building. The classroom is perhaps the most important aspect of a student's school environment and the aspect over which the teacher has the most control. Teachers should do everything they can to provide a safe, comfortable, and nonthreatening environment in the classroom. However, the classroom is but one part of the total school environment. Teachers also should be an advocate for healthful school environment for their school building and their community. This, of course, is a cooperative undertaking involving many people. As health

Figure 3-4

School Food Services Reinforce Healthful Eating Behaviors

School food services should reinforce healthful eating behaviors by serving meals and snacks that reflect The Dietary Guidelines for Americans.

advocates, teachers will work with other school professionals, students, parents, and community organizations to bring about improvements in the total healthful school environment.

Student Involvement

Students need to take responsibility and become involved to create a healthful school and community environment. Before students can feel responsible, they must develop an attitude of ownership and pride in their school. Such feelings are more likely to develop when there is active student involvement in preserving healthful school environment as well as the community environment. There are many opportunities for student involvement. Here are a few suggestions:
- working on litter cleanup and recycling projects at school and in the community;
- serving on safety patrols;
- writing letters to community leaders about environmental health or safety concerns;
- attending city or county planning meetings to voice concerns about pressing environmental issues;
- forming student committees to address

environmental concerns at the school or in the community;

- fundraising activities for purchasing safe playground equipment.

Parent and Community Involvement

A comprehensive and effective program to improve and protect the health of youth in the United States will require active involvement of families as well as all parts of the community (American Medical Association, 1990). The basic responsibility for the health and vitality of children lies with the family, but families need the support of schools and other community agencies. Schools are an important part of the community that must rely and work cooperatively with other community agencies to meet the needs of students. Another important reason for emphasizing parental and community involvement in the school health programs is because it is highly effective. Because many of the health problems that youth face are complex and multifaceted, (e.g., sexual abuse, substance abuse, depression) they require comprehensive approaches. Countering these health problems requires that young people acquire services that are often outside the ability of the school system to provide, such as health care, mental health, and social welfare.

The focus of this teacher resource is on comprehensive school health education, and this teacher resource has stressed that the responsibility for health is shared with families and communities (Figure 3-5). In order for the comprehensive school health education program to work effectively, integration with community health promotion efforts is required. Successful integration requires careful planning, interaction, cooperation, and programming. The input of various community agencies, members, and leaders is fundamental to this process. This is often facilitated through forming school health advisory committees and community health councils. These coalitions can help build support for the school health program and pave pathways for successful school-community health promotion ventures. School-community health coalitions should strive to bring together organizations and agencies from several community sectors, including: education, government, voluntary health agencies, health care

Figure 3-5

The Responsibility for Health is Shared

School personnel, students, parents, families, community members, local government, and local health agencies must work together to protect the health of students.

providers, charitable organizations, businesses, and parents.

Providing a Safe School Environment

The potential for accidents happening in the school environment is a concern. Schools serve a large number of students for many hours a day. School personnel are responsible for the safety of students at school and during school activities. They share in the responsibility of keeping students safe as they travel to and from school. In addition, the safety of all people who work and visit the school must be protected.

Some school districts are able to employ a safety director or supervisor who can oversee the total school safety program. Other districts or individual schools form safety councils to supervise these activities. Safety councils are formed with representation from teachers, administrators, school support staff, parents, and students. Safety councils establish sound safety policies, procedures, and programs.

School Environment

Teacher Responsibilities

This section of the chapter discusses teacher responsibilities, safe school transportation, safe playgrounds, and disaster and emergency preparedness.

Classroom teachers have primary responsibility for instructing students about safety, but they also have other major responsibilities in the school safety program. These responsibilities are:

- properly reporting any accident or injury in or around the school;
- assessing and correcting potential safety hazards in the classroom and total school environment;
- providing proper first aid care to injured students or school employees;
- assisting students and other school personnel in the safe transportation of students and school employees to and from school;
- establishing safety procedures in the classroom;
- providing appropriate supervision of students at all times.

Liability Protection and Safety Guidelines Elementary and secondary teachers are increasingly becoming aware that the law defines, limits, and prescribes many aspects of a teacher's daily life. This is an age of litigation. As such, grievances are often brought forth against schools and teachers in the courts, and newly formed legislation seems to be regulating more of school life. In addition to the growing number of local, state, and federal laws, there is a confusing array of complex case law principles that add to the confusion.

The major aspect of safety liability cases stem from charges of negligence relating to a teacher's failure to supervise properly in accordance with his/her *in loco parentis* obligation (to act "in the place of the parents"), contractual obligation, and professional responsibility. **Negligence** is the failure to conduct oneself in conformity with standards established by law for the protection of others against unreasonable risk of injury. While courts of law do not expect teachers to protect students from "unforeseeable accidents" or "acts of nature," they do require teachers to act as a reasonably prudent teacher should in protecting students from possible harm or injury.

Teachers are responsible for exercising good judgment in providing adequate supervision of the students in his/her charge. A teacher may be found by a court not to have acted in a reasonably prudent manner when (s)he exercised his/her duties with carelessness, lack of discretion, or lack of diligence. When an injury results, the teacher may be held liable for negligence as the cause of the injury to the student.

There are several guidelines that teachers should follow in order to avoid injuries and civil liability:

- establish and enforce safety rules for all school activities;
- be familiar and informed about school, district, and state rules and regulations that pertain to student safety;
- enforce rules whenever violations occur;
- be familiar with the liability laws of the state in which the school is located;
- be aware of the type of insurance policy provided by the district by which the teacher is employed;
- if the school district has no policy, invest in a personal policy for personal protection (the National Education Association, American Federation of Teachers, and many insurance companies offer policies);
- become certified in first aid and maintain that certification;
- always provide adequate supervision of students for all school-related activities;
- provide higher standards of supervision when students are younger, handicapped, or when engaged in potentially dangerous activities;
- ensure that all equipment used in school activities is in correct working order and checked for safe operation;
- be at the assigned place at all times;
- make appropriate arrangements for supervision when it is necessary to leave the classroom or the assigned place of responsibility;
- inform substitute teachers about any unusual medical, psychological, or handicapping conditions of students placed under their supervision;
- plan field trips with great care and be sure to provide adequate supervision;
- do not send students on errands off the school grounds;
- be sure to file an accident report whenever an accident has occurred to a student under their supervision.

Figure 3-6

The Accident Report

Accident reports should provide the following information:
- name, age, grade level, and gender of injured student(s) or staff;
- home address of the injured person;
- specific date and time that the accident occurred;
- specific location where the accident occurred;
- detailed description of the nature and degree of the injury and how the injury occurred;
- description of what the injured person was doing, unsafe acts or unsafe conditions, equipment involved, etc.;
- who was present when the injury occurred;
- teacher or school professional in charge when injury occurred;
- whether parent or other individual was notified;
- immediate action taken;
- date of student's or employee's return to activity.

Reporting Accidents It is important for teachers and other school professionals to complete and file accident reports following any injury (Figure 3-6). Accident reports not only protect school and school employees in liability suits, but also can be helpful in identifying and correcting hazardous conditions at the schoolsite (Bever, 1992). Accident reports also are useful because they can provide information for evaluating the school safety program. Accident reports should provide the following information:
- name, age, grade level, and gender of injured student(s) or staff;
- home address of the injured person;
- specific date and time that the accident occurred;
- specific location where the accident occurred;
- detailed description of the nature and degree of the injury and how the injury occurred;
- description of what the injured person was doing, unsafe acts or unsafe conditions, equipment involved, etc.;
- who was present when the injury occurred;
- teacher or school professional in charge when injury occurred;
- whether parent or other individual was notified;
- immediate action taken;
- date of student's or employee's return to activity.

Witnesses of the accident should be noted and asked to sign the accident report. The signature of the school professionals completing the report and the principal also should be included on the report.

Safe School Transportation

Students travel to and from school by walking, riding bicycles, and riding in automobiles and school buses. School professionals must work in conjunction with students, parents, and the broader community to ensure safe school transportation. Schools and communities should consider the following suggestions in order to protect students as they travel to and from school (Bever, 1992; Wilson et al., 1991):

- place adult crossing guards at busy intersections;
- provide sidewalks and other walkways separated from traffic;
- design communities to minimize street crossing;
- prohibit parking where students are most likely to cross streets;
- provide students with reflectors and clothing that can be easily seen;
- use warning signs and speed bumps;
- provide crossings that are safer and easier, such as midblock traffic lights near schools;
- enforce speed limits in areas frequented by students;
- pass and/or enforce laws requiring traffic to stop when a school bus is taking on or discharging passengers;
- train students in street-crossing strategies;
- teach students not to dart out into the street between intersections;
- establish safe bike and walking routes;
- promote bicycle helmet use;
- institute school regulations requiring bicycle helmet use;
- make bicycle helmets inexpensive and easy to obtain;
- separate bicycle riders from motor vehicle traffic through the use of bicycle paths, bikeways, and physical barriers;
- provide bicycle safety training;
- discourage excessive speed, stunt riding, and riding double on bicycles;
- provide safe places where students can go if they get lost or are threatened with violence;
- support regulations requiring the installation of safety restraints on school buses;
- provide state-of-the-art safety features on school buses;
- carefully select and screen school bus drivers;
- provide adequate training for school bus drivers;
- conduct regular mechanical maintenance of school buses;
- avoid overcrowding and do not tolerate disruptive behavior on school buses;
- avoid locating bus stops in hazardous locations;
- train students in proper procedures for boarding and exiting school buses;
- prohibit teachers or other school professionals from transporting students in personal vehicles;
- promote safety restraints use when riding in motor vehicles.

A high proportion of school-related pedestrian fatalities occur as students either approach or leave a pickup or drop-off point. All schools should have well-developed plans for safe pickup and drop-off points and pedestrian crosswalks in the school vicinity. Pickup and drop-off of students should occur only at the curb or at an off-street location protected from traffic. Adequate supervision should be provided to assist students during boarding and exiting all vehicles by an adult who ensures that students are buckled into a safety restraint and are clear of the path of the vehicle after exiting (American Public Health Association and American Academy of Pediatrics, 1992).

Safe Playgrounds

More injuries occur to elementary students on the playground than in any other area of the school (Figure 3-7). Therefore, providing a safe school environment requires close attention to playgrounds and playground equipment. Schools are responsible for providing safe playground equipment, adequately supervising students on the playground, instructing students about safety on the playground, and providing prompt emergency care when students are injured.

The most common cause of playground equipment injuries is from falls or jumps from swings or slides to the surface below. The type of surface that students fall on is an important factor in the likelihood and severity of injury as is the height of the apparatus. Falls on pavement are much more likely to result in injury than falls on grass

Figure 3-7

Safety on Playgrounds

More injuries occur to elementary school students on the playground than in any other area of the school.

or dirt or specially designed protective surfaces. Other serious playground equipment injuries are those that involve strangulation by hanging in ropes or chains, falling onto a sharp protrusion, entrapment of a finger or head in a small space or angle, or impact with moving or collapsing equipment (Wilson et al., 1991).

School professionals should see that school playgrounds and playground equipment adhere to the following standards (Bever, 1992):
• adequate supervision is provided;

• horseplay and inappropriate behavior is discouraged;
• older and younger students are separated;
• students are instructed in the safe use of playground equipment;
• handrails or guardrails are provided for steps and platforms;
• surfaces on equipment are slip-resistant;
• energy-absorbing materials underneath climbing equipment are in place;
• the height of playground equipment is limited;
• equipment is inspected for protrusions that could injure a falling student or into which a student could run;

- moving equipment (i.e., swings) is arranged so that students cannot collide with it;
- all pieces of playground equipment are designed to guard against entrapment or situations that may cause strangulation;
- the velocity of moving equipment is controlled;
- enclosures on the top of high equipment are provided to avoid falls;
- any dangerous equipment is removed;
- the condition of playgrounds and playground equipment is maintained;
- comfortable seating for adults is provided to encourage close adult supervision;
- written policies for maintaining playground safety are developed that include procedures for supervision, playground rules, playground maintenance, and injury-reporting procedures;
- monthly routine inspections of playgrounds are conducted;
- play areas accessible to students who are handicapped are provided;
- the soil in play areas is tested to make sure that it does not contain any toxic chemicals or substances;
- coating or treating outdoor play equipment with toxic materials is avoided;
- the playground is checked daily for broken glass, trash, and other foreign materials.

An important resource for use in planning playgrounds is *Public Playground Handbook for Safety* from the U.S. Consumer Product Safety Commission. This handbook presents specific safety guidelines for playground equipment and is intended for use by school officials as well as others concerned with playground safety.

Disaster and Emergency Preparedness

Schools must be prepared to deal with a variety of natural or human-made emergencies: severe weather, fire or explosion, earthquake, a hostage crisis, bomb threat, and other unforeseen emergency situations. Every school must be ready to take action in the event of such emergencies. Planning in advance of an emergency situation is of paramount importance. This requires formal planning and testing of procedures to maximize the safety of students and staff. School districts are urged to develop emergency plans through the use of emergency planning committees. **Emergency planning committees** are committees established for the purpose of developing and implementing school emergency plans. Emergency planning committees function best when coordination and participation is from the:

- superintendent's office;
- Board of Education;
- principals from each of the levels of schools within the district;
- teachers;
- transportation personnel;
- buildings and grounds personnel;
- health services;
- food services;
- students;
- parents;
- community chief executive's office;
- fire department;
- emergency medical service;
- police agency.

School emergency plans should be developed at three levels: district, building, and classroom. A district-wide plan includes general procedures for district personnel to follow when an emergency affects any of the schools within the district's boundaries. The building-level plan should be consistent and compatible with the district-wide plan and specify school procedures to be utilized by an individual building's response to an emergency. At the classroom level, specific step-by-step procedures for teachers and staff during various kinds of emergencies should be detailed. Emergency preparedness plans should be periodically reviewed, tested, and updated (New York State Disaster Preparedness Commission, 1990).

After a plan is developed, students and staff should be trained in response techniques that are consistent with the emergency plan. Training should be provided for school staff who have been assigned specific roles and areas of responsibility in the emergency plan. This training should be conducted annually to ensure that school staff and students understand emergency procedures and to include any changes to school plans. Training also should be coordinated with local emergency management and emergency services personnel in the community. Many school districts use emergency simulations in training students and staff (New York State Disaster Preparedness Commission, 1990).

Special Concerns in Today's School Environment

School professionals face a number of emerging health concerns that professionals in the past did not face. This section addresses the following concerns in schools: violence, sexual harassment, drug use, environmental tobacco smoke, and bloodborne diseases.

Violence

Educators across the nation are grappling with the problem of protecting students and school staff from the violence surrounding them. Violence is now one of the foremost school concerns. Incidences of violence in schools are occurring more frequently. Educators are faced with the issues of assaults, rapes, suicide, gang membership, and weapon-carrying in their schools (Meeks, Heit, and Page, 1995).

Violence is not limited to secondary schools. Episodes of violence involving elementary students are also on the increase. It is a concern that is no longer limited to large urban areas, but extends to smaller cities and rural areas as well (Morganthau, 1992). An increasing number of students and adolescents are not only becoming victims of violence but also are routinely witnessing violence in their communities (Fitzpatrick, 1993). Four of every ten inner-city children age seven to nineteen say that they have actually witnessed a homicide (Morganthau, 1992). Seven of every ten inner-city Chicago students report that they have witnessed a murder, shooting, stabbing, or robbery—half of which involved friends, family members, classmates, or neighbors (Bell, 1991). Beyond the obvious threat that violence poses to student's personal safety, violence also poses another potential problem for schools. The threat of violence adversely interferes with student's development and learning potential. When students constantly confront the threat of violence at home, school, or in the community, they must learn to protect themselves by setting up defenses against their fears. These defenses take considerable emotional energy, thus depleting the energy needed for other developmental tasks including learning in school (Wallach, 1993). The presence of violence in the home is often associated with feelings of guilt and responsibility on the part of young people, with consequent feelings of being bad or worthless. These feelings are not compatible with a student's potential for learning, and commonly result in feelings that one is incapable of learning. This, in turn, contributes to a lack of motivation to achieve in school (Wallach, 1993).

Students who face the threat of violence or who have suffered trauma from violence have difficulty seeing themselves in meaningful future roles. Students who cannot perceive a positive and secure future for themselves are unable to give serious attention and energy to the tasks of learning and socialization. The unpredictability of violence contributes to a sense of little or no control over one's life. Such a sense of helplessness interferes with the development of autonomy, essential for healthful growth and maturation (Wallach, 1993).

Teachers increasingly report feeling threatened by the possibility of violence. These feelings of fear negatively impact their ability to teach effectively. It is estimated that one in five teachers has been threatened by students (Morganthau, 1992).

Figure 3-8

Goal Six of the National Education Goals for the Year 2000

Every school in the United States will be free of drugs, violence, and the unauthorized presence of firearms and alcohol and will offer a disciplined environment conducive to learning.

Today's schools must implement policies that build a violence-free school environment for students, staff, and others who come on school premises. Goal Six of *The National Education Goals for the Year 2000* (U.S. Department of Education) states that every school in America will be free of drugs and violence and will offer a disciplined environment conducive to learning (Figure 3-8). Schools that are capable of fostering learning and healthful development must be free from violence and crime, drugs and drug dealing, and students who carry weapons. For some school systems, this may mean providing such controls as locker searches, hiring police to patrol school premises, and having metal detectors that students must pass before entry. Some school systems have even created separate alternative schools for young people with a history of violent and abusive behavior. While this option is attracting attention as a

means to deal with violence, it is also controversial (Harrington-Lueker, 1992).

National health objectives target a reduction in the incidence of weapon-carrying by youth. When weapons, especially firearms, are carried into schools, the potential for violent episodes to occur escalates. There have been far too many violent episodes involving weapons on school campuses that have led to tragedy in recent years (Morganthau, 1992).

School security and law enforcement officials estimate that four of every five firearms that are carried into schools come from the students' homes. Often guns find their way into schools when young people bring one of their parent's firearms to show friends. Law enforcement officials also explain that firearms are easily accessible by other means. They are also readily borrowed from friends, bought by proxy, stolen, or even rented. Guns may be purchased on the street for as little as $25, an amount that many youth can easily afford. Once a gun is readily accessible, a youth can easily bring it to school (Harrington-Lueker, 1992). The ready access of firearms can be particularly dangerous for young people. Young people often use guns for solving seemingly trite problems that they face—a beef over something someone said, a fallout over a girl, a suspected slight, a pair of sneakers, a football jacket. (Harrington-Lueker, 1992) Guns also are increasingly being used by young people against older and/or larger students who had a history of bullying or intimidating them. Thus, guns are used as an "equalizer."

Sexual Harassment

Sexual harassment is not just a problem for adults at the worksite; it also occurs to children and adolescents in schools. Within schools, sexual harassment is not limited to adolescents; recent media accounts have focused on students in elementary grades being subjected to severe acts of harassment. **Sexual harassment** is unwanted and unwelcome sexual behavior. Sexual harrassment interferes with a student's right to get an education or to participate in school activities. Sexual behavior that constitutes harassment consists of conduct and words that sexually offend, stigmatize, or demean a student. Examples of sexual harassment include (Stein, 1993):

- touching, pinching, and grabbing body parts;
- sharing sexual notes or pictures;
- writing sexual graffiti;
- being cornered, forced to kiss someone, or coerced to do something sexual;
- making suggestive or sexual gestures, looks, verbal comments, or jokes;
- spreading sexual rumors or making sexual propositions;
- pulling someone's clothes off;
- pulling your own clothes off;
- attempted rape and rape.

Students deserve a school climate that does not tolerate sexual harassment. Students should be reassured that their school officials have taken steps to stop sexual harassment from happening in the first place and that, if it does happen, immediate actions will be taken to intervene. When school officials fail to respond appropriately, students may develop feelings that "they are incapable of standing up to injustice or acting in solidarity with peers who are being harassed or bullied" (Stein, 1993). The silence of adults in schools about sexual harassment constitutes negligence and violation of Title IX, a federal law prohibiting harassment and sexual discrimination in schools. Schools should develop and enact policies that clearly define what constitutes sexual harassment.

Students, staff, and parents should know exactly what constitutes sexual harassment and the consequences offenders will face. Students and parents should be informed of what actions to take if a student feels that (s)he is a target of harassment. Recommended actions for students to take include telling someone who will believe them, finding people who will support them (particularly parents), avoiding self-blame, maintaining a written record detailing incidents, saving any notes received from a harasser, reporting incidents to the person at their school responsible for dealing with sexual harassment, clearly informing the harasser that they do not like the behavior, and knowing their rights to file a complaint or lawsuit (Stein, 1993).

Drug Use

One of the eight *National Education Goals for the Year 2000* calls for all U.S. schools to be free of drugs. The best way that a school can prevent students from using drugs is simply to be a good school. This means having a challenging curriculum; high expectations for all students; dedicated, knowledgeable teachers; energetic administrators; high degree of parent involvement; and an orderly, disciplined learning environment.

In addition to offering a comprehensive drug prevention curriculum at all grade levels (see Chapter 2 for more information), schools should supplement and reinforce their drug-free curricula by: assessing drug-use problems, establishing and enforcing drug-free school policies; offering positive peer programs; offering drug-free activities; and establishing drug-free school zones.

Assessing Drug-Use Problems in Schools
School personnel should be informed about

the extent of drug use in their school. School boards, superintendents, and other public officials should support school administrators in their efforts to combat them. To guide and evaluate effective drug prevention efforts, schools need to take the following actions:

- conduct anonymous surveys of students and consult with local law enforcement officials to identify the extent of drug problems;
- bring together school personnel to identify areas where drugs are being used and sold;
- meet with parents to help determine the nature and extent of drug use;
- maintain records on drug use and sale in the school over time, for use in evaluating and improving prevention efforts. In addition to self-reported drug-use patterns, records may include information on drug-related arrests and school discipline problems.

School Policies Clear policies regarding use and possession of alcohol and other drugs both on and off school property are critical to all members of the school community. Parents, school officials, students, law enforcement officials, and drug and alcohol professionals should all be involved in the development of the policies to make them most effective. School policies should clearly establish that drug use, possession, and sale on the school grounds and at school functions will not be tolerated. These policies should apply both to students and to school personnel, and may include prevention, intervention, treatment, and disciplinary measures.

School policies should:
1. Specify what constitutes a drug offense by defining:
   - illegal substances and paraphernalia;
   - the area of the school's jurisdiction: for example, the school property, its surroundings, and all school-related events, such as proms and athletic events;
   - the types of violations (drug possession, use, and sale).
2. State the consequences for violating school policy. Punitive action should be linked to referral for treatment and counseling. Possible measures to deal with first-time offenders include the following:
   - a required meeting of parents and the student with school officials,

concluding with a contract signed by the student and parents in which they both acknowledge a drug problem and the student agrees to stop using drugs and to participate in drug counseling or a rehabilitation program;
- suspension, assignment to an alternative school, in-school suspension, afterschool or Saturday detention with close supervision, and demanding academic assignments;
- referral to a drug treatment expert or counselor;
- notification of police.

It is important that established policies are enforced fairly and consistently. Further, adequate security measures are needed to eliminate alcohol and other drugs from school premises and school functions. It is important that everyone understands the policy and the procedures that will be followed in case of infractions. Copies of the school policy should be made available to all parents, teachers, and students, and the policy should be throughout the school and community. In addition, strict security measures to bar access to intruders and to prohibit student drug trafficking should be imposed. Enforcement policies should correspond to the severity of the school's drug problem.

Positive Peer Programs Positive peer programs utilize student peers as role models, facilitators, helpers, and leaders for other students, particularly in grades seven through twelve. Programs such as these can provide help to young people who are having problems, who are undergoing normal adolescent stresses and want to confide in someone, and who want to participate in school and community service activities. School administrators must be prepared to provide extensive support and guidance in order to ensure successful implementation of peer programs.

Drug-Free Activities If students are expected to lead drug-free lives, schools must provide them with appealing alternatives. Activities can help relieve the boredom that tempts many young people to become involved with drugs, as well as provide them with responsible adult supervision. Another positive aspect of such activities is that they provide young people with a sense of camaraderie and community that can compete with the appeal of youth gangs and drug trafficking networks.

Figure 3-9

Drug-Free Activities

- Dances
- Rap contests
- Drama events
- Carnivals
- Lip sync contests

- Talent shows
- Food fairs
- Fashion shows
- Beautification projects
- Street fairs

Many schools have begun to offer alcohol- and drug-free after-prom parties, graduation parties, and other school-based celebrations that allow young people to have fun without exposing them to negative peer pressure. Local businesses also are an excellent source of support for alternative activities such as athletic teams or part-time jobs. Other ideas for drug-free activities include (Figure 3-9):
- after-school and weekend activities;
- dances;
- rap contests;
- drama events;
- carnivals;
- lip sync contests;
- talent shows;
- food fairs;
- fashion shows;
- beautification projects;
- street fairs.

Drug-Free School Zones Many communities have established drug-free zones around schools and other areas where young people congregate. A **drug-free school zone** is a defined geographic area around a school for the purpose of sheltering youth from the sale

School Environment

of controlled substances (Figure 3-10). Drug-free school zones show a united front of schools, students, parents, and communities in working together to establish drug-free schools and communities by decreasing drug trafficking around schools (Thomas, 1992).

Increased penalties for selling and using drugs have been established for drug-free school zones. The basis for drug-free school zones is the federal Drug-Free Schools and Communities Act which states:

> Any person who distributes or manufactures a controlled substance in or on, or within one thousand feet of a public or private elementary, vocational, or secondary school or a private college, junior college, or university, or within 100 feet of a playground, public or private youth center, public swimming pool, or video arcade facility, is punishable by a term of imprisonment, or fine, or both up to twice that authorized by existing federal law, and at least twice any term of supervised releases authorized by existing federal law for a first offense. (Section 845a[a]).

Establishing drug-free school zones is an important way to show drug dealers that drugs are not tolerated in a school and/or community. In many areas, drug-free school zones extend within and around a 1,000-foot perimeter of school property, school buses, and school bus stops and routes. Drug-free school zones are often designated by signs declaring areas as drug-free (Thomas, 1992).

Environmental Tobacco Smoke

Environmental tobacco smoke is the combination of sidestream smoke and the mainstream smoke exhaled by a smoker. There is consensus among medical scientists and public health professionals that environmental tobacco smoke (ETS) is a significant cause of health problems in nonsmokers. Environmental tobacco smoke is a cause of lung cancer and chronic obstructive pulmonary disease in healthful nonsmokers. More nonsmokers die as a result of exposure to environmental tobacco smoke than from exposure to any other pollutant. Approximately 50,000 deaths are attributed annually to environmental tobacco smoke. About 3,000 of these deaths are due to lung cancer.

The group most affected by environmental tobacco smoke is children. Children exposed to environmental tobacco smoke are at increased risk of respiratory and middle ear infections, reduced air flow, and asthma. The increased vulnerability of children to environmental tobacco smoke makes them a high priority for efforts to protect nonsmokers.

Local schools boards should enact regulations requiring all public elementary and secondary schools be 100 percent smoke-free. Teachers, school nurses, parents, and students can be advocates for tobacco-free school environments in localities that allow tobacco smoking at the schoolsite. A tobacco-free school environment is important for at least two reasons. First, a tobacco-free environment protects students during the time they spend at school. Second, a tobacco-free school environment reinforces anti-tobacco messages taught in the health classroom.

Over 90 percent of school districts have written policies with some restriction on smoking. Yet, only 40 percent of school districts have written policies that provide for a total ban of smoking on school grounds. While only a very small proportion of school districts (4 percent) allow students to smoke in areas designed for smoking, 43 percent permit staff members to smoke in such areas (D'Onofrio and Altman, 1993).

Bloodborne Pathogens

The Federal Occupational Safety and Health Administration (OSHA) requires employers to protect employees from occupational exposure to bloodborne pathogens. **Bloodborne pathogens** are pathogenic microorganisms that are present in human blood and can cause disease. The two most important bloodborne pathogens are the human immunodeficiency virus (HIV) and the hepatitis B virus (HBV). **Occupational exposure** is the reasonably anticipated skin, eye, mucous membrane, or parenteral contact with blood or other potentially infectious materials that may result from the performance of an employee's duties. **Parenteral contact** is the piercing of mucous membranes or the skin barrier through such events as needlesticks, human bites, cuts, and abrasions (scrapes). The American Public Health Association and American Academy of

Figure 3-10
A Drug-Free School Zone

A **drug-free school zone** is a defined geographic area around a school for the purpose of sheltering youth from the sale of controlled substances.

Pediatrics (1992) point out the potential risk of various body fluids:

...blood and direct blood-derived fluids (such as watery discharges from injuries) pose the highest potential risk, by virtue of containing the highest concentration of viruses. In addition, hepatitis B virus can survive in a dried state in the environment for at least a week and perhaps even longer. Some other body fluids–may contain live virus (with hepatitis B virus) but at lower concentrations than are found in blood itself. Other body fluids, including urine and feces,

do not pose a risk with these bloodborne diseases unless they are visibly contaminated with blood, although these fluids do pose a risk with other infectious diseases...

OSHA requires that employers, including school districts, institute a comprehensive program to decrease employee exposure to bloodborne pathogens. This requires adopting universal precautions as an approach to infection control. **Universal precautions** are the steps taken to prevent the spread of disease by treating all human blood and certain body fluids as if they are known to be infectious for HIV, HBV, and other bloodborne pathogens. Universal precautions are applicable for anyone who may be exposed to blood or other potentially infectious body fluids. The OSHA regulations that are required of employers include:

- developing a written exposure control plan and making it available to all employees;
- reviewing and updating the exposure control plan at least annually;
- preparing an exposure determination that lists all of the work tasks and procedures in which occupational exposures occur and a list of all job classifications in which employees in those job classifications have occupational exposures;
- providing annual training during regular work hours to all employees who potentially could be exposed to blood or other potentially infectious materials;
- providing appropriate personal protective equipment to employees at no cost to the employees (examples of protective equipment are gloves, gowns, face shields or masks and eye protection, and mouthpieces, resuscitation bags, pocket masks, or other ventilation);
- providing handwashing facilities that are readily accessible to employees;
- ensuring that employees wash their hands immediately or as soon as feasible after removal of gloves or other personal protective equipment;
- ensuring that employees wash hands and any other skin with soap and water, or flush mucous membranes with water immediately or as soon as feasible following contact of such body areas with blood or other potentially infectious material;
- prohibiting contaminated needles and other contaminated sharps to be bent, recapped, or removed (recapping of needles is only allowed if accomplished through the use of a mechanical device or a one-handed technique);
- ensuring that contaminated reusable sharps be placed in puncture-resistant and leak-proof containers that are labeled or color-coded in accordance with OSHA regulations;
- prohibiting food and drink storage in refrigerators, in freezers, on shelves, in cabinets, or on countertops where blood or other potentially infectious materials are possibly present;
- ensuring that the workplace is maintained in a clean and sanitary condition;
- ensuring that all equipment and environmental and working surfaces shall be cleaned and decontaminated after contact with blood or other potentially infectious material;
- making available the Hepatitis B vaccine and vaccination series to all employees (at no cost to employees) who have occupational exposure.

Health Promotion for Staff

Most of the focus in this teacher resource has been on the health and vitality of students. Another important aspect of comprehensive school health education, however, is the health and well-being of school employees. Like healthy students, healthy school employees are better able to participate in the learning process. Schoolsite employee health promotion is a supportive environmental condition because healthy employees serve as positive role models reinforcing the health principles that students learn in health education. This section of the chapter focuses on the rationale for health promotion for staff as well as on planning and implementing health promotion programs.

Rationale for Health Promotion for Staff

Health care costs have increased at an astronomical rate in recent years. In response to rising health care and health insurance costs, there has been a rapid proliferation of health promotion programs offered at the worksite. By keeping employees and their families healthy, worksite health promotion programs have the potential to lower employee health care costs, reduce absenteeism, improve morale, and increase job satisfaction (Figure 3-11).

Schools are one of the largest employers in our nation. Like business and industry, schools are interested in controlling health care costs and in saving taxpayer dollars spent on education. The prospect of saving health care dollars has motivated some school systems to implement health promotion programs for employees. Health promotion programs are also offered as a means of improving employee morale and reducing burnout and stress in educators (Allegrante and Michela, 1990).

Additional reasons for offering school worksite health promotion programs are offered by the Health Insurance Association of American and American Council of Life Insurance (1985) report titled *Wellness at the School Worksite:*

Wellness at the school worksite programs can help reduce absenteeism and improve performance on the job—in and out of the classroom. A healthier staff gets more done. Fewer substitutes in the classroom means more time on task for the students and thus more learning. Reduced incidence of job burnout and turnover also contributes to keeping educational resources focused where they should be.

School staff are role models for our students, major influences on young people during their formative years when goals, values, and personal habits are being established for a lifetime.

And in these areas—personal goals, value, and habits—what school staff do in and out of the classroom often makes a stronger impression than what they say. We all invoke the cliche, "Do as I do, not as I say" to make just this point: in some cases, students may be more responsive to the hidden curriculum of implied values, attitudes, and feelings than to the announced lesson plan.

It follows that active school staff involvement in wellness programs is likely to have far greater impact on promoting good health habits in students than will occasional classroom units devoted to discussing health.

Planning and Implementing Health Promotion Programs

The school is an ideal place for implementing teacher/staff health promotion programs because necessary facilities and personnel are usually in place. It is natural for health edu-

Figure 3-11

Worksite Health Programs

Worksite health programs have the potential to lower employee health care costs, reduce absenteeism, improve morale, and increase job satisfaction.

cation teachers to participate in the planning and operation of school-based health promotion programs as well as administrators, nurses, guidance counselors, food service personnel, family life (home economics) teachers, physical educators, and other staff member groups. School buildings have adequate space for instruction, screening, and physical fitness programs. As with any aspect of the school program, administrator support is fundamental to success. The following suggestions focus on identifying needs, identifying program components, and maximizing participation.

Identifying Needs The particular health promotion needs within a particular school or school district can be identified by conducting employee surveys, conducting health risk appraisals, and reviewing health care utilization and cost data. Identifying relevant needs allows program planners to offer program components that will best serve school employees.

Program Components Most school systems provide an employee health insurance program. Other health promotion components that school worksite programs offer include:

91

- worksite hazard identification and reduction;
- health risk appraisal;
- medical screenings and surveillance;
- medical management and/or referral;
- smoking cessation;
- employee assistance programs for substance abuse and personal counseling;
- fitness and exercise;
- nutrition and weight control;
- stress management;
- injury prevention;
- CPR and first aid training;
- wise use of medical benefits;
- cancer risk reduction;
- self-care.

Maximizing Participation High health program participation rates are necessary for maximizing benefits within a school system. This can be achieved by permitting employees to participate during working hours, offering a variety of activities, and maximizing convenience. A promotion and education campaign can increase program visibility and aid in recruiting program participants. Incentives and awards for regular participation or achievement can help motivate people to continue participation. Employee involvement in planning and managing the program can also be important to program success. Special efforts should be made to target high-risk employees (U.S. Department of Health and Human Services, 1991).

Schools also are an ideal site for community health promotion centers. Many schools extend the use of their facilities and health promotion program personnel to families of students and other community members. This is a wise use of school facilities that may otherwise stand idle as many as two days and several evenings a week and for three months during the summer. Community- and school-based health promotion programs are one means of making complete use of publicly supported facilities. Also, in the process, the role of schools as centers of community life are reinforced.

Bibliography

Allegrante, J.P., and Michela, J.L. (1990) Impact of a school-based workplace health promotion program on morale of inner-city teachers. *Journal of School Health,* 60:25–28.

American Medical Association. (1990) *America's Adolescents: How Healthy Are They?* Chicago, IL: American Medical Association.

American Public Health Association and American Academy of Pediatrics. (1992) *Caring for Our Children—National Health and Safety Performance Standards: Guidelines for Out-of-Home Child Care Programs.* Washington, DC: American Public Health Association.

Bell, C. (1991) Traumatic stress and children in danger. *Journal of Health Care for the Poor and Underserved,* 2:175–188.

Bever, D.L. (1992) *Safety: A Personal Focus.* St. Louis, MO: Mosby.

Della-Giustina, D.E. (1988) Planning for School Emergencies. Reston, VA: American Alliance For Health, Physical Education, Recreation and Dance.

Reston, VA: American Alliance for Health, Physical Education, Recreation and Dance. D'Onofrio, C.N., and Altman, D.G. (1993) Children and youth. In T.P. Houston (Ed.), *Tobacco Use: An American Crisis—Final Conference Report and Recommendations from America's Health Community.* (pp. 32–42). Chicago: American Medical Association.

Fitzpatrick, K.M. (1993) Exposure to violence and presence of depression among low-income, African-American youth. *Journal of Consulting and Clinical Psychology,* 61:528–531.

Harrington-Lueker, D. (1992) Blown away by school violence. *American School Board Journal,* 179:20–26.

Health Insurance Association of America and American Council of Life Insurance. (1985) *Wellness at the School Worksite: A Manual.* Washington, DC: Health Insurance Association of America and American Council of Life Insurance.

Morganthau, T. (1992) It's not just New York...Big cities, small towns: More and more guns in younger hands. *Newsweek,* March 9, 25–29.

National Dairy Council. (1992) Hunger and undernutrition in America. *Dairy Council Digest,* 63(2):7–12.

———. (1993) Breakfast: Its effects on health and behavior. *Dairy Council Digest,* 64(2): 7–12.

New York State Disaster Preparedness Commission. (1990) *Planning Manual and Guidelines for School Emergency/Disaster Preparedness.* Albany, NY: New York State Department of Education.

Nordland, R. (1992) Deadly lessons. *Newsweek,* March 9, 22–24.

Page, Randy (1990) High school size as a factor in adolescent loneliness. *The High School Journal,* 73:150–153.

———. (1991) Adolescent use of alcohol, tobacco, and other psychoactive substances: Relation to high school size. *American Secondary Education,* 19: 16–20.

Stein, N. (1993) Stop sexual harassment in schools. *USA Today,* May 18, 11A.

U.S. Consumer Product Safety Commission. (no date listed) *Public Playground Handbook for Safety.* Washington, DC: U.S. Consumer Product Safety Commission.

U.S. Department of Health and Human Services. (1991) *Healthy People 2000: National Health Promotion and Disease Prevention Objectives.* Publication No. PHS 91-50213.

Van Leer, T., and Thomson, L. (1993) Some Utah schools now serve up breakfasts for hungry students. *Desert News,* October 24, B2.

Wallach, L.B. (1993) Helping children cope with violence. *Young Children,* May, 4–11.

Wilson, M.H., Baker, S.P., Teret, S.P., Shock, S., and Garbarino, J. (1991) *Saving Children: A Guide to Injury Prevention.* New York: Oxford University Press.

Figure 4-1

Teaching Life Skills for Health

Teachers have the opportunity to teach students skills that will enhance the quality of their lives for years to come.

Chapter 4

THE COMPREHENSIVE SCHOOL HEALTH EDUCATION CURRICULUM: *Teaching Life Skills*

The **comprehensive school health education curriculum** is an organized, sequential K-12 plan for teaching students the information and skills they need to become health literate and maintain and improve health, prevent disease, and reduce health-related risk behaviors. Your role in implementing the comprehensive school health education curriculum is challenging. Because health is essential to the quality of life, you have the opportunity to teach your students skills that will enhance the quality of their lives for years to come (Figure 4-1). Ultimately, students must assume responsibility for practicing these life skills.

This chapter will acquaint you with the comprehensive school health education curriculum. It begins with a discussion of educational reform including health literacy, The National Health Education Standards, and performance indicators. It explains why these are important in designing a curriculum. Next, the chapter focuses on curriculum design. It describes the philosophy for the curriculum. It includes a discussion of *The Scope and Sequence Chart* (in *The Curriculum Guide* in Section 5). It explains how each of the following is used to formulate a blueprint for the curriculum: the components of health literacy, The National Health Education Standards, the performance indicators, the content areas and life skills, and the health topics. Also included in this chapter are innovative ways to teach life skills and evaluation techniques.

Educational Reform

Today, there is great emphasis on educational reform. The purpose of educational reform is to examine what knowledge and skills young people should learn in school to prepare them for the twenty-first century. **Chapter 1. A Nation At Risk: The Need for Comprehensive School Health Education** provided a rationale as to why young people need knowledge and skills for health. But, what knowledge and skills do they need? Most educators agree that young people need to develop literacy. Therefore, the comprehensive school health education curriculum should focus on health literacy. The Joint Committee on Health Education Standards was formed to develop national health education standards designed to help young people become health literate. It is believed that The National Health Education Standards will also (1) ensure commonality of purpose and consistency of concepts in health instruction; (2) improve student learning across the nation; (3) provide a foundation for assessment of student performance;

(4) provide a foundation for curriculum development and instruction; and (5) provide a guide for enhancing teacher preparation and continuing education (The Joint Committee on Health Education Standards, 1995). Performance indicators were developed to assess student mastery of The National Health Education Standards. The following discussion will examine health literacy, The National Health Education Standards, and the performance indicators that were identified and explain how these might be used to develop comprehensive school health education curricula.

Health Literacy

Health literacy is competence in critical thinking and problem solving, responsible and productive citizenship, self-directed learning, and effective communication (The Joint Committee on Health Education Standards, 1995). A **health literate individual** is a critical thinker and problem solver, a responsible and productive citizen, a self-directed learner, and an effective communicator (The Joint Committee on Health Education Standards, 1995).

Imagine a health literacy continuum. At one end of the continuum would be the health literate individual. By examining a description of the skills that this person has, it will become obvious what skills are lacking in the individual at the opposite end of the continuum.

Critical Thinking and Problem Solving Skills Young people who are critical thinkers and problem solvers are able to examine personal, national, and international health problems and formulate ways to solve these problems. They gather current, credible, and applicable information from a variety of sources and assess this information before making health-related decisions. They approach health promotion with creative thinking and use responsible decision-making and goal setting as tools.

Responsible and Productive Citizenship Young people who are responsible and productive citizens feel obligated to keep their community healthful, safe, and secure. They are committed to the expectation that all citizens deserve a high quality of life. They recognize that their behavior effects the quality of life for others and they avoid behaviors that threaten their personal health, safety, and security and that of others. They work collaboratively with others to maintain and improve health for all citizens.

Self-Directed Learning Young people who are self-directed learners recognize that they need to gather and use health information throughout life as the disease prevention knowledge base will change. They gain skills in literacy, numeracy, and critical thinking and expect to gather, analyze, and apply new health information throughout their lives. They embrace learning from others and have the interpersonal and social skills to do so. They internalize self-directed learning and use this process to grow and mature toward a high level of wellness.

Effective Communication Young people who are effective communicators are able to express and convey their knowledge, beliefs, and ideas through oral, written, artistic, graphic, and technological media. They demonstrate empathy and respect for others and encourage others to express their knowledge, beliefs, and ideas. They listen carefully and respond when others speak. They are advocates for positions, policies, and programs that promote personal, family, and community health.

The National Health Education Standards

The Joint Committee on Health Education Standards is a committee whose purpose was to identify The National Health Education Standards that incorporate the knowledge and skills essential to the development of health literacy. Members of The Joint Committee on Health Education Standards consisted of professionals representing 1) The American School Health Association, 2) The Association for the Advancement of Health Education, 3) The School Health Education and Services Section, American Public Health Association, and 4) The Society of State Directors of Health, Physical Education, Recreation and Dance. There also were representatives from institutions of higher education, state education associations (SEAs), and local education associations (LEAs), as well as classroom teachers.

The Joint Committee on Health Education Standards established the following definition and description for health education standards: ***Health education standards*** *are standards that specify what students should know and be able to do. They involve the knowledge and skills essential to the development of health literacy. Those "skills" include the ways of communicating, reasoning, and investigating which characterize health education.*

Health Education Standard #1: *Students will comprehend concepts related to health promotion and disease prevention* (The Joint Committee on Health Education Standards, 1995). To be health literate individuals who are self-directed learners, young people must be able to comprehend health promotion and disease prevention concepts including how their bodies function, ways to prevent diseases and other health problems, how their behavior influences their health status, and ways to promote health. As they grow and develop, they must be able to comprehend ways in which physical, mental, emotional, and social changes influence their health status.

Health Education Standard #2: *Students will demonstrate the ability to access valid health information and health-promoting products and services* (The Joint Committee on Health Education Standards, 1995). To be health literate individuals who are responsible and productive citizens, young people must be able to recognize and use reliable and credible sources for health information. They must be able to assess health products and services. To do so, they need to develop skills in critical thinking, organization, comparison, synthesis, and evaluation.

Health Education Standard #3: *Students will demonstrate the ability to practice health-enhancing behaviors and reduce health risks* (The Joint Committee on Health Education Standards, 1995). To be health literate individuals who are critical thinkers and problem solvers, young people must be able to recognize and practice health enhancing behaviors that contribute to a positive quality of life. They must recognize and avoid risk-taking behaviors. They must assume responsibility for personal health.

Health Education Standard #4: *Students will analyze the influence of culture, media, technology, and other factors on health* (The

Joint Committee on Health Education Standards, 1995). To be health literate individuals who demonstrate critical thinking, problem solving, and responsible and productive citizenship, young people must be able to recognize, analyze, evaluate, and interpret the influence that a variety of factors have on health and on society. These factors include but are not limited to culture, media, and technology.

Health Education Standard #5: *Students will demonstrate the ability to use interpersonal communication skills to enhance health* (The Joint Committee on Health Education Standards, 1995). To be health literate individuals who demonstrate effective communication, young people must be able to interact in positive ways with family members and people in the workplace, school, and community. They must be able to resolve conflict in healthful ways.

Health Education Standard #6: *Students will demonstrate the ability to use goal-setting and decision-making skills that enhance health* (The Joint Committee on Health Education Standards, 1995). To be health literate, young people must be able to make responsible decisions and set and reach goals. These skills make it possible for young people to apply health knowledge and develop a healthful lifestyle. They are valuable tools that can be used when working with other citizens to improve the quality of life in families, schools, and communities.

Health Education Standard #7: *Students will demonstrate the ability to advocate for personal, family and community health* (The Joint Committee on Health Education Standards, 1995). To be health literate individuals who are effective communicators and responsible citizens, young people must have health advocacy skills. They must be able to recognize when and how they might serve as advocates for positive health in their communities.

The Performance Indicators

The Joint Committee on Health Education Standards coined the term performance indicators for use in assessing the National Health Education Standards. **Performance indicators** *are a series of specific concepts and skills students should know and be able to do in order to achieve each of the broader*

National Health Education Standards (The Joint Committee on Health Education Standards, 1995). For each of the seven health education standards, there are several performance indicators. The Joint Committee further delineated which performance indicators would be used to assess mastery of the health education standards at the completion of grades four, eight, and eleven.

Curriculum Development and The National Health Education Standards

Traditionally, state departments of education, local departments of education, and school districts organized curricula around seven to twelve health content areas. More recently, a change occurred when The Centers for Disease Control and Prevention identified the six categories of risk behaviors. Educators began to organize curricula around these six categories. Yet, some health topics did not seem to fit as easily under one of the six categories of risk behaviors as they had under one of the traditional content areas. For example, most educators include dental health topics such as brushing and flossing of teeth, making healthful diet choices, and having regular dental checkups in their curriculum. Given the six categories of risk behaviors (unintentional and intentional injuries; tobacco use; alcohol and other drug use; sexual behaviors that result in HIV infection, other STDs, and unintended pregnancy; dietary patterns that contribute to disease; and insufficient physical activity), under which category of risk behaviors would these dental health topics be included? Perhaps it would be less confusing to include these health topics within the content area of Personal Health.

Another example might be helpful. Many children and adolescents experience the harmful effects of too much stress. Under which of the six categories of risk behaviors would health topics focusing on stress be included? Harmful coping or too much stress contributes to each of the six categories of risk behaviors. Perhaps the discussion of stress might be included in the content area of Mental and Emotional Health and then reemphasized when each of the risk behaviors is included in other content areas.

For practicality in curriculum implementation, many educators see the need to combine content areas and the six categories of risk behaviors. While the purpose of The National Health Education Standards initiative was to organize curricula around the health education standards that promoted health literacy, it is understood that the health topics included in curricula will be derived from both the content areas and the six categories of risk behaviors (The Joint Committee on Health Education Standards, 1995). The performance indicators will serve as guidelines for assessing mastery of the health education standards at the completion of grades four, eight, and eleven.

The rest of this chapter will describe how to develop, implement, and evaluate a curriculum that (1) has a clear philosophy, (2) promotes health literacy, (3) identifies The National Health Education Standards, (4) identifies the performance indicators, (5) is derived from both the content areas and the six categories of risk behaviors and teaches life skills, (6) can be taught in an innovative way, and (7) can be evaluated using the performance indicators.

The Philosophy of the Curriculum

A **philosophy** is an overall vision of the purpose of the curriculum and it explains the meaning of health and its value. A philosophy should reflect the attitudes and values of society about the purpose of education and the contribution of comprehensive school health education. The following discussion examines the domains of health, *The Wellness Scale*, health knowledge, healthful behaviors and risk behaviors, healthful situations and risk situations, healthful relationships and destructive relationships, responsible decision-making skills, resistance skills, protective factors and risk factors, resiliency, health literacy, and *The Model of Health and Well-Being*.

The Domains of Health

Health is the quality of life that includes physical, mental-emotional, and family-social health. The **domains of health** refer to the three kinds of health: physical, mental-emotional, and family-social. **Physical health**

Figure 4-2

The Wellness Scale

Factors that Influence Health and Well-Being

Lack of health knowledge	Possession of health knowledge
Risk behaviors	Wellness behaviors
Risk situations	Healthful situations
Destructive relationships	Healthful relationships
Irresponsible decision-making	Responsible decision-making
Lack of resistance skills	Use of resistance skills
Lack of protective factors	Possession of protective factors
Lack of resiliency	Having resiliency
Lack of health literacy	Having health literacy

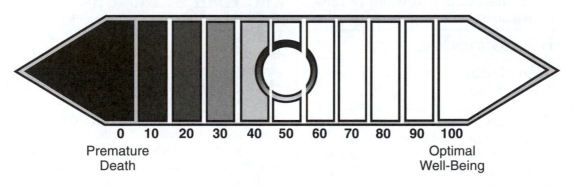

0	10	20	30	40	50	60	70	80	90	100

Premature
Death

Optimal
Well-Being

Health status is the sum total of the positive
and negative influence of these factors.

is the condition of a person's body. Eating healthful meals and getting exercise and sleep are examples of ways to keep the body in good condition. **Mental-emotional health** is the condition of a person's mind and the ways that a person expresses feelings. The mind requires as much, if not more, conditioning than the body. Assessing new information, having challenging conversations, and deciding on ways concepts from different areas can be synthesized are examples of ways the mind is kept in top condition. Taking the time to understand feelings, express them in healthful ways, and meet needs without interfering with the rights of others are ways to keep emotional health in condition. **Family-social health** is the condition of a person's relationships with others. Focusing on expressing oneself clearly and listening intently when others are speaking are ex-

amples of ways to keep family-social health in good condition. Learning to give affection in appropriate ways and to receive the affection of others also is an aspect of family-social health.

The Wellness Scale

Wellness is another way to describe the quality of life. **Wellness** is the quality of life that includes physical, mental-emotional, and family-social health. *The Wellness Scale* (Figure 4-2) depicts the ranges in the quality of life from optimal well-being to high level wellness, average wellness, minor illness or injury, major illness or injury, and premature death. There are at least nine factors that influence health and wellness over which a person has some degree of control. **Health**

status is the sum total of the positive and negative influence of:

1. The level of health knowledge a person has;
2. The behaviors a person chooses;
3. The situations in which a person participates;
4. The relationships in which a person engages;
5. The decisions a person makes;
6. The resistance skills a person has;
7. The protective factors a person possesses;
8. The degree to which a person is resilient;
9. The degree of health literacy a person has achieved.

Each influence can be either positive or negative. When an influence is positive, it is viewed as a plus (+). When an influence is negative, it is viewed as a minus (-). A person's health status fluctuates on *The Wellness Scale* depending on whether these influences are positive or negative.

Health Knowledge

Health knowledge consists of information that is needed to develop health literacy, maintain and improve health, prevent disease, and reduce health-related risk behaviors. There are ten content areas of health in this teacher resource book. Health knowledge is needed in each of these content areas. Knowledge in these content areas contributes to the achievement of the performance indicators identified for each of The National Health Education Standards. Each of the six categories of risk behaviors is included within one or more of these ten content areas, therefore, health knowledge will be obtained for each of the six categories of risk behaviors. The ten content areas are:

1. Mental and Emotional Health
2. Family Living
3. Growth and Development
4. Nutrition
5. Personal Health
6. Alcohol, Tobacco, and Other Drugs
7. Communicable and Chronic Diseases
8. Injury Prevention and Safety
9. Consumer and Community Health
10. Environmental Health

Healthful Behaviors and Risk Behaviors

Health knowledge is essential to evaluate behavior to determine whether or not it promotes health status. **Healthful behaviors** or **wellness behaviors** are actions that promote health, prevent illness, injury, and premature death, and improve the quality of the environment. Examples of healthful behaviors include eating a balanced breakfast, reducing the amount of saturated fat in the diet, wearing a safety belt, and recycling products. **Risk behaviors** or **harmful behaviors** are voluntary actions that threaten health, increase the likelihood of illness and premature death, and destroy the quality of the environment. Examples of risk behaviors include smoking cigarettes, sunbathing without a sunscreen having an adequate sun protective factor (SPF), walking into the street between parked cars, and burning trash.

Healthful Situations and Risk Situations

Most people recognize that health knowledge assists in evaluating behaviors, but it also is essential in evaluating the situations in which someone chooses to be. **Healthful situations** or **wellness situations** are circumstances that promote health, prevent illness, injury, and premature death, and improve the quality of the environment. Examples of healthful situations are attending drug-free parties, sitting in nonsmoking sections of restaurants, being a passenger in a car driven by someone who obeys safety rules, and living in a home with a safe radon level. **Risk situations** or **harmful situations** are circumstances that threaten health, increase the likelihood of illness, injury, and premature death, and destroy the quality of the

environment. Examples of risk situations include traveling to another country without having had the recommended immunizations and being in a room where people are smoking cigarettes.

Healthful Relationships and Destructive Relationships

Healthful relationships are relationships that promote self-esteem and productivity, encourage health-enhancing behavior, and are free of violence and drug misuse and abuse. Examples of healthful relationships might be those in which people identify strengths in each other, encourage each other to complete projects, support each other's exercise or diet plans, and motivate each other to be energetic. Sidney Jourard, psychologist and author of *Transparent Self*, says healthful relationships "inspirit" people (Jourard, 1971). People feel lifted up and energized as a result of being in healthful relationships.

Destructive or **unhealthful relationships** are relationships that destroy self-esteem, interfere with productivity and health, and may include violence and drug misuse and abuse. Examples of destructive relationships are those in which one or both people unjustly criticize each other, interrupt each other's work, encourage each other to engage in risk behaviors, and drain each other of energy. Sidney Jourard says destructive relationships "dispirit" people. There appears to be a relationship between relationships which "dis-spirit" people and the likelihood that these people will suffer from "dis-ease."

Responsible Decision-Making Skills

Health knowledge also is needed to make responsible decisions, a fifth factor which influences health status. *The Responsible Decision-Making Model* (Table 4-3) is a series of steps to follow to assure that the decisions a person makes lead to actions that:
1. promote health,
2. protect safety,
3. protect laws,
4. show respect for self and others,
5. follow guidelines set by responsible adults such as parents and guardians,
6. demonstrate good character.

Table 4-3

The Responsible Decision-Making Model

1. **Clearly describe the situation you face**. If no immediate decision is necessary, describe the situation in writing. If an immediate decision must be made, describe the situation out loud or to yourself in a few short sentences. Being able to describe a situation in your own words is the first step in clarifying the question.

2. **List possible actions that can be taken**. Again, if no immediate decision is necessary, make a list of possible actions. If an immediate decision must be made, state possible actions out loud or to yourself.

3. **Share your list of possible actions with a responsible adult such as someone who protects community laws and demonstrates character**. When no immediate action is necessary, sharing possible actions with a responsible adult is helpful. This person can examine your list to see if it is inclusive. Responsible adults have a wide range of experiences that can allow them to see situations maturely. They may add possibilities to the list of actions. In some situations, it is possible to delay decision-making until there is an opportunity to seek counsel with a responsible adult. If an immediate decision must be made, explore possibilities. Perhaps a telephone call can be made. Whenever possible, avoid skipping this step.

4. **Carefully evaluate each possible action using six criteria**. Ask each of the six questions to learn which decision is best.
   a. Will this decision result in an action that will promote my health and the health of others?
   b. Will this decision result in an action that will protect my safety and the safety of others?
   c. Will this decision result in an action that will protect the laws of the community?
   d. Will this decision result in an action that shows respect for myself and others?
   e. Will this decision result in an action that follows guidelines set by responsible adults such as my parents or guardian?
   f. Will this decision result in an action that will demonstrate that I have good character?

5. Decide which action is responsible and most appropriate. After applying the six criteria, compare the results. Which decision best meets the six criteria?

6. Act in a responsible way and evaluate the results. Follow through with this decision with confidence. The confidence comes from paying attention to the six criteria.

Resistance Skills

After developing the skill of responsible decision-making, a person recognizes when it is necessary to say NO to an action or situation because (s)he wants to say YES to good health. But someone may want to say NO and not be able to do so. Being able to use resistance skills when appropriate is a sixth factor that influences health status. **Resistance skills** are skills that are used when a person wants to say NO to an action and/or leave a situation. *The Model for Using Resistance Skills* (Table 4-4) contains a list of suggested ways for effectively resisting pressure to engage in actions that:

1. threaten health,
2. threaten safety,
3. break laws,
4. result in lack of respect for self and others,
5. disobey guidelines set by responsible adults,
6. detract from character.

Protective Factors and Risk Factors

Protective factors are ways that a person might behave and characteristics of the environment in which a person lives that promote health, safety, and/or well-being. The greater the number of protective factors a person possesses, the more likely that health status will be optimal. Characteristics of the environment that serve as protective factors include (Benard, 1992):

1. caring and support provided by a caring parent, a confident and positive teacher, supportive and caring peers, or social links within the community;
2. high expectations including positive parental attitudes, high academic and behavioral expectations at school, and clear community expectations and values;
3. active participation including responsibilities at home, involvement in school and extracurricular activities, and opportunities for participation in useful tasks in the community.

Risk factors are ways that a person might behave and characteristics of the environment in which a person lives that threaten health, safety, and/or well-being. When a person does not have a caring and supportive environment, is confused as to the

---

Table 4-4

The Model for Using Resistance Skills

1. **Use assertive behavior.** There is a saying, "You get treated the way you 'train' others to treat you." Assertive behavior is the honest expression of thoughts and feelings without experiencing anxiety or threatening others. When you use assertive behavior, you show that you are in control of yourself and the situation. You say NO clearly and firmly. As you speak, you look directly at the person(s) pressuring you. Aggressive behavior is the use of words and/or actions that tend to communicate disrespect. This behavior only antagonizes others. Passive behavior is the holding back of ideas, opinions, and feelings. Holding back may result in harm to you, others, or the environment.

2. **Avoid saying, "NO, thank you."** There is never a need to thank a person who pressures you into doing something that might be harmful, unsafe, illegal, or disrespectful or which may result in disobeying parents or displaying a lack of character.

3. **Use nonverbal behavior that matches verbal behavior.** Nonverbal behavior is the use of body language or actions rather than words to express feelings, ideas, and opinions. Your verbal NO should not be confused by misleading actions. For example, if you say NO to cigarette smoking, do not pretend to take a puff of a cigarette in order to resist pressure.

4. **Influence others to choose responsible behavior.** When a situation poses immediate danger, remove yourself. If no immediate danger is present, try to turn the situation into a positive one. Suggest alternative, responsible ways to behave. Being a positive role model helps you feel good about yourself and helps gain the respect of others.

5. **Avoid being in situations in which there will be pressure to make harmful decisions.** There is no reason to put yourself into situations in which you will be pressured or tempted to make unwise decisions. Think ahead.

6. **Avoid being with persons who choose harmful actions.** Your reputation is the impression that others have of you, your decisions, and your actions. Associate with persons known for their good qualities and character in order to avoid being misjudged.

7. **Resist pressure to engage in illegal behavior.** You have a responsibility to protect others and to protect the laws of your community. Demonstrate good character.

Figure 4-5

The Model of Health and Well Being

To maintain and improve health prevent disease, and reduce health-related risk behaviors, students must assume personal responsibility and:

1. **develop health knowledge,**
2. **choose healthful behavior,**
3. **participate in healthful situations,**
4. **develop healthful relationships,**
5. **make responsible decisions,**
6. **use resistance skills,**
7. **possess protective factors,**
8. **demonstrate resiliency,**
9. **achieve health literacy.**

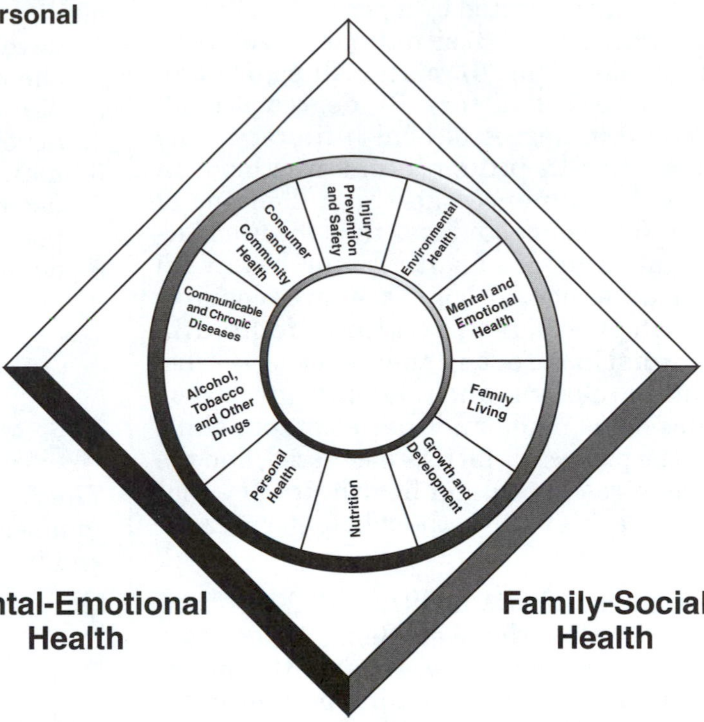

Physical Health

Mental-Emotional Health

Family-Social Health

Injury Prevention and Safety

Consumer and Community Health

Environmental Health

Communicable and Chronic Diseases

Mental and Emotional Health

Alcohol, Tobacco and Other Drugs

Family Living

Personal Health

Nutrition

Growth and Development

---

expectations set by adults, or is unable to actively participate in school and extracurricular activities, the likelihood of health-compromising choices is increased (Benard, 1992).

Resiliency

Resiliency is the ability to prevent or to recover, bounce back, and learn from misfortune, change, or pressure. Resiliency, the capacity for mental health despite exposure to adversity, is innate in all human beings and is accessible (Mills, 1993). The Health Realization Approach to resiliency focuses on reconnecting people to the health in themselves and then directing them in ways to bring forth health in others (Mills, 1993). This reconnecting process strengthens a person and contributes to optimal health status. A person who is not resilient and who has not been reconnected to his/her health potential may experience a sense of hopelessness and a compromised health status.

Health Literacy

The following definitions regarding health literacy and a health literate individual will be included again. **Health literacy** is competence in critical thinking and problem solving, responsible and productive citizenship, self-directed learning, and effective communication. (Joint Committee on Health Education Standards, 1995). A **health literate individual** is a critical thinker and problem solver, a responsible and productive citizen, a self-directed learner, and an effective communicator (The Joint Committee on Health Education Standards, 1995).

The degree of health literacy a person has achieved influences his/her health status. A person who is described as being a health literate individual is more likely to make choices that promote optimal health status than is a person who is not described as being a health literate individual.

The Model of Health and Well-Being

The Model of Health and Well-Being (Figure 4-5) shows the relationship among the three domains of health, the health content areas, and the nine factors that influence health status. The three domains of health—physical health, mental-emotional health, and family-social health—provide the structure for the outside of the Model. In the center of the Model, there is a Well-Being Wheel. The Well-Being Wheel is composed of the ten areas that are affected by a person's 1) knowledge, 2) behaviors, 3) situations, 4) relationships, 5) decisions, 6) relationships, 7) number of protective factors, 8) degree of resiliency, and 9) degree of health literacy. The areas of health influence one another. In turn, they influence the three domains of health. The connectedness that the nine factors that influence health status have with the ten areas of health and the three domains of health is referred to as **holistic health.** The **holistic effect** is the effect of the behaviors, situations, and relationships chosen; the decisions made and the resistance skills used, the protective factors possessed, and the degree of resiliency and health literacy that has been achieved, on the whole person.

To visualize holistic health and the holistic effect, visualize the Well-Being Wheel as a large jar of water. All of the health content areas and the three domains of health are contained within the jar. Now take a drop of red food coloring. Drop it into the jar. The red food coloring represents one or more of the following positive influences on health status: wellness behaviors, wellness situations, healthful relationships, responsible decisions, resistance skills, protective factors, resiliency, and health literacy. Red is used because it is the color of blood and represents "life-giving" behavior. Soon, the entire jar of water becomes red even though only one drop of red food coloring was placed inside. There has been a holistic effect. The whole person has been affected.

Now take another jar of water. This time put a drop of blue food coloring in the jar. The blue food coloring represents one or more of the following negative influences on health status: risk behaviors, risk situations, destructive relationships, irresponsible decisions, harmful pressure from others, risk factors, lack of resiliency, and lack of health literacy. Blue is used to denote illness, injury, and premature death. Soon, the entire jar of water becomes blue even though only one drop of blue food coloring was placed inside. There has been a holistic effect.

The philosophy of the comprehensive school health education curriculum is illustrated by *The Model of Health and Well-Being.* To maintain and improve health, prevent disease, and reduce health-related risk behaviors, students must assume personal responsibility and:
1. develop health knowledge,
2. choose healthful behavior,
3. participate in healthful situations,
4. develop healthful relationships,
5. make responsible decisions,
6. use resistance skills,
7. possess protective factors,
8. demonstrate resiliency,
9. achieve health literacy.

The Scope and Sequence Chart

The Scope and Sequence Chart is a chart that serves as a blueprint for the curriculum and it includes the components of health literacy, The National Health Education Standards, the performance indicators, the content areas and life skills, and the health topics. In this teacher resource book, *The Scope and Sequence Chart* (in *The Curriculum Guide* in Section 5) illustrates how the ten content areas (with the six categories of risk behaviors included in one or more of each of the content areas) are used to support the more important framework that includes health literacy, The National Health Education Standards, and performance indicators. Each of the following is described as it appears in *The Scope and Sequence Chart* (in *The Curriculum Guide* in Section 5): the components of health literacy, The National Health Education Standards, the performance indicators, the content areas and life skills, and the health topics.

The Components of Health Literacy

The components of health literacy (critical thinking and problem solving, responsible and productive citizenship, self-directed learning, and effective communication) are identified in the introduction to *The Scope and Sequence Chart* (in *The Curriculum Guide* in Section 5). This makes the emphasis on health literacy clear to those who will use *The Scope and Sequence Chart* (in *The Curriculum Guide* in Section 5) to implement the comprehensive school health curriculum.

The National Health Education Standards

The National Health Education Standards are identified in the first column of *The Scope and Sequence Chart* (in *The Curriculum Guide* in Section 5). The seven health education standards provide the framework for identifying what students should know and be able to do:

1. Students will comprehend concepts related to health promotion and disease prevention.
2. Students will demonstrate the ability to access valid health information and health-promoting products and services.
3. Students will demonstrate the ability to practice health-enhancing behaviors and reduce health risks.
4. Students will analyze the influence of culture, media, technology, and other factors on health.
5. Students will demonstrate the ability to use interpersonal communication skills to enhance health.
6. Students will demonstrate the ability to use goal setting and decision-making skills that enhance health.
7. Students will demonstrate the ability to advocate for personal, family, and community health.

The Performance Indicators

The performance indicators that will be used to assess student mastery of each of the broader National Health Education Standards at grades four, eight, and eleven are identified in the second column of *The Scope and Sequence Chart* (in *The Curriculum Guide* in Section 5).

When developing the performance indicators, The Joint Committee on Health Education Standards subscribed to the principle that true learning occurs when students function at all levels of cognition identified in Bloom's Taxonomy: knowledge, comprehension, application, analysis, synthesis and evaluation (The Joint Committee on Health Education Standards, 1995). To better understand the performance indicators, the following information on understanding the relationship to behavioral objectives, developing behavioral objectives, and classifying behavioral objectives is included.

Understanding the Relationship to Behavioral Objectives Traditionally, educators designed curricula using carefully stated behavioral objectives. A **behavioral objective** is a statement of what a student should be able to do after completing a learning experience. Most likely, you are familiar with behavioral objectives and with curricula that have been designed around behavioral objectives. This approach to curricula design is based on the classic work of Benjamin Bloom. *Bloom's Taxonomy of Educational Objectives* is still widely used today. The performance indicators also are statements of what a student is expected to do. The difference between behavioral objectives and performance indicators is the performance indicators are specifically correlated to the National Health Education Standards. However, if you want to know how to develop and classify performance indicators, you might examine how to develop and classify behavioral objectives. The skills are similar.

Developing Behavioral Objectives A behavioral objective is a statement of what a learner should be able to do after a learning experience. There are five rules for writing behavioral objectives.

Rule #1: A behavioral objective needs to be stated in a way that makes it clear that the expectation is for the student. It would be correct to say, "The *student* will..." It would be incorrect to say, "The *lesson* describes..." or "The *teacher* will..." The first part of a behavioral objective is referred to as the WHO.

Rule #2: A behavioral objective must specify the kind of behavior that will be accepted as evidence. Some words that specify evidence of student behavior are *to list, to compare, to identify, to differentiate, to solve, to write,* and *to recite*. Words which are incorrect because there is no evidence of behavior are to know, to understand, to have faith in, to believe, to really understand, and to appreciate. Part two of a behavioral objective is referred to as the BEHAVIOR.

Rule #3: A behavioral objective must include content about the specific learning experience. The student will identify *the effects of alcohol on the body.* Part three of the behavioral objective is referred to as the CONTENT.

Rule #4: A behavioral objective describes the important conditions under which the behavior will be expected to occur. Some examples of conditions are: *with textbook open, after seeing a film, using a model of a heart,* and *given a 50-minute time period.* Part four of the behavioral objective is referred to as the CONDITION.

Rule #5: A behavioral objective must specify the criteria for acceptable performance by describing how well the learner must perform to be acceptable. Thus, the objective, "The student will write an essay on the danger signals of heart disease," would not be an example of an objective with acceptable criteria. Correctly stated, the objective with criteria would read, "The student will write an essay about heart disease *that includes at least two danger signals.*

Constructing A Behavioral Objective (Table 4-6) provides examples of two behavioral objectives. Each of the behavioral objectives is broken down into the 1) who, 2) behavior, 3) content, 4) condition, and 5) criteria.

Classifying Behavioral Objectives In addition to constructing behavioral objectives correctly, you will want to be able to differentiate between desirable student behaviors. Student behaviors can generally be described as thinking behaviors, feeling or attitudinal behaviors, or action behaviors. These three different categories of behavior make it necessary to classify objectives into three domains: the cognitive domain, the affective domain, and the psychomotor or action domain.

The **cognitive domain** is a category of objectives dealing with thinking behavior. Objectives in the cognitive domain emphasize learning and problem solving tasks and are divided into six classifications (Kibler, Barker, and Miles, 1970).

Low Level

   1. **Knowledge objectives** are objectives that require students to reproduce or recall something that they have experienced previously in the same or similar form. Words used in writing knowledge

---

Table 4-6

Constructing a Behavioral Objective

With an open textbook, the student will write a balanced menu for one day that includes the correct number of servings from The Food Guide Pyramid.

Who:	the student
Behavior:	will write
Content:	a balanced menu for one day
Condition:	with an open textbook
Criteria:	that includes the correct number of servings from The Food Guide Pyramid

After viewing the film on self-protection, the student will write a pamphlet on child abuse that identifies at least five signs and symptoms of physical abuse.

Who:	the student
Behavior:	will write
Content:	a pamphlet on child abuse
Condition:	after viewing the film
Criteria:	that identifies at least five signs and symptoms of physical abuse

objectives might include: define, recall, describe, identify, list, match, name, and recite.

2. **Comprehensive objectives** are objectives that require students to reproduce or recall something previously experienced in a new form. Words used in writing comprehensive objectives might include: explain, summarize, interpret, rewrite, estimate, confer, infer, translate, rearrange, and paraphrase.

Higher Level

3. **Application objectives** are objectives that require students to use previously experienced procedures or knowledge in new situations. Words used in writing application objectives might include: change, compute, demonstrate, operate, show, use, and solve.

4. **Analysis objectives** are objectives that require students to break down into its component elements something which they have not broken down previously. Words used in writing analysis objectives might include: outline, break down, subdivide, deduce, discriminate, diagram, order, categorize, and distinguish.

5. **Synthesis objectives** are objectives that require students to put something together which they have not put together previously. Words used in writing synthesis objectives might include: combine, compile, compose, create, design, rearrange, plan, and produce.

6. **Evaluation objectives** are objectives that require students to render judgments regarding something for which they have not rendered judgment previously. Words used in writing evaluation objectives might include: justify, appraise, criticize, compare, support, conclude, and contrast.

Low Level

1. **Receiving objectives** are objectives that require students to recognize and receive certain phenomenon and stimuli.

2. **Responding objectives** are objectives that require students to demonstrate a wide variety of reactions to stimuli.

Higher Level

3. **Valuing objectives** are objectives that require students to display a behavior with sufficient consistency.

4. **Organizing objectives** are objectives that require students to organize values into a system, determine the interrelationships among them, and establish dominant and pervasive ones.

5. **Characterizing objectives** are objectives that require students to act consistently in accordance with the values they have internalized at this level.

The **affective domain** is a category of objectives dealing with feelings and attitudes. Objectives in the affective domain contain the behaviors that have emotional overtones and encompass likes and dislikes, attitudes, values, and beliefs and are divided into five classifications (Bloom, 1956).

The **psychomotor domain** is the category of objectives dealing with action behavior. Objectives in the psychomotor domain emphasize some muscular or motor skill, some manipulation of materials or objects, or some act which requires neuromuscular coordination and are divided into four classifications (Kibler, Barker, and Miles, 1970).

Low Level

1. **Gross bodily movement objectives** are objectives that require students to move entire limbs.

2. **Finely coordinated movement objectives** are objectives that require students to coordinate movements of the extremities, usually with the eye and ear.

Higher Level

3. **Nonverbal communication objectives** are objectives that require students to convey a message to a receiver without the use of words.

4. **Speech objectives** are objectives that require students to communicate through speech, such as public speaking.

107

The CSHE Curriculum

The Content Areas and Life Skills

The content areas in the curriculum appear as headings for *The Scope and Sequence Chart* (in *The Curriculum Guide* in Section 5). Notice that the health education standards and the performance indicators appear under each of the content areas. This design is used in order to illustrate appropriate content areas that can be taught to meet each of the health education standards and performance indicators. Each of the six categories of risk behaviors are included in one or more of these ten content areas and therefore are correlated to the health education standards and the performance indicators. The ten content areas are:

1. Mental and Emotional Health
2. Family Living
3. Growth and Development
4. Nutrition
5. Personal Health
6. Alcohol, Tobacco, and Other Drugs
7. Communicable and Chronic Diseases
8. Injury Prevention and Safety
9. Consumer and Community Health
10. Environmental Health

Life skills have been identified for each of the ten content areas. **Life skills** are actions that promote health literacy, maintain and improve health, prevent disease, and reduce health-related risk behaviors that are learned and practiced for a lifetime. Life skills are stated as "I will..." because they indicate that the student is willingly and willfully choosing to be committed to practicing them. The primary purpose of comprehensive school health education is to help students develop and practice life skills that are correlated to the health education standards and the performance indicators. In *The Scope and Sequence Chart* (in *The Curriculum Guide* in Section 5), ten life skills are identified for each of the content areas.

Life skills should be stated as specifically as possible. Life skills help students know what is expected of them. They help students recognize what they need to do to become health literate, maintain and improve health, prevent disease, and reduce health-related risk behavior. When life skills are practiced, stu-

dents begin to take responsibility for their health. The youth in this nation are less at risk because they have begun to replace health-related risk behaviors with health-enhancing behaviors.

The Health Topics

Health topics are the subjects within each of the content areas that need to be taught in order that students might have the health knowledge needed to practice life skills that enable them to master the performance indicators for the health education standards. Consider the health education standards and performance indicators to be achieved after grade eight. One of the health education standards is: *Students will demonstrate the ability to use goal setting and decision-making skills that enhance health.* One of the performance indicators for this health education standard is: *Demonstrate the ability to apply a decision-making process to health issues and problems individually and collaboratively.*

This health education standard and the related performance indicator might be covered in the content area identified as Mental and Emotional Health. Consider the third life skill for this content area: *I will make responsible decisions.* Directly under this life skill is a list of health topics that provide the knowledge and skills needed for mastery of the performance indicator that was identified for the health education standard. The health topics include: *proactive decision-making, reactive decision-making, inactive decision-making, the responsible decision-making model, and ways to demonstrate character and social values.*

It is very important to select health topics carefully. The **scope** is the depth or degree of difficulty of each of the health topics to be covered. When developing the scope, the focus is on WHAT health topics should be taught. An important question that might be asked is, "WHAT do students need to know to practice life skills and master the performance indicators?"

The **sequence** is the order in which the health topics will be covered including what will be covered by the different grade levels. When developing the sequence, the focus is on WHEN to teach different health topics. This includes when to introduce, emphasize, and reinforce the different health topics. The performance indicators are very important when determining the sequence. Remember, there are performance indicators for grades four, eight, and eleven. This means specific health topics must be covered by these respective grade levels in order that students might accomplish the performance indicators for each of the health education standards. With regard to sequence or the WHEN to teach, the readiness of students is important. Health topics should be placed in a sequence that fosters a preventive approach. For example, if research indicates that students are likely to experiment with drinking alcohol by the fifth grade, then there are important considerations when introducing, emphasizing, and reinforcing health topics designed to promote the life skill "I will not drink alcohol." Alcohol-related health topics might be introduced in grades K–4, emphasized in grades 5–9, and reinforced in grades 10–12. Whenever research is available to indicate the age at which students are likely to begin experimenting with a risk behavior, it is appropriate to introduce related health topics at least two years prior to this age.

The Scope and Sequence Chart (in *The Curriculum Guide* in Section 5) must take into consideration specific needs of the school district, community, and state as well as the needs that have been identified for the nation. For example, hurricanes are more likely to occur in some communities than in others. Although students in communities where hurricanes are unlikely need this information, the emphasis placed on this health topic and the related life skills would be greater in states where hurricanes pose a threat.

Innovative Ways to Teach Life Skills

Self-responsibility for health is the priority that a person assigns to being health literate, maintaining and improving health, preventing disease, and reducing health-related risk behaviors. One of the goals of comprehensive school health education is to motivate students to assume self-responsibility for health. **Health promotion** is the informing and motivating of students to become health literate, maintain and improve health, prevent disease, and reduce health-related risk behaviors. Health promotion involves the environmental constructs and supports that enable students to act on knowledge and skills.

Health promotion also involves classroom instruction. Teachers are involved in health promotion when they make the classroom a laboratory where students develop and practice life skills for health. There are several innovative ways to help students develop and practice life skills: health behavior inventories, teaching strategies, and health behavior contracts. There also are ways a teacher can assist by using staying motivated incentives.

Health Behavior Inventories

You can promote health in students by helping them to be more aware of what they are currently doing. A **health behavior inventory** is a personal assessment tool that contains a list of actions to which a student responds positively (+), "I practice this action," or to which the student responds negatively (-), "I do not practice this action." A positive response indicates that a student has made a choice to practice a life skill that results in an action that promotes health literacy, maintains and improves health, prevents disease, and reduces health-related risk behaviors. A negative answer indicates that the student chooses actions that may

interfere with health literacy, harm health, and increase the risk of disease or injury and premature death. *The Health Behavior Inventory* (Table 4-7) is an example of how an inventory might look. Notice that the actions included in *The Health Behavior Inventory* were derived from the life skills by omitting the word "will." *The Health Behavior Inventory* (Table 4-7) assesses what the student is doing right now. You might choose to design a health behavior inventory to be given to students after you have covered a content area to assess what the students intend to do. In this situation, you might use "will" and ask students what they intend to do as a result of what they have just learned. In this case, you are assessing intended actions, not current actions.

When you ask students to complete a health behavior inventory, it is important to explain that the actions that are being assessed are not of equal value. For example, "I do not use tobacco products," is of greater value to well-being than "I volunteer in school clubs and community organizations and agencies that promote health." Although both of these actions are desirable, choosing not to use tobacco products is of greater value in becoming health literate, maintaining and improving health, preventing disease, and reducing health-related risk behaviors than is choosing to volunteer in school clubs and community organizations.

After students complete a health behavior inventory, have them summarize what they have learned about their behavior. For example, in *The Health Behavior Inventory* (Table 4-7), appears the statement "I listen to music at safe levels." Suppose a student responds with "no." The student might have had different reasons for giving this response. Perhaps the student is unaware of what a "safe" level might be. If this was the reason for the "no" response, the student needs health knowledge about safe levels of noise. Perhaps the student responded with "no" because (s)he enjoys loud music. If this was the reason for the "no" response, the student needs to be motivated to change his/her behavior. The student also might be encouraged to complete a health behavior contract. Health behavior contracts are discussed later in this chapter.

Table 4-7

Health Behavior Inventory

Directions: Read each statement carefully. If the statement describes you, place a (+) in front of it to indicate a positive action that promotes health literacy, maintains and improves health, prevents disease, and reduces health-related risk behaviors. If the statement does not describe you, place a (-) in front of it to indicate your actions interfere with health literacy, harm health, promote disease, and increase health-related risk behaviors.

Mental and Emotional Health
(   ) 1. I cope with stress in healthful ways.
(   ) 2. I express feelings in healthful ways.

Family Living
(   ) 3. I avoid discriminatory behaviors and prejudice.
(   ) 4. I handle disagreements without fighting.

Growth and Development
(   ) 5. I practice behaviors that contribute to healthful aging.
(   ) 6. I share my feelings about dying and death.

Nutrition
(   ) 7. I read food labels.
(   ) 8. I select foods that reduce my risk of heart disease.

Personal Health
(   ) 9. I care for my skin, hair, and nails daily.
(   ) 10. I have a plan for physical fitness.

Alcohol, Tobacco, and Other Drugs
(   ) 11. I do not use tobacco products.
(   ) 12. I do not drink alcohol.

Communicable and Chronic Diseases
(   ) 13. I use sunscreen to protect myself from the sun.
(   ) 14. I have information about my family's history of disease.

Injury Prevention and Safety
(   ) 15. I have a list of emergency telephone numbers.
(   ) 16. I wear a safety restraint when riding in a car.

Consumer and Community Health
(   ) 17. I have a budget that I follow.
(   ) 18. I participate in school clubs and community activities that promote health and safety.

Environmental Health
(   ) 19. I recycle.
(   ) 20. I listen to music at safe levels.

Figure 4-8

A *Totally Awesome Teaching Strategy*™

Instructional Strategies

It is important to use a variety of teaching strategies when teaching health. An instructional strategy is a technique used by a facilitator or teacher to help a student 1) understand a particular concept, and/or 2) develop and practice a specific life skill. This teacher resource book contains one type of instructional strategy, the *Totally Awesome Teaching Strategy*™.

Totally Awesome Teaching Strategies™

A Totally Awesome Teaching Strategy™ (Figure 4-8) is a creative and motivating teaching strategy that includes:

* *Clever Title*. A clever title is set in boldfaced type in the center of the page.

* *Designated Content Area*. The content area for which the teaching strategy is designed appears in the upper left-hand corner: Mental and Emotional Health; Family Living; Growth and Development; Nutrition; Personal Health; Alcohol, Tobacco, and Other Drugs; Communicable and Chronic Diseases; Injury Prevention and Safety; Consumer and Community Health; and

Environmental Health. The six categories of risk behaviors identified by The Centers for Disease Control and Prevention are included within one or more of the content areas: behaviors that result in unintentional and intentional injuries; tobacco use; alcohol and other drug use; sexual behaviors that result in HIV infection, other STDs, and unintended pregnancies; dietary patterns that contribute to disease; insufficient physical activity.

* *Designated Grade Level*. The grade level for which the teaching strategy is appropriate appears directly beneath the designated content area in the upper left-hand corner.

* *Infusion into Curriculum Areas Other Than Health*. **Infusion** is the integration of a subject area into another area(s) of the curriculum. Teaching strategies are designed to be infused into several curriculum areas other than health education: art studies, foreign language, home economics, language arts, physical education, math studies, music studies, science studies, social studies, and visual and performing arts. The curriculum area into which the teaching strategy is designed to be infused is designated by a symbol that appears to the right of the clever title that is set in boldfaced type.

The CSHE Curriculum

- *Health Literacy.* **Health literacy** is competence in critical thinking and problem solving, responsible and productive citizenship, self-directed learning, and effective communication. (The Joint Committee on Health Education Standards, 1995). The teaching strategies are designed to promote competency in health literacy. Four symbols are used to describe the health literate individual: critical thinker, responsible citizen, self-directed learner, and effective communicator. The symbol designating one of the four components of health literacy appears to the right of the symbol designating curriculum infusion.

- *Health Education Standard(s).* **Health education standards** are standards that specify what students should know and be able to do. They involve the knowledge and skills essential to the development of health literacy (The Joint Committee on Health Education Standards, 1995). The health education standard(s) are listed under the boldfaced subheading.

- *Performance Indicator(s).* **Performance indicators** are the specific concepts and skills students should know and be able to do in order to achieve each of the broader health education standards (The Joint Committee on Health Education Standards, 1995). The performance indicator(s) for the teaching strategy are listed under the boldfaced subheading.

- *Life Skill(s).* **Life skills** are actions that promote health literacy, maintain and improve health, prevent disease, and reduce health-related risk behaviors. The life skill(s) that are reinforced by using the teaching strategy are listed under this boldfaced subheading.

- *Materials.* The **materials** are items that are needed to do the teaching strategy. The materials used in the teaching strategies are readily available and inexpensive. They are listed under this boldfaced subheading.

- *Motivation.* The **motivation** is the step-by-step directions to follow when doing the teaching strategy. The motivation includes a creative way to teach the health knowledge and skills students need to master the health education standards, performance objectives, and life skills. The motivation is listed under this boldfaced subheading.

- *Evaluation.* The **evaluation** is the means of measuring the students' mastery of the health education standards, the performance indicators, and the life skills. The evaluation is listed under this boldfaced subheading.

- *Multicultural Infusion.* **Multicultural infusion** is the adaptation of the teaching strategy to include ideas that promote an awareness and appreciation of the culture and background of different people. Suggestions for adapting the teaching strategy to incorporate learning about people of varied cultures and backgrounds are included under this boldfaced subheading.

- *Inclusion.* **Inclusion** is the adaptation of the teaching strategy to assist and include students with special learning challenges and may include enrichment suggestions for the gifted and reteaching ideas for students who are learning disabled. Suggestions for adapting the teaching strategy to assist students with special learning challenges are included under this boldfaced subheading.

The effectiveness of comprehensive school health education is very much dependent upon the quality and creativity of the teaching strategies that are utilized in the classroom. You will want your lessons to be motivating and challenging. Section 3. *Totally Awesome Teaching Strategies*™ contains *Totally Awesome Teaching Strategies*™ that can be used in the classroom.

Health Behavior Contracts

A **health behavior contract** is a plan that is written to develop the habit of following a specific life skill. A health behavior contract includes: 1) the life skill for which a habit needs to be formed, 2) a few statements describing the importance of this life skill to optimal well-being, 3) a plan for practicing this life skill, 4) an evaluation including a method of reporting progress, and 5) a statement of the results experienced from practicing this life skill. Remember, the life skills in *The Scope and Sequence Chart* (in *The Curriculum Guide* in Section 5) are correlated to the health education standards and the performance indicators. Therefore, the health behavior contract becomes another tool designed to help students master the health education standards and the performance indicators. *The Health Behavior Contract* (Figure 4-9) is an example of how a contract might look.

Using health behavior contracts to help students take responsibility for health can help them develop a process that can be used for the rest of their lives. Whenever a new life skill is desired, or whenever a healthful habit needs to be formed, they can design a health behavior contract. Making a health behavior contract is helpful for several reasons.

First, the life skill that is desired is written on paper. Most of the research completed on goal setting emphasizes that people who write down what they want to accomplish are more likely to accomplish it. Writing down the life skill helps people focus on their commitment. In Figure 4-9, the life skill for the health behavior contract is, "I will select the appropriate number of servings from The Food Guide Pyramid."

Second, the health behavior contract allows for an individualized plan to be made to practice the life skill. For example, students might individualize their plans for practicing the life skill in *The Health Behavior Contract* (Figure 4-9). For example, students who have a vegetarian diet might select different foods from Meat, Poultry, Fish, Dry Beans, Eggs, and Nuts Group than students who do not have a vegetarian diet. This individualization also allows for multicultural sensitivity as students with different cultural backgrounds may select varied ethnic foods.

Third, health behavior contracts allow for monitoring progress. Part of taking self-responsibility for health is being aware of one's behavior and making constant choices for positive behavior. By completing a chart or writing in a journal to monitor

---

Figure 4-9

The Health Behavior Contract

Life Skill: I will select the appropriate number of servings from The Food Guide Pyramid.

Effect on My Well-Being:  Selecting the appropriate number of servings from The Food Guide Pyramid will help me have a balanced diet. Eating the recommended number of servings will help me to get the nutrients my body needs each day. Choosing the appropriate number of servings will help me to maintain a healthful weight, reduce my risk for diseases such as heart disease and cancer, and eat a diet low in fat content.

My Plan:  Each day, I will choose the appropriate number of servings of food The Food Guide Pyramid recommends. I will choose 6-11 servings from the Bread, Cereals, Rice, and Pasta Group; 3 to 5 servings from the Vegetable Group; 2 to 4 servings from the Fruit Group; 2 to 3 servings from the Meat, Poultry, Fish, Dry Beans, Eggs, and Nuts Group; 2 to 3 servings from the Milk, Yogurt, Cheese Group; and eat foods from the Fats, Oils, and Sweets sparingly.

Evaluating My Progress: I will complete the following chart to indicate the number of servings from The Food Guide Pyramid I have eaten each day.

Group From The Food Guide Pyramid	Recommended Number Servings	Servings I Have Have Eaten
Bread, Cereals, Rice And Pasta	6 - 11	✓✓✓✓✓
Vegetable	3 - 5	✓✓✓✓
Fruit	2 - 4	✓✓✓
Meat, Poultry, Fish, Dry Beans, Eggs, and Nuts	2 - 3	✓✓
Milk, Yogurt, Cheese Group	2 - 3	✓✓
Fats, Oils, and Sweets	use sparingly	✓

Results:

I have more energy.
I do not feel as tired.

The CSHE Curriculum

progress, awareness of health behavior is brought into focus. For example, if a student lists the foods that (s)he has chosen for a day, (s)he can become aware of whether or not (s)he was eating the recommended number of servings from the Food Guide Pyramid. The student might learn that (s)he is not getting the appropriate number of servings of fruits and vegetables.

Fourth, health behavior contracts enable students to analyze the results of following life skills. They are asked to record ways in which following a specific life skill improves their physical, mental-emotional, and family-social well-being. Because the life skills have been correlated with the health education standards, they learn ways in which mastery of the health education standards will benefit them.

Fifth, family members can become involved when students make and follow health behavior contracts. Teachers can duplicate a sample health behavior contract with directions for its completion and have students take it home to share with their families. Family members might become involved. For example, family members might become committed to practicing the life skill identified in *The Health Behavior Contract* (Figure 4-9). This may change the foods that are served at family meals and the snacks that are kept in the home.

A final note about health behavior contracts is needed. When evaluating health behavior contracts, it is important to evaluate the process and not the results. In other words, the health behavior contract is another means by which students learn about their behavior and are motivated to make positive changes. Suppose a student was working on the *Health Behavior Contract* (Figure 4-9). Perhaps the student was working to change his/her diet. When asked to process this experience, the student identified obstacles to this plan. The student might have gained much insight into his/her behavior. As a result, much learning has taken place. Teachers need to be supportive and to reward attempts to improve and maintain positive behavior. They also need to encourage honesty. If students are penalized for failing to meet their goals, they may not be honest or insightful.

Staying Motivated Incentives

There is a saying, "Your success is measured by your ability to complete the things you say you will do." Another way to say this is, "A winner is a finisher." What are some strategies that you can use in your classroom to help students stay motivated to practice life skills and to follow health behavior contracts to make new life skills a habit?

- *Use reminders.* Have students write the life skill they want to develop on a few index cards. Have them place the cards in locations where they will be reminded of the life skill and the health behavior contracts they have made.

- *Share progress made on plans.* Set aside time for students to share their progress on their plans with their classmates. This will allow students the opportunity to receive feedback on what they are doing. Of course, you will want to respect confidentiality and not ask students who would rather keep their contracts in confidence to share their contracts and results with classmates.

- *Develop support systems.* Suggest that students working on similar life skills form support networks. For example, students desiring to lose weight might have a meeting time to share their obstacles and feelings and to encourage one another. Students desiring to ride bicycles to engage in aerobic exercise might plan some bicycling trips together. Usually, it is easier to stay motivated when there are others on whom you can count for support and encouragement.

- *Use role models as encouragers.* You might use resource people who practice specific life skills to share their experiences and health behavior contracts with your class. These people can be those who have been committed to a life skill such as distance walking who can explain how practicing a life skill improved their lifestyle. They also might be people who have abandoned old habits for new ones. For example, a person who used to eat poorly who became serious about eating healthfully and maintaining ideal weight might be a role model.

- *Reward progress.* Examine ways students can be rewarded for their progress in making a life skill a habit. For example, students who are trying to reduce their weight might buy a new pair of shorts for exercise after sticking to their diets for two weeks. Another way of rewarding students is to give bonus points for progress. Teachers can individually contract with students for bonus points to be rewarded for progress toward making a life skill a end habit.

Evaluation Techniques

Evaluation is the procedure used to measure the results of efforts toward a desired goal. The emphasis on accountability in education has made evaluation increasingly important in recent years. With regard to comprehensive school health education, there are at least four foci for evaluation. First, evaluation must measure the efforts that schools, communities, institutions of higher education, and state and national education agencies are making to implement The National Health Education Standards.

The following discussion describes The Opportunity-to-Learn Standards designed for this purpose. Second, the curriculum must be evaluated. The following discussion provides a checklist that can be used to evaluate the curriculum. Third, there must be evaluation of students' mastery of the health education standards and the performance indicators. Several techniques that can be used to measure progress and mastery are described. Fourth, teacher effectiveness must be evaluated. Several techniques for measuring teacher effectiveness are described in the following section of this chapter.

Evaluation of The Opportunity-to-Learn Standards

The Opportunity-to-Learn Standards *are standards that specify directions for the policies, resources, and activities to be conducted in schools, communities, institutions of higher education, and state and national education agencies in order to implement The National Health Education Standards* (The Joint Committee on Health Education Standards, 1995). The Opportunity-to-Learn Standards are identified for:
1. Local Education Agencies
2. Community Education Agencies
3. State Education Agencies
4. Teacher Preparation Institutions
5. National Health Agencies

A copy of The Opportunity-to-Learn Standards for each of the above is included in the Appendix.

Evaluation of the Curriculum

The comprehensive school health education curriculum is an organized, sequential K-12 plan for teaching students the information and skills they need to become health literate, maintain and improve health, prevent disease, and reduce health-related risk behaviors. The curriculum should be evaluated regularly. *The Comprehensive School Health Education Checklist* (Table 4-10) might be used as an evaluation tool.

Evaluation of Students

With the current emphasis on the health education standards and the performance indicators, it is important to identify ways that student progress and mastery can be evaluated. There are different techniques that might be used.

Observation Perhaps the most obvious method involves direct observation. Performance indicators describe what students will be able to do. Teachers can observe students to see what they are doing. What choices are they making for school lunches? Are they following school guidelines for safety? Are students being reported for breaking guidelines involving the use of alcohol and other drugs? Although this technique of evaluation is subjective, it is important for teachers to be keen observers to learn what students are doing. Teachers might share their observations, in confidence, with students. This would allow a teacher and a student to discuss new ways of behaving that might be more healthful.

Health Behavior Contracts Health behavior contracts require the students to report data about their health behavior and changes or improvements in their health behavior. There has been increasing emphasis on using health behavior contracts as an evaluation technique. Students are not evaluated on their mastery of the life skill. Instead, they are evaluated on the effort with which they attempt to master the life skills. The teacher may require the students to write a paper that provides insight into their experience. For example, a student might attempt to complete a health behavior contract whose life skill focuses on achieving a desirable level of fitness. The student might outline an

aerobic exercise plan such as walking several times a week.

Now suppose the student does not achieve the desired results and fitness level. When writing this paper, the student gives insights as to why (s)he did not walk on some of the days that (s)he had planned to walk. The student discusses the roadblocks or obstacles that (s)he experienced while attempting to complete his/her plan. A great deal of learning has taken place. The teacher evaluates the student's paper using the quality of the insights as a criterion. Some teachers are skeptical about evaluating summary papers completed for health behavior contracts. They recognize that students must be honest in their self-reporting efforts. In order to become self-directed learners (a component of health literacy), students must develop self-reporting skills and must have trusting relationships with those who help them.

Participation **Cooperative learning** is an instructional strategy in which students work together to understand a particular concept or develop a life skill. Cooperative learning provides the opportunity for students to practice interpersonal skills and learn about other students. It also provides the opportunity for students with different skills to share these skills as they work on a project. For example, a student who has difficulty reading but who excels in art might be involved in a cooperative learning project with a student who excels at reading. Together, they may work on

Table 4-10

The Comprehensive School Health Education Checklist

_____1. *Adheres to a plan in which an adequate amount of time is spent on health education.* The Society of State Directors of Health, Physical Education, and Recreation recommends at least two hours per week of health instruction for the elementary grades. The Society recommends a daily period of health instruction for at least two semesters in the middle and junior high school. For high school, the Society recommends a daily period of health instruction for at least two semesters. These are the minimal recommendations of the Society.

_____2. *Focuses on the health education standards and mastery of performance indicators by grades 4, 8, and 11.* Those responsible for designing and implementing the curriculum keep the primary focus on mastery of performance indicators designed to meet the health education standards.

_____3. *Provides a foundation of health knowledge.* The content areas, life skills, and health topics that are included in the curriculum are selected to promote mastery of the performance indicators and health education standards.

_____4. *Focuses on health literacy.* Health literacy is infused into the lessons so that students become critical thinkers and problem solvers, responsible and productive citizens, self-directed learners, and effective communicators.

_____5. *Uses teaching strategies that are motivating and highly interactive.* The classroom is set up as a laboratory in which students learn concepts and develop and practice life skills. "Seeing is believing" and "experiencing is believing" are more than cliches when referring to curriculum implementation. A "hands-on," interactive, skill-based approach to learning is used.

_____6. *Provides for right and left brain learning.* Research indicates that learning may be influenced by the right brain as well as the left brain. Students who learn best from right brain activities learn more easily with visual lessons including art and music projects. Students who learn best from left brain activities are more suited to traditional styles of teaching. However, all students respond to variety and involvement and need the challenge of both right and left brain learning. By varying teaching style, the classroom remains stimulating.

_____7. *Provides opportunities for inclusion of students with special needs.* As teaching strategies are designed to promote mastery of health education standards and performance indicators, provisions are made for students with special needs. For example, a student who has diabetes might complete a health behavior contract in which a daily menu is planned differently than a student who does not have special diet considerations. A student who has a physical disability might be given assistance in learning ways to achieve the benefits from aerobic exercise from sports and games in which (s)he can participate given his/her limitations. In addition, provisions are made for students with different learning challenges. Students who are able to achieve easily may be given challenging tasks labeled as "challenge" or "enrichment" in the curriculum. When there are students who have difficulty learning, the teacher can focus on reteaching. **Reteaching** is the teaching that occurs when a teacher uses an alternate strategy for instruction after students were not able to garner the concept or life skill from the first instructional strategy.

(Continued)

_____8. *Uses a multicultural approach.* The curriculum is multiculturally sensitive. Family health practices vary depending on cultural backgrounds. For example, students may belong to families with different ethnic backgrounds and may have learned to eat specific foods. When teaching about nutrition, examples of diets and food choices typical of the students' families are included. A multicultural approach to curriculum makes health education more relevant and it expands the awareness students have of those people around them.

_____9. *Provides opportunities for infusion into subject areas other than health.* The teaching strategies are designed to be infused into several curriculum areas other than health education: art studies, foreign language, home economics, language arts, physical education, math studies, music studies, science studies, social studies, and visual and performing arts. Curriculum infusion reinforces learning and helps students understand ways in which educational goals overlap.

_____10. *Includes the family.* The family is actively involved. Parents and guardians are kept current on the health issues studied in the classroom. A family newsletter keeps parents and guardians informed as to what students are learning and provides up-to-date health knowledge. Parents and guardians are invited to participate in health behavior contracts. They support the efforts of their children and may, in turn, complete health behavior contracts themselves.

_____11. *Uses community resources.* Professionals in the community serve as resources by donating time, supplies, and materials; speaking; and serving on committees. Teachers call national and local health agencies and ask for samples of materials.

_____12. *Uses a positive approach.* The attitude of those responsible for health education permeates what happens in the curriculum and then in the classroom. Approaching health and well-being with the attitude that it is rewarding, exciting, and fun to be healthful is more desirable than emphasizing illness and injury. Research indicates that students are more likely to be motivated by a positive approach than by a scare tactic approach. Positive wording is important. For example, it is better to say, "Most young people do not smoke" than it is to say "Many young people smoke." It is better to use audiovisuals depicting young people engaging in wellness behaviors than audiovisuals depicting young people engaging in risk behaviors. A picture is worth a thousand words and students should identify with wellness behaviors and healthful situations, not risk behaviors and risk situations.

_____13. *Includes technology.* **Technology** is the use of computers, CD-Rom, interactive video, medlines, and other forms of high-tech equipment used to communicate and to assimilate, synthesize, analyze, and evaluate information. Those responsible for the curriculum make suggestions for the use of technology within the classroom. The technology should facilitate mastery of the health education standards and performance indicators.

a class presentation on risk factors for heart disease. The student who excels in art may help the other student design posters to share with the class. The student who excels in reading may help the other student when they go to the library to find research articles from which they will gather facts. The students help one another develop and practice skills.

Teachers can observe ways in which students communicate during cooperative learning exercises and provide students with important feedback. Teachers also can encourage students to give each other feedback in a constructive manner. In this way, the teacher evaluates health literacy (being an effective communicator).

Tests The current emphasis in comprehensive school health education is on student mastery of performance indicators. Health knowledge is essential to this task. Assessment of student health knowledge can take place through the use of teacher constructed tests—either in the form of short answers (objective) or essay.

The teacher should keep the following principles in mind when constructing an examination:

1. Test construction must take into account the use to be served by the test.
2. The types of test items used should be determined by the specific outcomes to be measured.
3. Test items should be based on a representative sample of the course content and the specific learning outcomes to be measured.
4. Test items should be of the proper level of difficulty.
5. Test items should be constructed so that extraneous factors do not prevent the student from responding.
6. Test items should be constructed so that the student obtains the correct answer only if (s)he has attained the desired learning outcome.
7. The test should be constructed so that it contributes to improved teacher-learning practices (Grunland, 1971).

Most educators believe that it is helpful to use a variety of examinations. Student performances vary depending on the type of examination administered. *Construction of Examinations to Measure Knowledge* (Table 4-11) provides helpful hints for designing tests.

Portfolio Assessments The **portfolio** is a collection of student works, which can help the teacher evaluate a student's attainment of knowledge, attitudes, and skills (Cleary, 1993). Portfolios have become increasingly popular as assessment devices. In a classroom portfolio designed for student assessment, student pieces are selected (primarily by the student) and reflected upon to show student progress and help the student, teacher, and parents or guardians make evaluations.

When designing a portfolio assessment program, the teacher must first determine the purpose of the portfolio. If the purpose of the portfolio is to track student progress, the teacher must determine which learner goals will be assessed, what samples can demonstrate achievement of these goals, and what criteria will be used to evaluate the contents of the portfolio (Montana Office of Public Instruction, 1993).

Table 4-11

Construction of Examinations to Measure Knowledge

Essay Examinations

Advantages of essay examinations:
1. They are easy to construct since few questions need be asked.
2. They allow students the opportunity to be creative and show organizational skills.
3. They can be used for any topic in the health education curriculum.
4. They allow students to apply knowledge.

Disadvantages of essay examinations:
1. They are difficult to grade.
2. It is sometimes difficult to word them.
3. There is low reliability in scoring them.
4. Students with better writing ability and less knowledge may score well.
5. It is time consuming to grade them.

Hints in the construction of essay examinations:
1. In writing an essay examination, be specific. For example, a nonspecific item would be: Do you feel that smoking in public places should be banned? A student might write a simple "yes" or "no" and provide an accurate response. A better item would be: Select a position, pro or con, on whether smoking should be banned in public places and provide at least five reasons for your position.
2. Always make the criteria for acceptable performance clear. In the previous essay item, students were asked to provide "at least five reasons for your position." If this criterion were not identified, those students who provided one reason and those who provided five would have fulfilled what the teacher had asked. It would be unfair to grade them differently.
3. If you plan to count spelling, grammar, creativity, convincing evidence, etc., be certain to state this on the exam. State

how many points each aspect is worth.
4. Assign a point value to each essay item. This will enable students to set priorities in allocating their time when writing answers to more than one question.
5. Take the exam or have a student take the exam before it is given to the class to determine a reasonable amount of time in which it should be completed.

Hints for grading essay examinations:
1. Prior to grading essay examinations, make a checklist of the items you plan to evaluate and the number of points each is worth. In the previous example given, your checklist might include: 1) provides at least five reasons (5 points), 2) provides convincing evidence (4 points), 3) is grammatically correct (2 points), etc. As you read the essay answers, use your checklist for grading. If possible, duplicate this checklist and give it to students before they write their essays.
2. Read only several papers during a time period. During the reading of essay examinations, especially those requiring many pages of writing, you may begin by grading objectively and then tire of reading the same kinds of answers. After a while all grades may become similar. Short breaks between sets of papers, such as every five papers, will minimize this effect.

True-False Examinations

Advantages of true-false examinations:
1. They are easy to construct since each question consists of only one statement.
2. They can be graded objectively.
3. They are easy to score.
4. There is no confusion over correct and incorrect responses.

(Continued)

Disadvantages of true-false examinations:
1. Students have a 50-50 chance of a correct guess.
2. Questions are often ambiguous or tricky.
3. It is difficult to measure a higher thought process.

Hints for the construction of true-false examinations:
1. Avoid using value judgments in the wording, such as, "Children under the age of 12 should not drink alcohol." Use statements to avoid controversy. "It is harmful to health for children under the age of 12 to drink alcohol."
2. Avoid questions which use the words "always," "never," "all," or "none." Students are conditioned to answer false to these statements.
3. Avoid double negatives.
4. Avoid using compound sentences and long sentences.

Hints for grading true-false examinations:
1. Use a separate answer sheet instead of having students write their answers on the examination. Then the examinations can be used for different classes.
2. Rather than having students write *t* for true and *f* for false have them write *T* or + for true and *F* or - for false. It is easier to read these answers correctly. As an alternative, have a *T* and an *F* for each statement and have students circle their choice.

Multiple Choice Examinations

Advantages of multiple choice examinations:
1. There is a lower chance of guessing correctly than on true-false examinations.
2. It is easy to grade multiple choice examinations.
3. Students must critically examine several alternatives.

Disadvantages of multiple choice examinations:
1. It is time consuming to prepare them.

2. There must be several responses that are feasible for them to be valid.
3. Students may still guess at answers.

Hints in the construction of multiple choice examinations:
1. When writing the directions, use "Select the best answer" to protect against students finding reasons that more than one choice is correct.
2. Make each possible answer a worthy choice. When one or more of the choices can be ruled out right away, students are guided toward the correct choice without demonstrating mastery of knowledge.
3. Use four or five choices. More than five becomes too cumbersome and confusing and less than four increases the chance of a correct guess.

Hints for grading multiple choice examinations:
1. Have students write answers in capital letters. This minimizes errors in interpreting script.
2. Distribute an answer sheet upon which the student can circle the correct choice.

Advantages of matching examinations:
1. The scoring is easy and reliable.
2. Student guessing is minimized.
3. Students are required to discriminate in a more rigorous manner than on other kinds of examinations.
4. These tests are highly valid.

Disadvantages of matching examinations:
1. They can be difficult to construct.
2. They may take too long a period to complete.
3. The answers may be correct or incorrect in pairs.
4. There may be several answers for one question.

(Continued)

Hints for constructing matching examinations:

1. Do not include more than ten nor less than five or six items. Too many choices may lead to confusion and too few items may lead to "correct guessing."
2. The alternatives from which to choose should exceed the number of items by one or two. This eliminates the student automatically matching the remaining items if there is but one alternative left.

Hints for grading matching examinations:

1. A grading key can be made and placed next to student answers for quick grading.

Completion Examinations

A completion examination requires students to add missing information to a sentence fragment.

Advantages of completion examinations:

1. This type of examination requires students to know all aspects of a subject.
2. It is difficult to guess on this type of examination.
3. This type of examination allows students to organize information.
4. It is easy to write this type of examination.

Disadvantages of completion examinations:

1. Several answers may correctly complete each item.

2. It takes more time to grade because of the number of possible correct answers.
3. Students will select answers they believe the teacher wants rather than ones they might select.

Hints for constructing completion examinations:

1. Word completion items so that only one response will be correct. For example, "Hashish is more potent than marijuana" can be completed with other answers. However, "Hashish which is made from the resin of the hemp plant, is more potent than marijuana" is completed only with hashish.

Hints for grading completion examinations:

1. When grading completion answers, place a line through the incorrect answer and not through the question number. This prevents the student from changing the original answer and saying the item was graded incorrectly.
2. If an answer is left blank by a student, place a line through it also. This prevents the student from filling in the blank when the examination is returned and saying the item was misgraded.

Table 4-12

Teacher As A Role Model

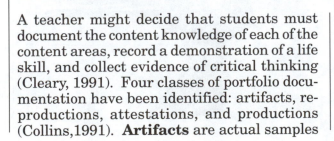

I'd rather see a sermon
than hear one any day;
I'd rather one should walk
with me than merely
show the way.
The eyes a better pupil,
and more willing than the ear;
Fine counsel is confusing,
but examples always clear.

I soon can learn to do it,
if you'll let me see it done;
I can see your hands in
action, but your tongue
too fast may run.
And the lectures you deliver
may be very fine and true.
But, I'd rather get my lesson
by observing what you do.
For I may misunderstand you
and the high advice you give,
But, there's no
misunderstanding how
you act and how you live.

A teacher might decide that students must document the content knowledge of each of the content areas, record a demonstration of a life skill, and collect evidence of critical thinking (Cleary, 1991). Four classes of portfolio documentation have been identified: artifacts, reproductions, attestations, and productions (Collins,1991). **Artifacts** are actual samples of student works. A health education artifact could be a research paper on a health-related topic, a copy of a test given by the teacher, or a brochure designed to educate about a health-related agency. **Reproductions** are tangible evidence of student participation. Examples of health education reproductions include photographs of a student's involvement in a community cleanup campaign and photographs of a student working at a booth at a school health fair.

Attestations are documents written about the work of the student by someone other than the student. Attestations might include a letter from the organizer of a health fair to thank the student for participating, or a letter describing a student's involvement in a volunteer program at a hospital. **Productions** are works prepared by the student to document knowledge and skills. Productions may include a student's written reflection of the portfolio's contents, and captions attached to each document describing the piece and what knowledge or skills the student gained while completing the piece (Cleary, 1993).

One disadvantage of portfolio assessment is the potential difficulty in evaluation. For example, how can a teacher weight and evaluate different documents in each student's portfolio? Should the portfolio be evaluated as a whole or should each component in the portfolio be evaluated separately? Portfolios are not meant to stand alone as evaluation tools, and standardized tests and other traditional measures are still necessary to accurately gauge student progress (Cleary, 1993). However, the portfolio can provide an in-depth, personalized picture of student progress and an assessment tool that provides hands-on involvement of students, teachers, and parents or guardians. Self-reflection or self-evaluation, an important component of the portfolio, requires that students select their best work, determine strengths and weaknesses of their own samples, and suggest ways they could improve (Montana Office of Public Instruction, 1993).

Evaluation of Teachers

Socrates said, "The unexamined life is not worth living." Perhaps teacher evaluation begins with the teacher examining himself or herself to ascertain whether (s)he is committed to being a role model for students. Students are very interested in having teachers who are committed and who "practice what they preach." *Teacher as Role Model* (Table 4-12) is a poem that speaks to the importance of the teacher making a commitment to following the life skills that were identified in *The Scope and Sequence Chart* (in *The Curriculum Guide* in Section 5).

There is no doubt that students want to admire their teachers. They want to know that their teachers believe and are committed to what they are teaching. Therefore, an important aspect of teacher evaluation is the teacher's self-evaluation. This is not to imply that if a teacher's behavior is not perfect (s)he will not be effective. What it means is that if the teacher takes responsibility for his/her health and practices life skills, it will have a positive influence on students. The teacher should take the time to regularly evaluate his/her performance of these life skills. If (s)he is not engaging in specific life skills, a health behavior contract can be used to reinforce the habit of doing so. Teachers should discuss their commitment to practicing life skills and making health behavior contracts with their students.

A teacher also should model a commitment to lifelong learning. When a teacher regularly reads up-to-date health knowledge, enrolls in courses, or takes courses for professional recertification, this sends a message to students that lifelong learning is important. Because health knowledge changes, this message is especially important. Students need to know how important it will be for them to continue learning health knowledge after they finish school. They need to have role models for self-directed learning, an important component of health literacy.

Table 4-13
Likert Scale to Measure Teacher Effectiveness

SA A N D SD 1. The teacher was interested in the subject matter.

2. The teacher motivated me to practice life skills.

3. The teacher had knowledge of health.

4. The teacher answered my questions.

5. The teacher communicated subject matter in a meaningful way.

6. The objectives for health were clear to me.

7. I knew which life skills were important for me to follow.

8. The tests that were given were fair.

9. The teaching strategies used helped me understand health information and practice life skills.

10. The assignments for this class contributed to my learning about health.

Additional comments: _____

_____

_____

_____

_____

_____

Table 4-14
Semantic Differential to Measure Teacher Effectiveness

Directions: I would like to learn how you describe our health education class. Below there is a heading. A list of pairs of words follows. Place a circle around the letter that describes how you feel about the heading.

Your Teacher

Caring	A B C D E	Uncaring
Well prepared	A B C D E	Not prepared
Healthy	A B C D E	Not healthy
Well informed	A B C D E	Not informed
Open minded	A B C D E	Opinionated

The Unit on Nutrition

Learned a lot	A B C D E	Did not learn much
Learned life skills	A B C D E	Did not learn life skills
Fair test	A B C D E	Unfair test
Good activities	A B C D E	Boring activities
Included family	A B C D E	Did not include family
Made me think	A B C D E	Did not make me think

Comments: _____

_____

_____

_____

Likert Scales Besides being a role model for students, teachers will want to demonstrate teaching effectiveness. A **Likert scale** is a technique used to measure beliefs and attitudes in which students react to statements with a response of strongly agree, agree, neutral, disagree, and strongly disagree. *Likert Scale to Measure Teacher Effectiveness* (Table 4-13) might be used by teachers to gain valuable feedback.

Semantic Differentials A **semantic differential** is a technique used to measure beliefs and attitudes in which students are asked to circle a letter from A-B-C-D-E to indicate their preference on a continuum. *Semantic Differential to Measure Teacher Effectiveness* (Table 4-14) might be used.

Bibliography

Association for the Advancement of Health Education, (1991) "Report of the Joint Committee on Health Education Terminology," *Journal of Health Education*, Vol. 22(2), 104.

Bloom, Benjamin S., et al. (1956) *Taxonomy of Educational Objectives-The Classification of Educational Goals, Handbook II: Affective Domain.* New York: David McKay Company, Inc.

Cleary, Michael (1993) Using portfolios to assess student performance in school health education. *Journal of School Health Education*, 63:377–380.

Collins, A. (1991) Portfolios for biology teacher assessment. *Journal of School Personnel Evaluation Education*, 5:147-167. Quoted in Cleary, Michael (1993) Using portfolios to assess student performance in school health education. *Journal of School Health Education*, 63:377–380.

Grunland, Norman E. (1971) *Measurement and Evaluation in Teaching.* New York: Macmillan.

Jourard, Sidney. (1971) *The Transparent Self.* New York: D. Van Nostrand.

Kibler, R. J., and Barker, L., and Miles, D. (1970) *Behavioral Objectives and Instruction.* Boston: Allyn and Bacon.

The Joint Committee on Health Education Standards. (1995) *The National Health Education Standards: Achieving Health Literacy.* Questions about *The National Health Education Standards* might be directed to The American Cancer Society; The American School Health Association; The Association for The Advancement of Health Education; The School Health Education and Services Section, American Public Health Association; and The Society of State Directors of Health, Physical Education, Recreation, and Dance. For copies of *The National Health Education Standards,* call or write The American Cancer Society, 1599 Clifton Road NE, Atlanta, Georgia 30329 (1-800-ACS-2345).

Figure 5-1

Instructional Strategies and Technologies

Effective teachers select creative ways for their students to learn.

Chapter 5

INSTRUCTIONAL STRATEGIES AND TECHNOLOGIES:
Motivating Students to Learn

It has often been said that teaching is an art. Most likely, this is because effective teachers select creative ways for their students to learn (Figure 5-1). They recognize the importance of preparing lessons with the same passion and energy that ballerinas, pianists, actors, and actresses have as they prepare for a first-class performance. Effective teachers are indeed artists who recognize the variety of ways in which students learn. They design learning experiences that are challenging, motivating, creative, and captivating. They design learning experiences that help students become health literate and master the performance indicators identified for The National Health Education Standards. This chapter will discuss instructional strategies and instructional technologies that can be used in the classroom.

Instructional Strategies

Instructional strategies are teaching methods that help students 1) understand a particular concept, and/or 2) develop and practice a specific life skill. In the previous chapter, *Totally Awesome Teaching Strategies*™ were discussed. *Totally Awesome Teaching Strategies*™ are one type of instructional strategy. They serve as creative, challenging, and motivating mini-lessons. A *Totally Awesome Teaching Strategy*™ contains a clever title, designated content area, designated grade level, suggestions for infusion into

curriculum areas other than health, health literacy, health education standards, performance indicators, life skills, materials, motivation, evaluation, suggestions for multicultural infusion, and suggestions for inclusion. This section of the chapter will focus on other types of instructional strategies: lecture, lecture and discussion, role play, brainstorming, buzz groups, panel discussions, debate, cooperative learning, decision-making, self-appraisals and health behavior inventories, student presentations, field trips, demonstrations, and guest speakers.

Lecture

Lecture is an instructional strategy involving a verbal presentation. Lecture is often used when many facts need to be covered in a short period of time. The lecture method of teaching can accommodate a large group of students. The following suggestions can increase the effectiveness of lecture:

1. Plan the lecture so that there is a motivating beginning, a presentation of the factual content, and a summary. The beginning and the summary should help students recognize how the material helps them become health literate and master the performance indicators.

2. Use audiovisuals such as overhead transparencies or slides to provide visual support for the verbal presentation and to clarify concepts and facts. Before using

Instructional Strategies and Technologies

audiovisuals, be certain they can be seen and read by students sitting at the back of the classroom.

3. Make the lecture more interesting and personal by adding anecdotes, humor, and fascinating stories.

4. When using notes for lecture, write them on one side of separate sheets or cards so that you can slide from one to the next with ease. Turning pages can be distracting.

5. Give students an outline upon which they can take notes on the lecture material. Collect the students' notes periodically and review them to make suggestions. Students who take detailed and organized notes usually retain more information and perform better on tests.

6. Select specific students to gauge the pace of your lecture. Observe these students to determine if they have enough time to grasp the information and take notes. Adjust your pace if necessary.

7. Vary your pace, posture, and voice to avoid monotony. Be certain that you can be heard at the back of the classroom. If your voice cannot be heard, use a microphone.

Lecture and Discussion

Lecture and discussion is an instructional strategy combining a verbal presentation with student dialogue. Student interaction is included when discussion is added to the lecture method. Students have the opportunity to interact with other students as well as with the teacher. Students also have the opportunity to listen to other students. Adding discussion to the lecture method increases the likelihood that students will gain skills needed to become health literate. The following suggestions can increase the effectiveness of lecture and discussion:

1. Plan the lecture so that there is a motivating beginning, a presentation of the factual content, and a summary. The beginning and the summary should help students recognize how the material helps them become health literate and master the performance indicators. As you plan the lecture, appropriate enough time for student discussion.

2. Use audiovisuals such as overhead transparencies or slides to provide visual support for the verbal presentation and to clarify concepts and facts. Before using audiovisuals, be certain that they can be seen and read by students sitting at

the back of the classroom. Ideas generated during student discussion can be written on a blank overhead transparency using a water-base marker. Be certain to write large enough for students sitting in the back of the classroom to read what has been written.

3. Make the lecture more interesting and personal by adding anecdotes, humor, and fascinating stories. Ask students to share experiences they have had that pertain to the material that is being covered.

4. When using notes for lecture, write them on one side of separate sheets or cards so that you can slide from one to the next with ease. Turning pages can be distracting.

5. Insert questions for students in your notes. By doing so, you can generate discussion of points you believe to be important. You can motivate students to use critical thinking skills needed to become health literate.

6. Give students an outline upon which they can take notes of the material to be presented. Include space where students can record what other students have said. Collect the students' notes periodically and review them to make suggestions. Students who take detailed and organized notes usually retain more information and perform better on tests.

7. Encourage students to participate in discussion. Recognize and affirm students for their participation. When a student

asks a question that is not relevant at the time, give a short answer and assure the student that you will answer the question in greater detail at the appropriate time. When a student asks a question that you are not able to answer, say that you cannot answer the question and offer to find the answer.

8. Have guidelines for participation in order to maintain classroom control. Explain that students must raise their hands and be acknowledged before speaking. Only one student is to speak at a time while other students listen. Students are to be courteous when they disagree with what is being said.

9. Have a plan of action to use when one or a few students dominate student discussion. For example, you might ask students who have participated to wait until others have had a chance to participate before they speak again.

10. During student discussion, keep students focused upon the topic being addressed. Keep to the allotted time frame so that the lecture material is covered.

Role Play

Role play is an instructional strategy in which students use assigned roles to show how they might act in specific situations. There are two different kinds of role plays. In one kind of role play, students are assigned roles and given specific scripts. During role play, they act according to the specific scripts they have been given. In another kind of role play, students are given assigned roles and a situation. During role play, they act according to the role they have been assigned but the script is spontaneous and depends on what they choose to say. The following suggestions can increase the effectiveness of role play:

1. Use role play to master specific life skills and performance indicators and be certain the script and summary discussion stay focused. For example, suppose role play is used to reinforce the life skill, "I will not drink alcohol." When the script for the role play is designed, it might call for one student to be assigned the role of trying to persuade another student to drink alcohol. Another student might be assigned the role of being the person who is pressured to drink alcohol. The script for the role play might give instructions for the student to resist the pressure. This role play would clearly keep the focus on the life skill, "I will not drink alcohol." Now suppose the role play was designed differently. Suppose the student who was assigned the role of being the student who was pressured was not given instruction to resist the pressure but was asked to respond spontaneously to the first student. Suppose that this student did not resist the pressure but agreed to drink the alcohol. At the end of the role play, the discussion must immediately be focused on why this action was not responsible behavior. When role play is used, it must always culminate in a responsible message that reinforces life skills. Students should never be given a mixed message.

2. Role play should be limited to three minutes. When role play lasts longer, students often become disinterested and forget the situation and the responses that need to be processed.

3. Sometimes students are given scripts that contain false information or they make false or misleading statements when they act in their assigned roles. Correct all misinformation immediately. For example, given the previous situation to use

in role play, the student assigned the role of pressuring another student to drink might say, "Drinking one beer will not harm health." At the culmination of this role play, the teacher must refocus on this false statement and give correct information. The teacher might ask, "How might drinking one beer effect health?" The response might be, "Drinking even one beer slows reaction time. A person is more likely to have an accident when reaction time is slowed."

4. Allow students to volunteer for role play. When selecting students for role play, give them the opportunity to switch roles or to decline. It is difficult to know what life experiences all students have had. Some role plays may include scripts that are too similar to a student's life experience and this student may feel embarassed or uncomfortable being assigned a role and having to act this role in front of classmates.

5. Create role plays that help students develop health literacy. A role play might be designed so that students assigned certain roles must think critically and respond quickly to a lifelike situation. This gives students the opportunity to test their skills without experiencing the consequences. A role play might be designed so that students assigned certain roles might practice using words and nonverbal communication to respond to life-like situations. For example, role play is very effective in helping students practice their use of resistance skills. When students practice their use of resistance skills during role play, they are practicing skills needed for effective communication, another component of health literacy. A role play might be designed so that students are assigned roles in which each responds differently to the same situation. The follow-up discussion can focus on which response demonstrated responsible citizenship, still another component of health literacy.

6. Use role reversal within a role play to help students gain an appreciation of how one's role can influence one's perceptions and feelings. **Role reversal** is a technique used during role play in which the role assigned to one student is exchanged with the role assigned to another student in the middle of the role play. For example, in the situation given previously, the student who is assigned the role of pressuring the other student to drink beer is exchanged in the middle of the role play. This student then has the assigned role of being pressured to drink beer. At the culmination of the role play, the students who were assigned the role reversals can share how they felt as they played each role. A variation might be the following. A student might be assigned the role of using resistance skills when pressured to drink beer. During the beginning of the role play, the student is not given a script and must rely on himself/herself to resist the pressure. After several moments, the student might be given a list of reasons to use when resisting the pressure to drink beer. After the role play, this student might be asked which assigned role was most effective. Most likely, the student would recognize that it was easier to use resistance skills when (s)he had the list. This role play might be used to reinforce the need to prepare ahead to say NO to pressure to act in harmful, unsafe, and illegal ways.

Brainstorming

Brainstorming is an instructional strategy in which a variety of responses to the same question, problem, or trigger statement are requested. There are two ways to use brainstorming. The teacher can state the question, problem, or trigger statement for which responses are requested and then facilitate the brainstorming session to generate responses. The teacher can state the question, problem, or trigger statement for which responses are requested and then ask students to break into small groups and generate the list of responses. When brainstorming is done in small groups, the students in each of the small groups should select a leader to record responses. Brainstorming is an appropriate instructional strategy for helping students learn how to make responsible decisions. Brainstorming can be used to help students think creatively and explore several options. The following suggestions can increase the effectiveness of brainstorming. These suggestions might be adapted when the class is divided into small groups for the brainstorming session.

1. During a brainstorming session, record the responses so that students can see them and refer back to them during

a discussion. Write the responses on the chalkboard. Write the responses large enough so that students who are sitting in the back of the classroom can read them.

2. Record the responses in the order they are given by students. Do not judge or evaluate the responses by rank ordering them in any way. This can be done at the culmination of the brainstorming and will allow for careful and consistent evaluation.

3. Encourage all students to participate when generating the list of responses. If some students do not respond, ask them if a response was given that they might have given. If some students dominate the brainstorming session, ask them to wait to respond further until others have given responses.

4. Have guidelines for the brainstorming session in order to maintain classroom control. Explain that students must raise their hands and be acknowledged before speaking. Only one student is to speak at a time.

5. When using brainstorming to reinforce responsible decision-making skills, give students a situation and ask them to identify as many options as possible. Ask them not to judge or evaluate the options, but merely to brainstorm a list. After brainstorming the options, be clear as to the criteria that will be used to evaluate each option. Use *The Responsible Decision-Making Model* (Table 4-3). Have students evaluate each option asking whether the option is healthful, safe, legal, respectful of self and others, follows the guidelines of responsible adults such as parents or guardians, and demonstrates character.

Buzz Groups

A **buzz group** is an instructional strategy in which a small group of students discusses a topic or issue. Buzz groups are also referred to as small group discussions. Buzz groups provide one of the best opportunities for students to practice skills in effective communication, a component of health literacy. The following suggestions can increase the effectiveness of buzz groups:

1. Have a carefully planned strategy for deciding how to place students in buzz groups. Capitalize on this opportunity for students to practice communication skills. Rather than having students belong to buzz groups to which their friends belong, place them in groups with students they do not know as well. Consider the present communication skills of students. Balance the groups allowing for at least one student who has good communication skills to be in the group and one student who has fewer skills. By balancing groups in this way, students might learn from one another.

2. Give students a written copy of the topic or issue to be addressed. Give them specific instructions as to how they should proceed. For example, you might ask that each group selects a group leader or facilitator. Tell students how long they will have for discussion and what they should accomplish during the allotted time. For example, you might say they are to discuss what they would do if someone tried to pick a fight with them. At the end of a five minute time period, they are to summarize the suggestions of the group.

3. Never give directions for a buzz group that require members of the group to come to a consensus on a controversial issue. Parents and guardians have the responsibility for teaching children their value system. It is not appropriate to have students take a position on an issue that is contrary to the position of their parents or guardian.

4. When giving instructions for the buzz groups, discuss ways students might communicate effectively in their groups. Discuss the need to stay on task. Emphasize the importance of encouraging all group members to actively participate and listen.

5. While students are participating in buzz groups, demonstrate your interest and involvement by interacting with each group. Provide suggestions to groups who are having difficulty staying on task or getting started with their discussion.

6. After the allotted time, ask the leader or facilitator from each group to share the responses of the group with the entire class. Refocus on the life skill that prompted your use of the buzz group. For example, in the situation given, the life skill might have been, "I will practice conflict resolution skills." After the students summarized what group members would do if someone tried to pick a fight with them, the discussion would focus on conflict resolution skills.

7. Allow time for students to evaluate their use of communication skills in the buzz groups. This can be done within the buzz groups or with the class as a whole.

Panel Discussions

A **panel discussion** is an instructional strategy in which two or more students research and report on a topic or issue. Panel members may speak for a set amount of time or they may interact with each other and the audience. The following suggestions can increase the effectiveness of panel discussions:

1. Before assigning panel discussions, discuss how to gather and evaluate health information. Introduce students to reliable sources of health information. Review ways to use the library to obtain information.

2. Give students written instructions for the panel discussions. Clearly state the topic or issue to be addressed. Identify the number of sources that must be used when gathering information. Explain the role of

different panel members. Identify time lines for completion of tasks prior to having the panel discussion in the classroom.

3. Provide class time for at least the first planning session. Ask members of the panel to develop a plan, outline the panel discussion, and assign responsibilities to panel members. Review the plan and make suggestions.

4. After the members of the panel discussion have had time to complete their plans and practice their presentations, meet with them to be certain they are ready for the class presentation. This avoids wasting valuable class time.

5. After the panel presentation, review and clarify information presented. Refocus on the life skill and the performance indicators to be mastered.

Debate

A **debate** is an instructional strategy in which an issue is presented and students identify and defend an approach, solution, or choice. Debate provides the opportunity for students to recognize the importance of being well-informed. The following suggestions can increase the effectiveness of debate:

1. Select appropriate issues for debate. For example, students might debate the following, "For a first offense, any student who starts a fight on school premises should be required to attend a class in conflict resolution training for three successive Saturdays." One student might support or defend this as a helpful solution to reducing the incidence of fighting at school. Another student might

challenge this and be supportive of mandatory three day suspension for the first offense for fighting on school premises.

2. Recognize that some topics are not appropriate for debate in the school setting. For example, students should not be asked to debate whether or not abortion should be legal. Parents and guardians are responsible for influencing the value systems of their children. The topic of abortion and the many issues surrounding this topic should be addressed at home. A further example might be helpful. Students should not be asked to debate whether marijuana use should be made legal. Marijuana use is against the law. Most parents and guardians do not want their children spending time in school developing strategies to defend illegal behaviors.

3. Give students written instructions for the debate. Clearly state the issue to be debated. If students are to select an issue to be debated, screen the issues they select carefully. Adhere to the guidelines in suggestion #2. Identify the number of sources that must be used when gathering information for the debate. Identify time lines for completion of tasks prior to having the debate in the classroom.

4. Provide class time for at least the first planning session for students who will debate the same issue. Ask students to develop a plan, outline possible topics to cover during the debate, and assign responsibilities to those students who will debate the issues. Review the plan and make suggestions.

5. After students have had time to research the issue to be debated and have practiced their presentations, meet with them to be certain they are ready to debate the issue in the classroom. This avoids wasting valuable class time.

6. Before the debate, give specific directions to other students. Ask students to write the issue to be debated at the top of a sheet of paper. Have them fold the paper into two columns and label the columns FOR and AGAINST. Ask students to identify reasons that are FOR and reasons that are AGAINST the issue being debated. Under each reason, they are to make a notation whether or not the reason was supported with sufficient evidence. After the debate, have students share what they have written. Discuss the importance of documenting sources of health information and of being well-informed on health issues. The processing discussion after the debate should help students learn to evaluate the reliability of information presented by people addressing health issues, a skill needed to meet one of the health education standards.

Cooperative Learning

Cooperative learning is an instructional strategy in which students work together to understand a particular concept or develop a life skill. Cooperative learning provides the opportunity for students to practice communication skills which promote health literacy. Cooperative learning affords the opportunity for students with diverse backgrounds to dialogue and gain further understanding of one another. It also provides the opportunity for students with different skills to share these skills as they work together. The following suggestions can increase the effectiveness of cooperative learning:

1. Select cooperative learning experiences carefully. They should be learning experiences that provide an opportunity for students of varied abilities to work together and to succeed. Carefully select students who will be paired together. Assess their varied skills when making selections. Place students who have difficulty learning with students who will be encouraging and supportive.

2. Give specific instructions for the task to be completed. Ask students to develop a plan to complete the task that involves each student. Emphasize the need to combine their strengths and to practice communication skills.

3. When the task is complete, ask students to share what they have learned. Ask students to discuss what they have gained from working together as a team. Ask students to identify the many ways they must work as a team in situations outside of the school setting.

4. Avoid using cooperative learning as a basis for grading. When students are aware that a task will be graded, they often focus on the grade rather than on combining their talents. One or two students may do most of the project because of their concern about the grade.

Instructional Strategies and Technologies

Decision-Making

Decision-Making is an instructional strategy in which students are given a situation for which a choice must be made and asked to apply a series of steps to determine which choice leads to actions that are responsible. The authors of this book have developed *The Responsible Decision-Making Model* (Table 4-3) for use with this instructional strategy. *The Responsible Decision-Making Model* (Table 4-3) is a series of steps to follow to assure that the decisions a person makes lead to actions that: 1. promote health, 2. protect safety, 3. protect laws, 4. show respect for self and others, 5. follow guidelines set by responsible adults such as parents and guardians, and 6. demonstrate character. Being able to make responsible decisions is a skill needed to become health literate. The following suggestions can increase the effectiveness of responsible decision-making:

1. Help students distinguish between problem-solving and responsible decision-making. The difference focuses upon the first step. In problem-solving, the first step is "Identify the problem." In responsible decision-making, the first step is "Identify the situation." For example, the student may be asked to examine this scenario, "You are at a party and someone offers you an alcoholic beverage." Using the problem-solving approach, this scenario would be stated as being the "problem." Students would be asked to "Identify the problem." Given the responsible decision-making approach, students would be asked to "Clearly describe the situation they face." The responsible decision-making approach helps students to be more empowered for the following reason. In the problem-solving approach, they are told they have a problem that must be solved. In the responsible-decision making approach, they are told they are facing a situation. If they make a decision that results in a responsible action, they avoid having a problem.

2. Emphasize the importance of using the six criteria that are stated in step 4 of *The Responsible Decision-Making Model* (Table 4-3). Explain that these criteria help them to be objective and to avoid being convinced that a decision or action is responsible when it is not. For example, given the previous example, suppose several of their friends decided to drink an alcoholic beverage. The actions of their friends would not be an acceptable reason for choosing to drink an alcoholic beverage. It is not one of the criteria to be used to decide if an action or decision is responsible.

3. Emphasize the importance of gathering and evaluating information in making responsible decisions (a health education standard). When using *The Responsible Decision-Making Model* (Table 4-3), a student may need to gather and evaluate information to learn if a particular decision will result in an action that meets the six criteria. Given the previous example, the following information is helpful. Drinking alcohol irritates the stomach lining (interferes with health). Drinking alcohol slows reaction time (interferes with safety). Drinking alcohol is against the law for minors (against the law). Drinking alcohol depresses the central nervous system and interferes with judgment (may result in actions that do not show respect for self or others). Most parents and guardians do not want their minor children drinking alcohol (against family guidelines). Drinking alcohol is against school rules (shows a lack of character).

Self-Appraisals and Health Behavior Inventories

A **self-appraisal** or **health behavior inventory** is a personal assessment tool that contains a list of actions to which a student responds positively (+), "I practice this action," or to which the student responds negatively (-), "I do not practice this action." A positive response indicates that a student has made a choice to practice a life skill that results in an action that promotes health literacy, maintains and improves health, prevents disease, and reduces health-related risk behaviors. A negative answer indicates that the student chooses actions that may interfere with health literacy, harm health, and increase the risk of disease or injury and premature death. The following suggestions can increase the effectiveness of a health behavior inventory:

1. When you ask students to complete a health behavior inventory, explain that the actions that are being assessed are not of equal value. For example, the

following two statements might appear on the same health behavior inventory: "I do not use tobacco products," and "I volunteer in school clubs and community organizations and agencies that promote health." Although both of these actions are desirable, choosing not to use tobacco products is of greater value in becoming health literate, maintaining and improving health, preventing disease, and reducing health-related risk behaviors than is choosing to volunteer in school clubs and community organizations.

2. If you choose to design a health behavior inventory to be given to students after you have covered a content area to assess what the students intend to do, add the word "will" to each statement. For example, a statement might be "I will not use tobacco products." Students then respond YES or NO to indicate what they intend to do as a result of what they have just learned. In this case, you are assessing intended actions, not current actions.

3. After students complete a health behavior inventory, have them summarize what they have learned about their behavior.

4. Some health behavior inventories contain statements that may be an invasion of family and student privacy. Be certain to follow school policy when selecting health behavior inventories for use in the classroom.

Student Presentations

A **student presentation** is an instructional strategy in which a student makes an oral presentation or demonstration on a health topic that (s)he has researched in-depth. This instructional strategy helps students develop effective communication skills and gather and evaluate health information. The following suggestions can increase the effectiveness of student presentations:

1. Work with students to select topics that directly support mastery of the health education standards. For example, health education standard #4 is "Students will analyze the impact of culture, media, technology, and other influences on health" (The Joint Committee on Health Education Standards, 1995). A student might make an oral presentation on the impact the media has on the incidence of violence. When students are selecting topics, be certain that they know why they are appropriate.

2. Give students the criteria for acceptable performance (grading) before they give student presentations. A written list of criteria is helpful and usually improves the performance of students. For example, the student presentation may be worth twenty-five points. You may award five points for a creative presentation style, ten points for having used accurate sources of information, and ten points for having made at least three relevant points about the impact of the media on the incidence of violence. By establishing the criteria prior to the student presentations, you will not be swayed by the halo effect and reward students who are entertaining but who have not adequately evaluated health information and made relevant points. You will not unjustly penalize students who were not entertaining but who did adequately evaluate health information and make relevant points.

3. Encourage students to practice their presentations and to develop an effective communication style. Offer to help them prior to their presentation. Suggest practicing the student presentation at home with their families or in front of a mirror. Encourage students to use audiovisuals such as posters, photographs, slides, or overhead transparencies.

Field Trips

A **field trip** is an instructional strategy in which students visit a site outside the school to gather information or develop a life skill. A field trip might involve a visit to a health museum, a health agency, a waste treatment plant, or a fire department.

1. Be aware of school district policy regarding field trips. For example, a school district may require that parents or guardians sign a consent form that has been approved by the school board. There may be a requirement as to how many adults must be available to supervise students during a field trip. Check the school district policy covering liability. Check your personal liability or professional liability coverage. Remember, the consent of parents or guardians does not waive the teacher from being responsible for protecting the health and safety of students.

2. After discussing the proposed field trip with the individuals at the site, follow with a letter. State the purpose of the field

Instructional Strategies and Technologies

trip, the number of students who will attend, and describe your expectations. In most cases, individuals are better prepared to meet the needs of your students when they have this information clearly stated in writing.

3. Prepare students for the field trip. Give them relevant information. Clarify your reasons for taking the field trip and your expectations. If students are to write reaction papers or complete other learning experiences after the trip, tell them before the trip. Set guidelines for student behavior for the field trip and identify consequences for breaking guidelines.

4. After the trip, process the learning experience. Have students write thank you notes to the individuals who participated at the field trip site and to parents, guardians, or other adults who assisted with the trip. Write a letter to the individual(s) with whom you planned the trip and provide appropriate feedback.

Demonstrations

A **demonstration** is an instructional strategy in which the teacher or other appropriate person demonstrates a concept or life skill. A teacher may want to depict a form of physical abuse. The teacher might take two eggs. The teacher breaks the first egg into a bowl. The egg yolk will be visible. The teacher might say this is the brain of a child. Then the teacher might shake the second egg vigorously and explain that shaking a child is a form of physical abuse. The teacher then breaks the egg into a bowl. The yolk will be scrambled and can be used to show what might happen to the brain as a result of the vigorous shaking. Students can observe the brain damage that often results from this kind of child abuse. Teachers also can demonstrate life skills such as brushing and flossing teeth. The following suggestions can increase the effectiveness of demonstrations:

1. Be certain to have all the materials needed for the demonstration. Try the demonstration before using it with students. Have the materials organized and ready to avoid wasting class time.

2. Adequately prepare students for the demonstration. For example, in the demonstration using the two eggs, the teacher might ask students to note the difference between the two egg yolks.

3. After the demonstration, process the information or the life skill that was presented. When appropriate, such as when a life skill has been demonstrated, have students repeat the demonstration.

Guest Speakers

A **guest speaker** is a person who will speak to students on his/her expertise or experience regarding a health topic or life skill. A guest speaker might also demonstrate a concept or life skill. There usually are many qualified guest speakers in a community.

Health care professionals and health educators at health agencies often are available as guest speakers. Guest speakers may have audiovisuals or other resources that the teacher may not have available to him/her. Using a guest speaker can provide a change of pace for the students and peak their interest. The following suggestions can increase the effectiveness of using a guest speaker in the classroom:

1. Have a specific purpose in mind when using a guest speaker as an instructional strategy. Carefully select the guest speaker. Whenever possible, select guest speakers who are highly recommended by other competent teachers and who have spoken to students of this specific age level previously.

2. When contacting a guest speaker, be specific as to the purpose for which you are inviting the person to your classroom, the expected outcomes, the date and time

period, the location, and the age and number of students. Share any concerns or school district policies related to the topic or life skill to be addressed. For example, if a guest speaker is contacted to address the topic of suicide prevention, it may be helpful for the guest speaker to be aware of the curriculum guidelines for this topic at the grade level of the students to whom (s)he is speaking. In addition, if there has been a recent suicide or suicide attempt in the school, the guest speaker should be informed so (s)he will be prepared should students begin to share feelings. Ask the guest speaker if (s)he has any specific requests for audiovisual equipment or room set up.

3. Prepare students for the guest speaker. Collect questions for the speaker ahead of time and send them to the speaker. Have students prepare questions for the class period. Explain your expectations for the class time to be spent with the guest speaker.

4. After the guest speaker's visit, process the learning experience. Obtain feedback from students. Ask students to write thank you notes to the guest speaker. Their thank you notes should provide specific feedback to the guest speaker. For example, a student might share something that (s)he learned or a reason that (s)he is now motivated to practice a specific life skill.

5. Keep a file on guest speakers. After having a guest speaker, summarize feedback from the students and record it. Make notations as to whether or not the guest speaker's visit to the classroom met expectations. Refer back to your file before inviting a guest speaker for another visit to the classroom.

Instructional Technologies

Instructional technologies or **educational technologies** are teaching methods that involve the use of high-tech equipment including computers, CD-Rom, interactive laserdisc systems, online telecommunications, modems, and online networks. Instructional technologies help students communicate in a variety of ways, gather sources of health information, apply critical thinking skills, and solve problems. Newer educational technologies will continue to be available for classroom purposes in the future (Gilder, 1994). Teachers are challenged to keep up with available instructional technologies because of the fast rate at which they are being developed. This section of the chapter describes multimedia technologies including CD-Rom and interactive laserdisc systems, as well as telecommunications technologies including online networks.

Multimedia Technologies

Multimedia technologies are technologies in which computers are used to combine video, sound, graphics, still photography, and animation into interactive communication systems. Today, students can select, edit, and play back educational material as a result of having multimedia technologies. The levels of interaction within different multimedia systems vary considerably with the cost.

Multimedia technologies also make it possible for students to develop their own communication systems. Students can create their own multimedia presentations using scanning devices, videos, photographs, and video clips. Students can be involved in group projects and cooperative learning experiences in which they are assigned one or more of the following roles: writer, producer, camera operator, and editor.

A typical multimedia set-up consists of a computer with a CD-Rom drive. A **CD-Rom drive** is a drive that reads small optical discs capable of storing and playing back high-quality still and video images, sound, and text. CD-Rom stands for compact disc-read only memory. Most CD-Rom discs can store more information than most computer hard drives

Instructional Strategies and Technologies

(650 megs) or about the equivalent of about 500 floppy discs. The storage capacity of a CD-Rom disc is the equivalent of 250,000 pages of text, 15,000 color images, or 15 hours of audio.

Multimedia technologies in schools may involve the use of interactive laserdisc technology. **Interactive laserdisc systems** are interactive communication systems in which a computer interfaces with a laserdisc player. Instruction is provided to students through still or moving video pictures, printed material, computer graphics, and/or by sound. Students interact with the program by using a keyboard, pointing a lighted pen at a computer monitor, touching the monitor screen, speaking to the computer, or by using a mouse. A **mouse** is a hand device that directs the computer. This type of technology is possible through development of the interactive laserdisc. An **interactive laserdisc** is an optical disc that is capable of storing and playing back up to 54,000 still frames or 30 minutes of motion picture video and two channels of audio that can be played back by means of a laserdisc player. Any frame can be displayed within a maximum of five seconds. Teachers can now access technology that allows them to develop and put their own programs on to laserdiscs.

Telecommunication Technologies

Telecommunication technologies are technologies with the capacity to link students and teachers to each other and to others so they can see and talk with each other without being physically present at the same time (Farrington and Eleey, 1994). Students can already access resources from multiple sources while they are sitting in their own classrooms. Linkages with cable television and satellite systems allow interactive, two-way communication between students and teachers, regardless of location. In some schools, students are being taught by instructors located in places far away from their classroom. Through the use of computer-operated video and audio equipment that is run through fiber optic telephone lines, students and teachers in various locations can enjoy live, face-to-face, interactive instruction.

Online telecommunication is an innovative way to access and disseminate information.

Online telecommunication or **tele-computing** is a way in which people communicate through computers, telephone lines, and modems. **Modems** are devices that link computers to telephone lines. Online telecommunication allows access to a vast array of resources and permits people who are great distances apart to communicate and collaborate with each other. Online research allows students to gain access to hundreds of libraries without ever leaving the place where the computer is located. Teachers can also use electronic bulletin boards and information services that provide up-to-the minute information.

Online Networks Working online through a computer can open the world to the classroom. Access to information is often available through the Internet and other systems. The **Internet** is an online telecommunication system funded by The National Science Foundation that connects millions of people worldwide. Internet is a system that links most online networks worldwide. The Internet is growing at a pace of about 15 percent a month (Gilder, 1994). Most colleges and universities are connected to the Internet and many school districts are gaining access. To gain access, an account on a network is needed. Schools often get accounts on local university systems or pay to join commercial online services. In the future, there will be a faster and more spacious information superhighway. In 1991, Congress authorized nearly 3 billion dollars for the development of the National Research and Education Network (NREN). This vast network will incorporate the Internet as it provides access to electronic information for schools, libraries, researchers, universities, and other agencies. NREN also will access interactive online multimedia.

The most commonly used Internet service is E-mail. **E-mail** is an instantaneously delivered electronic message. Through E-mail students can transmit electronic messages to experts. The experts can respond and transmit electronic messages back. Students can also communicate and work collaboratively on projects with students in other parts of the world or country.

Another online computer network that is used in schools is KIDSNET, a network designed for school-age children. Children who are enrolled in schools with access are given an

140

account number to use the network. Through KIDSNET, children can gain access to the Internet and they can download free software and files from The Smithsonian Institute and interact with student bulletin boards and a talk-line (Herndon, 1994). There are other commercial networks available for curricular projects that teachers and students can join.

Teachers in some areas of the country can sometimes connect easily and inexpensively to their own telecommunication networks. For example, TENET connects schools in Texas, Big Sky Telegraph connects Montana schools, and NYCENET connects schools in New York City. TENET links all Texas school districts and thousands of Texas schools. Managed by the University of Texas, it will eventually provide online communications to more than 200,000 teachers and 3 million school children (Herndon, 1994).

Bibliography

Farrington, G.C., and Eleey, M. (1994) Penn's plans for integrating Emerging Technologies. *Technological Horizons in Education*, 22, 104–106.

Gilder, G. (1994) The convergence of the twain: Computers and fiber optics are coming together in cheap and powerful ways. *Electronic Learning*. 13(8), 30–31.

Graumann, P.J. (1994) The road to the information superhighway: Are we almost there yet? *Technology and Learning*, 14(2), 28–34.

Herndon, J.P. (1994) School as waystation on the information highway. *Technological Horizons in Education*, 22, 78–82.

The Joint Committee on Health Education Standards. (1995) *The National Health Education Standards: Achieving Health Literacy*. Questions about *The National Health Education Standards* might be directed to The American Cancer Society; The American School Health Association; The Association for The Advancement of Health Education; The School Health Education and Services Section, American Public Health Association; and The Society of State Directors of Health, Physical Education, Recreation, and Dance. For copies of *The National Health Education Standards,* call or write The American Cancer Society, 1599 Clifton Road NE, Atlanta, Georgia 30329 (1-800-ACS-2345).

Thomas, S.B. (1987/1988) Microcomputer telecommunications: Basic principles for health education research. *Health Education*, December/January, 16–19.

Wiist, W.H. (1987/1988) Update on computer-assisted video instruction in the health sciences. *Health Education*, December/January, 8–12.

Section 2

HEALTH CONTENT

Figure 6-1
Life Skills for Mental and Emotional Health

1. I will strive to have optimal health.

2. I will gain health knowledge.

3. I will make responsible decisions.

4. I will use resistance skills when appropriate.

5. I will practice life skills for health.

6. I will choose behaviors to promote a healthy mind.

7. I will develop positive self-esteem.

8. I will commmunicate with others in healthful ways.

9. I will express feelings in healthful ways.

10. I will practice stress management and suicide prevention skills.

Chapter 6

MENTAL AND EMOTIONAL HEALTH

Mental and Emotional Health is the area of health that focuses on gaining health knowledge and practicing life skills, making responsible decisions, using resistance skills when appropriate, choosing behaviors to promote a healthy mind, developing positive self-esteem, communicating with others in healthful ways, expressing feelings, and coping with stress in healthful ways. The content in this chapter provides the health knowledge that is needed to teach young people important life skills for mental and emotional health (Figure 6-1).

Life Skill #1

I will strive to have optimal health.

Health and Wellness

The term health means a lot more than the absence of a disease. **Health** is the quality of life that includes physical, mental-emotional, and family-social health. In other words, health involves and concerns every part of a person's life. Another term that describes health is wellness. **Wellness** is the quality of life that includes physical, mental-emotional, and family-social health.

The Domains of Health

Physical Health **Physical health** is the condition of a person's body. Eating the right kinds of foods, exercising, and getting enough

sleep are ways to care for physical health so that the body will be in the best possible condition. Having regular medical checkups so that there is a record of how the body functions, not only when a person is ill but also when a person is well is another indication of caring for physical health.

Mental-Emotional Health **Mental-emotional health** is the condition of a person's mind and the ways that a person expresses feelings. It is important to recognize that a person's mind needs care and conditioning just as the physical body does. Reading, having interesting conversations, and learning new skills or languages are examples of ways to exercise the mind. Emotional health is closely tied to mental health. When a person understands the emotions (s)he is experiencing and can express those emotions in healthful ways, (s)he is taking care of emotional health.

Family-Social Health **Family-social health** is the condition of a person's relationships with others. Focusing on expressing oneself clearly and listening intently when others are speaking are examples of ways to care for and nurture family-social health. Learning to give affection in appropriate ways and to receive the affection of others is an important aspect of family-social health.

The Wellness Scale

It is helpful to think of the possible ranges of health by using *The Wellness Scale*. *The Wellness Scale* depicts the ranges in

Figure 6-2
The Wellness Scale
Factors that Influence Health and Well-Being

Lack of health knowledge	Possession of health knowledge
Risk behaviors	Wellness behaviors
Risk situations	Healthful situations
Destructive relationships	Healthful relationships
Irresponsible decision-making	Responsible decision-making
Lack of resistance skills	Use of resistance skills
Lack of protective factors	Possession of protective factors
Lack of resiliency	Having resiliency
Lack of health literacy	Having health literacy

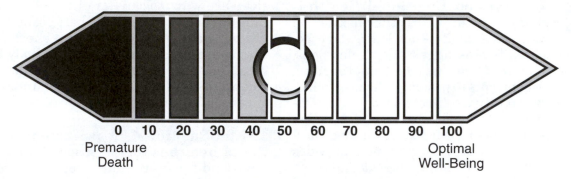

0 10 20 30 40 50 60 70 80 90 100

Premature
Death

Optimal
Well-Being

Health status is the sum total of the positive
and negative influence of these factors

the quality of life from optimal well-being to high level wellness, average wellness, minor illness or injury, major illness or injury, and premature death (Figure 6-2). There are at least nine factors that influence health and wellness over which a person has some degree of control. **Health status** is the sum total of the positive and negative influence of:

1. the level of health knowledge a person has;
2. the behaviors a person chooses;
3. the situations in which a person participates;
4. the relationships in which a person engages;
5. the decisions a person makes;
6. the resistance skills a person has;
7. the protective factors a person possesses;
8. the degree to which a person is resilient;
9. the degree of health literacy a person has achieved.

Each influence can be either positive or negative. When an influence is positive, it is viewed as a plus (+). When an influence is negative, it is viewed as a minus (-). A person's health status fluctuates on *The Wellness Scale* depending on whether these influences are positive or negative.

Health Knowledge Health knowledge consists of information that is needed to become health literate, maintain and improve health, prevent disease, and reduce health-related risk behaviors. Health knowledge is discussed further in Life Skill #2: I Will Gain Health Knowledge.

Behaviors People choose behaviors that determine their lifestyles and influence the quality of their lives. They can choose behaviors that either promote their health or threaten their health. **Healthful behaviors** are actions that promote health; prevent

146

illness, injury, and premature death; and improve the quality of the environment. Examples of healthful behaviors are exercising regularly, wearing a safety belt, eating healthful foods, getting enough sleep, and using prescription drugs according to directions.

Risk behaviors are voluntary actions that threaten health, increase the likelihood of illness and premature death, and destroy the quality of the environment. Examples of risk behaviors are riding a motorcycle without wearing a helmet, using tobacco, drinking alcohol, skipping meals, and using illegal drugs. The Centers for Disease Control and Prevention has identified six categories of risk behaviors in today's students:
1. Behaviors that result in unintentional and intentional injuries
2. Tobacco use
3. Alcohol and other drug use
4. Sexual behaviors that result in HIV infection, other STDs, and unintended pregnancy
5. Dietary patterns that contribute to disease
6. Insufficient physical activity

Situations Just as there are consequences of behavior choices, there are consequences of various situations to consider. **Healthful situations** are circumstances that promote health; prevent illness, injury, and premature death; and improve the quality of the environment. Examples of healthful situations are sitting in nonsmoking areas in restaurants, being a passenger in a car driven by someone who has not been drinking alcohol, and attending drug-free parties.

Risk situations are involuntary circumstances that threaten health; increase the likelihood of illness, injury, and premature death; and destroy the quality of the environment. Examples of risk situations are being in a location where illegal drugs are sold, sitting in a smoke-filled room, and being in the presence of someone who has a gun.

Relationships Relationships are the connections a person has with other people. Relationships exist in families, at school, at work, and in recreational activities. **Healthful relationships** are relationships that promote self-esteem and productivity, encourage health-enhancing behavior, and are free of

violence and drug misuse and abuse. Examples of healthful relationships are those in which people encourage one another to set and reach personal and academic goals, help one another cope with difficult situations, and encourage one another to avoid risk behaviors.

Destructive relationships are relationships that destroy self-esteem, interfere with productivity and health, and may include violence and drug misuse and abuse. Examples of destructive relationships are those with people who tell lies, who are abusive, and who encourage the use of alcohol or the use or sale of illegal drugs.

Decision-Making A **decision** is a choice. Everyday decisions influence the quality of a person's health as well as the lives of others. Young people may not stop to think about the possible consequences of a decision they are about to make. They may see only the immediate benefits; yet a decision that is made hurriedly may have negative consequences that last a lifetime.

Resistance Skills **Peer pressure** is the pressure that people of similar age or status exert on others to encourage them to make certain decisions or behave in certain ways. Peer pressure can be positive or negative. Negative peer pressure should be resisted by using resistance skills. **Resistance skills** are skills that are used when a person wants to say NO to an action and/or leave a situation.

Protective Factors Protective factors are ways that a person might behave and characteristics of the environment in which a person lives that promote health, safety, and/or well-being. The greater the number of protective factors a person possesses, the more likely that health status will be optimal. Characteristics of the environment that serve as protective factors include (Benard, 1992):
1. caring and support provided by a caring parent, a confident and positive teacher, supportive and caring peers, or social links within the community;
2. high expectations including positive parental attitudes, high academic and behavioral expectations at school, and clear community expectations and values;
3. active participation including responsibilities at home, involvement in school and extracurricular activities, and

opportunities for participation in useful tasks in the community.

Risk factors are ways that a person might behave and characteristics of the environment in which a person lives that threaten health, safety, and/or well-being. When a person does not have a caring and supportive environment, is confused as to the expectations set by adults, or is unable to actively participate in school and extracurricular activities, the likelihood of health-compromising choices is increased (Benard, 1992).

Resiliency **Resiliency** is the ability to prevent or to recover, bounce back, and learn from misfortune, change, or pressure. Being resilient strengthens a person and contributes to optimal health status. A person who lacks resiliency and who has not been reconnected to his/her health potential may experience a sense of hopelessness and a compromised health status.

Health Literacy **Health literacy** is competence in critical thinking and problem solving, responsible and productive citizenship, self-directed learning, and effective communication (Joint Committee on Health Education Standards, 1995). A **health literate individual** is a critical thinker and problem solver, a responsible and productive citizen, a self-directed learner, and an effective communicator (The Joint Committee on Health Education Standards, 1995).

Life Skill #2

I will gain health knowledge.

Health Knowledge

Health knowledge consists of information that is needed to become health literate, maintain and improve health, prevent disease, and reduce health-related risk behaviors. What a person does today will influence his/her health tomorrow. A person can plan to take care of his/her health now. To do that, a person will need health knowledge. Sources of health knowledge include classroom lessons; observation of others' behaviors, and media such as magazines, newspapers, and television.

The Ten Areas of Health

The ten areas of health are Mental and Emotional Health; Family Living; Growth and Development; Nutrition; Personal Health; Alcohol, Tobacco, and Other Drugs; Diseases and Disorders; Consumer and Community Health; Safety and Injury Prevention; and Environmental Health. It is important to have knowledge in these ten areas of health in order to make responsible decisions and to evaluate behavior and situations that involve risks.

Mental and Emotional Health **Mental and Emotional Health** is the area of health that focuses on gaining health knowledge and practicing life skills; making responsible decisions; using resistance skills when appropriate; choosing behaviors to promote a healthy mind; developing positive self-esteem; communicating with others in healthful ways; expressing feelings; and coping with stress in healthful ways.

Family Living **Family Living** is the area of health that focuses on developing relationship skills; avoiding discrimination; practicing conflict resolution skills; striving for healthful family relationships; making healthful adjustments to family changes; forming healthful and responsible friendships; recognizing harmful relationships; identifying resources to improve relationships; developing skills to prepare for future family life; and practicing life skills to support abstinence.

Growth and Development **Growth and Development** is the area of health that focuses on caring for the body systems; recognizing changes during growth periods; accepting maleness/femaleness; accepting physical appearance; accepting one's learning style; achieving appropriate developmental tasks; learning about the beginning of a new life; recognizing the needs of people of different ages; preparing for aging; and sharing feelings about dying and death.

Nutrition **Nutrition** is the area of health that focuses on planning a healthful diet and includes choosing foods from The Food Guide Pyramid; adhering to dietary guidelines;

reading food labels; making healthful food selections to reduce the risk of disease; making healthful selections when dining out; considering food safety; maintaining desirable weight; eating for healthful reasons; and recognizing eating disorders.

Personal Health **Personal Health** is the area of health that focuses on making a personal health management plan that includes being well-groomed; caring for the body; having regular checkups; following a dental health plan; obtaining adequate rest and sleep; and achieving a desirable level of physical fitness.

Alcohol, Tobacco, and Other Drugs **Alcohol, Tobacco, and Other Drugs** is the area of health that focuses on kinds of drugs and their safe use; understanding the risk factors and protective factors associated with drug misuse and abuse; preventing the misuse and/or abuse of alcohol, tobacco, and controlled substances; recognizing how drug use increases the likelihood of HIV infection; seeking help for personal or family drug misuse or abuse; being aware of school and community intervention and treatment resources; choosing to be safe and drug free; and using resistance skills when pressured to use drugs.

Communicable and Chronic Diseases **Communicable and Chronic Diseases** is the area of health that focuses on recognizing communicable and noncommunicable diseases; keeping the immune system healthy; preventing the spread of pathogens; reducing the risk of infection with common communicable diseases, STDs, and HIVs; obtaining a family history for diseases; reducing the risk of cardiovascular diseases and cancer; and recognizing ways to manage chronic diseases.

Injury Prevention and Safety **Injury Prevention and Safety** is the area of health that focuses on following safety rules in the home, school, and community; following safety guidelines for different weather conditions and natural disasters; being able to get help for emergency situations; being skilled in basic first aid procedures; reducing the risk of violence; protecting oneself from those who are dangerous; and staying safe while riding in a car and when enjoying exercise.

Consumer and Community Health **Consumer and Community Health** is the area of health that focuses on choosing sources of health-related information and products and services; analyzing advertising, recognizing and reporting quackery; spending money and time wisely; using school nurse and school health services when appropriate; using health care providers and health care facilities; cooperating with people in the community who protect health and safety; and volunteering in school clubs and community organizations and agencies that promote health.

Environmental Health **Environmental Health** is the area of health that focuses on showing concern about environmental issues, keeping the air clean, keeping the water clean, keeping the indoor environment free of pollution, keeping noise at a healthful level, protecting oneself from radiation, disposing of solid wastes properly, recycling, being aware of the effects of overcrowding, and cooperating with environmental protection agencies.

Health Behavior Inventories

A **health behavior inventory** is a personal assessment tool that contains a list of actions to which a student responds positively, "I practice this action," or to which a person responds negatively, "I do not practice this action." *The Health Behavior Inventory* (Table 6-3) is an example of how an inventory might look. The behaviors included on *The Health Behavior Inventory* are stated as healthful or wellness behaviors. A positive answer indicates that the student is engaging in behavior that promotes well-being. A negative answer indicates that the student is engaging in behavior that promotes illness, injury, or premature death.

It is important to explain to students that the listed behaviors are not of equal value. For example, "I do not use tobacco products," is of greater value to well-being than "I volunteer in school clubs and community organizations and agencies that promote health." Although both of these actions are desirable, choosing not to use tobacco products is of greater value in becoming health literate, maintaining and improving health, preventing disease, and reducing health-related risk behaviors than is choosing to volunteer in school clubs and community organizations.

Life Skill #3

I will make responsible decisions.

Decision-Making Styles

Most people usually make decisions using a particular decision-making style. Other people may use a combination of three decision-making styles–inactive, proactive, or reactive. An **inactive decision-making style** is a decision-making style in which a person fails to make choices, and this failure determines what will occur. A person who uses an inactive decision-making style usually procrastinates. **Procrastination** is the act of delaying something until a future time. People who use the inactive decision-making style often put off making decisions when they are faced with something difficult. They do not know what they want to do. They may

---

Table 6-3

Health Behavior Inventory

Directions: Read each statement carefully. If the statement describes you, place a (+) in front of it to indicate a positive action toward optimal health. If the statement does not describe you, place a (-) in front of it to indicate your actions interfere with health literacy, harm health, and increase the risk of disease, injury, and premature death.

Mental and Emotional Health
(   )   1. I cope with stress in healthful ways.
(   )   2. I express feelings in healthful ways.

Family Living
(   )   3. I avoid discriminatory behavior and prejudice.
(   )   4. I handle disagreements without fighting.

Growth and Development
(   )   5. I practice behaviors that contribute to healthful aging.
(   )   6. I share my feelings about dying and death.

Nutrition
(   )   7. I read food labels.
(   )   8. I select foods that reduce my risk of heart disease.

Personal Health
(   )   9. I care for my skin, hair, and nails daily.
(   ) 10. I have a plan for physical fitness.

Alcohol, Tobacco, and Other Drugs
(   ) 11. I do not use tobacco products.
(   ) 12. I do not drink alcohol.

Communicable and Chronic Diseases
(   ) 13. I use sunscreen to protect myself from the sun.
(   ) 14. I have information about my family's history of disease.

Injury Prevention and Safety
(   ) 15. I have a list of emergency telephone numbers.
(   ) 16. I wear a safety restraint when riding in a car.

Consumer and Community Health
(   ) 17. I have a budget that I follow.
(   ) 18. I participate in school clubs and community activities that promote health and safety.

Environmental Health
(   ) 19. I recycle.
(   ) 20. I listen to music at safe levels.

---

never make a decision and their options cease to exist. Unfortunately, people who use this style have little control over the direction their lives take. Because of this, they have difficulty developing the self-confidence they might gain from feeling that they have taken responsibility for their decisions.

A **reactive decision-making style** is a decision-making style in which a person allows others to make decisions for him/her. People who use this style are easily influenced by what others think, do, or suggest. They are easily pressured by peer pressure. They lack self-confidence, and have a need to be liked by others. They give the control of their destiny to others.

A **proactive decision-making style** is a decision-making style in which a person examines the decision to be made, identifies and evaluates actions that can be taken, selects an action, and assumes responsibility for the consequences. People who use this decision-making style are not driven by circumstances and conditions or others' influence. People who use this decision-making style have principles, such as integrity, fairness, honesty, and human dignity, that guide their decisions and thus their behavior. People who use the proactive decision-making style are empowered. To be **empowered** is to be inspired because of the belief that a person has some control over the direction of his/her life. People who are empowered believe they have the capacity to make responsible decisions; change their habits, if necessary; develop and uphold morals, keep promises and trusts; exercise courage; and treat others with kindness and respect. They are willing to accept responsibility.

The Responsible Decision-Making Model

The Responsible Decision-Making Model (Table 6-4) is a series of steps to follow to assure that the decisions a person makes lead to actions that:
- promote health,
- protect safety,
- protect laws,
- show respect for self and others,
- follow guidelines set by responsible adults such as parents and guardians,
- demonstrate good character.

Table 6-4

The Responsible Decision-Making Model

1. **Clearly describe the situation you face**. If no immediate decision is necessary, describe the situation in writing. If an immediate decision must be made, describe the situation out loud or to yourself in a few short sentences. Being able to describe a situation in your own words is the first step in clarifying the question.

2. **List possible actions that can be taken**. Again, if no immediate decision is necessary, make a list of possible actions. If an immediate decision must be made, state possible actions out loud or to yourself.

3. **Share your list of possible actions with a responsible adult such as someone who protects community laws and demonstrates character**. When no immediate action is necessary, sharing possible actions with a responsible adult is helpful. This person can examine your list to see if it is inclusive. Responsible adults have a wide range of experiences that can allow them to see situations maturely. They may add possibilities to the list of actions. In some situations, it is possible to delay decision-making until there is an opportunity to seek counsel with a responsible adult. If an immediate decision must be made, explore possibilities. Perhaps a telephone call can be made. Whenever possible, avoid skipping this step.

4. **Carefully evaluate each possible action using six criteria**. Ask each of the six questions to learn which decision is best.
   a. Will this decision result in an action that will promote my health and the health of others?
   b. Will this decision result in an action that will protect my safety and the safety of others?
   c. Will this decision result in an action that will protect the laws of the community?
   d. Will this decision result in an action that shows respect for myself and others?
   e. Will this decision result in an action that follows guidelines set by responsible adults such as my parents or guardian?
   f. Will this decision result in an action that will demonstrate that I have good character?

5. Decide which action is responsible and most appropriate. After applying the six criteria, compare the results. Which decision best meets the six criteria?

6. Act in a responsible way and evaluate the results. Follow through with this decision with confidence. The confidence comes from paying attention to the six criteria.

There are many benefits that result from using *The Responsible Decision-Making Model*. Because the *Model* contains guidelines for what is responsible behavior, a person always knows how to evaluate a situation. Then the person identifies possible actions to take and asks the following questions.

Will this decision result in an action that:
1. will promote my health and the health of others?
2. will protect my safety and the safety of others?
3. will protect the laws of the community?
4. shows respect for myself and others?
5. follows guidelines set by responsible adults such as my parents or guardians?
6. will demonstrate good character?

By using these guidelines, decisions can be made in a rational manner rather than in an impulsive manner. The person will not be tempted to choose what might seem best for the moment but will think about his/her future.

People can use these guidelines to tell peers when they do not want to do something they are being pressured to do. They can state why they are saying NO. For example, if peers are urging a young person to be sexually active, (s)he can say, NO, I want to respect myself and others." If peers are urging a young person to use tobacco, (s)he can say, "NO, I want to protect my health and also the health of others."

Life Skill #4

I will use resistance skills when appropriate.

Resistance skills are skills that are used when a person wants to say NO to an action and/or leave a situation that threatens health, threatens safety, breaks laws, results in lack of respect for self and others, disobeys guidelines set by responsible adults, or detracts from character. Resistance skills are sometimes called refusal skills and can be used to resist peer pressure when it is negative. **Peer pressure** is pressure that people of similar age or status place on others to encourage them to make certain decisions or

---

Table 6-5

The Model for Using Resistance Skills

1. **Use assertive behavior.** There is a saying, "You get treated the way you 'train' others to treat you." Assertive behavior is the honest expression of thoughts and feelings without experiencing anxiety or threatening others. When you use assertive behavior, you show that you are in control of yourself and the situation. You say NO clearly and firmly. As you speak, you look directly at the person(s) pressuring you. Aggressive behavior is the use of words and/or actions that tend to communicate disrespect. This behavior only antagonizes others. Passive behavior is the holding back of ideas, opinions, and feelings. Holding back may result in harm to you, others, or the environment.

2. **Avoid saying, "NO, thank you."** There is never a need to thank a person who pressures you into doing something that might be harmful, unsafe, illegal, or disrespectful or which may result in disobeying parents or displaying a lack of character.

3. **Use nonverbal behavior that matches verbal behavior.** Nonverbal behavior is the use of body language or actions rather than words to express feelings, ideas, and opinions. Your verbal NO should not be confused by misleading actions. For example, if you say NO to cigarette smoking, do not pretend to take a puff of a cigarette in order to resist pressure.

4. **Influence others to choose responsible behavior.** When a situation poses immediate danger, remove yourself. If no immediate danger is present, try to turn the situation into a positive one. Suggest alternative, responsible ways to behave. Being a positive role model helps you feel good about yourself and helps gain the respect of others.

5. **Avoid being in situations in which there will be pressure to make harmful decisions.** There is no reason to put yourself into situations in which you will be pressured or tempted to make unwise decisions. Think ahead.

6. **Avoid being with persons who choose harmful actions.** Your reputation is the impression that others have of you, your decisions, and your actions. Associate with persons known for their good qualities and character in order to avoid being misjudged.

7. **Resist pressure to engage in illegal behavior.** You have a responsibility to protect others and to protect the laws of your community. Demonstrate good character.

behave in certain ways. Peer pressure can be positive or negative. When a peer encourages a student to stay in school, the pressure is positive. When a peer urges a student to join a gang, the pressure is negative.

Someone may want to say NO, but may not know how to say NO in an assertive manner and to stick to the decision. By using *The Model for Using Resistance Skills*, a person can practice ways to reinforce decisions. ***The Model for Using Resistance Skills*** (Table 6-5) is a list of suggested ways for effectively resisting pressure to engage in actions that threaten health, threaten safety, break laws, result in lack of respect for self and others, disobey guidelines set by responsible adults, and detract from character.

The Model for Using Resistance Skills helps young people master potential life crises and gain confidence in themselves. In order to gain emotional maturity, young people must learn to make decisions and take responsibility for the consequences. Learning to delay gratification is an important step in this process. **Delayed gratification** is the act of allowing oneself to sacrifice in the present so that a benefit will be achieved in the future. For example, a young person may delay purchasing a sporting equipment item until money is earned for the purchase. Learning to delay gratification when appropriate enables young people to master the art of coping successfully.

Life Skill #5

I will practice life skills for health.

Life Skills

Life skills are actions that promote health literacy, maintain and improve health, prevent disease, and reduce health-related risk behaviors. Life skills are stated as "I will...." because they indicate that the person is willingly and willfully choosing to commit himself/herself to doing them. For people to practice life skills, they must first have the knowledge that is required so that they can make a commitment. Examples of life skills are "I will cope with stress in healthful ways" and "I will select the correct number of servings from The Food Guide Pyramid."

Self-Responsibility and Self-Discipline

Practicing life skills helps young people assume self-responsibility for their health. **Self-responsibility for health** is the priority that a person assigns to being health literate, maintaining and improving health, preventing disease, and reducing health-related risk behaviors. One of the goals of comprehensive school health education is to motivate students to assume self-responsibility for health. **Self-discipline** is the effort or energy with which a person follows through on what (s)he intends or promises to do. Self-discipline is necessary for a person to develop self-responsibility. Teachers can help students develop self-responsibility for health by engaging in health promotion with health behavior inventories, teaching strategies that promote life skills, health behavior contracts, and incentives to stay motivated.

Health Behavior Contracts

A **health behavior contract** is a plan that is written to develop the habit of following a specific life skill. A health behavior contract includes: 1) the life skill for which a habit needs to be formed; 2) a few statements describing the importance of this life skill to optimal well-being; 3) a plan for practicing this life skill; 4) an evaluation including a method of reporting progress; and 5) a statement of the results experienced from practicing this life skill. *The Health Behavior Contract* (Figure 6-6) is an example of how a contract might look.

A contract is a valuable tool in changing behavior or adopting new behaviors. Most of the research completed on goal setting emphasizes that people who write down what they want to accomplish are more likely to accomplish it. Writing down the life skill helps a person focus on what is desired. Other benefits of making a contract are:

- the plan for practicing the life skill is individualized;
- progress in practicing the life skill can be monitored;
- the individual is able to analyze the results of following the life skill.

Incentives, Support Systems, and Rewards

It is important to stay motivated to practice life skills. Students can follow health behavior contracts to make new life skills a habit. Some form of reminding students is helpful. For example, students can write the life skill from the contract on several index cards. Then the cards can be placed in locations where the students will find them and be reminded of the commitment they made. Another incentive might be to contact resource people who can serve as role models. A role model might be a person who was successful in changing

Figure 6-6

The Health Behavior Contract

Life Skill: I will select the appropriate number of servings from The Food Guide Pyramid.

Effect on My Well-Being:

Selecting the appropriate number of servings from The Food Guide Pyramid will help me have a balanced diet. Eating the recommended number of servings will help me to get the nutrients my body needs each day. Choosing the appropriate number of servings will help me to maintain my healthful weight, reduce my risk for diseases such as heart disease and cancer, and eat a diet low in fat content.

My Plan:

Each day, I will choose the appropriate number of servings of food The Food Guide Pyramid recommends. I will choose 6 to 11 servings from the Bread, Cereals, Rice, and Pasta Group; 3 to 5 servings from the Vegetable Group; 2 to 4 servings from the Fruit Group; 2 to 3 servings from the Meat, Poultry, Fish, Dry Beans, Eggs, and Nuts Group; 2 to 3 servings from the Milk, Yogurt, Cheese Group; and eat foods from the Fats, Oils, and Sweets sparingly.

Evaluating My Progress: I will complete the following chart to indicate the number of servings from The Food Guide Pyramid I have eaten each day.

Group From The Food Guide Pyramid	Recommended Number Servings	Servings I Have Have Eaten
Bread, Cereals, Rice And Pasta	6 - 11	✓✓✓✓✓✓
Vegetable	3 - 5	✓✓✓✓
Fruit	2 - 4	✓✓✓
Meat, Poultry, Fish, Dry Beans, Eggs, and Nuts	2 - 3	✓✓
Milk, Yogurt, Cheese Group	2 - 3	✓✓
Fats, Oils, and Sweets	use sparingly	✓

Results:

I have more energy every day.

I don't feel as tired.

a harmful habit. This person may be willing to work with students who want to develop the same habit.

Students who are practicing the same life skill can form support networks. For example, students desiring to lose weight might have a meeting time to encourage one another and share their feelings and frustrations. Usually, it is easier to stay motivated when there are others on whom a person can depend for support and encouragement.

Rewards are important and may make the difference with some students in staying motivated. A reward may be bonus points in a grading system for progress toward making a life skill a habit. Or perhaps students in support groups might design a progress report in the form of a chart just for their group.

Life Skill #6

I will choose behaviors to promote a healthy mind.

Mental Alertness

To be alert is to be quick to perceive and act, to be watchful and intelligent. People who are alert are interested in what is going on in their lives. They understand that they will have problems and disappointments but they do not allow those problems and disappointments to overwhelm them. People who are mentally alert understand that their minds need exercise just as their bodies do. They read for fun and for information. They challenge themselves with word puzzles or jigsaw puzzles. They read newspapers to be aware of what is going on in their neighborhood and in the world. They never stop learning about new ideas and new ways of doing things. They choose to promote their mental health.

Mental Disorders

Mentally healthy people are people who generally feel good about themselves, have satisfying relationships, and set realistic goals for themselves. Their life experiences are not always positive, but they learn to cope. Some people are not able to cope and they suffer from some form of mental illness. The difference between mental health and mental illness is often very slight. Symptoms of many forms of mental illness can be controlled with medicines so that people can continue to function normally in society. Other mental disorders are more serious and the treatment and recovery are more complicated.

Anxiety Disorders Anxiety disorders are disorders in which real or imagined fears occur so often that they prevent a person from enjoying life. Some people feel anxious, tense, and fearful most of the time. There is no specific object or situation that produces the fear. Other people experience phobias. A **phobia** is the excess fear of a situation, object, or person. The source of the fear is usually not dangerous in itself. A phobia is usually related to some past experience that was very upsetting to the individual. For example, a person who was accidentally locked in a closet when (s)he was a child was so terrified by the experience that (s)he developed claustrophobia, a fear of closed places. However, not everyone who experiences such a situation develops a phobia.

Depression **Depression** is the feeling of being sad, unhappy, discouraged, and "down in the dumps." It is a feeling of hopelessness and helplessness. Everyone experiences feelings like these at times. Usually these times are short. However, feelings of depression that are prolonged and persistent are not normal. Symptoms include loss of sleep, loss of interest, loss of appetite, loss of energy, and loss of ability to concentrate. People who are depressed tend to withdraw from others.

Manic-Depressive Disorder **Manic-depressive disorder** is a mood disorder in which a person's moods vary from being very high to being very depressed. The manic phase is the high mood. During the manic phase, a person experiences great joy for no reason. The person may laugh, sing, or talk all the time. The manic phase also may be a restless stage with outbursts of intense anger. This anger may turn into violence making the person dangerous to himself/herself or to others.

During the depressive phase, the person experiences a passive mood and has very little energy. At this stage, the person may be suicidal and must be observed. The depressive phase ends when behavior swings back in the other direction—the manic phase. With professional help, psychotherapy, and/or drug therapy, a person should be able to learn to balance his/her feelings rather than experience these opposite behaviors.

Obsessive-Compulsive Disorder **Obsessive-compulsive disorder** is behavior that is characterized by unreasonable thoughts and actions that are rigid, inflexible, and repetitive. Suppose a person want to be a marathon runner. Every day, this person plans activities around a training schedule. Eventually, running interferes with this person's studying and other activities. (S)he has no time for family and friends. This behavior is obsessive. The person has become so obsessed with running that other commitments are overlooked.

Compulsive behavior involves repeating a behavior when it is unneccessary. For example, a person reads in the newspaper about a burglary in his/her neighborhood. This person checks to see that the doors in his/her home are locked. This is a healthful response. However, if a person checks the doors over and over again, the behavior is compulsive.

Seasonal Affective Disorder **Seasonal affective disorder** is a type of depression that is associated with winter months when the amount of sunshine is decreased. Characteristics of this disorder are an increase in appetite along with a decrease in physical activity, irritability, and general depression. These moods may be the result of chemical imbalances due to the absence of sunlight. People living in the northern parts of the United States are more apt to experience this disorder. Special light therapy for short periods every day relieves many of the symptoms in a short period of time.

Schizophrenia **Schizophrenia** is a mental disorder in which there is a split or breakdown in logical thought processes. The split results in unusual behavior. Actions, words, and emotions are confused and inappropriate for whatever the occasion is. A person suffering with this disorder may appear desperate and withdraw into an inner world of fantasy. Treatment for this disorder requires professional help. The patient is usually hospitalized. There is no cure for this disorder.

Addictive Behaviors

Addictive behavior is behavior associated with repeated and continual connection with an activity or object that results in unhealthful effects on the person. These activities or objects may seem to have beneficial short-term effects but in the long run, they are harmful. Addictive behavior is a form of coping and may be associated with the use of drugs, with food, or with work. Addictive behavior differs from a habit. A person can change a habit by becoming mentally aware of the behavior and determining to control it and change it. Addictive behavior is different in that it is compulsive behavior that cannot be changed easily because the person does not have control over the behavior. In fact, a person who is addicted usually denies that the behavior is out of control.

In many cases, people who become addicted are seeking escape from situations or responsibilities that are painful or difficult. These people seek to experience a more pleasurable mood and will do whatever is required to attain it. In the process, they are not aware of the harm they are causing themselves or the effect on their families and friends. Kinds of addictions include codependence; money, clothes, and shopping addictions; gambling addiction; workaholism; exercise addiction; relationship addiction; and eating disorders.

Codependence **Codependence** is a mental disorder in which a person loses personal identity, has frozen feelings, and copes ineffectively. People who are codependent often grow up in dysfunctional families in which members do no interact in healthful and responsible ways. Their behavior is addictive. The messages that a person who is codependent learns from such a family include the following:
- I should not talk to others about family problems.
- I should get others to believe that everything in my family is fine.
- I would be better off continuing to behave the way that I am than attempting to deal with the dysfunction in my family.
- I am safer if I keep my feelings to myself.
- I do not deserve to be treated with respect.
- I am better off being dishonest because if

I told others the truth they might not like me.
- I am more comfortable being serious than playful and having fun.
- I cannot trust others.

These messages make it impossible to form healthful relationships with anyone outside the family. Young people often choose risky behavior to experience temporary relief from the difficult and painful issues that face them. Violence, alcohol and other drug use, and sexual experimentation are much more common in young people who have difficult family relationships. Violent behavior may be a way to express anger. Alcohol and drug use may be an attempt to numb painful feelings. Sexual experimentation may be an attempt to make up for the affection that is lacking at home. Sexual violence may be an attempt to control others because of powerlessness that is experienced at home. Any relief that is felt from these risk behaviors is temporary.

Money, Clothes, and Shopping Addiction
Some people exhibit addictive behavior about spending money. They compulsively spend money on items they do not need or want. They enjoy the feelings of power when they purchase items. They are compulsive shoppers. They buy clothes they may never wear. The danger is that they go into debt to satisfy their needs.

Gambling Addiction
Gambling addiction is an addictive behavior in which a person is unable to control the urge to gamble. Most people who gamble do so for entertainment and can stop any time they wish. However, a person with a gambling addiction is unable to control the urge to gamble even at the risk of losing money, going into debt, alienating family members and friends, losing a job, losing possessions, and even risking health.

Workaholism
Workaholism is an addictive behavior in which a person devotes an inappropriate amount of time to his/her job with the result that family, friends, and personal interests suffer. Workaholics are driven by the need for approval and success that goes beyond the normal desires to develop skills, perform well, and find satisfaction in a job well done. Because people with workaholism work so compulsively, they run the risk of developing physical and mental health problems.

Exercise
While a regular exercise routine is beneficial to a person's health, addictive exercise can be damaging and destructive. As with other addictions, exercise addictions can result in alienation from family and friends and in physical health problems.

Relationships
Normally, relationships with others are a source of companionship and intimacy in which people trust and respect each other. Addictive behavior in relationships is driven by a need for attention and is dominated by fear and jealousy, not by love. People addicted to relationships desire that a single person will be everything to them. They want the devotion of that person and are unable to cope with being rejected. **Sexual addiction** is compulsive behavior involving sexual activity without any commitment to the sexual partner. People with a sexual addiction may participate in several forms of sexual behavior, such as prostitution, masturbation, exhibitionism, rape, or incest.

Eating Disorders
An **eating disorder** is a food-related dysfunction in which a person changes eating habits in a way that is harmful to the mind or body. Eating disorders, such as overeating, anorexia nervosa and bulimia, fit the pattern of addictive behavior because they are compulsive behavior patterns that are destructive and have dangerous consequences.

Multiple Addictions
A **multiple addiction** is a condition in which a person is addicted to more than one source of addiction at one time. Multiple addictions are common. For example, some young people are addicted to both alcohol and cigarettes. Other young people are addicted to both exercise and to an eating disorder.

Treatment and Recovery

Enablers An **enabler** is a person who knowingly or unknowingly supports a person who has an addiction by protecting this person and making it easy for him/her to continue in the addiction. People who are codependent often are enablers. Enablers are usually sincere in their efforts and may be motivated by loyalty to or by love for the person with an addiction. Even when enablers become aware of their relationship with a person who is addicted, they may not take any action. They may be afraid of the person. They may not know how to handle the situation. They may be embarrassed to acknowledge the problem.

Intervention People who have addictions need help and often do not want it. One method of helping a person with an addiction face his/her problem is by intervention. **Intervention** is a confrontation by people, such as parents, spouses, or friends, who wish to help a person with an addiction. The purpose of the intervention is to make the person who is addicted face the problem and to stop denying that there is a problem. The person with an addiction must understand that his/her lifestyle must be changed. It is important to plan an intervention ahead of time so that everyone involved understands what to expect and what needs to be accomplished.

Treatment Addiction may never be cured, but it can be checked if the person with the addiction is willing to cooperate. Many forms of treatment are available, such as individual therapy, family therapy, group therapy, and Twelve Step programs. Individual therapy involves one-on-one contact with a trained professional. Family therapy involves the entire family in the process of helping the person who is addicted recover. However, family therapy also helps family members who may have become codependent or enablers. Group therapy is a step beyond individual therapy in which a person with an addiction has an opportunity to relearn relationship skills.

There are several Twelve Step groups that offer people with addictions peer support. Alcoholics Anonymous was the first group to use a Twelve Step program and others are patterned after their program. The steps suggest guidelines for recovery and encourage addicts to honestly face up to their situation. People who attend Twelve Step support programs do so while maintaining their anonymity. The meetings are not threatening and their is no pressure for anyone to take part.

Relapse For many people who are addicted, treatment may help only temporarily, and then they experience a relapse. **Relapse** is the return to an addiction after a period of abstaining from an addiction.

Life Skill #7

I will develop positive self-esteem.

Self-Esteem

Self-esteem is what a person thinks or believes about himself/herself. Self-esteem is an important indicator of a person's mental health. When people have positive self-esteem, they feel confident that they can handle problems. They are more likely to make responsible decisions and to be resilient. People who have positive self-esteem engage in self-loving behavior. When people have negative self-esteem, they are more likely to engage in self-centered and self-destructive behavior.

Self-Loving Behavior **Self-loving behavior** is healthful and responsible behavior that indicates a person believes himself/herself to be worthwhile and lovable. Self-loving behavior protects a person from negative peer pressure and from abuse because the person values himself/herself.

Self-Centered Behavior **Self-centered behavior** is behavior in which a person acts in ways that fulfill his/her needs and wishes with little regard for the needs and wishes of others. Self-centered people are selfish in that they "want what they want when they want it." Being self-centered is risky behavior.

Self-Destructive Behavior **Self-destructive behavior** is behavior in which a person harms himself/herself. People who engage in this type of behavior are self-destructive. They may become involved in violence in which they are harmed, and they involve others who may be harmed.

Responsibility and Self-Esteem

Responsibility is being reliable and dependable. People who have positive self-esteem value their relationships with others. They not only respect themselves, but they also respect others and choose behavior that strengthens their relationships. In doing so, they prove to themselves and others that they are reliable and dependable.

Developing Positive Self-Esteem

A person can actively do the following to improve and maintain positive self-esteem.

1. *Set goals and make plans to reach them.* It is important that a person sets realistic goals that (s)he can reach because doing tasks well boosts self-esteem. When the first goals are met, others should be set.

2. *Develop a skill or talent.* A person can identify a skill or talent that (s)he enjoys and then work to improve that skill or talent. Practicing a skill, such as playing the guitar or cooking, gives this person the opportunity to experience personal progress.

3. *Make a list of things (s)he does well.* It is helpful for a person to keep a list of things (s)he does well so that (s)he can focus on strengths. This is especially important to boost self-confidence when working to master a new skill. The list will help a person persist when things get difficult, because (s)he will remember how hard (s)he worked to learn skills now done well.

4. *Work to do his/her best in school.* Doing well in school improves self-esteem. This includes attending school regularly, keeping track of assignments or other responsibilities,

studying, handing in all homework assignments and participating in class.

5. *Be involved in school clubs and community activities.* Self-esteem is improved through the experience of belonging at school, a feeling of being a part of what is happening. Joining a club or a team and getting involved helps improve self-esteem.

6. *Develop a trusting relationship with at least one adult.* Adults who are positive role models can be very important to self-esteem.

7. *Choose friends who encourage others to do their best.* It is important to spend time with friends who are responsible. Friends who have high standards for their own behavior encourage others to try their best as well..

8. *Spend time with friends and adults who provide support.* Friends and adults who support a person's best efforts are a tremendous boost to a person's self-esteem.

9. *Volunteer to help another person.* Helping others will give a person a sense of his/her own value.

10. *Keep a neat appearance.* A neat appearance helps a person feel good about himself/herself and influences others' perceptions of the person. This, in turn, influences self-image.

Life Skill #8

I will communicate with others in healthful ways.

Communication

Communication is the sharing of feelings, thoughts, and information with another person. The way a person expresses and shares feelings, thoughts, and information influences how well this person relates with others. If a person expresses feelings in healthful ways, (s)he is more likely to have a healthy mind and body. If a person expresses feelings in harmful ways or keeps feelings bottled up inside, (s)he may not relate well with others. When a person is unable to express feelings, this person's health may be affected.

Difficulty in Communicating Many young people do not learn to recognize and express their feelings as they mature. For example, children who grow up in dysfunctional families often find it difficult to express their feelings. They may not understand what they are feeling or why. Instead, they learn to deny what they are feeling. **Denial** is a condition in which a person refuses to recognize what (s)he is feeling because it is extremely painful. Denial can take many forms, such as minimizing problems; blaming problems on others; making excuses for problems; pretending that a problem does not exist; changing the subject to avoid threatening topics; and avoiding issues. Recognizing and expressing feelings can help an individual understand and cope with negative feelings such as anger, anxiety, and jealousy.

I-Messages and You-Messages An **I-message** is a statement that contains (1) a specific behavior or event, (2) the effect that the behavior or event has on the individual, and (3) the feeling that resulted. I-messages are a healthful way of expressing feelings. When a person uses I-messages, (s)he assumes responsibility for sharing feelings because I-messages refer to the person speaking, his/her feelings, and his/her needs. An example of an I-message is "When you picked me up late for the game, we were late, and I was angry with you." The use of an I-message gives the other person an opportunity to respond without being on the defensive. For example, in response to the I-message, the other person might say "I understand why you are angry with me. I would feel the same way." A **you-message** is a statement that blames or shames another person instead of expressing feelings. A you-message puts down the other person and puts him/her on the defensive. This kind of message would provoke a much different response.

Active Listening An important part of learning to communicate effectively is to learn to listen carefully. Listening carefully shows interest in the other person. **Active listening** is a type of listening in which a person lets others know (s)he heard and understood what was said. There are four ways to use active listening: clarifying responses; restating responses; summarizing responses, and confirming responses. A **clarifying response** is a response in which a person asks for more information. Perhaps in response to the I-message, the person could ask a question, such as "Will you give me another chance to pick you up for an event so that I can show you that I will be on time?" A **restating response** is a response in which a person repeats what the speaker has said in his/her own words. This kind of response allows the listener to confirm that the meaning is understood. An example might be "So what you are telling me is that you are angry with me because I picked you up late." A **summarizing response** is a response to review the major idea or ideas expressed. An example might be "I can see that the problem is that you missed part of the game because I picked you up late. A **confirming response** is a response to acknowledge the feelings that the speaker expressed and to show appreciation for the expression of the feelings. For example, "I don't blame you for feeling angry and I appreciate that you told me how you feel."

Nonverbal Communication

Nonverbal communication is the use of behavior rather than words to express feelings. Examples of nonverbal communication are a nod of the head, a hug, a smile, a frown, or a tap of the foot. When verbal and nonverbal communication is combined, these two kinds of behavior should match so that the message is clear. A **mixed message** is a message in which verbal and nonverbal behavior do not match. Suppose there is someone in class that a student would like to get to know better. (S)he smiles but when there is an opportunity to speak to another person, (s)he walks away without speaking. The other person might be confused as to which message is the real message. Mixed messages are difficult to understand.

Passive, Aggressive, and Assertive Behavior

Three methods of communicating messages are passive, aggressive, and assertive

160

behavior.. These methods can be nonverbal and verbal. **Passive behavior** is the holding back of ideas, opinions, and feelings. People who behave passively have difficulty expressing their concerns. They often make unnecessary apologies and excuses for what they have said or done. They might look away or even laugh when they are trying to express serious feelings. People who behave passively usually keep angry feelings inside rather than expressing them.

Aggressive behavior is the use of words and/or actions that show disrespect toward others. People who behave aggressively might call other people names and make loud and sarcastic remarks. They interrupt others and monopolize conversations. They are domineering and threaten and intimidate others. Aggressive, nonverbal behaviors include glaring at another person, using threatening hand gestures, and assuming a rigid position.

Assertive behavior is the honest expression of thoughts and feelings without experiencing anxiety or threatening others. Assertive behavior is more healthful than passive or aggressive behavior. People who are assertive are more likely to make and maintain healthful relationships because they communicate clearly and confidently. An example of nonverbal assertive behavior is maintaining comfortable eye contact with another person.

Life Skill #9

I will express feelings in healthful ways.

Feelings

Feelings are emotions such as excitement, sadness, happiness, or anger. Learning to cope with emotions is important to an individual's mental health. We experience a wide range of emotions and children and adolescents often have a difficult time identifying and expressing their feelings. In order to feel close to another person, there must be a mutual sharing of feelings. If someone does not share feelings or shares them in hostile ways such as by shouting or throwing objects, it would be difficult to become close to that person. A person who is able to express feelings in healthful ways uses I-messages and engages in active listening.

Life Crises

Most people experience difficult life crises. A **life crisis** is an emotionally significant event or change in a person's life. Parents have the responsibility of preparing their children for life crises by teaching them coping skills. These parents allow their children the opportunity to struggle through difficult situations so that they can grow emotionally. They do not try to shelter their children from life crises.

Elisabeth Kübler-Ross was a pioneer in the study of coping skills needed when a person faces death or faces the death of a loved one. She identified five stages that are experienced in a crisis. However, these five stages also are stages that a person experiences when dealing with other life crises. The stages are denial, anger, bargaining, depression, and acceptance (Kübler-Ross, 1975). Suppose a young person learns that his/her family is going to move to a different city. At first, this young person may respond with denial and not discuss the move. (S)he pretends that the move will not actually occur. Then his/her family begins to make plans to move. The young person realizes that (s)he will no longer live near friends. (S)he becomes angry and doesn't believe it is fair for his/her family to do this. The young person might begin to bargain. (S)he offers to get a part-time job to earn money to help the family so they will not have to take a new job and move. When this doesn't work, the young person becomes sad. After all, (s)he will miss friends, his/her school, and the activities in which (s)he participates. Eventually, the young person works through the sadness and reaches acceptance. The young person pitches in and helps the family. (S)he begins to think of ways to meet new friends and to join activities at the new school.

This situation is not as difficult as some life crises that a person might experience. A student might experience separation or divorce of parents or stepparents. A family member may be sick. Property may be damaged by a tornado, fire, or earthquake. Anyone who experiences a life crisis must learn to express feelings during difficult times in order to mature emotionally.

Sharing Anger, Disappointment, and Grief

Anger is the feeling of being irritated, annoyed, and/or furious. Anger is usually a response to being hurt or frustrated. The hurt might be emotional, psychological, social, and/or physical.

Anger Triggers and Anger Cues **Anger triggers** are thoughts or events that cause a person to become angry. Perhaps someone is hit and feels physical pain. Or, a person may be frustrated over a situation or is rejected by peers and becomes angry. **Anger cues** are changes in the body that are signs that a person is angry. When a person is angry, the anger response begins, which is fight or flight. The anger response causes body changes such as the following to occur: rapid breathing; increase in heart rate; rise in blood pressure; increased sweating; and dryness of the mouth.

Disappointment and Grief Disappointment and grief are two emotions that are associated with difficult life crises. Sometimes it is difficult for an individual to express these emotions and to work through the feelings. If these feelings are not expressed and shared, hidden anger may develop. **Hidden anger** is anger that is not recognized or is expressed in a harmful way and may result in inappropriate behavior and poor health. Some signs of hidden anger are being negative; making cruel remarks to others, being flippant, and being depressed. When these feelings are not recognized and expressed, they usually increase. Hidden anger builds and eventually cannot be kept hidden and is expressed in outbursts, temper tantrums, or fights.

Sharing Feelings Promotes Resiliency To be **resilient** is to be able to prevent or to recover, bounce back, and learn from misfortune, change, or pressure. Young people who are reared in functional families have opportunities to observe their parent(s) struggle with difficult situations. These young people are taught that there are benefits to expressing and sharing difficult times and feelings. When young people are helped to master life crises, they gain confidence. They recognize that if they stay with solving a problem they gain perseverance. Adults who allow children to share feelings prevent their children from feeling stuck or living in a constant state of denial, anger, and/or depression. Young people who feel stuck or young people who live with others who feel stuck find it difficult to be resilient.

Life Skill #10

I will practice stress management and suicide prevention skills.

Stress Management

Stress is the response of the body to the demands of daily living. Stressors are the sources or causes of stress. A **stressor** is a demand that causes changes in the body. Stressors cause the body to respond. A stressor can be physical, mental, or social. For example, a deadline to get an assignment done might cause a mental response of worry, fatigue, or frustration. Having an argument with a friend might affect the relationship.

Eustress and Distress **Eustress** is a healthful response to a stressor that produces positive results. For example, a person might diligently train for a race, and win the race. This person would feel terrific and gain confidence that (s)he accomplished a goal. **Distress** is a harmful response to a stressor that produces negative results. A person may postpone efforts to meet a deadline and end up not completing the assignment. A person might be so angry at himself/herself for getting a poor grade that (s)he compounds his/her disappointment by not doing other assignments.

Stress Response Everyone experiences stress. It is impossible for people to avoid having demands placed on them. The response can be either healthful or harmful. The body responds to stress in a series of changes. The **general adaptation syndrome (GAS)** is a series of changes that occur in the body when stress occurs. The GAS occurs in three stages: the alarm stage, the resistance stage, and the exhaustion stage. The **alarm stage** is the first stage of the GAS in which the body gets ready for action. During this stage, adrenaline is released into the bloodstream. **Adrenaline** is a hormone that helps the body get ready for an emergency. The heart rate and blood pressure increase, digestion slows, muscles contract, respiration and sweating increase, and mental activity increases. The pupils dilate so the person can see sharply, and hearing sharpens as well. There is a burst of quick energy. Sometimes this response is called the fight-or-flight response because a person is ready to take action or to flee. The **resistance stage** is the second stage of the GAS in which the body attempts to regain balance and return to normal. The body is no longer in a state of emergency and attempts to regain a state of internal balance. Adrenaline is no longer secreted. Heart rate and blood pressure decrease, digestion begins again, muscles relax, respiration returns to normal, and sweating stops. Sometimes the state of internal balance is not restored. Because the body is not capable of being ready for an emergency for long periods of time, the body eventually will become exhausted. The **exhaustion stage** is the third stage of the GAS in which there is wear and tear on the body, lowered resistance to disease, and an increased likelihood of disease or death. This third stage of the GAS is usually not experienced if people know and practice stress management skills.

Sources of Stress Stress can result from the accumulation of daily hassles as well as from life crises. **Daily hassles** are the day-to-day stressors of normal living. Hassles may include concerns about physical appearance, relationships with peers, worries about school assignments or grades, being criticized, or losing belongings.

Stress Management Skills

If a person does not learn to manage stress, health may be affected. Long periods of stress cause the body to work too hard by keeping blood pressure and heart rate higher than normal. The muscles tire from being tensed for long periods of time. In addition, the immune system does not function as efficiently as it should. The **immune system** is the body system that fights disease.

Stress management skills are techniques that can be used to cope with the harmful effects produced by stress. One type of skill focuses on doing something about the cause of stress. Learning and using responsible decision-making skills can help solve the stressor that is causing stress. A second type of skill focuses on keeping the body healthy and relieving anxiety. Exercising and eating a healthful diet are ways to keep the body healthy and to relieve anxiety. Consider the following stress management skills.

1. *Using responsible decision-making skills.* Refer to the earlier discussion of *The Responsible Decision-Making Model* in this chapter. When the steps in the *Model* are applied to a difficult situation, a person will feel less anxious and more in control. (S)he will develop confidence to cope both with everyday hassles and with life crises.

2. *Getting enough rest and sleep.* Without rest and sleep, a person will find it difficult to reduce stress levels. When a person is resting, blood pressure lowers, heart rate slows, and muscles relax. After sleep, a person feels invigorated and ready to face the day's challenges.

3. *Participating in physical activities.* Physical activity relieves tension by providing a physical outlet for the energy that builds up with stress.

4. *Using a time management plan.* If a person is overwhelmed by the number of tasks to complete in a day, this person should try keeping a daily calendar. The person should write down what (s)he needs to do and the order to follow to complete the list. It is sometimes best to tackle the more difficult tasks first.

5. *Writing in a journal.* Writing is a healthful way to express feelings and it may help a person work through stress. A person may choose to share a journal with a parent, mentor, or trusted friend or (s)he may not.

6. *Having close friends.* When a person is with friends, (s)he can share feelings and experiences without being judged. Friends can listen and offer suggestions that might help ease stress.

7. *Talking with parents and other trusted adults.* Parents or other trusted adults can listen and offer encouragement and suggestions from their own life experiences.

8. *Helping others.* Helping others can provide a different outlook on a situation. Helping people less fortunate than oneself can make stressful situations seem less important.

9. *Expressing affection in appropriate ways.* Expressing affection in appropriate ways provides a feeling of closeness, which in turn will relieve stressful feelings.

10. *Caring for pets.* Taking care of and holding a pet is comforting and relaxing. The physical contact involved in the care helps reduce feelings of stress.

11. *Changing outlook.* A person might change his/her outlook and view life's obstacles as challenges. **Reframing** is changing one's outlook in order to see a situation in a more positive way.

12. *Keeping a sense of humor.* A good laugh is a positive way to manage stress. A hearty laugh relaxes a person and lowers heart rate, blood pressure, and muscular tension.

Suicide Prevention

Suicide is the intentional taking of one's own life. Suicide is a permanent solution to temporary problems. Suicide is the third-ranked cause of death among people ages fifteen to twenty-four. **Parasuicide** is a suicide attempt in which a person does not intend to die. It usually is a cry for help by people who are in pain and depressed. The following facts should be considered in suicide prevention.

Thoughts, Attempts, and Completions
At least once in their lives, many people think about suicide. For most of these people, the thought is a fleeting one. However, many people dwell on the thought. Each year, almost one-half million young people attempt suicide for reasons such as being alienated from family and friends; having difficulty coping with body changes and sexuality; or experiencing the death of a parent. Most of these people do not receive help and so continue life in the same pattern, which often is one of depression and withdrawal from others. Approximately 5,000 people ages 15 to 24 commit suicide each year (National Center for Health Statistics, 1993). The number may be higher because of unreported suicides.

Suicidal Tendencies Characteristics of people who are at risk for making a suicide attempt are as follows: excessive perfectionism, aggressive behavior, hopelessness, low self-esteem, inadequate social skills, mental disorders, and depression.

Signs of Suicide

Young people who are thinking about suicide often provide warning signs. Young people who are thinking about suicide might do some of the following: make a direct statement about killing themselves, lose interest in personal appearance, withdraw from family and others, have a change in personality and lose interest in personal appearance, use alcohol and other drugs, run away from home, or have a preoccupation with death and dying.

Suicide Prevention Skills

Suicide prevention skills are techniques that can be used to help prevent a person from thinking about, attempting, and completing suicide.

1. *Knowing suicide hotline numbers.* Keep hotline numbers available. One national suicide hotline service is the National Youth Suicide Hotline. The toll-free phone number is 1-800-621-4000. This 24-hour hotline is available to all young people. The phones are staffed by trained volunteers who listen to problems and offer support and help. They provide information on resources, youth programs, and support groups available in the community.

2. *Knowing what to do when a person feels depressed.* A person should try to determine what is the source of the depression. (S)he might make a list of strengths and the positive aspects of his/her life. This person should decide on a plan of action that will relieve the feelings.

3. *Building a network of support.* A support network may include people who care, such as family members, friends, school counselors, clergy, and teachers. They will listen, offer advice, and help during difficult times.

4. *Getting involved in rewarding activities.* Rewarding activities provide an opportunity to be productive. A person's self-esteem will be raised and (s)he will feel rewarded.

5. *Knowing what to do if someone shows warning signs.* It is important to get help for anyone who is depressed or demonstrates other suicidal tendencies:
   - Do not ignore any signs or take them lightly.
   - Ask a responsible adult for help.

- Let the person know you care. Be concerned and show respect.
- Listen and try not to be shocked by what the person says.
- Ask the person directly if (s)he is considering suicide. The person will either be relieved or will deny such thoughts.
- Help the person think of better ways to solve problems.
- Identify other supportive people with whom the person can talk.
- Get professional help. Call a suicide hotline or school officials, the person's parents and physician, clergy, or the police.
- Do not leave the person alone. Stay with the person, at least until professionals take over.
- Use a contract for life. A contract for life is a written agreement in which a suicidal person promises not to hurt himself/herself for a certain period of time and/or until (s)he receives professional help.

Figure 7-1
Life Skills for Family Living

1. I will develop relationship skills.

2. I will avoid discrimination.

3. I will practice conflict resolution skills.

4. I will strive for healthful family relationships.

5. I will make healthful adjustments to family changes.

6. I will form healthful and responsible friendships.

7. I will recognize harmful relationships.

8. I will identify resources to improve relationships and family communication.

9. I will develop skills to prepare for future relationship choices—dating, marriage, parenthood, and family life.

10. I will practice life skills to promote abstinence.

Chapter 7

FAMILY LIVING

Family Living is the area of health that focuses on developing relationship skills, avoiding discrimination, practicing conflict resolution skills, striving for healthful family relationships, making healthful adjustments to family changes, forming healthful and responsible friendships, recognizing harmful relationships, identifying resources to improve relationships, developing skills to prepare for future family life, and practicing life skills to promote abstinence. The content in this chapter provides the health knowledge that is needed to teach young people important life skills for family living (Figure 7-1).

Life Skill #1

I will develop relationship skills.

Kinds of Relationships

Relationships are the connections people have with other. Positive interpersonal relationships are essential to a person's health. They can be a source of happiness and can affect self-esteem in positive ways. Feeling respect and worth from others reinforces positive feelings about oneself. Relationships also can be the source of sadness and pain and can affect self-esteem in negative ways. Feeling isolated, worthless, and frustrated reinforces negative feelings about oneself.

Healthful and Harmful Relationships

Healthful relationships are relationships that promote self-esteem and productivity, encourage health-enhancing behavior, and are free of violence and drug misuse and abuse. Examples of healthful relationships might be those in which people identify strengths in each other, encourage each other to complete projects, support each other's exercise or diet plans, and motivate each other to be energetic.

Destructive or **unhealthful relationships** are relationships that destroy self-esteem, interfere with productivity and health, and may include violence and drug misuse and abuse. Examples of destructive relationships are those in which one or both people unjustly criticize each other, interrupt each other's work, encourage each other to engage in risk behaviors, and drain each other of energy.

Social Skills

Social skills are skills that can be used to relate well with others. Family relationships usually provide the foundation for what people know about love and what people expect from themselves and others in relationships. A person raised in a loving family environment has experiences that help develop social skills needed to form healthful and responsible relationships. A person raised in a family that lacked loving relationships may not have developed such social skills. Social skills which enhance a relationship include:

1. *Using manners.* Using good manners makes a lasting impression. Saying please, thank you, excuse me, and pardon me shows others respect. Listening without interrupting show respect for others.

2. *Asking for help.* A person who is in a difficult situation should think about people who might help them. One of these people might be asked for help. This person needs to know about the problem. The situation should be described clearly. Suggestions can be requested. The suggestions should be considered, and the person thanked for the help.

3. *Giving and following instructions.* The following are guidelines for giving instructions: say what needs to be done; tell who should do it; explain how it is to be done; tell when it must be completed; and explain why it must be done. When the guidelines have been followed, the person who has given the instructions should ask if the instructions are clear, and if the other person has questions. The following are guidelines for following instructions: listen carefully; repeat the instructions to yourself and write them down, if necessary; ask questions if you are not clear; imagine yourself following the instructions before you begin; and set a time for getting things done.

4. *Expressing affection.* Expressing affection in appropriate ways is an important social skill. First, a person should determine if (s)he has warm, caring feelings for another. Then a person must consider if the other person would like to know about these feelings. The most appropriate way, place and time to express feelings should be considered.

5. *Expressing and responding to a complaint.* Before a complaint is expressed, it is important to identify the problem and determine who is responsible. Consider ways to solve the problem. The problem should be explained to the appropriate person and ideas for solving it included. The people involved should work together to solve the problem, including specific steps to take.

6. *Dealing with rejection.* Being rejected can be a painful experience. When a person is rejected, (s)he should not attack or harm the person or persons who rejected him/her. Instead, positive actions should be taken, such as: learning why the rejection occurred, brainstorming a list of ways to deal with the situation, discussing ways to deal with the situation with a trusted adult or close friend.

7. *Dealing with a stressful conversation or event.* When a stressful conversation or event is anticipated, a mental rehearsal can be helpful. A **mental rehearsal** is a technique that involves imagining oneself in the stressful conversation or situation, pretending to say and do specific things, and imagining how the other person will respond.

8. *Dealing with shyness.* Most shy people do not like to be called shy. They do not like to be forced to participate or for others to call attention to their shyness. They prefer to be encouraged gently with praise or helpful suggestions. When they decide to participate, they like to succeed the same way others do. Feelings of shyness usually lessen with time as a person gains more social experience. People who are shy should be encouraged to talk with a trusted adult if feelings of shyness do not lessen.

9. *Responding to the feelings of others.* **Empathy** is the ability to share in another person's emotions or feelings. Empathy is more than understanding another person's point of view. It involves caring. Showing empathy for another person includes the following: paying attention to the person's actions and words; trying to understand what the person is feeling; and expressing thoughts and feelings in a warm and sincere way.

10. *Dealing with excessive fear.* Some people have such excessive fear that they avoid specific objects, situations, or people. Sometimes fears are not appropriate and there may not be a valid reason for being afraid. A person with excessive fear should talk to a trusted adult about the fear. They may choose to seek professional help.

Social Competence

Social competence is the effective use of social skills. By practicing social skills in the family and then with friends, young people develop social competence and understand how to begin relationships. They have positive relationship with peers. They are aware that new relationships develop gradually. They do not expect to be accepted by others right away. They avoid forcing themselves on others and when they experience difficulties in a relationship, they talk things over with parents or other trusted adults. As young people mature, they have a need to feel close to others, to belong. Knowing and practicing social skills helps them relate well with others. Belonging to a school team or playing in a summer league are healthful ways to feel a part of a group. Being in a school play or singing in a choir also creates a sense of belonging. **Alienation** is the feeling that one is apart from others. Young people can feel this way even when they are around others. This feeling is very painful. They experience loneliness. **Loneliness** is an anxious, unpleasant, and painful feeling that results from having few friends or from being alienated. Most young people feel lonely at times. Lonely young people lack self-confidence when they are unable to gain acceptance from their peers.

Life Skill #2

I will avoid discrimination.

Discriminatory Behavior

People differ in age, gender, racial and ethnic heritage, socioeconomic class, and sexual orientation. However, all people are alike in that they want the respect of others. Everyone wants to be treated fairly. Some people single out certain people or groups of people and treat them unfairly and disrespectfully. **Discriminatory behavior** is behavior that makes a distinction in treatment or shows favor or prejudice against and individual or group of people. **Prejudice** is suspicion, intolerance, or irrational hatred directed at an individual or group of people. Both discriminatory behavior and prejudice divide people. These kinds of behavior are

learned. Training in how to treat and respect other people begins early in life. **Isms** is beliefs, attitudes, assumptions, and actions that subject individuals or people in a particular group to discriminatory behavior. Common isms include ageism, sexism, racism, and heterosexism. **Ageism** is behavior that discriminates against people in a specific age group. **Sexism** is behavior that discriminates against people of the opposite sex. **Racism** is behavior that discriminates against members of certain racial or ethnic groups. **Heterosexism** is behavior that discriminates against people who are gay, lesbian, or bisexual. Any behavior that sets one group apart from another can cause people to discriminate against others and to be prejudiced. Although there are laws that guarantee all people the same rights regardless of their differences, these laws are not enough. Individuals must willingly treat others fairly and with respect.

Discriminatory behavior and prejudice often result in violence. People who practice such behavior are at risk for being both perpetrators and victims of violence. A **perpetrator** is a person who commits a violent act. A **victim** is a person who is harmed by violence. **Hate crimes** are crimes motivated by religious, racial, ethnic, sexual orientation, or other bias. Hate crimes are sometimes called bias crimes and include violent attacks, intimidation, arson, and other kinds of property damage.

People who experience discrimination and prejudice are likely to become angry. They may try to contain their anger. **Hidden anger** is anger that is not recognized or is expressed in harmful ways and may result in inappropriate behavior and poor health.

Eventually, the anger will not be contained and may be directed at self or others. Unfortunately, the confrontations that occur often result in serious injury and death to those involved.

Avoiding Discrimination

When people show respect for others, the likelihood that others will be at their best and contribute to society is increased. For this reason, it is important to avoid discriminatory behavior. In order to avoid this kind of behavior, it is important to recognize this type of behavior and challenge anyone who chooses this behavior:

1. *Challenge stereotypes.* A **stereotype** is a prejudiced attitude that assigns a specific quality or characteristic to all people who belong to a particular group. It is unfair to make generalizations about people based on stereotypes. Although people belong to a specific racial, religious, ethnic, or gender group share much in common, they are different in other ways. It is important that people avoid believing that everyone who belongs to the same group is exactly the same. Fair treatment of everyone promotes nonviolence.

2. *Create synergy through diversity.* When people enjoy, appreciate, and respect all people in their environment, the result is synergy. **Synergy** is a positive outcome that occurs when different people cooperate and respect one another and, as a result, more energy is created for all. **Diversity** is the quality of being different or varied. When there is synergy, people with different backgrounds, talents, and skills work together to produce better solutions than would be possible if everyone were exactly alike. Synergy promotes nonviolence.

3. *Show empathy for all people.* **Empathy** is the ability to share in another's emotions or feelings. When people have empathy for individuals, they not only try to understand what other individuals are feeling, but also express understanding when appropriate. Having empathy includes being interested in everything that concerns others.

4. *Avoid discriminatory comments.* Words often cause emotional wounds that are more difficult to heal than physical wounds. People who think before speaking are less likely to make comments that may be hurtful to others. People should avoid making jokes or snide remarks about other people.

5. *Ask others to stop discriminatory behavior.* When people allow others to behave in a discriminatory way, they have their passive approval. Instead, people should share their feelings about discriminatory behavior with others. When someone makes a snide remark or tells a joke about an individual, they should express disapproval without sounding self-righteous. They can remind the other person that his/her behavior is hurtful.

6. *Learn about people who are different.* As people learn more about others, they will appreciate their talents. They can learn about others who are different by studying a foreign language in school, or by reading about other races or cultures in the library. They might get to know a student in their school or community who comes from a different country. This will help them see others as being valuable.

Life Skill #3

I will practice conflict resolution skills.

Conflict occurs in all relationships. A **conflict** is a disagreement between two or more people or between two or more choices. Strong emotions often accompany conflicts. **Conflict resolution skills** are skills a person can use to resolve a disagreement in a healthful, safe, legal, respectful, and nonviolent way.

Sources of Conflict

Conflicts often are centered on different needs and values that people have. They often involve availability of resources, fulfillment of psychological needs, upholding of personal values, and maintaining self-preservation. **Resources** are available assets and may include time, money, and material possessions. When there are not enough resources, conflicts often occur. **Psychological needs** are things that are needed to feel important and secure and may include friendships, belonging, accomplishments, and status. If something happens that interferes with people getting what they need, conflicts can occur. **Values** are the beliefs, goals, and standards held by people. When decisions must be made, and people approach those decisions with different values and standards, conflicts can occur. **Self-preservation** is the inner desire to keep oneself and others safe from harm and may include preserving physical, mental, and social health. When people threaten to harm others, conflicts can occur.

Types of Conflict

There are four types of conflict: intrapersonal conflict, interpersonal, intragroup conflict, and intergroup conflict. An **intrapersonal conflict** is a conflict that occurs within a person. For example, a person may have to make a decision about the available time (s)he has when (s)he want to go to the movies with friends, and (s)he a homework assignment to do. (S)he wants to go to the movies, but (s)he also wants to hand in the assignment on time. An **interpersonal conflict** is a conflict that occurs between two or more people. For example, a person may think that (s)he was the first in line to buy a ticket but someone else thinks (s)he was first. The two people argue about it.

An **intragroup conflict** is a conflict that occurs between people who identify themselves as belonging to the same group. When a class at school wants to celebrate an occasion and there are different plans proposed, class members may get involved in an intragroup conflict. An **intergroup conflict** is a conflict that occurs between two or more groups of people. The conflict may involve different families, schools, gangs, racial groups, religious groups, and/or nations. For example, when teams from two rival schools are playing a game, a player from one team may bump into a player from the other team. The one team may argue that the bump was intentional and was meant to put the player out of the game. The other team may argue that it was an accident.

Conflict Response Styles

A **conflict response style** is a pattern of behavior a person demonstrates when a conflict occurs. Usually, people choose one of three styles. They avoid conflicts, they confront conflicts, or they resolve conflicts.

Conflict Avoidance **Conflict avoidance** is a conflict response style in which a person

denies that there is a conflict and/or attempts to please others at his/her expense. If a person chooses not to acknowledge that a conflict exists, (s)he is allowing others to resolve the conflict in their way. As a child grows, conflict avoidance often is learned in a family where disagreements are avoided at any cost. The child learns the message, "It is not all right to disagree." In this way, there is a denial that any conflict exists.

A child also may learn to avoid conflict if (s)he grows up in a family in which one or more significant adults becomes out of control or abusive and threatens the safety of family members. As a result, the child learns the message, "If I avoid disagreements, I will be safer." In other families, children get the message, "If you agree with me and do what I tell you to do, I will love you." If there is agreement, there is approval. If there is disagreement, there is disapproval and withholding of love and support. The child learns the message, "The way to be loved and lovable is to allow others to have their way even if they do things that I do not want them to do."

Conflict Confrontation **Conflict confrontation** is a conflict response style in which a person attempts to settle a disagreement in a hostile, defiant, and aggressive way. People who choose this behavior style view conflict as a win-lose situation. A person with this style wants to win or be right at any cost and refuses to consider any other side to the issue.

Children who observe this behavior style in a significant adult in their family learn that this person was always right. Any disagreement was met with verbal and/or physical retaliation. The children observe a great deal of hostility and, as a result, view relationships as being hostile and argumentative. When these children become adults, they are likely to be confrontational in their relationships in order to resist being dominated by others.

Conflict Resolution **Conflict resolution** is a conflict response style in which a person uses conflict resolution skills to resolve a disagreement in a healthful, safe, legal, respectful, and nonviolent way. **Conflict resolution skills** are skills a person can use to resolve a disagreement in a healthful, safe, legal, respectful, and nonviolent way. People who choose to use conflict resolution skills view conflict as a win-win situation. They view conflict as a natural part of life. They are rational and think clearly.

Children who observe this behavior pattern see that significant adults in their family respect the rights and needs of others and attempt to work through disagreements in healthful and responsible ways. These adults were more concerned about resolving a situation and allowing everyone involved to maintain his/her integrity and dignity. They did not avoid the conflict but viewed conflict as necessary and important. Children who grow up observing this behavior style gain self-confidence as they learn to resolve disagreements with others.

Risks Associated with Conflict

Threats to Health In many cases, people who choose to avoid conflict are glad that the conflict is over and they do not have to deal with it. However, this is not always the case. The conflict may have been avoided, but some people remain in a constant state of inner conflict about the situation. As they continue to bury their feelings, they develop hidden anger. **Hidden anger** is anger that is not recognized or is expressed in a harmful way. On the outside, the person may appear as if nothing is wrong but on the inside (s)he may be very angry and hostile. **Hostility** is a feeling of ill will and antagonism.

People who choose conflict confrontation show outward signs of hostility and aggression and often are passive-aggressive. **Passive-aggressive** is the appearance of being cooperative and pleasant on the outside while feeling angry and hostile. People who are hostile have a high risk of developing severe, life-threatening illnesses because their bodies are in a constant state of emergency. They may experience increased heart and respiration rates and are more likely to have headaches, stomachaches, restlessness, sleeplessness, irritability, and heart and respiratory diseases.

Threats to Relationships People who practice conflict avoidance and conflict confrontation are more likely to experience destructive relationships because they are often dishonest with others. Because they do not share their true feelings, close relationships are pre-

vented from developing because there are no opportunities to respond. It is difficult to feel safe in a relationship when people are hostile and aggressive.

Threat of Violence Both conflict avoidance and conflict confrontation are associated with increased risks of violence because of feelings of anger and hostility. People who avoid conflict are often passive-aggressive, which means that while they appear outwardly passive, they continue to be irritated, annoyed, and furious on the inside. Such a person can suddenly reach a boiling point and become violent.

Conflict Resolution Skills

It is possible for people to change their way of responding to conflict and to learn conflict resolution skills. A guiding principle of conflict resolution is the concept of win-win.
1. *Remain calm.* It is important that all parties remain calm. If the parties are not calm, have a time-out before proceeding.
2. *Set the tone.* Each person in a conflict has the goal of meeting his/her own needs. The tone should be set so that the communication will be positive. Avoid blaming and interrupting; be sincere; avoid put downs; reserve judgment; avoid threats; separate the person from the problem; help others save face; use positive nonverbal messages.
3. *Define the conflict.* It may be helpful to define the conflict in writing so that both sides can be heard in full. The conflict should be described briefly and clearly. The focus should be on the conflict and not on the people involved.

4. *Take responsibility for personal actions.* Each person involved in the conflict should take responsibility for his/her own behavior. Harming another person is not appropriate behavior unless this behavior occurs as a result of defending oneself or others from personal harm and injury. It is important that each person takes responsibility for personal actions, recognizes what (s)he may have done, and apologizes when (s)he is wrong.

5. *Use I-messages to express needs and feelings.* An **I-message** is a statement that contains (1) a specific behavior or event, (2) the effect that the behavior or event has on the individual, and (3) the feeling that resulted. When a person expresses feelings rather than calling the other person a name, it is easier to work out the problem and reach a win-win solution.

6. *Listen to the needs and feelings of others.* It is important for each person to share his/her needs and feelings. The other person should not interrupt or judge. Usually when people feel they have the opportunity to clearly express themselves and are being taken seriously, they are more open to reaching a solution in a peaceful manner.

7. *List and evaluate possible solutions.* Brainstorm as many solutions as possible to resolve the conflict. Discuss each suggested solution and predict the outcome. How might each solution affect the people involved? Will the solution be a win-win solution for both? Will the solution result in actions that are healthful, safe, legal, show respect for all involved, and be nonviolent?

8. *Agree on a solution.* Both people should agree on one of the solutions. The solution may be put in writing so that the agreement can be viewed later.

9. *Follow the agreement.* Both people should genuinely agree to do what they say they will do. Some people need help in keeping their word. However, good faith is very important in conflict resolution.

10. *Ask for the assistance of a trusted adult or obtain peer mediation if the conflict cannot be resolved.* When an interpersonal conflict cannot be resolved, the people involved might talk with a trusted adult or seek professional help. A trusted adult can arrange for peer mediation.

Peer Mediation

When people are unable to resolve disputes using conflict resolution skills, peer mediation can be helpful. A **peer** is a person who is similar in age or status. To **mediate** is to bring together people who are in conflict. **Peer mediation** is a process used to resolve conflicts, in which a person helps peers resolve disagreements in healthful, safe, legal, respectful, and nonviolent ways. A **peer mediator** is a person who helps the people who are in conflict reach a solution. Many schools have peer mediation programs. The process of peer mediation involves several steps:

1. *The peer mediator introduces himself/herself and explains that (s)he will maintain a neutral position.* The peer mediator is responsible for arranging a meeting place that is agreeable and neutral. (S)he explains that (s)he has no authority over the people involved in the conflict and that it is their responsibility to resolve their disagreement.

2. *The peer mediator establishes ground rules and the peers in conflict agree to follow them.* The people who are in a disagreement often express hostility and suspicion for each other. By following ground rules, they are more likely to focus on the conflict rather than on their feelings toward one another. Appropriate ground rules include telling the truth; committing to resolve the conflict; avoiding blame, putdowns, and threats; avoiding sneering, pushing, and hitting; reserving judgment; and listening without interruption.

3. *Each of the people in disagreement clearly defines the conflict.* The people involved need to clearly identify and describe the reason for the conflict. The peer mediator uses his/her skills to focus the discussion on the conflict by asking questions or summarizing what has been said so that the conflict is clearly defined and everyone is focusing on the same issue.

4. *Each of the people in conflict expresses his/her needs and feelings about the conflict.* The people involved need to share what they believe led to the conflict. They need to share their current feelings using I-messages and following the ground rules. They need to express how their needs might be met.

5. *Each of the people in conflict identifies possible ways to resolve the conflict.*

The peer mediator assists with brainstorming and with identifying as many solutions as possible before evaluating each one. Both people involved should feel comfortable offering suggestions.

6. *The peer mediator offers additional ways to resolve the conflict.* The peer mediator may identify solutions that the people involved have not identified.

7. *Each of the suggested solutions is evaluated.* It is important to use the same criteria when evaluating each solution. The peer mediator assists by identifying the following criteria to be used. Will the solution result in actions that are:
   • healthful?
   • safe?
   • legal?
   • respectful of all people involved?
   • nonviolent?
   When these criteria are used to evaluate each solution, appropriate actions will result.

8. *The people in conflict attempt to resolve the conflict by agreeing to a solution. If this is not possible, the peer mediator negotiates an agreement.* The peer mediator may meet separately with the people involved. During these meetings, the peer mediator may suggest making trade-offs in order for everyone involved to experience a compromise that is viewed as win-win. This step of peer mediation may take time. The peer mediator may need to remind the people involved about their commitments to the mediation process.

9. *An agreement is written and signed by all people.* A written agreement should be designed stating what those involved in the conflict will do. The people involved should have time to read the agreement and to ask any questions they might have. Then both they and the peer mediator should sign and date the document. Each person should have a copy of the signed agreement.

10. *A follow-up meeting is set to discuss the results of following the agreement.* The people who signed the agreement should mutually decide about when to have a follow-up meeting. The purpose of the meeting might be to review how well the agreement is working. If the agreement is not working, the process of peer mediation might begin again.

I will strive for healthful family relationships.

Family Relationships

Family relationships are the connections one has with family members, including extended family members. **Extended family members** are family members in addition to parents, brothers, and sisters. Extended family members might include stepparents, stepbrothers, stepsisters, grandparents, aunts, uncles, and foster brothers and sisters. There may be other significant adults in the home who would be included also.

The Family Continuum

The Family Continuum is a scale marked in units ranging from zero to 100 that shows the quality of relationships within a family (Figure 7-2). A dysfunctional family is toward the zero end of *The Family Continuum*. A **dysfunctional family** is a family in which feelings are not expressed openly and honestly, coping skills are lacking, and family members do not trust each other. The quality of the relationships within a dysfunctional family is low. A healthful family is toward the 100 end of *The Family Continuum*. A **healthful family** is a family in which feelings are expressed openly and honestly, coping skills are adequate, and family members trust each other. A family does not have to be at one end or the other of the *Continuum*, but could be somewhere in between. For example, a family might demonstrate some of the items listed under the dysfunctional family and at the same time demonstrate items listed under the healthful family. If such a family demonstrated more items of a healthful family, it would be closer to the 100 end of *The Continuum*. In a healthful family, family members show respect for each other; trust each other; follow guidelines for responsible behavior; experience consequences when they do not follow guidelines; spend time with each other; share feelings in healthful ways; practice effective coping skills; resolve conflict in nonviolent ways; avoid alcohol and other drugs; and use kind words and actions.

Figure 7-2
The Family Continuum

The Family Continuum depicts the degree to which a family promotes skills needed for loving and responsible relationships.

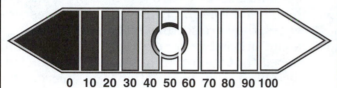

0 10 20 30 40 50 60 70 80 90 100
Dysfunctional Families   **Healthful Familes**

Dysfunctional Families

1. do not show respect for each other;
2. do not trust each other;
3. are confused about guidelines for responsible behavior;
4. are not punished or are punished severely for wrong behavior;
5. do not spend time with each other;
6. do not share feelings or do not share feelings in healthful ways;
7. do not have effective coping skills;
8. resolve conflicts with violence;
9. abuse alcohol and other drugs;
10. abuse each other with words and actions.

Healthful Families

1. show respect for each other;
2. trust each other;
3. follow guidelines for responsible behavior;
4. experience consequences when they do not follow guidelines;
5. spend time with each other;
6. share feelings in healthful ways;
7. practice effective coping skills;
8. resolve conflict in nonviolent ways;
9. avoid alcohol and other drugs;
10. use kind words and actions.

Young people who grow up in a dysfunctional family do not learn to express themselves openly and honestly. They do not learn coping skills and they do not trust each other. In a dysfunctional family, one or more of the family members:

- do not show respect for each other;
- do not trust each other;
- are confused about guidelines for responsible behavior;
- are not punished severely for wrong behavior;
- do not spend time with each other;
- do not share feelings or do not share feelings in healthful ways;
- do not have effective coping skills;
- resolve conflicts with violence;
- abuse alcohol and other drugs;
- abuse each other with words and actions.

Life Skill #5

I will make healthful adjustments to family changes.

Family relationships are constantly changing and these changes can be very stressful for everyone in the family, especially young people.

Death

Even though death is inevitable for each person, talking about death is often avoided. Some people die unexpectedly and their families have no advance notice. As a result, the death can be very stressful. In other cases, a family member may have a terminal illness. A **terminal illness** is an illness that is incurable and will eventually cause death. A person with a terminal illness will experience psychological stages of dying. Five emotional stages and feelings have been identified and described (Kübler-Ross, 1975). The five stages are denial, anger, bargaining, depression, and acceptance. Understanding the stages of dying can help both the dying person and the family realistically cope with death. At such a time, it is helpful if family members can talk together and support each other through the difficult time.

It is important to learn to express feelings during difficult times such as a death in the family.

Separation

All married couples struggle at times to maintain a meaningful relationship. During such times, some couples continue to live together while others decide to separate. A **separation** is an agreement between a married couple to live apart but remain married while working out their problems. Some married couples reunite after a separation while others decide to legally end their marriage.

A separation creates stress in a family. Each family member is affected. Adolescents are especially affected because they are striving to develop their own personal and sexual identity. They need the effective role modeling of both parents in a loving, lasting relationship. When this is no longer available to them, they may become confused, angry, and depressed. Being able to talk with their parents or with counselors will help. Changes in a family require adjustments, patience, and a desire to make the situation better.

Divorce

A **divorce** is a legal way to end a marriage in which a judge decides the conditions of the settlement. Divorce has a profound effect on the security and safety that children and adolescents need to have as they grow and develop physically, mentally, emotionally, and socially. When parents remain emotionally and psychologically close even though they are divorced, children in the family seem to adjust well. These children may not like the fact that their parents are divorced, but they still feel close to their parents. However, when divorced parents do not remain emotionally and psychologically close, children in the family can feel abandoned. It is important that children and adolescents of divorced parents have the opportunity to express their feelings with their parents or with a professional counselor.

Parental Dating

Feelings of abandonment are vital to children's adjustment when a divorced parent starts to date again. Young children find parental dating disruptive if they believe they will be abandoned if the parent connects into a new relationship. This is especially true if the new relationship demands a great deal of time, thereby reducing the time that the parent spends with the child.

Adolescents often have difficulty with parents dating because adolescents are at the developmental stage where this is appropriate behavior for them. During their adolescent years, they are sorting out their own feelings about opposite sex relationships. They had hoped that their parents would be in a comfortable and stable relationship. In order for a healthful adjustment to be made, honest and open dialogue is needed within the family.

Remarriage

A **remarriage** is a marriage in which at least one of the two persons has been married before. A remarriage creates new family relationships and, as a result, an adolescent will likely experience mixed feelings. (S)he may be happy for the natural parent, yet saddened that his/her parents will not get back together. It is important to realize that it is worthwhile to give support and effort to the new relationship.

Stepfamilies

Stepfamilies are blended families. A **blended family** is a family that includes the newly married adults and their children from any previous marriage. The greatest source of conflict in a blended family is integrating the children into one set of values and rules. Parents who remarry may think that if their new relationship is comfortable and loving, children will have the same feelings about the new stepfamily. However, research indicates that it may take seven years for children and adolescents to feel a comfortable bond with the new family unit. Young people tend to have an easier time adjusting if their natural parents spend some quality time alone with them and provide them with emotional support.

New Baby in the Family

When a baby is born into a family, everyone in the family has to make adjustments.

The new baby needs to be fed, clothed, cared for and loved. At the same time, everyone else in the family must have his/her needs met. One of these basic needs is to be nurtured within the family. Nurturing involves loving, supporting, paying attention to, and encouraging everyone in the family. Sometimes it is difficult for other children in the family to share their parents' attention when a new baby is born into the family. It is important that parents understand the needs of the other children as well as the new baby. It also is important that the other children have the opportunity to help in the care of the new baby so that they will feel needed.

Life Skill #6

I will form healthful and responsible friendships.

Being a Friend and Making Friends

A **friend** is someone known well and liked. There is an old saying that "A friend is a gift you give yourself." Good friends share interests; help you solve problems; teach you new things; and help you feel good about yourself. Friends support each other through happy as well as difficult times. Meaningful friendships contribute to optimal health and help a person to feel accepted. The number of friends a person has is not as important as the quality of the friendships.

There is an old saying "To have a friend, you must be a friend." Making new friends takes time and effort, but it is worth it. There are skills that can be practiced to help make new friends. The following skills help a person become a good friend:
• listening carefully and keeping confidences;
• avoiding gossip;
• telling the truth;
• sharing joys and sorrows;
• being able to say "I am sorry."
• being a good companion;
• sharing with the other person;
• accepting mistakes the other person makes;
• praising the other person when (s)he does something well;

• helping the other person when (s)he needs assistance.

Two characteristics, shyness and loneliness, make it difficult for people to make new friends. **Shyness** is a condition characterized by discomfort, inhibition, and awkwardness in social situations. Shy young people withdraw from interacting and expressing themselves with others. As shy young people are encouraged to interact with others, small successes will increase their self-confidence.

Loneliness is a condition that is characterized by unpleasant, painful, or anxious feelings as a result of having fewer or less satisfying relationships than desired. Feelings of loneliness often are temporary. However, many young people feel alienated and lonely because of changes in their personal lives, such as the separation or divorce of their parents, or moving away from their friends.

Making Choices with Friends

Being accepted by peers is critically important in satisfying young people's needs for belonging and helping counteract feelings of alienation and loneliness. **Peer pressure** is pressure that people of similar age or status place on others to encourage them to make certain decisions or behave in certain ways. Peer pressure plays an important role in the decisions a person makes about his/her behavior. Young people should be advised to use *The Responsible Decision-Making Model* (Table 6-3) when making choices with friends.

Ending Friendships

Changing friends is part of growing up. Friendships change for many different reasons. A friend may move away and not keep in touch. A friend may break a confidence and the friendship is never the same again. Sometimes interests change, and new friends replace old ones. However, there are times when a person needs to be objective about a friend and decide if that person truly is a friend. For example, the friend might encourage wrong actions or actions contrary to values. It might be time to end the friendship.

Life Skill #7

I will recognize harmful relationships.

Recognizing Harmful Relationships

Healthful relationships are relationships that enhance self-esteem, foster respect, develop character, and promote health-enhancing behavior and responsible decision-making. On the other hand, **harmful relationships** are relationships that threaten self-esteem, are disrespectful, indicate a lack of character, threaten health, and foster irresponsible decision-making. When a person is made to feel unimportant, worthless, isolated, and frustrated, it is time to evaluate the relationship. The relationship may be abusive, violent, or codependent.

Abusive Relationships A relationship in which a person is abusive toward another is a harmful relationship. **Abuse** is the harmful treatment of a person. Abuse includes the following behavior: neglect, sexual abuse, physical abuse, and emotional abuse.

Violent Relationships **Violence** is the threatened or actual use of physical force to injure, damage, or destroy others, or property. Violent behavior is usually learned early in life by observing the ways parents and other adults act. Young people who have observed violent behavior at home are likely to be aggressive as they grow. Eventually, this behavior affects their relationships.

Codependent Relationships Codependence is a mental disorder in which a person loses personal identity, has frozen feelings, and copes ineffectively. Codependent people learn not to talk to others about family problems. They learn that they do not deserve to be treated with respect. They cannot trust others. Obviously, these feelings destroy their ability to form healthful relationships.

Being Attracted to Gangs

All young people need and want supportive adults present in their lives. Unfortunately, many young people are not reared in healthful families. Many young people do not have stable, loving adults in their lives. These young people may be uninvolved in school activities and youth groups and may not have jobs where they might interact with supportive adults. If young people do not have responsible adult role models, they are at risk for joining gangs or spending time with friends who get into trouble. Young people who spend time with friends who are involved in gang-related activity are at risk for being involved in gangs themselves.

Self-protection strategies are strategies that can be practiced to protect oneself and to decrease the risk of becoming a victim. People may think that they have little control over their environment. However, they probably have more control than they realize. They can learn to protect themselves. There are three keys to self-protection. First, people should always trust their feelings about people and situations. When they have a gut feeling that a particular relationship is not healthful, they should trust this feeling. They should recognize that the relationship is harmful and break off the relationship.

Second, people should always be on the alert. They should pay close attention to the people who are near them and know what they are doing. Third, they should avoid being in risk situations. **Risk situations** are circumstances that increase the likelihood that something negative will happen to one's health, safety, and/or well-being. When people are in risk situations, they are not practicing self-protection.

People who have been harmed by abusive, violent, and codependent relationships need help to fully recover. If they do not get help, they will likely be unable to form healthful relationships. Recovery from harmful relationships always involves dealing with painful issues and learning to express feelings and getting needs met in healthful ways. If victims of harmful relationships do not learn ways to protect themselves, they continue to be at risk.

I will identify resources to improve relationships and family communication.

Mentors

Because many young people grow up in harmful relationships within their families, they lack a stable, long-term adult presence in their lives. Adult mentors can play a vital role in helping a young person stay safe. **Mentors** are adults who guide and help younger people. Mentors can be helpful in helping young people recognize what they are feeling, why they are feeling the way they do, and what are some healthful ways of coping with their feelings. It can be very reassuring to have trusting adults understand their feelings.

Twelve Step Programs

Twelve Step Programs are programs that focus on twelve steps to take to recover from the past and gain wholeness. Originally, the Twelve Step Program was developed for people with alcoholism, but it has now been expanded to include people who have an excessive dependency on people or things. Some of these excessive dependencies include drugs, gambling, food, perfectionism, exercise, and sexual addictions. The programs change behavior by focusing on strengthening relationships—relationships with self, others, and one's personal beliefs.

Counseling

Getting professional help can be an important step to recovery from harmful relationships.

There are many different areas of mental health for which professional counseling programs are available. The programs are designed to help people gain skills in recovering from their dependency. Counseling may be on an individual basis, a group basis, or a family basis. Victims of harmful relationships may need not only counseling but also protection and care. In many cities, shelters have been established to help particular groups of victims such as abused spouses and their children.

I will develop skills to prepare for future relationship choices–dating, marriage, parenthood, and family life.

Dating

Preadolescents' social life usually involves same-sex group activities, mostly with close friends. Group activities still interest young teens. However, the groups may now consist of both males and females. Gradually, members of the group begin to date each other. **Dating** is the sharing of social activities and time with members of the opposite sex. Dating is an extension of friendship. Adolescents need to learn to develop and sustain successful and satisfying dating relationships in order to prepare for more important decisions regarding commitment and marriage. Dating provides the opportunity for young people to

learn more about themselves and others. Dating affords adolescents the opportunity to:

- *Strengthen self-esteem.* Being liked and accepted by members of the opposite sex is especially important during adolescence. Asking someone to share an activity and having this person accept affirms a young person's belief about his/her attractiveness and desirability. Feeling good about a dating experience allows an adolescent to gain confidence in the way that (s)he is managing his/her social life.

- *Improve social skills.* Dating provides an opportunity to practice social skills, such as meeting the date's parents or guardian for the first time, making a mutual decision about what to do on a date, using manners, and taking part in conversations.

- *Becoming secure with one's masculinity or femininity.* Two important adolescent developmental tasks focus on accepting body changes that occur as the result of puberty and becoming comfortable with one's sex role. Adolescents have many questions about their sex roles. Dating affords them the opportunity to express different aspects of their personalities, to have a wide variety of interests, and to gain acceptance. This reinforces their comfort level with regard to their masculinity or femininity.

- *Develop skills in intimacy.* **Intimacy** is the term used to describe a deep and meaningful kind of sharing between two people. Skills needed to have intimate relationships can be learned and practiced. A sense of trust and a sense of caring is important in the development of intimacy.

- *Understand personal needs.* In a healthful relationship, people develop an understanding of one another's needs and they desire to meet these needs in healthful ways.

Evaluating Dating Relationships

It is essential that adolescents have a gauge or measure that they can use to evaluate the behavior of others, especially in a dating relationship. Adolescents need to know the answers to questions such as: "What behavior should I expect from others? How do I know that someone is behaving toward me in a respectful manner?"

Prior to dating, an adolescent should ask himself/herself the questions from the following list. Does the person I am interested in dating:

1. Demonstrate self-loving behavior?
2. Express feelings in healthful ways?
3. Adhere to family guidelines?
4. Set goals and make plans to reach them?
5. Balance time between family, friends, and other commitments?
6. Avoid abusive behavior?
7. Avoid abusing and misusing alcohol and other drugs?
8. Recognize the benefits of abstinence?

Preparing for Marriage

When two people choose to marry, they are choosing to share their lives with one another. Since intimacy plays such a vital role in a marriage relationship, adolescents need to understand that for a marriage to be sustained over the years, there are four kinds of intimacy that are of particular importance: philosophical intimacy, psychological intimacy, creative intimacy, and physical intimacy.

Philosophical Intimacy **Philosophical intimacy** is the sharing of one's beliefs, philosophy of life, and life principles. In other words, it is the sharing of what is important in a person's life. Philosophical intimacy provides important information about how each person makes decisions and how values and beliefs influence lifestyle. Assessing the compatibility of one's values and beliefs with that of a potential marriage partner should be done while considering marriage rather than waiting until after marriage.

Psychological Intimacy **Psychological intimacy** is the sharing of one's needs, drives, weaknesses, strengths, intentions, emotional feelings, and deepest problems. Attaining psychological intimacy with another individual usually occurs gradually because this kind of sharing evolves after a level of trust is developed. The greater the level of trust, the greater the likelihood of psychological intimacy.

Creative Intimacy **Creative intimacy** is the sharing in the work or development of a project, task, or creation of something new. In creative intimacy, two persons explore their ability to cooperate with one another, to operate as a team.

Physical Intimacy **Physical intimacy** is the sharing of physical expressions of affection.

180

When preparing for marriage, it is important for a couple to assess the warmth and closeness that each partner feels for the other and if each partner is comfortable expressing affection. However, expressing affection should not be confused with having sexual intercourse.

Maintaining a Healthful Marriage

A healthful marriage is a marriage in which both partners share both the responsibilities and privileges of married life. Maintaining a healthful marriage requires sustained effort. A marriage is not static but dynamic–marriage is constantly changing because the marriage partners are in the process of growing and changing. A **healthful relationship** is a relationship that promotes self-esteem and productivity, encourages health-enhancing behavior, and are free of violence and drug misuse and abuse. A **healthful marriage** is a healthful relationship between marriage partners that is based on equality, trust, communication, and commitment. Each marriage partner feels the other's needs, goals, and feelings are as important as his/her own and is supportive of the personal identity and growth of the other. Trust is needed for each partner to feel secure in the marriage. Effective communication includes expressing thoughts and feelings, listening actively, and having empathy for what the other person communicates. Commitment to one another and commitment to the marriage contract is needed to maintain a healthful marriage. Partners who have a commitment to one another recognize the benefits of a monogamous marriage. A **monogamous marriage** is a marriage in which both persons remain sexually faithful to one another. Responsible adults agree that the greatest opportunity for joy that is not accompanied by penalty, guilt, or destruction of self or others is sex within marriage. A monogamous marriage offers a sense of security.

Understanding the Risks of Adolescent Marriage

More than 75 percent of adolescent marriages end in divorce. The reasons are many, but they are all related to the fact that adolescents have not had enough time to master the following developmental tasks:

1. *Achieving mature relationship with age-mates of both sexes.* Adolescent marriage disrupts the time needed to master the developmental task of forming mature relationships. Adolescents who marry are less likely to have a support network of mature friends who will be helpful during the stressful first years of marriage.

2. *Achieving a masculine or feminine social role.* Dating allows adolescents to learn how they respond to members of the opposite sex. They are robbed of the time they need to become comfortable with their masculine or feminine social role and to learn appropriate ways of behavior. They also pass up much of the fun that their peers have engaging in normal social activities.

3. *Accepting one's physique.* Adolescents' bodies are growing and developing at different rates and secondary sex characteristics are evident. The hormonal changes that accompany adolescence not only initiate these physical changes but also result in new emotions. Adolescents need time to understand the emotions that result from these hormonal changes. Adolescents who marry may do so because they had a strong sexual attraction for one another. Without the skills needed to differentiate between love and strong infatuation, adolescents can make mistakes when choosing a mate.

4. *Achieving emotional independence from parents and other adults.* Adolescents normally bounce back and forth from being dependent on parents to challenging their authority. Their behavior is indicative of an attempt to achieve emotional independence from their parents. However, they still need the safety and security of their parents while they are testing their independence. Adolescents who marry are faced with adulthood without the safety and security of parents.

5. *Preparing for marriage and family life.* Adolescents who marry miss the opportunity to sign up for high school courses

that include such courses as relationships, marriage, and parenting.

6. *Preparing for an economic career.* Adolescents need to gain an education that will enable them to enter college and/or the job market. The end goal is to become gainfully employed in order to be financially independent and to have the resources necessary to support a family. Adolescents who marry usually disrupt their education and, as a result, they are less educated and have fewer skills to enable them to be competitive in the job market. They are usually financially disadvantaged and run the risk of staying that way. Often feelings of "being trapped" are associated with limited financial resources.

7. *Acquiring a set of values and an ethical system as a guide to behavior–developing an ideology.* During adolescence, when adolescents are attempting to achieve emotional independence from parents, they have an opportunity to test their own standards and values. They become confident when they move from "this is what my parents say" to "this is what I believe." Adolescents who marry may do so before they are certain of their own standards and values.

8. *Developing a social conscience.* Adolescence can be described as the "me" period of life. Toward the end of adolescence, adolescents are looking more objectively at the world around them and thinking of ways they can help. Adolescents gain positive self-esteem by contributing to society. Adolescents who marry miss the experiences of helping others. Survival becomes their focus.

Being a Responsible and Caring Parent

Parenting involves more than having loving feelings for a child. Being a responsible and caring parent is not an easy task. It involves developing intimacy with a child, nurturing the child as (s)he grows and develops, and helping the child develop self-control and self-discipline. Responsible and caring parents:
• spend quality time with a child;
• set realistic expectations;
• teach children about health and safety;
• give love and affection;
• teach a positive attitude, avoiding condemnation and criticism;

• teach moral and ethical values;
• teach self-discipline and self-control;
• provide economic security;
• recognize and respect their rights;
• provide a stable, secure family that is free from all forms of abuse.

Understanding the Risks of Adolescent Parenthood

Adolescents are not ready for the responsibility of parenthood. There are many risks associated with adolescent parenthood:

1. *Estimated federal costs of adolescent childbearing.* In 1990, the United States single year cost for adolescent childbearing exceeded $25 billion, an increase of 16 percent over the previous year.

2. *Health risks to the adolescent mother.* During pregnancy, adolescents are at a much higher risk than older women of suffering from serious medical complications, including anemia, pregnancy-induced hypertension, toxemia, cervical trauma, and premature delivery. This not only results in higher medical costs associated with pregnancy, but also has an impact on the present and future health

of the adolescent. The maternal mortality rate for mothers under age fifteen is 60 percent greater than for women in their twenties. Adolescents tend to delay or forego prenatal care and this contributes to increased health risks.

3. *Health risks to the baby of a adolescent mother.* The infant mortality rate in the United States is strongly related to the number of infants born at low birth weights. A low birth weight is a weight that is less than 5.5 pounds at birth. Low birthweight babies are more apt to have developmental problems, both physical and mental, than babies of normal weights. Even normal-birthweight infants of adolescent mothers have a higher rate of rehospitalization than infants of older mothers.

4. *Educational risks to the adolescent mother and father.* Adolescent mothers are less likely than their childless peers to have the education and skills needed to become economically independent. Eighty percent of adolescent mothers drop out of school and only 56 percent ever graduate from high school. A female who begins parenting in her teens earns half the lifetime wages of a female who waits until she is twenty to have her first child.

5. *Economic consequences of adolescent parenthood.* Two-thirds of adolescent parents fifteen to nineteen years of age, and almost all adolescent parents fourteen years or younger, are unmarried, increasing the likelihood that they will need public assistance. Even when adolescent mothers are married, their husbands likely did not complete high school and their unemployment rate is higher than their male peers.

6. *Parenting skill deficiencies in adolescent parents.* Adolescents who are parents are suddenly faced with the awesome responsibility of shaping the lives and characters of their children at a time when they themselves are in the midst of overwhelming and confusing physical and emotional developmental tasks. Not only is their own development interrupted by parenthood, but also their children are all to often negatively affected as well.

7. *Impact of fatherhood on adolescent males.* Adolescent fathers are much more likely to be high school dropouts than other male adolescents. Approximately 84 percent of the fathers of children born to adolescent mothers live apart from their children.

I will practice life skills to promote abstinence.

Affection is a fond or tender feeling that a person has toward another person. Affection is a feeling of emotional warmth or closeness. Being able to give or receive affection is important in any relationship. During adolescence, relationships with the opposite sex include not only affection but also the added dimension of sexual feelings. **Sexual feelings** are feelings that result from a strong physical and emotional attraction to another person.

Abstinence is choosing not to engage in sexual intercourse. Most parents want schools to teach the many benefits of abstinence. These benefits can be examined using the criteria for responsible decision-making from *The Responsible Decision-Making Model* (Table 4-3).

Benefits of Abstinence

1. *Abstinence is healthful and safe.* Serious consequences may result from permissive sexual involvement. Statistics prove that the risks are great for becoming infected with an STD or with HIV. The suicide rate of adolescent mothers is ten times greater than the general population. Child abuse and neglect are prevalent among adolescent parents.

2. *Abstinence protects the laws of the community.* In most states, sexual involvement with a person under the legal age of consent can be considered corruption of a minor. The legal age of consent is that age when a person is considered responsible for his/her sexual actions. For persons who are mentally disabled, the age of consent may be different.

3. *Abstinence shows respect for self and others.* Making the decision to wait to have sexual intercourse involves self-discipline and the willingness to delay gratification, which in turn maintains self-respect and respect for others.

4. *Abstinence follows guidelines set by responsible adults such as parents and/or*

guardians. As many as 97 percent of parents in a poll want abstinence taught in schools.

5. *Abstinence demonstrates good character and moral values.* Sexual union without commitment and a sense of continuity may contribute to inner turmoil that weakens self-confidence. Educating young people about the benefits of keeping sexual intercourse within a monogamous marriage helps protect them from permissive sexual relationships.

6. *Other advantages of choosing abstinence.* When adolescents become sexually involved, the intensity of the physical experience may make it difficult for them to focus on other aspects of a relationship and they are not able to learn necessary skills. During adolescence, relationships are intermittent. As a result, many relationships that are thought to be serious by one or both partners eventually break up. At best, the broken relationship may leave one or both partners very disappointed and hurt. However, when sexual intercourse has been a part of a relationship, the trauma of breaking up is intensified. The partner who has been abandoned often feels that (s)he has been used. Feelings of distrust and worthlessness are common. It is traumatic for most people to imagine a former partner being sexually intimate with a new partner.

Life Skills to Support Abstinence

Choosing abstinence is difficult. Adolescents are under great pressure to behave as other peers do in order to be accepted. The media—videotapes, movies, television, and magazines promote permissiveness. Adolescent heroes engage in permissive lifestyles than flaunt lack of moral character and good judgment. The consequences of permissiveness are not portrayed realistically. Adolescents who desire to choose abstinence need to practice life skills so that they are armored with personal strength to resist the pressures they will experience. They can:

1. *Be involved in activities that promote self-worth.* School and community activities help adolescents develop feelings of self-worth, a sense of accomplishment, and a sense of doing something for others. In turn, feeling good about themselves is important in developing the self-confidence to resist peer pressure. Activities also help adolescents have a feeling of belonging. Feelings of alienation or being left out are associated with early sexual involvement.

2. *Establish goals.* It is much easier to employ self-discipline and to delay gratification when adolescents identify the benefits of doing so. Adolescents can examine how an unwanted pregnancy, adolescent marriage, or a sexually transmitted disease might interfere with achieving their goals.

3. *Develop loving family relationships.* Peer relationships are important during adolescence but they are not a substitute for nurturing family relationships. Family relationships provide a sense of belonging and reinforce values. When adolescents feel supported by their families, they are less likely to turn to sex to meet their needs for intimacy.

4. *Be assertive and use decision-making skills.* It is important for adolescents to be assertive, to stand up for what they believe, and to express their beliefs clearly to others. One way to do this is to think ahead about situations in which there may be pressure to be sexually active. It is helpful to role-play possible situations in which adolescents need to say NO to negative peer pressure.

5. *Establish relationships with trusted adults.* When adolescents have established relationships with trusted adults, they have the opportunity to examine their goals in life with someone who is older and wiser. A trusted adult can add future perspectives and help adolescents adhere to their values.

6. *Select friends who choose abstinence.* Adolescents have strong sexual feelings. Abstinence is a difficult choice. Selecting friends who are sexually active adds additional stress because they may not support the decision to be abstinent.

7. *Date people who have chosen abstinence.* Having a relationship with someone who has also chosen abstinence relieves much of the pressure to become sexually active. A couple can discuss ways to support their decision and each one can assume responsibility for his/her actions.

8. *Avoid situations that are tempting.* Some situations intensify sexual feelings and increase temptation. When adolescents

realize that they are tempted in certain situations, they should avoid those situations.

9. *Abstain from the use of alcohol and other drugs.* Alcohol and many other drugs depress the parts of the brain that control judgment and reason, making it more difficult to say NO and mean it.

10. *Select entertainment that promotes sex within a monogamous marriage.* Movies, soap operas, videos, CDs, magazines, and other media highlight people engaged in sexual relationships without commitment. They do not show negative consequences. They are totally unrealistic. There is danger in filling the mind with entertainment that portrays unrealistic relationships.

Figure 8-1

Life Skills for Growth and Development

1. I will care for my body systems.

2. I will recognize how my body changes as I grow.

3. I will accept my maleness/femaleness.

4. I will accept my physical uniqueness.

5. I will accept and develop my learning style.

6. I will achieve developmental tasks for my age group.

7. I will learn about conception, pregnancy, and childbirth.

8. I will recognize the needs of people of different ages.

9. I will practice behaviors that contribute to healthful aging.

10. I will share my feelings about death and dying.

Chapter 8
GROWTH AND DEVELOPMENT

Growth and Development is the area of health that focuses on caring for the body systems, recognizing changes during growth periods, accepting maleness/femaleness, accepting physical appearance, accepting one's learning style, achieving appropriate developmental tasks, learning about the beginning of new life, recognizing the needs of people of different ages, preparing for aging, and sharing feelings about dying and death. The content in this chapter provides the health knowledge that is needed to teach young people important life skills regarding growth and development (Figure 8-1).

Life Skills #1

I will care for my body systems.

Understanding the Human Body

A person can help his/her body perform at its best by learning about the body and by knowing how to take care of it. For a person's body to achieve the best possible performance, the body systems must work at their highest levels. It is important to understand that the body functions as a result of all body systems working together.

Support and Control Systems

Skeletal System The **skeletal system** is a body system composed of bones, cartilage, ligaments, and tendons (Figure 8-2) Over 200 bones serve as the framework for the body and protect body organs. For example, the bones of the skull protect the brain. Ribs protect the heart and lungs. Bones support and withstand not only great weights but also forces. Bones work with muscles to provide movement of the body. Another important function of bones is the production of red blood cells and white blood cells in the marrow of long bones. **Marrow** is a soft substance in the center of bones. A **joint** is the point where two or more bones meet. There are different types of joints in the body. Immovable joints are found in the skull where the bones are joined at seams, called sutures. Most of the joints in the body are freely movable. The hips and the shoulders are examples of ball and socket joints. These joints allow a wide range of motion. The elbows and knees are examples of hinge joints, which allow motion in a single plane. The joint at which the skull meets the spine is a pivot joint, which provides rotary movement. The wrists and ankles are examples of gliding joints. The bones in these joints glide over each other. **Ligaments** are bands of tough connective tissue that hold bones together at joints. **Tendons** are bands of tough connective tissue that attach muscles to bones at joints. **Cartilage** is connective tissue that is tough but flexible. Cartilage forms the external ears and the tip of the nose. Cartilage cushions many joints, such as the knee.

It is important to keep bones strong. Milk and other dairy products are good sources of the minerals calcium and phosphorus that

Growth and Development

are needed for bone formation. In addition, vitamin D is essential for the most efficient use of calcium and phosphorus. Sources of vitamin D are fish oils, eggs, and liver. A lack of calcium in a person's diet combined with a lack of exercise may cause osteoporosis when a person is older. **Osteoporosis** is a bone disease in which bone tissue becomes brittle.

Muscular System The **muscular system** is a body system in which there are three types of muscles—skeletal, smooth, and cardiac (Figure 8-3). **Skeletal muscles** are muscles that are attached to bones, and with the bones provide body movement. Skeletal muscles are sometimes called voluntary muscles because they can be controlled by conscious effort. **Smooth muscles** are muscles that line internal organs, such as the stomach and intestine. Smooth muscles are sometimes called involuntary muscles because they function without conscious effort. **Cardiac muscles** are muscles found only in the heart.

Movement in the body is controlled by a network of over 600 muscles. All muscle cells have the unique ability to contract, or shorten, and then to return to their original state. This ability allows body movement. When a skeletal muscle contracts, the bone(s) to which it is attached is pulled toward the muscle. Contraction of smooth muscle in the digestive tract moves food through the digestive organs allowing the food to be digested. Cardiac muscle has some characteristics of both skeletal and smooth muscles but it is considered as a distinct kind of muscle. The heart contracts and relaxes rhythmically and automatically and involuntarily to pump an average of seventy times each minute, forty million times each year, for as long as a person lives. A balanced diet and regular exercise are essential in keeping muscles strong and efficient. This is particularly important for the heart muscle. Regular exercise improves the efficiency of the heart by increasing the amount of blood pumped with each beat. This, in turn, results in the heart beating less often with more rest between each beat.

Integumentary System The **integumentary system** is a body system composed of the skin, hair, nails, and glands (Figure 8-4). It is the largest system in the body and covers and protects the body. **Skin** is the outermost covering of body tissue, which protects internal organs. The skin protects against injury and helps keep microorganisms from getting into the body. The skin also functions in maintaining body temperature. When the body produces excess heat during exercise, sweat glands produce perspiration, which evaporates from the surface of the skin and cools the body.

The skin is composed of two main layers, the epidermis and the dermis. The **epidermis** is the first layer of skin; the outer cells of this layer are dead. These cells are continually sloughing off and being replaced by new cells. Fingernails and toenails are formed by the epidermis and grow from a base called the nail bed, which continually produces new nails. The **dermis** is the deeper layer of skin containing cells that are well supplied with blood vessels and nerve cells.

The dermis contains hair follicles and glands. Hairs grow out of the follicles, which extend from the dermis to the surface of the epidermis. Two major kinds of glands are in the dermis—sebaceous glands and sweat glands. **Sebaceous glands** are glands that produce sebum, which is an oily substance that lubricates the hairs and the surface of the skin. Most of the skin contains sweat glands. **Sweat glands** are glands that secrete a fluid that is mostly water, but also contain small amounts of salts and other waste materials.

Nervous System The **nervous system** is a body system composed of a network of nerve cells that carry messages, or impulses, to and from the brain and spinal cord to all parts of the body (Figure 8-5). The nervous system consists of the brain, the spinal cord, and nerves that branch from the brain and spinal cord. Individual nerve cells are called neurons. **Neurons** are nerve cells that relay impulses to and from the brain and spinal cord. They may vary slightly in size and shape. The nervous system is composed of two main parts–the central nervous system (CNS) and the peripheral nervous system (PNS). The **central nervous system (CNS)** is the part of the nervous system that consists of the brain and spinal cord. The brain

188

is considered to be the most complex part of the CNS and is protected from injury by the skull. The brain also is protected and nourished by the meninges. **Meninges** are the three membranes that cover and protect the brain and spinal cord. The spinal cord consists of a column of neurons that extends from the base of the brain through the vertebral column.

The three main sections of the brain are the brain stem, the cerebrum and the cerebellum. The brain stem is the connection of the brain and spinal cord and is responsible for many important involuntary functions, such as heart rate, breathing, swallowing and coughing. The cerebrum is the largest area of the brain and functions in interpreting impulses from sense organs, in initiating voluntary muscular activity, and in memory. The cerebrum also is the center of personality and intelligence. The cerebellum is the area of the brain that controls and coordinates muscular activity and the balance of the body.

The **peripheral nervous system (PNS)** is the part of the nervous system that consists of the nerves that branch from the central nervous system to the periphery, or outer areas, of the body. Twelve pairs of cranial nerves branch from the brain and transmit information to and from the eyes, ears, nose, and tongue. Cranial nerves also control muscles in the face and neck. Thirty-one pairs of spinal nerves branch from the spinal cord. Spinal nerves transmit impulses to and from all other parts of the body. **Sensory neurons** are neurons that carry impulses from the sense organs to the brain and spinal cord. Neurons that carry impulses from the brain and spinal cord to muscles and glands are **motor neurons**. Two subdivisions of the PNS are the somatic nervous system and the autonomic nervous system. The **somatic nervous system** is the sudivision of the nervous system that controls the skeletal muscles responsible for voluntary movement. For example, if a person touches a sharp instrument, sensory neurons carry the impulse to the CNS, which interprets the message and motor neurons carry the impulse to the muscles of the person's hand, and (s)he lifts the hand. The **autonomic nervous system** is the subbdivision of the nervous system that is concerned with the automatic regulation of internal body functioning. This system controls involuntary actions and regulates heart rate and body temperature.

Energy and Transport Systems

Digestive System The **digestive system** is a body system that breaks down food so that nutrients can be absorbed by the cells in the body (Figure 8-6). Food is the source of energy for the body so that the body can function and be active. **Digestion** is the process by which food is chemically changed to a form that can pass through cell membranes. The main organs of the digestive system form a continuous tube or tract through which food moves as the result of involuntary muscle contractions called **peristalsis**.

Digestion starts in the mouth when food is chewed and mashed by the teeth and moistened by saliva. **Saliva** is the watery, slightly alkaline fluid secreted into the mouth. Saliva contains an enzyme that starts the chemical breakdown of carbohydrates. An **enzyme** is a chemical that speeds up a chemical reaction. Other enzymes are produced in the stomach and small intestine to complete the process of digestion as food moves through those organs. Digestion is completed in the small intestine, which is a coiled tube measuring approximately twenty-three feet in length. The digested food is absorbed through cell membranes in the lining of the small intestine into blood vessels that are present around cells in the lining. Food that is not digested passes into the large intestine, which is also called the colon. The **colon** is the major part of the large intestine. The cells that form the lining of the colon absorb water from the undigested material and return it to body tissues. This is an important factor in maintaining the body's water balance. The remaining undigested material forms a semi-solid mass called **feces**, which is excreted through the anus.

The liver, gallbladder, and pancreas are other body organs that are involved in the process of digestion. They are not part of the continuous digestive tract. The **liver** is the largest gland in the body and produces bile. **Bile** is a liquid secreted by the liver. Bile is essential in the digestion of fat in foods because it breaks fat particles into smaller droplets that will pass through cell membranes. Bile produced in the liver moves through tubes called hepatic ducts to the gallbladder where it is stored. When food is present in the stomach, bile is released from the gallbladder, moves through the common bile duct, and empties into the small intestine.

The **pancreas** is an elongated, tapered, gland that lies across the back of the abdomen. The pancreas produces enzymes that are necessary for the complete digestion of carbohydrates, proteins, and fats. These enzymes flow through a duct that empties into the common bile duct. The pancreas produces an important hormone also, which will be discussed later in this chapter. Anything that upsets the body's ability to process food affects the entire body. It is important to get medical help for any chronic or lasting ailment that affects digestive organs.

Cardiovascular System The **cardiovascular system** is a body system that consists of the heart, blood vessels, and blood (Figure 8-7). The **heart** is a muscular pump that beats continuously and rhythmically to send blood to the body. The heart is surrounded and protected by a sac called the pericardium. The **pericardium** is a membraneous bag that completely envelops the heart. Within the heart are four chambers, two atria and two ventricles. A wall called the septum separates the two sides. The atria are upper chambers and receive blood returning to the heart. The **ventricles** are lower chambers that pump blood from the heart. The heart beats an average of seventy to eighty times per minute. **Blood pressure** is the force exerted by the flowing blood against the walls of the arteries. The pumping action of the heart creates the force. Every time the heart beats, the pressure increases. When the heart muscle relaxes between beats, the pressure decreases.

Blood is continually circulating from the left ventricle to all body cells and back to the right atrium. This blood that is rich in oxygen is pumped through the aorta. The **aorta** is the main artery of the body. This blood circulates to all body cells providing them with nutrients and oxygen. At the same time, carbon dioxide, which is a waste product of cell metabolism, and other wastes move from the cells through cell membranes into the circulating blood. This blood returns to the right atrium through large veins, the superior and inferior vena cava. This is systemic circulation.

Blood also is continually circulating from the right ventricle to the lungs and back to the left atrium. This is pulmonary circulation. Blood returning to the right atrium in systemic circulation flows into the right ventricle, which contracts and pumps the blood to the lungs. In the lungs, an exchange of gases occurs. This blood, which is rich in carbon dioxide, moves through cell membranes into lung cells and at the same time oxygen moves from lung cells into the circulating blood. The oxygen in the lung cells is the result of a person's inhaling. The blood now rich in oxygen returns to the left atrium and flows into the left ventricle and systemic circulation starts again. As the person exhales, carbon dioxide is removed from the body. There are three main types of blood vessels—arteries, veins, and capillaries. **Arteries** are blood vessels that carry blood away from the heart. In **systemic circulation**, blood flows through the aorta and other arteries to all parts of the body. In **pulmonary circulation**, blood flows through the pulmonary artery to the lungs. Near the heart, arteries are large, muscular, and have thick walls. Away from the heart, large arteries continually subdivide into smaller arteries called arterioles. An **arteriole** is a blood vessel that branches off an artery to link it to a capillary. A **capillary** is a microscopic, thin-walled blood vessel through which materials can be exchanged with the blood. Capillaries connect arterioles to small veins called venules. Blood flowing through venules and veins is being returned to the right and left atria.

Blood is the fluid that supplies essential substances to all body cells and removes waste products from all body cells. **Plasma** is the fluid part of blood that remains if the blood cells are removed. Plasma is about 90 percent water. Red blood cells, white blood cells, and platelets are immersed in the plasma. Red blood cells contain hemoglobin. **Hemoglobin** is a substance that combines with oxygen and gives blood its red color. **Red blood cells** are the most numerous cells in blood and they carry oxygen. New red cells are continually being produced in bone marrow. **White blood cells** are cells that destroy pathogens that enter the body.

They are produced in bone marrow and in lymph nodes. The number of white blood cells increases when pathogens enter the body. White blood cells surround and destroy pathogens. **Platelets** are small fragments in the blood, shaped like disks, that help prevent blood loss from injured blood vessels. Platelets help form clots, which seal holes in blood vessels and stop bleeding.

Since blood pressure varies from person to person and within the same person, it is essential to have blood pressure checked. A person can have high blood pressure and not know it. Continued high pressure is the most common disease affecting the heart and blood vessels and can lead to serious health problems. Ways to take care of the cardiovascular system are to avoid smoking, reduce the amount of fat and salt in the diet, and get enough exercise and rest.

Respiratory System The **respiratory system** is the body system that consists of the nasal cavity, the pharynx, larynx, trachea, bronchi, and the lungs (Figure 8-8). The primary function of the respiratory system is to provide oxygen to the body and remove carbon dioxide from the body. **Respiration** is the exchange of gases between a person's body and the environment. Respiration is both external and internal. **External respiration** is the exchange of oxygen and carbon dioxide between circulating blood and inhaled air in the lungs. **Internal respiration** is the exchange of oxygen between body cells and blood circulating near them.

Inhalation is the process of taking air into the lungs. An adult inhales about twelve times each minute when resting, inhaling about one pint of air each time. Inhaled air is cleaned, warmed, and moistened as it moves to the lungs. Sticky mucus and tiny hairs in the nose and throat moisten and clean the air. It is warmed by blood circulating in the area of the nose and throat. During inhalation, rib muscles contract, causing the rib muscles to be pulled up and out. At the same time, the diaphragm also contracts and moves downward. This results in the chest cavity being enlarged and the lungs being filled with air, equalizing the pressure inside the lungs with the outside air pressure. **Exhalation** is the process of forcing air out of the lungs. During exhalation, rib muscles relax and the ribs move downward and inward. The diaphragm re-

laxes and moves upward, increasing the pressure around the inflated lungs and forcing air from the lungs. If the inhaled air contains dust or other particles over a long period of time, lung tissue can be affected. As a result, the lungs do not function efficiently. This kind of problem is the result of smoking or inhaling polluted air over a long period of time.

Urinary System The **urinary system** is the body system that consists of the kidneys, ureters, bladder, and urethra (Figure 8-9). These organs remove wastes from the body and help control the balance of fluid in the body. The **kidney** is the organ responsible for filtering the blood and excreting waste products and excess water in the form of urine. The two kidneys lie on either side of the body near the lowest ribs. Blood circulation through the kidneys is extensive. As blood circulates, the kidneys filter out waste materials, which leave the body as urine. **Urine** is a body fluid through which waste materials are dissolved. It is about 95 percent water. Urine flows from the kidneys through the ureters. The **ureters** are tubes that extend from each kidney to the bladder. The **bladder** is the organ that stores the urine temporarily until it becomes full, at which time nerve impulses stimulate both voluntary and involuntary muscles to release urine through the urethra. The **urethra** is a narrow tube that extends from the bladder to the outside of the body. Drinking sufficient water is essential to the health of the urinary system.

Endocrine System The **endocrine system** is the body system that consists of glands that secrete chemical substances called hormones (Figure 8-10). **Hormones** are groups of chemicals, each of which is released into the bloodstream by a particular gland or tissue to have an effect elsewhere in the body. The hormones are secreted directly in the bloodstream and act on specific activities of the body. In other words, specific glands produce specific hormones that affect specific activities. The glands of the endocrine system and the hormones they produce are the:
* *Pituitary gland.* The **pituitary gland** is a gland located at the base of the brain and is called the master gland because it not only produces a growth hormone but also produces hormones that control other endocrine glands. The effects of this gland will be discussed in the following section of this chapter.

Growth and Development

- *Thyroid gland.* The **thyroid gland** is a gland that consists of two lobes located below the larynx on either side of the trachea. Although the thyroid gland produces several hormones, thyroxin is the major one. **Thyroxin** is a hormone that regulates metabolism, which is all chemical activity within body cells.

- *Parathyroid glands.* The **parathyroid glands** are two pairs of oval, pea-sized glands located adjacent to the two lobes of the thyroid gland in the neck. There are four parathyroid glands that lie under the surface of the thyroid gland. These glands control the amount of calcium and phosphorus in the body.

- *Adrenal glands.* The two adrenal glands are located at the top of each kidney. The **adrenal glands** are a pair of glands that secrete hormones directly into the bloodstream. Each gland consists of two distinct parts–the outer portion, which is the cortex, and the inner portion, which is the medulla. The cortex is the part of the adrenal gland that produces several hormones that are involved in regulating water balance in body tissues and in increasing blood sugar levels. The medulla is the part of the adrenal glands that produces the hormone epinephrine, more commonly called adrenaline. Adrenaline helps the body respond to stressful or emergency situations by increasing heart rate and blood pressure and also blood sugar level.

- *Pancreas.* The **pancreas** is an elongated, tapered gland that lies across the back of the abdomen, behind the stomach. Certain cells, called the Islets of Langerhans, in the pancreas produce two hormones–glucagon and insulin. These hormones function primarily in regulating the level of glucose, in the blood. **Insulin** is a hormone that stimulates the liver to convert glucose to glycogen, which is a storage form of carbohydrate. **Glucagon** is a hormone that stimulates the liver to convert glycogen to glucose. In this way, the level of glucose in the blood is maintained.

- *Ovaries and testes.* The **ovaries** are reproductive organs that secrete the female hormone estrogen. The **testes** are reproductive organs that secrete the male hormone testosterone. These hormones will be discussed in the following section of this chapter.

Reproductive System The **reproductive system** is a body system that functions to produce offspring. Although this body system is not vital to the survival of an individual, it is vital to the survival of the human race. The reproductive system also will be discussed in the following section of this chapter.

Life Skill #2

I will recognize how my body changes as I grow.

Being Comfortable with Body Changes

Adolescence is the period of time between childhood and adulthood, usually occurring between the ages of twelve and nineteen. A unique aspect of adolescence is the onset of puberty. **Puberty** is the time of sexual development when males and females become physically capable of reproduction. The **secondary sex characteristics** are the changes that occur during puberty and are the result of hormones produced by endocrine glands. Females usually experience these changes before males.

Female secondary sex characteristics include the development of breasts; the development of pubic and underarm hair; a widened pelvis; increased amount of fat tissue in the buttocks and thighs; and the onset of sexual desire. Male secondary sex characteristics include development of facial, pubic, and underarm hair; broadened shoulders; longer and heavier bones; deepened voice; increased muscle tissue development; and onset of sexual desire. Both females and males also experience a period of physical growth during adolescence when all of these other changes are taking place. Sometimes these changes contribute to feelings of awkwardness and they intensify concerns about appearance. Adolescents

192

often are self-conscious and overly concerned with what others think of them.

It is important to remember that adolescence is a period of change in areas other than physical growth and secondary sex characteristics. Adolescence is a time of developing intellectually, learning skills, and maturing socially. These are the reasons that it is helpful to be aware of changes that occur during adolescence and the reasons for the changes. By being informed, an adolescent can recognize and accept that these changes are normal and that they are essential for a fulfilling adulthood.

Endocrine System

As stated earlier, the endocrine system consists of glands that secrete chemical substances called hormones (Figure 8-10). **Hormones** are groups of chemicals, each of which is released into the bloodstream by a particular gland or tissue to have an effect elsewhere in the body.. Hormones are secreted directly into the bloodstream and act on specific activities of the body.

Pituitary Gland Two of the hormones produced by the pituitary gland are the follicle-stimulating hormone (FSH) and the luteinizing hormone (LH). FSH in females activates the development of ova (egg cells) in the reproductive organs, the ovaries, and the production of other female sex hormones called estrogens by the ovaries. In males, FSH activates the reproductive organs, the testes, to produce sperm. LH in females activates ovulation, the release of a mature ovum from an ovary and the production of progesterone, another female hormone. **Estrogen** is a hormone essential for normal female sexual development and for the healthy functioning of the reproductive system. Estrogen controls the development and maintenance of female secondary sex characteristics and reproductive organs, and the menstrual cycle. In males, LH activates the testes to produce testosterone, a male hormone. **Testosterone** is the male hormone that stimulates bone and muscle growth and sexual development.

Reproductive System

The Female Reproductive System The external parts of the female reproductive system are the genitalia, or genitals (Figure 8-11). The **genitals** are the reproductive organs. They include the mons veneris, the labia, and clitoris. The **mons veneris** is a rounded fatty pad of tissue that lies over the pubic bone. The **labia** are liplike, fatty tissues that surround the opening of the vagina. The labia also cover the opening of the urethra, which is the tube that extends from the bladder to the outside of the body. The **clitoris** is a small knob of erectile tissue in the front of the vaginal opening. Although the breasts are not reproductive organs, they have reproductive significance. They consist of fatty tissue and mammary gland tissue, which produces milk after the birth of a baby.

The internal reproductive organs include the ovaries, the Fallopian tubes, the uterus, and the vagina. The **ovaries** are two glands that produce both hormones and ova. At birth, a female may have as many as 250,000 ovocytes (immature follicles) in her ovaries. Approximately 400 of these will mature during a female's lifetime. The **Fallopian tubes** (sometimes called oviducts) are two tubes that transport ova from each ovary to the uterus. The Fallopian tubes do not make direct contact with the ovaries. However, the open ends of the tubes expand to form a funnel shape. These open ends are lined with cilia, which are hairlike projections that beat and draw an ovum into a Fallopian tube. Once inside the tube, the ovum is moved by peristaltic contractions of the tube. The ovum moves at a rate of one inch every twenty-four hours. The **uterus** is the organ that prepares each month during a female's reproductive years to receive a fertilized ovum, to support the fertilized ovum during pregnancy, and to contract during childbirth to force the delivery of the baby. The uterus is a hollow, muscular, pear-shaped organ in the pelvic cavity, that is located between the bladder and the rectum. In the nonpregnant state, the uterus is about three inches long and two inches wide at the top, narrowing to the cervix where it is normally about one-half to one inch in diameter. The **cervix** is the lowest part of the uterus. The cervix opens into the vagina. The **vagina** is a muscular passageway that lies between the bladder and the rectum and serves as the female organ of intercourse, the passageway for sperm to the uterus, the birth canal, and the passageway for the menstrual flow.

The Menstrual Cycle Sometime between the ages of eight and thirteen, the menstrual cycle will start. The **menstrual cycle** is a rhythmic cycle of approximately one month in which hormone levels fluctuate to prepare a female's body for the possibility of pregnancy. During the menstrual cycle, one ovary produces a mature ovum and the lining of the uterus is prepared to receive a fertilized egg because of the action of hormones. The first menstrual cycle is called the **menarche**. Usually, the menstrual cycle occurs in regular phases. During one phase, the pituitary hormone FSH stimulates the growth and development of follicles in an ovary. As the follicle matures, it produces and releases estrogen, which stimulates the lining of the uterus to grow and thicken in preparation to receive a fertilized ovum. **Ovulation** is the release of a mature ovum from an ovary. The ovum moves through a Fallopian tube to the uterus. Ovulation generally occurs on the fourteenth day prior to the first day of the next menstrual cycle.

Following ovulation, part of the follicle left in the ovary changes and forms the corpus luteum. The **corpus luteum** is a temporary gland that secretes the hormones estrogen and progesterone, which cause the endometrium, the inner layer of the uterus, to thicken. If fertilization occurs, the corpus luteum continues to produce progesterone during pregnancy. If fertilization does not occur, the corpus luteum breaks down and hormone production ceases. Cells in the endometrium gradually die. This dead tissue and the unfertilized egg pass out of the body through the vagina. **Menstruation** is the process by which the lining of the uterus is expelled each month that pregnancy does not occur. Menstruation occurs each month about two weeks after ovulation and usually lasts from three to seven days. During menstruation, approximately 50 to 60 ml of blood and tissue are expelled. Every female's cycle differs in the length of time between menstruation and how long the menstrual flow lasts. **Menopause** is the cessation of the monthly menstrual cycle pattern. It usually occurs somewhere between the ages of forty-eight and fifty-two.

Female Reproductive Health It is important for each female to assume responsibility for her health. Cleanliness is a major requirement. Other requirements are performing necessary self-examinations, and having routine medical examinations. A **breast self-** examination is a cancer screening procedure in which a female visually examines her breasts, palpates them to detect any lumps, and squeezes her nipples to check for a clear or bloody discharge. A female should begin self-examination as soon as she begins to menstruate regularly. Although problems are rare in early adolescence, the practice of doing this self-examination will help an adolescent become familiar with her body, will promote self-acceptance, and will establish a lifelong habit. In addition to breast self-examinations, a female will have her breasts examined during her regularly scheduled checkups and especially if she finds any lumps or changes. The best time to do a breast self-examination is a few days after menstruation, when any swelling has subsided. The examination should be done at the same time each month. The visual part of the examination should be done in front of a mirror: the palpating part should be done while in the shower or while lying down.

Mammography is a highly sensitive x-ray screening test used to detect breast lumps and is a highly effective tool in the early detection of cancer. A **mammogram** is the image of the breast tissue created by mammography and is read by a qualified physician. The American Cancer Society recommends that: a female should have a baseline mammogram between the ages of thirty-five and forty; a female should have a routine mammogram every one to two years during her forties; A female should have a yearly mammogram after the age of fifty. Each month, there is a buildup of fluid and fibrous tissue in a female's breasts in preparation for pregnancy. When a pregnancy does not occur, the body must reabsorb these unneeded substances by draining and emptying them into lymph nodes. Occasionally, the drainage causes congestion and cysts and fibroadenomas are formed. A **cyst** is a sac that is formed when fluid becomes trapped in a lymph duct. A **fibroadenoma** is a lump that is formed when fluid becomes trapped in a lymph duct. The result is **fibrocystic breast condition**, a condition in which cysts and fibroadenomas cause lumpiness, breast tenderness, and discomfort. The exact causes of this condition are unknown, but are believed to be hormonally related.

A female should have regular examinations to detect cancer cells in her cervix. A **Pap smear** is a screening test for cervical

Growth and Development

cancer in which cells are scraped from the cervix and examined for abnormalities. If cancer cells are found, a female may have a hysterectomy. A **hysterectomy** is the surgical removal of the uterus and cervix, but not the ovaries. If cancer cells are present in one or both ovaries, the ovaries usually are surgically removed and radiation and drugs used. **Vaginitis** is an irritation or inflammation of the vagina usually accompanied by a discharge. The most common type of vaginitis is a yeast infection. Normal secretions are altered and the vagina and vulva become irritated and itchy. **Cystitis** is the inflammation of the urinary bladder. Because the opening of the urethra is near the vagina and near the anus, fecal bacteria and infectious agents from sexual contact are easily transmitted from the anus to the urethra. **Endometriosis** is a condition in which the endometrial tissue grows somewhere other than in the lining of the uterus, such as in the ovaries, Fallopian tubes, vagina or cervix. Endometriosis is a serious condition because it may result in sterility if left untreated. Treatment usually involves hormone therapy and/or surgery. There are other conditions associated with menstruation. **Dysmenorrhea** is painful menstruation with symptoms such as breast tenderness, cramping, nausea, and fluid retention. **Premenstrual syndrome (PMS)** is a chronic menstrual disorder characterized by emotional, behavioral, and physical symptoms. These symptoms usually occur a week prior to the onset of menstruation. **Toxic shock syndrome (TSS)** is a disease caused by the presence of dangerous bacteria that grow rapidly in the vagina of a menstruating female.

The Male Reproductive System The organs and structures of the male reproductive system include the scrotum, testes, seminiferous tubules, epididymis, vas deferens, seminal vesicles, ejaculatory duct, prostate gland, bulbourethral (Cowper's) glands, urethra, and penis (Figure 8-12). The **scrotum** is a sac-like pouch that holds the testes and regulates the temperature of the testes. The scrotum has two compartments, each of which contains a testis. The scrotum is suspended from the body so that the testes have a lower temperature than the rest of the body. The testes must be approximately 1.5 to 2 degrees cooler than the rest of the body in order to produce sperm. The scrotum contains

muscles that contract in cold weather and pull the scrotum closer to the body to increase the temperature. In warm weather, these muscles relax so that the testes move further away from the body to lower the temperature.

The **testes** are reproductive organs that secrete the male hormone testosterone and produce sperm. Testosterone is the male hormone that is responsible for male secondary sex characteristics.

The **seminiferous tubules** are a coiled network of tubes that fill each testis and in which sperm are produced. The **epididymis** is a comma-shaped structure found on the back and upper surface of each testis in which sperm are stored. The **vas deferens** are two long, thin cords that extend from the epididymis in the scrotum, and serve as a passageway for sperm. The vas deferens wind upward in the scrotum to the abdominal cavity and then turn downward to form the ejaculatory duct with the seminal vesicles. The **seminal vesicles** are two small glands at the ends of the vas deferens that secrete a fluid that nourishes and enables the sperm to move. The **ejaculatory duct** is a short, straight tube that passes into the prostate gland and opens into the urethra. The **prostate gland** is a gland that produces an alkaline solution that neutralizes acid in the male urethra and the acidic environment of the vagina. The **bulbourethral (Cowper's) glands** are two small, pea-shaped glands located on each side of the urethra and secrete a lubricating fluid. When a male becomes sexually excited, these glands secrete a slippery fluid, which is visible at the tip of the penis. These droplets may contain sperm.

The **urethra** is a tubelike passageway that extends from the urinary bladder to the tip of the penis and the outside of the body. The urethra serves as a passageway for semen and urine. The **penis** is the male organ for sexual intercourse, reproduction, and urination. The reproductive function of the penis is to deposit sperm in the female vagina during sexual intercourse. The penis is composed of erectile tissue. **Erection** is an involuntary process that occurs when spongy layers inside the penis are engorged with blood and cause the penis to swell and elongate. **Ejaculation** is the sudden expulsion of seminal fluid from an erect penis. Normally, three millileters of semen are expelled during

© Copyright by Meeks Heit Publishing Company.

195

ejaculation. Each milliliter contains about 120 million sperm. After ejaculation, the penis returns to the flaccid or nonerect state.

Male Reproductive Health It is important for each male to assume responsibility for his health. Cleanliness of the genital organs is a major requirement. Another important requirement is testicular self-examinations. **Testicular self-examination** is observation and palpation of the testicles to locate any mass or tenderness. The examination should be performed after a hot shower or bath when the scrotal skin is relaxed and the testes are descended. Any sign of a mass or of tenderness should be reported to a physician immediately. A mass may be a sign of cancer or a cyst. Tenderness may be a sign of an infection or of a sexually transmitted disease.

In the eighth or ninth month of fetal life, the testes of the fetus pass through the inguinal canal and become located in the scrotum. The inguinal canal closes to prevent other tissues from descending into the scrotum. If the inguinal canal fails to close or for some reason opens again, other contents of the abdominal cavity may pass through. **Herniation** is the protrusion of the contents of one of the body's cavities through an abnormal opening in the cavity wall. An **inguinal hernia** is a condition in which some of the intestine pushes through the inguinal canal. This condition is potentially dangerous because of the possibility of strangulation of the blood supply to the intestine. Inguinal hernia usually requires corrective surgery. As males age, the prostate gland commonly becomes enlarged. The American Cancer Society recommends that men over the age of forty have an annual digital rectal examination, in which a physician examines the prostate and rectum with a finger for signs of cancer.

Life Skill #3

I will accept my maleness/femaleness.

Being a Male or Female

Sexuality includes the feelings and attitudes a person has about his/her body, sex role, and sexual orientation as well as his/her feelings and attitudes regarding the bodies, sex roles, and sexual orientation of others. During adolescence, young people are forming their sexual identity. Two important developmental tasks of adolescence focus on accepting the body changes of puberty and becoming comfortable with one's sex role. A **sex role** is the way a person acts and the feelings and attitudes a person has about being a male or female as well as the expectations (s)he has for other males and females. Early sex roles are influenced by families. Regardless of being a male or female, a person should feel free to express a variety of emotions and participate in a variety of activities. Being able to express several aspects of one's personality and being able to have a wide variety of interests and to gain acceptance reinforce one's comfort level with regard to masculinity and femininity. A person who likes and accepts his/her sex role is more likely to accept the masculinity and femininity of others.

A male's sexuality and self-esteem are influenced by his attitude toward and acceptance of his body. Males need the opportunity to test their feelings about the masculine sex role. Is it masculine to express feelings? Is it masculine to cry? A female's sexuality and self-esteem also are influenced by her attitude toward and acceptance of her body. Females also need the opportunity to test their feelings about the feminine sex role. Is it feminine to be strong-willed? Is it feminine to be independent? Is it feminine to play sports? Is it feminine to express emotions? As part of this acceptance, it is important for adolescents to strengthen their self-esteem. Being liked and accepted by members of the opposite sex is especially important. Young people tend to model the examples that have been set for them in their families. A young person who has learned sex-role stereotyping may continue those attitudes and behaviors and make it difficult for another young person who is learning to express his/her femininity or masculinity and sex role.

Sexual Orientation

Sexual orientation is a person's sexual attraction to people of the opposite sex, same sex, or both sexes. A person who is **heterosexual** is a person who has a sexual preference for someone of the opposite sex.

A person who is **homosexual** is a person who has a sexual preference for someone of the same sex. A person who is **bisexual** has a sexual interest in people of both sexes.

I will accept my physical uniqueness.

Heredity

Heredity is the transmission of features from one generation to the next. No two people are alike. In fact, each person is unique. Genetics is the scientific study of the processes of heredity.

Growth Spurts Growth spurts in the muscular and skeletal systems occur in adolescence and are controlled by hormones. In females, growth spurts usually occur between the ages of eleven and thirteen and in males between the ages of thirteen and fifteen. Males may experience a growth spurt that results in a growth of five or more inches in a one year period. Some adolescents do not finish growing until their late teens.

Inherited Characteristics Parents and offspring have many features in common. **Genes** are the functional units of heredity and contain the codes for the reproduction and development of body cells. Genes are part of a cell structure called a chromosome. A **chromosome** is a distinct body in a cell nucleus that becomes apparent during cell division. Humans normally have forty-six chromosomes in each body cell. These chromosomes are arranged in pairs. One chromosome of each pair comes from each parent. One of the twenty-three pairs contains the genes that determine the sex of an individual. Each pair of chromosomes has a pair of genes that determines a particular trait, such as eye color.

Body Types Heredity influences body type, the size of the bones, and muscular structure. Generally, a person inherits a tendency toward one of three body types. An **ectomorph** is a person who is long-boned and has a lean body build. A **mesomorph** is a person who has a muscular body build. An **endomorph** is a person who has a greater percentage of fat tissue and a flabby appearance.

Body Image **Body image** is the perception a person has of how his/her body appears. Many people think that extreme overweight or extreme underweight is undesirable, aside from the health risks. For many people, looking in a mirror gives a realistic and valid evaluation of body image. However, for some people it is difficult to be objective about their own bodies.

I will accept and develop my learning style.

Different Ways of Learning

Every person has his/her own unique learning style. However, everyone needs to develop certain skills in order to cope with his/her environment and to be able to communicate with others. Acquiring basic skills involves the ability to perceive and process sights and sounds, to concentrate, and to remember.

Learning Disabilities

Many students find it difficult to develop necessary skills. For example, they may have attention problems and fail to focus on the important factors. These students often develop behavior problems that become another interference to learning. These students may not be able to continue with a task for a length of time. They have a learning disability. A **learning disability** is a physical and/or psychological disorder that causes a person to have difficulty learning. Learning disabilities are expressed in many different ways. Some students have difficulty distinguishing among different shapes. Some do not perceive letters and numbers correctly or they do not understand the meaning of what they see. These kinds of problems make it difficult to learn to read. Some students have difficulty understanding parameters of time and sequence, which makes it difficult to follow directions. Some students have difficulty organizing their time which makes it difficult to complete homework assignments. Some students have speech difficulties that impede their learning ability. Students from dysfunctional homes often lack stimulation and communication skills and this affects their ability to learn.

Dyslexia Dyslexia is a learning disability in which a person has difficulty learning to read despite conventional instruction, adequate intelligence, and sociocultural opportunity. Some common symptoms of dyslexia are substituting one consonant for another; changing the order of letters and numbers; confusing upper case and lower case letters; reversing letters; and writing illegibly. The exact cause(s) of dyslexia is unknown. Although students with dyslexia may respond to different educational approaches, they will not outgrow this learning disability. Dyslexia has no cure.

Attention Deficit Hyperactivity Disorder According to the American Psychiatric Association, Attention Deficit Disorder (ADD) is indicated when students display inappropriate inattention, impulsivity, and sometimes hyperactivity. According to the same Association, Attention Deficit Hyperactivity Disorder (ADHD) is diagnosed when a student displays, for six months or more, at least eight of the following characteristics prior to age seven:
- fidgets, squirms, or seems restless;
- has difficulty remaining seated;
- is easily distracted;
- has difficulty awaiting turn;
- blurts out answers;
- has difficulty following instructions;
- has difficulty sustaining attention;
- shifts from one uncompleted task to another;
- has difficulty playing quietly;
- talks excessively;
- interrupts or intrudes on others;
- does not seem to listen;
- often loses things necessary for tasks;
- frequently engages in dangerous actions.

Possible causes of ADHD are genetic, prenatal, or physical. Some students respond to medication. However, there currently is no cure for ADHD. Students with ADHD need to be included with the regular class. However, they should not be seated near high traffic areas, doors, windows, or other sources of distraction. They should be helped at home by having a regular place at home to do their homework and an established time in which to do homework.

I will achieve developmental tasks for my age group.

Developmental tasks are achievements that are necessary to be made during a particular period of growth in order that a person can continue growing toward maturity. For adolescents, the following developmental tasks have been identified:

- Task 1: Achieving a new and more mature relationship with age mates of both sexes.
- Task 2: Achieving a masculine or feminine social role.
- Task 3: Accepting one's physique.
- Task 4: Achieving emotional independence from parents and other adults.
- Task 5: Preparing for marriage and family life.
- Task 6: Preparing for an economic career.
- Task 7: Acquiring a set of values and an ethical system as a guide to behavior–developing an ideology.
- Task 8: Developing a social conscience.

I will learn about conception, pregnancy, and childbirth.

Conception

As part of a female's normal menstrual cycle, an ovary releases a mature ovum once each month. The mature ovum moves through a Fallopian tube to the uterus. **Conception**, or fertilization, is the union of an ovum and a sperm and this union usually takes place in a Fallopian tube when a sperm penetrates an ovum and forms a zygote. A **zygote** is a single cell that contains genetic material from each parent. A zygote divides to form two cells about 18 to 39 hours after conception. The two cells divide to form four cells, which divide to form eight cells, and so on to form a multi-celled mass called an **embryo**, which becomes implanted in the wall of the uterus.

Infertility **Fertility** is the capability to produce offspring. **Infertility** is the inability to produce offspring. A person who is infertile still has the same sexual desires as others do. Both males and females can be infertile. Certain diseases, such as mumps and sexually transmitted diseases, may affect male fertility. In addition, the use of drugs, including alcohol, can alter fertility. The failure to produce a mature ovum during her menstrual cycle is a common reason for female infertility. Side effects of infections may block the Fallopian tubes and prevent the ovum from passing through to the uterus.

Alternate Methods of Fertilization

Artificial insemination is a procedure in which sperm are introduced into the vagina or uterus by artificial means so that conception can occur. **In vitro fertilization** is a procedure in which mature ova are removed from a female's ovary and placed in a lab dish to be fertilized by sperm. After forty-eight to seventy-two hours, the developing embryo is placed directly into the female's uterus for implantation.

Pregnancy

Pregnancy is the period from conception to birth. The first sign that indicates a pregnancy is the absence of a menstrual period when it is expected. However, this sign may signify another condition. Other symptoms of pregnancy include nausea, breast tenderness, and fatigue. Human pregnancy is considered in terms of three-month periods called trimesters. Nine months (forty weeks) is the average length of a human pregnancy.

Development of the Fetus
The mass of cells that is the embryo moves to the uterus and becomes implanted in the wall of the uterus about ten to twelve days after conception. The outer walls of the embryo form the placenta, which attaches the embryo to the inner wall of the uterus. The umbilical cord develops within the first four weeks after conception and attaches to the placenta and the developing embryo. Oxygen, nutrients, and waste between the mother and the developing embryo pass into the arteries and veins that run through the umbilical cord. Through the second month of growth, the developing cells are called an embryo. By the end of the second month, the embryo is recognizable as a human and is called a **fetus**. By the end of

the first trimester, the fetus is about four inches long and weighs about one ounce. At the end of the second trimester, the fetus begins to open its eyes, It is about 12 inches long and weighs approximately 1.5 pounds. A fetus at the end of the third trimester may be 19 to 21 inches long and weigh up to 7.5 pounds.

Prenatal Care **Prenatal care** is the care given to both the mother and her developing fetus before birth. Prenatal care should begin as early as possible after a pregnancy is confirmed in order to prevent problems. Another benefit of early prenatal care is detection of complications that need immediate attention. Prenatal care includes regular medical checkups as soon as a pregnancy is confirmed. Two other very important aspects of prenatal care for which the mother must take primary responsibility are nutrition and the avoidance of any risk behaviors, such as the use of drugs including alcohol and tobacco, that will adversely affect the embryo and fetus.

Atypical Conditions A **miscarriage** is a spontaneous abortion or natural expulsion of the fetus or embryo before it has reached the point of development at which it can survive outside the mother's body. A **premature birth** is the birth of a baby before the thirty-seventh week of the pregnancy. A premature baby is usually not fully developed. The lower the birthweight of a premature infant, the lower the chance of survival. An ectopic pregnancy occurs when a fertilized ovum implants itself in a place other than in the wall of the uterus. In most cases, the ovum implants in the Fallopian tube and cannot be carried full term. Some embryos spontaneously abort and disintegrate. However, if the embryo has begun to grow and stretches the tube, the tube may rupture. Surgery is required in such a case to preserve the tube and to prevent rupture. Multiple births also are considered atypical. **Identical twins** are twins who develop from a single ovum fertilized by a single sperm that divides after fertilization and forms two zygotes rather than one. Since they inherit the same genetic material from the parents, identical twins are always the same sex. **Fraternal twins** are twins who develop from two separate ova that are fertilized by two different sperm. **Siamese twins** are twins who are physically joined at birth. This joining occurs when a cell mass does not separate completely.

Birth Defects Birth defects can be physical or mental or both. **Fetal alcohol syndrome (FAS)** is a birth defect related to the mother's use of alcohol during pregnancy. Effects on the baby include damage to the brain and nervous system, facial abnormalities, abnormally small head size, below normal I.Q., poor coordination, and behavior problems. Many babies are born each year with congenital heart defects. One cause is known to be the rubella virus. **Rubella** is a form of measles. If a pregnant female is infected with this virus during the first three months of pregnancy, the fetus is at great risk to be born with a heart defect.

Childbirth

Preparing for Childbirth **Childbirth** is the process by which an infant is moved from the uterus to the outside world. Many pregnant females and their mates attend classes to learn about the birth process. In these classes, the parents become aware of what will occur during labor and delivery. There are many advantages in taking classes. The pregnant female will be educated about what to expect when it is time to give birth. This will help remove the fear some females have about childbirth. It also prepares the father to understand and share the birth process.

Stages of Labor The delivery of a baby from the mother's uterus is an extremely complex process that may take several hours. During the last weeks of pregnancy, a female can feel mild muscular contractions. When contractions become intense and occur at regular intervals, labor has begun. **Labor** is a series of three stages that result in the birth of the baby. The first stage is the latent phase. The latent phase is the stage of labor during which contractions of the uterus cause the cervix and the cervical opening to dilate or stretch. This allows the head of the baby to enter the birth canal, the vagina. During this time, muscular contractions of the uterus become stronger and more frequent. The second stage of labor consists of strong uterine contractions that move the baby through the birth canal. The third stage is the expulsion of the placenta. The baby has been delivered, and the placenta and other membranes that supported the fetus do not remain in the uterus.

Problems in Childbirth Approximately 99 percent of all babies adopt a longitudinal position in the uterus during birth. And most of those babies have a cephalic, or head first, presentation. In this position, the baby is delivered head first with the face rotated to the side as the rest of the body emerges from the birth canal. Four percent of all longitudinal births are breech, or buttocks first, presentations. If the attending physician is aware that the fetus is in a breech position, he or she may try to manipulate the baby's body so that the head will present first. In approximately one in one hundred births, the fetus may lie across the birth canal in what is known as the transverse position, the shoulder, arm, or hand entering the birth canal first. Some babies cannot be delivered through the birth canal and a Cesarean section must be performed. A **Cesarean section** is the surgical removal of the fetus through an incision made in the mother's abdomen and uterus. Some of the reasons for a Cesarean section include a pelvis too small for the baby to pass through the vagina, breech or transverse presentation of the fetus, failure of the cervix to dilate, premature separation of the placenta from the uterus, infection in the vaginal tract, exhaustion of the mother, fetal distress, incapacitation of the mother because of injury or trauma.

Life Skill #8

I will recognize the needs of people of different ages.

Stages of Growth and Development

Eric Erikson is a developmental psychologist who identified eight stages of growth and development. Erikson believed each stage involved events and crises that must be experienced in order for a person to grow. The eight stages extend from infancy to old age.

1. *Infancy.* The most rapid and dramatic growth in human occurs during the first year of life. Growth during infancy is rapid and not necessarily uniform. Physical growth is influenced by many factors including genetics, state of health, and nutrition. On the average, an infant grows about an inch per month during the first six months and half an inch per month throughout the rest of the first year. Body weight typically doubles at five months and triples by age one. By age one, most babies have achieved the developmental tasks of learning to walk and talk and to eat solid food.

2. *Early Childhood.* The time after infancy before a child attends kindergarten is generally regarded as the early childhood period. The rate of growth is slower than during infancy but normally continues in a sequential and orderly fashion. The age of three may best be described as the age of doing. Three-year-olds have achieved the developmental tasks of learning to run, jump, go up and down stairs, and ride a tricycle. They also have learned to control their bladders and bowels.

3. *Preschool.* Large muscle coordination is much improved by age five. Preschool children can run, jump, and climb with confidence. At this age, children are very inquisitive and initiate cooperative play. A five-year-old loves to hear and tell stories and even likes the same ones over and over again. This is important because repetition enhances learning.

4. *Elementary*. Development in this stage varies greatly. Physical growth continues. Children at this stage should be physically active because skeletal muscles are developing and need regular exercise. Rapid muscular growth may result in awkwardness. During this stage, children become increasingly influenced by peers.

5. *Adolescence*. Adolescence is a physical, emotional, and social transition from childhood to adulthood. Puberty occurs in females most often between the ages of eleven and thirteen and in males between the ages of thirteen and fifteen. This is a period of rapid physical growth and striking individual differences. Body parts do not necessarily have a growth spurt at the same time and this results in awkwardness for many adolescents. Adolescents are very self-conscious and worry about what others think of them. There is a growing awareness of maleness and femaleness. Reasoning skills and intellectual maturity are gained during this stage.

6. *Early Adulthood*. Early adulthood is the period between the ages of eighteen and forty. During this period, young adults are able to be financially independent of their parents. They set career goals and work toward those goals. They accept more responsibility for their own lives. Emotionally, they are mature and form meaningful relationships with long-lasting commitments. Many young adults start their families.

7. *Middle Adulthood*. Adults in this stage are forty to sixty years of age. Many of these adults are satisfied with their accomplishments and look forward to the second half of their lives with anticipation and interest. Others find it difficult to adjust to the fact that their families are maturing and leaving home. They may realize that some of their dreams may never be accomplished. Some adults in this stage may resist changes, yet changes are a major part of this stage.

8. *Late Adulthood*. Adults in this stage are over sixty. Old age no longer has the negative connotation that it previously had. Today, many people in their seventies and eighties are still very active and in good health. Although sixty-five is still considered the age of retirement, many people continue to work past that age. Many people in late adulthood are interested in being physically fit. They exercise regularly and pay attention to their diets so that they get the proper nutrition. They also make plans for their care in the event that they will need some assistance. For some, however, late adulthood is accompanied by looking back and regretting that they did not use their years more productively, or accomplish certain goals.

Life Skill #9

I will practice behaviors that contribute to healthful aging.

There are many theories concerning aging. **Gerontology** is the study of aging. Some gerontologists believe aging begins the day a person is born. Others believe aging begins when a person's growth stops around the age of twenty-five. Many people feel that old age is a state of mind and not a specific period of life. Perhaps the saying, "You are as old as you feel" is the most practical way to define the word old.

Causes of Aging

Gerontologists have developed the following theories about the causes of aging:

- The wear-and-tear theory maintains that, like any machine, the human body simply wears out.
- The waste-product theory is based on the belief that waste products accumulate in body cells. These waste products damage body cells and cause them to lose their normal ability to function.
- The anti-immune theory proposes that the body's immune system attacks healthy cells instead of foreign substances that enter the body. Consequently, the body loses its ability to distinguish between healthy cells and foreign material.
- The cell-error theory maintains that as body cells divide, errors are introduced into the genetic material. As cells divide, the errors are reproduced. More and more cells accumulate errors, resulting in aging.
- The brain theory suggests that the brain initiates and control the aging process by a mechanism not completely understood.

The Aging Process

Physical Changes Physical changes occur to everyone at different times in the life cycle. Some physical changes, such as baldness, are observable and often occur early in life. However, for most people, wrinkled skin occurs later in life. Internal changes also occur. Blood may not circulate as efficiently. Reactions to stimuli may be slower. The ability to hear or to see may be diminished. Chronic diseases such as heart disease and arthritis cause many changes in a person's ability to cope. It is important to keep in mind that the occurrence of many chronic diseases can be traced to the effects of a person's lifestyle rather than the aging process.

Mental Changes The aging process does not always have negative mental effects. Personality and intellectual capacity do not necessarily deteriorate as a person ages. A person who practices a healthful lifestyle and remains mentally and socially active may remain mentally healthy throughout his/her life. When mental ability is impaired, a person may have dementia. **Dementia** is a condition in which the thinking processes are impaired. It is a general term used to describe the gradual development of mental impairment. **Senility** is the loss of mental faculties associated with old age. Characteristics of this condition are a short attention span, confusion, memory loss, inability to handle simple math problems, and loss of concept of time and place.

Social Changes Some older people find themselves isolated when their aging friends and/or spouses die. They become lonely. It is important to recognize that older people have many of the same social needs of younger people. They need friends with whom to talk and do things, someone to love, someone to listen, and someone to love them.

Concerns of the Elderly

Nutrition As adults age, their nutritional needs and interests change as energy requirements are decreased. However, their interest in food may be influenced by other factors, such as loss of income, loneliness, chronic health problems or tooth decay and loss. It is especially important that older people eat the kinds of foods that provide them with the essential nutrients.

Alcohol and Other Drugs The use of alcohol, no matter what age a person is, is a risk behavior. With older people, it may be a behavior they started in their early years, or it may be a behavior they adopted in later years as a way of coping with the stresses of growing older. In either case, the use of alcohol can compound other physical conditions and cause problems for families. Use of prescription drugs may present a problem. Older people may take prescribed medications in the wrong amounts or at the wrong times. They may fail to tell a physician what medications they are already using when the physician prescribes a new drug. These kinds of omissions can cause serious reactions and problems.

Supplements As the amounts and kinds of foods that elderly people eat change, they need to be sure that they are getting adequate minerals and vitamins. For example, elderly people may not get enough calcium because they do not consume as many dairy products as they once did. A lack of calcium can cause osteoporosis and other bone disorders. Osteoporosis is a condition in which the bones become brittle and break easily.

Alzheimer's Disease Alzheimer's disease is a degenerative disease of the central nervous system characterized by premature senility. Indeed, although it is generally believed that Alzheimers is a specific disease and not a specific consequence of aging, it is not yet clear whether that is actually the case. Alzheimers disease is a chronic brain disorder. Early symptoms include forgetfulness, memory loss, and lack of interest. Then there are radical changes in behavior, such as forgetting how to use a familiar machine, repeating the same story over without being aware of the duplication, and becoming disoriented in familiar places. The disease progresses to the point where the person can no longer take care of himself/herself and needs constant care for even the most basic needs. The cause of Alzheimer's disease is not known. One theory is that the problem is genetic. Experimental drugs have helped some people, but any benefits are only temporary. Many of the drugs have serious side effects and are no longer used.

Care There are many concerns associated with the care of elderly people. The need for health care increases, for example, as chronic problems persist and intensify. In many cases, the costs of health care deplete their savings, making them dependent on other family members. As people grow older, they may need for assistance with everday tasks. For example, some older people are no longer able to drive and may need assistance with transportation.

Planning to Age Healthfully

People who establish healthful behavior at an early age will most likely continue in the same pattern as they grow older. On the other hand, people who engage in risk behavior will probably continue that behavior as they grow older. This is the reason that it is essential to choose healthful options such as: being active both physically and intellectually, taking time to relax, balancing work and play, eating healthful foods, learning new skills, volunteering in community services as a way of helping others, and avoiding tobacco use.

Life Skill #10

I will share my feelings about death and dying.

Defining Death

There is no simple answer to the question: when does death occur? Formerly, it was thought that death occurred when the heart and lungs failed to function. Now, life support machines can keep the heart beating and the lungs functioning. The Uniform Determination of Death Act of 1981 states: an individual who has sustained either (1) irreversible cessation of circulatory and respiratory functions, or (2) irreversible cessation of all functions of the entire brain, including the brain stem, is dead.

The Stages of Dying and Death

Many people die unexpectedly and have no advance notice of death. However, some people, for example those people who are terminally ill, have time to prepare for their death. These people experience psychological stages of dying that describe emotional feelings most dying people experience. Five

stages of dying have been identified (Kübler-Ross, 1975). They include denial, anger, bargaining, depression, and acceptance. Dying people do not necessarily go through the stages in the same order. They may skip a stage, go back to a previous stage, or remain in one stage for an extended time. The five stages are:

1. *Denial*. People in this stage do not want to accept that they are terminally ill. This is the "It can't be me" stage. They believe a cure will be found in time to help them or that they will be the exception and they will survive.

2. *Anger*. This is the "Why me?" stage. People in this stage realize that they are going to die and they are angry, impatient, bitter, and/or feel helpless. Their anger may be directed at family, friends, or their medical support system.

3. *Bargaining*. People in this stage may try to make deals with with their physicians, or with their friends. They may promise to change some habit if they recover.

4. *Depression*. Depression occurs when bargaining does not produce desired results and hope for recovery dims. People in this stage begin to feel the loss of family and friends and, they may go through their own grieving stage.

5. *Acceptance*. Acceptance occurs when the person who is dying acknowledges the situation and feels a sense of serenity. People in this stage are willing to talk about their impending death.

Decisions About Death

Most people, including the person who is dying, wish to feel some control over decisions that affect them. Decisions about the care of a person who is dying should be made so that the person will feel comfortable with the arrangements, feel valued and can die with dignity.

Wills A **will** is a legal document that describes how a person's possessions are to be distributed. A will also may include directions for the care of surviving family members. If a person dies without a will, the courts will decide how possessions are to be divided.

Organ Donation Many people make a decision to donate their organs as a "gift of life" to be used for transplants. The demand for transplant organs and tissues has greatly increased. People interested in donating their organs carry a Uniform Donor Card so that in case of an accident, their wishes will be known.

Hospice In some cases, if the dying person has been in the hospital, (s)he may choose to die at home. In other cases, the dying person needs special medications and 24-hour care that cannot be provided in a home environment. In such cases, a hospice setting may be chosen. A hospice is a facility or program of caring for terminally ill people and of counseling their families.

Grief and Loss

Grief is the distress caused by the death of another person. Grief is a normal reaction to a death. Individual reactions to grief vary widely. People who are grieving may experience shock, numbness, disbelief, depression, and loneliness. Experiencing and accepting these feelings are important in the recovery process. Eventually, the person who is grieving will reach a point in the recovery process where the loss is integrated into his/her life experience. A person who is grieving may be isolated from friends and family members who feel awkward around him/her. The following suggestions may be helpful when dealing with a person who is grieving:

1. Do something thoughtful for the person. Make a phone call, send a card, attend the funeral, offer help with practical matters such as meals, and errands.
2. Be a good listener. Make yourself available to talk. Simply being a good friend is important.
3. Do not minimize the loss. Avoid using cliches such as "Time heals all wounds."
4. Allow the person the opportunity to grieve and express emotions.
5. Accept your own limitations. Many situations can be difficult to handle. Seek advice from professionals and/or support groups if necessary.

Figure 8-2
The Skeletal System

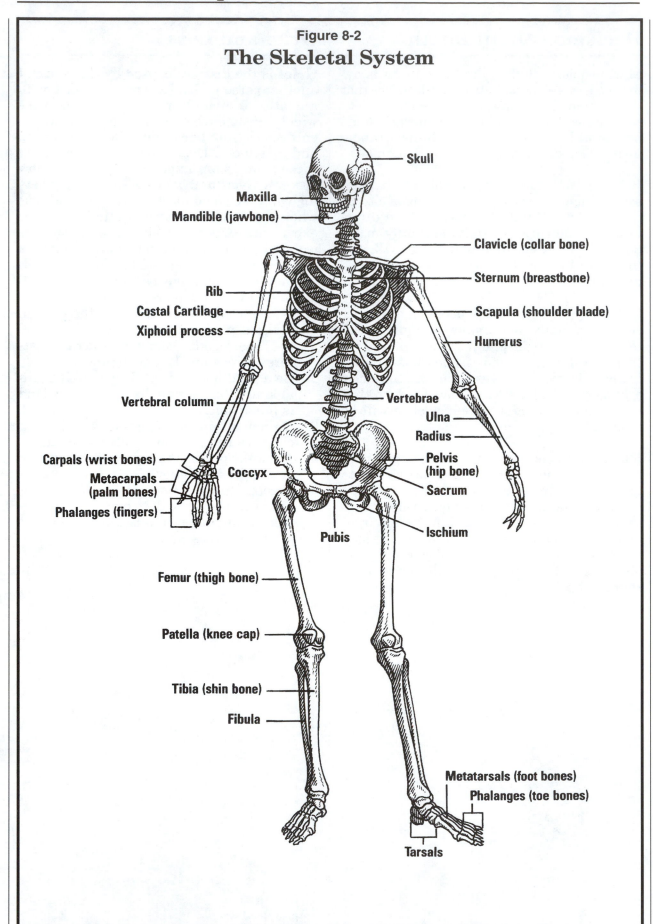

Skull

Maxilla

Mandible (jawbone)

Clavicle (collar bone)

Sternum (breastbone)

Rib

Costal Cartilage

Scapula (shoulder blade)

Xiphoid process

Humerus

Vertebral column

Vertebrae

Ulna

Radius

Carpals (wrist bones)

Coccyx

Pelvis (hip bone)

Metacarpals (palm bones)

Sacrum

Phalanges (fingers)

Ischium

Pubis

Femur (thigh bone)

Patella (knee cap)

Tibia (shin bone)

Fibula

Metatarsals (foot bones)

Phalanges (toe bones)

Tarsals

Figure 8-3
The Muscular System

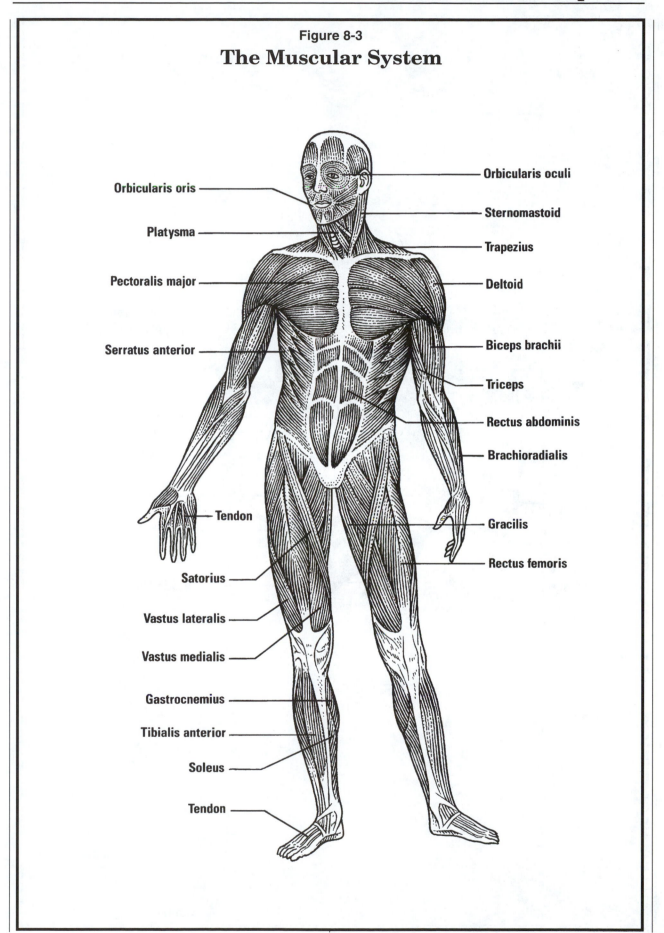

Orbicularis oris

Platysma

Pectoralis major

Serratus anterior

Tendon

Satorius

Vastus lateralis

Vastus medialis

Gastrocnemius

Tibialis anterior

Soleus

Tendon

Orbicularis oculi

Sternomastoid

Trapezius

Deltoid

Biceps brachii

Triceps

Rectus abdominis

Brachioradialis

Gracilis

Rectus femoris

Figure 8-4
The Integumentary System

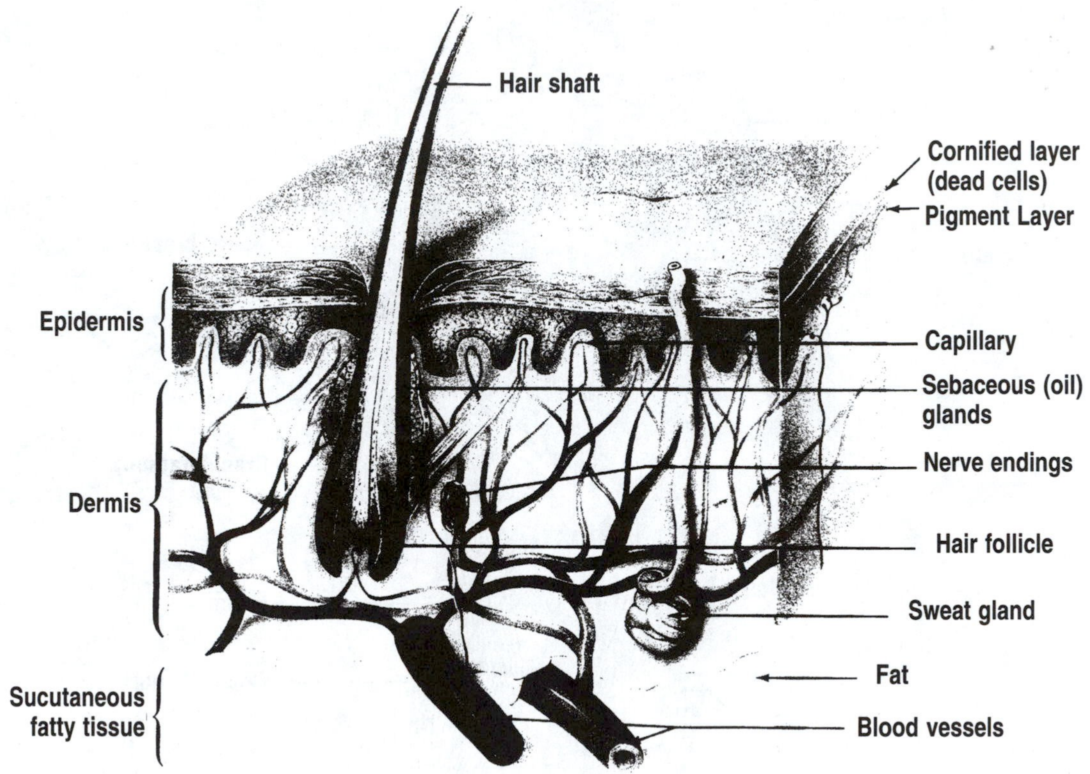

Hair shaft

Cornified layer (dead cells)

Pigment Layer

Epidermis

Capillary

Sebaceous (oil) glands

Nerve endings

Dermis

Hair follicle

Sweat gland

Fat

Sucutaneous fatty tissue

Blood vessels

Figure 8-5

The Nervous System

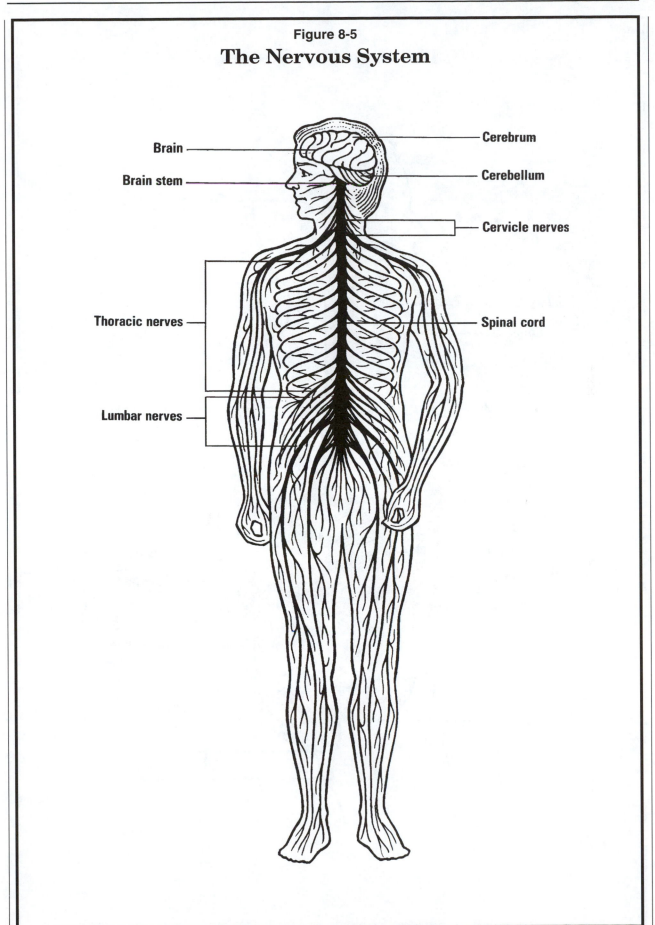

Brain

Brain stem

Cerebrum

Cerebellum

Cervicle nerves

Thoracic nerves

Spinal cord

Lumbar nerves

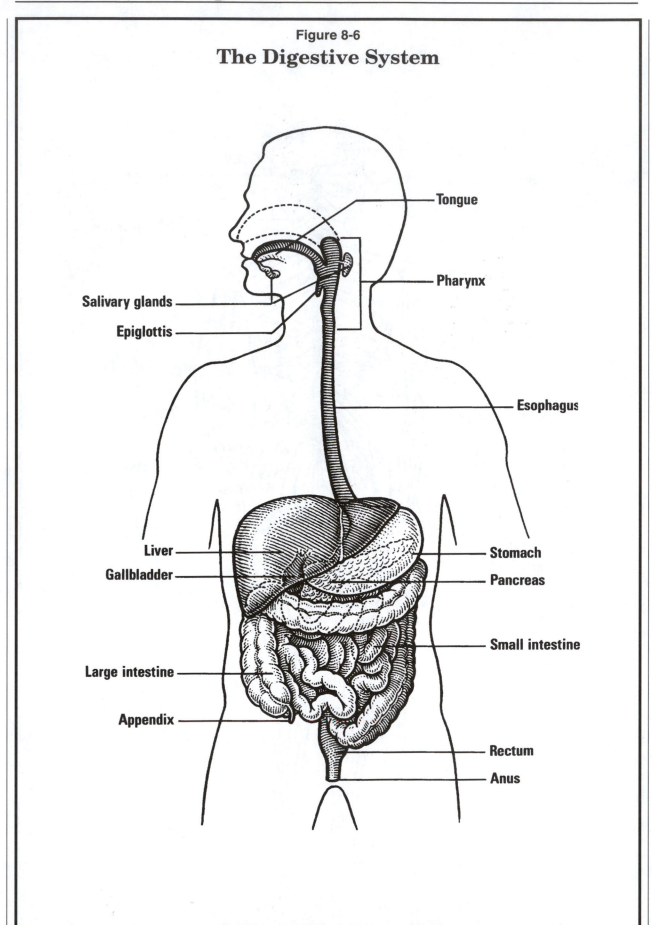

Figure 8-6
The Digestive System

Tongue

Pharynx

Salivary glands

Epiglottis

Esophagus

Liver

Stomach

Gallbladder

Pancreas

Small intestine

Large intestine

Appendix

Rectum

Anus

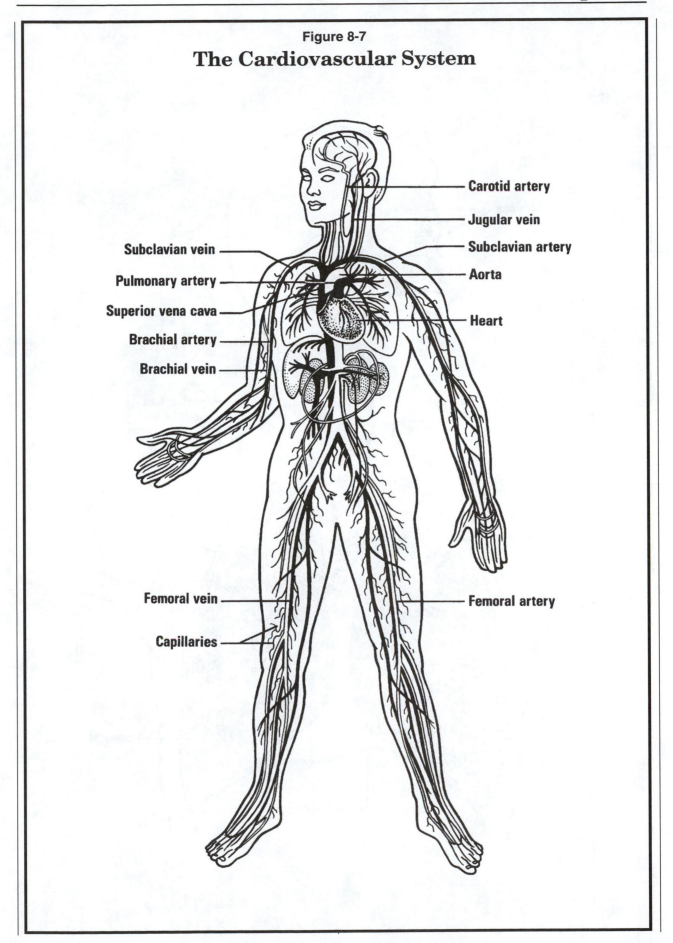

Figure 8-7

The Cardiovascular System

Carotid artery

Jugular vein

Subclavian vein

Subclavian artery

Pulmonary artery

Aorta

Superior vena cava

Heart

Brachial artery

Brachial vein

Femoral vein

Femoral artery

Capillaries

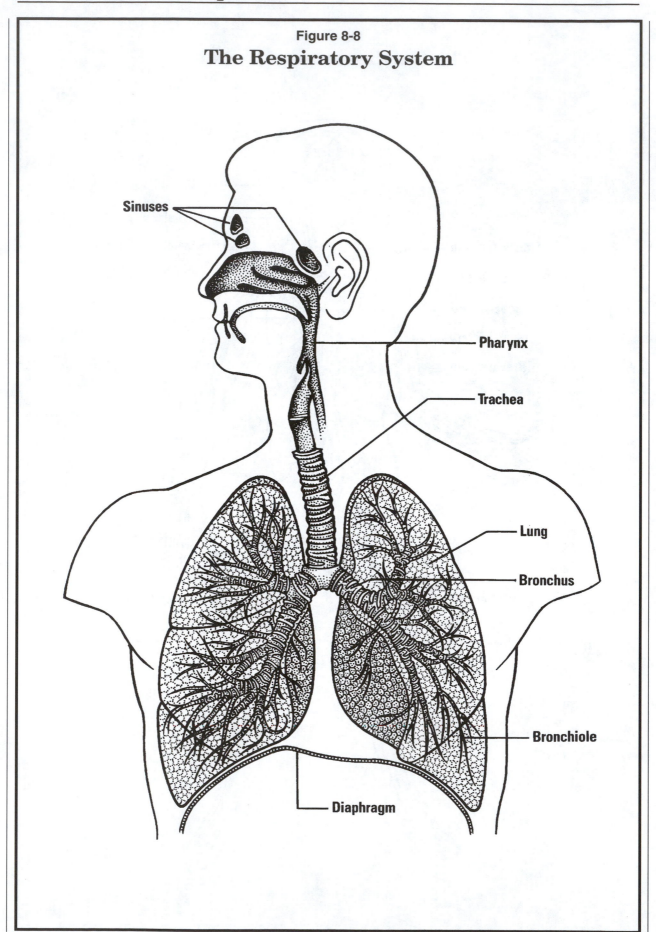

Figure 8-8
The Respiratory System

Sinuses

Pharynx

Trachea

Lung

Bronchus

Bronchiole

Diaphragm

Figure 8-9
The Urinary System

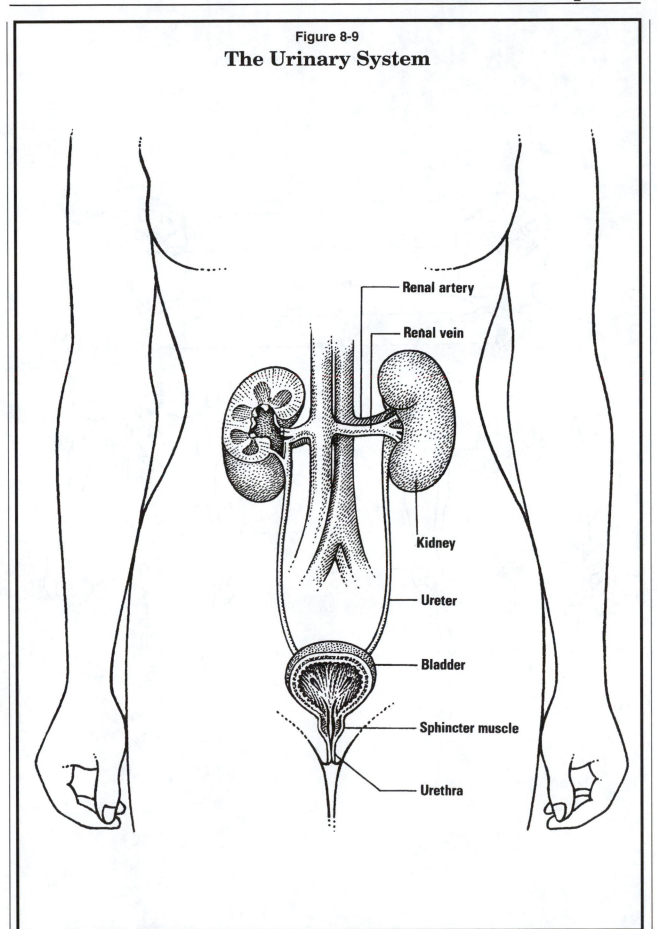

Renal artery

Renal vein

Kidney

Ureter

Bladder

Sphincter muscle

Urethra

Figure 8-10

The Endocrine System

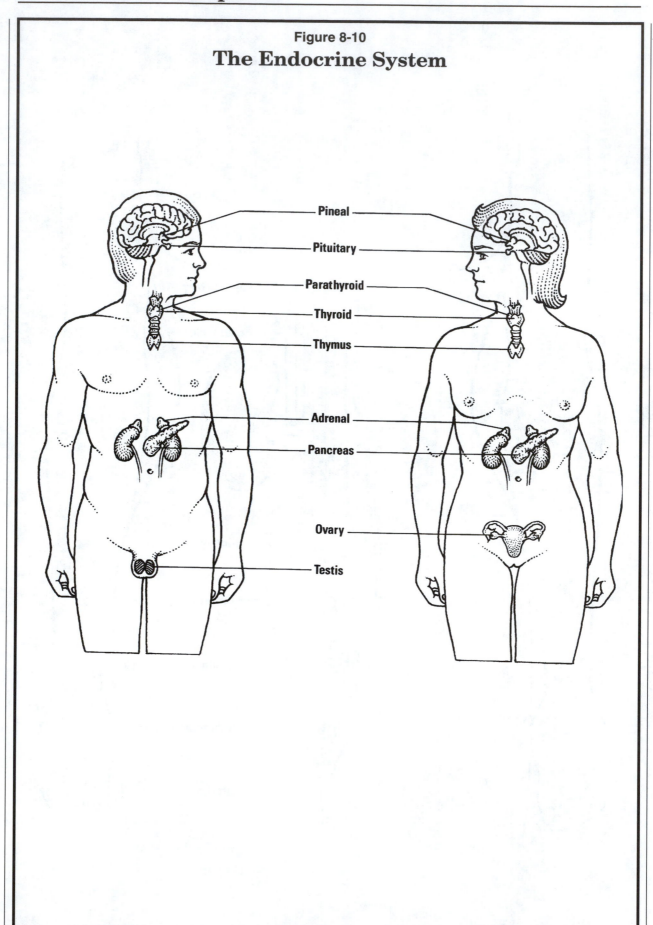

Pineal

Pituitary

Parathyroid

Thyroid

Thymus

Adrenal

Pancreas

Ovary

Testis

214

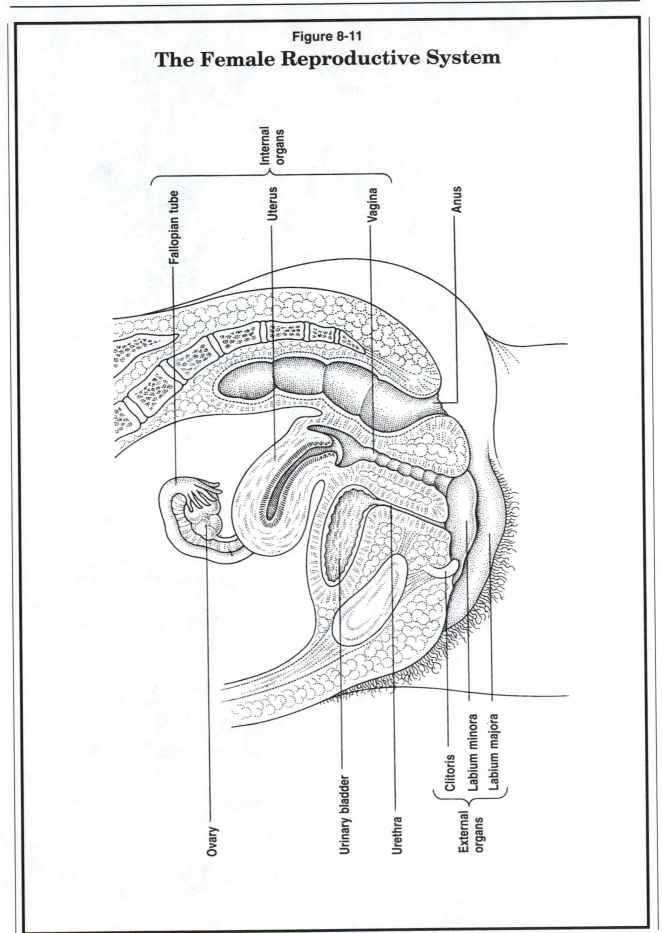

Figure 8-11
The Female Reproductive System

Figure 8-12
The Male Reproductive System

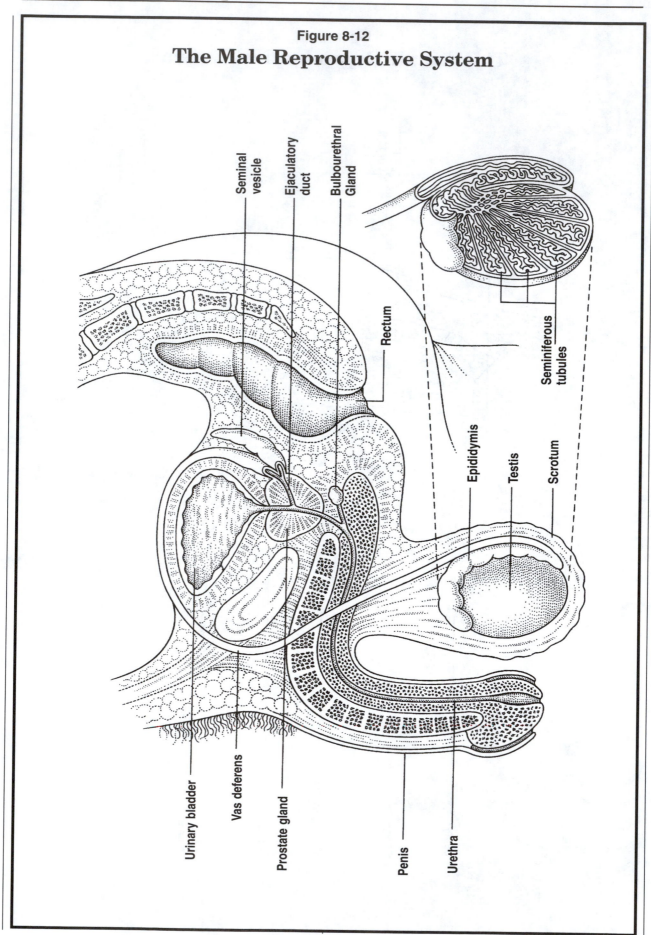

Seminal vesicle

Ejaculatory duct

Bulbourethral Gland

Rectum

Seminiferous tubules

Epididymis

Testis

Scrotum

Urinary bladder

Vas deferens

Prostate gland

Penis

Urethra

Figure 9-1
Life Skills for Nutrition

1. I will recognize foods that contain the six major nutrients.

2. I will select the appropriate number of servings from The Food Guide Pyramid.

3. I will follow the dietary guidelines.

4. I will read food labels.

5. I will make food selections that reduce my risk of disease.

6. I will make healthful selections when dining out.

7. I will consider food safety when making food selections.

8. I will maintain my desirable weight.

9. I will eat for healthful reasons.

10. I will recognize signs of eating disorders.

Chapter 9

NUTRITION

Nutrition is the area of health that focuses on planning a healthful diet and includes choosing a variety of foods from The Food Guide Pyramid, adhering to dietary guidelines, reading food labels, making food selections to reduce the risk of disease, making healthful selections when dining out, considering food safety, maintaining desirable weight, and avoiding harmful eating patterns, and recognizing eating disorders. The content in this chapter provides the health knowledge that is needed to teach young people important life skills for nutrition (Figure 9-1)

Life Skill #1

I will recognize foods that contain the six major nutrients.

Nutrients

Nutrients are chemical substances in foods that furnish body fuel for energy, provide materials needed for building and maintenance of body tissues, and/or supply substances that function in the regulation of body processes. No one food contains all nutrients in the amounts needed for health. There are six basic classes of nutrients: proteins, carbohydrates, fats, vitamins, minerals, and water.

Proteins **Proteins** are nutrients that are essential for the growth, development, and repair of all body tissues. Proteins form parts of muscles, bones, blood, cell membranes. They also form the hormones and enzymes used to regulate body processes. Protein also may be used as a source of energy. Surplus protein may be converted into body fat. Proteins are made of amino acids. **Amino acids** are the building blocks of proteins. There are approximately twenty-two different amino acids that the body needs for good health. The body can produce several of those amino acids. However, some amino acids, called essential amino acids, must come from food. **Essential amino acids** are eight amino acids that the body does not produce. Meat, poultry, fish, dried beans, eggs, and nuts are examples of good sources of protein.

Proteins that contain all the essential amino acids are called **complete proteins**. Animal sources of protein, such as meat, fish, chicken, turkey, and eggs are examples of complete proteins. An **incomplete protein** does not contain all the essential amino acids. Examples of sources of incomplete proteins are nuts, seeds, and beans. Since different incomplete proteins contain different essential amino acids, it is possible to get the essential amino acids in the diet by combining different incomplete proteins.

Carbohydrates **Carbohydrates** are nutrients such as starches and sugars that provide energy to the body. There are two main types of carbohydrates–simple and complex.

Nutrition

Simple carbohydrates are carbohydrates that enter the bloodstream rapidly and provide quick energy. Simple carbohydrates are sometimes referred to as simple sugars because of their chemical structure. Fruits and honey are sources of simple carbohydrates. **Complex carbohydrates** are carbohydrates that have a more complex chemical structure and provide a long-lasting source of energy. Plant foods, such as rice, wheat, and oats are examples of sources of complex carbohydrates. Approximately half of the daily energy intake should be derived from complex carbohydrates. Sources of complex carbohydrates are generally low in fat content.

Fiber is the indigestible material in grains and plant foods. Fiber also is a complex carbohydrate. Since fiber is not digested, it is not a source of energy and is not considered a nutrient. However, fiber is an essential component of a diet because it helps keep the digestive track healthy. Fiber is sometimes referred to as roughage. All plant foods contain some dietary fiber. Wheat, bran, cereals, fruits, and vegetables can be good sources of fiber.

Fats Fats are nutrients that are a source of energy and are essential for making certain vitamins available to the body. Fats are stored as fat tissue and surround and cushion the internal organs, such as the heart, liver, and kidneys. The chemical composition of fats is the basis for their division into two types—saturated fats and unsaturated fats. Most fats in the body are in the form of triglycerides. Triglycerides contain three fatty acids. Fatty acids are composed of chains of atoms of the chemical elements carbon and hydrogen. Fatty acids are commonly referred to as fats. **Saturated fatty acids** are fatty acids that are composed of chains that contain all the hydrogen atoms they can hold. **Saturated fats** are fats that contain a high proportion of saturated fatty acids. All fats are composed of chains of atoms of the chemical elements carbon and hydrogen. Saturated fats are present in meat and dairy products, and are usually solids at room temperature. Saturated fats contribute to the blood cholesterol level. **Cholesterol** is a fat-like substance made by the body and found in many foods. Cholesterol can accumulate on the walls of the arteries. This is a major cause of hardening of the arteries. Cholesterol is found in foods such as such as meat, poultry,

milk products, and egg yolks. While the body needs a certain amount of cholesterol, cholesterol levels that are too high is a risk for heart disease. **Unsaturated fats** are fats that are composed of chains that are able to add more hydrogen atoms to their structure. Sources of unsaturated fats are plant products, such as corn oil, and are usually liquids at room temperature. Unsaturated fats contain both polyunsaturates and monosaturates. Polyunsaturated fats are found in oils such as sunflower oil, safflower oil, and corn oil. Monounsaturated fats are found mainly in olive, canola, and peanut oils. **Trans-fatty acids** are fatty acids that are produced when polyunsaturated oils are hydrogenated. Trans-fatty acids raise cholesterol and are thought to contribute to certain types of cancer.

Vitamins Vitamins are organic substances needed in very small amounts to facilitate chemical reactions in the body. Vitamins do not supply energy, but many vitamins help release energy from carbohydrates and fats. **Fat-soluble vitamins** are vitamins that can be stored in the body. They include vitamins A, D, E, and K. Fat-soluble vitamins are stored primarily in the liver. **Water-soluble vitamins** are vitamins that cannot be stored by the body in significant amounts. Vitamin B complex and vitamin C are water-soluble vitamins.

People who do not eat a balanced diet may experience vitamin deficiencies. Symptoms of vitamin C deficiency include loosened teeth and gum disease. Symptoms of vitamin D deficiency include rickets, poor teeth, and soft bones in adulthood. Diseases associated with vitamin deficiency are rare in the United States and are most common in underdeveloped countries. Many people take vitamin supplements. **Vitamin supplements** are usually synthetic forms of particular vitamins. However, a person who eats a balanced diet that contains all the food groups will get adequate amounts of vitamins from foods. There have been many claims that vitamin supplements will improve health. Certain groups of people such as the elderly, athletes, or people who have illnesses that affect normal digestion might benefit from supplements. However, foods are the best source of nutrients. One danger of taking supplements is that people tend to think that if a small amount of vitamins is what is needed,

220

taking a larger amount of vitamin supplements will multiply the benefits. Instead, high doses of many vitamins can be toxic.

Minerals Minerals are inorganic substances in food that are needed by the body in small amounts. Many minerals assist in the regulation of chemical reactions in the body. Three important minerals are iron, calcium, and sodium. **Iron** is a mineral that is an important component of hemoglobin. It functions as a carrier of oxygen in the body. Iron deficiency can lead to anemia. **Anemia** is a condition in which the body is unable to produce sufficient red blood cells. A person who does not get enough iron is susceptible to illnesses and infection, and may have a poor appetite, feel weak, and be continually tired. This results in a decrease in the ability of the body to transport oxygen. The best way to get an adequate amount of iron is to eat a variety of foods, such as seafood, green leafy vegetables, lean red meats, and whole grain breads.

Calcium is a mineral that is needed for building bones and teeth and for maintaining bone strength. Calcium also functions in the contraction of muscles and in blood clotting. All cells in the body need calcium. Good sources of calcium are milk and milk products, dark green leafy vegetables, calcium-fortified orange juice, and dried beans. **Sodium** is a mineral that regulates and maintains the balance of fluids in the body. Table salt is a major source of sodium. Sodium also occurs naturally in many foods and is added to many processed foods, such as salted snacks and canned foods. In most cases, requirements of sodium in the diet can be met without adding extra salt to food.

Water Water is a nutrient that helps make up blood, helps the process of digestion and removal of body wastes, and regulates body temperature. Approximately 60 percent of the body is made up of water. Intake of water is needed to replace the body water lost in urine and sweat. Drinking the equivalent of six to eight glasses of water every day will meet daily requirements of water. Water has no calories. While drinking juices and sodas may add to the water intake, they also can have high calorie content. Many foods, such as fruits, also contain significant amounts of water. Many consumers who are concerned

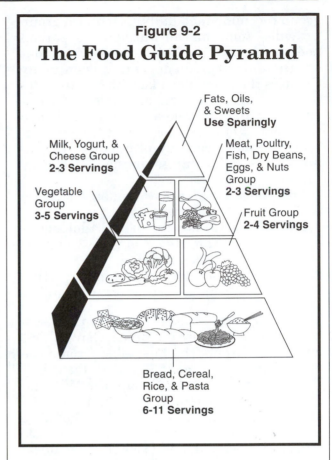

Figure 9-2
The Food Guide Pyramid

Fats, Oils, & Sweets
Use Sparingly

Milk, Yogurt, & Cheese Group
2-3 Servings

Meat, Poultry, Fish, Dry Beans, Eggs, & Nuts Group
2-3 Servings

Vegetable Group
3-5 Servings

Fruit Group
2-4 Servings

Bread, Cereal, Rice, & Pasta Group
6-11 Servings

about the safety of their water supply choose to drink bottled water. However, many brands of bottled water have not been tested or purified and may pose the same risks of water that has not been bottled.

Life Skill #2

I will select the appropriate number of servings from The Food Guide Pyramid.

The Food Guide Pyramid

The Food Guide Pyramid is a food-group guide that recommends daily guidelines to ensure a balanced diet. The Food Guide Pyramid is based on research from the United States Department of Agriculture and the Department of Health and Human Services. (Figure 9-2). The Food Guide Pyramid provides information about what foods Americans eat and how to make the best food choices. The Food Guide Pyramid also stresses the number of servings of each major food

Nutrition

group recommended daily. Each food group provides some of the nutrients a person needs each day. The number of servings that are right for a person depends on how many Calories the person needs, which in turn depends on age, sex, size, and levels of activity. A **Calorie** is a measure that indicates the amount of energy obtained from a food. The National Academy of Sciences recommends the following guidelines for energy intake:

1,600 Calories: Sedentary women and some older women
2,200 Calories: Most children, adolescent females, active women, sedentary men
2,800 Calories: Adolescent females, active men, very active women

The major food groups discussed in this section of the chapter are the Bread, Cereal, Rice, and Pasta Group; the Vegetable Group; the Fruit Group; the Meat, Poultry, Fish, Dry Beans, Eggs, and Nuts Group; the Milk, Yogurt, and Cheese Group; and the Fats, Oils, and Sweets Group. The foods that should be eaten in the largest amounts are at the bottom of the pyramid, and foods that should be eaten sparingly are at the top of the pyramid.

Breads, Cereals, Rice, and Pasta Group

The Bread, Cereals, Rice, and Pasta Group is composed of grain products. This food group contributes complex carbohydrates, vitamins, minerals, and fiber to the diet. Some people think that grain products are high in calories and are fattening. This is not necessarily true.

According to The Food Guide Pyramid, a person should choose the most servings from the Bread, Cereal, Rice, and Pasta Group–6 to 11 servings every day. One serving might include:
- 1 slice of bread
- 1 ounce of ready-to-eat cereal
- 1/2 cup of rice or pasta

Vegetable Group The Vegetable Group provides vitamins, such as vitamins A and C, and minerals, such as iron and magnesium. This group is naturally low in fat and also provides fiber. Different types of vegetables differ in the amount of nutrients they provide so it is important to eat a variety of vegetables. The Food Guide Pyramid recommends 3 to 5 servings of vegetables each day. One serving might include:

- 1 cup of raw leafy vegetables
- 1/2 cup of cooked or raw vegetables
- 3/4 cup of vegetable juice

To preserve nutrients as much as possible, vegetables should be eaten as soon as possible after purchasing. Reducing the amount of cooking and preparation of vegetables also helps preserve nutrients–raw or lightly steamed vegetables have the highest nutritional value. Adding salad dressings, dips, and sauces increases the Calorie and fat content.

Fruit Group The Fruit Group provides important amounts of vitamins A and C and the mineral potassium. Fruits are low in fat and sodium. The Food Guide Pyramid recommends 2 to 4 servings of fruits each day. One serving might include:
- 1 medium apple
- 1 banana or orange
- 1/2 cup of chopped, cooked, or canned fruit
- 3/4 cup of 100 percent fruit juice

Only 100 percent fruit juices should be counted toward the Fruit Group. Other fruit drinks, "ades," and punches contain only a little fruit juice and are mostly water and sugar. Fruits canned or frozen in heavy sauces or syrups may add extra calories and sugar to the diet.

Meat, Poultry, Fish, Dry Beans, Eggs, and Nuts Group This group provides protein, B vitamins, and the minerals iron and zinc. Dry beans, eggs, and nuts are similar to meats in providing protein and most vitamins and minerals.

The Food Guide Pyramid suggests 2 to 3 servings each day from this group. One serving might include:
- 2 to 3 ounces of cooked lean meat, poultry, or fish
- 1/2 cup of cooked dry beans
- 1 egg
- 2 tablespoons of peanut butter

Most Americans eat more products from this group than they need. To control fat content, choose lean meat, poultry without skin, fish, and dry beans and peas. Foods should be broiled, roasted, or boiled rather than frying. Egg yolks are high in cholesterol, so they should be limited. Nuts and seeds tend to have a high fat content, and should be eaten in moderation.

Milk, Yogurt, and Cheese Group Milk products provide protein, vitamins, and minerals. Milk, yogurt, and cheese are good sources of calcium. The Food Guide Pyramid recommends 2 to 3 servings of milk, yogurt, and cheese each day. Adolescents, young adults, and pregnant females should have 3 servings. One serving might include:
- 1 cup of milk
- 1 1/2 ounces of natural cheese
- 2 ounces of processed cheese

Many products that are good sources of calcium also have a high fat content. Drinking skim (nonfat) or low-fat milk, eating low-fat cheese and low-fat or nonfat frozen yogurt can contribute calcium to the diet without adding a large amount of fat.

Fats, Oils, and Sweets This group includes foods such as salad dressings and oils, cream, butter, margarine, sugars, soft drinks, candies, and sweet desserts. These foods provide calories and little or no vitamins or minerals. They should be eaten sparingly. Fats should not exceed 30 percent of total Calories each day. No more than 10 percent of total Calories should come from sugar. Fat intake can be reduced by limiting intake of fat-laden foods such as fried foods, foods that contain oils high in saturated fat, and whole milk and cheese products. Sugar intake could be reduced by drinking water and fruit juices instead of sodas, and limiting candy, cookies, and other sweets.

Alternative Diets

Vegetarian diets A vegetarian diet is a diet that excludes meat, fish, and other animal products. Strictly speaking, a vegetarian diet avoids all foods that have animal origin. However, there are a variety of kinds of vegetarian diets. A **semi-vegetarian diet** is a diet that does not include meat but does include plant foods, dairy products, and often a selection of seafood, eggs, and poultry. A **lacto-vegetarian diet** is a diet that does not include meats but does include dairy products. An **ovo-vegetarian diet** is a diet that includes eggs. A **lacto-ovo-vegetarian diet** is a diet that includes both dairy products and eggs. A **pesco-vegetarian diet** is a diet that includes fish, dairy products,

and eggs. It is important to carefully plan a vegetarian diet to ensure adequate nutrients in the diet. Vegetarians need to be sure to obtain enough protein, iron, vitamin D, calcium, iron, and zinc. Eating foods such as grains, nuts, and legumes is important since the proteins that are usually obtained in animal products are lacking.

Ethnic diets While eating habits in America are blended from many different traditions, ethnic diets and foods are considered those that have maintained their distinctiveness in America. Ethnic diets consist of foods and eating customs from other cultures. Ethnic diets reflect not only particular foods but also ways of combining them and cooking them. Many Americans eat a variety of ethnic foods, with Italian, Chinese, and Mexican among the most popular. Food traditions have been introduced to our society through immigrants who bring their own eating practices. Every type of ethnic cooking has its own nutritional benefits and potential disadvantages. For example, benefits of the traditional Chinese diet include low fat intake, a high proportion of plant products and low proportion of animal proteins. However, many foods in Chinese restaurants in America have a high sodium content, and when cooked in oil or fried may be high in fat content. Food served in Mexico features rice and beans, which are low in fat and high in protein. However, many meals that Americans eat at Mexican restaurants feature meat, cheese, and sour cream, which are very high in fat.

Figure 9-3
The Dietary Guidelines

1. Eat a variety of foods

2. Maintain a healthful weight.

3. Choose a diet low in fat, saturated fat, and cholesterol.

4. Choose a diet with plenty of vegetable, fruits, and grain products.

5. Use sugars only in moderation.

6. Use salt and sodium only in moderation.

7. Do not drink alcoholic beverages.

Life Skill #3

I will follow the dietary guidelines.

The Dietary Guidelines for Americans are recommendations for diet choices for healthy Americans two years of age or more (Figure 9-3). The guidelines are the result of research by the United States Department of Agriculture and the Department of Health and Human Services. By following the Dietary Guidelines, a person can improve the chance of having better health and reduce the chance of getting certain diseases. The guidelines are: eat a variety of foods; maintain healthful weight; choose a diet low in fat, saturated fat, and cholesterol; choose a diet with plenty of vegetables, fruits, and grain products; use sugars only in moderation; use salt and sodium only in moderation; and if you drink alcoholic beverages, do so only in moderation.

Eat a Variety of Foods

It is important to eat a variety of foods that contain nutrients for good health. No single food can supply all nutrients in the amounts that a person needs. It also is important to eat a variety of foods from each food group shown on the Food Guide Pyramid.

Maintain a Healthful Weight

It is possible to be too fat or too thin. Both situations have risks of health problems. Being overweight is linked to high blood pressure, heart disease, and diabetes. Being underweight is linked to eating disorders and nutrient deficiency. Desirable weight is the weight and body composition that is recommended for a person's age, height, sex, and body build.

Choose a Diet Low in Fat, Saturated Fat, and Cholesterol

Fat in foods contains over twice the Calories of equal amounts of carbohydrates or proteins. The amount of fat in a diet should be limited to 30 percent or less of total Calories.

Choose a Diet With Plenty of Vegetables, Fruits, and Grain Products

Vegetables, fruits, and grain products are good sources of complex carbohydrates, fiber,

Use Sugars Only in Moderation

Sugars add Calories to foods but are limited in nutrients. Eating too many foods that have a high sugar content can contribute to tooth decay.

Use Salt and Sodium Only in Moderation

Sodium is an important nutrient that is needed by the body, but only in moderation. Table salt is the major source of sodium in the diet. Approximately 1/4 teaspoon of salt daily provides the amount needed. Most people eat about ten times this amount. Foods that tend to be very high in sodium content include luncheon meats, salty snack foods, cheeses, and many fast food products. Using salt and sodium in moderation helps reduce the risk of high blood pressure.

If You Drink Alcoholic Beverages, Do So Only in Moderation (Adults Only)

Alcoholic beverages contain Calories, but little or no nutrients. An adult who drinks alcoholic beverages should do so only in moderation. Moderation is defined as one ounce of pure alcohol or less per day. Drinking alcohol can lead to many health problems and dependence. Alcohol should not be consumed by young people or by pregnant females.

Life Skill #4

I will read food labels.

Food Labels

Food labels are designed to assist consumers with making healthful food choices. In 1992, the federal government enacted new guidelines for food labels. These guidelines require food manufacturers to provide nutritional information that will be accurate, complete, and useful to the consumer (Figure 9-4). It is important to remember that the informa-

Figure 9-4

The Food Label

tion about particular percentages and amounts of the product are based on a daily diet that provides 2,000 Calories.

The Five Key Features on the Nutrition Panel

Nutrition Facts The title of the new label is "Nutrition Facts." The required information includes the following, always in this order:

- Total Calories
- Calories from fat
- Total fat
- Saturated fat
- Cholesterol
- Sodium
- Total carbohydrate
- Dietary fiber
- Sugars
- Protein
- Vitamin A
- Vitamin C
- Calcium
- Iron

Serving Size The nutrition facts are based on serving sizes that reflect amounts that people eat. The serving sizes are standardized.

Nutrition

Percent Daily Values Dietary standards are expressed as percent daily values and are based on a daily diet of 2,000 Calories. These figures tell how much of a day's worth of the nutrients is provided in the food product.

Vitamins and Minerals Amounts of vitamins A and C and the minerals iron and calcium are required on the label because deficiencies can cause serious health problems. Amounts are expressed as percentages. Other listings of vitamins and minerals may be included on the label.

Daily Values Daily amounts of nutrients that are necessary for health are calculated as follows: fat based on 30 percent of Calories; saturated fat based on 10 percent of Calories; carbohydrate based on 60 percent of Calories; protein based on 10 percent of Calories; and fiber based on 11.5 grams of fiber for every 1,000 Calories. For some nutrients, there are recommended upper limits such as less than 65 grams of fat, less than 20 grams of saturated fat, less than 300 milligrams of cholesterol, and less than 2,400 milligrams of sodium.

The Ingredients Listing

Food manufacturers must list all the ingredients by weight in their products, beginning with the one that is present in the greatest amount. For example, if a soup label lists tomatoes first, that means that by weight the soup contains more tomatoes than any other ingredient. The ingredients list should be read carefully to determine the true amount of an ingredient. For example, a food may consist of mainly sugar, but the sugar content may be broken down into smaller amounts and listed as sucrose, fructose, and glucose.

Dictionary of Terms

The new label requirements include restricted use of certain terms, such as "low fat." **Low fat** is a label for a product that contains 3 grams or less of fat per serving. Other terms and their meanings, according to the new labels include:

free — no amount of (or a trivial amount) of fat, saturated fat, cholesterol, sodium, sugars, and Calories

low Calorie	- 40 Calories or less per serving
lean	- less than 10 grams fat
reduced	- 25 percent less of a nutrient or of Calories than the regular product
good source	- one serving contains 10 to 19 percent of the daily value for a particular nutrient
low sodium	- 140 grams or less per serving

Special Categories

Some foods are exempted from the new label requirements. These include fresh fruits and vegetables, restaurant foods and foods served in hospitals and airplanes; bakery, deli, and candy products; foods sold by vendors and in vending machines, and coffee, tea, and spices.

Life Skill #5

I will make food selections that reduce my risk of disease.

Heart Disease

Diet plays a major factor in the risk of heart disease. Diets high in saturated fat and cholesterol greatly increase the risk of heart disease. The American Heart Association recommends that no more than 30 percent of the daily Calorie total should come from fat, with only 10 percent of that from saturated fat. The goals for reduced fat in a diet do not apply to children under the age of two. At approximately two years of age, children should be encouraged to eat foods that are lower in fat and that provide the Calories and nutrients they need for normal growth. Research also has linked vitamin intake to the risk of heart disease. **Antioxidants** are the substances that protect cells from being damaged by oxidation. Antioxidants, which include vitamins C and E and beta-carotene also may lower the risk of heart disease.

Cancer

Diets high in fat content also increase the risk of certain types of cancer. Most Americans consume more fat in their diets than is recommended for cancer prevention. A 1992 study published in the journal, *Nutrition and*

Here is your order: 65 grams of fat, and 700 mg of sodium

Cancer, found a link between the protective role of fruits and vegetables in preventing cancers of the lung, stomach, colon, bladder, pancreas, mouth, larynx, cervix, ovary, and breast. Foods rich in fiber also may have protective effects against colon cancer, the second leading cause of death from cancer in the United States. The National Cancer Institute recommends that the public increase dietary fiber levels to 20 to 30 grams a day. Other research suggests a link between antioxidants and lowered risk of cancer. The American Cancer Society suggests the following nutrition guidelines to reduce the risk of cancer.

• Avoid being overweight.
• Reduce your total fat intake.
• Eat high-fiber foods.
• Eat foods rich in vitamins A and C.
• Eat cruciferous vegetables such as cabbage and broccoli.
• Eat limited amounts of salt-cured products such as ham.
• Do not drink alcohol.

Diabetes and Hypoglycemia

Diabetes is a disease in which the body is unable to process the sugar in foods in normal ways. Diabetes occurs when the pancreas gland does not produce enough insulin,

which is a hormone that regulates the level of sugar in a person's blood. Diabetes also results if insulin is produced, but it does not function as it should. It is important that a person with diabetes chooses a balanced diet that includes an abundance of complex carbohydrates and is high in fiber and low in sodium and fat, which will help keep the level of blood sugar in a normal range. **Hypoglycemia** is a condition in which the pancreas produces too much insulin and blood sugar levels decrease. People with hypoglycemia may become weak, dizzy, or irritable. People with hypoglycemia should eat small regular meals that are high in protein. They also should avoid sweets, which cause a rapid rise in blood sugar levels, because their bodies cannot regulate blood sugar levels properly.

Life Skill #6

I will make healthful food selections when dining out.

Fast Foods

Fast foods are foods that can be served quickly and are prepared in walk-in or drive-through restaurants. Fast food restaurants are popular in this country for their convenience. All fast foods are not junk foods–foods that supply extra Calories and are usually high in fat and in salt content. However, a typical fast food meal of a cheeseburger, order of fries, and soft drink has a very high fat and sodium content. Some fast foods, such as vegetable-topped pizzas, may be healthful choices. Many fast food restaurants now offer low-fat items on their menus, such as salads with low-fat dressings, grilled chicken sandwiches, and low-fat frozen yogurt. Many fast food restaurants post the nutrients in their food items, or will make this information available to their customers.

Foods also should be chosen carefully when eating out in a restaurant. Foods that are broiled, baked, or steamed rather than fried can be more healthful choices. Asking for salad dressing or sauces on the side helps a person control the amount of potentially high-fat foods. Many restaurants now offer lighter or low-fat menu options, and honor special requests for food preparation.

Nutrition

I will consider food safety when making food selections.

Pesticides and Processing

A **pesticide** is any substance that is used to kill or control the growth of unwanted organisms. Pesticides are used both on farms and in homes. On farms, pesticides are used to control the growth of pests that affect crops. In homes, pesticides are used to keep out insects and other organisms. It is possible for traces of pesticides to cling to fruits and vegetables when they are harvested. If trace amounts of pesticides accumulate in a person's body, they can cause illness. This is the reason it is important to wash fresh fruits and vegetables before eating or cooking them. Many consumers choose to purchase organic foods to avoid potential pesticides. **Organic foods** are foods that are produced without any chemicals throughout the process.

Additives

Additives are substances added to foods to improve the flavor or appearance or to increase the nutritional content. Sometimes additives are added to food to replace nutrients lost during processing. Common examples are adding calcium to fortify orange juice, and vitamin C to fruit drinks. Some additives can pose a risk to consumers. Some additives have been linked to certain forms of cancer. In the United States, the Federal Government regulates the use of additives in foods.

Artificial Sweeteners

There are several sugar substitutes available in this country. One artificial sweetener is saccharin, which has been used in the United States for many years, primarily in soft drinks. Saccharin is also used as a sweetener in tea or coffee and in other daily uses. Aspartame is a sweetener that has seen a rise in popularity. Artifical sweeteners contain either no Calories or few Calories. Some sweeteners can be used in cooking. It is generally recommended that artificial sweeteners be used only in moderation.

Fake Fat

Fat substitutes, or "fake fat," can help to lower fat intake. Fat substitutes are now common in foods such as ice cream, mayonnaise, and salad dressings. However, it is important to recognize many light versions of food contain little or no nutrients, and to avoid eating larger portions of these foods.

Food Irradiation

Food irradiation is a process to protect foods in which the foods are treated with gamma radiation. Irradiation kills microorganisms and prolongs the life of the food without making the food radioactive. However, it does damage to the molecular structure of the food. There are many critics of this process as the long-term effects of irradiation are not completely known yet.

Food-Borne Infections

Food-borne infections are illnesses caused by eating food that has been contaminated with virus, bacteria, worms, or other organisms. Preventing food-borne infections begins when foods are purchased and continues as they are stored, prepared, cooked, and served at home. The bacteria that cause food-borne illnesses are usually colorless, odorless, and

tasteless and require warmth, moisture, time, and food to grow. Government inspection and standards help keep food supply safe, but it is important for the individual to take additional precautions. Symptoms of food-borne illness include diarrhea, nausea, vomiting, and cramps. In most people, symptoms last only a day or two. However, occasional cases of food-borne illnesses can cause life-threatening illness and even death. Examples of food-borne illnesses are salmonella infection, clostridum botulinum, and escherica coli. **Salmonella** is a bacterial infection that contaminates many foods, particularly undercooked chicken, eggs, and processed foods. Symptoms of salmonella infection include severe diarrhea, fever, vomiting, and cramps. Salmonella may cause death. **Botulism** is a acterial infection that results primarily from improperly canned foods. Botulism is rare, but can be fatal. *Escherichia coli (E. Coli)* is a bacteria that is usually harmless, but of which a certain strain can cause food-borne illness. Illness from the bacteria *Escherichia coli* is rare but can be fatal. Food-borne illnesses are generally treated by drinking water and other liquids, frequent washing of hands, and rest. A physician's care is recommended.

There are several important requirements to prevent food-borne infections:
- Wash your hands before handling food.
- Refrigerate the food when necessary.
- Do not thaw frozen food on the kitchen counter.
- Wash your hands, utensils, and counters after contact with raw meat and poultry.
- Keep hot foods hot and cold foods cold.
- Thoroughly cook raw meat, poultry, and fish.
- Freeze or refrigerate leftovers promptly.

Food Allergies

Food allergies are overreactions by the body to normally harmless ingredients in foods. Symptoms of food allergies are difficulty in breathing, loss of consciousness, hives, swelling, and a drop in blood pressure. It is estimated that food allergies affect less than 2 percent of adults and 2 to 8 percent of children. People who experience food allergies have to alter their lifestyles and be careful to avoid the food or foods that have caused them allergy symptoms. These people will probably have to avoid those foods all their lives. Food allergies can be diagnosed through testing by a trained allergist. Nuts, wheat, shellfish, and milk are some of the most common substances that cause these reactions. More common than food allergy is food intolerance. **Food intolerance** is a reaction to food by people who lack the digestive chemicals needed to break them down. People with food intolerance can eat small amounts of certain foods without experiencing symptoms, but become sensitive to these foods in larger amounts. A common example of food intolerance is lactose intolerance. **Lactose intolerance** is caused by a deficiency of the enzyme lactase that is necessary to digest all the lactose (milk sugar) that is consumed. Other examples include intolerance to caffeine, alcohol, and MSG.

Life Skill #8

I will maintain my desirable weight.

Calories

A **Calorie** is a measure that indicates the amount of energy obtained from a food. As the body uses the food that has been eaten, energy is released for daily activities. The number of Calories a person needs depends on his/her age, sex, body build, and the amount of daily physical activity. A person who is physically active needs more daily Calories from food than a person who is not physically active. In addition to physical activity, the body uses Calories to maintain the body systems such as respiration, circulation, and digestion.

Desirable Weight

Desirable weight is the weight and body composition that is recommended for a person's age, sex, height, and body build. The body is composed of two types of tissues—fat tissue and lean tissue. Total body weight may be an indicator of health risks, but the more important indicator is body composition. **Body composition** is the percentage of fat tissue and lean tissue in the body. When a low percentage of body fat is maintained, a person is at lower risk of many diseases and illnesses.

Hunger, Satiety, and Set Point

Hunger is the physiological need for food. **Appetite** is the desire for food that is determined by environmental and psychological factors. Weight management includes balancing eating for health with satisfying appetite. **Satiety** is the feeling of being full after eating. It is the internal feeling that a person has that it is time to stop eating. **Set point** is a theory that states that the body has a control system for keeping weight at a point at which it is comfortable. A person may easily gain or lose five to ten pounds around this set point weight. To gain or lose more than that may be difficult. This theory may explain why many people who lose weight regain about the same amount.

Gaining Weight

Gaining weight is basically the result of gaining more Calories than the body needs or spends. When people eat more than they need, their body stores the extra nutrients as either glycogen or fat. **Glycogen** is a temporary reserve supply of energy in the form of sugar and is stored in the liver and muscles. Glycogen is constantly being used and restored in the body. Fat is different. Fat is stored in fat cells throughout the body. Fat is a more permanent type of stored energy. A person who wants to gain weight should seek a physician's advice, which may include choosing high-Calorie foods from the Food Guide Pyramid while maintaining a balanced diet and participating in resistance training for muscle development.

Losing Weight

Losing weight is usually the result of reducing the number of Calories and increasing physical activity. There is no one answer to what makes one person lose weight more easily than another. People who are trying to lose weight should look at many factors, including lifestyle, exercise habits, family history, and psychological factors. A person who wants to lose weight should be realistic and recognize that it is not wise to try to lose weight too quickly. A weight loss of one to two pounds per week is reasonable. Weight loss may be more permanent if the weight is lost slowly over a period of time. People who are interested in losing weight should discuss weight-loss methods with a physician. Fad diets, dietary supplements such as diet shakes and bars, and over-the-counter diet pills can be harmful to a person's health.

Obesity

Obesity is excessive body fat. An adult male is considered to be obese when he has a body fat percentage of 20 or more. An adult female is considered to be obese when she has a body fat percentage of 30 or more. Obesity may be caused by factors other than overeating, such as heredity and lack of physical activity. Obesity is associated with health risks including high blood pressure, cardiovascular disease, and diabetes. Health risks of obesity generally increase with severity.

Life Skill #9

I will eat for healthful reasons.

Extreme Dieting

Extreme dieting includes skipping meals, taking diet pills, and inducing vomiting after eating. It has been estimated that about 30 percent of adolescent females consider themselves to be overweight. They look for a way to lose weight quickly, which means that they often choose extreme methods. Because these extreme dieting methods reduce the nutrients that every person needs, the function of body systems and organs can be affected. Fasting is associated with blood sugar imbalance, headaches, fatigue, intolerance to cold, dehydration, kidney failure, and weight gain. Extreme dieting patterns often lead to yo-yo dieting. **Yo-yo dieting** is a cycle of weight loss and weight gain. The repeated stress of yo-yo dieting on the body may be as harmful as being overweight. Most serious of all, extreme dieting may lead to anorexia nervosa and bulimia, which will be discussed later in this chapter.

Binge Eating

Binge eating is an eating pattern in which a person eats in an uncontrollable fashion. Usually, foods eaten are convenience foods that are high in Calories and consumed in great quantities. Individuals with this eating disorder feel that they lose control of themselves and do not stop eating until they are uncomfortably full. Binge eating is a characteristic of a person who has bulimia.

Cravings

Food cravings are intense and urgent desires for certain kinds of food. Many food cravings are normal and are not harmful. However, some food cravings can be a sign of an illness, for example continual thirst is a sign of diabetes. Other food cravings are a sign of a nutritional need. Research suggests that food cravings may be linked to brain chemistry, biological and psychological factors.

Eating and Emotions: Reward, Anger, Depression

Because good behavior in childhood is often rewarded by food, many children grow up connecting food with positive thoughts. As adults, they may continue to use foods as their way of rewarding themselves, especially if their lives are not fulfilling in other respects.

If people do not learn to express their anger in healthful ways, they may turn to food as a way of responding to their angry feelings. This type of behavior can be very harmful since the angry feelings will still be there, and the eating habit may lead to overweight. Some people reward themselves with food. Some people use food to relieve the emotions they experience when they are depressed. These types of eating habits are never satisfying because they do nothing to alleviate the causes of anger or depression.

Life Skill #10

I will have a healthful body image and recognize signs of eating disorders.

Body Image

Body image is the perception that a person has of his or her body's appearance. Many Americans, including children and adolescents, are overly preoccupied and dissatisfied with their body image. Some people who are dissatisfied with their body image also have a distorted body image, focusing on the negative aspects of their bodies. Preoccupation with body image and distorted body image can lead to feelings of low self-worth and low self-esteem.

Sexual Identity

As young people mature and become aware of their body images, they will also become aware of sexual identity. As young people grow, they need to be encouraged to feel comfortable with the changes taking place in their bodies. Not being comfortable with sexual identity is linked with a dissatisfaction with body image, low-self esteem, and eating disorders. An **eating disorder** is a food-related dysfunction in which a person changes eating habits in a way that is harmful to the mind or body.

Anorexia Nervosa

Anorexia nervosa is an eating disorder characterized by self-starvation and a weight of 15 percent or more below normal. It is self-starvation. The person experiences unhealthful and extreme weight loss that affects the way the body functions, not only physically, but also mentally. Even after losing extreme amounts of weight, people with anorexia nervosa are convinced they are overweight. Food and weight become obsessions. Adolescent females are most apt to become obsessed with problems of weight and sexuality and thus have anorexia nervosa. People with anorexia nervosa need medical and psychological help. Extreme cases of anorexia nervosa can result in death due to malnutrition and starvation.

Bulimia

Bulimia is an eating disorder in which a person has uncontrollable urges to eat excessively and then to rid the body of the excess Calories. A person does this by various forms of purging, such as vomiting, abusing laxatives or diuretics, taking enemas, or exercising obsessively. Bulimia is known as the "secret eating disorder" because these individuals can hide their binge eating and purging habits from others. The binges often are tied to times of anger, loneliness, depression, or fear. Bulimia can lead to muscle spasms, digestive tract disorders, rotting teeth, fatigue, and heart palpitations. Both habits of binge eating and purging can cause damage to a person's health. Medical and psychological help are needed to treat bulimia.

Figure 10-1

Life Skills for Personal Health

1. I will be well-groomed.

2. I will care for my ears and eyes.

3. I will have regular checkups.

4. I will follow a dental health plan.

5. I will obtain adequate rest and sleep.

6. I will participate in movement and exercise.

7. I will follow guidelines to prevent injuries during exercise.

8. I will learn correct first aid procedures for exercise injuries.

9. I will achieve a desirable level of physical fitness.

10. I will improve my skill-related fitness.

Chapter 10

PERSONAL HEALTH

Personal Health is the area of health that focuses upon making a personal health management plan that includes being well-groomed, caring for the body, having regular checkups, following a dental health plan, obtaining adequate rest and sleep, and achieving a desirable level of physical fitness. The content in this chapter provides the health knowledge that is needed to teach young people important life skills for personal health (Figure 10-1).

I will be well-groomed.

Grooming

Grooming consists of taking good care of the body by following practices that help people look, smell, and feel their best. Good grooming practices require the regular cleansing of the body including the care of the skin, hair, nails, and feet, as well as wearing clean clothes. Good grooming practices help keep a physical body healthy by reducing the spread of germs from one part of the body to another part and from one person to another. Grooming practices also affect social and emotional well-being. Young people who are not well-groomed may be subjected to rejection and ostracism by their peers. This lowers feelings of self-worth. On the other hand,

being well-groomed and having a neat and clean appearance enhances self-confidence and fosters peer and adult acceptance.

Posture

Posture is the relative position of different parts of the body at rest or during movement. Good posture means that the head is directly in line with the shoulders, which are directly in line with the pelvis. Correct posture promotes optimum functioning of internal body organs. A person with poor posture is more likely to suffer back pain, neck pain, headaches, and other discomforts. When the spine is kept in alignment, a person is less likely to experience back discomfort or related problems. Posture may also indicate feelings of self-worth and self-confidence. Poor posture may be interpreted by other people as being unenthusiastic and having low self-esteem. Good posture may indicate self-confidence and positive self-esteem.

Maintaining Good Posture
Maintaining proper alignment is important as people age and have a natural tendency to slouch. Young people should be instructed to stand so that they can draw an imaginary line through their neck,

shoulders, lower back, pelvis and hip, knee, and ankle joints. In addition, they should be taught to sit so that the hips and back of the thighs support weight. When crossing legs, they should be encouraged to cross them at the ankle. Chairs that give support to the lower part of the back help keep good posture.

Poor posture is sometimes seen in tall children and adolescents who are self-conscious about their height who slouch to compensate. When poor posture is detected, the problem should be investigated to ensure that there is no developmental deformity. More is needed to correct poor posture than merely telling young people to stand or sit up straight. Instead, they should be encouraged to exercise regularly because good posture requires overall muscle strength to keep the skeleton supported and maintain alignment. What is needed are exercises that specifically strengthen the upper body (Pacelli, 1991). Sitting in one spot for much of the day can contribute to poor posture. Giving the back a chance to change position by getting up frequently to walk around or stretch can relieve the back strain that contributes to poor posture. Excess weight and chronic fatigue also are factors that contribute to poor posture.

Curvatures of the Spine Curvature of the spine accounts for a small proportion of the poor posture that is seen in young people. Screening programs in schools can help in detecting these conditions early. Regular exercise is often helpful for students with curvature of the spine. In severe cases, surgery is necessary.

Three types of curvatures of the spine are kyphosis, lordosis, and scoliosis. **Kyphosis** is an excessive rounding of the back. This curvature of the spine creates a humpback appearance with the shoulders rounded. **Lordosis** is a curvature of the spine that creates a "swayback" appearance. **Scoliosis** is lateral or S-shaped curvature of the spine that is found in approximately one in fifty people. Scoliosis is more common in females than males and occurs most frequently during the ages of ten to sixteen. Untreated scoliosis can lead to permanent disfigurement. Detection of scoliosis during the late elementary years or early adolescent years and appropriate referral and treatment often prevents the need for surgery. The most accurate method of determining scoliosis is an X-ray examination.

Care for the Skin

Skin is considered to be the largest organ in the body. The average-sized adult has seventeen square feet of skin. Skin protects the body from invasion of microbial agents and ultraviolet rays from the sun. It serves a sensory function by relaying messages from the outside world to the brain. Skin also helps to eliminate toxins and wastes from the body through perspiration. Within skin are millions of cells that make up nerve endings, blood vessels, and sweat glands. Because skin is a complex organ it requires good care. Important aspects of caring for skin are cleansing the skin, controlling body odor, controlling acne, and sun protection.

Cleansing the Skin and Nails One of the most important aspects of good skin care is keeping the skin clean. Cleansing the skin daily with soap and water helps remove bacteria, oil, perspiration, and dirt through a bath or shower. Hand and face washing should be done a few times a day. Soap cleans the skin more effectively than any other cleansing product. Some people react to soaps that are alkaline and can dry out and irritate skin. In such cases, it is wise to switch to a pH-balanced soap. Excessive washing or bathing can also dry out and irritate skin, especially in winter months. Care should also be taken to be sure that soap is thoroughly rinsed with adequate amounts from the skin after washing. People with oily skin may need to wash their skin more frequently than other individuals. Another part of correct grooming is having clean, trimmed fingernails and toenails. Nails that are dirty and broken are unattractive and unhealthy. Fingernails can collect dirt and bacteria. They should be cleaned and trimmed often.

Controlling Body Odor Controlling body odor is an important part of skin care. It is important to understand that perspiration or sweat has no odor. Body odor results when bacteria interact with perspiration. Therefore, an important aspect of controlling body odor is keeping the skin clean through washing. Washing helps reduce body odor by removing bacteria from the skin. Body odor may also be controlled by the use of deodorants and antiperspirants. Because the sweat glands become more active during puberty, control of body odor can be a problem for adolescents.

Controlling Acne Another important skin care problem for many adolescents is acne. Acne is also a problem for many adults. The psychological effects of acne are often severe because of the embarrassment that it causes. Although acne cannot be prevented or cured it can be controlled and minimized. The American Academy of Pediatrics recommends the following guidelines for teenagers in treating acne:

1. Wash skin two or three times per day with mild soap and water. Acne is not caused by dirt and excessive scrubbing will not improve it; often it worsens the condition.
2. Use a mild soap. Special acne soaps often are not necessary.
3. Gently massage soap into skin with clean fingers or a washcloth.
4. Use hot water to wash, cool water for rinsing.
5. Gently pat skin dry.
6. Avoid using hard soaps or abrasive soaps.
7. Use topical benzoyl peroxide in 5 percent strength gel. This is available without a doctor's prescription and available from drugstores and supermarkets. If after four to six weeks the acne isn't better, increase to a 10 percent strength gel.
8. If improvement is not seen after using the 10 percent strength gel, see a doctor. Doctors can prescribe stronger treatments and advise in proper use of these treatments.
9. Avoid touching and picking acne because these practices can irritate the acne and result in spreading to other areas of the body.
10. Use cosmetics sparingly, particularly those with oily creams can worsen acne. Oil-free or water-based cosmetics are best for individuals prone to acne.
11. Dietary restrictions are usually not necessary. Despite prevailing misconceptions, foods like chocolate, french fries, nuts, or cola drinks do not aggravate acne.

Protecting the Skin from the Sun

Although a sun tan is often associated with images of health, it actually accelerates the aging process. Overexposure to the sun can result in premature aging of the skin, cataracts, and skin cancer. Prolonged exposure to ultraviolet rays in tanning salons or under sun lamps also increases aging of the skin and the risk of developing skin cancer. One in six Americans will develop skin cancer and the incidence of skin cancer is increasing nearly 4 percent annually (Gormon, 1993). The rising incidence is believed to be linked to overexposure to the sun.

Protecting the skin from the sun includes avoiding prolonged exposure to the sun and staying away from tanning salons and sun lamps. In the summer, exposure to the sun should be limited during the hours of 10 a.m. and 3 p.m. When a person must be in direct sun, (s)he should wear lightweight, long-limbed clothing with a wide-brimmed hat and sunglasses to protect against the sun's rays. Sunscreens provide some protection from ultraviolet rays. While sunscreens appear to be effective in blocking ultraviolet B (UVB) rays that cause sunburns, many sunscreen products provide little protection against ultraviolet A (UVA) rays. Both UVB and UVA appear to cause premature aging and skin cancer. Therefore, sunscreen products that provide protection against both UVA and UVB rays should be selected. Unfortunately, sunscreen products are only rated according to the protection they provide against UVB rays. Sunscreen products are rated

according to the sunburn protection they provide; the higher the number the greater the protection. Individuals with fair skin who sunburn easily need a higher sun protection factor (SPF) than people with darker skin. Sunscreens should be applied in generous amounts and care should be taken to cover all skin areas exposed to the sun. Water-resistant sunscreens should be selected, however, sunscreens should be reapplied frequently during sun exposure because sweat and water can wash them away.

Care for the Hair

In addition to skin care, hair care is another important grooming need. Dirt and oils should be removed frequently for a healthful, shiny appearance. Washing the hair at least twice a week with shampoo will remove dirt and oil. Individuals who are active, perspire heavily, or have an oily scalp, may need to shampoo daily. Using a shampoo also helps to control dandruff. It is sometimes necessary to experiment with several types of shampoo to find the type best suited for a particular individual. Combs and brushes must be kept clean and clear of accumulated hair. Brushing hair daily helps keep it neat and clean. Brushing not only removes loose dirt but also gives hair a natural shine. Brushing wet hair may damage the hair shaft. A comb should be used on wet hair rather than a brush. Special care should be taken when blow drying or using heat on hair. The temperature should be set low when blow drying hair because too much heat can cause hair to become dry, brittle, and to have split ends. Split ends may also be caused by the overuse of chemicals, such as hair sprays or hair colorings, on the hair.

Care for the Feet

Wearing comfortable shoes of the correct size, washing feet daily, and keeping toenails cut straight across are practices that promote the health of the feet. If feet are not cared for, problems such as blisters, calluses, corns, and ingrown toenails may result. A **blister** is a sore that may be caused by irritation due to the foot rubbing against the shoe. When a blister develops, cover with an adhesive bandage or a light coating of petroleum jelly. If the blister breaks and releases fluid, clean the area with an antiseptic and cover with a sterile bandage. **Calluses** are extra layers of skin that form due to excess rubbing on the foot. When the source of rubbing is removed, a callus will generally heal itself. **Corns** are painful growths that can result from excess rubbing of the shoe against the foot. Special pads may be used to relieve pain, and over-the-counter medications often remove corns. If a corn persists, a physician should be consulted. An **ingrown toenail** is when a toenail grows into the skin. If swelling or infection occurs, medical help should be sought.

Life Skill #2

I will care for my ears and eyes.

Care for the Eyes

Eye problems can be detected by regular eye examinations. Young people ages five to fifteen should have their eyes examined every eighteen months to two years. From ages nineteen to forty, eye examinations are only needed if a person experiences symptoms of eye problems. From age forty to sixty, eye examinations should be every five years with glaucoma tests. After age sixty, eye examinations should be conducted every two or three years which include testing for glaucoma. Eye examinations for young people should include a review of health and vision history and tests for nearsightedness, farsightedness, astigmatism, color perception, lazy eye, crossed-eyes, eye coordination, depth perception, focusing ability, and general eye health. Eye examinations can be performed by either ophthalmologists or optometrists. **Ophthalmologists** are medical doctors who specialize in the medical and surgical care and treatment of the eye. These professionals can diagnose and treat all types of eye disorders, test

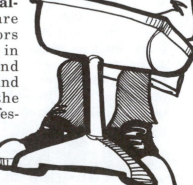

vision, and prescribe corrective lenses. **Optometrists** are specially trained health care practitioners who are trained in schools of optometry. These professionals are not medical doctors. They can test vision and prescribe corrective lenses. Technicians who fill prescriptions for glasses and contact lenses are **opticians**.

In addition to having eye examinations, eye care involves the wearing of protective glasses or goggles. Some sports, like racquetball and tennis, pose potential risk of injury to the eyes because of the possibility of being hit in the eye by a ball or racquet. Because chlorine and other substances in water can irritate the eyes, goggles will help protect the eyes when swimming. Safety goggles should also be used whenever working with harmful chemical substances such as bleaches, insecticides, and cleansing products that could splash into the eyes. Other suggestions for good eye care include the wearing of sunglasses and hats to protect the eyes from sunlight, avoiding eyestrain, and resting the eyes frequently. Young people should also be instructed about the potential dangers of playing with objects such as BB guns, slingshots, and fireworks that could cause damage to the eyes.

Refractive Errors The most common eye problems are refractive errors that impair visual acuity and are generally easy to correct. **Refractive errors** are defects in the shape of eye structures that result in the inability of images to focus on the retina and interfere with visual acuity. **Visual acuity** is sharpness of vision. Common refractive errors are myopia, astigmatism, hyperopia, and presbyopia. **Myopia** is a refractive error of the eye, usually due to an elongated-shaped eyeball, that causes nearsightedness (distant objects are fuzzy). **Astigmatism** is irregular curvature of the cornea that results in blurred vision. **Hyperopia** is a refractive error that results in farsightedness (close-up vision is blurred). **Presbyopia** is an impaired ability to change focus as a result of weakened eye muscles and rigidity of the lens. Presbyopia is a condition that develops with age that causes difficulty with reading (farsightedness).

Correcting Refractive Errors All the focusing problems that result from refractive errors can generally be remedied with corrective lenses. About half of the population wears some form of corrective lenses, either eyeglasses or contact lenses (Health Letter Associates, 1991). Contact lens wearers who notice any unusual redness, blurring or sudden change in vision, or persistent pain in or around an eye, should remove the lenses and consult their optometrist or ophthalmologist.

Eye Conditions While refractive errors are the most common problems that affect the eyes, there are other important eye conditions. **Conjunctivitis** is an inflammation of the membrane lining the eyelids and covering the eyeball (conjunctiva). Commonly known as "pinkeye," conjunctivitis is a highly contagious condition most often caused by bacterial infection. However, it can also be caused by allergies, certain drugs, or from irritation from foreign objects. Conjunctivitis is rarely serious unless infection progresses to the deeper tissues of the eye, in which case, vision may be affected. Recognition of this condition is most often through observation of redness and swelling of the eyes along with significant tearing. A discharge may also be present. Young people with conjunctivitis may complain of a "gritty" feeling in the eyes and that their eyelids stick together upon waking from sleep. Two eye conditions that develop in older adults are glaucoma and cataracts. **Glaucoma** is a disease of the eyes marked by increased pressure within the eyeball that can ultimately damage the optic nerve. Glaucoma affects two million Americans (Health Letter Associates, 1991). Although it cannot be prevented, if it is detected early enough it can be treated by surgery or laser treatment. As a result, blindness may be averted. A **cataract** is clouding of the lens of the eye that obstructs vision and can lead to blindness.

Eye Injuries If dirt or a small object is in the eye, the eye should not be rubbed as this may damage the linings of the eye. By lifting the upper lid over the lower lid, the lashes can brush the object off the inside of the upper eyelid. Blinking can also be helpful in removing small particles from the eye. If these techniques are unsuccessful, the eye should be kept closed and medical help should be obtained. The prompt and correct care of a serious eye injury can prevent the loss of sight. Whenever an eye is injured, medical help should be sought as soon as possible. There are some general guidelines to follow in the case of eye injuries. When there is a blow to the eye, an ice cold compress should be immediately applied and an ophthalmologist should be consulted. Both eyes should be bandaged in the case of cuts of the eye and/or lids or when an object has become imbedded in an eye. This will minimize eye movement and further damage to the eye. When there is a serious injury to the eye, there should be no attempts to wash the eye or remove objects stuck in the eye. If chemicals are splashed into the eye, the eye should be immediately flushed with water and the eye should not be bandaged.

Care for the Ears

Care of the ears is important. The outer ear should be frequently cleaned with a soft, clean washcloth. Objects of any size, including cotton-tipped swabs, should never be inserted into the ear because these objects might puncture the eardrum. A puncture would allow dirt or microorganisms to get into the ear and cause infection. Proper cleansing of the outer ear also helps avert wax accumulation and buildup in the ear canal. After bathing or swimming, the ears should be thoroughly and gently dried with the corner of a clean towel. The wearing of earplugs prevents water from entering into the ear and can help prevent ear infections such as swimmer's ear. **Swimmer's ear** is painful and itchy bacterial infection of the external ear canal that develops after long periods of swimming or bathing. If an infection develops in the ear, scratching or inserting cotton swabs into the ear will only aggravate the condition. A physician should be consulted whenever an ear becomes infected because infections of the middle ear can affect hearing.

Avoiding loud noises is a critical part of ear care. Loud noises can cause permanent loss of hearing. The wearing of ear plugs andother ear protection devices can protect the hearing of people who work around loud equipment. Hearing can also be protected by not exposing the ears to loud music. Special care should be taken to not play walkabout stereos and "boom boxes" at loud levels because these devices can be played at levels that greatly exceed safety levels for noise. People who must be exposed to high noise levels at work, should give their ears a break from noise during their leisure time.

Hearing Loss Hearing loss ranges from mild to profound deafness. There many causes of hearing loss. Some causes of hearing loss occur very early in life, such as being prenatally exposed to drugs or infection, being born prematurely, experiencing respiratory distress upon birth, having a birth defect, or being infected with certain viral diseases early in life. Middle ear infections, high fevers, injuries, and exposure to loud music also can lead to hearing loss. Severe middle ear infections may cause an eardrum to rupture and lead to hearing loss.

Mild or moderate hearing impairment can often be detected by observation. The signs of hearing loss in young people include inattentiveness, turning the head to hear, talking loudly or in monotone, failure to respond to questions, frowning when trying to hear, or reports of dizziness, ringing in ears, or earache.

Hearing examinations are necessary to confirm hearing loss. The most frequently used test for hearing loss is audiometer testing. The **audiometer** is a machine that assesses the range of sounds that a person can hear at various frequencies and intensities. Hearing loss is classified as either conductive or sensioneural. **Conductive hearing loss** is faulty transportation of sound from the outer to the inner ear. The causes of conductive hearing loss are excessive ear wax buildup, damage or malformation of ear structures due to injury, or middle ear infection. Hearing aids are most often used to remedy conductive hearing loss and surgery is often necessary to alleviate situations where damaged or malformed ear structures result in conductive hearing loss. **Sensioneural hearing loss** is a disorder in which sounds that reach the inner ear fail to be transmitted to the brain because of damage to the structures within the inner ear or to the acoustic nerve which connects the inner ear to the brain. Sensioneural hearing loss also is known as perception deafness. Frequently, little can be done to correct this type of hearing loss. However, recent advances have been made in the development of electrical implants known as cochlear implants that sometimes allow people to hear some sounds.

I will have regular checkups.

Physical Exams

It is advisable for people to have checkups from a physician every year or two between the ages of two and twenty. Adults who have special health conditions such as a chronic disease or a pregnancy should schedule regular checkups with their physician. For other adults, annual physical examinations are not usually recommended. However, if any unusual or abnormal symptoms appear, a person should promptly visit a physician. Prompt, medical care means early diagnosis and treatment. A **symptom** is a change in a body function from a normal pattern. A symptom may be an indication of a health problem. Some symptoms, such as constant headaches, interfere with usual daily routines. A person may not feel like eating or exercising properly. The headaches may interfere with sleep. In such cases, a person should seek help from a physician to relieve the symptoms and/or the health problem that is causing the symptoms. Symptoms that require medical attention include:

- shortness of breath after mild activity;
- loss of appetite for no obvious reason;
- cold symptoms that last more than a week;
- blood in urine or bowel movement;
- blood coughed up;
- a constant cough;
- fever of 100 degrees F (37.7 degrees C) or higher for more than one day;
- swelling, stiffness, or aching in the joints;
- severe pain in any body part;
- frequent or painful urination;
- sudden weight gain or loss;
- dizziness or fainting;
- any warning signs of cancer;
- any warning signs of heart attack or stroke.

A first visit to a physician includes completing a health history. A **health history** consists of a questionnaire that gathers information about lifestyle, past health conditions, past medical care, allergies and drug sensitivities, and family health history. The health history is an important tool the physician uses to provide the best possible health care. With every appointment, a person may be asked to update his/her health history. Knowing one's health history and family health history provides important insight into the type of care that a person should be receiving.

The extent of a physical examination can vary. The following are typically checked during a physical examination: height, weight, body temperature, pulse rate, body temperature, respiratory rate, blood pressure, general appearance, eyes, ears, nose, oral cavity, neck, lungs, heart, breasts, lymph nodes, back, abdomen, sex organs, rectum, legs, feet, bones and joints, and reflexes. A physical examination may also include the following laboratory tests: urinalysis, blood cell count, blood chemistry, tests for syphilis and tuberculosis, and Pap smear. After the physical examination, the physician will discuss the results of the tests with the patient. If the tests reveal problems, the physician will recommend appropriate treatments. This is an important part of personal health care. Patients need to feel comfortable to ask questions. This is an optimal time to make a plan to achieve and maintain optimum health.

Screening Tests

Healthy individuals should receive certain screening tests for particular diseases at regular intervals. People with certain lifestyles, occupations, or family histories may require more frequent screening tests than the number recommended for the general population. People who are eighteen years of age and older should have their blood pressure and total cholesterol level checked every one to three years. In addition, females should have an annual pelvic exam and breast exam. Females should also have a Pap smear performed every one to three years. The **Pap smear** is a test to detect abnormal changes in the cells of the cervix and thus to prevent the development of cervical cancer. Females should have a mammogram at about age thirty-five and from age forty and up they should have an annual mammogram. A **mammogram** is a low-dose X-ray used to detect breast cancer.

Personal Health

It is recommended that people who are forty and over have a digital rectal exam annually. A **digital rectal exam** is an examination of the lower bowel and, in men, the prostate, in which a physician inserts a gloved finger into the anal opening. This exam is used to detect rectal cancer and enlargement of the prostate gland in men. Screening tests for visual acuity, glaucoma, and hearing should also be performed every three years after age forty until age sixty-five. After age sixty-five, these tests should be performed every year. People who are fifty and over should have a proctosigmoidoscopy and fecal occult blood test. A **proctosigmoidoscopy** is a visual inspection of the colon and rectum by use of a fiber-optic tube that detects cancer of the colon and rectum. The **fecal occult blood test** checks for blood in feces. The presence of blood in the feces is a possible indicator of colon and rectal cancer.

Childhood Immunizations

An important part of personal health care is making sure that all childhood immunizations are received. Immunizations can be obtained from personal physicians and often (at reduced cost) from local public health clinics. **Childhood immunizations** include the following shots: DPT, MMR, HiB, OPV, and Hepatitis B. **DPT** is a combination inoculation against tetanus, diphtheria, and pertussis (whooping cough). It is given at two, four, six, and fifteen to eighteen months, with a booster between four and six years. **HiB** immunizes against the *Hemophilus influenza type B*, which is the leading cause of bacterial meningitis. Depending on the brand of vaccine, HiB is given in either three or four doses by the time a child is twelve to eighteen months old. It has recently been combined with the DPT vaccine to reduce the number of shots needed. **MMR** immunizes against measles, mumps, and rubella (German measles) and is given in two doses, at fifteen months and again between four and six years or before junior high or middle school. **OPV** stands for oral polio vaccine and it should be given in a series of three oral-vaccine doses two, four, and fifteen to eighteen months, and again between four and six years. **Hepatitis B vaccine** should be given in a shot at birth, another one to two months, and a third at six to eighteen months. Hepatitis vaccine has been recommended for all newborns only since 1992.

I will follow a dental health plan.

Dental health problems can usually be avoided by following a dental health plan. A **dental health plan** is a plan for taking care of the teeth and gums that includes frequent brushing and flossing, reduction of cavity-promoting foods, avoidance of tobacco, protecting the teeth from injury, regular dental checkups, and cleaning of the teeth by a dental hygienist.

Types of Teeth

At about six months of age, teeth begin to appear in the mouth of babies and by age two a complete set of teeth known as "baby teeth" is present. These teeth will be replaced by thirty-two permanent teeth. There are four different types of permanent teeth. **Incisors** are the eight teeth in the front and center of the mouth that have a flat, sharp edge that cuts up food. **Cuspids** are the four teeth in the corners of the mouth that have a long, heavy root and a pointed cusp that tears food. **Bicuspids** are the eight teeth in back of the cuspids with two cusps and one or two roots that tear and crush food. **Molars** are the twelve teeth in the back of the mouth with several cusps and two or three roots that grind food.

Dental Problems

Dental emergencies are injuries or disorders of the teeth or gums that require immediate treatment because of severe pain and/or because delay could lead to further complications. Universal precautions should be followed for dental emergencies. **Knocked-out teeth** are teeth that have been knocked out of their sockets. If a tooth does get knocked out, the tooth should not be washed and should be placed in a cup of milk or water if milk is not available. See a dentist immediately as the sooner the tooth is placed back inside the socket, the better the chance it can be saved. With proper treatment, most knocked-out teeth can be saved. A **toothache** is pain that comes from a tooth or from the gums. A toothache may be the sign of one of the following dental disorders. A common cause of dental disorders is the formation of plaque. **Plaque** is a rough, sticky coating on the teeth that consists of saliva, bacteria, and food debris. It is the chief cause of tooth decay. Daily toothbrushing and flossing help remove plaque. **Tartar buildup** occurs when plaque is not removed and it hardens. Plaque formation and tartar buildup lead to dental caries. **Dental caries** are areas of tooth decay (cavities). Dental caries are the result of acids produced by bacteria attacking and dissolving the enamel and dentin of the tooth. It takes about twenty-four hours for the plaque to buildup to a sufficient amount to begin causing damage to teeth. A **filling** is the material that a dentist uses to repair the cavity of a tooth. Sometimes tooth decay progresses into the pulp of the tooth. The **pulp** is the living tissue within a tooth The pulp can become damaged irreversibly or die. If this occurs, a root canal must be performed by a dentist. A **root canal** is a dental procedure performed to save a tooth in which the pulp has died or become untreatably diseased.

Plaque formation and acid production by bacteria in the plaque can also lead to peridontal or gum disease, the main cause of tooth loss in adults. **Periodontal disease** is a disease of the gums and other tissues that support the teeth. A high proportion of people over forty have some periodontal disease. The disease often begins in young people with plaque or calculus buildup when brushing and flossing are neglected.

The early stage of peridontal disease is called gingivitis. **Gingivitis** is an inflammation that often results in redness, swelling, and bleeding of the gums. If gingivitis is not treated, the disease usually progresses. The gums pull away from the teeth, forming pockets between the teeth and gums. Plaque, calculus, and pus collect in the pockets causing bad breath and infection. Food particles are trapped in the pockets and begin to decay. The supporting bones and ligaments that connect the root of the tooth to the bone are destroyed. The teeth loosen and may fall out. If this occurs, a bridge may be needed. A **bridge** is a partial denture or replacement that is used to take the place of one or more teeth. The natural teeth that surround the bridge support it. A complete **denture** is a full set of false teeth.

Malocclusion Malocclusion is the abnormal fitting together of teeth when the jaws are closed. Malocclusion may be caused by heredity, by jaw size, from early loss of primary teeth, or from injury to the teeth. When teeth do not fit together properly, extra stress is placed on the jaw. The teeth grind together unnecessarily and plaque is more likely to collect and cause cavities. Malocclusion is corrected by removing teeth or applying braces. **Braces** are devices that are cemented or bonded to the teeth and wired together to bring the teeth into correct alignment. Young people wear braces from eighteen to twenty-four months. Adolescents and adults usually wear them longer. After the braces are removed, a retainer is usually worn. A **retainer** is a plastic device with wires that keeps the teeth from moving back to their original places.

Care for the Teeth and Gums

Plaque formation is inhibited by frequent and proper brushing and flossing. Teeth should be brushed after every meal and should be flossed every day. Flossing once a day, preferably at bedtime, is necessary because the plaque and food that is between teeth cannot be reached by brushing alone. Proper brushing and flossing are habits that can be established early in life. The use of a soft-bristled toothbrush and fluoridated toothpaste is the best defense against dental decay. By age nine, most children have the cognitive and motor skills to assume total responsibility for brushing and flossing. Children younger than this require assistance and guidance because they lack the fine motor control to brush and floss their teeth thoroughly. Because adolescence is the time during which dental cavities are most likely to occur, adolescents especially need to practice good brushing and flossing practices.

A visit to a dentist or dental hygienist twice a year for checkups and cleaning is a good dental health practice. These visits should be made even if a person does not have any symptoms of dental problems or discomfort. These dental health professionals often spot problems before they become painful or apparent. The early treatment of dental problems is usually less painful, traumatic, and expensive than problems that are allowed to fully develop. Cleaning of the teeth by a dental hygienist is also an important part of dental care that should be performed at least twice a year. Certain practices carry the risk of causing damage to the teeth or structures in the mouth. Risky practices include: smoking cigarettes, chewing tobacco, or using oral snuff; chewing on ice and other hard objects; and failing to protect the teeth from injury. To maintain good oral health these practices should be avoided. Some suggestions for protecting the teeth from injury are the wearing of protective mouthguards when participating in sports and wearing safety belts while traveling in motor vehicles.

Life Skill #5

I will obtain adequate rest and sleep.

To keep mentally alert, maintain a good disposition, stay physically well, and maintain proper growth, adequate rest and sleep are essential. **Rest** refers to periods of relaxation. Rest can be a conscious or unconscious state. **Sleep** is a state of profound relaxation during which the eyes are closed and there is little movement or consciousness. Rest and sleep help the body rebuild itself and reenergize. While asleep, several changes occur in the body. Heart rate slows by about ten to fifteen beats per minute, blood pressure decreases, and fewer breaths per minute are taken. Muscles lose tension during sleep. Growth hormone is released into the blood so that growth occurs during rest and sleep. There are two kinds of sleep. **Rapid eye movement (REM) sleep** is the period of sleep during which the most vivid and virtually all dreaming occurs that is characterized by rapid eye movements behind closed eyelids. Only about one-fourth of a night's sleep is spent in REM sleep, the rest is nonrapid eye movement sleep. **Nonrapid eye movement (NREM) sleep** is the period of sleep in which the eyes are relaxed. NREM sleep can range from very light sleep to very deep sleep.

Getting Adequate Sleep

Young people who are not getting enough sleep lack the vitality and concentration needed to perform well in school and other pursuits. Lack of sleep also increases susceptibility to minor illnesses and increases the potential for accidents. The amount of sleep needed varies from person to person according to activity levels and other unknown factors. The amount of sleep usually decreases with age. Infants spend most of their time sleeping. First and second graders usually sleep for eleven to twelve hours; sixth graders may average nine or ten hours. Adolescents often require extra sleep and rest due to their rapid physical growth and in order to deal with the demands of a busy lifestyle. Adolescents will usually need nine or ten hours of sleep. Most adults need about eight hours of sleep, but the range of normal sleep for adults ranges from five to ten hours. Feeling rested and energetic during the day is a good sign that a person has had enough sleep. However, too much sleep can make a person feel sluggish, so more is not always better.

Adequate sleep can be encouraged by establishing a regular bedtime and time for getting up in the morning. Quiet activities such as reading, taking a warm bath, or listening to relaxing music can help the transition between wakefulness and sleep. Nightly rituals such as brushing teeth, setting the alarm clock, and organizing materials needed for the next day can facilitate sleepiness. Napping during the day is a good way of catching up on sleep, but sometimes this practice makes it hard to fall asleep at night. Having a quiet and comfortable place to sleep is necessary for a good night's sleep. A medium-hard mattress for the bed supports a person's back and makes it easier to follow asleep and sleep restfully. Certain substances, when taken into the body make falling to sleep difficult. Excessive liquid intake is disruptive to sleep because of the need to get up and empty the bladder. Caffeinated beverages should be avoided in the evening because they can induce wakefulness. By suppressing rapid eye movement (REM) sleep, alcoholic beverages and some sleeping medications disrupt normal sleep stages causing sleep to not be restful. The nicotine in cigarettes is a stimulant and can make falling to sleep difficult. Eating large amounts of food just before going to bed can interfere with sleep. Occasionally not being able to fall asleep is normal. But, failure to fall asleep may be insomnia. **Insomnia** is when the inability to get to sleep becomes a pattern. Insomnia has many causes—stress being the leading cause. People with insomnia should seek medical help for the condition. Stress reactions in young

244

people are sometimes linked to sleeping problems or insomnia.

Ways to Relax and Rest

Being able to relax and rest is important in counteracting physical and mental fatigue and in coping with stress. One way to relax and rest is for a person to take time for the things (s)he enjoys doing. Participating in enjoyable activities such as hobbies, interests, and entertainment can be rejuvenating. By providing a diversion away from work, school, and other responsibilities these activities promote relaxation and can be restful. Certain activities also promote relaxation by providing a physical outlet for stress such as playing sports, exercising, and going for a walk.

Life Skill #6

I will participate in movement and exercise.

Movement and exercise contributes to physical fitness. **Physical fitness** is the condition of the body as a result of participating in exercises that promote muscular strength, muscular endurance, flexibility, cardiovascular endurance, and a healthful percentage of body fat. A person who has achieved a level of muscular strength, muscular endurance, flexibility, and cardiovascular endurance is **physically fit**. Physical fitness is achieved by the regular movement of muscles through a variety of exercises. Maintaining physical fitness is a lifelong process and should always be part of a healful lifestyle. People with disabilities can also reach a measure of physical fitness by doing exercises appropriate for their conditions. There are many benefits of being physically fit.

Benefits of Physical Fitness

There are numerous health benefits derived from obtaining a desirable level of physical fitness. Being physically fit:

1. *Promotes cardiovascular health.* There are numerous ways in which being physically fit can promote cardiovascular health. When a person exercises, the heart muscle becomes stronger. This has a positive effect on cardiac output. **Cardiac output** is the amount of blood pumped by the heart to the body each minute. Another way of saying this is, cardiac output is equal to the heart rate multiplied by stroke volume. **Heart rate** is the number of times that the heart beats each minute forcing blood into the arteries. **Stroke volume** is the amount of blood the heart pumps with each beat. To become physically fit, a person engages in exercises that promote cardiovascular endurance. These exercises strengthen the heart muscle enabling the heart to pump more blood with each beat. This lowers resting heart rate and allows the heart an opportunity to rest between beats. This is accompanied by a reduction in blood pressure which means there is less wear and tear on artery walls. Exercises that promote cardiovascular endurance have an additional benefit in promoting cardiovascular health. Participating in these exercises for at least twenty minutes, three days per week, increases the ratio of high-density lipoproteins in the bloodstream to low-density lipoproteins in the bloodstream. **Lipoproteins** are fats in the bloodstream. **High-density lipoproteins** or **HDLs** are fats that transport excess cholesterol to the liver for removal from the body. **Low-density lipoproteins** are fats that form deposits on the artery walls and contribute to the development of atherosclerosis.

2. *Reduces the incidence of cancer.* Many people are aware of the health benefits of exercise with regard to cardiovascular disease while not as many are aware of the health benefits with regard to cancer. One of the risk factors for cancer is being overweight. People who exercise regularly are better able to control their weight. Regular exercise also benefits people who have or have had cancer. Researchers have found that people undergoing treatment for cancer were better able to tolerate their treatment and maintained a more optimistic attitude if they were involved

in an exercise program. Regular exercise also benefitted those patients who had surgery and needed to regain muscular strength. Exercising with others also was beneficial as it provided for fellowship and support while simultaneously deriving health benefits.

3. *Helps to control the effects of stress.* Participating in an exercise program for physical fitness helps reduce the harmful effects of stress. Regular exercise helps reduce stress by generating overall feelings of well-being and by using the adrenaline that was secreted into the bloodstream during the stress response. After a person participates in an exercise program for at least twenty-five minutes, three times per week for seven to ten weeks, his or her body will release beta-endorphins during exercise and continue to release these substances for ninety minutes following completion of exercise. **Beta-endorphins** are substances produced in the brain that help reduce pain and create a feeling of well-being. These substances have been linked to the "runner's high" that some runners report having after running at a steady pace for twenty-five minutes or more.

4. *Promotes weight management.* Participating in an exercise program for fitness helps with weight management in a number of ways. The **energy equation** states that Caloric intake needs to equal Caloric expenditure for weight maintenance. With regard to children and adolescents, overweight has been linked to inactivity rather than overeating. A regular program of exercise changes the energy equation. During exercise, more Calories are expended. It is also possible that the metabolic rate continues to be increased for up to six hours following exercise. People who exercise regularly tend to eat less. Regular exercise also affects body composition by decreasing the percentage of body fat and increasing the amount of lean tissue. A person has more muscle tone and looks trimmer.

5. *Improves the strength and condition of the bones, muscles, and joints.* Participating in an exercise program for fitness improves the strength and condition of bones, muscles, and joints. The weight bearing bones become more dense as a result of regular exercise. As a person

ages, (s)he is less likely to develop osteoporosis. **Osteoporosis** is a disease in which the bones become brittle and break easily. Regular exercise improves the strength and condition of the muscles. People with strong muscles are less likely to become injured when lifting, pulling, or pushing objects. They are more likely to maintain healthful sitting, standing, and walking posture and they are less vulnerable to back pain as they age. The joints also benefit from regular exercise. **Osteoarthritis** is a condition in which there is erosion in the moveable parts of a joint. Regular exercise in which the joints are moved through the full range of motion reduces the effects of this condition in old age.

Participating in Physical Activity

Young people are often inactive and passive about physical activity as a result of the dramatic increase in television viewing and video games, combined with budgetary cutbacks in recreation and physical education programs in schools. Also, many young people are kept indoors after school and during summers because their neighborhoods are not safe or they have working parents who want to know where their children are. Almost half of young people from low-income families do not participate in any extracurricular activities (Brodkin, 1993). Children find great enjoyment moving, climbing, jumping, and running and seem to have boundless energy. However, children have largely become socialized and reinforced into quiet, sedentary behavior when restricted by adults who want them quiet, "out of trouble," or in front of the television. By the time that young people reach high school, the spontaneous expression of physical activity has often been curtailed (Glover and Shepherd, 1989). Despite the barriers of participating in physical activity, there are many ways in which adults can encourage physical activity. Most importantly, adults should be good role models for young people of a physically active lifestyle. In addition, adults can encourage young people to participate in the organized sports and dance activities that are offered within a community. Because many community youth sports and exercise programs rely on volunteers, adults can volunteer as coaches and youth leaders. On a more informal basis, adults can organize the playing of games with young people in neighborhoods, schools, and other settings.

Physical education classes are an important vehicle for improving the fitness of young people. Unfortunately, not all school districts provide daily physical education. Adults should be advocates for daily physical education. In addition, physical education classes should focus on lifetime sports. **Lifetime sports** include sports activities that can be continued as young people grow older. Some examples of lifetime sports are swimming, bicycling, cross-country skiing, and playing tennis.

Types of Exercises

There are different types of exercises that can be used when making a physical fitness plan. A person can choose from a variety of aerobic, anaerobic, isokinetic, isometric, and isotonic exercises. An **aerobic exercise** is one in which oxygen is required continually for an extended period of time. These exercises must be performed at target heart rate for at least twenty minutes, at least three times per week. An **anaerobic exercise** is one in which the body demands more oxygen than is available and a person begins to pant for air. Playing basketball, running sprints,

playing soccer, and playing tag are examples of anaerobic exercises. An **isometric exercise** is one in which a muscle is tightened for about five to six seconds and there is no body movement. Pushing against a wall would be an example. An **isokinetic exercise** is one in which a weight is moved through a full range of motion. The exercise machines at health centers and in training rooms provide for isokinetic exercise. An **isotonic exercise** is one in which there is a muscle contraction and a movement of body parts. Lifting weights and pushups are examples of isotonic exercise.

Life Skill #7

I will follow guidelines to prevent injuries during exercise.

Training Principles

Training principles are guidelines to follow to derive the maximum benefits from an exercise plan and to prevent injuries. The **principle of warming up** involves three to five minutes of light exercise to gradually begin increased blood flow to prepare joints and muscles for harder exercise. The **principle of cooling down** involves three to five minutes of reduced exercise to slow the heart beat rate and body temperature down and to return normal blood flow to the heart. The **principle of specificity** involves selecting a specific exercise or activity to provide a specific benefit. The **principle of overload** involves increasing activity levels to develop an increased fitness level. The **principle of progression** involves planning a fitness program in which the intensity and duration of exercise are gradually increased. The **principle of frequency** involves exercising frequently enough to derive the desired benefits.

Special Considerations While Exercising

Special considerations must be taken when exercising in certain environmental and weather conditions in order to avoid injury and prevent illness. Exercising in hot weather requires the circulatory system to shift substantial quantities of blood to the skin. This allows heat to be released in the form of sweat. The skin and blood circulating near the skin is cooled as a result. The need to cool the body places an increased demand upon an exercising body because the muscles require large quantities of blood in order to persist in the activity. Because the body loses water rapidly in the form of sweat (as much as one to three quarts an hour), water needs to be replaced. The loss of body fluids is a serious health hazard to people who exercise strenuously in hot weather. Loss of body fluids can lead to muscle cramping, heat exhaustion, and heat stroke. To avoid heat-related injuries and illness: exercise at times of the day when the temperature is lowest, drink fluids before exercise and during prolonged exercise, avoid highly vigorous activity on extremely hot and humid days, wear clothing that allows for the circulation of air around the body, and slow down or cease any exercise if there is any dizziness, disorientation, or muscle weakness.

The most important consideration in exercising in cold weather is being properly clothed. Failure to consider the wind-chill factor can place a person who is exercising in a situation in which (s)he is ill-prepared for the cold. However, overdressing leads to excessive sweating and severe perspiration can lead to chilling. To avoid this from happening, a person who is exercising should dress in layers of clothing. The first layer should be made of a material such as polypropylene or thermax which takes moisture away from the skin. Over this layer should be a layer of dacron or polyester fleece which serves as a good insulator, even if it becomes wet. On the top should be a windbreaker, made from a waterproofing material that keeps moisture out but allows perspiration to filter out. Gloves and hats can help protect the fingers and ears.

Safety Precautions

Exercise-related injuries can plague people who engage in exercise activities. Many of these activities can be avoided by adhering to the following suggestions. Wear properly fitting equipment and equipment designed to prevent sports-related injuries (for example, mouthguards, protective helmets, knee and elbow pads). Wear shoes designed for the particular activity. Warmup up sufficiently and include some stretching before engaging in the activity. Also, include a cool-down after the activity. Be aware of the safety rules for specific activities (e.g., walking and running, bicycling, swimming and diving).

Life Skill #8

I will learn correct first aid procedures for exercise injuries.

The most common conditions and injuries that accompany exercise and sport programs include: athlete's foot, blisters, bruises, joint injuries, muscle cramps, muscle strain, side aches, sprains, and stress fractures. **Athlete's foot** is a fungal infection that grows between the toes when feet are not kept dry. It can be treated with a powder or ointment that kills the fungus. **Blisters** are an accumulation of fluid between the layers of the skin that are usually caused from friction from poorly fitting shoes or improper use of equipment. Small blisters should be covered and a first aid cream applied. Large blisters should be lanced by a physician and covered. **Bruises** are discolorations from hemorrhaging resulting from blows to the muscles or bones. Applying ice helps reduce bleeding and swelling. **Joint injuries** are injuries to the tissues that surround the joints. Poorly fitting shoes and jarring during exercise contribute to joint injuries. Applications of ice and a period of rest are recommended. **Muscle cramps** are sharp pains that occur when muscles contract involuntarily usually because muscles have not been stretched before hard exercise. Stretching and massaging the muscle can alleviate the soreness. **Muscle strain** is injury and hemorrhaging in muscle tendons that is accompanied by a loss of muscular strength. Applying ice, stretching, and resting the muscle from hard exercise are recommended. **Side aches** are dull sharp pains in the side that occur when there has been inadequate warmup. Because side aches indicate too much too soon, slowing or taking a break is helpful. **Sprains** are injuries to ligaments that usually occur from twisting particularly the knees and ankles. Applying ice and resting are recommended. **Stress fractures** are hairline breaks in a bone caused by undue stress on or a blow to a bone. Stress fractures can be serious, especially if the fracture is through a large segment of the bone. But often, the fracture is not detectable on an X-ray. Some runners suffer stress fractures to bones in the leg or foot due to pounding on the bones caused by running. The treatment for stress fractures depends on the severity and the area that is affected. Sometimes a cast is placed around the injured body part.

Life Skill #9

I will achieve a desirable level of physical fitness.

Components of Physical Fitness

The components of physical fitness are:

1. *Muscular strength*. **Muscular strength** is the amount of force the muscles can exert against resistance. When muscles are used regularly, they become strong. Muscles help in lifting, pulling, jumping, twisting, turning, and bending. Having muscular strength can keep a person from being easily fatigued. It can keep muscles from becoming sore or injured when doing things like shoveling snow or mowing the lawn. Strong muscles help in standing, sitting, and walking easily. When a person has strong abdominal and back muscles, (s)he is less likely to have lower back pain. Muscular strength improves performance in sports. Individuals are able to throw a softball farther and hit a tennis ball harder and with more control when muscles are strong. There is a difference in muscle size in males and females. Even if size, weight, and activity were equal, females would not develop as much muscle mass as males.

2. *Muscular endurance*. **Muscular endurance** is the ability to use muscles for an extended period of time. When a person has muscular endurance, the muscles are able to perform repeated movements for long periods of time without becoming tired. Many daily activities as well as many sports activities require muscular endurance. Carrying a heavy load of books home from school requires muscular strength to lift the books from a desk, but walking home from school and continuing to carry the books uses muscular endurance to hold the books. Muscular endurance also helps to maintain correct posture. Muscular endurance is important in many sports. To repeatedly hit a tennis ball, swing a golf club, or roll a bowling ball, muscular endurance is needed. This is the reason arm and shoulder muscles may become tired when first practicing these sports. Muscular endurance is also needed to hike, ride a bicycle, or swim long distances.

3. *Flexibility*. **Flexibility** is the ability to bend and move the joints through a full range of motion. When a body is flexible, it does not get stiff easily. Flexibility makes it less likely to injure muscles or have lower back pain. Inactive people are less flexible than people who enjoy a variety of activities in which movement is required. Active people stretch their muscles more than inactive people. If most of the day is spent sitting, muscles connected to the knee, hip, and elbow joints begin to shorten. To remain flexible the muscles must be stretched. Many fitness experts claim that stretching for twenty minutes a day helps prevent the stiffness that accompanies aging. Flexibility is important in many sports. A gymnast shows flexibility as (s)he moves through a range of motion. A drum major shows flexibility twirling a baton, reaching, and bending.

4. *Cardiovascular endurance*. **Cardiovascular endurance** is the ability to do activities which require increased oxygen intake for extended periods of time.

Examples of activities for which individuals need cardiovascular endurance include: taking a long bike trip or hike, swimming several laps in a pool, and walk up and down stairs for an extended length of time. The ability to gain cardiovascular endurance depends on the frequency, intensity, and length of time spent in training. It also depends on the condition of the body and heredity.

5. *Healthful body composition.* The body is made up of two types of tissues–fat tissue and lean tissue. **Body composition** is the percentage of fat tissue and lean tissue in the body. As a person becomes physically fit, the ratio changes. The percentage of fat tissue decreases and the percentage of lean tissue increases. **Healthful body composition** is a high ratio of lean tissue to fat tissue. The body uses fat tissue every day. Fat is used as the body stores and uses nutrients. Everyone has fat stored beneath the skin and around the internal organs. The number of fat cells a person has is determined at a very young age. Fat cells can become smaller, but they cannot be lost. Females have more stored fat in their bodies than males. The total percentage of body weight that is fat is usually 16 to 19 percent for males and 22 to 25 percent for females.

Muscles, bones, cartilage, connective tissue, nerves, skin, and internal organs are lean tissue. The percentage of body weight that is lean tissue varies. The amount of muscle and size of the bones are factors that most greatly influence the percentage of the body that is lean tissue. As many people age, their level of physical activity decreases. By using less energy, muscle tissue decreases and a larger percentage of body weight becomes fat. Heredity influences body composition, the size of bones, and muscle structure. The type and frequency of exercise also influences body composition. When exercising to develop cardiovascular endurance and become physically fit, the ratio of fat tissue and lean tissue changes. The percentage of fat tissue decreases and the percentage of lean tissue increases. For example, marathon runners may have only 6 to 10 percent fat tissue.

Exercises That Promote Physical Fitness

There are a variety of exercises and physical activities that promote fitness. Aerobic exercises promote cardiovascular endurance because they require a continuous use of oxygen over an extended period of time. This usually means at least 15 to 30 minutes of continuous exercise. Some examples of aerobic exercise include aerobic dancing, distance running and jogging, bicycling at a steady pace, distance swimming, and speed walking. Aerobic exercises also help in developing some flexibility and muscular strength. In addition, aerobic exercises promote healthful body composition. Muscular strength and muscular endurance is promoted by isometric, isotonic, and isokinetic exercises. To some extent these exercises can also promote flexibility, cardiovascular endurance, and healthful body composition.

Isometric exercises are exercises that involve tightening muscles for five to ten seconds without moving body parts. Pushing against the wall is an example of an isometric exercise. Tightening the abdomen while lying on the back with the knees bent and standing on a jump rope and pulling the rope ends as hard as possible are other isometric examples. It is important for a person to not hold their breath while doing isometric exercises. These exercises make the muscles attached to bones larger and stronger. However, they are of limited value in building flexibility and muscular endurance and are of little value in promoting cardiovascular endurance. Isometric exercises may cause a sudden increase in blood pressure and should not be selected by people with heart problems.

Isotonic exercises are exercises that involve contraction and movement of muscles. Swimming, walking, running, bicycle, and sports activities are isotonic exercises. Push-ups, curl-ups, and jumping jacks are all isotonic. Weight lifting is an another example of isotonic exercise. When beginning to do isotonic exercises, it is important to increase the amount of exercise gradually. Muscles need to be strengthened in order to build endurance. Isotonic exercises help build muscular strength and improve flexibility. Some isotonic exercises may improve cardiovascular endurance if performed at a certain intensity for a specified amount of time.

Isokinetic exercises are exercises that involve the movement of weight through an entire range of motion. Machines with weight plates, popular at exercise clubs, utilize isokinetic exercises that promote muscular strength, muscular endurance, and flexibility. An extra feature of machines with weight plates is that resistance can be varied. While resisting the weight plates, heart rate increases. Maintaining this heart rate level promotes cardiovascular endurance.

Stretching exercises are exercises that promote flexibility. Many fitness experts claim that stretching for 20 minutes a day helps prevent the stiffness that accompanies aging. Stretching should be done slowly and the bouncing movement that forces the muscles into a greater stretch must be avoided to prevent injury. It is also a good idea to warm up the muscles with a brief warmup activity such as light jogging before any intense stretching.

Making a Physical Fitness Plan

Because of the many health benefits derived from being physically fit, it is recommended that all people develop a complete plan for physical fitness. The exercises that an individual chooses for working out depend upon health status, body build, current level of physical fitness, and personal preferences. A physical fitness plan can be individualized. Exercises that meet personal needs and preferences should be selected. Keeping a record of progress and results is important. A physical fitness plan should contain:

1. *Exercises for warming up.* Three to five minutes of exercises that prepare the joints and muscles for strenuous activity should be planned. Stretching exercises and aerobic exercises done at a reduced level should be included.

2. *Exercises for flexibility.* Stretching exercises to improve and maintain the range of movement in muscles and joints should be included.

3. *Exercises for cardiovascular endurance and body composition.* The American College of Sports Medicine recommends 15 to 60 minutes of continuous aerobic activity at an individual's target heart rate. **Target heart rate** is between 60 and 90 percent of the difference between resting heart rate and maximum heart rate. **Maximum heart rate** is 220 minus your age. Aerobic dancing, swimming distances, running distances, bicycling distances, and walking distances are examples of aerobic exercises. The number of minutes that an activity should be performed depends on the intensity of the activity and a person's fitness level.

4. *Exercises for muscular strength and endurance.* Exercises which strengthen and tone muscles should be included in the physical fitness plan. Isotonic, isometric, and isokinetic exercises accomplish this purpose. Exercises for all major muscle groups and joints should be included.

5. *Exercises for cooling down or warming up.* Three to five minutes of reduced exercise should be done at the end of the workout session. During this time, the heart rate slows, the body temperature lowers, and muscles help return blood to the heart and brain. Stretching exercises and aerobic exercises done at a reduced level should be included.

Life Skill #10

I will improve skill-related fitness.

In addition to the health-related components of fitness, there are skill-related components. **Skill-related fitness components** refer to the components of fitness that contribute to sports performance and make participating in sports activities more enjoyable. Skill-related fitness is performance-oriented and contributes to athletic success. To a large extent, skill-related fitness is influenced by heredity. However, training and practice can result in improvement in most people.

The skill-related fitness components include power, agility, reaction time, speed, balance, and coordination. **Power** is the ability to perform sudden bursts of energy. Jumping, throwing, and kicking are examples of activities that require power. **Agility** is the ability to quickly change position while controlling movement. Football and downhill skiing are examples of sports activities requiring agility. **Reaction time** is the amount of time it takes to begin moving after making a decision to do so. Reaction time is important in baseball, softball, football, sprinting, and several other sports. **Speed** is the ability to cover a distance or perform movement in a short period of time. Track, field hockey, and soccer are examples of sports requiring speed. **Balance** is the ability to maintain or regain equilibrium while moving or standing still. This is an important skill in football and gymnastics. **Coordination** is the ability to synchronize more than one muscular task or sense at the same time. Coordination is needed for many sports. Tennis, baseball, soccer, basketball, and volleyball are examples of sports requiring coordination.

Figure 11-1

Life Skills for Alcohol, Tobacco, and Other Drugs

1. I will use over-the-counter and prescription drugs in responsible ways.

2. I will recognize the risk factors and protective factors associated with drug misuse and abuse.

3. I will not drink alcohol.

4. I will not use tobacco products.

5. I will not misuse or abuse controlled substances.

6. I will reduce my risk of HIV infection by not using intravenous drugs or drugs that dull my decision-making skills.

7. I will seek help for personal or family drug misuse or abuse.

8. I will become aware of school and community resources for intervention and treatment.

9. I will remain safe and drug-free.

10. I will use resistance skills when pressured to use drugs.

Chapter 11

ALCOHOL, TOBACCO, AND OTHER DRUGS

Alcohol, Tobacco, and Other Drugs is the area of health that focuses on kinds of drugs and their safe use; understanding the risk factors and protective factors associated with drug misuse and abuse; preventing the misuse and abuse of alcohol, tobacco, and controlled substances; recognizing how drug use increases the likelihood of HIV infection; seeking help for personal or family drug misuse or abuse; being aware of school and community intervention and treatment resources; choosing to be safe and drug-free; and using resistance skills when pressured to use drugs. The content in this chapter provides the background information needed to teach young people life skills pertaining to the use of alcohol, tobacco, and other drugs (Figure 11-1).

Life Skill #1

I will use over-the-counter drugs and prescription drugs in responsible ways.

A **drug** is a substance that is introduced into the body, excluding food, that alters the function of the body. A **medicine** is a drug that is used to treat, prevent, or diagnose illness. Medicines can be either over-the-counter or prescription drugs.

How Drugs Enter the Body

There are four major ways drugs enter the body. Drugs can be taken orally, by injection, by inhalation, or by absorption. The most common method of taking drugs is oral administration. Drugs taken by oral administration include tablets, capsules, or liquids taken into the mouth. Drugs can be injected directly into a vein, into muscle tissue, or just below the skin's surface. Drugs taken by injection are absorbed rapidly into the bloodstream. Drugs administered by inhalation are absorbed into the bloodstream by passing through the lungs. Drugs can also enter the body through use of a suppository. A **suppository** is a wax-coated form of a drug that is inserted into the anus and held in place until the wax melts, the drug is released, and the drug is absorbed.

Prescription Drugs

A **prescription drug** is a drug that can be legally obtained only by a prescription from licensed health professionals and dispensed through registered pharmacists. A **prescription** is an instruction written by a physician that directs a pharmacist to dispense a particular drug in a specific dose. A **pharmacist** is a professional who has been trained to prepare and dispense drugs. Prescription drugs are usually more powerful than

over-the-counter drugs. Since each prescription is personalized for an individual's particular needs, it is important to know as much as possible about the drug that is being taken. The use of the drug should not be discontinued, without consulting with the appropriate health care provider, just because the user is feeling better. Drugs should only be taken by the person for whom the drugs were prescribed.

Brand Name and Generic Drugs. Some drugs are sold only under a brand name; many are sold under both generic and brand names. A **brand name drug** is a registered name or trademark given to a drug by a pharmaceutical company. A **generic name drug** is the chemical and/or biological equivalent of a specific brand name drug.

Over-the-Counter Drugs

An **over-the-counter drug** is a drug that is approved for legal purchase and use without a prescription from a doctor. Over-the-counter drugs are often self-prescribed and self-administered for the relief of symptoms of self-diagnosed illness. Over-the-counter drugs are used to treat a wide variety of ailments. No medication, over-the-counter or prescription, is safe or effective unless it is used responsibly by consumers. Before buying and/or using any over-the-counter product, it is wise to seek advice from a physician or pharmacist regarding the drug. By federal law, manufacturers of over-the-counter drugs are required to place specific information on product labels. To ensure proper use, consumers should read labels before using

any over-the-counter drugs and strictly adhere to directions for use. Most over-the-counter drug labels warn users about possible side effects and the length of time a person should take a drug before seeing a physician for a particular condition.

Life Skill #2

I will recognize the risk factors and protective factors associated with drug misuse and abuse.

Drug use is the use of alcohol and other drugs in any form, legal or illegal, whether by prescription or for "recreational" purposes. All drugs, legal as well as illegal, have the potential for misuse or abuse. **Drug misuse** is the inappropriate use of drugs including prescribed or nonprescribed medicines. **Drug abuse** is the use of drugs that results in impairment of a user's ability to function normally or that is harmful to the user or others. Drug abuse can involve both legal and illegal drugs. **Polydrug abuse** is the simultaneous abuse of more than one drug.

Risk Factors for Drug Misuse and Abuse

Successful comprehensive school health education programs must focus on skills that lessen the impact of risk factors that tend to make young people vulnerable to irresponsible and harmful drug use. **Risk factors** are ways that a person might behave and characteristics of the environment in which a person lives that threaten health, safety, and/or well being. Risk factors refer only to the statistical probability that young people will engage in irresponsible and harmful drug use; they do not predict an adverse outcome for any particular child or adolescent. These factors are listed in *Risk Factors that Make Young Persons Vulnerable to Drug Use* (Figure 11-2).

Protective Factors and Resiliency

Comprehensive school health education must provide young people with armor to protect

Figure 11-2

Risk Factors that Make Young Persons Vulnerable to Drug Use

- Being reared in a dysfunctional family
- Having negative self-esteem
- Being unable to resist peer pressure
- Having difficulty mastering developmental tasks
- Being economically disadvataged
- Having a genetic background with a predisposition of chemical dependency
- Experiencing family disruption
- Experiencing depression
- Having difficulty achieving succeed in athletics
- Having attention deficit hyperactivity disorder
- Having immature character disorder

Figure 11-3

Protective Factors that Serve as a Coat of Armor and Promote Resiliency

- Being reared in a loving, functional family
- Being involved in school activities
- Having positive self-esteem
- Having clearly defined goals and plans to reach them
- Having close friends who do not abuse drugs
- Feeling a sense of accomplishment at school
- Having adult role models including parents who do not abuse drugs
- Having a healthful attitude about competition and athletic performance
- Being committed to following the rules of the community
- Having a plan to cope with life stressors

them or keep them invulnerable when they are exposed to situations in which they might use drugs. **Protective factors** are ways that a person might behave and characteristics of the environment in which a person lives that promote health, safety, and well-being. Young people who are armed with protective factors are more likely to resist drugs and demon-

strate resiliency. **Resiliency** is the ability to recover from or adjust to misfortune, change, pressure, and adversity. Any successful health education program must focus on protective factors that promote resiliency. These factors are listed in *Protective Factors that Serve as a Coat of Armor and Promote Resiliency* (Figure 11-3).

Alcohol, Tobacco, and Other Drugs

I will not drink alcohol.

Alcohol is a psychoactive drug that depresses the central nervous system. It depresses the activity of the nerve cells of the brain. **Ethyl alcohol** is the type of alcohol that is found in alcoholic beverages. It is produced by a process called fermentation. **Fermentation** is the process that occurs when yeast cells act on sugar in the presence of water producing a chemical change. The yeast recombines sugar and water into ethyl alcohol and carbon dioxide. **Wine** is made from the fermentation of grapes or other fruits. **Beer** is an alcoholic beverage that is made from the fermentation of grains such as barley, corn, or rye. **Distilled spirits** are alcoholic beverages that have concentrations of alcohol higher than those reached by fermentation alone. The alcohol is concentrated by the process called distillation. **Proof** is a measure of the amount of alcohol in any alcoholic beverage, and is double the percent of alcohol content in a beverage.

Reasons Why Young People Drink

One influential factor that encourages drinking among young people is easy access to and availability of alcoholic beverages. Another influential fact is alcohol use by parents and peers. Alcohol is used to cope with such negative feelings as awkwardness, loneliness and shyness, being upset, hopelessness, and boredom. Adolescents are vulnerable to these feelings as part of their development and establishment of a personal identity. Another profound influence is alcohol advertising (Grube and Wallack, 1994). Advertisements for alcohol on television and in magazines effectively portray drinking alcohol as glamorous, "cool," and fun. It is clear that alcohol advertisements target young people. However, the consequences that alcohol often brings (for example accidents, family violence, alcohol dependency) are different from the fantasy and fun depicted in the advertisements.

Benefits of Not Drinking Alcohol

Choosing to not drink alcohol has many benefits. Single episodes of drinking, persistent alcohol abuse, and alcohol dependence can result in adverse consequences. Virtually no part of the body is spared the effects of excessive alcohol consumption. Individuals with alcohol-related problems require more general health care, are less productive at their jobs, and are overrepresented among those who commit acts of interpersonal violence and suicide. Because alcohol use dulls alertness, being alcohol-free enhances a young person's chances of achieving academic and vocational goals. Avoiding alcohol contributes to the development of effective problem-solving skills. Adolescents who are alcohol-free learn how to have fun and to handle social situations successfully without drinking alcohol. Making responsible decisions about alcohol promotes self-respect and shows respect and concern for others.

Absorption and Oxidation of Alcohol

Within minutes after alcohol is consumed, it is absorbed into the bloodstream. When alcohol reaches nerve cells, they are numbed. This action slows nerve messages from the brain to all parts of the body. Alcohol acts as a relaxant or tranquilizer when one or two drinks are taken. When larger amounts are consumed, the nerve centers in the brain that govern judgment, memory, speech, reaction time, coordination, muscular control, and brain activity are impaired.

Oxidation is the breakdown of alcohol by enzymes in the liver, converting alcohol into carbon dioxide and water at the rate of about half an ounce of alcohol per hour. Drinking more alcohol than this causes the blood-alcohol concentration to rise. A **drink** of alcohol is defined as one-half ounce of ethyl alcohol. This is roughly the amount of alcohol in one can of beer, four ounces of wine, or one mixed drink. Generally, the liver can process about one drink per hour.

Whether or not alcohol will have an effect on a person is dependent on a number of factors. These include the alcohol concentration in a drink, the rate at which the alcohol is consumed, the amount of alcohol consumed, the amount of food in the stomach, the body size, genetic makeup, and age of the person. The use of alcohol is a particular concern, especially among young drivers.

Blood-Alcohol Concentration

Blood-alcohol concentration (BAC) is the ratio of alcohol in a person's blood to the person's total amount of blood and is expressed as a percent. BAC can be measured through urine, breath, or blood samples. Legal levels of intoxication are determined by a person's BAC. Intoxication is defined in the law as a certain BAC. The legal standard of intoxication in most states is a BAC of 0.10; in a few states it is 0.08. When BAC is at the level of 0.10, muscular coordination, reaction time, judgment, and perception are seriously impaired, making driving extremely dangerous.

Alcohol and Driving

The risk of a fatal crash, per mile driven, may be at least eight times higher for an intoxicated driver (BAC of 0.10 or greater) than for a sober one. A BAC of 0.10 significantly affects a person's ability to drive by impairing vision, perception, judgment, reaction time, and the ability to brake and control speed. Approximately half of all traffic crashes involve alcohol. During 1990, alcohol-related crashes killed 22,084 people; one-third were innocent victims. In addition to these fatalities, which account for almost two million potential years of life lost, 1.2 million people were injured in alcohol-related crashes.

Because adolescents are especially susceptible to the effects of alcohol, drinking and driving is particularly hazardous for adolescent drivers and passengers of adolescent drivers. The leading cause of death in adolescents and young adults is alcohol-related highway accidents.

Alcohol and Violence

Alcohol, more than any other drug, has been linked with a high incidence of violence and aggression. Acute and chronic alcohol consumption is associated with high rates of homicides, suicides, sexual assaults, spouse abuse, and child abuse. Laboratory research has produced evidence of links between the pharmacologic effects of alcohol and aggressive behavior.

Alcohol and Sexual Decision-Making

Alcohol impairs the ability to think clearly and reduces inhibitions and defenses. A person under the influence of alcohol has more difficulty sticking to the choices (s)he has made for himself/herself and for his/her body. An alcohol-free mind is a protective factor against making unwise choices.

Alcohol use increases the risk of sexually transmitted diseases, pregnancy, and sexual assault because of impaired judgment. A male may feel powerful and become more aggressive under the influence of alcohol. He is less able to control himself and less aware of the consequences of his actions. A female who has been drinking also is less able to control herself and less aware of the consequences of her actions. Females who have been drinking alcohol are more vulnerable to sexual assault than females who have not been drinking.

Alcohol and Health Consequences

Alcohol use is associated with several health consequences. Because the liver is the primary site of alcohol metabolism, it can be severely affected by heavy alcohol use. There are three major types of alcohol-induced liver damage: fatty liver, alcoholic hepatitis, and cirrhosis. Fatty liver and alcoholic hepatitis are reversible with abstinence; cirrhosis is not. **Cirrhosis** is a disease in which alcohol destroys liver cells and plugs the liver with fibrous scar tissue and can lead to liver failure and death.

The long-term use of alcohol can directly damage heart tissue, which can result in abnormal heart functioning. Alcohol damage to the heart muscle may result in cardiomyopathy and cardiac arrhythmia. **Cardiomyopathy** is a degeneration of the heart muscle that is characterized by severe enlargement of the heart and inability of the damaged heart to pump blood effectively. **Cardiac arrhythmia** is an irregular heartbeat. Chronic alcohol consumption is also associated with a significant increase in high blood pressure and stroke.

Alcohol causes significant damage in the stomach, which is exposed to higher concentrations of alcohol than any other site, with the possible exception of the mouth and esophagus. Alcohol often injures the inner lining of the stomach, especially when combined with aspirin. Regular alcohol consumption may

precipitate inflammation of the esophagus and make existing peptic ulcers worse. Heavy alcohol consumption is also a leading cause of acute and chronic pancreatitis and pancreatic cancer. **Pancreatitis** is inflammation of the pancreas that increases the risk of diabetes. The neurological complications of heavy alcohol consumption include dementia, blackouts, seizures, hallucinations, and nerve destruction throughout the body. **Alcohol dementia** is brain impairment that is characterized by overall intellectual decline, due to the direct toxic effects of alcohol.

Alcoholism

Another serious consequence of alcohol abuse is alcoholism. **Alcoholism** is a complex disease that is characterized by a preoccupation with drinking alcohol that has progressed to serious physical, social, occupational, and/or family consequences for an individual. It is a complex disease because there are social, family, psychologic, genetic, and physiological causes of alcoholism. Alcoholism has consequences not only on the dependent person directly involved but also on the children of parents who are dependent on alcohol. Children of parents with alcoholism have an increased risk of abusing alcohol themselves.

Fetal Alcohol Syndrome

Heavy use of alcohol can result in fetal alcohol syndrome. **Fetal alcohol syndrome (FAS)** is a characteristic pattern of severe birth defects present in babies born to mothers who drink alcohol during their pregnancy. Among the abnormalities are small eye slits, small head circumference, facial abnormalities, growth retardation, and mental retardation. FAS is the leading known cause of mental retardation, surpassing even Down syndrome and spinal bifida. **Fetal alcohol effects (FAEs)** are birth defects in prenatally alcohol-exposed babies that do not meet the criteria for an FAS diagnosis but may be categorized as having suspected effects. FAEs often include impaired memory, brief attention span, poor judgment, and limited capacity to learn from experience.

Life Skill #4

I will not use tobacco products.

Tobacco use is a leading cause of death and disability in the United States and worldwide. Tobacco use is responsible for more than one in every six deaths in the United States and is the most important single preventable cause of death and disease. An estimated 48 million adults (Centers for Disease Control and Prevention, 1994) and 3.1 million adolescents smoke (United States Department of Health and Human Services, 1994).

Reasons Why Young People Use Tobacco Products

There are factors in the lives of young people that influence whether or not they will use tobacco products. The family exerts a powerful influence. Parents and older siblings who use tobacco influence younger siblings to use tobacco products. Social pressures play an important role in influencing young people to begin tobacco use. In particular, the peer groups of young people play an important role in decisions to use tobacco products. Tobacco advertisements also influence young people. Tobacco advertisements appear on billboards, in magazines, and in newspapers. Tobacco use is portrayed as glamorous. Tobacco products are also promoted by tobacco companies through the sponsoring of athletic events, motor vehicle racing, and cultural events. Another way that tobacco products are advertised to young people is through the use of t-shirts, caps, sweatshirts, and other apparel bearing tobacco product logos.

Components of Tobacco Smoke

The estimated number of chemical compounds in tobacco smoke exceeds 4,000. As many as 400 to 500 vaporous compounds are emitted into the air from a cigarette that is being smoked. **Tar** is a sticky, dark mixture in tobacco smoke that contains at least 3,500 chemicals. Tar produces chronic irritation of the respiratory system and is a major cause of lung cancer. The most abundant chemical compound found in the particulate matter of cigarette smoke is nicotine. **Nicotine** is the active psychoactive agent found naturally in tobacco and is responsible for the addictive behavior of tobacco smokers. All forms of tobacco contain nicotine. Nicotine is a mood-altering drug that can provide pleasurable effects. Nicotine stimulates the adrenal glands and the cerebral cortex of the brain. Nicotine acts first as a stimulant, then as a tranquilizer. It causes physical dependence characterized by a withdrawal syndrome that usually accompanies abstinence from nicotine. Other actions of nicotine include a dulling of the taste buds, constriction of blood vessels, and an increase in blood pressure and heart rate.

Nicotine addiction appears to begin early in young people's use of tobacco (Kelder et al., 1994). Of the addictive behaviors such as the use of alcohol or other drugs, cigarette smoking is most likely to become established during adolescence. Young people who begin to smoke at an earlier age are more likely than later starters to develop long-term nicotine addiction. Adolescents who try to quit smoking report withdrawal symptoms similar to those reported by adults.

Health Effects of Tobacco Smoking

More than 400,000 people die each year from smoking-related causes. Smoking is a major cause of lung cancer and a major risk factor for cancers of the larynx, pharynx, oral cavity, esophagus, pancreas, and bladder. Smoking is also a known or suspected cause or risk factor for the following diseases and health conditions: chronic bronchitis, emphysema, coronary heart disease, stroke, atherosclerotic peripheral disease, osteoporosis, facial wrinkling, intrauterine growth retardation, and low birthweight babies.

Research in recent years has determined that secondhand smoke is a cause of disease in healthy nonsmokers, including lung cancer. The children of parents who smoke have an increased frequency of respiratory infections.

Health Consequences of Tobacco Use Among Young People

Smoking by young people is associated with significant health problems during childhood and adolescence and with increased risk factors for health problems in adulthood. Cigarette smoking during adolescence appears to reduce the rate of lung growth and the level of maximum lung function that can be achieved. Young people who smoke are likely to be less physically fit than young people who do not smoke. Adolescents who smoke report that they are more likely than their nonsmoking peers to experience shortness of breath, coughing spells, phlegm production, wheezing, and overall diminished physical health. Cigarette smoking during childhood and adolescence poses a clear risk for respiratory symptoms and problems during adolescence; these health problems are risk factors for other chronic conditions in adulthood, including chronic bronchitis and emphysema (U.S. Department of Health and Human Services, 1994).

Cardiovascular disease is a leading cause of death among adults in the United States. Cigarette smoking has been shown to be a primary risk factor for coronary heart disease, arteriosclerotic peripheral vascular disease, and stroke. Smoking by children is associated with an increased risk of early atherosclerotic lesions and increased risk factors for cardiovascular diseases. If sustained into adulthood, these patterns significantly increase the risk for early development of cardiovascular disease (U.S. Department of Health and Human Services, 1994).

Tobacco use is associated with a range of problem behaviors during adolescence. Smokeless tobacco or cigarettes are generally the first drug used by young people in a sequence that can include tobacco, alcohol, marijuana, and other illegal drugs. This pattern does not imply that tobacco use causes other drug use, but rather that other drug use rarely occurs before the use of tobacco. Cigarette smokers are also more likely to get into fights, carry weapons, attempt suicide, and engage in high-risk sexual behaviors. These problem behaviors can be considered a syndrome, since involvement in one behavior increases risk for involvement for other behaviors (U.S. Department of Health and Human Services, 1994).

Smokeless Tobacco Use

Smokeless tobacco includes both chewing tobacco and snuff. Smokeless tobacco is regaining popularity, especially among young adults. In some parts of the United States, as many as 25 to 40 percent of adolescent males report current use of smokeless tobacco. Young people may think that smokeless tobacco is harmless because smoke is not drawn into the lungs. But there is strong evidence that smokeless tobacco is extremely dangerous. Whether the smokeless tobacco is in the form of **snuff**, a powdered form of tobacco, or **chewing tobacco**, a plug or loose form of tobacco, it is hazardous. It rots the teeth because it causes the roots of the teeth to be exposed; it causes the enamel of the teeth to be worn. Use of smokeless tobacco can cause **leukoplakia**, a white, patchy lesion on the lining of the mouth that can lead to cancer. There are some indications that use of smokeless tobacco is responsible for the development of cancer in other sites in the body. Smokeless tobacco users are more likely than nonusers to become cigarette smokers.

Benefits of Not Using Tobacco Products

Tobacco use is a serious threat to good health, both now and in later years. Avoidance of lung cancer, emphysema, chronic bronchitis, oral cancer, dental problems, and heart disease are convincing reasons for choosing to avoid tobacco products. Tobacco users have discolored teeth and bad breath. Using tobacco products is expensive. If a one-pack a day smoker spends an average of $2.25 on a pack of cigarettes, (s)he would spend $821.26 in one year. Over a twenty-year period the accumulated cost of cigarettes would be $16,425 or the cost of a moderately-priced new car.

Smoking Cessation and Discontinuing Use of Smokeless Tobacco

There are many ways to break the tobacco habit. Many organizations, such as the American Lung Association, sponsor smoking cessation programs. These programs are conducted by leaders who have been trained to help people stop smoking. Programs can be successful only if the person is committed to changing behavior. The first step in breaking the tobacco habit is an awareness that tobacco use is harmful to health. However, knowing about the dangers is not always enough to persuade a person to quit. Other incentives are often needed. Regardless of the type of program, studies show that the most successful way for a person to quit using tobacco is to quit immediately and completely and do it on his/her own.

Life Skill #5

I will not misuse or abuse controlled substances.

The misuse or abuse of some drugs threatens the health of the user and may cause behaviors that threaten the health and safety of others. These drugs include several types of controlled substances. A **controlled substance** is a drug that is illegal without a prescription. The possession, distribution, manufacture, and sale of these substances are controlled by the law. **Illicit drug** is another term used to describe a controlled substance—a drug which is illegal. Many controlled substances are psychoactive drugs. A **psychoactive drug** is a substance that acts on the central nervous system and alters a user's moods, perceptions, feelings, personality, or behavior.

Cocaine

Cocaine is a drug that stimulates the central nervous system and often results in dependence. Cocaine can be absorbed through any mucous membrane, and is circulated in the blood to the heart, lungs, and other body organs. Inhaled through the nose, it reaches the brain in three minutes; injected, in fifteen seconds; smoked, in seven seconds. Many users of cocaine inhale it through the nose, or "snort" it. Inhaled, the drug's effects peak in fifteen to twenty minutes, and disappear in sixty to ninety minutes. Another way cocaine is administered is by placing a small amount of freebase on a piece of foil, which is heated from below with a match or lighter. **Freebase** is the purified base form of cocaine processed from the hydrochloride salt using volatile chemicals, usually ether. The rising wisps of smoke are inhaled. Some users inject a cocaine solution under the skin, into a muscle, or into a vein. Intravenous use is often preferred, as it is the only route of introduction yielding 100 percent absorption of the drug. The result is an intense high that crests in three to five minutes and wanes over thirty or forty minutes.

Cocaine is a vasoconstrictor, narrowing the blood vessels. Heart rate, blood pressure, and respiration are quickened, and the body's metabolism is stepped up. The user's appetite is deadened, and (s)he cannot sleep while "wired" on the drug. Cocaine is metabolized rapidly in the blood and liver. Its actions on the sympathetic nervous system mimic the body's fight-or-flight response to fear or challenge. The effects are similar to those of amphetamines. As the euphoria and excitement wear off, the user slides into physiological depression.

Other adverse effects of cocaine use include the following:
- loss of interest in work and other responsibilities;
- delusions, hallucinations, and/or paranoia;
- anxiety and insomnia;
- chronic fatigue;
- burns and sores on the nasal membranes, including perforation of the nasal septum;
- rupturing of blood vessels;
- induction of epilepsy in people with no previous history of epilepsy;
- heart attacks and strokes;
- increased aggressiveness or impulsiveness;
- crystal formation in the retina of the eyes;
- malnutrition leading to increased susceptibility to infectious disease;
- increased risk of hepatitis, HIV, and other infections from contaminated needles;
- increased involvement in crime in order to buy, sell, or secure cocaine;
- psychological and physical dependency;
- depression and suicide;
- overdose and sudden death.

Crack Crack is a purified form of cocaine that produces a rapid and intense reaction. It is named for the sound it produces when smoked. It has been described as looking like slivers of soap but having the general texture of porcelain. It is usually smoked in a pipe and sold in quantities that are relatively inexpensive. Crack is the most accessible and powerful form of cocaine. The effects of crack are said to be ten times greater than that of snorted cocaine. A crack user can become addicted to the drug in as little as six weeks.

Amphetamines and Methamphetamine

Amphetamines are stimulants that speed up the central nervous system. They were used at one time as diet pills. They are no longer used for this purpose because of possible harmful effects. **Methamphetamine** is a stimulant drug that falls within the amphetamine family. The use of methamphetamine produces behavioral and psychological effects similar to cocaine and other stimulants. These effects include euphoria, increased alertness, the perception of improved self-esteem and self-confidence, impaired judgment, and impulsiveness.

Look-Alike Drugs A **look-alike drug** is a tablet or capsule manufactured to resemble amphetamines and mimic their effects. It is frequently sold as an appetite suppressant or anti-fatigue medication. Look-alike drugs typically contain legal stimulants such as caffeine, ephedrine, and phenylpropanolamine, either alone or in combination.

New-Generation Stimulants New-generation stimulants, such as crank, ice, and CAT, have emerged in the drug scene. **Crank** is an amphetamine-like stimulant. Crank's effects last longer than those of crack or cocaine. **Ice** is a smokeable form of pure methamphetamine that is gaining popularity in the United States. As with cocaine, smoking methamphetamine compounds the effects and promotes rapid addiction. Ice is a much longer-acting drug than crack. The intense high from smoking ice lasts from four to fourteen hours. Repeated use of ice is associated with significant accumulation of methamphetamine in the body. Prolonged use has resulted in serious lung and kidney damage and psychological dysfunction that has lasted for as long as two years after last use. Episodes of aggressive behavior and the birth of severely addicted babies are associated with its use.

Designer Drugs

A **designer drug** is any one of a group of drugs that are made in labs to imitate well-known drugs. Designer drugs are also called analog drugs. These drugs were originally designed to circumvent the law banning controlled substances by producing a drug that was chemically slightly different from a particular controlled substance. However, in 1986 the Controlled Substance Analogue Act, which bans designer drugs, was passed. Designer drugs are manufactured from raw materials that are easily available. Designer drugs are particularly dangerous because they can be far more potent than the drugs they imitate. Common designer drugs include Ecstasy and China White.

Hallucinogens

Drugs that create illusions and distort a user's senses are psychedelic or hallucinogenic drugs. A **hallucinogenic drug** is a substance that has the major effect of producing marked distortions in perception. With the exception of phencyclidine (PCP), which was used as an anesthetic until it was discontinued because of hallucinogenic side effects, hallucinogenic drugs have not been approved for use in general medicine.

In addition to producing marked distortions in perception, hallucinogens also cause euphoria, impair short-term memory, increase pulse rate, seem to make time pass very slowly, and produce significant disturbances in judgment. Hallucinogens have many severe adverse effects, the major effect being the "bad trip." Three kinds of bad trips include panic attacks; severe episodes of depression; and psychotic incidents that resemble schizophrenia Tand are characterized by anxiety, delusions, and hallucinations. Another side effect is the production of flashbacks. **Flashbacks** are manifestations of one or more of the acute effects of the drug that recur after it was taken. Flashbacks are generally brief, lasting only a few seconds, but they have been reported to reappear years after the drug was taken.

LSD LSD is a synthetic drug that produces hallucinations. LSD is the abbreviation for lysergic acid diethylamide. Hallucinations may include seeing imaginary bright colors and having altered perceptions of what is real. LSD is a clear, tasteless, colorless liquid that usually is taken orally and rapidly absorbed into the bloodstream. LSD users often use blotter acid. **Blotter acid** is blotter-like paper that has been impregnated with LSD and cut into small squares. The blotter acid is swallowed or chewed briefly. LSD also comes in other forms. **Microdots** are tablets of LSD that are less than an eighth of an inch in width. **Windowpanes** are tiny, thin gelatin chips of LSD. LSD is an extremely potent drug. LSD sometime produces "bad trips" in which a person experiences panic, fear, and physical symptom. Flashbacks have been reported to reappear years after the drug was taken.

PCP Phencyclidine, known as **PCP**, is a hallucinogen that may be manufactured as a tablet or capsule, but also can be smoked, swallowed, or sniffed. It was originally marketed as an anesthetic drug, and its use for this purpose was later discontinued because it caused states of confusion, agitation, disorientation, delirium, and bizarre behavior in patients who had been anesthetized. PCP is much different from other hallucinogenic drugs because it also has stimulant, depressant, and pain-relieving properties.

In some users, PCP evokes feelings of power, strength, and invulnerability, followed by depression. PCP may cause agitation and confusion, feelings of grandiosity, impaired coordination, and incoherent speech. Small doses produce a feeling of intoxication, with staggering gait, slurred speech, numbness of extremities, and lowered sensitivity to pain. Increasing doses can cause a person to become fully anesthetized. Heart rate and blood pressure are elevated, and there may be sweating, drooling, fever, and muscular rigidity. At higher doses, convulsions, coma, heart failure, lung failure and strokes may occur.

The greatest danger of PCP is its resulting in behavioral toxicity. **Behavioral toxicity** is the transformation of people into insane people who become violent. They may get sudden bursts of energy and feel as if they have superior strength. The unpredictability of PCP makes it a very dangerous drug.

Mescaline Mescaline is a hallucinogenic drug from the Mexican peyote cactus. Mescaline can be taken by chewing peyote buttons from the cactus or grinding peyote into powder and taking it orally. Mescaline is also produced synthetically. The psychoactive effects of mescaline are very similar to LSD but it is 1000 to 3000 times less potent than LSD. Synthesizing or obtaining mescaline costs more than making LSD; as a result, most of the "mescaline" sold on the streets is actually diluted LSD.

Psilocybin Psilocybin is a hallucinogenic drug derived from a specific type of mushroom that alters mood and perception. Its effects are similar to LSD and mescaline. Psilocybin is also made synthetically; however, like mescaline, what is sold on the street as psilocybin is rarely, in fact, actually psilocybin.

Inhalants

Inhalants are chemicals that produce vapors resulting in psychoactive effects. The substances most likely to be abused by young people for psychoactive effects are household chemicals including aerosols, airplane glue, cleaning fluids, paint thinners, spray-can propellants, and petroleum products such as kerosene and gasoline. These substances are inexpensive and readily available to children and adolescents—often within a young person's home or garage. Others can easily be acquired at stores.

Inhalants can be administered in a variety of ways. The simplest method is to inhale vapors directly from a cup or glass filled with the substance. **Huffing** is sniffing the vapors from a rag or cloth that has been soaked or had a solvent poured on it. **Bagging** is putting the solvent in a bag or spraying an aerosol into a bag, placing the bag over the mouth and nose, and inhaling deeply. This can be risky if loss of consciousness should occur because the user could be suffocated. Because inhaled chemicals rapidly travel to the brain, a very quick "high" is produced, even faster than with alcohol. However, the "high" is short-lived, with intoxication lasting only a few minutes, while some of the effects may be felt for about thirty minutes. Pleasurable effects are frequently followed by nausea, headache, and amnesia. The effects that occur during intoxication by inhaled substances include: exhilaration, disorientation, invincibility, unconsciousness, sedation, hallucinations, and time and space distortions. Inhalant use can be dangerous and adverse effects can include: respiratory impairment by coating the lungs; kidney failure; accidents; seizures; liver damage; brain and nerve damage; muscle weakness; reduced blood cell formation; and heart arrhythmia.

Nitrous Oxide Nitrous oxide is a colorless gas known for its powerful analgesic and weak anesthetic effect that is abused as an inhalant drug. Known as "laughing gas," nitrous oxide can produce the following effects: exhilaration; sense of warmth; light-headedness; visual hallucinations; detachment from reality; sensation of flying or floating; loss of motivation; silliness and giddiness; reduced social inhibitions; loss of consciousness with continued inhalation; and loss of motor control. Often, a serious consequence of nitrous oxide use is accidents. Other potential health-compromising effects of nitrous oxide abuse are: decreased oxygen level in the blood leading to brain damage; respiratory depression; coma; shortness of breath; loss of hearing; nausea; disturbances in heart rhythm; kidney and liver disease; spontaneous miscarriage; and depressed bone marrow function.

Alcohol, Tobacco, and Other Drugs

Marijuana

Marijuana is a drug containing THC that impairs short-term memory and changes mood. The effects of marijuana are dependent on the amount of its active ingredient, **tetrahydrocannabinol**, or **THC**. It is usually smoked in the form of a cigarette, or joint. In low doses, marijuana use can result in altered perceptions, increased heartbeat rate, and dry mouth and throat. Marijuana use affects the nervous system by impairing coordination. Blood pressure can be increased. Use of marijuana can impair the immune system, thereby leaving a person more susceptible to infections. Perhaps one of the more significant results of marijuana is the development of amotivational syndrome. **Amotivational syndrome** is a lack of desire by people to become motivated to perform daily responsibilities. THC remains in the blood for several weeks.

Hashish is a drug that consists of the drug-rich resinous secretions of the cannabis plant. These secretions are collected, dried, and then compressed into a variety of forms, such as balls, cakes, or cookie-like sheets. **Hashish** is frequently smoked, either alone or mixed with tobacco, as well as baked in cookies and candies. **Hashish oil** is a variation of hashish, produced by a process of repeated extraction of cannabis plant materials to yield a dark viscous liquid. A drop or two of this liquid on a cigarette is equal to a single "joint" of marijuana. Some users place a drop of hashish oil on hot tinfoil and inhale the smoke.

Narcotics

Narcotics are drugs that depress the central nervous system and inhibit the perception of pain. Narcotics are highly addictive. They are used medically for **analgesia** or relief of pain. Narcotics may be natural or synthetic substances. Natural narcotic drugs are also called **opiates** because of their derivation from or chemical similarity to opium. Opiates include opium, morphine, and codeine. Synthetically made narcotics are called **opioids**.

Narcotic use and abuse often leads to a short-lived state of euphoria. In addition to pain relief, narcotics reduce anxiety and depression, sedate, dry secretions in the nose and mouth, decrease respiration, suppress the cough reflex, and cause constipation. Narcotic drugs tend to induce pinpoint pupils and reduced vision, drowsiness, apathy, and decreased physical activity. A large dose may induce sleep and increase the possibility of nausea, vomiting, and depression.

Continuous use of narcotic drugs, even for relatively short periods of time, causes physical dependence. Deprivation of a narcotic drug in an addict can result in typical flu-like narcotic withdrawal symptoms. Without treatment, visible symptoms of withdrawal continue for seven to ten days, but may take weeks for the body to return to normal functioning. Craving for heroin or other narcotics is often described by chronic users long after the body has returned to normal. Since people who are chronic abusers tend to become preoccupied daily with obtaining and taking drugs, they often neglect themselves and may suffer from malnutrition, infections, and unattended diseases or injuries. People who are chronic abusers are at risk of hazardous overdose reactions to large amounts of narcotics, with effects ranging from breathing difficulties to coma and possible death, caused by suppression of the brain center that regulates respiration.

Opium is a natural derivative of the opium poppy plant that may be smoked or sniffed as a powder. The two substances that can be extracted from opium are morphine and codeine. **Morphine** is a drug that is used to control pain. When it is prescribed, a patient begins to have an altered perception of pain. Usually, the relief of the pain is due more to the perception than the actual physical effect. **Codeine** is a narcotic painkiller produced from morphine. Although it is weaker than morphine, it still is prescribed as a painkiller. **Heroin** is a narcotic drug derived from morphine. Heroin has no approved medical use in the United States. It is a white powder with a bitter taste that is often mixed with sugars, starch, powdered milk, and quinine as common diluents. In most cases, heroin is injected intravenously. Heroin abuse is a major health problem in many countries.

Sedative-Hypnotic Drugs

Sedative-hypnotic drugs are central nervous system depressants. **Sedatives** are

Alcohol, Tobacco, and Other Drugs

drugs that have a calming effect on behavior. **Hypnotic drugs** induce drowsiness and encourage sleep. Having useful medical purposes, they are especially dangerous when self-administered or administered without medical supervision and direction. Like alcohol, which is also a central nervous system depressant, sedative-hypnotics have a high potential for abuse. Use of sedative-hypnotics can result in psychological and physical dependence and tolerance.

Barbiturates **Barbiturates** are depressant drugs that are used to induce sleep and relieve tension. When used in small dosages, barbiturates can cause a decrease in the ability to be responsive and loss of muscle coordination. With increased dosage, they can result in slurred speech, decreased breathing rate, slowed heartbeat, and possible unconsciousness and death. They are extremely dangerous when taken with alcohol because they potentiate the barbiturate's respiratory depressant effects. Once a person is physically dependent on barbiturates, medical supervision is needed for withdrawal.

Benzodiazepines The **benzodiazepines** are a class of drugs that is widely used as anti-anxiety agents or tranquilizers. These drugs have become popular because they reduce anxiety with fewer of the typical sedative-hypnotic side effects such as impaired coordination. They are also preferred to sedative-hypnotics because they have a much greater margin of safety. Benzodiazepines are rarely fatal, even if taken in very large doses. However, they can be dangerous if taken in combination with other sedatives such as alcohol or with narcotics. Benzodiazepines are among the most widely prescribed drugs in America. One problem resulting from long-term use of benzodiazepines is the development of physical dependence from therapeutic doses.

Anabolic Steroids

One drug of major concern to school-age students is anabolic steroids. **Anabolic steroids** are powerful derivatives from the male hormones that produce muscle growth and can change health and behavior. Steroids have been used by athletes, both male and female, to build muscles and thus to improve performance. However, they are now illegal and have been banned from use in sporting events.

The continued use of anabolic steroids poses serious health consequences for both males and females. Males may experience testicular shrinkage and reduced sperm production. Females may experience breast reduction and sterility. Both males and females may experience liver tumors, kidney damage, and heart disease. Behavioral changes including aggression and violence accompany steroid use. Even when the use of steroids is discontinued, the effects of steroids often cannot be reversed. Long-term use of steroids may result in addiction. Steroid users often describe a euphoric state produced by anabolic steroids. Users also claim that steroids anesthetize the body, enabling the user to work out intensely without feeling pain. However, when the user stops taking steroids, muscles and especially joints become very sore. Some users say that feelings of power become so associated with steroid use that they begin to use steroids for social situations in which they feel insecure. For example, adolescents may take steroids before going to a party because they feel nervous, and the steroids give them a sense of being able to handle difficult situations. In these cases, the drugs address basic feelings of inadequacy.

Steroid abuse is sometimes associated with a withdrawal syndrome that is similar to stimulant addiction. Steroid withdrawal symptoms include: depression and sometimes suicide attempt; loss of appetite; difficulty sleeping; tiredness; anxiety and restlessness; and decreased sexual drive. Anabolic steroids have been used by professional and amateur athletes to improve athletic performance. However, drug testing for the presence of anabolic steroids has resulted in a decreased use by athletes. Athletes who test positive for anabolic steroids can be banned from competing for life.

Caffeine

Caffeine is a legal drug that is found in chocolate, coffee, tea, some soda pops, prescription drugs, and over-the-counter drugs. Caffeine is not a controlled substance. However, because it is the world's most widely used stimulant, people should be aware of this drug and its effects. Caffeine is a powerful central nervous stimulant, producing "pick-me-up" effects.

Caffeine is also a cardiac stimulant, causing heart rate to increase and increasing the force of the heart's contractions. In some people, caffeine appears to contribute to irregular heart beats and heart rhythms. This can be risky for people with heart disease. Another important effect of caffeine is its stimulation or excitation of spinal nerves and the areas of the brain that control breathing. This stimulation accounts for an increase in breathing rate, muscle tremors or shakiness, and skeletal muscle tension. Caffeine also has a powerful diuretic effect. The diuretic effect causes a loss of even more fluids than were consumed in the caffeinated beverage.

By causing a constriction of blood vessels in the brain, caffeine lessens pain and gives some relief from certain types of headaches. For this reason, caffeine is a common ingredient in many over-the-counter headache remedies. Another side effect of caffeine is irritation of the stomach. Because caffeine stimulates an increase in the production of stomach acids, consumers often experience upset stomachs. The release of these acids can be particularly troublesome for individuals who are prone to ulcers. It is important to note that decaffeinated coffee also stimulates stomach acid secretions.

Caffeinism is a condition of chronic caffeine toxicity or poisoning associated with very heavy use and preoccupation with caffeine. Some signs and symptoms of caffeinism are: disruption of sleep and insomnia; mood changes; anxiety; tremulousness and muscle twitching; restlessness; headache; lethargy and depression; ringing in the ears; dryness of the mouth; increased urinary output; nausea, vomiting, or stomach pain; diarrhea; gastric ulcer; palpitations and irregularities in heartbeat; and irritability.

Life Skill #6

I will reduce my risk of HIV infection by not using intravenous drugs and drugs that dull my decision-making skills.

A high proportion of HIV (human immunodeficiency virus) infections and AIDS cases are linked to drug abuse. Intravenous injection is linked to HIV in a number of ways. **Intravenous** is within a vein. Intravenous drug users inject ("shoot") drugs directly into their veins through syringes and needles. The sharing of syringes and needles is a risky practice because HIV-infected blood can be spread from person to person. In addition to HIV, other infectious diseases such as hepatitis B are spread through intravenous drug abuse. For this reason, total avoidance of intravenous drug use is recommended. HIV can also be spread through sexual activity. Drug users who have become infected with HIV through the sharing of needles are likely to spread the infection to their sexual partners. Crack and other drug addicts have a difficult time affording drugs. Some turn to prostitution. The exchange of sex for drugs places these people at increased risk of having sex with a person infected with HIV.

Another way that HIV infection is linked to drug abuse is through the dulling of decision-making skills. Under the influence of alcohol or other drugs, judgment and decision-making capacity is poor.

Life Skill #7

I will seek help for personal or family drug misuse or abuse.

Drug Dependence

Drug dependence is compulsive use of a drug (or drugs) despite adverse psychological, physiological, or social consequences. The lives of people who are dependent on drugs become dominated by obtaining and using drugs. Drug dependence leads people to do things that are often contrary to their values, their judgment, and their common sense in order to use drugs. Drug dependence is an illness that requires treatment. Drug dependence is believed to develop in 10 to 20 percent of those who use mood altering (psychoactive) drugs (Trapold, 1990). Compared to adults, adolescents and children appear to have increased susceptibility or vulnerability to drug dependence. **Chemical dependency** is another term used to describe drug dependence.

Physical dependence is a physiological process in which repeated doses of a drug cause the body to adapt to the presence of the drug. Physical dependence includes the development of tolerance or of withdrawal symptoms. **Tolerance** is a condition in which the body becomes adapted to a drug so that increasingly larger amounts of the drug are needed to produce the desired effect. **Withdrawal symptoms** are unpleasant symptoms experienced by individuals who are physically dependent on a drug when deprived of that drug. Physical dependence on a drug is not always a prerequisite of chemical dependency. **Psychological dependence** is a condition characterized by a pervasive desire or "craving" to achieve the effects produced by a drug. This type of dependence may or may not be accompanied by physical dependence.

Codependency and the Family

Codependence is a mental disorder in which a person loses personal identity, has frozen feelings, and copes ineffectively. People who have codependence are called **codependent**. Children reared in families in which adults are chemically dependent and codependent may copy this behavior. They may begin to use chemicals such as alcohol or marijuana. They may behave in codependent ways and lose their personal identity, deny their feelings, and cope ineffectively. Codependents often need treatment to overcome these problems.

Getting People Who Are Drug-Dependent into Treatment

Few people who are drug-dependent decide to seek treatment on their own. Quitting substance-abusing behavior is extremely difficult. Treatment programs are often demanding and difficult experiences. In addition, treatment programs are directed at denying people who are addicted their single greatest source of pleasure and comfort— the drugs to which they are addicted. Another reason it is difficult to get people into treatment is that they are likely to be in a state of denial of their drug problem. Those who feel they have a problem avoid treatment by promising themselves that they will get help for themselves—tomorrow.

The overwhelming majority of people who are drug-dependent must be "jolted" into drug treatment and induced to stay there by some external force—the criminal justice system, employers who have discovered their drug use, spouses who have threatened to leave, parents who are mandating it, or the death of a friend who used drugs. It is important to take action to get people who are drug-dependent into treatment. Because drug-dependent people are not likely to seek help, supportive others should seek out appropriate treatment resources for the person who is drug-dependent. Drug abuse can lead to life-threatening situations unless quick and proper action is taken.

Treatment Approaches

Detoxification is often the first stage of drug treatment. **Detoxification** is the process by which a drug is withdrawn from the body. This is essential because the person must learn to cope with the craving and depression of withdrawal from drugs. Because withdrawal from certain drugs can be life-threatening, withdrawal should be supervised by qualified health care professionals. Detoxification is the first step toward further treatment.

Different approaches have been developed to help people who are addicted permanently kick their habit. Programs can be offered either on an inpatient or an outpatient basis. Most inpatient programs are housed in hospitals or live-in treatment centers. Most are

Parents

Employers

Friends

Courts

Families

Alcohol, Tobacco, and Other Drugs

very expensive. A therapeutic community is a special type of inpatient treatment program. A **therapeutic community** consists of trained professionals and individuals who were formerly drug-dependent who help counsel the individual who has a drug problem. The individual seeking treatment often will live in a restricted environment and receive professional counseling as well as social support. Many people who are drug-dependent now receive treatment on an outpatient basis. Outpatient programs are popular because they are usually less expensive, more available, and less disruptive to the lives of treated individuals. Community programs are often offered on an outpatient basis. Treatment approaches such as family therapy, group therapy, and psychotherapy are offered in both outpatient as well as inpatient programs.

One of the most popular approaches to drug treatment is self-help groups. **Self-help groups** are groups that offer fellowship and support and are based upon a Twelve Step treatment model. The Twelve Step treatment model originated from Alcoholics Anonymous, which is the largest self-help group. This model has been incorporated into many community-based and professionally-sponsored treatment programs.

I will become aware of school and community resources for intervention and treatment.

The types of school and community resources available for the intervention and treatment of drug use will vary from locale to locale. A valuable tool in locating available community resources is the telephone directory. Many drug treatment programs are listed in the yellow pages. Public-supported programs and facilities will be listed under city, county, or state services. Other sources of information about community resources include health teachers, school counselors, clergy, and public health departments. Intervention and treatment services are provided by charitable organizations, law enforcement agencies, private corporations, psychologists, universities, and public health and social service agencies.

Schools may offer services for high-risk students: drug-free activities, resistance training, positive peer programs, and student assistance programs. A **student assistance program** is a school-based approach to the prevention and treatment of alcohol and other drug abuse. In addition, student assistance programs use a referral process for getting appropriate help for a troubled student. Students can also refer themselves to program services. Support groups also may be helpful. **Parent support groups** are formed by parents to help one another cope with alcohol and drug problems in their neighborhoods and families. **Student support groups** consist of groups of students who are struggling to cope with certain life problems. There are many types of support groups throughout communities. These groups provide needed social support to people needing assistance.

Life Skill #9

I will remain safe and drug-free.

Risks of Drug Use and Abuse

There are many risks involved in using drugs. Some examples of impairment or harm resulting from drug abuse are:
- scholastic failure or underachievement;
- motor vehicle injuries;
- cirrhosis of the liver (from chronic use of alcohol);
- lack of emotional development;
- suicide or suicide attempts;
- drug overdose;
- impaired social relationships;
- social withdrawal;
- abusive relationships;
- fetal alcohol syndrome;
- financial difficulties;
- relationship difficulties;
- impaired driving ability;
- loss of self-esteem;
- risk of HIV infection;
- family problems;
- arrest for drug possession;
- drug dependence.

270

© Copyright by Meeks Heit Publishing Company.

Benefits of Being Drug-Free

A person is **drug-free** when (s)he does not use harmful and illegal drugs. A person may choose not to be drug-free. A person may choose to drink an alcoholic beverage before driving an automobile. The alcohol may affect the person's judgment and ability to drive. This person is engaging in behavior and decision-making that jeopardize his/her health and safety and that of others.

Many of the dangers associated with drug use and abuse can be alleviated when a person chooses a drug-free lifestyle. A **drug-free lifestyle** refers to a lifestyle in which people do not use harmful and illegal drugs. Choosing a drug-free lifestyle allows individuals to take full advantage of their opportunities and potential. Choosing a drug-free lifestyle averts the many problems associated with using and abusing drugs that have been discussed in this chapter.

Staying drug-free is healthful to both body and mind. Drug-free individuals do not risk becoming dependent upon drugs. The body is not destroyed by dangerous chemicals. There is no risk of overdosing on drugs. Family and social relationships are not as likely to be disrupted. There is a reduced likelihood of violence. More information on violence prevention can be found in **Violence Prevention:** *Totally Awesome*™ **Teaching Strategies for Safe and Drug-Free Schools** (1995), by L. Meeks, P. Heit, and R. Page.

Being drug-free is a lifestyle that promotes obeying laws. People who experiment with drugs and become involved in drug trafficking, risk criminal sanctions. Being arrested for drug abuse can do more than cause embarrassment. Using and selling drugs are criminal activities which carry legal penalties. Penalties for drug offenses vary from state to state, but offenses can mean being fined, going to jail, and/or other penalties. A police record may interrupt plans and opportunities for the future. Some employers do not hire a person with a police record.

Life Skill #10

I will use resistance skills when pressured to use drugs.

Peer pressure plays an enormous role in influencing young people to try alcohol or other drugs. Young people need practical social skills to be able to handle such pressure. Having resistance skills can help young people resist peer pressure to participate in a range of risky or criminal behaviors. Saying NO to drugs is an indication of strength, not weakness. Saying NO is an indication of self-confidence. A detailed discussion of resistance skills and *The Model for Using Resistance Skills* (Table 4-4) are included in Chapter 6.

Figure 12-1

Life Skills for Communicable and Chronic Diseases

1. I will recognize that some diseases are communicable while others are noncommunicable.

2. I will keep my immune system healthy.

3. I will choose behaviors to prevent the spread of pathogens.

4. I will choose behaviors to reduce the risk of infection with common communicable diseases.

5. I will choose behaviors to reduce the risk of infection with STDs.

6. I will choose behaviors to reduce the risk of HIV infection.

7. I will obtain information about my family's history of disease.

8. I will choose behaviors to reduce my risk of cardiovascular disease.

9. I will choose behaviors to reduce my risk of cancer.

10. I will recognize ways to manage chronic diseases.

Chapter 12

COMMUNICABLE AND CHRONIC DISEASES

Communicable and Chronic Diseases is the area of health that focuses on recognizing communicable and noncommunicable diseases; keeping the immune system healthy; preventing the spread of pathogens; reducing the risk of infection with common communicable diseases, STDs, and HIV; obtaining a family history for diseases; reducing the risk of cardiovascular diseases and cancer; and recognizing ways to manage chronic diseases. The content in this chapter provides background information needed to teach young people life skills for communicable and chronic diseases (Figure 12-1).

Life Skill #1

I will recognize that some diseases are communicable while others are noncommunicable.

Communicable diseases, also called **infectious diseases**, are illnesses caused by pathogens that enter the body through direct or indirect contact. **Pathogens** are disease-causing organisms. For example, a person develops a cold when pathogens that cause the common cold enter his/her body. Other diseases, such as heart disease, are noncommunicable diseases. **Noncommunicable diseases**, are illnesses that are not caused by a pathogen. They are also called noninfectious diseases. For example, heart disease may result from hereditary factors, improper diet, smoking, and other risk factors. It is not caused by direct or indirect contact with another person.

Life Skill #2

I will keep my immune system healthy.

Immune System

The **immune system** is the body system that fights disease. Every person has inborn defenses against pathogens that may enter the body. The skin is the first line of defense against pathogens. Acting as a barrier, unbroken skin helps prevent pathogens from entering the body. Other inborn defenses include the oils produced by the body and perspiration. These kill many of the pathogens with which they come in contact. Pathogens can enter the body in other ways. Tears contain chemicals that kill many of the pathogens that may enter through the eyes. Pathogens can also enter through the nose and mouth. Nasal mucus and hairs that line the inside of the nose trap many of these pathogens so that they cannot travel into the lungs. Pathogens traveling through the nose and mouth can be trapped by cilia in the windpipe, thus preventing them from entering the lungs.

The Lymphatic System

Another part of the body that helps protect it from pathogens is the lymphatic system. The **lymphatic system** is a part of the immune system that includes lymph vessels, lymphocytes, lymph nodes, the thymus gland, tonsils, and the spleen. The lymphatic system carries fluid away from body tissues to the circulatory system, helping maintain fluid balance in the body. The lymphatic system also filters blood and lymph so that pathogens are removed from the body. **Lymphocytes** are white blood cells that are formed primarily in the lymph glands. They circulate throughout the lymphatic system to help the body fight pathogens. **Neutrophiles** are white blood cells that are produced in the bone marrow. They also fight pathogens. Pus is made up mostly of neutrophiles. **Pus** is a fluid found at the site of bacterial infection.

Helper T cells and B cells are two types of lymphocytes inside the lymphatic system. **Helper T cells** are white blood cells that signal B cells to make antibodies. **B cells** are the blood cells that produce antibodies. **Antibodies** are proteins produced by B cells that help destroy pathogens inside the body.

Immune System Response to a Pathogen

Suppose a virus such as the chickenpox virus enters a person's body. Certain reactions begin to take place. Helper T cells are activated and the immune system response begins to occur. B cells are signaled, and they begin to produce antibodies. Antibodies travel throughout the lymph vessels and attach themselves to the pathogens so that they are more easily engulfed and digested by macrophages. A **macrophage** is a large cell that acts as a scavenger by engulfing and destroying pathogens.

Suppose this person comes in contact with the chickenpox virus again at a future time. The chickenpox antibody would already be in the bloodstream. Thus, the person would be protected from developing chickenpox again in his/her lifetime.

Keeping the Immune System Healthy

The following life skills can help people to keep their immune system healthy.

1. *Avoid alcohol, tobacco, and other drugs.* Drugs including alcohol and tobacco impair the ability of the immune system to protect the body from disease.
2. *Reduce stress levels.* Too much stress can reduce the efficiency of the immune system.
3. *Get enough rest.* Sleep is a way for the body to replenish its energy level and to keep the immune system strong.
4. *Develop good nutritional practices.* Good nutritional practices are essential in order to keep the immune system strong.
5. *Get appropriate immunizations.* Immunizations can provide protection against certain diseases.

Immunizations

An **immunization** is a vaccine that provides immunity to a certain infectious disease. Most immunizations consist of an altered, weakened, or dead form of a microorganism that is introduced into the body. Protein or carbohydrate components (antigens) of the microorganism stimulate the body's immune system to produce protective antibodies that are needed to prevent disease caused by that specific organism. After processing the antigens, a memory system is established by the immune system that allows the immune system to recall which antibodies are needed to counter the organism if later exposures occur.

Childhood immunizations are immunizations that are given to children to protect them against potentially serious infectious diseases. These immunizations include immunizations against diphtheria, whooping cough, tetanus, measles, mumps, rubella (German measles), polio, hepatitis B, and *Haemophilus influenzae* type B. Because the immunity to some of these diseases wanes over time, some of these immunizations may need to be repeated as children grow older.

Disorders of the Immune System

The immune systems of some people overreact to certain substances in the environment and result in allergies. The immune systems of others may mistakenly attack the body's own cells for foreign invaders and result in autoimmune diseases.

Allergy An **allergy** is a hypersensitive reaction by the immune system to a foreign antigen. Allergies are ususally harmless. An **allergen** is a substance that provokes the immune system to produce antibodies to harmless substances in the environment such as pollen, dust, or mold. Then, a subsequent encounter with the same allergen triggers histamine which, in turn, contributes to the allergic reaction. **Histamine** is a chemical released by the body in allergic reactions that causes itching, constriction of smooth muscle in the bronchial tubes, and leakiness of blood vessels. Other chemicals released during allergic reactions are potent constrictors of the small airways in the lungs.

Asthma is an allergic disease of the lungs manifested by constrictions of the small air passages called bronchioles. When the airways narrow, a person experiences coughing, wheezing, and difficulty in breathing. Some allergens known to provoke asthma attacks are grasses, house dust, and foods. Asthma may also be caused by other factors such as infections, exercise, emotional stress, and cold air.

Treating allergic diseases usually involves the careful management of the environment to avoid contact with substances and factors that trigger reactions. Effective drugs are now available to help in the management of allergies.

Autoimmune Disorder An **autoimmune disorder** is a condition in which the immune system produces autoantibodies that launch an attack on the body's own cells. Systemic lupus erythematosus, rheumatoid arthritis, and myasthenia gravis are examples of autoimmune diseases. Treatment usually involves correcting any major deficiencies by replacing missing blood components or hormones, and reducing the activity of the immune system.

Life Skill #3

I will choose behaviors to prevent the spread of pathogens.

Types of Pathogens

When pathogens enter the body, they can cause illness. Pathogens include viruses, bacteria, rickettsia, fungi, protozoa, and parasitic worms.

Viruses are the smallest known pathogens. Viruses consist of chains of nucleic acid covered by a protein coat. They are unable to reproduce on their own. Examples of viral infections include the common cold, measles, chickenpox, influenza, herpes, and HIV. Antibiotic drugs do not have any effect on viruses.

Bacteria are single-celled microorganisms that can produce illness. Examples of infections caused by bacteria are strep throat, tuberculosis, syphilis, and gonorrhea.

Rickettsia are disease-causing microorganisms that grow inside living cells and resemble bacteria, although they are much smaller. Two infections that are caused by rickettsia are Rocky Mountain spotted fever and typhus.

Fungi are single-celled or multicellular plantlike organisms, such as yeasts and molds, that are capable of causing diseases of the skin, mucous membranes, and lungs. Examples of infections caused by fungi are athlete's foot, ringworm, jock itch, thrush, and candidiasis.

Protozoa are tiny, single-celled organisms that produce toxins that are capable of causing disease. Examples of infections caused by protozoa are malaria, African sleeping sickness, and amoebic dysentery. Giardia is a protozoa that infects people who drink impure water in the United States.

Parasitic worms are the largest pathogens that can enter the human body to cause infection. Examples of parasitic worms are intestinal parasites such as tapeworms, pinworms, and hookworms. Trichina are nematode worms that in the larval stage are parasitic in muscles.

Susceptibility to Pathogens

Exposure to a pathogen does not necessarily mean a person will become ill. For a disease to occur, a person must have a susceptibility to infection. Susceptibilty to infection can be increased by: not taking care of one's body, aging, being sick, and failing to receive immunizations.

Communicable and Chronic Diseases

Transmission of Pathogens

Communicable diseases are spread through direct or indirect contact. Kissing, touching, and sexual intercourse are some major ways communicable diseases are spread from person to person by direct contact. Pathogens are also spread by indirect contact. For example, pathogens can be spread by inhaling germ-laden mists resulting from a sneeze, or by coming in contact with something that has been touched by an infected person, such as an infected person's toothbrush, eating utensils, clothes, or food. Sharing contaminated needles is a way that infections such as HIV and hepatitis B are transmitted.

Pathogens also can be spread through contaminated water and contaminated food. They can also be transferred by insects that carrying pathogens from one place to another. For example, an insect may land on sewage and then land on food. If this food is eaten, a disease may be transmitted. Animals such as mice and rats can indirectly spread disease.

Reducing the Spread of Pathogens

Some simple precautions can reduce the spread of pathogens. People with infections, such as the common cold and influenza, should avoid other people during the contagious stage. Young people with these illnesses should not attend school. Personal items such as towels, toothbrushes, and eating utensils should not be shared. Careful laundering and dishwashing can help reduce the spread of pathogens to others in the home. Hands should be washed frequently. Foods should be prepared, served, and stored under sanitary conditions. Only water that has been properly treated should be used for drinking. Immunizations can greatly reduce the incidence of disease and thus reduce the spread of disease.

Avoiding certain risk behaviors can also reduce the spread of disease. Because some infections can be spread through sexual contact, decisions about sexual behavior are very important in reducing the spread of pathogens. Abstaining from sexual intercourse provides young people with protection from infections that are spread from person to person during intercourse. Avoiding injecting drugs can reduce the spread of infections like HIV and hepatitis.

Common Cold

Many people have an average of three colds a year. The **common cold** is a viral infection of the upper respiratory tract. The common cold is caused not by just one virus but by hundreds of different viruses. Its symptoms include a runny nose, coughing, sneezing, sore throat, watery eyes, and headache. Viruses that cause colds can be transmitted through direct or indirect contact. Immunity against a cold is not possible. Thus, the only way to prevent getting a cold is to avoid contact with another person who has a cold, especially during the first twenty-four hours because that is the most contagious period. High stress levels can increase a person's chances of catching a cold.

There is no cure for the common cold. Some people believe that large doses of vitamin C will prevent colds; others do not. However, medications such as cough syrups and nasal decongestants are available to relieve the symptoms of a cold. Coldlike symptoms can sometimes be a signal of a more serious disorder. The early stages of measles and strep throat begin with cold symptoms.

Chickenpox

Chickenpox is a highly contagious and common childhood viral illness that produces fever, tiredness, and skin blisters. The symptoms of chickenpox are usually mild, but there is significant discomfort because the skin blisters itch and ooze a clear fluid. Most people develop chickenpox during their

childhood and thus acquire a lifelong immunity to chickenpox. However, the chickenpox virus (herpes zoster) remains hidden in body tissues in some people. During adulthood, the herpes zoster virus may become reactivated and result in shingles. **Shingles** is an infection caused by the herpes zoster virus that affects only a small segment of the population, usually over the age of fifty.

Measles

Measles is a potentially deadly viral illness that produces an itchy rash on the face and body, tiredness, high fever, coughing, and runny nose. Serious complications develop in 10 to 15 percent of those who contract measles. These complications include diarrhea, ear infections, pneumonia, and inflammation of the brain. An effective measles vaccination is available. Measles affects primarily children. **German measles** or rubella is a viral disease that is a milder form of measles. Usually it is not a threat to young people. However, mothers who were infected with rubella during early pregnancy may give birth to babies that are deaf, blind, mentally retarded, or have heart defects. All females should be immunized against rubella before becoming pregnant.

Mumps

Mumps is a viral disease of children that results in a swelling of the salivary glands. Mumps can cause serious complications such as sterility in males and hearing loss. It is not common today because an effective mumps vaccine is available.

Influenza and Pneumonia

Influenza is a viral disease that affects the respiratory system. Also known as flu, its symptoms include fever, chills, muscle pains, headaches, coughing, sore throat, and runny nose. Flu-causing viruses can be easily spread by coughing or sneezing. People with flu can affect others before their own symptoms appear.

There are three main types of flu, which are labeled A, B, and C. Each type is caused by many strains or kinds of viruses. Because each of these strains is quite different, it is difficult to find one vaccine that would prevent all types of flu. When a certain strain is identified, a specific vaccine can be given to help prevent it. Since the initial symptoms of flu are similar to those of a cold, people tend to treat them the same. For many people, this means taking aspirin. Caution must be taken when using aspirin, especially with children. There appears to be an association between taking products containing aspirin to relieve symptoms of flu and the onset of Reye's syndrome. **Reye's syndrome** is a disease which may follow influenza and chickenpox in children and adolescents, that is characterized by swelling of the brain and destruction of liver tissue. Reye's syndrome generally develops in children just when they appear to be recovering from their flu illness. Many victims of Reye's syndrome suffer permanent brain damage or die.

Pneumonia is an inflammation of the lungs accompanied by fever, shortness of breath, headache, chest pain, and coughing. Flu complications often lead to pneumonia. Laboratory tests, X-rays, and a physical examination are used to diagnose pneumonia. Pneumonia can be caused by viruses, bacteria, or other organisms. If caused by bacteria, pneumonia can be treated with prescribed antibiotics. The viral pneumonia may be treated by other drugs.

Hepatitis

Hepatitis is a viral infection that causes enlargement and pain in the liver. As the virus destroys liver cells, bile enters the bloodstream and causes a yellowing, or jaundice, of the skin. Hepatitis is most common in children, young adults, and the elderly. Signs of this disease are pain in the upper part of the abdomen, fever, chills, loss of appetite, headache, nausea, diarrhea, aching joints, and muscle pains. Five different viruses have been identified that cause hepatitis. These types are referred to as hepatitis A, B, C, D, and E.

Hepatitis A is commonly known as "infectious hepatitis" and is the least serious form of hepatitis. The major mode of transmission is through fecal contamination of food or water. The virus enters the body primarily through the mouth. Poor sanitation often plays a role in the transmission of the disease. In the United States, hepatitis A frequently is spread in day-care centers by workers who fail to wash their hands after changing dirty diapers. Eating raw shellfish is another source of hepatitis A transmission.

Hepatitis B is a potentially deadly disease that is passed through blood and other body fluids, including semen, mucus, and saliva. Hepatitis B is often spread by sexual intercourse and the sharing of contaminated needles. Needle-stick accidents can also spread hepatitis B to health care workers. All children as well as health care workers and others at risk should be immunized against hepatitis B.

Hepatitis C and D appear to be spread in the same ways as hepatitis B. Hepatitis D is present only with hepatitis B. Hepatitis E is rare in the United States. It appears to be spread through feces-contaminated water.

General treatment for all types of hepatitis is bed rest and fluid intake to prevent dehydration. No effective medication is available at present.

Mononucleosis

Mononucleosis is a viral infection that occurs most frequently in those in the fifteen- to nineteen-year-old age group; it is also known as "mono." It is sometimes called the "kissing disease" because it is transmitted primarily by oral contact.

Symptoms of mononucleosis are swollen glands, fever, sore throat, enlargement of lymph nodes (especially in the neck), chills, headache, and extreme fatigue. Mononucleosis can affect body organs such as the liver and spleen, and is diagnosed through blood tests. Recuperation from mononucleosis requires a few weeks of bed rest and good nutrition. Antibiotics are effective in treating secondary bacterial throat infections, but they are not effective in the treatment of mononucleosis itself.

Life Skill #5

I will choose behaviors to reduce the risk of infection with STDs.

Sexually transmitted diseases (STDs) are diseases caused by pathogens that are transmitted from an infected person to an uninfected person during intimate sexual contact. At present, there are about 20 microorganisms that are known to be transmitted sexually. These organisms are responsible for causing about 50 different syndromes, or set of symptoms.

The organisms that cause STDs are transmitted in similar ways because they all have an affinity for mucous membranes such as those that line the reproductive organs. Transmission usually requires direct contact of genital areas. Mucous membranes provide an ideal environment for these organisms to grow and multiply. They also grow and multiply in the bloodstream.

More than 12 million new cases of STDs are reported each year inthe United States, including 4 million cases of chlamydia, 1.3 million cases of gonorrhea, 500,000 to 1 million cases of genital warts, 200,000 to 500,000 cases of genital herpes, and 134,000 cases of syphilis (Randall, 1993; Willis, 1993). About 30 million Americans are estimated to have genital herpes infections, and as many as 40 million people may be infected with the virus that causes genital warts (Erickson and Trocki, 1992). Adolescents have the highest rate of STDs of any age group (Goldsmith, 1993). Two-thirds of all STDs occur in people less than twenty-five years old and the incidence is rising. Each year, one of every six adolescents acquires an STD, accounting for 3 million adolescent cases.

Using drugs and alcohol increases a person's chances of getting STDs because these substances can interfere with judgment and ability to use preventive measures (National Commission on AIDS, 1994). The more sexual partners that a person has, the higher the chance of being exposed to an STD, because it is difficult to know whether a partner is infected or has had sex with people who are infected (Willis, 1993). Thirty-six percent of high school students report having more than two sexual partners; 19 percent report having more than four (Goldsmith, 1993).

Young people should see a doctor or go to a health clinic if they have any of the following STD symptoms: discharge from vagina, penis, or rectum; pain or burning during urination; pain in the abdomen, testicles, buttocks, or legs; blisters, open sores, warts, rash, or swelling in the genital or anal areas or mouth; or persistent flu-like symptoms including fever headache, aching muscles, or swollen glands.

Chlamydial Infections

Chlamydial infections are STDs caused by the bacterium *Chlamydia trachomatis*. They result in inflammation of the urethra and epididymis in males and inflammation of the vagina and cervix in females. Chlamydial infections are spread through sexual contact; however, they can also be transmitted from an infected mother to her baby during vaginal delivery.

Chlamydial infections are quite prevalent in the United States and have serious consequences. Chlamydial infections are often referred to as "silent" STDs because symptoms are often either very mild or absent.

In females, chlamydial infections involve the vagina and cervix. Symptoms, if present, include irritation and itching in the genital area, burning during urination, and a vaginal discharge. If the infection is not treated, the upper reproductive tract may also be involved. **Pelvic inflammatory disease (PID)** is an infection of the upper reproductive tract. Chlamydia is a leading cause of PID. Symptoms of PID include fever, abdominal pain, nausea, and disrupted menstrual periods. Ectopic pregnancy and sterility have been linked to PID. In males, chlamydial infections involve the urethra and epididymis, and cause discharge and burning during urination. Infection may be symptomless for years. Meanwhile, internal organs are being infected and damaged, and sterility may result. Chlamydia can be successfully treated with antibiotics such as tetracycline or erythromycin. The infected person and his/her sex partner both should be treated.

Gonorrhea

Gonorrhea is an STD caused by the bacterium *Neisseria gonorrhoeae*, which infects the linings of the genital and urinary tracts of males and females. Symptoms, when they occur, are increased vaginal discharge, genital irritation, and pain during urination. There may be frequent urination, abnormal menstrual bleeding, and abdominal tenderness.

If left untreated, gonorrhea will spread to the uterus, ovaries, and Fallopian tubes. A common cause of sterility in females, it can be life-threatening if left untreated.

More males than females show signs and symptoms of gonorrhea infection. However, as many as 40 percent show no symptoms. Symptoms include a discharge from the penis, pain, and frequency of urination. Early symptoms often disappear, but the bacteria are still present, and the male can infect others. A male can be cured at any time. However, if left untreated, the infection will spread and potentially be serious enough to cause permanent sterility. Penicillin has been an effective treatment for gonorrhea. Recently, there has been evidence of strains of gonorrhea that are resistant to penicillin, requiring treatment with other antibiotics.

Syphilis

Syphilis is an STD caused by the *Treponema pallidum* bacterium, which penetrates mucous membranes and abrasions of the skin and causes lesions that may involve any organ or tissue. A **chancre** is a hard, round, painless sore with raised edges resulting from syphilis. Chancres appear mostly in the genital area three weeks or longer after exposure. They may also appear on the lips, tongue, fingers, or nipples. A chancre may be the size of a dime or as small as a pimple. In females, chancres usually appear on the labia or within the vagina or cervix. Because chancres are painless, they often go unnoticed if they develop in internal areas of the body. In males, chancres usually appear on the penis, the scrotum, or in the pubic area. Chancres heal and disappear without treatment within a few weeks, giving the infected person the mistaken impression that the condition has cured itself. The infected person may have no further symptoms for a period of time after a chancre has disappeared. However, this infected, symptomless person can infect others during this time.

The secondary stage of syphilis is characterized by a skin rash and lesions that appear on the palms of the hands and the soles of the feet. The rash may cover the entire body; it does not itch. The infected person experiences fever, weight loss, swollen lymph nodes, and even hair loss. These secondary stage symptoms will subside without treatment after a few weeks, and the person again may think that the disease has been cured without treatment. An infected person is very contagious in the secondary stage. The secondary stage lasts about a year.

A latent stage may follow the secondary stage. During latent syphilis, there are usually no obvious symptoms in infected people, even though syphilis bacteria are affecting tissues and organs in the body. Many people who have syphilis stay in the latent stage for the remainder of their lives. Without treatment during the primary and secondary stages, syphilis will likely progress to the third stage. During the tertiary stage, symptoms include blindness, paralysis, liver damage, and mental problems. The tertiary stage of syphilis may result in death.

Congenital syphilis is syphilis that is transmitted to a fetus from an infected pregnant female who has untreated primary or secondary syphilis. Most pregnancies in infected females end in miscarriage or stillbirth. If carried to term, a baby may be born with congenital syphilis. Congenital syphilis can cause mental disturbance or retardation and other birth defects.

Treatment with antibiotics is usually effective for the primary and secondary stages of syphilis. Unfortunately, any organ damage acquired during the tertiary stage may be irreversible. Untreated syphilis may result in heart disease, central nervous system disease, and musculoskeletal diseases and disorders.

Genital Herpes

Genital herpes is a highly contagious STD that is caused by two forms of the herpes simplex virus (HSV), HSV-1 and HSV-2. HSV-1 generally causes cold sores or fever blisters in the mouth or on the lips. HSV-2 is generally associated with sores or lesions in the genital area. However, HSV-1 is known to cause genital lesions and HSV-2 is known to cause oral lesions.

A person with genital herpes is highly contagious when lesions are present. The virus can be transmitted when a lesion on an infected person erupts and releases fluid containing the virus particles. These virus particles enter a partner's body during sexual contact. Transmission can also occur by touch alone or during kissing if contact is made with a lesion. Personal hygiene is especially important when lesions are present.

During the active stage, males and females develop characteristic skin lesions on their genitals. These skin lesions appear as shallow, ulcerated blisters. These blisters may rupture during urination, sexual intercourse, or irritation from clothing and cause acute pain and itching. Other symptoms include fever, headaches, tiredness, and swollen lymph nodes. Females may also have a whitish discharge. Eventually the blisters heal and disappear and the other symptoms vanish. The genital herpes enters the latent stage. During the latent stage, there are no signs and symptoms of genital herpes although the virus is still present in the body. Genital herpes tends to recur spontaneously. Females who are infected with genital herpes are at increased risk for developing cervical cancer and should have regular Pap smears and pelvic examinations. Males and females who are infected with genital herpes and have an outbreak of the blisters are at increased risk of becoming infected with HIV from an HIV-infected partner during sexual contact. HIV can enter the body through the broken blisters.

There is no known cure for genital herpes. Prompt treatment is recommended. One drug, acyclovir, is helpful on a short-term basis for relieving some of the symptoms, and may also keep the virus from reproducing.

Genital Warts

Genital warts are dry wartlike growths that are caused by the human papilloma virus (HPV). The warts are painless and have a cauliflower shape. Genital warts are spread through direct sexual contact and through contact with infected bed linen, towels, and clothing. The presence of genital warts has been associated with cervical cancer.

No treatment is available to eradicate HPV completely. The usual treatment involves the use of topical medications to erode the warts. Laser surgery can be used to remove warts. Warts may be destroyed by freezing them with liquid nitrogen. None of these treatments will assure that the warts will not recur because the virus remains in the body.

Bacterial Vaginosis

Bacterial vaginosis is an STD caused by the *Gardnerella vaginalis* bacterium. Normally found in small amounts in the vagina, an increase in their growth produces typical symptoms of the disease. Symptoms, when present, in females include a foul-smelling discharge, possible irritation of vaginal tissue, and burning during urination. Symptoms in males include inflammation of the foreskin, urethra, and bladder.

Candidiasis

Candidiasis is an STD caused by a fungus, *Candida albicans*. It is commonly called a yeast infection or moniliasis. The *Candida albicans* organism is normally in the vagina of many females and will begin to multiply when the environment is altered. The altered environment can be a result of several factors, such as pregnancy, the use of birth control pills, the use of antibiotics or the presence of diabetes. Frequent douching also increases the likelihood of candidiasis.

Candidiasis is spread from an infected female to an uninfected male through sexual intercourse. The fungus causing candidiasis can be found under the foreskin of the penis and can be transmitted from male to female during sexual intercourse. Symptoms of candidiasis in females include a white, foul-smelling discharge and itching. Males with candidiasis may experience itching and burning during urination.

Trichomoniasis

Trichomoniasis is an STD caused by a parasitic protozoan, *Trichomonas vaginalis*. This STD affects about 10 to 15 percent of people who are sexually active. In addition to being transmitted sexually, trichomoniasis can also be transmitted nonsexually by the sharing of infected towels. The protozoa may survive for twenty-four hours on damp towels. Females who use vaginal sprays and douches may change the natural flora of their vagina enough to create a favorable environment for this parasite to flourish.

Approximately half of the females who are infected with trichomoniasis are asymptomatic for the first six months. When symptoms appear, there is a frothy, greenish-yellow vaginal discharge that has an odor. Vaginal tissue may become inflamed. There may be itching, burning, and pain during urination. Most infected males show no symptoms. A male with symptoms usually suffers from urethritis and pain and burning during urination. Trichomoniasis can often be treated successfully with antifungal medications.

Nongonococcal Urethritis

Nongonococcal urethritis (NGU) is an STD caused by pathogens other than *Neisseria gonorrhoeae*. It causes an infection and inflammation of the urethra. NGU is more common than gonorrhea. NGU can be spread from an infected partner to an uninfected partner during sexual intercourse.

Symptoms, if present, in females are usually mild, and include itching and burning during urination. If left untreated, a female may develop pelvic inflammatory disease (PID) and cervical inflammation. As many as two million males may be infected each year with NGU. Symptoms of NGU in males include painful and frequent urination as well as a purulent urethral discharge.

The symptoms may disappear temporarily without treatment. Penicillin is not effective against NGU, so other antibiotics such as tetracycline or erythromycin are the usual treatment.

Pediculosis Pubis

Pediculosis pubis refers to infection with *Phthirus pubis*, pubic or crab lice. Lice are parasitic insects that are yellowish-grey in color and about the size of a pinhead. The lice attach themselves to pubic hairs and burrow into the skin where they feed on blood. An infected person will feel intense itching where the lice are attached. Female lice produce eggs, called nits, that attach to body hair. The eggs hatch in six to eight days and mature in twenty-one days. Since each female lays as many as fifty eggs, an infection can increase in a very short time.

Lice can be transmitted from one person to another through close sexual contact. Since lice can live outside the body for as long as a day, it is possible for a person to become infected by sleeping on infected sheets, wearing infected clothing, sharing infected towels, and sitting on a toilet seat that has been used by an infected person. When a person is infected with pediculosis pubis, (s)he should avoid sexual intimacy and close contact until after treatment. All clothing, towels, and bed linen should be disinfected by thorough washing in hot water or by dry cleaning. Toilet seats that have been used by the infected person should be disinfected. Pubic lice can be effectively treated with prescription medications. A follow-up checkup should occur to be certain that the lice have been eradicated.

Hepatitis B

Hepatitis B is a common type of viral hepatitis. The hepatitis B virus is found in blood, blood products, saliva, semen, and vaginal secretions. People at most risk for infection with hepatitis B have had multiple sex partners, have used intravenous drugs, are routinely exposed to blood or blood products as a health care provider, or have a family member with hepatitis B. At one time, hepatitis B was spread through blood transfusions. Today, blood is carefully screened and the potential for infection through the use of contaminated blood products is minimal. A vaccine is available to prevent hepatitis B. Everyone who is exposed to hepatitis B is encouraged to get the vaccine.

Life Skill #6

I will choose behaviors to reduce the risk of HIV infection.

The **human immunodeficiency virus (HIV)** is the pathogen that destroys the body's immune system allowing the development of acquired immunodeficiency syndrome (AIDS). **Acquired immunodeficiency syndrome (AIDS)** is a disorder of the human immune system in a person infected with HIV, characterized by severe breakdown of the immune system that leaves a person very susceptible to opportunistic infections. An **opportunistic infection** is an infection that would probably not have the opportunity to invade the body if a person's immune system were healthy.

HIV Infection

A virus is one of the smallest pathogens that can cause disease. Like other viruses, HIV cannot replicate by itself. However, when HIV enters a person's body, it attaches to a part of the helper T cell, takes control of the helper T cell, and reproduces its genetic material in the helper T cell. The virus multiplies inside the helper T cell, causing an interruption in the signals for help in the form of antibodies. The result is an unchecked spread of HIV and the eroding of the ability of the immune system to defend itself against other pathogens.

Most people do not have any symptoms when they are first infected with HIV, and do not know they are infected until they have an HIV test. It may take anywhere from a few weeks to many years for symptoms to appear. Symptoms of HIV infection usually include fever, diarrhea, weight loss, tiredness, and enlarged lymph nodes.

Transmission of HIV

Two major ways that infection with HIV can occur are through sexual intercourse with an infected person and by sharing needles with an infected person. Also, females infected with HIV can pass the virus to their babies during pregnancy or during childbirth. They can also transmit it when breast-feeding. In the past, some people have become infected with HIV by receiving blood transfusions and through organ transplants. With blood screening, these latter possibilities have been greatly reduced.

Sexual Transmission HIV can be spread through sexual intercourse. People with STDs who have accompanying open lesions and engage in sexual behaviors are especially vulnerable to infection with HIV. The more sexual partners one has, the greater chance of encountering an infected partner and of becoming infected.

HIV may be in an infected person's blood, semen, or vaginal secretions. HIV can enter the body through cuts or sores in the skin or the moist lining of the vagina or penis. Some of these cuts or sores are so small that people do not know they are there.

The only way to completely avoid sexual transmission is to abstain from sexual intercourse or to engage in sexual intercourse only with an uninfected partner who is committed to a monogamous relationship. Latex condoms have been shown to help reduce the risk of transmission with HIV and other sexually transmitted diseases, especially when used in combination with a spermicide.

Needle Transmission Sharing needles to inject intravenous drugs is the most dangerous form of needle sharing. HIV from an infected person can remain in a needle or syringe and then be injected directly into the bloodstream of the next person who uses it. Sharing needles for other purposes may also transmit HIV. These types of needles include those used to inject steroids and those used for tattooing or piercing ears. Only qualified people using sterile equipment should be consulted for these services.

Mother-to-Baby Transmission A female infected with HIV can spread the virus to her baby during pregnancy, while giving birth, or when breast-feeding. If a female is infected before or during pregnancy, her child has about one chance in three of being born with HIV infection. There is no known way to prevent this transmission. Any female who is considering having a baby and who has ever engaged in any risk behavior for HIV should first seek counseling and testing for HIV infection to help her make informed choices.

Blood Transfusion Transmission Currently in the United States, because of blood screening, there is little chance of infection with HIV through a blood transfusion. A person cannot become infected with HIV from giving blood at a blood bank or other certified blood collection center. For this purpose, only sterile needles are used, and once they are used they are immediately destroyed.

Organ Transplants Although transmission of HIV has occurred through organ transplants in the past, new testing procedures have made this form of transmission highly unlikely.

Ways That HIV is Not Transmitted Because HIV infection leads to AIDS, it is important to know about ways that HIV is not transmitted as well as about ways that HIV is transmitted. HIV infection is not caught like a cold or flu, and is not spread by coughs or sneezes. A person becomes infected with HIV by receiving infected blood, semen, or vaginal fluids from another person. Some ways that HIV is not transmitted are as follows:

- HIV is not transmitted through everyday contact with infected people at school, work, home, or anywhere else.
- HIV is not transmitted by touching clothes, phones, or toilet seats. It cannot be passed on by things like forks, cups, or other objects that someone who is HIV-infected has used.
- HIV is not transmitted from eating food prepared by a person who is infected with HIV.
- HIV is not transmitted by a mosquito bite. HIV does not live in a mosquito. Neither is it transmitted by lice, flies, or other insects.
- HIV is not transmitted through sweat or tears.
- HIV is not transmitted through a simple kiss. Experts are not completely certain about HIV transmission through deep, prolonged, or open mouth kissing.

Testing for HIV

The only way for a person to know if (s)he is infected with HIV is to take an HIV-antibody blood test. The tests available to detect HIV infections are among the most accurate medical tests known. Two separate tests for HIV (called ELISA and Western blot), when used together, are correct more than 99.9% of the time.

When a person becomes infected with HIV, the body makes substances called antibodies. These HIV antibodies usually show up in the blood within three months after infection, and almost all people who are infected will show antibodies within six months. The tests detect these antibodies, not the virus itself. A negative HIV test means that no antibodies were found and that a person is probably not infected with HIV. However, if a person engaged in risk behavior less than six months before the test, (s)he may need to be retested later to be sure (s)he is not infected.

Progression of HIV Infection and AIDS

While many people do not experience initial signs and symptoms of HIV infection, others may exhibit a mononucleosis-like illness that lasts only a few days. The most prominent kind of symptom is **lymphadenopathy**, the presence of swollen lymph glands throughout the body. A sore throat, skin rash, or fever may also be present. These signs and symptoms will disappear and the infected individual then becomes asymptomatic. The asymptomatic period may last for ten or more years. The individual may feel healthy, but all the time HIV is attacking the T cells inside the body. The person is also able to infect others.

After the initial asymptomatic period, a person infected with HIV may experience any number of symptoms. One symptom is called the wasting syndrome. The **wasting syndrome** is an unexplained loss in body weight of more than ten percent of the total body weight. A person may also experience fevers and night sweats. A high fever of up to 106 degrees Fahrenheit is not uncommon. Diarrhea may also accompany these signs and symptoms.

The lymph glands in the head and neck, groin, and armpits may be swollen and may or may not be accompanied by pain. Harm to the nervous system may also occur. Physical damage to the brain may cause mental functioning to be impaired. Depression and impaired social interaction may occur. The spinal cord can swell, causing the limbs to weaken.

When HIV has attacked the immune system beyond a certain point a person is said to have AIDS. A person with AIDS often gets many types of infections, and those infections happen more often and get worse. Some infections that may occur include yeast infections in the mouth or throat and serious infections caused by the herpes viruses. Other common problems that occur when a person develops AIDS are a certain pneumonia (*Pneumocystis carinii*) that causes coughing, fever, and difficult breathing and a form of cancer (Kaposi's sarcoma) that produces purple blotches on the skin. Tuberculosis is also common among people with AIDS.

Living with HIV Infection and AIDS

Many people who are infected with HIV have received early treatment, have continued to stay healthy, and are able to lead productive lives. For this reason, it is important for people infected with HIV to take care of themselves physically and emotionally. It is also important for them to receive support from their families, friends, and the community.

A positive test for HIV does not mean that a person has AIDS. Rather it means that this person is infected with HIV and that this virus will remain in the body for the remainder of his/her life. It also means that this person can now infect others with whom (s)he has an intimate relationship involving the exchange of body fluids.

Learning that an HIV test is positive leads to many types of feelings. Some people feel angry, while others feel depressed, sorry, or resentful. Some people may feel relieved to finally know their health status after having engaged in risk behaviors and suspecting that they may have become infected with HIV. A positive test result may help people take more definite actions such as deciding to refrain from becoming sexually active with another person in order to prevent infecting others. Regardless of one's feelings, it is important to plan for the rest of one's life. A person infected with HIV can help his/her immune system function at its best. The immune system can be protected and bolstered by: avoiding alcohol, tobacco, and other drugs; reducing stress levels; getting enough rest; avoiding exposure to sunlight; obtaining medical advice before receiving a vaccine; being careful around pets; and eating a nutritious diet.

There is no cure for HIV infection. Once a person is infected, the infection will remain for a lifetime. A drug known as AZT can relieve the signs and symptoms of AIDS, but this drug is not a cure.

Responsibility for Preventing the Spread of HIV

Responsible behavior helps to protect and promote one's health and the health of others. Each of the risk behaviors and risk situations identified in *Risk Behaviors and Risk Situations for HIV infection* (Table 12-2) should be avoided. Teachers can help young people choose responsible behavior by promoting positive self-esteem, teaching facts about HIV/AIDS, identifying risk behaviors and risk situations, teaching resistance skills

Figure 12-2

Risk Behaviors and Risk Situations for HIV Infection

1. Having sexual intercourse with an HIV-infected person.
2. Having sexual intercourse with multiple sex partners or sexual intercourse with a person who has had multiple sex partners.
3. Having sexual intercourse with a prostitute.
4. Having sexual intercourse with a person who has hemophilia and has not been tested for HIV infection.
5. Having sexual intercourse with a person who has had a blood transfusion between 1978-1985 and who has not been tested for HIV.
6. Having sexual intercourse with an IV drug user.
7. Being an IV drug user and sharing needles or syringes when injecting drugs.
8. Having sexual contact with a person who has open lesions caused by an STD and who is HIV-infected.
9. Having open lesions due to an STD and having sexual contact with a person who is HIV-infected.
10. Being born to an HIV-infected mother.
11. Not following sterilization procedures with the result that needles used for ear piercing or tattooing may contain blood that is HIV-tainted.
12. Performing a ceremony such as blood sister/brother in which HIV-infected blood is exchanged.
13. Being exposed to needle-stick injuries in a health care setting.
14. Not following precautions when caring for a person who has AIDS.
15. Using mind-altering drugs such as marijuana or alcohol that change the ability to make responsible decisions.

for HIV prevention, and encouraging honest communication within relationships.

Life Skill #7

I will obtain information about my family's history of disease.

Heredity and Disease

People from the same biological family share common physical characteristics, such as eye color, skin tone, or body structure. These characteristics are passed by genes from generation to generation in a family. **Genes** are special structures that transmit inherited characteristics. They also contain the code for the reproduction and development of body cells. Genes not only influence physical makeup but also can contain codes that result in genetic disorders and diseases. **Genetics** is the scientific study of genes and how they determine and control development.

Sometimes an individual inherits the genes for a specific genetic disease. Some genetic diseases are apparent at birth while others do not express themselves until later in life. Many inherited genes do not cause disease by themselves. Rather, the inherited genes make it more likely for a disease to occur in a person. Individuals who are genetically at risk for a disease can often avoid or delay the development of a disease by adhering to certain health habits. For example, a person who is genetically at risk for coronary heart disease can eat low-fat foods, abstain from smoking, and stay physically active.

Some diseases tend to occur frequently within biological relatives. Examples are cardiovascular diseases, many forms of cancer, and diabetes.

Genetic Diseases

Muscular Dystrophy Muscular dystrophy is a disease that is characterized by weakness due to the deterioration of muscle fibers. The symptoms appear slowly and may vary from one person to another. Because there is no known cure for muscular dystrophy, treatment focuses on physical therapy.

Hemophilia Hemophilia is a genetic disease characterized by the absence of a protein factor necessary for the clotting of blood. Thus, a minor injury can result in severe blood loss. People with hemophilia may be treated with blood transfusions and other blood products. There is no cure.

Sickle-Cell Anemia Sickle-cell anemia is a blood disease that gets its name from the shape of the abnormal red blood cell. The cell is elongated and sickle-shaped rather than being disc-shaped. It is also rigid and brittle. The sickle-shaped cell has difficulty passing through small blood vessels in the body. Consequently, these cells clump together and prevent oxygen from reaching parts of the body.

People with sickle-cell anemia may experience severe pain and tissue damage. Other complications may include frequent infections and damage to body organs. Physical activity may be extremely limited, and the person's life span may be shortened. However, the effects of sickle-cell anemia vary. Some patients become very ill while others rarely experience difficulties. Sickle-cell disease is most prevalent among people of African descent. However, sickle-cell disease is found among ethnic groups of African, Mediterranean, and Asian ancestry.

Sickle-cell anemia can not be cured. However, being aware of the symptoms of sickle-cell anemia will enable affected individuals to promote their own good health. People who are concerned that they might have sickle-cell trait should be tested for its presence. After testing, these individuals may be counseled about their status.

Cystic Fibrosis Cystic fibrosis is a genetic disease that affects the mucous and sweat glands. It is the most common genetic disease that affects the white American population in the United States. A person with cystic fibrosis secretes a thick and sticky mucous that blocks the passageways of different parts of the body, including air passages. As a result, the person has difficulty breathing. Cystic fibrosis can be detected by checking the salt content of a person's perspiration. However, tests to accurately check for

carriers of this disease are lacking. A person with cystic fibrosis has a 50 percent chance of living to adulthood if the disease is detected and treated early.

Tay-Sachs Tay-Sachs is a genetic disease caused by the absence of a key enzyme needed to break down fats in the body. The result is an accumulation of fatty materials in the brain that leads to mental retardation, blindness, and death by the age of three or four years. Most individuals with Tay-Sachs disease are from Jewish families of eastern European descent. Carriers of Tay-Sachs disease can be identified by blood tests and may choose to undergo genetic counseling.

Down Syndrome Down syndrome is a genetic disease that is the result of an extra chromosome. A child born with Down syndrome has forty-seven instead of forty-six chromosomes. Characteristics of a child with this disease are folds around the eyes that make the eyes appear slanted; a broad, flat nose; mental retardation; and sometimes a heart defect. Many individuals with Down syndrome live into the adult years. Down syndrome is more likely to occur in children born to mothers over the age of thirty-five.

Gathering Information about a Family's History of Disease

Sources of information about family history of disease include conversations with older family members and family records. The

occurrence in one or more biological relatives of the following diseases should be noted: alcoholism, allergies, anemia, asthma, hay fever, blood disorders, cancer, diabetes, eating disorders, emphysema, epilepsy, hearing disorders, heart disease, high blood pressure, kidney disease, liver disease, lupus, mental illness, migraine headache, multiple sclerosis, obesity, osteoporosis, rheumatic fever, sickle-cell anemia, stroke, thyroid disease, ulcers, visual problems, inherited genetic disorders, and other problems. This information enables people to become aware of the specific diseases that tend to occur in their family. It also gives insight into which health practices they can follow to reduce the risk of getting the same disorders as family members.

Life Skill #8

I will choose behaviors to reduce my risk of cardiovascular disease.

Cardiovascular disease is a group of diseases of the heart and blood vessels. It is the leading cause of death in the United States. **Coronary heart disease** is the broad term used to describe damage or malfunction of the heart caused by blockage of the coronary arteries. The coronary arteries supply blood to the heart. **Arteriosclerosis** is a general term used to describe several conditions that cause hardening and thickening of arteries. Often, underlying coronary heart disease is **atherosclerosis** which is a form of arteriosclerosis in which fatty substances are deposited on artery walls. Blockage of the coronary arteries often causes angina pectoris. **Angina pectoris** is chest pain that results from narrowed blood vessels in the heart. If the blockage is severe enough, a myocardial infarction may result. **Myocardial infarction** or heart attack is a condition that results in damage to the heart muscle because of interruption of blood flow. Some other forms of cardiovascular disease include **arrhythmia** or irregular heartbeat, **hypertension** or high blood pressure, and **stroke**, a break or block in a blood vessel in the brain.

Each year, 1.5 million Americans have a heart attack and about 500,000 of these heart attack victims die. Three in five of these deaths occur before a heart attack victim reaches a hospital. About half of all heart attack victims wait more than two hours after the start of symptoms before getting help (Gunby, 1993).

Risk Factors for Heart Disease

Risk factors for developing heart disease can be categorized into one of two groups; risks that an individual cannot control and risks that an individual can control. There are four risk factors for heart disease that are not voluntarily controlled:

1. *Heredity*. Individuals with a parent or sibling who had a premature heart attack are at increased risk of coronary heart disease. A **premature heart attack** is one that occurs before age 55 in men and before age 65 in women.

2. *Sex*. Males have a higher risk of developing cardiovascular disease than do females until the age of 40. It is rare for a female to have a heart attack before she reaches menopause. But once a female reaches the age of 65, heart disease becomes the number one cause of death.

3. *Race*. African-Americans are two times more likely than white Americans to develop high blood pressure. An increased blood pressure is related to an increased risk of developing heart disease. African-Americans also have a greater family history of developing heart disease.

4. *Age*. The risk of developing heart disease increases with age. About 80 percent of people who develop heart disease do so after age 65.

Many risk factors for heart disease can be controlled, including:

1. *Smoking*. Cigarette smoking is the single most preventable cause of death in the United States. Smokers have a significantly higher risk of developing cardiovascular disease than do nonsmokers. Smoking increases the risk that a person who has a heart attack will die from that attack. Smoking is a risk factor because the ingredients in the smoke of a burning cigarette affect the heart in particular. Nicotine in tobacco smoke causes the heart to pump more often. Carbon monoxide in the smoke displaces the oxygen in the bloodstream. The heart is denied

adequate amounts of oxygen. Cigarette smoke also harms the inside of the coronary arteries so that cholesterol can build up more easily, causing narrowing of the arteries and restricted blood flow.

2. *Diet and high blood cholesterol.* Diet plays a significant role in the health of the heart. Foods high in cholesterol and saturated fat lead to increases in the buildup of fatty deposits in the coronary arteries. It is recommended that a person keep blood cholesterol within a healthful range. Total cholesterol is recommended to be below 200 mg of total cholesterol per deciliter of blood (mg/dL). A person who has a total cholesterol level of 201 to 239 is considered borderline and thus at moderate risk of developing heart disease. Levels over 240 are considered high, and dietary and/or medical interventions are needed. For every 1 percent reduction in blood cholesterol level, there is a 2 to 3 percent decline in the risk of heart attack. Diet is also a factor in the amount of fats (lipids) in the bloodstream. These lipids are called lipoproteins. There are two kinds of lipoproteins in the body. **High-density lipoproteins (HDL)** are fats that transport excess cholesterol to the liver for removal from the body. The higher the HDLs in the blood, the lower the risk of developing heart disease. People who exercise regularly and quit smoking increase their HDL levels. **Low-density lipoproteins (LDL)** are fats that form deposits in artery walls and continue the development of atherosclerosis. What is most important to understand about HDLs and LDLs is their ratio to total cholesterol. The higher the ratio of HDLs to total cholesterol, the lower the heart attack risk. A male is at increased risk if the percentage of HDL is less than 20 percent. A female is at risk if the ratio is less than 25 percent. The best way to control cholesterol is to reduce the intake of foods high in fat.

3. *Hypertension.* About 50 million Americans have high blood pressure, which is a serious risk factor for stroke and heart attack. Hypertension forces the heart to work harder than it should. The heart must force blood into arteries with increased resistance. Thus, the heart can become diseased, and the arteries also may become diseased and burst. In addition to being controlled through medication, blood pressure can be controlled through exercise and by limiting intake of sodium, calories, and alcohol.

4. *Lack of exercise.* Exercise helps a person maintain a desirable body weight, increases HDLs, decreases the tendency of the blood to form clots, moderates stress, helps the body to use insulin, and lowers blood pressure. Regular aerobic exercise is important in reducing the risk of heart disease. Even physical activity that is low in intensity such as walking and gardening, if done regularly and long-term, can decrease risk of heart disease.

5. *Obesity.* Having a high percentage of body fat and being obese increase a person's risk for developing heart disease. The heart must work harder if a person is overfat and obese than if a person has a lean body and a desirable weight. Obesity also increases the risk for high blood cholesterol, hypertension, and diabetes, which further increases coronary heart disease risk. Another important factor is how fat is distributed in the body. Individuals who carry fat around the waist in a "pot-bellied" or "apple-shaped" manner have a greater chance of developing heart disease than people whose excess weight has accumulated on the hips (pear-shaped).

6. *Diabetes.* Noninsulin dependent diabetes mellitus (NIDDM) is another important risk factor for coronary heart disease. NIDDM can often be managed by weight control and exercise.

Treatment of Heart Disease

People who have heart disease can often be treated successfully. Drugs such as calcium blockers can lower blood pressure and control arrhythmias. **Beta-blockers** are drugs that can slow the heartbeat rate and reduce the force of the heart's contractions.

One of the more common treatments for coronary artery disease is coronary bypass surgery. **Coronary bypass surgery** is an operation in which a vein from another part of the body, often the leg, is grafted into a coronary artery so that blood is detoured around a blockage. Coronary bypass surgery is not a panacea since a large number of people who have this surgery develop blockages up to ten years later. Doctors now often use the internal mammary artery instead of a vein because that graft tends to stay open longer. Another method for treating a blocked coronary artery is the use of balloon angioplasty. **Balloon angioplasty** is a procedure in which an artery is unclogged by catheterization. A dye is injected into the arteries so that the clog shows up on a monitor. A balloon is then inflated so that the artery is widened. The balloon is then deflated so that normal blood flow can resume.

Life Skill #9

I will choose behaviors to reduce my risk of cancer.

Cancer is a group of diseases in which there is uncontrolled multiplication of abnormal cells in the body. Cancer is the second leading cause of death in the United States. Often, the development of cancer is manifest in the growth of malignant tumors. A **malignant tumor** is a cancerous tumor. This is in contrast to a **benign tumor**, which is a noncancerous tumor.

Causes of Cancer

Why a normal cell develops into a cancerous cell is not known. There may be a combination of factors involved such as viruses, chemicals, radiation, or a combination of these or other factors:

- *Heredity.* There seems to be a link that some kinds of cancers are related to a person's genetic makeup. Cancers of the breast, ovary, pancreas, and colon appear to run in families.
- *Viruses.* There is some link between viruses and the development of certain kinds of cancers such as leukemia.
- *Tobacco.* People who smoke cigarettes and use smokeless tobacco have an increased risk of developing cancer. Cigarette smoke contains carcinogens and is therefore related to the development of lung cancer.
- *Ultraviolet Radiation.* There is a definite link between exposure to ultraviolet radiation, whether from the sun's rays or tanning beds, and the development of cancer, particularly skin cancer. Skin cancer is the most common form of cancer. Examples

are basal and squamous cell carcinomas. Most skin cancers can be treated successfully if diagnosed early. But there is now evidence that exposure to ultraviolet radiation is responsible for **malignant melanoma**, the most serious of the skin cancers. Malignant melanoma is highly invasive so that early detection and immediate treatment are essential if it is to be treated successfully.

Detecting Cancer

Detecting cancer in an early stage increases the chances that it can be successfully treated. The American Cancer Society advocates that people learn seven early warning signs of cancer, the beginning letter of each warning sign corresponding to a letter in the word CAUTION:

Change in bowel or bladder habits
A sore that does not heal
Unusual bleeding or discharge
Thickening or lump in a breast or elsewhere
Indigestion or difficulty in swallowing
Obvious change in a wart or mole
Nagging cough or hoarseness

One sign of malignant melanoma is a change in the color of a lesion. The color may be in multiple shades of brown or black, red, white, and blue, and spread to the surrounding skin. There may be an enlargement of the lesion. The shape of the lesion may change so that the surrounding border may develop an irregular shape. The lesion may appear raised and scaling, and may ooze. Crusting may result. If there is itching and pain as well as a softening or other change in texture, medical help is indicated.

An important procedure helpful in detecting early breast cancer is for females to have **mammogram**, special X-rays of the breast. There should be one baseline X-ray between the ages of thirty-five and thirty-nine, and then one every one to two years between the ages of forty and forty-nine. A yearly mammogram should be given after age fifty. For early detection of uterine cancers, all females who are sexually active or who have reached eighteen years of age should have a Pap test and pelvic exam yearly. After the age of forty, both males and females should have a digital rectal examination each year. They should have a proctoscopic examination every three to five years after the age of fifty, following two initial negative tests one year apart. A stool blood test is also recommended every year after age fifty. These tests are for detection of colon and rectal cancers.

Cancer Treatment

A variety of cancer treatment methods are available. Surgery is the most common treatment method. If tumors are confined to a particular site, surgery can be used independently to accomplish a cure. A large number of cancer patients receive radiotherapy. **Radiotherapy** is the treatment of cancer via the use of radiation. In this treatment, X-rays are used to kill cancer cells. For other cancer patients, chemotherapy may be the method of treatment. **Chemotherapy** is the use of drugs to kill cancer cells inside the body. Chemotherapy has many different side effects that may include nausea, hair loss, weight loss, and fatigue. When the usual drugs used in chemotherapy do not work, some patients may receive experimental drugs that may cause serious side effects. In many cases, a combination of treatments are used. Chemotherapy might be combined with radiotherapy and/or surgery.

Life Skill #10

I will recognize ways to manage chronic diseases.

Diabetes

Diabetes is a disease in which the body is unable to process the sugar in foods in normal ways. It occurs when the pancreas either does not produce enough insulin or produces insulin that does not help the cells break down sugar. This results in too much sugar or glucose in the bloodstream. Diabetes cannot be cured, but it can be controlled.

There are two types of diabetes. One type is insulin-dependent diabetes, formerly called juvenile diabetes because it appears most often in young people. **Insulin-dependent diabetes** is diabetes in which the pancreas produces little or no insulin. People with this type of diabetes must have daily injections of insulin to stay alive. The second type of diabetes

is noninsulin-dependent diabetes, formerly called adult- or maturity-onset diabetes. **Noninsulin-dependent diabetes** is diabetes in which the pancreas produces some insulin, but the body cells are not able to properly use it. This type of diabetes is most likely to affect people who are over age 40, physically inactive, and overweight. This type of diabetes can be controlled with oral medication. Many people control this type of diabetes through a program of diet and exercise.

Both forms of diabetes have obvious symptoms. Among them are frequent urination, abnormal thirst, weakness, fatigue, drowsiness, blurred vision, tingling and numbness in the hands and feet, and slow healing of cuts. Not all of these symptoms appear at the same time.

People with diabetes must realize that they need a lifelong commitment to control this disease. It is a leading cause of other diseases. Complications of diabetes are blindness and poor circulation, which can lead to gangrene and amputation of the extremities. Of particular concern are the millions of Americans who are unaware that they have diabetes. Thus, it continues to cause irreversible damage inside the body. Once the symptoms are recognized, healthful behaviors can be followed to prevent its harmful effects.

Ulcerative Colitis and Diverticulosis

Ulcerative colitis and diverticulosis are disorders of the walls of the intestines. **Ulcerative colitis** is an inflammatory disease of the walls of the large intestine. Individuals suffering from ulcerative colitis may experience several episodes of bloody diarrhea each day. Additionally, colitis causes stomach cramping, nausea, sweating, fever, and weight loss. This disease baffles medical experts because it tends to go away and then recur for no apparent reason. People with ulcerative colitis experience a high rate of colorectal cancer and are likely to develop irritable bowel syndrome. **Irritable bowel syndrome (IBS)** is a condition in which a person experiences nausea, gas, pain, attacks of diarrhea, and cramps after eating certain foods. The cause of ulcerative is unknown. High levels of stress and reactions to certain foods are believed to play a role. Doctors recommend that colitis patients increase the amount of fiber in their diets. Certain medications are sometimes prescribed to relieve the symptoms of colitis.

Diverticulosis is a disease in which the intestinal walls develop outpouchings called diverticula. Diverticulosis most often occurs in the small intestine, although it can occur in any intestinal wall. Pain and discomfort is felt as fecal material fills into the diverticula, causing irritation and infection. Diverticulosis can be life-threatening if bleeding and blockage occurs. It can occur at any age, but is most likely to occur in middle or older age. Lower abdominal pain that does not go away is a possible sign of diverticulosis.

Arthritis

Arthritis is a general term that includes over one hundred diseases, all of which involve inflammation. Out of the millions of people who have this disease, most suffer from two kinds. The first kind of arthritis is osteoarthritis. **Osteoarthritis** is a wearing down of the moving parts of a joint. It usually occurs due to wear and tear. Some cases of osteoarthritis appear to be hereditary. Other cases are caused by physical damage, such as sports injuries. Being overweight can be a factor in the disease since it is believed that extra weight adds stress on a joint.

Treatment for osteoarthritis often consists of aspirin and other pain relievers. Exercise can sometimes improve movement in a joint area. In some cases, surgery is needed to implant new joints. These joints are usually made of plastic or metal and are joined to the bone with special cements.

The second kind of arthritis is rheumatoid arthritis. **Rheumatoid arthritis** is a serious disease in which joint deformity and loss of joint function occurs. This type of arthritis most often affects people between the ages of twenty and fifty-five, but it can also affect young people. It is important for people with this kind of arthritis to carefully follow a prescribed exercise plan. Once movement in a joint is lost, it is difficult to regain. Certain medications, including aspirin, can be used to treat rheumatoid arthritis. At other times, cortisone is prescribed to reduce swelling and ease pain. However, cortisone has strong side effects and often cannot be used on a regular basis.

Sometimes, surgery is needed to relieve pain and improve movement in the joint.

Systemic Lupus

Systemic lupus erythematosus (SLE) is a chronic disease of unknown cause that affects most of the systems in the body. In particular, SLE affects the skin, kidneys, joints, muscles, and central nervous system. In SLE, antibodies are formed that attack various tissues in the body. SLE can progress to bleeding in the central nervous system, kidney failure, or heart failure. The outlook for SLE patients has improved greatly in the past decade. The onset of SLE most often occurs in late adolescence and it is more common in females than males. SLE runs in families.

Treatment for SLE varies depending upon which specific body tissues are involved. Medications such as cortical steroids, aspirin or nonsteroidal inflammatory agents, antibiotics, diuretics, and immunosuppressive drugs may be given. The complications from long-term cortical steroid use are a serious concern among SLE patients. These complications include bone disease, muscle wasting, cataracts, and short stature.

Chronic Fatigue Syndrome

Chronic fatigue syndrome (CFS) is a condition in which fatigue comes on suddenly and is relentless or relapsing, causing debilitating tiredness in someone who has no apparent reason for feeling this way. People diagnosed with CFS often describe its onset as sudden but not alarming because its symptoms mimic those of the flu. The symptoms include headache, sore throat, low-grade fever, fatigue and weakness, tender lymph glands, muscle and joint aches, and inability to concentrate. Unlike the flu which goes away in a few weeks, CFS symptoms persist or recur frequently for more than 6 months.

For many people, CFS begins after an acute illness such as the flu, bronchitis, hepatitis, or gastrointestinal illness. In adolescents and young adults, it follows a mononucleosis infection that temporarily saps the energy. In a smaller number of people, CFS develops more gradually and seemingly with no apparent cause. The illness may begin when an individual is feeling highly stressed.

Communicable and Chronic Diseases

In recent years, scientists have considered the Epstein-Barr virus (EBV) as a possible cause of CFS. Some researchers believe that EBV may cause CFS in people who never recovered from mononucleosis, or in whom the virus has somehow been reactivated. Newer evidence indicates that the EBV cannot, however, explain all cases of CFS.

Currently, no proven effective treatment for CFS exists. Health experts recommend that people with CFS try to maintain a healthful lifestyle by eating a balanced diet and getting adequate rest. Physical conditioning should be preserved by exercising regularly as much as can be tolerated short of causing more fatigue. People with CFS learn to pace themselves physically, emotionally, and intellectually. Too much stress can exacerbate the symptoms.

Managing Chronic Diseases

Individuals with chronic diseases often have to cope with their diseases over long periods of time. They need to take special care of themselves daily. They may have to adhere to medication regimens or follow special diets. They may require assistance with daily activities and home health care. They may need periodic health care visits throughout their lives. Living with a chronic disease often necessitates working through feelings about death, fear, anxiety, and isolation. To cope with these concerns, many people with chronic diseases turn to support groups that help people living with chronic diseases and their families learn to live each day as fully and completely as possible. These groups can help individuals with chronic diseases improve their outlook on life and live with hope and optimism for the future.

Figure 13-1

Life Skills for Injury Prevention and Safety

1. I will follow safety rules in my home.

2. I will follow safety rules at school.

3. I will follow safety rules in my community.

4. I will follow safety guidelines for different weather conditions and natural disasters.

5. I will be able to get help for emergency situations.

6. I will be skilled in basic first aid procedures.

7. I will choose behaviors to reduce my risk of violence.

8. I will protect myself from people who might harm me.

9. I will stay safe while riding in a car.

10. I will stay safe while exercising.

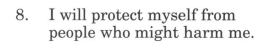

Chapter 13

INJURY PREVENTION AND SAFETY

Injury Prevention and Safety is the area of health that focuses on following safety rules in the home, school, and community; following safety guidelines for different weather conditions and natural disasters, being able to get help for emergency situations; being skilled in basic first-aid procedures; reducing the risk of violence; protecting oneself from those who are dangerous; and staying safe while riding in a car and when enjoying exercise. **Injury prevention** is actions that are taken for the purpose of preventing injuries. **Safety** is the condition of being protected from injuries. The content in this chapter provides the background information needed to teach young people life skills for injury prevention and safety (Figure 13-1).

Life Skill #1

I will follow safety rules in my home.

Accidents are sudden, unexpected events that often result in injury. The term accidents implies that accidents are random, uncontrollable acts of fate over which there is little control, or a result of carelessness or ignorance. Approximately one-third of all accidents occur in the home. The number of fatal accidents in the home is second only to the number of deaths from automobile accidents. The home is the most likely place for accidents to occur to young children. The leading causes of injury fatality in the home are falls, fires, poisonings, firearms, suffocation, and drownings.

Preventing Falls

More people die at home as a result of falls than from any other type of home accident. Many more people are permanently disabled. Although elderly people are most at risk of suffering serious injury or death from falls, falls are also a common problem of other age groups, especially young children. Babies and young children are likely to fall from cribs, high chairs, tables, decks, and porches, and to fall down stairs. Another potential location for serious falls is in bathtubs and showers.

Falls can be avoided by taking the following precautions:
- placing rubber mats in bathtubs and showers;
- placing a nonskid backing on floor rugs;
- keeping objects, such as toys, off walkways and stairways;
- installing handrails along stairways;
- adequately lighting stairway areas;
- using safety gates to block children's access to stairs;
- placing window guards in upper-story windows to which children may have access;
- clearing ice and snow from steps and sidewalks;
- not leaving a baby unattended in a high chair;

- making sure that ladders are in good condition.

Fire Safety

More than half of all fire fatalities involve children under the age of four. Most fires in the home are the result of carelessness. Some examples of carelessness that could lead to a fire are:
- falling asleep in a bed or on a couch with a lighted cigarette;
- overloading outlets;
- running electrical cords under rugs;
- playing with matches or cigarette lighters;
- leaving food cooking on the stove;
- improperly storing flammable materials;
- not regularly checking electrical systems for defects.

All homes should be equipped with smoke detectors or heat detectors. When properly installed, placed in an appropriate location, and maintained in good working order, these devices can detect smoke or gases before the flames reach people. When smoke or gases are detected, a loud alarm is sounded, alerting people to the danger and waking them from their sleep. Many people who die in fires have been overcome by smoke and are unconscious or are already dead before the flames reach them.

Another important fire safety procedure is the family fire drill plan. Family members should prepare a plan for how to safely and quickly escape from the home in the event of a fire. Plans should also be made to meet at a precise location outside and a safe distance from the home. Fire drills should be practiced frequently and regularly so that all family members remain aware of how to act. Family members should be instructed never to attempt to stay in a burning house or to reenter a burning house. When exiting a smoke-filled room or house, they should stay as low as possible in order to breathe any available fresh air. The mouth and nose should be covered with a wet cloth, if possible. They should not stop to collect any belongings or to telephone anyone. Bedroom doors should be closed while the family is sleeping in order to keep out smoke, heat, and dangerous gases. In case of fire, the door should be checked to see if it is hot. If hot, the door should not be opened. Escape through a window or another exit.

People should be taught that if their clothing or hair catches fire, they should use the Stop, Drop, and Roll method. The Stop, Drop, and Roll method includes the following steps: Immediately stop where you are, drop to the ground, and roll over and over to smother the flames. Rolling up in a blanket, coat, or other heavy material also can smother and extinguish flames.

The following fire safety tips can help to prevent home fires:
- don't smoke in bed;
- check around furniture for burning cigarettes, cigars, and pipes;
- make sure electrical circuits are not overloaded;
- always replace a blown fuse with one of the proper size;
- check electric cords for cracks, exposed wire, broken plugs, and poor connections;
- use proper size light bulbs in lamps and light fixtures;
- don't leave food that is cooking unattended on the stove;
- don't wear robes or other loose-fitting clothing when cooking;
- have the heating systems professionally checked once a year;
- keep matches and lighters away from children;
- place upholstered furniture away from stoves, fireplaces, and other heat sources;
- have chimneys and fireplaces inspected regularly for cracks, crumbling bricks, obstructions, and other potential problems.

Poisoning

Poisoning is the entry into the body of a substance that disrupts the structure or function of cells. Eight out of every ten poisoning cases occurs in the home. The poisonous substances most often involved are household chemicals such as bleaches, disinfectants, detergents, herbicides, insecticides, polishing agents; medications; and certain household plants. Young people can often readily gain access to these poisonous substances because they are often stored in locations that young people can reach. Simple precautions such as storing these substances out of their reach or the use of childproof containers can prevent many poisonings. Mr. Yuk or Officer Ugh stickers should be placed on containers of poisonous substances to help children identify them.

Adults are also subject to poisoning. Taking overdoses of prescription drugs, mixing certain medications, or taking the wrong medication account for a large number of poison-related accidents. Poisonous gases and vapors from gas leaks and faulty cooking and heating equipment in the home are another source of accidental poisoning.

Firearm Safety

Firearm-related homicides, suicides, and accidental shootings account for approximately 38,000 deaths a year in the United States (Buchsbaum, 1994). A **firearm** is a weapon from which gunpowder is discharged. Among adolescents fifteen to nineteen years of age and young adults twenty to twenty-four years of age, one of every four deaths is by a firearm. One of every eight deaths in children ten to fourteen is by a firearm.

Many firearm accidents among young people occur in the home. Young people are curious about guns. For this reason, firearms should be locked away from children and stored unloaded. Ammunition should be locked away and stored separately from the firearm. The handling of firearms should be done only under the close supervision of a responsible adult. Adolescents who are planning to hunt should be taught how to properly use and carry firearms. Firearms should be treated as if they are loaded at all times, and they should never be pointed at another person or at oneself. Most firearm accidents can be avoided if simple safety precautions are observed.

Preventing Suffocation Injuries

Suffocation is a condition in which there is a lack of oxygen due to an obstruction to the passage of air into the lungs. Children often put objects in their mouth, which can lead to suffocation. Toys, marbles, buttons, and coins are objects that, if swallowed, can block the airway passage. Food items such as carrots, hot dogs, grapes, and hard candy can also lead to choking or suffocation, especially in small children. Plastic bags, pillows, and blankets can also cause suffocation in very small children. Small toys and objects should be kept out of reach of small children. Food should be cut up in small pieces, and children should

not be allowed to run and play while eating. Children under the age of five should not be given food items on which they could choke.

Self-Protection When at Home

A **burglary** is an unlawful entry of a structure to commit a theft. Every ten seconds there is a burglary. People attempting to commit burglary may enter a home, intending to do more than take valuables. They may plan to commit an assault, kidnapping, rape, or murder. A plan is needed to protect oneself when at home and protect the contents of the home. *Self-Protection When At Home* (Table 13-2) provides a list of guidelines to follow for safety at home.

Life Skill #2

I will stay safe at school.

Playground Safety

Serious injuries can occur on the playground. About three-fourths of playground-related emergency room visits involve falls. Four of every five of these falls were from playground equipment and from seesaws and swings. Certain materials such as sand and some artificial materials, if properly installed and maintained, can reduce the severity of many playground injuries. Falling and striking playground equipment is the second most common cause of playground injuries. Other causes include colliding with equipment while running and being struck by moving equipment such as swings and merry-go-rounds (National Commission for Injury Prevention and Control, 1989).

Many playground injuries could be prevented with adequate supervision and by separating older students from younger students during play. Having certain safety features such as handrails or guardrails on steps and platforms can help prevent falls. Playground equipment should be age-appropriate and should be well maintained.

Table 13-2

Self-Protection When At Home

1. Keep window and doors locked at all times, even when you are home.
2. Make sure your home has extra-security deadbolts on all entry doors.
3. Be aware that chain locks are easily ripped off a door.
4. Consider having a home security alarm system installed.
5. Consider getting a dog and placing a "Beware of Dog" sign on your property.
6. Do not give out your house key to anyone other than a trusted friend.
7. Do not hide your extra keys outside your home.
8. Consider having a one-way viewer or peephole in your door.
9. At night, leave one or more lights on.
10. Have your mail, newspaper delivery, and other services discontinued when you leave for an extended period of time.
11. Ask a trusted neighbor to check you home and vary the position of the drapes.
12. Always have your keys ready before going to your door.
13. If there are signs that someone has entered your home, do not go inside. Go to a safe place and call the police.
14. Never let a stranger into your home unless you are sure it is safe to do so.
15. When speaking on the phone or answering the door, always give the impression someone else is in the home with you.
16. Ask to see identification before allowing a repair person to enter you home.
17. Do not open the door when someone asks to come in and make an emergency phone call. You can always make the call yourself if you want to do so.
18. Report any stranger who does not have identification to the police.
19. Be cautious about giving out information on where you live to people in person, on the phone, or by mail.
20. If you receive a crank phone call, do not talk to the person. Hang up immediately.
21. Report continuous, obscene, or bothersome phone calls to the telephone company and police.
22. Keep a list of emergency phone numbers such as the number for the police and fire departments by the phone.

Violence and Gangs at Schools

Violence is the threatened or actual use of physical force to injure, damage, or destroy oneself, others, or property. Examples of physical violence are slapping, punching, stabbing, and shooting. **Youth gangs** are groups of young people who band together and participate in violent, unlawful, or criminal behavior. Gang activity in schools increases violence. Gangs often stake out an area of the school as their turf. When rival gang members or other students enter this area, fighting begins. Often young people are harmed in these turf battles. In some schools, gang members have forced students to pay them money to stay safe. Students may not be able to walk safely in a certain place without paying a fee. Gang activity also may involve selling drugs to students at school. Drug-related debts or arguments can result in violence.

Weapons at Schools

One in 20 high school students has reported carrying a gun. Reasons students reported they carried a gun include it safeguarded them from being jumped or assaulted by others, it gave them recognition and status, and it was their only protection against older and larger people who bullied them. Many schools have taken security measures to prevent students from carrying guns to school. They may require students to carry see-through backpacks to school. Students may have to pass through metal detectors as they enter the school. There may be unannounced locker searches. Extra police may be hired for extra security on school grounds. These security measures are costly. Walk-through metal detectors often cost $10,000. X-ray equipment may cost as much as $17,000. The hiring of extra security also is expensive.

Drug & Weapon Free Zone

Weapon-Free or Gun-Free Zones

Weapon-free zones or **gun-free zones** are areas near schools in which it is illegal to carry a firearm. In 1990, the U.S. Congress made it a felony offense to bring a gun within 1,000 feet of any school. In addition to this federal legislation, some state and local lawmakers have passed additional legislation that bans guns in and near schools.

Drug-Free School Zones

A **drug-free school zone** is a defined area around a school for the purpose of sheltering young people from the sale of drugs. Increased penalties for using and selling drugs have been set for drug-free school zones. School officials and law enforcement officers pay particular attention to the drug-free school zones to reduce the risk of violence.

Life Skill #3

I will stay safe in my community.

Pedestrian Safety

Although walking is the safest and most reliable form of transportation, more than 8,000 pedestrians are killed each year in the United States. The highest rates of pedestrian accidents and fatalities occur among children ten years of age and younger. Young children have difficulty judging vehicle distances, anticipating the speed of vehicles, and understanding traffic signals and signs. Small children are often effectively taught to look to the left and the right before crossing the street, but then still proceed into oncoming traffic. While elementary school students can be effectively taught specific traffic safety, the ability to judge vehicle motion and spatial relationships can only develop over time. The safety of elementary students can be enhanced by stationing adults at busy intersections to assist them as they come to or leave school, and emphasizing that they cross streets only at intersections.

The following actions increase a pedestrian's risk of being hit by a moving motor vehicle and should therefore be avoided:

- entering a street between two parked cars;
- attempting to cross a street as a traffic signal is changing;
- playing miniaturized stereo radio-tape players while walking or jogging in busy traffic areas;
- not using sidewalks and crosswalks;
- walking along the side of a road with the traffic;
- wearing darkly colored clothing at dusk or when it is dark;
- hitchhiking.

Animal Safety

The most common victims of animal bites are children. The animal most likely to bite people is the domestic dog. Each year about twenty people die of dog bites. Half of these dog bite deaths are from pit bull terriers (Powers, 1990). Young people should be cautioned not to approach strange animals or to try to feed them. Adults should be careful not to leave young children unattended near dogs. When a bite does occur, immediate medical attention should be obtained.

Self-Protection Strategies for Public Places

Most people visit many different places in the course of their daily lives. *Self-Protection When In Public Places* (Table 13-3) provides a list of guidelines to follow for safety when in public places.

Table 13-3

Self-Protection When In Public Places

1. Avoid walking alone at night or in high-risk areas.
2. Stay on well-lighted streets and avoid deserted areas, alleys and staircases when walking alone.
3. Keep your distance if someone in a car stops to ask you for directions. Ignore the person or call out the directions to them.
4. Never accept a ride from a stranger or someone you do not trust.
5. Never hitchhike.
6. Wear comfortable shoes that allow you to run from trouble.
7. Do not talk to strangers who approach you.
8. Seek help in a nearby store or building with other people. Walk briskly with your head up, and move in a confident manner if you think you are being followed.
9. Carry a loud siren, whistle, or buzzer to get attention if you need it.
10. Avoid using bank money machines whenever possible. If you use a money machine, do so during the day.
11. Stay away from areas where there are gangs.
12. Carry a chemical spray such as tear gas to use in case you are attacked.
13. Carry a flashlight at night and use it to light up potentially dangerous areas. It

also can be used as a weapon in an emergency.

14. Carry your purse tucked under your elbow and hold it firmly with one hand. (instead of carrying a purse, consider wearing a waist pack and carrying only what you need.
15. Avoid using alcohol or other drugs so that you think clearly and make wise decisions about what you should do.
16. Wait only in safe and well-lighted areas for public transportation. After boarding, stay with a group of people or sit near the driver if possible.
17. Do not go into places that are deserted.
18. Yell, scream, or shout loudly for help if someone is bothering you in a public place.
19. Be sure to vary your walking route if you routinely walk to and from school or work.
20. Speed up, cross the street, turn around, run, or do whatever you feel is necessary if you feel a person may be following you.
21. Do not turn your back toward a street or a lobby when you are using a public telephone; turn you back toward the telephone.
22. Use pay telephones only when they are in well-lighted places where there are many other people.

Weapons in the Community

Today, guns are readily available. Many people have them illegally, do not know how to use them, misuse them and have accidents, or intend to use them to harm others. In about one-half of all households, someone owns a gun. In one-quarter of all households, someone owns a handgun. Many young people to obtain a gun from their homes without their parents or guardians knowing. Young people can buy guns on the street, from drug dealers, and from pawnshops. In fact, more than half of students in grades six through twelve said they could "get a gun if they wanted one" (*Newsweek*, 1993). Guns can be purchased for as little as ten dollars. Young people also may be able to borrow guns from questionable sources. Many

young people disobey the law and carry a weapon. Carrying a weapon, particularly a gun, increases the risk that they will be seriously injured or murdered. It increases the risk that they will seriously injure or murder another person. Young people who carry guns are more likely to be involved in gangs, drug trafficking, and crime.

Gangs in the Community

Youth gangs are groups of young people who band together and participate in violent, unlawful, or criminal behavior. Gangs usually have names and are territorial. They use graffiti to mark their turf. Gang members associate together and often commit crimes against other youth gangs or against the general population. Most gang members adopt certain colors or a clothing style that is recognized as belonging to their gang. Gang members often refer to the groups to which they belong as "crews" or "posses." Gang activity is increasing rapidly in many communities. There is much concern over violent gang members moving from large cities, such as Los Angeles and Chicago, to smaller cities. Another concern is the increasing involvement of females in gangs.

Belonging to a gang can be very risky. Gang members are more likely to be around illegal drugs and weapons. They get into fights more often. They are more likely to get arrested and spend time in jail. Family members of active gang members are at risk for harm as well. Their property may be stolen or damaged. Belonging to a gang often means being with young people who have enemies. Rivalry exists among gangs. Gang rivalry and hatred results in fighting and other acts of violence. Gang members are injured and some are murdered. Gang members often get criminal records. Then, it is difficult for these gang members to get jobs.

Drugs in the Community

Drug trafficking is the purchasing and selling of illegal drugs. Drug trafficking is a crime and is associated with increased incidence of violence. Innocent people can be injured directly or indirectly in communities ridden with drug trafficking. Innocent people are injured in accidents caused by people who abuse drugs. Many families have experienced the tragedy of having a family member injured or killed by a drunk driver. Drug use destroys families, interrupts school systems, and places a heavy burden on community drug treatment services and law enforcement personnel.

Life Skill #4

I will follow safety guidelines for different weather conditions and natural disasters.

Hot Weather Safety

Heat exhaustion is a condition in which the body loses large amounts of salt and water

through sweating. **Heat stroke** is a condition that occurs when the body becomes so overheated that it no longer can sweat to cool off. It is more serious than heat exhaustion. This is a life-threatening condition. Safety precautions in hot weather include drinking a lot of water and other fluids and avoiding overexertion. Avoiding any heavy activity in hot weather that can overheat the body. Clothing choices during hot weather should include lightweight, loose-fitting clothing that allows the circulation of air around the body, helping to cool it.

Cold Weather Safety

Cold temperatures can cause injury and emergency problems for the unprotected individual. Continued exposure to cold and dampness can progress to a serious condition known as hypothermia. **Hypothermia** is low body temperature. It will cause death if the body is not warmed up. Another serious condition due to cold temperatures is frostbite. **Frostbite** is a freezing of parts of the body.

The best way to prevent these injuries is to wear proper clothing when outdoors in cold temperatures. Layers of clothing provide more protection than a single thick layer. Boots or gloves that are too tight can decrease blood circulation to toes and fingers, that is needed to warm these body areas. Wet and damp clothing allows the body to cool and freeze more quickly than dry clothing. Whenever outdoors, individuals should be aware of the wind-chill factor. The **wind-chill factor** is a measure of the air temperature which takes into account the chilling effect of the wind.

Lightning Safety

Lightning kills about 150 people every year and injures another 250 people. During storms in which there is lightning:
- do not stand under a tree or out in the open during an electrical storm. If caught out in the open, try to find a ravine or low spot for shelter;
- if swimming, immediately get out of and away from the water;
- stay away from metal objects and avoid using the telephone;

Injury Prevention and Safety

- unplug electrical appliances during a severe thunderstorm and stay away from the fireplace.

Tornado Safety

Tornadoes are violent, rapidly spinning windstorms that have funnel-shaped clouds. Tornadoes can destroy everything in their paths; they are responsible for about 100 deaths each year. Tornadoes are more common in midwestern and southern states, and most occur in the spring and early summer months. A **tornado watch** is a caution issued by the National Weather Service that the weather conditions are such that a tornado is possible. This means that people in the area should be alert and prepared for possible danger. A **tornado warning** is a caution that a tornado has been sighted. It will be announced and broadcast over radio and television stations.

For the greatest protection against visible tornadoes, individuals should seek shelter in a basement or underground cellar whenever possible. If no basement is available, they should move to the center of the ground floor, into a room with no windows such as a closet or bathroom. If possible, they should crawl under something strong such as a heavy piece of furniture. If a person is trapped outside, (s)he should seek shelter in a depression such as a ravine, gully, or ditch.

Hurricane Safety

Hurricanes are tropical storms with heavy rains and winds in excess of 74 miles per hour. Hurricanes are the most dangerous of all storms because they have the potential to kill large numbers of people and destroy great amounts of property. The southern Atlantic states are at the greatest risk of hurricane damage in the United States. Most hurricanes occur during the months of August, September, and October. The National Hurricane Service tracks hurricanes and provides advance warnings to potential hurricane victims. The most important safety procedure is to follow and heed the warnings issued by the National Hurricane Service, which are issued over television and radio stations. In the event of a serious hurricane, people may be instructed to evacuate the area.

Earthquakes

One of the most destructive of natural disasters is the earthquake. **Earthquakes** are violent shakings of the earth's surface caused by the shifting of the plates that make up the earth's crust. Movements in the earth can cause the foundations of buildings to give way. This may cause parts of buildings to collapse. The greatest number of injuries from earthquakes occurs from falling debris. Some of the most devastating earthquakes have killed hundreds of thousands of people. Geologists estimate that most areas of the United States are at risk for earthquakes.

In the event of an earthquake, it is important to follow these guidelines for safety:
- stay calm and do not panic;
- stay clear of any objects that can fall;
- move into an open space if outside;
- stay away from broken power lines;
- if inside a building, get under a table or desk;
- stay away from windows which may shatter;
- if driving in a car, stop as soon as possible and get out;
- if on a bridge, get off as soon as possible.

Life Skill #5

I will be able to get help for emergency situations.

When an emergency situation occurs it is important to know where to call to get help. In many communities, calling 9-1-1 will reach assistance for fire, police, and medical emergencies. The local phone book will tell whether a community has a 9-1-1 emergency assistance number. If a 9-1-1 system is not available, the appropriate emergency numbers will be listed. When a call is made to 9-1-1, a dispatcher will answer the phone. A person calling 9-1-1 should:
1. remain calm and speak clearly;
2. describe the exact location of the emergency;
3. provide the exact address and any landmarks that will assist emergency personnel in getting to the location;
4. state his/her name, what happened, the number of people involved, the condition

of any injured people, and the help that has been given;

5. the telephone number of the phone being used should be given to the dispatcher. This makes it possible for the dispatcher to call back if more information is needed;

6. the phone should not be hung up until the dispatcher hangs up.

Life Skill #6

I will be skilled in basic first aid procedures.

Importance of First Aid

First aid is the immediate and temporary care given to a person who has been injured or suddenly becomes ill. Knowing first-aid procedures enables people to save themselves and others from possible serious injury or death. Knowing how to perform first aid also promotes safety awareness. Individuals are more cautious and take steps to eliminate hazards that increase the risks of having accidents. They follow universal precautions.

General Directions for Giving First Aid

The plan of action to follow in giving first aid depends on the circumstances surrounding the accident or illness. Sometimes, prompt action is needed to save a life. Assuming that someone needs medical care quickly, it is important to know how to summon help. (Use the instructions for getting help that were given in the previous section.) After help has been summoned, the situation should be further evaluated. Standard first-aid priorities to help a victim of an accident or illness include:
• following universal precautions;
• prompt rescue, if necessary;
• checking for open airway;
• controlling severe bleeding;
• checking for signs of poison.

When life-threatening situations have been controlled, the victim's condition should be assessed. Check for a Medic Alert tag. A **Medic Alert tag** is a medical identification that provides important information about the person wearing it. It is usually worn as a necklace or bracelet.

It is important to give an ill or injured person psychological first aid. **Psychological first aid** is the process of helping people deal with the emotional aspects related to physical injury or illness. This kind of first aid can be administered at the same time as physical first aid. An example of psychological first aid would be to tell a victim who is suffering severe pain that medical help is on the way and that steps will be taken as soon as possible to relieve the pain.

Respiratory Emergencies

Respiratory emergencies are emergencies in which a person has limited breathing or has stopped breathing. Among these are drowning, heart failure, electric shock, drug overdose, and carbon monoxide poisoning. **Asphyxiation** is stoppage or limit of breathing. When a person is asphyxiated, it is important that breathing be restored quickly through artificial respiration. **Artificial respiration** is a term that includes many techniques that are used by one person on another to restore breathing. A mouth protector should always be used. In mouth-to-mouth or mouth-to-nose respiration, the rescuer inflates the victim's lungs by forcing air into them. The following steps should be used in deciding whether or not to give artificial respiration:

1. Determine if the victim is responsive.
2. Tap the victim on the shoulder and ask, "Are you OK?" If there is no response, place the victim on his or her back.

3. If a spinal injury is suspected, do not move the victim .
4. Check for breathing by looking for chest movement and listening for air movement.

Airway obstruction is a condition in which breathing is partly or completely prevented by a blockage in the part of the air passages known as the larynx. Choking on a piece of food or an object is a common and potentially dangerous occurrence in the school setting. In almost all cases, the object will become dislodged by itself. But on occasion, a student may choke on something and not be able to dislodge it by himself/herself. The student may cough or attempt to cough and may show the universal distress signal. The **universal distress signal** is a warning demonstrated by a person clutching at the throat with one or two hands.

A student may have a partial airway obstruction or a complete airway obstruction. A student who has a partial airway obstruction may be able to inhale and exhale but will gasp for air. If the airway is completely obstructed, the student will not be able to speak, breathe, or cough. The student also may have cyanosis. **Cyanosis** is a condition that results from the lack of oxygen to body tissues, and manifests itself as bluishness around the lips and mouth.

The **Heimlich Maneuver** is a technique that makes use of abdominal thrusts to dislodge an object in the air passage of a conscious person who is choking. Before using the Heimlich Maneuver, ask the student if (s)he is choking. If the student can speak or cough easily, do not do anything. If the student cannot speak, breathe, or cough, stand behind him/her and wrap your hands around his/her waist. Make a fist with one hand and place the thumb side of the fist into the student's abdomen above the navel and below the rib cage. Grab your fist with the other hand and give quick upward thrusts into the abdominal area. Repeat these thrusts until the object is dislodged. Each thrust should be separate and distinct.

If the object is not dislodged, the student may become unconscious. Call an emergency medical service immediately. Open the student's airway by grasping the lower jaw and tongue. Lift the jaw. Using what is called a finger sweep, attempt to dislodge and remove the object by sweeping it out with your finger. Use a hooking action with your finger. If nothing happens, while tilting the student's head and lifting the chin and, with appropriate mouth protection, give the student two full breaths. If air does not get into the lungs, the airway is still blocked. Give six to ten abdominal thrusts. To give abdominal thrusts, straddle the student's thighs. Place the heel of one hand on the student's abdomen just above the navel but below the tip of the breastbone. Place your other hand on top of the fist. Make sure the fingers of your hands point toward the student's head. Give quick, upward thrusts. If nothing happens after six to ten thrusts, do another finger sweep. Then give two full breaths. If you cannot get breaths into the student, repeat the same procedures—thrusts, finger sweeps, and two breaths. Do this sequence until emergency medical personnel arrive.

If a person experiences an obstructed airway and no one else is around, (s)he can perform this technique on himself/herself by pressing his/her own fist into the upper abdomen and giving a quick, upward thrust or by leaning forward over a chair and pressing the abdomen quickly down on the edge of the chair.

If an infant or child has an obstructed airway, the procedure should be performed differently. The infant or child should be placed face up with the face lower than the rest of the body. Four chest thrusts should be given. For an infant, pressure should be applied on the chest by using two fingers on the sternum between the nipples.

Cardiopulmonary Resuscitation

Cardiopulmonary resuscitation (CPR) is an emergency procedure that is used with mouth-to-mouth resuscitation when the heart has stopped beating. CPR should never be done on a conscious person or on someone who has a heartbeat. Only persons trained in CPR should administer these techniques. Universal precautions should be followed.

The ABCs of CPR are general procedures that should be known:
A—Airway. Always be sure the victim's airway is open. The tongue is the most common

cause of airway obstruction in an unconscious victim;

B—Breathing. After making sure the airway is open, check to see if the person is breathing. CPR should not be performed if the person is breathing;

C—Circulation. Always check the victim's pulse to determine if chest compressions will be necessary.

If necessary, CPR is performed by placing the victim on his/her back. If an adult victim or large child has no pulse or is not breathing, a trained person will perform CPR. The trained person will follow the steps.

1. Find the lower part of the breastbone (xiphoid process) and measure up the width of two fingers from that point.
2. Place the heel of the hand on the sternum next to the fingers. (S)he will then place the hand used to find the xiphoid process on the top of the hand on the sternum. By interlocking the fingers of the two hands, the trained person keeps the fingers off the chest of the victim.
3. Lock the elbows and bring the shoulders directly over the hands so that pressure is forced straight down. This person will exert enough pressure to depress the breastbone one and one-half to two inches. Each compression forces blood from the heart to other parts of the body.

Compressions should be given at a rate of 80 per minute. After every 15 compressions, the person trained in CPR will give two full breaths. This cycle is to be repeated until respiration and circulation are restored or until medical help arrives.

It is important for teachers to become trained in CPR. Information about CPR training can be obtained by contacting a local chapter of the American Red Cross or the American Heart Association.

Controlling Bleeding

A **wound** is any break in the continuity of the body's tissues. An **open wound** is a wound in which the skin is broken, and there is injury to underlying tissues. A **closed wound** is one in which the skin is not broken. An open wound presents unique problems. The first is the possibility of infection. Even the smallest break in the skin can permit the entrance of bacteria into the body. The second problem is the loss of blood. The type of wound and its severity determine the extent of bleeding.

When someone is bleeding, follow universal precautions. The priority is to stop the bleeding and prevent germs from entering the wound. A person with a wound may bleed to death in a matter of minutes. The application of direct pressure is one way to stop bleeding. Direct pressure is applied by pressing the palm of the hand on a clean dressing directly over the wound. In most cases, this step will be enough to stop bleeding. If blood soaks through the dressing, do not remove it. Removing the dressing can promote more bleeding by pulling away clots that may be forming. Instead, more layers of dressing should be added. In addition to direct pressure, the wounded body part should be elevated above the level of the heart. This helps reduce blood flow to the area. If a foreign object is lodged deep in the tissue of the wound, it should not be removed. This can cause further bleeding and serious damage.

A second method of stopping bleeding is the use of pressure on a supplying artery. If direct pressure and elevation do not stop bleeding, the pressure point technique may be required. The pressure point technique compresses the main artery that supplies blood to the affected body part. The two pressure points recommended by the American Red Cross are under the arm (the brachial artery) and inside the groin area (the femoral artery). It is important to remember that if the use of pressure points is necessary, it should be used with direct pressure and elevation. Using pressure points to stop bleeding is not a substitute for direct pressure.

A third method of stopping bleeding is the use of a tourniquet. A **tourniquet** is a band that is applied to stop blood flow to a wound. Using a tourniquet is dangerous because severe tissue damage may result from lack of blood and oxygen if the tourniquet is left on too long. A tourniquet is a last resort and should be used only for severe, life-threatening bleeding that cannot be controlled by other means. If a tourniquet is applied, it should not be loosened. A note showing the location and time of application of the tourniquet should be attached to the victim's clothing in a visible location. The tourniquet should be visible at all times. A physician should be seen immediately.

Poisoning

A **poison** is any substance that can cause illness or death when introduced into the body. Poisons can enter the body through ingestion (swallowing), inhalation, injection, or absorption through the skin or mucous membranes. The first step in the treatment of a poison victim is to determine immediately the poison ingested. If a container is nearby, the first aid directions on the label should be followed. Additional clues can be obtained by asking others what they think happened. The local Poison Control Center or a physician should be called for further information. Medical help for the victim should be sought immediately.

An unconscious victim should never be forced to vomit. Also, a victim who has swallowed a corrosive substance such as lye, bleach, or a petroleum product such as gasoline or kerosene should not be forced to vomit. Vomiting these products can cause further damage to the digestive tract. Rather, the victim should swallow milk or eat mashed potatoes so that the stomach can be coated and the poison neutralized.

Shock

Shock is a condition in which the rate of the functions of the vital organs of the body slows. Any serious injury or illness can result in shock. A person who goes into shock will have characteristic signs and symptoms. In the early stages of shock, blood flow to the skin is reduced, resulting in a lowered body temperature. The skin may appear bluish and feel cold and clammy to the touch. The pulse may be too weak to detect at the wrist. Breathing rate may increase and nausea may occur. These early stages of shock may last for a period of time after which the signs and symptoms of the late stages of shock appear.

During the late stages of shock, the victim may not be responsive. The eyes may be sunken and the pupils dilated. Body temperature and blood pressure may continue to fall to a low level. The victim may lose consciousness and perhaps die if treatment does not begin immediately.

It is important to improve the circulation of a shock victim. This means keeping the airway open or administering artificial respiration or CPR. It is also important to maintain body temperature. To accomplish this, the person should be kept lying down. The head should be level with the body and the lower extremities raised about eight to twelve inches above the level of the heart. However, the victim's feet should not be raised if there is a head injury or fracture in one or both legs. If the victim is having difficulty breathing, the head and shoulders should be raised. The victim should be allowed to get adequate oxygen and kept warm with a blanket. Heat should not be added, but the body temperature should be maintained. Unless medical assistance will be delayed more than six hours, nothing should be given by mouth.

Heart Attack and Stroke

Heart attack and stroke are leading causes of death in the United States. However, many victims of these conditions might be saved each year if first-aid techniques were administered. Before giving first aid for a heart attack victim, it is important that certain signs and symptoms be recognized.

A person having a heart attack may experience uncomfortable pressure, squeezing, fullness, tightness, or pain in the center of the chest or in the left arm. The pain may spread to the shoulders, arm, neck, or jaw. Pain may be accompanied by sweating, nausea, weakness, and shortness of breath. If a heart attack victim is conscious, (s)he should be placed in a semireclining position. Any tight clothing should be loosened. Reassurance should be provided and help summoned for immediately. If the victim is not breathing, artificial respiration should be administered. Medical help is needed immediately.

A stroke victim may be conscious or unconscious. Breathing rate may be slow and pupils in the eyes may be unequal in size. The victim may have slurred speech and paralysis on one side of the body. First aid for a stroke victim consists of keeping the person lying down with the head and shoulders raised to relieve the force of blood on the brain. The victim's air passage should be kept open. The victim should be kept calm and medical help summoned immediately.

Fractures, Dislocations, Sprains, and Strains

A **fracture** is a break or a crack in a bone. Sometimes a fracture is not easy to detect because its signs and symptoms may be similar to those of a sprain. A person who has a fracture should receive immediate medical help. The displaced bone should not be moved. A **sprain** is a partial or complete tearing of ligaments at a joint. An X-ray of the sprain is usually performed to exclude the possibility of a fracture. Treatment for a sprain consists of applying an ice pack to reduce swelling, wrapping the joint with a compression bandage, resting it in a raised position until the pain and swelling begin to subside, and taking analgesics to relieve the pain. If uncertain whether a fracture or sprain exists, an injury should be treated as if it were a fracture.

People who are active in sports involving physical contact often suffer dislocations. A **dislocation** is the displacement of a bone from its joint. Dislocations often are accompanied by stretched ligaments. Muscle strain is another common injury. **Strain** is an overstretching of muscles and tendons. One of the most common strains involves the muscles of the back.

Burns

Each year, over two million burn accidents occur in the United States. Burns may result from contact with various sources: a fire, a hot stove, an exposed electrical wire, chemicals, and exposure to the sun. Burns produce significant problems. They cause pain since nerve endings in the skin are harmed. The burned area may become swollen. In severe burns, there may be a loss of body fluids as well as severe infection caused by the destruction of skin tissue. Severely burned victims who initially survive an accident may die because of infection that results from their burns.

There are three different types of burns: first-degree burns, second-degree burns, and third-degree burns. **First-degree burns** are burns that cause reddening of the skin and affect only the top layer of the skin. **Second-degree burns** are burns that damage deeply, causing blisters. Second-degree burns generally will heal without scarring. **Third-degree burns** are burns that destroy the full skin thickness. The affected area will look white or charred, and, if the burn is very deep, muscles and bones will be exposed.

Follow universal precautions when giving first aid. Immerse minor burns in cold running water. A cold-water compress can be applied until the pain diminishes. Any watches, rings, or constrictive clothing should be removed from the area in case of swelling. The burned area should be dressed with a clean, sterilized, nonfluffy (if possible) material. For major burns, any clothing should not be removed from the burned area. Any exposed area should be covered with a dry, clean, nonfluffy cloth to stop infection. Immediate medical attention should be sought.

Nosebleeds

Nosebleeds are loss of blood from the mucous membranes that line the nose. Nosebleeds can result from injury, vigorous nose blowing, or dry nasal membranes. When helping someone with a nosebleed, follow universal precautions. To stop a nosebleed, a person should either stand or sit and lean forward. The nose should be pinched with the thumb and forefinger just below the cartilage or hard part of the nose for ten minutes. If bleeding does not stop within a reasonable time, a small clean pad of gauze should be inserted into one or both nostrils. Pressure should again be applied.

Nosebleeds can be prevented by keeping nasal membranes moist. This can be accomplished by applying petroleum jelly inside of the nose daily. A vaporizer will also increase the humidity of the air that is breathed and reduce dryness. The nose should also be protected against injury. After a nosebleed has stopped, an individual should not blow the nose for several hours. Whenever a person experiences regular nosebleeds or one that persists, a physician should be seen. Recurrent nosebleeds may indicate a health problem that requires further medical attention.

Snakebites

About 45,000 people are bitten each year by snakes in the United States. Over half of all snakebites occur in Texas, North Carolina, Florida, Georgia, Louisiana, and Arkansas. Among the poisonous snakes in the United States are the coral snakes and pit vipers, such as rattlesnakes, water moccasins, and copperheads.

Symptoms of snakebite can be mild, moderate, or severe. Mild to moderate symptoms

Injury Prevention and Safety

include mild swelling and pain or discoloration at the site of the wound. Rapid pulse, dimmed vision, nausea, vomiting, and shortness of breath are also mild to moderate symptoms. Severe symptoms may include rapid swelling and numbness followed by severe pain at the wound site. The victim may also have constricted pupils, slurred speech, shock, and paralysis. These symptoms may be followed by difficulty in breathing and unconsciousness.

The victim of a snakebite should be taken to a hospital immediately. Meanwhile, the following first aid procedures should be performed.

1. Keep the victim still and as calm as possible. This will help reduce the speed with which toxins will circulate in the body.
2. Keep the bitten extremity at or below the level of the heart. If the victim will be in a hospital within four or five hours and no further symptoms develop, no further first aid measures need by taken.
3. For victims who develop mild to moderate symptoms, apply a constricting band two to four inches above the bite but not around a joint or the head, neck, or trunk. The band should be three-fourths to one and one-half inches wide, yet loose enough for a finger to be slipped underneath.
4. Victims who develop severe symptoms and stop breathing should receive mouth-to-mouth resuscitation. If there is no pulse or heartbeat, individuals trained in CPR should give CPR.

A person who has been bitten by a snake needs medical attention as soon as possible. To prevent being bitten by a snake, the follow precautions should be taken:

- do not disturb snakes;
- avoid areas where snakes are found;
- wear heavy midcalf boots and long trousers when entering areas infested with snakes.

Poisons from Plants

Among the plants that may cause severe irritation if touched or contacted are poison ivy, poison oak, and poison sumac. People should learn how to recognize these plants so that contact with them can be avoided. These plants are even hazardous in the winter when they have dropped their leaves. Contact with a poisonous plant may cause a skin reaction accompanied by redness, swelling, itching, or burning. Blisters may form and seep or ooze a watery substance. A reaction may be prevented if contaminated clothing is removed, the exposed area is washed with soap and water, and alcohol and calamine lotion are applied.

Rashes from poisonous plants can be treated with over-the-counter gels and liquids. If the rash is spread over large parts of the body, applications of cool saltwater compresses (two teaspoons of salt per quart of water) will be helpful in relieving itching. Scratching of affected areas should be avoided because infection may occur and delay healing. Itching may be relieved through medication or cold compresses, but a skin reaction may continue for as long as two weeks. A physician may need to be seen if the affected area covers a large part of the body.

Insect Stings and Bites

Insect stings and bites are often painful, but pain and discomfort are usually the most serious effects. Among the more common insects that sting people are bees, hornets, wasps, and yellowjackets. Hornets, wasps, and yellowjackets can sting repeatedly. They inject venom with each thrust of their tails. A bee stings once and usually leaves its stinger with its sac of venom in the victim's skin. A sting will usually produce a burning sensation followed by reddening and itching at the site. Swelling and pain may also occur. For people who are allergic to insect bites, a sting from an insect poses a serious problem that may result in death. A person who is sensitive to these stings may develop headaches, nausea, stomach pains, go into shock, and have swollen vocal cords. This may result in respiratory failure. These individuals can be given special medications to fight the effect of stings.

Preventive measures can be taken to help avoid being stung. If in the area where there are bees, individuals should avoid wearing bright colors, strong perfumes and lotions, and scented soap. All of these products attract bees. Other safeguards against bee stings include wearing shoes when outdoors and covering food at a picnic.

Insect stings are often painful, but pain and discomfort are usually the most serious

308

effects. If a student is stung by an insect, the stinger needs to be removed from the skin. The stinger should be scraped away from the skin with your fingernail or a thin and sturdy object such as a plastic credit card. The stinger should not be removed with tweezers because there is usually a sac with venom attached to the stinger. The squeeze of the tweezers against the sac can force venom into the body. After the stinger is removed, the affected area should be washed with soap and water. The area should be kept clean. An ice pack should be applied to the area to help reduce pain and swelling.

Some students will suffer from allergic reactions when stung by an insect. Every student who is stung by an insect should be observed for thirty minutes for reactions. Many students who are allergic to stings carry special medication, or the school nurse has made arrangements with a student's family for treatment procedures. Immediate treatment is needed if there is an allergic reaction.

Objects in the Eye

Foreign bodies, such as dust or small dirt particles, often lodge in the eyes. These eye problems can usually be treated at home. Generally, these dust particles are found under the upper lid and can be irritating. The eye should not be rubbed because further injury can result. Assistance should be obtained from someone to help lift the upper lid. If the pain is not relieved, the object is probably sticking to the inside of the eyelid. The object may be removed by pulling the upper lid over the lower lid. When the object is seen, remove it with a clean, moist, cotton swab. If the object is seen on the clear surface of the eye, it can be dislodged by blinking or flushing the eye very carefully with water.

Particular attention should be paid to an object lodged on the cornea. The **cornea** is the front part of the outer shell of the eyeball. The object can scratch the cornea and cause vision damage. If a speck of dirt or dust is not removed from the cornea through rinsing, medical attention should be sought.

Table 13-4

Protective Factors That Prevent Violence

Protective Factors are ways that a person might behave and characteristics of the environment in which a person lives that promote health, safety, and/or well-being.

1. Recognizing violent behavior.
2. Having positive self-esteem.
3. Being reared in a healthful family.
4. Living in a nurturing environment.
5. Using social skills.
6. Practicing anger management skills.
7. Practicing stress management skills.
8. Participating in physical and recreational activities.
9. Practicing suicide prevention strategies.
10. Practicing conflict resolution and peer mediation skills.
11. Avoiding discriminatory behavior.
12. Making responsible decisions.
13. Practicing resistance skills.
14. Avoiding alcohol and other drugs.
15. Practicing responsible behavior around weapons.
16. Resisting gang membership.
17. Respecting authority and abiding by laws.
18. Practicing self-protection strategies.
19. Participating in recovery if a victim.
20. Changing behavior if a juvenile offender.

Life Skill #7

I will choose behaviors to reduce my risk of violence.

Protective Factors

Protective factors are ways that a person might behave and characteristics of the environment in which a person lives that promote health, safety, and well–being. Some protective factors that prevent violence are listed in *Protective Factors That Prevent Violence* (Figure 13-4). **Violence** is the threatened or actual use of physical force to injure, damage, or destroy oneself, others, or property. Protective factors refer only to the statistical probability that one's health, safety, and well-being will be protected. There is a chance that something outside of one's control will affect health, safety, and/or well-being in negative ways. For example, a young person might be a victim of random violence such as a drive-by shooting. However, the more protective factors that apply to a person, the more likely (s)he is to be protected from violence.

Risk Factors

Risk factors are ways that a person might behave and characteristics of the environment in which a person lives that threaten health, safety, and/or well-being. Some risk factors that promote violence are listed in *Risk Factors that Promote Violence* (Table 13-5). Risk factors refer only to the statistical probability that something negative will happen. This does not necessarily mean that a young person will actually behave in violent ways or be harmed by others. Young people have varying degrees of control over different risk factors. For example, a young person has control over whether or not to carry a weapon to school. However, there is no control over the family in which a person is reared. Recognizing risk factors is an important step in being violence-free.

Life Skill #8

I will protect myself from people who might harm me.

A **perpetrator** is a person who commits a crime or violent act. A perpetrator can be either a stranger or a person who is known to the victim. Some perpetrators of violent acts are family members. A **victim** is a person who is harmed by violence.

Self-Protection Against Sexual Abuse

Child sexual abuse is any sexual act or acts performed by an adult with a person under eighteen years of age. **Incest** is child sexual

---

Table 13-5

Risk Factors That Promote Violence

Risk Factors are ways that a person might behave and characteristics of the environment in which a person lives that threaten health, safety, and/or well-being

1. Failing to recognize violent behavior.
2. Having negative self-esteem.
3. Being reared in a dysfunctional family.
4. Living in an adverse environment.
5. Lacking social skills.
6. Being unable to manage anger.
7. Being unable to manage stress.
8. Not participating in physical and recreational activities.
9. Having suicidal tendencies.
10. Resolving conflict in harmful ways.
11. Practicing discriminatory behavior.
12. Lacking responsible decision-making skills.
13. Being unable to resist negative peer pressure.
14. Using alcohol and other drugs.
15. Carrying a weapon.
16. Belonging to a gang.
17. Challenging authority and breaking laws.
18. Being in risk situations.
19. Avoiding recovery if a victim.
20. Repeating violence if a juvenile offender.

---

abuse involving a close relative of the child. Incest is the most common form of sexual abuse.

The most commonly reported form of incest involves an adult male family member and a female child. The adult male may be a father, grandfather, stepfather, uncle, or older brother. The most commonly occurring form of incest involves siblings. Incest may occur among unrelated siblings within blended families because these siblings have not been conditioned against sexual attraction to one another from an early age. Perpetrators of incest abuse their power and position in a family by taking advantage of a child's dependence, trust, ignorance, and love.

Guidelines for young people to follow to avoid and stop child sexual abuse are:
1. Refuse sexual activity with adults and family members.

Table 13-6

Self-Protection When In Social Situations

1. Stay away from places where you will be alone when you are with a person you do not know well or whom you do not trust.
2. Do not go anywhere with a stranger even if you are supposed to meet other people.
3. Trust your gut feelings about other people.
4. Choose to be with other people when you socialize with someone the first few times.
5. Do not use alcohol or other drugs.
6. Set limits for expressing affection and communicate these limits to others.
7. Do not pressure another person to drink alcohol or to express affection beyond limits. Know that a person who has been drinking is accountable for sexual behavior.
8. Avoid behavior that might be interpreted as sexually teasing or seductive.
9. Respect the limits other people have set for expressing affection. Never pressure someone beyond limits.
10. Ask the other person to tell you clear limits when you are confused or feel you are getting mixed messages.
11. Do not assume you and another person want to express affection in the same ways or have the same limits.
12. Use physical force if someone continues sexual behavior after you have set limits.
13. Attend workshops, seminars, or classes to be clear on issues regarding acquaintance rape.
14. Pay attention to warning signs that indicate a person might harm you: disrespectful attitude toward you, dominating attitude, extreme jealousy, unnecessary physical roughness, and/or a history of violent and/or abusive behavior.

---

2. Avoid situations in which you might be alone with the adult whom you do not trust or whom you know is abusive.
3. Do not ignore feelings of discomfort.
4. If abuse occurs, write down the date, time, and situation and exactly what happened.
5. Share any situations in which abuse occurred with a parent, stepparent, or trusted adult who believes you.
6. If the first adult you tell does not believe you, tell another trusted adult who will take action to prevent sexual abuse from occurring again.
7. Call local hotlines or child welfare agencies for help.

Self-Protection When in Social Situations

Most individuals face many social situations. *Self-Protection When in Social Situations* (Table 13-6) provides a list of guidelines to follow when in social situations. A common social situation is meeting new people. At other times, socializing is with friends and other people who are already known. Most people do not expect to be harmed, especially when socializing with people whom they know. Unfortunately, a perpetrator might be an acquaintance, such as someone who is known from school, or a neighbor. A perpetrator might be someone with whom one has had only a few dates. One type of violence that occurs frequently is acquaintance rape. **Acquaintance rape** is rape that is committed by someone known to the victim.

Self-Protection When Sexually Harassed

Sexual harassment is unwanted sexual behavior that ranges from making sexual comments to forcing another person into unwanted sex acts. Sometimes sexual harassment occurs in the workplace. It may occur when someone at the workplace says sexual things to another person that are not appropriate, when someone tries to force another to kiss him/her, or when a person touches another in a way that the other person does not want.

Sexual harassment may also occur at school. The most common types of sexual harassment at school are sexual comments and sexual jokes; inappropriate gestures; staring up and down; and touching, grabbing, and pinching in sexual ways. Many students report having been forced to do something sexual other than kissing. Males as well as females are victims of sexual harassment. Students who have been sexually harassed often do not want to attend school. They are likely to stay home or cut classes to avoid further harassment. *Self-Protection When Sexually Harassed* (Table 13-7) provides a list of guidelines for young people to follow when they have been sexually harassed.

Self-Protection When Being Stalked

Stalking is harassing someone, typically by following the person around, with the intent to threaten or harm that person. Approximately 200,000 cases of stalking occur each year. Most of the people being stalked are female (Friedman, 1994). Typically, people who stalk others are trying to form a relationship with the person. They may feel that by stalking, they are able to get the other person's attention. The stalker may fantasize a relationship with a person and decide to take action. Stalking also may begin when a relationship has just ended. The stalker is upset and wants to scare the victim into continuing the relationship. *Self-Protection When Being Stalked* (Table 13-8) provides a list of guidelines for young people to follow when they are being stalked.

Life Skill #9

I will stay safe while riding in a car.

Motor Vehicle Safety

More people die of motor vehicle injuries than any other cause of injury. Accidents in motor vehicles account for about half of all fatal accidents and about 20 percent of all injuries leading to disability. Factors that contribute to motor vehicle injuries and deaths are: alcohol consumption; failure to use seat belts and safety restraints; speeding and reckless driving; poor driving conditions (for example, heavy rainstorms, icy roads, reduced visibility); disregarding traffic rules (for example,

---

Table 13-7

Self-Protection When Sexually Harassed

1. Ask the person who is harassing you to stop. Be direct about what behavior is bothering you. Describe the situation and behavior that made you uncomfortable.
2. Keep a record of what happened. Write down the date and time, describe the situation and behavior, and explain how you handled the situation. Save any notes, letters, or pictures.
3. Check to see if there are guidelines; if at work, check work guidelines.
4. Report the harassment to the appropriate person in charge. This may be a boss, teacher, or school counselor.
5. Determine if you want to take legal action.

---

failure to yield the right of way to traffic, failure to signal, failure to stop at stop signs); and poorly maintained motor vehicles (for example, defective tires, brakes, windshield wipers, lights). Motor vehicle accidents often involve collisions between motor vehicles or with fixed objects such as walls or guardrails.

To reduce the risk of motor vehicle injuries, a person should follow these guidelines. First, a person should avoid drinking and driving. Second, a person should avoid excessive speed. The faster one drives, the greater the chances of an accident. Third, a person should heed warning signs. This means that one must drive defensively. To drive defensively means to anticipate what others might do. Fourth, a person should drive only when at his/her physical best. For example, a person should avoid operating a motor vehicle when taking a medication that may produce drowsiness. Fifth, a person should use available safety devices such as safety restraints in automobiles and helmets when riding motorcycles.

Alcohol-Related Crashes According to the National Highway and Traffic Safety Administration, alcohol is a factor in about half of all fatal accidents. Alcohol-related motor vehicle deaths occur more frequently among fifteen- to twenty-four-year-olds than among any other age group. Because alcohol is a central

Table 13-8

Self-Protection When Being Stalked

1. Check the laws of your state regarding stalking. Thirty-seven states currently have antistalking laws. Know your rights and the best way to protect your rights. Know the limits of your protection as well.

2. Contact the police department to report the stalking. Consider pressing charges against the person who is stalking you. This may be enough to frighten and stop the person.

3. Keep a record of each case of stalking. Write down the date, time, what was said, and what happened. Save any evidence, including notes and letters that may have been written to you.

4. Try to obtain a restraining order. A restraining order is an order by a court that forbids a person from doing a particular act.

5. Tell your parents and school officials what is happening. They should be told everything so they can do what they can to help protect you.

6. Seek appropriate counseling or join a support group for victims of stalking.

nervous system depressant, it is dangerous to drive while under its influence. Alcohol impairs judgment and motor skills, slows reaction time, blurs vision, and reduces coordination. Driving impairment increases as the amount of alcohol in the bloodstream increases. In most states, a blood alcohol level of 0.10 is set as the legal level of intoxication.

Safety Restraints The use of seat belts and child safety restraints is now required by law in many states. Although required by law, most people do not regularly "buckle up." Reasons commonly cited for failure to buckle their safety belts include feelings that seat belts are inconvenient and uncomfortable. Many people also have misconceptions about the effectiveness of seat belts. Despite the fact that seat belts greatly reduce the chances of death or accidental injury, misconceptions abound that one would be better off unrestrained even if thrown from a car. A motor vehicle occupant's chances of being killed are twenty-five times greater when thrown from a car than when the occupant remains in the car. Also, very few motor vehicle accidents involve a car plunging into water or catching on fire, situations in which it would be necessary to make a quick getaway from the vehicle. When a seat belt is worn, a motor vehicle occupant is more likely to be alert, uninjured, and alive, thus making a quick getaway possible, than in situations where no seat belt is used.

Wearing a seat belt reduces the chance of being killed by 60 to 70 percent and the chance of being seriously injured by 50 percent. Seat belts are effective because they prevent or reduce the "human collision." The **human collision** is a forceful collision experienced when an unbelted occupant is thrown against the motor vehicle's interior components—dashboard, windshield, steering wheel, etc. Such collisions are often responsible for serious injury and death. Seat belts also prevent occupants from being ejected from a car as well (usually after being thrown through the windshield). Lap and shoulder belts used together (newer models have combination lap and shoulder belts) are much more effective in saving lives and preventing injuries than lap belts alone. Less than one-fourth (24.3 percent) of high school students "always" use safety belts when riding in a car or truck driven by someone else. An additional 23 percent of students use safety belts "most of the time," and 13.4 percent report "never" using seat belts (Centers for Disease Control, 1992).

Air Bags Air bags are also effective motor vehicle safety devices. **Air bags** are cushions that inflate when activated by sensors in the dashboard and front bumpers within a fraction of a second between the first collision and the "human collision." They cushion the occupants in the front seat and prevent dangerous collisions with the car's interior components. The greatest advantage of air bags over seat belts is that air bags work automatically without the assistance of the occupants. Many new cars are equipped with air bags.

Self-Protection Strategies While Driving and Riding in Cars

There is a need for self-protection while driving or riding in a car with others. Some people

Injury Prevention and Safety

pose as good Samaritans and assault people who have car trouble. Other people hitchhike and rob or assault people who stop and give them a ride. In recent years, there has been concern about carjackings. A **carjacking** is a car theft that occurs while the driver and/or passengers are in or near the vehicle. Thousands of carjacking victims have been injured, kidnapped, raped, or killed. *Self-Protection While Driving and Riding in Cars* (Table 13-9) provides a list of self-protection strategies to follow while driving and riding in cars.

Life Skill #10

I will stay safe while exercising.

Sports Safety

Many injuries occur each year from participation in sports activities. Injuries may be caused by a lack of knowledge of the rules of the sport or lack of adequate adult supervision. They may also result from improper use of equipment or lack of appropriate equipment. Sports that appear to be safe can, in fact, be dangerous. The number of basketball injuries reported each year is higher than injuries reported from football and baseball (Consumer Product Safety Commission in 1991). More than 70 percent of softball injuries result when players slide into a base. Research has shown that the majority of recreational and professional baseball and softball injuries could be prevented by replacing existing bases with newer break-away bases. A **break-away base** is a base that pops loose when a sliding runner collides with it.

Many people younger than age twenty-five receive emergency room treatment for injuries associated with playground equipment, children's vehicles, skateboards, and roller skates. More than 58,000 head injuries are sustained annually from these recreational activities—30 percent of them involve playground swings. Because head injuries from these activities are almost as common as head injuries in people ages five to fourteen years who were bicycling and far more common in younger children, protective headgear or helmets appear to be appropriate for these activities (Baker et al., 1994).

Another way that young people may be harmed during sports activities is from violence during or after games. Emotions can run high during athletic contests because of the drive to win. Frustration can lead to episodes of violence.

Bicycle Safety

Bicycle riding is gaining in popularity. Besides being an economical means of transportation, bicycling helps a person develop cardiovascular fitness. The most dangerous bicycle accidents are those that involve collisions with motor vehicles. About one-half of all collisions occur at intersections and are the result of failure by the bicyclist to obey a traffic law. Most of the people killed in bicycle accidents are between the ages of five and twenty-four. Head injuries account for most bicycle-related deaths. Bicycle helmets can prevent an estimated 60 to 85 percent of fatal bicycle-related head injuries. In spite of this fact, fewer than 10 percent of riders in fatal bicycle accidents were wearing helmets at the time of the accident. Only 2.3 percent of high school students wear bicycle helmets when riding a bicycle "always" or "most of the time" (Centers for Disease Control and Prevention, 1992; Skolnick, 1993).

A person can reduce the risk of being injured while riding a bicycle by:
- increasing visibility by using lights, reflectors, or reflective tape during times of darkness or low visibility;
- learning and obeying traffic rules for all motor vehicles;

Table 13-9

Self-Protection While Driving and Riding In Cars

1. Always park in a safe and well-lighted area where there are other people and other cars.
2. Take special note of exactly where you are parked in a large parking lot.
3. Lock your car at all times and keep your keys with you.
4. Have someone walk with you to your car whenever possible.
5. Check the front and back seats to make sure that no one is hiding inside before getting in your car.
6. Never leave infants or small children in an unattended car even if you are leaving only for a brief time.
7. Never leave the keys in the ignition or the engine running.
8. Always take your keys with you when leaving your car.
9. Keep wallets, purses, unattached stereos, and other valuables out of sight.
10. Do not allow yourself to run out of gas.
11. Plan ahead and fuel your car only during daylight hours.
12. Keep your car in good condition to prevent breakdowns.
13. Try to drive in safe, well-lighted areas, especially at night.
14. Install a car phone to use in case of emergency.
15. Keep a sign in your car that says "Send Help" to display if your car breaks down.
16. Keep a flashlight and road flares in your trunk.
17. Stay in your car, keep your doors locked and windows rolled up, keep a lookout for passing police cars, and honk your horn if you see a police car when your car breaks down.
18. Do not get out of the car if someone other than a police officer stops and offers help. Roll the window down only a crack and ask the person to call the police.
19. Drive to a nearby phone and call 9-1-1 if you see someone in need of help.
20. Never pick up a hitchhiker.
21. Do not drive home if you think you are being followed. Go to a store, police station, or well-lighted area where there are other people. Call the police and report that you were being followed.
22. Be cautious of anyone approaching your car when it is stopped.
23. Keep your car doors locked and windows rolled up at all times to prevent carjacking. If you need ventilation, roll the windows down only a crack. Keep your sunroof closed. Avoid driving in a convertible with the top down.
24. Keep your car in gear when at a stoplight or stop sign. Allow enough distance between your car and the car ahead to drive away.
25. If a person armed with a weapon demands your car or your keys, do not resist.
26. Do not give out your keys to other people.
27. Consider getting an inside latch for your trunk. If you are ever forced into the trunk you could escape.
28. Do not rent cars that are marked as rental cars.
29. Be a courteous driver on the street. If another driver makes you angry, ignore this person. Never begin a fight.

- always keeping bikes in good working order;
- wearing a helmet;
- always wearing shoes while riding;
- avoiding riding two or more abreast in traffic;
- properly signaling before turning;
- watching out for suddenly opening car doors when approaching parked cars;
- watching out for cars and trucks backing out of driveways;
- watching out for pedestrians;
- watching out for sewer grates that run parallel to the direction of travel; the narrow tires of some bicycles can drop through a grate, bring the bicycle to a sudden stop, and result in throwing the rider over the top of the handlebars;
- keeping to the right and riding with the traffic;
- using crosswalks to walk a bicycle across busy intersections;
- not grabbing onto another moving vehicle.

Motorcycle and Motorbike Safety

Motorcycles have special appeal to young people. They provide a sense of freedom and exhilaration from the feeling of openness and the speeds that can be achieved. Motorcycles are also portrayed as a source of excitement in movies, television shows, and magazine articles and advertisements. Unfortunately, motorcycles pose serious risks to safety. The chances of being killed or injured are much higher for motorcycle riders than for automobile passengers. Motorcycle drivers and their passengers are left relatively unprotected when they collide with another vehicle or object, or when they are thrown from the motorcycle. Nearly nine of every ten motorcycle accidents result in serious injury or death for the drivers and passengers compared to about only one in ten automobile occupants.

Many motorcycle accidents are due to another motorist's violating the motorcycle driver's right of way. In other words, many accidents are the fault of other motorists on the road. A common reason cited by motorists who have collided with motorcycles is that they did not see the motorcycle. Unsafe driving practices and failure to obey traffic regulations account for many accidents.

People riding motorcycles should wear appropriate rider protection gear including a helmet, goggles; have a face shield or a windshield; and wear clothing such as heavy gloves, jackets, and pants that can provide protection against weather and slides across pavement during a fall.

Water Safety

Any activity in or around water, including swimming, carries with it the risk of drowning. **Drowning** is suffocation in water. It is the second most common cause of accidental death in people ages one to twenty-four years, after motor vehicle accidents. About two-thirds of all drownings are alcohol-related.

The following guidelines will help to prevent drowning:
• know how to swim;

• read and follow all posted instructions near swimming areas;
• never swim alone;
• swim only where a lifeguard is on duty;
• when boating or waterskiing, always use life jackets;
• do not swim if overtired, overheated, or chilled;
• leave the water if muscle cramps develop;
• stay out of the water during thunderstorms;
• know and respect swimming limitations;
• avoid drinking alcohol;
• avoid swimming in unlighted bodies of water.

All swimmers and nonswimmers who spend time near water should learn drownproofing. **Drownproofing** is a technique that allows an individual to stay afloat without a life jacket during a swimming emergency. During drownproofing, an individual takes a deep breath, sinks below the surface of the water, and breathes out slowly. By moving the hands up and down and kicking the legs, the person returns to the surface. Then another breath is taken. These steps are repeated until help arrives.

Prompt action is necessary in order to assist a person who may be drowning. Attempts to swim out to the person should be made only as a last resort and only by a person trained in water rescue. This is essential because double drownings can easily occur when another person attempts to assist a person struggling in water. When possible, attempt to throw a flotation device to the person or extend a hand or an object such as a towel or stick for the person to grab. If the person is farther out, take a boat, if one is available, and reach out to the person.

Diving accidents are a major cause of spinal cord injuries. Diving accidents typically occur when people dive into water that is too shallow. Water depth should always be known before diving. Other water-related accidents occur while boating. Close to 1,000 people are killed each year in boating accidents. Many boating accidents result from collisions. In many of these accidents, alcohol is involved.

Self-Protection While Exercising Outdoors

Many people enjoy jogging or walking for exercise. Other people enjoy activities such as rollerblading. However, people exercising outdoors are potential victims of violence. People who exercise outdoors should make a plan. *Self-Protection While Exercising Outdoors* (Table 13-10) provides a list of self-protection strategies to follow while exercising outdoors.

Table 13-10

Self-Protection While Exercising Outdoors

1. Avoid exercising alone, at night, and at places where there are few other people.
2. Pay attention to your feelings and avoid areas that do not seem safe.
3. Vary routes and routines (change route, time of day, etc.) because people may stalk their victims and plan their attacks.
4. Avoid paths where a person could be hiding in bushes or trees and quickly grab you.
5. Run or walk quickly in the opposite direction and run to a place where there are other people if you are harassed by someone in a car.
6. Carry a personal siren, personal protection alarm, or whistle.
7. Consider taking a large dog with you when you exercise.
8. Do not use personal stereos with headphones because you will be less likely to hear someone approach you.
9. Keep your distance from strangers.
10. Carry identification and change to make a telephone call.
11. Always let someone you trust that you will follow. Tell this person what time you expect to return.

Figure 14-1

Life Skills for Consumer and Community Health

1. I will choose sources of health-related information, products, and services wisely.

2. I will analyze the effects of advertising on my choices.

3. I will recognize and report quackery.

4. I will spend money wisely.

5. I will spend time wisely.

6. I will use school nurse and school health services when appropriate.

7. I will use health care providers when appropriate.

8. I will use health care facilities when appropriate.

9. I will cooperate with people who protect my health and safety.

10. I will volunteer in school clubs and community organizations and agencies that promote health.

Chapter 14

CONSUMER AND COMMUNITY HEALTH

Consumer and Community Health is the area of health that focuses on choosing sources of health-related information, products, and services wisely; analyzing advertising; recognizing and reporting quackery; spending money and time wisely; using school nurse and school health services when appropriate; using health care providers and health care facilities; cooperating with people in the community who protect health and safety; and volunteering in school clubs and community organizations and agencies that promote health. The content in this chapter provides the background information needed to teach young people life skills for consumer and community health (Figure 14-1).

Life Skill #1

I will choose sources of health-related information, products, and services wisely.

A **consumer** is a person who chooses sources of health-related information and buys or uses health products and services. It is estimated that more than fifty cents of every dollar are spent on health products and services. A wise consumer makes sound decisions about the purchase of health products and services. **Consumerism** is the practice of carefully analyzing health-related information, getting value for money spent on health products and services, and making comparisons between alternative products and services. Wise health consumerism not only helps individuals save money and time, but also helps them avert illness. Unwise decisions, based on misinformation, can have serious health and financial consequences. Examples of the consequences of unwise health consumerism include decisions that delay the detection and treatment of an illness, expose people to dangerous health products, and place them in serious financial difficulty because of inadequate health insurance coverage. Being well-informed provides important protection against being cheated in the marketplace. Avoiding being taken advantage of in the marketplace requires assertiveness—standing up for consumer rights and actively seeking answers to questions and concerns.

319

Consumer and Community Health

Sources of Health-Related Information

People must rely on various sources of information about health. Health-related information (and misinformation) can be obtained from many sources. Many legitimate health agencies and organizations disseminate accurate health information. Examples of agencies that disseminate reliable health information are the American Heart Association, American Cancer Society, March of Dimes Foundation, and American Diabetes Association. These and similar organizations distribute public information through such channels as public service announcements on radio and television, pamphlets and information sheets, and films and videotapes.

The local public health department is an excellent source of health-related information. Many health departments have resource rooms and/or pamphlet files that are stocked with reliable sources of health information for the public. A health information specialist or health educator may be on staff. This person can provide accurate information on a variety of health topics. State health agencies are also good sources of health information. In addition, federal agencies such as the Food and Drug Administration, Department of Education, Department of Agriculture, and Department of Health and Human Services provide reliable health information.

Available through a multitude of outlets are books, magazines, and journal articles on various health topics and issues. Judging the reliability of the information is critical. Inaccurate material can influence individuals to make unwise consumer health decisions. Reliable health information is based solely on scientific research and information. It does not attempt to influence consumers by trying to sell products and services for self-interest or profit. Accurate health information does not include testimonials.

A good place to look for accurate health information is physicians' and dentists' offices. Talking to health professionals in these offices is a good way to get accurate information. Another source of information is the variety of patient education pamphlets available in waiting areas. Health information from friends, family, and media can be accurate, but should be accepted only with caution. Family and friends may be well-meaning, but can still pass on misinformation. Consumers should be particularly wary of media advertisements. The purpose of advertisements is to promote the sale of products and services rather than to inform. All health information appearing in the mass media should be critically evaluated, including news stories and features.

Evaluating Health-Related Information

Health information can be evaluated by asking questions. What is the source of the information? What are the qualifications of the organization, author, or speaker? What is the purpose of disseminating the information—to inform, to sell? Is the information based on up-to-date research and scientific knowledge? Is the information accepted as valid by reputable health care professionals? Does the information make claims of unusual remedies for incurable conditions? Is the information based on testimonials or the opinions of only a few individuals? Does the information rely on the use of emotional appeal?

Life Skill #2

I will analyze the effects of advertising on my choices.

The Advertising Industry

The advertisements in magazines and newspapers and the commercials on television are all designed to influence individuals. **Advertising** is a form of selling in which individuals are informed of products and services. An **advertisement** is a paid announcement. A **commercial** is an advertisement on television or radio.

Companies pay large sums of money to place their advertisements in a variety of media so they can tell people about their products and/or services. **Media** are the various forms of mass communication such as television, radio, magazines, and newspapers. The advertisements appear in places most likely to be seen or heard by the consumer who is most likely to desire and buy the product. For example, toys and games are shown in commercials during children's television shows. Clothes for adolescents are advertised in magazines that are likely to be read by people in that age group.

Types of Appeals in Advertising

Sellers use a variety of techniques in their advertisements to try to convince consumers that their products and services are more desirable than those of their competitors. There are ten different kinds of appeals the advertising industry uses to be convincing.

- *Bandwagon Appeal.* The bandwagon appeal tries to convince consumers that everyone else wants a particular product or service and they should too.
- *Brand Loyalty Appeal.* The brand loyalty appeal tells consumers that a specific brand is better than the rest, and that they would be cheating themselves to use anything but this brand.
- *False Image Appeal.* The false image appeal attempts to convince consumers that they will give a certain impression if they use the product.
- *Glittering Generality Appeal.* The glittering generality appeal contains statements that greatly exaggerate the benefits of the product.
- *Humor Appeal.* The humor appeal uses a slogan, jingle, or cartoon to keep the consumer's attention.
- *Progress Appeal.* The progress appeal tells consumers that a product is a new and better product than one formerly advertised.
- *Reward Appeal.* The reward appeal tells consumers that they will receive a special prize or gift if they buy a product.
- *Scientific Evidence Appeal.* The scientific evidence appeal gives consumers the results of survey or laboratory tests to provide confidence in a product.
- *Snob Appeal.* Snob appeal convinces consumers that they are worthy of a product or service because it is the best.
- *Testimony Appeal.* Testimony appeal includes a promotion by a well-known person who says that a product or service is the best one for the consumer.

Analyzing Advertisements Carefully

A wise consumer is able to differentiate a product or service that is needed and is a responsible use of time and money from one that might be purchased because of an advertising appeal. This requires being able to accurately analyze advertisements before purchasing a product or service. To analyze advertisements objectively, a person must recognize that the purpose of advertising is to influence people to purchase a product or service. Individuals should also recognize that companies spend large sums of money on advertisements in order to influence purchases. It is very important to remain objective about a product or service and not be affected by the emotional appeal of the advertisement. What is the real message in the advertisement? Is the message realistic? What appeals are being used? For example, does it imply that the consumer will be more popular, more attractive, or have more fun if the consumer purchases the product? Being able to accurately assess the message of the advertisement and recognize the advertising appeals that are used helps one to avoid being manipulated by the advertisement.

321

Consumer and Community Health

I will recognize and report quackery.

Fear of illness, pain, aging, and death strongly influences a consumer's choices. These fears may prompt a consumer to select an ineffective or harmful health product or service that wastes both money and time. **Quackery** is consumer fraud that involves the practice of promoting and/or selling useless products and services, especially health products and services. A **quack** is a person who markets inaccurate health information, unreliable health care, or useless health products.

Quackery Involving Weight Loss and Diet Scams

Looking for quick and easy solutions to their weight problems, Americans spend an estimated $30 billion a year on all types of diet programs and products, including diet foods and drinks. Many succumb to quick-fix claims like "Eat all you want and still lose weight!" or "Melt fat away while you sleep!" and they invest their hopes and money in all manner of pills, gadgets, and programs that hold the promise of a slimmer, happier future. An estimated 50 million Americans go on diets each year. However, only about 5 percent will manage to keep off lost weight in the long run. The weight-loss industry is a booming industry (Food and Drug Administration, 1992).

Searching for "Magic Bullets" Some people who are dieting base their hopes for weight loss on pills and capsules that promise to "burn," "block," "flush," or otherwise eliminate fat from the system. However, science has yet to find a low-risk "magic bullet" for weight loss. Some pills may help control the appetite, but they can have serious side effects. For example, amphetamines are highly addictive and can have an adverse impact on the heart and central nervous system. Other pills are totally ineffective.

The Federal Trade Commission (FTC) and a number of state Attorney Generals have successfully brought cases against marketers of pills claiming to absorb or burn fat. The Food and Drug Administration (FDA) has banned over 100 ingredients once found in over-the-counter diet products. None of these substances, which include alcohol, caffeine, dextrose, and guar gum, have been proved to be effective in weight loss or appetite suppression (Food and Drug Administration, 1992).

Phony Devices and Gadgets Phony weight-loss devices range from those that are simply ineffective to those that are truly dangerous to health. At a minimum they are a waste of money.

Diet Programs Approximately 8 million Americans a year enroll in some kind of structured weight-loss program involving liquid diets, special diet regimens, or medical or other supervision. More than 8,500 commercial diet centers are in operation across the nation, many of which are owned by a half-dozen or so well known national companies (Food and Drug Administration, 1992).

Before a consumer joins a diet program, (s)he should realize that relatively few participants succeed in keeping off weight in the long term. Also, before signing up with a diet program, a consumer should ask the following questions (Food and Drug Administration, 1992):
1. What are the health risks?
2. What data prove that the program actually works?
3. Do customers keep off weight after they leave the program?
4. What are the costs of membership, weekly fees, food, supplements, maintenance, and counseling? What's the payment schedule? Are any costs covered under health insurance? What, if any, refunds will be made if the person decides not to continue the program?
6. Is there a maintenance program? Is it part of the package or does it cost extra?
7. What kind of professional supervision is provided? What are the credentials of these professionals?
8. What are the program's requirements? Are there special menus or foods, counseling visits, or exercise plans?

Quackery Involving Unproven Treatments and Products

Each year, Americans spend about $30 billion on unproven medical treatments and products, many of which are worthless and even harmful (Lange, 1993). Promoters of unproven treatments often claim that their products prevent aging and such conditions as heart disease, arthritis, and Alzheimer's disease.

Payments for unproven medical treatments can drain a person's economic resources, particularly elderly people with limited resources. Besides being medically useless, some unproven treatments can cause serious injuries or illness. Another danger is that people who rely on these products may delay or reject proven treatments. This is particularly dangerous in the case of cancer because delays in detection and treatment may advance a patient past the point where proven treatments can help (Napier, 1994).

Herbal products are often promoted as cures of a variety of ailments. Herbal products do not have to meet the same standards as over-the-counter medications because they are sold as foods rather than drugs. As a result, claims about healing disorders cannot be made on labels. However, magazines, pamphlets, and people make widespread claims about the healing properties of herbal products (Short, 1994). Herbal products are available in various forms including teas, capsules, and tablets. Some, such as chamomile tea, lobelia, and comfrey, are potentially hazardous. Chamomile tea can cause a severe allergic reaction in people allergic to ragweed. Lobelia can causes vomiting, breathing problems, convulsions, coma, and death if used in large amounts. People with heart disease are particularly susceptible to the effects of lobelia. Comfrey can cause liver disease (Napier, 1994).

Avoiding Quackery and Consumer Fraud

A quack or fraud may promote products or services by promising quick cures, miracles, and/or new formulas of which no one has heard. Quacks are often successful in promoting fraudulent health services and products because they tell people what they want to hear. The quack may sell door-to-door or by telephone rather than in conventional ways. The consumer may be provided with testimonials from people who claim that several illnesses or ailments were remedied by a product or service. Responsible consumers should avoid purchases in these instances because, almost always, consumer fraud is indicated.

To recognize quackery, the following additional questions should be asked and evaluated. Does the seller of the product or service claim that the medical profession does not recognize this product or service? Does the seller claim that traditional medical treatment is more harmful than healthful? Is the product available only through a post office box number? Is the product or service promoted by a person or group of people about whom little or nothing is known? Does the seller use scare tactics that play on fears and emotions? Does the seller guarantee a quick cure or a cure for an incurable disease?

The FDA and Arthritis Foundation advise consumers to be very suspicious of any remedy not prescribed by a physician that (Napier, 1994):
- has celebrity endorsements;
- contains inadequate labeling (a legitimate nonprescription medication is labeled with indications for use, as well as directions for its use, and cautions about when to seek medical help);
- makes claims that the product works by secret formula;
- is promoted only in the back pages of magazines, over the phone, by direct mail, in newspaper advertisements in the format of news stories, or 30-minute commercials in talk show format;

- claims that it is effective for a wide variety of disorders such as cancer, arthritis, and sexual dysfunction;
- claims to be all-natural, inexpensive, has no side effects, works immediately and permanently, and/or it is not necessary to talk to a doctor about it.

To protect against quackery, consumers should gather information about health products and services, keep records and/or receipts of all purchases, and contact consumer protectors if there are suspicions about the practices of any sellers or providers of health care products or services.

Life Skill #4

I will spend money wisely.

Making a Budget

An important strategy for managing money effectively is to have a budget. Having a budget and living within that budget also tend to influence health, happiness, and stress level. A **budget** is a plan for spending and saving money. A budget involves planning for income, expenses, and savings. **Income** is the money that is received from a variety of sources. A young person may receive an allowance for mowing the grass, washing the dishes, or helping with other household chores. (S)he may also have a part-time job. **Expenses** are the costs of items that are needed and wanted to be purchased. Young people sometimes use earned money to help with family expenses. If old enough to drive, an adolescent may need to purchase gasoline and car insurance. Money may be needed for dating and entertainment. Money may also be set aside to give to charitable organizations. **Savings** is the money set aside for future use. A person may be saving to buy a new pair of running shoes in the near future. A young person may be saving to help pay for technical school or college expenses or to buy a car sometime in the future. Savings may be planned for the time when a young person will be living on his/her own. It is important to consider savings for use in the near future as well as the distant future.

People who have a budget are less likely to purchase unnecessary items and more likely to have savings. The ability to make a budget and follow it closely today is helpful for the future. Young people who have an understanding of their family's budget will gain insight into how to budget money as an adult. Having a budget helps to develop some skills of responsible consumership. A wise consumer makes a budget and lives within that budget. The person attempts to buy the best products and services affordable with the given resources.

Most family budgets include expenses for groceries, medical care, clothing, and entertainment. Other important items to include in a budget are housing, utilities, household furnishings, child care, insurance, and transportation expenses. A family should also budget for savings. Savings may be used to cover future educational expenses for children.

Shopping Wisely

Shopping wisely involves examining priorities and needs, evaluating financial resources, taking a little extra time to gather information about products, and shopping around for the best values. Consumers should recognize that prices on many items vary from store to store. They should compare prices and become familiar with particular stores which have a reputation for offering the best buys on certain items; watch for advertisements in the newspaper, television, and other sources announcing special sales; learn to buy certain items at the time of year when they go on sale; and stock up on items that will be needed in the future when prices are reduced. However, a consumer should not be persuaded to make a purchase simply because an item is on sale.

It is important to stay aware of differences in quality. A brand name item may have a higher price than a generic name product. Some brands offer better quality. However, sometimes a particular brand has a higher price more for the brand name than for quality. For example, the only difference in some jeans other than the price is the label. Carefully read labels, tags, and consumer information before making purchases.

It is important to be particularly careful about impulse buying. Having a budget helps to clearly distinguish between needs and wants and to avoid impulse buying. To avoid impulse buying at the grocery store, a person should not go to the store when hungry or thirsty. It is important to keep control of credit purchases. Impulse buying can greatly reduce the bank balance and ruin a credit rating.

At the grocery store, unit prices should be compared to save money. Read food labels to find out exactly what is being purchased. A grocery list should be made and only items on the list should be purchased to avoid overspending. Coupons might be used, but only for items that are on the grocery list.

Shopping Addiction Most people occasionally spend money on impulse, but are able to control their spending urges. Some people become shopping addicts. A **shopping addict** is a person who lacks control of spending urges and repeatedly engages in impulse buying. For these people, spending money provides a sense of excitement or euphoria that allows them to temporarily escape painful feelings of depression and/or anxiety. Shopping sprees are most likely to occur when the shopping addict is feeling upset or depressed. Individuals suffering from this condition often have a strong need for approval. As a result, many of their purchases are for other people. Underlying this behavior is the hope that they will gain approval. Obviously, this disorder creates immense difficulties for individuals and families. A family can easily be financially ruined, and relationships can be shattered. Individuals with shopping addiction need professional treatment. New ways of coping with emotional problems must be developed.

Spending Money on Entertainment

Having money for entertainment can add to the enjoyment of life. Entertainment can be relaxing or be stimulating. Finding the right balance of entertainment can add to the quality of life and provide an outlet for stress. Because there are so many fun things on which to spend money, it is easy to spend beyond one's means.

Budgets should include entertainment expenses. Then, discipline is required to stay within the constraints that have been set. This can be difficult for young people because entertainment costs are often high. Going to a movie costs approximately $5, a concert $20 to $30, or a ball game $10 to $30. Purchasing refreshments greatly increases the cost of attending one of these events. Buying a compact disc costs $10 to $20. Young people who are unable to control their urges to spend money on entertainment can easily get into financial trouble.

Entertainment choices should be discussed with parents. Parents can provide guidelines for avoiding situations and forms of entertainment media that are not healthful. Television, films, rock music, videos, books, and magazines may provide images, messages, and role models of inappropriate behavior for youth. Too many of these forms of media have violent content, use violent behavior to solve interpersonal problems, show females who are dressed provocatively, and show sexual intimacy. Videos and cable television provide access to more violent, X-rated, and pornographic films than were available in past generations. In the midst of this access, it is essential to properly supervise young people and help them make wise choices in spending money and choosing leisure time activities.

Paying for Health Care

The average American spends in excess of $625 a year on health care. Consumers pay for health care directly out of their pockets, through local, state, and federal taxes, and through health insurance. **Health insurance** is a financial agreement between an insurance company and an individual or group for the payment of health care. The consumer pays a premium to the insurance company for a health insurance policy and, in turn, the health insurance company pays for specific benefits. Health insurance policies differ in their coverage, making it necessary for consumers to be well-informed prior to purchasing a policy and prior to expecting benefits to be paid for the specific health care. Usually, there is a deductible. A **deductible** is an amount to be paid by the insurance policy holder before the health insurance company makes any payment. Usually there are fixed indemnity benefits. **Fixed indemnity benefits** are specific amounts that an insurance company pays for specific procedures.

Often, there are exclusions. **Exclusions** are certain items and services that are not covered by the health insurance policy.

Types of Health Insurance. Health insurance is obtained in three major ways:
1. individual or group policies;
2. managed care;
3. government programs.

Individual policies are insurance policies arranged between a consumer and a health insurance company. Individual policies are usually more expensive than group plans and may provide less coverage. **Group policies** are insurance policies available through organizations that employ or to which people may belong (e.g., professional associations, social organizations, unions). They are arrangements between a health insurance company and the organization.

Because of rising health care costs, there has been an emergence of managed care health insurance systems. **Managed care** is a set of procedures used by health insurers to control health care costs by controlling which medical services consumers are entitled to receive and by limiting reimbursement for certain services. For example, a consumer may be required to get a second opinion before surgery can be performed. Two types of managed care are: health maintenance organizations and preferred provider organizations. **Health maintenance organizations (HMOs)** are health care delivery plans in which subscribers prepay a fixed monthly fee for coverage from member health care providers. HMOs usually provide comprehensive health care as well as preventive care. This arrangement encourages people to use member health care providers. These health care providers work together, allowing for cost containment. One drawback of the HMO is the lack of personal patient/health care provider relationship. The patient sees many different health care providers rather than developing a constant relationship with one. **Preferred provider organizations (PPOs)** and **preferred provider associations (PPAs)** are health care delivery plans in which arrangements have been made by a third party (e.g., a union, insurance company, self-insured business) for consumers to select health care providers from a list of "preferred providers." In turn, consumers receive health care services at a discounted rate. If consumers choose to go to health care providers outside of the system, then they will pay more than if they stay within the system.

The government is also involved in paying for health care. **Medicare** is a governmental health insurance to which people contribute during their working years in exchange for some of their health care costs being covered after age 65. **Medicaid** is a governmental health insurance plan in which people receiving other types of public assistance receive medical and hospital coverage. There is no age requirement for Medicaid. Before a state can receive federal Medicaid monies it must match the federal funding. As a result, states set income eligibility requirements, and these requirements vary from state to state.

Life Skill #5

I will spend time wisely.

Making a Time Management Plan

Consumers need to be careful about the use of time. An individual is more likely to achieve balanced physical, mental-emotional and family-social health when time is valued and used wisely. Just as a budget is needed to plan wisely for spending and saving, a time management plan is needed. A **time management plan** is a plan that indicates how time will be spent on daily activities and leisure. An effective time management plan includes blocks of time set aside to promote physical, mental-emotional and family-social health. To make a time management plan, a person identifies all daily activities on a calendar showing the hours of the day. Then a person might examine the activities and assess whether or not attention has been given to all areas of well-being. People who manage their time well and who attempt to balance their time and include activities to promote all areas of health, tend to be healthier and happier and report fewer harmful effects of stress. Time is not wasted.

After completing a time management plan, the effectiveness of the plan should be evaluated. Are activities completed that must be done? Is time allocated for activities that promote each dimension of physical, mental-emotional, and family-social health?

Analyzing How Time Is Spent

To develop an effective time management plan it may be helpful to analyze how time is spent. An effective way to do this is to develop an assessment form that divides the day into fifteen-minute segments. This form can be used to record how each fifteen-minute segment is spent throughout the day. All activities should be recorded for several days. When this record is completed, the manner in which time is spent can be evaluated. It will become apparent how time is being spent and what activities dominate the time spent. Based on this analysis, goals can be set for modifying how time is spent if it is not spent wisely. One good way to make changes is to develop a contract that includes rewards for making desired changes in time-use practices.

Watching Too Much Television One way that young people waste a lot of time is watching television. Young people spend an enormous amount of time watching recreational television. Children and adolescents average over twenty hours per week viewing commercial or cable television (Dietz, 1990). Additional hours are spent watching videocassettes and playing video games. More time is spent watching television than is spent in any activity other than sleep. Many young people actually spend more time viewing television than they do in school. The time spent watching television is time that is not spent in other activities such as physical activity, social interaction, and reading.

Television viewing is associated with increased body fatness and poor physical fitness in children and adolescents (Robinson et al., 1994). Because television viewing is a sedentary activity, there is likely to be reduced caloric expenditure among those who watch television for extended periods of time. Young people are also susceptible to eating high-calorie snacks of poor nutritional quality while viewing television. These eating practices tend to be reinforced by the fact that young people are exposed to television commercials for high-calorie foods.

Watching television can affect young people in other negative ways. The portrayal of violence on television and in other media is pervasive. Watching violence desensitizes young people to the violence. **Desensitization** is the effect of reacting less and less to exposure to violence or other shocking experiences. As a result, young people come to accept with little emotional reaction things that should result in feelings of shock, anger, sadness, or fear. Some have become so desensitized that they laugh or enjoy seeing violence. It is estimated that the average youth between the ages of five and fifteen years has witnessed 13,400 people killed in the media by violent acts. In one year, the ABC television network averaged twenty-four acts of violence per hour; NBC and CBS showed seventeen acts of violence per hour (Powell, 1991).

Entertainment Addiction Entertainment is an important source of pleasure and enjoyment for people. But some young people develop a type of entertainment addiction. **Entertainment addiction** is an extreme need to be entertained at the expense of taking care of physical, social, emotional, and/or mental needs. Perhaps the most common form of entertainment addiction is television addiction. In this condition, television viewing has become the primary activity, and large amounts of time are spent in front of the television. Physical activity is avoided at the expense of television viewing. Social skills are not exercised. Friendships are not developed. Schoolwork is neglected. Schedules revolve around favorite shows. Television becomes a mechanism for escape. Problems are forgotten by indulgence in the fantasy world of television and video movies.

Life Skill #6

I will use school nurse and school health services when appropriate.

The School Nurse

School nurses are trained to help students, school personnel, and teachers with many

Consumer and Community Health

health needs. If a student becomes ill at school, the school nurse should be notified immediately. The school nurse will examine the student to determine if there is a need for prompt or emergency medical care. If needed, the school nurse will initiate the care or make arrangements for the student to receive appropriate medical care. Parents will be notified whenever the student becomes ill at school. Sometimes a parent will be called and asked to pick the student up from school.

School nurses do much more than assist students who become ill at school. Much of what they do focuses on trying to keep students healthy. This includes maintaining health records and histories for each student, providing information about community health resources, and conducting health appraisals and screenings. School nurses conduct screenings for such health conditions as scoliosis, head lice, vision, and hearing. When necessary, school nurses are available to provide emergency first aid for injuries sustained at school. They also counsel parents, students, and teachers about special health concerns. When a student suffers from a chronic disease, students and parents can rely on school nurses for assistance. Many school nurses have training in how to manage chronic diseases such as asthma, heart conditions, epilepsy, and diabetes.

School Health Services

Health services are expensive. In order to provide more students with needed services, many schools now rely on community linkages with outside agencies. This allows schools to offer a broader range of services to meet the health needs of students and families. Students and parents in need of the services that are available through school-community linkages should be notified. These linkages can make the following services available to students and their families: physical examinations and screenings, immunizations, treatment of minor injuries and illness, prenatal care for pregnant females, parenting classes for adolescent parents, dental care, vision services, and substance abuse and mental health counseling.

I will use health care providers when appropriate.

Selecting Health Care Providers

Consumers seek health care providers for screening, preventive measures, consultation, diagnosis, and treatment. Selecting a competent health care provider is an important task. After an initial visit, several questions can be asked: Was I comfortable with this person? Was I able to communicate? Did this person listen to me? Were all my questions answered in an understandable and reassuring way? Did this person show concern for my well-being? Does this person seem interested in having me as a client? Is this person's training and specialty area a match for my needs? Is this person associated with professional associations or hospitals that are credible? Is this person's policies for payment compatible with my ability to pay? What are the hours that this person is available? Will my needs be met if there is an emergency? Will I receive prompt responses to my telephone calls?

Physicians

A **physician** is a person licensed to practice medicine and surgery in all branches of medicine. The two types of physicians in the United States who follow the principles of modern science are medical doctors and osteopaths. A **medical doctor** is a physician trained in a medical school, with the doctor of medicine (M.D.) degree. An **osteopath** is a physician trained in a college of osteopathic medicine, with the doctor of osteopathy (D.O.) degree.

Medical doctors and osteopathic physicians can choose either to work in primary care or to become a specialist. An **anesthesiologist** is a physician who specializes in the administration of drugs to prevent pain and induce unconsciousness during surgery. A **cardiologist** is a physician who specializes in the treatment of disorders of the heart and blood vessels. A **dermatologist** is a physician who specializes in the medical care of the skin. A **gastroenterologist** is a physician who specializes in the treatment of disorders of the digestive tract. A **geriatrician** is a physician who specializes in the medical care of the elderly. A **neurologist** is a physician who specializes in the diagnosis and treatment of diseases of the brain, spinal cord, and nerves. An **obstetrician** is a physician who specializes in the care of females during pregnancy and after delivery. A **gynecologist** is a physician who specializes in treatment of disorders of the female reproductive system. An **ophthalmologist** is medical doctor who specializes in the medical and surgical care and treatment of the eye. An **orthopedist** is a physician who specializes in the surgical care of muscle, bone, and joint injuries and disorders. A **pediatrician** is a physician who specializes in the care of children and adolescents. A **plastic surgeon** is a physician who specializes in surgery to correct, repair, or improve body features. A **psychiatrist** is a physician who specializes in the diagnosis and treatment of mental and emotional problems. A **urologist** is a physician who specializes in treatment of urinary disorders and the male reproductive system.

Specialized and Allied Health Professionals

In addition to medical doctors, there are also health care practitioners. A **health care practitioner** is a health care professional whose practice is restricted to a specific area of the body. A **podiatrist** is a health care professional trained and licensed as a doctor of podiatric medicine (D.P.M.), specializing in problems of the feet. Podiatrists are licensed to prescribe drugs and perform surgery on the feet. An **optometrist** is a health care professional trained and licensed as a doctor of optometry (O.D.), examining the eyes and detecting vision and eye problems. They can prescribe eyeglasses and contact lenses and use diagnostic drugs but do not perform

surgery. A **dentist** is a health care professional trained and licensed as either a doctor of dental surgery (D.D.S.) or as a doctor of medical dentistry (D.M.D.), providing dental care. Dentists may choose to work either in general practice or in a specialty such as orthodontics (correction of irregularities of teeth) or pediatric dentistry (dental care of children).

Allied health professionals are scientifically trained practitioners who practice under some degree of medical supervision. Allied health professionals include nurses and many other types of practitioners. A **registered nurse (R.N.)** is an allied health professional who possesses either an associate degree or a bachelor's degree (B.S.N.) and is certified either for general practice or for any one of several nurse specialties such as anesthesia, midwifery, public health, or intensive care. Registered nurses who pursue further training can become nurse practitioners. A **nurse practitioner** is a specially trained registered nurse who can function as a primary care provider in some states. A **licensed practical nurse (L.P.N.)** and a **licensed vocational nurse (L.V.N.)** are licensed and trained nurses who provide nursing care under the direction of registered nurses or medical doctors.

Other examples of some of the more than 70 types of allied health professionals are audiologists, dental hygienists, medical technologists, occupational therapists, pharmacists, physical therapists, physician's assistants, registered dietitians, respiratory therapists, and speech pathologists. An **audiologist** is an allied health professional who screens people for hearing problems and makes recommendations for hearing devices. A **dental hygienist** is an allied health professional who provides oral health services such as cleaning teeth and education about proper care of teeth. A **medical technologist** is an allied health care professional who performs laboratory tests used in the detection of disease and medical supervision of patients. An **occupational therapist** is an allied health care professional who helps people with disabilities learn to adapt to their disabilities and to relearn skills needed for daily living. A **pharmacist** is an allied health care professional who dispenses medications in accordance with a physician's prescription. A **physical therapist** is an allied health care professional who works with people with physical disabilities and ailments to restore function. A **physician's assistant** is an allied health care professional who works closely under the direction of a physician in performing physical examinations, counseling patients, and prescribing medication. A **registered dietitian** is an allied health care professional who counsels patients about healthful dietary principles and performs dietary planning for patients in health care institutions. A **respiratory therapist** is an allied health care professional who tests for and treats breathing disorders according to physician's orders. A **speech pathologist** is an allied health care professional who helps people overcome speech disorders.

Life Skill #8

I will use health care facilities when appropriate.

Prior to using health facilities, responsible consumers learn about them. They learn the exact services performed and the costs for those services. They check into methods of payment. They make comparisons to using other types of facilities. There are a variety of facilities of which consumers need to be aware.

Hospitals

Hospitals can be private, public, or voluntary. A **private hospital** is a hospital facility owned by private individuals and operated for profit. Private hospitals are not supported with tax dollars, thus they are usually used by people who are able to pay for all services. A **public hospital** is a governmental or tax-supported hospital. This type of hospital usually provides services to low-income people as well as to others. Frequently, they are teaching hospitals. A **voluntary hospital** is a nonprofit public institution, usually owned by the community. Voluntary hospitals are supported by patient fees and contributions. Fraternal groups and charitable organizations often run them. A current trend is for these hospitals to have wellness centers.

Outpatient Centers

Consumers can often save money when necessary surgery is performed at outpatient surgery centers. An **outpatient surgery center** is a clinic or other facility that offers an alternative to overnight hospital stay for patients in need of certain surgeries. Fees for surgeries performed in these centers generally are lower than standard hospital fees. These facilities are generally not suitable for major surgery that requires general anesthesia or extensive postoperative care.

Emergency Centers

Many people rely on hospital emergency rooms as their primary health facility because it is the only way that they can access the health care system. Many come in for health conditions that would not be considered emergencies. Many lack health insurance. As a result, many emergency rooms, particularly in large cities, have become very crowded and have difficulty serving all the people who come in for health care. The fees for services rendered at emergency rooms are substantially higher than for office visits made to physicians. Emergency room visits for routine health care may not be covered by health insurance. An alternative to hospital emergency rooms are freestanding emergency centers. A **freestanding emergency center** is a facility, not part of a hospital, that provides prompt care for accidents or illnesses which occur when a personal physician is not available or a person does not have a personal physician. Freestanding emergency centers do not require an appointment and are open most hours of the day. Their fees are lower than those of hospital emergency rooms but higher than those for visits to a physician's office.

Life Skill #9

I will cooperate with people who protect my health and safety.

Because the health industry is such big business and the potential harm and cost to people is great, there are a variety of federal, state, and local agencies as well as professional associations who serve as consumer protectors.

Professional Associations

Professional associations help the consumer by monitoring the credentials of their members and their actions. The **American Medical Association (AMA)** is an association that sets standards for the education and conduct of medical physicians. The AMA has a Department of Investigation and a Department of Health Education to assist the consumer and to investigate complaints. The **American Dental Association (ADA)** is an association that sets standards for the education and conduct of dentists.

Private Organizations

There are other kinds of consumer protectors. The **Better Business Bureau** is a nonprofit, voluntary, self-regulating organization that monitors unfair competition and misleading advertisements for private firms. Although this organization has no legal power, businesses want to have a favorable reputation and usually comply with its recommendations. The **Consumers' Research** and **Consumers' Union** are private groups that test products and provide ratings for consumers to make comparisons with regard to products' performance and safety. Both groups are supported by private donations and by the sale of their publications. The Consumers' Union publishes the widely read *Consumer Reports*, a monthly magazine that provides readers with information on a wide range of consumer products and topics, including health products and services. The **Center for Science in the Public Interest (CSPI)** is a private organization that publishes information about foods and food choices, including the monthly *Nutrition Action Healthletter*.

Federal Governmental Agencies

The federal government plays a vital role in consumer protection. The **Food and Drug Administration (FDA)** is a federal agency within the Department of Health and Human Services that monitors the safety and effectiveness of medical devices and new drugs and the safety and purity of cosmetics and foods. The FDA also publishes a consumer health magazine entitled *The FDA Consumer*, which provides information on a wide variety of topics. The **Federal Trade Commission (FTC)** is an independent agency that monitors the advertising of foods, drugs, cosmetics, devices, and advertising that appears on television. The **United States Postal Service** is the federal agency that protects the public when products, devices, and services are sold through the mail. The **Office of Consumer Affairs** is the federal agency that serves as the liaison between the President and all consumers. This office coordinates investigations into consumer problems, coordinates research, and conducts seminars to inform the public. The **Consumer Product Safety Commission** is the federal agency that distributes information and receives complaints about the safety of products. The commission also enforces uniform safety standards for products whose use could result in injuries or illness. **The National Health Information Center** is a federal agency that operates a toll-free hotline through which it refers consumers to organizations that can provide reliable health information. The **United States Department of Agriculture (USDA)** is a federal agency that enforces standards for ensuring that food is processed safely and also oversees the distribution of food information to the public.

State and Local Agencies and Personnel

State and local agencies and associations are also valuable consumer protectors. The state health department usually has a consumer affairs office that investigates complaints and takes actions when harmful products or services are sold in the state. The local or city health department may also have a consumer affairs office that investigates complaints and takes actions when harmful products or services are sold at the city or local level.

Police and fire personnel work hard in communities to protect the health and safety of citizens. They often risk their own lives in trying to protect members of the community. Police work to prevent crime and apprehend criminals. Many police are actively involved in school and community violence and substance abuse prevention programs. Besides fighting fires, fire fighters check fire-alarm boxes and fire hydrants to make sure they work properly. They also check buildings for fire hazards and install smoke detectors. Fire fighters give talks on fire safety.

Life Skill #10

I will volunteer in school clubs and community organizations and agencies that promote health.

Much of the emphasis in health education is on personal responsibility for health. However, there are many health problems that can be solved only by individuals working together and serving the needs of others. Trained health professionals and community health agencies cannot confront community health problems alone. Community health is a shared responsibility. When individuals become active participants in community health, great strides can be made to improve the health of community members.

Responsible community health citizenship entails respecting and following health laws, making financial donations, staying informed on community health issues, and voting on community health issues once voting age is reached. A very important part of community health is volunteering in school clubs and community organizations and agencies that promote health. In this section, several organizations in which a person can volunteer his/her efforts to promote health are reviewed.

School Clubs and Organizations

Young people can volunteer service in school clubs and organizations. Service clubs perform a variety of services that meet the needs of various community members. Fundraising activities often provide funding for needy people or organizations that serve people who are handicapped, elderly, or sick. Service projects may include such activities as visiting elderly residents of a nursing home, starting a recycling program, or teaching younger students about the dangers of drug use.

Other opportunities for student involvement include peer leader programs (e.g., Natural Helpers), Students Against Drunk Driving (SADD) clubs, and safety patrols.

Community Health Agencies

There are many types of community health agencies. Some are governmental organizations while others are not. There are international, national, state, and local community health agencies. The **World Health Organization (WHO)** is an agency of the United Nations and is headquartered in Geneva, Switzerland, that strives to improve the quality of health throughout the world by planning, providing, and coordinating health services. WHO works with many nations to solve health problems, often assisting in training personnel to carry out health services with the goal that the need for outside help be reduced. WHO works collaboratively with other international organizations such as the United Nations Children's Fund (UNICEF), the Food and Agriculture Organization (FAO), and the International Labor Organization (ILO).

The health agency that plays a principal role at the federal level is the **U.S. Public Health Service** within the **Department of Health and Human Services**. The **Centers for Disease Control and Prevention (CDC)** is the federal agency within the Public Health Service responsible for tracking disease incidence and trends, coordinating disease control efforts with other nations, taking action in response to outbreaks, epidemics, and natural disasters, and working with states and communities in developing and operating disease control programs. Also within the U.S. Public Health Service are: Substance Abuse and Mental Health Services (SAMSA), the Food and Drug Administration (FDA), the Indian Health Services (IHS) and the National Institutes of Health (NIH), among others.

The health agency that plays a principal role at the state level is the state health department. A **state health department** is the official state agency that has responsibility for the health of people residing in the state. This agency is supported by tax funds and is recognized as a governmental agency. State health departments typically administer a wide range of health services and programs.

The **local health department** is the official agency that has responsibility for the health of people residing within a community. Services typically offered by state and local health departments include: collection, compilation, and dissemination of vital and health statistics; communicable disease control; maternal and child health services and programs; chronic disease control; mental health promotion; environmental health protection; health education; health planning; consumer protection; public health nursing; emergency medical services; and programs for children who are handicapped.

Voluntary Health Organizations

There are many voluntary health associations that assist in providing community health services. **Voluntary health organizations** are agencies supported by funding other than taxes, that usually focus on a specific disease, health problem, or body organ. Examples of voluntary health associations are: American Cancer Society, American Heart Association, American Diabetes Association, American Lung Association, National Society for Prevention of Blindness, March of Dimes, American Red Cross, National Safety Council, Arthritis Foundation, Mothers Against Drunk Driving, Students Against Drunk Driving, and National Kidney Foundation. These agencies seek to educate the public and health care professionals about particular health conditions. They also raise funds for research and community health programs. Many of these agencies rely heavily on volunteers.

Figure 15-1

Life Skills for Environmental Health

1. I will be concerned about environmental issues.

2. I will keep the air clean.

3. I will keep the water clean.

4. I will keep my indoor environment free of pollution.

5. I will keep noise at a healthful level.

6. I will protect myself from radiation.

7. I will dispose of solid waste properly.

8. I will recycle.

9. I will be aware of the effects of overcrowding and poverty.

10. I will cooperate with environmental protection agencies.

Chapter 15

ENVIRONMENTAL HEALTH

Environmental health is the area of health that focuses on being concerned about environmental issues, keeping the air clean, keeping the water clean, keeping the indoor environment free of pollution, keeping noise at a healthful level, protecting oneself from radiation, disposing of solid waste properly, recycling, being aware of the effects of poverty and overcrowding, and cooperating with environmental protection agencies. The content in this chapter provides the background information you will need to teach young people the following life skills for environmental health (Figure 15-1).

Life Skill #1

I will be concerned about environmental issues.

Environment is the multitude of dynamic conditions that are external to a person. For a person to achieve optimal health, the environment must be healthful. A healthful environment enhances the quality of life and allows people to achieve the highest levels of physical, mental-emotional, and family-social health.

Environmental Interest Groups

Concerned citizens have formed organizations to increase public awareness of environmental issues and to solve related problems. Goals of these organizations include preserving natural areas, protecting wildlife and its habitats, eliminating or limiting pollution, educating the public, confronting groups that harm the environment, and influencing legislation. Some of the larger and better-known environmental organizations are the Sierra Club, the National Audubon Society, the National Wildlife Federation, the Nature Conservancy, and Greenpeace.

Environmental Issues

Americans are concerned about environmental issues and environmental quality. These issues include:
- ozone layer deterioration;
- global warming;
- hazardous waste;
- oil spills;
- air pollution;
- acid rain;
- solid waste disposal;
- nuclear waste;
- contaminated water;
- forest destruction;
- endangered species and threats to wildlife;
- pesticide use;
- world population;
- radon gas;
- natural disasters;
- indoor air pollution.

The Ozone Layer

The **ozone layer** is a layer of the upper atmosphere that filters out the sun's ultraviolet rays. Depletion of the ozone layer caused by release of chlorofluorocarbons and halogens into the air is a major concern. **Chlorofluorocarbons** are odorless nonpoisonous chemicals that are used as aerosol propellants and refrigerants. They are also used to make plastic foam found in disposable food containers. **Halogens** are a group of related chemicals that are used for various purposes, among them to extinguish fires. When these substances are released into the air, they can remain there for thirty or more years and destroy the ozone layer through chemical reactions. As the ozone layer thins, more of the sun's ultraviolet rays penetrate through the atmosphere to reach the Earth's surface. This has increased the risk of skin cancer and eye cataracts, and damage to forests and crops.

The Greenhouse Effect and Global Warming

Scientists worldwide are concerned about the increased warming of the Earth. The **greenhouse effect** is an increase in the carbon dioxide concentration in the atmosphere that reduces heat loss from the Earth and increases atmospheric temperature. When light rays from the sun strike the surface of the Earth or the tops of clouds, they are reflected as heat energy that is absorbed by the atmosphere. The increase of carbon dioxide causes greater absorption of heat. As a result, the average temperature of the Earth may rise several degrees over a period of decades. This can create serious consequences. The polar ice caps can melt when there is a rise of the Earth's atmospheric temperature of only a few degrees. Flooding of coastal regions of the Earth can result. Some scientific research indicates that by around the year 2050, the average temperature of the Earth will increase between three and nine degrees. This increase can reduce water levels in rivers and lakes. Droughts will be more common. Evidence indicates that there will be decreased winter ice cover.

I will keep the air clean.

Air Pollution

An estimated 66 percent of the U.S. population lives in communities that fail to meet one or more federal air quality standards. The **Environmental Protection Agency (EPA)** is a federal agency that is responsible for alleviating and controlling environmental pollution. The EPA measures air quality by the pollutant standard index. The **pollutant standard index (PSI)** is a standardized measure of air quality based on the sum of the levels of five different pollutants relative to regulatory standard maximums. The regulatory standard maximums are assigned a value of 100 and are determined from the influence they have on health status. When a maximum permissible level of air quality determined by the EPA is exceeded, the EPA advises against strenuous outdoor work or recreational exercise because exercising exposes the lungs to increased pollutants. The American Lung Association cautions people not to engage in vigorous outdoor activity when the PSI for ozone exceeds 70 (Schultz, 1994).

Sources of Air Pollution

Air is needed to sustain life. Unfortunately, the air in many places in the world is polluted. Air pollution is one of the greatest environmental risks to human health. Health problems brought on or exacerbated by airborne pollutants include: lung diseases, such as chronic bronchitis and pulmonary emphysema; cancer, particularly lung cancer; bronchial asthma; and eye irritation. Certain major air pollutants and conditions are dangerous to health.

Carbon Monoxide **Carbon monoxide** is an odorless, tasteless, colorless, poisonous gas. It results from the incomplete combustion of organic materials. Automobiles are the principal source of carbon monoxide in the environment.

When carbon monoxide enters the body, it becomes attached to red blood cells. Because carbon monoxide combines chemically with hemoglobin more readily than oxygen, it displaces oxygen in the blood so that oxygen cannot reach various body cells including the lungs. **Hemoglobin** is the oxygen-transporting component of blood. Long-term exposure to carbon monoxide may lead to decreased physical health. There is some concern that people who are driving trucks or autombiles and who are exposed to high levels of carbon monoxide may have reduced ability to react to accident situations.

Sulfur Oxides **Sulfur oxides** are pollutants that result from the combustion of fuels containing sulfur and from sulfur from volcanoes that combine with oxygen to form sulfur oxides. When people inhale sulfur oxides, their respiratory system becomes irritated. Research studies are currently examining the relationship between breathing sulfur oxides and acquiring other lung diseases.

Nitrogen Oxides **Nitrogen oxides** are gases produced by the high-temperature combustion of energy sources such as coal and oil. The most significant source of nitrogen oxides in the atmosphere is the exhaust from automobiles. Nitrogen oxides cause irritation of the eyes and respiratory passages. Prolonged exposure results in damage to the respiratory tract and the development of lung diseases. Cigarette smoke contains large amounts of nitrogen dioxide. When the smoke is combined with nitrogen oxides from other sources, the harm to the body is greater.

Hydrocarbons **Hydrocarbons** are chemical compounds that contain only carbon and hydrogen. The most abundant hydrocarbon pollutants are propane, benzene, and ethylene. Hydrocarbons are a major contributor to smog. Motor vehicles account for approximately one-quarter of hydrocarbon emissions.

Ozone **Ozone** is a chemical variant of oxygen that is classified as a photochemical because it is created in the presence of hydrocarbons, nitrogen oxides, and sunlight (Schultz, 1994). Ozone is a gas and is the most widespread air pollutant. It is dangerous to a person's health: causing irritation of the eyes, lungs, and throat and producing headaches, coughing, and shortness of breath. Ozone also damages plants and harms animals. It is a major cause of damage to products such as the cracking of rubber.

Approximately 60 percent of Americans live in areas that exceed the current National Ambient Air Quality Standards for ozone level. In some parts of the country, ozone levels approach twice the standard. In healthy, nonsmoking adults, exposure to this concentration of ozone in the air for two hours causes acute inflammation of the lungs and bronchial tubes, and outdoor exercise even at levels below the standard can impair lung function. Young people appear to be at even greater risk for lung impairment from ozone exposure than adults (Schultz, 1994).

Particulates **Particulates** are particles in the air. Soot, ashes, dirt, dust, and pollen are examples of particulates. They are more prevalent in larger cities. However, rural areas with unpaved roads and extensive wood burning also have high particulate matter levels.

Particulates can harm the surfaces of the respiratory system. Although not all particulates in the air are toxic to a person's health, some particulates, such as asbestos, are dangerous. The cilia can be damaged so that they are less effective in keeping foreign matter from getting into the lungs. Research studies show that being exposed to high particulate levels increases the likelihood of having persistent coughs, respiratory illnesses, and severe asthmatic attacks (Schultz, 1994).

Thermal Inversion **Thermal inversion** is a condition that occurs when a layer of warm air forms above a cooler layer. Within the cooler layer, the lack of air circulation causes pollutants to become very highly concentrated. When pollutants cannot escape, smog develops. **Smog** is a combination of smoke and fog. In the presence of sunlight, smog that contains pollutants from automobile emissions can form photochemical products such as ozone and other irritants. Periods of thermal inversion can seriously threaten the health of people with respiratory disease and people who are elderly.

Denver and Los Angeles often experience thermal inversions because of their topography. During thermal inversions, people often are warned to avoid jogging. Some localities have passed ordinances regulating the use of wood-burning stoves during thermal inversions (Green and Ottoson, 1994).

Motor Vehicle Emissions **Motor vehicle emissions** are products created from the

Environmental Health

combustion of motor fuels such as gasoline and diesel fuel. They include carbon monoxide, airborne lead, sulfur oxides, and nitrogen oxides. The Clean Air Act was passed in 1979 to reduce motor vehicle emissions. The switch to unleaded gasoline and greater use of oxygenated fuels in motor vehicles resulted in a decrease in lead emissions. Decreases in sulfur dioxide, nitrogen oxides, particulate matter, and volatile organic compounds have been smaller (Schultz, 1994). This is largely a result of more motor vehicles on the road and longer commutes (American Lung Association, 1994).

Acid Rain

Acid rain is precipitation (rain, snow, sleet, hail) that contains high levels of acids formed from sulfur oxides, nitrogen oxides, and moisture in the air. When precipitation such as rain or snow falls, lake or river water, land vegetation, and human-made structures such as buildings are damaged.

Air pollution is a source of acid rain production. Acid rain can result from air pollution from human activities or from natural events. The burning of coal is the major contributor to acid rain. The smokestacks of coal-burning industries emit waste products that travel for hundreds of miles causing acid rain to fall in communities that have no industry. The acid rain in Canada is largely caused by pollution from the United States (Green and Ottoson, 1994). Acid rain can also result from volcanic activity and forest fires. When acid rain falls in water, algae growth increases and oxygen in water blocks sunlight. As a result, fish die.

Life Skill #3

I will keep the water clean.

Water Pollution

After air, water is the most essential requirement of the human body. Humans can live without water for only a few days. Drinking clean water is essential to maintaining health. On the average, each person in the United States drinks 3 1/2 to 7 pints and uses 125 gallons of water each day.

Water pollution is a health hazard. In many parts of the world, dysentery is a major problem. **Dysentery** is a severe infection of the intestines, causing diarrhea and abdominal pain. Visitors to a foreign country such as Mexico are aware of dysentery. Pollution increases the sodium content of the water so that people with high blood pressure can be at risk. People can also be exposed to toxic chemicals, such as mercury, that accumulate in fish and shellfish taken from contaminated waters. Polluted water is also be unsightly.

Sources of Water Pollution

There are many sources of water pollution including population growth, urbanization, suburbanization, industrial expansion, and increased use of technology.

Water Runoff Water runoff from farming, landfill areas, urban areas, mining, forestry, and construction contaminates water supplies, rivers, and lakes. Runoff may carry oil and gasoline; agricultural pesticides, herbicides, and fungicides; heavy metals and other toxic substances; bacteria and viruses; silt; nutrients; and oxygen-demanding compounds.

Sewage and Animal Waste Sewage and waste from animals and agricultural chemicals are a concern because these substances increase the amount of nitrates in water. Nitrates can accumulate in ground water, which supplies wells. Infants who drink water contaminated with nitrates can suffer from blood diseases. Polluted ground water can also cause other diseases and may cause cancer in adults.

338

PCBs PCBs are polychlorinated biphenyls, a class of organic compounds containing chlorine. The presence of PCBs in the water supply has caused much concern. Until 1977, PCBs were used as insulating materials in high-voltage electrical transformers and capacitors. Discarded electrical equipment at dump sites have broken open and released PCBs into surrounding groundwater and drinking water supplies. PCBs tend to accumulate in the fatty tissues of the body and the liver. Exposure to PCBs may be associated with birth defects, reproductive disorders, liver and kidney damage, and cancerous tumors.

Thermal Pollution Thermal pollution is pollution of water with heat resulting in a decrease in the water's oxygen-carrying capacity. Less oxygen in the water creates an imbalance in the aquatic environment, killing fish and aquatic plants. Thermal pollution often results from dumping heated water used to cool steam turbines in power plants into the environment.

Trihalomethanes Most water treatment systems in the United States use chlorine as a disinfectant for water purification. **Trihalomethanes** are chemical by-products containing halogens, formed when chlorine attacks biological contaminants in water. Any drinking water supply that contains added chlorine is likely to have these substances. The trihalomethanes include the following chemical substances: chloroform, bromoform, and dichlorobromomethane. Chloroform may slightly increase the risk of bladder and rectal cancer, birth defects, and central nervous system disorders.

The trihalomethane byproducts cannot be avoided by drinking only bottled water. They are volatile organic compounds that are released into the air from shower heads and toilet bowls.

Mercury The element mercury and most of its compounds are toxic. In the early 1970s, a factory in Japan released industrial waste containing mercury compounds into the Pacific Ocean. The mercury reached humans through the food chain. People in a nearby fishing village ate the fish that contained mercury. They suffered from mental retardation, numbness of body parts, loss of vision and hearing, and emotional disturbances. Some of these people died. Because of this and similar tragedies, most industrialized nations have taken steps to prevent mercury dumping.

Pesticides Pesticides are important in farming because they destroy insects and weeds that kill crops. **Pesticides** are substances used to kill or control the growth of unwanted organisms. Pesticides can be used on farms or in homes. They often contaminate water supplies through water runoff. **DDT** is a pesticide that was banned because it was found in food products after harvest. DDT is dangerous because it accumulates in fat tissues of humans and increases cancer risk. Pesticides can kill wildlife that feeds on crops. Wildlife may also die after eating fish from bodies of water contaminated by runoff. Pesticide residues also cling to fresh fruits and vegetables and are consumed when these foods are eaten.

Dioxins Dioxins are a group of chemicals belonging to the chlorinated hydrocarbons and used as insecticides. Dioxin is no longer manufactured for commercial use in the United States because it is considered one of the most toxic waste products in the environment. However, dioxins still occur as an unintended by-product of incineration, the manufacture of chlorinated chemicals, and chlorine bleaching of pulp and paper. Dioxins can accumulate in fish that live downstream from paper and pulp mills. These fish are a serious threat to people who eat them (Upton and Graber, 1993).

Very small amounts of dioxins are produced naturally by forest fires and volcanic eruptions. Dioxin is also the chemical that is believed to have caused health problems in Vietnam veterans. **Agent Orange** is a substance containing dioxin that was sprayed on vegetation to kill it. Health problems thought to be produced by Agent Orange are cancer, depression, liver damage, and miscarriages.

Lead The highest risk of lead in the water supply is from lead pipes and water lines in older urban housing. The EPA is working aggressively with communities to reduce lead contamination of drinking water.

Ways to Keep Water Clean

In 1974, Congress passed the Safe Drinking Water Act in response to growing concern about the quality of drinking water. This Act covers all public water systems that serve 25 or more people. It requires the EPA to determine and issue safe levels for drinking water pollutants. The EPA is charged with making sure that public water systems keep pollutants within safe levels. The Safe Drinking Water Act requires that operators of water systems notify customers when they violate one or more of the standards. Since most operators have ignored this regulation, individuals are advised to call the water treatment system serving them to find out what the pollutant levels are. If there is a violation, the EPA should be notified.

In addition to ensuring that laws and regulations are enforced, individuals can take actions to keep water clean:
- avoid dumping garbage or any kind of chemical in lakes, streams, rivers, or ditches;
- avoid pouring or spilling harmful chemicals onto the ground; they can seep into ground water supplies;
- never pour toxic chemicals down the drain; instead, dispose of them at a hazardous waste collection center.

If drinking water from a faucet has an orange or red hue, it could be contaminated. Contact the public health department to have it tested. Until assured that it is safe, it is wise to drink bottled water. Home-water treatment systems are available, but consumers should evaluate these systems carefully to be sure that they work effectively before purchasing one. To reduce lead ingestion through drinking water, the tap should be run for several minutes before taking water for drinking or cooking.

Ways to Conserve Water

In some areas of the world, water supplies are scarce. Water is a precious resource and should be used conservatively. **Water conservation** is a set of actions taken to avoid wasting water and to prevent water contaminations. Clean water is needed for good health and for many household, agricultural, industrial, and recreational uses. Adequate water consumption is important to proper functioning of body systems and organs. Approximately two-thirds of the human body is made up of water. Without water, a human will die within days.

Individuals who practice water conservation can save thousands of gallons of water. Simple measures such as these can be taken:
- Turn water off while brushing teeth or washing hands.
- Take short showers instead of baths.
- Install a low-flow shower head.
- Check faucets and pipes for leaks.
- Run washing machines and dishwashers only when they contain a full load.
- Water lawns only when needed and at the coolest times of the day.

Life Skill #4

I will keep my indoor environment free of pollution.

Sick Building Syndrome

On the average, people spend 90 percent of their time indoors. In order to save energy, homes and commercial and institutional buildings are more airtight and better insulated than in the past. This results in less air circulation from outdoors and greater accumulation of indoor pollutants. **Sick building syndrome (SBS)** is illness that results from indoor air pollution. SBS generally includes some or all of the following symptoms: headaches, irritated eyes, nausea, dizziness, lethargy, respiratory discomfort, and hoarseness. In SBS, symptoms usually diminish or disappear when affected people spend time away from the building and the agent causing the symptoms.

Indoor air pollution is particularly risky for the following groups: the elderly; pregnant females; infants; heart disease patients; people with allergies, asthma, or other respiratory disorders; or anyone who spends a great deal of time indoors. Many different kinds of pollutants can be found indoors. The three most dangerous indoor air pollutants are tobacco smoke, radon, and asbestos.

Sources of Indoor Air Pollution

Chemicals in the Home The indoor environment contains pollution-creating products. Household cleaning agents and insecticides are used to kill organisms and to clean items and various parts of the home. Hobby supplies and other products also release noxious fumes each time they are used (American Lung Association, 1994).

Asbestos Asbestos is a heat-resistant mineral that is found in building materials. It has been linked to lung and gastrointestinal cancer. These cancers may not develop until twenty to thirty years after exposure to lead. If the asbestos becomes airborne, the fibers can be trapped in the lungs, causing lung cancer. Because of dangers, asbestos use has been prohibited. Because it was once widely used for structural fireproofing, it is often found in heating systems, floor and ceiling tiles, shingles, and household pipes in older homes. Removing asbestos can be dangerous and expensive. When asbestos-containing material is damaged or disintegrates with age, microscopic fibers are dispersed into the air and can be inhaled. If asbestos is found within a home, call on certified experts for testing, advice, and possible removal or sealing. In some cases, it is safer to leave asbestos-containing material in place if it is intact, and seal it rather than remove it.

Lead Lead is an element that is found in many products used inside and outside the home. Lead is released into the atmosphere from automobile exhausts. Lead poisoning is a risk for young children. About three million children in the United States suffer permanent neurological damage caused by lead poisoning. Children may ingest lead by eating lead-containing paint chips. Another source of lead is drinking water contaminated through the corrosion of plumbing materials, such as lead solders and lead service lines.

Lead-containing dust and soil indoors is another source.

Health effects of highly elevated lead levels include coma, convulsions, profound irreversible mental retardation and seizures, and death. Even low levels of exposure can result in persistent impairment of the central nervous system, especially in children. Adverse effects include delayed cognitive development, reduced intelligence, shortened attention span, learning difficulties, short-term memory loss, impaired hearing and sight, reduced blood production, and diminished growth. Fetuses may be affected adversely by prenatal exposure to lead. In adults, lead in the blood may interfere with hearing, increase blood pressure and, at high levels, kidney damage and anemia. Government regulations have curtailed the use of lead in many products, such as paints, that are used inside the home. Government action has encouraged some removal of lead-based paint from homes. Lead paint abatement can be very costly, and many homeowners cannot afford the extensive home repair or renovation necessary to reduce lead exposure. Houses that need abatement are often located in low-income neighborhoods.

Carbon Monoxide Carbon monoxide is an air pollutant that is produced by incomplete fuel combustion. Sources of carbon monoxide emission in the home are gas ranges, furnaces, and smoke from cigarettes. Breathing small amounts of carbon monoxide can make a person sick, and long-term exposure can cause headaches, tiredness, and sleepiness. Carbon monoxide pollution in the home increases during the winter months because storm windows, weather stripping, and sealers are in regular use, and windows are rarely opened. The carbon monoxide level can build up quickly when an automobile is idling in a garage. If the garage is attached to a house, carbon monoxide can seep into the house. Fumes from a fireplace, charcoal grill, or improperly vented gas stove can raise significantly the carbon monoxide levels in a home (Health Letter Associates, 1991).

Formaldehyde Formaldehyde is a colorless gas with a pungent odor. It was once widely used in the manufacture of particle board, plywood, and other wood products found in homes and furniture. High formaldehyde levels are found in the air of mobile homes because they contain large quantities of plywood and particle board. Formaldehyde can be found in insulation, cosmetics, upholstery, carpets and other floor coverings, and exhaust from household appliances. It is emitted from cigarette smoke. Formaldehyde is known to cause breathing problems (shortness of breath, tightness of the chest, coughing), dizziness, eye irritation, headaches, nausea, skin irritations, asthma attacks, and cancer.

Radon Radon is an odorless, colorless radioactive gas that is emitted from bricks, concrete materials and from rocks and other substances below the Earth. Because radon is odorless and colorless, people may not be aware of it inside the home. Radon can enter homes from below the ground. As many as one of every twelve homes has a dangerous radon level above the danger level. Radon enters a home through cracks in the floors or walls in basements and through drains and sump pumps. Radon tends to be higher in newer homes because these homes are built with better insulation.

Homes containing a high concentration of radon may be found in low-radon areas. The only way to know the radon level is to make a test (American Lung Association, 1994). Testing is inexpensive and easy. Many stores and agencies sell radon testing kits. These kits have specific directions for ways to measure radon levels. If radon levels are high, a homeowner can seal all cracks and install fans in strategic locations to vent radon from the home.

If young people live in the home, radon testing is highly recommended. Young people are at higher risk than adults from indoor radon because they receive more radiation from a given volume of radon than adults. Further, young people tend to be more sensitive to the carcinogenic (cancer-causing) effects of radiation. People who were exposed to radon before age twenty appear to have a higher risk of developing lung cancer than those exposed later in life. If high levels of radon exposure are avoided in childhood, risk of lung cancer before middle age may be substantially reduced. (U.S. Department of Health and Human Services, 1991).

The radon gas enters the lungs when it adheres to dust particles that are inhaled. Radon is believed to be the second leading cause of lung cancer, following cigarette smoking (Schultz, 1994). Lung cancer risk is greatly increased when radon exposure is coupled with cigarette smoking. The combined risk of smoking and radon exposure is greater than the sum of the individual risks.

Secondhand Cigarette Smoke **Secondhand cigarette smoke** is a mixture of the smoke given off by the burning end of a cigarette, pipe, or cigar and the smoke exhaled from the lungs of smokers. This mixture contains more than 4,000 substances, more than 40 of which are known to cause cancer, and many of which are strong irritants. **Environmental tobacco smoke (ETS)** is another term for secondhand smoke. **Involuntary smoking** or **passive smoking** is exposure to secondhand smoke.

Secondhand smoke has been identified by the EPA as a known cause of lung cancer in humans. It causes lower respiratory tract infections in infants and children, and aggravates asthma in young people. Passive smoking also causes thousands of children to develop asthma each year (Environmental Protection Agency, 1993).

In order to reduce the health risks of passive smoking at home, a person should not smoke in the house or allow others to do so. If a family member insists on smoking indoors, ventilation in the area where smoking takes place should be increased. Windows or exhaust fans should be used. Smoking should not be permitted when children are present, particularly infants and toddlers, because they are very susceptible to the effects of passive smoking.

The EPA recommends that every workplace have a smoking policy that effectively protects nonsmokers from involuntary exposure to tobacco smoke. Many businesses and organizations already have smoking policies in place, but these policies vary in effectiveness. If a workplace does not have a smoking policy that effectively controls secondhand smoke, one can be established by working with appropriate management and labor organizations. Merely separating smokers from nonsmokers within the same area, such as a cafeteria, may reduce exposure, but nonsmokers will still be exposed to recirculated or drifting smoke. Prohibiting smoking indoors or limiting smoking to rooms that have been specially designed to prevent smoke from escaping are two options that effectively protect nonsmokers. The costs associated with establishing properly designed smoking rooms vary from building to building, and are likely to be greater than the outright banning of smoking. Nonsmokers should not have to use the smoking room for any purpose. It should be located in a non-work area that people are not required to enter as part of their work responsibilities. Employer-supported smoking cessation programs are an important part of any smoking policy.

Woodstove Smoke Many people use woodstoves for heating homes. Woodstoves emit significant amounts of particulates, carbon monoxide, and sulfur dioxide. Levels of these pollutants in the home can exceed the healthful maximum if woodstoves are not properly installed, vented, and maintained. One way to reduce the emission of pollutants is to burn properly aged wood. Woodstoves that lack emission controls emit significantly higher levels of pollutants into the outdoor air.

Ways to Keep Indoor Air Free of Pollution

One of the most important ways to keep indoor air free from pollution is to ban tobacco smoking in homes or buildings. Indoor areas should be adequately ventilated with fresh outdoor air or recirculated filtered air. The sources of pollutants should be removed. Appliances and heating systems should be kept in good repair and checked frequently for proper operation. Homes and other buildings should be checked for asbestos and radon. If these hazardous substances are detected, they should be safely and properly eliminated, as much as possible. Asbestos removal should never be attempted without the help of an abatement specialist.

Life Skill #5

I will keep noise at a healthful level.

Noise is a major concern in the environment. **Noise** is sound that produces discomfort or annoyance. Noise has numerous detrimental effects on health. Exposure to loud noise can result in an increase in blood pressure, constriction of blood vessels in parts of the body, and a possible increase in blood cholesterol levels. Exposure to very loud sounds can cause permanent loss of hearing. Because noise increases stress levels, people exposed to it experience headaches, tension, sleep disturbances, and increased anxiety. Exposure to noise causes a lack of concentration and can cause irritability and aggressiveness. Loud noises decrease the likelihood of hearing safety warnings and increase the risk of being involved in an accident. Joggers, for example, have had accidents when running while listening to music on headsets because they were not able to hear traffic sounds.

Sources of Noise Pollution

A **decibel** is a unit used to measure sound intensity. The smallest difference in sound intensity detectable by the human ear is one decibel. The sound intensity of leaves rustling is about 10 decibels, and 20 decibels is the level of a quiet whisper. Sound levels at 90 decibels can result in hearing damage after about eight hours, at 100 decibels after about fifteen minutes, and at 110 decibels about one minute. The following are examples of decibel levels produced by various sounds: jet engine, 140; shotgun firing, 130; chain saw and jackhammer, 110; garbage truck/cement mixer, 100; lawn mower, 90; and food blender, 90.

Many young people listen to walkabout stereos. Through earphones, these devices are often operated at levels that exceed safety limits and can contribute to permanent hearing loss. Noise at a high-decibel level for long

periods of time increases the risk of hearing loss. Rock concerts, personal sound systems (such as "boom boxes" or walkabout stereos), and "boom cars" also pose a serious risk of hearing loss. The decibel levels at rock concerts often reach 110 to 140 decibels. Personal sound systems can play music that reaches 115 decibels. "Boom cars" are cars equipped with very loud music systems. These music systems can reach a decibel level of 145, which is louder than a jet engine.

Ways to Protect Against Noise Pollution

A few simple measures can protect the ears from noise pollution. When listening to music through headphones, music should be kept low enough to be able to hear clearly someone speaking in a normal conversation. When attending concerts, sit at a safe distance. Wear hearing protection devices such as ear plugs or earmuffs when exposed to loud noise. Have hearing checked regularly for hearing loss by a medical professional.

Life Skill #6

I will protect myself from radiation.

Electromagnetic Radiation

There are many sources of radiation in the environment. **Radiation** is a term that is applied to the transmission of energy through space or through a medium. Commonly, radiation refers to the electromagnetic spectrum. The **electromagnetic spectrum** is the electromagnetic radiation ranging from the longest to the shortest wavelength. The spectrum includes all types of electromagnetic radiation. From the longest wavelength to the shortest wavelength, the spectrum includes sonic and ultrasonic, radio and television, microwave, infrared, visible light, ultraviolet, X-ray, gamma, and cosmic waves.

Sources of Radiation

Radiation is classified into two types—ionizing and nonionizing. **Ionizing radiation** is the part of the electromagnetic spectrum that contains the shortest wavelengths—radiation that ionizes atoms or molecules. Ionizing radiation is emitted by X-ray machines, nuclear power plants and nuclear weapons, and other radioactive materials. Large doses of ionizing radiation can severely damage body tissue and cause cancer.

Nonionizing radiation is the part of the electromagnetic spectrum that contains the longer wavelengths. Nonionizing radiation is emitted by microwave ovens, video display terminals, heaters, car phones, and electric blankets. Many of these sources are inside the home. Video display terminals (VDTs) have been suspected of increasing reproduction problems and causing cataracts. However, most studies have shown that radiation measurements from VDTs are below dangerous levels. Microwaves are a form of radiation, but there is little evidence that microwaves in the environment pose a health risk to people.

Ultraviolet radiation is a type of nonionizing radiation that comes mainly from the sun. There are two types of ultraviolet radiation—UVA and UVB. Exposure to ultraviolet radiation is associated with wrinkling of the skin, skin cancer, and cataract formation. The best advice for protection against ultraviolet radiation exposure is to simply stay out of the sun. When exposed to sunlight, a person should use a sunscreen that blocks ultraviolet radiation and wear protective clothing. Ultraviolet-ray-blocking sunglasses help protect against cataract formation.

Life Skill #7

I will dispose of solid waste properly.

Sources and Disposal of Solid Waste

Solid waste is substances such as trash, unwanted objects, and litter that threaten the environment. Chicago creates more than 7,500 tons of garbage each day. Each day, New York City produces more than 25,000 tons, and Los Angeles County produces more than 50,000 tons. The average person in the United States generates about four pounds of solid waste per day, more than twice as much as people in other industrialized countries (with the exception of Canada) (U.S.

Department of Health and Human Services, 1991). Some cities use landfills to dispose of solid waste. A **landfill** is a method of waste disposal in which waste is buried between layers of soil, often building up low-lying areas in the process. Landfills that serve some of our nation's major cities are filled beyond capacity, and solid waste is shipped to other parts of the country because existing landfills cannot accept the waste. Some waste is dumped illegally. For example, used syringes and medical waste have washed ashore on some northeastern beaches.

When disposed of improperly, common household waste can create noxious smoke from burning trash and breeding grounds for rats, flies, and mosquitos. In addition, household waste can contribute to air and water pollution because small quantities of toxic substances such as pesticides, paints, or solvents are sometimes dumped with other household trash. Rain water seeping through the buried waste can dissolve pollutants as it percolates down through the soil. This contaminates ground water. Other organic waste, such as garbage and paper products, decomposes and can form explosive methane gas. Methane, like carbon dioxide, absorbs heat from sunlight and contributes to global warming. Methane is the second leading type of "greenhouse" gas, behind carbon dioxide and ahead of chlorofluorocarbons. Therefore, in addition to reduction of solid waste production, careful monitoring to ensure proper land disposal is important (U.S. Department of Health and Human Services, 1991).

Some communities use incineration to dispose of solid waste. **Incineration** is a method of waste disposal in which waste is burned to ashes. This practice is expensive and controversial. If incinerators are improperly designed and maintained, toxic air pollution can result. For example, cadmium and cadmium compounds can be released through incineration. Once cadmium is released into the air, human exposure can occur through food, water, or inhalation. Exposure causes many adverse health effects. Short-term inhalation of high levels of cadmium causes severe irritation to the lungs. Long-term exposure to lower levels of cadmium damages the kidneys, lungs, liver, testes, immune system, and blood (U.S. Department of Health and Human Services, 1991).

Sources and Disposal of Hazardous Waste

Greater use of industrial chemicals has led to an increase in hazardous waste. **Hazardous wastes** are harmful substances that are difficult to discard safely.

Many kinds of hazardous waste are biodegradable. A **biodegradable substance** is a substance that decomposes through natural or biological processes into harmless materials. Other hazardous waste that may be biodegradable may not break down for many years. Others are not biodegradable at all. The toxic waste disaster of Love Canal, a community near Niagara Falls, New York, is one example of health problems caused by hazardous wastes. A chemical and plastics company dumped waste around Love Canal between 1947 and 1952 and covered it with dirt to form a landfill. Soon, a new community was developed on the landfill. But, in 1978, heavy rains caused the buried contents to surface. An increase in the number of birth defects linked to mothers living around the canal was associated with this waste. Many other physical disabilities were discovered. Over 200 families had to be evacuated while the federal government worked to make the area safe for living again.

Today, the EPA is extremely concerned about the dumping of waste that is toxic or poisonous. When buried underground, toxic waste may leak from containers and threaten groundwater supplies. The EPA has enacted several laws to safeguard the public from exposure to hazardous waste. These laws place regulations on the transport, buying, and containment of toxic waste.

Some household products are toxic or can become toxic. Some materials deteriorate with age; some may deteriorate if not stored properly. Labels should give information about proper storage and usage. These instructions should be followed closely.

Life Skill #8

I will recycle.

People can help reduce pollutants in the air, water, and soil by acting on their convictions: encourage schools, businesses, and employers to purchase recycled products; avoid products

overpackaged with paper, plastic, plastic foam, or other materials; use reusable tableware; encourage local restaurants to avoid throwaway tableware; make a compost pile for lawn trash; and avoid one-use consumer goods (e.g., disposable razors, cigarette lighters, etc.). Recycling may also help reduce air, water, and soil contamination. **Recycling** is the process of reforming or breaking down waste products to their basic components so that they can be used again. Recycling involves collecting and separating reusable material from waste, and processing, marketing, and reusing the raw material for products which may or may not be similar to the original products.

Materials currently recovered for reuse include motor oil, newspapers, corrugated boxes, office papers, mixed papers, ferrous metals, glass containers, aluminum cans, plastic soft drink and milk containers, and lead-acid automobile batteries. Recycling, when compared to energy use and contaminant production of original manufacture, results in lower energy consumption, reduced water use, and less air and water pollution. Recycling one ton of paper is estimated to preserve about twenty trees (which produce oxygen and reduce accumulation of greenhouse gases), two barrels of oil,

7,000 gallons of water, and 4,100 kilowatt hours of electricity (enough energy to power the average American home for five months). Recycling prevents emission of 60 additional pounds of toxic agents into the air and saves three cubic yards of landfill space. Recycling currently accounts for only 13 percent of garbage treatment, although experts believe that as much as 90 percent of solid waste is recyclable (U.S. Department of Health and Human Services, 1991).

Life Skill #9

I will be aware of the effects of overcrowding and poverty.

Population Growth

Human health is greatly affected by population growth. More than 5 billion people inhabit the world, and the current rate of growth exceeds a net population gain of over 90 million people per year. By the year 2029, there will be a doubling of the world's population unless something is done to slow population growth (Caplan, 1990).

The governments of areas of the world with such rapid population growth are unable to provide for the basic services of the populace and are overwhelmed by the demand. Two-thirds of the people of the world lack sufficient food, and millions are severely malnourished. When there is starvation, there is rampant disease. Attempts to provide clean water, sewage facilities, transportation, police, and public health services are far from adequate. This has led to large aggregations of poor people in cities with problems such as sickness, pollution, starvation, drug abuse, and crime. Many young people living in poverty die from these conditions each day.

Large population increases create intense competition for the world's resources. A growing population produces more environmental pollution and uses more natural resources. Hydrocarbons in the atmosphere from automobile exhausts contribute to ozone depletion and global warming. Demand for lumber and population movement into forested areas leads to deforestation. Solid and hazardous waste disposal and air pollution problems emerges as the population increases. Crop destruction results from acid rain and threatens the food supply.

Adverse Socioeconomic Conditions

Adverse socioeconomic environmental conditions, such as poverty, overcrowding, and poor housing, are linked to poor health conditions. Poverty is related to increased occurrence of depression, hostility, psychological stress, inadequate medical care, poor nutrition, infant mortality, child abuse, and crowded and unsanitary living conditions. Risky health practices, such as cigarette smoking, poor diet, physical inactivity, and substance abuse, are linked to poverty (Adler et al., 1994). Children who grow up under these adverse environmental conditions show a higher risk of developing a pattern of problems in adolescence—doing poorly in school, dropping out, becoming adolescent parents, becoming delinquent, and using alcohol and/or other drugs as part of a cycle of misery and hopelessness (Kazdin, 1993). The sheer volume of risk factors these youth endure puts them at high risk for serious life problems. It is important to point out that high-risk youth are certainly not restricted to those who come from adverse environments (Dougherty, 1993). Programs that attempt to help high-risk youth from adverse environments should concentrate on helping them develop the skills to break out of the cycle of school failure, delinquency, drug use, adolescent pregnancy, and chronic underemployment.

Four million youth in the United States live in neighborhoods that are characterized by poverty, unemployment, and school dropout. These 4 million youth represent about 6 percent of the nation's children. One-half of these youth live in the six largest states—New York, California, Texas, Ohio, Illinois, and Michigan. However, rural states in the deep south have some of the highest percentages of youth living in troubled neighborhoods. One in five U.S. youth lives in poverty (Usdansky, 1994).

Poverty and Violence The occurrence of interpersonal violence is closely related to poverty and high rates of unemployment. Youth in the lowest socioeconomic levels of society are the most likely to be victims and perpetrators of violence. Urban area dwellers, and especially inner-city residents, tend to experience much higher rates of interpersonal victimization and perpetration than do those who live in suburban and rural areas (Ropp et al., 1992). This is especially true for urban areas characterized by low socioeconomic status, poor housing, high population density (overcrowding), and high unemployment rates. It is believed that the feelings which often accompany these conditions, such as hopelessness about life options and anger about poverty, account for the increase in violent behavior. Being poor in America often means living in crime-ridden neighborhoods, growing up in a family without a father, and going to schools where most students fail and are expected to fail (Prothrow-Stith and Weissman, 1991).

Research has identified several environmental conditions that are related to violence (Panel on High-Risk Youth, 1993; Reiss and Roth, 1993). These include: the large and increasing number of families who are living in or near poverty; the concentration of poor families in some urban and rural neighborhoods; the increase in the numbers of severely deprived neighborhoods; racial and ethnic discrimination in employment, housing, and the criminal justice system; high residential mobility and population turnover; overcrowding; weak intergenerational ties in families and communities; the location of illegal markets for drug distribution and firearms in communities and the increase in illegal marketing of drugs and guns; increased gang activity; and weak control of street-corner peer groups; few social resources; and high levels of family disruption from divorce, desertion, and female-headed families; and diminished numbers of community elders who take responsibility for local youth or who have moved away from urban communities.

Life Skill #10

I will cooperate with environmental protection agencies.

Environmental Protection Agencies

Environmental protection agencies help protect the quality of the environment and human health. Environmental protection agencies are regulatory agencies. A **regulatory agency** is an agency that enforces laws on behalf of the general public. These agencies are found at the federal, state, and local levels of government. The **Environmental Protection Agency** (EPA) is a federal agency that has the responsibility for alleviating and controlling environmental pollution. The EPA attempts to maintain and improve environmental quality by setting standards, monitoring conditions, and providing education and research activities. Examples of environmental concerns with which the EPA deals include: safe drinking water, air and water quality, groundwater and wetland protection, solid and hazardous waste, pesticides, and radon. The **Occupational Safety and Health Administration (OSHA)** and the **National Institute for Occupational Safety and Health (NIOSH)** are federal agencies responsible for environmental regulations in the workplace.

At the state or provincial level is usually a department of environmental quality or environmental protection. The exact names of these agencies vary from state to state. On the local level, the public health department serves as the environmental regulatory agency for most communities. Local public health departments enforce environmental standards and regulations. They are responsible for inspecting restaurants and food service establishments, sewage disposal, public water supplies, and other related functions. Local public health departments provide information about such environmental concerns as safe disposal of toxic materials, home radon exposure, and proper installation of septic tanks.

Bibliography for Health Content

Adler, N. E., Boyce, T., Chesney, M. A., Cohen, S., Folkman, S.,Kahn, R. L., and Syme, S. L. (1994) Socioeconomic status and health: The challenge of gradient. *American Psychologist*, 49:15–24.

American Academy of Pediatrics. (1989) Acne vulgaris: Pathway to the adolescent. *Adolescent Health Update: A Clinical Guide for Pediatricians*, 2:1-8.

American Lung Association. (1994) *Your Lungs: An Owner's Manual*. New York: American Lung Association.

Baker, S. P., Fowler, C., Guohua, L., Warner, M., and Dannenberg, A. L. (1994) Head injuries incurred by children and young adults during informal recreation. *American Journal of Public Health*, 84:649–652.

Bart, P. B., and O'Brien, P. H. (1985) *Stopping Rape*. New York: Pergamon Press.

Brodkin, M. (1993) *Every Kid Counts: 31 Ways to Save Our Children*. New York: HarperCollins.

Buchsbaum, H. (1994) Guns r us. *Scholastic Update*, February 11:18–19.

Caplan, R. (1990) *Our Earth, Ourselves*. New York: Bantam.

Castleman, M. (1994) Beach bummer. *Annual Editions: Health*, 1994/1995, 38–42.

Centers for Disease Control and Prevention. (1994) Cigarette smoking among adults—United States, 1992, and changes in definition of smoking.

———. (1994) Prevalence of adults with no known major risk factors for coronary heart disease——Behavioral risk factor surveillance system, 1992. *Morbidity and Mortality Weekly Report*, 43:61–63, 69.

———. (1992) Safety-belt and helmet use among high school students—United States, 1990. *Morbidity and Mortality Weekly Report*, 41:111–114.

———. (1992) Trends in alcohol–related traffic fatalities, by sex—United States. *Morbidity and Mortality Weekly Reports*, 189:195–197.

Consumers Union. (1994) Alternative medicine. *Consumers Report*, 1:51–53.

Cornacchia, H.J., and Barrett, S. (1993) *Consumer Health: A Guide to Intelligent Decisions*. St. Louis, MO: Mosby.

Dietz, W. H. (1990) You are what you eat: What you eat is what you are. *Journal of Adolescent Health Care*, 11:76–81.

Dougherty, D. (1993) Adolescent health: Reflections on a report to the U.S. Congress. *American Psychologist*, 48:193–201.

Environmental Protection Agency. (1993) *Secondhand Smoke: What You Can Do About Secondhand Smoke as Parents, Decisionmakers, and Building Occupants*. Washington, DC: U.S. Environmental Protection Agency.

Erickson, K. P., and Trocki, K. F. (1992) Behavioral risk factors for sexually transmitted diseases in American households. *Social Science Medicine*, 34:843–853.

Fein, J. (1993) *Exploding the Myth of Self-Defense: A Survival Guide for Every Woman*. Sebastopol, CA: Torrance.

Finklehor, D., and Dzuiba-Leatherman, J. (1994) Victimization of children. *American Psychologist*, 49:173–183.

Food and Drug Administration. (1992) *The Facts about Weight Loss Products and Programs*. DHHS Publication No. (FDA) 92-1189. Rockville, MD: Food and Drug Administration.

Fox, J. A., and Pierce, G. (1994) American killers are getting younger. *USA Today Magazine*, January:24–26.

Gibb, N. (1993) Hell on wheels. *Time*, August 16:44–46.

Glover, B., and Shephard, J. (1989) *The Family Fitness Handbook*. New York: Penguin Books.

Goldsmith, M. F. (1993) 'Invisible' epidemic now becoming visible as HIV/AIDS pandemic reaches adolescents. *Journal of the American Medical Association*, 270:16–19.

Gormon, C. (1993) Does sunscreen save your skin? *Time*, May 24:69.

Green, L. W., and Ottoson, J. M. (1994) *Community Health*. St. Louis, MO: Mosby.

Bibiliography for Health Content

Grube, J. W., and Wallack, L. (1994) Television beer advertising and drinking knowledge, beliefs, and intentions among schoolchildren. *American Journal of Public Health*, 84:254–259.

Gunby, P. (1993) Two new reports help put nation's no. 1 killer disease challenges into perspective for 1993. *Journal of the American Medical Association*, 269:449–450.

Hammond, W. R., and Yung, B. (1993) Psychology's role in the public health response to assaultive violence among young African-American men. *American Psychologist*, 48:142–154.

Health Letter Associates. (1991) *The Wellness Encyclopedia*. Boston: Houghton Mifflin.

Henney, J. E. (1993) Combatting medical fraud. *New York State Medical Journal*, 93:86–87.

Kazdin, A. E. (1993) Adolescent mental health: Prevention and treatment programs. *American Psychologist*, 48:127–141.

Kelder, S. H., Perry, C., Kleppm, K., and Lytle, L. L. (1994) Longitudinal tracking of adolescent smoking, physical activity, and food choice behavior. *American Journal of Public Health*, 84:1121–1126.

Kusinitz, I., and Fine, M. (1995) *Your Guide to Getting Fit*. Mountain View, CA: Mayfield.

Lange, R. H. (1993) Wolves in sheep's clothing. *New York State Medical Journal*, 93:85–86.

Larson, E. (1994) *Lethal Passage: How the Travels of a Single Handgun Expose the Roots of America's Gun Crisis*. New York: Crown Publishers.

Lowry, R., Holtzman, D., Truman, B. J., Kann, L., Collins, J. L., and Kolbe, L. J. (1994) Substance use and HIV-related sexual behaviors among U.S. high school students: Are they related? *American Journal of Public Health*, 84:1116–1120.

McCabe, P. P. (1991) Low level lead toxicity. *Childhood Education*, Winter:88–92.

McIntosh, K. (1994) Transmissibility of HIV infection: What we know in 1993. *Journal of School Health*, 64:14–15.

Meeks, L., Heit, P., and Burt, J. (1993) *Education for Sexuality and HIV/AIDS: Curriculum and Teaching Strategies*. Blacklick, OH: Meeks Heit Publishing Company.

Meeks, L., Heit, P., and Page, R. (1995) *Drugs, Alcohol, and Tobacco: Totally Awesome™ Teaching Strategies*. Blacklick, OH: Meeks Heit Publishing Company.

————. (1995) *Violence Prevention: Totally Awesome™ Teaching Strategies for Safe and Drug-Free Schools*. Blacklick, OH: Meeks Heit Publishing Company.

Mizell, L. R. (1993) *Street Sense for Women: How to Stay Safe in a Violent World*. New York: Berkeley Books.

Monroe, J. (1994) CAT and LSD: Designer Drugs. *Current Health* 2, September, 13–15.

Napier, K. (1994) Unproven medical treatments lure elderly. *FDA Consumer*, March:33–37.

Natale, J. A. (1994) Roots of violence. *American School Board Journal*, March:33–40.

National Center for Health Statistics. (1993) Annual summary of births, marriages, divorces, and deaths: United States, 1992. *Monthly Vital Statistics Report* 41(13). Hyattsville, MD: U.S. Public Health Service.

National Commission on AIDS. (1994) Preventing HIV/AIDS in adolescents. *Journal of School Health*, 64:39–51.

National Commission for Injury Prevention and Control (1989) *Injury Prevention: Meeting the Challenge*. New York: Oxford University Press.

Pacelli, L. C. (1991) Straight talk on posture. *The Physician and Sportsmedicine*, 19:124-127.

Panel on High-Risk Youth of the National Research Council. (1993) *Losing Adolescents: Adolescents in High-Risk Settings*. Washington, DC: National Academy Press.

Pangrazi, R., and Dauer, R. P. (1995) *Dynamic Physical Education for Elementary School Children*. Needham Heights, MA: Allyn and Bacon.

Phalon, R. (1994) New support for old therapies. *Forbes*, December 20:254–255.

Poppy, J. (1993) The purist's guide to tap water. *Health*, September:71–75.

Powell, E. (1991) *Talking Back to Sexual Pressure: What to Say To Resist Pressure, To Avoid Disease, To Stop Harassment, To Avoid Acquaintance Rape*. Minneapolis, MN: CompCare Publishers.

Powers, R.D. (1990) Taking care of bite wounds. *Emergency Medicine*, 22:131–139.

Price, J. H., Desmond, S. M., and Smith, D. (1991) Inner city adolescents' perceptions of guns—a preliminary investigation. *Journal of School Health,* 61:255–259.

Prothrow-Stith, D., and Weissman, M. (1991) *Deadly Consequences.* New York: HarperCollins.

Quarles, C. L. (1989) *School Violence: A Survival Guide for School Staff.* Washington, DC: National Education Association.

Randall, T. (1992) Driving while under influence of alcohol remains major cause of traffic violence. *Journal of theAmerican Medical Association,* 268:303–304.

————. (1993) New tools ready for chlamydia diagnosis, treatment, but teens need education most. *Journal of the American Medical Association,* 269:2716–2717.

Reis, A. J., and Roth, J. A. (1993) *Understanding and Preventing Violence: Panel on the Understanding and Control of Violent Behavior.* Washington, DC: National Academy of Sciences.

Roberts, S. V., and Watson, T. (1994) Teens on tobacco: Kids smoke for reasons all their own. *U.S. News and World Report,* April 18:38 and 43.

Robinson, T. N., Hammer, L. D., Killen, J. D., Kraemer, H. C., Wilson, D. M., Hayward, C., and Taylor, C. B. (1993) Does television viewing increase obesity and reduce physical activity? Cross-sectional and longitudinal analyses among adolescent girls. *Pediatrics,* 91:273–280.

Ropp, L., Visintainer, P., Uman, J., and Trelor, D. (1992) Death in the city: An American tragedy. *Journal of the American Medical Association,* 267:2905–2910.

Schlaadt, R.G., and Shannon, P. T. (1994) *Drugs: Use, Misuse, and Abuse.* Englewood Cliffs, NJ: Prentice Hall.

Schultz, D. (1994) *Lung Disease Data, 1994.* New York: American Lung Association.

Seiger, L. H., and Hesson, J. (1994) *Walking for Fitness.* Dubuque, IA: Brown and Benchmark.

Short, S. H. (1994) Health quackery: Our role as professionals. *Journal of the American Dietetic Association,* 94:607–611.

Simons-Morton, B., Taylor, W. C., Snider, S. A., and Huang, I. W. (1993) The physical activity of fifth-grade students during physical education classes. *American Journal of Public Health,* 83:262-264.

Skolnick, A. A. (1993) Injury prevention must be part of nation's plan to reduce health care costs, say control experts. *Journal*

of the American Medical Association, 270:19–24.

Smolowe, J. (1993) Danger in the safety zone: As violence spreads into small towns, many Americans barricade themselves. *Time,* August 23:29–32.

Trapold, M. (1990) Adolescent chemical dependency. In S. W. Henggler and C. M. Borduin (Eds.), *Family Therapy and Beyond: A Multisystemic Approach to Treating the Behavioral Problems of Children and Adolescents.* Pacific Grove, CA: Brooks/Cole.

Upton, A. C., and Graber, E. (1993) *Staying Healthy in a Risky Environment.* New York: Simon & Schuster.

Usdansky, M. L. (1994) 4 million kids on wrong side of track. *USA Today,* April 25:2A.

U. S. Department of Agriculture, U.S. Department of Health and Human Services. *Dietary Guidelines for Americans,* 3rd edition.

————. *The Food Guide Pyramid,* Home and Garden Bulletin, Number 252.

U. S. Department of Agriculture/Human Nutrition Information Service, *Good Sources of Nutrients,* January 1990

U. S. Department of Health and Human Services. (1991) *Healthy People 2000: National Health Promotion and Disease Prevention Objectives.* DHHS Publication No. (PHS) 91-50213. Washington, DC: U.S. Government Printing Office.

U. S. Department of Health and Human Services. (1994) *Preventing Tobacco Use Among Young People: A Report of the Surgeon General.* Washington, DC: U.S. Government Printing Office.

Williams, R. D. (1994) Kids' vaccinations get a little easier. *FDA Consumer,* March, 13–17.

Willis, J. L. (1993) Preventing STDs. *FDA Consumer,* June, 33–35.

Wilson, M. H., Baker, S. P., Teret, S. P., Shock, S., and Garbarino, J. (1991) *Saving Children: A Guide to Injury Prevention.* New York: Oxford University Press.

Section 3

TOTALLY AWESOME TEACHING STRATEGIES™

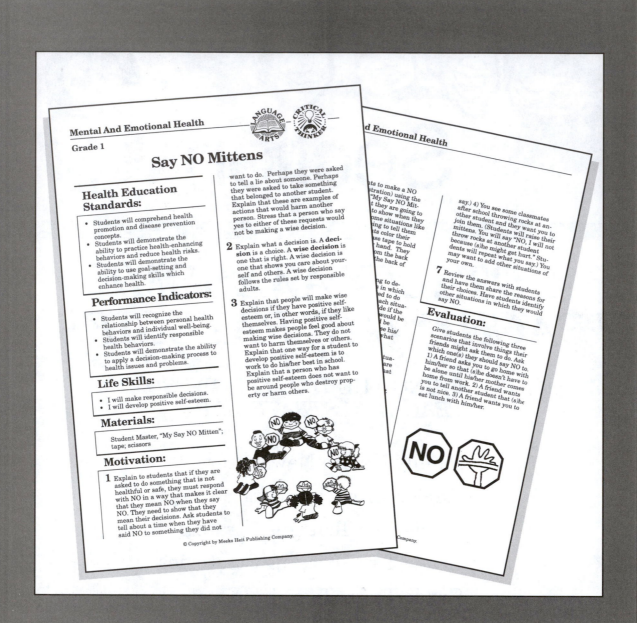

Figure 16-1

Totally Awesome Teaching Strategies™

Totally Awesome Teaching Strategies™ are designed to help students become health literate and master the performance indicators established for each of The National Health Education Standards.

Chapter 16

USING THE *TOTALLY AWESOME TEACHING STRATEGIES*™

A **teaching strategy** is a technique used by a facilitator or teacher to help a student 1) understand a particular concept, and/or 2) develop and practice a specific life skill. *Totally Awesome Teaching Strategies*™ are teaching strategies that contain a clever title, designated content area, designated grade level, suggestions for infusion into curriculum areas other than health, health literacy, health education standard(s), performance indicator(s), life skill(s), materials, motivation, evaluation, suggestions for multicultural infusion, and inclusion. *Totally Awesome Teaching Strategies*™ are designed to help students become health literate and master the performance indicators established for each of The National Health Education Standards (Figure 16-1). This chapter contains *Totally Awesome Teaching Strategies*™. The following discussion describes their unique design.

The Design of *The Totally Awesome Teaching Strategies*™

The Totally Awesome Teaching Strategies™ include:
- *Clever Title.* A clever title is set in bold-faced type in the center of the page.
- *Designated Content Area.* The content area for which the teaching strategy is designed appears in the upper left-hand corner: Mental and Emotional Health; Family Living; Growth and Development; Nutrition; Personal Health; Alcohol, Tobacco, and Other Drugs; Communicable and Chronic Diseases; Injury Prevention and Safety; Consumer and Community Health; and Environmental Health. A teaching strategy may include content from more than one content area. The additional content area(s) for which the teaching strategy is appropriate are identified in parenthesis next to the life skill(s). The six categories of risk behaviors identified by The Centers for Disease Control and Prevention are included within one or more of the content areas: behaviors that result in unintentional and intentional injuries; tobacco use; alcohol and other drug use; sexual behaviors that result in HIV infection, other STDs, and unintended pregnancies; dietary patterns that contribute to disease; insufficient physical activity.
- *Designated Grade Level.* The grade level for which the teaching strategy is appropriate appears directly beneath the designated content area in the upper left-hand corner.
- *Infusion into Curriculum Areas Other Than Health.* **Infusion** is the integration of a subject area into another area(s) of the curriculum. Teaching strategies are designed to be infused into several curriculum areas other than health education: art studies, foreign language, home economics, language arts, physical education, math studies, music studies, science studies, social studies, and visual and performing arts.

The curriculum area into which the teaching strategy is designed to be infused is designated by a symbol that appears to the right of the clever title that is set in boldfaced type. (Figure 16-1)

- *Health Literacy*. **Health literacy** is competence in critical thinking and problem solving, responsible and productive citizenship, self-directed learning, and effective communication. (The Joint Committee on Health Education Standards, 1995). The teaching strategies are designed to promote competency in health literacy. Four symbols are used to describe the health literate individual: critical thinker, responsible citizen, self-directed learner, and effective communicator. The symbol designating one of the four components of health literacy appears to the right of the symbol designating curriculum infusion. (Figure 16-2)

- *Health Education Standard(s)*. **Health education standards** are standards that specify what students should know and be able to do. They involve the knowledge and skills essential to the de-

velopment of health literacy (The Joint Committee on Health Education Standards, 1995). The health education standard(s) are listed under this bold-faced subheading.

- *Performance Indicator(s)*. **Performance indicators** are the specific concepts and skills students should know and be able to do in order to achieve each of the broader health education standards (The Joint Committee on Health Education Standards, 1995). The performance indicator(s) for the teaching strategy are listed under this boldfaced subheading.

- *Life Skill(s)*. **Life skills** are actions that promote health literacy, maintain and improve health, prevent disease, and reduce health-related risk behaviors. The life skills for the primary content area are listed first under this boldfaced subheading. Life skills for other content areas covered in the teaching strategy appear in italics and are identified in parenthesis.

- *Materials*. The **materials** are items that are needed to do the teaching strategy. The materials used in the teaching strategies

---

Figure 16-1

Curriculum Infusion

Symbols used to designate the curriculum areas into which the teaching strategies are infused.

are readily available and inexpensive. They are listed under this boldfaced subheading.

- *Motivation*. The **motivation** is the step-by-step directions to follow when doing the teaching strategy. The motivation includes a creative way to teach the health knowledge and skills students need to master the health education standards, performance objectives, and life skills. The motivation is listed under this boldfaced subheading.

- *Evaluation*. The **evaluation** is the means of measuring the students' mastery of the health education standards, the performance indicators, and the life skills. The evaluation is listed under this boldfaced subheading.

- *Multicultural Infusion*. **Multicultural infusion** is the adaptation of the teaching strategy to include ideas that promote an awareness and appreciation of the culture and background of different people. Suggestions for adapting the teaching strategy to incorporate learning about people of varied cultures and backgrounds are included under this boldfaced subheading.

- *Inclusion*. **Inclusion** is the adaptation of the teaching strategy to assist and include students with special learning challenges and may include enrichment suggestions for the gifted and reteaching ideas for students who are learning disabled. Suggestions for adapting the teaching strategy to assist students with special learning challenges are included under this boldfaced subheading.

The effectiveness of comprehensive school health education is very much dependent upon the quality and creativity of the teaching strategies that are utilized in the classroom. You will want your lessons to be motivating and challenging. Section 3. *Totally Awesome Teaching Strategies*™ contains *Totally Awesome Teaching Strategies*™ that can be used in the classroom.

Figure 16-2

Health Literacy

Symbols used to designate the category of health literacy promoted by the teaching strategies.

Family Health NEWSLETTER

Dear Parent,

Your child will be learning life skills for health in school. Life skills are actions that promote health literacy, maintain and improve health, prevent disease, and reduce health-related risk behaviors. Life skills are learned and practiced for a lifetime.

Your child will practice other skills as he or she learns life skills for health. My health lessons are creative and meaningful. They help your child develop skills in art, language arts, visual and performing arts, foreign languages, social studies, math, music, physical education, home economics, and science. They also help your child to become a critical thinker and problem solver, a responsible and productive citizen, a self-directed learner, and an effective communicator. I have included lessons to help your child gain an appreciation of people who are different from him or her.

I will teach your child how to make wise choices. I will encourage your child to:
- Make choices that are healthful.
- Make choices that are safe.
- Make choices that follow school laws and school rules.
- Make choices that show you care about others.
- Make choices that follow family rules.

I also will teach your child ways to say NO when (s)he is pressured by others to do something harmful, unsafe, illegal, or something that harms others or is against family rules.

From time to time, I will be sending you a Dear Parent Letter. Each Dear Parent Letter will tell you what your child is learning. I also will be sending you a copy of a Health Plan. A Health Plan is a plan that helps your child develop a healthful habit. For example, your child might have a Health Plan that asks him or her to brush and floss the teeth each day. You can help your child develop this habit. You can go over the Health Plan with your child. You can encourage your child to complete the Health Plan.

I want to work with you to keep your child healthy and safe. Should you have any questions, please write them on the back of this letter. Have your child return the letter to me. I will be in touch with you.

I hope today finds you and your family in good health.

Warm regards,

Family Health *NEWSLETTER*

Dear Parent,

Your child will be learning life skills for health in school. Life skills are actions that promote health literacy, maintain and improve health, prevent disease, and reduce health-related risk behaviors. Life skills are learned and practiced for a lifetime. Your child will practice other skills as he or she learns life skills for health. My health lessons are creative and meaningful. They help your child develop skills in art, language arts, visual and performing arts, foreign languages, social studies, math, music, physical education, home economics, and science. They also help your child to become a critical thinker and problem solver, a responsible and productive citizen, a self-directed learner, and an effective communicator. I have included lessons to help your child gain an appreciation of people who are different from him or her.

I will use *The Responsible Decision-Making Model* to help your child learn how to make responsible decisions. I will encourage your child to evaluate each possible decision by asking:
- Will this decision result in an action that promotes my health and the health of others?
- Will this decision result in an action that promotes my safety and the safety of others?
- Will this decision result in an action that is legal?
- Will this decision result in an action that shows respect for myself and others?

- Will this decision result in an action that follows the guidelines of responsible adults including my parent(s) or guardian?

I also will teach your child resistance skills he or she can use when pressured by peers to engage in actions that are harmful, unsafe, illegal, and which show disrespect for others and for family guidelines.

From time to time, your child will bring home Health Behavior Contracts. A Health Behavior Contract is a written guide that helps your child develop a healthful habit. For example, your child might have a Health Behavior Contract that asks him or her to eat four servings of vegetables each day. You can help your child develop this habit. You can review the Health Behavior Contract with your child. You can discuss ways to get these four servings each day. You can encourage your child to have a healthful diet.

I want to work with you to keep your child healthy and safe. Should you have any questions, please write them on the back of this letter. Have your child return the letter to me. I will be in touch with you.

I hope today finds you and your family in good health.

Warm regards,

Family Health *NEWSLETTER*

Dear Parent,

More than likely you are aware that many young people participate in risk behaviors with devastating results. Risk behaviors threaten self-esteem, harm health, and increase the likelihood of illness, injury, and premature death. The Centers for Disease Control and Prevention has identified six categories of risk behaviors of special concern:

1. Behaviors that result in unintentional and intentional injuries;
2. Tobacco use;
3. Alcohol and other drug use;
4. Sexual behaviors that result in HIV infection, other STDs, and unintended pregnancy;
5. Dietary patterns that contribute to disease;
6. Insufficient physical activity.

These risk behaviors usually are established at a young age and continue into adulthood. Fortunately, they can be prevented. One way to prevent risk behaviors is to educate young people and help them develop life skills for health. This is the purpose of the health education course your child is taking. Your child will gain health knowledge and develop life skills in many areas of health: Mental and Emotional Health; Family Living; Growth and Development; Nutrition; Personal Health; Alcohol, Tobacco, and Other Drugs; Communicable and Chronic Diseases; Injury Prevention and Safety; Consumer and Community Health; and Environmental Health. Hopefully, your child will make a commitment to being healthy and:

- Use health knowledge
- Choose wellness behaviors instead of risk behaviors.
- Choose to be in healthful situations.
- Choose to have healthful relationships.
- Make responsible decisions that promote health, protect safety, protect laws, show respect for self and others, follow your guidelines, and demonstrate good character.
- Use resistance skills and say NO to peers when pressured to do something harmful, unsafe, illegal, disrespectful, or in conflict with the guidelines you have set.
- Possess protective factors including a supportive and nurturing environment.
- Be resilient or capable of recovering, bouncing back, and learning from misfortune, change, or pressure.
- Be health literate and have competency in critical thinking and problem solving, responsible and productive citizenship, self-directed learning, and effective communication.

I want to work closely with you, as I believe the home and school are important in educating students about health. Should you have any questions or suggestions, please contact me.

I hope today finds you and your family in good health.

Warm regards,

My Choices

Health Education Standards:

- Students will comprehend health promotion and disease prevention concepts.
- Students will demonstrate the ability to practice health-enhancing behaviors and reduce health risks.
- Students will demonstrate the ability to use goal-setting and decision-making skills that enhance health.
- Students will demonstrate the ability to use effective interpersonal communication skills that enhance health.

Performance Indicators:

- Students will recognize the relationship between personal health behaviors and individual well-being.
- Students will identify responsible health behaviors.
- Students will demonstrate the ability to apply a decision-making process to health issues and problems.
- Students will demonstrate refusal skills.

Life Skills:

- I will make responsible decisions.
- I will use resistance skills when appropriate.

Materials:

Student Master "Make Wise Choices To Be At Your Best"; Student Master "Say NO"; red construction paper; green construction paper

Motivation:

1 Give each student a copy of the Student Master "Make Wise Choices To Be At Your Best." Explain the importance of making wise choices. Wise choices are healthful. Have students point to the girl eating the apple. She makes a healthful choice. Have students tell you another healthful choice.

2 Have students point to the boy who is skating. Explain that he is careful when he skates. He does not skate in the street. He wears a helmet, knee pads, and elbow pads. Wise choices are safe. Have students tell you another safe choice.

3 Have students point to the boy who is holding his baby sister. Explain that he holds his sister because he cares about her. Wise choices show that a person cares about others. Have students tell ways they can show they care about others.

4 Have students point to the boy who is holding the stop sign. He is on the safety patrol at his school. He helps boys and girls follow school rules. He helps them cross the street. Wise choices follow laws and school rules. Have students tell other choices that follow laws and school rules.

5 Have students point to the girl setting the table for dinner. She is following family rules. All families have rules. The rules may tell what time the children must be in bed. Children who follow this rule are ready for bed at this time. The rules may tell children where toys are to be kept. Children who follow this rule put their toys back in this place when they are done playing. Have students share a rule from their families.

6 Explain to students that some choices are not wise. It would not be wise for the boy to skate in the street. It would not be wise for him to skate between parked cars. It would not be wise to talk to a stranger. It would not be wise to smoke a cigarette. If someone tries to get you to do something that is not a wise choice, say NO.

7 Give each student a copy of the Student Master "Say NO." Explain that when someone tries to get them to do something that is not a wise choice, they can say NO. Go over the steps on the Student Master "Say NO."

Evaluation:

Give each student a sheet of red construction paper and a sheet of green construction paper. They can print NO on the red construction paper and YES on the green construction paper. Explain that you are going to ask them to make choices that demonstrate responsible decisions. If the choice is wise, they should hold up the green paper and say YES. If the choice is not wise, they should hold up the red paper and say NO, showing that they are using their resistance skills. Then they should tell you why they said NO.

1. Let's eat an apple. (YES)
2. Let's run across the street. (NO. It is not safe.)
3. Let's call your parent to say you came to my house to play. (YES)
4. Let's ride double on my bike. (NO. It is not safe. It is against the law.)
5. Let's wait until the light is green to cross the street. (YES)
6. Let's push to get ahead in line to go down the slide. (NO. It is not safe. It does not show I care about others.)
7. Let's play inside my house. No grownup is home. (NO. It does not follow my family rules.)
8. Let's smoke a cigarette. (NO. It is not good for my health.)
9. Let's call someone an ugly name. (NO. It does not show I care about others.)
10. Let's play with matches. (NO. It is not safe.)

Multicultural Infusion:

Have students do the same evaluation. This time, teach them how to say YES and NO in other languages. For example, in French YES is OUI (sounds like "we") and NO is NON (sounds like "nawh"). When students hold up the green paper, they will say OUI. When students hold up the red paper, they will say NON.

Student Master
Make Wise Choices To Be At Your Best

Make choices that are healthful.

Make choices that follow laws and school rules.

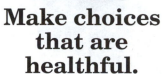

Make choices that are safe.

Make choices that show you care about others.

Make choices that follow family rules.

Student Master

Say No

SAY NO

1. Look at the person.

2. Say NO.

3. Tell them why you are saying NO.

4. Do not change your mind.

Family Living

Kindergarten

My Family

Health Education Standards:

- Students will comprehend health promotion and disease prevention concepts.
- Students will demonstrate the ability to use effective interpersonal communication skills which enhance health.
- Students will demonstrate the ability to practice health-enhancing behaviors and reduce health risks.

Performance Indicators:

- Students will describe how the family influences the health of individuals.
- Students will identify the most common health problems of children.
- Students will recognize that many injuries and illnesses can be prevented and treated.
- Students will develop injury prevention strategies for personal health.
- Students will describe characteristics needed to be a responsible friend and family member.

Life Skills:

- I will strive for healthful family relationships.
- *I will follow safety rules in my home. (Injury Prevention and Safety)*

Materials:

Student Master, "My Family"; crayons; small paper bags; old magazines

Motivation:

1 Introduce the term family. A **family** is a group of people who are related

or who live together. Bring old magazines to class and cut out pictures that show families engaged in healthful activities. Be sure to show different kinds of families such as single-parent families, families with both parents, families with one or several children, families with grandparents, and families of different cultures.

2 Show the class the pictures of families. For each picture, have students tell what they think the people in the family are doing to enjoy themselves and each other. Have students also tell how the families differ.

3 Explain to students that there are many different kinds of families and that all family members can spend meaningful times with each other. Explain that each member of a family has a responsibility to keep other members safe, regardless of the activity the family is enjoying. For example, you might show a family at a cookout and point out that the young children in the family are kept away from the fire so that they do not become harmed.

365

4 Emphasize that parents or guardians have a responsibility to help protect their children from harm. Children should appreciate the decisions or choices their parents or guardians must make to help keep them safe.

5 Distribute copies of the Student Master "My Family" and have students draw a picture that shows them doing something with one or more of their family members. Emphasize that their pictures should show they are doing something enjoyable and also safe.

6 After students complete their pictures, have them share what they have drawn. Students should explain not only what they are doing but also when it is safe to do this activity. Give each student a small paper bag. Decorate your own bag first and explain to students that they will make a family member puppet. Students can color the different parts of the face and draw facial features such as eyes and ears. The puppet will represent a family member they like. When they finish their puppets, they will introduce the puppet to the class. Students are to pretend that the puppet is the family member. They are to talk as if they are the puppet and tell why they are a good family member. Begin this activity by demonstrating your own puppet. Place the paper bag on your hand in order to show students the hand puppet. Say something like, "Hi, I'm Mother Puppet and I love everyone in my family. I help my children do their homework. I talk to them when they are sad." Select students to take turns with their puppets.

Evaluation:

Have students share information about family activities that give them an opportunity to do things with members of their family and a chance to get to know one another better. Also have them share how their family members influence them to make responsible or wise choices. For example, a parent may insist that when riding a bicycle, a helmet must be worn.

Multicultural Infusion:

Have students share activities they do with family members that are common to their cultural background. For example, students may go to certain places with family members on special occasions. They may celebrate certain holidays, or eat certain foods.

My Family

Name _____

Draw your family.
Show your family doing something fun and
safe.

Being Sensitive Toward Others

Health Education Standards:

- Students will comprehend health promotion and disease prevention concepts.
- Students will demonstrate the ability to practice health enhancing behaviors and reduce health risks.

Performance Indicators:

- Students will describe mental, emotional, social, and physical health during childhood.
- Students will develop an awareness of personal health needs.
- Students will identify the most common health problems of children.

Life Skills:

- I will accept and develop my personal learning style.
- I will recognize the needs of people of different ages.

Materials:

Student Master, "Being Helpful To Others"; paper; writing instruments; blindfolds; a book that can be read to the class

Motivation:

1 Explain to students that as they grow, they have different things they need. Students need food, friends, help from family members and an education. Have students brainstorm the kinds of things they need every day.

2 Explain to students that sometimes people are not able to perform activi-

ties in the same way as others because their learning styles and needs may be different. Some people learn by reading and others are more visual learners. Some have learning problems. Some have bodies that may not work in the same ways as others. For example, some people have a visual impairment. They cannot see clearly or see at all. Some people have a hearing impairment. They may not be able to hear as well as others or they may not be able to hear at all.

3 This activity will help students develop a sensitivity toward people who have special needs. Ask students to take a sheet of paper and draw a simple picture. Next give students blindfolds or ask them to close their eyes if you do not have blindfolds. Keeping their eyes closed, students are to try to find a sheet of paper and something with which to write. Continuing to keep their eyes closed, students are to draw the same pictures as they did when their eyes were open.

4 Discuss with students how it felt to try to do tasks when their eyes were closed. Students will say they were scared or frustrated. Explain that there are many people who either were born with a visual impairment or lost their sight at some time during their lives. These people learn and continue to make adjustments so they can perform tasks.

5 Take a book and begin to read it to the class. As you read it, gradually lower your voice so that it is barely heard. However, keep your lips moving so that it appears you are still talking. Have students share how they felt when they could not hear what you were saying. Explain that a person who has a hearing impairment may be able to hear only slightly or may not be able to hear at all. Yet these people have many of the same needs as everyone else.

6 Tell students that people who are not able to see or hear still have the same needs as everyone else. In addition, these people may sometimes need help. Ask students to share how they might help others who may have visual or hearing impairments. For example, a student might help a person who has a visual impairment by offering his/ her arm to guide the person. A student might speak more slowly and look at a person who has a hearing impairment so that person can read their lips. **Lip reading** is watching another person's lips as (s)he forms words.

7 Distribute the Student Master "Being Helpful To Others." Explain that the person in the wheelchair has a disability. This person cannot walk. A friend helps the person in the wheelchair move to another place. Have students color the picture. Students can share their pictures and tell how they would help a person in a wheelchair.

Evaluation:

Walk into class and pretend that you have a visual impairment. Tell students that you need to perform certain tasks and that they are to tell you how they would help you. For example, you may say that you need to find a pencil or that you need to walk to the back of the room. You might have students practice what they would actually do to help you. You can also pretend that you have a hearing impairment. How might students talk to you? What other ways might students help communicate to you? Ask students how they might help older family members who have visual and/or hearing impairments? How might they help other students who have physical disabilities? How might they help another student who has a learning style that is different than their own? It is also important for students to understand that people who may have disabilities need to have the opportunity to perform tasks without the help of others. All people need a sense of accomplishment.

Student Master

Being Helpful To Others

Name _____

Be Helpful To Others

Healthful Foods Help Me Grow

Health Education Standards:

- Students will comprehend health promotion and disease prevention concepts.
- Students will demonstrate the ability to practice health-enhancing behaviors and reduce health risks.
- Students will demonstrate the ability to use goal-setting and decision-making skills that enhance health.

Performance Indicators:

- Students will recognize the relationship between personal health behaviors and individual well-being.
- Students will identify responsible health behaviors.
- Students will demonstrate strategies to improve or maintain personal health.
- Students will recognize that many injuries and illnesses can be prevented and treated.
- Students will set a personal health goal and make progress toward its achievement.

Life Skills:

- I will recognize foods that contain the six major nutrients.
- I will follow the dietary guidelines.
- I will make food selections that reduce my risk of disease.
- *I will choose behavior to reduce my risk of cardiovascular disease. (Communicable and Chronic Diseases)*
- *I will choose behavior to reduce my risk of cancer. (Communicable and Chronice Diseases)*

Materials:

Student Master, "Healthful Food Choices"; Student Master, "Healthful Foods I Like"; paper plates for each student; scissors; old magazines; crayons

Motivation:

1 Cut out pictures from magazines that show different kinds of foods. Cut out pictures that show healthful foods such as fruits and vegetables as well as foods that are not healthful such as candy and cake. Explain to students that certain kinds of foods are important in helping them grow. These foods are the fruits such as oranges, grapes, and apples. Other healthful foods are vegetables. Some examples of vegetables include carrots, lettuce, and broccoli. Fruits and vegetables come from plants. Other kinds of foods that may be healthful come from another group that is made up of milk, yogurt, and cheese. Some foods come from animals and are kinds of meats including chicken and fish. Yet other kinds of foods come from breads, cereal, rice, and pasta. (It is not necessary for students at this age group to identify the six major nutrients found in these foods—water, proteins, carbohydrates, fats, vitamins, and minerals. However, healthful foods will contain some or all of these nutrients.) The purpose of this strategy is to have students select foods from the USDA Food Guide Pyramid that are healthful and to try to avoid foods that are made up mostly of fats, oils, and sweets.

2 After reviewing the material about healthful foods, explain to students that certain foods such as candy or cake may not be healthful because they contain sugar and oils. Fried foods may contain large amounts of fat. (You may choose to demonstrate the presence of oil or fat in food by taking a slice of a sponge cake or fried potato and pressing a tissue upon it. Students will see the oil.) Eating fatty foods can lead to cardio-vascular disease. Some foods may also contribute to cancer. Explain to students that they can substitute healthful foods for foods high in fats, oils, and sweets.

3 Distribute paper plates and scissors to each student. Distribute a copy of the Student Master "Healthful Food Choices." Have students color the healthful foods the appropriate colors (1 red tomato, 2 orange carrots, and 3 brown breads). They are to put an X through the food that is not healthful (the slice of cake). In addition, they are to trace the corresponding numbers that reflect the number of items in each box. After completing the colors and numbers, students are to cut around the box and place their healthful foods on the plate. Students can be selected to identify their healthful foods and the number of healthful foods in the pictures. They can also identify the food they would avoid (the one with the X placed through it).

4 You can expand this activity to identify other healthful foods and other foods that can be avoided. You can also have students look through magazines and identify foods that are healthful and foods that can be avoided because they may not be nutritious.

Evaluation:

Give examples of different kinds of foods to students. You may cut out pictures of foods from maga-zines and show them to students, or you may tell examples to the class. For each food identified, have students give a "thumb's up" signal if the food is healthful or a "thumb's down" signal if the food is not healthful. Have them identify foods that have been fried and can contribute to clogged arteries and perhaps even cancer. You also can evaluate the student responses on the Student Master to indicate if they were able to distinguish between healthful and harmful foods. Distribute the Student Master "Healthful Foods I Like." In each of the four boxes, ask students to draw a healthful food and to color that food. Stu-dents are to share their masters with others.

Multicultural Infusion:

Explain that certain cultures have a basic food that is eaten. For example, rice has been a basic food of Asia and wheat bread has been a basic food of Europe throughout history. In certain cultures, red meats are not eaten but fish is. Students may bring in foods that are common in a cer-tain culture. Students may share these foods with the class. As each food is identified it can be categorized, such as coming from a plant or an animal, or belonging to a group such as fruits, veg-etables, milk, or cereal.

Student Master

Healthful Food Choices

Name_____

Color the food.
Trace the number.
Draw an X through the picture of the food that
is not healthful.

...1.. **red
tomato**

2.. **orange
carrots**

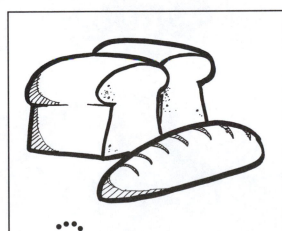

3 **brown
breads**

...1.. **slice of
cake**

Healthful Foods I Like

Name _____

Draw one healthful food in each box.
Color the four foods.

A Restful Experience

Health Education Standards:

- Students will comprehend health promotion and disease prevention concepts.
- Students will demonstrate the ability to practice health-enhancing behaviors and reduce health risks.
- Students will demonstrate the ability to use goal-setting and decision-making skills that enhance health.

Performance Indicators:

- Students will develop an awareness of personal health needs.
- Students will demonstrate strategies to improve or maintain personal health.
- Students will recognize that many injuries and illnesses can be prevented and treated.
- Students will set a personal health goal and make progress toward its achievement.

Life Skills:

- I will obtain adequate rest and sleep.
- I will achieve a desirable level of physical fitness.
- *I will choose behavior to reduce my risk of cardiovascular disease. (Communicable and Chronic Diseases)*

Materials:

Student Master, "Whose Heart Works Hard?"; any battery-operated toy

Motivation:

1 Bring a battery-operated toy to class. Show students the toy and explain that the toy can operate only if the battery inside the toy is charged. Show students the battery. Start up the toy and let students see how the toy operates. Explain that the battery inside the toy serves as energy for that toy. The battery gives the toy its energy to work.

2 Explain to students that they need energy to do everything. Have students share what they do every day. They may say they play with their friends, they read, and they go to school. Explain that they need **energy** to do these activities. Explain that they get their energy from food, whereas the toy gets its energy from the battery.

3 Explain that the human body needs to rest after it has used energy. The more energy the body uses, the more important it is to rest. For example, if someone is involved in an activity for an hour, that person may feel tired. It is important to rest when feeling tired.

4 The following activity will demonstrate that rest is needed. Have students make a tight fist. Explain that you are going to ask them to open their fists wide and then shut them tight. You are going to count from one to ten with each opening and closing of the fist. At the count of one, students will open their fists. At the count of two, students will close their fists. At the count of three, they will open their fists again, and so on. As students open and close their fists, they are to count from one through ten with you. Students will do sets of opening and closing their fists four times. Each time, you are to speed up the count.

5 After the fourth time, students will notice that their hands feel tired.

At this point, have students rest their fists. Explain that they need to rest because they feel tired. Emphasize that when they feel tired they need to rest, otherwise an injury may occur. Explain that if you had not given them a rest, eventually they would not have been able to open and close their fists continually. At first, students would have noticed that they began to open and close their fists more slowly before stopping completely. Explain that by resting, students are allowing their bodies to return to a more energized state so that they can continue to perform activities again.

6 Explain that there are different ways to rest. Students can sleep. They can sit quietly and color in a coloring book. They can watch an educational show on television.

7 Next, introduce the function of the heart. Explain that the **heart** works somewhat like a fist in that it always moves as it pumps blood throughout the body. The harder a person exercises, the faster the heart beats. When a person is at rest, the heart beats more slowly. Point to your ribs and explain that the heart is located underneath. Emphasize that resting one's body also allows the heart to

beat fewer times in a given period of time. Explain that the heart rests between beats but it can rest in a different way by beating fewer times when you rest. Emphasize that exercise helps the heart become healthier and promotes physical fitness. By exercising and resting, a person can help keep healthy.

8 Distribute the Student Master "Whose Heart Works Hard?" to students. Give students instructions to color the circles red if the person is resting and the heart is not working hard. Tell students to color the circles green if the person is physically active and the person's heart is working hard.

Evaluation:

Students are going to identify ways they can rest. Tell them you are going to begin a sentence. The sentence is "I rest by... ." Have students complete the sentence by telling ways they rest. Also have students explain how adequate rest and sleep in combination with exercise promote physical fitness and reduce the risk of cardiovascular disease.

Student Master

Whose Heart Works Hard?

Name _____

Color the circles green if the heart works hard.
Color the circles red if the heart rests.

Which Is Which?

Health Education Standards:

- Students will comprehend health promotion and disease prevention concepts.
- Students will demonstrate the ability to practice health-enhancing behaviors and reduce health risks.

Performance Indicators:

- Students will recognize the relationship between personal health behaviors and individual well-being.
- Students will develop an awareness of personal health needs.

Life Skills:

- I will use over-the-counter and prescription drugs in responsible ways.
- *I will cooperate with people who protect my health and safety. (Consumer and Community Health)*

Materials:

Student Master, "Medicine Or Food?"; poster paper; glue; four different types of over-the-counter (OTC) pills or capsules that may also look like candy; four different kinds of candy that can be mistaken as pills or capsules

Motivation:

1 Divide a large sheet of poster paper into eight equal sections. In four different sections, glue an OTC pill or capsule. In four other sections, glue a piece of candy. Under each OTC medicine and each candy, write if that product is a medicine or candy. Temporarily, cover what is written with a strip of paper.

2 Tell students they are going to try to guess which items are medicines and which are candies. Students will find that it may be difficult to distinguish between the two. Hold up each section and, as volunteers guess, remove the strip of paper to reveal whether each is a medicine or candy.

3 Review the answers students gave. It will become obvious that students will not always be able to distinguish between what is a medicine and what is a candy. Explain that if they took the medicine and thought they were taking a candy, they might harm their bodies. They might become dizzy. They might feel tired or drowsy. They might experience a rapid heart rate.

4 Stress to students that a person should not distinguish between products like medicines and candy by appearance only. This is the reason it is important never to take something from another person if there is doubt about what that product is. Suppose a person finds something in his/her home, and the person does

not know what that product is. That person should not put that product in his/her mouth. The product may be a medicine. Emphasize also that a person should never take something from a stranger. A stranger may not care about the student's health and might give him/her something that could be harmful to the body.

5 From your medicine cabinet at home, select about five different OTC medicines and prescription drugs and bring only the empty containers or boxes. Also select five different foods that may be in packages. Try to get an assortment of different packages. For example, you may have small jars or paper packages. Make sure all packages are closed tight and cannot be easily opened by students. Do not permit students to take the packages to their desks. Have them look at the different packages. Ask them to differentiate between drugs (medicines) and candy. They may indicate that some products, most likely candy, may be easily identified because they saw these products in the supermarket. Explain that the drugs are purchased in a special area of a supermarket or in a store such as a drug

store. Show students the labels of the different products such as the word "warning" or the word "tablets." Select other words students can see and recognize. Show students that medicines may be packaged differently. For example, some bottles have special caps.

6 After students begin to differentiate between medicines and foods, distribute the Student Master "Medicine Or Food?" Instruct students to draw a circle around the word "medicine" or "food" in each picture to identify the appropriate substance. Have students share their answers.

Evaluation:

Describe different situations for the students and ask them what they would do if they were in these situations. In this way, students can show whether they are responsible and are cooperating with people who want to keep them healthy and safe. For example, while walking in the playground, you find a bottle with what looks like candy inside. What would you do? (Bring it to a responsible adult and do not take what is inside.)

Student Master

Medicine Or Food?

Name _____

Look at the picture.
Circle the correct word.

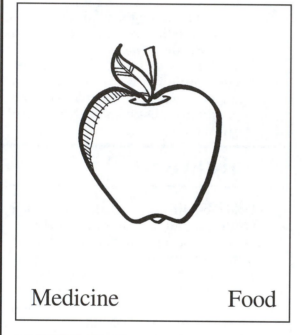

Medicine   Food

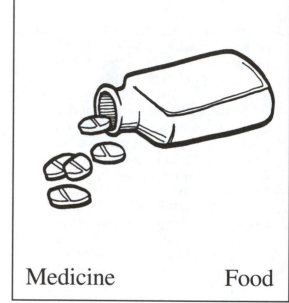

Medicine   Food

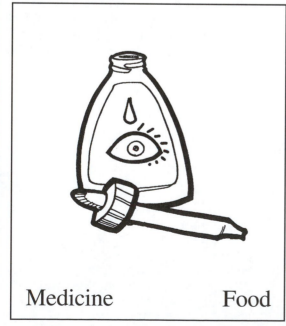

Medicine   Food

Medicine   Food

Your Germs Are Spreading

Health Education Standard:

- Students will comprehend health promotion and disease prevention concepts.

Performance Indicators:

- Students will recognize that many injuries and illnesses can be prevented and treated.
- Students will identify the impact of the environment on personal health.
- Students will describe the influence of culture on personal health practices.

Life Skills:

- I will choose behaviors to reduce the risk of infection with common communicable diseases.
- *I will be aware of the effects of overcrowding and poverty. (Environmental Health)*

Materials:

Family Master, "Cold Tips"; dark colored felt; chalk dust or powder; two hand puppets

Motivation:

1 Explain to students that germs are spread through the air in many different ways. Explain that most people their age get a cold at least two times in a year. In other words, between one birthday and the next, most people their age will have two colds.

2 Review the signs and symptoms of a cold. Explain to students that they might know they have a cold when their nose feels stuffy. They may have a runny nose and their eyes may have a large number of tears. They may have a sore throat or they may have a headache. Not all people who have colds experience the same kinds of symptoms.

3 Explain that a cold is a disease that is spread from one person to another. A disease is being ill or not feeling well. There are many different kinds of diseases, but you are going to talk only about the common cold. Explain that the cold is common because many people get colds. Explain that one way people get colds from other people is through coughing or sneezing. For example, if you have a cold and you cough into the face of another person, that person can breathe in or inhale your germs. When these germs get into the other person's body, that person can then become ill.

4 To demonstrate how germs spread through the air when a person coughs, take the dark piece of felt and tape it to the wall or chalkboard. Place a hand puppet on each hand. Place chalk dust or powder in the mouth of one puppet. Hold the puppets in front of the felt. As the puppets are talking to each other, pretend to cough. As you manipulate the puppet, cough sideways across the mouth of the puppet that has the powder in its mouth. When you do this, students will notice that specks of chalk dust or powder splatter on the felt. Explain to the class that the chalk dust or powder represents germs. Have the students notice that the "germs" are now near the puppet that did not cough. Explain that the "germs" may enter the body of the other puppet. Ask the class how this can happen. (When the other puppet breathes in or inhales, the germs can enter the body. When this happens, the person may also become ill.)

5 Explain to students that the puppet who was not ill could have been better protected. Ask students how this could have happened. (The puppet who was ill could have placed its hand over its mouth when it coughed. This would have slowed the spread of the germs.) Emphasize to students that if they have a cold, they can help protect others by covering their mouth when they cough. They can also cover their nose when they sneeze. These actions will help reduce the spread of germs throughout the air. It is always helpful to provide students with healthful hints. For example, when people sneeze, they should not pinch their nostrils shut. The air

from a sneeze needs to leave the nose, otherwise a person may create health problems in other parts of the body such as the ears.

6 Distribute the Family Master "Cold Tips" and have students take it home to share with a parent.

Evaluation:

Select students to try your puppets. Under the same circumstances (the cough), have students tell you what they should do to stop the spread of germs from a cough. Students should demonstrate that they know how to help prevent colds from spreading. Point out that crowded conditions increase the risk of spreading a cold to others. Review student answers for accuracy.

Student Master

Cold Tips

Dear Parent,

Your child is learning how to protect himself/herself if (s)he has a cold or is around others who have a cold. Speak with your child and review the tips on this sheet.

1. Always carry tissues or a handkerchief if you have a cold and are sneezing or coughing.

2. Cover your mouth and nose when you cough or sneeze.

3. Try to avoid going near others when you have a cold.

4. Wash your hands if you touch the same object that the person who has a cold has touched.

5. Get rest and drink plenty of healthful fluids if you have a cold. Water and fruit juices are good fluids to drink.

6. Do not take aspirin if the cold may actually be the flu. A person who has muscle aches, fever, or a sore throat may have the flu. Taking aspirin if a person really has the flu can cause an illness called Reye's Syndrome.

7. See a doctor if the signs of a cold last more than five days and you do not feel better.

8. Do not leave used tissues around because someone else may touch them and catch the germs from the sick person.

9. Do not play sports or engage in heavy physical activity.

10. Avoid close contact with others until signs of the cold disappear.

Avoid That Car

Health Education Standards:

- Students will demonstrate the ability to practice health-enhancing behaviors and reduce health risks.
- Students will demonstrate the ability to access valid health information and appropriate health products and services.

Performance Indicators:

- Students will generate ways to avoid threatening situations.
- Students will explain how to get assistance in threatening circumstances.
- Students will demonstrate the ability to locate school and community health helpers.

Life Skills:

- I will protect myself from people who might harm me.
- *I will cooperate with people who protect my health and safety. (Consumer and Community Health)*

Materials:

Teaching Master "What Do You Remember?"; transparency projector; a cardboard carton from the grocery or appliance store; chair; scissors; pencil

Motivation:

1 Ask students if they have ever been walking down the street when a car with a stranger inside stopped and the stranger wanted to ask a question. Ask students to describe what they did. Some students may say that they approached the car. Others might say that they did not approach the car and ran away. Explain that most people who are traveling in cars and who stop to ask someone a question are nice. But you cannot tell if a person inside a car is nice or not. Tell students that the following activity will describe what they can do if they are approached by a stranger in a car.

2 Cut one of the large sides from a carton. Then draw an outline of a car in the shape of a convertible, and cut around the outline. You will need this shape because you will place a chair behind it so it appears that you are driving. You also will be able to reach out from the side of the car.

3 Select a student to stand ten feet away from the car. Tell this student to pretend (s)he is walking down the street and to do what you say. Pretend you have a photograph of a puppy and say to the student, "Excuse me. I lost my puppy and I have a picture of her. Could you come over here so I can show you her picture? She is lost and I want to know if you saw her." As the student approaches the car, reach out and grab him/ her by the arm. Then tell the class that if you were a stranger who wanted to harm this person, you easily could have dragged him/her into the car.

4 With this example in mind, emphasize that you should never approach a car with a stranger inside. Reinforce the concept that most strangers are nice people; however, there are certain rules that need to be followed in situations involving strangers, and keeping away from strangers in automobiles is one of those rules.

5 Explain to students that when approached by a stranger inside a car, they should run in the direction OPPOSITE to the car's direction. They are to run in the opposite direction because if a person inside the car wanted to attack them, the car would need to travel backward or turn around and that would be difficult to do. If a person were to run away in the same direction as the car was traveling, it would be much easier for the stranger to catch this person. Explain to students that it is also important to remember as much as possible about the car and the stranger. For example, the student could remember the color of the car, what kind of car it is, and what the stranger was wearing. You can practice this aspect of the activity by drawing and attaching a license plate to the car. Do not tell the class what you have done. Then have another student volunteer to be walking along the street. Pretend that you stopped your car and asked this student to come closer to see the photograph of your lost puppy. Tell the student to act in the correct way. (Run away in the opposite direction the car is traveling.)

Evaluation:

Have students tell what they would do if they were walking down the street and were approached by a stranger in a car. (They would run away in the direction opposite to the direction in which the car was traveling.) By running away, the student is protecting him/herself from a person who might harm him/her and is cooperating with people who are concerned with the student's safety. Tell students to close their eyes and to try to remember certain facts such as the numbers on your license plate and three things about you (the stranger). They may think about such items as the color of your dress or shirt, your hair color, if you were wearing glasses, etc. Then tell students to to tell what they remember without looking up to see you or the car. Review student answers to your questions for thoroughness and accuracy. Make a transparency of the Teaching Master "What Do You Remember?" Do not tell students what you have in mind. Show the transparency and after ten seconds, turn off the transparency projector, then ask students to tell you what they remembered about the picture. Assess how many facts about the person or the car students remembered. Students should remember the sex of the driver (male), his characteristics (mustache), his clothing (hat with the letter) and the car (two door sedan).

Teaching Master

What Do You Remember?

Protectors

Health Education Standards:

- Students will demonstrate the ability to access valid health information and appropriate health products and services.
- Students will demonstrate the ability to advocate for family and community health.

Performance Indicators:

- Students will demonstrate the ability to locate school and community health helpers.
- Students will identify community agencies that advocate for healthy individuals, families, and communities.

Life Skills:

- I will use school nurse and school health services when appropriate.
- I will use health care providers when appropriate.
- I will use health care facilities when appropriate.

Materials:

Old magazines with pictures; scissors

Motivation:

1 Explain that there are many people in a home, school, and community who can help young people if they have any concerns about which they need to talk. These people are interested in protecting young people from harm.

2 You can explain that a **teacher** can help protect boys and girls in school. Adults in a family help keep children in the family safe and secure. A teacher helps children learn how to cross the street safely. A teacher also helps children learn how to solve problems by talking with them. A firefighter helps boys and girls be safe from harm by fire and smoke. A police officer helps boys and girls keep safe from others and from danger. A member of the clergy helps boys and girls and their families solve problems.

3 Cut pictures from magazines that show people in the family, school and community who protect health and safety. You may cut out a picture of a parent and a baby. You may cut out a picture of a guard at a school crossing guiding children across the street as they walk to school. Cut out several pictures that show different people helping boys and girls.

4 Show the pictures you have cut out to the class. When you show each picture, have a volunteer imagine and tell a story about the picture. The story should include how the picture illustrates a responsible adult who is protecting health by following school rules and laws.

Evaluation:

Have students name a responsible adult in their community who helps protect them and keep them safe. They are to tell how this person helps keep them safe. In doing so, they should demonstrate that they will seek help from people who will protect their physical and emotional health and their safety.

Multicultural Infusion:

Show people of different cultures doing something to help protect the health and safety of boys and girls. Explain that no matter what country people come from, there are responsible adults who care about the safety of children.

My Friend, My Home

Health Education Standard:

- Students will comprehend health promotion and disease prevention concepts.

Performance Indicator:

- Students will identify the impact of the environment on personal health.

Life Skills:

- I will keep the air clean.
- I will keep the water clean.

Materials:

The poem, *My Friend, My Home*; globe; art paper; crayons or markers

Motivation:

1 If possible, take students to sit outside during this lesson. Talk to students about the difference between things made by nature and things made by people. Ask students to name things that they can see that are made by nature (trees, grass, flowers). Tell students that air and water are also part of nature. Explain that all living things—people, plants, and animals—need air and water to live. Ask students to name ways they use air and water everyday. (We breathe the air. We drink water and wash in it.)

2 Read the poem *My Friend, My Home* aloud. Have students act out these ideas as you say them: playing in the air and the shining sun; tiny creatures running; putting toes in running water; rain coming down

and flowers growing; students being kind to the Earth. Tell students that these activities are what the poem is about. Have students close their eyes and ask them to imagine each activity as you slowly read the poem again.

3 Have students name the parts of nature they heard in the poem (air, sun, breeze, water, flowers). Ask students what the poet was referring to as "my friend, my home." (Earth) Then ask why they think the poet called the Earth "my friend, my home," and a living place. (Students might say because we live here; because Earth takes care of us; because people, plants, and animals live here.) Explain that people need to take care of the Earth and all living things. Ask students to tell ways that they might take care of things made by nature. (water the grass, stay out of flower gardens, be careful and kind to animals)

4 Tell students that keeping air and water clean is also important. Explain that clean air and water help all living things live and grow. Point out that people everywhere are working very hard to keep the Earth safe and clean. Ask students what they might do to help keep the world clean. (Throw litter away in trash cans; ask people they know to keep the world clean.) Tell them that another way students can help keep the Earth safe and clean is to ask an adult before throwing something away or spraying something in the air. Explain that litter, especially sprays and liquids, can be washed into rivers and streams by the rainfall.

Evaluation:

When you return to the classroom, have each child make an "I Love You Earth" card. It should include these words and include a picture showing activities that promote clean air and clean water. Display the cards on classroom walls with a globe nearby.

My Friend, My Home

The air,
the shining sun,
a place where tiny creatures run.

The quiet breeze
across my face—
the Earth is such a living place.

Clear water runs
across my toes,
rains down
to make the flowers grow.

My friend, my home
for every day—
I'll keep it safe in every way.

You Are So Very Special

Health Education Standards:

- Students will demonstrate the ability to practice health-enhancing behaviors and reduce health risks.
- Students will demonstrate the ability to use effective interpersonal communication skills that enhance health.

Performance Indicators:

- Students will develop an awareness of personal health needs.
- Students will demonstrate strategies to improve or maintain personal health.
- Students will differentiate between negative and positive behaviors involving conflict.

Life Skills:

- I will develop positive self-esteem.
- *I will avoid discrimination.*
  (Family Living)

Materials:

Student Master, "I Am Special"; shoe box; decorative paper such as scrap wallpaper; tape; small pocket mirror

Motivation:

1 To prepare for this lesson, prepare a special box that you will bring to class. Take a shoe box for which you no longer have use. Decorate the cover and all sides of the shoe box by pasting decorative paper to it. In the inside bottom of the shoe box, place a mirror that is held in place by tape.

2 Stand in front of your class, holding the shoe box so that it is visible to everyone. For several seconds, do not say a word to the class. Students will begin to wonder what is inside the shoe box. After several seconds, tell the students that each of them will have the opportunity to see what is inside the shoe box. Tell students there are two rules to follow when you do this activity. First, they cannot tell anyone else what is inside the box. Second, they must identify what is special about what is inside the box. Explain to students that what is inside the box is very special. Approach each student and give him/her the opportunity to see what is inside the box.

3 As you approach each student, tilt the box so that(s)he will see his/her face as (s)he peeks inside. Reiterate to each student that it is important to remember what is special about what (s)he sees inside the box. (Emphasize that you are asking students "What is special about what you see inside the box?" not "What do you see inside the box?" This way you will avoid having students give responses such as "I saw myself inside the box.")

4 After students have had the opportunity to see their faces reflected in the mirror inside the box, they are to share what was so special about what they saw. You can add that what is inside the box is a special gift. Discuss the concept that people like receiving gifts and that gifts help make people feel good. Explain that you can be a gift to others. You can share happy feelings with people and give the gift of helping them to feel good about themselves. You also can talk about what makes you special and important. You can discuss how you look and what you like to do with others. You can discuss qualities students have that others like.

5 Distribute the Student Master "I Am Special." Explain that there is a mirror inside the bottom of the shoe box. Each student is to pretend that (s)he is looking inside the box and sees a reflection of his/her face. Students are to draw their faces and show their picture to the class. Then they are to share how they are special.

Evaluation:

On the chalkboard, write the following incomplete statement. "I feel good about myself because...." Go around the room and have students tell a characteristic they have that makes them feel good about themselves. An optional activity is to show students a picture of a person who looks happy. Students in the class can brainstorm ideas about why the person in the picture feels happy. They can make up a story about a situation that happened to that person that made him/her feel special and important. You can then have students relate these stories to their own experiences. For example, they may indicate that the person in the picture has a birthday and received a new toy. Receiving a new toy can help make a person feel happy and special. Students can then share an experience they have had in which they received a toy and why that helped them to feel happy.

Multicultural Infusion:

You can choose to show pictures from magazines depicting people of different cultures. These pictures will show people who appear happy and often there may be something in the picture that will show why this person appears happy. For example, a person may be eating a particular ethnic food, and this person is smiling because (s)he likes this food. This is a good opportunity to infuse different cultural aspects about health and how these aspects impact a person's health.

I Am Special

Name

Pretend this is a box with a mirror taped to the bottom. Pretend you look inside. Draw your face. Tell why you are special.

One, Two, A Friend For You

Health Education Standards:

- Students will demonstrate the ability to use effective interpersonal communication skills that enhance health.
- Students will demonstrate the ability to practice health-enhancing behaviors and reduce health risks.

Performance Indicators:

- Students will describe characteristics needed to be a responsible friend, and family member.
- Students will demonstrate ways to communicate care, consideration, and respect of self and others.
- Students will explain how to get assistance in threatening circumstances.

Life Skills:

- I will develop relationship skills.
- I will form healthful and responsible friendships.
- I will recognize harmful relationships.

Materials:

Student Master, "Friendly Faces"; paper; pencils

Motivation:

1 Ask students if they have ever heard of the nursery rhyme, "One, Two, Buckle My Shoe." You can tell students the first few lines for this nursery rhyme. It is as follows:

> One, two,
> Buckle my shoe;
> Three, four,
> Shut the door;

> Five, six,
> Pick up sticks;
> Seven, eight,
> Lay them straight;

2 Tell students that they are going to learn a new version of this nursery rhyme. However, this new version will emphasize the importance of being a good friend. Have students sing the song using the new words. The new words for this song are as follows:

> One, two,
> I like you;
> Three, four,
> I'll smile more;
> Five, six,
> I'll eat a mix;
> Seven, eight,
> Of foods that are great;

3 Distribute the Student Master "Friendly Faces." Students are to draw friendly faces next to each number so that the number of friendly faces matches the number to its left. For example, a student will draw one friendly face next to the number 1, two friendly faces next to number 2, and so on. Collect the papers and check that the drawings match the numbers.

4 You can continue this activity with extended math instruction. For example, you can point to the number 8 and ask students, "How many faces would remain if two of the friendly faces went away?" (Six friendly faces) You can present math problems that will correspond to the ability of your students.

Evaluation:

Have each student select a number from one through five. You can have them pick from random numbers in an envelope. For each number, students are to tell ways to be a good friend. For example, a student who selects the number three will tell three ways to be a good friend; a student who selects the number five will tell five ways to be a good friend, and so on.

Friendly Faces

Name _____

Look at each number.
Draw the correct number of faces by each number.

1.

2.

3.

4.

5.

6.

7.

8.

Unique Me

Health Education Standard:

- Students will demonstrate the ability to practice health-enhancing behaviors and reduce health risks.

Performance Indicators:

- Students will develop an awareness of personal health needs.
- Students will demonstrate strategies to improve or maintain personal health.

Life Skills:

- I will accept my physical uniqueness.
- *I will develop positive self-esteem. (Mental and Emotional Health)*

Materials:

Student Master, "This Is Me"; markers or crayons; ink pad; index cards; a card for each student

Motivation:

1 Distribute an index card to each student. Tell each student to draw a picture of himself/herself that includes as many unique features as possible. The picture is to be a drawing of the student without a head, but have students leave space so that they can add a head later. Have several students share their headless drawings with the class and indicate what is special about their drawings.

2 Have students press their thumbs on the ink pad to make a thumbprint where their heads should be on their pictures. Each student will now

have a complete body. Students are to write their names on their cards. Post each card on the bulletin board.

3 Explain to students that the "heads" on the cards may look alike from a distance. However, there is something unique about each of the "heads." Have students closely observe the details of the "heads." Then ask students to indicate what they observed. Students will indicate that each "head" is different because each fingerprint is unique. Explain that no two people have the same fingerprints. Fingerprints are a physical feature that makes one person different from another. Have students share other ways people differ from each other because of their physical features. Emphasize that although people may look similar from a distance, on closer inspection they are different. For example, thumbprints look alike from a distance but on close inspection, they are different. Explain that people have other unique features with which they were born. A person has

no control over these features and it is these unique features that help make each person special.

4 Discuss the different kinds of features people have and how each of these features may differ. For example, people have eyes. But some people have brown eyes, others have green eyes, and yet others have blue eyes. Tell students about hair. Have students identify different color hair. Discuss the kind of hair people have, such as long or short or curly or straight. Introduce other physical features such as tall or short. Distribute the Student Master "This Is Me." Have students draw a full picture of themselves. Then have them fill in the blanks. You can review the blanks and help them fill in the missing information.

Evaluation:

Randomly distribute the cards that were displayed on the bulletin board. Be sure that each student has another student's card. Each student is to go to the student whose card he or she has and tell that student two features observed on the card that make that student special.

This Is Me

Name _____

Draw a picture of yourself from head to toe.
Answer the questions.

My hair color is _____ .

My eye color is _____ .

My hair is _____ .

Healthful Food Grab Bag

Health Education Standards:

- Students will demonstrate the ability to practice health-enhancing behaviors and reduce health risks.
- Students will demonstrate the ability to use goal-setting and decision-making skills which enhance health.

Performance Indicators:

- Students will identify responsible health behaviors.
- Students will demonstrate strategies to improve or maintain personal health.
- Students will set a personal health goal and make progress toward its achievement.

Life Skills:

- I will recognize foods that contain the six major nutrients.
- I will follow the dietary guidelines.
- I will make food selections that reduce my risk of disease.

Materials:

Student Master, "A Smile Or A Frown"; Student Master, "My Fruit Diary"; one orange; slice of bread; banana; grains of rice; tomato; corn flakes; a brown paper bag

Motivation:

1 In this activity, students will learn how they can identify foods by using only the sense of touch. They will learn that they may identify a food by how soft or hard a food may feel, how a food is shaped, or by the texture of a food. They also will learn that foods that are nutritious will provide the body with energy and contain substances needed for the maintenance of body tissues and the regulation of body processes. Six major classes of nutrients are used by the body. The following descriptions of these nutrients are included for the teacher's reference: Proteins are nutrients that are essential for growth and development and the repair of all body tissues. Some foods that contain protein are meat and cheese. Carbohydrates are nutrients that are the main source of energy for the body. Examples of carbohydrates are starches that are found in pasta. Fats are nutrients that provide additional energy and help the body store certain vitamins. Fats that are healthful for the body can be found in animals that fly or swim, such as poultry and fish. Vitamins are nutrients that help chemical reactions that take place inside the body. Many different kinds of foods contain specific kinds of vitamins. Minerals are nutrients that regulate the many chemical reactions in the body. Foods such as leafy green vegetables contain minerals. Water, although not considered a food, is a nutrient that makes up about sixty percent of the body mass.

2 Introduce the term nutritious to the class. Explain that foods that are nutritious are healthful. They help the body grow. Explain that some foods are not nutritious. They contain a large amount of sugar or other substances such as saturated fats that are not healthful for the body. Explain that these foods may include different kinds of candy, potato chips, and ice cream. Emphasize to students that they should make healthful selections whenever possible.

3 Explain that students can use their sense of touch to identify many healthful kinds of foods. Explain that you are going to play a game called "Feel the Food." You will place different foods, one at a time, inside a bag. You will select several student volunteers to come to the front of the room. Each student will place one hand inside the bag. Students may not look at what is inside the bag. They will feel what is inside the bag. They are to describe what they feel inside the bag. Then the student should guess what the food is in the bag. If the student is not able to guess, the other students in the class can try to guess the name of the food based upon the description of that food given by the student whose hand is in the bag. For example, the student may be feeling the tomato. That student may say that it feels very smooth, it is soft, and it is round.

4 Explain to students that only nutritious foods will be inside the bag. You want students to begin to develop an awareness of those foods that are nutritious and are as free as possible from substances such as sugar, saturated fats, and salt. This also is an opportunity for students to begin to describe the characteristics of nutritious foods.

Evaluation:

Students can pretend they have identified a healthful food that is in a bag. Select one student at a time to close his/her eyes and pretend his/her hand is inside the bag. That student is to think of a food and describe it to the class. The class must identify the food imagined by the student. Be sure that students only identify healthful foods. You can also distribute the Student Master, "A Smile Or A Frown." Students are to take this master home and complete it with a parent. Have students return their masters the next day and review their answers. Emphasize the importance of eating healthful foods. Distribute the Student Master, "My Fruit Diary." Explain that a diary is a record a person keeps to tell what (s)he is doing. Have students keep a diary that shows how many fruits they eat for one week. The recommended number of servings from the fruit group for students of this age group is three servings each day. Have students write the names of fruits they eat each day. Their parent can help them keep track of the fruits eaten by helping them record the information. Review the student diaries after a week.

Student Master

A Smile Or A Frown

Name _____

Dear Parent,

Your child is learning about healthful foods to eat. Your child is learning that foods high in sugar, fats, and salt should be avoided and that healthful foods should be eaten. There are many different kinds of foods listed on this sheet. Have your child determine whether the food pictured is healthful and nutritious or harmful and not nutritious. Next to each food is a face that has no mouth. Have your child draw a smile (‿) for the mouth if the food is healthful. Have your child draw a frown (⁀) for the mouth if the food is not nutritious. Have your child provide you with reasons why (s)he made his/her particular choice.

Apple   **Carrot**

Potato Chips   **Skim Milk**

Bread   **Chocolate**

Student Master

My Fruit Diary

Name _____

Write the names of the fruits you eat each day.
Ask a parent or adult to help you.
Try to eat 3 fruits each day.

Monday _____

_____

Tuesday _____

_____

Wednesday _____

_____

Thursday _____

_____

Friday _____

_____

Saturday _____

_____

Sunday _____

_____

Teeth With A Bite

Health Education Standards:

- Students will comprehend health promotion and disease prevention concepts.
- Students will demonstrate the ability to use goal-setting and decision-making skills that enhance health.

Performance Indicators:

- Students will recognize the relationship between personal health behaviors and individual well-being.
- Students will recognize that health problems should be detected and treated early.
- Students will set a personal health goal and make progress toward its achievement.

Life Skills:

- I will follow a dental health plan.
- *I will care for my body systems. (Growth and Development)*

Materials:

Student Master, "Which Do My Teeth Need?"; Student Master, "How I Care for My Teeth"; transparency projector; carrot; a large photo from a magazine that highlights the face of a person who has a nice smile with teeth very evident (make two transparencies of this picture and in one of the transparencies, darken several teeth so it appears that this person lost some teeth)

Motivation:

1 Tell the class that you are going to review three reasons why having

healthy teeth is important. Begin by having a student come to the front of the room. Ask this student to take a bite of the carrot and then chew what is insider his/her mouth. Then tell this student to pretend (s)he has no teeth and to take another bite of the carrot. To pretend that this student has no teeth, ask him/her to place his/her lips over his/her front teeth. Then ask this student to take another bite of the carrot. The student not be able to bite the carrot because the teeth are covered by his/her lips. Explain to the students that they just observed what it would be like not to be able to bite due to missing teeth. Ask the students, "What is one purpose of teeth?" (One purpose of teeth is to help people chew food.)

2 Discuss the second purpose of teeth. Show students the transparency of a person who has a wide smile with bright, clean teeth. Ask students, "What do you notice about this person?" (Students will indicate this person has a nice smile or a nice appearance.) Then show the students the next transparency of the same person. Explain that this person decided not to care for his/her teeth, as shown by the darkened spaces that show missing teeth. Then ask the students, "What do you think about this person's appearance?" (Students will probably laugh at first and then say this person does not have a nice appearance.) Explain that another purpose of teeth is to help people have a nice appearance. It is important to recognize that many students in your class have lost or are losing teeth. Remind students that everyone loses their baby or primary teeth. Emphasize that this is normal and that boys and girls who lose their teeth still look cute. But you want your students to understand that it is important to

405

keep their adult or permanent teeth. The person in the picture lost his/her permanent teeth.

3 Review the third purpose of teeth. Tell students you want them to say the following tongue-twister. "She sells seashells by the seashore." Have the class repeat this statement with you. Now have students pretend they lost their teeth and place their lips over their front teeth. After students do this, have them repeat the tongue-twister again. Then ask students, "Why couldn't I understand what you were saying?" (Students will indicate that they could not speak clearly when they had teeth missing.) Thus, you can indicate that another purpose of teeth is to help people speak clearly.

4 You can use this activity to reinforce that there are behaviors students can follow to help insure that their teeth remain healthy. Emphasize that students should brush their teeth after meals, floss every evening, avoid sticky and sweet foods that stick to the teeth, and eat dairy products such as milk and yogurt that help keep teeth hard.

5 Distribute the Student Master "How I Care for My Teeth" and encourage students to record their healthful dental practices.

Evaluation:

Provide students with a copy of the Student Master "Which Do My Teeth Need?" Have students color the products that are healthful for teeth. Have students place an X through those products that are not healthful for teeth. Evaluate the students' papers for accuracy. Also, have students share their masters with a parent.

"She sells seashells by the seashore."

Which Do My Teeth Need?

Name _____

Dear Parent,
Your child is learning about dental health. Your child has learned healthful behaviors that are important for dental health. (S)he has learned that it is important to brush twice each day, floss each day, eat foods high in calcium such as milk products including yogurt and cheese, and avoid foods that contain large amounts of sugar and that stick to teeth. Check your child's work on this page. Your child should color the pictures that show something healthful related to teeth, and your child should place a large X through the pictures that show something that is not healthful for teeth.

Dental Floss　　**Toothbrush**　　**Candy**

Milk　　**Marshmallows**

Cheese

How I Care For My Teeth

Name _____

Dear Parent,
Your child is learning the importance of following good dental health practices. Your child should brush his/her teeth at least two times each day and eat foods high in calcium, such as foods that contain milk. Help your child keep this diary by helping him/her enter the requested information. Keep this diary for one week.

Place a check in the appropriate block each time you brush your teeth that day.

Monday	Tuesday	Wednesday	Thursday	Friday	Saturday	Sunday

List the names of foods you eat each day that help your teeth.

Monday _____

Tuesday _____

Wednesday _____

Thursday _____

Friday _____

Saturday _____

Sunday _____

Bagged Lungs

Health Education Standards:

- Students will demonstrate the ability to practice health-enhancing behaviors and reduce health risks.
- Students will demonstrate the ability to use effective interpersonal communication skills that enhance health.

Performance Indicators:

- Students will identify behaviors that are safe, risky, or harmful to self and others.
- Students will demonstrate refusal skills.

Life Skills:

- I will not use tobacco products.
- I will remain safe and drug-free.
- I will use resistance skills when pressured to use drugs.

Materials:

Teaching Master, "Smoky Lungs"; transparency projector; cigarettes; two clear plastic sandwich bags; two straws; cotton balls; tape

Motivation:

1 Explain to students they will observe how harmful ingredients from cigarette smoke can harm the lungs. To review how the lungs function, take a clear plastic sandwich bag and stuff cotton balls inside. Insert a straw through the top of the bag. Wrap the top of the bag around the bottom of the straw about one inch from the bottom of the straw. Tape the wrapped bag around the straw to form a lung (bag) with the windpipe (straw) going inside. At this point, the connection between the straw and the bag should be airtight.

2 To prepare for this experiment, construct another plastic bag lung at home. Find a person who smokes. When (s)he is ready to smoke a cigarette, ask that person to smoke the cigarette without inhaling the smoke. Do not use a cigarette that has a filter tip. Have the person blow the smoke from the cigarette through the straw into the bag with cotton. Each time the person blows smoke into the bag, squeeze the bag so that the smoke is released. After doing this procedure for two cigarettes, you will notice that the cotton balls become brown due to the deposit of tar from the cigarette smoke. Bring this bag to class.

3 Show students the clean plastic bag lung containing fresh cotton. Explain to students how a lung works. Explain that the cotton balls represent air sacs inside the lungs and that the air sacs hold fresh air that is carried throughout the body by the blood. The bag is the lung and the straw is the windpipe. Blow a puff of air into the lungs through the windpipe. Have students observe how the lung inflates or becomes bigger. You can also have the class observe how you inhale and notice that your chest cavity expands. Now squeeze the air out of the lung through the windpipe. Students will notice that the lung deflates and becomes smaller. Have students observe how you exhale and how your chest becomes smaller because the air is escaping from your lungs. Explain that the lung you have shown students is clean. The lung has not been exposed to tobacco, not specifically cigarette smoke.

4 Show the bag you prepared with cigarette smoke to the class and have students observe this lung. Students will notice that the cotton inside is brown. Explain that the cotton, or air sacs, inside that lung changed colors due to smoke that entered the lungs from a cigarette. Explain that cigarette smoke contains tar which is a dark, sticky substance. Explain that the smoke from only two cigarettes was blown into the lung. Tell students that when a person smokes, the tar from the cigarette smoke begins to cover the lungs. This can cause a person to have difficulty breathing. It also can cause a person to develop many kinds of illnesses.

5 You can pass the bag representing the smoker's lung around the room and ask students to smell the contents of the lung through the opening of the straw. Students will notice that an awful odor is emitted. Explain to students that the lung you passed around contained the ingredients from only two cigarettes. Tell students that smokers may smoke a pack or more of cigarettes each day for many years. A pack of cigarettes contains twenty cigarettes. Have students imagine how the lungs of someone who smokes a pack of cigarettes each day might look.

6 Review the harmful effects of tobacco on the body. Explain that it harms the lungs. It causes many different kinds of illnesses. You can also mention that smoking harms the heart as well as the throat and many other body parts. It makes the teeth yellow and it causes an unpleasant odor.

7 Show the Teaching Master "Smoky Lungs." Have students visualize smoke from a cigarette entering the lung by moving from the mouth, down the windpipe, and into the lungs.

Evaluation:

Take a large trash bag and tell students to imagine you are holding a large lung. Provide each student with a sheet of white paper. Tell students you would like them to draw a picture of something healthful a person could do instead of smoking. They might also draw a picture showing the use of resistance skills to say NO to pressure to use tobacco. Students are to write their name on their paper. Then have each student roll the sheet of paper around so that it appears they have made a large cigarette. Tell students you want them to roll their papers so that their pictures are on the inside. Tape the students' papers so that they stay in the shape of a cigarette. Explain to students that they have just created cigarette tips. They are to place their "cigarette tips" inside the large trash bag. Have each student pick out a cigarette from the bag (lung). They are to read the name of the person whose picture they have chosen and then describe what "healthful tip" is inside the picture. Use this opportunity to have students share positive activities people can do instead of smoking.

Teaching Master
Smoky Lungs

Friend Or Foe?

Health Education Standards:

- Students will comprehend health promotion and disease prevention concepts.
- Students will demonstrate the ability to practice health-enhancing behaviors and reduce health risks.

Performance Indicators:

- Students will identify the most common health problems of children.
- Students will recognize that many injuries and illnesses can be prevented and treated.
- Students will demonstrate strategies to improve or maintain personal health.

Life Skills:

- I will recognize that some diseases are communicable while others are noncommunicable.
- I will choose behaviors to reduce my risk of cancer.

Materials:

The poem, *Friend or Foe?;* sunglasses; hat; two umbrellas; long-sleeved shirt that buttons up the front; sunscreen with SPF; a sheet of yellow construction paper that has been cut into the shape of the sun; a white sheet of paper cut into the shape of the moon; a grey sheet of paper cut into the shape of a large raindrop

Motivation:

1 Begin the lesson by taping the paper sun, moon, and large raindrop on the chalkboard. Explain to students that

these are three of their friends. Ask them why each is a friend. Why is the sun a friend? (The sun can keep you warm. You can play outside when it is sunny. You might go swimming when it is sunny.) Why is the moon a friend? (When the moon shines, you can see the sky. It is beautiful. The moon means it is bedtime and you can get some sleep.) Why is rain your friend? (The rain gives flowers and grass a drink of water. The rain fills up lakes and rivers with water. Some people like to swim in the lake. Some people take boats on the lake.)

2 Explain to students that you are going to read them a poem about one of these three friends. The poem is called *Friend or Foe?* A foe is someone who might harm you. Ask them to listen carefully to guess which of these friends might also harm them. After you have read the poem, ask the students if the foe was the sun, the moon, or the raindrop. (The sun can be both a friend and a foe.) What might harm them? (The sun's rays might harm them.) The sun's rays can harm the skin. The skin covers the body and is made of cells. A cell is the smallest part of a person's body. The sun can change the cells in harmful ways. Then a person gets skin cancer. Skin cancer is harmful changes in the skin.

3 Explain that there are ways to keep the skin safe from too much sun. Show students the following: hat, umbrella, long-sleeved shirt, and sunscreen with SPF. Explain how each of these keeps the sun from the skin. Although there is hair on the head, the sun's rays can still reach the skin. The hat covers the head and keeps the skin on the head from getting too much sun. The hat also keeps sun off the face. (Put the hat on.) The umbrella can also keep the sun away from the skin. Look at how much of my skin is covered by the umbrella. If I put on this long-sleeved shirt, I also keep the sun from my skin. The long-sleeved shirt keeps my arms, shoulders, and back from getting too much sun. (Put on the long-sleeved shirt.)

4 Now show students the sunscreen. Show them the letters SPF. Explain that **SPF** means sun protection factor. SPF is something in sunscreen that keeps the sun from harming the skin. An SPF rating is a number. It might be an 8, or a 15, a 25, or a 30. The higher the number the more it keeps the sun from harming the skin. (Thirty keeps more sun from the skin than does 8.) Take a drop of sunscreen and rub it on your arm. Tell the students that using sunscreen when you are going to be outside on sunny days keeps the sun from harming your skin.

5 Finally, explain that they will want to protect their eyes from the sun too. Too much sun can harm the eyes. You can put on the sunglasses.

Evaluation:

Divide the students into five groups. Give each group one of your props: hat, long-sleeved shirt, sunglasses, umbrella, and sunscreen. Begin with group one and say, "I am going to be in the sun so I will wear..." They are to answer, "My hat." Then begin again, "I am going to be in the sun so I will wear..." Groups one and two say, "My hat." And group two is to add, "and long-sleeved shirt." Begin again, "I am going to be in the sun so I will wear..." Groups one, two, and three say, "My hat and long-sleeved shirt." And group three adds, "and my sunglasses." Repeat. Groups one, two, three, and four will say, "My hat, my long-sleeved shirt, and my sunglasses." Group four will add, "my umbrella." Repeat, and groups one, two, three, four, and five will say, "My hat, my long-sleeved shirt, my sunglasses, and my umbrella." Group five will add, "and, my sunscreen." Repeat again, "I am going to be in the sun so I will use..." All five groups will respond, "My hat, long-sleeved shirt, sunglasses, umbrella, and sunscreen."

Friend Or Foe?

❖❖❖❖❖❖❖

I greet you in the morning
and watch you through the day.
When you look and see me,
you want to come and play.

I give you warmth and light
and help you tell the time.
I like to see you run and jump
and be a friend of mine.

But if you stay and play
and spend some time with me,
you must take special care
or you'll be unhappy.

Because while I mark the time
and keep you nice and warm,

You cannot keep safe from me
or the rays I send that harm.

Staying Below The Smoke Line

Health Education Standard:

- Students will demonstrate the ability to practice health-enhancing behaviors and reduce health risks.

Performance Indicators:

- Students will develop injury prevention strategies for personal health.
- Students will distinguish between threatening and nonthreatening circumstances.

Life Skills:

- I will follow safety rules in my home.
- I will follow safety guidelines for different weather conditions and natural disasters.
- *I will be concerned about environmental issues. (Environmental Health)*

Materials:

Student Master, "Five Fire Facts"; several mats from the gymnasium (or you may take your class to the gymnasium)

Motivation:

1 Ask students if they have ever seen smoke from a fire or smokestack. Ask students what they noticed about the smoke. Students should say smoke usually rises. Explain that warm air rises. Smoke is in the air. Smoke rises with the air. Explain that this lesson is about being safe when in a fire. Explain that many deaths due to home fires result not from burns, but from smoke that is inhaled. Therefore, it is important to know what to do in case students may need to escape from a fire and its smoke.

2 Have students imagine they are surrounded by smoke. Ask them what they should do. Students would need to keep low to the ground so that they are below the line of smoke. Bring mats to class (or bring your students to the gymnasium.) Lay several mats on the floor. Explain to students that they are to get down on their hands and knees (demonstrate this) and crawl. Have students pretend that they are escaping from a fire and there is smoke above. Tell students to crawl on their hands and knees from one end of the mats to the other.

3 There are many other safety rules students should know if they are trying to escape from a fire. If they are trying to get out of a room but must open a door to do so, explain that they need to feel the door before they open it. If the door feels hot, they are not to open it. Fire could burst into where they are if they open the door. If they can, they should get to a window. They can scream "fire." Each student's family should also have fire escape plans for their homes and practice family fire drills at least twice each year. People need to practice escape routes and plan a place to meet outside the home. If people meet at the assigned place, everyone will know that all people have escaped safely. If someone is not at the meeting place, firefighters can be told that someone may yet be inside the home.

4 Review the following poem with students and have them say it with you. The title of the poem is "Five Fire Facts."

Five fire facts can help you be,
Fabulous, safe, and healthy.

First, you need to understand,
In smoke you crawl and do not
stand.

Second, you don't open a door
that's hot,
For escaping from fire, you will
not.

Third, you need to have a plan,
So you can escape as quickly as
you can.

Fourth, you'll need to pick a spot,
Outside the house, where it's not
fiery hot.

Fifth, and finally, have fire drills,
So you can practice your fire escape
skills.

5 This poem is on the Student Master "Five Fire Facts." Have students take the master home and share with their parents and other significant adults what they have learned in school. Students can encourage their parents to practice fire safety in the home.

Evaluation:

Read the first line of each part of the poem to students. Then have students say the second line. As they say this, they will be reinforcing the safety tips they learned. Ask students what conditions might cause fires in the home. (unsafe wiring, heaters, open flames, natural disasters such as earthquakes that cause gas leaks, etc.) Also ask them to identify sources of smoke in their community and to make suggestions for reducing the amount of smoke.

Student Master

Five Fire Facts

Dear Parent,

Your child has been learning about fire safety. The poem that follows has been used in class to teach about fire safety. Specifically, this poem focuses on escaping from a fire. Read this poem aloud with your child and review the five facts in this poem with him/her. It is important that you and your family have a fire escape plan for your home. It is recommended by firefighters to practice fire drills in your home. Take this opportunity to work with your child to make a fire escape plan for your home.

"Five Fire Facts"

Five fire facts can help you be,
Fabulous, safe, and healthy.

First, you need to understand,
In smoke you crawl and do not stand.

Second, you don't open a door that's hot,
For escaping from fire, you will not.

Third, you need to have a plan,
So you can escape as quickly as you can.

Fourth, you'll need to pick a spot,
Outside the house, where it's not fiery hot.

Fifth, and finally, have fire drills,
So you can practice your fire escape skills.

Don't Forget To Floss

Health Education Standards:

- Students will demonstrate the ability to access valid health information and appropriate health products and services.
- Students will analyze the impact of culture, media, technology, and other factors on health.

Performance Indicators:

- Students will identify factors that determine the reliability of health information, products, and services.
- Students will compare health information from a variety of appropriate sources.
- Students will describe ways technology can influence health.

Life Skills:

- I will choose sources of health-related information, products, and services wisely.
- *I will be well-groomed. (Personal Health)*
- *I will follow a dental health plan. (Personal Health)*

Materials:

Student Master, "A Flossing I Will Go"; a shoe box; thick colorful strip of yarn that is about 18" in length; scissor; a gumdrop

Motivation:

1 To prepare for this strategy, make a model set of teeth from a shoe box. Take the bottom of a shoe box and turn it on its side. On the actual bottom side of the shoe box, trace teeth from one end to the other.

Then cut slits between the teeth so that the bottom of the shoe box becomes a set of teeth. Bring the shoe box to class.

2 Discuss the importance of brushing teeth. It is also important to discuss the fact that when people eat food, they get food caught between their teeth. Sometimes brushing with a toothbrush cannot remove food that is lodged between the teeth. Explain that one way to remove food that is stuck between teeth is to use dental floss. **Floss** is a thin, stringlike substance that is slid between teeth. Using floss helps loosen and remove food trapped between teeth.

3 Tell students that you are going to demonstrate how to use floss by using yarn and the shoe box that you made into a set of teeth. Show students a strip of yarn that is approximately 18" in length. Explain that they can use floss in strips of about the same length as the yarn. Wrap the floss several times around each index finger and slide it between two teeth. First, slide the floss up and down the side of one tooth pulling the floss slightly in the direction of that tooth. Then slide the floss along the side of the other

tooth pulling it slightly to the side of that tooth. To make your demonstration easier, you can ask a student to help you by holding the shoe box as you demonstrate the flossing technique.

4 Explain that there are different kinds of floss. Some people have very tight teeth so that they may need a kind of floss that is waxed. Other people may want a kind of floss that does not have wax and can be used when teeth are not as close to one another.

5 Select student volunteers to come up to the front of the room and demonstrate the proper flossing technique that you demonstrated. Be sure they slide the floss up and down the side of the teeth.

Evaluation:

Distribute the Student Master "A Flossing I Will Go." Have students complete a smiling face on each tooth in the master for each day they floss. They are to draw a smile if they flossed or a frown if they did not floss. One tooth is drawn for each day of the week. Ask students to describe the proper way to floss teeth. Then ask them why flossing is important. (Their teeth will be clean, and students will be practicing good dental health.)

Student Master

A Flossing I Will Go

Name _____

Draw a smile (⌣) on the tooth if you flossed that day.
Draw a frown (⌢) on the tooth if you did not floss that day.

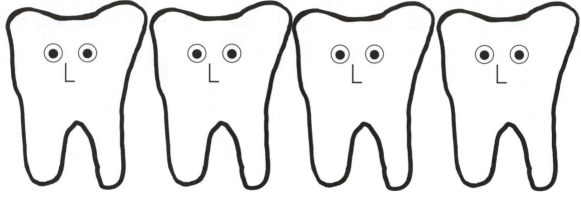

Monday   **Tuesday**   **Wednesday**   **Thursday**

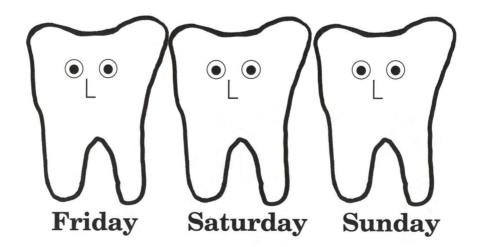

Friday   **Saturday**   **Sunday**

Messy Things

Health Education Standard:

- Students will comprehend health promotion and disease prevention concepts.

Performance Indicator:

- Students will identify the impact of the environment on personal health.

Life Skill:

- I will dispose of solid waste properly.

Materials:

The poem, *Messy Things*; globe; 3" x 5" index cards; crayons or markers; butcher paper

Motivation:

1 Show students a globe and tell them it is a model of the Earth. Let students examine the globe as you point out the areas that show water and the areas that show land. Explain that we often refer to the world as our home. Ask students what they think that means. (We live on Earth. All people share a home.) Ask students what they might do to take care of their home and keep it clean. (They might clean up after themselves; they might not litter.) Point out that it is easier to get sick or have accidents in a messy home.

2 Read the poem aloud. Ask students to name messy things they have seen around the school. (papers on the streets, bottles and cans left on the ground). Ask students what might

happen if no one cared about keeping the Earth clean. (It might get messier and messier). Explain that people use trash cans to help keep the Earth clean. Tell students that putting trash where it belongs helps keep the world clean.

3 Take students on a short nature walk around the school neighborhood. Have them pay attention as they breathe in the fresh air. Explain that people, plants, and animals need fresh air and clean water to grow. Then send students on a litter patrol around the school. Tell students to observe what kinds of trash they see around the school grounds. Tell students not to touch the trash. (It is important that students do not touch any items they see on the ground because the items may be harmful.) When you return to the classroom, make a class list of the kinds of trash they saw.

4 Write the word pollution on the board. Read it aloud and then invite the class to read it along with you. Explain that pollution is dirt and gases that make the Earth's water and air unsafe. Allow students who know examples of pollution to share what they know. Ask students what might happen if the air and water are dirty. (People might get sick. Plants and flowers might die.)

Evaluation:

Review the list of kinds of litter students saw. Have students draw a picture using color markers or crayons of one of the pieces of litter that is on the list, or of another piece of litter that might be found on the ground. While students are drawing, tape a large piece of butcher paper on the wall. On the butcher paper draw a picture of a large trash can. Over the trash can write "Our class

knows where litter belongs!"
or "Our class helps keep the Earth
clean!" Have each student tape his/
her picture of litter inside the trash
can to show that they know the
proper way to dispose of solid waste.
Also have students discuss which
types of trash are suitable for
recycling.

Messy Things

❖❖❖❖❖

Messy things do bother me—
A can along the street,
a wrapper on the ground.
It's sad to think the Earth
   should see
Such messy things around.

My friends and I can keep
   things clean—
the bottles with the glass,
the litter where it goes.
We want the world all blue and
   green
So that its beauty shows.

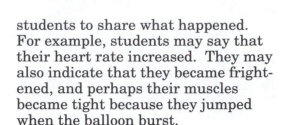

Physical Stress

Health Education Standards:

- Students will comprehend health promotion and disease prevention concepts.
- Students will demonstrate the ability to practice health-enhancing behaviors and reduce health risks.

Performance Indicators:

- Students will identify the most common health problems of children.
- Students will develop ways to manage common sources of stress for children.

Life Skills:

- I will practice stress management and suicide prevention skills.
- *I will keep my immune system healthy. (Communicable and Chronic Diseases)*

Materials:

Teaching Master, "The Effects Of Stress on the Body"; transparency projector; inflated balloon; a pin

Motivation:

1 Before the class enters, blow up a balloon and keep it under your desk out of sight of your students. After the students are sitting at their desks and are quiet, reach under your desk. Using a pin, burst the balloon. Obviously, there will be a loud noise and the students will be startled momentarily.

2 Explain to students that when the balloon burst, certain things happened inside their bodies. Ask

students to share what happened. For example, students may say that their heart rate increased. They may also indicate that they became frightened, and perhaps their muscles became tight because they jumped when the balloon burst.

3 Explain that when the balloon burst, they were temporarily stunned and reactions occurred inside their bodies. They were feeling the effects of stress. Explain that certain physical changes such as increased heart rate occur with stress. Explain that everyone experiences stress and that the body changes when stress occurs. Other physical signs that indicate a person is feeling stress may be sweating, having a dry mouth, feeling tired, and not being able to go to sleep.

4 Explain that there are many different causes of stress. Have students share ways stress may be caused in their lives. For example, they may have an argument with a friend; they may argue with a family member; their parents may have an argument; they may be moving to another neighborhood; they may be called a name by a friend. These are some reasons that a person may feel stress.

5 Explain that there are ways to deal with stress. How stress is handled may depend on the cause of the stress. For example, if a student has an argument with a friend, (s)he can speak to the friend to settle their differences. A counselor at school may help a student who is feeling the effects of stress. Ask students what they would do if they were called names by friends. Some answers may center around telling a friend that you feel hurt when you are called a name and asking the friend to stop. You may choose to discuss other reasons why a person might feel stress and how stress can be handled healthfully.

6 Show the Teaching Master "The Effects Of Stress On The Body." Review the physical effects of stress on the body, shown on the Teaching Master. The pupils of the eyes widen. The **pupil** is the dark circle in the eye that opens and closes to control light. The heartbeat rate speeds up. The person may sweat. The stomach may feel tied up in knots. The muscles in the body may tighten. The mouth becomes dry. Explain that these all are signs of stress.

Evaluation:

Identify different situations that might cause stress for the students. Some examples may be: forgetting to

do homework, not having enough money to buy something that is needed; having feelings hurt by a friend; worrying about a family member who is ill; having a new baby in the family. Have students share ways to deal with each of these stressors. Remind students that dealing effectively with stress helps them maintain good health.

Inclusion:

Students with special needs can identify stressors they experience and share healthful ways to manage these stressors. For example, a student who is hearing impaired might feel stress when students place their hands in front of their mouths and talk. It is difficult to read lips. The student might ask other students to speak clearly, look directly at him/her, and avoid having anything in front of the mouth.

The Effects Of Stress On The Body

The pupils of the eyes widen.

The mouth becomes dry.

The muscles tighten.

The heartbeat rate increases.

The stomach feels tied up in knots.

Peaceful Flakes

Health Education Standards:

- Students will demonstrate the ability to practice health-enhancing behaviors and reduce health risks.
- Students will demonstrate the ability to use effective interpersonal communication skills that enhance health.

Performance Indicators:

- Students will generate ways to avoid threatening situations.
- Students will explain how to get assistance in threatening circumstances.
- Students will utilize nonviolent procedure to resolve conflicts in school.

Life Skills:

- I will practice conflict resolution skills.
- I will recognize harmful relationships.

Materials:

Teaching Master, "Handling Disagreements"; transparency projector; empty cereal box (or shoe box) for each student; crayons; construction paper

Motivation:

1 To prepare for this strategy, have students bring an empty cereal box from home. (An empty shoe box also could be used.)

2 Introduce the term conflict. A **conflict** is a disagreement between two or more people or between two or more choices. Explain that it is common for people to have occasional disagreements. The important thing is to learn how to respond to disagreements in healthful and responsible ways. A person can learn skills to resolve disagreements without getting angry and getting into a fight.

3 Explain that you are going to suggest some skills for handling disagreements without getting into a fight. Use the Teaching Master "Handling Disagreements," to discuss these skills with students:

- **Stay calm.** Speak softly. Do not get excited.
- **Be polite.** Show others that you want to treat them respectfully.
- **Take time to cool down.** If you are feeling angry, take time to get over the anger before you do anything.
- **Share your feelings.** Tell the other person why you feel the way you do about the disagreement.
- **Don't use putdowns.** A putdown is a remark about another person that is not nice.
- **Listen to the other person.** Listen and try to understand why the other person disagrees with you.
- **Pretend you are the other person.** Imagine that you are the other person. This often helps to understand that person's feelings.
- **Ask an adult to help.** Adults, such as a parent or a teacher, are available to help settle a disagreement.
- **Let others know when you are wrong.** If you take time to stay calm or to cool down, you may realize that you have made a mistake. When you admit that you are wrong, the disagreement will be ended.
- **Run away if someone threatens you or insists on fighting.** Realize that you might be harmed if you continue the disagreement.

4 Explain to students that they are going to design a box for a new kind of cereal. The name of the cereal is "Peaceful Flakes." Explain that the "Peaceful Flakes" are going to represent ways of handling disagreements without fighting. Give a sheet of construction paper to each student. Students are to design the words and pictures that will appear on the box for the new cereal, including the name and the kinds of "flakes," which are skills to handle disagreements without fighting. After they have finished their designs, they will paste the new design on one side of their empty cereal box. Students may add additional "flakes." Ask for volunteers to share their new cereal boxes with the class.

Evaluation:

Share examples of disagreements, such as two students who want the same book from the school library. As you state each example, call on students to choose a "flake" that would be a way to handle the disagreement without fighting. Students should demonstrate that they recognize harmful relationships and that they seek to resolve conflicts.

Teaching Master

Handling Disagreements

1. Stay calm.

2. Be polite.

3. Take time to cool down.

4. Share your feelings.

5. Do not use putdowns.

6. Listen to the other person.

7. Pretend you are the other person.

8. Ask an adult for help.

9. Let others know when you are wrong.

10. Run away if someone threatens you or insists on fighting.

My Puppy

Health Education Standards:

- Students will demonstrate the ability to use effective interpersonal communication skills that enhance health.

Performance Indicators:

- Students will express needs, wants, and feelings appropriately.
- Students will demonstrate ways to communicate care, consideration, and respect of self and others.

Life Skill:

- I will share my feelings about death and dying.

Materials:

The poem, *My Puppy*; construction paper; paper; crayons or markers; stapler

Motivation:

1 Ask students what happens when something dies. (Students might say it stops breathing, it stops growing, it is not alive anymore). Explain to students that dying is a natural part of life. Point out that the cycle of life is that living things are born (or sprout), grow, and die.

2 Read the poem aloud and ask students how they would feel if their puppy died. (Students might say sad, lonely.) Ask students what the child in the poem did in order feel better. (Students will say the child talked to a friend and told her how (s)he missed the dogs.) Explain that often when

we feel sad, talking and/or crying helps us to feel better. Point out that when something very sad happens, such as when a pet dies, it is healthy to cry.

3 Tell students that when a person has sad feelings, sharing those feelings is the best way to start to feel better. Ask students why they think this might be true. (Students might say that other people have had sad feelings too and they might help, or that sometimes just talking about what happened can help us understand it better.)

Evaluation:

Write the poem on the board. Provide several sheets of paper for students and have them draw a picture to illustrate the poem. Help students copy the appropriate lines of the poem under the picture they drew. Have students use another sheet of paper to draw a picture of a person who they can talk to about their questions about death. Staple the sheets of paper inside a construction paper cover and have students design a cover for their book. Allow time for students to share their books and their ideas with a friend.

My Puppy

I loved my puppy.

A sunny, yellow, friendly dog.

and then one day, he died.

I didn't know

I didn't know

My yellow dog would die and go.

And when I knew,

I cried.

I found a friend

a gentle, caring kind of friend.

She listened and I let her.

I talked to her.

I talked to her.

I said I missed my puppy's fur

And when she knew,

I felt better.

Pyramid Relay

Health Education Standards:

- Students will comprehend health promotion and disease prevention concepts.
- Students will demonstrate the ability to advocate for family and community health.

Performance Indicators:

- Students will recognize the relationship between personal health behaviors and individual well-being.
- Students will identify methods of health promotion.
- Students will describe a variety of methods to convey accurate health information and ideas.

Life Skills:

- I will select the appropriate number of servings from The Food Guide Pyramid.
- I will maintain my desirable weight.

Materials:

Student Master, "The Food Guide Pyramid"; tape; legal size envelopes; two paper bags, index card (two sets, each set a different color); markers; chalk

Motivation:

1 Use the Student Master "The Food Guide Pyramid" as a guide for this teaching strategy. Review the information about how different foods are grouped. Then follow the outline of the Food Guide Pyramid by drawing the outline of the food triangle on the chalkboard. Label the names of the food groups on the outside of the pyramid as shown on the master. Inside the pyramid that is drawn on the chalkboard, write the correct number of servings of foods needed each day. Within each of six areas on the pyramid, tape a legal size envelope.

2 Write the names of the following foods on index cards, using one card per food. Write the name of each food twice—once on one color index card, and once on the other color card. The cards will correlate to the correct number of servings for foods in each of the areas on the pyramid. You will have eleven index cards for the Bread, Cereal, Rice, and Pasta Group. The eleven food items for this group would include: brown rice, whole wheat bread, corn flakes, oatmeal, spaghetti, pita bread, lo mein noodles, barley, cracked wheat, bagel, and tortilla. The five servings in the Vegetable Group would include: carrots, potatoes, broccoli, green beans, and peas. Four servings from the Fruit Group would include: grapes, apples, kiwi fruit, and banana. Three servings from the Milk, Yogurt, and Cheese Group would include: skim milk, yogurt, and cheddar cheese. Three servings from the Meat, Poultry, Fish, Dry Beans, Eggs and Nuts Group include: beef, turkey, and cashew nuts. Foods eaten sparingly in the Fats, Oils, and Sweets Group would include: chocolate candy, cookies, and potato chips.

3 Place each set of index cards into a grocery bag. The two grocery bags will be in the front of the room. Divide the class into two teams. Team 1 and Team 2 will line up in single file. When you say, "go," the race will begin. The first student in each team will run to the bag in front of his/her line. The student will pull a card from the bag, read it, and place it in the correct envelope. (If a student cannot read a word, you may help that student.) Thus, a student who pulls "banana" will place this card in the envelope that is attached to the fruit group. When the student completes this task, (s)he will run back to the line and tag the next student in line. This continues until one team finishes.

4 The envelopes are now checked to be sure the foods were placed in the correct food groups. The team that finished first will get fifteen points and the team that finished second will get ten points. In addition, each food placed in the correct envelope will earn two points for that team. (You can determine the team who earns or loses points by checking the color of the index card.) For each card placed incorrectly in the envelope, you will subtract two points from the team's total points. As you check each envelope, review the foods and the correct food groups. Some foods identified are less common than other foods. Allow students to ask questions about the different kinds of foods with which they may not be as familiar. Remember to include information about the foods in the Fats, Oils, and Sweets Group. Explain that foods from this groups should be eaten sparingly.

Evaluation:

Distribute a copy of the Student Master "The Food Guide Pyramid" to each student. Each student is to draw pictures of different foods his/her family eats so that the food falls inside the correct group on the master. Have students share their pictures. This is a good time to discuss the number of servings and how to maintain desirable weight. It is also a good time to identify foods that may be specific to different cultures. You may follow up by having a "healthful snack day" and have students bring foods to class that are healthful. You also may follow up by having a "foods from different cultures day" and have students bring ethnic foods related.

Inclusion:

If you have a student in your class who is in a wheelchair, ask another student to serve as a runner. The student in the wheelchair will stay near the bag and will tell the runner where to place the card.

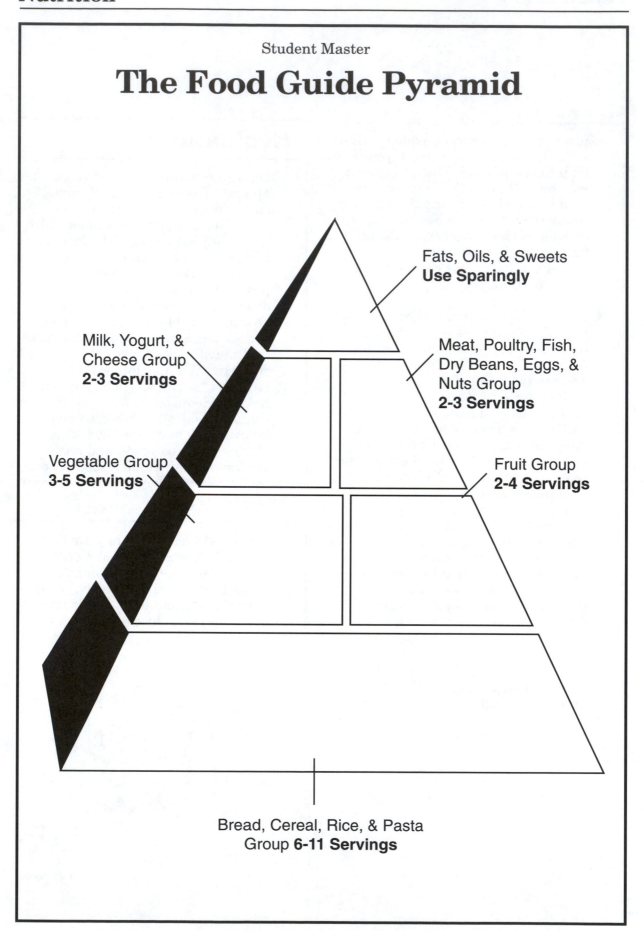

The Food Guide Pyramid

Fats, Oils, & Sweets
Use Sparingly

Milk, Yogurt, &
Cheese Group
2-3 Servings

Meat, Poultry, Fish,
Dry Beans, Eggs, &
Nuts Group
2-3 Servings

Vegetable Group
3-5 Servings

Fruit Group
2-4 Servings

Bread, Cereal, Rice, & Pasta
Group **6-11 Servings**

Check Me Out

Health Education Standards:

- Students will demonstrate the ability to access valid health information and appropriate health products and services.
- Students will demonstrate the ability to practice health-enhancing behaviors and reduce health risks.

Performance Indicators:

- Students will demonstrate the ability to locate school and community health helpers.
- Students will develop an awareness of personal health needs.
- Students will demonstrate strategies to improve or maintain personal health.

Life Skills:

- I will care for my ears and eyes.
- I will have regular checkups.
- *I will use school nurse and school health services when appropriate. (Consumer and Community Health)*

Materials:

The poem, *Check Me Out*; Student Master, "The Checkup"; pencils or crayons

Motivation

1 Tell students you are going to read them a poem titled *Check Me Out*. This poem is about having a checkup. A **checkup** helps a doctor learn about the health of your body. Read the poem out loud. Ask students if they have had a checkup.

2 Give students a copy of the Student Master "The Checkup." Read the

poem again. After you read each of the following lines, stop. Have students find the correct picture on "The Checkup" and circle it.

- waiting while I get weighed (circle the scale)
- sitting for my pressure (circle the blood pressure cuff)
- I'm still with the thermometer (circle the thermometer)
- looks at my throat (circle the tongue depresser)
- She listens to my breath (circle the stethoscope)
- She looks in my ears (circle the otoscope)

3 Review the following information about checkups with students. When you go to the doctor, the doctor may measure you. **Height** is a measure of how tall you are. The doctor wants to know how fast you are growing. **Weight** is a measure of how heavy you are. The doctor wants to know if

you are at a healthful weight. The doctor shines a light into your eyes to check them. The doctor may ask you to read letters on a chart to learn how well you see. The doctor shines a light into your ears to check them. The doctor will look to see if there is too much wax in your ears. This can keep you from hearing. The doctor may ask you to listen for sounds and raise your hand when you hear them. The doctor wants to know if you can hear well. The doctor will listen to your lungs. You will be asked to take a deep breath and blow out. The doctor also listens to your heart to see if your heart is healthy.

Evaluation

Tell students that they will want to have regular medical checkups. Have students use the Student Master "The Checkup." Ask them to tell what a doctor does during the checkup. They are to take turns pointing to one of the pictures on the Student Master and saying one of the following: checks to see how much I weigh, listens to my blood pressure, takes my temperature, looks in my throat, listens to my lungs, checks my ears.

Check Me Out

by Patricia M. Dashiell

Sitting and waiting,
that's what I do.
Sitting and waiting,
outside on the chairs,
inside on the table.

It's boring on the chairs.
It's cold on the table.
I sit, and I wait.

Sitting and waiting,
that's what I do,
sitting and waiting.
Then, she walks in,
No more waiting!

Sitting and waiting,
that's what I do,
sitting and waiting,
waiting while I
get weighed,
sitting for my blood pressure
　(and my temperature).

I don't move on the scale.
I'm still with the
thermometer.
I sit, and I wait.

I say, "Ahhhhh."
She looks at my throat.
I cough.
She listens to me breathe.
I look right.
I look left.
She shines a light at me.
She looks in my ears.
She thumps my back.
She taps my knees.

Sitting and waiting,
that's mostly
what I do
whenever I come here.
I sit, and I wait,
wait for the doctor
to check me out!

Teaching Master
The Checkup

**Stethoscope
(Heart)**

**Tongue Depressor
(Tongue)**

**Scale
(Body Weight)**

**Otoscope
(Ear)**

Thermometer

**Blood Pressure
Cuff (Arm)**

Medicine Safety

Health Education Standards:

- Students will demonstrate the ability to access valid health information and appropriate health products and services.
- Students will demonstrate the ability to practice health-enhancing behaviors and reduce health risks.

Performance Indicators:

- Students will identify factors that determine the reliability of health information, products, and services.
- Students will identify a variety of resources from the home, school and community that provide reliable health information.
- Students will develop an awareness of personal health needs.

Life Skills:

- I will use over-the-counter and prescription drugs in responsible ways.
- *I will choose sources of health-related information and products wisely. (Consumer and Community Health)*

Materials:

Teaching Master, "A Prescription Drug Label"; Student Master, "Medicine Safety Rules"; transparency projector; examples of containers for over-the-counter and prescription drugs

Motivation:

1 Introduce the word drug. A **drug** is something that will change the way a person's body works. Explain that some kinds of drugs such as medicine can be helpful. A **medicine** is a drug that is given to help a person feel better if (s)he is ill. There are many different kinds of medicines. Some medicines are pills. Some are given in shots, or injections. Some medicines can be breathed in or inhaled, such as medicine sprays. Other medicines can be placed on the skin in the form of a patch. The patch has medicine that is absorbed or goes through the skin. From the skin, the medicine goes into the blood where it is carried throughout the body.

2 Explain that just as medicine can be helpful, it can also be harmful. Place containers for different kinds of medicine on your desk. Place containers for some over-the-counter (OTC) medicines on your desk. Explain that **over-the-counter medicines**, or **OTCs**, are medicines that an adult can buy off the shelf in a place such as a drugstore or supermarket. Show the class a container for a prescription drug. Explain that a **prescription drug** is a medicine that is recommended by a physician. When a physician thinks that a certain type of drug will help a person, the physician writes a special note called a prescription. The prescription is taken to a special worker called a pharmacist. A **pharmacist** is a person who fills the prescription. Explain that prescription drugs are more powerful than OTC drugs.

3 Explain to students that regardless of the type of medicine, a medicine should be given to students only by a responsible adult. Students should not take either OTCs or prescription drugs by themselves. Emphasize that medicines can be dangerous. Read the warnings on these labels to the class. For example, some warnings may indicate that the medicine can cause rashes. Other medicine can cause drowsiness and sleep. Some medicines can cause serious harm.

4 Have students differentiate between OTC labels and prescription labels. Pick up containers for different medicines and have students tell you if it is an OTC or prescription drug. Then, distribute the Student Master "Medicine Safety Rules." You can review the information on this master before distributing it. In addition, review safety tips for taking medicine. These are: 1) Take medicine only from a responsible adult. 2) Ask an adult to help you read the label so that the medicine is taken according to directions. 3) Tell a responsible adult if the medicine produces a harmful effect such as a rash. Stop taking the medicine and have the responsible adult contact a physician to find out what to do. 4) Never take another person's medicine because, while it can help to the other person, it can harm you. 5) Medicine should be placed away from the reach of small children so that they do not take it by mistake.

5 Show the Teaching Master "A Prescription Drug Label" and have students observe certain parts of the label. For example, point out that the name of the person for whom the medicine is prescribed is on the label. The physician's name is on the label. There is a place that shows a warning. Show students the directions one must follow in using the medicine. Emphasize that only the person for whom the medicine is intended should be taking the medicine.

Evaluation:

Have students take the Student Master "Medicine Safety Rules" home to share with a parent. Students are then to share ways they practice medicine safety in their homes. Students can also share tips with others for protecting them from being harmed by medicine.

Student Master

Medicine Safety Rules

Dear Parent,

Your child has learned about medicines. Your child has learned the difference between an over-the-counter (OTC) medicine and a prescription drug. A copy of each label is shown below. Show your child OTC medicines and drugs that are in your home. Tell your child not to take any medicine unless it is given by you. Go over the medicine safety rules with your child.

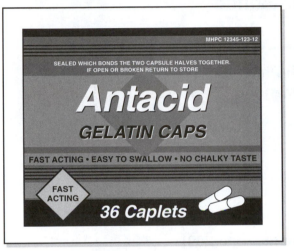

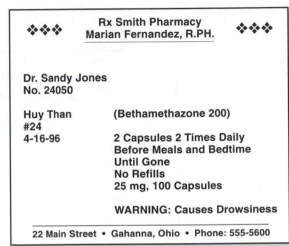

Medicine Safety Rules

1. Take medicine only from a parent or another responsible adult.

2. Read the label with an adult and follow the directions.

3. Tell an adult if a medicine produces a harmful effect such as a rash. Stop taking the medicine and have the responsible adult contact a physician to find out what to do.

4. Never take another person's medicine. It can help the other person but it may harm you.

5. Keep medicine away from small children so they do not take it by mistake.

Teaching Master
A Prescription Drug Label

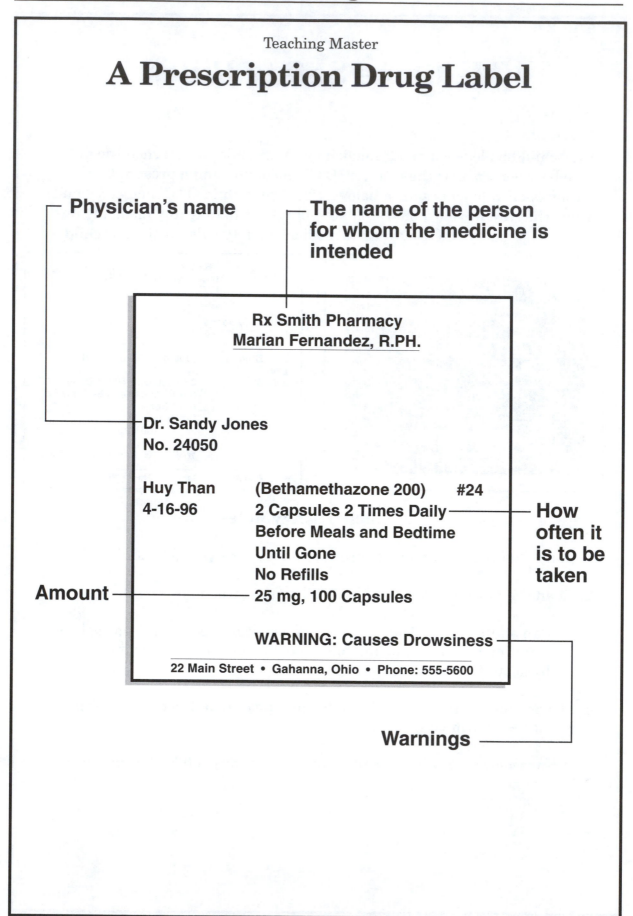

Physician's name

The name of the person for whom the medicine is intended

Rx Smith Pharmacy
Marian Fernandez, R.PH.

Dr. Sandy Jones
No. 24050

Huy Than   **(Bethamethazone 200)**   **#24**
4-16-96   **2 Capsules 2 Times Daily**
                      Before Meals and Bedtime
                      Until Gone
                      No Refills

How often it is to be taken

Amount   **25 mg, 100 Capsules**

                      WARNING: Causes Drowsiness

22 Main Street • Gahanna, Ohio • Phone: 555-5600

Warnings

Your Handshake Is Glittering

Health Education Standard:

- Students will comprehend health promotion and disease prevention concepts.

Performance Indicators:

- Students will identify the most common health problems of children.
- Students will recognize that many injuries and illnesses can be prevented and treated.

Life Skills:

- I will recognize that some diseases are communicable while others are noncommunicable.
- I will choose behavior to reduce the risk of infection with common communicable diseases.
- *I will be well-groomed. (Personal Health)*

Materials:

Student Master, "Avoiding Other People's Germs"; glitter

Motivation:

1 Begin this strategy by showing the class you have glitter. Empty a small amount of glitter on your right hand. Spread it all over your hand and ask for a volunteer who would like to shake your hand. Shake hands with this person and make sure the handshake is tight and held for a few seconds so the glitter is transferred to the student's hand.

2 Ask this student to do the same with another student, who then shakes

hands with another student, and so forth. Stop when five students in the class have had an opportunity to shake hands. Then, ask the last student who has had his/her hand shaken to show the class his/her hand. The class will notice that this student has glitter on his/her hand.

3 Explain that the glitter represented germs and that you were the first person who had the germs. Explain that five persons later, your germs showed up. Emphasize that if a person is ill, that person has germs in and on his/her body. Through touch, the germs are spread to others. Suppose the people who had glitter on their hands (all five) touched their mouths with the hand with germs on it. The germs would have gotten inside their bodies and caused them to become ill.

4 Explain that one person can infect another person without even touching him/her. For example, the fifth person who got the teacher's germs never even touched the teacher. Yet that person got the teacher's germs. This is one reason why a person who is ill, for example with the common cold, can infect many others without directly touching them.

5 Explain that the most common way germs are spread is through touch. The germs from one person's hands can be spread to another person when they touch or when they share an object. You can use another demonstration with the class to show how germs are spread. Ask to use another person's pencil. Take the pencil. Pretend to sneeze and cover your nose with the hand holding the pencil. The pencil now has the germs. Now hand the pencil back to the student. Suppose that student were to place his/her hand in his/her mouth. That student might become infected with your germs. That student might become ill.

6 Explain to students that if they are not feeling well, it may be important for them to stay home. If they have a cold and come to school, they can spread their cold germs to others.

Evaluation:

Distribute the Student Master "Avoiding Other People's Germs." Have students share this Student Master with a parent. It contains tips for avoiding the germs of other's. Students can work with a parent to add ways to avoid the germs of others. Have students share their health tips with the class.

Student Master

Avoiding Other People's Germs

Dear Parent,

Your child has been learning about ways germs are spread. This master contains a list of ways your child can avoid the germs of others. It lists ways your child can keep from spreading germs. Help your child add to the list.

1. I will not go near other people who are ill.
2. I will wash my hands after I use the restroom.
3. I will wash my hands with soap and water after I sneeze or cough.
4. I will not drink from the same cup as someone else.
5. I will cover my mouth when I cough.
6. I will cover my mouth when I sneeze.
7. I will stay home from school when I have a cold.
8. I will wash my hands before handling food.
9. I will not handle objects that a person who has a cold has touched.
10. I will not touch a used tissue.

11. _____

12. _____

13. _____

14. _____

15. _____

445

Who's Calling?

Health Education Standard:

- Students will demonstrate the ability to practice health-enhancing behaviors and reduce health risks.

Performance Indicators:

- Students will distinguish between threatening and nonthreatening circumstances.
- Students will generate ways to avoid threatening situations.
- Students will explain how to get assistance in threatening circumstances.

Life Skills:

- I will follow safety rules in my home.
- I will be able to get help for emergency situations.
- I will protect myself from people who might harm me.

Materials:

Telephone (not hooked up)

Motivation:

1 Explain to students that it is not possible to tell from looking at or listening to a person if that person might try to harm them. Explain that one way to protect themselves is to be especially careful around strangers. A **stranger** is a person you do not know. Students need to know that most strangers will not harm children. However, some strangers may try to harm children. These strangers may not look different from other people and they may seem to be very friendly. Explain that it is important for students to learn to protect themselves.

2 Explain that you are going to illustrate one particular way that a person might try to harm a child. Ask for a volunteer to help you with a demonstration. Pretend you are a stranger who is calling the student. Share the following script with the volunteer so that (s)he will answer your questions in the way that a typical student might answer the telephone. Pretend to have the telephone ring and then proceed with the following conversation.

Student: Hello.
Stranger: Hi! Who is this?
Student: This is Fran.
Stranger: Hi, Fran. This is Mr. Smith. Is your mother at home?
Student: No.
Stranger: Do you know when she will be home?
Student: No.
Stranger: Is anyone else at home?
Student: No.
Stranger: Fran, I have a package your mom wanted me to deliver to your house and I lost your address. Would you give me your address and I'll stop by in a little while to deliver her package?
Student: Sure. I live at 1234 5th Street.
Stranger: Thanks. When I come over, just open the door and I'll give you the package.

3 Ask students to identify the different items of information that were given to you, the stranger. They should list the child's name, the fact that the mother was not home, that the child did not know when she would be home, that no one else was at home, and the address. Explain that if the stranger was a person who wanted to harm a child, the student would be in possible danger.

4 With a volunteer, demonstrate another telephone conversation with the student giving the following different answers.

Student: Hello.
Stranger: Hello. Who is this?
Student: With whom do you wish to speak?
Stranger: Is your mother at home?
Student: She's busy right now and can't come to the phone. Can I take a message?
Stranger: I need to deliver a package for her and I lost your address. Will you please give me your address so that I can deliver the package for her?
Student: If you leave me your name and phone number, my mother will call you back shortly.
Stranger: Never mind. Goodbye.

5 Discuss with students the reason that the second conversation protects the safety of the student. At the end of the conversation, the stranger had no information about the student. If the stranger was a person who wanted to harm a child, this student would be safe.

Evaluation:

Ask students to identify the information that was not given to the stranger in this conversation. They should say the child's name; that the mother was not home; and the address. Repeat this activity with different students and evaluate their responses. Review telephone safety rules.

Don't Fall For It

Health Education Standards:

- Students will demonstrate the ability to access valid health information and appropriate health products and services.
- Students will analyze the impact of culture, media, technology, and other factors on health.

Performance Indicators:

- Students will identify factors that determine the reliability of health information, products, and services.
- Students will compare health information from a variety of appropriate sources.
- Students will describe how the media seeks to influence thought, feelings and behaviors.

Life Skills:

- I will choose sources of health-related information, products, and services wisely.
- I will recognize and report quackery.

Materials:

Student Master, "Make the Better Deal"; two paper cups; any two health-related products that can be purchased from a supermarket such as aspirin—but one name brand and the other a generic brand, each with the exact same ingredients and weight but with different prices

Motivation:

1 Begin this strategy by telling the class that you just discovered the most exciting product in the world. Tell students the name of this product is called Incredible Ears. Bring two cups to class. However, tell students that while these two objects may look like cups, they are not. Explain that you just got these cups from a friend of yours who saw them advertised on television. Tell students that they will have the opportunity to buy a set of Incredible Ears too, but first you want to provide them with information so they know what they will be purchasing.

2 Begin by telling students that the Incredible Ears help people learn better because they help the brain understand any information very easily. Tell the class that other students who use Incredible Ears get A's in school. Incredible Ears have the ability to make any schoolwork easy to understand. And Incredible Ears work very easily. Show students how they work by placing a cup over each ear and holding them in place with your hands. Tell students that if they want a pair, they will need to bring twenty-five cents from home tomorrow. If they do not, they will not be able to get a pair, because Incredible Ears will no longer be sold. Tell students that if they buy Incredible Ears, they will probably get all A's every year in school.

3 Ask students, by a show of hands, who plans to bring in twenty-five cents to school the next day. Many students will probably raise their hands.

4 Process the information you have just told to the class. Ask students why they would want to buy Incredible Ears. Students may indicate that they believe what you have said. They particularly believe you because you are the teacher. Explain that every day, many famous people such as movie stars and athletes appear on television to try to sell products. This is called an endorsement. However, an endorsement does not mean that the product being sold is something that may really be needed.

5 Explain to students that you made many false claims. Explain that there is no product that is capable of making students understand everything and thus making it easy to get A's. The only way to get A's is to do all schoolwork and study hard. Even this will not guarantee that people will get A's. No product you can buy will help them to automatically get A's. Explain that you made a false claim. A **false claim** is a lie that is told to others so that they will buy a product.

6 Tell the class that you also mentioned that you needed the money by tomorrow because after that time Incredible Ears will no longer be available. Explain that when some people try to sell products, they say things like "the products will be available for only a short period of time." This pressures people into making choices without having the time to think about whether or not these products really work.

7 Explain to students that they have just seen how companies try to get people to buy their products. Most companies do not lie or pressure people to buy their products. However, some do. And people do not know if the products work. As a result, many people spend money on products they do not need or do not work. Explain to students that as they grow older, they will make decisions about products. They will need to analyze the information they receive about the product and determine if they need the product, or if there is another product that may be a better purchase. Show the students the two products you purchased at the supermarket. Explain that the products are exactly the same but that one is the popular or name brand product, and the other is the generic or store brand product. Read the labels to students. Read the claims made on the products. Tell them how many items of each of the products are in the package. Then tell them the price. Have students tell you which product they should buy and why. Review why buying one product is a wiser choice than buying the other product.

Evaluation:

Distribute the Student Master "Make The Better Deal." Have students complete the master.

Student Master
Make The Better Deal

Name _____

Look at the two products. Answer the questions about the products. Decide which product is a better deal.

FLAKEYS
Champion Swimmer Liz Whiz Loves Them!
Flakeys Makes Me Swim Faster!
12oz. $3.00

CRUNCHIES
A Whole-Grain Cereal
No Sugar Added!
100% of the Recommended Daily Allowance of Vitamins
18oz. $3.29

1. Which product contains an endorsement?

_____

_____

2. Which product has a false claim?

_____

_____

3. Which product has healthful ingredients?

_____

_____

4. Which product is a better deal? Why?

_____

_____

That's A Litter Bit Better

Health Education Standard:

- Students will comprehend health promotion and disease prevention concepts.

Performance Indicators:

- Students will identify the impact of the environment on personal health.
- Students will identify methods of health promotion.

Life Skills:

- I will dispose of solid wastes properly.
- I will recycle.

Materials:

A large trash bag containing enough of the following items so that each student can have at least one item: crumpled papers, tissues, soda cans, candy wrappers, empty cereal boxes

Motivation:

1 Before coming to class, take a trash bag and place different disposable items in it. The items should be clean and may include clean tissues, newspaper pages, sheets of paper, candy wrappers, and empty cereal boxes. Be sure to have at least one item for each of the students in the class.

2 Bring the filled trash bag to class. Before you begin this strategy, be sure the classroom is clean. Have students look around the room and notice how clean it looks. Emphasize that the room is clean. Tell students that you are going to have a grab bag.

Explain that in this grab bag, students will have the opportunity to select something from the bag you brought to school. Go around the room and have each student select an item and place that item on his/her desk. Students will probably wonder why they are picking the items you have brought to class. Explain to students that they do not need to keep their items on their desks. Tell students that they should place their items on the floor. They do not need to place these items in the trash basket in the room.

3 Once students have placed their items on the floor, have them observe how the room now looks. Students will share that the room looks dirty. Ask them if they would mind if the room stayed like it is. Students may say that they do not wish to be in a room with trash all over. Explain to students that what they just did was litter. To **litter** means to throw trash in places that are not made to hold garbage. Explain that it is against the law to litter. Products such as crumpled papers and cereal boxes need to be disposed of, or thrown away, properly.

4 Have students pick up their litter and then place it in your trash bag. Tell students you will dispose of the litter. Explain to students that when they are in their community, they have a responsibility to dispose of trash in a responsible manner. This means throwing trash in litter baskets or garbage cans. It also means recycling. To recycle is to use something again.

5 Explain that litter can be harmful to health. For example, food that is thrown on the ground attracts insects and rodents such as flies and rats. Flies and rats carry germs that can cause people to become ill. For example, a fly is an insect. A fly can land on food or on other products that may contain germs. The fly then lands on a piece of food you will eat. The germs from the fly can enter your body when you eat that food and you can become ill. Tell students that litter can cause harm. Suppose the soda can has soda inside and it spilled on the floor in the classroom. A person walking by might fall because the floor would be slippery.

Evaluation:

Have students take a small strip of paper and write the name of an item of waste that they may have seen on the street in their community. They are then to come to the front of the room and throw their crumpled paper in the trash. But they must first say the name of the item, for example, "This is an orange peel and it belongs in the trash." After each student has a turn, name the most common forms of litter and discuss what people can do to dispose of each of these properly. Ask students to name items that can be recycled.

452

Putting Your Best Foot Forward

Health Education Standards:

- Students will demonstrate the ability to practice health-enhancing behaviors and reduce health risks.
- Students will demonstrate the ability to use goal-setting and decision-making skills that enhance health.

Performance Indicators:

- Students will demonstrate strategies to improve or maintain personal health.
- Students will list the steps in setting personal health goals.
- Students will set a personal health goal and make progress toward its achievement.

Life Skills:

- I will strive to have optimal health.
- I will practice life skills for health.

Materials:

One pair of shoes for each student

Motivation:

1 On the day before you teach this strategy, ask students either to bring an extra pair of shoes from home or to wear a pair of shoes that they wore to a meaningful event and they wore when they performed a healthful action. For example, a pair of shoes may have been worn at a birthday party at which family members who had not visited for a long time gathered together and shared wonderful memories. The shoes chosen can be any type such as athletic shoes, dress shoes, or tap dance shoes.

2 Explain to students that it is important to be at their best to maintain and improve health status. Introduce the phrase "putting your best foot forward." Have students share what they think this phrase means. Explain that "putting your best foot forward" means to do the very best you can at all times. This means doing your best when you perform tasks, interact with others, and make decisions.

3 Tell the class that student volunteers are going to participate in an activity called "Putting Your Best Foot Forward." Ask for each student volunteer, in turn, to wear his/her chosen pair of shoes and come to the front of the room. Each student volunteer is to show his/her pair of shoes to the class, and describe a situation in which the shoes were worn.

4 Discuss the situations in which the shoes were worn. Why was it important for them to "put their best foot forward" in each of these situations?

Evaluation:

Ask students to name three life skills they will practice. Have them tell how each life skill shows a way to "put their best foot forward."

Multicultural Infusion:

Have students wear or bring a pair of shoes that has a cultural significance. Perhaps it is a shoe that was purchased in another country. The shoes might have been a part of the clothing worn by people of another culture during a celebration or on a particular holiday. Have students share a life skill practiced by people of a specific culture.

Want Ad: A Friend

Health Education Standards:

- Students will demonstrate the ability to use effective interpersonal communication skills that enhance health.
- Students will demonstrate the ability to advocate for family and community health.

Performance Indicators:

- Students will describe characteristics needed to be a responsible friend and family member.
- Students will demonstrate the ability to influence and support others in making positive health choices.

Life Skills:

- I will form healthful and responsible friendships.
- I will recognize harmful relationships.

Materials:

Student Master, "Want Ad: A Friend"; Teaching Master, "Making Responsible Decisions With Friends"; transparency projector; paper and pencil; newspaper; chalkboard; chalk

Motivation:

1 Discuss friendship. A **friend** is a person who is known well and liked. Ask students to share qualities they feel are important in a friend. Student responses may include characteristics and behaviors such as: tells the truth, does things with me, shares feelings with me, does not say unkind things about me, helps me, and is kind.

2 Introduce the idea of a want ad. Explain that a want ad is a printed notice that a person may write in order to find someone or sell something. You might explain that if a school is looking for a teacher, the principal may place a want ad in a newspaper. The want ad will be a printed notice in the newspaper that will tell people who read that newspaper that a teacher is needed. The word "ad" is short for advertisement.

3 Explain that students are going to write their own want ads. Distribute the Student Master "Want Ad: A Friend." Open a newspaper to the Help Wanted section. Read several Help Wanted advertisements. Explain to students that the ads in this section are notices for people who are needed for jobs. Read some of the copy in the ads. Have students notice the kinds of qualities for which companies are looking. Explain that the companies note specific qualities that are needed.

4 Tell students they also are going to have the opportunity to write want ads. But, they are going to write want ads for a friend. Tell students that they are to think about the characteristics they would want in a good friend. A **characteristic** is a special quality or feature a person has. A characteristic might be that a person is funny or friendly. Other characteristics a friend may have might be caring about others or always sharing with others. Tell students to write five characteristics they think a good friend should have. They are to write these characteristics in the lines provided.

5 After students write their characteristics, they are to share what they have written. Write the students' responses on the chalkboard. Do not list responses already mentioned. Afterwards, have students read silently what you have written on the chalkboard. Then have the students discuss what they think might be the most important characteristics they feel a friend should have. Eliminate those characteristics that do not appear to be among the most important.

Evaluation:

Have students identify the five most important characteristics a friend should have. Then they are to tell ways to tell if a friend has these characteristics. Have students discuss how a good friend would treat them. Tell students that it is also important for them to choose friends who make responsible decisions. Explain that a **decision** is a choice. A responsible decision is a decision that protects health, safety, and laws; shows respect for self and others; follows guidelines set by responsible adults such as parents

and guardians; and demonstrates good character and moral values. You can review responsible decision-making by showing the Teaching Master "Making Responsible Decisions With Friends." Have students relate the importance of being a good friend and making responsible decisions.

Inclusion:

Emphasize that being a good friend is not related to how a person looks or what physical qualities a person has. Explain that being a good friend is related to how people treat each other. Explain that people who make fun of others or treat them unfairly because of how they look are not the kind of people who would make good friends. Good friends show respect for others. To show **respect** means to treat someone as if that person is important. Tell students that every student in the class is important. Everyone has characteristics that make him/her special.

Want Ad: A Friend

Write five characteristics you would want a good friend to have.

1. _____

_____

2. _____

_____

3. _____

_____

4. _____

_____

5. _____

_____

Teaching Master

Making Responsible Decisions With Friends

Your actions should:

- be safe

- be healthful

- follow family rules

- follow school rules and laws

- show respect

All Of Me

Health Education Standard:

- Students will demonstrate the ability to practice health-enhancing behaviors and reduce health risks.

Life Skill:

- I will accept my physical uniqueness.

Performance Indicator:

- Students will develop an awareness of personal health needs.

Materials:

The poem, *All of Me*; butcher paper (a five-foot length for each student and longer sheet for any guest speakers); scissors; crayons or markers; blindfolds for half the students

Motivation:

1 Read the poem *All of Me* to students. Assign students to pairs. Have one student in each pair wear a blindfold for fifteen minutes. Have students do an activity in pairs, such as work on a math problem or write a story. The student who is not blindfolded should provide help and guidance as the student who is blindfolded works. Then have partners change roles. Ask students the following questions: What do you think would be different if you could not see?

2 Tell students that a physical challenge changes the body, not the person. Reread the poem with the class and ask students to explain why the speaker is sad. Dim the lights and ask children to close their eyes as you read the poem aloud. Invite students to explain what the poem is saying. Ask students how the boy without sight learns. Have students describe how the two children are alike and how they are different.

3 Tell students that everyone has feelings, thoughts, and challenges. Define the word challenges. **Challenges** are tasks that are stimulating or difficult. Ask the class to name challenges the two children in the poem are facing. Explain that a physical challenge can be very noticeable (such as needing a wheelchair) or almost invisible (such as a learning disability). Help students brainstorm the kinds of physical challenges a person might face. Point out that people can react to a challenge differently. Have a student read the poem aloud and ask the class how each child reacted to his personal challenge. Allow students time to speculate as to why the two young people feel so differently about their challenges.

4 Give a five-foot length of butcher paper to each student. Have students work in pairs to trace their bodies to make life-size cutouts. Have students draw their faces on their cutouts. Have students also draw a t-shirt on their cutouts. Discuss with students the variety of characteristics people have. (Students might say physical characteristics such as their face or body; students might say personality characteristics such as friendly or funny.) Then ask students to write some of the traits, skills, and talents they have on the t-shirt of their cutouts. Once students begin writing, add traits and skills to each student's list. Encourage students to add traits and skills to other student's lists. Display the cutouts on walls throughout the classroom. Encourage students to add to their lists as they think of other traits and skills they have. Guide students to recognize that they are more than what they can do.

5 Tell students people with physical challenges are just that—people. Have a Challenge Day for the class. Invite people with disabilities to visit the class to talk about their lives, their friends, and what they want to tell people about their disabilities. Before guests arrive, have the class prepare a list of questions to share with the visitors. Guide students to include questions about guests' thoughts and feelings. Then have groups of students help guests make their own life-size butcher-paper figures and lists for the classroom wall.

Evaluation:

Have small groups work together to make up a play about a child with a physical challenge. Ask students to use their plays to show how all people have feelings, thoughts, and challenges.

All of Me

❖❖❖❖❖❖❖❖

I have a friend, whose eyes are dark—
who sees all of me.
His heart and mind see even more
than two bright eyes might see.

When he takes my hand to walk,
He says, "Your sadness shows."
And when I ask, "How could you tell?"
He says, "Oh, I just know."

And if we're at a baseball game,
He sees just how I feel.
And when I hate my wheelchair,
He says, "Some feet are wheels."

I have a friend whose eyes are dark—
who sees all I can be.
And when I ask, "How do *you* see?"
He says, "With all of me."

❖❖❖❖❖❖❖❖

Balloon Toss Veggies

Health Education Standards:

- Students will comprehend health promotion and disease prevention concepts.
- Students will demonstrate the ability to practice health-enhancing behaviors and reduce health risks.

Performance Indicators:

- Students will recognize the relationship between personal health behaviors and individual well-being.
- Students will demonstrate strategies to improve or maintain personal health.

Life Skills:

- I will make food selections that reduce my risk of disease.
- *I will choose behavior to reduce my risk of cardiovascular disease. (Communicable and Chronic Diseases)*
- *I will choose behavior to reduce my risk of cancer. (Communicable and Chronic Diseases)*

Materials:

Balloon

Motivation:

1 Explain to students that their health habits today will influence how healthy they will be as adults. This means that it is important to eat correctly now and continue to eat correctly throughout life. Introduce the word habit. Explain that a **habit** is an action that is repeated so that it becomes automatic. Students may have picked up harmful habits in the past. For example, students who play sports may have developed habits that continue. When a habit continues, it can be hard to break. Perhaps a student may not dribble a ball correctly. The longer a person dribbles incorrectly, the more difficult it becomes to dribble correctly. It can take a lot of time and practice to change an old habit.

2 Explain that eating healthfully can become a habit. If this habit is started early in life, it is easy to continue. But if a students has harmful eating habits now, these eating habits may continue throughout adulthood. The harmful eating habits may be difficult to break in adulthood. Emphasize that is important to have healthful eating habits now. One way to start is to eat healthful foods. One group of healthful foods is the vegetable group.

3 Explain that this strategy will help students name the many different kinds of vegetables they can eat.

4 Divide the class in half and have the students form two equal lines. They are to face each other and line up in single file. Explain to students that they are going to play a game called Balloon Toss Veggies. The game goes as follows: You will begin by standing in front of one line. Tap the balloon high in the air to the first student in the line. The student to whom the balloon is tapped must name a vegetable and tap the balloon to the first student in the other line. This student must then name another vegetable and tap it back. After a student taps the balloon and names a vegetable, (s)he goes to the back of his/her team's line. The balloon gets tapped back and forth from student to student and must remain in the air. Students cannot repeat the name of a vegetable that has already been named. If a student incorrectly names or repeats the name of a vegetable, that student is out of the game and must leave the line and sit down. A team wins when it has the last student remaining.

5 There are any number of vegetables that can be named. Among these are: artichokes, asparagus, green beans, lima beans, navy beans, waxed beans, beets, broccoli, brussels sprouts, cabbage, carrots, cauliflower, celery, chard, corn, cucumber, dandelion greens, eggplant, kale, kohlrabi, leeks, lettuce, mushrooms, okra, onion, parsnips, peas, peppers, potatoes, radishes, rutabagas, sauerkraut, spinach, squash, sweet

potatoes, tomatoes, turnips, yams, and zucchini.

6 You can adapt this strategy to any of the different groups from the Food Guide Pyramid. For example, you can ask students to name different fruits or meats.

Evaluation:

Keep count of the number of different vegetables students name. Then name the vegetables on the list in Step 5 that have not been given. You can have students repeat this activity and compare the number of vegetables named the first time the game was played with the number of vegetables named the second time.

O Two My CO$_2$

Health Education Standards:

- Students will demonstrate the ability to practice health-enhancing behaviors and reduce health risks.
- Students will demonstrate the ability to use goal-setting and decision-making skills that enhance health.

Performance Indicators:

- Students will demonstrate strategies to improve or maintain personal health.
- Students will set a personal health goal and make progress toward its achievement.

Life Skills:

- I will participate in movement and exercise.
- I will achieve a desirable level of physical fitness.

Materials:

Five index cards on which "O$_2$" is written; five index cards on which "CO$_2$" is written; five index cards on which "CO" is written; fifteen-foot strip of yarn

Motivation:

1 Tell students they are going to play a game called the Exchange Game. The game will be played as follows: Take a fifteen-foot strip of yarn and place it on the floor to form an outline of a lung. Select five students to line up single file around the inside of the lung. Hand each student standing inside the lung an index card that says CO$_2$. Have five more students line up in single file around the lung. These students are to hold cards that say O$_2$.

2 Students often have difficulty understanding the exchange of gases inside the lungs. Explain to students that they are holding cards that represent gases in the air. These gases are used in the body. The cards that have O$_2$ written on them represent oxygen. **Oxygen** is a gas in the air that is inhaled into the lungs and is carried by the blood to the cells. CO$_2$ represents carbon dioxide. **Carbon dioxide** is a gas that is released as a waste product after oxygen is used by the cells. Carbon dioxide is carried away from the cells to the lungs by the blood and released from the body when a person exhales.

3 Explain to students that the following game will demonstrate how the exchange of gases in the lungs occurs. Have each student outside the lung holding an O$_2$ card enter the lung and line up opposite a student lining the inside of the lungs. The students should be facing each other. Have them exchange cards with their partners. Now have the students who walked from the outside of the lungs to the inside step outside the lung again. The O$_2$ cards will remain with the students who are inside the lung. The CO$_2$ cards are now with the students who are outside the lungs.

4 Tell students that when a person inhales, oxygen is absorbed into the lining of the lungs. The oxygen is stored in the air sacs or **alveoli** of the lungs. The blood then picks up the oxygen and carries it to the cells. At the same time, blood brings CO$_2$ to the lungs to be exhaled. This exchange of gases was demonstrated by the students who walked into the lungs holding O_2 cards and left holding CO_2 cards.

5 Explain that physical exercise can keep the heart and lungs healthy. A healthful exercise for the heart is called aerobic exercise. **Aerobic exercise** is exercise in which oxygen is required continually for an extended period of time. For example, running for twenty minutes without becoming out of breath is an aerobic exercise. People who participate in aerobic exercise should do so without becoming out of breath.

6 Repeat the Exchange Game, but this time make the exchange of cards faster. You begin this activity by leading the class in clapping hands at the rate of about 70 beats per minute. As the class claps to your lead, students will step in and out of the lung and exchange their cards. Then introduce an aerobic exercise such as running, walking, or bicycle riding. Explain that when people exercise, the heartbeat rate increases. More blood is pumped by the heart, more oxygen is needed and must be sent to the cells inside the body. Clap your hands to approximately one hundred beats per minute so that students now must move much faster to exchange their cards. Explain that the heart muscle is working harder. It gets stronger with exercise.

7 Now demonstrate what happens when a person smokes. Use another five students. Three of these students will be given CO cards and two will be given O_2 cards. CO is **carbon monoxide,** which is a poisonous gas in cigarette smoke. CO takes the place of oxygen in the blood. Since the body cells cannot get the same amount of oxygen when CO enters the body, the heart must beat faster than normal to get the same amount of oxygen in the blood. Repeat the activity, but this time students will exchange their cards at a fast pace. Clap at a pace of about eighty-five beats per minute. Students will notice that the heart beats move often when a person smokes. The heart beats about fifteen more times each minute. Emphasize the importance of not smoking and of engaging in aerobic exercises.

Evaluation:

Have students identify different kinds of exercises in which they participate that strengthen the heart muscle. Have students share examples of exercises in which they participate. You can use this opportunity to have students develop a log to record how often they exercise. They can identify the exercises they do, the amount of time spent exercising, and how often they exercise. Have students share their logs with the class.

Cigarette Tips

Health Education Standards:

- Students will demonstrate the ability to practice health-enhancing behaviors and reduce health risks.
- Students will comprehend health promotion and disease prevention concepts.

Performance Indicators:

- Students will identify behaviors that are safe, risky, or harmful to self and others.
- Students will recognize that many injuries and illnesses can be prevented and treated.

Life Skills:

- I will not use tobacco products.
- *I will choose behavior to reduce my risk of cardiovascular disease. (Communicable and Chronic Diseases)*
- *I will choose behavior to reduce my risk of cancer. (Communicable and Chronic Diseases)*

Materials:

Teaching Master, "How Smoking Affects Health"; transparency projector; old shoe box; sheets of paper; cellophane tape; pencil or pen; magazines; scissors

Motivation:

1 Explain to students that tobacco use is a major health concern. **Tobacco** is a plant that contains a product called nicotine. **Nicotine** is a drug in tobacco that causes the parts inside the body to work harder than they normally should. Drugs that increase the speed at which the body parts work are called **stimulants**.

2 Review the harmful effects of cigarette smoke on the body. Explain that cigarette smoke contains nicotine, and that when a person smokes, nicotine enters the lungs. The smoke from the cigarette replaces the oxygen in the lungs. There is less oxygen in the lungs for the blood to carry to the body parts. Yet the body parts need oxygen. The nicotine also enters the blood. These actions cause the heart to work harder. The heart beats more often. This places stress on the heart.

3 Explain that tobacco also contains tar. **Tar** is a dark, sticky substance in tobacco that is very harmful. Tar can stick to the lining of the lung. The surface of the lungs has tiny air sacs that supply blood with oxygen. Tar can destroy these air sacs. Tar also can cause diseases of the lungs as a person grows older.

4 Explain that the smoke from a smoker's cigarette also is harmful. Tell students that if they are inside a room with people who are smoking, they will inhale the smoke. Explain that people who breathe smoke become ill more often than people who do not breathe smoke.

5 Present the following strategy to the class. Have students decorate a shoe box as if it were a large cigarette pack. The box should have a warning statement that says cigarettes are harmful. Students can cut pictures from magazines and combine these pictures to create sayings or pictures that show that smoking is harmful.

6 Give students a sheet of paper. Tell them to write a statement that indicates why smoking is harmful. They can also be given the option of writing a jingle about the dangers of cigarette smoking or why a person should never smoke.

7 After students write their statements, tell them to roll their sheets of paper into what appears to be a long cigarette. Use tape to attach the paper at the edge so that it remains closed. The paper will now look like a cigarette. Have students place their "cigarettes" into the shoe box (cigarette box). Explain that the shoe box now contains cigarette tips. Have each student select a "cigarette

tip" from the box and read it to the class. Write the different kinds of facts students identified on the chalkboard. Do not repeat similar tips.

Evaluation:

Have students identify the harmful effects of cigarette smoking on the body. You can then show the Teaching Master "How Smoking Affects Health" and compare student responses to the responses on the teaching master. Have students add additional items they would place on this list.

Teaching Master

How Smoking Affects Health

People who smoke...

- have yellow teeth.

- get tired easily.

- have increased heartbeat rate.

- are more likely to have diseases of the heart and blood vessels.

- increase their chances of getting diseases of the lungs.

- have clothes and breath that smell of stale smoke.

- cause nonsmokers to inhale the smoke from their cigarettes.

- can cause fires with their cigarettes.

- spend their money on cigarettes when they can spend it on more useful products.

- have more colds and respiratory diseases than people who do not smoke.

Steady Flow

Health Education Standards:

- Students will demonstrate the ability to access valid health information and appropriate health products and services.
- Students will analyze the impact of culture, media, technology and other factors on health.

Performance Indicators:

- Students will identify a variety of resources from the home, school, and community that provide reliable health information.
- Students will describe the influence of culture on personal health practices.

Life Skills:

- I will obtain information about my family's history of disease.
- I will choose behavior to reduce my risk of cardiovascular disease.

Materials:

Teaching Master, "Health Habits For My Heart"; transparency projector; straw; hollow coffee stirrer

Motivation:

1 Explain to students that heart disease is the leading cause of death. Often, heart disease is due to the health habits a person follows throughout life. Show students the Teaching Master "Health Habits For My Heart." Review the health habits a person can follow to reduce the risk of heart disease.

2 Explain that sometimes a person cannot completely control the risk of

heart disease. For example, a person who belongs to a family that has a history of heart disease has a greater chance of getting heart disease. Explain that a "history of heart disease" means that one or more family members have had heart disease. For example, a person's mother and grandfather may have died at an early age from heart disease. That person may now be at greater risk of having heart disease than a person who does not have a family history of heart disease. Introduce the term "risk." **Risk** means chance. A person who has a high risk of having heart disease has a greater chance.

3 Explain that there are different causes of heart disease. The most common cause is when the artery gets narrow. **Arteries** are blood vessels that carry blood away from the heart. The narrower an artery is, the less blood can pass through it. To show what is meant by "narrow," hold your thumb and forefinger (pointer finger) so that a circle is formed. (This is the same shape as when someone gives an OK sign using the thumb and forefinger.) Now, close up the circle by sliding the forefinger lower down the thumb. Show students that the opening is narrower. Explain that if they were looking inside an artery, they would notice that the opening can change sizes.

4 To demonstrate the difference between the flow of blood through a narrow and a healthy artery, ask for two students. Fill two identical beverage glasses to the halfway point with water. Give each student a beverage glass. Give one student a straw and the other student a hollow coffee stirrer. At your signal, have both students begin

468

together to drink the water. They are to race to determine who can finish first. Stop the activity as soon as one person has emptied his/her glass. Now show the class what happened. (The student who used the straw finished drinking the water much sooner than the student who sipped the water through the stirrer.)

Evaluation:

Have the class discuss why the student using the straw finished sooner than the student using the stirrer. (The opening of the straw is wider than the opening of the coffee stirrer. More water was able to pass through it.) Now have students make an analogy to the functioning of the heart. (Narrowed arteries cannot allow as much blood to pass through them as arteries that are open.) Review the Teaching Master "Health Habits For My Heart" and have students give examples of how they can keep their heart and arteries healthy. For example, "Exercise each day," may include answers such as "ride a bicycle" or "run."

Teaching Master
Health Habits For My Heart

I will...

- exercise each day.

- eat a healthful diet.

- have a medical checkup each year.

- eat few fatty foods.

- cope with stress.

- know my family history of heart disease.

- never smoke cigarettes.

- stay away from places where people are smoking.

- never use illegal drugs.

Biking Safely

Health Education Standards:

- Students will demonstrate the ability to practice health-enhancing behaviors and reduce health risks.
- Students will analyze the impact of culture, media, technology and other factors on health.

Performance Indicators:

- Students will distinguish between threatening and nonthreatening circumstances.
- Students will explain how to get assistance in threatening circumstances.
- Students will describe the influence of culture on personal health practices.

Life Skills:

- I will follow safety rules in my community.
- *I will follow guidelines to prevent injuries during exercise. (Personal Health)*

Materials:

The poem, *A-Safe Biking I Will Go;* Student Master, "Bicycle Safety"; a bicycle with the parts labeled correctly

Motivation:

1 Begin this strategy by asking students how many of them ride bicycles. Most students will probably raise their hands. Explain that there are important rules to follow when a person rides a bicycle.

2 Give each student a copy of the poem *A-Safe Biking I Will Go*. Read the poem aloud and have the students listen.

3 Each section of the poem has information about bicycle safety. As you read each part of the poem, use the bicycle to point out many important safety facts. The first fact relates to the need to have a reflector on the bike. Explain that a **reflector** allows lights from a car to bounce off it, creating light that a driver can see. The light from the car's headlights lights up the reflector. Most reflectors are red. The next important fact relates to brakes. Explain that before riding, students should make sure the brakes on their bikes are in good working order. They should try to use brakes before they ride too fast or far.

4 The next safety fact concerns seats. It is important for the seat to be just the right height. Explain that the balls of a person's toes should be resting on the ground when seated on the bike with both feet fully stretched to the ground. The distance to the handlebars should feel comfortable. The handlebars should be set straight ahead and kept tight.

5 Explain that the tires should have enough air inside them because, unlike a car, one does not carry a spare tire on a bike. If the tires feel soft when squeezed, they may need air. Ask an adult to help put air in a tire. Do not use an air pump at a gas station to put air inside the tire. The air pumps at gas stations pump with a great deal of force. Gas station air pumps can cause a tire to burst.

6 Explain that their bikes should have a chain guard to prevent clothing from getting caught in the chain, thus causing them to fall. If a bike does not have a chain guard, encourage students not to wear clothing that could become caught inside the chain. This means not wearing pants with loose cuffs.

Evaluation:

Distribute the Student Master "Bicycle Safety." Have students look at the picture of the bicycle and write a safety tip for each part. Collect student masters and review their answers. Have them take the master home to their parents.

A-Safe Biking I Will Go

❖❖❖❖❖❖❖❖❖

A-safe biking I will go,
as my reflectors will glow.

My brakes will stop me in time.
In fact, they'll stop on a dime.

My seat will be set just right.
And my handlebars will be straight and tight.

The tires will have air,
for I do not carry a spare.

The chain guard will help stop,
my chances of taking a flop.

It's to everyone's liking,
when safely I go biking.

❖❖❖❖❖❖❖❖❖

Student Master
Bicycle Safety

Look at the parts of the bicycle. Write a safety tip for each part.

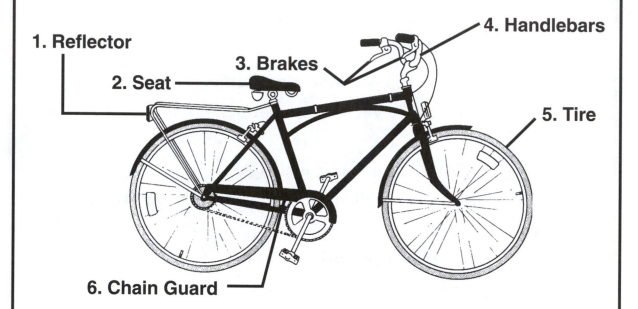

1. Reflector

2. Seat

3. Brakes

4. Handlebars

5. Tire

6. Chain Guard

1. _____

2. _____

3. _____

4. _____

5. _____

6. _____

A Hardening Experience

Health Education Standard:

- Students will demonstrate the ability to access valid health information and appropriate health products and services.

Performance Indicators:

- Students will identify factors that determine the reliability of health information, products, and services.
- Students will identify a variety of resources from the home, school and community that provide reliable health information.
- Students will compare health information from a variety of appropriate sources.

Life Skills:

- I will choose sources of health-related information and products wisely.
- *I will follow a dental health plan. (Personal Health)*

Materials:

Teaching Master, "The Structure Of A Tooth"; transparency projector; two eggs; white vinegar; two beverage glasses; water with fluoride

Motivation:

1 Prepare one day before you teach this strategy in class. Place a whole egg in a glass that contains vinegar; place another egg in a glass that contains water that contains fluoride.

2 Tell students that it is important for them to follow dental health practices. Explain that there are many ways to care for teeth. They have

learned about brushing and flossing. But it is also important to choose dental health products that promote healthy teeth.

3 Review the anatomy of a tooth. Show the Teaching Master "The Structure Of A Tooth." Explain that you will review the different parts of a tooth and what the different parts of a tooth do. As you describe what each part does, have students write the information you present. You can also write the information on your overlay. The following is the information you will need to share with students.
- *Crown* — The crown is the surface of the tooth that is at the top.
- *Root* — The root is the part of the tooth that holds the tooth to the jawbone.
- *Enamel* — The enamel is the hard tissue that covers the tooth and protects it.
- *Dentin* — The dentin is the hard tissue that forms the body of the tooth.
- *Pulp* — The pulp is the soft tissue that contains the nerves and blood vessels.
- *Cementum* — The cementum is the hard tissue that covers the root portion of the tooth.

4 Review the importance of the enamel in protecting the tooth and preventing **decay** or holes in the teeth. Explain to students that they need to use toothpaste that contains fluoride. **Fluoride** is a mineral that is added to water and helps protect teeth from decay. Show students the two eggs in the glasses. Explain that the shell of the egg is somewhat like the enamel on the teeth. The shell protects the egg just like the enamel protects the inside of the tooth. Tell students that one egg is in fluoride and the other is not. Remove the eggs, wipe them dry, and then have students feel them. Students will notice that one egg (the one in the vinegar that was not given fluoride) has a shell that is soft, if not dissolved. Explain that if this was a tooth, it would not be protected from decay.

5 Show the egg that was inside the fluoride. Explain that this egg has a hard shell. It is protected from decay. Emphasize that fluoride protects teeth from decay. Students should read the printing on tubes of toothpastes to see that the toothpaste contains fluoride. If you wish, you can bring a tube of toothpaste to class and show students where fluoride is printed on the label.

Evaluation:

Point to the different parts of the tooth on the Teaching Master "The Structure Of A Tooth." Have students name each part and identify what each part does. They can also check their toothpaste at home to make sure it contains fluoride. Students can come to class and tell the brand they use and whether it contains fluoride.

Teaching Master

The Structure Of A Tooth

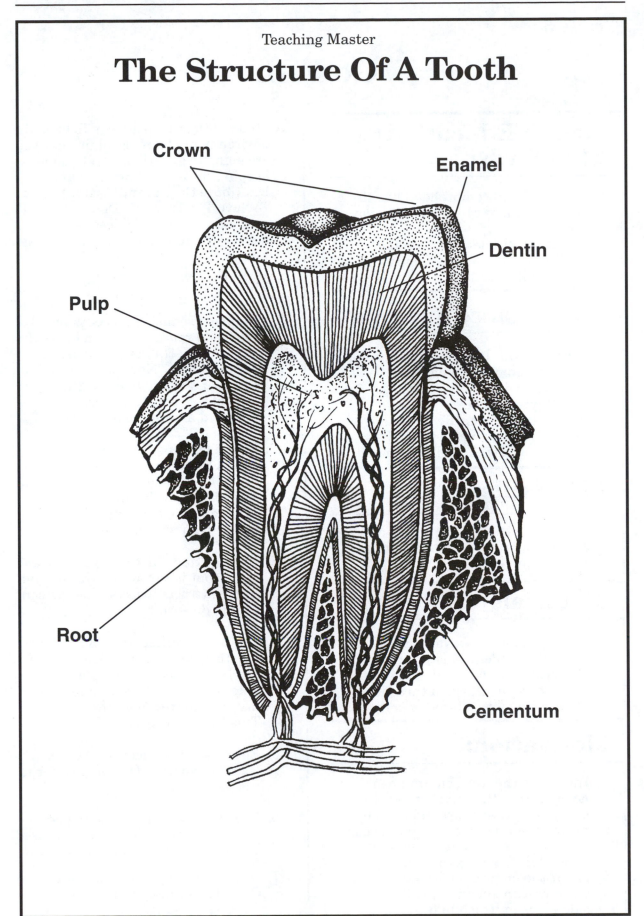

Crown

Enamel

Dentin

Pulp

Root

Cementum

Go Fish

Health Education Standards:

- Students will comprehend health promotion and disease prevention concepts.
- Students will demonstrate the ability to advocate for family and community health.

Performance Indicators:

- Students will identify the impact of the environment on personal health.
- Students will identify methods of health promotion.
- Students will identify community agencies that advocate for healthy individuals, families, and communities.

Life Skills:

- I will recycle.
- I will cooperate with environmental protection agencies.

Materials:

Family Master, "Ways To Save The Planet"; Student Master, "Fish Pattern"; a paper clip; a stick at least three feet long; a three-foot string; magnet; a large paper bag

Motivation:

1 Introduce the word environment. Explain that the **environment** is everything that is around us. This means the products we use, the cars we ride in, and the televisions we view. Tell students this activity is about the environment and the many ways we can keep it a healthful and safe place in which to live.

2 Share with students ways to keep the environment clean. Explain that you are going to give them ten tips for keeping the environment clean. Distribute the Parent Master "Ways To Save The Planet." Define "planet" as the Earth on which people live. Review the ten tips with students as well as the information highlighted about each tip. The tips are as follows:

1. Recycle products. To **recycle** means to reuse. Jars can be used to store objects instead of being thrown away. Newspapers can be saved and taken to **recycling centers**. The newspapers are collected and the paper is reused.

2. Ride a bike instead of riding in a car. A bike does not use gasoline. Gasoline is burned by cars. Chemicals created by burning gasoline can make the air dirty. This does not happen with a bike.

3. Do not litter. **Litter** is garbage and trash that is thrown on the ground. Litter attracts insects. Insects can spread disease.

4. Use paper rather than plastic bags. Plastic cannot be recycled. Paper can be recycled. Using plastic helps cause trash to accumulate faster than it would otherwise. This takes up space.

5. Encourage your parent(s) to fix leaks in faucets. Dripping water is wasted water.

6. Use sponges rather than paper towels to clean. Sponges are reused but paper towels are thrown away.

7. Use a cloth bag when shopping. Cloth bags can be reused.

8. Shut off the faucet when brushing teeth. This way, water is not used needlessly.

9. Use products that do not have aerosol sprays. Use pump sprays instead of aerosol sprays. Aerosol sprays such as those used in air fresheners have harmful products that pollute the air.

10. Use both sides of scrap paper. You can save paper this way.

3 Give each student two copies of the Student Master "The Fish Pattern." On one copy, have each student write a tip to help save the environment on the fish. On the other copy, students are to decorate the fish. Give each student a paper clip. Have students cut out and glue each fish with a tip written on it to a decorated fish from the other sheet. As they do this, have them place the paper clip between the two parts of each fish to make a mouth for the fish.

4 Divide the class into two teams. Each team will select one person to be the person fishing. A stick will serve as a pole and a string as the line of the fishing pole. At the end of the string is a magnet. The person will "fish" for a tip on how to save the planet. When a student gets a fish attached to the line by the magnet, another person on the team who is assigned to be the helper will remove the fish from the line. As the fish is removed, the helper reads the tip to the student fishing. The student who is fishing must identify a way to follow that tip. These tips are from the Parent Master "Ways To Save The Planet." A team gets one point for a correct tip. If a student selects a decorated fish and answers the question correctly, his/her team gets three points. An incorrect answer will earn no points. If an answer is missed, the next person in line on the other team gets a chance to answer.

Evaluation:

The number of correct answers will serve as a way to assess what students know. After students have taken the Parent Master home and shared it with a parent, ask them ways their families can help care for the environment.

Family Master

Ways To Save The Planet

Dear Parent:

Your child is learning ways to care for the environment. Review these tips together.

1. Recycle products. To **recycle** means to reuse. Jars can be used to store objects instead of being thrown out. Newspapers can be saved and taken to **recycling centers** where the newspapers are collected and reused.

2. Ride a bike instead of riding in a car. A bike does not use gas. Gas is burned in cars and the air can become dirty. This does not happen with a bike.

3. Do not litter. **Litter** is garbage that is thrown on the ground. Litter attracts insects. Insects can spread disease.

4. Use paper bags rather than plastic bags. Plastic cannot be recycled. Paper can be recycled. Using plastic helps cause garbage to pile up faster than need be. This takes up space.

5. Encourage your parent to fix leaks in faucets. Dripping water is wasted water.

6. Use sponges rather than paper towels to clean. Sponges are reused but paper towels are thrown away.

7. Use a cloth bag when shopping. Cloth bags can be reused.

8. Turn off the faucet when brushing teeth. This way, water is not used needlessly.

9. Use products that do not have aerosol sprays. Use pump sprays instead of aerosol sprays. Aerosol sprays such as those used in air fresheners have harmful products that pollute the air.

10. Use both sides of scrap paper. You can save paper this way.

Student Master
The Fish Pattern

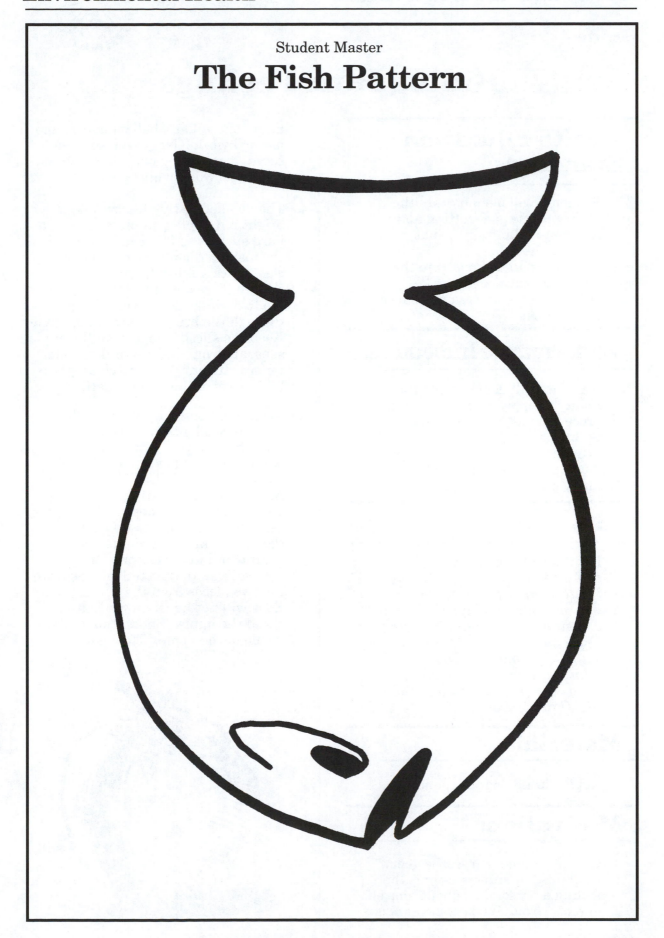

Hiding Hurt Feelings

Health Education Standards:

- Students will demonstrate the ability to use goal-setting and decision-making skills that enhance health.
- Students will demonstrate the ability to practice health-enhancing behaviors and reduce health risks.

Performance Indicators:

- Students will demonstrate the ability to apply a decision-making process to health issues and problems.
- Students will demonstrate strategies to improve and maintain personal health.

Life Skills:

- I will develop positive self-esteem.
- *I will identify resources to improve relationships and family communication. (Family Living)*
- *I will develop skills to prepare skills to prepare for future relationship choices—dating, marriage, parenthood and family life. (Family Living)*

Materials:

Apple; knife; paper; pencil

Motivation:

1 Introduce the term "self-esteem." Explain that **self-esteem** is the feeling a person has about himself/herself. **Positive self-esteem** is liking oneself and believing that one is worthwhile. **Negative self-esteem** is not liking oneself or believing one is worthwhile.

2 The day before this lesson, take a bright red apple and hit it once on a hard surface so it becomes bruised on the inside. About one hour before class, slice a fairly large wedge-shaped piece out of the apple from top to bottom. Make sure the slice is through the bruised part of the apple. Keep the sliced wedge from the apple separate from the rest of the apple. Before students come to class, place both parts of the apple together.

3 Begin this lesson by showing the apple to students. Ask them to describe it to you. Students will make statements such as, "It looks bright red" or "I'd like to eat it." After a number of students have had the opportunity to describe the apple, ask who would like to take a bite of the apple. Many students may volunteer, but choose only one. As you walk up to the student, separate the two pieces from the apple. The class will not have known that you sliced the apple. Show students the inside of the apple. The inside of the

apple will look bruised. It will also have turned brown, and students will say that they would not want to take a bite of the apple.

4 Explain that this apple was bruised inside, and therefore what they saw on the outside was not representative of what the inside was like. Now make the analogy that people may appear to be feeling one way on the outside, but on the inside they may feel differently. This is a good opportunity to emphasize to students that sometimes people want others to think they feel great, so they act very cheerful and pretend that nothing is wrong. Yet, they may be angry, sad, depressed, or disappointed.

5 This also is a good opportunity to discuss the importance of sharing feelings with a trusted adult. Explain that a **trusted adult** is a person such as a parent whom the student knows will offer help. Explain that not feeling well or not sharing certain feelings can harm a person's health. A person may feel more stress. A person may feel nervous or not be able to concentrate. A person may feel angry or may start

fights easily. This can also cause people not to feel good about themselves and have low self-esteem. There are many different people in school or in the community who can be of help. For example, in school, the teacher or the school nurse is available to help with different concerns. You can also identify other people in the school such as counselors who can be of help. Help students identify people in the community who can help such as workers in community health agencies or clergy.

6 Emphasize to students that help is available to them if they ever need it. Have students work in small groups. Each group is to identify sources of anger, sadness, depression, and disappointment in people their age. Then they are to discuss healthful ways to share these feelings.

Evaluation:

Have students fold a sheet of paper in half to create two columns. In the first column, they are to list "Five Ways Young People Get Bruised Inside." In the second column, they are to list "Five Ways to Deal with Bruised Feelings."

Older And Wiser

Health Education Standard:

- Students will demonstrate the ability to use effective interpersonal communication skills that enhance health.

Performance Indicator:

- Students will demonstrate ways to communicate care, consideration, and respect of self and others.

Life Skills:

- I will strive for healthful family relationships.
- *I will practice behaviors that contribute to healthful aging. (Growth and Development)*
- *I will share my feelings about death and dying. (Growth and Development)*

Materials:

Petroleum jelly; pair of old glasses; wooden tongue depressors; tape; strip of cellophane about five inches long; tape recording of muffled sounds; tape recorder

Motivation:

1 Introduce the word aging. Explain that **aging** means getting older. Make an analogy of aging to older, beautiful trees in the community. Explain that as trees get older, they have more branches and their trunks become larger. This is an indication that a tree is aging. Explain that people age also. As people get older, their bodies grow bigger, but then they stop growing. For males, this may be up to about age twenty, but for females it may be through age eighteen or nineteen. This varies with different people. Explain that people age in other ways. They age mentally. That is, they learn more and have had many different experiences throughout life that make them more aware of their surroundings.

2 Explain that as people grow older, they have many different physical changes. For example, a tree that is older may have branches that may break easily. As a person ages, that person's body may have changes such as bones breaking more easily.

3 One part of the body that may be affected by aging is vision. Explain that **vision** is the ability to see. The following activity can help students become more aware of what it might feel like to begin to lose vision. Take the old pair of glasses and smear petroleum jelly on the outside of the lenses. Then ask a student volunteer to wear the glasses and try to read a book or look at an object at a distance. Have that student share what that experience may feel like. The student will probably indicate that his/her vision is not clear. The student probably cannot read the book. You can explain that many older people get blurred vision as they grow older. This happens because the muscles around the eye do not work as well as they once did and objects are not focused. This causes a person to wear glasses to correct the vision problems.

4 Have students cover their ears with their hands. Then play the tape recording of muffled sounds. After students listen to the muffled tape, ask them to share how they felt trying to understand the sound. Students will feel frustrated.

You can make an analogy that people who are older may experience a hearing loss.

5 Take the tongue depressor and the piece of cellophane tape. Ask for a student volunteer. Put the tongue depressor behind one finger, and then tape two fingers together. Ask the student to try to do simple things like tying shoes or eating with a fork using the taped hand. Introduce the word arthritis. Explain that **arthritis** is a condition in which the joints are difficult to move. Arthritis is more common in older people than in younger people.

6 Explain to students that they have just experienced three different scenarios that a person who is aging may experience. Emphasize that the majority of people who are older than sixty-five do not have many of these conditions and that, in fact, these people are healthy. But it is important to be sensitive to the needs of older adults, especially family members who may have some of these conditions. Explain that there are many ways to be sensitive to older adults. Suppose a person cannot see clearly. Ask students what they might do to help this person. Answers may be: "Help to make sure enough light is present when that person is reading," "Help by reading to someone," and "Answer any questions this person may have." Suppose a person has difficulty hearing. One may speak more slowly, loudly, and clearly. A person who has arthritis may have difficulty moving. This person can be assisted to perform certain tasks or be helped to move around.

7 Ask students if they have known someone who has died. Explain that it is normal to feel a deep sense of loss and sadness when someone they care about dies. Tell students that it is helpful to talk to other people about their loss.

Evaluation:

This is a good opportunity to have students identify physical or mental health concerns an older adult, perhaps someone in their families, may experience. Some of these conditions are mentioned in the strategy. Others may be conditions such as feeling tired often, not speaking clearly, dropping objects easily, or falling easily. Have students identify actions they can take when they are around an older person who has health problems. Emphasize to students that when they are helpful to others, they are also helpful to themselves. They have good feelings when they are helpful to other people. Have them tell you what they would say to a friend or adult if someone they care about dies. Have students write papers on "The Special Gifts and Special Needs of Older People."

Disjointed Movements

Health Education Standards:

- Students will comprehend health promotion and disease prevention concepts.
- Students will demonstrate the ability to use goal-setting and decision-making skills that enhance health.

Performance Indicators:

- Students will describe the human body systems.
- Students will set a personal health goal and make progress toward its achievement.

Life Skill:

- I will care for my body systems.

Materials:

Teaching Master, "The Skeletal System"; transparency projector; a coin such as a dime

Motivation:

1 Explain to students that one major system of the body about which they will learn is the skeletal system. The **skeletal system** is the body system that is made up of all of the bones. The collection of bones inside the body helps give the body support. Explain that the bones serve as a frame. You can make an analogy of a building being constructed. Explain to students that usually a frame is built. The frame helps to support everything. The frame gives support for a roof. The frame also helps support the walls. The bones inside the body serve as a frame. The **skeleton** is another name for the bony frame of the body. The skeleton helps a person stand straight. It also helps a person move.

2 Explain that people can move because their bones have joints. A **joint** is a part of the body where two bones meet. Show students examples of different kinds of joints. Bend your knee. Bend your elbow. Explain that these joints can bend back and forth. Hold your arms straight out to the side. Now rotate your arms. Explain to students that you can do this because the joints in the shoulders enable you to move in many different directions such as in a circular fashion. Emphasize that different kinds of joints can help the bones move in different directions.

3 Have students pretend what their bodies would be like if they did not have any joints. Have students seated at their desks. Then ask them to stand while trying not to bend their knees. Students will observe that a simple task like standing is difficult. Have students try to pick up a coin from the floor while keeping the joints in their fingers locked. Students will not be able to do this. Students will develop an appreciation for how the joints help them move.

4 Explain that bones have functions in addition to supporting the body. Bones also contain a center part called marrow. **Bone marrow** is a part inside the bones that helps produce red blood cells. **Red blood cells** are cells that carry oxygen to the different parts throughout the body.

5 The following activity will enable students to help identify the major bones inside the body. Show the Teaching Master "The Skeletal

System." Use a transparency of this master to review the location of different bones inside the body, pointing to the corresponding areas on your body as you point to the bones.

6 After reviewing the bones on the master, tell the class you are going to play "Simon Says." You can review the rules if students do not know how this game is played. The rules of this version will be similar. While keeping the transparency projected, you will point to areas of the body that contain different kinds of bones. When you point to the area on the master, you will name the corresponding bone. For example, you may say "Simon Says touch your patella." and students will point to their knee area. Following the rules of "Simon Says," students will be eliminated if they do not point to the area which you name or if they point to that area when you do not preface your statement with "Simon Says."

Evaluation:

By playing "Simon Says," you will be able to determine how well students understand the names of the different bones in the body and where they are located. You can also use the same transparency but cover the names. Identify certain bones inside the body and ask students to identify the location of the particular bones on the projected image. You can also assign a number to each bone while covering up the name. You may choose ten bones students will need to identify. Students can number down the side of a paper from one through ten. Students must write the correct name of the bone that corresponds to the number on the transparency. This can be used as a test. Have students point to bones on their bodies that are most often injured in accidents, and ask them what they can do to prevent injury to these bones. In a discussion of taking care of their bones, students should indicate that proper nutrition is essential to bone growth and to the healing of bones should one of their bones be broken.

Teaching Master

The Skeletal System

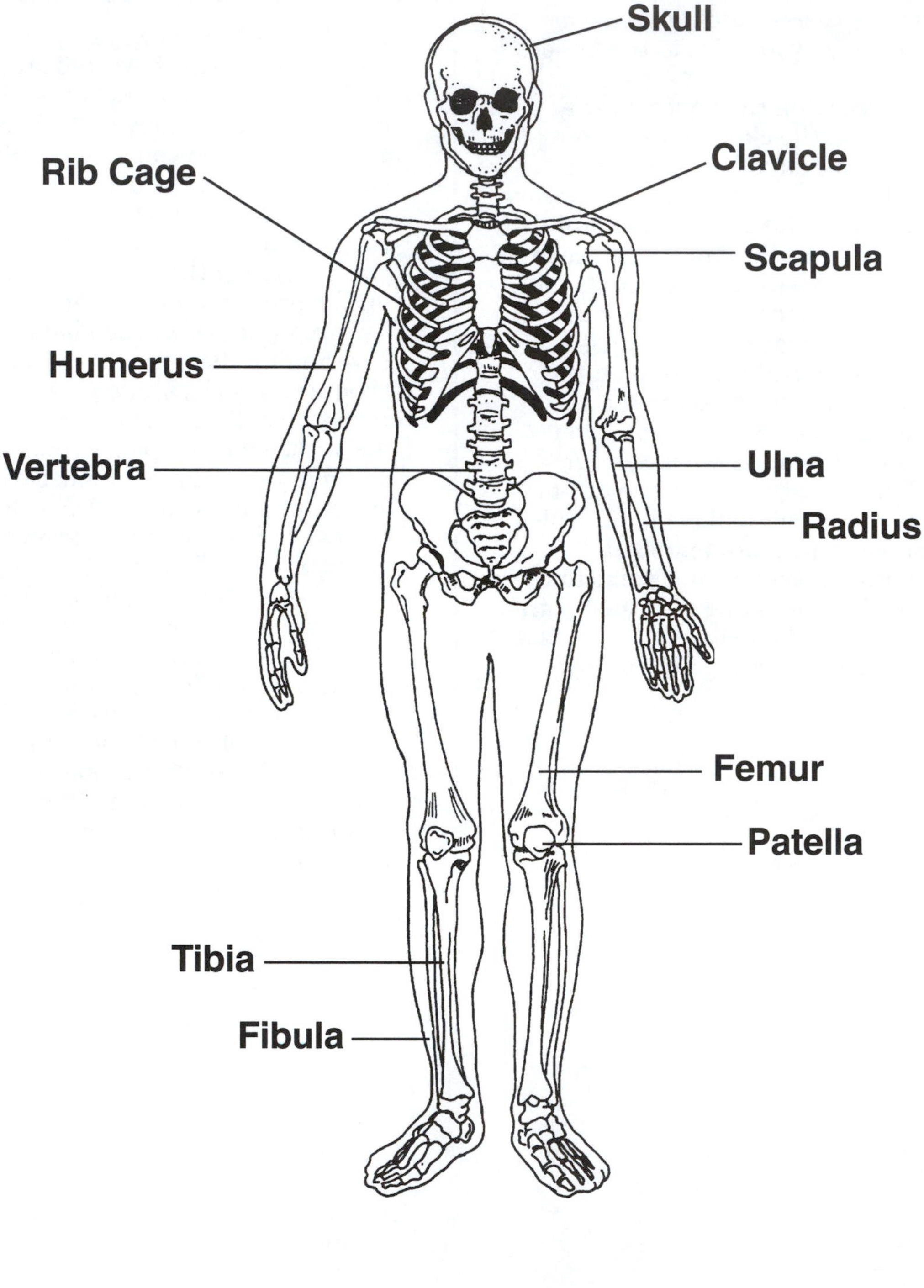

Skull

Clavicle

Rib Cage

Scapula

Humerus

Vertebra

Ulna

Radius

Femur

Patella

Tibia

Fibula

Mineral Match

Health Education Standards:

- Students will comprehend health promotion and disease prevention concepts.
- Students will demonstrate the ability to practice health-enhancing behaviors and reduce health risks.

Performance Indicators:

- Students will recognize the relationship between personal health behaviors and individual well-being.
- Students will identify responsible health behaviors.

Life Skills:

- I will recognize foods that contain the six major nutrients.
- I will make food selections that reduce my risk of disease.
- *I will choose behaviors to reduce my risk of cardiovascular disease. (Communicable and Chronic Diseases)*

Materials:

Teaching Master, "Important Minerals"; transparency projector

Motivation:

1 Begin by asking students how a car would travel if it did not have gasoline in its tank. Students will indicate that the car would not be able to get anywhere if there was no gas in the tank because there would not be anything to power the engine. Explain that just like a car, people need something to power their bodies. But unlike a car, people do not use gasoline. They use food. If people did not have food, they would not be able to live. They would not have anything to provide them with a source of energy. Their bodies would not be able to perform.

2 Explain that just having food is not enough. People need to have foods that contain nutrients. A **nutrient** is a substance in food that is used by the body. Nutrients are a source of energy. Explain to students that there are six kinds of nutrients. These six nutrients are proteins, carbohydrates, fats, minerals, vitamins, and water.

3 Review the major points about each kind of nutrient. Begin with proteins. Explain that **proteins** are nutrients that help build and repair cells in the body. Proteins are also a source of energy. Among the kinds of foods that contain proteins are dairy products such as milk; meat such as beef, poultry, and fish also contain proteins.

4 Introduce the word carbohydrate. **Carbohydrates** are nutrients that serve as a main source of energy for the body. The two kinds of carbohydrates are starches and sugars. **Starches** are foods such as bread, rice, and potatoes that provide energy over a long period of time. **Sugars** are carbohydrates that provide very quick energy for the body. Some sugars are natural in that they are contained in healthful foods such as oranges, kiwi, and apples. Other foods contain sugar that is added. Sugars that are added to foods are called **processed sugars.** Cake and candy contain processed sugars. It is best to limit the intake of processed sugars.

5 Introduce the word "fats." **Fats** are nutrients that help provide energy to the body as well as help the body to store vitamins. There are two kinds of fats. **Saturated fats** are fats in foods that come mostly from animals. Some examples of foods that contain saturated fats include pork, steak, eggs, whole milk, and butter. **Unsaturated fats** are fats more healthful than saturated fats and are found in vegetables, nuts, and fish. Emphasize that eating too much saturated fat is related to the development of heart disease.

6 Explain that minerals are another kind of nutrient. **Minerals** are nutrients that regulate many of the chemical reactions in the body. Minerals help the body grow and develop. Green leafy vegetables and meat contain different kinds of minerals. Distribute the Teaching Master "Important Minerals." Make a transparency of this chart and review content with students. Explain that you are going to play a game called "Mineral Match" with the class. After reviewing the material in the chart, have students put their charts away. Cover the last two columns on the chart. Only the names of the minerals and the headings in the other two columns should be showing. Identify content in one of the columns. For example, you may say that, "This mineral helps a person grow and stay alert." The students will have to answer, "Zinc." You may say, "Bananas and green leafy vegetables are examples of this nutrient. Students will respond, "potassium." Do this activity so that all of the information in the chart is covered.

7 Explain that another nutrient is vitamins. **Vitamins** are nutrients that help other chemical reactions in the body take place. Some people think they have to take vitamin pills to get all the vitamins they need. But most people following a healthful diet should not need to take vitamins in the form of pills.

8 Introduce the final nutrient, water. **Water** is a nutrient that is needed for all body processes. An important function of water is controlling the temperature of the body. Emphasize to students that they should have the equivalent of between six to eight glasses of water each day. Many foods such as fruits and vegetables are made up of large amounts of water.

9 Explain that food should be prepared in ways that help keep the nutrients in them. Share some hints about helping to keep proteins in foods. Among these are: keep foods cold, cook vegetables for a short period of time to avoid nutrient loss, do not soak vegetables before cooking, and eat foods fresh rather than keeping them around for long periods of time.

Evaluation:

Review the facts about minerals by giving students a blank chart similar to the one used in the strategy. Then have students fill in the blank areas inside the chart. Have students develop a daily menu for a week that includes breakfast, lunch, dinner, and snacks. Be sure they include food and beverage selections that indicate they are aware of diseases that can be caused by nutrient excesses and deficiencies.

Teaching Master
Important Minerals

Name of Mineral	Purpose of Mineral	Examples of Foods
Iron	Helps produce red blood cells	dried beans, peas, liver
Sodium	Helps muscles relax and contract	salt, beets
Calcium	Helps build strong bones and teeth, helps blood clot	milk, yogurt, green vegetables
Potassium	Helps cells maintain a balance of water	bananas, green leafy vegetables
Zinc	Promotes growth and alertness	wheat bran, eggs, oatmeal
Iodine	Helps make the thyroid hormone and provides energy	iodized salt, seafood

The Benefits Of Fitness

Health Education Standards:

- Students will comprehend health promotion and disease prevention concepts.
- Students will demonstrate the ability to practice health-enhancing behaviors to reduce health risks.

Performance Indicators:

- Students will recognize the relationship between personal health behaviors and individual well-being.
- Students will demonstrate strategies to improve or maintain personal health.

Life Skills:

- I will participate in movement and exercise.
- I will achieve a desirable level of physical fitness.
- I will improve my skill-related fitness.

Materials:

Teaching Master, "Bee Wise And Exercise"; transparency projector; straw; small glass of water

Motivation:

1 Start with a glass of water and a straw. Ask a student to drink a small amount of water through the straw. The student will notice that the water moved smoothly through the straw. You can make an analogy that the straw is like a healthy blood vessel in that this blood vessel was not clogged, and water (analogous to the blood) flowed easily.

2 Then pinch the straw and twist it around. Now ask the same student to drink the water through the straw. The student will notice that the water does not flow easily through the straw. Explain that this straw (blood vessel) is not healthy. The water (blood) could not flow through it easily.

3 Tell students that people who do not exercise and who participate in unhealthful behaviors can have problems with their circulation. Their blood vessels may be clogged and not allow blood to flow easily. Explain that being physically fit helps the blood vessels as well as the heart to stay healthy. Define **physical fitness** as the condition of the body as a result of participating in exercises that promote muscular strength, muscular endurance, flexibility, cardiovascular endurance, and a healthful percentage of body fat.

4 Explain that there are many benefits of physical fitness. Discuss these benefits by showing the Teaching Master "Bee Wise And Exercise." Provide students with the opportunity to add benefits to this list.

5 Explain that to get one's body into top condition, it is important to develop the components of physical fitness. They are muscular endurance, muscular strength, cardiovascular endurance, flexibility, and a heathful percentage of body fat.

6 Introduce the term muscular endurance. **Muscular endurance** is the ability to use muscles for an extended period of time. A person who swims for a mile or who runs two miles demonstrates muscular endurance. Muscular endurance can be developed by participating in activities that require long periods of work. For example, a marathon runner will need to run many miles almost every day to develop the endurance needed to run a marathon.

7 Introduce the term musclar strength. **Muscular strength** is the ability of muscles to perform tasks with power such as pulling and pushing. For example, a person may be able to lift heavy weights, thereby showing that the muscles are strong.

8 **Cardiovascular endurance** is the ability to do exercises that require increased oxygen intake for an extended period of time. Aerobic exercises such as riding a bicycle over a long distance without getting tired indicates that a person has heart fitness.

9 **Flexibility** is the ability to bend easily at the joints and stretch muscles without too much effort. Touching your toes with your fingertips while your knees are locked straight shows you have flexibility. Being flexible helps keep

the muscles in the body free from injury.

10 The reduction of body fat is important in becoming physically fit. Everyone has fat tissue, but some people have more fat tissue than others. **Lean tissue** is body tissue that has little or no fat. Becoming physically fit helps reduce the amount of fat tissue and increase the amount of lean tissue in the body. Aerobic exercises such as speed walking and long distance running help reduce the amount of fat tissue.

Evaluation:

After reviewing the five components of physical fitness, have students identify activities they can do to develop each one. For example, they may do toe touches each day to improve flexibility.

Teaching Master

Bee Wise and Exercise

Bee Wise says that exercise will:

...help you cope with stress.

...help improve your self-concept.

...help you feel rested and sleep well.

...help your muscles become strong.

...help you get along well with others.

...help you concentrate in school more easily.

...help reduce the chances of developing heart disease.

...help the lungs work more easily.

...help you have a healthful appearance.

...help you perform better in many kinds of sports.

It's A Difficult Task

Health Education Standards:

- Students will recognize the relationship between personal health behaviors and individual well-being.
- Students will demonstrate the ability to practice health-enhancing behaviors and reduce health risks.

Performance Indicators:

- Students will recognize the relationship between personal health behaviors and individual well-being.
- Students will identify behaviors that are safe, risky, or harmful to self and others.

Life Skills:

- I will not misuse or abuse controlled substances.
- I will remain safe and drug-free.

Materials:

One pair of old eyeglasses; petroleum jelly; needle with tape covering the point; thread

Motivation:

1 Explain that the use of illegal drugs can be harmful to many parts of the body. Opiates such as heroin and morphine are types of illegal drugs that can be abused. These drugs slow the actions of the central nervous system. Drugs that slow body actions are called depressants. Other drugs called stimulants speed up the actions of the body. Cocaine, amphetamines, and crack are stimulants. Stimulants can speed up actions of the body so much that a person can experience heart failure.

Marijuana is a drug that is prepared from crushed leaves of the cannabis plant. People who smoke marijuana may experience amotivational syndrome. **Amotivational syndrome** is a syndrome in which people lack the desire to perform common everyday tasks such as doing homework.

2 Explain that many body parts are affected when a person uses illegal drugs. The following activity will demonstrate how drugs affect muscle coordination and the ability of the brain to control muscle activity.

3 Place a light coating of petroleum jelly on the lenses of an old pair of eyeglasses. Select a volunteer to come to the front of the class. Give the volunteer a needle and a piece of thread. Tape should cover the point of the needle. Ask the volunteer to try to thread the needle while (s)he is wearing the eyeglasses. The volunteer will have difficulty performing the task.

Evaluation:

Have the students in the class explain how using drugs might be compared to wearing eyeglasses that are coated with petroleum jelly. Explain that the blurred vision caused by the petroleum jelly prevented the student from threading the needle. (Using illegal drugs can interfere with vision, which makes the completion of simple tasks difficult.) Responses should indicate that students understand the many effects that different types of drugs can have on the body and that they will avoid the use of illegal drugs in any form.

Wheel Of Misfortune

Health Education Standards:

- Students will demonstrate the ability to practice health-enhancing behaviors and reduce health risks.
- Students will demonstrate the ability to practice health-enhancing behaviors to reduce health risks.

Performance Indicators:

- Students will recognize that many injuries and illnesses can be prevented.
- Students will recognize the relationship between personal behaviors and individual well-being.
- Students will demonstrate strategies to improve or maintain personal health.

Life Skills:

- I will recognize that some diseases are communicable while others are noncommunicable.
- I will keep my immune system healthy.
- I will choose behaviors to prevent the spread of pathogens.
- I will choose behaviors to reduce the risk of infection with common communicable diseases.

Materials:

Student Master, "Terms Related to Communicable and Chronic Diseases"; paper; writing marker

Motivation:

1 Explain to students that they will play a game called "Wheel of Misfortune." Explain that the game will focus on diseases that, unfortunately, many people have. Terms related to diseases will also be given.

2 Explain that this game is played like the television show, *Wheel of Fortune*. The class can be divided into teams. Each member of the team will have only one turn to select a letter and try to guess the disease or related term. Explain that the diseases will be either communicable or noncommunicable. You will need enough sheets of paper to hold the individual letters that will spell the words or terms that you use. The words or terms may be diseases that have been covered in previous lessons or they may be related terms or diseases or disorders that are listed on the Teaching Master "Terms Related To Communicable And Chronic Diseases." You can choose to distribute copies of this master to students and have them review the information on it. But students should not use this master to find answers to the words or terms. You can choose to assign certain categories for the diseases such as "A Communicable Disease" or "A Disease That Affects Children."

3 You can play several rounds of this game and declare the team that guesses the most words as the winner.

Evaluation:

You can use the information from the teaching master to design a quiz on the different kinds of diseases and terms related to these diseases and their definitions and characteristics.

497

Student Master

Terms Related To Communicable And Chronic Diseases

Allergy – a hypersensitive reaction by the immune system to a foreign antigen (protein).

Alzheimer's Disease – a degenerative disease of the central nervous system characterized by premature senility.

Antibiotic – a medicine used to treat certain diseases.

Antibody – protein produced by B cells that helps destroy pathogens inside the body.

Arthritis – a general term that includes over 100 diseases, all of which involve inflammation.

Athlete's Foot – a fungal infection that grows between the toes when feet are not kept dry.

Bacteria – single-celled microorganisms that can produce illness.

Cancer – a group of diseases in which there is uncontrolled multiplication of abnormal cells in the body.

Chronic Disease – a disease that lasts a long time or recurs frequently

Common Cold – a viral infection of the upper respiratory tract.

Communicable Disease – illness causes by pathogens that enter the body through direct or indirect contact.

Cystic Fibrosis – a genetic disease that affects the mucous and sweat glands.

Diabetes – a disease in which the body is unable to process the sugar in foods in normal ways.

Disability – a physical or mental impairment.

Epilepsy – a condition in which there is a disturbance of impulses in the brain leading to seizures.

Fungi – single-celled or multicellular plant-like organisms, such as yeasts and molds, that are capable of causing disease to the skin, mucous membranes, and lungs.

Hives – small, itchy bumps on the skin.

Hypertension – high blood pressure.

Immunity – the body's protection from disease.

Influenza – a viral disease that affects the respiratory system.

Leukemia – cancer of the blood.

Mononucleosis – a viral infection that occurs most frequently to those in the 15- to 19-year-old age group; it is also known as "mono."

Pathogen – disease-causing organism.

Pneumonia – an inflammation of the lungs accompanied by fever, shortness of breath, headache, chest pain, and coughing.

Protozoa – tiny, single-celled organisms that produce toxins that are capable of causing disease.

Reye's Syndrome – a serious condition, which may follow influenza and chickenpox in children and adolescents, that is characterized by swelling of the brain and destruction of liver tissue.

Rheumatic Fever – disease in which there is an acute fever, the joints swell, and the body temperature rises.

Sickle-cell Disease – a blood disease that gets its name from the shape of the abnormal red blood cell.

Symptom – a change in a body function from a normal pattern.

Tay-Sachs Disease – a genetic disease caused by the absence of a key enzyme needed to break down fats in the body.

I Guard My Eyes

Health Education Standard:

- Students will demonstrate the ability to practice health-enhancing behaviors and reduce health risks.

Performance Indicators:

- Students will develop injury prevention strategies for personal health.
- Students will generate ways to avoid threatening situations.

Life Skills:

- I will stay safe while exercising.
- *I will choose sources of health-related information and products wisely. (Consumer and Community Health)*
- *I will follow guidelines to prevent injuries during exercises. (Personal Health)*

Materials:

Two unpeeled hard-boiled eggs; crayons; marble; glass of water; plastic wrap; magazines; posterboard; glue; paints

Motivation:

1 Show the unpeeled eggs to students. Explain that each of the eggs represents an eye. Use a crayon or marker to draw the parts of the eye on each of the hard boiled eggs. Place one of the hard-boiled eggs in a clear glass. Pour water over the egg so that water is barely covering the egg. Explain that a real eyeball is in a protected area. This protected area is the eye socket. Explain that an eyeball is protected by fluids also.

2 Take a marble and drop it on the egg that is in the glass of water. Students will notice that the shell on the egg cracks. Explain that this egg, or eyeball, was not protected. If this were a real eyeball and the marble hit it, the eyeball could have been injured. Vision could have been harmed. Vision could have been lost.

3 Remove the cracked hard-boiled egg from the glass of water. Replace this egg with the other hard-boiled egg. Cover the top of the glass with clear plastic wrap. Again, drop the marble above the glass. This time, students will notice that the marble hit the plastic wrap and bounced off. The marble did not penetrate the plastic wrap and get to the egg or eyeball. Explain that the eyeball was protected. Explain that in some respects, the cellophane wrap acted like an eyeguard. Eyeguards protect eyes just as the plastic wrap protected the egg. Eyeguards prevent objects from entering the eyes.

4 Explain to students that they are consumers. A **consumer** is a person who buys and uses products and services and who makes choices about how to spend time. Consumers need to make wise choices about products that help protect the health of individuals. For example, your students may participate in many different kinds of sports. They need to keep themselves protected from injury when they play these sports. They may need to buy special products that help protect them from injury when they play sports. One part of the body that needs protection is the eyes. Not only do the eyes need protection during sports but they also need protection when doing other activities.

5 Explain to students that thousands of people each year lose some vision or are blinded because they injured their eyes doing certain activities. In most of these cases, loss of vision could have been avoided had the person been wearing eyeguards for protection.

6 Identify certain situations in which eyeguards would be recommended. For example, in certain sports such as racquet sports, eyeguards can offer protection from a ball that can hit the eyeball. Suppose a person has already suffered an eye injury; that person would need to protect his/her eye from further harm. Ask students if they watch basketball on television. They may wonder why some basketball players wear eyeguards. Explain that some of these players may already have suffered an eye injury. They do not want another person's fingers or the ball coming in contact with their eyes. They wear the eyeguards for protection.

7 Tell students that they need to wear eyeguards at certain times. Some situations that call for the use of eyeguards are using sharp tools, being around areas where there may be flying substances such as wood chips flying when a power saw is being used, or playing a sport such as racquetball, or using power lawn equipment.

Evaluation:

Have students brainstorm different activities they do or are around that may necessitate the use of eyeguards. Students can also share where they can purchase eyeguards. For example, sporting goods stores or hardware stores sell eyeguards. Have students make a commitment to use eyeguards when necessary to protect their vision.

Quack, Quack, Quack

Health Education Standards:

- Students will demonstrate the ability to access valid health information and appropriate health products and services.
- Students will analyze the impact of culture, media, technology, and other influences on health.

Performance Indicators:

- Students will explain the impact of advertising on the selection of health resources, products, and services.
- Students will describe how the media seeks to influence thought, feelings, and behaviors.

Life Skills:

- I will analyze the effects of advertising on my choices.
- I will recognize and report quackery.
- I will spend money wisely.

Materials:

Construction paper; writing markers; scissors; variety of empty cans and bottles; children's clothes

Motivation:

1 Distribute construction paper, scissors, and writing markers to students. Have students draw two ducks on the construction paper and cut them out.

2 Explain to students that they are going to learn about quackery. Explain that **quackery** is the selling of products or services using false information. Explain that **products**
are materials that people may buy, such as cans of food or medicines. **Services** are ways that people are helped. For example, visiting a physician for a checkup is a service for which a person will pay.

3 Present the following tips that students should know to help identify quackery:
- Someone tells you that a product is a miracle cure for something.
- Someone tells you that there is a secret ingredient in a food or product.
- Someone comes to your door to sell you a product that should be sold in a supermarket or drug store.
- Someone tells you that a product will cure many different illnesses.
- Someone tells you that you can be just like someone else if you buy the product.

4 Explain to students that you are going to sell them products. If they think you are using methods that a quack would use to sell products, they are to hold up their ducks and say, "quack, quack, quack."

5 The following are examples of products and ways to sell them:
- Hold up an empty bottle. "This miracle drug will make you grow up to be very tall." (quack, quack, quack)
- "This cereal has no sugar." Show a cereal high in sugar. (quack, quack, quack)
- "I am coming to your door because this food is so new that no one has the secret recipe yet to make it. You can be the first to try it." (quack, quack, quack)
- "If you wear this clothing, you will be just like... ." Name a famous person students will admire. (quack, quack, quack)
- "If you wear these sneakers you will play basketball like an all-star." (quack, quack, quack)

501

6 Have students discuss the criteria they used in determining whether something was quackery or legitimate. Students can also share examples of quackery they have observed and tell why they considered something or someone as being associated with quackery.

Evaluation:

Divide the class into small but equal groups and have each group select a product from a magazine or make up its own product. Have half of the groups develop "quack" commercials that they will present to the rest of the class. Have the other half of the groups present an actual advertisement from the magazine. Have students determine which are the quack presentations and which are valid advertisements. Students are to discuss their reasons for their choices.

QUACK!
QUACK!

Environmental Smash CD

Health Education Standards:

- Students will comprehend health promotion and disease prevention concepts.
- Students will demonstrate the ability to advocate for personal, family, and community health.

Performance Indicators:

- Students will identify the impact of the environment on personal health.
- Students will identify methods of health promotion.
- Students will express ideas and opinions on health issues.
- Students will demonstrate the ability to influence and support others in making positive health choices.

Life Skills:

- I will be concerned about environmental issues.
- I will cooperate with environmental protection agencies.

Materials:

Poster paper; color markers; glue

Motivation:

1 Explain to students that they are going to have the opportunity to use their creative talents to identify ways they can make the environment a more healthful place in which to live. Give students enough poster paper so they can glue two pieces together. They should form a thick poster that is to resemble a CD but it will be much bigger so they can have room to write. Explain to students that they are to pretend that they are music producers and that they are going to have the opportunity to produce a hit CD. However, the CDs they produce will be related to making the environment a more healthful place in which to live.

2 Tell students to think up a title for their CD and to use their markers to write the title on their CD poster. They should create a title that will focus on making the environment a healthful one for them. For example, they may create a title such as, "Sweet Surroundings." Or, another title might be "Clean and Green." They are to create a name of a group that has recorded the songs. One example of a fictitious group might be Ozzie and the Ozones. Another example of a group might be Robby Reuse and the Recyclers. Students are then to design a cover for their album, focusing on a picture of the environment.

3 Tell students they are to take a sheet of paper and use it as sheet music. They are to write a ten-line song that identifies five facts that show the environment is important. Students should give their songs a title. If students wish, they can cut their paper in the form of a CD and write their song on it.

4 An alternate way to do this exercise is to have the students work in teams. Within teams, they can sing a song, thereby presenting different facts to the class. The students in the class must focus on what is being said so they can identify important information about the environment.

Evaluation:

You can take notes about the different facts presented by the different groups that have presented. Use your notes to quiz students about the different facts related to the environment. Ask students to identify environmental problems and issues in their community. Have students suggest the names of agencies they might contact to learn more about these problems and issues and to learn if and how students can be of help in addressing some of these.

Stress Test

Health Education Standard:

- Students will demonstrate the ability to practice health-enhancing behaviors and reduce health risks.

Performance Indicator:

- Students will develop ways to manage common sources of stress for children.

Life Skills:

- I will practice stress management and suicide prevention skills.
- *I will recognize the risk factors and protective factors associated with drug misuse and abuse. (Alcohol, Tobacco, and Other Drugs)*

Materials:

Student Master, "Health Behavior Contract"; ruled paper; pencil; chalk and chalkboard

Motivation:

1 Prior to beginning this strategy, students should not know what topic you plan to cover because the element of surprise is important. As soon as your class begins, place students in the following stressful situation. Tell students, "Take out a sheet of paper and number down the left-hand side from one to twenty. I told you that you were responsible for reading (whatever you are working on currently). I am going to see if you completed this assignment. And by the way–this test is going to be worth 50 percent of your grade for the course." Proceed to give students

questions that will be almost impossible to answer. For example, you can say, "The first question has three parts. Name three effects of stress on the cerebral cortex." Choose another three difficult questions before stopping.

2 Tell students, "This is not a real test. However, when I told you that I was giving you a test, certain reactions occurred inside your body. What are some reactions that occurred?" Students will most likely mention increased heart rate, sweating, dry mouth, etc.

3 Define the words stress and stressor. **Stress** is the response of a person's mind or body to stressors. A **stressor** is a physical, mental, emotional, social, or environmental demand. In the illustration that was used, an example of stress was the increase in heart rate. This was one of the body's responses to the stressor. The stressor was the unannounced and difficult test. The test was a mental-emotional demand.

4 Review information regarding the general adaptation syndrome. The **general adaptation syndrome,** or **GAS,** is the body's response to a stressor. During the **alarm stage of GAS,** the body prepares for quick action as adrenaline is released into the bloodstream, heart rate and blood pressure increase, digestion slows, blood flows to muscles, respiration increases, pupils dilate, and hearing sharpens. The body is prepared to meet the demands of the stressor. As the demands are met, the resistance stage of GAS begins. During the **resistance stage of GAS,** pulse, breathing rate, and blood pressure return to normal. The pupils contract and muscles relax. If the demands of the stressor are met unsuccessfully, the GAS continues, and the exhaustion stage of GAS begins. During the **exhaustion stage of GAS,** the body becomes fatigued from overwork and a person becomes vulnerable to diseases.

5 Explain that people respond to stressors in different ways. **Eustress** is successful coping or a healthful response to a stressor. When a person experiences eustress, the resistance stage is effective in establishing homeostasis in the body because the demands of the stressor are met. **Distress** is unsuccessful coping or a harmful response to a stressor. The exhaustion stage often accompanies distress.

6 Emphasize the importance of using stress management skills. **Stress management skills** are techniques that can be used to cope with stressors and to lessen the harmful effects of distress. Stress management skills used to cope with stressors include talking with responsible adults about difficult life events and daily hassles, using The Responsible Decision-Making Model and resistance skills, and writing in a journal. Exercising, eating a healthful diet, and spending time with caring people also help with stress.

7 Outline reasons why using harmful drugs increases stress rather than relieving stress. Harmful drugs such as stimulants increase the body's response to stress. The heart beats faster, respiration increases, digestion slows, and the pupils dilate. Harmful depressant drugs such as barbiturates and alcohol depress the reason and judgment centers of the brain. It becomes more difficult to make choices about what to do about the stressors.

Evaluation:

Have students complete the Student Master "Health Behavior Contract" on the topic of Stress Management. Have students discuss the effects of drug misuse and abuse on the ability of people under stress to cope with stressors.

Multicultural Infusion:

Ask students to describe stressors that they experience and that they believe are specific to their culture. Have the class brainstorm stress management skills that might be used to ease the stress that may be caused by these stressors. Write students' ideas on the chalkboard. How might classmates help students with cultural stressors relieve stress?

Inclusion:

Ask students with special needs to describe stressors that they experience as a result of their specific disabilities. Have the class brainstorm stress management skills that might be used to lessen the stress that may be caused by these stressors. Write students' ideas on the chalkboard. How might classmates help students with special needs relieve stress?

Student Master

Health Behavior Contract

Name _____

Life Skill: I will practice stress management skills.

**Effect On
My Health:**

_____

_____

_____

_____

**My Plan
To Manage
Stress:**

_____

_____

_____

_____

**How My
Plan Worked:**

_____

_____

_____

_____

_____

My Relationships, My Future

Health Education Standard:

- Students will demonstrate the ability to use effective interpersonal skills that enhance health.

Performance Indicators:

- Students will describe how the behavior of family and peers contributes to one's physical, mental, emotional, and social health.
- Students will demonstrate ways to communicate care, consideration, and respect of self and others.

Life Skills:

- I will develop relationship skills.
- I will strive for healthful family relationships.
- I will form healthful and responsible friendships.

Materials:

A broomstick or yardstick that is about three feet in length; cellophane tape; pen; two small pieces of paper about one inch square

Motivation:

1 Begin this strategy by introducing the term relationship skills. Define **relationship skills** as the ability people have to communicate and get along well with others. People who have good relationship skills help promote the health of others. They help others make responsible decisions.

2 Take a broomstick or yardstick and two small pieces of paper that are about one inch square. On one piece of paper, write, "Your present" and tape that paper to the bottom of the broomstick (or yardstick). On the other sheet of paper, write "Your future." Tape this piece to the top of the broomstick. Then ask for a volunteer to come up to the front of the room. Explain that you want this person to balance the broomstick on one finger. However, you are going to place certain restrictions on this task. The person must hold out a hand at about waist height and balance the stick on the finger only looking at where the broom meets the finger. Emphasize that the eyes must be focused on where the broomstick meets the finger. Tell the class that this yardstick represents a person and that this person must have a balanced life. The balanced life is indicated by how long this "life" can be balanced on the finger. Now ask the volunteer to begin to balance this "life" on a finger, looking only where the finger and broomstick meet. Count the number of seconds the person keeps the broomstick balanced. The class will observe that the broomstick, or "life," falls rather quickly.

3 Now have the volunteer repeat the task but this time, the volunteer can place his/her eyes anywhere. Tell the class they are to observe this person the second time and see what happens. The class will notice that the volunteer raised his/her eyes toward the top of the broomstick and that the "life" was balanced for a much longer period of time.

4 Explain what took place by asking students what they observed. Students will indicate that when the volunteer looked up, the "life" became balanced for a much longer period of time. Explain that when the volunteer looked up or ahead, (s)he was looking at "your future." When the volunteer looked only where the broomstick met the finger, (s)he was looking at "your present." The yardstick or life became unbalanced very quickly when the volunteer looked only at "your present."

5 Introduce this concept to indicate that people who make decisions based only on what might feel good "right now" are not looking at the implications of their behavior for the future. But when people make decisions looking at the implications for the future, they are more balanced. They have looked at "your future."

6 Have students describe how they make decisions with friends and family members. For example, if a student agrees to the pressures from friends to smoke a cigarette, this student may think that it is all right for now to try to smoke. But, choosing to smoke now may be a stepping stone for beginning to smoke as a regular habit. This student can look at the implications of smoking now

by being aware that smoking can upset the balance of health because it is easy to become dependent on cigarettes. To be **dependent** means to need to do something. Thus, by thinking that smoking might seem harmless now, the risk remains that smoking will become a regular habit. This regular habit can cause many health problems. Emphasize to students that they must look at the future results of their present actions.

7 Explain that people who have good relationship skills with others will be able to communicate in healthful ways. They will also support healthful actions for their friends and family members. This presents a good opportunity to have students discuss how they can deal with people who encourage them to engage in harmful behaviors. Have students share specific ways to handle some of the different pressures they may face. For example, ask students what they would do if they had a friend who wanted them to try to smoke. Discuss using resistance skills to avoid harmful behaviors. Discuss walking away from the situation and telling a family member or trusted adult who would be in a good position to provide guidance.

Evaluation:

Divide the class into two equal groups. Have one group identify a situation that people their age might face. The situation should involve family or friends. They are to present that situation to the other group. That group must identify ways to handle that situation in a healthful way. Then have the groups reverse roles so that the first group will respond to a situation that is given and the second group presents a different situation for consideration. Assess the responses given to indicate the use of responsible decision-making.

The Body Systems Game

Health Education Standard:

- Students will comprehend health promotion and disease prevention concepts.

Performance Indicator:

- Students will describe how body systems are interrelated.

Life Skill:

- I will care for my body systems.

Materials:

Twenty-five 3" x 5" index cards; tape; one red marker; one green marker; pencil or pen

Motivation:

1 To prepare for this activity, you will need twenty-five 3" x 5" index cards. On each of these cards, you are to print the following body systems and the parts associated with each of these systems. Print the names of the body systems in red. The parts that belong under these body systems can be printed in green.

- circulatory system – heart, arteries, veins, blood
- digestive system – liver, small intestine, stomach, large intestines
- respiratory system – lungs, bronchial tubes, alveoli, bronchi
- nervous system – axon, dendrite, neuron, brain
- skeletal system – bones, knee cap, ribs, skull

2 Define the term body systems. A **body system** is a group of body organs that work together to perform certain functions. The **circulatory system** is the body system that provides all body tissues with a regular supply of oxygen and nutrients and carries away carbon dioxide and waste products. The **digestive system** is the body system that breaks food down into chemicals that the body can use for energy and to maintain cells and tissues. Included in this system are the stomach, liver, small intestine, and large intestine. The **respiratory system** is the body system responsible for carrying oxygen from the air to the bloodstream and for expelling the waste product carbon dioxide. Included in this system are the lungs, bronchial tubes, alveoli, and bronchi. The **nervous system** is the body system that gathers information from the external environment, stores, and processes it, and initiates appropriate responses. Included in this system are the brain, axons, dendrites, and neurons. The **skeletal system** is the body system that forms a framework to support the body and to help protect internal soft tissues of the body. Included in this body system are the bones, knee cap, ribs, and skull. You may want to review these five body systems with students before playing "The Body Systems Game."

3 Tell students that they are going to play a game called "The Body Systems Game." Explain to students that they will form a single line on one side of you. When they come up to you, they are to turn their backs so that you can tape a card with a name of a body system or the name of a part of that body system on their backs. Explain that they will not know what part of the body system is taped on their backs. One objective of this activity is for students to guess what is printed on the card on their backs. They are to do this by approaching other students. When they approach other students, they are to turn their backs so the person can read the card. Then the person will turn and ask a question. However, only a question that receives a "yes" or "no" response can be asked. For example, a student cannot approach another student and ask, "Am I above or below the waist?" Rather, the student is to ask, "Am I above the waist?" After receiving an answer, the student must then approach another person. Explain that only one question is allowed to be asked each person. Explain that when the word on the back is correctly identified, that student is to tape the card in the front of his/her body. This will indicate to others that the student guessed what was printed on his/her card. However, this student must still be available to help others who have not guessed what is on their backs.

4 When most of the students have guessed what is on the card on their backs, stop the activity. Ask students who have not guessed what is on their backs to now take their cards and tape them to their fronts. Next, explain that they are to remain completely nonverbal. Explain to students that they each belong to one of five groups. Without being allowed to talk, have students sort themselves into the groups to which they belong. Have groups assemble across the room so that the groups are distinct.

5 After students assemble into groups, explain that you helped them assemble themselves into body systems by printing the names of

the body systems in red and the names of the parts of each body system in green.

6 Now that students are in groups, explain that their group is going to have a task to perform. Tell students that they are going to look at ways to care for the body system their group represents. They can introduce any health facts they desire but these facts must be presented as lyrics to a song. For example, students may sing about a body system using the lyrics they have written and singing to the tune of a popular song or nursery rhyme. Give students about fifteen minutes to prepare for this assignment. Explain that they are to think of a name for their group and a title for their song. Then, they will come to the front of the room and sing the words to their song. Their song is to be from eight to ten lines in length. You can give students an example of how this would work by presenting the following example about the nervous system. You can say, "The name of our group is Denny and the Dendrites and we are here today to sing the newest single from our CD titled 'I'm Nervous About That Impulse.'" The lyrics to the song may go as follows:

The nervous system has a brain.
If I touch something sharp, I'll feel the pain.
Hot and cold, soft and rough.
When my nervous system is healthy, I sure am tough.

7 Have each group present its song. The class is to remember as many facts as possible. You can then use the information with the class to review facts about the care of the different body systems.

Evaluation:

Collect the index cards from students that were used to play the game the first time. Play the game again but, this time, make sure students have different cards. Compare the length of time it took for students to guess what was on their backs and get into groups the second time you did this activity with the first time. Assess how accurate the students were in selecting into groups. This will give you the opportunity to determine how familiar students are with the different body parts and the body systems to which they belong. In addition, you can also assign students another body system. Have them write at least five facts about that body system and include at least one way to care for that body system.

Read That Label

Health Education Standards:

- Students will demonstrate the ability to access valid health information and appropriate health products and services.
- Students will demonstrate the ability to practice health-enhancing behaviors and reduce health risks.
- Students will demonstrate the ability to advocate for personal, family, and community health.

Performance Indicators:

- Students will evaluate health information from multiple sources.
- Students will analyze various communication methods to accurately express health information and ideas.
- Students will demonstrate strategies to improve or maintain personal of family health.

Life Skills:

- I will follow the dietary guidelines.
- I will read food labels.
- I will make food selections that reduce my risk of disease.
- *I will choose behaviors to reduce my risk of cancer. (Communicable and Chronic Diseases)*

Materials:

Teaching Master, "Nutrition Facts Label"; transparency projector; five different boxes of cereals; napkins; scissors

Motivation:

1 Obtain five different boxes of cereal. Sometimes if you ask the manager of a large supermarket for damaged boxes of products such as cereals you might get them for free. (You might also save and ask friends to save cereal boxes with one serving of cereal left in each one.) For this strategy, you will need the cereal from five different cereal boxes placed on five separate napkins on your desk. Do not let students know which cereal came from which box. Ask students if they can identify the most healthful cereal, the second most healthful cereal, etc. Students will not be able to do this task. Ask them why they cannot do it. Students will probably respond that they have no information about the cereal since they do not have the cereal boxes available.

2 Explain that information about different products can be obtained from the labels on their containers. If students had seen the labels, they would be able to answer the question regarding the most nutritious cereals. Explain to students you are going to review information about the food labels that are included on all packages. Show the Teaching Master "Nutrition Facts Label" to the class. Explain that this label is required on food products. Tell students that this label contains important information about the foods inside of a package.

3 Use the Teaching Master "Nutrition Facts Label" to review information about the product. Begin with the top line that says "serving size." The **serving size** is the amount of food that most people would eat, or a portion. Explain that the serving size comes in two measurements. On this label, serving size is written in cups (1 cup). But serving size can be written in grams (228g). Using grams is a more precise way to measure the amount. Indicate that the number of servings in the package (2) is identified.

4 Point out that nutrients are listed next to the Calories. A **Calorie** is a unit of energy. The label tells the number of Calories in a serving. The label also tells the number of Calories that come from fat. Explain that a person should have 30 percent or less fat from Calories each day. For example, a person who eats 100 Calories should have no more than 30 Calories come from fat.

5 Explain that after the Calories, nutrients are listed next. Explain that fats, cholesterol, and sodium are on the label because they are to be eaten in moderation. Eating a diet high in fats, cholesterol, and sodium is related to the development of heart disease. Explain that the percents given at the ends of the lines for each nutrient make it easy to tell if a serving is high or low in nutrients. Usually, 5 percent or less is considered low.

6 After cutting the Nutrition Facts labels from the five cereals, divide the class into five equal groups. Each group will get one label. Cut an additional area from each cereal box around the space where the label was cut out so that students cannot match the labels with the boxes on the basis of the cutout label shape. Also, pass the cereal boxes to each group and have the groups read them. Then, you can have the class pass the boxes from one group to another group after reviewing the information on the boxes for three minutes. Students are to match the labels to the correct cereal boxes by analyzing the nutrients listed on the label and the information on the cereal box. Have students share how they came to conclusions about

matching the labels to the correct cereal boxes.

Evaluation:

Follow this activity by saving five labels and food packages. Hand out the labels to different students and ask them to match the labels to the correct food packages. Evaluate students' knowledge by how accurately they match the labels to the food packages. Ask students to name diseases they might develop if they fail to make wise dietary choices.

Nutrition Facts Label

Nutrition Facts

Serving Size 1 cup (228g)
Servings Per Container 2

Amount Per Serving

Calories 250 Calories from Fat 110

% Daily Value*

Total Fat 12g	**18%**
Saturated Fat 3g	**15%**
Cholesterol 30mg	**10%**
Sodium 470mg	**20%**
Total Carbohydrate 31g	**10%**
Dietary Fiber 0g	**0%**
Sugars 5g	
Protein 5g	

Vitamin A 4%	•	Vitamin C 2%
Calcium 20%	•	Iron 4%

* Percent Daily Values are based on a 2,000
calorie diet.

Medical And Dental Checkups

Health Education Standards:

- Students will comprehend health promotion and disease prevention concepts.
- Students will demonstrate the ability to access valid health information and appropriate health products and services.

Performance Indicators:

- Students will identify ways to reduce risks related to health problems of adolescents.
- Students will analyze methods of health promotion and disease prevention.
- Students will demonstrate strategies to improve or maintain personal and family health.

Life Skills:

- I will be well-groomed.
- I will care for my ears and eyes.
- I will have regular checkups.
- I will follow a dental health plan.
- *I will use health care providers when appropriate. (Consumer and Community Health)*
- *I will use health care facilities when needed. (Consumer and Community Health)*

Materials:

Teaching Master, "How To Floss"; Teaching Master, "A Healthy Body"; transparency projector; classified telephone directory; paper; pencils

Motivation:

1 Begin this strategy by asking students to open up a book and begin to read. As they are reading, turn the lights off in the room and close the shades on the windows. Students will say that they cannot read. Explain to students that their sight is very important and they need to take steps to protect their vision.

2 Tell students that they need to protect their eyes, and that one way to do this is to have vision screening. **Vision screening** is having an eye exam to help detect any eye disorders. Emphasize to students that even if they think their eyes are healthy, they need eye checkups each year so that if any problems are present, they can be corrected. The sooner a health problem is detected, the more effectively it can be treated. Explain that there are many health helpers in the community who can help protect people's eyes. An **ophthalmologist** is a physician who can examine eyes and prescribe glasses and contacts as well as do surgery. An **optometrist** is a health-care professional trained and licensed as a doctor of optometry, examining the eyes, and detecting vision and eye problems. An **optician** is the person who fills prescriptions for glasses and contact lenses.

3 Explain to students what happens during an eye examination. A medical professional can ask a person to read a special chart to see if objects can be seen clearly. The inside of the eyeballs may also be examined. By looking at the blood vessels and other areas in the eyeball, the health of the eyes can be determined. Explain that eyes may be checked for nearsightedness and farsightedness. A person who is **nearsighted** can see objects up close clearly but distant objects are fuzzy. A person who is **farsighted** sees objects that are far away clearly but objects that are close are blurred. Distribute the Teaching Master "A Healthy Body" and review the tips for keeping the eyes healthy.

4 Begin to read and then lower your voice. Continue to lower your voice until it is no longer audible. Eventually you will be moving your lips and not saying anything. Explain to students that if they suffered hearing loss, they would not be able to hear sounds. Many young people suffer hearing loss but are not aware of it. Explain that hearing screening is important to help keep the ears healthy.

5 Introduce the word audiologist. An **audiologist** is a person who tests hearing. An **audiometer** is a machine that assess the range of sounds that a person can hear at various frequencies and intensities. The audiometer works by sending sounds through headphones that the person wears. At first the sounds are loud. Then they are made softer. The point at which no sound can be heard indicates to the audiologist how well a person can hear. Explain that there are many reasons for hearing loss. Among these might be damage to the eardrum from listening to constant, loud sounds or from infection. Pathogens also can enter the ears from the throat.

6 Explain that dental screening is important in helping to protect the teeth. Have students open a book and ask them to read aloud. Then have them stop and pretend they have no teeth. They can simulate this by puckering their mouths so that their lips are folded over their teeth. Now, ask them to read again. Students will notice that they cannot speak clearly. Explain that

if they did not have teeth, they would not be able to speak clearly or to chew food. Explain that there are many people in the community who help protect teeth. A **dentist** is a person who is trained to provide care for the teeth, ranging from giving medical examinations to repairing teeth that are decayed. A **dental hygienist** is a person who cleans teeth, takes X-rays, and provides information about ways to care for the teeth.

7 Explain what happens during a dental exam. X-rays are often taken of the teeth. This helps determine how healthy teeth are on the inside. The teeth are inspected with certain instruments, as are the gums. Twice a year, a person should have his/her teeth cleaned. This helps remove calculus. **Calculus** is hardened plaque. **Plaque** is the sticky substance on the teeth that consists of saliva, bacteria, and food debris. Explain that not caring for teeth can result in dental disease. **Gingivitis** is a condition in which the gums bleed easily. Gingivitis can be caused by improper brushing and not flossing. Show the Teaching Master "How To Floss" and review the steps in flossing. Explain that another problem related to poor dental health is periodontal disease. **Periodontal disease** is a disease of the gums and other tissues that support the teeth. If the teeth lose their supporting tissue and underlying bone, they can fall out.

8 Introduce the word braces. **Braces** are devices that are placed on the teeth to straighten them. Sometimes teeth are crowded and teeth must be pulled to reduce overcrowding in the mouth. Usually braces are put on by an orthodontist. An **orthodontist** is a person who specializes in repositioning the teeth with braces.

9 Discuss grooming. **Grooming** is taking care of the body by following practices that help people look, smell, and feel their best. Explain to students that they should bathe regularly and keep themselves clean in order to reduce the risk of infection and disease.

Evaluation:

Students need to be aware of resources in the community that they can use to obtain medical care. Using the classified pages of the telephone directory, have students work in groups to make a list of health professionals in their community. It is also important to share with students the health services that may be available at their school. Have students make a health directory.

Teaching Master
A Healthy Body

Tips For Keeping Eyes Healthy
- Have regular eye checkups.
- Avoid rubbing the eyes.
- Do not use another person's washcloth.
- Avoid using sharp objects near the eyes.
- Give your eyes a rest when they feel tired.
- Wear sunglasses when in bright sunlight or when playing sports in which you look into the sun at times.
- Keep some lights on in a room when you watch television.

Tips For Keeping Ears Healthy
- Have regular hearing checkups
- Do not place objects in the ears.
- Do not use headphones when listening to loud music.
- Keep the outer ear clean by using a washcloth.
- Allow a health professional to remove wax from the ears.
- Protect the eardrum by wearing a safety helmet when involved in contact activities.
- Seek medical help if sounds become more difficult to hear.

Tips For Dental Health
- Have a dental exam every six months.
- Contact a dentist if teeth are sensitive to hot or cold.
- Always brush after meals with a toothpaste that contains fluoride.
- Floss regularly.
- Eat foods such as cheese that contain calcium to harden teeth.
- Avoid foods that contain sugar and stick to teeth, such as marshmallows.

Teaching Master
How To Floss

1. **Wrap dental floss around two fingers.**

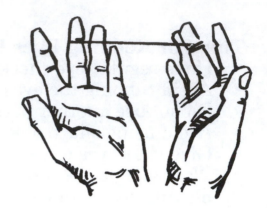

2. **Gently move floss between teeth to gum line.**

3. **Wrap floss around tooth and slide up and down.**

Trying To Think Straight

Health Education Standards:

- Students will demonstrate the ability to access valid health information and appropriate health products and services.
- Students will demonstrate the ability to practice health-enhancing behaviors and reduce health risks.

Performance Indicators:

- Students will research the availability of community health information, products, and services that can help adolescents and their families.
- Students will analyze the short-term and long-term consequences of safe, risky, and harmful behaviors.

Life Skills:

- I will not drink alcohol.
- I will become aware of school and community resources for intervention and treatment.
- I will remain safe and drug-free.

Materials:

Teaching Master, "How Alcohol Affects Well-Being"; transparency projector; sheet of paper; pencil

Motivation:

1 Begin this strategy by asking students on a sheet of paper to write their names clearly in cursive. After they have written their names, ask them to move their chairs so that they can extend one foot in front of them. Their foot should be extended so that the knee is locked. They can use either the right or left foot to do

this activity. Tell students that while their foot is extended, they are to turn it in a wide circle continuously until you tell them to stop.

2 While students are turning their feet in a continuous circle, ask them to write their names in cursive again underneath the name they wrote earlier. As students are doing this, observe their foot. You will notice that they are no longer turning their foot in a circle. Rather, they are moving their foot up and down and side to side. Say, "I see that you are having trouble keeping your foot going in a circle. Please move it in a circle while you are writing your name."

3 Students will be confused and probably laugh at the difficulty they are having. After students have completed this task, discuss what happened. Ask the following questions. "Was it easier to write your name the first time or the second time?" (the first time) "Did writing your name the first time take more or less time?" (less) "Did your name appear neater or sloppier the first time?" (neater) "What happened when you tried to keep your foot going in a circle while writing your name?" (the foot went side to side or up and down)

4 Explain to students that the task of writing a name became very difficult when they were asked to do a second task at the same time, such as moving the foot in a circle. The foot could not move in a circle and the ability to perform an easy task such as writing a name became a problem. Explain to students that they just experienced what it might be like to function if they had alcohol in their body. Define alcohol. **Alcohol** is a harmful drug such as beer or wine that slows down how the body functions. Alcohol is classified as a depressant. A **depressant** is a drug that slows down the actions of the body. Explain to students that had they tried to perform tasks under the influence of alcohol, they would have had great difficulty. This is one reason why people who drink have many accidents and often become injured.

5 Show the Teaching Master "How Alcohol Affects Well-Being," and review the many ways alcohol harms health. All ten areas of health are affected by the use of alcohol.

6 Introduce the word alcoholism. **Alcoholism** is a disease that causes a person to be physically and mentally dependent on alcohol. In the case of alcohol and other drugs, to be **dependent** means to have a need for a drug. Alcohol causes two kinds of dependence. **Physical dependence** is a bodily need for a drug. **Psychological dependence** is a mental need for a drug. Explain that in many families, alcoholism is a problem. About 15 million families in the United States have a member who suffers from alcoholism; this results in many problems for the family. People who have alcoholism often become violent. They cause stress to family members. Children may be afraid to bring friends home because they feel embarrassed. Children may also feel guilty because they do not have the skills to know how to cope or stop the person from drinking. Schoolwork may suffer.

7 Explain to students that help is available for people who have alcoholism and for families who suffer the effects of a member who has alcoholism. Explain that **Alcoholics Anonymous (AA)** is a support group that helps people who have drinking

problems. **Al-Anon** is a support group for family members or friends of someone with alcoholism.

Alateen is a support group for teens who are affected by a friend or family members' drinking. To familiarize students with resources in the community, show them a telephone directory that lists community agencies that offer help. Tell students that they can also see a counselor at school if they have concerns about alcohol and a family member.

Evaluation:

Identify an area of health that appears on the Teaching Master "How Alcohol Affects Well-Being" and have students identify how

using alcohol can have an affect on this area. It is also important for students to understand the importance of being alcohol-free. Divide the class into groups of about five, and have each group write five tips to help people avoid the use of alcohol. For example, if they are at a party, they can leave if they notice someone drinking. Each group in the class is to present five tips to remain alcohol-free. These tips might include suggestions for school and community resources that could be used should there be a need for intervention and treatment. Make a list of these tips and write them in order from the tips most often given down to the one tip least often given. Make a note of how many times each tip was given.

Teaching Master

How Alcohol Affects Well-Being

Mental and Emotional Health:
- Decreases learning and performance in school
- Intensifies moods and feelings
- Interferes with responsible decision-making
- Causes various brain disorders including organic mental disorder
- Intensifies stress

Family Living:
- Interferes with effective communication
- Intensifies arguments
- Increases the likelihood of violence
- Causes fetal alcohol syndrome (FAS).
- Creates codependence and enmeshment

Growth and Development:
- Destroys brain cells
- Decreases performance of motor skills
- Lowers body temperature
- Dulls the body senses
- Increases heartbeat rate and resting blood pressure

Nutrition:
- Interferes with healthful appetite
- Interferes with vitamin absorption
- Causes niacin deficiency
- Causes thiamine deficiency

Personal Health:
- Decreases athletic performance
- Interferes with coordination
- Increases likelihood of sports injuries

Alcohol, Tobacco, and Other Drugs:
- Depresses the brain and respiratory center
- Causes physical and psychological dependency
- Causes dizziness when combined with tranquilizers
- Can cause coma and/or death when combined with narcotics

Communicable and Chronic Diseases:
- Causes cirrhosis of the liver
- Causes heart disease
- Increases the risk of cancers of the mouth, esophagus, larynx, and pharynx when combined with cigarette smoking
- Increases the risk of kidney failure

Consumer and Community Health:
- Is an expensive habit to maintain
- Is taxed heavily in most states

Injury Prevention and Safety:
- Is linked to most violent crimes
- Is linked to many suicides and suicide attempts
- Increases the risk of being injured, drowning, or falling
- Is linked to many fires

Environmental Health:
- Is costly due to an increased need for treatment centers and law enforcement
- Is linked to many missed days of work
- Contributes to environmental pollution

Stuck For Life

Health Education Standards:

- Students will comprehend health promotion and disease prevention concepts.
- Students will demonstrate then ability to practice health-enhancing behaviors and reduce health risks.

Performance Indicators:

- Students will explain the relationship between positive health behaviors and the prevention of injury, illness, disease, and premature death.
- Students will analyze the short-term and long-term consequences of safe, risky, and harmful behaviors.

Life Skills:

- I will choose behaviors to prevent the spread of pathogens.
- I will choose behaviors to reduce the risk of HIV infection.
- *I will reduce my risk of HIV infection by not using intravenous drugs that dull my decision-making skills. (Alcohol, Tobacco, and Other Drugs)*

Materials:

Teaching Master, "How HIV Attacks The Immune System"; transparency projector; two apples—one shiny and one bruised; a needle; red food coloring

Motivation:

1 Make the following preparation for the lesson without students seeing what you are doing. Place the needle into the container of red food coloring. After removing the needle from the container, some of the red food coloring should remain on it. Then stick the needle into the shiny apple. Be certain that some of the red food coloring gets inside the apple.

2 Define HIV, AIDS, and intravenous drug use. **HIV,** or **human immunodeficiency virus,** is a pathogen that causes AIDS. **AIDS,** or **acquired immune deficiency syndrome,** is the final stage of HIV infection during which there is a significant decrease in the disease fighting cells inside the body. **Intravenous drug use** refers to the injection of a drug into a vein. Explain that people sharing needles for intravenous drug use are engaging in a risk behavior for becoming infected with HIV. Review how HIV affects the immune system by reviewing the Teaching Master "How HIV Attacks The Immune System."

3 Show students the two apples—one shiny and one bruised. Explain that each of the apples represents a person. Ask the class which one they believe is infected with HIV. In many cases, most students in the class will say that they believe the bruised apple is the one infected with HIV. Explain that appearance alone will not indicate whether or not a person is infected with HIV. It is not a person's appearance, gender, or race that puts a person at risk. Rather, it is a person's behavior.

4 Cut a piece from the shiny apple near the spot where you inserted the needle with the red food coloring on it. Explain what you did earlier— that you stuck the apple with the needle that had previously been in the container of red food coloring. Further explain that you did this to demonstrate what happens when people share needles for intravenous drug use.

5 Discuss the transmission of HIV through intravenous drug use. The transmission of HIV through intravenous drug use occurs when people who use drugs share needles. The sharing of needles, whether used for anabolic steroids or narcotics, increases the risk of HIV infection. The process in which the needle is used, whether it be skin popping or subcutaneous, intramuscular (such as injecting steroids), or mainlining (directly into a vein), makes no difference in a person's chances of becoming infected with HIV. HIV can enter the syringe when the drug user draws back on the plunger to see if the needle is inside the vein. A vein is tapped when blood is easily drawn into the syringe. Even if only a small amount of blood is trapped inside the syringe, this blood can contain a large amount of HIV when drawn from an infected person. Even if this blood is "shot up," there will remain traces of HIV. If another person uses the same syringe, there is a high probability that HIV will be transmitted and cause infection.

One of the reasons for the high probability of infection is the fact that HIV is pumped directly into the bloodstream rather than through the skin.

6 Explain that in the case of the apple that was stuck with red food coloring, enough of the apple might be cut off to get rid of the food coloring. But, this is not true of people who are stuck with an HIV-infected needle. Once a person is infected with HIV, (s)he is infected for life. Students should also explain that a person's appearance, race, religion, and sexual orientation are not risk factors, rather it is a person's behavior choices. They also should explain the importance of HIV testing for people who have engaged in risk behavior.

7 Cut off pieces from the bruised apple in several places. Explain to students that even though the bruised apple did not look as healthful or appealing as the shiny apple, it is not infected with HIV.

8 Discuss the importance of testing people who have shared needles and/or other injection equipment for intravenous drug use for HIV infection. The test most commonly used to detect HIV infection is called the ELISA test. **ELISA** is a test that detects antibodies developed by the human immune system in response to the presence of HIV. The **Western Blot Test** is a blood test that is used to confirm the results of a positive ELISA.

Evaluation:

Have students write a paper with the theme "Stuck For Life." Students should include a discussion of how HIV transmission occurs when needles and/or injection equipment is shared. They should explain that once a person is infected with HIV, (s)he will always be infected. Students should also explain why appearance, race, and sexual orientation are not risk factors, but the risk factor is a person's behavior choices. They also should explain the importance of HIV testing for people who have engaged in risk behavior.

Inclusion:

Have students write a paper including at least ten sentences with the following theme "Stuck for Life." Provide these students with the following list of facts to include in their papers:

1. Intravenous drug use is a risk behavior for HIV infection.
2. A needle that is shared may have droplets of HIV-infected blood on it.
3. You cannot tell by appearance if a person is infected with HIV.
4. A person is not HIV positive because of his/her race, appearance, or sexual orientation.
5. A person who has engaged in risk behavior should be tested for HIV.
6. There are two tests for HIV—ELISA and Western Blot.
7. If a person is infected with HIV, (s)he will always be infected.

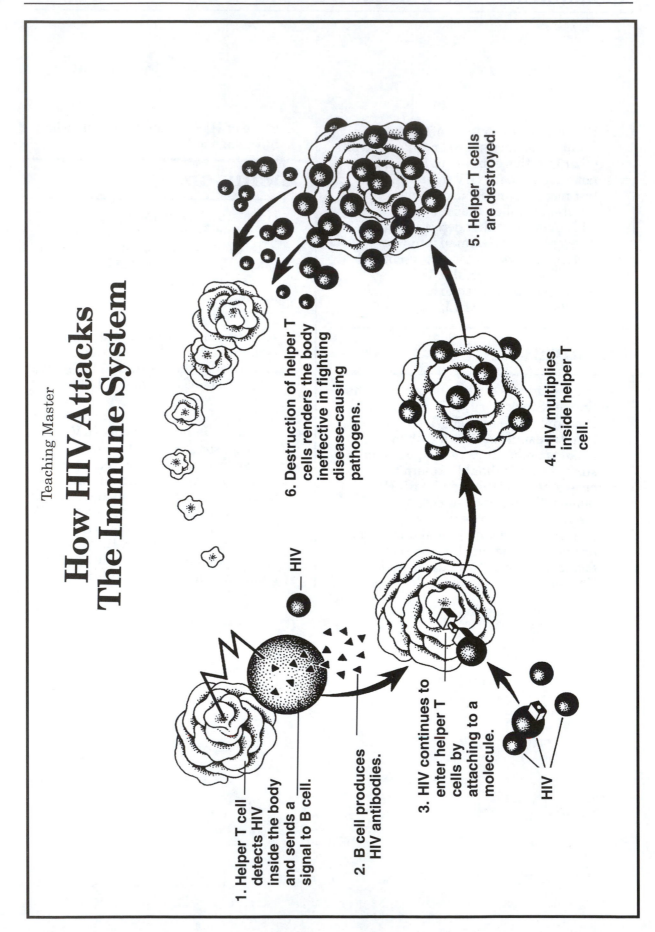

Teaching Master

How HIV Attacks
The Immune System

1. Helper T cell detects HIV inside the body and sends a signal to B cell.

2. B cell produces HIV antibodies.

3. HIV continues to enter helper T cells by attaching to a molecule.

4. HIV multiplies inside helper T cell.

5. Helper T cells are destroyed.

6. Destruction of helper T cells renders the body ineffective in fighting disease-causing pathogens.

HIV

HIV

Get That Breathing Started

Health Education Standard:

- Students will demonstrate the ability to practice health-enhancing behaviors and reduce health risks.

Performance Indicator:

- Students will develop injury prevention strategies for personal health.

Life Skills:

- I will be able to get help for emergency situations.
- I will be skilled in basic first aid procedures.

Materials:

Teaching Master, "The Heimlich Maneuver"; transparency projector; a one-gallon plastic milk container; cork; a mannequin designed to practice rescue breathing; two mouth protectors

Motivation:

1 Before beginning this strategy, prepare the following: Draw a pair of lungs on the surface of a one-gallon plastic milk container. Bring a cork that is big enough to fill the opening on the top of the milk container.

2 Begin this strategy by asking, "How many of you have ever been chewing some food and have had it lodge in your throat?" Many students will answer, "Yes." Explain that almost everyone experiences having food stuck in the throat at some time. In almost all cases, the food will dislodge by itself and the air passage will open.

3 Explain that sometimes people are not so fortunate. On occasion, a piece of food that is stuck inside the throat may not become dislodged by itself. In this case, a person needs help to breath. One method used to help a person breathe is the use of the Heimlich maneuver. The **Heimlich maneuver** is a technique in which pressure is placed in the abdominal area to remove a blockage in the air passage.

4 Provide students with the following scenario. They are at a restaurant eating with a friend. The friend suddenly appears to be choking. In the majority of choking situations, the person choking will place a hand on his/her throat. The lips may be turning blue. If this person cannot cough, speak, or breathe, the Heimlich maneuver can be used. Show the Teaching Master "The Heimlich Maneuver." Use a student to demonstrate the position of the hands for the Heimlich maneuver. However, you will not want to perform the thrust on the student and you will not want the students in the class to do this with each other. Explain that in performing the Heimlich maneuver, the person performing the maneuver is to move behind the standing or seated person and wrap his or her hands around the victim's waist. Place the thumb side of the fist against the victim's abdomen just below the tip of the breastbone and slightly above the navel. Grasp the fist with the other hand and press into the victim's abdomen with four quick upward thrusts. Each sharp thrust forces air out of the lungs; the air will push the object out. You can repeat giving thrusts if the initial attempts do not dislodge the object.

5 Show students the milk container with the cork that represents the food lodged inside the throat to demonstrate the result of the Heimlich Maneuver. Squeeze the milk container until the cork flies out. This mimics what would happen if food were actually stuck in the air passage.

6 Explain that sometimes a person stops breathing because of illness or injury. In this case, rescue breathing is needed. **Rescue breathing** is a first aid procedure in which a person who has stopped breathing is given assistance to restore breathing. Rescue breathing is also known as artificial respiration or mouth-to-mouth resuscitation. Use the mannequin to simulate a victim to demonstrate rescue breathing. Describe and demonstrate the following steps:

Step 1 – Check the victim's chest to see if it is moving up and down. Place your ear next to the victim's nose and mouth to feel for air being exhaled. If the victim's chest is not moving and there is no air coming from the nose and mouth, the person is not breathing and needs rescue breathing.

Step 2 – Place the victim on his/her back and turn the head to the side. Remove anything that is inside the person's mouth.

Step 3 – Place your hand underneath the victim's neck and rest your other hand against the forehead. Pull the neck up slightly and press the forehead down. This allows the passage into the lungs to be opened.

Step 4 – Pinch the victim's nostrils closed. This will stop the air you will breathe into the victim from escaping through the nose. Take a deep breath and seal your mouth using the mouth protector over the victim's mouth and blow air into it. You will notice that the victim's chest rises.

Step 5 – Place your ear by the victim's mouth so that you can listen for the exhaled air. If breathing resumes, do not blow any more air into the victim's mouth. If breathing did not continue, resume blowing air into the victim's mouth every four seconds until the person breathes on his/her own or until emergency help has arrived. If emergency help is needed, ask someone else to call the emergency service while you continue to monitor the person's condition.

Evaluation:

Have students practice the steps of rescue breathing. Have a student practice the steps on the mannequin. Have the other students identify the steps while the student demonstrates. It is important that the student volunteer uses a clean mouth protector while demonstrating rescue breathing. Ask students how they will get emergency help if it is needed. Assess the order of the steps and the accuracy of the information given by the students.

The Heimlich Maneuver

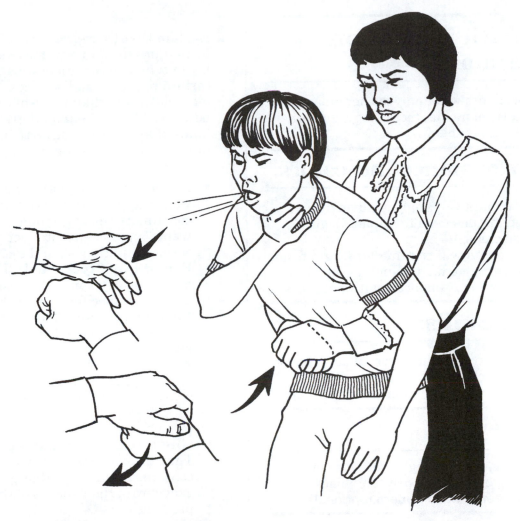

- **Wrap your arms around the person's waist.**
- **Make a fist.**
- **Place the thumb side of the fist on the middle of the person's abdomen just above the navel and well below the lower tip of the breastbone.**
- **Grasp the fist with your other hand.**
- **Press the fist into the person's abdomen with a quick upward thrust.**

Before I Buy

Health Education Standard:

- Students will analyze the impact of culture, media, technology, and other factors on health.

Performance Indicators:

- Students will analyze advertising techniques used to impact health decisions.
- Students will critique messages from culture, media, technology, and other factors that impact health practices.

Life Skills:

- I will analyze the effects of advertising on my choices.
- I will recognize and report quackery.

Materials:

Newspapers; magazines; art supplies, including poster board and black markers; video camera (optional)

Motivation:

1 Ask students to name their favorite advertisements. (Student answers will vary). Discuss with them what they like about the advertisements they named. (Students might mention humor which makes ads more interesting; information they learn about the product). Remind students that the purpose of advertising is to sell a product. Then ask students whether they have ever bought an advertised product and been disappointed. (Students will probably say yes). Allow time for students to elaborate on their responses.

2 Explain that there are a variety of techniques used in advertisements to try to convince consumers that certain products and services are more desirable than those of competitors. There are ten different kinds of appeals the advertising industry uses to be convincing.

- **Bandwagon Appeal.** The bandwagon appeal tries to convince consumers that everyone else wants a particular product or service and they should too.
- **Brand Loyalty Appeal.** The brand loyalty appeal tells consumers that a specific brand is better than the rest, and that they would be cheating themselves to use anything but this brand.
- **False Image Appeal.** The false image appeal attempts to convince consumers that they will give a certain impression if they use the product.
- **Glittering Generality Appeal.** The glittering generality appeal contains statements that greatly exaggerate the benefits of the product.
- **Humor Appeal.** The humor appeal uses a slogan, jingle, or cartoon to keep the consumer's attention.
- **Progress Appeal.** The progress appeal tells consumers that a product is a new and better product than one formerly advertised.
- **Reward Appeal.** The reward appeal tells consumers that they will receive a special prize or gift if they buy a product.
- **Scientific Evidence Appeal.** The scientific evidence appeal gives consumers the results of survey or laboratory tests to provide confidence in a product.
- **Snob Appeal.** Snob appeal convinces consumers that they are

worthy of a product or service because it is the best.

- **Testimony Appeal.** Testimony appeal includes a promotion by a well-known person who says that a product or service is the best one for the consumer.

3 Read the poem aloud and ask students what the narrator's message is. (Students might say that the narrator wants advertisers to tell the truth). Ask students whether they think 100 percent of the claims in advertising are true. (Students will answer no).

4 Give small groups of students old magazines, newspaper, and art supplies. Have them cut out ads and write down television and radio jingles for health products, such as cold remedies or diet products. Have them glue the ads to the posterboard and decorate their work to make a collage.

5 When groups are finished, have them present their collages to the class. Work with the class to find claims in the ads that are exaggerated or untrue. Allow group members to use a black marker to write "NOT!" on any ad that has such claims. Ask students how such ads might be dangerous to a person's health. (Students may say that people might substitute going to a doctor with using a product).

6 Point out that commercials and ads usually have an underlying message that implies that the product has many benefits. Ask students to give examples of how ads do this. (For example, students might mention a potato chip commercial that shows young people playing at the beach and say that it implies that if they eat these potato chips they will be popular). For homework, ask students to write down three more examples of underlying messages in advertising. (Student answers will vary, but should show they understand the hidden message an ad is sending, such as a commercial for perfume that implies that a person wearing it will be irresistible).

Evaluation:

Have students work in pairs to present or videotape a hard-sell commercial for a common school item, such as a pencil. They are to include at least two of the appeals discussed in class. When students share their commercials with the class, have the class point out which statements were factual and which were misleading or false appeals.

Before I Buy

❖❖❖❖❖❖❖❖

Ads in my magazines!
Commercials on TV!
Ads in the newspapers!
Bombarding me!

This will make you perfect!
This will make you thin!
This will make you stronger!
Send your money in!
Here's a cure for sickness!
Won't you even try it?
Melt that fatty fat away!
Buy our ice cream diet!
I won't be a target
for every ad I see.
Before I buy your product,
prove it works for me.

❖❖❖❖❖❖❖❖

Environmental Draw-And-Guess

Health Education Standard:

- I will be concerned about environmental issues.

Performance Indicators:

- Students will identify the impact of the environment on personal health.
- Students will identify methods of health promotion.
- Students will express ideas and opinions on health issues.
- Students will demonstrate the ability to influence and support others in making positive health choices.

Life Skills:

- I will keep the water clean.
- I will protect myself from radiation.
- I will dispose of solid wastes properly.
- I will recycle.
- I will cooperate with environmental protection agencies.

Materials:

Student Master, "Glossary of Environmental Terms"; chalkboard; chalk

Motivation:

1 Before beginning this strategy, distribute the Student Master "Glossary of Environmental Terms." This master contains many terms that will be used in this strategy. Have students silently read the vocabulary words and terms.

2 Explain to students that they are going to play a version of a well-known game. This game will be called Environmental Draw-and-Guess. Explain to students that they will need to identify a term based upon another person's drawing that relates to that term.

3 Divide the class into two equal groups. Begin by asking one member from each team to come to the front of the room. Use a coin toss to indicate which person goes first. Show that person a term that is related to the environment. You can use any of the terms on the Student Master, or you may add terms. Tell students if you have added terms they can use.

4 After a student sees the term, (s)he is to draw a picture that will help his/her teammates identify the term. The student's team will have one minute to identify the term. If it is not identified in the time allotted, the other team will have the opportunity to guess the term. The team that correctly guesses the term will receive one point. The teams will take turns drawing pictures. Each person on a team will have one turn to draw a picture.

5 You can adapt this game by playing a special round of Environmental Draw-and-Guess. In this round, one team decides on the term that the other team must guess. Give each team one point for identifying the term correctly. If a team does not guess correctly, the team providing the term will receive the point.

Evaluation:

You can evaluate this activity by evaluating the students' ability to

535

identify the terms during the game.
You can also use the Student Master
to develop a vocabulary test by selecting terms and having students spell
and define them. Also, you can ask
students to tell ways they can protect the environment, using the
terms in the Glossary.

Glossary of Environmental Terms

acid rain: precipitation (rain, snow, sleet, hail) that contains high levels of acids formed from sulfur oxides, nitrogen oxides, and moisture in the air

air pollution: dirty air

asbestos: a heat-resistant mineral that is found in building materials

biodegradable: able to be decomposed through natural or biological processes into harmless materials

decibels: a unit used to measure sound intensity

Environmental Protection Agency (EPA): a federal agency that is responsible for alleviating and controlling environmental pollution

fluorocarbons: chemicals used as propellants in aerosol-spray cans

hazardous waste: harmful substances that are difficult to discard safely

lead: an element that is found in many products used inside and outside the home

noise pollution: loud noises in the environment

ozone: a chemical variant of oxygen that is classified as a photochemical because it is created in the presence of hydrocarbons, nitrous oxides, and sunlight

particulate: particle in the air

pesticide: any substance that is used to kill or control the growth of unwanted organisms

radiation: term applied to the transmission of energy through space or through to a medium

recycling: the process of reforming or breaking down waste products to their basic components so that they can be used again

solid waste: substances such as trash, unwanted objects, and litter that threaten the environment

thermal inversion: a condition that occurs when a layer of warm air forms above a cooler layer

thermal pollution: pollution of water with heat resulting in a decrease in the water's oxygen-carrying capacity

water pollution: dirty water

Stormy Weather

Health Education Standards:

- Students will demonstrate the ability to practice health-enhancing behaviors and reduce health risks.
- Students will demonstrate the ability to use goal-setting and decision-making skills that enhance health.

Performance Indicators:

- Students will explain the importance of assuming responsibility for personal health habits.
- Students will demonstrate the ability to apply a decision-making process to health issues and problems individually and collaboratively.
- Students will analyze the role of individual, family, community, and cultural values when making health-related decisions.
- Students will explain how decisions regarding health behaviors have consequences for self and others.

Life Skills:

- I will make responsible decisions.
- I will use resistance skills when appropriate.

Materials:

Student Master, "The Responsible Decision-Making Model"; Student Master, "The Model for Using Resistance Skills"; umbrella; construction paper; scissors; markers; tape; two chairs; index cards

Motivation:

1 To prepare for this strategy, cut six large raindrops from the construction paper. Label each of the six large raindrops with one of the categories of risk behaviors identified by The Centers for Disease Control and Prevention (label with the underlined words only):
1) Behaviors that result in unintentional and intentional injuries—<u>injuries</u>; 2) Tobacco use—<u>tobacco</u>; 3) Alcohol and other drug use—<u>drugs</u>; 4) Sexual behaviors that result in HIV infection, other STDs, and unintended pregnancy—<u>HIV, STDs, pregnancy</u>; 5) Dietary patterns that contribute to disease—<u>diet</u>; and 6) insufficient physical activity—<u>lack of exercise</u>. Cut six long strips of paper and label each with one of the six criteria from The Responsible Decision-Making Model:
1. healthful, 2. safe, 3. legal, 4. respect for self and others, 5. follows guidelines of responsible adults, 6. demonstrates character.

2 Give each student a copy of the Student Master "The Responsible Decision-Making Model." **The Responsible Decision-Making Model** is a series of steps to follow to assure that the decisions a person makes lead to actions that: promote health, promote safety, protect laws, show respect for self and others, follow guidelines set by responsible adults such as parents and guardians, and demonstrate good character. Explain that there are many benefits that result from using The Responsible Decision-Making Model. Because the Model contains guidelines for what is responsible behavior, students will always know how to evaluate behavior. Ask students to memorize the six questions asked to evaluate behavior.

3 Ask for two student volunteers. Have them sit next to one another in two chairs in front of the class. Give one of the students the umbrella. Explain that the two students are preparing for life. In the last lesson, "The Web of Health," they learned that life skills are actions that promote health literacy, maintain and improve health, prevent disease, and reduce health-related risk behaviors. An important life skill is "I will make responsible decisions."

4 Explain that the student with the umbrella is prepared for the storms of life. This student makes responsible decisions and uses the six questions to evaluate his/her behavior. Review

these six questions as you tape them to the top of the umbrella. Explain that the other student does not practice responsible decision-making. This student does not ask these six questions to evaluate behavior before making decisions.

5 Further explain that they are at an age when they will have many decisions to make. These decisions will involve whether or not to participate in risk behaviors. **Risk behaviors** are voluntary actions that threaten self-esteem, harm health, and increase the likelihood of illness, injury, and premature death. Discuss the six categories of risk behaviors identified by The Centers for Disease Control and Prevention. (These are identified in step 1 of this motivation.) Show students each of the six large raindrops that represent the six categories of risk behaviors.

6 Ask students what will happen when each of these students encounters the storms of adolescence and must make responsible decisions. Demonstrate the following. Drop the raindrops on the student without the umbrella. Explain that this student might be affected by these risk behaviors because (s)he does not practice the life skill "I will make responsible decisions." Collect the raindrops and allow them to drop over the student protected by the umbrella. This student is protected because (s)he practices the life skill, "I will make responsible decisions."

7 Give each student a copy of the Student Master "The Model For Using Resistance Skills." Explain that in addition to practicing responsible decision-making, students will need to practice the life skill "I will use resistance skills when appropriate." **Resistance skills** are skills that are used when a person wants to say NO to an action and/or leave a situation. **The Model for Using Resistance Skills** is a list of suggested ways for effectively resisting pressure to

engage in actions that threaten health, threaten safety, break laws, result in lack of respect for self and others, disobey guidelines set by responsible adults, and detract from character. Review and demonstrate the use of resistance skills.

Evaluation:

Give each student an index card. Ask students to write a situation on the index card that necessitates a decision. For example, a student might write, "A friend asks me to a party where there will be beer." Collect the index cards. Read them and discard inappropriate situations. Place the rest of the index cards in a pile. Have students take turns coming in front of the class and selecting an index card from the pile. Students are to evaluate the decision to be made using the six questions from The Responsible Decision-Making Model. Then they are to role-play with you how they would resist pressure to participate in the risk behavior.

Student Master

The Responsible Decision-Making Model

1. Clearly describe the situation you face.

2. List possible actions that you can take.

3. Share your list of possible actions with a responsible adult.

4. Carefully evaluate each possible action. Ask questions. Will this decision result in an action that:
   - is healthful?
   - is safe?
   - is legal?
   - shows respect for self and others?
   - follows the guidelines of responsible adults such as my parents or guardian?
   - demonstrates that I have good character?

5. Decide which action is responsible and most appropriate.

6. Act in a responsible way and evaluate the results.

The Model For Using Resistance Skills

1. Use assertive behavior.

2. Avoid saying, "NO, thank you."

3. Use nonverbal behavior that matches verbal behavior.

4. Influence others to choose responsible behavior.

5. Avoid being in situations in which there will be pressure to make harmful decisions.

6. Avoid being with people who choose harmful actions.

7. Resist pressure to engage in illegal behavior.

Gift Of Friendship

Health Education Standards:

- Students will demonstrate the ability to use effective interpersonal communication skills that enhance health.
- Students will demonstrate the ability to advocate for personal, family, and community health.

Performance Indicators:

- Students will describe how the behavior of family and peers contributes to one's physical, mental, emotional, and social health.
- Students will demonstrate ways to communicate care, consideration, and respect of self and others.
- Students will identify barriers to effective communication of information, ideas, feelings, and opinions on health issues.

Life Skills:

- I will develop relationships skills.
- I will form healthful and responsible friendships.
- I will practice life skills to promote abstinence.

Materials:

A shoe box for each student; wrapping paper; tape; ribbon; index cards; pens

Motivation:

1 Initiate a discussion about relationships and about friendship. **Relationships** are the connections a person has with other people. Friendship is a special relationship. A **friend** is a person who is known well and liked. Friends provide supportive relationships in which we can learn about ourselves and try new ways of interacting in order to grow personally. There are two important ingredients in friendship—affection and respect. **Affection** is a fond or tender feeling that a person has toward another person. It is experienced as emotional warmth or closeness. **Respect** is having esteem for someone's admirable characteristics and responsible and caring actions. In a healthful friendship, there is both affection and respect.

2 Identify some of the admirable characteristics and responsible and caring actions that make a young person of this age worthy of respect:
- demonstrates self-loving behavior;
- is trustworthy and honest;
- expresses feelings in healthful ways;
- adheres to family guidelines;
- sets goals and makes plans to reach them;
- demonstrates interdependence;
- demonstrates balance when managing time for family, school, hobbies, and friends;
- avoids abusive behavior;
- is committed to a drug-free lifestyle;
- practices abstinence.

3 Brainstorm other characteristics and responsible and caring actions that are important in friendship. Students may mention behaviors such as "keeps thoughts I share in confidence" and "encourages me to do well in school." Students may also mention qualities that they enjoy in others such as "has a sense of humor" and "has good listening skills." Sharing interests can bring people closer together. Explain that varied interests are a bonus to friendship.

4 Give each student a shoe box, wrapping paper, and tape (or have each student bring these items from home). Have students wrap their boxes. They should wrap the top and the bottom of the box separately so they can put something in the box later.

5 Give each student five index cards. Ask students to reflect for a moment on the characteristics and interests that they have that are valuable to a friendship. For example, a student might be a very loyal person. Another student might be a very cheerful person. Another student might have very clear values and behave very responsibly. Another student might be very athletic and enjoy playing sports with others. Another student might enjoy sharing his/her love of music. Ask students to make a list of the characteristics and interests that they have that are valuable to a friendship. From this list, they are to select five items. They are to print each of the five items selected on a separate index card.

6 Have the students place the index cards in their wrapped boxes. Now have students tie a colorful ribbon around their boxes. Collect the boxes and place them in the center of the room.

7 Have each student take a box other than the one that belonged to him/her. Explain that each student has just received a gift. Ask students to describe what is meant by "gift." A **gift** is something special that is given to another person. It involves

the act of giving or putting forth effort. A gift is only of value to a person if it is received. So, a gift also involves the act of receiving.

8 Have students open the friendship boxes and read the index cards to learn about the gifts each has received. Then ask students to select one of the five gifts in their boxes. They are to tell the class which gift they selected as most valuable to them and why they would like to receive this gift from a friend.

Evaluation:

Have students identify five gifts of friendship that they have to give and five gifts of friendship that they would like to receive. You might also explain that a gift of friendship includes not pressuring another person to do something that is a risk or harmful to physical, mental, or emotional health. You may have students discuss abstinence as a gift of friendship.

Multicultural Infusion:

Initiate a discussion on the importance of having friends from different cultures. Have students share with classmates special gifts they possess because of their cultural heritage. Prior to this sharing, you may want to have students discuss the positive aspects of their cultural heritage with their parents.

Happy Birth-Day

Health Education Standards:

- Students will comprehend health promotion and disease prevention concepts.
- Students will demonstrate the ability to practice health-enhancing behaviors and reduce health risks.

Performance Indicators:

- Students will explain the relationship between positive health behaviors and the prevention of injury, illness, disease, and premature death.
- Students will explain the importance of assuming responsibility for personal health habits.

Life Skill:

- I will learn about conception, pregnancy, and childbirth.

Materials:

Sock; small baby doll that can fit through the opening of the sock; scissors

Motivation:

1 Explain to the class that you will describe how childbirth occurs. You can review the role of the uterus in the development of a baby. Explain that the uterus is the organ that prepares each month during a female's reproductive years to receive a fertilized ovum, to support the fertilized ovum during pregnancy, and to contract during childbirth to force delivery of the baby. Point to the approximate position of the uterus. Hold up a sock containing a small baby doll. Explain that the sock represents a uterus. Explain that the baby inside the uterus is ready to come out from the woman's body after growing and developing for about nine months.

2 Tell the class that muscles in the uterus are going to become tight. The body does this automatically when the baby is to be born. This tightening of the muscles of the uterus is called a contraction. When a baby is ready to be born, there are many contractions, one after another. Explain that the contractions push the baby down through the opening of the uterus. Push the baby slightly through the uterus, or sock. Explain that the opening of the sock represents the opening of the uterus, or cervix. As the baby's head pushes through the uterus, the opening of the uterus becomes fully widened or dilated. The baby then moves completely through the uterus and into the birth canal, or vagina.

3 You can modify this strategy to use the neck of the sock as the vaginal canal. Explain that just as the neck of the sock stretches to allow the baby to pass through, so do the walls in the vagina stretch to allow a baby to pass through. Explain that, on occasion, the vaginal opening may not be able to stretch enough to allow the baby's head to pass through. You can use the sock to demonstrate an episiotomy. Cut a slit in the neck of the sock. Explain that this cut, or incision, widens the opening of the vagina so that the vagina will not overstretch. Then the neck of the sock, or vaginal opening, can be stitched. It is important to emphasize that the use of an episiotomy is not nearly as common today as years ago. Explain that episiotomies were performed unnecessarily in the past. In most cases, episiotomies are not needed.

4 You might also use this activity to explain a Cesarean section. In this surgical procedure, an opening is made through the abdomen into the uterus. The baby is removed through this opening. A Cesarean section is performed when vaginal delivery might be difficult for the baby. For example, if the baby is not in a position to pass through the vagina easily, a Cesarean section may be performed.

Evaluation:

Select a student to come to the front of the class. Ask this student to imagine that (s)he is a physician who delivers babies. Tell the class that this kind of physician is called an obstetrician. Give the student the sock with the baby doll inside. Have the student use this visual aid to explain the process of childbirth, naming as many facts as possible. After completing this task, the class is to identify additional facts that this student may not have mentioned. You may want to include a discussion of conception at this time.

Pyramid Hopscotch

Health Education Standards:

- Students will demonstrate the ability to practice health-enhancing behaviors and reduce health risks.
- Students will demonstrate the ability to use goal-setting and decision-making skills that enhance health.

Performance Indicators:

- Students will demonstrate strategies to improve or maintain personal and family health.
- Students will formulate a personal wellness plan which addresses adolescent needs and health risks.

Life Skills:

- I will select the appropriate number of servings from The Food Guide Pyramid.
- I will follow the dietary guidelines.

Materials:

Teaching Master, "Food Guide Pyramid"; transparency projector; old magazines that contain pictures of food; scissors; masking tape

Motivation:

1 Review the basic information about the Food Guide Pyramid. The Food Guide Pyramid is an outline of what to eat each day based upon the Dietary Guidelines for Americans. Define the **Dietary Guidelines for Americans** as recommendations for diet choices for healthy Americans two years of age or older. Explain the seven steps in the Dietary Guidelines: 1) Eat a variety of foods.

2) Maintain a healthful weight. 3) Choose a diet low in fat, saturated fat, and cholesterol. 4) Choose a diet with plenty of vegetables, fruits, and grain products. 5) Use sugars only in moderation. 6) Use salt and sodium only in moderation 7) If a person drinks alcoholic beverages, (s)he should do so only in moderation.

2 Show the Teaching Master "Food Guide Pyramid," and explain to students that, for their age group, they need the following number of servings: 9 Bread Group servings; 4 Vegetable Group servings; 3 Fruit Group servings; 2–3 Milk Group servings; and 2 Meat Group servings for a total of 6 ounces.

3 Divide the class into groups of five. Have each group use masking tape to outline a large Food Guide Pyramid on the floor using the Teaching Master "Food Guide Pyramid" as a guide. Each group is to cut pictures from the magazines that would fulfill the amount of each food needed for a day. For example, the group will cut out pictures of four vegetables and place them in the appropriate box on the pyramid. After each group has completed this task, it is to share its results with the class. The students will have an idea of what they need to eat each day to fulfill the serving

requirements recommended in the Food Guide Pyramid.

4 Set up a game called "Pyramid Hopscotch." Using masking tape or chalk, outline three large Food Guide Pyramids on the floor. Do not label the different food groups on the pyramid. Students will need to guess what each food group is. Divide the class into three equal teams. Each team forms a line behind each pyramid. When you say "Go," the first student will hop into each food group on the pyramid. For each food group on into which students hop, they are to name a healthful food that belongs to the group. For example, the base of the pyramid is the Breads, Cereal, Rice, and Pasta Group. A student will hop into this food group, say, "spaghetti," and then hop to another food group, say, "lettuce," move to another area, say, "apple," and so forth. Explain that a student must stay on one foot at all times. If a food is named incorrectly, the student is out and the next team member goes. A team gets one point for each time a player goes through the pyramid correctly naming a food from each food group. If the player fails to stand on one foot, (s)he is eliminated.

Evaluation:

In this activity, you will be able to evaluate the number of different foods identified as well as the accuracy with which foods were placed into the different food groups on the Food Guide Pyramid. At the end of this activity, students can make a list of the different foods they can eat within each of the different food group of the Food Guide Pyramid.

Multicultural Infusion:

You can encourage students to identify ethnic foods and place them into the different food groups in the Food Guide Pyramid. Students should be encouraged to name foods identified with certain cultures, such as Italian, French, Mexican, Vietnamese, Cambodian, Korean, Chinese, Spanish, Lebanese, and others.

Inclusion:

You may have students in your class who have physical disabilities and cannot hop from space to space on the Food Guide Pyramid. These students can play the game, but you can assign different students to hop while the student who has a physical disability names the foods.

Teaching Master

Food Guide Pyramid

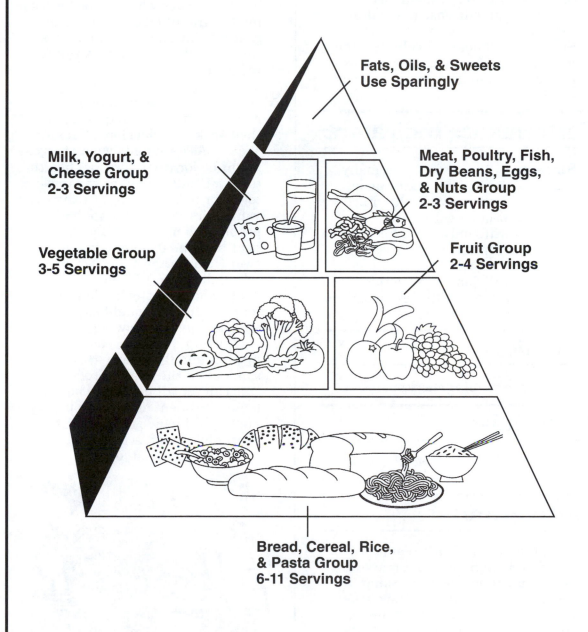

Fats, Oils, & Sweets
Use Sparingly

Milk, Yogurt, &
Cheese Group
2-3 Servings

Meat, Poultry, Fish,
Dry Beans, Eggs,
& Nuts Group
2-3 Servings

Vegetable Group
3-5 Servings

Fruit Group
2-4 Servings

Bread, Cereal, Rice,
& Pasta Group
6-11 Servings

When I Grow Up

Health Education Standards:

- Students will comprehend health promotion and disease prevention concepts.
- Students will demonstrate the ability to access valid health information and appropriate health products and services.

Performance Indicators:

- Students will recognize that many causes of premature death can be prevented by positive health practices and appropriate health care.
- Students will analyze methods of health promotion and disease prevention.
- Students will demonstrate the ability to locate health resources and services.

Life Skill:

- I will have regular checkups.

Materials:

The poem, *When I Grow Up*; copies of a blank team roster form

Motivation:

1 Ask students to define teamwork. (Students might say that teamwork is a group of people all working toward the same goal.) Have students give examples of teamwork they have experienced. (Student answers might include sports teams, band, dance groups, or speech teams.) Ask students if all members on a team have the same job. (Students will say no.)

2 Have students explain why team members often have different jobs. (Students might say that each team member may be good at different things; by specializing, a team can have members who are good working toward all facets of the team's goal.) Point out that teammates rely on each other to work toward the same good goal.

3 Distribute copies of a blank team roster to students. Explain that their task is to develop a "Health Team." Ask students what the goal might be for their personal health team. (Students might say to work together to keep them healthy.) Ask volunteers to give examples of people who might be part of their health team. (Students might answer their doctor, their parents, the school dietician.) Then ask students what a doctor's role is on the team. (Students might say to check on how they are growing; to find early symptoms of disease; to treat injuries and illnesses.) Have them think of all the health professionals who can contribute to the health team. (Student answers will vary but might include doctor, dentist, dental hygienist, school nurse, school psychologist, etc.)

4 Read the poem *When I Grow Up* aloud and ask students why they should consider their doctor to be their friend. (Students may say because the doctor takes care of their health, he is on their team). Reread the poem and have students name examples from the poem that show the doctor's role. (Students will mention the following: help people live healthful lives, keep people safe, is available in an emergency.) Ask students to name their role as a member of the health team. (Students will say they must eat right, get enough sleep, get regular checkups, and have a checkup when they are sick.)

Evaluation:

Have groups of four or five students make up a cheer for their personal health team. In their cheers, they are to mention why they will have regular checkups. They are to name members of their health care team. Allow time for groups to perform their cheers for the class.

When I Grow Up

❖❖❖❖❖❖❖

I want a job
where I can
help folks
live their lives;
where I can
keep them
safe and healthy;
where I can
save them
from disease.
When I grow up,
I will be a doctor.
And you can call me
anytime,
day or night.
I will be there.
You can call me
to fix
what you've broken.
You can call me
to fix
what hurts.
You will call me
doctor,
but I hope
you will call me friend.

❖❖❖❖❖❖❖

I Can't Understand You

Health Education Standard:

- Students will demonstrate the ability to practice health-enhancing behaviors and reduce health risks.

Performance Indicator:

- Students will analyze the short-term and long-term consequences of safe, risky, and harmful behaviors.

Life Skill:

- I will not drink alcohol.

Materials:

A bag of marshmallows

Motivation:

1 Review some of the possible physical effects that result when a person drinks alcohol. Examples are slurred speech, poor coordination of body muscles, liver damage, inability to think clearly, drowsiness, dizziness, and injury due to increased risk of accidents.

2 The following activity will demonstrate how alcohol affects coordination of body muscles. Select a volunteer to come to the front of the class and read a paragraph aloud from a book that is an appropriate reading level. Ask the class how clear the reading was. Most students should be able to follow what was read.

3 The volunteer will read the paragraph aloud again, but this time (s)he will have a marshmallow in his/her mouth. This student cannot chew or eat the marshmallow; the marshmallow is to remain in the person's mouth. Again, ask the class how clear the reading was. Were they able to understand what the volunteer was reading? Students will indicate that the student was difficult to understand. The words were slurred.

4 Explain that the tongue is a muscle and that many muscles help the mouth move to form words. When a person drinks too much alcohol, muscles cannot work in a coordinated manner. Trying to read with a marshmallow in his/her mouth simulated how a person who drinks too much alcohol might sound.

5 You can have the class try another experiment. Have the students pair off. First, one partner will try reading to his/her partner with a marshmallow in his/her mouth. Then the partner will take a turn. Students might also remark that they felt frustrated as they tried to read with a marshmallow in their mouths. Explain that drinking alcohol also can cause a person to become frustrated.

Evaluation:

Have students name other activities requiring the use of coordinated muscles. Then have students share how drinking alcohol will interfere with the coordination needed for these activities.

Defend That Line

Health Education Standards:

- Students will comprehend health promotion and disease prevention concepts.
- Students will demonstrate the ability to practice health-enhancing behaviors and reduce health risks.

Performance Indicators:

- Students will describe how heredity and micro-organisms are related to the cause or prevention of disease and other health problems.
- Students will analyze methods of health promotion and disease prevention.
- Students will analyze the short-term and long-term consequences of safe, risky, and harmful behaviors.

Life Skills:

- I will keep my immune system healthy.
- I will choose behavior to reduce the risk of HIV infection.

Materials:

Posterboard cut out in the shape of t-shirts; marker; string; strips of posterboard with the names of opportunistic infections written on them

Motivation:

1 On each of five sheets of posterboard, draw an outline of a t-shirt with a marker. Punch two holes in the t-shirt on each side of the neck and insert string through each hole so that you can wear the t-shirt like a billboard. On the front of each of the t-shirts in large letters should be written one of five terms. The five terms are skin, helper T cell, B cell, antibody, and macrophage. Written on the back of each poster should be information about each term. For skin, you may state, "I'm the first line of defense." Helper T cell will state, "I send a signal to B cells to tell them to make antibodies." B cell will state, "I produce antibodies." Antibody will state, "I destroy pathogens so that macrophages can digest them." And macrophage will state, "I will surround pathogens and digest them." Be sure to number each t-shirt so it looks authentic. You can number the following: skin #40, helper T cell #58, B cell #60, antibody #65, and macrophage #72.

2 Select five students to come to the front of the room. Each is to wear a t-shirt. The teacher will introduce the t-shirt team and, as each member is introduced, state the function of each. Students may refer to the information on the back of the posters.

3 Ask for a volunteer and designate this volunteer as a non-HIV pathogen. First, line up the team in single file in the following order: skin, helper T cell, B cell, antibody, and macrophage. Have this volunteer gently try to "get into the body" by breaking through the skin. The skin is to prevent the person from getting through. Tell the class that the skin is the first line of defense in protecting us from pathogens. Then have the volunteer pretend to get through the skin, and have the helper T cell hug the pathogen to simulate that this type of cell will multiply and prevent harm by this pathogen. Have B cells arrive, produce antibodies, and the macrophage then digests the pathogen.

4 Now have another volunteer try to enter the body. Designate this volunteer as HIV. HIV breaks through the skin and attacks the helper T cell. Antibodies to HIV are produced, but the helper T cells are destroyed by HIV. Have three other students in the class pretend to be HIV that has multiplied in the body. Now that HIV has multiplied, they begin to call in their friends. To represent the friends of HIV, make opportunistic infection signs. Among the signs you can make up on strips of paper are pneumocystis carinii pneumonia (a type of pneumonia), Kaposi's sarcoma (a type of cancer), and AIDS dementia complex (a mental disorder caused by the destruction of brain cells). Explain to the class that HIV destroys the helper T cells. The reduction in the number of helper T cells causes the immune system to become susceptible to the development of opportunistic infections and leads to the development of AIDS. Eventually, the opportunistic infections cause death.

5 You can modify this activity to introduce the roles played by B cells.

Explain to the class that when a pathogen enters the body, helper T cells signal B cells to stimulate the production of antibodies. Suppose you were talking about the chickenpox virus. The antibodies to this virus would remain inside the body to prevent chickenpox from occurring again if that virus were to enter. But when HIV enters, helper T cells are destroyed, thereby interfering with the functioning of B cells. HIV multiplies and destroys the immune system. Even though HIV antibodies are present, they cannot protect the body from the increased multiplication of HIV that, in turn, destroys the immune system.

Evaluation:

Have the class divide into small groups of about five. Each group is to develop a skit that demonstrates how the immune system functions to protect the body and what happens to the immune system once it becomes infected with HIV. Have students identify the important facts they have included in their skits.

Introducing Maxine And The Matches

Health Education Standard:

- Students will demonstrate the ability to practice health-enhancing behaviors and reduce health risks.

Performance Indicator:

- Students will manage a range of situations involving injury.

Life Skill:

- I will be skilled in basic first aid procedures.

Materials:

Teaching Master, "First Aid: What You Should Know"; transparency projector; paper; pencil

Motivation:

1 Begin this strategy by asking students if they have ever become suddenly ill or injured. Have students share what happened and how people responded to their situation. After students have shared their situations, explain that they probably received first aid. **First aid** is the immediate care given to an injured or ill person.

2 Explain that there are many different situations in which first aid may be given. To help present the information, show the Teaching Master "First Aid: What You Should Know." This master presents information about common emergencies, their causes, descriptions, signs and symptoms,

and first aid procedures to follow.

3 After reviewing the information on this master, divide the class into groups of about five. You can assign a different first aid situation to each group. In turn, each group is to work together to develop a song that uses information from the master. The song that students in each group develop is to be accompanied by a title and the name of the group who sang it. The group name is to relate to first aid or an injury associated with first aid. After students develop the lyrics to their songs, they are to sing their songs to the tune of a popular song. Or, students can choose to create poetry and have a poetry reading. If they do choose to have a poetry reading, they also should give the poet a name. All of the students can sing or read the poetry together or different students can read different parts. Students should have between twenty to thirty minutes to prepare.

4 Tell students you want them to have ten lines to their poems or songs. Within the ten lines, they are to have at least five facts. You can give students the following as an example of a poem:

Burned To A Degree
by Maxine and the Matches

We're here today to tell you a way,
That burns can make for an awful
    day.

We thought we would cook, that's
    certainly no sin
Until that pot of boiling water poured
    onto our skin.

Those second-degree burns, made our
    skin so red,
 The pain was so severe, we thought
    we were dead.

Those blisters and swelling were
    certainly bold,
But we relieved the pain by applying
    something cold.

So a word of advice we want to say,
Be careful around heat and you'll
    have a great day!

5 After giving students the example of the poem, you can ask related questions such as, "What are the signs and symptoms of second-degree burns?" or "What can cause a second-degree burn?" For extra credit, you can have each group identify five questions the group can ask students about its poem or song.

Evaluation:

Have students present their songs and/or poems to the class. You can assess students' knowledge about the different first aid situations by listening for the five facts in their songs or poems. You can also develop questions based on the group presentations.

Teaching Master
First Aid: What You Should Know

SHOCK
Definition: A condition in which the rates of functions of the important organs in the body slow down.

Causes: Any injury or illness can cause shock. These include blood loss, a fracture, or sudden illness.

Signs and Symptoms: The early stages of shock will be evident by reduced blood flow to the skin that results in lowered body temperature. The skin may appear cold and clammy. The pulse may feel weak and the breathing rate may increase. A person may feel nauseous. In the later stages of shock, a person may appear unresponsive. They eyes may appear sunken and the pupils of the eyes may be dilated.

First Aid: It is important to maintain body temperature. Keep the person lying down. Keep the head level with the body and raise the lower extremities about eight to twelve inches above the level of the heart. Do not raise the victim's feet if there is a head injury or a fracture in the leg. Keep the victim warm by covering him/her with a blanket. Do not give the victim anything to eat or drink and allow a medical professional to further treat the victim.

FRACTURE
Definition: A fracture is a break or a crack in a bone.

Causes: A blow to a bone or a movement in an awkward position.

Signs and Symptoms: There may be pain, swelling, and loss of movement in the affected area. The injured area may be deformed. If the fracture is serious, the bone may protrude through the skin.

First Aid: Treat for bleeding and shock if necessary. Prevent the injured part from moving. For head injuries, keep the person still. Apply ice to prevent swelling and get medical help immediately.

BLEEDING
Definition: A condition in which blood escaped from the vessels that naturally contain it.

Causes: Any accident in which the skin is opened.

Signs and Symptoms: A loss of blood from the injured area.

First Aid: Since blood carries oxygen and nutrients, a person needs to have the blood loss stopped as soon as possible. The most common way to stop bleeding is the application of direct pressure. Direct pressure is the force placed directly over the wound. This is done by placing a clean cloth over the cut and pressing down. If the cut is on a finger or arm, raise the body part above the level of the heart and apply direct pressure. If bleeding does not stop, place pressure on a supplying artery. A supplying artery is a major blood vessel that supplies blood to the affected part. The two supplying arteries recommended by the Red Cross are under the arm and inside the groin area.

HEAT CRAMPS

Definition: Heat cramps are muscle spasms that occur most often in the legs and arms due to excessive fluid loss through sweating.

Causes: Extended activity during warm weather can cause muscle cramps.

Signs and Symptoms: A sharp pain will be felt around the muscle and it may be observed contracting. The muscle may also feel very hard.

First Aid: Heat cramps are easily treated with rest. Light massage to the affected area also is helpful. It is important to drink plenty of fluids during strenuous physical activity.

HEAT EXHAUSTION

Definition: Heat exhaustion is extreme tiredness due to the inability of the body temperature to be regulated.

Causes: Excessive physical activity at high temperatures.

Signs and Symptoms: A person will feel dizzy and have pale, cool, dry, skin. Body temperature will be normal or above normal.

First Aid: Move the person to a cool, dry place and lay him/her down. Give the person cool liquids and cool the body by applying cool water with a sponge.

HEAT STROKE

Definition: Heat stroke is a sudden illness brought on by exposure to high temperatures.

Causes: The inability of the body to sweat causes it to have an elevated temperature.

Signs and Symptoms: The skin may be hot, red, and dry. The person may feel weak and have a headache.

First Aid: Move the person into the shade and sponge the skin with cool water. The person should be taken to the hospital immediately.

FROSTBITE

Definition: Frostbite is the freezing of parts of the body. The parts of the body most often affected are the extremities such as the toes, fingers, and ears.

Causes: Frostbite is caused by overexposure to very cold temperatures.

Signs and Symptoms: At first, there is a tingling sensation in the affected body part. Pain may also be present. The body part may be numb and look waxy. A white, cold spot may appear.

First Aid: Place the affected body part in warm water for twenty minutes. Afterwards, it should be kept dry; medical attention should be sought.

HYPOTHERMIA

Definition: Hypothermia is a low body temperature.

Causes: Excessive exposure to cold, moisture, and wind for an extended period of time will cause hypothermia. The temperature can be as warm as 50 degrees Fahrenheit, yet still cause a person to suffer from hypothermia.

Signs and Symptoms: A person may begin to feel chilled and eventually may become disoriented and weak.

First Aid: Bring the victim indoors and replace the clothing with clean, warm, and dry clothing. Give the victim warm fluids to drink.

The One

Health Education Standard:

- Students will analyze the impact of culture, media, technology, and other factors on health.

Performance Indicator:

- Students will analyze advertising techniques used to impact health decisions.

Life Skill:

- I will analyze the effects of advertising on my choices.

Materials:

The poem, *The One;* transparency projector; Teaching Master, "Advertising Appeals"; advertisements cut from newspapers and magazines

Motivation:

1 Ask students to bring in copies of advertisements for their favorite products. Then share the Teaching Master "Advertising Appeals" with the class. Have students determine which appeals each advertisement uses to convince consumers to buy the product.

2 Read the poem *The One* aloud. Have students use the chart to determine how the poet is making each purchase mentioned in the poem. (Students might say that the shampoo advertisement uses false image appeal; the jeans advertisement uses the brand loyalty appeal; the soft drink advertisement uses the glittering generality appeal.)

3 Point out to students that the underlying purpose of any advertisement is not to inform, but to get consumers to buy. Ask students why advertisers use such a variety of ways to promote their products. (Students might say that different appeals will attract different consumers; that they want to try many ways to get consumers to buy.)

4 Explain that wise consumers analyze advertising to ensure that their purchases are a responsible use of money and that will benefit them and meet their needs. Ask students to name examples of ways they can be responsible consumers of advertisements. (Students might mention that they can read ads and product labels before buying products; they can be aware of appeals to which they are vulnerable.)

Evaluation:

Have students find ads for three similiar products and compare the ads for their type of appeal and for the information they give. Then have them explain which of the three products they would buy and on what basis they made that selection.

The One

❖❖❖❖❖❖❖

How do I choose
which shampoo I use?
Is it the ads on TV?

How do I know
it will make my hair glow?
How is it working on me?

How do I decide
which jeans I will try?
Do I decide by the fit?

If I saw the same tag
on any old rag,
would I make a point to buy it?

Why do I think
my favorite soft drink
tastes better than all the rest?

So many to try.
So why do I just buy
the one whose commercials are best?

❖❖❖❖❖❖❖

Teaching Master

Advertising Appeals

Bandwagon Appeal
Tries to convince consumers that everyone else wants a product and they should too.

Brand Loyalty Appeal
Tells consumers that a brand is better than the rest.

False Image Appeal
Convinces consumers that people who use the product give off a certain image.

Glittering Generality Appeal
Greatly exaggerates the benefits of the product.

Humor Appeal
Uses a slogan, jingle or cartoon to keep consumers' attention.

Progress Appeal
Tells consumers that a product is new and improved compared to other versions.

Reward Appeal
Tells consumers that they will get a prize or gift if they buy the product.

Scientific Appeal
Gives consumers evidence of a survey or test that proves the product is effective or reliable.

Snob Appeal
Tells consumers that they are worthy of the best products or services.

Testimony Appeal
Uses a well-known personality to say that a product or service is the best.

Environmental Mural

Health Education Standards:

- Students will comprehend health promotion and disease prevention concepts.
- Students will demonstrate the ability to advocate for personal, family, and community health.

Performance Indicators:

- Students will analyze the interrelationship between the environment and personal health.
- Students will express ideas and opinions on health issues.
- Students will demonstrate the ability to influence and support others in making positive health choices.

Life Skills:

- I will be concerned about environmental issues.
- I will cooperate with environmental protection agencies.

Materials:

Five-foot sheet of butcher paper; cellophane tape; colored markers; plastic trash bag with examples of trash that is clean and safe to handle and commonly found on streets; such as candy wrappers; soda cans; and crumpled tissues

Motivation:

1 Begin this strategy by laying a five-foot strip of butcher paper on the floor. Tell students that they are going to make a mural of the environment. Explain that this mural should consist of scenery that shows the environment at its best. That is, it should be free from any pollutants. Define **pollutants** as anything that makes the environment dirty, such as smoke or trash. Students can draw pictures of mountains, lakes, streams, people swimming, trees, and any other scene that is pleasing to the eye. Have students use the colored markers to draw the mural.

2 Pick up the completed mural from the floor and tape it to the chalkboard or other long area at the front of the room. Have students observe the mural of the clean environment and provide you with feedback about how nice this environment looks.

3 Show students the bag of trash you have. Tell students that they are going to have the opportunity to select items from the trash bag. Explain that the trash inside your bag consists of items that are clean and safe to handle. Have each student select an item. They will select items such as crumpled tissue papers, candy wrappers, aluminum soda cans, and other examples of discarded items. Explain that these items represent litter. **Litter** is trash that is thrown on the street, ground or other places in the environment. Have each student take a piece of cellophane tape and attach his/her piece of trash to the mural. Have students describe how their mural of the environment looks now. Students will indicate that the environment looks dirty. Explain that the litter made the environment appear dirty. Explain that litter also attracts rodents and insects, which can carry disease. Encourage students to dispose of litter in litter cans or in other appropriate areas.

4 Explain that there are other sources of pollution in the environment. **Air**

pollution is dirty air that is caused by automobile exhaust or other matter burned in the environment. Explain that the **Environmental Protection Agency (EPA)** is a federal agency that is responsible for alleviating and controlling environmental pollution. By following rules such as disposing of trash properly, they can help keep the environment clean. Explain that **water pollution,** which is dirt or waste in water, can be caused by the dumping of waste in rivers, lakes, and streams. Sometimes the water is so dirty that swimming must be prohibited. Explain that it is important to avoid going into polluted water because pathogens from the water can enter the body. **Solid waste pollution** is the throwing away of substances such as trash, litter, and unwanted objects, some of which may be very large, in the environment. Many communities have solid waste buried in sanitary landfills. A **sanitary landfill** is an area where layers of solid waste are dumped and covered by layers of dirt. Introduce the word pesticide. A **pesticide** is any substance used to kill or control the growth of unwanted organisms. For example, a spray can of pesticide may be used to kill insects on a house plant. Explain that the pesticide can be harmful if inhaled or swallowed. While pesticides can be helpful in controlling insects that harm the environment, they can harm the environment by seeping into lakes and streams when it rains. This can kill fish and aquatic plants.

Evaluation:

Have students look through newspapers and magazines for one week and keep a log of different environmental issues that are described in news articles and editorials. In their logs, have students identify the type of pollution identified, the issue(s) involving this type of pollution, and what is being done to solve the issue(s). You can grade students' papers by referring to the number of articles they found and their summaries about the issues and solutions.

Wiping Stress Away

Health Education Standards:

- Students will comprehend concepts related to health promotion and disease prevention.
- Students will demonstrate the ability to use interpersonal communication skills to enhance health.

Performance Indicators:

- Students will describe ways to reduce risks related to adolescent health problems.
- Students will demonstrate strategies to manage stress.
- Students will demonstrate healthy ways to express needs, wants, and feelings.

Life Skills:

- I will practice stress management and suicide prevention skills.
- I will express feelings in healthful ways.
- *I will choose behaviors to reduce my risk of cardiovascular diseases. (Communicable and Chronic Diseases)*

Materials:

Teaching Master, "General Adaptation Syndrome"; tissue; two blank transparency overlays; transparency projector; one blue oil-base writing marker; one red water-base marker; balloon

Motivation:

1 Begin this strategy by asking students to define stress. After several students

have given their definitions, review the correct definition. **Stress** is the response of the body to the demands of daily living. Explain that stressors are the sources or causes of stress. A **stressor** is a demand that causes changes in the body. Stressors cause the body to respond. A stressor can be physical, mental, or social. Give examples of stressors, such as having an argument with a friend, being chased by a dog, and worrying about a test. Ask students to give other examples.

2 Explain to students that they do not always have the same response to stressors. Sometimes their responses are positive while at other times they are not. **Eustress** is a healthful response to a stressor that produces positive results. For example, a student might experience stress before being in the school play. The student experiences excitement and performs very well. This is an example of eustress. Ask students to share examples of eustress they have experienced. Then explain distress. **Distress** is a harmful response to a stressor that produces negative results. For example, a student might experience stress before a test and during the test be so anxious that (s)he performs poorly. Ask students to share examples of distress they have experienced.

3 Explain that everyone experiences stressors. It is impossible to avoid stressors. Therefore, it is important to know how to manage stress. Make a transparency of the Teaching Master "General Adaptation Syndrome." Review the general adaptation syndrome. The **general adaptation syndrome** is a series of changes that occur in the body when stress occurs. Refer to the written words on the left side of the figure.

Explain that these are the responses of the body during the alarm stage of the GAS. The alarm stage is the first stage of the GAS in which the body gets ready for action. During this stage, adrenaline is released into the bloodstream. Adrenaline is a hormone that helps the body get ready for an emergency.

4 Refer to the written words on the right side of the figure. Explain that these are the responses of the body during the resistance stage of the GAS. The **resistance stage** is the second stage of the GAS in which the body attempts to regain balance and return to normal.

5 Explain that there is a third stage of the GAS. The **exhaustion stage** is the third stage of the GAS in which there is wear and tear on the body, lowered resistance to disease, and an increased likelihood of disease and death. People who experience the exhaustion stage frequently have a higher incidence of cardiovascular diseases and certain kinds of cancer.

6 Explain the importance of managing stress. **Stress management skills** are techniques that can be used to cope with the harmful effects produced by stress. Do the following activity. Select one student who does not practice stress management skills. Name this student "I. M. Stressed." Select another student who practices stress management skills and name this student "Stress Manager." Take two blank transparency overlays and place them on your desk. Give I. M. Stressed a blue, oil-base writing marker and give Stress Manager a red, oil-base writing marker. Ask the other students to identify at least eight stressors. As each stressor is identified, I. M. Stressed and Stress Manager are

to list ways the body responds during the alarm stage of the GAS on the transparency.

7 Now explain that I. M. Stressed is going to show the class the importance of practicing stress management skills. Give I. M. Stressed a tissue. Ask I. M. Stressed to "wipe away" the effects of the alarm stage of the GAS with the tissue. The effects cannot be wiped away. I. M. Stressed's body does not experience the resistance stage of the GAS, but instead the exhaustion stage of the GAS begins. Now give Stress Manager a tissue. Tell the class that you are going to identify stress management skills that Stress Manager practices. Stress Manager is to wipe away one of the body's responses to the alarm stage of the GAS each time you mention a stress management skill. The following are stress management skills you might say: 1) using responsible decision-making skills; 2) getting enough rest and sleep; 3) participating in physical activities; 4) using a time management plan; 5) writing in a journal; 6) having close friends; 7) talking with parents and other trusted adults; 8) helping others; 9) expressing affection in appropriate ways; 10) caring for pets; 11) changing outlook; 12) keeping a sense of humor. Stress Manager wipes away the alarm stage of the GAS. His/her body enters the resistance stage of the GAS and returns to normal. Review the importance to good health.

Evaluation:

Divide the class into groups of three students. For this cooperative learning experience, you may want to put students with strong language arts skills with those who need more help. Explain that each group is

going to develop a ten-line poem that
provides at least five stress management skills. Give the groups an
appropriate amount of time to write
their poems. Have a poetry reading
in which each group reads its poem.
Have the class review the stress
management skills included in each
poem. Explain that situations that
result in certain feelings, such as
anger, disappointment, and worry are
stressors because they elicit the GAS.
Have students list five stress management skills they might practice
when they experience these feelings.
Explain that they will need to work
through these feelings as well as
practice stress management skills.

Teaching Master

General Adaptation Syndrome

During the **ALARM STAGE,**
the **SYMPATHETIC NERVOUS
SYSTEM** prepares to meet the
demand of
the stressor.

During the **RESISTANCE STAGE,**
the **PARASYMPATHETIC NERVOUS
SYSTEM** attempts to return the
body to a state of homeostasis.

ALARM STAGE

RESISTANCE STAGE

Pupils dilate

Pupils constrict

Hearing sharpens

Hearing is normal

Saliva decreases

Saliva increases

**Heart rate
increases**

Heart rate decreases

**Blood pressure
increases**

Blood pressure decreases

Bronchioles dilate

Bronchioles constrict

Digestion slows

**Intestinal secretions
increase to normal**

**Blood flow to
muscles increases**

**Blood flow to muscles
decreases**

Muscles tighten

Muscles relax

Positive Parenting

Health Education Standards:

- Students will demonstrate the ability to use interpersonal communication skills to enhance health.
- Students will comprehend concepts related to health promotion and disease prevention.

Performance Indicators:

- Students will demonstrate ways to communicate care, consideration, and respect for self and others.
- Students will describe how family and peers influence the health of adolescents.
- Students will demonstrate healthy ways to express needs, wants, and feelings.

Life Skills:

- I will develop skills to prepare for future relationship choices—dating, marriage, parenthood, and family life.
- I will make healthful adjustments to family changes.
- *I will protect myself from people who might harm me. (Injury Prevention and Safety)*

Materials:

Student Master, "Children Learn What They Live"

Motivation:

1 Begin this strategy by introducing the saying, "Do as I say, not as I do." Have students describe the meaning of this saying and give examples.

You can clarify this saying by explaining that people may engage in risk behavior and at the same time express that risk behavior is inappropriate. For example, a person might admonish another person for starting a fight. Yet, when this same person becomes angry, (s)he may settle a disagreement by fighting. What the person says and what the person does are not the same. The person is inconsistent. Another example might be illustrative. Explain that a person might say that (s)he is on a weight-loss diet. This same person might order a hamburger, French fries, and a milkshake for lunch. What the person says (I am on a weight-loss diet) and what the person does (order a high-Calorie lunch) are not the same.

2 Ask students why it is important to practice the saying, "Do as I do." Explain that this saying implies that a person needs to be consistent in what (s)he says and does. This is because what a person does sends a very strong message. Most of us have more meaningful learning experiences when we observe what someone does than when we listen to what someone says. Introduce the term role model. A **role model** is a person who teaches others by demonstrating specific behaviors. There are two types of role models. A positive role model demonstrates healthful and responsible behavior. A negative role model demonstrates harmful and irresponsible behavior. A negative role model demonstrates risk behavior.

3 Explain that the most significant role models in children's lives are their parents, guardians, or other people who raise them. Young children learn by observing their behavior. Ask students to imitate you and then do the following: clap your hands, wave "bye-bye," stomp your feet. Ask students if they have ever seen a baby do what they have just done. Now ask students if they have ever seen a small child scold a doll or treat another small child in the same way that an adult has treated them.

4 Give each student a copy of the Student Master "Children Learn What They Live." Divide the class into twelve groups of students. (There may only be two students in each group.) Assign each group one of the lines from the poem. Make these assignments randomly and do not let the entire class know which group has which line. The students in each group are to develop a non-verbal skit to demonstrate the line it was assigned. After an appropriate amount of preparation time, each group is to nonverbally act out its line for the other students in the class. The other students are to guess which line is being acted out. Be certain not to have the students act out the lines in the same order as the lines in the poem. After all groups have presented, discuss each line.

5 Explain that as they are developing and maturing, they are learning from the significant role models in their lives. Discuss the kinds of relationships they are observing: male-female relationships, marriage relationships, parent-child relationships (significant adult-child). It is important for them to analyze the messages that they are learning. For example, they are learning ways that significant adults respond to family changes, such as having a new family member or having an ill family member. They are learning ways that significant adults rear children.

6 Explain that some significant adults may not be skilled in relationships.

Refer to the student master. Significant adults who are not skilled in relationships may be critical and hostile. They may shame or ridicule others. They may be abusive. **Child abuse** is the harmful treatment of a person under the age of eighteen and includes physical abuse, emotional abuse, sexual abuse, and neglect. Further explain that young people who are treated in these ways may repeat these behaviors if they choose to be parents. This is why it is important to understand the effects of the behaviors of significant role models.

7 Identify other behaviors that might be modeled by significant adults. For examples, some adults might be drug-free while others might misuse or abuse drugs. Some adults might exercise regularly and practice stress management skills while others might be couch potatoes and be stressed.

Evaluation:

Have students write a "Positive Parenting Pledge" in which they identify at least ten behaviors they believe a parent should role model. Select students to read their pledges to the class. Have students share their pledges and their copies of "Children Learn What They Live" with the significant adults in their families.

Multicultural Infusion:

Use a globe or world map. Have several students point to different countries. After you have named different countries, introduce the concept that families around the world have much in common. The significant adults in all families are important role models. Have students identify five behaviors that they believe significant adults in families from all cultures might role model for their children.

Inclusion:

Explain how the behaviors and attitudes of significant adults effect young people with disabilities. When significant adults are patient and accepting, young people who with disabilities develop positive self-esteem and are accepting of themselves.

Children Learn What They Live

by Dorothy Law Nolte

If a child lives with criticism, (s)he learns to condemn.

If a child lives with hostility, (s)he learns to fight.

If a child lives with ridicule, (s)he learns to be shy.

If a child lives with shame, (s)he learns to feel guilty.

If a child lives with tolerance, (s)he learns to be patient.

If a child lives with encouragement, (s)he learns
confidence.

If a child lives with praise, (s)he learns to appreciate.

If a child lives with fairness, (s)he learns justice.

If a child lives with security, (s)he learns to have faith.

If a child lives with approval, (s)he learns to like
herself/himself.

If a child lives with acceptance and friendship,
(s)he learns to find love in the world.

Steps Toward Maturity

Health Education Standards:

- Students will comprehend concepts related to health promotion and disease prevention.
- Students will demonstrate the ability to use goal-setting and decision-making skills that enhance health.

Performance Indicators:

- Students will describe how personal health goals are influenced by changing information, abilities, priorities, and responsibilities.
- Students will describe ways to reduce risks related to adolescent health problems.
- Students will describe the interrelationship of mental, emotional, social, and physical health during adolescence.

Life Skills:

- I will achieve developmental tasks for my age group.
- I will accept my maleness/femaleness.
- I will accept my physical uniqueness.
- I will accept and develop my learning style.

Materials:

Teaching Master, "Developmental Tasks of Adolescence"; transparency projector; four wastebaskets; eight sheets of paper plus one sheet of paper for each student; pencils; chalk

Motivation:

1 Make a transparency of the Teaching Master "Developmental Tasks of Adolescence." Review the information on the master with the students. Explain that **developmental tasks** are achievements that are necessary to be made during a particular period of growth in order that a person can continue growing toward maturity. The eight tasks identified on the transparency are the eight tasks which they are now attempting to master.

2 Divide the class into eight groups of students, one for each of the developmental tasks. Each group is to select one student to be its leader. The leader is to write the assigned developmental task on a sheet of paper and crumple it into a ball. For example, the leader in group one would write "Achieving a new and more mature relationship with age mates of both sexes" on a sheet of paper and then crumple this sheet of paper into a ball.

3 Use chalk to make a starting point on the floor. In a direct line, place the first wastebasket three feet from the starting point. Place the second wastebasket six feet from the starting point. Place the third wastebasket nine feet from the starting point and the fourth wastebasket twelve feet from the starting point.

4 Ask the eight group leaders to line up in order of the developmental tasks (Task 1, Task 2, etc.) at the starting point. Explain that the wastebasket that is furthest from the starting point represents mastery of each of the developmental tasks written on the crumpled sheets of paper. The waste baskets in between are "steps toward maturity" because they lead to toward mastery of the developmental tasks. Begin with the group leader who has Task 1 written on the

574

crumpled sheet of paper. Ask this student to toss the crumpled sheet of paper into the wastebasket that is twelve feet from the starting point. If the student misses, have the student pick up the crumpled paper. Repeat, asking the second student to follow the same directions. Repeat, having the remaining students representing their groups as leaders toss their crumpled sheets of paper into the furthest wastebasket. In many cases, none of the students will successfully toss their crumpled sheets of paper into the wastebasket.

5 Now begin again with different directions. The student who is the leader for Task 1 is to toss the crumpled paper into the wastebasket that is three feet from the starting point. If (s)he is successful, then (s)he is to remove the crumpled paper. Standing at the first wastebasket, (s)he is to toss it into the second waste basket. If (s)he is successful, (s)he is to stand at the second wastebasket and toss it into the third wastebasket. Finally, if (s)he is successful, (s)he is to toss the crumpled paper into the fourth wastebasket. If the student misses, (s)he is to remain at the basket at which (s)he missed. Repeat having the other students who are leaders for different tasks follow the same directions.

6 Finally, allow students who missed additional attempts so that they can move from one wastebasket to the next to get to the final wastebasket.

7 Explain that you have just demonstrated how to master the developmental tasks for their age group. Very few, if any, students were able to toss their crumpled sheets of

paper into the furthest wastebasket on the first try. Yet many students were successful when they followed the second set of directions and were allowed to progress from one wastebasket to the next. Explain that this is how developmental tasks are mastered—by taking one step at a time. For example, Task 6 involves preparing for an economic career. This is not done quickly. It requires several steps, such as doing homework, attending school regularly, child sitting or mowing lawn to earn money, etc. Further explain, that sometimes it is difficult to master a task and practice helps. Some students missed the wastebaskets in between. You gave them additional tries. This is because trying is very important. For example, they may try to do math homework and some of their answers may be incorrect. They will want to do these math problems again.

Evaluation:

Have students work in their assigned groups. Explain that a **goal** is something toward which a person works. The long-term goal of each group is to master the developmental task it was assigned. To reach this long-term goal, the group is to identify three short-term goals. (Long-term goal: Task 6. Preparing for an economic career; Short-term goals: Complete homework assignments, get good grades, graduate from high school). Have each group leader present the short-term goals by repeating the previous activity using the wastebaskets. Then have students use paper and pencils for the following evaluation. Have them list the eight developmental tasks and next to each identify an action they can take to move toward mastery.

Inclusion:

Have students with different learning styles, such as Attention Deficit Hyperactivity Disorder and dyslexia, work on an independent project with their parents. They are to set a long-term goal for their education and identify at least three short-term goals that will help them master their long-term education goal.

Teaching Master

Developmental Tasks of Adolescence

Developmental tasks are achievements that are necessary to be made during a particular period of growth in order that a person can continue growing toward maturity. For adolescents, the following developmental tasks have been identified:

Task 1:	Achieving a new and more mature relationship with age mates of both sexes.

Task 2:	Achieving a masculine or feminine social role.

Task 3:	Accepting one's physique.

Task 4:	Achieving emotional independence from parents and other adults.

Task 5:	Preparing for marriage and family life.

Task 6:	Preparing for an economic career.

Task 7:	Acquiring a set of values and an ethical system as a guide to behavior—developing an ideology.

Task 8:	Developing a social conscience.

Nutrient Match Up

Health Education Standards:

- Students will comprehend concepts related to health promotion and disease prevention.
- Students will demonstrate the ability to practice health-enhancing behaviors and reduce health risks.

Performance Indicators:

- Students will explain the relationship between positive health behaviors and the prevention of injury, illness, and premature death.
- Students will explain the importance of assuming responsibility for personal health behaviors.

Life Skills:

- I will recognize foods that contain the six major nutrients.
- I will select the appropriate number of servings from The Food Guide Pyramid.

Materials:

Teaching Master, "The Six Basic Classes of Nutrients"; Teaching Master, "The Food Guide Pyramid"; transparency projector; slips of paper; tape; red pen; blue pen

Motivation:

1 Before beginning this strategy, you will need to prepare slips of paper with nutrients written on them. You will prepare six slips of paper by using a red pen to write one of the six basic classes of nutrients on each: proteins, carbohydrates, fats, vitamins, minerals, and water. Then you will use a blue pen to prepare the

other slips of paper. You will write examples of each of the six basic classes of nutrients on each slip of paper. The six basic classes of nutrients are listed below with the examples that you can use for the other slips of paper.

Proteins	Carbohydrates	Fats
meat	wheat bread	ice cream
chicken	rice	whole milk
tuna	pasta	french fries
dried	macaroni	butter
beans	noodles	corn oil
steak	cereal	
eggs	oatmeal	
nuts		

Vitamins	Minerals	Water
Vitamin A	calcium	drinking
Thiamine	chlorine	water
Riboflavin	iodine	bottled water
Niacin	iron	fruit juice
Folic Acid	magnesium	soups
Ascorbic	phosphorous	fruits
Acid		celery

2 Explain to students that they are going to be reviewing the nutrients and the importance of obtaining the nutrients they need for optimal health. Define nutrients. **Nutrients** are chemical substances in foods that furnish fuel for energy, provide materials needed for building and maintenance of body tissues, and/or supply substances that function in the regulation of body processes. Explain that no one food contains all nutrients in the amounts needed for health. Identify the six basic classes of nutrients: proteins, carbohydrates, fats, vitamins, minerals, and water.

3 Use the Teaching Master "The Six Basic Classes of Nutrients" to review important information about each of the nutrients.

4 Tell students that they are going to play "Nutrient Match Up." The directions for this activity are as follows. Students will form a line in front of you. They will turn so their backs are facing you. Tape a slip of paper on each of their backs. The slip of paper will have a word or words written on it. The word or words will either be the name of one of the six basic classes of nutrients or an example of one of the nutrients. Explain to students that they are not to look at the slip of paper taped to their backs. Instead, they are to guess what is written on the slip of paper by asking their classmates questions. They can only ask their classmates questions that can be answered with "yes" or "no." For example, a student can ask, "Am I a carbohydrate?" The student could not ask, "What kind of nutrient am I?" In addition, they can only ask each student one question. If they guess what is written on the slip of paper on their back, they are to take it off their back and tape it someplace on the front of them. Allow students five to ten minutes for this part of the activity.

5 After enough time has been allowed, have students who have not guessed what was written on the slip of paper on their back, to take it from their back, read it, and tape it on the front of them. Explain that they are now ready for the second part of this activity. Further explain that each student belongs in a group. Have the six students who have the six basic classes of nutrients written in red ink on the slips of paper taped to them stand in front of the class. Without talking, the remaining students are to join one of these six students and form a group.

6 Some students may have more difficulty finding their correct groups. Explain that some words

belong to more than one group. For example, steak contains fat, but it is also a source of protein. Check to see that students are in the groups identified in step 1 of this strategy.

Evaluation:

Ask students to write a song for their evaluation. Each student is to contribute at least one line to the group's song. The line should contain a fact pertaining to the word written on the slip of paper that the student has taped on him/her. After an appropriate amount of time, have students sing their songs for the class. Use the Teaching Master "The Food Guide Pyramid." **The Food Guide Pyramid** is a food-group guide that recommends daily guidelines to ensure a balanced diet. Explain that the Food Guide Pyramid provides information about what foods Americans eat and how to make the best food choices. The Food Guide Pyramid also stresses the number of servings of each major food group that is recommended daily. Each food group provides some of the nutrients a person needs each day. Have students name foods they enjoy eating that belong to each of the food groups illustrated.

Multicultural Infusion:

Place students in groups. Each group is to appoint a recorder. The recorder should fold a sheet of paper lengthwise to make two columns. The first column should be labeled "foods" and the second column should be labeled "food groups." Each group is to brainstorm a list of foods from different cultures. The recorder will

list these in the first column. Then
each group is to identify the food
group to which each food belongs.
The food group should be written on
the same line as the food, but in the
second column.

Inclusion:

Students who are gifted might be
placed into a group for a cooperative
learning experience. They are to use
a foreign language dictionary, such
as Spanish, and create the slips of
paper for each of the six basic classes
of nutrients.

Teaching Master
The Six Basic Classes of Nutrients

NUTRIENT	FACTS	SOURCES
Proteins	• Essential for the growth, development, and repair of all body tissues • Form parts of muscle, bone, blood, cell membranes • Form hormones and enzymes • Made of amino acids	• Meat, chicken, tuna, dried beans, eggs, nuts
Carbohydrates	• Provide energy • Simple carbohydrates, such as fruit, enter the bloodstream rapidly for quick energy • Complex carbohydrates, such as rice, provide long-lasting energy	• Bread, wheat, rice, pasta, macaroni noodles, cereal, oatmeal
Fats	• A source of energy • Essential for making certain vitamins available • Stored as fat tissue which surrounds and protects organs • Saturated fats, such as those in meat or dairy products, raise cholesterol levels • Unsaturated fats are found in plant products	• Ice cream, milk, cheese, butter, margarine, yogurt, meat, egg yolks, corn oil
Vitamins	• Facilitate chemical reactions	
	Vitamin A—night vision; bone formation	Carrots, sweet potatoes
	Thiamine—appetite	Nuts, cereals, peas, beans
	Riboflavin—metabolism; energy production; eyes and skin	Whole milk, cottage cheese, eggs
	Niacin—normal digestion, appetite, nervous system	Cereals, fish, peanuts
	Folic Acid—blood formation, enzyme function	Whole grain bread, broccoli
	Ascorbic Acid—helps body resist infection, strengthens blood vessels	Oranges, limes, tomatoes

Nutrition

NUTRIENT	FACTS	SOURCES
Minerals	• Assist in the regulation of chemical reactions	
	Calcium—strong bones and teeth, heartbeat	Milk, cheese, cottage cheese
	Chlorine—aids in digestion, keeps body limber	Table salt
	Iodine—energy, mental alertness, growth, manufacture thyroid	Table salt, seafood
	Iron—forms red blood cells, growth, prevents fatigue	Oatmeal, red meat, liver
	Magnesium—fights depression, insomnia, nervousness	Dark green vegetables, apples
	Phosphorus—healthy gums and teeth, growth and repair of cells	Whole grains, fish, poultry
Water	• Makes up blood • Helps the process of digestion • Helps remove the body wastes • Helps regulate body temperature	• Drinking water, bottled water, juices, soups, vegetables such as celery

Teaching Master

The Food Guide Pyramid

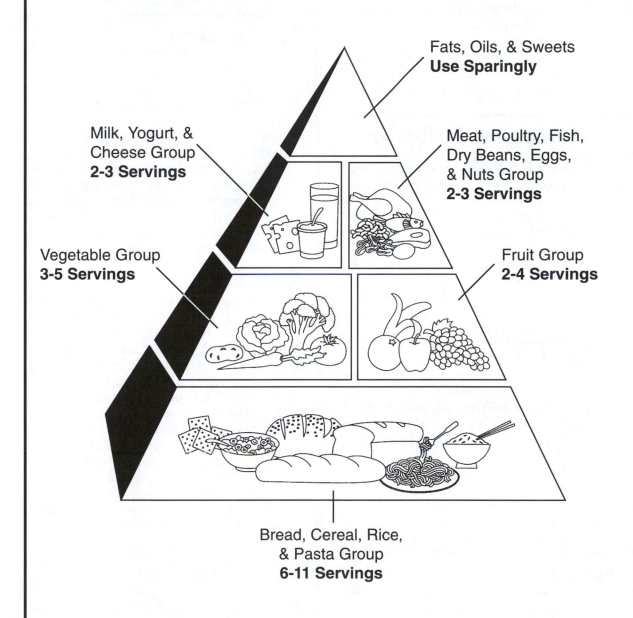

Fats, Oils, & Sweets
Use Sparingly

Milk, Yogurt, &
Cheese Group
2-3 Servings

Meat, Poultry, Fish,
Dry Beans, Eggs,
& Nuts Group
2-3 Servings

Vegetable Group
3-5 Servings

Fruit Group
2-4 Servings

Bread, Cereal, Rice,
& Pasta Group
6-11 Servings

Grooming Products Auction

Health Education Standards:

- Students will comprehend concepts related to health promotion and disease prevention.
- Students will demonstrate the ability to access valid health information and health promoting products and services.

Performance Indicators:

- Students will explain the importance of assuming responsibility for personal health behaviors.
- Students will analyze the validity of health information, products, and services.
- Students will compare the costs and validity of health products.
- Students will analyze how media influences the selection of health products and services.

Life Skills:

- I will be well-groomed.
- *I will choose sources of health-related information, products, and services wisely. (Consumer and Community Health)*
- *I will spend money wisely. (Consumer and Community Health)*
- *I will analyze the effects of advertising on my choices. (Consumer and Community Health)*

Materials

Teaching Master, "Persuasion"; transparency projector; play money; grooming products or pictures of items such as cotton swabs, tissues, dental floss, toothbrush, powder, toothpaste, mouthwash, antiperspirant, lipstick, cotton balls, razor, soap, shampoo, nail file, nail polish, comb, brush, deodorant, perfume, after shave, conditioner, nail polish remover, nail polish, eyeliner, skin makeup, tweezers, toe clippers, cuticle scissors; magazines; calculators (optional)

Motivation:

1 Introduce the topic of grooming. **Grooming** is the practice of caring for the body in order to look, smell, and feel one's best. Good grooming practices require the regular cleansing of the body including the care of the skin, hair, nails, and feet, as well as wearing clean clothes. Good grooming practices help keep the physical body healthy by reducing the spread of germs from one part of the body to another part and from one person to another.

2 Explain to students that there are many products for grooming. They are consumers when they make decisions about purchasing these products. A **consumer** is a person who chooses sources of health-related information and buys or uses health products and services. Explain that more than fifty cents of every dollar is spent on health products and services. It is important for them to learn to spend their money wisely. Companies that produce grooming products often advertise. **Advertising** is a form of selling in which individuals are informed of products and services. A **commercial** is an advertisement on television or radio.

3 Explain to students that sellers use a variety of techniques in their advertisements to try to convince consumers that their products and services are more desirable than those of their competitors. Use the Teaching Master "Persuasion" to review different advertising appeals that are used.

4 Place the grooming products on a desk or table. Have students select one of the grooming products for the Grooming Products Auction. They will be asked to auction off this product when the auction begins. Give students time to prepare for the auction. Remind them that they can use one or more of the appeals from the Teaching Master "Persuasion." They may also tell the class facts about their products. For example, a student might auction off the tissues and suggest that the tissues are a good buy because they can be used when a person sneezes to prevent the spread of germs.

5 Give each student play money. Explain that they are to make the best buys possible. They need to decide which health products for grooming are most needed and to bid for these health products.

6 Select a student to begin the Grooming Products Auction. This student is to auction off his or her grooming product to the highest bidder. The student should try to get the highest price possible by convincing the bidders that the product is necessary and appealing.

7 After the auction, have students discuss the grooming products upon which they bid. Which products demanded the highest price? Why? Which products were not in demand? Why? What were some of the ways the auctioneers tried to persuade the bidders to raise their bids? Which appeals were most convincing?

Evaluation:

Have students bring a magazine advertisement for a grooming product from their homes. If students do not have magazines in their homes, you might ask those who do to share with those who do not. Students are to staple their advertisements to a sheet of notebook paper. They are to write two paragraphs on the notebook paper. The first paragraph is to include a discussion of how this product is used for grooming. The second paragraph is to analyze the information and appeals used in the advertisement.

Multicultural Infusion:

If possible, obtain a foreign magazine that has an advertisement for a grooming product(s). The advertisement should be written in a language other than English. Ask students who are proficient in the other language not to tell the students what is written. Now have students describe the appeal in the advertisement from the visual effect only. After they have had the opportunity to give answers, tell them the written words or have students who are proficient in the language read the words to them. Ask students if the same advertising appeals are used in magazines of different languages.

Inclusion:

Give students the opportunity to practice using calculators. As students bid on products, have them record the lowest bids and the highest bids. Then have them use the calculators to determine the difference.

Teaching Master

Persuasion

Bandwagon Appeal. The bandwagon appeal tries to convince consumers that everyone else wants a particular product or service and they should too.

Brand Loyalty Appeal. The brand loyalty appeal tells consumers that a specific brand is better than the rest, and that they would be cheating themselves to use anything but this brand.

False Image Appeal. The false image appeal attempts to convince consumers that they will give a certain impression if they use the product.

Glittering Generality Appeal. The glittering generality appeal contains statements that greatly exaggerate the benefits of the product.

Humor Appeal. The humor appeal uses a slogan, jingle or cartoon to keep the consumer's attention.

Progress Appeal. The progress appeal tells consumers that a product is a new and better product than one formerly advertised.

Scientific Evidence Appeal. The scientific evidence appeal gives consumers the results of a survey or laboratory tests to provide confidence in a product.

Snob Appeal. The snob appeal convinces consumers that they are worthy of a product or service because it is the best.

Reward Appeal. The reward appeal tells consumers that they will receive a special prize or gift if they buy a product.

Testimony Appeal. The testimony appeal includes a promotion by a well-known person who says that a product or service is the best one for the consumer.

Stuck In The Middle

Health Education Standards:

- Students will comprehend concepts related to health promotion and disease prevention.
- Students will demonstrate the ability to use interpersonal communication skills to enhance health.
- Students will demonstrate the ability to use goal-setting and decision-making skills that enhance health.

Performance Indicators:

- Students will demonstrate the ability to apply a decision-making process to health issues and problems individually and collaboratively.
- Students will predict how decisions regarding health behaviors have consequences for self and others.
- Students will describe ways to reduce risks related to adolescent health problems.
- Students will demonstrate refusal and negotiation skills to enhance health.

Life Skills:

- I will not drink alcohol.
- I will not use tobacco products.
- I will not misuse or abuse controlled substances.
- I will use resistance skills when pressured to use drugs.
- *I will make responsible decisions. (Mental and Emotional Health)*

Materials:

Student Master, "The Consequences of Harmful Drug Use"; transparency of the Teaching Master, "Resisting Harmful Drug Use"; transparency projector; twelve marshmallows

Motivation:

1 Make copies of the Student Master "The Consequences of Harmful Drug Use" for each student. Have students review the information on the Student Master. Emphasize the consequences of harmful drug use. For example, violence may occur from the use of PCP.

2 Use a transparency made from the Teaching Master "Resisting Harmful Drug Use." Emphasize the importance of using resistance skills when pressured to use drugs. **Resistance skills** are skills that are used when a person wants to say NO to an action and/or leave a situation that threatens health, threatens safety, breaks laws, results in lack of respect for self and others, disobeys guidelines set by responsible adults, or detracts from character.

3 Ask for two student volunteers. Have each of these students extend one arm and place the palm of the hand up. Place six marshmallows in the palm of each student's hand. The marshmallows represent peers. Explain that one student will use resistance skills when pressured by peers to use drugs. The other student will not. Ask the class to begin to pressure both students to use drugs. The one student will use resistance skills when pressured. The other will close the palm of the hand and squeeze tighter and tighter each time (s)he is pressured. Have the class continue the pressure for several minutes.

4 Explain that the one student was able to withstand the pressure of peers by using resistance skills. This student has the six marshmallows in his/her hand. Although (s)he is around peers, (s)he made responsible decisions about drug use. Now have the student who made a tight fist open the fist. The marshmallows will be stuck together. Explain that this student did not use resistance skills. Now (s)he is "stuck with the consequences" of what peers wanted him/her to do. Have students name some of the consequences. They can refer to the Student Master "The Consequences of Harmful Drug Use."

Evaluation:

Have students make their own "Top Ten Reasons for Not Misusing or Abusing Drugs" list. Explain that they are to recall at least ten facts from the Student Master "The Consequences of Harmful Drug Use."

Inclusion:

Students who have difficulty learning may use the Student Master when they make their "Top Ten" list.

Student Master

The Consequences of Harmful Drug Use

SAY
NO

Life Skill: I will not use alcohol.

Alcohol is a psychoactive drug that depresses the central nervous system. It slows reaction time and increases the likelihood of accidents. It intensifies feelings, increasing the risk of violence. **Cirrhosis** is a disease in which alcohol destroys liver cells and plugs the liver with fibrous scar tissue. It can lead to liver failure and death. **Alcohol dementia** is brain impairment that causes intellectual decline. **Alcoholism** is a complex disease that is characterized by a preoccupation with drinking alcohol that has progressed to serious physical, social, occupational, and family consequences for the individual.

Life Skill: I will not use tobacco products.

Tobacco products include cigarettes and smokeless tobacco that contain many harmful ingredients. The estimated number of chemical compounds in tobacco smoke exceeds 4,000. **Tar** is a sticky, dark mixture in tobacco smoke that produces chronic irritation of the respiratory system and causes lung cancer. **Nicotine** is the active psychoactive agent in tobacco. It increases heart rate and blood pressure and is addicting. Cigarette smoking causes lung cancer, emphysema, chronic bronchitis, and cardiovascular diseases. Use of smokeless tobacco causes oral cancer.

Life Skill: I will not misuse or abuse controlled substances.

A **controlled substance** is a drug that is illegal without a prescription. Many controlled substances are psychoactive drugs. A **psychoactive drug** is a substance that acts on the central nervous system and alters a user's moods, perceptions, feelings, personality, and behavior.

Cocaine is a drug that stimulates the central nervous system and causes dependence. People using this drug get a quick high, but then slide into physiological depression. They may lose interest in work and other responsibilities, have delusions and hallucinations, experience anxiety and panic. **Crack** is a form of cocaine that produces a rapid and intense reaction. The effects are believed to be ten times greater that cocaine.

Amphetamines are stimulants that speed up the central nervous system. They may produce euphoria, increased alertness, impaired judgment, and impulsiveness. They increase heart beat rate and blood pressure. **Methamphetamines** are stimulant drugs that fall within the amphetamine family. They produce behavioral and psychological effects similar to cocaine and other stimulants. **Crank** is an amphetamine-like stimulant with effects that last longer than crack or cocaine. **Ice** is an amphetamine-like drug that is smoked. Prolonged use of this drug results in serious lung and kidney damage.

Alcohol, Tobacco, and Other Drugs

A **hallucinogenic drug** is a substance that has the major effect of producing marked distortions in perception. Hallucinogens can cause euphoria, impair short-term memory, increase pulse rate, seem to make time pass very slowly, produce significant disturbances in judgment, and cause flashbacks. A **flashback** is the recurrence of the effects of a drug after it was taken. **LSD** is a synthetic drug that produces hallucinations. It is extremely potent and may produce "bad trips" in which a person experiences panic, fear, and physical symptoms. Flashbacks have been reported to reappear years after the drug was taken. **PCP** is a hallucinogen that is manufactured as a tablet or capsule, but it also can be smoked, swallowed, or sniffed. Small doses produce a feeling of intoxication, with staggering gait, slurred speech, numbness of extremities, and lowered sensitivity to pain. Increased doses may cause convulsions, coma, heart failure, lung failure, and stroke. People who use PCP often become violent. **Mescaline** is a hallucinogenic drug that comes from the Mexican peyote cactus. Its effects are similar to LSD. **Psilocybin** is a hallucinogenic drug derived from a specific type of mushroom that alters mood and perception. Its effects are similar to LSD.

Inhalants are chemicals that produce vapors, which cause psychoactive effects. The substances most likely to be abused include household chemicals such as aerosols, airplane glue, cleaning fluids, paint thinners, spray-can propellants, and gasoline. Inhalants are very dangerous. They travel quickly to the brain and cause disorientation, unconsciousness, sedation, and hallucinations. They may also harm the respiratory system, damage the kidneys and liver, produce seizures, and irregular heartbeat. **Nitrous oxide** is a colorless gas that is abused as an inhalant.

Marijuana is a drug containing THC that impairs short-term memory and changes mood. This drug affects the nervous system by impairing coordination. It raises blood pressure and impairs the immune system. Use of marijuana may result in amotivational syndrome. **Amotivational syndrome** is a lack of desire by people to become motivated to perform daily responsibilities. **Hashish** is a drug that consists of the drug-rich resinous secretions of the cannabis plant. It is more potent than marijuana.

Narcotics are drugs that depress the central nervous system and block the feeling of pain. They are highly addictive. **Morphine** is a drug that is used to control pain. It is sometimes prescribed for the relief of pain. **Codeine** is a narcotic painkiller produced from morphine. **Heroin** is a narcotic drug derived from morphine that has no approved medical use. Heroin is injected into the vein. Sharing needles to inject heroin is a way that HIV is spread.

Sedative-hypnotic drugs are central nervous system depressants. **Sedatives** are drugs that have a calming effect on behavior. **Hypnotic drugs** are drugs that cause drowsiness and sleep. Use of these drugs can cause dependence. **Barbiturates** are depressant drugs used to induce sleep and relieve tension. They are extremely dangerous when taking with alcohol. People who become dependent on these drugs need medical supervision to stop taking them.

Teaching Master

Resisting Harmful Drug Use

1. Use assertive behavior.

Look directly at the person who is pressuring you.
Say NO clearly and firmly.
Give a reason.
Repeat the reason if necessary.
Do not change your mind.

2. Avoid saying, "NO, thank you."

Never thank someone for pressuring you to do something
harmful, unsafe, illegal, disrespectful, or which may
disobey your parents or display a lack of character.

3. Use nonverbal behavior that matches verbal behavior.

Do not pretend to take a sip of beer or a puff from
a cigarette. This behavior sends a mixed message to
others. It can also get you in trouble. Others may
believe you did something wrong.

4. Influence others to choose responsible behavior.

When a situation poses immediate danger, leave right
away. But, suppose you are invited to a party in which
there will be drugs. Say NO and encourage those who
ask you to consider responsible behavior. Give them
reasons why attending the party is not responsible.

5. Avoid being in situations in which there will be pressure to make harmful decisions.

Always think ahead. When you know that drugs might be
used, stay away.

6. Avoid being with peers who use drugs.

Peers who use drugs will pressure you to do
the same. When you are with peers who use
drugs, others may believe that you use them too.
You also are at risk for being involved in violence.

7. Resist pressure to engage in illegal behavior.

You have a responsibility to follow laws and
to be a responsible citizen.

591

STD Scrabble

Health Education Standards:

- Students will comprehend concepts related to health promotion and disease prevention.
- Students will demonstrate the ability to practice health-enhancing behaviors and reduce health risks.

Performance Indicators:

- Students will explain the relationship between positive health behaviors and the prevention of injury, illness, disease, and premature death.
- Students will describe how lifestyle, pathogens, family history, and other risk factors are related to the cause or prevention of disease and other health problems.
- Students will distinguish between safe, risky, and harmful behaviors in relationships.

Life Skills:

- I will choose behaviors to reduce the risk of infection with STDs.
- *I will practice life skills to promote abstinence. (Family Living)*

Materials:

Student Master, "STDs"; chalk; chalkboard

Motivation:

1 Make a copy of the Student Master "STDs" for each student. Review the facts about each of the following STDs: chlamydial infections, gonorrhea, syphilis, genital herpes, genital warts, bacterial vaginosis, candidiasis, trichomoniasis, pediculosis pubis, and hepatitis B.

2 Review the facts by playing "STD Scrabble." Using the chalk, print SEXUALLY TRANSMITTED DISEASES on the chalkboard. Then divide the class into two teams. Explain that the teams will take turns adding on letters to make words. The words must all be related to STDs. For example, letters may be added vertically below the S to make syphilis. Then "ice" can be added to the "l" in syphilis to form the word "lice" (see the illustration). Each time letters are added to form a word, the student must use the word in a sentence. For example, suppose a student added the letter to form the word "syphilis." Then this student might say, "Syphilis is an STD caused by a bacterium that penetrates the mucous membranes." Teams receive one point for a correct word and one point for a correct statement. They alternate turns.

3 Explain to students that they have just reviewed the facts regarding STDs. But, there is another fact that they should know. The best way for them to avoid becoming infected with an STD is to practice abstinence. **Abstinence** is choosing not to engage in sexual intercourse. Encourage students to choose the following behaviors that support abstinence:

1. Be involved in activities that promote self-worth.
2. Establish goals.
3. Develop loving family relationships.
4. Be assertive and use decision-making skills.
5. Establish relationships with trusted adults.
6. Select friends who choose abstinence.
7. Date people who have chosen abstinence.
8. Avoid situations that are tempting.

9. Abstain from the use of alcohol and other drugs.
10. Select entertainment that promotes sex within a monogamous marriage.

Evaluation:

Explain to students that they have a pen pal who is their age. This pen pal lives in another area of the country. Many young people in this area are infected with STDs. Their pen pal writes them and expresses concern about STDs. They are to write back to the pen pal and explain why abstinence is a responsible choice and tell behaviors which support abstinence.

Inclusion:

You might modify "STD Scrabble." You can give some students a list of words that they might use. For example, the list might include: trichomoniasis, chancre, inflammation, urethra, culture, penicillin, etc. Students with special needs might use this list to locate words that will attach to a letter.

STDs

CHLAMYDIAL INFECTIONS

Cause: the bacterium *Chlamydia trachomatis*
Transmission: sexual intercourse; from an infected mother to her baby during vaginal delivery
Symptoms in females: usually none; if symptoms occur, irritation and itching in the genital area, burning during urination, and a vaginal discharge
Symptoms in males: usually none; if symptoms occur, discharge and burning during urination; after many years, sterility
Diagnosis: microscopic examination of vaginal and urethral discharges
Treatment: antibiotics

GONORRHEA

Cause: the bacterium *Neisseria gonorrhoeae*
Transmission: sexual intercourse; from an infected mother to her baby during vaginal delivery
Symptoms in females: none; increased vaginal discharge, genital irritation, pain during urination
Symptoms in males: a discharge from the urethra, pain, increased urination
Diagnosis: culture test of mucous membranes in infected areas
Treatment: Penicillin (there are some resistant strains)

SYPHILIS

Cause: the bacterium *Treponema pallidum*
Transmission: sexual intercourse; from a pregnant female to her fetus through the placenta
Symptoms in females and males: a chancre appears in the first stage and then goes away; a rash appears in the second stage and then goes away; in the late stage, organs such as the liver, heart, and brain are damaged
Diagnosis: culture of chancre in first stage; blood test
Treatment: Penicillin G and doxycycline

GENITAL HERPES

Cause: herpes simplex virus
Transmission: sexual intercourse; contact with blisters
Symptoms in females and males: blisters in the genital area, fever, headaches, tiredness, swollen lymph nodes
Diagnosis: inspection and culture of fluid from the blisters
Treatment: no known treatment; genital herpes recurs; acyclovir relieves the symptoms

Communicable and Chronic Diseases

GENITAL WARTS

Cause: the human papilloma virus (HPV)
Transmission: sexual intercourse; direct contact with infected
  bed linen, towels, and clothing
Symptoms in females and males: warts which are painless and have
  a cauliflower shape appear on the genitals
Diagnosis: clinical inspection
Treatment: no treatment eradicates them completely; topical
  medications can be applied by a physician

BACTERIAL VAGINOSIS

Cause: the bacterium *Gardnerella vaginalis*
Transmission: sexual intercourse
Symptoms in females: a foul-smelling discharge, possible irritation
  of vaginal tissue, and burning during urination
Symptoms in males: inflammation of the foreskin, urethra,
  and bladder
Diagnosis: microscopic examination of discharge
Treatment: the antibiotic metronidazole

CANDIDIASIS

Cause: the fungus *Candida albicans*
Transmission: sexual intercourse
Symptoms in females: white, foul-smelling discharge and itching
Symptoms in males: itching and burning during urination
Diagnosis: examination by physician
Treatment: a cream, tablet, or vaginal suppository

TRICHOMONIASIS

Cause: a parasitic protozoan, *Trichomonas vaginalis*
Transmission: sexual intercourse; increased growth in vagina;
  sharing infected towels
Symptoms in females: half have none; frothy greenish-yellow
  discharge that has an odor, itching, and burning
Symptoms in males: usually none
Diagnosis: microscopic examination of discharges
Treatment: metronidazole, a prescription drug

PEDICULOSIS PUBIS

Cause: the crab louse, *Phthirus pubis*
Transmission: close sexual contact; wearing infected clothing;
  sleeping in infected sheets; sharing infected towels
Symptoms in females and males: little black spots
Diagnosis: clinical inspection by physician
Treatment: lindane, a prescription drug

HEPATITIS B

Cause: hepatitis B virus
Transmission: sexual intercourse; sharing needles for IV drugs
Symptoms in females and males: profound fatigue, jaundice, nausea,
  abdominal pain; fatal in about 4 percent of cases; 5 to 10 percent
  become chronic carriers
Diagnosis: blood tests for hepatitis antibodies
Treatment: no effective treatment; bed rest and fluid intake;
  antibiotics treat secondary infections

The Weather Channel

Health Education Standards:

- Students will demonstrate the ability to practice health-enhancing behaviors and reduce health risks.
- Students will demonstrate the ability to advocate for personal, family, and community health.

Performance Indicators:

- Students will develop injury prevention and management strategies for personal and family health.
- Students will analyze the influence of technology on personal and family health.

Life Skills:

- I will follow safety guidelines for different weather conditions and natural disasters.
- *I will cooperate with people who protect my health and safety. (Consumer and Community Health)*

Materials:

Student Master, "Weather Watch"; computer with online service (optional); cable television (optional); weather forecast in the newspaper; map of the United States; index cards

Motivation:

1 Explain to students the importance of practicing the life skill, "I will follow safety guidelines for different weather conditions and natural disasters." Make a copy of the Student Master "Weather Watch" for each student. Review the information on the master. Explain that the guidelines on this master will help them to practice the life skill.

2 Explain that there are people with whom they can cooperate who protect their safety. If you have a computer with online service available, have students locate the weather service to learn weather conditions in different locations. Specifically, you may want them to find the weather forecast for your area for the next several days. If you have cable television in your school, have students locate the weather channel and listen to the forecast. Emphasize that these are services provided by people who help them protect their health and safety. If you do not have these options available, you may want to discuss them. Perhaps students can use the computer online service at home. They may have cable television at home. Show students the weather forecast in the newspaper.

3 Divide the class into seven groups. Assign each group one of the following: hot weather, cold weather, lightning, tornados, earthquakes, hurricanes, floods. Explain that each group is going to prepare a report for "The Weather Channel." Each group is to select one person to be the meteorologist who will give the report. The group is to select an area in the country. When it presents its report, the group can use your map to show the location. The meteorologist is to give the weather report and then explain the safety guidelines to follow. Allow an appropriate amount of time for group work.

4 Have students present their reports. Discuss the different weather conditions and the recommended safety guidelines. Ask students to name the person(s) in your community who are responsible for the weather report.

Evaluation:

Write each of the following on an index card: hot weather, cold weather, lightning, tornados, earthquakes, hurricanes, floods. Place the index cards face down on your desk. Have students take turns selecting an index card and reviewing the safety guidelines to follow aloud for the class.

Inclusion:

Ask students who have difficulty learning to write the index cards for you. This allows them a further opportunity to review these weather conditions and natural disasters. Students also will feel good about helping you.

Weather Watch

HOT WEATHER SAFETY

Heat exhaustion is a condition in which the body loses large amounts of salt and water through sweating. **Heat stroke** is a condition that occurs when the body becomes so overheated that it no longer can sweat to cool off. To prevent these conditions:

1. Drink plenty of fluids.
2. Avoid overexertion.
3. Wear lightweight, loose-fitting clothing.
4. Stay in the shade or in the coolest area of an apartment, house, or building.

COLD WEATHER SAFETY

Hypothermia is low body temperature. **Frostbite** is a freezing of parts of the body. To prevent these conditions:

1. Wear layers of clothing.
2. Keep clothing as dry as possible.
3. Wear boots and gloves that are loose enough to allow circulation of blood.
4. Stay inside when the wind chill factor is very low. The wind chill factor is a measure of the air temperature which takes into account the chilling effect of the wind.

LIGHTNING SAFETY

Lightning is the flashing of light caused by a discharge of electricity in the atmosphere. To stay safe during lightning:

1. Do not stand under a tree or out in the open during an electrical storm. If caught out in the open, try to find a ravine or low spot for shelter.
2. If swimming, immediately get out of and away from the water.
3. Stay away from metal objects and avoid using the telephone.
4. Unplug electrical appliances during a severe thunderstorm and stay away from the fireplace.

HURRICANE SAFETY

Hurricanes are tropical storms with heavy rains and winds in excess of 74 miles per hour. The southern Atlantic states are at risk for hurricanes. Most hurricanes occur during August, September, and October. Some hurricane safety precautions are:

1. Follow and heed the warnings issued by the National Hurricane Service, which are issued over television and radio stations.
2. In the event of a serious hurricane, evacuate the area if possible.

Injury Prevention and Safety

TORNADO SAFETY

Tornados are violent, rapidly spinning windstorms that have funnel-shaped clouds. Tornados are more common in Midwestern and Southern states, and most occur in the spring and early summer months. A **tornado watch** is a caution issued by the National Weather Service that the weather conditions are such that a tornado is possible. People in the area should be alert and prepared for possible danger. A **tornado warning** is a caution that a tornado has been sighted. It will be announced and broadcast over radio and television stations. Some tornado safety precautions are:

1. Seek shelter in a basement or underground cellar whenever possible. If no basement is available, move to the center of the ground floor, into a room with no windows such as a closet.
2. If possible, crawl under something solid such as a heavy piece of furniture.
3. If outside, seek shelter in a depression such as a ravine, gully, or ditch.

EARTHQUAKES

Earthquakes are violent shakings of the earth's surface caused by the shifting of the plates that make up the earth's crust. The greatest number of injuries occur from falling debris. Most areas of the United States are at risk for earthquakes. Some earthquake safety precautions are:

1. Stay calm and do not panic.
2. Stay clear of any objects that can fall.
3. Stay away from broken power lines.
4. If inside a building, get under a table or desk.
5. Stay away from windows which may shatter.
6. If riding in a car, stop and get out as soon as possible.
7. If riding or walking on a bridge, get off as soon as possible.

FLOODS

A **flood** is a rising and overflowing of a body of water onto normally dry land. Areas that receive heavy rainfall and are near a body of water are at risk for flooding. Some flood safety precautions are:

1. Leave your home and community if warned to do so by officials.
2. Keep a supply of batteries, flashlights, and a radio nearby.
3. Learn the safest and quickest route to take from your home to shelter.
4. Keep supplies of fresh water and food that do not need refrigeration or heat.
5. Turn off all electrical circuits in the home if a flood occurs.
6. Close all gas lines that lead into the home.
7. Move all valuables to the top floors in a home to help prevent them from being destroyed.
8. Maintain the family car in good working order and keep the gas tank filled so that you can leave the area quickly.
9. Have a first aid kit available.
10. Do not drive where water is over the road.

You Can Count On Me

Health Education Standards:

- Students will demonstrate the ability to advocate for personal, family, and community health.
- Students will demonstrate the ability to access valid health information and health promoting products and services.

Performance Indicators:

- Students will demonstrate the ability to influence and support others in making positive health choices.
- Students will analyze the validity of health information, products, and services.
- Students will analyze the influence of technology on personal and family health.

Life Skills:

- I will volunteer in school clubs and community organizations and agencies that promote health.
- I will spend time wisely.

Materials:

Family Master, "Being A Volunteer"; Student Master, "Health Behavior Contract"; computer with online service (optional); recording of "You Can Count On Me," an oldie by the Jefferson Starship (optional); compact disc or cassette player; chalk and chalkboard.

Motivation:

1 Before teaching this strategy, refer to your school district's policy on outside assignments such as volunteering.

You may need to obtain school board clearance to use the Health Behavior Contract.

2 On the chalkboard, write the following: physical health; mental-emotional health; family-social health; no benefit. Be certain to write these high enough on the chalkboard so that you will be able to make a list under each. Introduce the topic of time management. Ask students to brainstorm ways that they spend their time. As a student identifies a way that (s)he spends time, ask the student if there is a benefit to physical health, mental-emotional health, family-social health, or no benefit to health. Write the activity under the appropriate heading on the chalkboard.

3 Have students analyze the activities that are listed on the chalkboard. Students may learn that they have a balance of activities that promote health. They may learn that they neglect an area of their health. Introduce the idea that they are consumers when they make decisions about how to spend time. This is an important responsibility in the area of consumer health. To be a responsible consumer, they may want to have a time management plan. A time management plan is a plan that indicates how time will be spent on daily activities and leisure. An effective time management plan includes blocks of time set aside to promote physical, mental-emotional, and family-social health. To make a time management plan, a person identifies all daily activities on a calendar showing the hours of the day. Then a person might examine the activities and assess whether or not attention has been given to all areas of well-being.

4 Have the students review the lists on the chalkboard again. Explain that much of the emphasis in health education today is placed on personal responsibility for health. However, there are many health problems that can be solved only by individuals working together and serving the needs of others. A volunteer is a person who undertakes or expresses a willingness to provide a service.

5 Divide the class into equal groups of students. Have each group brainstorm a list of ways that young people might volunteer to serve the health needs of others and/or the community. Give examples such as volunteering in school clubs, community organizations, and health agencies. Have students ways they might volunteer to help individuals such as a person who is shut-in or disabled. If your school has computers with online service available, have students locate volunteer opportunities. For example, many services provide a special area for young people that contains online information they might use to locate volunteer opportunities. After an appropriate amount of time, have each group share its list with the class.

5 Give each student a copy of the Student Master "Health Behavior Contract" and the Family Master "Being A Volunteer." Explain to students that they are going to make a health behavior contract to volunteer in a school club, community organization, or agency to promote health or to help a specific individual or family. They are to give their parent/guardian the Family Master "Being A Volunteer" and obtain permission to perform the volunteer service identified in the "Health Behavior Contract." Set a date for completion of the Health Behavior Contract.

6 (Optional) If you are able to obtain the recording, "You Can Count On Me," by the Jefferson Starship, play it for the class. Discuss the words...."You can count on me, count on my love." Emphasize that we show love for others by providing those in need with service. Extending our love to others in this way helps us to feel more loving. It promotes self-esteem. It also helps others to feel more loved.

Evaluation:

For the evaluation, students will submit the two-page summary reports described on the "Health Behavior Contract." Check to see that students identified specific tasks they performed while volunteering. Check to see that students have identified ways that volunteering benefits them and why volunteering is a wise use of a consumer's time.

Multicultural Infusion:

An appropriate volunteer activity might be for a student to help a younger child who is not proficient in English with homework and with reading. This volunteer activity promotes Mental and Emotional Health. It promotes positive self-esteem. It also benefits the child by helping the child with mental alertness. The student can be a positive role model. In addition, it helps students to be more aware of the challenges that people who are not proficient in English face.

Inclusion:

Students with special needs, such as those who have a physical disability or a learning disability, might volunteer to work with younger children who also have special needs. They can be role models of ways to promote physical, mental-emotional, and family-social health. For example, a student who uses a wheelchair might exercise with a child who uses a wheelchair. Explain that this relationship can be special for both the student and the child.

Family Master

Being A Volunteer

Dear Parent/Guardian:

In our health class, I have emphasized the importance of taking personal responsibility for health. However, there are many health problems that can be solved only by individuals working together and serving the needs of others. We have been focusing on the importance of having volunteers in the community. I have explained to your child that a volunteer is a person who undertakes or expresses a willingness to provide a service. A young person might volunteer to visit elderly residents in a nursing home, read to someone who is visually impaired, or carry groceries for someone with a disability. A young person might also volunteer in a school club, community organization or agency. Our class discussed a number of ways that young people might volunteer. Ask your child to share some of these ways with you.

As a follow-up to our lesson, I have asked your child to commit himself/herself to several hours of volunteer service. Your child is designing a Health Behavior Contract. I have asked your child to go over the Health Behavior Contract with you and to get your permission to perform volunteer service.

Please return this letter to me so that I know that you are aware of the volunteer service and are in approval. If you have any questions or suggestions, please write them on the back of this letter and I will contact you.

I hope today finds you and your family in good health.

Sincerely,

My child has selected the following volunteer service:

_____

My signature indicates that I approve:

_____

Student Master

Health Behavior Contract

Name_____

Life Skill: I will volunteer my services to a school club, community organization or agency or to an individual or family to help promote health.

Effect On My Well-Being: There are many volunteer services that promote the health of individuals, families, and communities. When I participate in volunteer services, I promote the level of health for myself and others. I am a responsible, productive citizen. I feel good about myself. I help someone else by showing my care and concern. I learn about others.

My Plan: I will make a list of volunteer activities, such as visiting elderly residents of a nursing home, starting a recycling program, or teaching younger students about the dangers of drug use. I will speak with people in the community such as those at organizations and agencies to learn about volunteer possibilities. I will examine possible ways that I might help my neighbors. Then I will decide upon a service I want to perform, discuss it with my parent/guardian, and obtain approval. I will write the volunteer service I have selected in the space below.

_____

Evaluating Progress: I will commit to performing _____ hours of service.

I will write the dates and times I will perform service in the space below.

_____   _____
_____   _____
_____

Results: I will keep a diary to record what I did and any insights that I had. I will write a two-page summary report identifying the tasks that I performed and how I felt performing them. I will describe ways in which volunteering benefited my health and ways it promoted the health of another person(s) and/or my community.

Environment Calendar

Health Education Standards:

- Students will comprehend concepts related to health promotion and disease prevention.
- Students will demonstrate the ability to advocate for personal, family, and community health.

Performance Indicators:

- Students will analyze how environment and personal health are interrelated.
- Students will express information and opinions about health issues.
- Students will demonstrate the ability to influence and support others in making positive health choices.

Life Skills:

- I will be concerned about environmental issues.
- I will keep the air clean.
- I will keep the water clean.

Materials:

Construction paper; markers; paint; stapler; magazines that contain pictures of healthful environments; photos students have taken (optional); transparency of the Teaching Master, "Sources of Air Pollution"; transparency of the Teaching Master, "Sources of Water Pollution"; transparency projector; computer with online service (optional); literature from environmental groups (optional); calendar with photo of landscape or ocean

Motivation:

1 Introduce the strategy by showing students the photo in the calendar.

Ask students to imagine that they are in the surroundings depicted in the photo. Have them describe their feelings. Ask students how these surroundings might effect their health. Define environment. The **environment** is the multitude of dynamic conditions that are external to a person. A healthful environment enhances the quality of life and allows people to achieve the highest levels of physical, mental-emotional, and family-social health.

2 Explain that concerned citizens have formed organizations to increase public awareness of environmental issues. These citizens want to guarantee that the environment is as depicted in the photo in the calendar that you showed them. Identify some of the issues about which these citizens are concerned: ozone layer deterioration; global warming; hazardous waste; oil spills; air pollution; acid rain; solid waste disposal; nuclear waste; contaminated water; forest destruction; endangered species and threats to wildlife; pesticide use; world population; radon gas; natural disasters; indoor air pollution. If your school has computers with online services, mention that people interested in environmental issues have information networks. Have students link to these information networks.

3 Use the transparency of the Teaching Master, "Sources of Air Pollution" to discuss the life skill, "I will keep the air clean."

4 Use the transparency of the Teaching Master, "Sources of Water Pollution" to discuss the life skill, "I will keep the water clean."

5 Divide the class into groups. Give each group construction paper, magazines, and markers. Explain

606

that each group is going to make an Environmental Calendar. The calendar is to have twelve drawings, photos from magazines, and/or photos students have taken that depict a healthful environment. At least one of the photos or drawings should depict clean air while at least one other must depict clean water. Explain to students that a photo or drawing does not have to show a landscape, mountain, or ocean. A healthful environment might be depicted by a photo of plastic bag in which garbage has been collected. It might depict a clean bedroom or a clean school playground. Ask students to use their imaginations. Also,

direct students to have a caption for each of the twelve pages of the calendar. The caption should be a creative statement about health, such as "I get high on clean air."

Evaluation:

Explain that each group is going to give its calendar as a gift to a person or organization in the community. Each student in the group is to write a letter to accompany the calendar. In the letter, students are to explain their concern for environmental issues. They are to express ways to keep the air and water clean.

Teaching Master

Sources of Air Pollution

Life Skill: I will keep the air clean.

Air is needed to sustain life. Air pollution is one of the greatest
environmental risks to human health. It may cause chronic bronchitis, pulmonary emphysema, lung cancer, bronchial asthma, and
eye irritation. The major air pollutants are:

Carbon monoxide is an odorless, tasteless, colorless, poisonous gas.
Automobile exhaust is the main source. Carbon monoxide attaches to red
blood cells in the body. Then the red blood cells carry less oxygen to the
body's cells.

Sulfur oxides are pollutants that result from the combustion of fuels
containing sulfur and from sulfur from volcanos that combine with oxygen
to form sulfur oxides. This gas may cause lung diseases.

Nitrogen oxides are gases produced by the high-temperature combustion
of energy sources such as coal and oil. Automobile exhaust and cigarette
smoke are sources. This gas irritates the eyes and the respiratory tract
and causes lung diseases.

Hydrocarbons are chemical compounds that contain only carbon and
hydrogen. Motor vehicles account for most hydrocarbons. Hydrocarbons
are a major contributor to smog.

Ozone is a chemical variant of oxygen and is the most widespread air
pollutant. It causes irritation of the eyes, lungs, and throat. It produces
headaches, coughing, and shortness of breath. In healthy, nonsmoking
adults, two hours of exposure to ozone causes inflammation of the lungs
and bronchial tubes.

Particulates are particles in the air, such as soot, ashes, dirt, dust, asbestos, and pollen. They can harm the surfaces of the respiratory system and
increase the likelihood of persistent coughs, respiratory illness, and
asthma attacks.

Acid rain is precipitation (rain, snow, sleet, hail) that contains high levels
of acids formed from sulfur oxides, nitrogen oxides, and the moisture in
the air. The burning of coal is the major contributor to acid rain. When
acid rain falls in water, algae growth increases and oxygen in water blocks
sunlight. As a result, fish may die.

Teaching Master

Sources of Water Pollution

Life Skill: I will keep the water clean.

After air, water is the most essential requirement of the human body. Humans can live without water for only a few days. Water pollution is a health hazard. In many parts of the world, dysentery is a major problem. Dysentery is a severe infection of the intestines, causing diarrhea and abdominal pain. Polluted water is often high in sodium. Drinking polluted water poses a health risk for people with high blood pressure. Polluted water contains mercury which kills fish and shellfish. The major sources of water pollution are:

Water runoff from farming, landfill, areas, urban areas, mining, forestry, and construction contaminates water supplies, rivers, and lakes. It may contain oil, gasoline, pesticides, herbicides, fungicides, metals, bacteria, and viruses.

Sewage and animal waste increase the amount of nitrates in ground water. Infants who drink water contaminated with nitrates can suffer from blood diseases.

PCBs are a class of organic compounds that contain chlorine. PCBs have been used as insulating materials in high-voltage electrical transformers. Discarded electrical equipment at dump sites have broken open and released PCBs into surrounding groundwater and drinking water supplies. PCBs accumulate in the fatty tissues and liver. They cause birth defects, reproductive disorders, liver and kidney damage, and cancerous tumors.

Thermal pollution is pollution of water with heat resulting in a decrease in the oxygen in the water. It is caused by dumping heater water from power plants into the environment. Fish and aquatic plants die.

Trihalomethanes are chemical byproducts formed when chlorine attacks biological contaminants in the water. Any drinking water supply that has chlorine added contains these chemical byproducts. These byproducts slightly increase the risk of bladder and rectal cancer, birth defects, and central nervous system disorders.

Mercury is an element found in industrial waste. When people consume too much mercury through the food chain, they may suffer from mental retardation, numbness of body parts, loss of vision and hearing, and emotional disturbances.

Pesticides are substances used to kill or control the growth of unwanted organisms. **DDT** is a pesticide that was banned because it was found in food products after harvest. DDT accumulates in fat tissues and increases cancer risk.

Dioxins are a group of chemicals that were once used as insecticides. They are no longer produced for commercial use. However, they still occur because of incineration. **Agent Orange** is a substance containing dioxin that was sprayed on vegetation to kill it. It is believed to cause cancer, depression, liver damage, and miscarriages.

Lead is an element that may get into the water supply from lead pipes and water lines. Lead is also believed to cause mental retardation.

Bean Self-Disciplined

Health Education Standards:

- Students will comprehend concepts related to health promotion and disease prevention.
- Demonstrate the ability to use goal-setting and decision-making skills that enhance health.

Performance Indicators:

- Students will explain the relationship between positive health behaviors and the prevention of injury, illness, disease, and premature death.
- Students will develop a plan that addresses personal strengths, needs, and health risks.
- Students will apply strategies and skills needed to attain personal health goals.
- Students will describe how personal health goals are influenced by changing information, abilities, priorities, and responsibilities.

Life Skills:

- I will strive to have optimal health.
- I will gain health knowledge.
- I will practice life skills for health.

Materials:

Teaching Master, "The Wellness Scale" (transparency); Student Master, "Health Behavior Contract"; three bean bags; chalk; transparency projector

Motivation:

1 Define health. **Health** is the quality of life that includes physical, mental-emotional, and family-social health.

Another term that describes health is wellness. **Physical health** is the condition of a person's body. **Mental-emotional health** is the condition of a person's mind and the ways that a person expresses feelings. **Family-social health** is the condition of a person's relationships with others. Ask students to give examples of physical, mental-emotional, and family-social health.

2 Make a transparency of the Teaching Master "The Wellness Scale." Review the information on this master. **The Wellness Scale** depicts the ranges in the quality of life from optimal well-being to high level wellness, average wellness, minor illness or injury, major illness or injury, and premature death. Explain that there are at least nine factors that influence health and wellness over which a person has some degree of control. These factors are listed on The Wellness Scale. **Health status** is the sum total of the positive and negative influence of: 1) the level of health knowledge a person has; 2) the behaviors a person chooses; 3) the situations in which a person participates; 4) the relationships in which a person engages; 5) the decisions a person makes; 6) the resistance skills a person has; 7) the protective factors a person possesses; 8) the degree to which a person is resilient; and 9) the degree of health literacy a person has achieved.

3 Review the following definitions. **Health knowledge** consists of information that is needed to become health literate, maintain and improve health, prevent disease, and reduce health-related risk behaviors. **Healthful behaviors** are actions that promote health; prevent illness, injury, and premature death; and improve the quality of the environment. **Risk**

behaviors are voluntary actions that threaten health, increase the likelihood of illness and premature death, and destroy the quality of the environment. **Healthful situations** are circumstances that promote health; prevent illness, injury, and premature death; and improve the quality of the environment. **Risk situations** are involuntary circumstances that threaten health; increase the likelihood of illness, injury, and premature death; and destroy the quality of the environment. **Healthful relationships** are relationships that promote self-esteem and productivity, encourage health-enhancing behavior, and are free of violence and drug misuse and abuse. **Destructive relationships** are relationships that destroy self-esteem, interfere with productivity

and health, and may include violence and drug misuse and abuse. A **responsible decision** is a decision that is healthful, safe, legal, respectful of self and others, follows guidelines of responsible adults, and demonstrates character. **Resistance skills** are skills that are used when a person wants to say NO to an action and/or leave a situation. **Protective factors** are ways that a person might behave and characteristics of the environment in which a person lives that promote health, safety, and/or well-being. **Risk factors** are ways that a person might behave and characteristics of the environment in which a person lives that threaten health, safety, and/or well-being. **Resiliency** is the ability to prevent or to recover, bounce back, and learn from misfortune, change, or pressure. **Health literacy** is competence in critical thinking and problem solving, responsible and productive citizenship, self-directed learning, and effective communication.

4 Explain that people achieve a higher level of wellness on The Wellness Scale when they practice life skills for health. **Life skills** are actions that promote health literacy, maintain and improve health, prevent disease, and reduce health-related risk behaviors. Give examples of life skills: wearing a safety belt, maintaining desirable weight, being drug-free, using conflict resolution skills, having an escape plan for fire. Ask students to give examples of life skills they practice or want to practice.

5 Discuss the importance of being self-disciplined ("Bean Self-Disciplined"). **Self-discipline** is the effort or energy with which a person follows through on what (s)he intends or promises to do. It takes self-discipline to maintain desirable weight, wear a safety belt, maintain physical fitness, etc. A person who is "bean self-disciplined" recognizes that goals are achieved with effort. A **goal** is something desirable toward which a person works.

6 Have students identify a goal or life skill that want to achieve or practice. Now use chalk and draw the following on the floor of your classroom. Draw a starting line. Two feet from the starting line, draw a circle with a circumference of two feet. Then, draw another circle four feet from the starting line, another six feet from the starting line, and finally one eight feet from the starting line. Ask for three student volunteers. Give each a bean bag. Have each student take a turn. Each student is to stand at the starting line and throw the bean bag into the farthest circle (the one eight feet from the starting line). Most likely, one or more of the three students will miss.

7 Repeat, but this time give different directions. Each student is to throw

the bean bag into the first circle (two feet from the starting line). Then the student proceeds to the first circle, stands there, and throws the bean bag into the next circle which is two feet away. The student continues until (s)he successfully throws the bean bag into the farthest circle.

8 Explain that "Bean Self-Disciplined" often requires taking small steps toward a goal. For example, a person cannot lose ten pounds or become physically fit overnight. A person must identify a life skill (set a goal) and then make a plan that involves setting small steps toward the mastery of the life skill.

Evaluation:

Give each student a copy of the Student Master, "Health Behavior Contract." Students are to identify a life skill they want to master. They are to make a plan that involves setting small steps toward the mastery of the life skill. They are to write a two-page summary following the directions on the Health Behavior Contract.

Teaching Master

The Wellness Scale

Factors that Influence Health and Well-Being

Lack of health knowledge	Possession of health knowledge
Risk behaviors	Wellness behaviors
Risk situations	Healthful situations
Destructive relationships	Healthful relationships
Irresponsible decision-making	Responsible decision-making
Lack of resistance skills	Use of resistance skills
Lack of protective factors	Possession of protective factors
Lack of resiliency	Having resiliency
Lack of health literacy	Having health literacy

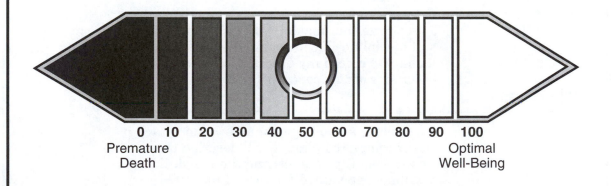

0 10 20 30 40 50 60 70 80 90 100

Premature
Death

Optimal
Well-Being

Health status is the sum total of the positive and negative influence of these factors.

Student Master

Health Behavior Contract

Life Skill:

I will practice life skills for health.

Effect On My Well-Being:

Life skills are actions that promote health literacy, maintain and improve health, prevent disease, and reduce health-related risk behaviors. Practicing life skills shows that I have assumed responsibility for my health. I use self-discipline and attain a higher level of well-being on The Wellness Scale. I function better and enjoy life more fully.

My Plan:

I will identify a life skill for health that I want to practice regularly. I will write this life skill in the space below.

_____

Evaluating My Progress:

I recognize that mastery of this life skill requires self-discipline. I will set smaller goals and design a chart to record my progress. *(You may use the other side of this contract.)*

Results:

I will write a two-page summary and attach it to my completed plan. I will describe the health benefits of practicing the life skill. I will describe any difficulties I had following my plan. I will describe my plan for continuing to follow my life skill.

My Signature:

_____

Rainbow of Diversity

Health Education Standards:

- Students will demonstrate the ability to use interpersonal communication skills to enhance health.
- Students will demonstrate the ability to practice health-enhancing behaviors and reduce health risks.

Performance Indicators:

- Students will demonstrate ways to avoid and reduce threatening situations.
- Students will analyze the possible causes of conflict among youth in schools and communities.
- Students will demonstrate strategies to manage conflict in healthy ways.

Life Skills:

- I will avoid discrimination.
- I will choose behaviors to reduce my risk of violence.

Materials:

Ten-foot roll of white paper; tape; red marker; green marker; blue marker; purple marker; yellow marker; orange marker; black marker

Motivation:

1 Tape a five foot roll of white paper across the chalkboard in the front of your classroom. Tape another five foot roll of white paper across the chalkboard directly beneath the first. Explain to students that they are going to create a rainbow with six hues. They will use a marker to create a rainbow on the top roll of white paper that is taped to the chalkboard. Give the red marker to a student. Ask this student to draw one of the lines for the rainbow. Then give the red marker to another student ask this student to draw another line for the rainbow. Repeat the previous directions asking four more students to draw lines for the rainbow. When the rainbow is completed, there will be five red lines to show the hues of the rainbow.

2 Now explain to students that they are going to create another rainbow. They will create this rainbow on the roll of paper that is directly beneath the first rainbow they created. Give the six markers (red, green, blue, purple, yellow, and orange) to six different students. Each is to take a turn drawing one of the lines on the rainbow. When the rainbow is completed, there will be six lines of color (red, green, blue, purple, yellow, and orange) to show the hues of the rainbow.

3 Ask students which rainbow they prefer and which one is most realistic. Although answers may vary, students will recognize that the rainbow with the six colors is more radiant and pleasing than the rainbow that is all red. In addition, they should recognize that the second rainbow is more realistic. Rainbows are multicolored, not just one color.

4 Explain that you have named the two rainbows. The first is called the "Rainbow of Duplication" while the second is called "The Rainbow of Diversity." Further explain that you created these rainbows to begin a discussion about the people with whom they interact. To duplicate means to copy. When students created the first rainbow, they duplicated the lines using the same color.

The lines turned out exactly alike. To be diverse means to be different. When students created the second rainbow, they used different colors to create the lines.

5 Explain that society is like the second rainbow–it is created with diverse or different people. People not only differ in color, they differ in age, gender, racial and ethnic heritage. (Depending on school district guidelines, you may want to mention that people differ in sexual orientation). However, all people are alike in that they want the respect of others. Everyone wants to be treated fairly. When people enjoy, appreciate, and respect everyone else in their environment, the result is synergy. **Synergy** is a positive outcome that occurs when different people cooperate and respect one another and, as a result, more energy is created for all. When there is synergy, people with different backgrounds, talents, and skills work together to produce better solutions than would be possible if everyone were exactly alike.

6 Explain that some people practice discriminatory behavior. They see themselves as belonging to the first rainbow. They accept others who belong to the first rainbow and who are just like them. When there are differences, they practice discriminatory behavior. **Discriminatory behavior** is behavior that makes a distinction in treatment or shows favor or prejudice against and individual or group of people. **Prejudice** is suspicion, intolerance, or irrational dislike directed at an individual or group of people. Both discriminatory behavior and prejudice divide people. These kinds of behavior are learned. Training in how to treat and respect people begins early in life.

7 Write "isms" on the red rainbow using the black marker. Explain that **isms** are beliefs, attitudes, assumptions, and actions that subject individuals or people in a particular group to discriminatory behavior. Common isms include ageism, sexism, and racism. As you define each of the following, use the black marker to write the term on the red rainbow. **Ageism** is behavior that discriminates against people in a specific age group. **Sexism** is behavior that discriminates against people of the opposite sex. **Racism** is behavior that discriminates against people of the opposite sex.

8 Explain that discriminatory behavior and prejudice often result in violence. People who practice such behavior might become perpetrators or victims. A **perpetrator** is a person who commits a violent act. A **victim** is a person who is harmed by violence. **Hate crimes** are crimes motivated by age, racial, ethnic sexual orientation, or other biases. Hate crimes are sometimes called bias crimes and include violent attacks, intimidation, arson, and other kinds of property damage. People who experience discrimination and prejudice may become angry. They may confront or fight back. This can result in serious injury.

9 Ask students to brainstorm ways to show respect for people who are different. Ask them how they might practice the life skill, "I will avoid discrimination." Suggest the following: 1) Challenge stereotypes. A **stereotype** is a prejudiced attitude that assigns a specific quality or characteristic to all people who belong to a particular group. 2) Create synergy through diversity. Having friends who are different can enrich one's life.

3) Show empathy for all people. **Empathy** is the ability to share in another's emotions or feelings. 4) Avoid discriminatory comments. Words often cause emotional wounds that are more difficult to health than physical wounds. 5) Ask others to stop discriminatory behavior. When people allow others to behave in a discriminatory way, they have their passive approval. 6) Learn about people who are different. As people learn about others, they gain appreciation.

Multicultural Infusion:

As an additional learning experience, have students discuss the diverse backgrounds of people in your community. Ask students if they have met someone who belongs to each culture, race, or age group mentioned. If not, ask students how they might have contact with people of diverse backgrounds in order to know and appreciate them.

Evaluation:

Ask students to write a "Personal Pledge to Avoid Prejudice." The students' pledges should contain types of prejudice (isms) they will avoid and at least five actions they can take. Encourage students to be creative in their writing style. Their pledges might be written as poems. They might be designed as a cheer or a rap. Have selected students present their Personal Pledges to their classmates. Select some students to present their Personal Pledges to other classes or to community groups.

Inclusion:

Discuss discriminatory behavior and prejudice that is directed at people who have special needs, such as people who are physically or mentally disabled. Have students include this type of prejudice on the first rainbow.

My Hero

Health Education Standards:

- Students will demonstrate the ability to use interpersonal communication skills to enhance health.
- Students will comprehend concepts related to health promotion and disease prevention.

Performance Indicators:

- Students will demonstrate healthy ways to express needs, wants, and feelings.
- Students will demonstrate ways to communicate care, consideration, and respect of self and others.
- Students will describe how personal health goals are influenced by changing information, abilities, priorities, and responsibilities.

Life Skills:

- I will share my feelings about death and dying.
- I will recognize the needs of people of different ages.

Materials:

Student Master, "My Hero"; transparency projector; five flashcards with one of the following words written on each: denial, anger, bargaining, depression, and acceptance; CD or cassette of the sound recording *The Wind Beneath My Wings* by Bette Midler (optional); compact disc or cassette player; paper; markers

Motivation:

1 Before beginning this strategy, prepare five large flashcards. On one side of each of the flashcards, print one of the following stages that appears in italics. On the other side, print the corresponding description for each stage.

Stage 1: *Denial*--People do not want to accept what is happening.

Stage 2: *Anger*--People are angry about what is happening.

Stage 3: *Bargaining*--People try to make deals thinking this will change the outcome.

Stage 4: *Depression*--People recognize that bargaining has not worked and begin to feel the loss and grieve.

Stage 5: *Acceptance*--People acknowledge the situation, talk about it, and feel a sense of peace.

2 Ask for a student volunteer. Explain that this student is moving and will no longer attend the same school. In fact, the student is moving such a distance that classmates will most likely never see him/her again.

3 Divide the class into pairs or triads of students. Each pair or triad is to brainstorm ways to say goodbye to the student volunteer. Each is to select one of the students in the pair or triad who will come in front of the class and speak directly to the student volunteer expressing feelings and saying goodbye. After an appropriate amount of time, have the sharing session. Follow up by asking the students who played the role of saying goodbye to share how they felt. Then ask students if they have ever had this experience. How did they feel when they said goodbye to someone close?

4 Show students the transparency "My Hero." Ask students to explain the meaning of the poem. The poem is about a person who knows that "my hero" is dying. Explain that when a person is dying, those around him/her begin to say goodbye. Saying goodbye and being "with you in your fight" involve sharing different feelings.

5 Explain that people who are dying and those who love them often experience psychological stages that describe emotional feelings. Elisabeth Kübler-Ross identified these five stages as denial, anger, bargaining, depression, and acceptance. Use the flashcards to review these five stages. Show the students the side of each flashcard which identifies the stage and the emotional feelings most people experience. Then refer to what is written on the back of each flashcard as you describe each stage. You may want students to take notes on the five stages.

6 Discuss the importance of saying goodbye to someone who is dying. Explain that in some cases a person cannot say goodbye directly to the person who is dying. The person may be in a coma or may have died unexpectedly. It is still important to say goodbye. A funeral or memorial service is often performed so that people can gather together to say goodbye and to share feelings with others who were close to the person who has died.

7 Explain that after a death, people may experience grief. **Grief** is the distress caused by the death of another person. Grief is a normal reaction to a death. People grieve in different ways. They may experience shock, numbness, disbelief, depression, and/or loneliness. These feelings are part of the recovery process. Ask students how they might show support for someone who is grieving. Give the following suggestions:
- Do something thoughtful for the person. Make a phone call, send a

card, attend the funeral or memorial service, run errands, help with chores, offer meals.
- Be a good listener. Make yourself available to talk. Simply being a good friend is important.
- Allow the person the opportunity to grieve and express emotions.
- Accept your own limitations. Many situations can be difficult to handle. Seek advice from professionals and/or support groups if necessary.

8 Discuss the importance of memories. Explain that although people die, memories of them continue. After a period of grieving, these memories become the focus. If you have a CD or cassette of *The Wind Beneath My Wings* by Bette Midler, play it for the class. Ask students why the person about whom Bette Midler sang was a hero. Ask students to describe the positive memories someone might have of such a hero.

9 Begin a discussion of people who are elderly. Explain the importance of sharing feelings with people of all ages, but especially of those who are elderly. It is important to share the positive memories experienced with these people.

Evaluation:

Have students design greeting cards to express their feelings to an elderly person about whom they care. Their message can be "I am glad you are here to share life's precious moments with me." They can write similar messages and then write personal notes. Show students the flashcards of the psychological stages that describe emotional feelings people experience when they are someone close to them are dying. On a sheet of paper, have students explain each of the five stages.

Student Master

My Hero

I've watched you all my life,
coming here and going there,
being everything to everyone,
a life the world could share.

I've seen you in my heart,
where you've found a place to live,
taking time to be my hero,
and there's nothing I can give.

Now I see you fading softly,
as you wander into the night.
It's my turn to be your hero—
I'll be with you in your fight.

Shake The Salt Habit

Health Education Standards:

- Students will comprehend the concepts related to health promotion and disease prevention.
- Students will demonstrate the ability to advocate for personal, family, and community health.

Performance Indicators:

- Students will explain the relationship between positive health behaviors and the prevention of injury, illness, disease, and premature death.
- Students will analyze various communication methods to accurately express health information and ideas.

Life Skills:

- I will follow dietary guidelines.
- I will read food labels.
- *I will recognize ways to manage chronic diseases. (Communicable and Chronic Diseases)*

Materials:

Teaching Master, "The Dietary Guidelines" (transparency); Teaching Master, "The Food Label" (transparency); transparency projector; one empty salt shaker (unbreakable is preferable); coin; paper; pens and markers; computers and computer paper (optional)

Motivation:

1 Review the dietary guidelines using a transparency of the Teaching Master "The Dietary Guidelines." The **Dietary Guidelines for Americans** are recommendations for diet choices for healthy Americans two years of age or more. The guidelines are a result of the research by the United States Department of Agriculture and the Department of Health and Human Services. Following the Dietary Guidelines, a person can improve the chance of having better health and reduce the chance of getting certain diseases.

2 Use the transparency of the Teaching Master "The Food Label" to explain ways that information on food labels can help people follow the dietary guidelines. Explain to students that the information on the food label for sodium tells how much salt is in the food. This food label is for a food that contains 20 percent of the Percent Daily Value for sodium in one serving size. The **Percent Daily Value** tells how much of a day's worth of the nutrient is provided in the food product for a 2,000 Calorie diet.

3 Remind students that it is important to use salt and sodium only in moderation. This helps reduce the risk of high blood pressure. High blood pressure is a chronic disease for many people. Have students brainstorm ways that they might reduce the amount of salt and sodium in their diets. Here are some suggested ways:

- Do not eat foods on which you can see the salt on them. (pretzels)
- Do not place a salt shaker on the table.
- Use spices such as garlic, herbs, lemon juice, and flavored vinegars, rather than salt to flavor food.
- Eat fresh foods rather than canned foods.
- If you eat canned foods, drain them, then rinse them for at least a minute. This removes almost 50 percent of the salt.

- Avoid eating cured, smoked, or highly processed foods.
- When dining in restaurants, ask that your food be prepared without salt.
- Taste your food before adding salt.
- Read food labels to determine the amount of sodium before purchasing foods.
- Purchase foods that are labeled "low sodium," "very low sodium," and "sodium free."
- Be aware that foods that are labeled "lite" or "reduced sodium" may still contain too much sodium; read the label for the actual Percent Daily Value.
- Identify foods that you eat that contain sodium and salt and eat these foods less often.

4 Divide the class into two teams. Ask the students on each team to select a team captain and to stand in line behind this captain. Toss a coin to see which team goes first. Give the team captain the salt shaker. Explain that the team will have a two minute time limit (you can vary this time limit depending on the number of students that are in your class). The team captain is to tell one way (s)he might "shake the salt habit" (I will not salt my popcorn), shake the empty salt shaker, and then hand the salt shaker to the next student in line on the team. The second student on the team is to name another way to "shake the salt habit" (I will choose foods labeled "low sodium"), shake the empty salt shaker, and pass the

salt shaker to the third student on the team. As the salt shaker is passed from student to student in the team line, each is to name a way to "shake the salt habit," however, no student can repeat what another team member has said. At the end of the two minute time limit, count the number of students who have responded. This is team 1's score. Now students on the other team have a turn. They follow the same directions. They can repeat some of the ways to "shake the salt habit" that team 1 named, however, they cannot repeat what one of their team members has said. At the end of the two minute time limit, count the number of students who have responded. This is team 2's score. Then have a second round. In the second round, team 2 goes first and then team 1. After the second round, compare the two team's scores.

Evaluation:

Have students create their own Family Health Newsletters to bring home to share with their families. They can use paper, pens, and markers. If your school has computers and computer paper available, this is an option. Their individual Family Health Newsletters should include a list and discussion of each of the Dietary Guidelines for Americans. They should include a personal plan for limiting the amount of sodium

and salt consumed by their family. Assess the individual Family Health Newsletters and allow students to make changes prior to taking them home to share with their families.

Multicultural Infusion:

Have students identify ethnic foods they enjoy. Refer to the dietary guidelines for Americans. Are these foods healthful? Which of these foods should be consumed in moderation? When students are writing their individual Family Health Newsletters, they can include a discussion of the ethnic foods their family enjoys. They can suggest limiting those which should be consumed in moderation.

Inclusion:

Mention that some students have difficulty with certain foods. For example, students with asthma may need to avoid specific foods that may increase respiratory problems. Students with geographic tongue may need to avoid very spicy foods to prevent the tongue from swelling. Students may volunteer to share foods they must eat in moderation to maintain optimal health. Although these dietary suggestions are not part of the Dietary Guidelines for Americans, they are important for the individual.

Teaching Master
The Dietary Guidelines

Eat A Variety of Foods

- No single food can supply all the nutrients you need.
- Select the appropriate number of foods from the Food Guide Pyramid each day.

Maintain a Healthful Weight

- Desirable weight is the weight and body composition that is recommended for a person's age, height, sex, and body build.
- Being overweight is linked to high blood pressure, heart disease, and diabetes.
- Being underweight is linked to nutrient deficiencies.

Choose a Diet Low in Fat, Saturated Fat, and Cholesterol

- Fat in foods contains over twice the Calories of equal amounts of carbohydrates or proteins.
- The amount of fat in your diet should be limited to 30 percent or less of total Calories.

Choose a Diet With Plenty of Vegetables, Fruits, and Grain Products

- Vegetables, fruits, and grains are good sources of vitamins and minerals.
- These foods are low in fat content.

Use Salt and Sodium Only in Moderation

- You need about 1/4 teaspoon of salt daily.
- Most people eat 10 times this much salt.
- Using salt and sodium in moderation helps reduce the risk of high blood pressure.

Do Not Drink Alcoholic Beverages (Children and Adolescents)

- Alcoholic beverages contain Calories, but few or no nutrients.
- Alcoholic beverages can alter the way you think, feel, and behave.
- Adults who drink alcohol should limit their consumption to one ounce of pure alcohol or less per day.

Teaching Master

The Food Label

Nutrition Facts

Serving Size 1 cup (228g)
Servings Per Container 2

Amount Per Serving

Calories 250   Calories from Fat 110

	% Daily Value*
Total Fat 12g	**18%**
Saturated Fat 3g	**15%**
Cholesterol 30mg	**10%**
Sodium 470mg	**20%**
Total Carbohydrate 31g	**10%**
Dietary Fiber 0g	**0%**
Sugars 5g	
Protein 5g	

Vitamin A 4%	•	Vitamin C 2%
Calcium 20%	•	Iron 4%

* Percent Daily Values are based on a 2,000 calorie diet.

I Can't See What You Say

Health Education Standards:

- Students will comprehend concepts related to health promotion and disease prevention.
- Students will demonstrate the ability to practice health-enhancing behaviors and reduce health risks.

Performance Indicators:

- Students will explain the relationship between positive health behaviors and the prevention of injury, illness, disease, and premature death.
- Students will explain how appropriate health care can prevent premature death and disability.
- Students will develop injury prevention and management strategies for personal and family health.

Life Skills:

- I will care for my ears and eyes.
- I will have regular checkups.
- *I will stay safe while exercising. (Injury Prevention and Safety)*

Materials:

Transparency of Teaching Master, "Knowing About Your Vision"; transparency projector; paper; pencils; chalk; chalkboard

Motivation:

1 To prepare for this strategy, draw a design on a sheet of paper. The design should consist of line drawings of several different geometric shapes placed randomly on the sheet of paper.

2 To begin the strategy, ask students to have a sheet of paper and a pencil to participate in the following task. Then ask for a student volunteer. Show the student volunteer the design you have drawn. Do not show the other students the design. Explain that the student volunteer will describe the design. As (s)he describes the design, the students are to draw what (s)he describes on their sheets of paper. They are to keep their eyes on their own papers and not ask fellow classmates for any help.

3 After this task is completed, share your design with the students. Then have students share the designs they have drawn. Are the designs exact duplications of your design? Whose design was most similar to yours? Why was it unlikely that one of the students would be able to duplicate your design with precision?

4 Explain that the students received information via the sense of hearing. The sense of hearing provided them with some information. Now have the students use the unused side of their sheets of paper. They can look at the design you have drawn as they draw the design again. Are there designs more similar to yours? Explain that the students received additional information via the sense of vision. Further explain the importance of caring for vision by protecting the eyes and having regular eye examinations. Define visually impaired. To be **visually impaired** is to have difficulty seeing or to be blind.

5 Use a transparency of the Teaching Master "Knowing About Your Vision" to review information about kinds of eye doctors, kinds of visual problems, kinds of eye conditions, and ways to care for the eyes.

Evaluation:

The following quiz can be used to assess student knowledge needed to perform the life skills. Answers are provided on the Teaching Master "Knowing About Your Vision."

1. Name two kinds of eye doctors and tell what they do.
2. What condition exists when a person cannot tell the difference between red and green?
3. What condition exists when a person cannot see clearly at night?
4. What visual problem does a person have if (s)he can see distant objects clearly, but objects close by are fuzzy?
5. What visual problem does a person have if (s)he can see close objects clearly, but distant objects are fuzzy?
6. What is astigmatism?
7. What would you do if you had a sty?
8. How might conjunctivitis or pinkeye be spread to others?
9. What would you do if you got hit in the eye with a baseball?
10. What would you do if you got a small piece of dirt in your eye?

Have students write a paragraph on ways to care for the eyes.

Inclusion:

Invite someone from a community agency to your class to discuss volunteer opportunities to help people who are visually impaired. You also may want to invite a person who is visually impaired to class to describe ways that young people might assist people who are visually impaired. For example, students might read to people who are visually impaired.

Teaching Master

Knowing About Your Vision

Kinds of Eye Doctors

- An **ophthalmologist** is a medical doctor who specializes in the medical and surgical care and treatment of the eye. This doctor can diagnose and treat all types of eye disorders, test vision, and prescribe corrective lenses.

- An **optometrist** is a doctor who can test vision and prescribe corrective lenses.

Kinds of Visual Problems

- **Nearsightedness** is a defect in the shape of the eye that causes distant objects to be fuzzy.

- **Farsightedness** is a defect in the shape of the eye that causes objects that are close to be fuzzy.

- **Astigmatism** is the irregular curvature of the cornea that causes blurred vision.

- **Night blindness** is a condition in which a person cannot see clearly at night.

- **Color blindness** is a condition in which a person cannot tell the difference between red and green.

628

Teaching Master (continued)

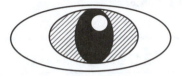 

Kinds of Eye Conditions

- A **sty** is an infection around the eyelash marked by swelling and pain; stys are treated by applying warm compresses to the eye. They usually heal in a week.

- **Conjunctivitis**, or pinkeye, is an inflammation of the membrane lining the eyelids and covering the eyeball. Pinkeye can be spread to others by sharing towels or washcloths. It is treated with medicines from a medical doctor.

- A **blow to the eye** should be treated immediately by applying an ice cold compress. An ophthalmologist should be seen.

- When **dirt or a small object** is in the eye, the eye should not be rubbed as this may damage the eye. By lifting the upper lid over the lower lid, the lashes can brush the object off the inside of the upper eyelid. Blinking can also be helpful in removing small particles from the eye. If this does not work, the eye should be kept closed until medical help is received.

Ways to Care for The Eyes

- Have regular eye checkups every eighteen months to two years. Wear corrective lenses (eyeglasses or contact lenses) if they have been prescribed for you. Follow guidelines for caring for eyeglasses and/or contact lenses. Contact lens wearers who notice any unusual redness, blurring or sudden change in vision, or persistent pain in or around the eye, should remove the lenses and consult with their eye doctor.

- Wear safety glasses when using tools, chemicals, or when near flying debris.

- Wear safety glasses when playing sports such as racquetball or lacrosse.

- Wear sunglasses to protect the eyes from the sun's rays. Never look directly into the sun.

629

Garbled

Health Education Standards:

- Students will comprehend concepts related to health promotion and disease prevention.
- Students will demonstrate the ability to access valid health information and health promoting products and services.

Performance Indicators:

- Students will describe ways to reduce risks related to adolescent health problems.
- Students will demonstrate the ability to locate health products and services.
- Students will describe how lifestyle, pathogens, family history, and other risk factors are related to the cause or prevention of disease and other health problems.

Life Skills:

- I will not drink alcohol.
- I will seek help for personal or family drug misuse or abuse.
- I will become aware of school and community resources for intervention and treatment.
- *I will obtain information about my family's history of disease. (Communicable and Chronic Diseases)*

Materials:

Transparency of the Teaching Master, "Codependency and The Family"; transparency projector; marshmallow; interesting book; pamphlets describing community resources for intervention and treatment of drug dependency; Yellow Pages of a telephone directory; paper and pens; computers and computer paper (optional)

Motivation:

1 Ask for a student volunteer to come forward and read from the interesting book that you have brought to class. Allow the student to read several paragraphs. Then ask the student volunteer to place the marshmallow in his/her mouth. Tell the student volunteer that (s)he is not to bite down on the marshmallow. Explain to the class that the student volunteer has been drinking alcohol. Now ask the student volunteer to continue reading. Allow the student to read several paragraphs. Most likely, the other students will begin to laugh as the words will be "garbled." Explain to students that this teaching strategy is called "garbled." To **garble** is to alter or distort; to change the meaning of something; to transmit in an inaccurate way. Further explain that the student volunteer began to garble as (s)he read the second time. Drinking alcohol has this effect.

2 Explain that the "garbling effect" increases as blood-alcohol concentration (BAC) increases. **Blood-alcohol concentration (BAC)** is the ratio of alcohol in a person's blood to the person's total amount of blood and is expressed as a percent. As BAC increases, a person becomes increasingly effected. A person who is drinking is more likely to have accidents and more likely to be involved in violence (homicide, suicide, abuse, fighting). A person is more likely to make irresponsible decisions about his/her sexual behavior.

3 Show students the transparency of the Teaching Master "Codependency and The Family." Explain that a person(s) in this family has alcoholism. **Alcoholism** is a complex disease that is characterized by preoccupation with drinking alcohol that has progressed to serious physical, social, occupational, and/or family consequences for an individual. Alcoholism has consequences not only on the dependent person directly involved but also on the children of parents who are dependent on alcohol.

4 Explain that alcoholism also has a "garbling" effect on the family. It distorts, alters, and changes family relationships. Family members may have codependence. **Codependence** is a mental disorder in which a person loses personal identity, has frozen feelings, and copes ineffectively. People who have codependence are called **codependent**. Have students discuss signs of codependence in these family members.

5 Refer to the young family member who abuses alcohol. Explain that children reared in families in which adults are chemically dependent may copy this behavior. They may abuse alcohol or other drugs. There is also research that indicates that the tendency for chemical dependency and alcoholism may be inherited.

This means that children whose parent(s) have alcoholism are at increased risk for this disease. The only way they can be certain not to have alcoholism is to never drink.

6 Introduce the topic of treatment. Explain that there are many different school and community resources for intervention and treatment. If you have them available, share pamphlets describing community resources. Show students how to locate resources in the Yellow Pages of a telephone directory. Discuss support groups that are available to help families. **Alcoholics Anonymous** or AA is a support group in which people with alcoholism meet regularly to support one another to abstain from drinking alcohol. **Al-Anon** is a support group in which people who are friends and family members with a person with alcoholism meet regularly to support one another and to change behaviors which are codependent. **Alateen** is a support group for teenagers who are friends and family members of a person with alcoholism. Members of Alateen meet regularly to support one another, to change codependent behavior, and to be drug-free.

Evaluation:

Have students develop pamphlets on alcoholism. They can use the library to gain information in addition to what was covered in class. If available, they can use computers to design their pamphlets and to assess information about alcoholism. Their individual pamphlets should include the following:

• A definition of the disease.
• A list of signs.
• An explanation of codependence including a list of codependent behaviors.
• A short description of treatment facilities in your community.
• A description of Alcoholics Anonymous, Al-Anon, and Alateen.

Inclusion:

Explain that automobile accidents involving a person who has been drinking alcohol are a leading cause of injuries that result in disabilities. In addition, many falls that result in disabilities occurred after a person had been drinking. Finally, violence that occurs do to drinking may result in people being disabled. Gunshot wounds have become a leading cause of disability. People who have been disabled in these ways have many lifestyle adjustments to make. Discuss ways to be supportive of people who disabled due to accidents caused by someone who had been drinking.

Teaching Master

Codependency and The Family

"I deny my drinking problem."

"I am overly responsible."

"I am sexually active to get the attention I need."

"I lie about my wife's drinking."

"I abuse alcohol and other drugs."

"I am very controlling because I am insecure."

Sweet Success

Health Education Standards:

- Students will comprehend concepts related to health promotion and disease prevention.
- Students will analyze the influence of culture, media, technology, and other factors on health.

Performance Indicators:

- Students will explain the relationship between positive health behaviors and the prevention of injury, illness, disease, and premature death.
- Students will describe how lifestyle, pathogens, family history, and other risk factors are related to the cause or prevention of disease and other health problems.

Life Skills:

- I will recognize ways to manage chronic disease.
- I will choose behaviors to reduce my risk of cardiovascular diseases.
- I will obtain information about my family's history of disease.

Materials:

Transparency of the Teaching Master, "Chronic Diseases"; transparency projector; test tube; sugar cubes or packets of sugar; water; small piece of felt; scissors

Motivation:

1 Before beginning this strategy, cut the piece of felt into a small circle. You may want to use the rim of an eight ounce glass for the pattern. The piece of felt will be used in the strategy to represent a body cell.

2 Begin the strategy, by showing the students the sugar cube. Ask students to name foods they eat that contain sugar. They may mention cakes, pies, and candy. They may mention other foods such as oranges, apples, and ice cream. Explain that something must happen to foods in order for the sugar in them to be used by the body's cells. Empty a packet of sugar into the test tube. Explain that the **pancreas** is a gland in the digestive system that secretes insulin. **Insulin** is a hormone that promotes the absorption of blood sugar (glucose) into the muscle cells where it is used for energy. Thus, the pancreas must produce insulin for blood sugar to be absorbed by the body's cells. Pour some water from the measuring cup into the test tube. Mix the water and sugar by placing your finger over the opening of the test tube and shaking it. Then pour the water-sugar mixture on one of the felt pieces that represents a muscle cell. The water-sugar mixture will absorb into the felt. Then squeeze the felt. The water will drip off. Explain that the muscle cell has absorbed (soaked up) the blood sugar (glucose) and produced energy.

3 Repeat the demonstration in a different way. Empty a packet of sugar into the test tube. Do not add the water. Then pour the sugar onto the other piece (dry) of felt that represents a muscle cell. Students will notice that without the water (insulin), the sugar cannot be absorbed by the cell. Squeeze the felt. Students will notice that the sugar cannot be used to produce energy. The sugar remains unchanged and falls off the piece of felt. No energy can be squeezed from the felt muscle cell. Use this demonstration to discuss diabetes. In the first demonstration, the pancreas produced insulin. The insulin helped the muscle cell absorb the glucose or blood sugar. Then the muscle cell could produce energy. In the second demonstration, the pancreas produced little or no insulin. The sugar in the bloodstream remained unchanged and could not be absorbed by the muscle cell. **Diabetes** is a disease in which the body is unable to process the sugar in foods in normal ways. It occurs when the pancreas does not produce enough insulin to help the cells break down and use the sugar.

4 Use the transparency of the Teaching Master "Chronic Diseases" to review other facts about diabetes. Explain that diabetes is a chronic disease. A **chronic disease** is a recurring or persistent disease. A **chronic health condition** is a recurring or persistent health condition. Review information about ulcerative colitis, diverticulosis, arthritis, systemic lupus, and chronic fatigue syndrome. Explain that people who have these chronic diseases and health conditions must learn to manage them. For example, a person who has insulin-dependent diabetes will take daily injections of insulin. This person may have a specific diet and exercise program. Managing his/her condition means being certain to get the injections and balance exercise and diet.

5 Explain to students that some chronic conditions and diseases are inherited. For example, diabetes can be inherited. Knowing one's family history of disease is important. It helps a person know his/her risk factors for developing specific diseases and conditions. For example, people who are at risk for developing diabetes need to practice certain health habits. They need regular physical examinations and blood

tests. They need to eat a diet low in sugar. They need to have a regular exercise program. Having diabetes is a risk factor for cardiovascular diseases. By following these health habits with a family history of diabetes reduces the risk of diabetes and cardiovascular diseases.

Evaluation:

Have students develop individual crossword puzzles using the terms on the Teaching Master "Chronic Diseases" and facts about them as glues. For example, the glue for osteoarthritis might be "may be caused by sports injuries or wear and tear on joints." Students must use ten of the eleven boldfaced words from the Teaching Master. Ask students how people with diabetes, irritable bowel syndrome, and chronic fatigue syndrome manage these chronic diseases.

Inclusion:

The evaluation might be completed as a cooperative learning activity. Pair students who might have difficulty designing an individual crossword puzzle with students who would not find this task to be demanding. Have them discuss a strategy for completing the evaluation as a team. What might each contribute to the task?

Teaching Master
Chronic Diseases

Diabetes

- **Diabetes** is a disease in which the body is unable to process the sugar in foods in normal ways. There are two types of diabetes.
- **Insulin-dependent diabetes** is diabetes in which the pancreas produces little or no insulin. People with this type of diabetes must have daily injections of insulin.
- **Noninsulin-dependent** diabetes is diabetes in which the pancreas produces some insulin, but the body cells are not able to properly use it. People control this type of diabetes with diet and exercise. Some people take oral medication.
- Symptoms of diabetes include frequent urination, abnormal thirst, weakness, fatigue, drowsiness, blurred vision, tingling and numbness in the hands and feet, and slow healing of cuts.
- Complications include blindness and poor circulation, which can lead to gangrene.

Ulcerative Colitis

- **Ulcerative colitis** is an inflammatory disease of the walls of the large intestine.
- Symptoms include daily episodes of bloody diarrhea, stomach cramping, nausea, sweating, fever, and weight loss.
- People with this condition have an increased risk of colorectal cancer and often develop irritable bowel syndrome.
- **Irritable bowel syndrome** is a condition in which a person experiences nausea, gas, pain, attacks of diarrhea, and cramps after eating certain foods.
- Ulcerative colitis and irritable bowel syndrome are treated with a diet high in fiber and with certain medications.

Diverticulosis

- **Diverticulosis** is a disease in which the intestinal walls develop outpouchings called diverticula. It most often occurs in the small intestine.
- Symptoms include fecal material filling into the diverticula causing pain, discomfort, and infection. It can be life-threatening if bleeding and blockage occurs.
- Diverticulosis is treated with surgery.

Communicable and Chronic Diseases

Arthritis

- **Arthritis** is a general term that includes over one hundred diseases, all of which involve inflammation. There are two kinds of arthritis.
- **Osteoarthritis** is a wearing down of the moving parts of a joint. It occurs because of wear and tear, overweight, sports injuries, and heredity. It is treated with aspirin and pain relievers as well as exercise. Sometimes new joints are implanted in the body.
- **Rheumatoid arthritis** is a serious disease in which joint deformity and loss of joint function occur. It affects people between ages twenty and fifty-five. A careful exercise plan must be followed to avoid loss of joint function. Aspirin is used for pain. Cortisone may be used for inflammation. Surgery may be required.

Systemic Lupus

- **Systemic lupus erythematosus (SLE)** is a chronic disease of unknown cause that affects most of the systems in the body. The skin, kidneys, joints, muscles, and central nervous system may be affected. The onset occurs late in adolescence. The disease may progress to bleeding in the central nervous system. There may be heart and kidney failure. Treatment for SLE depends on the organs involved. Medications including steroids are used. Unfortunately, long-term use of steroids may cause bone disease, muscle wasting, and short stature.

Chronic Fatigue Syndrome

- **Chronic fatigue syndrome (CFS)** is a condition in which fatigue comes on suddenly and is relentless or relapsing, causing tiredness in someone for no apparent reason. The symptoms include headache, sore throat, low-grade fever, fatigue, weakness, tender lymph glands, muscle and joint aches, and inability to concentrate. CFS symptoms recur frequently and may persist for years. Currently, there is no effective treatment. People with CFS must maintain a healthful diet, get adequate rest and sleep, manage stress, and exercise at a comfortable pace.

Sealed With Strength

Health Education Standards:

- Students will comprehend concepts related to health promotion and disease prevention.
- Students will demonstrate the ability to practice health-enhancing behaviors and reduce health risks.

Performance Indicators:

- Students will develop injury prevention and management strategies for personal and family health.
- Students will describe ways to reduce risks related to adolescent health problems.
- Students will demonstrate the ability to utilize resources from home, school, and community that provide valid health information.

Life Skills:

- I will choose behaviors to reduce my risk of violence.
- *I will identify resources to improve relationships and family communication. (Family Living)*

Materials:

Transparency of Teaching Master, "Protective Factors"; transparency projector; two rubber balls; sealant or patch; small air pump

Motivation:

1 Prepare for this strategy in the following way. Obtain two rubber balls similar to the ones that are used to play dodge ball. Put a small hole in one of the rubber balls. The other rubber ball should have air in it.

2 Show the two rubber balls to the class. Explain that each rubber ball is a young person. Allow the balls to drop to the floor. The ball with the small hole in it will not bounce back as high as the one without the hole. Explain that there is a difference between these two young people. The young person represented by the ball with the puncture or hole in it has been a survivor of violence. This young person has had the "wind knocked out of him or her."

3 Explain that a survivor of violence must participate in recovery in order to be "sealed with strength." Explain that when a person has experienced violence (s)he may:
- be highly emotional;
- feel depressed;
- cry often;
- not want to talk with others about what happened;
- neglect every day tasks;
- have difficulty paying attention;
- feel afraid;
- sleep often or have difficulty sleeping;
- have nightmares;
- have flashbacks about what happened;
- use alcohol and other drugs;
- choose to stay away from others;
- feel ashamed;
- behave in violent ways.

4 Further explain that although some survivors recover from physical injuries and emotional hurt without help, most do not. Often many experience difficulty for many years. **Post traumatic stress disorder (PTSD)** is a condition in which a person relives a stressful experience again and again. Emphasize that people who are survivors of violence are at risk for behaving in violent ways. For example, grownups who abuse children often were abused when they were children. Young people who commit crimes and who join gangs have often lived in homes where there has been domestic violence.

5 Further emphasize the importance of participating in survivor recovery if one has experienced violence. Define survivor recovery. **Survivor recovery** is a person's return to physical and emotional health after being harmed by violence. Place a seal over the puncture or hole in the rubber ball. As you mention each of the following suggestions for survivor recovery, pump a small amount of air into the ball:

- Talk about what happened;
- Get a complete medical examination;
- Seek counseling;
- Join a support group;
- Learn and practice self-protection strategies.

6 Bounce the rubber ball again. Explain that the rubber ball has been "sealed with strength" because this survivor of violence has participated in survivor recovery. Ask students to tell you what the strongest part of the ball is. They should recognize that the strongest part of the ball is the place where it has been sealed. Use this illustration to initiate a discussion about the importance of asking for and getting help. Emphasize that this is a sign of strength.

7 Explain that you have just covered one protective factor for violence. This protective factor is "I will participate in recovery if a survivor of violence." Define protective factors. **Protective factors** are ways that you might behave and characteristics of the environment in which you live that promote your health, safety, and/or well-being. Use the transparency of the Teaching Master "Protective Factors That Prevent Violence" to review other protective factors.

Evaluation:

Divide the class into two teams. Have each team form a line. Give one of the rubber balls to a student at the beginning of one of the two team lines. This student is to name a way for a survivor of violence to become "sealed with strength," then bounce the ball to the first person in line for the second team, and then go to the end of the line. The first person in line for the second team is to repeat what the first student did. (S)he is to name a way for a survivor of violence to become "sealed with strength," then bounce the ball back to the next person in line for the other team. Repeat. As you complete this evaluation activity, encourage students to be specific. For example, one survival skill is to "join a support group." A student might say, "join a support group at St. Stephens community center." You want students to identify specific people and places in your community.

Inclusion:

If possible, invite a person from your community who has been disabled as a result of violence to speak with your class. Violence is a leading cause of disability. Ask the person to speak about survivor recovery. What were his/her feelings following the incident? In what survivor recovery efforts did (s)he participate? You may also want to invite a person who has lost a family member or friend due to violence. Explain that this person is also a survivor of violence. (S)he has survived the death of a loved one. What were his/her feelings following the incident? In what survivor recovery efforts did (s)he participate?

Teaching Master

Protective Factors That Prevent Violence

Protective factors are ways that you might behave and characteristics of the environment in which you live that promote your health, safety, and/or well-being. Practicing the following life skills will help protect you.

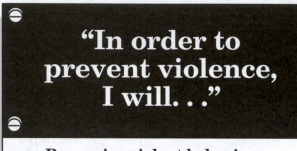

"In order to prevent violence, I will. . ."

- Recognize violent behavior.
- Develop positive self-esteem.
- Develop healthful family relationships.
- Overcome an adverse environment.
- Use social skills.
- Practice anger management skills.
- Practice stress management skills.
- Participate in physical and recreational activities.
- Practice suicide prevention strategies.
- Practice conflict resolution and peer mediation skills.
- Avoid discriminatory behavior.
- Make responsible decisions.
- Practice resistance skills.
- Avoid alcohol and other drugs.
- Practice responsible behavior around weapons.
- Resist gang membership.
- Respect authority and abide by laws.
- Practice self-protection strategies.
- Participate in recovery if I have been a survivor of violence.
- Change my behavior if I have been a juvenile offender.

Chewing The Fat

Health Education Standards:

- Students will demonstrate the ability to access valid health information and health promoting products and services.
- Students will comprehend concepts related to health promotion and disease prevention.

Performance Indicators:

- Students will analyze the validity of health information, products, and services.
- Students will analyze how messages from media and other sources influence health behaviors.
- Students will explain the relationship between positive health behaviors and the prevention of injury, illness, disease, and premature death.

Life Skills:

- I will choose sources of health-related information, products, and services wisely.
- I will spend money wisely.
- *I will follow the dietary guidelines. (Nutrition)*
- *I will make food selections that reduce my risk of disease. (Nutrition)*

Materials:

Teaching Master, "Saturated Sandwiches"; transparency projector; teaspoon; shortening; small clear plastic cup with lid; red food coloring; water

Motivation:

1 Write the following on the chalkboard: egg salad, turkey with mustard, grilled cheese, reuben, corned beef with mustard, vegetarian, ham with mustard, roast beef with mustard, BLT, turkey club, tuna salad, and chicken salad. Take the shortening, teaspoon, and small clear plastic cup with the lid. Explain that each of these sandwiches contains fat and saturated fat. Fat is an essential nutrient. Fat is needed to transport fat-soluble vitamins, to make hormones, and to regulate other body functions. However, too much fat, especially saturated fat, increases the risk of heart disease and cancer. **Saturated fats** are fats from animal origin such as beef and dairy products. Ask students to rank order the sandwiches written on the chalkboard beginning with the one that contains the least amount of saturated fat. Write the ranking given next to each sandwich.

2 Use the teaspoon, shortening, and clear plastic cup with a lid. Explain to students that one teaspoon of the shortening represents 4 grams of saturated fat. Place one half teaspoon of shortening into the clear plastic cup. Tell students that the sandwich with the least amount of saturated fat in it contained 2 grams of fat. Look to see which one they ranked as having the least amount of saturated fat. Tell them that the sandwich made with turkey and mustard had the least amount of saturated fat. Now add another one half teaspoon of shortening. Explain that there are now 4 grams of fat in the plastic cup. Then add four more teaspoons of shortening to the plastic cup. There will be a total of five teaspoons of shortening in the plastic cup or (5 x 4) 20 grams of fat. The sandwich with the greatest amount of saturated fat in it contained 20 grams of saturated fat. Which sandwich did the students rank as having the greatest amount of saturated fat?

Tell them that the reuben had 20 grams of saturated fat.

3 Use the transparency of the Teaching Master "Saturated Sandwiches" to review the amount of fat and saturated fat in the sandwiches listed on the chalkboard. Ask students if they were surprised at how the sandwiches ranked. Most people are surprised to learn the amount of fat and saturated fat in a tuna sandwich. Often, people rank it as one of the sandwiches with the least amount of fat and saturated fat. Tuna is healthful and low in fat and saturated fat. However, one tablespoon of mayonnaise is loaded with 11 grams of fat and 100 Calories. A person could eat 80 potato chips to have the equivalent of the tuna sandwich. One way to cut the amount of fat and saturated fat when eating a sandwich is to use mustard rather than mayonnaise.

4 Add water and red food coloring to the clear plastic cup. Explain that the plastic cup is an artery. The red colored water is the blood and the shortening is the saturated fat from the reuben. Explain to students that eating a diet high in saturated fat increases the risk of heart disease and cancer. Further explain that there are three ways to reduce the amount of fat in the blood. The first way is to reduce the intake of saturated fat. The Teaching Master "Saturated Sandwiches" offered information as to the amount of saturated fat that should be eaten. The other way is to engage in regular aerobic exercise. Cover the clear plastic cup with the lid and shake it vigorously. Note that some of the shortening dissolves. Explain that regular vigorous aerobic exercise clears some saturated fat from the bloodstream. A third way to lower the amount of fat in the bloodstream is to eat foods that are high in fiber. Whole grain breads contain fiber. It is healthful to eat sandwiches made with whole grain, low-fat breads.

Evaluation:

Have students write television commercials warning consumers to on reduce the number of "saturated sandwiches" they eat. Their commercials should encourage consumers to make healthful choices when ordering sandwiches at fast food restaurants. They should tell the number of grams of fat and saturated fat that adolescent females and males should eat to have a heart healthy diet.

Teaching Master

Saturated Sandwiches

The Center for Science in the Public Interest examined the fat content of twelve common sandwiches. The Food and Drug Administration recommends daily limits of 65 grams of total fat and 20 grams of saturated fat for adults eating 2,000 Calories a day. Adolescent females consume approximately 2,200 Calories per day. Their total fat should be less than 73 grams and their saturated fat should be 20 to 24 grams. Adolescent males consume approximately 2,800 Calories per day. Their total fat should be less than 93 grams per day and their saturated fat should be 25 to 31 grams.

Fat Content of Common Sandwiches

GRAMS	FAT GRAMS	SATURATED FAT
Turkey with mustard	6	2
Roast beef with mustard	12	4
Chicken salad	32	6
Corned beef with mustard	20	8
Tuna salad	43	8
Ham with mustard	27	10
Egg salad	31	10
Turkey club	34	10
BLT	37	12
Vegetarian	40	14
Grilled cheese	33	17
Reuben	50	20

My Fair Share

Health Education Standards:

- Students will comprehend concepts related to health promotion and disease prevention.
- Students will demonstrate the ability to practice health-enhancing behaviors and reduce health risks.

Performance Indicators:

- Students will analyze how environment and personal health are interrelated.
- Students will demonstrate strategies to manage stress.

Life Skills:

- I will be aware of the effects of overcrowding and poverty.
- *I will practice stress management and suicide prevention strategies. (Mental and Emotional Health)*
- *I will choose behaviors to reduce my risk of violence. (Injury Prevention and Safety)*

Materials:

Construction paper; marker; chalk; scissors; pencils or pens

Motivation:

1 Prepare for the strategy in the following ways. On a sheet of construction paper, use the marker to print the following words: water, food, shelter, sewage facilities, medical care. Using chalk, draw a large circle with a five foot diameter on the floor.

2 Ask for five student volunteers. Have the five student volunteers stand inside the circle. Give one of the

student volunteers the sheet of construction paper. Ask this student to read the words printed on the paper. Explain that these are resources available in the environment in which these five student volunteers live. The student who has the paper is to share these resources with the other four students in the circle. The student can share the resources by tearing the sheet into five pieces, keeping one of the pieces for himself/herself.

3 Now explain that the population is growing. There are going to be more people living in the environment and sharing the resources. Ask two more students to join the circle. Of course, they must have a share of the resources so two of the students who are already in the circle must tear off part of their torn sheets of paper and give them to the two new students. Allow two of the original five students to volunteer to share their resources.

4 Repeat step 3. Have two more students join the circle. Of course, two of the students in the circle must tear off part of their torn sheets of paper and give them to the two new students. The students in the circle will have to decide among themselves who shares resources and tears off a piece of their torn paper. Repeat step 3 again. Continue until there is no space left in the circle.

5 Process what happened as the group became larger and more crowded. Obviously, there were decisions to be made about who must give up resources (tear off their torn sheet of paper). And of course, there was the issue of how much paper to tear off or give away. Did everyone in the group agree as to how the resources were shared? Does anyone in the group feel cheated? Was anyone denied resources?

6 Explain that human health is greatly affected by population growth. More than 5 billion people inhabit the world, and the current rate of growth exceeds a net population gain of over 90 million people per year. By the year 2029, the world's population will double unless something happens to slow population growth.

7 Ask students to brainstorm ways that overcrowding and poverty will affect the environment. Explain that poverty, overcrowding, and poor housing, are linked to poor health conditions. Poverty is related to an increased occurrence of depression, hostility, psychological stress, inadequate medical care, poor nutrition, infant mortality, child abuse, and crowded and unsanitary living conditions. In poor environments, more people smoke cigarettes, have harmful diets, are physically inactive, and abuse alcohol and other drugs. Young people their age who are reared in overcrowded and poor environments show a higher risk of doing poorly in school, dropping out of school, becoming adolescent parents, becoming delinquent, and using alcohol and other drugs. Four million youth in the United States live in poor, overcrowded neighborhoods.

8 Explain that there is another serious health consequence that occurs frequently in poor and overcrowded environments—violence. Because there is a lack of resources, and an increase in substance abuse and stress, there is more conflict and crime. Young people living in poor and overcrowded environments need to practice behaviors to reduce the risk of being violent or being harmed by violence. Having an adult role model who can manage stress and who is nonviolent is essential. Learning to manage stress and communicate without fighting are important life skills. Participating in regular physical exercise, avoiding alcohol and other drugs, and keeping a sense of humor are helpful.

Evaluation:

Cut sheets of construction paper into four equal pieces. Give each student one of the pieces. On their sheets of paper, have students write as many words as possible to describe what it would be like to live in a poor and overcrowded environment. They are to crowd the words on the paper. Examples of words might be: stressful, dangerous, substance abuse, smoking cigarettes, drop out of school, adolescent parenthood, lack of medical care, lack of shelter, not enough food, inadequate sewage facilities, lack of water, depression, hostility, child abuse, infant mortality. After an appropriate amount of time, ask students to turn their sheets of paper to the unused side. Have them list at least three life skills, that might be practiced by young people living in poor and overcrowded environments. Their answers might include: having a role model who can manage stress, practicing stress management skills, expressing feelings without fighting, participating in physical exercise, avoiding alcohol and other drugs, keeping a sense of humor.

Internal Messages

Health Education Standard:

- Students will demonstrate the ability to practice health-enhancing behaviors and reduce health risks.

Performance Indicators:

- Students will analyze the role of individual responsibility for enhancing health.
- Students will develop strategies to improve or maintain personal, family, and community health.

Life Skills:

- I will choose behaviors to promote a healthy mind.
- I will develop positive self-esteem.

Materials:

Transparency of the Teaching Master, "Internal Messages Heard by People Who Are Codependent"; transparency projector; blank cassette tapes; cassette player; spotlight (a flashlight might be used)

Motivation:

1 Explain to students that they are going to be in the spotlight. Give them the following directions. One at a time, students are to come forward, step in the spotlight, and make a statement about doing something memorable they hope to do in the future. (A flashlight might be used if a spotlight is unavailable). For example, a student might come forward, step in the spotlight, and say, "I am graduating from high school." A student might come forward, step in

the spotlight and say, "I am shooting the winning basket in a basketball game." During their moment in the spotlight, they are to share something special that they picture themselves doing.

2 Explain to students that they have just shared a positive vision of themselves. Further explain that having a positive vision of oneself is essential to mental and emotional health. Self-esteem is what a person thinks or believes about himself/herself. Explain that there are ways to develop positive self-esteem:

- Set goals and make plans to reach them.
- Develop a skill or talent.
- Make a list of thinks you do well.
- Work to do your best in school.
- Be involved in school clubs and community activities.
- Develop a trusting relationship with at least one adult.
- Choose friends who encourage others to do their best.
- Spend time with friends and adults who provide support.
- Volunteer to help another person.
- Keep a neat appearance.

3 Explain that mentally healthy people are people who feel good about themselves, have satisfying relationships, set realistic goals for themselves, and behave in healthful ways. Some people struggle with their mental health. They may have addictive behavior. Addictive behavior is behavior associated with repeated and continual connection with an activity or object that results in unhealthful effects on the person. These activities or objects may seem to have beneficial short-term effects but in the long run, they are harmful. Addictive behavior is compulsive; a person does not have control over it. In fact, a person who is addicted usually denies that the behavior is out of control. Kinds of addictions include codependence; money, clothes, shopping, and gambling addictions; workaholism; exercise addiction; relationship addiction; and eating disorders.

4 Further explain codependence. Codependence is a mental disorder in which a person loses personal identity, has frozen feelings, and copes ineffectively. Their behavior is addictive. They usually learn and believe certain messages from their families. Review the transparency of the Teaching Master "Internal Messages Heard By People Who Are Codependent." Discuss why these messages interfere with self-esteem.

5 Explain that young people with positive self-esteem and who are mentally healthy have positive internal messages. It is as if a tape recording is playing inside their minds saying, "You are lovable. You are capable. You are trustworthy. It is safe to share your feelings. You can trust others." These messages are quite different than the messages that young people who are codependent hear. Their internal tapes are playing messages that interfere with positive self-esteem and with mental health.

Evaluation:

Have students make their own individual cassette tapes of positive internal messages that would contribute to their having positive self-esteem and mental health. These messages might be ones they hear or ones they would like to hear. The messages should include at least three of the ways to develop positive self-esteem that were stated in step 2. For example, a student might make a tape recording that says, "I have a good sense of humor. I am capable of doing well on tests. I keep a neat appearance. I am a member of the baseball team. I try my best." As students plan to make their cassette tapes of "Internal Messages," they may want to identify messages they want to reprogram. For example, a student who hears the internal message, "I am safer if I keep my feelings to myself" will want to place a different message on his/her tape. (S)he might record, "It is safe to share my feelings with others." Ask students to listen to their tapes frequently. Remind them that it is important for some people to reprogram their internal messages to delete negative messages and learn new positive messages.

Teaching Master

Internal Messages Heard By People Who Are Codependent

"I would be better off continuing to behave the way that I am than attempting to deal with the dysfunction in my family."

"I am better off being dishonest because if I told others the truth, they might not like me."

"I am safer if I keep my feelings to myself."

"I am more comfortable being serious than playful and having fun."

"I cannot trust others."

"I should not talk to others about family problems."

"I do not deserve to be treated with respect."

"I should get others to believe that everything in my life is fine."

Mentor Match

Health Education Standards:

- Students will comprehend concepts related to health promotion and disease prevention.
- Students will demonstrate the ability to use interpersonal communication skills to enhance health.

Performance Indicators:

- Students will analyze how the family, peers, and community influence the health of individuals.
- Students will demonstrate skills for communicating effectively with family, peers, and others.
- Students will demonstrate strategies for solving interpersonal conflicts without harming self or others.
- Students will demonstrate refusal, negotiation, and collaboration skills to avoid potentially harmful situations.

Life Skills:

- I will strive for healthful family relationships.
- I will recognize harmful relationships.
- I will identify resources to improve relationships and family communication.

Materials:

Transparency of the Teaching Master, "The Family Continuum"; transparency projector; puzzles made from the pattern, "Mentor Match"; cardboard paper; scissors; marker; paper; pencils

Motivation:

1 Prepare for this strategy in the following ways. Divide the number of students in your class by six to know the number of puzzles you will need to make. You will need to make six different sets of puzzles using the cardboard and scissors. Use a marker to outline the six pieces of each puzzle and to write the words on each of the six pieces. The first set of puzzles will be made by cutting out the piece on the pattern labeled "A." Therefore, you will have a puzzle with one missing piece. (Refer to illustration) The second set of puzzles will be made by cutting out the piece on the pattern labeled "B." The third set of puzzles will be made by cutting out the piece on the pattern labeled "C." The fourth set of puzzles will be made by cutting out the piece on the pattern labeled "D." The fifth set of puzzles will be made by cutting out the piece on the pattern labeled "E." The sixth set of puzzles will be made by cutting out the piece on the pattern labeled "F."

2 Use the transparency of the Teaching Master "The Family Continuum" to review family relationships. Explain the following. Family relationships are the connections one has with family members, including extended family members. Extended family members are family members in addition to parents, brothers, and sisters. The Family Continuum is a scale marked in units ranging from zero to 100 that shows the quality of relationships within a family. A dysfunctional family is toward the zero end of The Family Continuum. A dysfunctional family is a family in which feelings are not expressed openly and honestly, coping skills are lacking, and family members do not trust each other. The quality of the relationships within a dysfunctional family is low. A healthful family is toward the 100 end of The Family Continuum. A healthful family is family in which feelings are expressed openly and honestly, coping skills are adequate, and family members trust each other. A family does not have to be at one end or the other of the continuum, but could be somewhere in between. For example, a family might demonstrate some of the items listed under the dysfunctional family and at the same time demonstrate items listed under the healthful family.

3 Now divide the class into two groups. One group of students will consist of five-sixths of the class. Explain that they each will get a puzzle with a piece missing. Hand the puzzle to them with the blank side up. They will not see the outline of the pieces on the back. They will not read what the puzzles they are holding say. This group of students is to stand in one area of the classroom. The other one-sixth of the students are to be given one of the small puzzle pieces. Again, hand the pieces to the students with the blank side up. They are not to read the words on the other side. Explain to the students who are holding a puzzle with a missing piece that when you tell them to do so they are to find a student who has a small puzzle piece that will make their puzzle complete. They are to stand next to the person who has this piece. Allow an appropriate amount of time for students to find the matching pieces to their puzzles.

4 After students have found their matches, have them turn their puzzles over and read them. Explain the following. Each student who originally held the puzzle with a missing piece was holding a puzzle with five of the following six characteristics written on it: respect, trust, responsible behavior, no substance abuse, no violence, healthful communication. These students represented young people reared in families with many positive characteristics. Still, one of

the characteristics of relationships in a healthful family was missing. Explain that you asked them to find another student who was holding the piece their puzzle was lacking in order to be whole. What you had asked them to do was to locate a person outside the family who might serve as a mentor. A mentor is a person who guides and helps a younger person. The mentor, or missing piece, they found to make their puzzle whole is a person who helps them learn the characteristic written on the piece. This characteristic makes them better equipped to have healthful relationships with others. Emphasize the importance mentors can play in teaching them how to have healthful relationships.

5 Have students return to their desks. Explain that the strategy they have done focused primarily on families that had healthful relationships. After all, these families demonstrated five of the six positive characteristics. Healthful relationships are relationships that enhance self-esteem, foster respect, develop character, and promote health-enhancing behavior and responsible decision-making. Further explain that some young people are reared in dysfunctional families. They may have harmful relationships. Harmful relationships are relationships that threaten self-esteem, are disrespectful, indicate a lack of character, threaten health, and foster irresponsible decision-making. Ask students what might have appeared on the six puzzles pieces for a dysfunctional family. They might answer: lack of respect, distrust, irresponsible behavior, chemical dependency, violence, harmful communication. Emphasize the importance of mentoring for young people reared in families with these characteristics.

6 Identify resources to improve relationships and family communication.

650

Twelve Step Programs are programs that focus on twelve steps to take to recover from the past and gain wholeness. These programs change behavior by focusing on strengthening relationships—relationships with self, others, and one's personal beliefs. Getting professional help can also be an important step to recovery from harmful relationships. There are many different areas of mental health for which professional counseling programs are available.

Evaluation:

Have students develop individual "Family Relationship Checklists." Their checklists should include ten characteristics of healthful families. Encourage students to include at least five characteristics from The Family Continuum. However, they might also include other characteristics they deem to be important. For example, a student might say, "keeps a sense of humor."

Inclusion:

Have students add characteristics to their "Family Relationship Checklists" that are especially important when family members have disabilities. For example, a student might say, "compassion" and/or "patience."

Multicultural Infusion:

Ask students to assess the "Family Relationship Checklists" they have developed and comment as to whether families with members of various cultures would select the same characteristics. Explain that families may differ in some ways, however, characteristics of healthful families seem to transcend the issue of culture.

Teaching Master

The Family Continuum

The Family Continuum depicts the degree to which a family promotes skills needed for loving and responsible relationships.

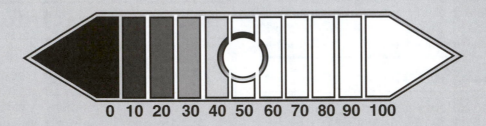

0 10 20 30 40 50 60 70 80 90 100

Dysfunctional Families   **Healthful Famlies**

Dysfunctional Families

1. do not show respect for each other;

2. do not trust each other;

3. are confused about guidelines for responsible behavior;

4. are not punished or are punished severely for wrong behavior;

5. do not spend time with each other;

6. do not share feelings or do not share feelings in healthful ways;

7. do not have effective coping skills

8. resolve conflicts with violence;

9. abuse alcohol and other substances;

10. abuse each other with words and actions.

Healthful Families

1. show respect for each other;

2. trust each other;

3. follow guidelines for responsible behavior;

4. experience consequences when they do not follow guidelines;

5. spend time with each other;

6. share feelings in healthful ways;

7. practice effective coping skills;

8. resolve conflict in nonviolent ways;

9. avoid alcohol and other substances;

10. use kind words and actions.

Mentor Match

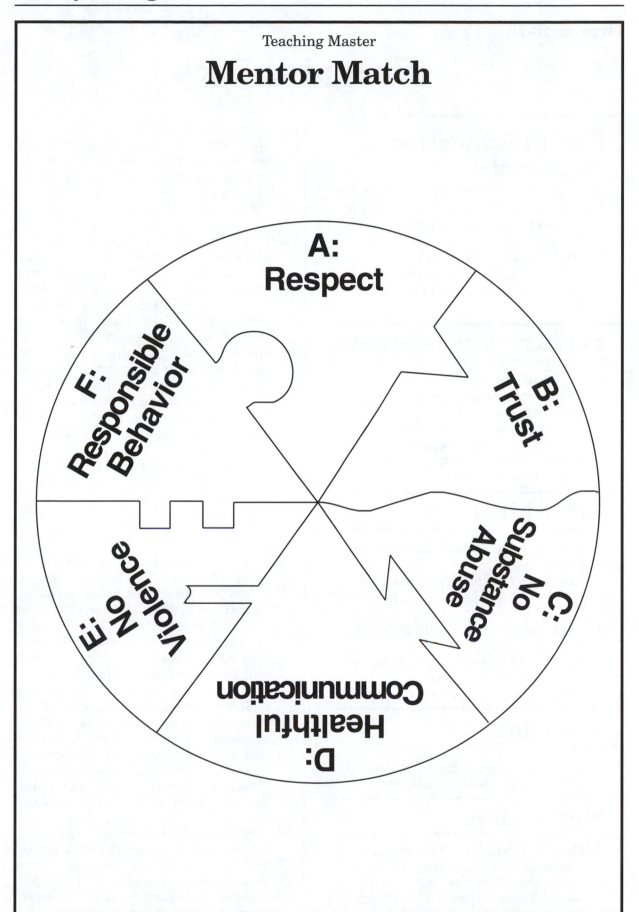

Snapping Back

Health Education Standards:

- Students will comprehend concepts related to health promotion and disease prevention.
- Students will demonstrate the ability to use interpersonal communication skills to enhance health.

Performance Indicators:

- Students will describe the interrelationships of mental, emotional, social, and physical health throughout adulthood.
- Students will analyze how the family, peers, and community influence the health of individuals.

Life Skills:

- I will achieve developmental tasks for my age group.
- *I will develop skills to prepare for future relationship choices. (Family Living)*
- *I will recognize harmful relationships. (Family Living)*
- *I will identify resources to improve relationships and family communication. (Family Living)*

Materials:

Two rubber bands (short in length); two pencils; chalk; chalkboard

Motivation:

1 Explain to students that they are in a growth spurt. During this growth spurt, they are changing in many ways. There are mental-emotional, physical, and family-social changes.

Define developmental tasks. Developmental tasks are achievements that are necessary to be made during a particular period of growth so that a person can continue growing toward maturity.

2 Identify one of the important developmental tasks of adolescence, "Task 4: Achieving emotional independence from parents and other adults." Use the following illustration to clarify the meaning of this task. Take one of the pencils. Place the rubber band so that one end is touching a side of the pencil while the other end is not (see illustration). Explain that during adolescence, young people want to "pull away" from their parents. Begin to pull one end of the rubber band away from the pencil. Explain that this "pulling away" is natural and healthful. In order for adolescents to achieve emotional independence from parents and other adults, they must "pull away."

3 Pull one end of the rubber band a little bit more. Then let it go so that it "snaps back" and hits the pencil. Explain that after a period of pulling away, adolescents often feel the need to "snap back." They will want to be very close to their parent(s). They will want their advice, help, and support. This is what adult intimacy is about—being independent and having feelings of closeness. Adolescents develop the ability to behave in this way over time. This is why "achieving emotional independence from one's parents" is considered a developmental task of adolescence.

4 Repeat the demonstration three times. As you repeat the demonstration, explain interdependence. Interdependence is a condition in which two people depend on each other yet have separate identities. During

654

adolescence, they are learning to depend more on themselves, yet they still depend on their parents and/or other adults. Further explain that this can be confusing and trying at times. During this period, they may struggle with parent(s) and/or other adults rearing them. At times, they will exert too much independence and their parent(s) will pull them back. At other times, they will want to depend heavily on parent(s). This is a part of growing to emotional maturity.

5 Further explain that this is also a growing period for their parent(s). Their parent(s) are adjusting to them "pulling away" and "snapping back." At times, their parent(s) will want the closeness when they do not. At other times, their parent(s) may expect them to make adultlike decisions, and they may or may not count on parent(s) to make the decisions. These adjustments in the parent-child relationships are necessary for adolescents to develop emotional maturity.

6 Now take the other pencil and wrap a rubber band very tightly around it (see illustration). Explain that this is

another kind of parent-child relationship. Notice that the rubber band is wrapped so tightly around the pencil that it cannot "pull away." Explain that this is not a healthful parent-child relationship. This is enmeshment. Enmeshment is a condition in which the identities of two people in a relationship have blended into one whereby at least one of the people cannot see himself/herself as having a separate identity. In the case of a parent/child relationship, either the parent or the child cannot see himself/herself as having a separate identity.

7 Ask one of the students to try to "pull away" the rubber band from the pencil. It will not be easy to do so. Explain that one or both people feel "strangled" when there is no opportunity to "pull away" and "snap back." It is difficult for adolescents in this kind of parent-child relationship to have a sense of their own feelings. They become too wrapped up in what the parent(s) think and feel. Use the following example:

A father was frustrated that he was not a good athlete. When his son was an adolescent, he began to pressure his son to excel in athletics. He wanted to live his dreams through his son's accomplishments. After a while, the

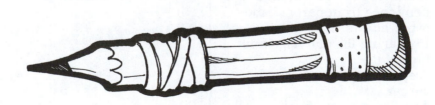

son had difficulty knowing whether he really enjoyed playing football. He could not "pull away" and see whether he was playing football for his own enjoyment. He was so enmeshed with his father that his inner self was giving him the messages that his father was giving him: "To be worthwhile, you must be a good athlete." It is impossible to be enmeshed and to master Task 4: Achieving emotional independence from parents and other adults. During adolescence, young people separate their thoughts and feelings from those of their parent(s). This does not mean that they will not have similar beliefs and attitudes to parent(s). It means that adolescents learn to own their own beliefs and attitudes.

8 Explain that the kind of parent-child relationship that was just illustrated was codependent. A person is codependent when (s)he has no sense of personal identity. There are many resources to improve relationships and family communication. There are Twelve Step Programs. There is individual counseling.

9 Using chalk, list all eight developmental tasks on the chalkboard and discuss each task.

Task 1: Achieving a new and more mature relationship with age mates of both sexes.

Task 2: Achieving a masculine or feminine social role.

Task 3: Accepting one's physique.

Task 4: Achieving emotional independence from parents and other adults.

Task 5: Preparing for marriage and family life.

Task 6: Preparing for an economic career.

Task 7: Acquiring a set of values and an ethical system as a guide to behavior—developing an ideology.

Task 8: Developing a social consequence.

Evaluation:

Have students keep individual relationship journals for a week. Each day have them write in their journals. They should describe times when they needed to "pull away" from parent(s) or other significant adults responsible for rearing them. They should write the feelings they experienced during these times. They also should describe times when they wanted a special closeness with parent(s) or other significant adults responsible for rearing them. They should write about the feelings they experienced during these times. Allow students to maintain privacy and confidentiality. Do not collect their journals. However, at the end of the week ask them to write a one- to two-page paper describing the importance and difficulty of mastering the developmental task of "Achieving emotional independence from one's parents." They are to include a discussion of how mastering this task will help them to prepare for future relationship choices. They also are to discuss ways that too much dependence or too little intimacy interferes with relationships. They might identify one place in the community that provides resources to improve family relationships. In addition, ask them to discuss one of the other developmental tasks covered in class.

Name That Food

Health Education Standards:

- Students will demonstrate the ability to advocate for personal, family, and community health.
- Students will demonstrate the ability to practice health-enhancing behaviors and reduce health risks.
- Students will demonstrate the ability to access valid health information and health promoting products and services.

Performance Indicators:

- Students will evaluate the effectiveness of communication methods for accurately expressing health information and ideas.
- Students will develop strategies to improve or maintain personal, family, and community health.
- Students will evaluate the validity of health information, products, and services.

Life Skills:

- I will read food labels.
- I will make food selections that reduce my risk of disease.
- *I will spend money wisely. (Consumer and Community Health)*

Materials:

Transparency of Teaching Master, "Name That Food"; transparency projector; chalk; chalkboard; marker; three grocery bags; purple and white licorice candy; artificial coffee sweetener; canned cat food; several food labels; paper; pencils

Motivation:

1 To prepare for this strategy, use the marker to label the grocery bags. Label the first bag "1," the second "2," and the third "3." Place the purple and white licorice candy in the first grocery bag. Place the artificial coffee sweetener in the second grocery bag. Place the can of canned cat food in the third grocery bag. You may want to ask students to collect food labels from empty cans or cartons and bring them to class.

2 Use the transparency of the Teaching Master "Name That Food." Explain to students that you are going to play "Name That Food." Tell the students that they are on a deserted island and they have three choices of foods to eat: food number 1, food number 2, and food number 3. You are going to give them a few minutes to choose one of these foods by examining the list of ingredients for each. You also want them to name the food after examining the ingredients.

3 After students have had time to examine the teaching master, write the following on the chalkboard: 1, 2, and 3. Then ask for a show of hands. Ask students how many of them would choose food number 1. Record the number next to the 1. Ask how many students would choose food number 2. Record the number next to the 2. Ask how many students would choose food number 3. Record the number next to the number 3.

4 Place the three grocery bags in view of the students. Begin with bag number 1. Ask students to name the food in this grocery bag. Have a student take the food out of the bag and show it to the class (purple and white licorice candy). Ask students to name the food in grocery bag number 2. Have a student take the food out of the bag and show it to the class (artificial coffee sweetener). Ask students to name the food in grocery bag number 3. Have a student take the food out of the bag and show it to the class (canned cat food). Many students will be surprised at the selections.

5 Ask students the basis for their food selections. They will respond that they made their selections based on the ingredients in the foods. Emphasize the importance of food labels. Food labels are designed to assist consumers with making healthful food choices. Food manufacturers must provide nutritional information that will be accurate, complete, and useful to consumers.

6 Give students copies of food labels. Have them look at the food labels as

you explain the following. The title of the label is "Nutrition Facts." The required information includes the following, always in this order:
- Total Calories
- Calories from fat
- Total fat
- Saturated fat
- Cholesterol
- Sodium
- Total carbohydrate
- Dietary fiber
- Sugars
- Protein
- Vitamin A
- Vitamin C
- Calcium
- Iron

7 Explain that food manufacturers must list all the ingredients by weight in their products, beginning with the one that is present in the greatest amount. The ingredients list should be read carefully to determine the true amount of an ingredient. Further explain that by reading the food label and the list of ingredients people can make food selections that reduce the risk of disease. For example diet plays a major factor in the risk of heart disease. Diets high in fat and saturated fat increase the risk of heart disease. Vitamins C and E and A may lower the risk of heart disease. Diets high in fat content also increase the risk of certain types of cancer. Diets that contain fiber and Vitamins A and C tend to lower the risk of cancer.

8 Write the following words on the chalkboard: low fat, free, low Calorie, lean, reduced, good source, and low sodium. Have students write the following definitions for each.
- **low fat** no amount of (or a trivial amount) of fat, saturated fat, cholesterol, sodium, sugars, and Calories

- **low Calorie** 40 Calories or less per serving

- **lean** less than 10 grams of fat

- **reduced** 25 percent less of a nutrient or of Calories than the regular product

- **good source** one serving contains 10 to 19 percent of the daily value for a particular nutrient

- **low sodium** 140 grams or less per serving

Evaluation:

Have each student write a Top Ten List of Reasons to read food labels. Their lists should include information as to what they will learn from reading food labels, such as "to learn the number of Calories from fat." Their lists might also include benefits from reading food labels, such as "to spend money wisely" and "to reduce my risk of cancer." Check their lists for accuracy. Have students share their lists with the class.

Name That Food

1

sugar, corn, syrup, wheat flour, molasses, caramel color, licorice extract, corn starch, salt, artificial colors (including yellow #6), resinous glaze, anise oil, canuba wax, artificial flavors

2

corn syrup solids, partially hydrogenated vegetable oil, (may contain one or more of the following oils: coconut, cottonseed, palm, palm kernel, safflower, or soybean), sodium caseinate, mono- and di-glycerides (prevent oil separation), dipotassium phosphate, artificial flavor, and annato color

3

tuna, water sufficent for processing, vegetable oil, dicalcium phosphate, sodium tripolyphosphate, tricalcium phosphate, sodium chloride, Vitamin A, B1, B6, E and D3 supplements, zinc sulfate, menadione soduim bisulfide, manganous sulfate, sodium nitrite, folic acid

Personal Health

Grades 9–12

Turn Off The Tube And MOVE!

Health Education Standards:

- Students will demonstrate the ability to practice health-enhancing behaviors and reduce health risks.
- Students will demonstrate the ability to use goal-setting and decision-making skills that enhance health.

Performance Indicators:

- Students will develop strategies to improve or maintain personal, family, and community health.
- Students will implement a plan for attaining a personal health goal.
- Students will formulate an effective plan for lifelong health.
- Students will evaluate progress toward achieving personal health goals.
- Students will develop injury prevention and management strategies for personal, family, and community health.

Life Skills:

- I will participate in movement and exercise.
- I will achieve a desirable level of physical fitness.
- *I will choose behaviors to reduce my risk of cardiovascular disease. (Communicable and Chronic Diseases)*
- *I will choose behaviors to reduce my risk of cancer. (Communicable and Chronic Diseases)*
- *I will choose behaviors to reduce my risk of violence. (Injury Prevention and Safety)*

- *I will maintain my desirable weight. (Nutrition)*

Materials:

Transparency of Student Master, "Facts About Exercise" (optional); Student Master, "Commitment to Exercise"; transparency projector (optional); five large index cards; notebook paper; pencils or pens; tape

Motivation:

1 To prepare for this strategy, reproduce the Student Master "Facts About Exercise." Cut the paper into five pieces so that each of the five facts about exercises are separate. Tape each to an index card.

2 Divide the class into five groups. Give each group an index card. Explain that each group is to identify three television programs that adolescents watch. The three programs are to be entertaining not educational. After the groups identify the three programs, they are to create a news story that will be used to interrupt one of the programs. The news story will focus on the latest facts about exercise. Each group has an index card that contains facts that it can use to create an informative and creative news story. The entire group can be part of the news story or the group can design the news story or the group can design the news story and one or more group members can present it. Allow an appropriate amount of time for the groups to develop their news stories.

3 Have each group present its news story in the following manner. One group member is to tell the class the name of a popular television show. Students in the class are to pretend they are viewing this show. Then the same member or another member of the group is to say, "We interrupt...(name of show)...to bring you the latest reasons why you should "Turn off the tube and MOVE!" Then the group is to present its creative and informative news story. Have each group present its news story in this way.

4 After each group has presented its news story, review the facts about exercise that were presented. Ask students to take notes using notebook paper. You may choose to make a transparency of the Student Master "Facts About Exercise" although you can conduct a review without doing so.

5 Make a copy of the Student Master "Commitment to Exercise" for each student or use a transparency of this Student Master and have students copy it. Review the five components of physical fitness that are defined in the "Effect On My Well-Being." Have the class brainstorm examples of exercises that improve each of the

five components of physical fitness. Set a date for students to complete this Health Behavior Contract.

Evaluation:

Collect the Health Behavior Contracts. Review them to evaluate whether or not students have identified exercises that develop each of the five components of physical fitness. Collect their journals to assess the benefits of exercise that they have identified.

Inclusion:

Have students with physical disabilities identify exercises they can do for each of the five components of physical fitness. If possible, invite a professional specializing in adaptive physical education to work with them on their physical fitness plans. Be certain that these plans have the support of parents/guardians and other health professionals.

Multicultural Infusion:

Divide students into groups. Allow each group to select a foreign country. The groups should research information about the exercise habits of people living in the country selected. What factors influence the exercise choices? For example, people from Switzerland may choose snow skiing as a form of exercise because of the Alps.

Facts About Exercise

EXERCISE. . .

Strengthens the heart muscle.

Regular exercise strengthens the heart muscle and increases cardiac output. Cardiac output is the amount of blood pumped by the heart to the body each minute. Another way to say this is cardiac output is equal to the heart rate multiplied by the stroke volume. Heart rate is the number of times that the heart beats each minute forcing blood into the arteries. Stroke volume is the amount of blood the heart pumps with each beat. When the heart muscle is strong, the heart pumps more blood with each beat. This lowers resting heart rate and allows the heart to rest between beats. This is accompanied by lower resting blood pressure. There is less wear and tear on the arteries.

Increases the ratio of HDLs to LDLs.

Exercises that strengthen the heart muscle increase the ratio of HDLs to LDLs in the bloodstream. Lipoproteins are fats in the bloodstream. High-density lipoproteins or HDLs are fats that transport excess cholesterol to the liver for removal from the body. Low-density lipoproteins are fats that form deposits on the artery walls and contribute to the development of atherosclerosis.

Reduces the risk of chronic diseases.

Regular vigorous exercise reduces the risk of breast cancer, especially when a regular exercise routine is begun before adulthood. Regular physical activity also appears to reduce the risk of heart disease, diabetes, and osteoporosis (Journal of National Cancer Institute, September 21, 1994).

Helps control the effects of stress.

Regular exercise helps reduce stress by generating overall feelings of well-being. It uses the adrenaline that is secreted during the stress response and that causes an increase in heart rate and blood pressure. When a person continues a vigorous exercise program for at least three times per week for seven to ten weeks, his or her body secretes beta-endorphins. Beta-endorphins are substances produced in the brain that help reduce pain and create a feeling of well-being. Regular exercise also reduces feelings of anger and thereby lessens the likelihood that someone will act out and be violent when feeling stressed.

Promotes weight management.

The energy equation states that Caloric intake needs to equal Caloric expenditure for weight maintenance. A regular program of exercise changes the energy equation. During exercise, more Calories are expended. People who exercise tend to burn more Calories and eat less. Their bodies are leaner.

Improves female reproductive health.

Females who exercise regularly have milder menstrual cramps and shorter menstrual periods. They are less likely to feel sad or depressed during their periods.

Commitment to Exercise: Health Behavior Contract

Life Skill: I will achieve a desirable level of physical fitness.

Effect On My Well-Being: Physical fitness is the condition of the body as a result of participating in exercises that develop muscular strength, muscular endurance, flexibility, cardiovascular endurance, and a healthful percentage of body fat. Muscular strength is the amount of force the muscles can exert against resistance. Muscular endurance is the ability to use muscles for an extended period of time. Flexibility is the ability to bend and move the joints through a full range of motion. Cardiovascular endurance is the ability to do activities which require increased oxygen intake for extended periods of time. Healthful body composition is a high ratio of lean tissue to fat tissue. Physical activity and fitness strengthens the heart muscle, increases the ratio of HDLs to LDLs, reduces the risk of chronic disease, helps control the effects of stress, provides a physical outlet for angry feelings reducing the risk of violent behavior, promotes weight management, and improves female reproductive health.

My Plan: I will identify exercises I can do for the different components of fitness on a weekly basis.

Muscular strength:_____

Muscular endurance:_____

Flexibility: _____

Cardiovascular endurance:_____

Lean and trim body:_____

Evaluating Progress: I will develop a progress chart showing the exercises I will do each day during the week and recording whether or not I did them.

Results: I will keep a journal in which I write about my efforts to follow my plan. I will identify obstacles to doing my exercises as well as benefits. I will describe any modifications I need to make in my plan.

My Signature:

_____

Sloppy Joe

Health Education Standards:

- Students will demonstrate the ability to practice health-enhancing behaviors and reduce health risks.
- Students will demonstrate the ability to use goal-setting and decision-making skills that enhance health.

Performance Indicators:

- Students will analyze the role of individual responsibility for enhancing health.
- Students will analyze the short-term and long-term consequences of safe, risky, and harmful behaviors.
- Students will predict immediate and long-term impact of health decisions on the individual, family, and community.

Life Skills:

- I will not drink alcohol.
- I will reduce my risk of HIV infection by not using intravenous drugs or drugs that dull my decision-making skills.
- *I will make responsible decisions. (Mental and Emotional Health)*
- *I will practice skills to promote abstinence. (Family Living)*
- *I will choose behaviors to reduce my risk of violence. (Injury Prevention and Safety)*

Materials:

Transparency of the Teaching Master, "Drugs and Sexuality"; transparency projector; watch with a second hand; paper; pencils; computers and computer paper (optional)

Motivation:

1 Use the following activity to demonstrate to students how alcohol affects reaction time. First, have students use their dominant hand and write, "I will not drink alcohol," in script on a sheet of paper while you time their efforts. It will take them approximately ten to twelve seconds.

2 Now explain that they did not follow this life skill. They drank alcohol at a party with peers. Then, have students use their other hand to write, "I will not drink alcohol," in script on the same sheet of paper while you time their efforts. It will take them approximately thirty to thirty-six seconds, or three times as long.

3 Discuss the results. Students should mention that after drinking alcohol they were not able to write as quickly or as neatly. In fact, they were a "Sloppy Joe" or "Sloppy Josephine" when it came to their writing ability. Explain that drinking alcohol results in a slower reaction time. Reaction time is the amount of time it takes to respond to a stimulus. Ask them to identify problems that may occur because of slowed reaction time. They might mention automobile accidents, injuries when playing sports, pedestrian accidents, falls, etc.

4 Then ask students to identify other ways that drinking alcohol affects the body. Mention the following:

- Liver damage. Cirrhosis is a disease in which alcohol destroys liver cells and plugs the liver with fibrous scar tissue and can lead to liver failure and death.
- Abnormal heart functioning. Cardiomyopathy is a degeneration

of the heart muscle that is characterized by severe enlarge ment of the heart and inability of the damaged heart to pump blood effectively. Cardiac arrhythmia is an irregular heartbeat. Chronic alcohol consumption is also associated with a significant increase in high blood pressure and stroke.

- Harms the stomach, mouth, and esophagus. Alcohol injures the inner lining of the stomach, especially when combined with aspirin. It may cause inflammation of the esophagus and make existing peptic ulcers worse.
- Causes pancreatitis. Pancreatitis is inflammation of the pancreas that increases the risk of diabetes.
- Causes neurological changes. Heavy alcohol consumption may cause dementia, blackouts, seizures, hallucinations, and nerve destruction throughout the body. Alcohol dementia is brain impairment that is characterized by overall intellectual decline, due to the direct toxic effects of alcohol.
- May result in alcoholism. Alcoholism is a complex disease that is characterized by a preoccupation with drinking alcohol that has progressed to serious physical, social, occupational, and/or family consequences for an individual.
- During pregnancy, may cause fetal alcohol syndrome. Fetal alcohol syndrome (FAS) is a characteristic pattern of severe birth defects present in babies born to mothers who drink alcohol during their pregnancy. Among the abnormalities are small eye slits, small head circumference, facial abnormalities, growth retardation, and mental retardation.

5 Use the following activity to demonstrate to students how alcohol affects decision-making. Have students use their dominant hand and write, "I will not be sexually active," in script on a sheet of paper while you time their efforts. It will take them approximately fifteen seconds.

6 Now explain that they decided to drink alcohol. Then they were in a situation in which they were encouraged to be sexually active. Have students use their other hand to write, "I will not be sexually active," in script on the same sheet of paper while you time their efforts. It will take them approximately three times as long and their writing will be sloppy.

7 Process what happened. Explain that after drinking alcohol, it was difficult to respond quickly with the life skill. After drinking alcohol, their decision-making was sloppy. It was not as clear that they were not going to be sexually active. Further explain that alcohol impairs the ability to think clearly and reduces inhibitions and defenses. A person under the influence of alcohol has more difficulty sticking to the choices (s)he has made for himself/herself and for his/her body. Alcohol use increases the risk of choosing behaviors that result in HIV infections, other STDs, and pregnancy because of impaired judgment. Alcohol use increases the risk of violence including sexual assault, suicide, and homicide because of impaired judgment. An alcohol-free mind is a protective factor against making unwise choices.

8 Use a transparency of the Teaching Master "Drugs and Sexuality" to review the importance of being

666

alcohol-free and drug-free. If you do not want to make a transparency, you can discuss the information on this Teaching Master with students while they take notes.

Evaluation:

Have students design a one page graphic that is an adaptation of The Wellness Scale showing a range of health from zero to 100. They are to provide their own clever title such as "The Alcohol and Other Drug Scale." At the zero end of the scale, they might use descriptors such as "liver damage," "pancreatitis," "sexual assault," "HIV infection," etc. At the 100 end of the scale, they might use descriptors such as "reduces risk of HIV infection," "responsible decisions,"

"mental alertness," etc. Explain to students that after completing this task they will be asked to share their Scales with the class. As they explain their Scales, they must show information covering the following four life skills:

- I will not drink alcohol.
- I will reduce my risk of HIV infection by not using intravenous drugs or drugs that dull my decision-making skills.
- I will make responsible decisions.
- I will practice skills to promote abstinence.
- I will choose behaviors to reduce my risk of violence.

If computers are available at your school or students have them in their homes, you may want to have them design their scales using computer graphics.

Teaching Master

Drugs and Sexuality

You can choose behaviors to reduce the likelihood that you will become infected with HIV and other STDs. You can choose behaviors to avoid being a teenage parent. You can choose behaviors to reduce the likelihood that you will be sexually assaulted and/or sexually assault another. Responsible behaviors include:

1. Be involved in activities that promote self-worth.

2. Establish goals.

3. Develop loving family relationships.

4. Select a mentor who is alcohol-free and drug-free and who has clear values when family relationships are not strong.

5. Select friends who are alcohol-free, drug-free and choose to wait to have sex.

6. Select people to date who are alcohol-free, drug-free and choose to wait to have sex.

7. Avoid being in situations and going to parties where there will be alcohol and other drugs.

8. Avoid being in situations where sexual feelings will be intense and you will be tempted to be sexually active.

9. Discuss pressure-packed situations and get advice from trusted adults.

10. Choose entertainment carefully avoiding movies, soap operas, music, and magazines that glamorize sex and drugs.

Just One Look

Health Education Standards:

- Students will comprehend concepts related to health promotion and disease prevention.
- Students will demonstrate the ability to practice health-enhancing behaviors and reduce health risks.

Performance Indicators:

- Students will analyze how behavior can impact health maintenance and disease prevention.
- Students will analyze how the prevention and control of health problems are influenced by research and medical advances.
- Students will develop strategies to improve or maintain personal, family, and community health.

Life Skills:

- I will choose behaviors to reduce my risk of cancer.
- *I will care for my ears and eyes. (Personal Health)*
- *I will stay safe while exercising. (Injury Prevention and Safety)*

Materials:

Transparency of the Teaching Master, "Cancer Clues"; transparency projector; several pairs of sunglasses; material to clean germs from sunglasses; several large mirrors; paper; markers

Motivation:

1 To prepare for this strategy, collect several pairs of sunglasses and mirrors or ask students to bring sunglasses and mirrors to class. Be certain that when the sunglasses are worn, at least one pair is dark enough so that it is difficult to see the eyes through the lenses. Do not tell students that there is a difference in the darkness of the sunglasses or they may have a clue as to purpose of this strategy.

2 Explain to students that you are going to have an sunglasses fashion show. Students can wear the sunglasses they have brought to class. If a student wears a pair of sunglasses you or another student has brought, be certain to clean the glasses before they are worn. The sunglasses fashion show will proceed as follows. Each student wearing sunglasses will parade in front of the class modeling the sunglasses for a few moments. The class will get "just one look" to determine how stylish the sunglasses are.

3 After each student wearing sunglasses has had a chance to parade in front of the class, have the class vote to determine which sunglasses they liked the best. Ask students to share the criteria they used for making their decisions. For example, they might say, "I liked metal frames" or "I liked the shape of the sunglasses" or "The sunglasses are the latest fashion."

4 Explain that there is an important factor to consider when choosing sunglasses. The sunglasses should block out ultraviolet radiation. Have students use the mirrors. Then ask them to look into the mirrors. Sunglasses should be dark enough to prevent the eyes from easily being seen. If not, they allow too much ultraviolet radiation through them and the eyes may be damaged. Have each student who modeled the sunglasses stand and share with the class whether or not the sunglasses they modeled blocked ultraviolet radiation. Emphasize the importance of wearing sunglasses that are dark enough to protect against ultraviolet radiation. Sunglasses should absorb at least 95 percent of UV-B rays and at least 65 percent of UV-A rays. Encourage students to purchase sunglasses that are rated by the American National Standards Institute (ANSI). ANSI ratings are determined by the amount of damaging UV rays that can penetrate the lens. Sunglasses rated "general purpose" are safe for most people while "special purpose" should be worn by those participating in sports for long periods of time. Discuss wearing sunglasses when exercising outdoors.

5 Explain that ultraviolet radiation is also a cause of skin cancer. There is a definite link between exposure to ultraviolet radiation, whether from the sun's rays or tanning beds, and the development of skin cancer. Despite warnings, an estimated 1 million Americans use tanning salons

daily (American Cancer Society). Side effects reported include burns, itching, dry skin, and nausea. Some young people go to tanning salons before taking a trip to a sunny area to get a base tan to protect their skin. However, the level of sun protection a salon "base tan" provides is the equivalent of wearing a suncreen with a protective factor of 4, which is not enough prtection from ultraviolet radiation. Recent studies suggest a higher likelihood of skin cancer for those who tan in the sun and with sunlamps than for those who are exposed to the sun only (American Cancer Society). There is now evidence that exposure to ultraviolet radiation is responsible for **malignant melanoma**, the most invasive of skin cancers.

6 Use the transparency of the Teaching Master "Cancer Clues" to review causes of cancer, the warning signs, and the kinds of treatment.

Evaluation:

Divide students into groups to design magazine advertisements for sunglasses. They are to design fashionable sunglasses. Their advertisements must creatively inform consumers that sunglasses must be worn to block ultraviolet radiation. They must encourage consumers to wear sunglasses when exercising outdoors. In a clever way, they can offer a free sunscreen containing a SPF of at least 15 with the purchase of a pair of sunglasses. Have students design individual crossword puzzles titled "Cancer Clues" the information using the information they recall from the Teaching Master by the same name. For example, a word in the crossword puzzle might be "bleeding" and the clue might be "a warning sign." Their individual crossword puzzles should contain at least ten facts from the Teaching Master.

Inclusion:

Discuss the relationship between the development of cataracts and overexposure to ultraviolet radiation. A cataract is a clouding of the lens of the eye that obstructs vision and can lead to blindness. It is now believed that people who have not protected their eyes from ultraviolet radiation over the years are at increased risk of becoming visually impaired because of cataracts.

Inclusion:

You might choose to have students paired for cooperative learning when developing the crossword puzzles to evaluate their recall of the "Cancer Clues" on the Teaching Master. Or, you may choose to copy the Teaching Master for specific students and allow them to use it as they design their crossword puzzles.

Teaching Master

Cancer Clues

Causes of Cancer

Heredity
- Cancers of the breast, ovary, pancreas, and colon appear to run in families.

Viruses
- There is some link between viruses and the development of certain kinds of cancers such as leukemia.

Tobacco
- People who smoke cigarettes and use smokeless tobacco have an increased risk of developing cancer.
- According to one study, males who begin smoking during adolescence are twice as likely to develop lung cancer; females who begin at age twenty-five or younger young are three times as likely.

Ultraviolet Radiation
- There is a definite link between exposure to ultraviolet radiation, whether from the sun's rays or tanning beds, and the development of cancer, especially skin cancer.

The Warning Signs

C hange in bowel or bladder habits

A sore that does not heal

U nusual bleeding or discharge

T hickening or lump in a breast or elsewhere

I ndigestion or difficulty in swallowing

O bvious change in a wart or mole

N agging cough or hoarseness

Kinds of Treatment

Surgery
- The most common treatment method.
- Used to confine cancer to a particular site.

Radiotherapy
- X-rays are used kill cancer cells.

Chemotherapy
- The use of drugs to kill cancer cells inside the body.

Combination
- Any combination of surgery, radiotherapy, and chemotherapy.

Buckle Up

Health Education Standards:

- Students will demonstrate the ability to practice health-enhancing behaviors and reduce health risks.

Performance Indicators:

- Students will demonstrate ways to avoid and reduce threatening situations.
- Students will analyze the role of individual responsibility for enhancing health.

Life Skills:

- I will stay safe while riding in a car.
- *I will not drink alcohol. (Alcohol, Tobacco, and Other Drugs)*

Materials:

Student Master, "Self -Protection While Driving and Riding in Cars"; enough clay to mold two balls the size of a softball; pencil or small stick; chalkboard; poster paper; markers

Motivation:

1 Ask for two student volunteers. Give each student a glob of clay to mold into a ball. Then give each student a pencil or small stick to use to carve a face into the ball. They can make the eyebrows, eyes, and a smiley face with teeth. You may choose to give each student extra clay to make a nose to mold into the face.

2 Have each student stand ten feet from the chalkboard. Explain to the class that they are about to witness two motor vehicle accidents. The two students are each holding a passenger in one of the motor vehicles that is involved in the accident. Neither is wearing a safety belt. Explain that a safety belt is a seat belt with a shoulder strap. Neither is riding in a motor vehicle that has an air bag. Explain that the first passenger is riding in a motor vehicle that is traveling fifty-five miles per hour. Have one student throw the clay ball as hard as (s)he can at the chalkboard. Retrieve the clay ball from the chalkboard and show it to the students. The students will notice the damage. The passenger has sustained many injuries. Most likely the face that was inscribed into the clay has been damaged.

3 Now ask students what will happen to a passenger who is an accident in a motor vehicle that is traveling only twenty-five miles per hour. Explain that many people do not wear safety belts when they are traveling at lower speeds such as while driving or riding in their neighborhoods. Have the second student gently toss his/her clay ball at the chalkboard. Retrieve the clay ball from the chalkboard and show it to the students. The students will notice the damage. Again, the passenger has sustained many injuries. Check the face that was inscribed into the clay. Most likely there are changes to the face.

4 Explain that more people die of motor vehicle injuries than any other cause of injury. Accidents in motor vehicles account for about half of all fatal accidents and about 20 percent of all injuries leading to disability. On the chalkboard list the factors that lead to motor vehicle injuries and deaths:
- alcohol consumption
- failure to use safety belts and seat belts (explain that newer cars have safety belts with seat belts and shoulder straps; older cars may have seat belts only)
- speeding and reckless driving
- poor driving conditions (heavy

rainstorms, icy roads, reduced visibility)
- disregarding traffic rules (failure to yield right of way)
- poorly maintained motor vehicle (defective brakes, etc.)

5 Brainstorm a list of guidelines to reduce the risk of motor vehicle injuries and deaths:
- Avoid drinking and driving.
- Avoid riding in a car with some one who has been drinking.
- Avoid excessive speed.
- Heed warning signs.
- Anticipate what other drivers will do.
- Always use available safety devices such as safety belts or seat belts and use safety restraints for small children.

6 Emphasize wearing a safety belt or seat belt, whichever is in the motor vehicle. Wearing a seat belt reduces the chance of being killed by 60 to 70 percent and the chance of being seriously injured by 50 percent. Seat belts are effective because they prevent or reduce the human collision. The human collision is a forceful collision experienced when an unbelted occupant is thrown against the motor vehicle's interior components—dashboard, windshield, steering wheel, etc. Seat belts also prevent occupants from being ejected from the motor vehicle. Safety belts (seat belts with a shoulder strap) are much more effective in saving lives and preventing injuries than seat belts alone. Air bags are also effective motor vehicle safety devices. Air bags are cushions that inflate when activated by sensors in the dashboard and front bumpers within a fraction of a second between the first collision and the "human collision." They cushion the occupants in the front seat and prevent dangerous collisions with the car's interior components.

7 Emphasize the importance of not drinking alcohol and driving, as well as not riding in a motor vehicle with someone who has been drinking. Explain that the risk of a fatal crash, per mile driven, may be at least eight times higher for an intoxicated driver than for a sober one. Drinking alcohol and driving affects a person's ability to drive by impairing vision, perception, judgment, reaction time, and the ability to brake and control speed. The leading cause of death in adolescents and young adults is alcohol-related highway accidents.

8 Give students a copy of the Student Master "Self-Protection While Driving and Riding in Cars," and review other ways to stay safe.

Evaluation:

Organize a motor vehicle safety campaign for the school and community. Explain to students that as their evaluation they will contribute to the campaign in two ways. Their first contribution will be done individually. They are to design a safety poster that focuses upon one of the six guidelines for reducing the risk of motor vehicle injuries and deaths. Their second contribution to the school and community campaign will be a cooperative learning experience in which there is group participation. Divide the class into groups. Each group is to prepare a short skit, presentation, or message to be presented to (1) another class of students in the high school, (2) a group of students at a younger grade level, (3) a community group such as a garden club, charity organization, etc. They should present in a clever and creative way at least three ways to stay safe while driving or riding in a car.

Student Master

Self-Protection While Driving and Riding in Cars

1. Always park in a safe and well-lighted area where there are other people and other cars.
2. Take special note of exactly where youare parked in a large parking lot.
3. Lock your car at all times and keep your keys with you.
4. Have someone walk with you to your car whenever possible.
5. Check the front and back seats to make sure that no one is hiding inside before getting in your car.
6. Never leave infants or small children in an unattended car even if you are leaving only for a brief time.
7. Never leave the keys in the ignition or the engine running.
8. Always take your keys with you when leaving your car.
9. Keep wallets, purses, unattached stereos, and other valuables out of sight.
10. Do not allow yourself to run out of gas.
11. Plan ahead and fuel your car only during daylight hours.
12. Keep your car in good condition to prevent breakdowns.
13. Try to drive in safe, well-lighted areas, especially at night.
14. Install a car phone to use in case of emergency.
15. Keep a sign in your car that says "Send Help" to display if your car breaks down.
16. Keep a flashlight and road flares in your trunk.
17. Stay in your car, keep your doors locked and windows rolled up, keep a lookout for passing police cars, and honk your horn if you see a police car when your car breaks down.
18. Do not get out of the car if someone other than a police officer stops and offers help. Roll the window down only a crack and ask the person to call the police.
19. Drive to a nearby phone and call 9-1-1 if you see someone in need of help.
20. `Never pick up a hitchhiker.

21. Do not drive home if you think you are being followed. Go to a store, police station, or well-lighted area where there are other people. Call the police and report that you were being followed.
22. Be cautious of anyone approaching your car when it is stopped.
23. Keep your car doors locked and windows rolled up at all times to prevent carjacking. If you need ventilation, roll the windows down only a crack. Keep your sunroof closed. Avoid driving in a convert ible with the top down.
24. Keep your car in gear when at a stoplight or stop sign. Allow enough distance between your car and the car ahead to drive away.
25. If a person armed with a weapon demands your car or your keys, do not resist.
26. Do not give out your keys to other people.
27. Consider getting an inside latch for your trunk. If you are ever forced into the trunk you could escape.
28. Do not rent cars that are marked as rental cars.
29. Be a courteous driver on the street. If another driver makes you angry, ignore this person. Never begin a fight.

Health Fair

Health Education Standards:

- Students will demonstrate the ability to advocate for personal, family, and community health.
- Students will demonstrate the ability to access valid health information and health promoting products and services.

Performance Indicators:

- Students will demonstrate the ability to work cooperatively when advocating for healthy communities.
- Students will demonstrate the ability to influence and support others in making positive health choices.
- Students will demonstrate the ability to adapt health messages and communication techniques to the characteristics of a particular audience.
- Students will demonstrate the ability to evaluate resources from home, school, and community that provide valid health information.

Life Skills:

- I will volunteer in school clubs and community organizations and agencies that promote health.
- I will cooperate with people who protect my health and safety.
- I will choose sources of health-related information, products, and services wisely.

Materials:

School board approval for having a health fair; parental permission for student participation in the a health fair; a list of local agencies that are willing to participate; paper; pencils; chalk

Motivation:

1 Allow a time period of two months to plan and prepare for this strategy. Careful planning will include:

- Obtaining school board approval for having a health fair involving students and voluntary and public health agencies.
- Obtaining parental permission for student participation in the health fair.
- Securing a place and date for the health fair such as the school cafeteria, gymnasium, or a place in the community such as a shopping center or supermarket.
- Identifying voluntary health agencies that are willing to participate and work with students to deliver the health fair. (Refer to The Health Resource Guide in Section 4 for ideas).
- Making and reproducing a copy of a list of the health agencies that are willing to participate, contact person, address, and telephone number. (Have this list approved by the appropriate people in your school district such as your school board to eliminate any conflicts of interest or controversy).
- Arranging for a contact person from each of the health agencies on the approved list to participate in a scheduled class period(s) to work with students.
- Identifying parents/guardians to help with supervision.
- Attending to all tasks associated with the health fair including, but not limited to transportation and liability.

2 Explain the following to students. Much of the emphasis in health education is on personal responsibility for health. However, there are

676

many health problems that can be solved or helped when individuals work together and serve the needs of others. A volunteer is a person who expresses a willingness to provide a service. Most voluntary health organizations need the services of volunteers. A voluntary health organization is an agency supported by funding other than taxes, that usually focuses on a specific disease, health problem, or body organ. These agencies seek to educate the public and health care professionals about particular health conditions. They also raise funds for research and community health programs. Examples of voluntary health agencies are:

- American Cancer Society
- American Heart Association
- American Diabetes Association
- American Lung Association
- National Society for Prevention of Blindness
- March of Dimes
- American Red Cross
- National Safety Council
- Arthritis Foundation
- National Kidney Foundation

3 Explain that voluntary health agencies need the services of volunteers particularly in the area of educating the public about particular health conditions and services provided. Further explain that voluntary health agencies often participate in health fairs. A health fair is a gathering designed to acquaint the public with health information and health services. Sometimes health screening is provided at a health fair. Health screening is an appraisal of a person's health status. For example, the American Heart Association or one of its state or local chapters may provide blood pressure screening at a health fair. Perhaps the health fair is being held at a shopping center.

People coming to the shopping center to shop may stop at a table or booth and have health screening to learn if their blood pressure is normal. If it is not, they are advised to see a physician. Further explain that information in the form of pamphlets and brochures is often given to people at a health fair.

4 Give students a copy of the list of voluntary health agencies that have agreed to participate in the health fair. Have students form groups based on their interests in doing volunteer work for a specific voluntary health agency. Explain that during the next class period a contact person from the voluntary health agency will be available to work with the group on plans for the health fair.

5 Have students meet in their groups with the contact person from the voluntary health agency. They are to collaboratively make decisions on the goals of the health fair and the target population. They need to decide upon the information that will be disseminated to the public. The students may decide to design pamphlets themselves. They may make posters. They may conduct interviews. They may assist people from the voluntary health agency who are providing health screening. All decisions must be approved by the contact person. Review each group's final plans.

6 Have a discussion involving all of the contact people representing the voluntary health agencies and all of the students in the different groups. You might discuss ways to advertise the health fair, as well as ways to evaluate the health fair.

7 Conduct the health fair at the scheduled time. Be certain that you have parents/guardians present to help with

677

supervision and unexpected situations. Provide time for students to visit the tables and booths of voluntary health agencies other than the one they chose for their group project.

8 Have a follow up class meeting in which group members meet with the contact person from the voluntary health agency with whom they worked. During this follow-up meeting, ask each group to share experiences from the health fair and to evaluate its success in accomplishing its goals.

Evaluation:

Use chalk to draw a large circle on the floor. The circle should be large enough so that all students might step inside it. (You may want to do this outside or in the gymnasium of your school.) Have students stand around the outside of the circle. Explain that the inside of the circle represents their community. As a

volunteer, they can step forward and get involved by expressing a willingness to provide a volunteer service. Taking turns, have each student identify a service that can be performed at one of the voluntary health agencies and step inside the circle. Ask students to avoid repeating what others have said. Explain that they can be very specific, such as "I could hand out a pamphlet on juvenile diabetes" or "I could collect money for the heart association." Pause after several students have joined the circle to remark that as more volunteered, the community gained more benefits. When the circle is full, explain that every member of a community has something to offer. Explain that as they volunteered they became closer to others in the community. They gained a sense of "community."

Environmental Link

Health Education Standards:

- Students will demonstrate concepts related to health promotion and disease prevention.
- Students will demonstrate the ability to advocate for personal, family, and community health.

Performance Indicators:

- Students will analyze how the environment influences the health of the community.
- Students will demonstrate the ability to influence and support others in making positive health choices.
- Students will develop strategies to improve or maintain personal, family, and community health.

Life Skills:

- I will be concerned about environmental issues.
- I will keep the air clean.
- I will keep the water clean.
- I will keep my indoor environment free of pollution.
- I will keep noise at a healthful level.
- I will protect myself from radiation.
- I will dispose of solid waste properly.
- I will recycle.
- I will be aware of the effects of overcrowding and poverty.
- I will cooperate with environmental protection agencies.

Materials:

Several sheets of colored construction paper (8 1/2" by 11"); stapler; scissors; blank white sheets of paper; pens or pencils; chalk

Motivation:

1 Prepare for this strategy in the following way. Cut each sheet of construction paper into four strips that are eleven inches long and two inches wide. You will need to have one strip of paper for each student.

2 Use this strategy to summarize what students have learned during other strategies focusing upon environmental health. List the ten life skills for environmental health on the chalkboard:
1. I will be concerned about environmental issues.
2. I will keep the air clean.
3. I will keep the water clean.
4. I will keep my indoor environment free of pollution.
5. I will keep noise at a healthful level.
6. I will protect myself from radiation.
7. I will dispose of solid waste properly.
8. I will recycle.
9. I will be aware of the effects of overcrowding and poverty.
10. I will cooperate with environmental protection agencies.

3 Divide the class into ten groups of students. Assign each group one of the ten life skills. The group is to brainstorm actions they can practice to support the life skill it was assigned. For example, a group might be assigned "I will keep the air clean." The group will brainstorm ways to keep the air clean such as "car pooling whenever possible" and "using roll-on deodorant rather than an aerosol." Allow the groups an appropriate amount of time to list as many actions as possible to promote the assigned life skills.

4 Give each student a strip of paper. Each student is to select an action that promotes the life skill his/her group was assigned and write it on the strip of paper. However, no two students in the same group can write the same action. For example, students in the group assigned the life skill, "I will keep the air clean" must each write a different action on the strip of paper they were given.

5 Form the "Environmental Link" as follows. Have the students stand and move about the room so that they are not standing with members of their assigned groups. Then begin with one student. This student is to identify the action written on his/her strip of paper and the life skill it will promote. Staple the strip of paper in a circle or link as the student holds it. Now have a second student identify the action written on his/her strip of paper and the life skill it will promote. Have the student place the strip of paper through the chain link of the first student and staple it together to make another link. Repeat with the rest of the students (see illustration). When the last student identifies the action written on his/her strip of paper and the life skill it will promote, (s)he will need to slip his/her strip of paper through the previous student's chain link as well as the very first student's chain link. This will link all students together.

6 Ask students to discuss the "Environmental Link" that has been created. Why are the ten life skills linked so closely? What would happen if one of the links or life skills was removed? Why is it important to influence the decisions that others make about behaviors

influencing the environment? How might they encourage others to practice these life skills?

Evaluation:

Erase the chalkboard so that students are not able to see the ten life skills. Give each student a blank sheet of paper. In the center of the paper, they are to draw or diagram aspects of their environment that they enjoy. In a creative way, they are to add the ten life skills to their drawings or diagrams illustrating their protective nature. For example, a student might draw his/her home. The ten life skills might be written on a picket fence that surrounds and protects the home.

682

Section 4

THE HEALTH RESOURCE GUIDE

Chapter 17: USING *THE HEALTH RESOURCE GUIDE*

THE HEALTH RESOURCE GUIDE

Figure 17-1

Using *The Health Resource Guide*

The Health Resource Guide contains a listing of the names and telephone numbers of organizations and agencies that provide resources for comprehensive school health education.

Chapter 17

USING *THE HEALTH RESOURCE GUIDE*

There are many other resources that can be used with this *Totally Awesome*™ Teacher Resource book on Comprehensive School Health Education. The materials in this teacher resource book are designed so that other resources can be easily integrated with them. The following discussion focuses on ways to use *The Health Resource Guide*.

Ways to Use *The Health Resource Guide*

The Health Resource Guide contains a listing of the names and telephone numbers (and in many cases the address) of organizations and agencies that provide resources for comprehensive school health education (Figure 17-1). This listing is divided into the following headings:
1. Mental and Emotional Health
2. Family Living
3. Growth and Development
4. Nutrition
5. Personal Health
6. Alcohol, Tobacco, and Other Drugs
7. Communicable and Chronic Diseases
8. Injury Prevention and Safety
9. Consumer and Community Health
10. Environmental Health

There is a separate section that provides a listing of the names, addresses, and telephone numbers of the professional organizations that were represented on The Joint Committe for Health Education Standards: The Ameri-can Cancer Society; The American School Health Association; The Association for the Advancement of Health Education; The School Health Education and Services Section, American Public Health Association; and The Society of State Directors of Health, Physical Education, and Recreation.

Several agencies and professional organizations that are listed in *The Health Resource Guide* provide free and/or inexpensive materials. They may provide pamphlets, curricula, kits, videos, and films. They also may provide services such as speakers' bureaus, support groups, and screening programs. They may have hotline numbers. Hotline numbers can be dialed to obtain immediate assistance. Teachers may want to share these hotline numbers with their students. They may want to have students write to these agencies and organizations to obtain further information when they are writing reports or preparing to give oral presentations. Teachers also may want to have students explore health careers available at these agencies and organizations.

The Health Resource Guide

Mental and Emotional Health

American Mental Health
Counselors Association
    800-345-2008

American Psychiatric Association
    1400 K Street, N.W.
    Washington, DC 20036
    202-965-7600

American Psychological Association
    750 First Street, N.W.
    Washington, DC 20002
    202-336-5500

National Alliance for the Mentally Ill
    2102 Wilson Boulevard
    Suite 302
    Arlington, VA 22201
    703-524-7600

National Clearinghouse for
Mental Health Information
    Public Inquiries Section
    5600 Fishers Lane
    Room 7C02
    Rockville, MD 20857
    301-443-4513

National Institute for Mental Health
    Science Communication Branch
    Public Inquiries Section
    5600 Fishers Lane
    Room 15C-17
    Rockville, MD 20857
    301-443-4513

National Mental Health Association
    1021 Prince Street
    Alexandria, VA 22314
    703-684-7722

National Self-Help Clearinghouse
    25 West 45th Street
    Room 620
    New York, NY 10036
    212-642-2944

Family Living

American Association of Marriage
and Family Therapy
    1717 K Street, N.W.
    Washington, DC 20006
    202-429-1825

Anti-Defamation League
    823 United Nations Plaza
    New York, NY 10017
    212-490-2525

Big Brothers/Big Sisters of America
    230 N. 13th Street
    Philadelphia, PA 19107
    215-567-7000

Displaced Homemakers Network
    1625 K Street, N.W.
    Suite 300
    Washington, DC 20006
    202-467-6346

Family Service America
    11700 West Lake Park Drive
    Milwaukee, WI 53224
    800-221-2681

National Institute Against
Prejudice and Violence
    31 S. Greene Street
    Baltimore, MD 21201

Parents of Murdered Children
    100 East 8th Street
    Suite B41
    Cinncinati, OH 45202
    513-721-5683

Parents Without Partners
    401 N. Michigan Avenue
    Chicago, IL 60611
    800-637-7974

Toughlove
    P.O. Box 1069
    Doylestown, PA 18901
    215-348-7090

686

Growth and Development

American Association of Retired Persons
601 E. Street, N.W.
Washington, DC 20049
202-434-2277

Alzheimer's Association
919 N. Michigan Avenue
Suite 1000
Chicago, IL 60611
312-335-8700

National Center for Education in
Maternal and Child Health
3520 Prospect, N.W.
Suite 1
Washington, DC 20057
202-625-8400

National Council on the Aging, Inc.
409 Third Street, N.W.
Suite 200
Washington, DC 20024

National Institute of Child Health
and Development
9000 Rockville Pike
Bethesda, MD 20014
301-496-4000

Nutrition

American Institute of Nutrition
9650 Rockville Pike
Bethesda, MD 20814
301-530-7050

American Dietetic Association
216 W. Jackson Blvd.
Suite 800
Chicago, IL 60606
312-899-0040

Center for the Treatment of Eating
Disorders and National Anorexic Aid, Inc.
1925 E. Dublin-Granville Road
Columbus, OH 43229
614-436-1112

Food and Nutrition Board
Institute of Medicine
2101 Constitution Avenue, N.W.
Washington, DC 20418
202-334-2238

Food and Nutrition Information Center
National Agricultural Library
Building
10301 Baltimore Blvd. Room 304
Beltsville, MD 20705
301-504-5719

National Dairy Council
Nutrition Education Division
O'Hare International Building
10255 West Higgins
Suite 900
Rosemont, IL 60019
708-803-2000

National Nutrition Education
Clearinghouse
Society for Nutrition Education
1700 Broadway, Suite 300
Oakland, CA 94612

North American Vegetarian Society
P.O. Box 72
Utica, NY 13329
518-568-7970

Nutrition Education Association
P.O. Box 20301
3467 Glen Haven
Houston, TX 77025
713-665-2946

United States Department of Agriculture
14th and Independence Avenue, S.W.
Washington, D.C 20250
202-720-2791

Personal Health

American Dental Association
211 East Chicago Ave.
Chicago, IL 60611
312-440-2500

Aerobics International Research Society
1200 Preston Road
Dallas, TX 75430
214-661-3374

American Physical Fitness
11796 Parklawn Drive
Rockville, MD 20852
301-340-0001

The Health Resource Guide

National Center for Health Services
Research
    Publications Branch
    5600 Fishers Lane
    Room 18-12
    Rockville, MD 20857
    301-443-2403

National Center for Health Statistics
    Scientific and Technical Information
    Branch
    Department of HHS
    6525 Belcrest Rd. Room 1064
    Hyattsville, MD 20782
    301-565-4167

National Institute of Dental Research
    Office of Communications
    9000 Rockville Pike
    Building 31, Room 2C35
    Bethesda, MD 20892

National Institutes of Health
    9000 Independence Avenue, S.W.
    Washington, DC 20201
    202-690-7536

Office of Health Information, Health
Promotion, Physical Fitness, and Sports
Medicine
    Department of Health and
    Human Services
    200 Independence Avenue, S.W.
    Washington, DC 20201

President's Council on Physical Fitness
and Sports
    701 Pennsylvania Avenue, N.W.
    Suite 250
    Washington, DC 20004

Women's Sports Foundation
    342 Madison Avenue
    Suite 728
    New York, NY 10018

Alcohol, Tobacco, and Other Drugs

Al-Anon Family Groups
    1372 Broadway
    New York, NY 10018
    212-302-7240

Alcohol and Drug Referral Line
    800-ALCOHOL

Alcoholics Anonymous
    307 Seventh Avenue
    Room 201
    New York, NY 10001
    212-647-1680

Alcohol, Drug Abuse, and Mental
Health Administration
    5600 Fishers Lane
    Rockville, MD 20857
    301-443-2403

Food and Drug Administration
    Office of Consumer Affairs,
    Public Inquiries
    5600 Fishers Lane (HFE-88)
    Rockville, MD 20857
    301-443-3170

Mothers Against Drunk Driving
    18935 I45
    Spring, TX 77388
    713-589-6233

National Clearinghouse for Alcohol
Information
    11426 Rockville Pike
    Rockville, MD 20852
    301-468-2600

Narcotics Anonymous
    P.O. Box 9999
    Van Nuys, CA 91409

National Clearinghouse for Alcohol
and Drug Information
    11426 Rockville Pike
    Rockville, MD 20852
    301-443-6500
    800-729-6686

National Cocaine Hotline
    800-COCAINE

National Coordinating Council on
Drug Education, Inc.
    1830 Connecticut Avenue, N.W.
    Washington, DC 20009

National Insitute on Drug Abuse
    5600 Fishers Lane
    Room 10A-39
    Rockville, MD 301-443-6245

PRIDE - Parents Resource Institute
for Drug Education
    10 Park Place South Suite 340
    Atlanta, GA 30303
    404-577-4500

688

Communicable and Chronic Diseases

American Allergy Association
P.O. Box 7273
Menlo Park, CA 94026
415-322-1663

American Cancer Society
1599 Clifton Road
Atlanta, GA 30329
404-320-3333

American Diabetes Association
1660 Duke Street
Alexandria, VA 22314
703-549-1500
800-496-3472

American Foundation for the Blind
15 West 16th Street
New York, NY 10011
212-502-7600

Alzheimer's Disease and Related
Disorders Association
70 East Lake Street
Chicago, IL 60601
800-621-0379

American Heart Association
7272 Greenville Avenue
Dallas, TX 75231
214-373-6300

American Kidney Fund
6110 Executive Blvd.
Suite 1010
Rockville, MD 20852
800-638-8299

American Lung Association
1740 Broadway
New York, NY 10019
212-315-8700

Arthritis Foundation
1314 Spring Street, N.W.
Atlanta, GA 30236
404-872-7100

Cancer Connection
R.A. Block Foundation
4410 Main
Kansas City, MO 64111

Cancer Information Service
National Cancer Institute
9000 Rockville Pike
Bethesda, MD 20205
800-4-CANCER

Center for Disease Control and Prevention
1600 Clifton Road, N.E.
Atlanta, GA 30333
404-639-3534

Center for Prevention Services
Centers for Disease Control
1600 Clifton Road, N.E.
Atlanta, GA 30333
404-639-3534

Center for Sickle-Cell Disease
2121 Georgia Ave., N.W.
Washington, DC 20059
202-806-7930

Epilepsy Foundation of America
4351 Garden City Drive
Landover, MD 20785
301-459-3700
800-221-4602

Juvenile Diabetes Foundation
International Hotline
800-223-1138

Leukemia Society of America, Inc.
600 Third Avenue
New York, NY 10016

Lupus Foundation of America
1717 Massachusetts Avenue, N.W.
Suite 203
Washington, DC 20036
800-558-0121

National AIDS Information Clearinghouse
800-458-5231

National Diabetes Clearinghouse
Box NDIC
9000 Rockville Pike
Bethesda, MD 20892
301-468-2162

National Down Syndrome Congress
1605 Chantilly Drive
Atlanta, GA 30324
800-221-4602

National Down Syndrome Society Hotline
666 Broadway
New York, NY 10012

National Federation for the Blind
1800 Johnson Street
Baltimore, MD 21230
410-659-9314

National Heart, Lung, and Blood Institute
9000 Rockville Pike
Building 31
Room 4A21
Bethesda, MD 20892
301-496-4236

National HIV/AIDS Hotline
800-342-AIDS
800-344-SIDA (Spanish)

National Institute of Arthritis and Musculoskeletal and Skin Disease Clearinghouse
P.O. Box 9782
Arlington, VA 22209

National Institute of Neurological and Communicative Disorders and Stroke
National Institute of Health
9000 Rockville Pike
Bethesda, MD 20892
301-496-4000

National Kidney Foundation
30 East 33rd Street
New York, NY 10016

National Psoriasis Foundation
6600 S.W. 92nd Avenue
Suite 300
Portland, OR 97223
503-244-7404

National Rehabilitation Information Center
8455 Colesville Road
Suite 935
Silver Springs, MD 20910
800-34-NARIC

National Reye's Syndrome Foundation
426 North Lewis
Bryan, OH 43506
800-233-7393

National Society to Prevent Blindness
500 E. Remington Road
Schaumburg, IL 60173
800-331-2020

National STD Hotline
800-227- 8922

Special Olympics
1350 New York Avenue, N.W.
Suite 500
Washington, DC 20005

Consumer and Community Health

Consumer Information
18th and S Street, N.W.
Room G142
Washington, D.C. 20405
202-501-1794

Consumer Education Research Center
350 Scotland Road
Orange, NJ 07050
201-443-3170

Council of Better Business Bureaus
703-276-0100

Environmental Protection Agency
PM 211-B
401 M Street NW
Washington, DC 20460
202-260-2080

Food and Drug Administration
Office of Consumer Affairs
Public Inquiries
5600 Fishers Lane (HFE-88)
Rockville, MD 20857
301-443-3170

U.S. Consumer Product Safety Commission Hotline
202-638-CPSC

Injury Prevention and Safety

Child Welfare League of America
440 First Street NW
Washington, DC 20001
202-638-2952

National Adolescent Suicide Hotline
800-621-4000

National Safety Council
444 North Michigan Avenue
Chicago, IL 60611
312-527-4800

National Burn Victim Foundation
32-34 Scotland Road
Orange, NJ 07050
201-676-7700

National Center for the Prevention and
Control of Rape
5600 Fishers Lane
Room 6C-12
Rockville, MD 20857
301-443-1410

National Committee for the Prevention
of Child Abuse
332 S. Michigan Ave.
Suite 1600
Chicago, IL 60604
312-663-3520

Poison Prevention Week Council
P.O. Box 1543
Washington, DC 20207
301-504-0580

Women Against Rape
P.O. Box 02084
Columbus, OH 43202
614-291-9751

Environmental Health

Council for a Livable World
110 Maryland Avenue, N.W.
Washington, DC 20002
202-543-4100

Environmental Protection Agency
Public Information Agency
PM 211-B
401 M Street S.W.
Washington, DC 20460

Hazardous Waste Hotline
800-424-9346

National Pesticide Telecommunications
Network
Texas Tech University
Thompson Room South 129
Lubbock, TX 79430
800-858-7378

Joint Committee on Health Education

American Alliance for Health, Physical
Education, Recreation, and Dance
1900 Association Drive
Reston, VA 22091
703-476-3400

American Public Health Association
(APHA)
1015 15th Street NW
Washington, DC 20005
202-789-5600

American School Health Association
7263 State Route 43
Kent, OH 44240
216-678-1601

National Association of School Nurses, Inc.
P.O. Box 1300
Scarborough, ME 04070
207-883-2117

Society of Public Health Education
(SOPHE)
2001 Addison Street
Suite 220
Berkeley, CA 94704
510-644-9242

Society of State Directors of Health,
Physical Education, and Recreation
Attn: Simon McNeely
9805 Hillridge Drive
Kensington, MD 20895
301-949-0709

Health Coalition

National School Health Education
Coalition (NaSHEC)
1001 G Street, NW
Suite 400 East
Washington, DC 20001
202-638-3556

The Health Resource Guide

Computer Online Resources

America Online
Commercial information service. Areas of interest to health educators include the Better Health and Medical Forum, Weather, Teacher's Information Network, and American Cancer Society Online.
800-827-3338

Apple Link
Offers a K–12 information area for educators.
20525 Mariani Avenue
Cupertino, CA 95014
800-800-2775

CompuServe
Commercial online service. Areas of interest to health educators include HealthNet, Human Sexuality Forum, and National Weather Service Reports.
800-848-8990

Consortium for School Networking
Networking resource for educators, government agencies, and students.
P.O. Box 65193
Washington, DC 20035-5193
202-466-6296
e-mail: info@cosn.org

FrEdMail Network
Networking for public agencies including schools, libraries, and community service organizations.
FrEMail Foundation
P.O. Box 243
Bonita, CA 91908
619-475-4852
e-mail: arogers@bonita.cerf.fred.org

GEnie
Commercial online service. Areas of interest to health educators include Medical Professional Center, Homework Help, and health support groups.
800-638-9636

Health Educators Electronic Forum (HEEF)
Computer communication service exclusively for health education/promotion. Offers information on all areas of health education, including a Job Bank.
Lousiana State Department of Education
P.O. Box 94064
Baton Rouge, LA 70804
504-342-1015
e-mail: 199.4.193.58 heef.doe.state.la

K12Net
Free international educational network available through bulletin board systems. Offers a forum dedicated to health educators.
Attn: Janet Murray
1151 SW Vermont Street
Portland OR 97219
503-280-5280
e-mail: jmurray@psg.com

National Geographic Kids Network
Offers a science-based curriculum focusing on environmental issues for students in grades 4 to 6.
National Geographic Society
Educational Services
Washington, DC 20036
800-368-2728

PBS Learning Link
Interactive communication network for K–12 educators and students.
PBS Learning Link
1320 Braddock Place
Alexandria, VA 22314
703-739-8464

Prodigy
Commercial online service. Areas of interest to health educators include the Health bulletin board, the Medical Support bulletin board, and the Homework Helper.
800-776-3449

SpecialNet
Information network focusing on special education issues.
GTE Educational Network Services
5525 MacArthur Boulevard
Suite 320
Irving, TX 75038
800-927-3000

Section 5

THE CURRICULUM GUIDE

Chapter 18:   USING THE CURRICULUM GUIDE

*THE COMPREHENSIVE
SCHOOL HEALTH EDUCATION
CURRICULUM GUIDE*

*THE SCOPE AND SEQUENCE
CHART*

Figure 18-1

Using *The Comprehensive School Health Education Curriculum Guide*

A curriculum committee can use *The Comprehensive School Health Education Curriculum Guide* to implement a successful and innovative program.

Chapter 18

USING THE CURRICULUM GUIDE

The **comprehensive school health education curriculum** is an organized, sequential K–12 plan for teaching students the information and skills they need to become health literate, maintain and improve health, prevent disease, and reduce health-related risk behaviors. This chapter identifies the components needed for a successful curriculum and includes a sample of a model curriculum, *The Comprehensive School Health Education Curriculum Guide.*

Components in a Successful Comprehensive School Health Education Curriculum Guide

The authors of this teacher resource book have worked closely with thousands of school districts throughout the United States as well as in a myriad of foreign countries to produce curricula that emphasize individual responsibility. The authors have identified the essential components to be included in a comprehensive school health education curriculum guide whose purpose is to teach students the information and skills needed to become health literate, maintain and improve health, prevent diseases, and reduce health-related risk behaviors. The following curriculum guide, *The CSHE Curriculum Guide,* includes:

- The Goals and Philosophy
- *The Responsible Decision-Making Model*
- *The Model for Using Resistance Skills*
- *Totally Awesome Teaching Strategies*™
- Children's Literature
- Curriculum Infusion
- Health Literacy
- Inclusion of Students With Special Needs
- Multicultural Infusion
- Family Involvement
- Evaluation
- *The Scope and Sequence Chart* with:
  - The National Health Education Standards
  - The Performance Indicators
  - Health Content Areas and Life Skills
  - Correlation to *Totally Awesome Teaching Strategies*™

The sample of a model curriculum guide, *The Comprehensive School Health Curriculum Guide,* follows. This *Guide* illustrates the importance of each of the aforementioned components.

Meeks Heit
Publishing Company

The Comprehensive School Health Education Curriculum Guide

The Goals and Philosophy...

The Comprehensive School Health Education Curriculum is an organized, sequential K–12 plan for teaching students the information and skills they need to become health literate, maintain and improve health, prevent disease, and reduce health-related risk behaviors. *The Umbrella of Comprehensive School Health Education* illustrates concepts which describe the purpose of the curriculum. *The Umbrella of Comprehensive School Health Education* protects young people from the six categories of risk behaviors identified by The Centers for Disease Control and Prevention:

1. Behaviors that result in unintentional and unintentional injuries
2. Tobacco use
3. Alcohol and other drug use
4. Sexual behaviors that result in HIV infection, other STDs, and unintended pregnancy
5. Dietary patterns that contribute to disease
6. Insufficient physical activity

At the top of the umbrella are three stripes, each of which illustrates an important component from which the comprehensive school health education curriculum is derived: Health Literacy, The National Health Education Standards, and The Performance Indicators. These might be defined as follows (The Joint Committee on Health Education Standards, 1995):

- **Health Literacy** is competence in critical thinking and problem solving, responsible and productive citizenship, self-directed learning, and effective communication. When young people are health literate, they possess skills that protect them from the six categories of risk behaviors.

- **The National Health Education Standards** are standards that specify what students should know and be able to do. There are seven health education standards. Young people are protected from the six categories of risk behavior when they:
  1. comprehend health promotion and disease prevention concepts;
  2. demonstrate the ability to access valid health information and appropriate health products and services;
  3. demonstrate the ability to practice health-enhancing behaviors and reduce health risks;
  4. analyze the impact of culture, media, technology, and other influences on health;
  5. demonstrate the ability to use effective interpersonal communication skills which enhance health;
  6. demonstrate the ability to use goal-setting and decision-making skills which enhance health;
  7. demonstrate the ability to advocate for personal, family, and community health.

- **The Performance Indicators** are a series of specific concepts and skills students should know and be able to do in order to achieve each of the broader National Health Education Standards. For each of the health education standards, there are several performance indicators. The performance indicators designate what students should know and be able to do by grades four, eight, and eleven. Young people need to exposed to a curriculum that helps them master these performance indicators at age-appropriate intervals.

The umbrella that protects young people is divided into ten sections. These ten sections represent content areas for which young people need to gain health knowledge and life skills. **Health knowledge** consists of information that is needed to become health literate, maintain and improve health, prevent disease, and reduce health-related risk behaviors. **Life skills** are actions that promote health literacy, maintain and improve health, prevent disease, and reduce health-related risk behaviors. The ten content areas for which students need to gain health knowledge and life skills are:

1. Mental and Emotional Health
2. Family Living
3. Growth and Development
4. Nutrition
5. Personal Health
6. Alcohol, Tobacco, and Other Drugs
7. Communicable and Chronic Diseases
8. Injury Prevention and Safety
9. Consumer and Community Health
10. Environmental Health

Students who participate in *The Comprehensive School Health Education Curriculum* and who master the performance indicators for The National Health Education Standards are enthusiastic, radiant, and energetic. They are confident and empowered because they:

- have health knowledge,
- choose wellness behaviors,
- choose to be in healthful situations,
- choose to have healthful relationships,
- make responsible decisions,
- use resistance skills when appropriate,
- possess protective factors,
- are resilient,
- are health literate.

698

The Umbrella of Comprehensive School Health Education

The comprehensive school health education curriculum is an organized, sequential K–12 plan for teaching students the information and skills they need to become health literate, maintain and improve health, prevent disease, and reduce health-related risk behaviors.

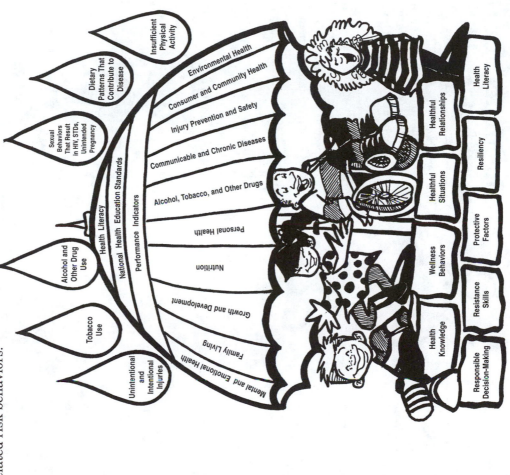

The Model For Using Resistance Skills . . .

The Comprehensive School Health Education Curriculum helps students learn to resist harmful peer pressure. *The Model for Using Resistance Skills* or "say NO" skills is taught at every grade level. Students practice the model as they:

* use assertive behavior,
* avoid saying "NO, thank you" to people who pressure them to behave in harmful, unsafe, illegal, or disrespectful ways (there is no need for them to thank people who want them to behave this way),
* use nonverbal behavior that matches verbal behavior,
* influence others to choose responsible behavior,
* avoid being in situations in which there will be pressure to make harmful decisions,
* resist pressure to engage in illegal behavior.

A Responsible Decision-Making Model . . . .

The Comprehensive School Health Education Curriculum helps students learn to make responsible decisions. *The Responsible Decision-Making Model* is taught at every grade level. The steps in the model are as follows:

* Clearly describe the situation.
* List possible actions that can be taken.
* Share the list of possible actions with a responsible adult such as someone who protects community laws and demonstrates character.
* Carefully evaluate each possible action using six criteria. A responsible action is one that is:
  1. healthful,
  2. safe,
  3. legal,
  4. respectful of self and others,
  5. consistent with guidelines of responsible adults such as parents and guardians,
  6. demonstrates character.
* Decide which action is responsible and most appropriate.
* Act in a responsible way and evaluate the results.

700

Totally Awesome Teaching Strategies™ . . .

Totally Awesome Teaching Strategies™ are creative teaching strategies designed to help students become health literate and master the performance indicators established for each of The National Health Education Standards.

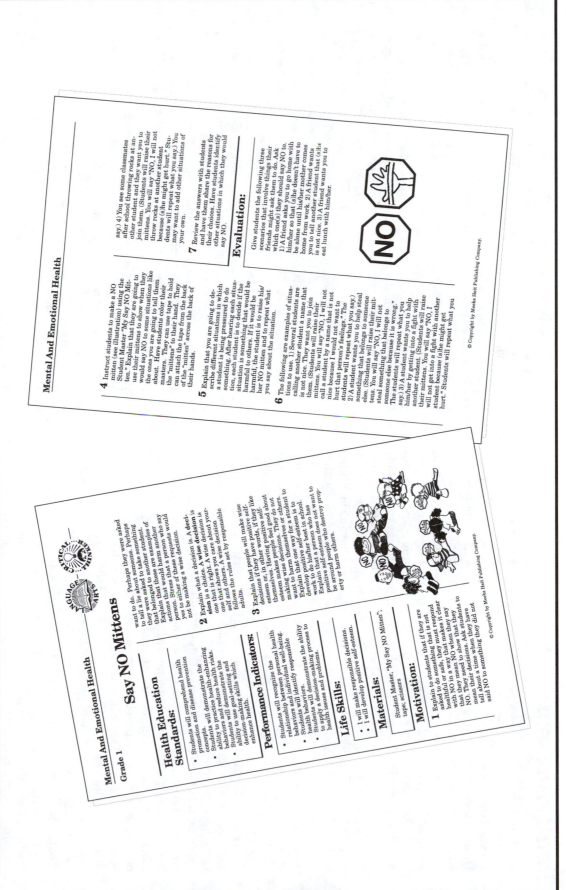

Mental And Emotional Health

Grade 1

Say NO Mittens

Health Education Standards:

- Students will comprehend health promotion and disease prevention concepts.
- Students will demonstrate the ability to practice health-enhancing behaviors and reduce health risks.
- Students will demonstrate and ability to use goal-setting and decision-making skills which enhance health.

Performance Indicators:

- Students will recognize the relationship between personal health behaviors and individual responsible health behaviors.
- Students will demonstrate the ability to apply a decision-making process in to health issues and problems.

Life Skills:

- I will make responsible decisions.
- I will develop positive self-esteem.

Materials:

Student Master, "My Say NO Mitten"; tape; scissors

Motivation:

1 Explain to students that if they are asked to do something that is not healthful or safe, they must respond with NO in a way that makes it clear that they mean NO when they say NO. They need to show that they NO. Ask students to tell about a time when they did not said NO to something they did not want to. Perhaps they were asked to tell a lie about someone. Perhaps they were asked to take something that belonged to another person. Explain that would harm who say actions Stress that a requests would yes or other of these decision.

2 Explain what a decision is. **A decision** is a choice. A **wise decision** is one that is right. A care about your one that shows you a wise decision self and others. A wise decision follows the rules set by responsible adults.

3 Explain that people will make positive self-esteem if they have positive self-esteem or others, in other words, self-esteem makes people feel good about themselves. They do not esteem wise decisions or others making wise decisions for a student is want to harm themselves or others to Explain positive self-esteem in school. develop positive for his/her best who has work to that a person does not want to positive self-esteem who destroy prop-be around people erty or harm others.

© Copyright by Meeks Heit Publishing Company.

Mental And Emotional Health

4 Instruct students to make a NO mitten (see illustration) using the Student Master "My Say NO Mitten." Explain that they are going to use their mittens to show when they would say NO to some situations like the ones you are going to tell them about. Have students color their masters. They can use tape to hold the "mittens" to their hand. They can attach the tape from the back of the "mitten" across the back of their hands.

5 Explain that you are going to describe different situations in which a student is being pressured to do something, is harmful to others. After hearing each situation, each student is to decide if the situation is something that would be harmful to others. If it would be her NO mitten and to raise his/her NO mitten and to repeat what you say about the situation.

6 The following are examples of situations to use. 1) Several students are calling another student a name that is not nice. They want you to join them. (Students will raise their mittens. You will say "NO, I will not call a student by a name because I would not want to hurt that person's feelings. "The 2) A student wants you to help steal something that belongs to someone else. (Students will raise their mittens. You will say "NO, I will not steal something that belongs to someone else because it is wrong." The students will repeat what you say.) 3) A student wants you to help another student by getting into a fight with another student. (Students will raise their mittens. You will say "NO, I will not get into a fight with another student because (s)he might get hurt." Students will repeat what you

say.) 4) You see some classmates after school throwing rocks at another student and they want you to join them. (Students will raise their mittens. You will say "NO, I will not throw rocks at another student because (s)he might get hurt." Students will repeat what you say.) You may want to add other situations of your own.

7 Review the answers with students and have them share the reasons for their choices. Have students identify other situations in which they would say NO.

Evaluation:

Give students the following three scenarios that involve things their friends might ask them to do. Ask which one(s) they should say NO to. 1) A friend asks you to go home with him/her so that (s)he doesn't have to be alone until his/her mother comes home from work. 2) A friend wants you to tell another student that (s)he is not nice. 3) A friend wants you to eat lunch with him/her.

© Copyright by Meeks Heit Publishing Company.

Totally Awesome
Teaching Strategies™ contain..

- **Clever Title.** A clever title is set in boldfaced type in the center of the page.

- **Designated Content Area.** The content area for which the teaching strategy is designed appears in the upper left-hand corner: Mental and Emotional Health; Family Living; Growth and Development; Nutrition; Personal Health; Alcohol, Tobacco, and Other Drugs; Communicable and Chronic Diseases; Injury Prevention and Safety; Consumer and Community Health; and Environmental Health. A teaching strategy may include content from more than one content area. The additional content area(s) for which the teaching strategy is appropriate are identified in parenthesis next to the life skill(s). The six categories of risk behaviors identified by The Centers for Disease Control and Prevention are included within one or more of the content areas: behaviors that result in unintentional and intentional injuries; tobacco use; alcohol and other drug use; sexual behaviors that result in HIV infection, other STDs, and unintended pregnancies; dietary patterns that contribute to disease; insufficient physical activity.

- **Designated Grade Level.** The grade level for which the teaching strategy is appropriate appears directly beneath the designated content area in the upper left-hand corner.

- **Infusion into Curriculum Areas Other Than Health.** Infusion is the integration of a subject area into another area(s) of the curriculum. Teaching strategies are designed to be infused into several curriculum areas other than health education: art studies, foreign language, home economics, language arts, physical education, math studies, music studies, science studies, social studies, and visual and performing arts. The curriculum area into which the teaching strategy is designed to be infused is designated by a symbol that appears to the right of the clever title that is set in boldfaced type.

- **Health Literacy.** Health literacy is competence in critical thinking and problem solving, responsible and productive citizenship, self-directed learning, and effective communication. (The Joint Committee on Health Education Standards, 1995). The teaching strategies are designed to promote competency in health literacy. Four symbols are used to describe the health literate individual: critical thinker, responsible citizen, self-directed learner, and effective communicator. The symbol designating one of the four components of health literacy appears to the right of the symbol designating curriculum infusion.

- **Health Education Standard(s).** Health education standards are standards that specify what students should know and be able to do. They involve the knowledge and skills essential to the development of health literacy (The Joint Committee on Health Education Standards, 1995). The health education standard(s) are listed under this boldfaced subheading.

- **Performance Indicator(s).** Performance indicators are the specific concepts and skills students should know and be able to do in order to achieve each of the broader health education standards (The Joint Committee on Health Education Standards, 1995). The performance indicator(s) for the teaching strategy are listed under this boldfaced subheading.

- **Life Skill(s).** Life skills are actions that promote health literacy, maintain and improve health, prevent disease, and reduce health-related risk behaviors. The life skills for the primary content area are listed first under this boldfaced subheading. Life skills for other content areas covered in the teaching strategy appear in italics and are identified in parenthesis.

- **Materials.** The materials are items that are needed to do the teaching strategy. The materials used in the teaching strategies are readily available and inexpensive. They are listed under this boldfaced subheading.

- **Motivation.** The motivation is the step-by-step directions to follow when doing the teaching strategy. The motivation includes a creative way to teach the health knowledge and skills students need to master the health education standards, performance indicators, and life skills. The motivation is listed under this boldfaced subheading.

- **Evaluation.** The evaluation is the means of measuring the students' mastery of the health education standards, the performance indicators, and the life skills. The evaluation is listed under this boldfaced subheading.

- **Multicultural Infusion.** Multicultural infusion is the adaptation of the teaching strategy to include ideas that promote an awareness and appreciation of the culture and background of different people. Suggestions for adapting the teaching strategy to incorporate learning about people of varied cultures and backgrounds are included under this boldfaced subheading.

- **Inclusion.** Inclusion is the adaptation of the teaching strategy to assist and include students with special learning challenges and may include enrichment suggestions for the gifted and reteaching ideas for students who are learning disabled. Suggestions for adapting the teaching strategy to assist students with special learning challenges are included under this boldfaced subheading.

702

Health Literacy . . .

A focus for educational reform has been the need for health literacy. A **health literate individual** is a critical thinker and problem solver, a responsible and productive citizen, a self-directed learner, and an effective communicator (The Joint Committee on Health Education, 1995). *The Totally Awesome Teaching Strategies*™ are designed to promote health literacy.

A **critical thinker** is an individual who is able to examine personal, national, and international health problems and formulate ways to solve problems. This individual gathers current, credible, and applicable information from a variety of sources and assesses this information before making health-related decisions.

A **responsible citizen** is an individual who feels obligated to keep his/her community healthful, safe, and secure. This individual avoids behaviors that threaten the personal health, safety, and security of self and others.

The **self-directed learner** is an individual who gathers and uses health information throughout life as the disease prevention knowledge base changes. This individual embraces learning from others and continues to do so.

The **effective communicator** is an individual who is able to express and convey his/her knowledge, beliefs, and ideas through oral, written, artistic, graphic, and technological media. This individual is able to demonstrate empathy and respect for others.

Children's Literature . . .

Several of the *Totally Awesome Teaching Strategies*™ contain children's literature. Students learn health knowledge and skills as they examine short stories and poems. Children's literature is another medium through which students develop health literacy.

Curriculum Infusion . . .

Skills needed to develop health literacy and to master the performance indicators for The National Health Education Standards are appropriately taught within the health education curriculum. However, today the trend in education is to infuse learning into many curriculum areas. Thus, the *Totally Awesome Teaching Strategies*™ are designed so that they might be infused into the following curriculum areas other than health education: art studies, foreign language, home economics, language arts, physical education, math studies, music studies, science studies, social studies, and visual and performing arts.

Family Involvement . . .

The family can be involved in *The Comprehensive School Health Education Curriculum*. A Family Letter can be sent home to familiarize the family with the life skills that will be covered. The *Totally Awesome Teaching Strategies*™ contain suggestions for family involvement. Family members can participate in health behavior contracts and read and study health knowledge together. The family plays a significant role in the degree of health literacy that is achieved.

Evaluation . . .

The Comprehensive School Health Education Curriculum can be evaluated in several ways. The *Totally Awesome Teaching Strategies*™ contain suggestions for measuring students' mastery of the health education standards, the performance indicators, and the life skills. Surveys might be developed and approved by the school board to gather information about students' behaviors. Portfolios and health behavior contracts might be used. Teachers might observe their students to determine attitudes and behaviors. Families might provide feedback as to attitudes and behaviors that are practiced and observed at home.

Inclusion of Students With Special Needs . . .

A current trend in education is to include students with special learning challenges as well as students who are gifted in the regular classroom. Inclusion is believed to promote health literacy as it gives students an opportunity to work together, socialize, and communicate. In order for inclusion to be effective, teachers may need to make adaptations to teaching strategies. These adaptations facilitate learning and bolster self-esteem in all students. Suggestions for inclusion accompany many teaching strategies.

Multicultural Infusion . . .

A current trend in education is to include opportunities for students to gain awareness and appreciation of the culture and background of different people. Multicultural infusion promotes health literacy by helping students recognize ways in which the strengths of people who are different can be blended to create synergy.

704

Meeks Heit
Publishing Company

The Scope and Sequence Chart

The Scope And Sequence Chart . . .

The Scope and Sequence Chart serves as a blueprint for *The Comprehensive School Health Education Curriculum* which is designed to help young people develop four kinds of health literacy: critical thinking and problem solving, responsible and productive citizenship, self-directed learning, and effective communication. *The Scope and Sequence Chart* is designed in five columns:

1. **The National Health Education Standards** are identified in the first column of the chart. The seven health education standards identify what students should know and be able to do.

2. The **performance indicators** that will be used to assess student mastery of each of the broader National Health Education Standards at grades four, eight, and eleven are identified in the next three columns of the chart.

3. The **content areas** appear as headings for the chart. There are 10 content areas. There are ten **life skills** for each of the content areas and these appear in the fifth column of the chart. These life skills are identified for the K–12 curriculum. It is important to note that some of the life skills are not appropriate at the earlier grade levels. Notice that the health education standards and the performance indicators appear to the left of the life skills for each of the content areas. This design is used in order to illustrate appropriate life skills from the content areas that can be taught to meet the health education standards and the performance indicators. Each of the six categories of risk behaviors are included in one or more of the life skills for the ten content areas and therefore are correlated to the health education standards and the performance indicators. Under each of the life skills identified for the ten content areas is a list of health topics.

706

MENTAL AND EMOTIONAL HEALTH

Health Education Standards	Performance Indicators	Performance Indicators	Performance Indicators	Life Skills And Health Topics
Students will:	**After health instruction in grades K-4, students will:**	**After health instruction in grades 5-8, students will:**	**After health instruction in grades 9-11, students will:**	**I will:**

1. comprehend concepts related to health promotion and disease prevention.	• describe relationships between personal health behaviors and individual well-being.
	
	• identify indicators of mental, emotional, social, and physical health during childhood.
		• explain the relationship between positive health behaviors and the prevention of injury, illness, disease, and premature death.
		
		• describe the interrelationship of mental, emotional, social, and physical health during adolescence.
			• analyze how behavior can impact health maintenance and disease prevention.	1. **strive to have optimal health.**
				  * health and wellness
				  * mental and emotional health
				  * family and social health
				  * physical health
				  * The Wellness Scale
				  * resistance skills
				  * self-esteem
				  * protective factors
				  * risk factors
				  * health status
				  * resiliency
				  * health literacy

3. demonstrate the ability to practice health-enhancing behaviors and reduce health risks.	• identify personal health needs.	• analyze a personal health assessment to determine health strengths and risks.	• evaluate a personal health assessment to determine strategies for health enhancement and risk reduction.	
4. analyze the influence of culture, media, technology, and other factors on health.			• analyze how cultural diversity enriches and challenges health behaviors.	
6. demonstrate the ability to use goal-setting and decision-making skills that enhance health.	• predict outcomes of positive health decisions.		• formulate an effective plan for lifelong health.	

707

MENTAL AND EMOTIONAL HEALTH

Health Education Standards	Performance Indicators	Performance Indicators	Performance Indicators	Life Skills And Health Topics
Students will:	**After health instruction in grades K-4, students will:**	**After health instruction in grades 5-8, students will:**	**After health instruction in grades 9-11, students will:**	**I will:**
1. comprehend concepts related to health promotion and disease prevention.			• analyze how behavior can impact health maintenance and disease prevention.	2. **gain health knowledge.** * ten areas of health * healthful behaviors and situations * risk behaviors and situations * health behavior inventories
3. demonstrate the ability to practice health-enhancing behaviors and reduce health risks.			• analyze the role of individual responsibility for enhancing health.	
4. analyze the influence of culture, media, technology, and other factors on health.	• explain how information from school and family influences health.			
6. demonstrate the ability to use goal-setting and decision-making skills that enhance health.		• develop a plan that addresses personal strengths, needs, and health risks.		

708

Health Education Standards	Performance Indicators	Performance Indicators	Performance Indicators	Life Skills And Health Topics
Students will:	**After health instruction in grades K-4, students will:**	**After health instruction in grades 5-8, students will:**	**After health instruction in grades 9-11, students will:**	**I will:**
1. comprehend concepts related to health promotion and disease prevention.	• describe relationships between personal health behaviors and individual well-being.			**3. make responsible decisions.** * proactive decision-making * reactive decision-making * inactive decision-making * The Responsible Decision-Making Model
3. demonstrate the ability to practice health-enhancing behaviors and reduce health risks.	• identify responsible health behaviors.	• explain the importance of assuming responsibility for personal health behaviors.		
6. demonstrate the ability to use goal-setting and decision-making skills that enhance health.	• demonstrate the ability to apply a decision-making process to health issues and problems.	• demonstrate the ability to apply a decision making process to health issues and problems individually and collaboratively.	• demonstrate the ability to utilize various strategies when making decisions related to health needs and risks of young adults.	
		• analyze how health-related decisions are influenced by individuals, family, and community values.	• analyze health concerns that require collaborative decision making.	
		• predict how decisions regarding health behaviors have consequences for self and others.	• predict immediate and long term impact of health decisions on the individual, family, and community.	
4. analyze the influence of culture, media, technology, and other factors on health.		• analyze how information from peers influences health.		**4. use resistance skills when appropriate.** * peer pressure * Model for Using Resistance Skills * delaying gratification
5. demonstrate the ability to use interpersonal communication skills to enhance health.	• demonstrate refusal skills to enhance health.	• demonstrate refusal and negotiation skills to enhance health.	• demonstrate refusal, negotiation, and collaboration skills to avoid potentially harmful situations.	

Health Education Standards	Performance Indicators	Performance Indicators	Performance Indicators	Life Skills And Health Topics
Students will:	**After health instruction in grades K-4, students will:**	**After health instruction in grades 5-8, students will:**	**After health instruction in grades 9-11, students will:**	**I will:**
3. demonstrate the ability to practice health-enhancing behaviors and reduce health risks.	• demonstrate strategies to improve or maintain personal health.	• demonstrate strategies to improve or maintain personal and family health.	• develop strategies to improve or maintain personal, family, and community health.	**5. practice life skills for health.** * life skills * self-responsibility * self-discipline * health behavior contracts
4. analyze the influence of culture, media, technology, and other factors on health.	• describe how culture influences personal health behaviors.	• describe the influence of cultural beliefs on health behaviors and the use of health services.		
6. demonstrate the ability to use goal-setting and decision-making skills that enhance health.	• set a personal health goal and track progress toward its achievement.	• apply strategies and skills needed to attain personal health goals. • describe how personal health goals are influenced by changing information, abilities, priorities, and responsibilities.	• implement a plan for attaining a personal health goal. • evaluate progress toward achieving personal health goals.	
3. demonstrate the ability to practice health-enhancing behaviors and reduce health risks.	• identify responsible health behaviors. • demonstrate strategies to improve or maintain personal health.	• explain the importance of assuming responsibility for personal health behaviors. • demonstrate strategies to improve or maintain personal and family health.	• analyze the role of individual responsibility for enhancing health. • develop strategies to improve or maintain personal, family, and community health.	**6. choose behaviors to promote a healthy mind.** * mental alertness * mental disorders * addictive behavior * kinds of addictions * treatment and recovery
3. demonstrate the ability to practice health-enhancing behaviors and reduce health risks.	• identify personal health needs. • demonstrate strategies to improve or maintain personal health.	• demonstrate strategies to improve or maintain personal and family health.	• develop strategies to improve or maintain personal, family, and community health.	**7. develop positive self-esteem.** * self-esteem * self-centered behavior * self-destructive behavior * self-loving behavior * responsibility and self-esteem

710

MENTAL AND EMOTIONAL HEALTH

Health Education Standards	Performance Indicators	Performance Indicators	Performance Indicators	Life Skills And Health Topics
Students will:	**After health instruction in grades K-4, students will:**	**After health instruction in grades 5-8, students will:**	**After health instruction in grades 9-11, students will:**	**I will:**
5. demonstrate the ability to use interpersonal communication skills to enhance health.	• distinguish between verbal and nonverbal communication. • demonstrate ways to communicate care, consideration, and respect of self and others. • demonstrate attentive listening skills to build and maintain healthy relationships.	• demonstrate effective verbal and nonverbal communication skills to enhance health. • demonstrate ways to communicate care, consideration, and respect of self and others. • demonstrate communication skills to build and maintain healthy relationships.	• demonstrate skills for communicating effectively with family, peers, and others. • demonstrate healthy ways to express needs, wants, and feelings. • demonstrate ways to communicate care, consideration, and respect of self and others.	**8. communicate with others in healthful ways.** * communication * I-messages and you-messages * active listening * nonverbal behavior * passive behavior * aggressive behavior * assertive behavior
7. demonstrate the ability to advocate for personal, family, and community health.		• identify barriers to effective communication of information, ideas, feelings, and opinions about health issues.	• utilize strategies to overcome barriers when communicating information, ideas, feelings, and opinions about health issues. • demonstrate the ability to adapt health messages and communication techniques to the characteristics of a particular audience.	
5. demonstrate the ability to use interpersonal communication skills to enhance health.	• demonstrate healthy ways to express needs, wants, and feelings. • differentiate between negative and positive behaviors used in conflict situations.	• demonstrate healthy ways to express needs, wants, and feelings. • analyze the possible causes of conflict among youth in schools and communities.	• demonstrate healthy ways to express needs, wants, and feelings. • analyze the possible causes of conflict in schools, families, and communities.	**9. express feelings in healthful ways.** * feelings * sharing positive feelings * life crises * sharing anger, disappointment and grief * anger management skills * feelings and resiliency

MENTAL AND EMOTIONAL HEALTH

Health Education Standards	Performance Indicators	Performance Indicators	Performance Indicators	Life Skills And Health Topics
Students will:	**After health instruction in grades K-4, students will:**	**After health instruction in grades 5-8, students will:**	**After health instruction in grades 9-11, students will:**	**I will:**
1. comprehend concepts related to health promotion and disease prevention. 3. demonstrate the ability to practice health-enhancing behaviors and reduce health risks.	• identify common health problems of children. • apply skills to manage stress.	• describe ways to reduce risks related to adolescent health problems. • demonstrate strategies to manage stress.	• evaluate strategies to manage stress.	**10. practice stress management and suicide prevention skills.** * stress management * eustress and distress * stress response * suicide prevention * signs of suicide

712

FAMILY LIVING

Health Education Standards	Performance Indicators	Performance Indicators	Performance Indicators	Life Skills And Health Topics
Students will:	After health instruction in grades K-4, students will:	After health instruction in grades 5-8, students will:	After health instruction in grades 9-11, students will:	I will:
1. comprehend concepts related to health promotion and disease prevention.	• describe how the family influences personal health.	• describe how family and peers influence the health of adolescents.	• analyze how the family, peers, and community influence the health of individuals.	1. develop relationship skills. * benefits of relationships * using manners * asking for help * giving and following instructions * expressing affection * expressing and responding to a complaint * dealing with rejection * dealing with stressful events * dealing with shyness * responding to the feelings of others * dealing with fear * social competence * belonging versus alienation
5. demonstrate the ability to use interpersonal communication skills to enhance health.	• describe characteristics needed to be a responsible friend and family member. • demonstrate ways to communicate care, consideration, and respect of self and others.	• describe how the behavior of family and peers affects interpersonal communication. • demonstrate ways to communicate care, consideration, and respect of self and others.	• demonstrate skills for communicating effectively with family, peers, and others. • analyze how interpersonal communication affects relationships. • demonstrate ways to communicate care, consideration, and respect of self and others.	
6. demonstrate the ability to use goal-setting and decision-making skills that enhance health.	• explain when to ask for assistance when making health-related decisions and setting health goals.			
7. demonstrate the ability to advocate for personal, family, and community health.	• demonstrate the ability to influence and support others in making positive health choices.	• demonstrate the ability to influence and support others in making positive health choices.	• demonstrate the ability to influence and support others in making positive health choices.	
5. demonstrate the ability to use interpersonal communication skills to enhance health.	• differentiate between negative and positive behaviors used in conflict situations. • demonstrate nonviolent strategies to resolve conflicts.	• analyze the possible causes of conflict among youth in schools and communities. • demonstrate strategies to manage conflict in healthy ways.	• analyze the possible causes of conflict in schools, families, and communities. • demonstrate strategies used to prevent conflict.	2. avoid discrimination. * discriminatory behavior * prejudice * ageism, sexism, racism, and heterosexism * hate crimes * hidden anger * avoiding discrimination

Health Education Standards	Performance Indicators	Performance Indicators	Performance Indicators	Life Skills And Health Topics
Students will:	**After health instruction in grades K-4, students will:**	**After health instruction in grades 5-8, students will:**	**After health instruction in grades 9-11, students will:**	**I will:**
3. demonstrate the ability to practice health-enhancing behaviors and reduce health risks.	• demonstrate ways to avoid and reduce threatening situations.	• demonstrate ways to avoid and reduce threatening situations.	• demonstrate ways to avoid and reduce threatening situations.	**3. practice conflict resolution skills.** * sources of conflict * intrapersonal conflict * interpersonal conflict * intragroup conflict * intergroup conflict * conflict response styles * conflict avoidance * conflict confrontation * conflict resolution * risks associated with conflict * conflict resolution skills * peer mediation
5. demonstrate the ability to use interpersonal communication skills to enhance health.	• differentiate between negative and positive behaviors used in conflict situations. • demonstrate nonviolent strategies to resolve conflicts.	• analyze the possible causes of conflict among youth in schools and communities. • demonstrate strategies to manage conflict in healthy ways.	• demonstrate strategies for solving interpersonal conflicts without harming self or others. • analyze the possible causes of conflict in schools, families, and communities. • demonstrate strategies used to prevent conflict.	
1. comprehend concepts related to health promotion and disease prevention.	• describe how the family influences personal health	• describe how family and peers influence the health of adolescents.	• analyze how the family, peers, and community influence the health of individuals.	**4. strive for healthful family relationships.** * family relationships * family continuum * healthful family relationships * dysfunctional family relationships
3. demonstrate the ability to practice health-enhancing behaviors and reduce health risks.		• demonstrate strategies to improve or maintain personal and family health.	• develop strategies to improve or maintain personal, family, and community health.	
5. demonstrate the ability to use interpersonal communication skills to enhance health.	• describe characteristics needed to be a responsible friend and family member.	• describe how the behavior of family and peers affects interpersonal communication.	• demonstrate skills for communicating effectively with family, peers, and others. • analyze how interpersonal communication affects relationships.	

FAMILY LIVING

Health Education Standards	Performance Indicators	Performance Indicators	Performance Indicators	Life Skills And Health Topics
Students will:	After health instruction in grades K-4, students will:	After health instruction in grades 5-8, students will:	After health instruction in grades 9-11, students will:	I will:
1. comprehend concepts related to health promotion and disease prevention.	• describe how the family influences personal health.	• describe how family and peers influence the health of adolescents.	• analyze how the family, peers, and community influence the health of individuals.	5. make healthful adjustments to family changes. * death * separation * divorce * parental dating * remarriage * stepfamilies * new baby in family
5. demonstrate the ability to use interpersonal communication skills to enhance health.	• demonstrate healthy ways to express needs, wants, and feelings.	• demonstrate healthy ways to express needs, wants, and feelings.		
4. analyze the influence of culture, media, technology, and other factors on health.		• analyze how information from peers influences health.		6. form healthful and responsible friendships. * characteristics of responsible friends * making friends * making choices with friends * peer pressure * ending friendships
5. demonstrate the ability to use interpersonal communication skills to enhance health.	• describe characteristics needed to be a responsible friend and family member.	• describe how the behavior of family and peers affects interpersonal communication.	• demonstrate skills for communicating effectively with family, peers, and others.	
			• analyze how interpersonal communication affects relationships.	
7. demonstrate the ability to advocate for personal, family, and community health.	• demonstrate the ability to influence and support others in making positive health choices.	• demonstrate the ability to influence and support others in making positive health choices.	• demonstrate the ability to influence and support others in making positive health choices.	

715

Health Education Standards	Performance Indicators	Performance Indicators	Performance Indicators	Life Skills And Health Topics
Students will:	**After health instruction in grades K-4, students will:**	**After health instruction in grades 5-8, students will:**	**After health instruction in grades 9-11, students will:**	**I will:**
1. comprehend concepts related to health promotion and disease prevention. 3. demonstrate the ability to practice health-enhancing behaviors and reduce health risks. 5. demonstrate the ability to use interpersonal communication skills to enhance health.	• describe how the family influences personal health. • demonstrate ways to avoid and reduce threatening situations. • demonstrate refusal skills to enhance health.	• describe how family and peers influence the health of adolescents. • demonstrate ways to avoid and reduce threatening situations. • describe how the behavior of family and peers contributes to one's physical, mental, emotional, and social health. • demonstrate refusal and negotiation skills to enhance health.	• analyze how the family, peers, and community influence the health of individuals. • demonstrate strategies for solving interpersonal conflicts without harming self or others • demonstrate refusal, negotiation, and collaboration skills to avoid potentially harmful situations	**7. recognize harmful relationships.** * abusive, violent, and codependent relationships * being attracted to gangs * practicing self-protection strategies
1. comprehend concepts related to health promotion and disease prevention. 2. demonstrate the ability to access valid health information and health promoting products and services. 6. demonstrate the ability to use goal-setting and decision-making skills that enhance health.	• describe how the family influences personal health. • explain when to ask for assistance in making health-related decisions and setting health goals.	• describe how family and peers influence the health of adolescents. • demonstrate the ability to utilize resources from home, school, and community that provide valid health information.	• analyze how the family, peers, and community influence the health of individuals.	**8. identify resources to improve relationships and family communication.** * mentors * Twelve Step Programs * counseling

FAMILY LIVING

Health Education Standards	Performance Indicators	Performance Indicators	Performance Indicators	Life Skills And Health Topics
Students will:	**After health instruction in grades K-4, students will:**	**After health instruction in grades 5-8, students will:**	**After health instruction in grades 9-11, students will:**	**I will:**
1. comprehend concepts related to health promotion and disease prevention. 5. demonstrate the ability to use interpersonal communication skills to enhance health.	• describe how the family influences personal health. • describe characteristics needed to be a responsible friend and family member. • demonstrate ways to communicate care, consideration, and respect of self and others.	• describe how family and peers influence the health of adolescents. • demonstrate ways to communicate care, consideration, and respect of self and others.	• analyze how the family, peers, and community influence the health of individuals. • demonstrate ways to communicate care, consideration, and respect of self and others.	**9. develop skills to prepare for future relationship choices—dating, marriage, parenthood, and family life.** * benefits and risks of dating * evaluating dating relationships * choosing behavior that promotes abstinence * preparing for marriage * maintaining a healthful marriage * risks of adolescent marriage * being a responsible and caring parent * risks of adolescent parenthood
1. comprehend concepts related to health promotion and disease prevention. 3. demonstrate the ability to practice health-enhancing behaviors and reduce health risks.	• describe relationships between personal health behaviors and individual well-being. • compare behaviors that are safe to those that are risky or harmful.	• explain the relationship between positive health behaviors and the prevention of injury, illness, disease, and premature death. • distinguish between safe, risky, and harmful behaviors in relationships.	• analyze how behavior can impact health maintenance and disease prevention. • analyze the short-term and long-term consequences of safe, risky, and harmful behaviors.	**10. practice life skills to promote abstinence.** * benefits of abstinence * life skills to support abstinence

GROWTH AND DEVELOPMENT

Health Education Standards	Performance Indicators	Performance Indicators	Performance Indicators	Life Skills And Health Topics
Students will:	**After health instruction in grades K-4, students will:**	**After health instruction in grades 5-8, students will:**	**After health instruction in grades 9-11, students will:**	**I will:**
1. comprehend concepts related to health promotion and disease prevention. 6. demonstrate the ability to use goal-setting and decision-making skills that enhance health.	• describe the basic structure and functions of the human body systems. • set a personal health goal and track progress toward its achievement.	• explain how health is influenced by the interaction of body systems.	• explain the impact of personal health behaviors on the functioning of body systems.	1. **care for my body systems.** * skeletal and muscular systems * integumentary system * nervous system * digestive system * cardiovascular system * respiratory system * urinary system * endocrine system
1. comprehend concepts related to health promotion and disease prevention. 3. demonstrate the ability to practice health-enhancing behaviors and reduce health risks.	• describe the basic structure and functions of the human body systems. • identify personal health needs.	• explain how health is influenced by the interaction of body systems.	• explain the impact of personal health behaviors on the functioning of body systems.	2. **recognize how my body changes as I grow.** * endocrine system * hormones * puberty * secondary sex characteristics * female reproductive system * menstrual cycle * male reproductive system
3. demonstrate the ability to practice health-enhancing behaviors and reduce health risks. 6. demonstrate the ability to use goal-setting and decision-making skills that enhance health.	• identify personal health needs.	• describe how personal health goals are influenced by changing information, abilities, priorities, and responsibilities.	• evaluate a personal health assessment to determine strategies for health enhancement and risk reduction.	3. **accept my maleness/femaleness.** * being a male * being a female * sexual orientation

718

GROWTH AND DEVELOPMENT

Health Education Standards	Performance Indicators	Performance Indicators	Performance Indicators	Life Skills And Health Topics
Students will:	**After health instruction in grades K-4, students will:**	**After health instruction in grades 5-8, students will:**	**After health instruction in grades 9-11, students will:**	**I will:**
3. demonstrate the ability to practice health-enhancing behaviors and reduce health risks.	• identify personal health needs.		• evaluate a personal health assessment to determine strategies for health enhancement and risk reduction.	**4. accept my physical uniqueness.** * heredity * body types * body image
6. demonstrate the ability to use goal-setting and decision-making skills that enhance health.		• describe how personal health goals are influenced by changing information, abilities, priorities, and responsibilities.		
1. comprehend concepts related to health promotion and disease prevention.	• identify common health problems of children	• describe ways to reduce risks related to adolescent health problems.		**5. accept and develop my learning style.** * different ways of learning * learning disabilities * dyslexia * Attention Deficit Hyperactivity Disorder
3. demonstrate the ability to practice health-enhancing behaviors and reduce health risks	• identify personal health needs		• evaluate a personal health assessment to determine strategies for health enhancement and risk reduction.	
1. comprehend concepts related to health promotion and disease prevention.	• identify indicators of mental, emotional, social and physical health during childhood	• describe the interrelation-ship of mental, emotional, social, and physical health during adolescence.	• describe the interrelation-ships of mental, emotional, social, and physical health throughout adulthood.	**6. achieve developmental tasks for my age group.** * developmental tasks of adolescence
3. demonstrate the ability to practice health-enhancing behaviors and reduce health risks	• identify personal health needs			

GROWTH AND DEVELOPMENT

Health Education Standards	Performance Indicators	Performance Indicators	Performance Indicators	Life Skills And Health Topics
Students will:	After health instruction in grades K-4, students will:	After health instruction in grades 5-8, students will:	After health instruction in grades 9-11, students will:	I will:
1. comprehend concepts related to health promotion and disease prevention.	• describe relationships between personal health behaviors and individual well-being	• explain the relationship between positive health behaviors and the prevention of injury, illness, disease, and premature death.	• analyze the role of individual responsibility for enhancing health.	7. **learn about conception, pregnancy, and childbirth.** * conception * infertility * pregnancy * development of the fetus * prenatal care * birth defects * childbirth * stages of labor
3. demonstrate the ability to practice health-enhancing behaviors and reduce health risks	• identify responsible health behaviors • identify personal health needs	• explain the importance of assuming responsibility for personal health behaviors.		
1. comprehend concepts related to health promotion and disease prevention.	• identify indicators of mental, emotional, social, and physical health during childhood	• describe the interrelationship of mental, emotional, social, and physical health during adolescence.	• describe the interrelationships of mental, emotional, social, and physical health throughout adulthood.	8. **recognize the needs of people of different ages.** * stages of development * infancy * early childhood * preschool * elementary * adolescence * early adulthood * middle adulthood * late adulthood
3. demonstrate the ability to practice health-enhancing behaviors and reduce health risks	• identify personal health needs			
6. demonstrate the ability to use goal-setting and decision-making skills that enhance health.		• describe how personal health goals are influenced by changing information, abilities, priorities, and responsibilities.		

GROWTH AND DEVELOPMENT

Health Education Standards	Performance Indicators	Performance Indicators	Performance Indicators	Life Skills And Health Topics
Students will:	After health instruction in grades K-4, students will:	After health instruction in grades 5-8, students will:	After health instruction in grades 9-11, students will:	I will:
1. comprehend concepts related to health promotion and disease prevention.	• describe relationships between personal health behaviors and individual well-being.	• explain the relationship between positive health behaviors and the prevention of injury, illness, disease, and premature death. • explain how appropriate health care can prevent premature death and disability.	• describe the interrelationships of mental, emotional, social, and physical health throughout adulthood.	9. **practice behaviors that contribute to healthful aging.** * causes of aging * the aging process * concerns of the elderly * planning to age healthfully
3. demonstrate the ability to practice health-enhancing behaviors and reduce health risks.	• identify personal health needs.			
5. demonstrate the ability to use interpersonal communication skills to enhance health.	• demonstrate healthy ways to express needs, wants, and feelings. • demonstrate ways to communicate care, consideration and respect of self and others.	• demonstrate healthy ways to express needs, wants, and feelings. • demonstrate ways to communicate care, consideration, and respect of self and others.	• demonstrate ways to communicate care, consideration, and respect of self and others.	10. **share my feelings about death and dying.** * defining death * the stages of dying and death * decisions about death * grief and loss

Health Education Standards	Performance Indicators	Performance Indicators	Performance Indicators	Life Skills And Health Topics
Students will:	**After health instruction in grades K-4, students will:**	**After health instruction in grades 5-8, students will:**	**After health instruction in grades 9-11, students will:**	**I will:**
1. comprehend concepts related to health promotion and disease prevention. 3. demonstrate the ability to practice health-enhancing behaviors and reduce health risks.	• describe relationships between personal health behaviors and individual well-being. • identify responsible health behaviors.	• explain the relationship between positive health behaviors and the prevention of injury, illness, disease, and premature death. • explain the importance of assuming responsibility for personal health behaviors.	• analyze the role of individual responsibility for enhancing health.	**1. recognize foods that contain the six major nutrients.** * proteins * carbohydrates * fats * vitamins * minerals * water
1. comprehend concepts related to health promotion and disease prevention. 3. demonstrate the ability to practice health-enhancing behaviors and reduce health risks. 6. demonstrate the ability to use goal-setting and decision-making skills that enhance health. 7. demonstrate the ability to advocate for personal, family, and community health.	• describe relationships between personal health behaviors and individual well-being. • demonstrate strategies to improve or maintain personal health. • describe a variety of methods to convey accurate health information and ideas.	• explain the relationship between positive health behaviors and the prevention of injury, illness, disease, and premature death. • analyze various communication methods to accurately express health information and ideas.	• implement a plan for attaining a personal health goal. • evaluate the effectiveness of communication methods for accurately expressing health information and ideas.	**2. select the appropriate number of servings from The Food Guide Pyramid.** * The Food Guide Pyramid * the bread, cereal, rice, and pasta group * the vegetable group * the fruit group * the meat, poultry, fish, dry beans, eggs, and nuts group * the milk, yogurt, and cheese group * the fats, oils, and sweets group * alternative diets

Health Education Standards — Students will:	Performance Indicators — After health instruction in grades K-4, students will:	Performance Indicators — After health instruction in grades 5-8, students will:	Performance Indicators — After health instruction in grades 9-11, students will:	Life Skills And Health Topics — I will:
1. comprehend concepts related to health promotion and disease prevention.	• describe relationships between personal health behaviors and individual well-being.	• explain the relationship between positive health behaviors and the prevention of injury, illness, disease, and premature death.		3. **follow the dietary guidelines.** * dietary guidelines
3. demonstrate the ability to practice health-enhancing behaviors and reduce health risks.	• demonstrate strategies to improve or maintain personal health.	• demonstrate strategies to improve or maintain personal and family health.		
6. demonstrate the ability to use goal-setting and decision-making skills that enhance health.	• set a personal health goal and track progress toward its achievement.	• formulate a personal wellness plan which addresses adolescent needs and health risks.	• implement a plan for attaining a personal health goal. • formulate an effective plan for lifelong health.	
3. demonstrate the ability to practice health-enhancing behaviors and reduce health risks.	• demonstrate strategies to improve or maintain personal health.			4. **read food labels** * nutrition facts * serving size * percent daily value * vitamins and minerals * daily values * ingredients * terms used on food labels * special categories of foods
7. demonstrate the ability to advocate for personal, family, and community health.	• describe a variety of methods to convey accurate health information and ideas.	• analyze various communication methods to accurately express health information and ideas.	• evaluate the effectiveness of communication methods for accurately expressing health information and ideas.	
1. comprehend concepts related to health promotion and disease prevention.	• describe relationships between personal health behaviors and individual well-being.	• explain the relationship between positive health behaviors and the prevention of injury, illness, disease, and premature death.		5. **make food selections that reduce my risk of disease** * diet and heart disease * diet and cancer * diet and diabetes * diet and hypoglycemia
3. demonstrate the ability to practice health-enhancing behaviors and reduce health risks.	• demonstrate strategies to improve or maintain personal health.	• demonstrate strategies to improve or maintain personal and family health.	• develop strategies to improve or maintain personal, family, and community health.	

723

NUTRITION

Health Education Standards	Performance Indicators	Performance Indicators	Performance Indicators	Life Skills And Health Topics
Students will:	**After health instruction in grades K-4, students will:**	**After health instruction in grades 5-8, students will:**	**After health instruction in grades 9-11, students will:**	**I will:**
1. comprehend concepts related to health promotion and disease prevention.	• describe relationships between personal health behaviors and individual well-being.	• explain the relationship between positive health behaviors and the prevention of injury, illness, disease, and premature death.	• analyze how behavior can impact health maintenance and disease prevention.	**6. make healthful selections when dining out** * fast foods
3. demonstrate the ability to practice health-enhancing behaviors and reduce health risks.	• demonstrate strategies to improve or maintain personal health.			
2. demonstrate the ability to access valid health information and health promoting products and services.	• identify characteristics of valid health information and health promoting products, and services.	• analyze the validity of health information, products, and services.	• develop strategies to improve or maintain personal, family, and community health.	**7. consider food safety when making food selections** * pesticides and processing * additives * artificial sweeteners * fake fat * food irradiation * food-borne infections * food allergies
3. demonstrate the ability to practice health-enhancing behaviors and reduce health risks.	• demonstrate strategies to improve or maintain personal health.	• demonstrate strategies to improve or maintain personal and family health.		
1. comprehend concepts related to health promotion and disease prevention.	• describe relationships between personal health behaviors and individual well-being.	• explain the relationship between positive health behaviors and the prevention of injury, illness, disease, and premature death.		**8. maintain my desirable weight.** * desirable weight * Calories * hunger, satiety, and set point * gaining weight * losing weight * obesity
3. demonstrate the ability to practice health-enhancing behaviors and reduce health risks.	• demonstrate strategies to improve or maintain personal health.	• demonstrate strategies to improve or maintain personal and family health.	• develop strategies to improve or maintain personal, family, and community health.	

724

NUTRITION

Health Education Standards	Performance Indicators	Performance Indicators	Performance Indicators	Life Skills And Health Topics
Students will:	**After health instruction in grades K-4, students will:**	**After health instruction in grades 5-8, students will:**	**After health instruction in grades 9-11, students will:**	**I will:**
1. comprehend concepts related to health promotion and disease prevention.		• describe ways to reduce risks related to adolescent health problems.	• analyze how behavior can impact health maintenance and disease prevention.	**9. eat for healthful reasons.** * extreme dieting * binge eating * cravings * eating and emotions * alcoholism
3. demonstrate the ability to practice health-enhancing behaviors and reduce health risks.	• identify personal health needs • compare behaviors that are safe to those that are risky or harmful.			
1. comprehend concepts related to health promotion and disease prevention.		• describe ways to reduce risks related to adolescent health problems.	• analyze how behavior can impact health mainte-nance and disease prevention.	**10. recognize signs of eating disorders.** * body image * sexual identity * anorexia nervosa * bulimia
3. demonstrate the ability to practice health-enhancing behaviors and reduce health risks.	• compare behaviors that are safe to those that are risky or harmful.			

PERSONAL HEALTH

Health Education Standards	Performance Indicators	Performance Indicators	Performance Indicators	Life Skills And Health Topics
Students will:	**After health instruction in grades K-4, students will:**	**After health instruction in grades 5-8, students will:**	**After health instruction in grades 9-11, students will:**	**I will:**
1. comprehend concepts related to health promotion and disease prevention. 3. demonstrate the ability to practice health-enhancing behaviors and reduce health risks.	• describe relationships between personal health behaviors and individual well-being. • identify responsible health behaviors. • demonstrate strategies to improve or maintain personal health.	• explain the relationship between positive health behaviors and the prevention of injury, illness, disease, and premature death. • explain the importance of assuming responsibility for personal health behaviors. • demonstrate strategies to improve or maintain personal and family health.	• analyze the role of individual responsibility for enhancing health. • develop strategies to improve or maintain personal, family, and community health.	**1. be well-groomed.** * grooming * posture * skin care * body odor * acne * care for the hair * care for the feet
1. comprehend concepts related to health promotion and disease prevention. 3. demonstrate the ability to practice health-enhancing behaviors and reduce health risks.	• describe relationships between personal health behaviors and individual well-being. • identify common health problems of children. • identify health problems that should be detected and treated early. • identify personal health needs. • demonstrate strategies to improve or maintain personal health.	• explain the relationship between positive health behaviors and the prevention of injury, illness, disease, and premature death. • describe ways to reduce risks related to adolescent health problems. • demonstrate strategies to improve or maintain personal and family health.	• develop strategies to improve or maintain personal, family, and community health.	**2. care for my ears and eyes.** * eye care * refractive errors * eye conditions * eye injuries * hearing examinations * signs of hearing loss * hearing aids * injuries and hearing loss

726

PERSONAL HEALTH

Health Education Standards	Performance Indicators	Performance Indicators	Performance Indicators	Life Skills And Health Topics
Students will:	**After health instruction in grades K-4, students will:**	**After health instruction in grades 5-8, students will:**	**After health instruction in grades 9-11, students will:**	**I will:**
1. comprehend concepts related to health promotion and disease prevention.	• identify health problems that should be detected and treated early.	• explain how appropriate health care can prevent premature death and disability.		**3. have regular checkups.** * physical exams * screening tests * keeping a health history * childhood immunizations
2. demonstrate the ability to access valid health information and health-promoting products and services.	• demonstrate the ability to locate school and community health helpers.	• demonstrate the ability to locate health products and services.	• analyze situations requiring professional health services.	
3. demonstrate the ability to practice health-enhancing behaviors and reduce health risks.	• identify personal health needs. • demonstrate strategies to improve or maintain personal health.	• analyze a personal health assessment to determine health strengths and risks.	• evaluate a personal health assessment to determine strategies for health enhancement and risk reduction.	
1. comprehend concepts related to health promotion and disease prevention.	• describe relationships between personal health behaviors and individual well-being. • identify health problems that should be detected and treated early.	• explain the relationship between positive health behaviors and the prevention of injury, illness, disease, and premature death.		**4. follow a dental health plan.** * types of teeth * brushing and flossing * plaque formation * tartar buildup * periodontal disease * gingivitis * regular dental checkups * dental cleaning * dental x-rays * dental sealants * first aid procedures
3. demonstrate the ability to practice health-enhancing behaviors and reduce health risks.	• demonstrate strategies to improve or maintain personal health.	• demonstrate strategies to improve or maintain personal and family health.	• develop strategies to improve or maintain personal, family, and community health.	
4. analyze the influence of culture, media, technology, and other factors on health.	• describe ways technology can influence personal health.	• analyze the influence of technology on personal and family health.		

PERSONAL HEALTH

Health Education Standards	Performance Indicators	Performance Indicators	Performance Indicators	Life Skills And Health Topics
Students will:	**After health instruction in grades K-4, students will:**	**After health instruction in grades 5-8, students will:**	**After health instruction in grades 9-11, students will:**	**I will:**
1. comprehend concepts related to health promotion and disease prevention.	• describe relationships between personal health behaviors and individual well-being.	• explain the relationship between positive health behaviors and the prevention of injury, illness, disease, and premature death.		**5. obtain adequate rest and sleep.** * rest and sleep * REM * dreams * sleep needs * factors that make sleep easier * factors that keep people awake * ways to relax and rest
3. demonstrate the ability to practice health-enhancing behaviors and reduce health risks.	• identify personal health needs. • demonstrate strategies to improve or maintain personal health.	• demonstrate strategies to improve or maintain personal and family health.	• develop strategies to improve or maintain personal, family, and community health.	
1. comprehend concepts related to health promotion and disease prevention.	• describe relationships between personal health behaviors and individual well-being.	• explain the relationship between positive health behaviors and the prevention of injury, illness, disease, and premature death.		**6. participate in movement and exercise.** * benefits of physical fitness * participating in physical activity * aerobic exercise * anaerobic exercise * isokinetic exercise * isometric exercise * isotonic exercise
3. demonstrate the ability to practice health-enhancing behaviors and reduce health risks.	• demonstrate strategies to improve or maintain personal health.	• demonstrate strategies to improve or maintain personal and family health.	• develop strategies to improve or maintain personal, family, and community health.	
6. demonstrate the ability to use goal-setting and decision-making skills that enhance health.	• set a personal health goal and track progress toward its achievement.		• implement a plan for attaining a personal health goal. • formulate an effective plan for lifelong health.	

Health Education Standards	Performance Indicators	Performance Indicators	Performance Indicators	Life Skills And Health Topics
Students will:	**After health instruction in grades K-4, students will:**	**After health instruction in grades 5-8, students will:**	**After health instruction in grades 9-11, students will:**	**I will:**
3. demonstrate the ability to practice health-enhancing behaviors and reduce health risks.	• identify responsible health behaviors. • develop injury prevention and management strategies for personal health.	• develop injury prevention and management strategies for personal and family health.	• develop injury prevention and management strategies for personal, family, and community health.	7. **follow guidelines to prevent injuries during exercise.** * training principles * principle of warming up * principle of cooling down * principle of specificity * principle of of overload * principle of progression * principle of frequency * dehydration * cramping * heat exhaustion * exercising in cold weather * safety during exercise
3. demonstrate the ability to practice health-enhancing behaviors and reduce health risks.	• develop injury prevention and management strategies for personal health.	• develop injury prevention and management strategies for personal and family health.	• develop injury prevention and management strategies for personal, family, and community health.	8. **learn correct first aid procedures for exercise injuries.** * athlete's foot * blisters * bruises * joint injuries * muscle cramps * muscle strain * side aches * sprains * stress fractures

PERSONAL HEALTH

Health Education Standards	Performance Indicators	Performance Indicators	Performance Indicators	Life Skills And Health Topics
Students will:	**After health instruction in grades K-4, students will:**	**After health instruction in grades 5-8, students will:**	**After health instruction in grades 9-11, students will:**	**I will:**

1. comprehend concepts related to health promotion and disease prevention.	• describe relationships between personal health behaviors and individual well-being.	• explain the relationship between positive health behaviors and the prevention of injury, illness, disease, and premature death.		**9. achieve a desirable level of physical fitness.**
				* components of physical fitness
				  * muscular strength
				  * muscular endurance
				  * flexibility
				  * cardiovascular endurance
				  * healthful body composition
				* making a physical fitness plan

3. demonstrate the ability to practice health-enhancing behaviors and reduce health risks.	• identify personal health needs. • demonstrate strategies to improve or maintain personal health.	• demonstrate strategies to improve or maintain personal and family health.	• develop strategies to improve or maintain personal, family, and community health.	
6. demonstrate the ability to use goal-setting and decision-making skills that enhance health.			• evaluate progress toward achieving personal health goals.	
1. comprehend concepts related to health promotion and disease prevention.	• describe relationships between personal health behaviors and individual well-being.	• explain the relationship between positive health behaviors and the prevention of injury, illness, disease, and premature death.		**10. improve my skill-related fitness.** * power * agility * reaction time * speed * balance * coordination
3. demonstrate the ability to practice health-enhancing behaviors and reduce health risks.	• demonstrate strategies to improve or maintain personal health.	• demonstrate strategies to improve or maintain personal and family health.	• develop strategies to improve or maintain personal, family, and community health.	

730

ALCOHOL, TOBACCO, AND OTHER DRUGS

Health Education Standards	Performance Indicators	Performance Indicators	Performance Indicators	Life Skills And Health Topics
Students will:	**After health instruction in grades K-4, students will:**	**After health instruction in grades 5-8, students will:**	**After health instruction in grades 9-11, students will:**	**I will:**
1. comprehend concepts related to health promotion and disease prevention. 3. demonstrate the ability to practice health-enhancing behaviors and reduce health risks.	• describe relationships between personal health behaviors and individual well-being. • identify personal health needs.	• explain the relationship between positive health behaviors and the prevention of injury, illness, disease, and premature death.	• analyze the short-term and long-term consequences of safe, risky, and harmful behaviors.	**1. use over-the-counter and prescription drugs in responsible ways.** * drugs and medicines * how drugs enter the body * prescription drugs * generic drugs * over-the-counter drugs
1. comprehend concepts related to health promotion and disease prevention. 3. demonstrate the ability to practice health-enhancing behaviors and reduce health risks.	• compare behaviors that are safe to those that are risky or harmful.	• describe ways to reduce risks related to adolescent health problems.	• analyze the role of individual responsibility for enhancing health. • analyze the short-term and long-term consequences of safe, risky, and harmful behaviors.	**2. recognize the risk factors and protective factors associated with drug misuse and abuse.** * drug use * drug misuse * drug abuse * polydrug abuse * risk factors for drug misuse and abuse * protective factors and resiliency
1. comprehend concepts related to health promotion and disease prevention. 3. demonstrate the ability to practice health-enhancing behaviors and reduce health risks.	• describe relationships between personal health behaviors and individual well-being. • compare behaviors that are safe to those that are risky or harmful.	• describe ways to reduce risks related to adolescent health problems.	• analyze the role of individual responsibility for enhancing health. • analyze the short-term and long-term consequences of safe, risky, and harmful behaviors.	**3. not drink alcohol.** * why young people drink * benefits of not drinking * absorption and oxidation of alcohol * blood-alcohol concentration * alcohol and driving * alcohol and violence * alcohol and health * alcohol and sexual decision-making * alcoholism * fetal alcohol syndrome

731

Health Education Standards	Performance Indicators	Performance Indicators	Performance Indicators	Life Skills And Health Topics
Students will:	**After health instruction in grades K-4, students will:**	**After health instruction in grades 5-8, students will:**	**After health instruction in grades 9-11, students will:**	**I will:**
1. comprehend concepts related to health promotion and disease prevention. 3. demonstrate the ability to practice health-enhancing behaviors and reduce health risks.	• describe relationships between personal health behaviors and individual well-being. • compare behaviors that are safe to those that are risky or harmful.	• describe ways to reduce risks related to adolescent health problems.	• analyze the role of individual responsibility for enhancing health. • analyze the short-term and long-term consequences of safe, risky, and harmful behaviors.	**4. not use tobacco products.** * why young people use tobacco products * components of tobacco smoke * effects of tobacco * smokeless tobacco use * smoking cessation programs
1. comprehend concepts related to health promotion and disease prevention. 3. demonstrate the ability to practice health-enhancing behaviors and reduce health risks.	• describe relationships between personal health behaviors and individual well-being. • compare behaviors that are safe to those that are risky or harmful.	• describe ways to reduce risks related to adolescent health problems.	• analyze the role of individual responsibility for enhancing health. • analyze the short-term and long-term consequences of safe, risky, and harmful behaviors.	**5. not misuse or abuse controlled substances.** * amphetamines * cocaine * designer drugs * hallucinogens * inhalants * marijuana * narcotics * sedative hypnotics * steroids * caffeine
1. comprehend concepts related to health promotion and disease prevention. 3. demonstrate the ability to practice health-enhancing behaviors and reduce health risks.	• compare behaviors that are safe to those that are risky or harmful.	• describe ways to reduce risks related to adolescent health problems.	• analyze the role of individual responsibility for enhancing health. • analyze the short-term and long-term consequences of safe, risky, and harmful behaviors.	**6. reduce my risk of HIV infection by not using intravenous drugs or drugs that dull my decision-making skills.** * intravenous drug use and HIV infection * drug use and sexual decision-making

ALCOHOL, TOBACCO, AND OTHER DRUGS

Health Education Standards	Performance Indicators	Performance Indicators	Performance Indicators	Life Skills And Health Topics
Students will:	**After health instruction in grades K-4, students will:**	**After health instruction in grades 5-8, students will:**	**After health instruction in grades 9-11, students will:**	**I will:**
1. comprehend concepts related to health promotion and disease prevention.	• describe how the family influences personal health.	• describe how family and peers influence the health of adolescents.		**7. seek help for personal or family drug misuse or abuse.** * drug dependence * codependency and the family * treatment of drug dependency
2. demonstrate the ability to access valid health information and appropriate products and services.	• demonstrate the ability to locate school and community health helpers.	• demonstrate the ability to locate health products and services.	• demonstrate the ability to access school and community health services for self and others.	
6. demonstrate the ability to use goal-setting and decision-making skills that enhance health.	• explain when to ask for assistance in making health-related decisions and setting health goals.			
7. demonstrate the ability to advocate for personal, family, and community health.		• demonstrate the ability to influence and support others in making positive health choices.	• demonstrate the ability to influence and support others in making positive health choices.	
2. demonstrate the ability to access valid health information and health promoting products and services.	• demonstrate the ability to locate resources from home, school, and community that provide valid health information. • demonstrate the ability to locate school and community health helpers.	• demonstrate the ability to utilize resources from home, school, and community that provide valid health information. • demonstrate the ability to locate health products and services.	• demonstrate the ability to access school and community health services for self and others.	**8. become aware of school and community resources for intervention and treatment.** * school resources * community resources * support groups
3. demonstrate the ability to practice health-enhancing behaviors and reduce health risks.	• compare behaviors that are safe to those that are risky or harmful.	• distinguish between safe, risky, and harmful behaviors in relationships.	• analyze the role of individual responsibility for enhancing health.	**9. remain safe and drug-free.** * risks of drug use * benefits of being drug-free
5. demonstrate the ability to use interpersonal communication skills to enhance health.	• demonstrate refusal skills to enhance health.	• demonstrate refusal and negotiation skills to enhance health.	• demonstrate refusal, negotiation, and collaboration skills to avoid potentially harmful situations	**10. use resistance skills when pressured to use drugs.** * resistance skills

733

Health Education Standards	Performance Indicators	Performance Indicators	Performance Indicators	Life Skills And Health Topics
Students will:	**After health instruction in grades K-4, students will:**	**After health instruction in grades 5-8, students will:**	**After health instruction in grades 9-11, students will:**	**I will:**
1. comprehend concepts related to health promotion and disease prevention.	• identify common health problems of children. • explain how childhood injuries and illnesses can be prevented or treated.	• describe how lifestyle, pathogens, family history, and other risk factors are related to the cause or prevention of disease and other health problems.	• analyze how the prevention and control of health problems are influenced by research and medical advances.	1. **recognize that some diseases are communicable while others are noncommunicable.** * communicable diseases * pathogens * noncommunicable diseases
1. comprehend concepts related to health promotion and disease prevention.	• identify common health problems of children. • explain how childhood injuries and illnesses can be prevented or treated.	• describe how lifestyle, pathogens, family history, and other risk factors are related to the cause or prevention of disease and other health problems.	• analyze how behavior can impact health maintenance and disease prevention.	2. **keep my immune system healthy.** * immune system * response to pathogens * keeping the immune system healthy * immunizations * allergies * asthma
1. comprehend concepts related to health promotion and disease prevention.	• describe relationships between personal health behaviors and individual well-being. • identify common health problems of children. • explain how childhood injuries and illnesses can be prevented or treated.	• explain the relationship between positive health behaviors and the prevention of injury, illness, disease, and premature death. • describe how lifestyle, pathogens, family history, and other risk factors are related to the cause or prevention of disease and other health problems.	• analyze how behavior can impact health maintenance and disease prevention.	3. **choose behaviors to prevent the spread of pathogens.** * types of pathogens * susceptibility to pathogens * transmission of pathogens * preventing the spread of pathogens
3. demonstrate the ability to practice health-enhancing behaviors and reduce health risks.	• demonstrate strategies to improve or maintain personal health.	• demonstrate strategies to improve or maintain personal and family health.	• develop strategies to improve or maintain personal, family, and community health.	

734

COMMUNICABLE AND CHRONIC DISEASES

Health Education Standards	Performance Indicators	Performance Indicators	Performance Indicators	Life Skills And Health Topics
Students will:	**After health instruction in grades K-4, students will:**	**After health instruction in grades 5-8, students will:**	**After health instruction in grades 9-11, students will:**	**I will:**
1. comprehend concepts related to health promotion and disease prevention.	• describe relationships between personal health behaviors and individual well-being.	• explain the relationship between positive health behaviors and the prevention of injury, illness, disease, and premature death.	• analyze how behavior can impact health maintenance and disease prevention.	4. **choose behaviors to reduce the risk of infection with common communicable diseases.** * common cold * chicken pox * measles * mumps * influenza and pneumonia * hepatitis * mononucleosis
	• identify common health problems of childrenn.	• describe how lifestyle, pathogens, family history, and other risk factors are related to the cause or prevention of disease and other health problems.		
	• explain how childhood injuries and illnesses can be prevented or treated.			
3. demonstrate the ability to practice health-enhancing behaviors and reduce health risks.	• demonstrate strategies to improve or maintain personal health.	• demonstrate strategies to improve or maintain personal and family health.	• develop strategies to improve or maintain personal, family, and community health.	

735

COMMUNICABLE AND CHRONIC DISEASES

Health Education Standards	Performance Indicators	Performance Indicators	Performance Indicators	Life Skills And Health Topics
Students will:	**After health instruction in grades K–4, students will:**	**After health instruction in grades 5-8, students will:**	**After health instruction in grades 9-11, students will:**	**I will:**
1. comprehend concepts related to health promotion and disease prevention.	• describe relationships between personal health behaviors and individual well-being. • explain how childhood injuries and illnesses can be prevented or treated.	• explain the relationship between positive health behaviors and the prevention of injury, illness, disease, and premature death. • describe ways to reduce risks related to adolescent health problems. • describe how lifestyle, pathogens, family history, and other risk factors are related to the cause or prevention of disease and other health problems. • distinguish between safe, risky, and harmful behaviors in relationships.	• analyze how behavior can impact health maintenance and disease prevention.	**5. choose behaviors to reduce the risk of infection with STDs.** * bacterial vaginosis * candidiasis * trichomoniasis * chlamydial infections * gonorrhea * nongonococcal urethritis * syphilis * genital herpes * genital warts * pediculosis pubis * viral hepatitis
3. demonstrate the ability to practice health-enhancing behaviors and reduce health risks.	• compare behaviors that are safe to those that are risky or harmful. • demonstrate strategies to improve or maintain personal health.			

COMMUNICABLE AND CHRONIC DISEASES

Health Education Standards	Performance Indicators	Performance Indicators	Performance Indicators	Life Skills And Health Topics
Students will:	**After health instruction in grades K-4, students will:**	**After health instruction in grades 5-8, students will:**	**After health instruction in grades 9-11, students will:**	**I will:**
1. comprehend concepts related to health promotion and disease prevention.	• describe relationships between personal health behaviors and individual well-being. • explain how childhood injuries and illnesses can be prevented or treated. • compare behaviors that are safe to those that are risky or harmful.	• explain the relationship between positive health behaviors and the prevention of injury, illness, disease, and premature death. • describe how lifestyle, pathogens, family history, and other risk factors are related to the cause or prevention of disease and other health problems.	• analyze how behavior can impact health maintenance and disease prevention. • analyze how the prevention and control of health problems are influenced by research and medical advances.	6. **choose behaviors to reduce the risk of HIV infection.** * HIV/AIDS * sexual transmission * needle transmission * mother-to-baby transmission * blood transfusion transmission * organ transplants * ways HIV is not transmitted * testing for HIV * progression of HIV infection * treatment of HIV infection * living with HIV infection * preventing infection
3. demonstrate the ability to practice health-enhancing behaviors and reduce health risks.	• demonstrate strategies to improve or maintain personal health.	• distinguish between safe, risky, and harmful behaviors in relationships.		

737

COMMUNICABLE AND CHRONIC DISEASES

Health Education Standards	Performance Indicators	Performance Indicators	Performance Indicators	Life Skills And Health Topics
Students will:	**After health instruction in grades K-4, students will:**	**After health instruction in grades 5-8, students will:**	**After health instruction in grades 9-11, students will:**	**I will:**
1. comprehend concepts related to health promotion and disease prevention.		• describe how lifestyle, pathogens, family history, and other risk factors are related to the cause or prevention of disease and other health problems.		7. **obtain information about my family's history of disease.** * risk factors and heredity * diseases and heredity * gathering a health history
2. demonstrate the ability to access valid health information and health-promoting products and services.	• demonstrate the ability to locate resources from home, school, and community that provide valid health information.			
3. demonstrate the ability to practice health-enhancing behaviors and reduce health risks.			• evaluate a personal health assessment to determine strategies for health enhancement and risk reduction.	
4. analyze the influence of culture, media, technology, and other factors on health.	• describe how culture influences personal health behaviors.	• describe the influence of cultural beliefs on health behaviors and the use of health services.		

738

COMMUNICABLE AND CHRONIC DISEASES

Health Education Standards	Performance Indicators	Performance Indicators	Performance Indicators	Life Skills And Health Topics
Students will:	**After health instruction in grades K-4, students will:**	**After health instruction in grades 5-8, students will:**	**After health instruction in grades 9-11, students will:**	**I will:**
1. comprehend concepts related to health promotion and disease prevention.	• describe relationships between personal health behaviors and individual well-being. • explain how childhood injuries and illnesses can be prevented or treated.	• explain the relationship between positive health behaviors and the prevention of injury, illness, disease, and premature death. • explain how appropriate health care can prevent premature death and disability. • describe how lifestyle, pathogens, family history, and other risk factors are related to the cause or prevention of disease and other health problems.	• analyze how behavior can impact health maintenance and disease prevention. • describe how to delay onset and reduce risks of potential health problems during adulthood. • analyze how the prevention and control of health problems are influenced by research and medical advances.	8. **choose behaviors to reduce my risk of cardiovascular disease.** * risk factors for heart disease * heredity * sex * race * age * smoking * diet and high blood cholesterol * hypertension * lack of exercise * obesity * diabetes * treatment of heart disease
3. demonstrate the ability to practice health-enhancing behaviors and reduce health risks.	• demonstrate strategies to improve or maintain personal health.			
6. demonstrate the ability to use goal-setting and decision-making skills that enhance health.	• set a personal health goal and track progress toward its achievement.			

COMMUNICABLE AND CHRONIC DISEASES

Health Education Standards	Performance Indicators	Performance Indicators	Performance Indicators	Life Skills And Health Topics
Students will:	**After health instruction in grades K-4, students will:**	**After health instruction in grades 5-8, students will:**	**After health instruction in grades 9-11, students will:**	**I will:**
1. comprehend concepts related to health promotion and disease prevention.	• describe relationships between personal health behaviors and individual well-being. • explain how childhood injuries and illnesses can be prevented or treated.	• explain the relationship between positive health behaviors and the prevention of injury, illness, disease, and premature death. • explain how appropriate health care can prevent premature death and disability. • describe how lifestyle, pathogens, family history, and other risk factors are related to the cause or prevention of disease and other health problems.	• analyze how behavior can impact health maintenance and disease prevention. • describe how to delay onset and reduce risks of potential health problems during adulthood. • analyze how the prevention and control of health problems are influenced by research and medical advances.	9. **choose behaviors to reduce my risk of cancer.** * causes of cancer * heredity and cancer * viruses and cancer * tobacco and cancer * ultraviolet radiation and cancer * detecting cancer * treatment for cancer
3. demonstrate the ability to practice health-enhancing behaviors and reduce health risks.	• demonstrate strategies to improve or maintain personal health.			
6. demonstrate the ability to use goal-setting and decision-making skills that enhance health.	• set a personal health goal and track progress toward its achievement.			

740

COMMUNICABLE AND CHRONIC DISEASES

Health Education Standards	Performance Indicators	Performance Indicators	Performance Indicators	Life Skills And Health Topics
Students will:	**After health instruction in grades K-4, students will:**	**After health instruction in grades 5-8, students will:**	**After health instruction in grades 9-11, students will:**	**I will:**
1. comprehend concepts related to health promotion and disease prevention.	• describe relationships between personal health behaviors and individual well-being. • explain how childhood injuries and illnesses can be prevented or treated.	• explain the relationship between positive health behaviors and the prevention of injury, illness, disease, and premature death. • describe how lifestyle, pathogens, family history, and other risk factors are related to the cause or prevention of disease and other health problems.	• analyze how behavior can impact health maintenance and disease prevention. • analyze how the prevention and control of health problems are influenced by research and medical advances.	**10. recognize ways to manage chronic diseases.** * diabetes * colitis and diverticulosis * arthritis * systemic lupus * chronic fatigue syndrome * managing chronic disease
3. demonstrate the ability to practice health-enhancing behaviors and reduce health risks.	• identify personal health needs. • demonstrate strategies to improve or maintain personal health.			

INJURY PREVENTION AND SAFETY

Health Education Standards	Performance Indicators	Performance Indicators	Performance Indicators	Life Skills And Health Topics
Students will:	**After health instruction in grades K-4, students will:**	**After health instruction in grades 5-8, students will:**	**After health instruction in grades 9-11, students will:**	**I will:**
1. comprehend concepts related to health promotion and disease prevention.	• identify common health problems of children.	• identify common health problems of children.		1. **follow safety rules in my home.** * falls * fire * poisoning * firearms * suffocation * self-protection for the home
	• explain how childhood injuries and illnesses can be prevented or treated.	• explain how childhood injuries and illnesses can be prevented or treated.		
3. demonstrate the ability to practice health-enhancing behaviors and reduce health risks.	• develop injury prevention and management strategies for personal health.	• develop injury prevention and management strategies for personal and family health.	• develop injury prevention and management strategies for personal, family, and community health.	
		• describe ways to reduce risks related to adolescent health problems.		
1. comprehend concepts related to health promotion and disease prevention.	• identify common health problems of children.			2. **follow safety rules at school.** * playground safety * avoiding violence * safe school zones
	• explain how childhood injuries and illnesses can be prevented or treated.			
3. demonstrate the ability to practice health-enhancing behaviors and reduce health risks.	• develop injury prevention and management strategies for personal health.	• develop injury prevention and management strategies for personal and family health.	• develop injury prevention and management strategies for personal, family, and community health.	
	• demonstrate ways to avoid and reduce threatening situations.		• demonstrate ways to avoid and reduce threatening situations.	
5. demonstrate the ability to use interpersonal communication skills to enhance health.		• analyze the possible causes of conflict among youth in schools and communities.	• analyze the possible causes of conflict in schools, families, and communities.	
			• demonstrate strategies used to prevent conflict.	

742

INJURY PREVENTION AND SAFETY

Health Education Standards	Performance Indicators	Performance Indicators	Performance Indicators	Life Skills And Health Topics
Students will:	**After health instruction in grades K-4, students will:**	**After health instruction in grades 5-8, students will:**	**After health instruction in grades 9-11, students will:**	**I will:**
1. comprehend concepts related to health promotion and disease prevention.	• explain how childhood injuries and illnesses can be prevented or treated.	• describe ways to reduce risks related to adolescent health problems.		**3. follow safety rules in my community.** * pedestrian safety * animal safety * self protection strategies
3. demonstrate the ability to practice health-enhancing behaviors and reduce health risks.	• demonstrate ways to avoid and reduce threatening situations.		• demonstrate ways to avoid and reduce threatening situations.	
4. analyze the influence of culture, media, technology, and other factors on health.	• describe how culture influences personal health behaviors.			
5. demonstrate the ability to use interpersonal communication skills to enhance health.		• analyze the possible causes of conflict among youth in schools and communities.	• analyze the possible causes of conflict in schools, families, and communities. • demonstrate strategies used to prevent conflict.	
1. comprehend concepts related to health promotion and disease prevention.	• explain how childhood injuries and illnesses can be prevented or treated.			**4. follow safety guidelines for different weather conditions and natural disasters.** * hot weather * cold weather * lightning * tornadoes * floods * hurricanes * earthquakes
3. demonstrate the ability to practice health-enhancing behaviors and reduce health risks.	• develop injury prevention and management strategies for personal health.	• develop injury prevention and management strategies for personal and family health.	• develop injury prevention and management strategies for personal, family, and community health.	
3. demonstrate the ability to practice health-enhancing behaviors and reduce health risks.	• develop injury prevention and management strategies for personal health.	• develop injury prevention and management strategies for personal and family health.	• demonstrate ways to avoid and reduce threatening situations.	**5. be able to get help for emergency situations.** * 9-1-1

743

INJURY PREVENTION AND SAFETY

Health Education Standards	Performance Indicators	Performance Indicators	Performance Indicators	Life Skills And Health Topics
Students will:	**After health instruction in grades K-4, students will:**	**After health instruction in grades 5-8, students will:**	**After health instruction in grades 9-11, students will:**	**I will:**
3. demonstrate the ability to practice health-enhancing behaviors and reduce health risks.	• develop injury prevention and management strategies for personal health.	• develop injury prevention and management strategies for personal and family health.	• develop injury prevention and management strategies for personal, family, and community health.	**6. be skilled in basic first aid procedures.** * respiratory emergencies * CPR * poisoning * shock * burns * fractures
1. comprehend concepts related to health promotion and disease prevention.		• describe ways to reduce risks related to adolescent health problems.		
3. demonstrate the ability to practice health-enhancing behaviors and reduce health risks.	• develop injury prevention and management strategies for personal health.	• develop injury prevention and management strategies for personal and family health.	• develop injury prevention and management strategies for personal, family, and community health.	**7. choose behaviors to reduce my risk of violence.** * protective factors * risk factors
	• demonstrate ways to avoid and reduce threatening situations.	• demonstrate ways to avoid and reduce threatening situations.	• demonstrate ways to avoid and reduce threatening situations.	
5. demonstrate the ability to use interpersonal communication skills to enhance health.		• demonstrate strategies to manage conflict in healthy ways.	• demonstrate strategies used to prevent conflict.	

744

INJURY PREVENTION AND SAFETY

Health Education Standards	Performance Indicators	Performance Indicators	Performance Indicators	Life Skills And Health Topics
Students will:	**After health instruction in grades K-4, students will:**	**After health instruction in grades 5-8, students will:**	**After health instruction in grades 9-11, students will:**	**I will:**
3. demonstrate the ability to practice health-enhancing behaviors and reduce health risks.	• develop injury prevention and management strategies for personal health. • demonstrate ways to avoid and reduce threatening situations.	• develop injury prevention and management strategies for personal and family health. • demonstrate ways to avoid and reduce threatening situations.	• develop injury prevention and management strategies for personal, family, and community health. • demonstrate ways to avoid and reduce threatening situations. • develop injury prevention and management strategies for personal, family, and community health.	**8. protect myself from people who might harm me.** * sexual abuse * social situations * sexual harassment * stalking
3. demonstrate the ability to practice health-enhancing behaviors and reduce health risks.	• develop injury prevention and management strategies for personal health. • demonstrate ways to avoid and reduce threatening situations.	• develop injury prevention and management strategies for personal and family health. • demonstrate ways to avoid and reduce threatening situations.	• demonstrate ways to avoid and reduce threatening situations.	**9. stay safe while riding in a car.** * self-protection in cars * motor vehicle safety
3. demonstrate the ability to practice health-enhancing behaviors and reduce health risks.	• develop injury prevention and management strategies for personal health. • demonstrate ways to avoid and reduce threatening situations.	• develop injury prevention and management strategies for personal and family health.	• develop injury prevention and management strategies for personal, family, and community health.	**10. stay safe while exercising** * water safety * exercising outdoors * bicycle safety * motorcycle safety

CONSUMER AND COMMUNITY HEALTH

Health Education Standards	Performance Indicators	Performance Indicators	Performance Indicators	Life Skills And Health Topics
Students will:	**After health instruction in grades K-4, students will:**	**After health instruction in grades 5-8, students will:**	**After health instruction in grades 9-11, students will:**	**I will:**
2. demonstrate the ability to access valid health information and health promoting products and services.	• identify characteristics of valid health information and health promoting products, and services. • demonstrate the ability to locate resources from home, school, and community that provide valid health information.	• analyze the validity of health information, products, and services. • analyze how media influences the selection of health information and products.	• evaluate the validity of health information, products, and services. • demonstrate the ability to evaluate resources from home, school, and community that provide valid health information.	**1. choose sources of health-related information, products, and services wisely.** * importance of being a wise consumer * sources of health-related information * distinguishing between accurate and inaccurate information
4. analyze the influence of culture, media, technology, and other factors on health.		• analyze how messages from media and other sources influence health behaviors.	• evaluate the effect of media, and other factors on personal, family, and community health.	
2. demonstrate the ability to access valid health information and health-promoting products and services.	• explain how media influences the selection of health information, products, and services. • explain how media influences thoughts, feelings, and health behaviors.	• analyze how messages from media and other sources influence health behaviors. • analyze how media influences the selection of health information and products.	• evaluate the effect of media, and other factors on personal, family, and community health.	**2. analyze the effects of advertising on my choices.** * the advertising industry * types of appeals in advertising * bandwagon appeal * brand loyalty * false image appeal * glittering generalities * humor appeal * progress appeal * reward appeal * scientific evidence appeal * snob appeal * testimony appeal * analyzing advertisements
4. analyze the influence of culture, media, technology, and other factors on health.				

Health Education Standards	Performance Indicators	Performance Indicators	Performance Indicators	Life Skills And Health Topics
Students will:	After health instruction in grades K-4, students will:	After health instruction in grades 5-8, students will:	After health instruction in grades 9-11, students will:	I will:
2. demonstrate the ability to access valid health information and health promoting products and services. 4. analyze the influence of culture, media, technology, and other factors on health.	• explain how media influences the selection of health information, products, and services. • explain how media influences thoughts, feelings, and health behaviors.	• analyze how messages from media and other sources influence health behaviors.	• evaluate the effect of media, and other factors on personal, family, and community health.	3. recognize and report quackery * quacks and quackery. * weight loss and diet scams * unproven treatments and products * avoiding quackery and consumer fraud
2. demonstrate the ability to access valid health information and health-promoting products and services. 4. analyze the influence of culture, media, technology, and other factors on health.	• identify characteristics of valid health information and health-promoting products, and services. • explain how media influences thoughts, feelings, and health behaviors.	• analyze the validity of health information, products, and services. • compare the costs and validity of health products. • analyze how messages from media and other sources influence health behaviors.	• evaluate the validity of health information, products, and services. • analyze the cost and accessibility of health care services.	4. spend money wisely. * making a budget * paying for health care * health insurance * shopping wisely * spending money on entertainment
2. demonstrate the ability to access valid health information and health-promoting products and services. 4. analyze the influence of culture, media, technology, and other factors on health.	• identify characteristics of valid health information and health-promoting products, and services. • describe ways technology can influence personal health.	• analyze the validity of health information, products, and services. • analyze the influence of technology on personal and family health.	• evaluate the validity of health information, products, and services. • evaluate the impact of technology on personal, family, and community health.	5. spend time wisely. * making a time management plan * analyzing how time is spent * watching television * entertainment addiction

Health Education Standards	Performance Indicators	Performance Indicators	Performance Indicators	Life Skills And Health Topics
Students will:	**After health instruction in grades K-4, students will:**	**After health instruction in grades 5-8, students will:**	**After health instruction in grades 9-11, students will:**	**I will:**
2. demonstrate the ability to access valid health information and health-promoting products and services.	• demonstrate the ability to locate school and community health helpers.	• demonstrate the ability to locate health products and services.	• demonstrate the ability to access school and community health services for self and others.	**6. use school nurse and school health services when appropriate.** * the school nurse * school health services
4. analyze the influence of culture, media, technology, and other factors on health.	• describe the influence that information from school and family has on health.			
1. comprehend concepts related to health promotion and disease prevention.		• explain how appropriate health care can prevent premature death and disability.		
2. demonstrate the ability to access valid health information and health-promoting products and services.	• demonstrate the ability to locate school and community health helpers.	• demonstrate the ability to locate health products and services.	• evaluate factors that influence personal selection of health products, and services.	**7. use health care providers when appropriate.** * selecting health care providers * physicians * specialized and allied health professionals
		• compare the costs and validity of health products.	• demonstrate the ability to access school and community health services for self and others.	
		• describe situations requiring professional health services.	• analyze the cost and accessibility of health care services.	
			• analyze situations requiring professional health services.	
7. demonstrate the ability to advocate for personal, family, and community health.	• identify community agencies that advocate for healthy individuals, families, and communities.			

748

CONSUMER AND COMMUNITY HEALTH

Health Education Standards	Performance Indicators	Performance Indicators	Performance Indicators	Life Skills And Health Topics
Students will:	**After health instruction in grades K-4, students will:**	**After health instruction in grades 5-8, students will:**	**After health instruction in grades 9-11, students will:**	**I will:**
1. comprehend concepts related to health promotion and disease prevention.		• explain how appropriate health care can prevent premature death and disability.		**8. use health care facilities when appropriate.** * hospitals * outpatient centers * emergency centers
2. demonstrate the ability to access valid health information and health-promoting products and services.		• compare the costs and validity of health products. • describe situations requiring professional health services.	• evaluate factors that influence personal selection of health products, and services. • analyze situations requiring professional health services. • analyze the cost and accessibility of health care services.	
4. analyze the influence of culture, media, technology, and other factors on health.	• describe ways technology can influence personal health.		• evaluate the impact of technology on personal, family, and community health.	
7. demonstrate the ability to advocate for personal, family, and community health.	• identify community agencies that advocate for healthy individuals, families, and communities.		• analyze how information from the community influences health.	

Health Education Standards	Performance Indicators	Performance Indicators	Performance Indicators	Life Skills And Health Topics
Students will:	**After health instruction in grades K-4, students will:**	**After health instruction in grades 5-8, students will:**	**After health instruction in grades 9-11, students will:**	**I will:**
2. demonstrate the ability to access valid health information and health promoting products and services.	• demonstrate the ability to locate school and community health helpers.		• analyze how public health policies and government regulations influence health promotion and disease prevention.	**9. cooperate with people who protect my health and safety.** * professional associations * private organizations * federal agencies * state and local agencies
4. analyze the influence of culture, media, technology, and other factors on health.		• analyze the influence of technology on personal and family health.		
6. demonstrate the ability to use goal-setting and decision-making skills that enhance health.	• explain when to ask for assistance in making health-related decisions and setting health goals.			
7. demonstrate the ability to advocate for personal, family, and community health.		• demonstrate the ability to work cooperatively when advocating for healthy individuals, families, and schools.	• demonstrate the ability to work cooperatively when advocating for healthy communities.	**10. volunteer in school clubs and community organizations and agencies that promote health.** * school clubs and organizations * community health agencies * voluntary health organizations
4. analyze the influence of culture, media, technology, and other factors on health.			• analyze how information from the community influences health.	
7. demonstrate the ability to advocate for personal, family, and community health.	• demonstrate the ability to influence and support others in making positive health choices.	• demonstrate the ability to influence and support others in making positive health choices.	• demonstrate the ability to influence and support others in making positive health choices. • demonstrate the ability to adapt health messages and communication techniques to the characteristics of a particular audience.	

ENVIRONMENTAL HEALTH

Health Education Standards	Performance Indicators	Performance Indicators	Performance Indicators	Life Skills And Health Topics
Students will:	After health instruction in grades K-4, students will:	After health instruction in grades 5-8, students will:	After health instruction in grades 9-11, students will:	I will:
1. comprehend concepts related to health promotion and disease prevention. 7. demonstrate the ability to advocate for personal, family, and community health.	• describe how physical, social, and emotional environments influence personal health. • express information and opinions about health issues. • demonstrate the ability to influence and support others in making positive health choices.	• analyze how environment and personal health are interrelated. • express information and opinions about health issues. • demonstrate the ability to influence and support others in making positive health choices.	• analyze how the environment influences the health of the community. • express information and opinions on health issues. • demonstrate the ability to influence and support others in making positive health choices.	1. be concerned about environmental issues. * environmental interest groups * environmental issues * ozone layer * greenhouse effect * global warming
1. comprehend concepts related to health promotion and disease prevention. 3. demonstrate the ability to practice health-enhancing behaviors and reduce health risks.	• describe how physical, social, and emotional environments influence personal health.	• analyze how environment and personal health are interrelated.	• analyze how the environment influences the health of the community. • develop strategies to improve or maintain personal, family, and community health.	2. keep the air clean. * sources of air pollution * carbon monoxide * nitrogen oxides * hydrocarbons * particulates * ozone * thermal inversion * motor vehicle emissions * acid rain
1. comprehend concepts related to health promotion and disease prevention. 3. demonstrate the ability to practice health-enhancing behaviors and reduce health risks.	• describe how physical, social, and emotional environments influence personal health.	• analyze how environment and personal health are interrelated.	• analyze how the environment influences the health of the community. • develop strategies to improve or maintain personal, family, and community health.	3. keep the water clean. * water pollution * sewage * lead * PCBs * pesticides * trihalomethanes * water conservation

751

ENVIRONMENTAL HEALTH

Health Education Standards	Performance Indicators	Performance Indicators	Performance Indicators	Life Skills And Health Topics
Students will:	**After health instruction in grades K-4, students will:**	**After health instruction in grades 5-8, students will:**	**After health instruction in grades 9-11, students will:**	**I will:**
1. comprehend concepts related to health promotion and disease prevention.	• describe how physical, social, and emotional environments influence personal health.	• analyze how environment and personal health are interrelated.	• analyze how the environment influences the health of the community.	**4. keep my indoor environment free of pollution.** * sick building syndrome * asbestos * lead * woodstove smoke * formaldehyde * carbon monoxide * radon * secondhand smoke * ways to keep indoor air free of pollution
3. demonstrate the ability to practice health-enhancing behaviors and reduce health risks.	• demonstrate strategies to improve or maintain personal health.	• demonstrate strategies to improve or maintain personal and family health.	• develop strategies to improve or maintain personal, family, and community health.	
1. comprehend concepts related to health promotion and disease prevention.	• describe relationships between personal health behaviors and individual well-being. • describe how physical, social, and emotional environments influence personal health.	• explain the relationship between positive health behaviors and the prevention of injury, illness, disease, and premature death. • analyze how environment and personal health are interrelated.	• analyze how behavior can impact health maintenance and disease prevention. • analyze how the environment influences the health of the community.	**5. keep noise at a healthful level.** * sources of noise pollution * ways to protect against noise pollution
3. demonstrate the ability to practice health-enhancing behaviors and reduce health risks.	• compare behaviors that are safe to those that are risky or harmful.			
1. comprehend concepts related to health promotion and disease prevention.	• describe how physical, social, and emotional environments influence personal health.	• analyze how environment and personal health are interrelated.	• analyze how the environment influences the health of the community.	**6. protect myself from radiation.** * electromagnetic radiation * sources of radiation
3. demonstrate the ability to practice health-enhancing behaviors and reduce health risks.	• compare behaviors that are safe to those that are risky or harmful.			

ENVIRONMENTAL HEALTH

Health Education Standards	Performance Indicators	Performance Indicators	Performance Indicators	Life Skills And Health Topics
Students will:	**After health instruction in grades K-4, students will:**	**After health instruction in grades 5-8, students will:**	**After health instruction in grades 9-11, students will:**	**I will:**
1. comprehend concepts related to health promotion and disease prevention. 3. demonstrate the ability to practice health-enhancing behaviors and reduce health risks.	• describe how physical, social, and emotional environments influence personal health.	• analyze how environment and personal health are interrelated.	• analyze how the environment influences the health of the community. • develop strategies to improve or maintain personal, family, and community health.	**7. dispose of solid waste properly.** * sources of solid waste * sources of hazardous waste
1. comprehend concepts related to health promotion and disease prevention. 3. demonstrate the ability to practice health-enhancing behaviors and reduce health risks.	• describe how physical, social, and emotional environments influence personal health.	• analyze how environment and personal health are interrelated.	• analyze how the environment influences the health of the community. • develop strategies to improve or maintain personal, family, and community health.	**8. recycle.** * recycling
1. comprehend concepts related to health promotion and disease prevention. 4. analyze the influence of culture, media, technology, and other factors on health.	• describe how physical, social, and emotional environments influence personal health. • describe the influence of culture on personal health practices.	• analyze how environment and personal health are interrelated.	• analyze how the environment influences the health of the community.	**9. be aware of the effects of overcrowding and poverty.** * population growth * adverse socioeconomic conditions * poverty and violence
1. comprehend concepts related to health promotion and disease prevention. 7. demonstrate the ability to advocate for personal, family, and community health.	• describe how physical, social, and emotional environments influence personal health. • identify community agencies that advocate for healthy individuals, families, and communities.	• analyze how environment and personal health are interrelated. • demonstrate the ability to work cooperatively when advocating for healthy individuals, families, and schools.	• analyze how the environment influences the health of the community. • demonstrate the ability to work cooperatively when advocating for healthy communities.	**10. cooperate with environmental protection agencies.** * environmental protection agencies

APPENDIX

THE OPPORTUNITY-TO-LEARN STANDARDS

The Opportunity-To-Learn Standards
for
LOCAL EDUCATION AGENCIES

For children and youth to achieve health literacy, local education agencies must provide for:

✔ **1.** collaborative planning among school personnel, students, families, related community agencies and business organizations to design, implement and assess health instruction for health literacy.

✔ **2.** the implementation of a plan including a budget that enables students to achieve the National Health Education Standards.

✔ **3.** the employment of elementary and secondary teachers professionally prepared to teach health education.

✔ **4.** ongoing professional development opportunities and incentives for persons responsible for teaching health education.

✔ **5.** leadership to create community awareness and support for health literacy through school health instruction.

✔ **6.** collaborative teacher planning and team building across curricular areas to make connections for health education.

✔ **7.** sufficient time for learning health education at the elementary and secondary school levels for students to achieve the National Health Education Standards.

✔ **8.** active family participation in fostering health literacy for students.

✔ **9.** utilization of information technologies in the delivery of health instruction.

✔ **10.** instruction based on the students' health needs, interests, strengths and culture.

✔ **11.** school policies that create a climate which promotes health literacy.

✔ **12.** use of multiple assessment strategies at grades four, eight, and eleven to determine student achievement of the National Health Education Standards.

✔ **13.** monitoring of implementation of the plan that supports students achievement of the National Health Education Standards.

✔ **14.** coordination of the comprehensive health education curriculum including assessment, materials and professional development.

✔ **15.** opportunities to conduct research and program evaluation related to student achievement of health literacy.

The Joint Committee on Health Education Standards, 1995

The Opportunity-To-Learn Standards
for
COMMUNITY AGENCIES

For children and youth to achieve health literacy, families and community agencies must:

✔ **1.** participate in planning with school personnel, students, governmental units and business organizations in order to design, implement, and assess health instruction for health literacy.

✔ **2.** support implementation of the local education agency plan including a budget that enables students to achieve the National Health Education Standards.

✔ **3.** create community awareness and support for school health instruction.

✔ **4.** provide learning opportunities at home and in the community that enhance and reinforce student achievement of the National Health Education Standards.

✔ **5.** support instruction based on the students' health needs, interests, strengths, and culture.

✔ **6.** foster community norms and programs that create a climate to promote child and adolescent health and health literacy.

✔ **7.** adopt public policies and social marketing programs advocating health literacy for all children, youth, and families.

✔ **8.** provide opportunities and incentive for ongoing health education for families, school personnel, and community members who work with children and youth.

✔ **9.** monitor implementation of the school plan that supports student achievement of the National Health Education Standards.

The Joint Committee on Health Education Standards, 1995

758

The Opportunity-To-Learn Standards
for
STATE EDUCATION AGENCIES

For children and youth to achieve health literacy, state education agencies and state health agencies must collaborate to:

✔ **1.** support planning at the state and local levels to achieve quality health instruction in schools.

✔ **2.** implement a state plan and budget supporting schools in their efforts to help children achieve the National Health Education Standards.

✔ **3.** establish health education as a core academic subject.

✔ **4.** employ professionally prepared school health educators within state agencies to provide leadership and assistance to local schools and communities.

✔ **5.** require adequate preservice professional preparation of all elementary teachers to teach toward the National Health Education Standards.

✔ **6.** require health instruction at the middle school/ junior high and high school levels be taught by professionally prepared school health educators.

✔ **7.** provide opportunities and incentives for ongoing professional development for teachers and other staff responsible for health education.

✔ **8.** increase community commitment to school health education.

✔ **9.** provide state mandates to insure adequate instructional time at the elementary and secondary school levels for students to achieve the National Health Education Standards.

✔ **10.** develop state guidelines to assist schools in implementing instruction based on relevant health needs, interests, strengths, and risks of students, families and communities.

✔ **11.** adopt public policies and social marketing programs advocating health literacy for all children, youth, and families.

✔ **12.** develop guidelines to assist schools in assessing the implementation of their plans to enable students to achieve the National Health Education Standards.

✔ **13.** develop guidelines to assist schools in assessing the implementation of their plans to enable students to achieve the National Health Education Standards.

✔ **14.** include health education concepts on the state teachers' examinations.

The Joint Committee on Health Education Standards, 1995

The Opportunity-To-Learn Standards
for
TEACHER PREPARATION INSTITUTIONS

For children and youth to achieve health literacy, teacher preparation institutions will:

✔ **1.** implement a plan and budget supporting professional preparation that prepares teachers to enable students to achieve the National Health Education Standards.

✔ **2.** provide health instruction programs directed by professionally prepared and experienced school health educators.

✔ **3.** prepare future school health educators consistent with the responsibilities and competencies specified by the National Commission on Health Education Credentialing, Inc.

✔ **4.** prepare future elementary and middle school teachers as specified in the AAHE/ASHA Health Instruction Responsibilities and Competencies for Elementary Classroom Teachers.

✔ **5.** provide leadership which will create public awareness and support for health education in schools.

✔ **6.** provide professional development incentives and opportunities for college and university faculty responsible for preparing teachers to help students achieve the National Health Education Standards.

✔ **7.** prepare future teachers to make health education connections across the curriculum.

✔ **8.** include in professional preparation programs content which addresses health needs, interests, and strengths of culturally diverse populations.

✔ **9.** provide leadership in health education research and evaluation.

✔ **10.** prepare future teachers to assess student achievement of the National Health Education Standards.

✔ **11.** monitor the institution's implementation of the Institution for Higher Education Teacher Preparation Standards.

✔ **12.** prepare administrators and other key school personnel to implement health education programs in school.

The Joint Committee on Health Education Standards, 1995

The Opportunity-To-Learn Standards
for
NATIONAL HEALTH AGENCIES

For children and youth to achieve health literacy, national health and education agencies and organizations must collaborate to:

✔ **1.** include health education as a core academic subject in **Goals 2000: Educate America Act.**

✔ **2.** support certification of the National Health Education Standards by the National Education Standards and Improvement Council.

✔ **3.** include health education concepts in national teacher examinations.

✔ **4.** foster public policies advocating health literacy for all children and youth.

✔ **5.** adopt a national plan and budget supporting schools, communities, and state and local agencies in their efforts to help children achieve the National Health Education Standards.

✔ **6.** develop guidelines for assessment of student progress in achieving the National Health Education Standards.

✔ **7.** adopt a national plan and budget supporting institutions of higher education which prepare teachers to implement the National Health Education Standards.

✔ **8.** support research in health education.

✔ **9.** employ professionally prepared health educators within national health and education agencies and organizations.

The Joint Committee on Health Education Standards, 1995

Appendix

GLOSSARY

Glossary

Glossary

A

abrasion: an injury when the skin is rubbed away.

abscess: localized collection of pus.

abstinence: choosing not to engage in sexual intercourse.

abuse: the harmful treatment of a person.

accident: sudden, unexpected events that often result in injury.

acid rain: precipitation (rain, snow, sleet, hail) that contains high levels of acids formed from sulfur oxides, nitrogen oxides, and moisture in the air.

acne: a skin disorder characterized by inflammation of skin glands and hair follicles and the eruption of pimples.

acquired immunodeficiency syndrome (AIDS): a disorder of the human immune system in a person infected with HIV, characterized by severe breakdown of the immune system that leaves a person very susceptible to opportunistic infections.

active listening: a type of listening in which a person lets others know (s)he has been heard and what was said has been understood.

addictive behavior: behavior associated with repeated and continual connection with an activity or object that results in unhealthful effects on the person.

additive: substance added to foods to improve the flavor or appearance or to increase the nutritional content.

adolescent pregnancy: pregnancy in the years between puberty and the end of the teen years.

adrenal gland: a pair of glands that secrete hormones directly into the bloodstream.

adrenaline: a hormone that helps the body get ready for an emergency.

advertising: a form of selling in which individuals are informed of products and services.

advertisement: a paid announcement.

aerobic exercise: exercise in which oxygen is required continually for an extended period of time.

affective domain: a category of objectives dealing with feelings and attitudes.

ageism: behavior that discriminates against people in a specific age group.

Agent Orange: a substance containing dioxin that was sprayed on vegetation to kill it.

aggressive behavior: the use of words and/or actions that show disrespect toward others.

agility: the ability to quickly change position while controlling movement.

AIDS (acquired immunodeficiency syndrome): a disorder of the human immune system in a person infected with HIV, characterized by severe breakdown of the immune system that leaves a person very susceptible to opportunistic infections.

air bags: cushions that inflate when activated by sensors in the dashboard and front bumpers within a fraction of a second between the first collision and the "human collision."

airway obstruction: a condition in which breathing is partly or completely prevented by a blockage in the part of the air passages known as the larynx.

alarm stage: the first stage of the GAS in which the body gets ready for action.

alcohol: a psychoactive drug that depresses the central nervous system.

alcohol dementia: brain impairment that is characterized by overall intellectual decline, due to the direct toxic effects of alcohol.

Glossary

Alcohol, Tobacco, and Other Drugs: the area of health that focuses on kinds of drugs and their safe use; understanding the risk factors and protective factors associated with drug misuse and abuse; preventing the misuse and/or abuse of alcohol, tobacco, and controlled substances; recognizing how drug use increases the likelihood of HIV infection; seeking help for personal or family drug misuse or abuse; being aware of school and community intervention and treatment resources; choosing to be safe and drug-free; and using resistance skills when pressured to use drugs.

alcoholism: a complex disease that is characterized by a preoccupation with drinking alcohol that has progressed to serious physical, social, occupational, and/or family consequences for an individual.

alienation: the feeling that one is apart from others.

allergen: a substance that stimulates the production of antibodies and subsequently results in allergic reactions.

allergy: a hypersensitive reaction by the immune system to a foreign antigen (protein).

allied health professional: scientifically trained practitioners who practice under some degree of medical supervision.

Alzheimer's disease: a degenerative disease of the central nervous system characterized by premature senility.

amblyopia: a condition characterized by dimness of vision in one eye.

American Dental Association (ADA): an association that sets standards for the education and conduct of dentists.

American Medical Association (AMA): an association that sets standards for the education and conduct of medical physicians.

amino acids: the building blocks of proteins.

amotivational syndrome: a lack of desire by people to become motivated to perform daily responsibilities.

amphetamines: stimulants that were used at one time as diet pills.

amping: an intense euphoria from a drug.

amyl nitrate: a clear yellowish liquid with a strong chemical smell that is used medicinally for the relief of chest pain known as angina pectoris.

anabolic steroids: synthetic derivatives of the male hormone testosterone.

anaerobic exercise: exercise in which the body demands more oxygen than is available and a person begins to pant for air.

analgesia: relief of pain.

analog drug: another name for a designer drug.

anaphylactic shock: a rare, severe, and life-threatening allergic reaction.

anemia: a condition in which the body is unable to produce sufficient red blood cells.

anesthesiologist: a physician who specializes in the administration of drugs to prevent pain and induce unconsciousness during surgery.

anger: the feeling of being irritated, annoyed, and/or furious.

anger cues: changes in the body that are signs that a person is angry.

anger trigger: thought or event that causes a person to become angry.

angina pectoris: chest pain that results from narrowed blood vessels in the heart.

antibodies: proteins produced by B cells that helps destroy pathogens inside the body.

anorexia nervosa: an eating disorder in which a person is preoccupied with being excessively thin.

antioxidant: a substance that protects cells from being damaged by oxidation.

anxiety disorder: disorder in which real or imagined fears occur so often that it prevents a person from enjoying life.

aorta: the main artery of the body.

appetite: the desire for food that is determined by environmental and psychological factors.

arrhythmia: an irregular heartbeat.

arteries: blood vessels that carry blood away from the heart.

arteriole: blood vessel that branches off an artery to link it to a capillary.

arteriosclerosis: a general term used to describe several conditions that cause hardening and thickening of arteries.

arthritis: a general term that includes over 100 diseases, all of which involve inflammation.

artifact: actual sample of student works.

artificial insemination: a procedure in which sperm are introduced into the vagina or uterus by artificial means so that conception can occur.

artificial respiration: a term that includes many techniques that are used by one person on another to restore breathing.

asbestos: a heat-resistant mineral that is found in building materials.

asphyxiation: stoppage or limit of breathing.

assertive behavior: the honest expression of thoughts and feelings without experiencing anxiety or threatening others.

asthma: an allergic disease of the lungs manifest by constrictions of the small air passages called bronchioles.

astigmatism: irregular curvature of the cornea that results in blurred vision.

atherosclerosis: a form of arteriosclerosis in which fatty substances are deposited on artery walls.

athlete's foot: a fungal infection that grows between the toes when feet are not kept dry.

Attention Deficit Hyperactivity Disorder (ADHD): a developmental disorder characterized by inattention, impulsiveness, hyperactivity, and inability to follow rules.

attestation: a document written about the work of the student by someone other than the student.

audiologist: an allied health professional who screens people for hearing problems and makes recommendations for hearing devices.

audiometer: a machine that assesses the range of sounds that children can hear at various frequencies and intensities.

autoimmune system: a condition in which the immune system produces autoantibodies that launch an attack on the body's own cells.

aura: a dreamlike state in which there are unusual bodily sensations.

aversion therapy: a technique in which a particular habit is made to be unpleasant.

B

B cells: the blood cells that produce antibodies.

bacteria: single-celled microorganisms that can produce illness.

bacterial vaginosis: an STD caused by the *Gardnerella vaginalis* bacterium.

bagging: putting the solvent in a bag or spraying an aerosol into a bag, placing the bag over the mouth and nose, and inhaling deeply.

balance: the ability to maintain or regain equilibrium while moving or standing still.

balloon angioplasty: a procedure in which an artery is unclogged by catheterization.

barbiturates: depressant drugs that are used to induce sleep and relieve tension.

beer: an alcoholic beverage that is made from the fermentation of grains such as barley, corn, or rye.

behavior modification: a technique in which one behavior is substituted with another more beneficial behavior.

behavioral objective: a statement of what a student should be able to do

Glossary

after completing a learning experience.

benign tumor: a noncancerous tumor.

benzodiazepines: a class of drugs that are widely used as anti-anxiety agents or tranquilizers.

beta-blockers: drugs that can slow the heartbeat rate and reduce the force of the heart's contractions.

beta-endorphins: substances produced in the brain that help reduce pain and create a feeling of well-being.

Better Business Bureau: a nonprofit, voluntary, self-regulating organization that monitors unfair competition and misleading advertising for private firms.

bicuspids: the eight teeth in back of the cuspids with two cusps and one or two roots that crush food.

biodegradable substance: a substance that decomposes through natural or biological processes into harmless materials.

bioequivalency: the ability of one drug to produce effects in the body similar to another drug.

bleeding: a condition in which blood escapes from the vessels that naturally contain it.

blended family: a family that includes the newly married adults and their children from any previous marriage.

blister: a sore that may be caused by irritation.

blood: the fluid that supplies essential substances to all body cells and removes waste products from all body cells.

blood-alcohol concentration (BAC): the ratio of alcohol in a person's blood to the person's total amount of blood; BAC is expressed as a percent.

bloodborne pathogens: pathogenic microorganisms that are present in human blood and can cause disease.

blood pressure: the force exerted by the flowing blood against the walls of the arteries.

blotter acid: blotter-like paper that has

been impregnated with LSD and cut into small squares.

body composition: the percentage of fat tissue and lean tissue in the body.

body image: the perception that a person has of his or her body's appearance.

bone injury: damage to bones that results from physical trauma.

braces: devices that are cemented or bonded to the teeth and wired together to bring the teeth into correct alignment.

brand name drug: a registered name or trademark given to a drug by a pharmaceutical company.

break-away base: a base that pops loose when a sliding runner collides with it.

bridge: a partial denture or replacement that is used to take the place of one or more teeth.

budget: a plan for spending and saving money.

bulbourethral (Cowper's) glands are two small pea-shaped glands located on each side of the urethra and secrete a lubricating fluid.

bruises: discolorations from hemorrhaging resulting from blows to the muscles or bones.

bulimia: an eating disorder in which a person has uncontrollable urges to eat excessively and then to rid the body of the excess Calories.

bullying: an attempt by a person to hurt or frighten people who are perceived to be smaller or weaker.

burglary: unlawful entry of a structure to commit a theft.

butyl nitrite: a liquid that has the same medicinal properties as amyl nitrite, but has never been used clinically.

C

caffeine: a legal drug that is found in chocolate, coffee, tea, some soda pops, prescription drugs, and over-the-counter drugs such as weight control aids, alertness pills, analgesic compounds, diuretics, and cold/allergy remedies.

caffeinism: a condition of chronic caffeine

toxicity or poisoning associated with very heavy use and preoccupation with caffeine.

calcium: a mineral that is needed for building bones and teeth and in maintaining bone strength.

calluses: extra layers of skin that form due to excess rubbing.

calorie: a measure that indicates the amount of energy obtained from a food.

cancer: a group of diseases in which there is uncontrolled multiplication of abnormal cells in the body.

candidiasis: an STD caused by a fungus, *Candida albicans*.

capillaries: any of the vessels that carry blood between the arterioles and the venules.

carbohydrates: nutrients such as starches and sugars that provide energy to the body.

carbon monoxide: an odorless, colorless gas present in the exhaust of automobiles as well as cigarette smoke.

cardiac arrest: a condition in which a person's heart has stopped beating.

cardiac arrhythmia: an irregular heartbeat.

cardiac muscles: muscles found only in the heart.

cardiac output: the amount of blood pumped by the heart to the body each minute.

cardiomyopathy: a degeneration of the heart muscle that is characterized by severe enlargement of the heart and inability of the damaged heart to pump blood effectively.

cardiologist: a physician who specializes in the treatment of disorders of the heart and blood vessels.

cardiopulmonary resuscitation (CPR): an emergency procedure that is used to revive a person whose heart has stopped beating.

cardiovascular disease: a group of diseases of the heart and blood vessels.

cardiovascular endurance: the ability to do activities which require increased oxygen intake extended periods of time.

cardiovascular system: a body system that consists of the heart, blood vessels, and blood.

carjacking: a car theft occurs while the driver and/or passengers are in or near the vehicle.

cartilage: connective tissue that is tough but flexible.

CAT: a form of methcathinone, the most active ingredient found in Khat, a naturally occurring stimulant.

cataract: clouding of the lens of the eye that obstructs vision and can lead to blindness.

Center for Science in the Public Interest (CPSI): a private organization that publishes information about foods and food choices, including the monthly newsletter, *Nutrition Action Healthletter*.

Centers for Disease Control and Prevention (CDC): federal agency within the Public Health Service responsible for tracking disease incidence and trends, coordinating disease control efforts with other nations, taking action in response to outbreaks, epidemics, and natural disasters, and working with states and communities in developing and operating disease control programs.

cervix: the lowest part of the uterus.

chancre: a hard, round, painless sore with raised edges resulting from syphilis.

chemical dependency: another term used to describe drug dependence.

chemotherapy: the use of drugs to kill cancer cells inside the body.

chewing tobacco: a plug or loose form of tobacco.

chickenpox: a highly contagious and common childhood viral illness that produces fever, tiredness, and skin blisters.

child abuse: the harmful treatment of a person under the age of eighteen and

Glossary

includes physical abuse, emotional abuse, sexual abuse, and neglect.

child sexual abuse: any sexual act or acts performed by an adult with a person under eighteen years of age.

childbirth: the process by which an infant is moved from the uterus to the outside world.

childhood immunizations: immunizations that are given to children to protect them against potentially serious infectious diseases.

childhood infectious diseases: abnormal body functions, usually in young persons, that are caused by microorganisms and viruses that are readily transmitted from one person to another.

"China White": the street name of a derivative of fentanyl, alpha methyl fentanyl, and has caused a number of overdoses from its very high potency.

chlamydial infections: STDs caused by the bacterium *Chlamydia trachomatis* that may result in inflammation of the urethra and epididymis in males and inflammation of the vagina and cervix in females.

cholofluorocarbons: odorless nonpoisonous chemicals that are used as aerosol propellants and refrigerants.

cholesterol: a fat-like substance made by the body and found in many foods.

chromosome: a distinct body in a cell nucleus that becomes apparent during cell division.

chronic fatigue syndrome (CFS): a condition in which fatigue comes on suddenly and is relentless or relapsing, causing debilitating tiredness in someone who has no apparent reason for feeling this way.

chronic health condition: a recurring or persistent health condition.

cirrhosis: a disease in which alcohol destroys liver cells and plugs the liver with fibrous scar tissue that can lead to liver failure and death.

clarifying response: a response in which a person asks for more information.

clostridium botulinum (botulism): a bacteria that results primarily from improperly canned foods.

cocaine: a strong stimulant that is derived from the leaves of the coca bush.

codeine: a narcotic analgesic drug.

codependence: a mental disorder in which a person loses personal identity, has frozen feelings, and copes ineffectively.

codependent: person who has codependence.

cognitive domain: a category of objectives dealing with thinking behavior.

cold-temperature-related emergencies: physical conditions that result from exposure to low temperatures, either below or above freezing.

colon: the major part of the large intestine.

commercial: an advertisement on television or radio.

commitment: a pledge or promise that is made.

common cold: a viral infection of the upper respiratory tract.

Communicable and Chronic Diseases: the area of health that focuses on recognizing communicable and noncommunicable diseases; keeping the immune system healthy; preventing the spread of pathogens; reducing the risk of infection with common communicable diseases, STDs, and HIV; obtaining a family history for diseases; reducing the risk of cardiovascular diseases and cancer; and recognizing ways to manage chronic diseases.

communicable diseases: illnesses caused by pathogens that enter the body through direct or indirect contact.

communication: the sharing or feelings, thoughts, and information with another person.

complete proteins: proteins that contain all the essential amino acids.

complex carbohydrates: carbohydrates that have a more complex chemical structure and provide a long-lasting source of energy.

comprehensive school health education: an organized, sequential K–12 plan for teaching students the information and helping them develop life skills that promote health literacy and maintain and improve health, prevent disease, and reduce health-related risk behaviors.

comprehensive school health program: an organized set of policies, procedures and activities designed to protect and promote the health, safety, and well-being of students and staff.

concave lenses: lenses that are curved or rounded inward like the inside of a bowl.

conductive hearing loss: faulty transportation of sound from the outer to the inner ear.

confirming response: a response to acknowledge the feelings that the speaker expressed and to show appreciation for the expression of the feelings.

conflict: a disagreement between two or more people or between two or more choices.

conflict avoidance: a conflict response style in which a person denies that there is a conflict and/or attempts to please others at his/her expense.

conflict confrontation: a conflict response style in which a person attempts to settle a disagreement in a hostile, defiant, and aggressive way.

conflict resolution: a conflict response style in which a person uses conflict resolution skills to resolve a disagreement in a healthful, safe, legal, respectful, and nonviolent way.

conflict resolution skills: skills a person can use to resolve a disagree-

ment in a healthful, safe, legal, respectful, and nonviolent way.

conflict response style: a pattern of behavior a person demonstrates when a conflict occurs.

congenital syphilis: syphilis that is transmitted to a fetus from an infected pregnant female who has untreated primary or secondary syphilis.

conjunctivitis: an inflammation of the membrane lining the eyelids and covering the eyeball (conjunctiva).

consumer: a person who chooses sources of health-related information and buys or uses health products or services.

consumerism: the practice of carefully analyzing health information, getting value for money spent on health products and services, and making comparisons between alternative products and services.

Consumer and Community Health: the area of health that focuses on choosing sources of health-related information and products and services, analyzing advertising, recognizing and reporting quackery, spending money and time wisely, using school nurse and school health services when appropriate, using health care providers and health care facilities, cooperating with people in the community who protect health and safety, and volunteering in school clubs and community organizations and agencies that promote health.

Consumer Product Safety Commission: the federal agency that distributes information and receives complaints about the safety of products.

Consumers' Research: private group that tests products and provides ratings for consumers to make comparisons with regard to products' performance and safety.

Consumer's Union: private group that tests products and provides ratings for consumers to make comparisons with regard to products' performance and

Glossary

safety.

controlled substance: a drug that is illegal without a prescription.

convex lenses: lenses that are curved or rounded like the exterior of a sphere or circle.

corpus luteum: a temporary gland that secretes the hormones estrogen and progesterone, which cause the endometrium, the inner layer of the uterus, to thicken.

cortex: the part of the adrenal gland that produces several hormones that are involved in regulating water balance in body tissues and in increasing blood sugar levels.

counseling, psychological, and social services: services that provide broad-based individual and group assessments, interventions, and referrals which attend to the mental, emotional, and social health of students.

cooperative learning: an instructional strategy in which students work together to understand a particular concept or develop a life skill.

coordination: the ability to synchronize more than one muscular task or sense at the same time.

corns: painful growths that can result from excess rubbing of the shoe against the foot.

coronary bypass surgery: an operation in which a vein from another part of the body, often the leg, is grafted into a coronary artery so that blood is detoured around a blockage.

coronary heart disease: the broad term used to describe damage or malfunction of the heart caused by blockage of the coronary arteries.

crack: a purified form of cocaine that produces a rapid and intense reaction.

crank: an amphetamine-like stimulant.

creative intimacy: the sharing in the work or development of a project, task, or creation of something new.

cuspids: the four teeth in the corners of the mouth that have a long, heavy root and a pointed cusp that tears food.

cyanosis: a condition that results from the lack of oxygen to body tissues and manifests itself as bluish color around the lips and mouth.

cyst: a sac that is formed when fluid becomes trapped in a lymph duct.

cystic fibrosis: a genetic disease that affects the mucous and sweat glands.

cystitis: the inflammation of the urinary bladder.

D

daily hassles: the day-to-day stressors of normal living.

dating: the sharing of social activities and time with members of the opposite sex.

DDT: a pesticide that was banned because it was found in food products after harvest.

death: the permanent cessation of brain, heart, and lung function.

decibel: a unit used to measure sound intensity.

decision: a choice.

deductible: an amount to be paid by the insurance policyholder before the health insurance company makes any payment.

delayed gratification: allowing oneself to sacrifice in the present so that a benefit will be achieved in the future.

dementia: a condition in which the thinking processes are impaired.

denial: a condition in which a person refuses to recognize what (s)he is feeling because it is extremely painful.

dental caries: areas of tooth decay (cavities).

dental emergencies: injuries or disorders of the teeth or gums that require immediate treatment because of severe pain and/or because delay could lead to further complications.

dental health plan: a plan for taking care of the teeth and gums that includes frequent brushing and flossing, reduction of cavity-promoting foods, avoidance of tobacco, protecting the teeth from injury, regular dental check-ups, and cleaning of the teeth by a dental hygienist.

dental hygienist: an allied health professional who provides oral health services such as cleaning teeth and education about proper care of teeth.

dental problems: nontraumatic tooth-related conditions that exist as a result of structure, infection, or diet.

dental sealants: thin plastic coatings that provide protection against dental decay to the chewing surfaces of teeth.

dentist: a health care professional trained and licensed as a either a doctor of dental surgery (D.D.S) or a doctor of medical dentistry (D.M.D.).

denture: a full set of false teeth.

dependence: a condition in which people have to have a drug or they experience withdrawal.

depression: the feeling of being sad, unhappy, discouraged, and "down in the dumps."

dermatologist: a physician who specializes in the treatment of disorders of the digestive tract.

dermis: the deeper layer of skin containing cells that are well supplied with blood vessels and nerve cells.

designer drug: any one of a group of drugs than are made in labs to imitate well-known drugs.

destructive relationship: relationship that destroys self-esteem, interferes with productivity and health, and may include violence and drug misuse and abuse.

developmental task: achievement that is necessary to be made during a particular period of growth in order that a person can continue growing toward maturity.

detoxification: the process in which a drug is withdrawn from the body.

diabetes: a disease in which the body is unable to process the sugar in foods in normal ways.

diabetes mellitus: a condition characterized by an excess of glucose in the blood, resulting when the pancreas produces too little or no insulin.

diabetic acidosis: a condition in which there is a production of two abnormal acids or a lowering of the alkali in the blood as a result of faulty metabolism.

Dietary Guidelines for Americans, The: recommendations for diet choices for healthy Americans two years of age or older.

digestion: the process by which food is chemically changed to a form that can pass through cell membranes.

digestive system: a body system that breaks down food so that nutrients can be absorbed by the cells in the body.

digital rectal exam: an examination of the lower bowel and, in men, the prostate, in which a physician inserts a gloved finger into the anal opening.

dioxins: group of chemicals belonging to the chlorinated hydrocarbons and used as insecticides.

direct pressure: the placement of pressure over the wound with the purpose of restricting blood flow and allowing normal clotting.

discipline: training that corrects and improves student behavior.

discriminatory behavior: behavior that makes distinctions in treatment or shows behavior in favor of or prejudiced against an individual or group of people.

dislocation: the separation of a bone from its joint.

dispiriting relationships: relationships that are characterized by a state of low spirits.

distilled spirits: alcoholic beverages that have concentrations of alcohol

Glossary

higher than those reached by fermentation alone.

distress: a harmful response to a stressor that produces negative results.

diversity: the quality of being different or varied.

diverticulosis: a disease in which the intestinal walls develop outpouchings called diverticula.

divorce: a legal way to end a marriage, in which a judge decides the conditions of the settlement.

domains of health: the three kinds of health: physical, mental-emotional, and family-social.

domestic violence: violence that occurs within the family or within other relationships in which people live together.

Down syndrome: a genetic disease that is the result of an extra chromosome.

DPT: a combination inoculation against tetanus, diphtheria, and pertussis (whooping cough).

drowning: suffocation in water.

drownproofing: a technique that allows an individual to stay afloat without a life jacket during a swimming emergency.

drug: a substance that is introduced into the body, excluding food, that alters the function of the body.

drug abuse: the use of drugs that results in impairment of a user's ability to function normally or that is harmful to the user or others

drug dependence: compulsive use of a drug (or drugs) despite adverse psychological, physiological, or social consequences.

drug free: when a person does not use harmful and illegal drugs.

drug-free lifestyle: a lifestyle in which persons do not use harmful and illegal drugs.

drug-free school zone: a defined geographic areas around a school for the purpose of sheltering young people

from the sale of controlled substances.

drug misuse: the inappropriate use of drugs including prescribed or nonprescribed medicines.

drug trafficking: the purchasing and selling of illegal drugs.

drug use: the use of alcohol and other drugs in any form, legal or illegal, whether by prescription or for "recreational" purposes.

dysentery: a severe infection of the intestines, causing diarrhea and abdominal pain.

dysfunctional family: a family in which feelings are not expressed openly and honestly, coping skills are lacking, and family members do not trust each other.

dyslexia: a learning disability manifested by difficulty in learning to read despite conventional instruction, adequate intelligence, and sociocultural opportunity.

E

earthquake: violent shakings of the earth's surface caused by the shifting of the plates that make up the Earth's crust.

eating disorder: food-related dysfunction in which a person changes eating habits in a way that is harmful to the mind or body.

ectomorph: a person who is long-boned and has a lean body build.

effective classroom management: the use of managerial skills by teachers to decrease disruptive behavior in the classroom and improve on-task behavior.

electromagnetic spectrum: the electromagnetic radiation ranging from the longest to the shortest wavelength.

Emergency Planning Committee: committee established for the purpose of developing and implementing school emergency plans.

emotional abuse: maltreatment that

774

involves assault in a nonphysical way.

emotional environment: the set of expectations, interpersonal relationships, and experiences that contribute to the development of the student by way of feeling and sensibilities.

emotional security: a feeling of freedom from anxiety in which individuals feel that they can present and express themselves without fear of ridicule, threat, or belittling.

empathy: the ability to share in another person's emotions or feelings.

empowered: to be inspired by the feeling that one has some control over his/her destiny.

enabler: a person who unwittingly supports a person who has an addiction by protecting the addict and making in easy for him/her to continue the addiction.

endometriosis: a condition in which the endometrial tissue grows somewhere other than in the lining of the uterus, such as the ovaries, Fallopian tubes, vagina, or cervix.

endomorph: a person who has a greater percentage of fat tissue and a flabby appearance.

energy equation: the Caloric intake needs to equal Caloric expenditure for weight maintenance.

entertainment addiction: extreme need to be entertained at the expense of taking care of physical, social, emotional, and/or mental needs.

environment: the multitude of dynamic conditions that are external to a person.

Environmental Health: the area of health that focuses on showing concern about environmental issues, keeping the air clean, keeping the water clean, keeping the indoor environment free of pollution, keeping noise at a healthful level, protecting oneself from radiation, disposing of solid wastes properly, recycling, being aware of the effects of overcrowding, and cooperating with environmental protection agencies.

Environmental Protection Agency (EPA): a federal agency that is responsible for alleviating and controlling environmental pollution.

environmental tobacco smoke: the combination of sidestream smoke and the mainstream smoke exhaled by a smoker.

enzyme: a chemical that speeds up a chemical reaction.

epidermis: surface layer of the skin; the outer cells of this layer of which is dead.

epilepsy: a condition in which there is a disturbance of impulses in the brain leading to seizures.

erection: an involuntary process that occurs when spongy layers inside the penis are engorged with blood and cause the penis to swell and elongate.

essential amino acids: eight amino acids that the body does not produce.

estrogen: a hormone essential for normal female sexual development and for the healthy functioning of the reproductive system.

ethyl alcohol: the type of alcohol that is found in alcoholic beverages.

eustress: a healthful response to a stressor that produces positive results.

evaluation: the means of measuring the students' mastery of the health education standards, the performance indicators, and the life skills. The procedure used to measure the results of efforts toward a desired goal.

exclusion: certain items and services that are not covered by the health insurance policy.

exhaustion stage: the third stage of the GAS in which there is wear and tear on the body, lowered resistance to disease, and an increased likelihood of disease or death.

expenses: the cost of items that are needed and wanted to be purchased.

external bleeding: bleeding that takes

place through a break in the skin.

extraction: surgical removal of a tooth.

F

fainting: the partial or complete loss of consciousness that occurs when there has been reduced blood flow to the brain.

fallopian tubes: two tubes that transport ova from each ovary to the uterus.

Family Living: the area of health that focuses on developing relationship skills, avoiding discrimination, practicing conflict resolution skills, striving for healthful family relationships, making healthful adjustments to family changes, forming healthful and responsible friendships, recognizing harmful relationships, identifying resources to improve relationships, developing skills to prepare for future family life, and practicing life skills to support abstinence.

family relationships: a scale marked in units ranging from zero to 100 that shows the quality of relationships within a family.

family-social health: the condition of a person's relationships with others.

fast food: food that can be served quickly and is prepared in walk-in or drive-through restaurants.

fat-soluble vitamin: vitamin that can be stored in the body.

fats: nutrients that are a source of energy and are essential for making certain vitamins available to the body.

fecal occult blood test: test to check for blood in feces.

Federal Trade Commission (FTC): an independent agency that monitors the advertising of foods, drugs, cosmetics, devices, and advertising of foods, drugs, cosmetics, devices, and advertising that appears on television.

fermentation: the process that occurs when yeast cells act on sugar in the presence of water producing a chemical change.

fertility: the capability to produce offspring.

fetal alcohol effects (FAEs): birth defects in prenatally alcohol-exposed babies that do not meet the criteria for an FAS diagnosis, but may be categorized as having suspected effects.

fetal alcohol syndrome (FAS): a characteristic pattern of severe birth defects present in babies born to mothers who drink alcohol during their pregnancy.

fiber: the indigestible material in grains and plant foods.

fighting: taking part in a physical struggle.

first aid: the immediate and temporary care given to a person who has been injured or suddenly becomes ill.

filling: the material that a dentist uses to repair the cavity of a tooth.

fixed indemnity: specific amounts that an insurance company pays for specific procedures.

flashback: manifestation of one or more of the acute effects of the drug that recursafter it was taken.

flexibility: the ability to bend and move the thorough a full range of motion.

flooding: the sudden, rather than gradual, exposure of a person to what causes the fear.

Food and Drug Administration (FDA): a federal agency within the Department of Health and Human Services that monitors the safety and effectiveness of medical devices and new drugs and the safety and purity of cosmetics and foods.

food allergy: overreaction by the body to normally harmless ingredients in foods.

food-borne infection: illness caused be eating food that has been contaminated with virus, bacteria, worms, or other organisms.

Food Guide Pyramid: a food-group guide that recommends daily guidelines to ensure a balanced diet.

food intolerance: negative effects of

consuming certain substances by people who lack the digestive chemicals needed to break them down.

food irradiations: a process to protect foods in which the foods are treated with gamma radiation.

footcandle: the amount of illumination from a standard candle on a surface at one foot of distance.

formaldehyde: a colorless gas with a pungent odor.

fracture: a break or a crack in a bone.

fraternal twins: twins who develop from two separate ova that are fertilized by two separate sperm.

freebase: the purified base form of cocaine processed from the hydrochloride salt using volatile chemicals, usually ether.

freestanding emergency center: a facility, not part of a hospital, that provides prompt care for accidents or illnesses which occurs when a person does not have a personal physician.

friend: a person who is known well and liked.

frostbite: the freezing of parts of the body.

fungi: single-celled or multicellular plant-like organisms, such as yeasts and molds, that are capable of causing disease to the skin, mucous membranes, and lungs.

G

gambling addiction: an addictive behavior in which a person is unable to control the urge to gamble.

general adaptation syndrome (GAS): a series of changes that occur in the body when stress occurs.

generic name drug: the chemical and/or biological equivalent of a specific brand name drug.

genes: special structures that transmit hereditary characteristics.

genetics: the scientific study of genes

and how they determine and control development.

genital herpes: a highly contagious STD that is caused by two forms of the herpes simplex virus (HSV), HSV-1 and HSV-2.

genital warts: dry, wartlike growths that are caused by the human papilloma virus (HPV).

geriatrician: a physician who specializes in the medical care of the elderly.

German measles: a viral disease that is a milder form of measles.

gerontology: the study of aging.

gingivitis: an inflammation that often results in redness, swelling, and bleeding of the gums.

glaucoma: a disease of the eyes marked by increased pressure within the eyeball that can ultimately damage the optic nerve.

glycogen: a temporary reserve supply of energy in the form of sugar and is stored in the liver and muscles.

gonorrhea: an STD caused by the bacterium *Neisseria gonorrhoeae*, which infects the linings of the genital and urinary tracts of males and females.

grand mal seizure: a major convulsive seizure during which a person drops to the ground, exhibits jerking motions, and stops breathing temporarily.

greenhouse effect: an increase in the carbon dioxide concentration in the atmosphere that reduces heat loss of the Earth and increases atmospheric temperature.

grooming: taking good care of the body by following practices that help people look, smell, and feel their best.

group policies: insurance policies available through organizations that employ or to which policyholders may belong.

Growth and Development: the area of health that focuses on caring for the body systems, recognizing changes during growth periods, accepting maleness or femaleness, accepting physical appearance, accepting one's learning style, achieving appropriate developmental tasks, learning about the beginning of a new life, recognizing the needs of people of different ages, preparing for aging, and sharing feelings about dying and death.

H

halogens: a group of related chemicals that are used for various purposes, among them to extinguish fires.

hallucinogenic drug: a substance that has the major effect of producing marked distortions in perception.

harmful behavior: voluntary action that threatens health, increases the likelihood of illness and premature death, and destroys the quality of the environment.

harmful relationship: relationship that threatens self-esteem, is disrespectful, indicates a lack of character, threatens health, and fosters irresponsible decision-making.

harmful situations: involuntary circumstances that threaten health, increase the likelihood of illness, injury, and premature death, and destroy the quality of the environment.

hashish: consists of the drug-rich resinous secretions of the cannabis plant, which are collected, dried, and then compressed into a variety of forms, such as balls, cakes, or cookie-like sheets.

hashish oil: a variation of hashish, produced by a process of repeated extraction of cannabis plant material to yield a dark viscous liquid.

hate crimes: crimes motivated by religious, racial, ethnic, sexual orientation, or other bias.

hazardous waste: harmful substances that are difficult to discard safely.

head injury: a traumatic physical event that involves the head.

health: the quality of life that includes physical, mental-emotional, and family-social health.

health behavior contract: a plan that is written to develop the habit of following a specific life skill.

health behavior inventory: a personal assessment tool that contains a list of actions to which a student responds positively, "I practice this action," or to which the student responds negatively, "I do not practice this action."

health care practitioner: a health care professional whose practice is restricted to a specific area of the body.

health education: a planned, sequential K–12 curriculum that addresses the physical, mental, emotional, and social dimensions of health.

health history: a questionnaire that gathers information about lifestyle, past health conditions, past medical care, allergies and drug sensitivities, and family health history.

health insurance: a financial agreement between an insurance company and an individual or group for the payment of health care.

health knowledge: information that is needed to develop health literacy, maintain and improve health, prevent disease, and reduce health-related risk behaviors.

health literacy: competency in critical thinking and problem solving, responsible and productive citizenship, self-directed learning, and effective communication. (Joint Health Education Standards Committee, 1994).

health literate individual: a critical thinker and problem solver, a responsible and productive citizen, a self-directed learner, and an effective communicator (The Joint Committee on Health Education Standards, 1994).

health maintenance organizations (HMOs): health care delivery plans in which subscribers prepay a fixed monthly fee for coverage from member health care providers.

health promotion: the informing and motivating of students to become health literate, maintain and improve health, prevent disease, and reduce health-related risk behaviors.

health promotion for staff: health promotion programs such as health assessments, health education, and health-related fitness activities that protect and promote the health of those on the school staff.

health services: services designed to appraise, protect, and promote the health of students.

health status: the sum total of the positive and negative influences of the level of health knowledge a person has, the behaviors a person chooses, the situations in which a person engages, the decisions a person makes, the resistance skills a person has, the protective factors a person possesses, the degree to which a person is resilient, and the degree of health literacy a person has achieved.

health topics: the subjects within each of the content areas that need to be taught in order that students might have the health knowledge needed to practice life skills that enable them to master the performance indicators for the health education standards.

healthful behavior: action that promotes health; prevent sillness, injury, and premature death; and improves the quality of the environment.

healthful body composition: a high ratio of lean tissue to fat tissue.

healthful family: a family in which feelings are expressed openly and honestly, coping skills are adequate, and family members trust each other.

healthful marriage: a healthful relationship between marriage partners that is based on equality, trust, communication, and commitment.

healthful relationships: relationships that promote self-esteem and productivity, encourage health-enhancing behavior, and are free of violence and drug misuse and abuse.

healthful situations: circumstances that promote health; prevent illness, injury, and premature death; and improve the quality of the environment.

healthy fitness zone: the range of test scores of a particular fitness test that are considered to be healthy for children at specific age levels.

hearing loss: the reduced ability to detect sound.

heart: a muscular organ that beats continuously and rhythmically to pump blood to the body.

heart rate: the number of times that the heart beats each minute forcing blood into the arteries.

heat cramp: painful muscle spasm that occurs most often in the legs and arms due to excessive fluid loss through sweating.

heat emergencies: physical conditions that result when a person is exposed to higher than normal temperatures for varying periods of time.

heat exhaustion: extreme tiredness due to the inability of the body temperature to be regulated.

heat stroke: a sudden attack of illness from exposure to high temperatures.

Heimlich maneuver: a technique that makes use of abdominal thrusts to dislodge an object in the air passage of a conscious person who is choking.

helper T cells: white blood cells that signal B cells to make antibodies.

hemophilia: a hereditary disorder characterized by the impaired ability of the blood to clot.

hepatitis: a viral infection that causes enlargement and pain in the liver.

hepatitis B: a common type of viral hepatitis.

hepatitis B vaccine: a vaccine for hepatitis B that should be given at birth, one to two months, and six to eighteen months.

herniation: the protrusion of the contents of one of the body's cavities through an abnormal opening in the cavity wall.

heroin: a narcotic drug that has no approved medical use in the United States.

heterosexism: behavior that discriminates against people who are gay, lesbian, or bisexual.

heterosexual: a person who has a sexual preference for someone of the opposite sex.

HiB: immunizes against the *Hemophilus influenza* type B, which is the leading cause of bacterial meningitis.

hidden anger: anger that is not recognized or is expressed in harmful ways and may result in inappropriate behavior and poor health.

high-density lipoproteins (HDLs): fats that transport excess cholesterol to the liver for removal from the body.

histamine: a chemical released by the body in allergic reactions that cause itching, constriction of smooth muscle in the bronchial tubes, and leakiness of blood vessels.

hit: one dose of LSD.

holistic effect: the effect of the behaviors, situations, and relationships chosen; the decisions made and the resistance skills used, the protective factors possessed, and the degree of resiliency and health literacy that has been achieved, on the whole person.

holistic health: the connectedness that the nine factors that influence health status have with the ten areas of health and the three domains of health.

homicide: the accidental or purposeful killing of another person.

homosexual: a person who has a sexual preference for someone of the same sex.

hormones: groups of chemicals, each of which is released into the bloodstream by a particular gland or tissue to have an affect elsewhere in the body.

hostility: a feeling of ill will with antagonism.

huffing: sniffing the vapors from a rag or cloth that has been soaked or had a solvent poured on it.

human collision: a forceful collision experienced when an unbelted occupant is thrown against the motor vehicle's interior components—dashboard, windshield, steering wheel, etc.

human immunodeficiency virus (HIV): the pathogen that destroys the body's immune system allowing the development of AIDS.

hunger: the physiological need for food.

hurricane: tropical storm with heavy rains and winds in excess of 74 miles per hour.

hydrocarbons: chemical compounds that contain only carbon and hydrogen.

hyperactivity: greater than normal physical restlessness.

hyperopia: a refractive error that results in farsightedness (close-up vision is blurred).

hypertension: high blood pressure.

hypnotic: drugs that induce drowsiness and encourage sleep.

hypoglycemia: a condition in which the pancreas produce too much insulin and blood sugar levels decrease.

hypothermia: low body temperature.

hysterectomy: the surgical removal of the uterus and cervix.

I

I-message: a statement that contains (1) a specific behavior or event, (2) the effect that the behavior or event has on the individual, and (3) the feeling that resulted.

ice: a smokeable form of pure methamphetamine that is gaining popularity in the United States.

identical twins: twins who develop from a single ovum fertilized by a single sperm that divides after fertilization.

illicit drug: a controlled substance—a drug which is illegal.

immune system: the body system that fights disease.

immunization: a vaccine that provides immunity to a certain infectious disease.

impetigo: a highly contagious bacterial infection of the skin.

in vitro fertilization: a procedure in which mature ova are removed from a female's ovary and placed in a lab dish to be fertilized by sperm.

inactive decision-making style: a decision-making style in which a person fails to make choices, and this failure determines what will occur.

incineration: a method of waste disposal in which waste is burned to ashes.

inclusion: the adaptation of the teaching strategy to assist and include students with special learning challenges and may include enrichment suggestions for the gifted and reteaching ideas for students who are learning disabled.

incest: child sexual abuse involving a close relative of the child.

incisors: the eight teeth in the front and center of the mouth that have a flat, sharp edge that cuts up food.

income: the money that is received from a variety of sources.

incomplete protein: a protein that does not contain all the essential amino acids.

individual policies: insurance policies arranged between a consumer and a health care insurance company.

infertility: the inability to produce offspring.

influenza: a viral disease that affects the respiratory system.

infusion: the integration of a subject area into another area(s) of the curriculum.

ingrown toenail: when a toenail grows into the skin.

inguinal hernia: a condition in which some of the intestine pushes through the inguinal canal.

inhalants: chemicals that produce vapors resulting in psychoactive effects.

inhalation: the process of taking air into the lungs.

injury prevention: actions that are taken for the purpose of preventing injuries.

Injury Prevention and Safety: the area of health that focuses on following safety rules in the home, school, and community; following safety guidelines for different weather conditions and natural disasters; being able to get help for emergency situations; being skilled in basic first aid procedures; reducing the risk of violence; protecting oneself from those who are dangerous; and staying safe while riding in a car and when enjoying exercise.

insomnia: a condition in which the inability to sleep becomes a pattern.

inspiriting relationships: relationships that lift the spirit and contribute to a sense of well-being.

insulin: a pancreatic hormone that regulated the sugar in the blood.

insulin-dependent diabetes: diabetes in which the pancreas produces little or no insulin.

integumentary system: a body system composed of the skin, hair, nails, and glands.

intergroup conflict: a conflict that occurs between two or more groups of people.

internal bleeding: bleeding within the body in which lost blood escapes into some internal cavity or into surrounding tissue.

interpersonal conflict: a conflict that occurs between two or more people.

intervention: a confrontation by people, such as parents, spouses, or friends, who are significant to the person who has an addiction

Glossary

intimacy: a deep and meaningful kind of sharing between two persons.

intragroup conflict: a conflict that occurs between people who identify themselves as belonging to the same group.

intrapersonal conflict: a conflict that occurs within a person.

involuntary smoking: exposure to secondhand smoke.

ionizing radiation: the part of the electromagnetic spectrum that contains the shortest wavelengths—radiation that ionizes atoms or molecules.

irritable bowel syndrome (IBS): a condition in which a person experiences nausea, gas, pain, attacks of diarrhea, and cramps after eating certain foods.

iron: a mineral that is an important component of hemoglobin.

isms: beliefs, attitudes, assumptions, and actions that subject individuals or people in a particular group to discriminatory behavior.

isokinetic exercise: exercise in which a weight is moved through a full range of motion.

isometric exercise: exercise in which a muscle is tightened for about five to six seconds and there is no body movement.

isotonic exercise: exercise in which there is a muscle contraction and a movement of body parts.

J

Joint Committee on Health Education Standards, The: a committee whose purpose was to identify The National Health Education Standards that incorporate the knowledge and skills essential to the development of health literacy.

joint: the point where two or more bones meet.

joint injuries: injuries to the tissues that surround the joints.

K

Khat: a stimulant that is found in the leaves of an evergreen plant that is sometimes chewed by people of East Africa and Southern Arabia.

knocked-out tooth: tooth that has been knocked out of its sockets.

kyphosis: an excessive rounding of the back.

L

labor: a series of three stages that result in the birth of a baby.

lactose intolerance: intolerance caused by a deficiency of the enzyme lactase that is necessary to digest all the lactose (milk sugar) that is consumed.

lacto-ovo-vegetarian diet: a diet that includes both dairy products and eggs.

lacto-vegetarian diet: a diet that does not include meats but does include dairy products.

landfill: a method of waste disposal in which waste is buried between layers of soil, often building up low-lying areas in the process.

lead: an element that is found in many products used inside and outside the home.

learning disability: a range of physical or psychological disorders that interfere with learning.

leukoplakia: a white, patchy lesion on the lining of the mouth that can lead to cancer.

licensed practical nurse: licensed and trained nurse who provides nursing care under the direction of registered nurses or medical doctors.

life crisis: an emotionally significant event or change in a person's life.

life skills: actions that promote health literacy, maintain and improve health, prevent disease, and reduce health-related risk behaviors.

lifetime sports: sports activities that can be continued as people grow older.

ligament: band of tough connective tissue that holds bones together at the joints.

Likert scale: a technique used to measure beliefs and attitudes in which students react to statements with a response of strongly agree, agree, neutral, disagree, or strongly disagree.

lipoproteins: fats in the bloodstream.

local health department: the official agency that has responsibility for the health of people residing within a community.

loneliness: an anxious, unpleasant, and painful feeling that results from having few friends or from being alienated.

look-alike drug: a tablet or capsule manufactured to resemble amphetamines and mimic their effects.

lordosis: a curvature of the spine that creates a "swayback" appearance.

low-density lipoproteins: fats that form deposits on the artery walls and contribute to the development of atherosclerosis.

low fat: a label for a product that contains 3 grams or less per serving.

LSD: a powerful hallucinogen that produces hallucinations, including bright colors and altered perceptions of what is real.

lyme disease: a bacterial disease transmitted through a tick.

lymphadenopathy: the presence of swollen lymph glands throughout the body.

lymphatic system: a part of the immune system that includes lymph vessels, lymphocytes, lymph nodes, the thymus glands, tonsils, and the spleen.

lymphocytes: white blood cells that are formed primarily in the lymph glands.

M

macrophage: a large cell that acts as a scavenger by engulfing and destroying pathogens.

malignant melanoma: the most serious of the skin cancers.

malignant tumor: a cancerous tumor.

malocclusion: the abnormal fitting together of teeth when the jaws are closed.

mammogram: a low-dose X-ray used to detect breast cancer.

managed care: a set of procedures used by health insurers to control health care costs by controlling which medical services consumers are entitled to receive and by limiting reimbursement for certain services.

manic-depressive disorder: a mood disorder in which a person's moods vary from being very high to being very depressed.

marijuana: a drug from the cannabis plant containing THC that impairs short-term memory and changes mood.

marrow: a soft substance in the center of bones.

materials: items that are needed to so the teaching strategy.

maximum heart rate: a heart rate that is calculated by subtracting your age from 220.

measles: a potentially deadly viral illness that produces an itchy rash on the face and body, tiredness, high fever, coughing, and runny nose.

media: the various forms of mass communication such as television, radio, magazines, and newspapers.

mediate: to bring together people who are in conflict.

medical technologist: an allied health care professional who helps people with disabilities learn to adapt to their disabilities.

Medicaid: a governmental health insurance plan in which people receiving other types of public assistance receive medical and hospital coverage.

Medicare: a governmental health insurance to which people contribute during their working years in exchange for some of their health care costs being covered after age sixty-five.

Medic Alert: a medical identification

Glossary

that provides important information about the person wearing it.

medicine: a drug that is used to treat, prevent, or diagnose illness.

menarche: the first menstrual cycle.

meninges: three membranes that cover and protect the brain and spinal cord.

menstrual cycle: a rhythmic cycle of approximately one month in which hormone levels fluctuate to prepare a female's body for the possibility of pregnancy.

Mental and Emotional Health: the area of health that focuses on gaining health knowledge and practicing life skills, making responsible decisions, using resistance skills when appropriate, choosing behaviors to promote a healthy mind, developing positive self-esteem, communicating with others in healthful ways, expressing feelings, and coping with stress in healthful ways.

mental-emotional health: the condition of a person's mind and the ways that a person expresses feelings.

mental rehearsal: a technique that involves imagining oneself in the stressful conversation or situation, pretending that one says and does specific things, and imagining how the other person will respond.

mentors: people who guide and help younger people.

mescaline: a hallucinogen native to the deserts of Mexico and the southwestern United States.

mesomorph: a person who has a muscular body build.

methadone maintenance: giving people who are addicted to drugs a legally-controlled, synthetic narcotic drug.

methamphetamine: a stimulant drug that falls within the amphetamine family.

microdots: tablets of LSD that are less than an eighth of an inch in width.

minerals: inorganic substances needed by the body in small amounts.

miscarriage: a spontaneous abortion or natural expulsion of the fetus or embryo before it has reached the point of development at which it can survive outside the mother's body.

mixed message: a message in which verbal and nonverbal behavior do not match.

MMR: immunizes against measles, mumps, and rubella (German measles) and is given in two doses, at fifteen months and again between four and six years or before junior high or middle school.

Model for Using Resistance Skills, The: a list of suggested ways for effectively resisting pressure to engage in actions that threaten health, threaten safety, break laws, result in lack of respect for self and others, disobey guidelines set by responsible adults, and detract from character.

Model of Health and Well-Being, The: shows the relationship among the three domains of health, the health content areas, and the nine factors that influence health status.

molars: the twelve teeth in the back of the mouth with several cusps and two or three roots that grind food.

monogamous marriage: a marriage in which both persons remain sexually faithful to one another.

mononucleosis: a viral infection that occurs most frequently to those in the fifteen- to nineteen-year-old age group; it is also known as "mono."

monovision contact lenses: lenses that provide correction for both nearsightedness and farsightedness in people who require bifocals.

morphine: a drug that is used to control pain.

motivation: the step-by-step directions to follow when doing the teaching strategy.

motor vehicle emissions: products

784

created from the combustion of motor fuels such as gasoline and diesel fuel.

MPPP: form of "designer heroin" that has been found to produce brain and nervous system damage in some users.

MPTP: form of "designer heroin" that has been found to produce brain and nervous system damage in some users.

multicultural infusion: the adaptation of the teaching strategy to include ideas that promote an awareness and appreciation of the culture and background of different people.

multiple addiction: a condition in which a person is addicted to more than one source of addiction at a time.

mumps: a viral disease of children that results in a swelling of the salivary glands.

muscle cramps: sharp pains that occur when muscles contract involuntarily usually because muscles have not been stretched before hard exercise.

muscle strain: injury and hemorrhaging in muscle tendons that is accompanied by a loss of muscular strength.

muscular dystrophy: a disease that is characterized by weakness due to the deterioration of muscle fibers.

muscular endurance: the ability to use muscles for an extended period of time.

muscular strength: the amount of force the muscles can exert against resistance.

muscular system: a body system in which there are three types of muscles—skeletal, smooth, and cardiac.

myocardial infarction: the common heart attack.

myopia: a refractive error of the eye, usually due to an elongated-shaped eyeball, that causes nearsightedness (distant objects are fuzzy).

N

narcotics: drugs that depress the central nervous system and inhibit the perception of pain.

National Health Education Standards, The: standards that specify what students should know and be able to do.

National Health Information Center: a federal agency that operates a toll-free hotline through which it refers consumers to organizations that can provide reliable health information.

neglect: maltreatment that involves lack of proper care and guidance.

negligence: the failure to conduct oneself in conformity with standards established by law for the protection of others against unreasonable risk of injury.

nervous system: a body system composed of a network of nerve cells that carry messages to the brain and spinal cord to all parts of the body.

neurologist: a physician who specializes in the diagnosis and treatment of diseases in the care of females during pregnancy and after delivery.

neutrophiles: white blood cells that are produced in the bone marrow.

nicotine: an odorless and colorless compound which is the active psychoactive agent found naturally in tobacco and is responsible for the addictive behavior of tobacco smokers.

nicotine-containing gum: a chewing gum that contains nicotine and a carbonate buffer to improve the absorption of nicotine.

nicotine transdermal patch: a polyethylene patch that delivers a relatively constant level of nicotine when placed on the skin.

nitrite inhalant: known for its vasodilation effects following inhalation that cause an increase in pressure in the brain, producing a euphoric effect or "high."

nitrogen oxide: gas produced by the high-temperature combustion of energy sources such as coal and oil.

nitrous oxide: a colorless gas known for its powerful analgesic and weak

Glossary

anesthetic effect that is abused as an inhalant drug.

noise: sound that produces discomfort or annoyance.

noncommunicable diseases: illnesses that are not caused by a pathogen.

nongonococcal urethritis (NGU): an STD caused by pathogens other than *Neisseria gonorrhoeae.*

noninfectious diseases: illnesses that are not caused by a pathogen.

noninsulin-dependent diabetes: diabetes in which the pancreas produces some insulin, but the body cells are not able to properly use it.

nonionizing radiation: the part of the electromagnetic spectrum that contains the longer wavelengths.

nonrapid eye movement (NREM) sleep: period of sleep in which the eyes are relaxed.

nonsupportive environmental conditions: circumstances and situations that detract from commitments for healthful behavior and could lead to injury, illness, or distress.

nonverbal communication: the use of behavior rather than words to express feelings.

nosebleed: loss of blood from the mucous membranes that line the nose.

nurse practitioner: a specially trained registered nurse who can function as a primary care provider in some states

nutrients: chemical substances in foods that furnish body fuel for energy, provide materials needed for building and maintenance of body tissues, and/or supply substances that function in the regulation of body processes.

Nutrition: the area of health that focuses on planning a healthful diet and includes choosing foods from The Food Guide Pyramid, adhering to dietary guidelines, reading food labels, making healthful food selections to reduce the risk of disease, making healthful selections when dining out, considering food safety, maintaining desirable weight, eating for healthful reasons, and recognizing eating disorders.

nutrition services: services that provide students with nutritionally balanced, appealing, and varied meals and snacks in settings that promote social interaction and relaxation.

nutritional environment: the set of conditions that include the school setting, facilities, food services, and attitudes toward good food habits that together contribute to the healthful development of the student by way of providing nourishment for growing and developing bodies and minds.

O

obesity: excessive body fat.

obsessive-compulsive disorder: behavior that is characterized by unreasonable thoughts and actions that are rigid, inflexible, and repetitive.

obstetrician: a physician who specializes in treatment of disorders of the female reproductive system.

occupational exposure: the reasonably anticipated skin, eye, mucous membranes,or parenteral contact with blood or other potentially infectious materials that may result from the performance of an employee's duties.

Office of Consumer Affairs: federal agency that serves as the liaison between the President and all consumers.

open wound: a wound in which the skin is broken, and there is an injury to underlying tissues.

ophthalmologists: medical doctors who specialize in the medical and surgical care and treatment of the eye.

opiates: natural narcotic drugs.

opioids: synthetically made narcotics.

opium: a natural derivative of the opium poppy plant that may be smoked or sniffed as a powder.

opportunistic infection: an infection that would probably not have the opportunity to invade if a person's immune system were healthy.

Opportunity to Learn Standards: standards that specify directions for the policies, resources, and activities to be conducted in schools, communities, institutions of higher education, and state and national education agencies in order to implement The National Health Education Standards (The Joint Committee on Health Education Standards, 1994).

ophthalmologist: medical doctor who specializes in the medical and surgical care and treatment of the eye.

opticians: technicians who fill prescriptions for glasses and contact lenses.

optometrists: specially trained health care practitioners who are trained in schools of optometry.

OPV(oral polio vaccine): a vaccine that should be given in a serious of three oral-vaccine doses two, four, and fifteen toeighteen months, and again between four and six years.

organic foods: foods that are produced without any chemicals throughout the process.

orthopedist: a physician who specializes in the surgical care of muscle, bone, and joint injuries and disorders.

osteoarthritis: a condition in which there is erosion in the moveable parts of a joint.

osteoporosis: a disease in which the bones become brittle and break easily.

outpatient surgery center: a clinic or other facility that offers an alternative to overnight hospital stay for patients in need of certain surgeries.

over-the-counter drug: a drug that is approved for legal purchase and use without a prescription from a doctor.

ovo-vegetarian diet: a diet that includes eggs but does not include meat.

ovulation: the release of a mature ovum from an ovary.

oxidation: the breakdowns of alcohol by enzymes in the liver, converting alcohol into carbon dioxide and water at the rate of about half an ounce of alcohol per hour.

ozone: a chemical variant of oxygen that is classified as a photochemical because it is created in the presence of hydrocarbons, nitrous oxides, and sunlight.

P

pancreas: an elongated, tapered, gland that lies across the back of the abdomen. The pancreas produces enzymes that are necessary for the complete digestion of carbohydrates, proteins, and fats.

pancreatitis: inflammation of the pancreas that increases the risk of diabetes.

Pap smear: a test to detect abnormal changes in the cells of the cervix and thus to prevent the development of cervical cancer.

parasitic worms: the largest pathogens that can enter the human body to cause infection.

parasuicide: a suicide attempt in which a person does not intend to die.

parathyroid gland: two pairs of oval, pea-sized glands located adjacent to the two lobes of the thyroid gland in the neck.

parent and community involvement: a dynamic partnership in which the school, parents, agencies, community groups, andbusinesses work collaboratively to address the health needs of children and their families.

parent support groups: formed by parents to help one another cope with alcohol and drug problems in their neighborhoods and families.

parenteral contact: the piercing of mucous membranes or the skin barrier through such events as needlesticks, human bites, cuts, and abrasions (scrapes).

particulates: particles in the air.

Glossary

passive behavior: the holding back of ideas, opinions, and feelings.

passive-aggressive: the appearance of being cooperative and pleasant on the outside while feeling angry and hostile.

pathogen: disease-causing organism.

PCBs: polychlorinated biphenyls, a class of organic compounds containing chlorine.

PCP: a hallucinogen that may be manufactured as a tablet or capsule, but it can also be smoked, swallowed, or sniffed.

pediatrician: a physician who specializes in the care of children and adolescents.

pediculosis: infestation with lice.

pediculosis pubis: infection with *Phthirus pubis*, pubic or crab lice.

peer: a person who is similar in age or status.

peer mediation: a process used to resolve conflicts, in which a person helps peers resolve disagreements in healthful, safe, legal, respectful, and nonviolent ways.

peer mediator: a person who assists the people who are in conflict to reach a solution.

peer pressure: pressure that people of similar age or status place on others to encourage them to make certain decisions or behave in certain ways.

pelvic inflammatory disease (PID): an infection of the upper reproductive tract.

penis: the male organ for sexual intercourse, reproduction, and urination.

Performance Indicators, The: a series of specific concepts and skills students should know and be able to do in order to achieve each of the broader National Health Education Standards.

pericardum: a membranous bag that completely envelops the heart.

periodontal disease: a disease of the gums and other tissues that support the teeth.

peripheral system (PNS) the part of the nervous system that consists of the nerves that branch from the central nervous system to the periphery, or outer areas, of the body.

permissiveness: the physical expression of sexual feelings with very little or no promise of intention to love and care for another.

perpetrator: a person who commits a crime or violent act.

Personal Health: the area of health that focuses upon making a personal health management plan that includes being well-groomed, caring for the body, having regular checkups, following a dental health plan, obtaining adequate rest and sleep, and achieving a desirable level of physical fitness.

pesco-vegetarian diet: a diet that includes fish, dairy products, and eggs.

pesticide: any substance that is used to kill or control the growth of unwanted organisms.

petit mal seizure: a minor seizure during which a person experiences a brief loss of consciousness.

peyote cactus: the hallucinogen mescaline, which is native to the deserts of Mexico and the southwestern United States.

pharmacist: an allied health care professional who dispenses medications in accordance with a physician's prescription.

philosophical intimacy: the sharing of one's beliefs, philosophy of life, and life principles.

philosophy: an overall vision of the purpose of the curriculum and it explains the meaning of health and its value.

phobia: the excess fear of a situation, object, or person.

physical abuse: maltreatment that harms the body.

physical activity: any bodily movement

produced by skeletal muscles that results in energy expenditure.

physical dependence: a physiological process in which repeated doses of a drug cause the body to adapt to the presence of the drug.

physical education: a planned, sequential K–12 curriculum that provides cognitive content and learning experiences in a variety of activity areas including basic movement skills; physical fitness, rhythms, and dance; games; team, dual, and individual sports; tumbling and gymnastics; and aquatics.

physical fitness: the condition of the body as a result of participating in exercises that promote muscular strength, muscular endurance, flexibility, cardiovascular endurance, and a healthful percentage of body fat.

physical health: the condition of a person's body.

physical intimacy: the sharing of physical expressions of affection.

physical therapist: allied health care professional who works with people with physical disabilities and ailments to restore function.

physically fit: a person who has achieved a level of muscular strength, muscular endurance, flexibility, and cardiovascular condition.

physician: a person licensed to practice medicine and surgical procedures.

pituitary gland: a gland located at the base of the brain and is called the master gland because it not only produces a growth hormone but it also produces hormones that control other endocrine glands.

plant poisoning: poisoning that results when a person either comes in contact with or eats certain plants or plant parts.

plaque: a rough, sticky coating on the teeth that consists of saliva, bacteria, and food debris.

plastic surgeon: a physician who specializes in surgery to correct, repair, or improve body features.

plaque formation: the buildup of an invisible, sticky film of bacteria on teeth especially near the gum line.

plasma: the fluid part of blood that remains if the blood cells are removed, which is about 90 percent water.

platelets: small fragments, shaped like disks, that help prevent blood loss from injured blood vessels.

pneumonia: an inflammation of the lungs accompanied by fever, shortness of breath, headache, chest pain, and coughing.

podiatrist: (**D.P.M.**) a health care professional trained and licensed as a doctor of podiatric medicine.

poison: any substance that can cause illness or death when introduced into the body.

poisoning: entry into the body of a substance that disrupts the structure or function of cells.

pollution standard index (PSI): a standardized measure of air quality based on the sum of the levels of five different pollutants relative to regulatory standard maximums are assigned a value of 100 and are determined from the influence they have on health status.

polydrug abuse: the simultaneous abuse of more than one drug.

portfolio: a collection of student works, which can help the teacher evaluate a student's attainment of knowledge, attitudes, and skills.

positive reinforcement: a training approach in which people are given positive reinforcers immediately following a desired behavior.

posture: the relative position of different parts of the body at rest or during movement.

power: the ability to perform sudden bursts of energy.

Glossary

preferred provider organizations (PPOs): health care delivery plans in which arrangements have been made by a third party (e.g. a union, insurance company, self-insured business) for consumers to select health care providers from a list of "preferred customer."

prejudice: suspicion, intolerance, or irrational hatred directed at an individual or group of people.

premature birth: the birth of a baby before the thirty-seventh week of the pregnancy.

premature heart attack: a heart attack that occurs before age fifty-five in men and before age sixty-five in women.

premenstrual syndrome (PMS): a chronic menstrual disorder characterized by emotional, behavioral, and physical symptoms.

prenatal care: the care given to both the mother and her developing fetus before birth.

presbyopia: an impaired ability to change focus as a result of weakened eye muscles and rigidity of the lens.

prescription: a very precise order from an appropriate health professional to a pharmacist to dispense a certain drug product to a patient.

prescription drug: a drug that can be legitimately obtained only by a prescription from licensed health professionals and dispensed through registered pharmacists.

pressure point: a location where an artery that is supplying blood to the area that is bleeding can be compressed.

principle of cooling down: three to five minutes of reduced exercise to slow the heart beat rate and body temperature down and to return normal blood flow to the heart.

principle of frequency: exercising frequently enough to derive the desired benefits.

principle of overload: increasing activity levels to develop an increased fitness level.

principle of progression: planning a fitness program in which the intensity and duration of exercise are gradually increased.

principle of specificity: selecting a specific exercise or activity to provide a specific benefit.

principle of warming up: three to five minutes of light exercise to gradually begin increased blood flow to prepare joints and muscles for harder exercise.

private hospital: a hospital facility owned by private individuals and operated for profit.

proactive decision-making style: a decision-making style in which you examine the decisions to be made, identify and evaluate actions that can be taken, select an action, and assume responsibility for the consequence.

procrastination: the act of delaying something until a future time.

proctosigmoidoscopy: a visual inspection of the colon and rectum by use of a fiber-optic tube that detects cancer of the colon and rectum.

productions: works prepared by the student to document knowledge and skills.

proof: a measure of the amount of alcohol in any alcoholic beverage, and is double the percent of alcohol content in a beverage.

protective factors: ways that a person might behave and characteristics of the environment in which a person lives that promote health, safety, and well-being.

proteins: nutrients that are essential for the growth, development and repair of all body tissues.

protozoa: tiny, single-celled organisms that produce toxins that are capable of causing disease.

psilocybin: a hallucinogenic drug that alters mood and perception in a manner similar to LSD and mescaline and is derived from a specific type of mushroom.

psychiatrist: a physician who specializes in surgery to correct, repair, or improve body features.

psychoactive drug: a substance that acts on the central nervous system and alters a user's moods, perceptions, feelings, personality, or behavior.

psychological dependence: a condition characterized by a pervasive desire or "craving" to achieve the effects produced by a drug.

psychological first aid: the process of helping people deal with the emotional aspects related to physical injury or illness.

psychological intimacy: the sharing of one's needs, drives, weaknesses, strengths, intentions, emotional feelings, and deepest problems.

psychological needs: things that are needed to feel important and secure and may include friendships, belonging, accomplishments, and status.

psychomotor domain: the category of objectives dealing with action behavior.

puberty: the time of sexual development when males and females become physically capable of reproduction.

public hospital: a governmental or tax-supported hospital.

pulmonary circulation: the process in which blood flows through the pulmonary artery to the lungs.

pulp: the living tissue within a tooth.

pus: a fluid found at the site of bacterial infection.

Q

quack: a person who markets inaccurate health information, unreliable health care, or useless health products.

quackery: a consumer fraud that in-volves the practice of promoting and/or selling useless products and services.

R

racism: behavior that discriminates against members of certain racial or ethnic groups.

radial keratotomy: the surgical correction of nearsightedness and astigmatism that involves tiny incisions on the surface of the cornea of the eye.

radiation: term applied to the transmission of energy though space or through to a medium.

radiotherapy: the treatment of cancer via the use of radiation.

radon: an odorless, colorless radioactive gas that is emitted form bricks, concrete materials and from rocks and other substances below the Earth.

rapid eye movement (REM) sleep: period of sleep during which the most vivid and virtually all dreaming occurs that is characterized by rapid eye movements behind closed eyelids.

reaction time: the amount of time it takes to begin moving after making a decision to do so.

reactive decision-making style: a decision-making style in which a person allows others to make decisions for him/her.

recycling: the process of reforming or breaking down waste products to their basic components so that they can be sued again.

red blood cells: the most numerous cells in the blood; and they carry oxygen.

refractive errors: defects in the shape of eye structures that results in the inability of images to focus on the retina that interfere with visual acuity.

reframing: changing your outlook in order to see a situation in a more positive way.

registered nurse: an allied health care professional who and is certified either

Glossary

for general practice or for any of the several nurse specialties such as anesthesia, midwifery, public health, or intensive care.

regulatory agency: an agency that enforces laws on behalf of the general public.

relationship continuum: a continuum that shows the range of relationships with dispiriting relationships at one end and inspiriting relationships at the other end.

relationships: the connections a person has with other people.

remarriage: a marriage in which at least one of the two persons has been married before.

reproductions: tangible evidence of student participation.

resiliency: the ability to recover from or adjust to misfortune, change, pressure, and adversity.

resistance skills: skills that are used when a person wants to say NO to an action and/or leave a situation that threatens health, threatens safety, breaks laws, results in lack of respect for self and others, disobeys guidelines set by responsible adults, or detracts from character and moral values.

resistance stage: the second stage of the GAS in which the body attempts to regain balance and return to normal.

resources: available assets and may include time, money, and material possessions.

respect: having esteem for someone's admirable characteristics and responsible and caring actions.

respiration: the exchange of gases between a person's body and the environment.

respiratory emergency: emergency in which a person has limited breathing or has stopped.

respiratory system: the body system that consists of the nasal cavity, the pharynx, larynx, trachea, bronchi, and the lungs.

respiratory therapist: an allied health

care professional who tests for and treats breathing disorders according to physician's orders.

responsible decisions: decisions that protect health, protect safety, protect laws, show respect for self and others, follow guidelines set by responsible adults such as parents and guardians, and demonstrate good character and moral values.

Responsible Decision-Making Model, The: a series of steps to follow to assure that the decisions a person makes lead to actions that promote health, promote safety, protect laws, show respect for self and others, follow guidelines set by responsible adults such as parents and guardians, and demonstrate good character.

responsibility: reliability and dependability.

rest: periods of relaxation.

restating response: a response in which a person repeats what the speaker has said in his/her own words.

retainer: a plastic device with wires that keeps the teeth from moving back to their original places.

reteaching: the teaching that occurs when a teacher uses an alternate strategy for instruction after students were not able to garner the concept or life skill from the first instructional strategy.

Reye's syndrome: a serious condition, which may follow influenza and chicken pox in children and adolescents, that is characterized by swelling of the brain and destruction of liver tissue.

rheumatoid arthritis: a serious disease in which joint deformity and loss of joint function occurs.

rickettsia: disease-causing microorganisms that grow inside living cells and resemble bacteria, although they are much smaller.

rigid gas permeable lenses: made from

a firm, durable plastic that allows oxygen through to the eye.

risk behaviors: voluntary actions that threaten self-esteem; harm health; and increase the likelihood of illness, injury, and premature death.

risk factors: ways that a person might behave and characteristics of the environment in which a person lives that threaten health, safety, and/or well being.

risk situations: involuntary circumstances that threaten health; increase the likelihood of illness, injury, and premature death; and destroy the quality of the environment.

rocky mountain spotted fever: a potentially life-threatening disease carried by a tick.

roid rages: episodes of aggressive and violent behavior associated with steroid use.

root canal: a dental procedure performed to save a tooth in which the pulp has died or become untreatably diseased.

safe and healthful school environment: an environment that attends to the physical an aesthetic surroundings, and psychosocial climate and culture that maximizes the health and safety of students and staff.

S

safety: the condition of being protected from injuries.

saliva: the watery, slightly alkaline fluid secreted into the mouth.

salmonella: a bacterial infection that contaminates many foods, particularly undercooked chicken, eggs, and processed foods.

sanitation: the protection of health and prevention of disease by means of freeing the environment form filth and infectious material.

satiety: the feeling of being full after eating.

saturated fats: fats that contain a high proportion of saturated fatty acids.

saturated fatty acids: fatty acids that are composed of chains that contain all the hydrogen atoms they can hold.

savings: money set aside for future use.

scabies: an infectious disease of the skin caused by small parasitic mites than burrow themselves under the skin.

schizophrenia: a mental disorder in which there is a split or breakdown in logical thought processes.

school health services: services designed to appraise, protect, and promote the health of students.

school-based health clinics: clinics that offers wide range of services including physical examinations and screenings, immunizations, treatment of minor injuries and illness, family life education, counseling for substance abuse and mental health, and referral services.

scoliosis: lateral or S-shaped curvature of the spine that is found in approximately one in fifty people.

scope: the depth or degree of difficulty of each of the health topics to be covered.

Scope and Sequence Chart: a chart that serves as a blueprint for the curriculum and it includes the components of health literacy, The National Health Education Standards, the performance indicators, the content areas and life skills, and the health topics.

scrotum: a sac-like pouch that holds the testes and regulates the temperature of the testes.

seasonal affective disorder: a type of depression that is associated with winter months when the amount of sunshine is decreased.

secondhand cigarette smoke: a mixture of the smoke given off by the burning end of a cigarette, pipe, or cigar and the smoke exhaled from the lungs of smokers.

sedative-hypnotic drugs: central nervous system depressants.

Glossary

sedatives: have a calming effect on behavior.

seizure: an episode during which a person experiences neurological disturbances.

self-centered behavior: behavior in which a person acts in ways that fulfill his/her needs and wishes with little regard for the needs and wishes of others.

self-destructive behavior: behavior in which a person harms himself/herself.

self-discipline: the effort or energy with which a person follows through on what (s)he
intends or promises to do.

self-esteem: the personal internal image that a person has about himself/herself.

self-help groups: groups that offer fellowship and support and are based upon a Twelve Step treatment model.

self-loving behavior: healthful and responsible behavior that indicates a person believes himself/herself to be worthwhile and lovable.

self-preservation: the inner desire to keep oneself and others safe from harm and may include preserving physical, mental, and social health.

self-protection strategies: strategies that can be practiced to protect oneself and to decrease the risk of becoming a victim.

self-responsibility for health: the priority that a person assigns to being health literate, maintaining and improving health, preventing disease, and reducing health-related risk behaviors.

semantic differential: a technique used to measure beliefs and attitudes in which students are asked to circle a letter from A-B-C-D-E to indicate their preference on a continuum.

semi-vegetarian diet: a diet that does not include meat but does include plant foods, dairy products, and sometimes a selection of seafood, eggs, and poultry.

seminal vesicles: two small glands at the ends of the vas deferens that secrete a fluid that nourishes and enables the sperm to move.

semniforous tubules: coiled network of tubes that fill each testis and in which sperm are produced.

senility: the loss of mental faculties associated with old age.

sensioneural hearing loss: a disorder in which sounds that reach the inner ear fail to be transmitted to the brain because of damage to the structures within the inner ear or to the acoustic nerve which connects the inner ear to the brain.

sensory neurons: neurons that carry impulses from the sense organs to the brain and spinal cord.

separation: an agreement between a married couple to live apart but remain married while working out their problems.

sequence: the order in which the health topics will be covered including what will be covered by the different grade levels.

set point: a theory that stated that the body has a control system for keeping weight at a point at which it is comfortable.

sex role: the way a person acts a the feelings and attitudes a person has about being male or female as well as the other expectations (s)he has for other males and females.

sexism: behavior that discriminates against people of the opposite sex.

sexual abuse: maltreatment that involves inappropriate sexual behavior between an adult and a child.

sexual addiction: compulsive behavior involving sexual activity without any commitment to the sexual partner.

sexual feelings: feelings that result from a strong physical and emotional attraction to another person.

sexual harassment: unwanted sexual behavior that ranges from making sexual comments to forcing another person into unwanted sex acts.

sexual orientation: a person's attraction to people of the opposite sex, same sex, or both sexes.

sexuality: the feelings and attitudes a person has about his/her body, sex role, and sexual orientations as well as his/her feelings regarding the bodies, sex roles, and sexual orientation of others.

sexually transmitted diseases (STDs): diseases caused by pathogens that are transmitted from an infected person to an uninfected person during intimate sexual contact.

shingles: an infection caused by the herpes zoster virus that affects only a small segment of the population, usually over the age of fifty.

shock: a condition in the rate of the functions of the vital organs of the body slows.

shopping addict: a person who lacks control of spending urges and repeatedly engages in impulse buying.

shopping wisely: examining priorities and needs, evaluating financial resources, taking a little extra time to gather information about products, and shopping around for the best value.

shyness: a condition characterized by discomfort, inhibition, and awkwardness in social situations.

Sick Building Syndrome: illness that results from indoor air pollution.

sickle-cell anemia: a blood disease that gets its name from the shape of the abnormal red blood cell.

side aches: dull sharp pains in the side that occur when there has been inadequate warm-up.

simple carbohydrates: carbohydrates that enter the blood stream rapidly and provide quick energy.

skeletal muscles: muscles that are attached to bones and, with the bones provide body movement.

skill-related fitness components: the qualities that enable sports performance and make participating in sports activities more enjoyable.

skin: the outermost covering of body tissue, which protects internal organs.

sleep: a state of profound relaxation during which the eyes are closed and there is little movement or consciousness.

smog: a combination of smoke and fog.

smokeless tobacco: includes both chewing tobacco and snuff.

Snellen chart: a chart used for testing visual acuity for distance, in which letters, symbols, or numbers are organized in decreasing size from the top to the bottom of the chart.

snuff: a powdered form of tobacco.

social competence: the effective use of social skills.

social skills: skills that can be used to relate well with others.

sodium: a mineral that regulates and maintains the balance of fluids in the body.

soft contact lenses: made from gel-like plastic which absorb water.

soft tissue injuries: injuries to the layers of skin, fat, and muscles.

solid waste: substances such as trash, unwanted objects, and litter that threaten the environment.

speed: the ability to cover a distance or performing movement in a short period of time.

sprain: a partial or complete tearing of ligaments at a joint.

state health department: the official state agency that has responsibility for the health of the people residing in the state.

stereotype: a prejudiced attitude that assigns a specific quality or characteristic to all people who belong to a particular group.

strabismus: misalignment of the eyes and commonly referred to as "crossed-eyes."

strain: a stretching or tearing of muscles, usually due to overexertion.

Glossary

stress: the response of the body to the demands of daily living.

stress fractures: hairline breaks in a bone caused by undue stress on or blow to a bone.

stress management skills: techniques that can be used to cope with the harmful effects produced by stress.

stressor: a demand that causes changes in the body.

stroke: a break or block in a blood vessel in the brain.

stroke volume: the amount of blood the heart pumps with each beat.

student assistance program: a school-based approach to the prevention and treatment of alcohol and other drug abuse.

student support groups: groups of students who are struggling to cope with certain life problems.

suicide: the intentional taking of one's own life.

suicide prevention strategies: techniques that can be used to help prevent a person from thinking about, attempting, and completing suicide.

sulfur oxides: pollutants that result from the combustion of fuels containing sulfur and from sulfur from volcanos that combines with oxygen to form sulfur oxides.

summarizing response: a response to review the major idea or ideas expressed.

supportive environmental conditions: those circumstances and situations that facilitate healthful choices and/or protect a student's well-being.

suppository: a wax-coated form of a drug that is inserted into the anus and held in place until the wax melts, the drug is released, and the drug is absorbed.

swimmer's ear: painful and itchy bacterial infection of the external ear canal that develops after long periods of swimming or bathing.

symptom: a change in a body function from a normal pattern.

synergy: a positive outcome that occurs when different people cooperate and respect one another and, as a result, more energy is created for all.

syphilis: an STD caused by the *Treponema pallidum* bacterium, which penetrates mucous membranes and abrasions of the skins and causes lesions that may involve any organ or tissue.

systematic desensitization: a process in which a person is gradually exposed to something that arouses fear and learns to respond less to it.

systemic lupus erythematosus (SLE): chromic disease of unknown cause that affects most of the systems in the body.

T

tar: a sticky, dark mixture of at least 3,500 chemicals in tobacco smoke.

target heart rate: between 60 and 90 percent of the difference between resting heart rate and maximum heart rate.

tartar buildup: occurs when plaque is not removed and it hardens.

Tay-Sachs: a genetic disease caused by the absence of a key enzyme needed to break down fats in the body.

teaching strategy: a technique used by a facilitator or teacherto help a student 1) understand a particular concept, and/or 2) develop and practice a specific life skill.

technology: the use of computers, CD Rom, interactive video, med-lines,and other forms of high-tech equipment used to communicate and to assimilate, synthesize, analyze, and evaluate information.

tendons: bands of tough connective tissue that attach muscles to bones to joints.

terminal illness: an illness that is incurable and will eventually cause death.

testes: reproductive organs that secrete the male hormone testosterone and produce sperm.

testicular self-examination: observation and palpation of the testicles to locate any mass or tenderness.

tetanus: a bacteria that grows in the body and produces a strong poison that affects the nervous system and muscles.

tetrahydrocannabinol (THC): the active ingredient in marijuana.

therapeutic community: trained professionals and individuals who were drug-dependent who help counsel an individual who has a drug problem.

thermal inversion: a condition that occurs when a layer of warm air forms above a cooler layer.

thermal pollution: pollution of water with heat resulting in a decrease in the water's oxygen-carrying capacity.

thyroid gland: a gland that consists of two lobes located below the larynx on either side of the trachea.

thyroxin: a hormone that regulates metabolism, which is all chemical activity inside the body.

time management plan: a plan that indicates how time will be spent on daily activities and leisure.

tobacco use: includes the use of cigarettes, pipes, cigars, and smokeless tobacco.

tolerance: a condition in which the body becomes adapted to a drug so that increasingly larger amounts of the drugs are needed to produce the desired effect.

toothache: pain that comes from a tooth or from the gums.

totally awesome teacher: a teacher who is committed to improving health literacy, improving health, preventing disease, and reducing health-related risk behaviors in students, and to creating a dynamic and challenging classroom where students learn and practice life skills for health.

tourniquet: a band that is applied to stop blood flow to a wound.

toxic shock syndrome (TSS): a disease caused by the presence of dangerous bacteria that grow rapidly in the vagina of a menstruating female.

training principles: guidelines to follow to derive the maximum benefits from an exercise plan.

trans-fatty acids: fatty acids that are produced when polyunsaturated oils are hydrogenated.

trichomoniasis: an STD caused by a parasitic protozoan, *Trichomonas vaginalis.*

trihalomethanes: chemical byproducts containing halogens, formed when chlorine attacks biological contaminants in water.

Twelve Step Programs: philosophical steps that are suggested guides to help people recognize the benefits of discovering and expanding their faith to recover from their past and gain wholeness.

U

ulcerative colitis: an inflammatory disease of the walls of the large intestine.

ultraviolet radiation: a type of nonionizing radiation that comes mainly from the sun.

unhealthful relationships: destroy self-esteem, interfere with productivity and health, and may include violence and drug misuse and abuse.

unintentional injuries: injuries that are accidental.

United States Department of Agriculture (USDA): a federal agency that enforces standards for ensuring that food is processed safely and also oversees the distribution of food information to the public.

United States Postal Service: the federal agency that protects the public when products, devices, and services are sold through the mail.

U.S. Public Health Service: health

agency that plays a principal role at the federal level.

universal distress signal: demonstrated by a person clutching at the throat with one or two hands.

universal precautions: the steps taken to prevent the spread of disease by treating all human blood and certain body fluids as if they are known to be infectious for HIV, HBV, and other bloodborne pathogens.

unsaturated fats: fats that are composed of chains that are able to add more hydrogen atoms to their structure.

urologist: a physician who specializes in treatment of urinary disorders and the male reproductive system.

uterus: the organ that prepares each month during a female's reproductive years to receive a fertilized ovum, to support the fertilized ovum during pregnancy, and to contract during childbirth to force delivery of the baby.

V

vagina: the muscular passageway that lies between the bladder and the rectum and serves as the female organ of intercourse, the passageway for sperm to the uterus, the birth canal, and the passageway for the menstrual flow.

vaginitis: an irritation or inflammation of the vagina usually accompanied by a discharge.

values: the beliefs, goals, and standards held by people.

vas deferens: two long, thin cords that extend from the epidymis in the scrotum, and serve as a passageway for the sperm.

vegetarian diet: a diet that excludes meat, fish, and other animal products.

ventricles: lower chambers that pump blood from the heart.

victim: a person who is harmed by violence.

violence: the threatened or actual use of physical force to injure, damage, or destroy oneself, others, or property.

viruses: the smallest known pathogens.

visual acuity: sharpness of vision.

visual disorders: conditions that adversely affect a person's sight.

vitamin supplements: usually synthetic forms of particular vitamins.

vitamins: organic substances needed in very small amounts to facilitate chemical reactions in the body.

voluntary health organizations: agencies supported by finding other than taxes, that usually focus on a specific disease, health problem, or body organ.

voluntary hospital: a nonprofit public institution, usually owned by the community.

W

wasting syndrome: an unexplained loss in body weight of more than ten percent of the total body weight.

water: a nutrient that helps make up blood, helps the process of digestion and removal of body wastes, and regulates body temperature.

water conservation: a set of actions taken to avoid wasting water and to prevent water contaminations.

water-soluble vitamins: vitamins that cannot be stored by the body in significant amounts.

wellness: the quality of life that includes physical, mental-emotional, and family-social health.

wellness behaviors: actions that promote health, prevent illness, injury, and premature death, and improve the quality of the environment.

Wellness Scale, The: depicts the ranges in the quality of life from optimal well-being to high level wellness, average wellness, minor illness or injury, major illness or injury, and premature death.

wellness situations: circumstances that promote health, prevent illness, injury, and premature death, and improve the quality of the environment.

white blood cells: cells that destroy pathogens that enter the body.

will: a legal document that describes how a person's possession are to be distributed.

windowpanes: tiny, thin gelatin chips of LSD.

wine: made from the fermentation of grapes or other fruits.

withdrawal symptoms: unpleasant symptoms experienced by individuals who are physically dependent on a drug when deprived of that drug.

workaholism: an addictive behavior in which a person devotes an inappropriate amount of time to his/her job with the result that family, friends, and personal interests suffer.

World Health Organization (WHO): an agency of the United Nations and is headquartered in Geneva, Switzerland, that strives to improve the quality of health throughout the world by planning, providing, and coordinating health services.

wound: any break in the continuity of the body's tissues.

Y

yo-yo dieting: a cycle of weight loss and weight gain.

you-message: a statement that blames or shames another person instead of expressing feelings.

youth gangs: groups of young people who band together and participate in violent, unlawful, or criminal behavior.

youth services centers: school-linked community–based centers that aspire to provide comprehensive services for the many problems young people face.

Glossary

INDEX

Index

Index

Index

and formaldehyde, 342
objectives, 16
Astigmatism, 65, 238, 239
Atherosclerosis, 245, 287
and smoking, 261
Athlete's foot, 248, 275
Atria, 190
Attendance. *See* School
attendance
Attention deficit disorder
(ADD), 198
Attention deficit hyperactivity
disorder (ADHD), 43
Attention span and lead
poisoning, 341
Attestations in student
portfolios, 124
Audiologist as health care
provider, 329
Audiometer machine, 54
Audiovisuals in teaching,
129–130
Aura and epilepsy, 53
Autoimmune disorders, 275,
291
Automobiles. *See* Motor
vehicles
Autonomic nervous system,
189
Avoidance of conflict, 171
Avulsions of the skin, 64

B

B cells, 274
Babies
of adolescent mothers, 183
and amphetamine
addiction, 264
and effect on siblings,
176–177
and HIV transmission,
56, 283
and sexually transmitted
diseases, 279, 280
and smoking, 261
and water pollution, 338
Bacteria. *See also*
Communicable disease;
Conjunctivitis ("pink
eye"); Impetigo; Infection;
Sexually transmitted

diseases (STDs)
and body odor, 236
and female disorders, 195
food-borne, 228–229
oral, 243
tetanus, 64
as type of pathogen, 275
Bad breath and smoking, 262
"Bad trips" and hallucinogens,
264
"Bagging" of inhalants, 265
Balance as fitness
component, 252
Balloon angioplasty, 289
Bandwagon appeal and
advertising, 320
Barbiturates, 267
Bargaining and life crises,
48, 161, 175, 204
Baseball injuries, 314
Basements and radon
pollution, 342
Basketball injuries, 314
Battery recycling, 346
Beans and Food Guide
Pyramid, 222
Bee stings, 308
Beer, 258
Behavior. *See also* Risk
behaviors
addictive, 156–157
and development of self-
esteem, 158–159
and emotional abuse, 53
healthful, 100, 146–147
and mental/emotional
health, 146–147, 155–156
passive, aggressive, and
assertive, 160–161
philosophy of the
curriculum, 100
Behavioral objectives,
105–107
Behavioral toxicity, 265
Benign tumor, 289
Benzene and air pollution,
337
Benzodiazepines, 267
Benzoyl peroxide, 237
Beta-blockers, 288
Beta-endorphins, 246
Bias crimes, 169

Bicuspids, 242
Bicycle safety, 314–315
and helmet use, 16, 80
Bile, 189–190
Binge eating, 231
Binge-purge syndrome, 44
Biodegradable substances,
345
Biological and chemical
agents, 24
Birth canal, 193. *See also*
Vagina
Birth control pills and
candidiasis, 281
Birth defects, 200
and chloroform, 339
and PCBs, 339
and sexually transmitted
diseases, 280
and toxic waste, 345
Birth process, 200–201
Birthweight, 21, 39
and adolescent mothers, 8
objectives, 17
and smoking, 261
Bisexuality, 197
Bites
dog, 299
insect, 59, 308–309
Biting and physical abuse, 61
Blackouts and alcohol, 260
Bladder, 191
cancer, 339
figure, 213, 215, 216
infection, 195, 281
Bleach and water pollution,
339
Bleeding, 43–44, 305.
See also Blood
Blended families, 176
Blindness, 65
and diabetes, 290
and sexually transmitted
diseases, 280
and Tay-Sachs disease, 286
Blisters, 238, 248
and chickenpox, 276
and plant poisoning, 308
and sexually transmitted
diseases, 277, 280
Blood, 190–191
and cadmium, 345

Index

Index

© Copyright by Meeks Heit Publishing Company.

Index

Index

Index

Index

Index

Index

Index

Money, 324–325
  addiction, 157
  spending as life skill, 28
Moniliasis, 281
Monogamous marriage, 181
Mononucleosis ("kissing disease"), 278
  and chronic fatigue syndrome, 291
Mons veneris, 193
Mood swings
  and drug abuse, 50
  and manic-depressive behavior, 156
  and marijuana, 7
Morphine, 266
Motivation
  and incentives, 114–115
  and instructional strategies, 111
  strategies and technologies, 129–141
Motor neurons, 189
Motor oil recycling, 346
Motor skills and alcohol, 313
Motor vehicles
  crashes, 12, 16
  exhaust, 336, 337–338
  and carbon monoxide, 341
  and population growth, 347
  injuries, 4
  safety, 312–314, 315
Motorbike safety, 316
Motorcycle safety, 316
  and helmet use, 16
Mouse, computer, 140
Mouth-to-mouth respiration, 303
  and snakebites, 308
Mouthguards, 248
Movement and exercise, 245–247
Movement objectives, 107
MSG intolerance, 229
Mucous and cystic fibrosis, 286
Mucous membranes, 60
  and bloodborne pathogens, 88
  and sexually transmitted diseases, 278, 279
Multicultural infusion and instructional strategies, 111, 118

Multimedia technologies, 139–140
Multiple addictions, 157
Multiple choice examinations, 121–122
Mumps, 46, 277
  immunization, 242
  objectives, 18
Muscle aches
  and chronic fatigue syndrome, 291–292
  and sexually transmitted diseases, 278
Muscle cramps, 248
Muscle pain
  and hepatitis, 277–278
  and influenza, 277
Muscle spasms, 54
Muscle strain, 64, 248, 307
Muscles
  and diet, 188
  and physical fitness, 249, 251
  and systemic lupus erythematosus, 291
Muscular dystrophy, 285–286
Muscular strength, 11
Muscular system, 188
  figure, 207
Music and hearing loss, 54, 72, 343, 344
Myasthenia gravis, 275
Myocardial infarction, 287
Myopia, 65, 239

N

Nails, 188, 236
Narcotics, 266
Nasal cavity, 191
National Academy of Sciences, 9
National Ambient Air Quality Standards, 337
National Audubon Society, 335
National Cancer Institute, 227
The National Education Goals for the Year 2000, 9, 21–22
  figure, 21

freedom from drugs, 85
freedom from violence, 84
The National Health Education Standards, 25, 95, 96–97
  and *The Scope and Sequence Chart,* 105
National Health Information Center, 331
National incentives and comprehensive school health, 9–21
National Institute for Occupational Safety and Health (NIOSH), 348
National Research and Education Network (NREN), 140
National Weather Service, 302
National Wildlife Federation, 335
Natural disasters, 27, 332
Natural resources
  conservation, 346
  and population growth, 347
Nature Conservancy, 335
Nausea
  and allergies, 41
  and colitis, 290
  and first aid, 308
  and food-borne infections, 229
  and formaldehyde, 342
  and heart attack, 306
  and heat emergencies, 54
  and hepatitis, 277–278
  and narcotics, 266
  and pregnancy, 199
  and shock, 63
  and sick building syndrome, 340
Nearsightedness, 238
Needles. *See* Intravenous drugs
Needs assessment and school environment, 72–73
Neglect, 5, 60. *See also* Child abuse
  and adolescent parents, 8
  objectives, 15
Negligence and liability, 78

Index

Osteoporosis, 188, 203
  and physical fitness, 246
  and smoking, 261
Outpatient centers, 330
Ova (egg cells), 193, 194
  and conception, 199
Ovaries, 192, 193, 214
  figure, 214, 215
  and menstrual cycle, 194
Over-the-counter drugs, 256
  and caffeine, 267
Overcrowding, 28, 347, 348
Overdose, drug, 303
Overload principle in
  exercise, 247
Overpopulation, 346–347
Overweight. *See* Weight
  management
Ovulation, 193, 194, 199
Oxidation of alcohol, 258
Oxygen
  and acid rain, 338
  and thermal pollution, 339
Ozone as pollutant, 337
Ozone layer, 336
  and population growth, 347

P

Pain
  abdominal, 62, 306, 338
  chest, 287, 306
  and chronic disease, 291
  and insect stings and bites,
    308
  and narcotics, 266
  and sexually transmitted
    diseases, 278, 279, 281
  and sickle-cell anemia, 286
  and spotted fever, 59
Paint
  and lead poisoning, 341
  and wall color, 71
Pancreas, 189, 190, 192
  and diabetes, 290
  and diet, 227
  figure, 210, 214
  and smoking, 261
Pancreatitis, 260
Panel discussions, 134
Panic attacks and
  hallucinogens, 264

Pap smear, 194–195, 241, 289
Paper and pulp bleaching,
  339
Paper recycling, 346
Paralysis
  and sexually transmitted
    diseases, 280
  and snakebites, 308
  and stroke, 306
Parasites
  mites, 62
  and STDs, 281
  worms, 275
Parasuicide, 6, 164
Parathyroid, 192, 214
  figure, 214
Parenteral contact and
  bloodborne pathogens, 88
Parenthood, 182–183
Parents
  determining drug use, 86
  and healthful school
    environment, 77
  involvement, 21, 24
  parental dating, 176
  and stress, 163
  and support groups, 270
Participation
  and evaluation of students,
    116, 119
  of students in the
    community, 147–148
Particulates, 337
  and woodstove smoke, 343
Passive-agressive behavior,
  171
Passive behavior, 160–161
Passive smoking, 342–343.
  See also Environmental
  tobacco smoke (ETS)
Pasta and Tood Guide
  Pyramid, 222
Pathogens, 273, 275–276
  bloodborne, 88–90
  HIV, 8, 55
  sexually transmitted
    diseases, 63
PCBs (polychlorinated
  biphenyls), 339
PCP (phencyclidine), 264
Pedestrian safety, 299
Pediatrician as health care

provider, 329
Pediculosis pubis (lice), 61,
  281–282
Peer mediation, 173–174
Peer pressure, 147, 152–163
  and choices with friends, 177
  and drugs, 271
Peer programs and drug use,
  86
Pelvic examinations,
  194–195, 241, 289
Pelvic inflammatory disease,
  279
Penalties for violating
  classroom rules, 75
Penis, 195–196
  and candidiasis, 216
  figure, 216
  and sexually transmitted
    diseases, 277, 279
Perfectionism and anorexia
  nervosa, 42
Performance indicators, 25
  and checklist, 117
  and health education
    standards, 97–98
  and instructional
    strategies, 111
  and *The Scope and
    Sequence Chart,*
    105–107, 108–109
Perfume and insects, 308
Pericardium, 190
Periodontal disease, 243
Peripheral nervous system
  (PNS), 189. *See also*
  Nervous system
Peristalsis, 189
Perpetration of crime, 347
Perpetrators of crime, 169,
  310, 311
Personal conflict, 171
Personal health, 27, 149,
  234–252
Personality changes and
  cocaine use, 7
Perspiration, 188
  and body odor, 236
  and exercising, 248
Pertussis. *See* Whooping
  cough (pertussis)
Pest control, 72

Index

Index

detectors, 5, 296

environmental tobacco smoke, 88, 261, 342–343

and incineration, 345

Smokeless tobacco, 6, 262

objectives, 12

Smoking, 6. *See also* Tobacco

and air pollution, 337

and carbon monoxide, 341

of crack, 263

and formaldehyde, 342

health effects of, 261

and heart disease, 287–288

and lung growth, 261

objectives for reducing, 12

and secondhand cigarette smoke, 342–343

and sleep, 244

and tooth damage, 244

Smooth muscles, 188

Snakebites, 307–308

Sneezing, 276, 277

Snellen chart, 65

Snob appeal and advertising, 320

"Snorting" cocaine, 7, 263

Snuff, 262

and tooth damage, 244

Soap and acne, 237

Social changes and aging, 203

Social competence, 168–169

Social conscience, 199

Social health domain, 99, 145

Social services, 24

Social skills, 167–168

and dating, 180

Socioeconomic conditions, 347–348

Soda pop. *See* Soft drinks

Sodium, 221

dietary guidelines, 225

and fast foods, 227

on food labels, 226

and water pollution, 338

Soft drinks, 227

and artificial sweeteners, 228

and caffeine, 267

and recycling, 346

Soft tissue injuries, 63–64

Softball injuries, 314

Solid waste, 28, 344–345

Solvents and solid waste pollution, 345

Somatic nervous system, 189

Sore throat

and chronic fatigue syndrome, 291–292

and influenza, 277

and mononucleosis, 278

Sores and sexually transmitted diseases, 277

Sound intensity, 343

Special concerns in today's school environment, 83–90

Specificity principle in exercise, 247

Speech

objectives, 107

slurred, 306, 308

Speech pathologist as health care provider, 330

Speed as fitness component, 252

Speeding and reckless driving, 312

Spending money, 324–325

Sperm

and anabolic steroids, 42

and conception, 199

and FSH, 193

production, 195

Spina bifida, 46

Spinal cord, 188–189

figure, 209

injuries, 16, 304

Spine

curvatures of, 236

deformity, 62

Spirits, distilled, 258

Spleen, 274

Sports, 24

and anabolic steroids, 42

and glasses, 239

injuries, 20

and promotion of physical activity, 246, 247

safety, 314

Spotted fever, 59, 275

Sprains, 64, 248, 307

Squinting and visual disorders, 65

Staff. *See* Employees

Stalking, 312

Standards

for drinking water, 340

environmental, 348

national health education, 25, 95, 96–97

The Opportunity to Learn Standards, 115

for playgrounds, 81–82

Starches, 219–220

Starvation, 232, 347

State agencies, 331–332, 348

State health departments, 332

STDs. *See* Sexually transmitted diseases (STDs)

Stealing and drug abuse, 50

Stepfamilies, 176

Stereos and noise pollution, 343

Stereotypes, 170

Sterility

and anabolic steroids, 42

and endometriosis, 195

and mumps, 277

and sexually transmitted diseases, 8, 279

Sternum, 305

Steroids, anabolic, 7, 13, 42, 267

Stiffness and aging, 249, 251

Stillbirth and sexually transmitted diseases, 280

Stimulant, caffeine as, 267–268

Stings and bites, insect, 59, 308–309

Stomach, 189

and alcohol, 259

and caffeine, 268

and colitis, 290

figure, 210

and insect stings, 308

Stool blood test, 290

Storms, 301–302

and motor vehicle safety, 312

Strabismus ("crossed-eyes"), 65, 238

Strain, 64, 248, 307

Strategies for teaching, 111–112, 129–139

checklist, 117

Index

Technologies, instructional, 139–141
  and health education, 118
Technology and water pollution, 338
Teeth. *See also* Dental health plan
  knocked-out, 60
  and tobacco, 262
Telecommunication technologies, 140–141
Telecomputing, 140
Telephones and self-protection, 300
Television viewing, 327
  and lack of physical activity, 246
Temper-tantrums, 43
Temperature
  of the body, 188, 190, 306
  in the classroom, 24, 71–72
Tendons, 187
  figure, 207
  and muscle strain, 248, 307
Tension and noise pollution, 343
Terminal illness, 175
Terms, dictionary of food, 226
Testes (testicles), 192, 214
  and anabolic steroids, 42
  and cadmium, 345
  figure, 214, 216
  and sexually transmitted diseases, 278
  and sperm production, 193, 195
Testicular self-examination, 196
Testimony appeal and advertising, 320
Testosterone, 195
  and male development, 193
  production, 192
Tests. *See* Examinations
Tetanus, 46, 64
  immunization, 242, 274
  objectives, 18
Tetrahydrocannabinol (THC), 7, 266
Therapeutic community, 270
Therapists
  occupational, 329

physical, 329–330
  respiratory, 330
Therapy, 158. *See also* Counseling
Thermal inversion, 337
Thermal pollution, 339
Third-degree burns, 307
Thirst and diabetes, 290
Throat and air pollution, 337
Thrush, 275
Thymus gland, *figure,* 214
Thyroid gland, 192, 214
  figure, 214
Thyroxin, 192
Ticks, 59
Time management
  spending as life skill, 28
  and stress, 163
Time management plan, 326–327
Time recommendations for health education, 117
Tiredness. *See also* Fatigue
  and carbon monoxide, 341
  and chickenpox, 276
  and HIV, 282
  and iron deficiency, 221
  and measles, 277
  and sexually transmitted diseases, 280
Tobacco, 254, 255, 260–262. *See also* Smoking
  and cancer, 289
  and health knowledge, 149
  and immune system, 274
  life skills and, 27
    objectives, 12
  and risk behavior, 6, 25
  and tooth damage, 244
Tobacco-free environments, 19, 88
Toenails, 188, 236
  care of, 238
Toilets and trihalemethane pollution, 339
Tolerance, 269
Tonsils, 274
Tooth abscess, 48
Toothache, 242–243
Toothbrushing, 243
  and pathogens, 276
Toothpaste, fluoridated, 243

Tornadoes, 302
Totally awesome strategies™, 50, 56
  figure, 111
Totally awesome teacher™
  definition, 3
  role of, 35
  and umbrella of protection, 29
Touching and pathogen transmission, 276
Tourniquet, 305
Toxemia and pregnancy, 39
Toxic air pollution, 345
Toxic chemicals and water pollution, 338, 340
Toxic shock syndrome (TSS), 195
Toxic waste, 345, 348
Toxicity, behavioral, 265
Toxin and snakebite, 308
Trachea, 191
  figure, 212
Traffic
  and bicycle safety, 314
  and motor vehicle safety, 312
  and pedestrian safety, 299
Training principles, physical, 247
Tranquilizer drugs, 267
Trans-fatty acids, 220
Transparent Self (Jourard), 101
Transport system of the body, 189–190
Transportation
  and population growth, 347
  safe school transportation, 80
  of students, 78
Trash. *See* Solid waste
Treatment
  for addictive behaviors, 158
  for drug dependency, 18, 268–270
Trees and recycling, 346
Trichina, 275
Trichomoniasis, 281
Triggers, anger, 162
Triglycerides, 220
Trihalomethanes, 339

Index

Management of Event Operations

Books in the series

Management of Event Operations
Julia Tum, Philippa Norton and J. Nevan Wright

Innovative Marketing Communications: Strategies for the Events Industry
Guy Masterman and Emma Wood

Events Management 2e
Glenn A J Bowdin, Johnny Allen, William O'Toole,
Rob Harris and Ian McDonnell

Events Design and Experience
Graham Berridge

Event Feasibility
William O'Toole

Marketing and Selling Destinations and Venues:
A Convention and Events Perspective
Tony Rogers and Rob Davidson

Management of Event Operations

Julia Tum, MBA MHCIMA
Philippa Norton, BA (Hons)
J. Nevan Wright, PhD

ELSEVIER
BUTTERWORTH
HEINEMANN

AMSTERDAM • BOSTON • HEIDELBERG • LONDON • NEW YORK • OXFORD • PARIS
SAN DIEGO • SAN FRANCISCO • SINGAPORE • SYDNEY • TOKYO

Butterworth-Heinemann is an imprint of Elsevier
The Boulevard, Langford Lane, Kidlington, Oxford, OX5 1GB
30 Corporate Drive, Suite 400, Burlington, MA 01803, USA

First edition 2006
Reprinted 2006, 2007, 2009

Notice
No responsibility is assumed by the publisher for any injury and/or damage to persons
or property as a matter of products liability, negligence or otherwise, or from any use
or operation of any methods, products, instructions or ideas contained in the material
herein. Because of rapid advances in the medical sciences, in particular, independent
verification of diagnoses and drug dosages should be made

British Library Cataloguing in Publication Data
A catalogue record for this book is available from the British Library

Library of Congress Cataloging-in-Publication Data
A catalog record for this book is available from the Library of Congress

ISBN: 978-0-7506-6362-5

For information on all Butterworth-Heinemann publications
visit our website at www.elsevierdirect.com

Transferred to Digital Printing in 2009

Working together to grow
libraries in developing countries

www.elsevier.com | www.bookaid.org | www.sabre.org

ELSEVIER   BOOK AID International   Sabre Foundation

Julia dedicates this book to Les Trois J
Nevan dedicates this book to Joy and their 25 years
Philippa dedicates this book to Simon, Samuel and Jake

Contents

Figures

Tables

Case studies

Series editors

Glenn A J Bowdin is Principal Lecturer in Events Planning at the UK Centre for Events Management, Leeds Metropolitan University where he has responsibility for managing events-related research. He is co-author of *Events Management*. His research interests include the area of service quality management, specifically focusing on the area of quality costing, and issues relating to the planning, management and evaluation of events. He is a member of the Editorial Boards for *Event Management* (an international journal) and *Journal of Convention & Event Tourism*, Chair of AEME (Association for Events Management Education), Charter Member of the International EMBOK (Event Management Body of Knowledge) Executive and a member of Meeting Professionals International (MPI).

Don Getz is a Professor in the Tourism and Hospitality Management Program, Haskayne School of Business, the University of Calgary. His ongoing research involves event-related issues (e.g. management, event tourism, events and culture) and special-interest tourism (e.g. wine). Recent books include *Event Management and Event Tourism* and *Explore Wine Tourism: Management, Development, Destinations*. He co-founded and is a member of the Editorial Board for *Event Management* (an international journal).

Professor Conrad Lashley is Professor in Leisure Retailing and Director of the Centre for Leisure Retailing at Nottingham Business School, Nottingham Trent University. He is also series editor for the Elsevier Butterworth-Heinemann series on Hospitality Leisure and Tourism. His research interests have largely been concerned with service quality management, and specifically employee empowerment in service delivery. He also has research interest and publications relating to hospitality management education. Recent books include *Organisation Behaviour for Leisure Services*, *12 Steps to Study Success*, *Hospitality Retail Management*, and *Empowerment: HR Strategies for Service Excellence*. He has co-edited *Franchising Hospitality Services* and *In Search of Hospitality: theoretical perspectives and debates*. He is the past Chair of the Council for Hospitality Management Education. He is a Chair of the British Institute of Innkeeping's panel judges for the NITA Training awards, and is advisor to England's East Midlands Tourism network.

The authors

Julia Tum is a Senior Lecturer in the UK Centre for Events Management at Leeds Metropolitan University. Her main areas of professional interest are in the field of operations management and strategic management. These are topics taught to undergraduates and MSc students and also from part of her outside work when contracted to external organizations. She led the development team for the Honours Degree in Event Management in 1996 and was Course Leader from 1996 until 2000. Prior to that, amongst her other commitments, she was the Course Leader for the MSc in Hospitality Management.

Philippa Norton works freelance within the events industry involved in operations management and marketing and is currently working on a project for Bradford Industrial Museum and the Imperial War Museum in connection with the 60th Anniversary of the ending of World War II. She has a first class honours degree in Events Management and has lectured part time at Leeds Metropolitan University. Philippa has a project administration background and has lived and worked in Namibia, Somalia and Pakistan. Throughout her life she always has been and still is involved in organizing local events on a voluntary basis.

Dr Nevan Wright is a Professor of Management at Auckland University of Technology in New Zealand, and is an Associate Member of Faculty at Henley Management College UK, where he lectures for several months each year. Prior to joining academia Nevan was a Director/General Manager for a group of multinational companies operating in New Zealand. He is a Justice of the Peace for New Zealand and an Associate Fellow of The New Zealand Institute of Management. Nevan is the author of several management books.

Series preface

The events industry, including festivals, meetings, conferences, exhibitions, incentives, sports and a range of other events, is rapidly developing and makes a significant contribution to business and leisure related tourism. With increased regulation and the growth of government and corporate involvement in events, the environment has become much more complex. Event managers are now required to identify and service a wide range of stakeholders and to balance their needs and objectives. Though mainly operating at national levels, there has been significant growth of academic provision to meet the needs of events and related industries and the organizations that comprise them. The English speaking nations, together with key Northern European countries, have developed programmes of study leading to the award of diploma, undergraduate and post-graduate awards. These courses focus on providing education and training for future event professionals, and cover areas such as event planning and management, marketing, finance, human resource management and operations. Modules in events management are also included in many tourism, leisure, recreation and hospitality qualifications in universities and colleges.

The rapid growth of such courses has meant that there is a vast gap in the available literature on this topic for lecturers, students and professionals alike. To this end, the *Events Management Series* has been created to meet these needs to create a planned and targeted set of publications in this area.

Aimed at academic and management development in events management and related studies, the *Events Management Series*:

- provides a portfolio of titles which match management development needs through various stages;
- prioritizes publication of texts where there are current gaps in the market, or where current provision is unsatisfactory;
- develops a portfolio of both practical and stimulating texts;
- provides a basis for theoretical and research underpinning for programmes of study;
- is recognized as being of consistent high quality;
- will quickly become the series of first choice for both authors and users.

Preface

The structure of this book is built around a proposed event operations management model, which has its origins in Wright (2001) and has been augmented for the events industry. The model provides a way of approaching how to plan and organize each event that is staged . . . from planning a series of recruitment interviews between two or more people to planning the Olympic Games. The approach is essentially the same. The authors believe that each event is in fact a project, and that the wealth of literature that is available on both operations and project management can be used to assist an event manager in the complex management of an event.

The aim of the book is to present a theoretical model which can be used by an event manager. The chapters in the book lead the reader gently through this management process, and enable reflection to take place as the different concepts become linked together.

There are four sections within the book, and each examines in depth the elements within the four stages of the event operations management model. At the start of each new section readers are reminded of the structure of the book, and where they are within the model. The start of each section therefore reintroduces the model, explains the importance of what has already been covered and how it leads onto the next section.

It is the growing importance of the event industry that has necessitated the writing of this book. The book brings together in one publication the intricacies and complexities of event management, and shows by using an event operations management model that the approach can become more structured. Bowdin et al. (2001) identify how the event industry dates back thousands of years. The Romans were masters at staging events. Many examples can be found throughout history – Greek and Roman gladiatorial games, the ancient Olympic Games (first held in 776 BC), events held in the Middle Ages which celebrated harvests, and events that celebrated Royal ceremonies and military feats. Getz (1997) identifies the world of event management covers a myriad of cultural, sport, political and business occasions.

Events have long played an important part in daily life. Shone and Parry (2004) offer the thought that in most societies the slightest excuse could be found for a good celebration and that routine daily activities were often interspersed with festivals and carnivals.

In more modern times, in the last century The Daily Mail Ideal Home Show was launched in 1908 and the first British Industries Fair was held at the Royal Agricultural Hall (now the Business Design Centre) in London in 1915 (Bowdin et al., 2001). Each one of these events was a project, managed by teams of people working towards common objectives.

Following the World Wars, celebrations became a thriving sector and existed alongside events celebrating cultures of new communities in the UK from the West Indies and South Asia. McKay (2000) highlights the emergence of festival culture with its origins in the 1950s.

The 1970s and 1980s saw a range of multi-purpose venues being built, funded by local authorities (Bowdin et al., 2001). Wood (1982) believes that governments used community festivals and festivities to provide a focus for society, and to enable social and economic regeneration.

Sporting events have risen in their prominence alongside corporate hospitality and entertainment. The 1984 Olympic Games in Los Angeles began a trend of blending sports, events and creative expression, bringing together production and marketing, media and an awareness of economic benefit (Bowdin *et al.*, 2001). In every detail these events are projects, and they need an event manager to be following an event operations management model to ensure successfully coordinated management.

The trend for professionally staged events continues into the twenty-first century, with increased funding from sponsors, local authorities, industry, government and private individuals. These all demand a return on their investment, and need to be assured that the event is well managed and realizing its objectives, and will be delivered both on time and within budget. It is this growth of events that has led to the emergence of an events industry, with its associated industry associations, training and education.

The companies within the event industry, like those in most other industries, are facing strong pressures on cost, whilst the market is demanding increased quality and service (Lee-Kelley, 2002). As Lee-Kelley (2002) cites, information and technology is now offering advanced communication possibilities. Improved communication also increases the expectations of our customers, and similarly our expectations of suppliers.

Journals, newspapers and advertisements can be scanned to see a myriad of different event companies offering a complete event service – from managing a wedding or planning an international conference, to the development of major sporting or charity events. On further investigation it can be seen that many of these companies do not directly employ the relevant specialists, skills and resources, but manage the event by the use of outsourced or subcontracted specialists. For example, catering, sound and lighting provision, security, stage and seating and possibly the venue itself may be hired by the event company for the duration of an event.

Thus it can be deduced that many event companies bring together and manage a variety of companies and services to produce the final event. These are complex projects, and the industry deserves an event operations management model that it can follow methodically to be assured that it is using well-researched best practices and concepts.

As rapidly as the event industry has emerged, so also has the need to be efficient in the many ways that money and time can be spent upon securing the right resources and delivering a successful event. O'Toole and Mikolaitis (2002) identify that, as growth in the demand for events has occurred and the events themselves have become increasingly complex, the event companies which are emerging have become increasingly professional. It is imperative that these companies are able to work methodically, be organized and can call upon the right resources to fulfil the needs of the event and enable a matching of the expectations of the various stakeholders.

Goldblatt (2002) indicates that hundreds or perhaps thousands of elements must be evaluated to produce a foolproof event. Coordination is critical to successful organization and management of any project, and no more so than for an event, which is distinctly time constrained and must be delivered and executed on time. Watt (1998) believes that good coordination comes from having a shared goal and common objectives, within an appropriate culture and structure.

O'Toole and Mikolaitis (2002) believe that one solution to reduce costly inefficiency is to introduce 'systematic methods for researching, designing, planning, co-ordinating and evaluating every event'. They argue that a systematic approach will improve efficiency and offer a higher rate of return on the investment of time, money and people. The event operations management model, which this book is based around, builds on some of their ideas and incorporates much from the general project management literature.

Dealing with a network of suppliers and multiple customer and client needs requires a total quality management approach to ensure a successful event. Crosby first proposed Total Quality Management (TQM) in the early 1980s. Before this, Total Quality

Control (TQC) and Company Wide Quality Control (CWQC) (Juran, 1969) had gained acceptance throughout the USA and Japan. Crosby (1979; 1984) proposed that work should have zero defects – i.e. total absence of failure. This approach, understandably, had a major impact on general management at that time, attracting attention to quality and influencing managers to commit themselves to quality (Kandampully, 2002).

Each event that is staged can be considered as a quality project, which requires the skills of a project manager to keep it on time and within budget while satisfying the expectations of clients and customers. Indeed, Getz (1997) identified that one-off events have a definite start and end date, and he advocates the use of project planning methods to create and launch an event. Once an event has started there are no second chances (Allen, 2000). This book looks at how an event manager can successfully manage the event process, and each chapter is dedicated to each stage in the process.

Mature industries such as building and construction have used a project management approach for many years (Webster, 1994; Cicmil, 1997). With these approaches comes a bank of tools and techniques that have been adapted and refined to meet the needs of the project manager, satisfy quality issues and enable all practices to be completed in a safe manner to budget and to time. This book will investigate some of the most relevant of these approaches and their associated techniques, and will apply them, within the proposed event operations management model, to the event industry.

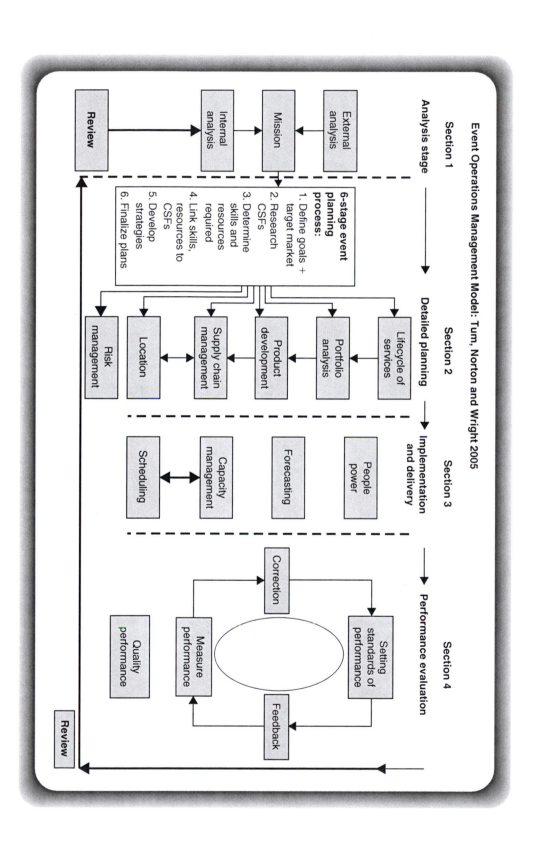

Event Operations Management Model: Tum, Norton and Wright 2005

Section 1

Analysis stage

External analysis

Mission

Internal analysis

Review

Section 2

Detailed planning

6-stage event planning process:

1. Define goals + target market
2. Research CSFs
3. Determine skills and resources required
4. Link skills, resources to CSFs
5. Develop strategies
6. Finalize plans

Lifecycle of services

Portfolio analysis

Product development

Supply chain management

Location

Risk management

Section 3

Implementation and delivery

People power

Forecasting

Capacity management

Scheduling

Section 4

Performance evaluation

Setting standards of performance

Correction

Feedback

Measure performance

Quality performance

Review

Section One
Analysis

Introduction

Within Section 1, the event operations management model is introduced and explained. The event operations management model provides the structure for the entire book, and the four sections within the book relate to the four stages of the model.

The importance of analysis is stressed in Chapters 1–6. An event manager must work with eyes, ears and mind open to activities that are going on around the organization – not only those that are close to the organization but also those that are thought to be remote and of no direct importance to the event. The concept that everything has a knock-on effect somewhere is very difficult to challenge.

This book identifies how, by using conventional operational management theory and project planning techniques, the event manager can be better equipped to manage events in the twenty-first century.

The chapters in Section 1 therefore concentrate upon internal and external analysis to identify the environments in which the event manager is working.

Chapter 1 introduces the development of the event operations management model. This model is proposed as the ideal process for an event manager. It is based on extensive research, and brings together aspects of previously published models. The model embraces all the aspects of managing an event, from concept through to implementation and review.

As alluded to in the preface, today's environment is dynamic, competitors are aggressive, and customers can be fickle and demanding. Many events organizations are small entrepreneurial companies, others are part of large companies often seeking to promote brands and excellence, and others are charitable or community based. None of these organizations can afford to make financial errors, lose reputation or fail to meet agreed objectives.

The event operations management model seeks to explore all the elements and issues that an event manager should be aware of as the event is considered from concept to completion.

Chapter 2 identifies some of the major terminology used within the operations management and the project management literature, which can clearly be applied to managers within the event industry. These previously very well researched and documented approaches are relevant and can be appropriately transferred to the event industry.

Critically, the importance of having a clear mission and objectives is discussed, as is the importance of knowing who the customers are and how their needs can be satisfied.

The notion of transformation of resources is introduced. This is the process whereby both tangible and intangible resources are utilized to create, and be consumed by, the event. Often creation and consumption is simultaneous.

The chapter concludes by examining the different formats that events can take. It is very important for an event manager to be able to consider the impact of these variances on costs, training needs, standardization and flexibility.

Chapter 3 considers in depth the external environment. It offers various techniques that can be used to appraise external factors, and explains the importance of both creating and understanding objectives set by and expected by a diverse range of people. In order to cover these points succinctly the importance of business policy is introduced, since this will have an impact on the event operations management model.

The chapter explores in depth many of the external issues and groups that influence organizations, and it offers a technique that can be used by an event manager to explore and analyse the impact of stakeholders on an organization.

Chapter 4 considers some aspects of marketing. This chapter provides a bridge between the internal and external environments. The main aim of the chapter is to demonstrate the importance of knowing what the customer wants and values. This is a significant aspect of the event operations management model.

The chapter considers specifications, consistency of provision, timeliness, flexibility, price and added value. The issues within this chapter are of considerable importance to the event manager.

Chapter 5 covers in depth the needs of the customers and the various stakeholders. It examines the amount of interaction between the organization and the customers, and the effect that different levels of contact can have on the management and control of the different elements of the event. Similarly, the chapter considers the degree of influence on the organization from the different stakeholders, and analyses the influence and impact that stakeholders can have on an event and how the event manager can aim to control this.

The concept of critical success factors is introduced and various techniques are explored to evaluate how well an organization is meeting the needs of its customers. This section culminates in exploring the concepts of gap analysis.

Chapter 6 focuses on the internal environment. This is an important part of the event operations management model. The chapter examines the culture of an organization and how this can influence quality decisions, what information systems are required and the importance of financial strength.

The chapter explores the efficient use of resources and the varied competencies of employees. A technique is offered which will enable the event manager to make efficient use of resources so as to provide the best possible customer satisfaction – i.e. the critical success factors (CSFs). The chapter closes with a discussion on the different management structures that organizations can create, and their varying advantages and limitations.

Hence, Section 1 offers a set of tools and techniques for events management, using a logical and clearly described event operations management model.

Chapter 1

Development of the proposed event operations management model

Learning Objectives

After reading through this chapter you will be able to:

- Define a project, and understand the various approaches to event operations and the management of a project
- Explain the importance of project management and its application to event operations management
- Appreciate how the event operations management model has been created
- Understand the four stages within the event operations management model.

Introduction

Tukel and Rom (2001) have researched various definitions of what a project is, and cite the work that has been put forward over a period of time by Kerzner (1994). Initially he offered three objectives for a project – that it should be:

1. Completed on time
2. Completed within budget
3. Completed at the desired level of quality.

It can be seen that these are only internally focused objectives, and are concerned with the success of the project from the organization's point of view.

By the late 1980s, after the introduction of Total Quality Management (TQM) into academic literature, Kerzner (1994) added a further two performance measurements:

4. Customer satisfaction and acceptance of the outcome
5. Customers allowing the contractor to use them as a reference.

This is an example of a trend by researchers to integrate customer involvement as a factor in determining project success.

Turner's (1999: 8) definition of a project starts to reflect some of the known and expected constraints and characteristics of a project:

> *... an endeavour in which human, financial and management resources are organized in a novel*
> *way to undertake a unique scope of work, of given specification, within constraints of cost and time,*
> *so as to achieve beneficial change defined by quantitative and qualitative objectives.*

This development of the definition is supported by Cicmil (2000), who argues that traditional project management had developed a range of specific techniques for planning, monitoring and control which used to be applied to industries such as construction, aerospace and defence. However, he also recognizes the limitations and challenges of modern projects. It is precisely those challenges that can often be present within virtual teams in the event industry – i.e. there exists complex and diverse customer–supplier chains and multiple stakeholders who have a complexity of expectations of an event.

It can be seen that project management is becoming more common and necessary as stakeholders and the business environment are demanding professional and commonly agreed standards. Bowdin *et al.* (2001) note that project management methodology is being used in fields as diverse as software management, business change management and event management.

Other work (Bubshait and Farooq, 1999) has focused on the person who is in charge of a project. This person is vital in providing, and often *being*, the main focal point. Gray and Larson (2000) advise project managers to innovate and adapt to changing circumstances in order to maintain control. Even well-planned projects in the event industry are likely to face unexpected challenges – customers' changing needs and numbers, variable weather conditions, road access closures, failures of suppliers etc. Cooke-Davies (1990) notes that any one of these changes may result in significant modifications being made to the project schedule and resource requirement. In the event industry, however, no changes can be made to the end time of the project, since this is the start time of the event. No slippage is possible, and there is only one opportunity to get it right. To quote from O'Toole and Mikolaitis (2002):

> *What separates the corporate event contract from others is the overriding importance of time.*

The dynamic nature of events and the way that the functional areas are so closely linked means that a small alteration in one area can result in crucial changes, and may affect the whole event (Bowdin *et al.*, 2001). Since an event has a start and an end point, it can also be defined as a project. It has a life expectancy, and the time from its inception to completion can be termed 'the event project life cycle'.

The work of Robbins and Coulter (1998), Cicmil (2000), Ibbs and Kwak (2000), Wright (2001), Grundy and Brown (2002), Wild (2002), Czuchry and Yasin (2003) and Slack *et al.* (2004) has been analysed in preparation for the following chapters regarding what they propose as an ideal project management methodology. The major elements, which are constantly highlighted as being essential, are to:

- Understand the external environment
- Establish a vision
- Define the nature and scope of the project and formulate clear objectives
- Plan, organize and manage the project
- Monitor and evaluate as the project develops
- Implement and control
- Take corrective action, review and learn.

Similarly, the works of Getz (1997), Goldblatt (1997), Watt (1998), O'Toole and Mikolaitis (2002) and Shone and Parry (2004) present ideal event management

processes. There are no major differences between them and, as before, although the words may differ, the essential concepts remain the same:

- Research
- Clarify aims and objectives and feasibility
- Design and present preliminary plan
- Organize and coordinate
- Implement
- Close down
- Review and evaluate.

Shone and Parry (2004) show that there are considerable similarities between the management of projects and the management of events, and they believe that there are techniques from the project management literature that can be adopted by event managers. These include:

- The use of work breakdown structures
- Identification of critical tasks and external dependencies
- Gantt charting, related to critical path analysis
- Risk assessment.

We will come to these techniques and others as we work through the event operations management model used in this book, and through the various sections. There are four stages within the event operations management model (see Figure 1.1), and hence there are four sections to this book:

1. Analysis
2. Detailed planning
3. Implementation and delivery
4. Performance evaluation.

The process presented in Figure 1.1 shows a linear progression through four stages. This is a useful method of presentation, as it enables us to see and understand each stage clearly. Each stage will be covered within the relevant section of the book.

Figure 1.2 shows the same event operations management model, but it is presented in an iterative format – i.e. where each stage is dependent upon another and *vice versa*. Using this model, the event manager should be flexible enough to return to any one stage and re-investigate changes as they occur. Due to the dynamic and changing nature of the external environment, analysis cannot be static and plans need to be constantly revisited to verify original assumptions.

Each of the four main stages is split into sub-sections, and each of these is discussed and applied to the event industry in the relevant sections and chapters within this book.

Analysis

The analysis stage is covered in Section 1 of this book, and it looks at both the environment external to the organization or specific event and the internal environment of the organization itself. Section 1 is concerned with introducing the event industry in greater depth, and examines the background of operational management theory in an event management context. All organizations should have clear objectives and goals, and these should be encompassed within the mission for that organization or for a particular event.

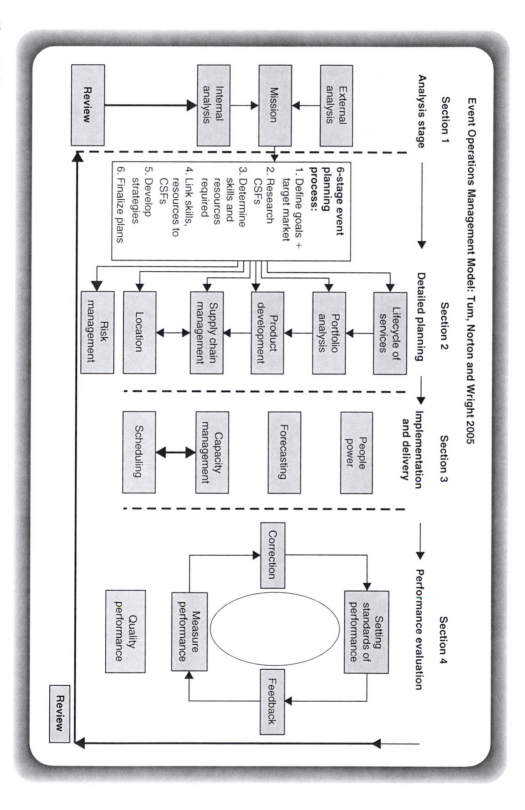

Figure 1.1 Event operations management model

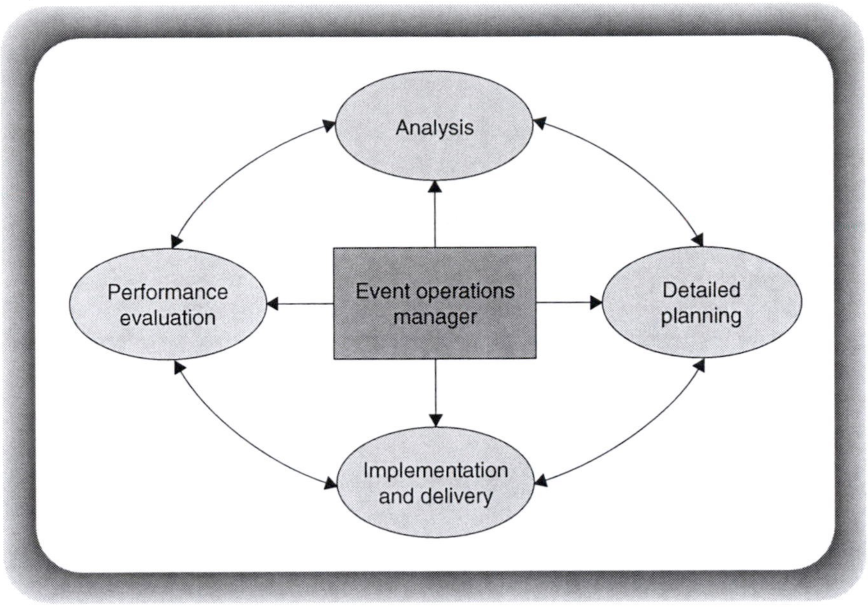

Figure 1.2 Event operations management model, shown as an iterative process

An analysis of both the internal capabilities, values and resources of the organization, and the external environment in which it operates, assists in determining the objectives for an organization. It is essential that a full analysis be undertaken prior to launching an event in order to move towards success.

Detailed planning

Section 2 looks in detail at all the planning activities that must be undertaken in order to stage an event. In some instances planning may take many years, as in the Olympics, and in other cases the planning may take just a week or even less. In each case many of the stages and techniques are the same, and these are detailed in the chapters. The topics cover the detail of the planning process and the management of the supply chain. Also within these chapters you will find work on choice of location for both the event organization and the events themselves. An important topic covered here is risk management. Although it sits within this section of the book, it should be understood that risk management should be considered throughout the life of the project.

Section 2 provides a basis for implementation, which is the next stage in our event operations management model.

Implementation and delivery

As its name suggests, Section 3 is concerned with the allocation of resources against the specifications designed for an event. Amongst other topics, this section of the book looks at motivation and the management of people, forecasting and planning for optimum capacity, and scheduling and coordination of all of the activities that bring an event to fruition.

Performance evaluation

Section 4 covers the last stage of the event operations management model, and it looks in detail at how the standard specification can be used in order to monitor and correct any stage of the operation both during and after the event. It is important that for future events, managers develop and learn from successes and mistakes of the past. The section also looks at how events can be evaluated, and offers various techniques to aid the event manager.

The important topic of quality is critically analysed within the last chapter. Although it is investigated here, quality should not be considered as a separate subject; it pervades every action and every stage of an event. Quality management is a fitting topic with which to conclude this book on event operations management.

Chapter summary and key points

This chapter has explored the varied definitions of a project that have developed over the years. In tandem with this investigation, the chapter has explored the various operations management models from both the general literature and the event management literature. It has been possible to consider the most relevant aspects of all these models and create a model that is appropriate for the management of an event operation. Incorporated into that model is an ideal model for managing an actual event, based on the project management literature.

The outcome is portrayed in this chapter, and is called the event operations management model. This has been shown in two formats; one linear and the other iterative. The linear approach is ideal to use as a structure for this book; the other is what will really happen in practice – i.e. as soon as one element of the model has been achieved and completed, before moving onto the next stage the event manager will invariably have to return to some earlier decision since the marketplace and the customer will be always changing. The model identifies that the event manager has to be nimble, and it also identifies that the event manager should be well organized and methodical.

Chapter 2

Event management: characteristics and definitions

Learning Objectives

After reading through this chapter you will be able to:

■ Appreciate the growth of the event industry and its different characteristics
■ Understand a range of useful definitions used within the operational management and project management literature
■ Explain the importance of having a clear mission and how this must translate in to 'making it happen' for the customer
■ Evaluate the need to match the environment, values and resources (i.e. EVR congruence)
■ Understand the transformation process and appreciate the use of resources, which are the inputs into the process, and services and products, which are the output of the process (i.e. the event itself).

Introduction

We are at the start of the event operations management model, and as such it is important to take stock of all that is happening around the organization and the event. This chapter identifies some basic definitions that are essential to understand before we proceed through the rest of the chapters. In particular, the chapter introduces terminology from the events industry, general management theory and operational management theory. It establishes the framework in which event managers work, looks at the constraints of policy, and shows how events are limited and affected by resources and the nature of the event. The chapter serves as an explanation for the need for external and internal analysis which is required for any event organization that is in the process of creating an event and having sustained business success. The analysis of these two environments is covered in depth in Chapters 3 and 6.

The different types of event operations are discussed, and also their implications for decision-making and event design.

Important definitions

First we will define the terms *industry, market* and *strategic group*. Evans *et al.* (2003) make an important distinction between markets and industries, and other competitors within the same strategic grouping. They believe that a *market* refers to the needs of the customers and potential customers, whereas the *industry* refers to a group of products linked by common technology, supply or distribution channels. A *strategic group* refers to those organizations that are identified as being the major competitors.

Modern organizations may operate in more than one industry, and in more than one market. For example, in the event industry, ThemeTraders is a vertically integrated UK-based art, design, and production company specializing in creative parties, themed events, road shows and motivational events. Its vertical integration within the *industry* comes from its own services and production of props, costumes and equipment. Each of these affiliated services can be hired separately to clients if wanted. It has clients in a variety of *markets*, including banks, media, car manufacturers, universities, retail establishments, television shows, hotels and airlines.

Each industry and market has its own distinctive structure and characteristics. Industries are centred on the supply of a product, while markets are concerned with demand.

Campbell *et al.* (2003) define the two concepts clearly:

● Industries *produce* goods and services – the supply side of the economic system
● Markets *consume* goods and services that have been produced by industries – the demand side of the economic system.

The event industry

A variety of authors (Getz, 1997; Goldblatt, 1997; Watt, 1998; Bowdin *et al.*, 2001; Shone and Parry, 2004) identify the extent of the event industry and create typologies in order to consider, in more manageable groupings, the diversity of the event industry, its sectors and its markets.

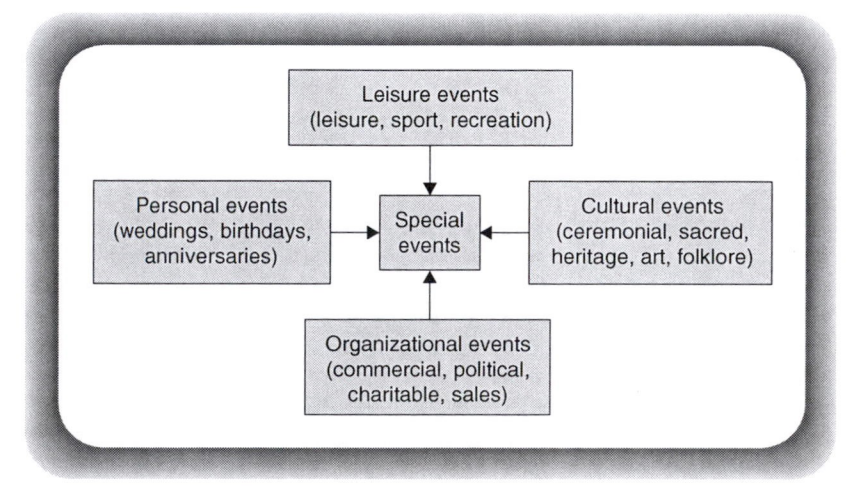

Figure 2.1 Shone and Parry typology of events (Shone and Parry, 2004)

Shone and Parry (2004) suggest a particular typology (Figure 2.1) which we use as a starting point in order to understand the breadth and variety of events. This approach is not offered as the definitive approach, but it does serve to highlight the diversity of event provision.

Getz's typology (Figure 2.2; Getz, 1997) is not dissimilar, but does include more detail within business and trade events, and also identifies educational and scientific events.

Another way the event industry could be split is into three sectors:

1. Public
2. Private
3. Voluntary.

Unlike commercial industries, events are not always driven by the need to make money, but may include a large number of personal, voluntary and charitable events. It is not difficult to think of worldwide examples for these categories but even in small communities illustrations of these three sectors can be found (see Case study 2.1).

All events are unique, and it is this uniqueness that makes them special and creates a challenge for the manager. Four different characteristics of events that are important to the event organizer are:

1. Size and volume of output
2. Complexity and variety of services/products offered to the consumer
3. Uncertainty of numbers attending, cost, time schedule and technical requirements
4. Interaction with the consumer, and degree of consumer and customer contact.

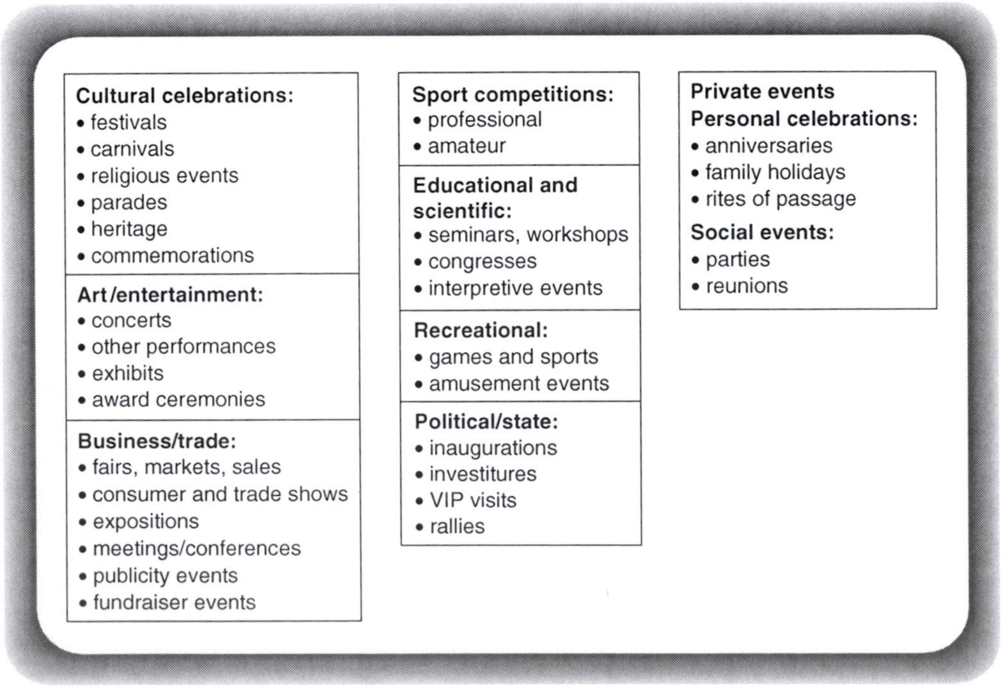

Cultural celebrations:	**Sport competitions:**	**Private events**
• festivals	• professional	**Personal celebrations:**
• carnivals	• amateur	• anniversaries
• religious events		• family holidays
• parades	**Educational and**	• rites of passage
• heritage	**scientific:**	
• commemorations	• seminars, workshops	**Social events:**
	• congresses	• parties
Art/entertainment:	• interpretive events	• reunions
• concerts		
• other performances	**Recreational:**	
• exhibits	• games and sports	
• award ceremonies	• amusement events	
Business/trade:	**Political/state:**	
• fairs, markets, sales	• inaugurations	
• consumer and trade shows	• investitures	
• expositions	• VIP visits	
• meetings/conferences	• rallies	
• publicity events		
• fundraiser events		

Figure 2.2 Getz's (1997) typology of events

Case study 2.1

Skipton

Skipton is a small, busy market town in North Yorkshire, England, situated on the southern edge of the Yorkshire Dales and with a population of 16 000. It has a castle, a canal, a bustling outdoor street market and many festivals and events, some of which are illustrated below.

Public sector event

Skipton Local Produce Festival was organized by the North Yorkshire County Council, Craven District Council and other local organizations as a method of promoting local produce.

The event was held over two days in October at the local Auction Mart, and included cookery demonstrations, music theatre, performance tent, roving performers, workshops, over ninety local produce stalls, and also producers from the Netherlands and Norway.

It was supported by the URBAL project, which is funded through the European Union INTERREG programme. The INTERREG project was launched in the Netherlands in June 2004, and includes partners from the Netherlands, Belgium, Norway, Germany, Sweden and the UK.

URBAL is designed to allow local producers to showcase their products at regional festivals with partner countries.

(Information printed by kind permission of Jochen Werres, Funding and Strategy Manager, Economic Development Unit, North Yorkshire County Council.)

Private sector event

Broughton Hall Country House Estate, Skipton, is still occupied by the Tempest family, and it is used in film and TV dramas. Besides being a country house it is a prestigious business park set in 3000 acres of parkland, and it holds events annually.

The 2004 annual fireworks and laser symphony concert held in July was entitled 'More sounds of the 70s'. This included a sixty-piece symphony orchestra and a vocal group. Audience members were invited to take their own picnics, although hot and cold refreshments as well as hospitality were provided.

(More information re. Broughton Hall Estate can be found at www.broughtonhall.co.uk.)

Voluntary sector event

The Skipton Charities Gala is held annually in July at Skipton, North Yorkshire. A gala – pronounced 'gayler' – in Yorkshire terms consists of a parade followed by activities for all the family, usually in a park; these would include games, funfair, demonstrations in an arena etc. There follows an extract from the Chairman's letter, cited in Skipton's Charity Gala programme.

> As usual we pray for dry weather, leaving the rest up to us. We as a committee work so hard trying to put everything into place for the big day. We would like to thank our volunteers who excel themselves each year, without them our gala would not exist. Last but not least to you our public who support us each year come rain or shine, making Skipton Charities Gala nothing but the best.
>
> Because of all this wonderful support we were able to donate over £1000.00 to local causes and charities so far this year. 'A Great Achievement', our sincere thanks go to you all.
>
> Mr and Mrs Dawson (Fred and Doreen), who have been the backbone of Skipton Gale for over seventy years, are going to do us the honour of opening the 2004 gala.
>
> Many thanks go to Marshall Waddington for the splendid firework display, which he donates year after year. Also a special thank you to Skipton Police for all their hard work and support, on and before gala day.

(More information on Skipton Gala can be found at www.skiptonweb.co.uk)

Reflective practice 2.1

1. Research examples of each events sector in your home city, town or village, and compare them with others from members of your study group.
2. What differences if any do you notice?
3. Why do you think this is?

These four characteristics are based on those proposed by Slack *et al.* (2004), and will be discussed more fully later in this chapter. However, it is important to understand the following concepts in advance.

Companies and organizations existing within the event industry

Event managers may work within a small or large event companies, or they may be employed within much larger organizations. The organization may be a multimillion-pound enterprise such as John Lewis, which employs social secretaries to organize anything ranging from small interview panels to their Annual Fun Day for 20 000+ Partners and their guests. Whatever their size, organizations and major events such as Children in Need (a charity fund-raising initiative in the UK) should have a mission – their *raison d'être*.

Mission

In event terms, the mission can be broadly separated into four areas:

1. The organization's task
2. The reason for staging the event
3. The event's stakeholders
4. The event's overall objectives.

These are usually defined by those who feel that the event should fulfil a need within their community, region, organization or company. The mission should then become the focus of the event, but be flexible enough so as not to stifle creativity and flexibility (see Case study 2.2; Getz, 1997; Bowdin *et al.*, 2001).

Different levels of management and decision-making

If we consider a company as being triangular in shape (Figure 2.3), we can see three different levels – strategic, business and operational. This approach is useful to improve our understanding of the different levels of decision-making – i.e. a long-term approach versus day-to-day management.

Case study 2.2

NYC & Company

NYC & Company (formerly known as the New York Convention & Visitors Bureau) is New York City's official tourism marketing organization. It lists among its goals the coordinating and/or facilitating of major promotional activities such as Restaurant Week, Paint the Town, CultureFest, OpSail, Broadway on Broadway, and the New York Marathon. It facilitates the expansion of convention and hospitality facilities, and provides support and resources to assist in obtaining major events, such as the 2012 Olympic Games, Grammys, and MTV Awards, for the city.

NYC & Company has the following mission statement:

> *NYC & Company, the city's official tourism marketing organization, is a private, membership-based non-profit organization dedicated to building New York City's economy and positive image through tourism and convention development, major events, and the marketing of the city on a worldwide basis.*

(Information supplied by courtesy of NYC and Company. For more information, see www. nycvisit.com.)

Reflective practice 2.2

1. Consider NYC & Company's mission statement in Case study 2.2, and discuss how it corresponds to the four areas of mission noted in this chapter.
2. What changes would you make?

Evans *et al.* (2001) believe that decisions taken at each of these levels differ from one another in terms of:

- Focus
- The level in the organization at which they are made

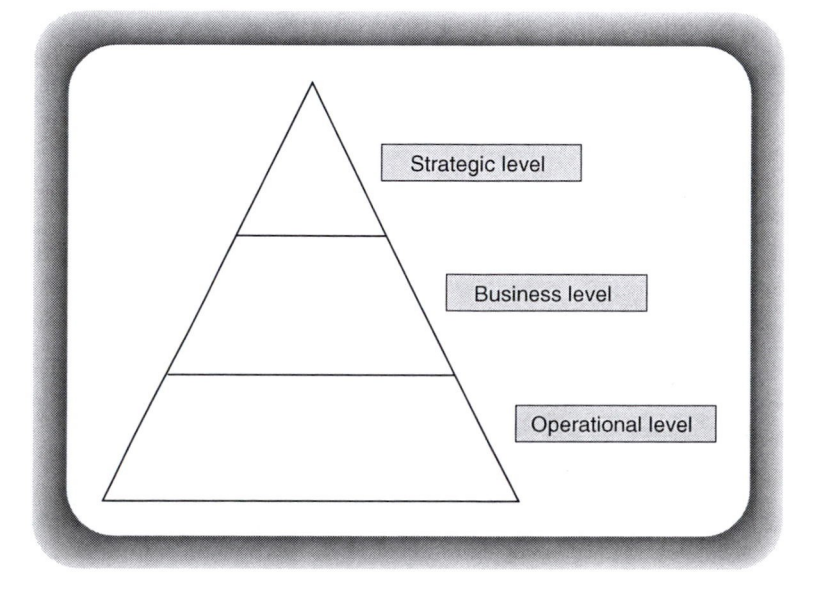

Figure 2.3 The triangle of management and decision-making

- Scope
- Time horizon
- Degree of certainty or uncertainty
- Complexity.

Strategic level decisions

Strategic level decisions are made by senior managers, and are concerned with long-term corporate objectives (i.e. a timescale usually greater than three years). These senior managers will create and evaluate strategies to achieve those objectives. Often these are incorporated into the mission statement.

Business level decisions

Within many companies there are specialized functions, and in many instances specific markets are sought and provided for.

The business decisions are dependent upon the strategic decisions, but only affect one part of the organization. They are medium-term in timescale – i.e. usually one to three years.

Operational level decisions

These are concerned with day-to-day management. It is where the implementation of the months of planning occurs, and where control and administration takes place.

The event manager is a decision-maker. As the event manager is at the hub of, and responsible for, making it happen, it follows that the most pressing decisions are of a day-to-day nature.

Certain influences will affect the decisions made by the event manager. The influences include the objectives of the organization, what is feasible with the resources available, the *structure* of the system, and the influences of the external environment, as our event operations management model shows.

Operational decisions are influenced by what is:

- *Desired* by the organization (mission and policy of the organization)
- *Feasible*, i.e. the availability, amount and quality of resources, both tangible and intangible, and the nature (in particular the structure) of the operating system being used
- *Possible*, due to the influence and impact of the external environment.

Figure 2.4 shows the constraints for an event manager. The mission and policy of the organization set the scope for the event manager; however, both the external and the internal environments influence the mission and, subsequently, any policies.

Once the policy has been decided, then what is desirable is expressed as the objectives of the organization, and the resources and structure of the organization may limit what is feasible. In Chapter 3 we will consider other external factors that limit what the event manager can provide – for example, the power and influence of the stakeholders.

The aim of the event manager will be to use resources as efficiently as possible to achieve the highest level of customer satisfaction within the constraints of policy objectives, available resources and the structure of the organization.

EVR congruence

Thompson (2001) indicates that a manager should fully appreciate the dynamics, opportunities and threats present in the external environment, and that these should match the organization's resources – both its strengths and its weaknesses. This concept can

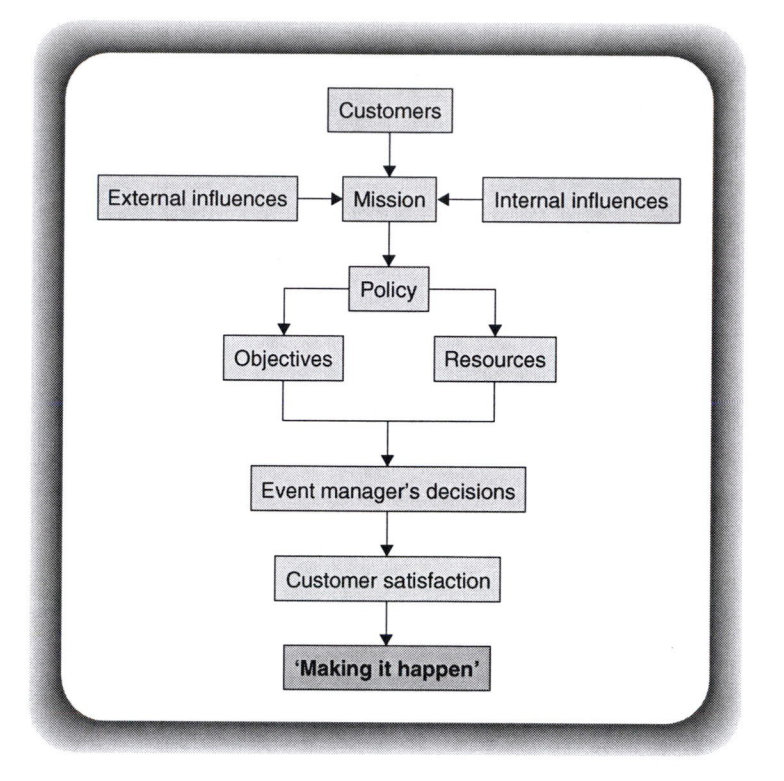

Figure 2.4 Influences on organizational decisions

also be expressed by saying that there should be a match between what the customer sees as being critical and the core competencies and resources being provided. However, it is also important that the values of the organization match both the needs of the environment and the critical success factors as determined by the customers. It is both the values and the culture that determine whether the environment and resources are currently matched, and whether they stay matched – i.e. congruent – in changing circumstances (Thompson, 2001). This is the notion of EVR congruence. There should be an overlap between the environment (critical success factors), the resources (tangible and intangible), and the values of the organization and its commitment to sustain this overlap (Figure 2.5).

If there is no overlap with any one of the three elements, the event manager should be in a position to address the situation and to achieve a suitable match that best addresses the organization and business.

Figure 2.6 shows an organization that has the desire, the skills and competencies, and the resources to move in a particular direction, but a direction that is not needed or valued by the consumer.

Figure 2.7 shows an organization that has the desire to move in a particular direction, and one that is appreciated and needed by consumers in a ready market. However, the organization does not have the skills and/or resources to deliver this particular product.

Figure 2.8 shows an organization that has the resources and skills to move in a particular direction, and one that is needed by the consumers. However, the culture and values of the staff within that organization do not want to move in that particular direction and with that product.

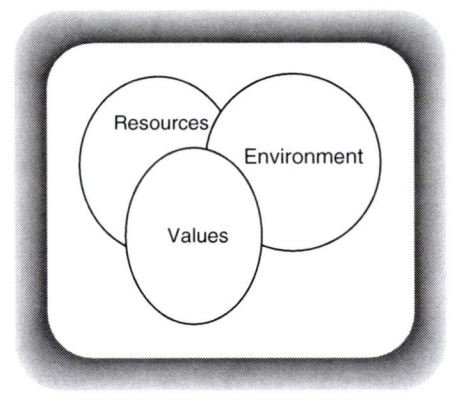

Figure 2.5 EVR showing an overlap of the three elements

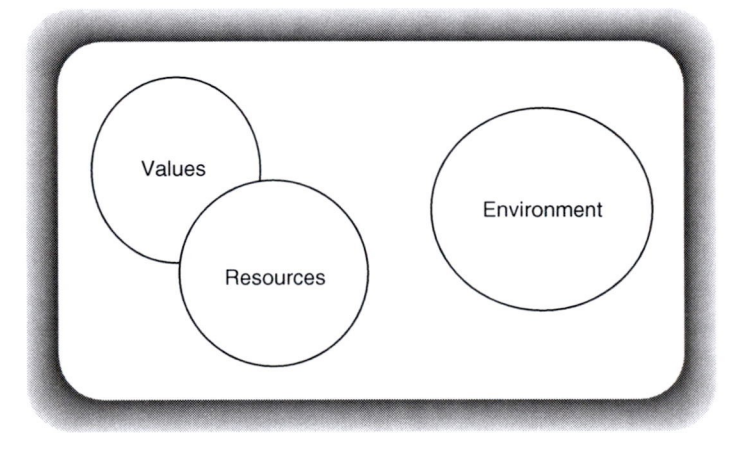

Figure 2.6 EVR showing an overlap of only the elements of values and resources

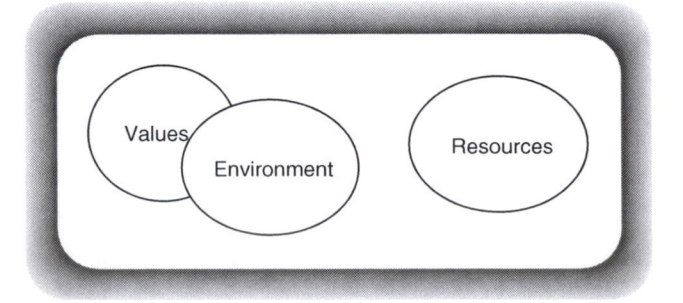

Figure 2.7 EVR showing an overlap of only the elements of values and the environment

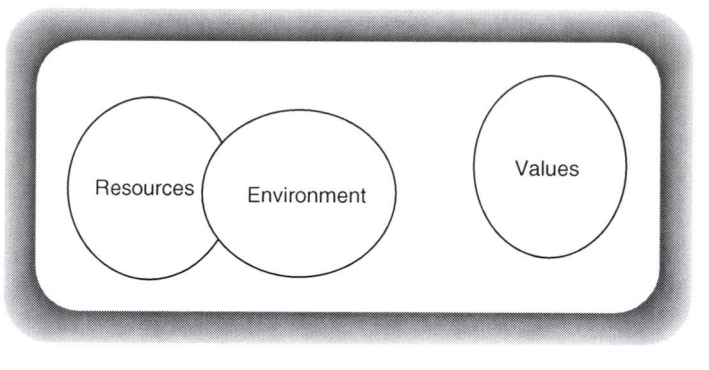

Figure 2.8 EVR showing an overlap of only the elements of the environment and resources

Important definitions

There are three further definitions that must be understood before proceeding further.

Service operations management

Service operations management is the function within a service organization that interacts with and delivers services to customers. Consequently, efficient operations management is crucial to the success of the organization. The role of a manager of an event operation is to manage an event and to provide customer satisfaction within the framework of the organization's policy, and to use resources as efficiently as possible.

Simply put, the event manager makes it, the mission, happen.

A further definition is provided by Wright (2001):

> operations management is the ongoing activities of designing, reviewing and using the operating system, or systems, to achieve service outputs as determined by the organization for customers.

Getz (1997), who has created a planning process for event operations, believes that it is the event manager who translates all of the key elements into the reality of an event (see Figure 2.9).

Campbell *et al.* (2003) see the operations function as being at the centre of the organization. It is that part of an organization which produces the output – the event itself. For example, for a product launch of a new perfume the operations function arranges coordination of an appropriate venue, reception staff, technical facilities and special effects, presentation scripts, an appropriate and relevant database of people to whom the product should be launched, and invitations to the relevant media. The actual launch and presentation is the output.

Service organization

A service organization is one where two or more people are engaged in a systematic effort to provide services to a customer. The objective is to serve a customer. For any service to be provided there has to be a customer. Without a customer, and interaction between customer and the service organization, the objective of providing service cannot happen. According to Wright (2001):

> A service organization exists to interact with customers and to satisfy customers service requirements.

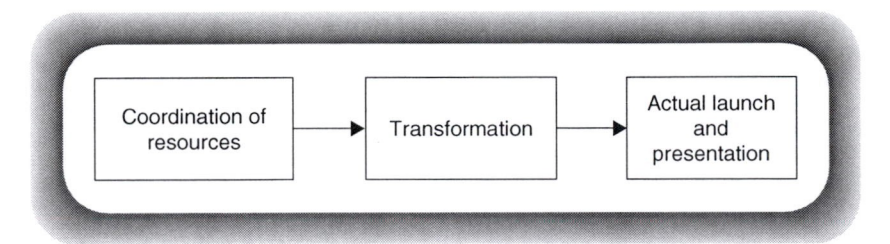

Figure 2.9 The transformation of resources into an event

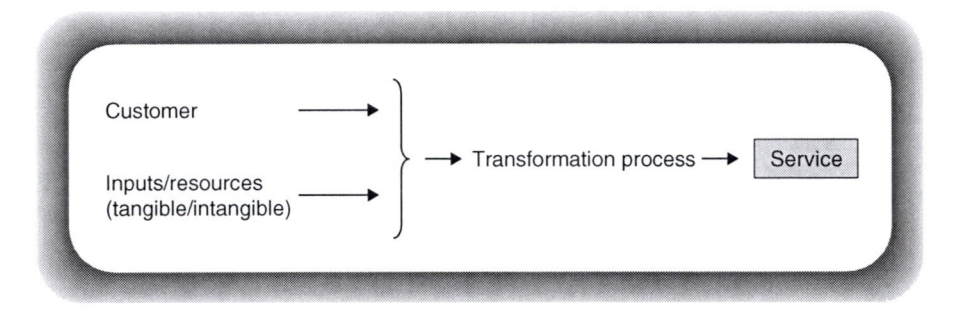

Figure 2.10 The transformation process

Service operating system

Slack and Lewis (2002) refer to a service operating system as the 'transformation process'. Wright (2001) defines it as follows:

> *A service operating system is the manner in which inputs/resources are organized and used to provide service outputs.*

Slack *et al*. (2004) recognize that there must be inputs to achieve an output. Within an operation, inputs/resources are transformed into outputs – for example, inputs could be raw food ingredients being transformed into a conference dinner (the output), or details about venues, room size and AV equipment availability being added to stored information to create a new improved database giving detailed information about the range of venues which are suitable for conferences (the output). The transformation process is the manipulation of the inputs/resources to produce an output i.e. service (Figure 2.10).

Inputs/resources

For ease and greater understanding in the events industry, we refer to the inputs as the resources needed and the outputs as service, or the event itself. Inputs can be tangible or intangible. Tangible inputs are physical, they can be seen and touched, and the amount or rate of use can be measured in quantifiable terms. Intangible inputs, which cannot be seen or touched, include:

- Time
- Information
- Innovative design

- Ideas
- Skills
- Sound, etc.

Measurement of the effective use of intangible resources is much more difficult than for the tangible resources. However, the amount of time and the information available are important issues for the event manager.

Without a customer the objective of service cannot be delivered, and therefore the customer must also be regarded as an input into the system that provides the service.

These inputs will be discussed in greater depth in Chapter 6.

Outputs

Service outputs include the following examples:

- A courtesy bus-shuttle service at an outdoor sculpture event taking passengers to different parts of the park, or 'Park and Ride' at an air show. A bus can travel on its advertised route, but until a passenger is picked up the function of the bus service is not carried out. Without a passenger the mission of the bus (i.e. to carry passengers) cannot be fulfilled. An empty bus travelling on the route is nothing more than an un-utilized, or 'stored', resource. Apart from the bus itself, other resources such as fuel and the time (wages) of the driver are being used.
- A hotel room. Until a guest checks in, the service function of the hotel cannot be performed. True the room can be 'serviced' and prepared in advance, but until a guest arrives there is no service output.

Case study 2.3

Royal Ascot, Ascot Racecourse

Royal Ascot is held annually in June at Ascot in Berkshire, UK.

The importance of intangible resources can be demonstrated by reactions to changes brought about by new management at Ascot Racecourse. In three years the Clerk of the Course and Chief Executive transformed attendance by concentrating on customer care. Richard Evans of the *Times*, quoted in *Ascot History*, said of the Royal Meeting that 'Ascot has gone out of its way to make customers feel welcome and wanted. Tradition and custom have not been sacrificed in the process and an air of relaxed formality has returned to the royal meeting'. Prior to these changes attendance had been faltering and information to customers on site had often been headed with the words 'By Order'.

(Magee, 2002)

Reflective practice 2.3

Consider Case study 2.3.

1. How could the terminology within signage affect the customer service of an organization?
2. Why would it?
3. What intangible resources are being affected here?

- A restaurant. With a restaurant it is possible for the chef to make up salads, and even to prepare and cook meals in advance, before any patron is seated. This may not be the policy (strategy) of a top-class restaurant, but nonetheless the decision (strategy) can be changed – i.e. it is not essential to have a customer before a meal is prepared. However, the mission of the restaurant is not to *prepare* meals, the mission is to *serve* meals, and the delivery of service cannot take place without the customer – it is not possible for the meal to be served unless there is a customer and the customer has placed an order.

In these three examples – the bus travelling on its route, the prepared hotel room and the partly prepared meal in the restaurant – there are stored resources waiting for the customer to arrive. However, without customer input no service output will be delivered.

The triangle of investigation

To summarize so far, we have:

- Noted the difference between industries and markets and strategic groups
- Considered the extent and diversity of the event industry
- Considered the importance of having a mission and appraised the three levels of decision-making within an organization
- Analysed the definitions and meanings of operational management, service organization, service operating system, and the transformation process.

It can be seen that in this chapter we ourselves have followed an inverted triangle of investigation (Figure 2.11) and moved from the general to the specific.

Now we are at the apex of the triangle. Who do we meet there? The customer!

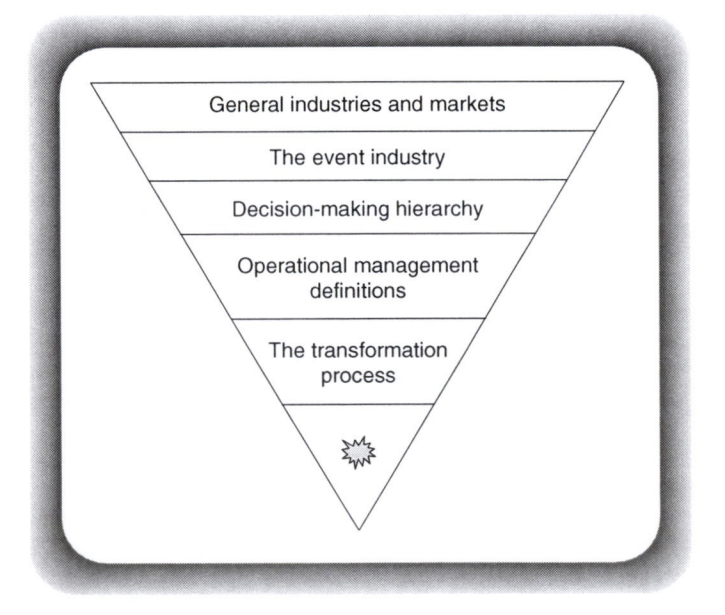

Figure 2.11 Inverted triangle of investigation, moving from the general to the specific

Who is the customer?

In events, customers can be the audience, a group of spectators, visitors, delegates or sponsors, or the individual client. From a commercial point of view, customers are the people who pay for the service. Kandampully (2002) categorizes customers into four groups:

1. External customers – a firm's end users
2. Internal customers – employees and managers of the firm
3. Competitors' customers – those the firm would like to attract
4. Ex-customers – those who have chosen to leave.

Similarly, in the events industry a distinction should be made between the paying customer and the end user.

In the majority of events the customer *pays* for the 'service' received – e.g. a paying customer at the Olympic Games in Athens, i.e. a spectator. Another example would be a ticket holder for a Pavarotti Concert. In fact, you might think you would be hard pressed to find a customer who does not pay. However, what about the audiences at the Queen's Golden Jubilee Celebrations, the audiences at major free outdoor local council events, and invited hospitality guests at annual dinners? What about incentive events and fabulous trips abroad? The distinction is that those who have attended and enjoyed these free spectaculars are 'end users'. In these instances, the customer is the one who pays for the service – so in the first example the customer of the Queen's Silver Jubilee is the Queen, or at least whoever holds her purse.

At local council events, is the customer the council, or perhaps the taxpayer or the consumer of the extravaganza?

Throughout this book, the term *customer* will be used. However, it should be remembered that this includes both the paying customer and the end user who does not pay but merely receives. Either way the customer is extremely important, and the customer's needs and impact on events feature heavily in this book. Chapter 5 analyses further the interaction between the customers, the stakeholders and how a company can start to measure its success in delivering all their diverse needs.

Different characteristics of operations and events

By now, you should understand a little more about the different characteristics of events. We know that, although the event operations management model (Figure 1.1) can be used for all different styles of events and is therefore transferable, decisions that are made about the characteristics and nature of the event have far-reaching consequences for the event operation manager.

We now consider these different characteristics and the different relationships we have with our customers.

We have seen that all operations involve a transformation process, where inputs are transformed into desired outputs – i.e. resources become transformed into services delivered; the event itself.

It is important to note the differences between types of operations and then to discuss the impacts that these differences have for the event manager and the organization.

Slack *et al.* (2004) believe that there are four important characteristics which can be used to identify different operations, and these distinctions are also useful and valid within the event industry:

1. The volume of service delivered at an event
2. The variety of the service delivered at an event
3. The variation in demand for the service delivered at an event
4. The degree of customer contact involved in producing the service delivered at an event.

Similar attributes to these were discussed earlier, although slightly amended. We remind you again of these four, adjusted by ourselves, to take into account the peculiarities of the event marketplace:

1. Size and volume of output
2. Complexity and variety of services/products offered to the consumer
3. Uncertainty of numbers attending, cost, time schedule and technical requirements
4. Interaction with the consumer, and degree of consumer and customer contact.

Size and volume of output

As an example, we can consider the thousands of applications from the public and many different charities to run in the annual London Marathon. The volume of enquiries and degree of processing of these enquiries enables a high degree of repeatability of actions for those staff who are concerned with the replies.

At the other end of the scale, imagine an event manager being involved with reviewing tender applications for extra seating for an indoor concert for 200 people from preferred suppliers. It can be seen that the volume of the similar task is very much lower, and the chance of employing more than one person to cover the second activity is remote. The staff involved in this small volume of administration will be employed to cover a wide range of other tasks, and therefore need to be much more flexible and highly trained in a variety of tasks. This may be more satisfying to the individual, but is less open to systemization.

With high-volume output, the task can become specialized and systematized and possibly warrant capital expenditure to enable the task to become more efficient – for example, by the use of computers and registration systems at a large exhibition.

The most important implication with high-volume activities is therefore that the unit cost can be much lower, since it can be spread over a large number of transformation processes/transactions.

Complexity and variety of services/products offered to the consumer

This dimension considers the variety of activities and tasks that the event manager can be called upon to perform during an event. In large events, different groups of staff are assigned to specific tasks – low variety, for example, being a steward at a particular entrance for an outdoor concert. (See Chapter 11 for more work on staff motivations.) However, at a small event – such as fifty-delegate seminar – the staff on duty could be asked a variety of questions regarding the provision of facilities and activities during the day, and be involved with a wide range of jobs.

A high degree of variety therefore determines the style of training required and the knowledge needed by individual staff. This means that flexibility comes at a price to the event manager.

Where variety is low, little flexibility is required and the tasks assigned can be standardized and regular. This lack of variety can result in relatively low costs, but may result in poor service if a member of staff becomes bored.

Uncertainty of numbers attending, cost, time schedule and technical requirements

Consider the demand pattern for a nightclub in a university town. When it is term time, the club will be full on certain nights and possibly would welcome even more space. However, during the summer months and at Christmas it may only use a fraction of its capacity.

If we consider a hotel close to a major road network and a tourist resort, it may be patronized by business conferences and business clientele during the week and by tourists at the weekends. It may find that its demand is virtually level. The consequence of this is that the hotel can plan its activities in advance and set out its staffing rotas.

Where there is low variation in demand, all activities can be planned in a routine and predictable manner. However, it may be that the range of activities varies between business and leisure guests.

The timeline does not have to be over one year, or over one week, but can show a variation in demand over one day. For example, can an event manager at an outdoor festival predict the demands on the bar over the course of a one-day event? How many staff should be employed for each hour of the day? Should it vary?

Would selling pre-paid tickets to a gala dinner confirm the number of diners? If so, the number of staff and amount of food can be pre-determined and this will ensure a high utilization of resources.

A low variation in demand enables routines to be established and for the required level of inputs to be predicted – whether over a one-day event or throughout a year.

A high variation in demand may prevent the organizer from knowing how many staff to employ and what capacity of space to make available, and may require greater flexibility from suppliers.

Case study 2.4 provides an example of a major annual event and the planning required.

Case study 2.4

The RHS Chelsea Flower Show

The RHS Chelsea Flower Show – the world's greatest flower show – is held annually for four days in May at the Royal Hospital, Chelsea. It has been held there since 1913, and the 2004 show was the eighty-second to be held at this site. Originally known as the Great Spring Show, it was first held in Kensington in 1862.

The Exhibitors
There are around 600 exhibitors in total. The 2004 show featured:

- Twenty-three show gardens
- Eight chic gardens
- Nine courtyard gardens
- Four city gardens

- Eight Sunflower Street gardens
- More than a hundred floral exhibitors.

International exhibitors came from countries as far away as the USA, Barbados, Kenya, Japan, Australia, Jamaica, South Africa and Trinidad & Tobago.

Some exhibitors, such as Nottcutt's, Kelways and McBean's Orchids, have exhibited at the show since its early days.

Exhibits are judged by specialist RHS Judging Panels before the show opens, and may be awarded Gold, Silver-Gilt, Silver and Bronze Medals.

Organization

RHS staff, exhibitors and contractors start planning for the show eighteen months in advance. Work is already underway for the show in 2005.

It takes 800 people three and a half weeks to build the show; construction includes 5 km of piping, 185 toilets, and enough canvas to cover 6 football pitches.

The floral pavilion covers nearly 12 000 square metres, and 7000 square metres of turf is relaid after the show. The showground covers 11 acres.

The visitors

There is a capped figure of 157 000 visitors to the show. This represents full capacity of the showground.

The RHS currently has over 300 000 members, and the Tuesday and Wednesday of the show are reserved for RHS members, although non-members may purchase tickets for the Wednesday afternoon and evening. Non-members can purchase tickets for Thursday and Friday.

Members of the Royal Family make a private visit to the show on the Preview Day (Monday).

Catering

During the course of the week, 6500 bottles of champagne, 18 000 glasses of Pimms, 5000 lobsters, 110 000 cups of tea and coffee, and more than 28 000 rounds of sandwiches are sold in the following restaurants:

- Ranelagh Seafood and Champagne – a large bistro-style restaurant serving seafood, salads, afternoon tea and strawberries; the champagne bar can also be found here. Open 10.30 am–7 pm.
- Ranelagh Restaurant – a large, seated catering area serving hot food, sandwiches, cakes and various beverages. Open 8 am–8 pm.
- Rock Bank Restaurant – a stylish seated restaurant offering full English breakfast, three-course lunches and late afternoon/early evening meals. This restaurant offers the best views of the show, overlooking some of the major gardens at the event. Tables in this restaurant can be pre-booked. Open 9 am–7.30 pm.
- Rock Bank Food Court – a large restaurant with some seating offering a range of hot and cold foods. This area includes a Pimms bar and a full bar facility. Open 8 am–8 pm.
- Thames View Restaurant – a small, seated restaurant overlooking the Thames, serving salads, pastries, baguettes, sandwiches and other cold foods together with hot and cold beverages. Open 8 am–8 pm.
- Western Avenue Food Court – this facility offers a wide range of hot and cold meals ranging from baguettes to jacket potatoes, crepes and ice cream. Open 8 am–8 pm.
- Champagne and Pimms – champagne and Pimms bars are located throughout the site. Open 8 am–8 pm.

(Reproduced by courtesy of the Royal Horticultural Society; more information can be found at www.rhs.org.uk/chelsea.)

Reflective practice 2.4

Consider the four characteristics of Slack *et al.* (2004)'s model, and outline the implications for The Chelsea Flower Show in terms of variety and volume of hospitality to customers and for employment of staff.

Interaction with the consumer, and degree of consumer and customer contact

Earlier it was noted that customer input is essential in any operation. Without the customer there would be no need for the operation. However, the event manager can make decisions on how much involvement the customer should have within the operation. For example, there are personal wedding planners who organize all of the details of the special day for the bride and groom – from organizing the flowers and photographer to discussing arrangements for the honeymoon, and booking hotels and transfers etc. On the other hand, the bride and groom may choose to use a wedding planning website and have no contact with a personal organizer.

With a high customer-contact event, the staff will need to have been trained in good customer skills and consequently the event will incur more costs than if it were a low-contact event.

In some events there will be a mixture of high-contact and low-contact activities – the event itself may have low contact with individual customers, but telephoning and reserving a seat will need high-contact skills from the operational staff.

Reflective practice 2.5

Looking at the table below, you should be able to give at least two examples of different events in the first and third columns for both the low and high dimensions of each of the typologies described.

High ⟶ Low

Event example	Typology	Event example
	Size and volume of output	
	Complexity and variety of services/products offered to the consumer	
	Uncertainty of numbers attending, cost, time schedule and technical requirements	
	Interaction with the consumer and degree of consumer and customer contact	

This exercise makes you realize the different types of events and their different characteristics.

However, more important is the next table, where you use the examples you have just cited and note the implications of these differences for the event manager. You will then see how making different choices regarding the design of the event and the customers' involvement has cost and planning implications for your organization. The types of implications that you should consider will be among the following alternatives:

- Repetition
- Systemization
- Unit costs
- Capital costs
- Flexibility
- Complexity
- Closely matching customer needs
- Flexibility of capacity
- Forecasted capacity
- Queuing
- Customer contact skills
- Standardization
- Centralization
- High staff utilization.

High ————————————————→ Low

Implications for your event example	Typology	Implications for your event example
	Size and volume of output	
	Complexity and variety of services/ products offered to the consumer	
	Uncertainty of numbers attending, cost, time schedule and technical requirements	
	Interaction with the consumer and degree of consumer and customer contact	

Chapter summary and key points

This chapter has covered the importance of analysis and how it can be executed within an organization. It is the first chapter of the book to describe this process, and its importance within the first section of the event operations management model. We have noted the difference between industries and the markets, and considered the extent and diversity of the event industry.

Within an organization it has been shown that there are three levels of decision-making, and we appraised the importance of having a mission. This concept was illustrated by examining three living applications of companies within the event industry and how they use the concept of mission as a communication tool.

The chapter has considered the definitions and meanings of several key phrases used within the general literature:

- Operational management
- Service organization
- Service operating system, internal and external constraints, and the transformation process.

We have also considered who the customer is.

These resources will be discussed in much greater depth when we progress to analysing internal resources in Chapter 6.

The chapter concluded with an overview of the four different types of organizations characterized by four different dimensions – volume, variety, variation in demand, and degree of customer contact – and the impact of these differences was the subject of an application exercise.

Chapter 3
Analysis of the external environment

Learning Objectives

After reading through this chapter you will be able to:

- **Understand the importance of objectives, and how event managers can cope within a changing and evolving environment**
- **Appreciate the importance of the customer**
- **Identify all other influencers on business policy**
- **Apply techniques that can assist event managers to understand and control their environment more objectively and effectively.**

Introduction

The content of this chapter is from the first stage of the event operations management model. It considers the external environment, and introduces the analysis process. In Chapter 2 (Figure 2.4), analysis of the external environment was considered an essential part of the overall process as outlined in the event operations management model (Figure 1.1). In this chapter, we can break that analysis down into various sub-headings.

In Chapter 2 we said that the role of the events manager is to arrange and use resources efficiently and effectively so as to achieve the goals or mission of the organization. We also said although events managers may not always be involved in determining goals and objectives, nevertheless they are the people responsible for turning the goals and objectives into realities, and 'making it happen'. Every business is now competing on the world stage, and to survive must strive to reach world-class standards. National and geographic boundaries no longer afford a protective barrier for competitors. Customers today are well travelled and well informed, and are quick to make value judgements on performance.

This chapter will consider how business policy is created, and how it often changes due to external influences.

Objectives of the event manager

Event managers have three key objectives:

1. To achieve the strategic objectives of the organization. For example, an event management company working within a local authority may have as its main objective to stage events, which assist

in achieving the overall aims of the authority. If the local authority wants to promote inclusiveness of all the community, then 'free street events' would be one way of bringing all of the community together.

2. To satisfy customers' wants. In this instance, the customers are those people who attend the event. Without customers, the organization will cease to exist.

3. To achieve efficient use of resources. If an organization cannot afford the level of service it is providing, it will soon go out of business. We will analyse how to use resources efficiently in Chapter 6.

All these objectives must be achieved simultaneously.

Tensions and issues for an event manager

An event manager with a changing and evolving business policy will have various tensions and issues to deal with. An events manager may be involved in shaping the corporate policy and objectives of the organization, establishing and acquiring resources, and setting specific operational targets. However, organizations seldom operate in an ideal fashion. The reality is that in many cases the event manager will inherit an existing structure. Problems may include the following:

- An event manager may be working within a small organization which has grown and expanded, so its structure is no longer ideal and may now be less than adequate.
- The principal objective, be it customer satisfaction or efficient resource utilization, may not be clearly defined in the business policy. Indeed, most organizations will have customer satisfaction and resource utilization as twin and equal objectives, without realizing that inherently there is a conflict between the two.
- Some organizations may have a clear mission and objectives, but the needs of the customers have changed. Some employees may reflect these changes in their work and others may not.
- Some organizations have tension occurring between the event manager and the person who secures future business and promises the impossible.
- Other states of tension exist between customer needs and what the stakeholders of the organization feel are appropriate or desirable.

The event manager has the task of making the seemingly impossible, possible. Consequently, the manager needs to be an optimist and adept at applying structured thinking as well as unstructured or lateral thinking to problems, so as to achieve the goals imposed on him or her.

Business policy

The business policy for an organization sets:

- The objectives of the organization
- The service to be provided
- The market to be served
- The way in which the service will be provided
- The level of quality to be aimed for
- The quantity and quality of resources that will be employed.

Business policy does not happen by accident; it is a conscious attempt by organizations to provide long-term goals and to plan resources to achieve those goals. As De Wit and Meyer (2004) explain, one of the difficulties for managers in today's environment is that both the business environment and the individual firms are constantly in flux, and

achieving a match between the two is an ongoing challenge. Business policy may start with the purpose of the organization – the very reason it exists (the *raison d'être*), and this is often referred to as the *vision* of the organization.

As explained by Dulewicz *et al.* (1995):

> *A vision depicts the aspirations of the company, a desired and attainable picture of how the company will appear in a few years' time, which can capture the imagination and motivate employees and others. The mission is to achieve the vision, expressing the commitment and will to do so. On the way decisions will have to be made according to the values of the company, as indicated in the decision-making behaviour of the board – according to what the board believes is good or bad, right or wrong from the company's point of view.*

Similarly, Thompson (2001) differentiates between vision and mission statements. He believes that vision statements should focus on those values to which the organization is committed, and that there should be appropriate measures in place to indicate progress towards those ideals. He sees the mission statement as addressing not what the company should do to survive, but what it has chosen to do to thrive.

Mission statement

As referred to in Chapter 2, the purpose of the business is often articulated in a mission statement. However, frequently what the mission statement says may be at variance with the true mission of the organization.

For example, we know of no organization with a mission statement that says 'our aim is survival, and to survive we will reduce our work force by 25 per cent', or 'we will aggressively advertise our service levels, but we will not spend any money on training our staff'. Such organizations are more likely to publish missions that proclaim 'we value and respect the importance of our highly trained and dedicated staff, and 'our aim is to provide outstanding world-class service'.

It is important for the event manager to understand what the true mission is, irrespective of what might be stated in the published mission. For instance, if survival is the mission (and this could well be a legitimate mission), this has to be understood and thus will shape the strategies to be employed.

Ackoff (1986) suggests that a good mission statement has five characteristics:

1. It contains a formulation of objectives that are measurable
2. It differentiates the company from its competitors
3. It defines the business that the company wishes to be in
4. It is relevant to all stakeholders and not just shareholders and managers
5. It is exciting and inspiring.

Case study 3.1 provides some examples of mission statements.

Holistic management

We should be aware that an organization does not operate in isolation. The event operations management model shows in the first stage that there are different environments that have an influence on it and should be analysed. These are the internal and external environments. Following analysis of these, it is then possible to develop the planning process. All organizations should work in partnership with their suppliers, customers and competitors (Thompson, 2001). An immediate impact is made on an organization by suppliers and customers, on whom it depends, and its competitors – both existing

Mission statements

The examples in these case studies illustrate mission statements from three different types of organizations involved with events. As can be seen, not all organizations use the word 'mission' when articulating the purpose of their business.

Melbourne Food and Wine Festival, Victoria, Australia

The Melbourne Food and Wine Festival is a unique event which operates on a not-for-profit basis. It commenced in 1993 with a simple programme of twelve events. It has grown annually, and the 2004 Festival included more than 120 events over a 3-week period from 19 March–4 April. The Festival is managed by a Board of Management and supported by a small team who are responsible for the successful coordination of its events.

Its mission is as follows:

> *The Festival's charter is to promote the quality produce, talent and lifestyle of Melbourne and the State of Victoria, and to reinforce Melbourne as the pre-eminent culinary city of Australia.*

(Printed by courtesy of Melbourne Food and Wine Festival. For more information see www. Melbournefoodandwine.com.au. Student information is also available on this site.)

Euro RSCG Skybridge, London, England

Euro RSCG Skybridge is an award-winning marketing solutions agency that works with the world's top companies to help them to achieve optimal performance. Their work includes experiential events and travel, communications strategies and innovative creative concepts. Information and video clips of events can be seen on their website (www.skybridge.com).

The events division consists of twenty full-time events professionals who organize and operate events on a global basis.

Their mission is as follows:

> *Our vision is to be the best international provider of marketing solutions, creating and adding value for our clients, employees, shareholders, business partners and the communities within which we work.*
>
> *We will achieve this through working in partnership with our clients to produce transformational performance and customer experiences that are appropriate to their needs, practical, easy to implement and that have a measurable impact on results.*

(For more information on RSCG Skybridge, see www.skybridgegroup.com.)

Clear Channel, San Antonio, Texas, USA

Clear Channel is a multinational organization started in 1972 by Lowry Mays and Red McCombs. They acquired their first Clear Channel radio station in 1975, entered television in 1988, and by 1995 owned 43 radio stations and 16 television stations. By 1998 they owned or programmed 204 radio stations, and had a worldwide outdoor advertising presence in 25 countries through the acquisition of More Group PLC. In 2000 they acquired SFX entertainment, one of the world's largest diversified promoters, producers and presenters of live entertainment events. They now either own or programme 1376 radio stations and approximately 700 000 outdoor advertising displays.

In 2001, Clear Channel Entertainment produced and marketed the three top grossing concert tours, and collectively Clear Channel divisions were operating in 65 countries worldwide.

In the UK, the music group exclusively runs six live entertainment venues and operates in nine European countries through the acquisition of concert promoters and other live entertainment

producers. It is also a dominant force within theatre and sports management of professional athletes.

Clear Channel's mission is as follows:

The Clear Channel Creed – It's What We Believe!

We are in the business of helping our customers grow their businesses. We do this effectively with our wide variety of media and entertainment products.

We believe in maximizing our customer's satisfaction, we will deserve and will earn their continued loyalty. Our goal is to have long-term, mutually profitable relationships.

We believe in providing superior value to customers through high quality, technologically advanced, fairly priced services designed to meet customer needs better than all the possible alternatives.

We believe Clear Channel's people are our most important asset. Our teams make the critical difference in how we perform, and their skills, talents and determination separate us from our competitors. We also believe people can achieve their full potential when they enjoy their work, so it is a priority to provide a workplace where growth, success and fun go hand in hand.

We believe we have an obligation for the well being of the communities in which we live. We further believe the future success of our communities and the industries where we do business is dependent upon the responsibility we feel, the high standards we set and the positive impact our actions have.

We believe excellence is the standard, and we seek to achieve excellence by encouraging and nourishing these core values:

- Respect for the individual
- Honest, open communication
- Individual development and satisfaction
- A sense of ownership in Clear Channel's success
- Participation, cooperation and teamwork
- Creativity, innovation and initiative
- Prudent risk-taking
- Recognition and rewards for achievement.

We believe success is measured by:

- Achieving leadership in the markets we serve
- Developing our own people to form the building blocks of our internal growth and expansion
- Maintaining the highest standards of ethics and integrity in every action we take and in everything we do.

We believe the ultimate measure of our success is to provide a superior value to our stockholders.

(Extracts from website. For more information on Clear Channel, see www.clearchannel.com.)

Reflective practice 3.1

Consider the organizations described in Case study 3.1.

1. How do the three examples given conform to the five characteristics that Ackoff (1986) says should be present within a mission statement?
2. Use the Internet to research the above organizations and determine whether they are practically applying their mission statements in the production/organization of their current events.
3. Are there any discrepancies, and if so, what criteria would you use to measure these?

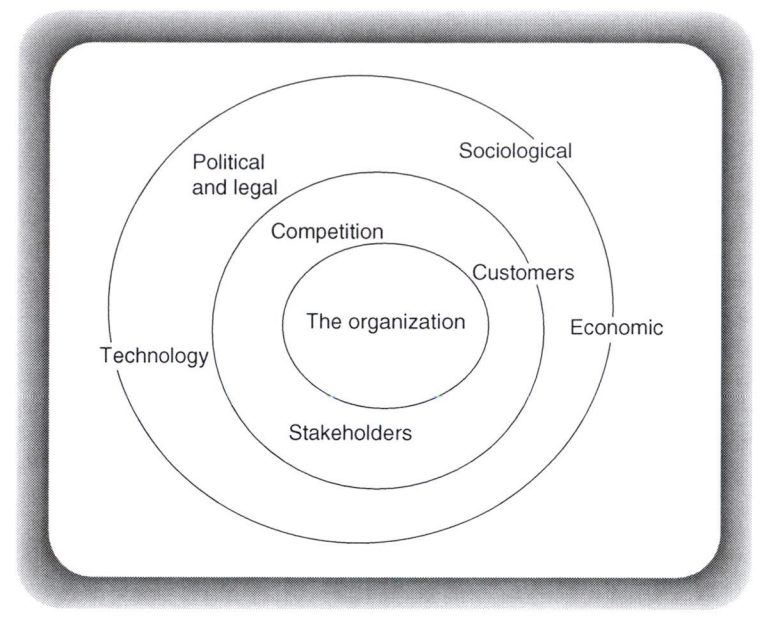

Figure 3.1 Environmental forces

ones and new ones joining the industry (see Figure 3.1). The influencers in the inner circle of the figure may be easier to control and manage than those in the outer circle.

Those in the outer circle are the wider environmental forces. These are commonly grouped together as PEST (political and legal, economic, sociological and technological) forces.

It is useful to think of all these forces in concentric circles, since they impact on every aspect of the organization and upon each other – sometimes equally and at other times with varying emphasis.

This chapter will seek to explore these environmental factors in greater depth, and to place them into context within the events industry.

A further diagrammatic representation of the influences within organizations is shown in Figure 3.2. This figure shows the customer firmly in the centre.

The importance of the customer

At the centre of Figure 3.2 is the customer. Without a customer, the organization will cease to exist. However, without suppliers the organization will not have sufficient resources, and without transforming those resources into a service an event cannot exist to be consumed.

Although the importance of satisfying the customer cannot be denied, it is important to appreciate that customer satisfaction is only one determinant of business policy.

As Wild (2002: 11) points out, 'many organizations have gone bankrupt despite having loyal and satisfied customers' (see Figure 3.3).

A company cannot achieve sustainable profits without the customer being satisfied. Sustained profits are totally dependent on customer satisfaction, but the reverse is not true (Kandampully, 2002). The event company equally should focus on the customers and improve their total experience. The whole organization should unify its approach in order to match, if not exceed, customer expectations, whilst organizing supply and use of resources in an efficient and controlled manner. In short, the level of customer

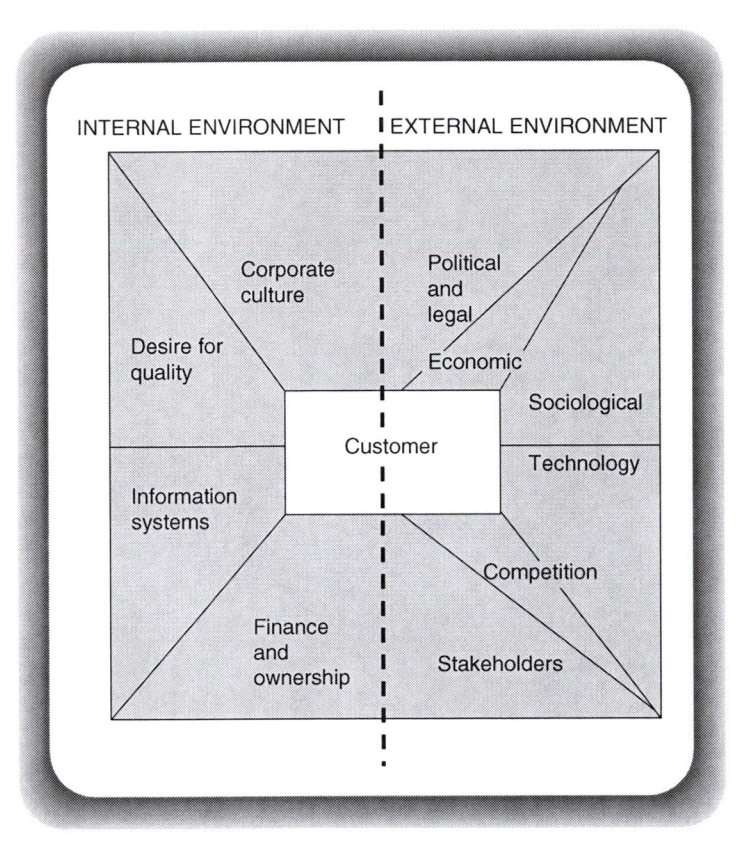

Figure 3.2 External and internal factors on the customer

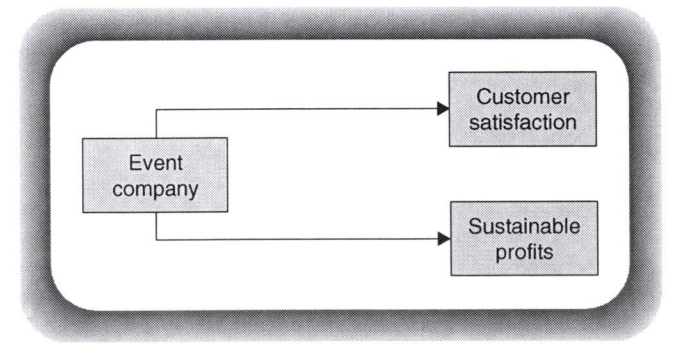

Figure 3.3 A company requires customer satisfaction and sustainable profits

satisfaction provided has to be *affordable* and *sustainable*. This will entail having an efficient and reliable supply chain – i.e. suppliers who provide the right resources, at the
right time, to the right place, at the right cost and in the right quantity.

Most organizations can provide a high level of customer satisfaction for a short
period, but the level offered has to be sustainable. In service industries customers will
be very aware if service levels drop or are inconsistent with what they expect based on
past experience.

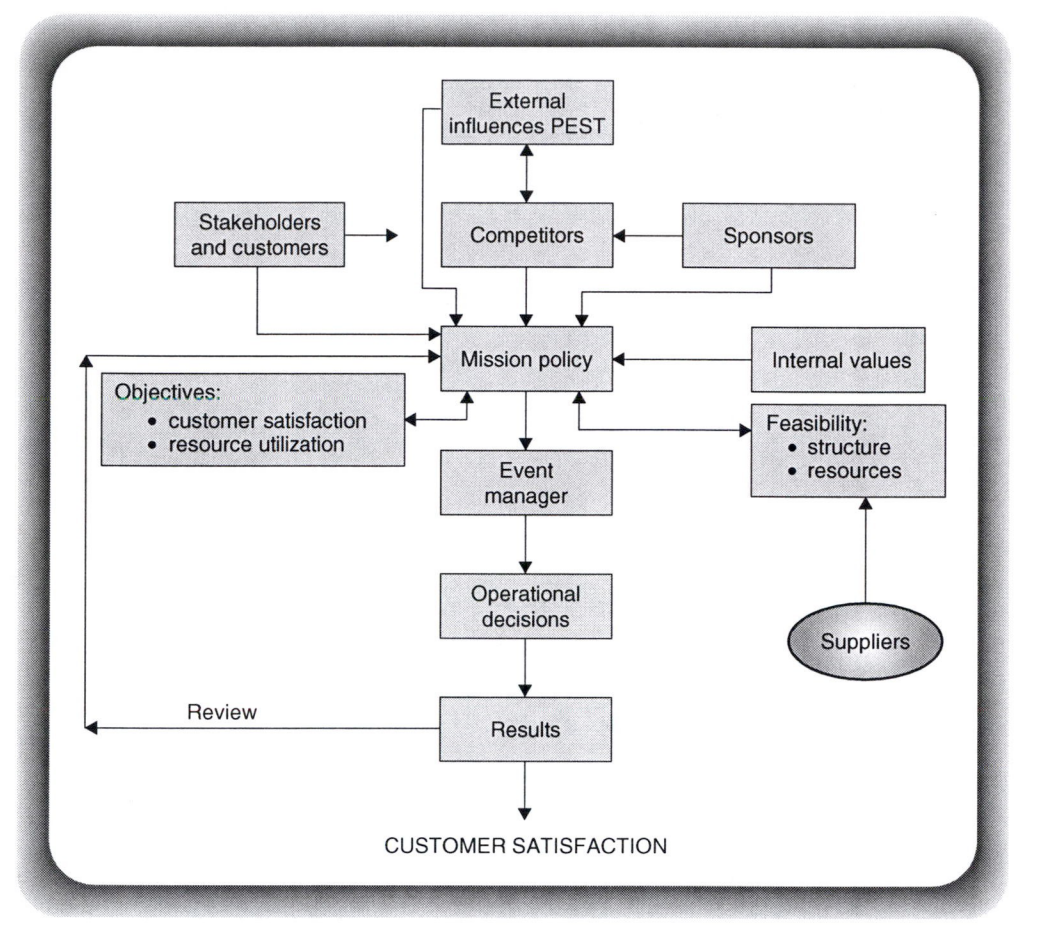

Figure 3.4 Interrelationships between the external environment and their impact on the mission of the company

Figure 3.4 above should be studied and understood, since it shows at a glance the interrelationships between the external environment and their impact on the mission of the company, and also the impacts from the customer and the suppliers on the desired structure of the operation and the resources available. It can be related to the first stage of the event operations management model.

Policy influencers

Figure 3.2 has an outer band, which includes (on the left-hand side):

- Corporate culture
- Desire for quality
- Information systems
- Finance and ownership.

These are certainly influenced by external factors, but they can be managed by actions from *within* the organization. You could think of these as being the *strengths* and *weaknesses* of the organization. Internal factors are covered in Chapter 6.

The other factors, shown on the right-hand side, are:

- Political and legal
- Economic
- Sociological
- Technology
- Competition
- Stakeholders.

These are all factors external to the organization, but which affect customer expectations and also, at another dimension, may limit what the organization is able to do. Often these influences are known as PEST factors. This handy phrase does however miss out the influence of competitors, which in no circumstances should be forgotten, and the importance of stakeholders.

You could think of PEST and competitors and stakeholders as providing *opportunities* or *threats*. To complicate this notion, some stakeholders may be internal to the organization.

In a traditional SWOT (strengths, weaknesses, opportunities and threats) analysis, the opportunities and threats are 'external' to the organization, and the strengths and weaknesses are 'internal' issues. Hence you can see that strengths and weaknesses are going to come from those aspects shown on the left-hand side of Figure 3.2, and the opportunities and threats from those aspects on the right-hand side of the figure.

Knowing the organization's own strengths and weaknesses will help determine feasibility, and will also indicate areas where corrective action should be taken. For the external factors, the aim is to determine opportunities and threats, and to determine how the organization is (or might be) affected by these external factors.

The work in this book will allow us to investigate how strengths can be used to maximize opportunities and reduce threats, and how opportunities can be used to minimize weaknesses. Griffin (2000) sees SWOT analysis as one of the most important steps in formulating strategy. Using the organization's mission as the context, managers can assess internal strengths and weaknesses as well as external opportunities and threats (Griffin, 2000). The goal is then to develop excellent service, which exploits opportunities and strengths, neutralizes threats and avoids weaknesses.

In Chapter 6 we will look at the internal factors as they might affect a company, but in this chapter we consider in detail the external factors (i.e. the opportunities and threats) facing an organization. To remind you, from Figure 3.2 these are:

- Political and legal factors
- Economic factors
- Sociological factors
- Technology
- Competition
- Stakeholders.

Political and legal factors

In the home market, laws and regulations might be seen as limitations; however, laws and regulations also serve to protect an organization. Whatever the laws are, it is important that an organization is aware of how they will affect the operations of the organization. Laws could limit the number of hours that staff work, the amount of maternity leave people are entitled to, and so on.

For our home market we should have a reasonable idea as to what is legally possible, what our health and safety responsibilities are, and how current fire regulations may affect our events. When providing services in other countries, or using performers from other countries elsewhere, it is essential that the organization makes the effort to find out what legal restraints exist and what is socially acceptable before committing to any actions. These should be communicated to all concerned.

Generally laws are for the benefit of people as a whole, and are enacted as the result of pressure from the people to add a safeguard. Thus it is useful to be aware of popular issues and to make adjustments to operations so as to be seen to be a responsible organization within the pervading culture, rather than waiting for legislators to take action as a result of public pressure. When a safeguard is made the subject of rules and regulations, it is likely to have more stringent conditions than when organizations or industries abide by their own self-imposed safeguards.

When we place this into the event context, the event manager should be considering (among other factors) the following:

- Health and Safety Executive
- Laws and regulations
- Licences
- Changes in politics and regimes across the world
- Different laws in countries where events take place, or from where suppliers originate
- The labour market, as affected by government training initiatives
- Financial opportunities and the cost of borrowing
- Alternative funding arrangements.

There is no limit to the list of factors that will influence organizations. However, it is essential that during the analysis only those aspects that could have a direct influence or indirect influence on your organization or on your competitor be considered. Organizations should spend time considering this list and expanding it in order to really delve into changes that are occurring, which are imminent or just remotely possible, and which could affect the organization.

Case study 3.2 provides an illustration.

Economic factors

The economy, exchange rates, interest rates, population growth and demographics, student population, the average wage, unemployment and other statistics relevant to the event industry are all areas of vital information when considering business policy (see Case study 3.3).

Economic conditions are influenced by politics and governments (Thompson, 2001). Governments decide who will be inside or outside the European Union; governments decide rates of interest, education policies and training schemes, and the power of trade unions; and governments may affect the expectations of shareholders.

The problem is to identify what is relevant to your event and locality, and to be aware of where to find information. It is essential to gather intelligence of all of the above, and to understand how you can manipulate the changes to your advantage. It is also useful to observe how your competitors are coping with the changes.

Sociological factors

Sociological trends and the sociocultural environment encapsulate demand and tastes, which vary with fashion and disposable income (Thompson, 2001). Over time, fashion and trends change and what was once a novelty becomes essential or no longer

Case study 3.2

Edinburgh Hogmanay Festivities, Scotland

The Edinburgh Hogmanay Festivities are held annually in Scotland on New Year's Eve. There follows an excerpt from an article published following its cancellation.

Edinburgh Hogmanay Party Cancelled

By Russell Fallis and Victoria Mitchell, Scottish Press Association

One of Britain's biggest New Year's Eve street parties was cancelled at the eleventh hour tonight, due to 'adverse weather conditions', organizers announced.

The high point of Edinburgh's Hogmanay celebrations was cancelled for public safety reasons after the Scottish capital was hit by bad weather.

An estimated 100 000 people had been expected to gather in the city centre for the focal point of the four-day festivities.

First, 8000 ticket-holders for a sell-out gig in Princes Street Gardens were informed that the concert, being headlined by pop duo Erasure, was cancelled as the strong winds had rendered the stage unsafe.

A spokeswoman for the event said: 'The Concert in the Gardens has been cancelled because of the high winds. The structure is starting to disintegrate and it is a dangerous situation.'

Reflective practice 3.2

Consider Case study 3.2.

1. What external factors influenced the organizers in their decision to cancel this event?
2. What cost implications are there?
3. How could these reasons affect other events in the future?
4. Could this have a lasting influence on large public events?

---

required. When this happens, pricing policies will need to change. Similarly, a particular style of event in the UK may not be appreciated elsewhere, or *vice versa*, dependent upon local fashion and trends.

Event organizations should be aware of demographic changes as the population changes in terms of age distribution, ethnic origins, affluence, numbers of people employed and leisure trends. As the changes occur, events should reflect the changes or be marking different products to changing markets. Threats to existing service styles might be increasing, and opportunities for differentiation and market segmentation emerging.

Technology

Customers will often be beguiled by technological promises and computer wizardry in virtual conferencing or laser light shows. On the other hand, an event organization will be limited by the technology that it has at its disposal. Keeping up to date with technology for the sake of keeping up is expensive. Companies may consider leasing or hiring in expensive and specialist equipment and know-how. It is best to be aware of changes and of what the competition is doing, and to offer a good service with the

Case study 3.3

Economic factors that can influence event costs

Below are listed the minimum hourly wages in the US, UK, Australia and New Zealand at press.

USA: The minimum wage in the US is $5.15, although Senator Kerry has proposed increasing this to $7.00. However, there are nine states where the current minimum wage is higher than the official US minimum, seven states where there is no minimum wage at all, and three states where the minimum wage is lower than the official US minimum.

UK: The minimum wage in the UK as of 1 October 2004 is as follows:

- Main (adult) rate for workers aged 22 and over, £4.85 (increased from £4.50).
- Development rate for workers aged 18–21 inclusive, £4.10 (increased from £3.80). **NB**: The development rate can also apply to workers aged 22 and above during their first 6 months in a new job with a new employer and who are receiving accredited training.
- For 16- and 17-year-olds, £3.00 (a new rate).

Australia: The adult minimum wage is $11.35, but an increase is wanted by the trade unions (Australian Council of Trade Unions).

New Zealand: The adult minimum wage is $9; that for 16- and 17-years-olds is $7:20.

(More information can be found on www.dol.gov, www.epionline.org, www.dti.gov.uk/, www.actu.asn.au/, www.worksite.govt.nz.)

Reflective practice 3.3

1. What implications do minimum wages have on the events industry?
2. Check the current exchange rates and calculate which of the countries listed in Case study 3.3 has the most favourable rate for employment if you were choosing the location for a new event.
3. What supplementary information do you need?

expertise that you have or can have available. The use of technology may be one way to secure competitive advantage.

Technology external to the organization may be captured and used. This may be influenced by government support and encouragement (Thompson, 2001). However, could your existing technology be rendered useless by breakthroughs used elsewhere? It is important to consider how costly new technology would be to install, and whether it requires extra investment in the form of training. However, it may be that the technical providers at many events are your own suppliers. In this case it is essential to be aware of the changes and to have good relationships with the suppliers.

The concept is rather like being on a treadmill at a gym (Figure 3.5); no sooner do you reach a comfortable speed than the trainer wants you to run faster. As you reach that new speed, you cannot keep up and you start to slide backwards. No sooner has a company or an event come up with a good idea than a competitor copies it. This can be more easily achieved by the competition if what is being copied is tangible (e.g. a desirable venue for a large conference, with varied and relevant facilities). However, it becomes more difficult to copy intangible resources (or competencies), which rely on staff values and corporate culture and a desire for quality.

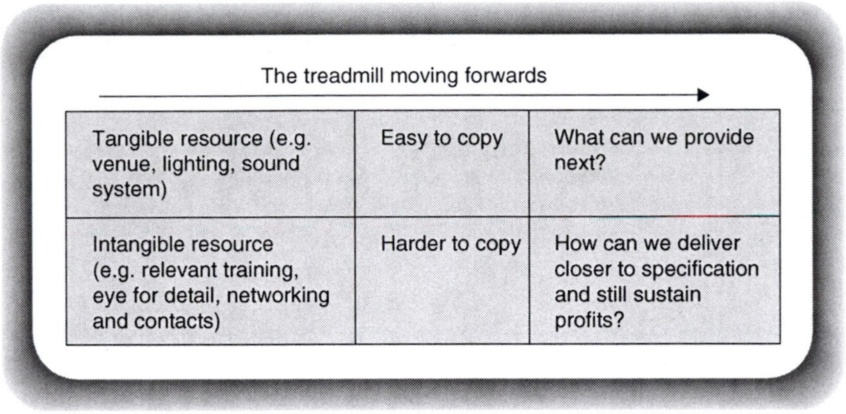

The treadmill moving forwards		
Tangible resource (e.g. venue, lighting, sound system)	Easy to copy	What can we provide next?
Intangible resource (e.g. relevant training, eye for detail, networking and contacts)	Harder to copy	How can we deliver closer to specification and still sustain profits?

Figure 3.5 The treadmill of change and competitor action

Competition

Competition is often a major threat. In the determination of the service and the level of quality to be offered, at the very least the organization has to meet the service provided by the competition. Today, competition is worldwide. No matter that we believe we are providing a service to a local market; people today are well travelled and very well informed, and our customers judge us by their perceptions of world-class standards. For any organization, competition, although not yet present, might only be days away. Technology and innovation provide no protection; technology can soon be copied, and new methods and systems are readily available to anyone (see Case study 3.4). Often customers are influenced by what the immediate competition *says* it can or will do. This might not be quite the same as what actually happens. Nonetheless, it is the perception of what the competition is offering that sets the market standards. Knowing what the competition is offering is only possible if it is known who the competition is, and who the likely new competition might be.

The factors described indicate only a selection of the external influences, and individual managers need to appreciate how these external forces affect their organization. The analysis is extremely useful in picking out emerging opportunities that your company could take advantage of, and the threats that could just affect your own company and not your competitors.

These external influences will affect different organizations in different ways, sometimes more forcefully than others and sometimes insignificantly. You must be aware which.

Stakeholders

Stakeholders are very much part of the external environment, and are therefore in the first stage of the event operations management model. They should be thought of as part of the external analysis. However, there are some internal stakeholders (for instance, the employees and the managers). Stakeholders are groups of people or individuals who have an influence on, or are influenced by, the activities of the organization. Shareholders form one group of stakeholders. It used to be part of economic theory that shareholders should be given first priority (Thompson, 2001), because there was a belief that owners (i.e. the shareholders) and managers were synonymous. Event managers are paid employees and, whilst concerned about profits, they also regard growth and

Case study 3.4

Internet technology

Internet technology allows businesses and individuals to access information worldwide at the touch of a button. The following information was taken from the websites of The Conference Centre at Church House, London, England; The Banff Centre, Banff, Canada; and The Melbourne Exhibition and Convention Centre, Melbourne, Australia. All are open all year round.

The Conference Centre at Church House, London, England
Inspiring people

You need to know what's inside our conference centre if you are considering holding an event here. But it's also the people at a conference centre that make an event successful; so we're going to tell you about the people inside ours too.

Many London-based conference centres suffer from the perpetual sound of traffic. Church House doesn't. It's position in the shadows of Westminster Abbey, within the tranquil setting of Dean's Yard, is a protection, and the noise of London simply fades away.

And it's a great location, close to both Charing Cross and Victoria Stations, allowing easy access via train and tube.

Whilst our building and its surroundings are steeped in history and tradition; our events draw on the latest equipment and the skills of an enthusiastic team. This refreshing combination creates a unique environment and is the reason for our many industry awards.

On-the-day success of every event is assured with the help of our dedicated Client Hosts. It is their job to manage your event as it happens, ensuring down to the finest detail that it unfolds in the way it was planned to.

We have seventeen spacious function and meeting rooms and can accommodate every type of event. Most of our rooms benefit from natural light and all enjoy the elegance and sophistication expected from a building of the 1930s.

The Conference Executive is responsible for event planning. This is a meticulous job that takes concentration, and requires faultless organization. The Conference Executive is the sole contact for the clients, liaising with them regularly on each facet of their event, booking rooms, preparing menus, briefing audiovisual staff, meeting suppliers, agreeing table layout and room decoration – the list can seem endless, the end result is seamless perfection.

We have advanced sound and lighting technology permanently on-site. All rooms are fitted with a network of Cat 5 cabling and ISDN. An infrared interpretation system to aid in international meetings is accessible to all halls and many of the small meeting rooms.

Lights and sound can make a room come to life. Our in-house technicians ensure they always do. They often manage major high-profile events, from clients as diverse as government to the media. They will work with you, carefully planning every stage of this critical aspect of your event, offering guidance and advice, to ensure the show you want is the show you get.

We are one of only a handful of conference centres that hold the Meetings Industry Association's accreditation, Hospitality Assured – Meetings, which ensures a commitment to the highest standard, and is a testament to the dedication and hard work of our people.

Committed people do not make an event successful; they make it outstanding. Only when people from all levels work together with a common purpose can the service delivery we offer be achieved. For us, success isn't when our clients notice the hard work we do, it's when their

event works so well and runs so smoothly that our role appears simple. After enjoying the day, they reflect and realize our efforts. This is when we are truly inspiring people.

(Extracts from website. For more information on Church House, see www.churchhouseconf. co.uk.)

The Banff Centre, Banff, Alberta, Canada

Experience The Banff Centre, offering unparalleled facilities with over 400 guest rooms, 60 exceptional meeting spaces, lecture theatres, and auditoriums to accommodate groups from 5 to 1000 people. It is an incubator for creativity that inspires and empowers artists, the mountain community and business leaders. The Banff Centre has a longstanding tradition of fostering innovation and new thoughts.

As experts in fostering fresh thinking, we realize the importance of your surroundings. That's why we offer over 60 exceptional meeting facilities, lecture theatres, and auditoriums to suit groups from 3 to 1000 participants. You can easily experience the full splendour of the Canadian Rockies from each meeting space, and you won't find a better sanctuary for your mind, body and spirit.

The Banff Centre welcomes you to the Business Centre, located in the main foyer of The Donald Cameron Hall. We handle guest and participant requests for faxing, photocopying, and computer use. The Business Centre respects copyright. The Banff Centre is licensed with Access Copyright (The Canadian Copyright Licensing Agency).

The Banff Centre provides free wireless access for individual browsing and email checking in several buildings on the property. To take advantage of this service, you must have wireless capability in your laptop that is preconfigured for DHCP.

Dedicated high-speed service for large groups, either via wireless access or by physical wiring, is also available. This must be prearranged with your Conferences Services Manager, who can provide you detailed information on computer requirements, locations and costs. Dial-up service can also be made available with advance notice.

A computer lab is also available. Featuring eleven new computers as of November 2003, each station is equipped with standard software including Windows XP, Norton Anti-Virus, Office XP Professional Suite, Adobe Acrobat Reader, Internet Explorer and QuickTime.

The Conference Management Package has been developed over a number of years and is designed to assist conference planners and organizers by assuming responsibility for several key components of the conference process. The emphasis is on a base package of services which are generally recognized as being the most timely or logistically challenging for many organizations. Complementing this base package is a shopping list of additional services that The Banff Centre offers to any clients who wish to incorporate them into their Conference Management Package for an additional fee.

Banff Centre Conference guests benefit from our graphic design capabilities and our partnership with The Document Source-Xerox. Consider using our on-site facilities to assist you with your production needs – from presentations, proposals and signage to a complete range of customized conference materials.

The video conference equipment located at The Banff Centre is a Tandberg Vision 5000 (ISDN based H.320 unit, capable of a six-channel, 384 kbps connection). The TELUS Video Conferencing Room is located in the Professional Development Centre and can seat a maximum of seven people at the table. For larger groups, the equipment can be moved to a larger meeting room, dependent upon available space. A document camera, VCR, and PC connection are available for use with the video conference unit. Fax and photocopy services are available at the Reception Desk in the main lobby of the Professional Development Centre. Water service is provided, and additional food and beverage service is available upon request. Further details and booking information is available, Monday to Friday, during regular office

hours. A technician will be provided for any video conference booked on any day, or time of day.

(Printed by courtesy of Banff Conference Centre; further information can be obtained from www.banffcentre.ca.)

The Melbourne and Exhibition Convention Centre, Melbourne, Victoria, Australia

A consistent winner of many prestigious 'Awards for Excellence', the MECC is renowned for providing national and international convention and exhibition organizers with the highest standards of personal service and event facilities.

The Centre was the very first to earn the distinction of being named the World's 'Best Congress Centre' by the principal professional body for congress centre managers – the Association Internationale des Palais de Congress (AIPC). Domestically, the MECC has also been a recipient of the Meetings Industry of Australia's highest accolade many times over.

The MECC offers a level of Quality Controls and flexibility that has made it popular with exhibition organizers and meeting planners alike. Whether it is the ease of access and loading dock facilities or the state-of-the-art theatres and meeting rooms, the Centre more than meets expectations – it exceeds them.

Few venues are better equipped to cater for your event requirements than the MECC. Our rooms all offer the highest level of sound, video and staging technology, as well as the latest telecommunications.

Our commitment to excellence also extends to Food and Beverage, where our team of highly skilled chefs, led by Executive Chef Frank Burger, prepare and serve meals that reflect the Centre's overall reputation for excellence.

The Melbourne Exhibition and Convention Centre offers a wide range of audiovisual and communications technology, including voice and data cabling, ISDN and Internet capabilities, a 750 extension PABX system and state-of-the-art fibre optics, all of which are discreetly linked to every area in the entire complex. So you can 'plug in' from any point.

The MECC has three theatres which are all fitted out with the latest audiovisual technology including high bandwidth video and data cabling infrastructure, and some meeting rooms feature built-in screens, electronic whiteboards and complete data and signal cabling for presentations and data transfers.

The Bellarine Rooms have a series of large-diameter conduits beneath the floor linking all existing cable trenches at each of their ends and at their midpoint.

With 30 000 sq m (322 500 sq ft) of single floor, pillarless space on offer at the Exhibition Centre, exhibitors also have access to a wide range of telecommunication services via floor pits, plant areas and a basement tunnel running the entire length of the building.

Essential services include single- and three-phase power, telephone, fax, computer and communication outlets. Each of the floor pits is fitted with six voice/data jacks that enable voice and data traffic at speeds of up to 10 Mb/s, web broadcasting and ISDN. Audio, voice and data cabling also runs throughout the Centre, allowing room-end to room-end connectivity.

At the Melbourne Exhibition and Convention Centre, we are committed to offering our clients the highest standards of personal service and support. We know that organizing events is not always easy, so our staff will be there every step of the way to offer their advice and experience to ensure everything goes smoothly.

Our staff are all highly trained in their particular field of expertise. Whether it is food and beverage, event planning, technical services or sales and marketing, you can be assured of receiving the very best service and attention to detail.

(Printed by courtesy of Melbourne Conference Centre; for more information see www.mecc.com.au.)

Reflective practice 3.4

1. Consider Case study 3.4, and compare the information contained in each example with the following criteria:
   - Presentation style of their message
   - Availability of the latest technology
   - The conveyance of intangible benefits to the customer.
2. Now rank each conference centre in order of preference for each of the criteria, and state why you have made these decisions.

security as important, and they will have their own agendas for success. Competitors and governments may have a restraining force, and companies should also create good relationships with their suppliers and partners.

A technique for considering the varying strengths and influences of the different stakeholders will be introduced in Chapter 5. This analysis is essential since the needs of the different stakeholders may not be consistent with each other, and they are extremely likely to vary in consideration of different factors and within different situations.

Sponsors

Sponsors form a further group of people from the external environment, and they should therefore be analysed within the event operations management model. They are stakeholders, but should be considered separately because they can have a major impact on an event company. Historically, sponsorship had its earliest modern origin in professional sport events (Goldblatt, 1997). Sponsorship allows different groups of people to reach certain markets, and assists event organizers to have access to additional funding to offset costs. However, events do not always easily attract sponsorship. Potential sponsors have to 'get something out' of the event. It is extremely unlikely that they will provide money or supplies unless there is a payback.

Shone and Parry (2004) have developed a list of those aspects that sponsors will be hoping to benefit from:

- Relevant market exposure
- Publicity and increased public relations
- Media exposure
- Free admission to the event/hospitality
- A heightened image, by association.

Sources of sponsorship identified by Shone and Parry (2004) are:

- In-kind arrangements, exchange of goods or activities
- Grants from local, regional or national governments, or the European Union
- Grants from charitable bodies, development agencies, arts, leisure or heritage bodies
- Lottery grants
- Fund-raising activities related to the event
- Commercial bank borrowing
- Trust funding.

Sponsors are very useful to an event manager, but may also be a source of limitation or inconvenience. One might wish to be the main sponsor, and cause confrontation with other sponsors or limit or change your own plans.

The sponsors may wish to influence the event in a way that is against your original objectives; you may have to adapt your event, and this might not be suitable. Also you should consider whether the sponsor has a reputation that will enhance your event, or whether it might endanger your project. In some instances a partnership should not be entered into.

Reflective practice 3.5

You are the organizer of a marathon in a large city, such as the New York Marathon.

1. What competitive, economic, political, legal, social and technological influences affect its organization?
2. How do you keep abreast of what is happening?

Chapter summary and key points

This chapter has covered in detail the external analysis of an organization. This is within the first stage of the event operations management model. The chapter has considered the importance of business policy, which sets the long-term objectives for an organization. The chapter has taken an organization-wide perspective and is concerned with the setting of goals and targets for the whole enterprise and the importance of determining the best use of the available resources. Business policy must take into account several factors, as shown in Figures 3.1–3.3.

The effective event manager will maintain a keen interest in all facets of the organization, and be aware of external trends and factors that could influence it. The manager, to be effective, must be aware of policy changes, and these should not come as a surprise. Ideally, the event manager should be sufficiently well informed of external pressures to make policy suggestions. Chapter 4, still within the first stage of the event operations management model, is concerned with the bridge between the external environment and the internal environment. As depicted in the event operations management model, both of these environments should be analysed and the next chapter looks at the relationship between the two.

Chapter 4
Defining service provision

Learning Objectives

After reading through this chapter you will be able to:

■ Understand the importance of the knowledge bridge between the analyses of the internal environment and the external environment
■ Know how to define the service that is to be provided
■ Discuss how to promote an event
■ Analyse the operational feasibility of an event.

Introduction

This chapter is essentially the interface between the external analysis and the internal analysis of the organization. It rests within the first stage of the event operations management model. Before an organization can attempt to satisfy the customer, it must first know the customer wants – i.e. the Critical Success Factors (CSFs) that make them purchase from one organization rather than another.

With regular scanning of key sources of information, it is possible to build a market intelligence database. This is a relatively cost-effective way to gain useful insights, and a precursor to an accurate forecasting system (Wood, 2004).

The primary function of marketing is to bring together buyers and sellers with the intention of exchanging products and services of mutual value (Kandampully, 2002). To be successful, the marketing department should analyse the expectations of each party. The three questions below constitute a knowledge bridge between the customer and the producer:

1. What does the customer want in terms of the service being offered (product)?
2. What price will customers be prepared to pay (price)?
3. Where will the service be provided (place)?

To complete the 'knowledge bridge', the marketing function will have the responsibility of promoting (advertising) the service. Traditionally, the marketing mix is made up of product, price, place and promotion – the 4Ps. However, these 4Ps do not address the distinctive characteristics of services and events; nor do they take into account the importance of the customer or the members of staff supplying the service. Other authors have added:

• People
• Process

- Physical evidence
- Performance
- Profit.

Event managers may focus on exciting and well-executed events, but neglect other areas such as quality, visitor satisfaction and evaluation before, during and after the event (Wood, 2002). A survey by the Meetings Industry Association (MIA) found that only 40 per cent of venues solicited the event organizers' opinions on their service, and fewer than 15 per cent of organizations and venues thought to ask the delegates or attendees (Tum, 2002; unpublished papers).

Defining the service to be provided

Service should be provided to conform to the following factors:

1. Specification
2. Consistency
3. Timeliness
4. Flexibility
5. Right price
6. Added value and little extras.

In many instances these different characteristics will have different weightings to different groups of people – to the customer, to the organization itself and to the stakeholders. It is this different emphasis that provides a daily challenge to the event manager.

The first and crucial issue is the specification. Unless the service fulfils the requirements of the customer, it will not be used. In Chapter 2 we discussed the courtesy bus service at a sculpture park, and we said that if the bus is not going from a to b then it would be of no use. The service offered might include other 'nice to have' attributes, but unless the basic service is right, the extras, the 'nice to have' features, become irrelevant. Therefore no matter how clean and comfortable the bus, or how polite the driver, unless the service is right (i.e. the bus stops somewhere close to the exhibits or the picnic spot) it is of no use and all the 'nice' extras are meaningless.

The second important issue is consistency. Customers expect service to be at the same level, or better, each time it is experienced. With the bus service we would expect the bus to arrive as stated on the arrival boards, and to follow the correct route. At an outdoor music event, the audience would expect the sound system and video screens to be working effectively throughout the event. Promoters of music events would expect their suppliers to be consistent throughout all of their events.

Once a level of quality of service has been promoted or actually provided, customers will be quick to notice if it is not achieved or sustained. There is no point in setting a high standard of service if the operation cannot consistently meet the standard.

The third issue is timeliness. Unless the tea and coffee is ready at the agreed coffee breaks at a conference, the delegate and the conference organizer will become disenchanted and may not return to that venue. Some conference venues for smaller meetings have break-out rooms adjacent to the seminar rooms where delegates can make their own coffees throughout the day. Here, exact timing for provision of hot drinks has been exchanged for total freedom for the delegates. However, timing for the venue is still important since the raw commodities (e.g. milk in a refrigerated environment and coffee and clean cups) should be available whenever needed.

Timing is of lesser importance when customers make appointments in advance. For example, for services from a wedding planning consultant, customers may be prepared to wait in order to see whoever is considered to give the best service, be it for advice, venue availability, or for a reputable and innovative lighting expert. It is past experience, promises and advertising that raise customers' expectations.

Fourth, flexibility is important in the service industry; there is no time for checking quality, no time for rehearsing the wedding photography – it has to be right first time. The moment the event is delivered it is consumed. Immediately, of course, we come across difficulties – customers can change their minds and want a slight change to the wedding arrangements, or rain will stop play at the Test Match at Lord's Cricket Ground, London, or there is a bomb threat in the outskirts of London and half the guests arriving for a major Annual Dinner and Ball are 45 minutes late so the meal and the entertainment have to be rescheduled. In all of these scenarios the event manager has to be flexible and to accommodate the changing situations. Customer expectations still have to be fulfilled despite changes in circumstances.

Fifth, determination of the right price can be agreed once the marketing team is satisfied that they know what the customer wants – the specification. This will determine the price that can be charged. What can be charged depends, of course, on what the customer is prepared to pay. The issue for the event manager will be 'can the service be provided to the given specification, including all those extras added by marketing, within the price set and still provide a profit?' Thus the event manager in achieving a defined level of customer satisfaction will simultaneously be required to minimize the use of resources and their costs to an affordable level.

In sixth position is 'added value and little extras'. Once the courtesy bus has met the basic requirements, then all the other 'extras' – such as cleanliness, comfort, plenty of seats, polite driver, waiting shelter, and perhaps even music interspersed with announcements from the driver – will add to the perception of quality and could provide the edge in a competitive environment.

Some specification issues are taken for granted by customers. Examples of this in the bus service are that the bus is roadworthy and the driver is licensed. Often what the customer takes for granted will be crucial to the whole operation, and will take a good deal of effort on behalf of the event manager to achieve – such as keeping the fleet maintained and roadworthy. These aspects are expected, and are not seen by the customer as added value extras.

Other 'requirements' of customers can be traced back to the marketing team 'selling' features that the customer had not previously considered important but which once sold will become to be expected by the customer. Carlzon (1989) calls this 'the olive in the martini'. In some service industries, for many customers the appearance and status will be every bit as important as the actual service received.

Case study 4.1 describes a major festival held in Miami, Florida.

Where the event will take place

The next issue to decide upon is where the event will take place. You may have a choice, and where you eventually choose to host your event can have an enormous effect on its success. This concept is explored more fully in Chapter 10, which is within the planning stage of the event operations management model. The location for the service provision is a marketing issue, and the decision will be affected by where the customers are and where the client wants the event to take place.

Case study 4.1

Carnaval Miami, Florida, USA

Carnaval Miami is the largest global showcase in the Hispanic Market with a festival that attracts the local community as well as people from around the world. For two weeks in March, the City of Miami transforms itself into the City of Carnaval. People from Europe, Asia, Central and South America all make the trip to participate in the festivities. The Kiwanis Club of Little Havana hosts a grand party with events full of colour, Latin music and international foods for the enjoyment of residents and tourists alike. Carnaval Miami's Calle Ocho is the culmination of many concerts, sports, culinary competitions and a Latin Jazz festival.

Calle Ocho celebrates its 26th Anniversary in 2004, inviting the entire community as one. The 'marquee' event of Carnaval Miami is 'the' largest celebration of Hispanic culture in the United States. 'El Festival de la Ocho', as commonly known to many, closes down SW 8th Street from 27th to 4th Avenues for twenty-three Little Havana city blocks. Over 40 stages are placed on intersecting avenues, featuring merengue, salsa, pop and Caribbean music. Ethnic food kiosks line the North and South sides of the street, while intersecting avenues showcase musical stages, youth sites, sampling pavilions and more. It offers a world of opportunities to show, test, taste and sample products.

The Kids Pavilion has become a 'festival within a festival', inviting children from all over Dade and Broward counties to be part of the celebration. Four city blocks between 8th and 4th Avenues are host to this kids' village of entertainment.

To celebrate the 'funtastic' party, the Guinness Book of Records record for the 'World's Largest Street Party' will be broken in the streets of Little Havana. Media blitzes and press conferences will be held prior to and on the day of event at a designated location. Major television networks, local Hispanic radio stations and newspaper partners will all be part of the festivities. Photographers from international newspapers, magazines and film-makers, visitors come from all over the US, Europe, Central & South America, a myriad of Latin music continuously performing throughout the 7 hours of Calle Ocho, all culminating with fireworks to say goodbye to another great year.

(The above comes from the Carnaval Miami website; for further information see www. carnaval-miami.org or search for 'Calle Ocho'.)

Reflective practice 4.1

Consider Carnaval Miami, described in Case study 4.1.

1. As an event manager responsible for the stage constructions, what logistical considerations are there?
2. How would you deal with these?
3. What problems could there be associated with the Guinness Book of Records attempt?

The location of services will have a great impact on operational decisions concerning supply, choice of suppliers, distribution, logistics, and health and safety issues.

Promotion of the event

Obviously marketing will advise on promotional strategies, but the overall thrust and philosophy of the promotional drive is very much a business policy decision. No

promotion activity should ever take place without the full involvement of the event manager. Marketing is not just about getting people in through the door, but also about ensuring that they get the kind of satisfaction from the event that they have been led to expect (Shone and Parry, 2004; see also Case study 4.2).

The more detailed the knowledge of each customer's requirements, the closer the organization can get to a customized offering, creating greater satisfaction and long-term customer relationships (Wood, 2004).

Case study 4.2

The golf club

A golf club advertised a free open day for prospective new members; the day chosen was a non-competition day when the course would be relatively free of club players. Noting that no play was scheduled for that day, and unaware of the open day, the green keepers made an early start on coring and re-sewing the greens, and temporary rough greens were cut. The overall impression gained by the prospective new members was not good, and the time and money spent on the promotion was to a large extent wasted.

Marketing mix and operational feasibility

It can be seen that the marketing team has a great influence on business policy. The team determines who the customer is, what the service offered will be (specification, time, place and price), and promotes the service and added value little extras. The event manager has to determine the overall feasibility – in other words, does the organization have the capacity to consistently provide the desired service and meet the expected demand and quality attributes within the price set and still return a profit? If not, what extra resources are required and what else could be done to make the impossible possible? In short, can the service, with all the desired features, actually be provided at the cost marketing suggests?

Case study 4.3 suggests a possible scenario.

Case study 4.3

Product launch

An important customer has tasked you with arranging an event for the launch of a new product. You plan a creative launch. In the lead up to the big day, starting six months in advance, you book a conference centre, arrange a lighting specialist (including lasers etc.), organize a sound system, hire a jazz band, and agree the guest list with your client – including local members of parliament, the mayor, sporting personalities and 500 other guests. You send out the invitations, arrange a television personality as the guest speaker, and contact the media to get

as much coverage as possible. You arrange caterers, and spend much time agreeing the menu. The client is responsible for providing gift baskets featuring a selection of their fine products for each of the guests. The event is timed to begin at 7 pm and to run through to about midnight. Two weeks out from the big day only 50 per cent of the guests have replied, and of those who have replied only a few have accepted the invitation. You find that the local sports team has got to the final of the league, and that the deciding match will be played in a neighbouring town starting thirty minutes after your scheduled event begins. The match will last at least ninety minutes. The excitement in the town is immense; never before has the local team got to the final. People are either going to the game, or watching the live broadcast on television. No one expected that this could happen six months ago when planning for your event began.

Reflective practice 4.2

Consider what you could do, bearing in mind that the television personality is only available for the night you booked. Likewise, the conference centre is also pre-booked for the next three months; however, you have it booked for three days – Friday for preparation, Saturday for the big event, and Sunday to clean up etc.

Chapter summary and key points

This chapter provides the bridge between external and internal analyses. In particular, the importance of an understanding of the marketing mix is discussed. The main focus of the chapter is the importance of knowing what the customer wants and values. Above all, if the end delivered product/service does not meet the basic specification, then other 'nice to have' features will not matter. Thus meeting specification is the first and overriding objective. Secondary objectives are to maintain consistency, to be on time, to be flexible, and to provide extras that delight the customer. All this has to be provided within the constraints of a given price. Finally, what is promised and agreed has to be feasible. Chapter 5, still within the first stage of the event operations management model, will examine more closely the needs of the customers and the stakeholders. This is an essential element within the event operations management model, since it is necessary to analyse the impact that these groups have on your future planning of the event and the shape and design it will have.

Chapter 5

Customers, stakeholders and gap analysis

Learning Objectives

After reading through this chapter you will be able to:

- Understand who the customer is, and appreciate the customer's needs, perceptions and what gives satisfaction
- Determine the stakeholders to the event and identify the challenges they present
- Undertake an analysis of what you can provide and what is expected by the stakeholders and customers
- Create competitive advantage using quality of service provision.

Introduction

This chapter pulls together some of the concepts in the earlier chapters and offers techniques regarding how to manage the interface between the needs of the customers, the impact of the stakeholders and the goals of the organization. It is within the analysis stage of the event operations management model, since it is not possible to start the planning stage until all the influences upon the event have been analysed. The chapter considers who our diverse customers are, the dimensions of customer satisfaction, resource utilization, and how by using the right resources it is possible to satisfy the needs of the customers and the varied stakeholders, keep within the strategic objectives of the organization and make a profit.

Wild (2002) notes that operations management is concerned with the achievement of both satisfactory customer service and resource utilization. He suggests that both of these objectives cannot always be maximized, and hence a satisfactory performance must be achieved on both and sub-optimization avoided. It is this conflict that often provides the challenge to event managers.

Who is the customer?

In Chapter 2 we established that the customer is an input into the process. Quite simply, without a customer no service can be performed. Kandampully (2002) believes that service quality can be

defined as the extent to which a service meets the expectations of customers. But who are our customers?

Kandampully divides customers into four broad groups:

1. Internal customers – employees and managers of the firm
2. External customers – a firm's end customers
3. Competitors' customers – those who the firm would like to attract
4. Ex-customers – those who are now going elsewhere (and therefore are no longer our customers).

Internal customers

In Chapter 16, within the implementation stage of the event operations management model, we discuss the philosophy of Total Quality Management (TQM) in greater detail. Proponents of TQM consider the importance of the customer to be vital in the operating process. For example, with TQM an event organizer passing a lighting specification to a lighting company would consider *that company* to be the customer. Consequently, the specification should be well written and unambiguous so that the lighting company knows exactly what to provide and when.

Some people believe that the TQM concept of the internal customer was always a contrivance, initially aimed to get factory workers on an assembly line to reduce waste and pass on a good job to the next operator in the process. It was easy to say that without customers we will not sell our goods, and without sales the factory will close, but for the operator wielding the screwdriver and faced with a seemingly never-ending assembly line, the customer was remote and faceless. Making the next person on the line the customer gave the 'customer' a face.

We applaud this approach, since anything that serves to make work more meaningful, gives people more esteem, and reduces costs has to be recommended. However, in reality it has to be accepted that the event steward has very little control over the quality of the event – the steward does not decide on the appropriateness of the lighting rigs used or decide on the sound system installed.

In the event industry we could engage with all participants of the supply chain – i.e. all the specialists who are providing part of the service that contributes to the final delivery of the event to the end customer. By encouraging them to deliver a service that will enable the delivery to be in line with the customer specification, it will help to achieve competitive advantage. The supply chain is covered further in Chapter 9, within the detailed planning stage of the event operations management model.

It can be argued that all staff engaged on an event receive and offer services to one another. The concept of all participants being both suppliers and customers within the process will encourage all 'actors' to consider the quality of the entire event. It will create an understanding of interdependency between suppliers and staff (Kandampully, 2002).

The degree of intensity of interaction between the customer and people of a service organization varies, and depends on the type of service offered. For example, an event manager providing advice to the Managing Director of a large company whilst organizing a touring product promotion will have a high degree of face-to-face interaction with the customer. Further down the scale, an event manager organizing a team-building day for twenty employees of a car dealership, or an event manager taking a small group of visitors around a pharmaceutical company on an induction programme, would have less face-to-face contact.

At the bottom of the scale, an example is where customers buy their own theatre tickets from an automatic machine point; here, customer interaction is purely with a machine.

Figure 5.1 shows a reducing degree of interaction between the event organizer and the customer. These different activities consequently have different influences for the

```
Consultant
        Interview
                Exhibition stand
                Conference
                        Charity fundraising event
                        Premiership football match
                                Attendance at a large outdoor music festival
                                Web-based services
                                        Automatic ticket dispenser point
    10..............................................................................................................................1
    High face to face                                              low face to face
```

Figure 5.1 The varying amounts of customer interaction

event manager in terms of customer relations and training, usage of time and opportunity to maintain standardization procedures. The greater the interaction with the customer, the greater will be the variances and the need for training in customer relations.

Irrespective of the level of face-to-face interaction, without some customer interaction service cannot be provided. Note, this does not mean that the customer always has to be present when the service is being provided. For example, when a stage is being erected for a classical outdoor concert the customer need not be present, but nonetheless without discussion with the relevant suppliers and without knowing the size of the audience, the acoustics available and the amount of set-up time, the staging company cannot provide a service.

External customers

External customers are sophisticated. Never before has the customer been more travelled, better informed or had higher expectations. Event customers now take it as a matter of right that they will get a reliable, high-quality product and courteous, well-informed service. World-class organizations know that new products or services and technological improvements are quickly copied and improved upon, and thus may offer only a short-term advantage in the marketplace. They also know that the 'competitive edge' comes from providing a higher level of customer satisfaction than does the competition.

It is therefore imperative, during this analysis stage of the event operations management model, to ascertain what the customers want at an event, since expectations have a great effect on subsequent levels of satisfaction. High expectations may sell more tickets for one event, but if those expectations are not met then future business will be lost (Wood, 2004). The expectations also need to be gleaned from those who did not attend, as market perceptions help to create an event's relative competitive position.

The quality of product and the level of service provided in a competitive market must at least equate to what the competition is providing or is perceived to be providing. Customers' expectations are influenced by what they have previously experienced, by what the competition is claiming to provide in advertisements, by what we are promising in our promotions, by what the media is saying, and sometimes by the promise of technological improvements.

Customer satisfaction

When introducing the concept of customer satisfaction, it has to be understood that the basic requirement of any service, for customers, is that the service must meet their specifications, secondly that it will meet cost expectations, and thirdly that it is timely.

Specification – providing customers with what they expect to receive or are prepared to accept – is the essential requirement. In consideration of Wild's (2002) dimensions, customers will also be concerned with the reliability of the service. For example, will it be as experienced before, does its reputation live up to the reality? Is the design of the event relevant and appropriate?

Regarding cost, the customer will evaluate the product or service received in terms of its overall expected costs, including any additional expenses.

As for time, is the timing of the event appropriate? What is the duration of the event? Is there a delay between agreeing on a brief for an event and it being confirmed in writing? Delay is often unacceptable to a customer, and reduces overall customer satisfaction.

Wild (2002) breaks down these three attributes into further dimensions, which are shown in Table 5.1 (opposite).

Assessing critical success factors

What is acceptable or reasonable will always be open to question, and will depend on how important the service is to the customer and the alternatives available.

Thompson (2001) says that one element of success is for an organization to meet the needs and expectations of its stakeholders. Therefore an event manager needs an understanding of what those needs are, and a mixture of common sense and competency in order to satisfy these needs. The critical success factors are those aspects that external customers consider essential in fulfilling their requirements.

Reflective practice 5.1

You are a conference company, planning events for a range of clients using a variety of venues across the country to match your clients' requirements. You have ascertained in detail what the client wants from an appropriate venue. These are the critical success factors (CSFs):

- Conference room availability for 300 people, theatre style
- Responsive staff willing to be flexible
- Audiovisual facilities including video conferencing and Hi-Fi
- Closeness to road and rail network, 10 minutes maximum
- Price within budget of client
- Good reputation.

As the event manager, you should ask the client to rate these CSFs on a scale of 1–5 as to which is the most important (5 being the most important). This cannot always be done quickly and may take a lot of research, but nevertheless it is a very useful exercise.

Next, plot the results of the research onto a chart as shown in Figure 5.2.

Usually customers will accept, or tolerate, a service that does not perfectly meet their requirements. The amount of tolerance will be dependent on what the competition is offering or, if there is no immediate competition, what the alternatives are. Customers might be prepared to trade some specification for cost or availability for specific dates.

Table 5.1 Customer requirements with subdimensions

Basic customer requirement	Further dimensions
Specification	Design
	Performance
	Reliability
Cost	Price
	Expenses
	Cost reliability
Timing	Delay
	Duration
	Timing reliability

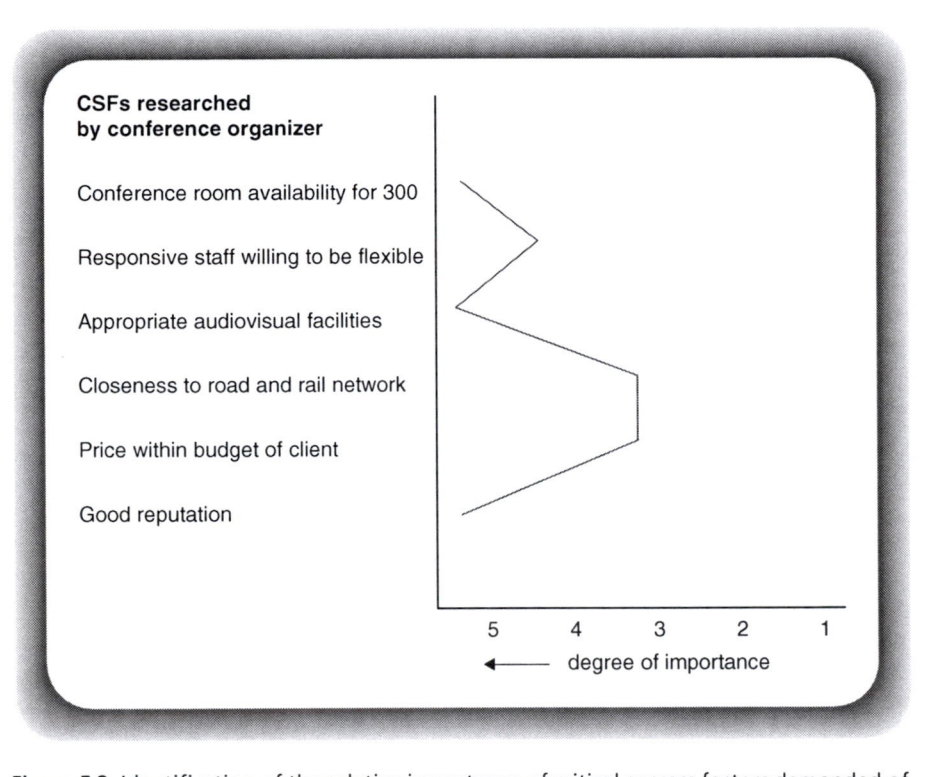

Figure 5.2 Identification of the relative importance of critical success factors demanded of a venue by conference delegates

The chart in Figure 5.2 can then be used further, by adding on the varied attributes of the various venues that are under consideration. This will show which venues match the desired characteristics, or critical success factors, demanded by the customer. Use different colours to highlight the client's requirements and the facilities of the different venues. This technique can be shown to the client so they can make an informed decision as to which venue to choose.

Case studies 5.1 and 5.2 illustrate various CSFs.

Case study 5.1

Edinburgh International Conference Centre (EICC), Scotland

Client: OSCE Parliamentary Assembly
Event: Thirteenth Annual Session
Date: 5–9 July 2004
Number of delegates: 650
More information: www.oscepa.org

Security is an issue for any conference, but when the conference is itself one of the world's leading forums on international security issues, special measures are obviously required.

When the Thirteenth Annual Session of the Organization for Security and Cooperation in Europe Parliamentary Assembly (OSCE PA) came to the EICC in July 2004, it also meant the arrival of 650 delegates, many of them parliamentary members from numerous nations around the globe.

The EICC made an ideal venue for this event for many reasons and, as a past venue for events such as the Commonwealth Heads of Government Meeting (1997), good security measures were clearly amongst its benefits.

During the five-day OSCE PA conference, visitors to the EICC had the reassurance of passing through airport-style screening. 'The delegates expect it', says Tracey Garratty, Delegation Secretary at the Overseas Office of the House of Commons. 'The UK approach is fairly low-key compared to parliamentary assemblies held elsewhere in the world, but it's very much about reassuring without intruding.'

With such an international audience – the OSCE PA prides itself on a membership ranging from Vancouver to Vladivostok – language and translation was also a key issue. 'The organization uses six official languages and the OSCE PA office in Copenhagen arranges the interpreters,' says Tracey, 'but you also have to find somewhere that has the capacity to allow six languages in simultaneous translation, and the EICC is able to do that.'

The conference, which involved fitting the entire Pentland Suite with desks for all the delegates, featured a busy programme, including a keynote speech from the Rt Hon. Peter Hain, Leader of the House of Commons and Secretary of State for Wales, and a wide range of committee and plenary sessions. The event culminated in delegates signing 'the Edinburgh Declaration' – a series of resolutions covering issues such as terrorism, racism and human trafficking.

Delegates also had the opportunity to continue networking over a busy social programme, including a reception at Holyrood Palace hosted by HRH the Duke of Kent and a dinner at the Museum of Scotland hosted by the Rt Hon. Michael Martin, Speaker of the House of Commons.

In 2005 the assembly moved on to Washington DC, but memories of Edinburgh remain warm, with the EICC's central location proving a major plus point.

'The size of Edinburgh gives it a big advantage,' says Tracey. 'Everything is within walking distance. There's a very good selection of hotels and they are all fairly close, which gives delegates the freedom to pop out and not feel isolated.'

'The feedback we have had about the EICC is also very positive,' she adds. 'People seem to like the set-up, the professionalism and the way it's been run. The staff are very helpful. They know what they are doing.'

(Case study printed by courtesy of Edinburgh International Conference Centre (EICC) and Whitel Light Media, Edinburgh. For further details of EICC, see www.eicc.co.uk.)

Case study 5.2

Dolce International Corporate Headquarters, Montvale, New Jersey, USA

Dolce International specializes in the meeting experience, and it is one of the leading global companies within the conference centre niche of the hospitality industry. It currently has twenty-six properties throughout the United States, Canada and Europe.

The Dolce brand of Conference & Resort Destinations includes properties in all six categories defined by the International Association of Conference Centres (IACC). The venues include:

- Executive conference centres
- Corporate conference centres
- University conference centres
- Resort conference centres
- Ancillary hotel conference centres
- Day meeting centres.

While the portfolio is varied in terms of location, type, and physical structure, they all offer Dolce's branded standards of service with meeting environments and service designed to provide the best meeting experience in the world.

One example is the Dolce Hayes Mansion, San José, California. This is an award-winning conference centre offering groups and individuals a unique blend of tranquillity, service and productivity.

The website describes the mansion in the following terms:

Opened to the public in 1994, the property quickly became the region's premier facility for meetings and events. An expansion and renovation programme, completed in 2002, enhanced the distinctive architectural characteristics of the original structure, and created even more additional meeting and event space.

Thoughtfully removed from the distractions of every day, Dolce Hayes Mansion is a place where absolutely no detail is left to chance. With over 33 000 square feet of dedicated meeting space, 22 specially designed and equipped conference rooms, and advanced multimedia capabilities, Dolce Hayes Mansion is the perfect destination to hold your next meeting. All meeting rooms are equipped with high-backed, fully adjustable executive conference chairs, individual lighting and heating/cooling controls and on-site audiovisual equipment. Skilled technicians and dedicated meeting professionals are always on hand to make sure your meeting runs smoothly from start to finish.

Vital statistics
  Meeting facility details: 33 000 sq ft
  Meeting rooms: 22
  Board rooms: 1
  Breakout rooms: 22
  Ballrooms: 6666 sq ft and 3000 sq ft

Rear screen capabilities: 1
Front screen capabilities: 22

Other facilities available:
Stage
Sound system
High-speed Internet access
Video conferencing
Basic LCD projectors included in the CMP
TV and video playback equipment
Overhead projectors
Lapel microphones
Handheld microphones
Ergonomic chairs
Hardtop work tables
Dolce e-café with computer workstations
Natural lighting in meeting rooms
AV staff on site
Whiteboards

(Printed by courtesy of Dolce International; further information can be obtained from www. dolce.com.)

Reflective practice 5.3

Consider Case study 5.2. What do you consider to be the critical success factors of Dolce International within the conference market?

Figure 5.3 compares the critical success factors and alternative providers. It can be seen that those venues that are closest to the customer's line may become the successful choice of the organizer.

Venue A did not have a conference room for 300 people; it is close to the rail and road networks and was less than required cost. Venue B exceeded the clients' needs, and was very expensive.

This technique is useful to measure how well a supplier or location can match the needs of the customer or the organization. Another technique is discussed in Chapter 10; which although shown as being very useful for choosing ideal locations for offices or for the event itself, could also be used to choose the sourcing of ideal resources.

The providers' perspective

From the perspective of a services provider, what is provided has to be what can be afforded, and must be at least up to the same standard as the competition. The determination of what to provide is based on economic considerations rather than altruism. Customers are needed for income, and in the long term the organization cannot afford to run at a loss. Many an organization has failed to survive although customers have received excellent service. The efficient use of resources is covered later in this chapter.

The technique of using the range of critical success factors demanded by your clients and plotting these against the resources available can be adapted by any organization that has undertaken extensive research into what the customer most desires and what is considered as being critical. As discussed earlier, the chart's use can be

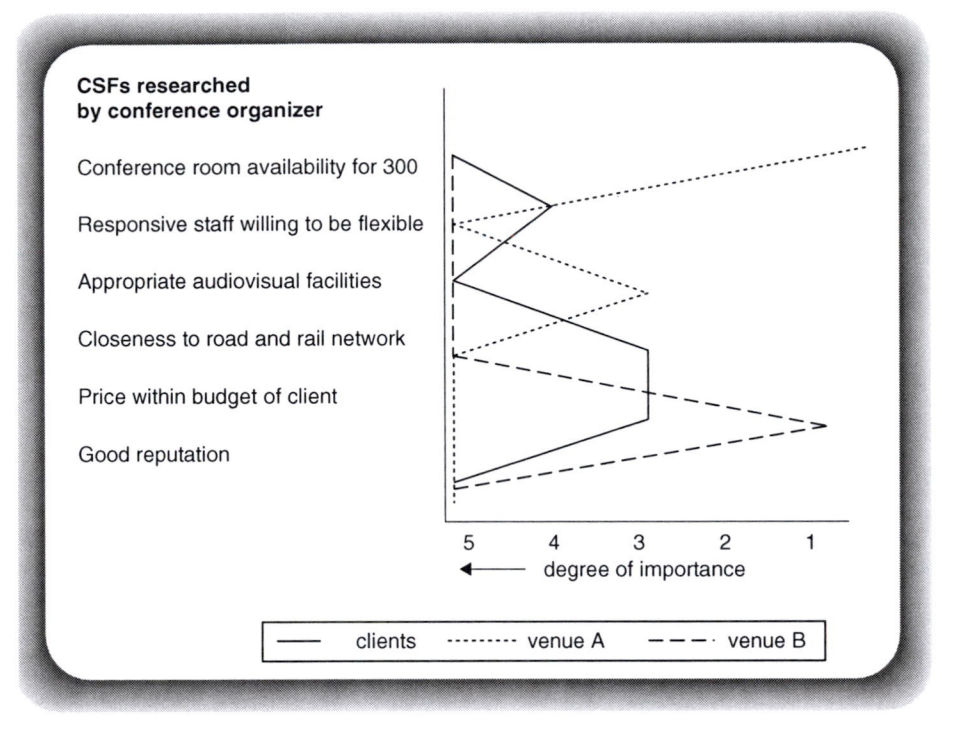

Figure 5.3 Comparison of critical success factors and alternative providers

extended and the attributes of the facilities changed and plotted to see the match (or otherwise) with the customer's requirements.

Further market research as to what the customer wants from an event company can also be plotted onto a similar graph. The organization should be highly critical and objective regarding where its own service and attributes would sit on the same scale. These attributes should also be plotted onto the same graph. To answer the question 'how well are *we* doing?', it is clear that the closer the organization's line to that which defines the customer's needs, the more the organization is in tune with those needs.

It can be seen that if the line drawn for an organization is to the left of what the customer wants then it is over-providing, and possibly spending more money and resources for a less valued attribute. If it is to the right, it is falling short of what the customer wants.

The next stage for the organizer is to analyse, in a similar way, what the competition is providing, and plot that onto the same chart.

The chart will now have a variety of lines, showing:

- What the customer wants
- What you believe you are providing
- What competitor A is providing
- What competitor B is providing
- What competitor C is providing.

Competitive advantage by using quality of service provision

As described earlier in this chapter, there is a need to emulate world-class standards in order to serve sophisticated customers. New services are quickly copied and improved

upon by the competition, and often the only competitive advantage will come from the level of service provided. Thus customer satisfaction goes past the basics of specification, time and cost to include the *quality* of service.

Quality has two dimensions, customer satisfaction and efficient use of resources. What constitutes quality, how it is judged and controlled, and the culture of quality is detailed in Chapter 16. However, in light of the importance of the quality of service in gaining a competitive edge, our discussion on customer service would be incomplete if we were to ignore the rudiments of what can be done to enhance the basic attributes of specification, time and cost.

In our example of choosing a conference venue, having offered a service that attracts customers and which meets the researched critical success factors, it is possible to look at ways of adding a perception of increased service without adding to the cost.

Adding value

Generally, some perception of added service can be provided at very little cost.

Using our conference venue as an example, and assuming that the CSFs meet the customers' basic needs, additional quality service attributes could include well-organized coffee and lunch breaks, cleanliness of the car park, friendly and well presented reception staff, and useful and meaningful signage. Well-organized service can be achieved by good planning, and should not cost the company any extra. Keeping the car park clean might add marginally to the cost (cleaning facilities and wages). Issuing the staff with smart uniforms will obviously be a cost, and training them in customer care will also incur some cost.

All such costs are minimal when compared to the overall operating cost of the conference venue. However, the general perception will be an improved service, although the critical success factors have not changed.

It is important to recognize that above all customers expect a reliable and a consistent service. A service that is sometimes excellent and sometimes indifferent will only confuse the customer. Once a service level has been established, then that standard must be maintained.

For any organization, increased service at little or no cost will require a special culture. The workforce has to be enthusiastic and must have some authority to make limited operational decisions. Creating a quality organizational culture, resulting in staff motivated to reduce inefficiencies and to give friendly and consistent service, is covered in Chapter 11, within the implementation stage of the event operations management model.

Summary

To recap, customer satisfaction involves several points:

- The service provided has to match the customers' expectations, but not always exactly.
- The company that exactly matches the critical success factors required by the customer will have the highest rating – providing the customer has found that company and knows exactly what is required in the first place.
- The perception of an improved quality service can be achieved at very little cost, and involves cleanliness, consistency, reliability, friendly and helpful frontline staff etc.
- If you provide attributes that are to the left of the line on your CSF matching chart, you may be spending more money and time on provision of service and facilities that the customer does not believe are important. If you are providing attributes that are to the right of the line, you are underachieving.
- What is offered has to be affordable and maintainable.

Wild (2002) reminds us that customers will have expectations, even to an extent that is in excess of their original specification, if that is what is being offered. Failure to meet

these expectations will cause dissatisfaction, but matching these expectations will give rise to satisfaction, and exceeding them may result in delight.

What are stakeholders?

We will now concentrate on determining who the stakeholders are, and how to rank the relative importance of the various requirements of customers and influential stakeholders. These were discussed briefly in Chapter 3, since many of the stakeholders are external to the organization. However, not all of them are, and it is essential to understand different techniques that can be used to assess their importance and influence.

Freeman (1984) defines a stakeholder as any person or group who can affect, or is affected by, the performance of the organization.

The word 'stakeholder' was coined in an internal memorandum at the Stamford Research Institute in 1963, and it referred to 'those groups without whose support the organization would cease to exist'.

De Wit and Meyer (2004) propose two definitions of stakeholder:

> *a wide sense, which includes groups who are friendly or hostile (trade associations, competitors, unions, employees, customer segments) who can affect the achievement of objectives or be affected by them … and a narrow sense, which aims to identify specific individuals or groups on which the organization is dependent upon for its survival (employees, certain suppliers, key government agencies, Health and Safety Executive and financial institutions).*

Wright (2001) believes that knowing who the stakeholders are and how their concerns might affect the operation of an organization is becoming more and more critical. He defines a stakeholder as anyone who has an interest in what an organization does. This might seem a very broad definition, and indeed it is.

Funds for an event may come from local authorities or charities initially investing in a fundraising event, or sponsors, racecourse venues etc. The body that provides the funds obviously has a stake in the efficiency of the operation. These stakeholders – the fund providers – should and increasingly do seek value for money. In their eyes, value for money includes not only providing a level of service to the customer, but also the efficient use of resources.

There are other stakeholders who do not directly provide money – for example, taxpayers – and who are also concerned that their money is being spent wisely (see Case study 5.3).

Determining who the stakeholders are

It can be seen that for any business, a stakeholder is anyone with a pecuniary interest in the organization (such as shareholders, banks, financiers, investors, suppliers of goods and services, the people who work in the organization and their families). Other more general stakeholders include investors in the share market, local bodies in the district of the operation, the venue/location where the event is being held, people who live and work in the general neighbourhood, and the Green movement. For government and quasi-government organizations, charitable trusts and other like bodies, stakeholders are fund providers, bankers, suppliers, people who work in the organization and their families, and the community at large. We should even include the competitors and the whole event industry.

Whereas before you thought you had to satisfy only the customers' needs and their CSFs, you can now see that all the stakeholders have different CSFs and priorities. What a challenge!

Case study 5.3

Carnival parades

Carnival parades are held worldwide, all the year round. In community-sponsored carnival parades, the end-users are those people who attend. A major stakeholder is the community itself (the major source of funds), which is concerned that there will be value for the money invested. However, do not forget the taxpayer who is funding the community. Other providers of funds may include product sponsors of branded goods (e.g. Coca-Cola™). All these groups are stakeholders, and they have a stake in the *quality* of the outputs.

There are still other stakeholders who do not directly provide funds for the event, but who will have a very real interest in its quality and safety. These might include shopping enterprises in the vicinity, local communities that may be affected, police, and road transport bodies.

Each stakeholder group is likely to have different priorities in judging the service provided, and will have varying levels of interest in the event. Some fund providers and taxpayers will be anxious that resources are being efficiently utilized (money is not being wasted), while others will be more concerned with the disruption that is being caused and still others with the safety and security of the event. Further groups might be interested in the content of the carnival parade and that it matches their expectations, or that it should bring more trade and economic value to the region.

Reflective practice 5.4

Choose a carnival and make a list of the different stakeholders, their needs and their priorities.

Case study 5.4 describes the Glastonbury Festival, which has many stakeholders.

Adaptation of matrix

Pareto analysis is a useful tool. Wilfredo Pareto was a nineteenth century Italian economist who concluded that 80 per cent of the wealth was held by 20 per cent of the population. The same phenomenon has often been found in businesses, where, for example, 80 per cent of the sales come from 20 per cent of the customers, or 20 per cent of the stock held accounts for 80 per cent of the inventory value. In other areas, 80 per cent of road accidents occur in localized areas (20 per cent of the roads have 80 per cent of the total accidents). In the early twentieth century, Lorenz produced a graph for demonstrating the cumulative dominance of the 20 per cent. Juran (1988) refers to the 80/20 phenomenon as the 'vital few and trivial many'.

When considering stakeholder satisfaction, Pareto analysis may indicate that a vital few of the stakeholders have a greater influence on the business. It may therefore be the case that the event organizer needs to take greater notice of these stakeholders.

Stakeholders such as banks and creditors (suppliers of goods and services) will generally only be interested in the financial security of the business. Other stakeholders (such as people living in the neighbourhood of the operation) will have different concerns (such as pollution, noise, and perhaps even heavy traffic flows). If local concerns are known in advance, then action can be taken to prevent offence. Actions that have to be taken as a result of protests or legal initiatives not only taint an organization's reputation, but also prove more costly than if the operation had been set up correctly and stakeholders' concerns addressed in the first place (see Case study 5.5).

Case study 5.4

The Glastonbury Festival, Somerset, England

Glastonbury Festival began on 19 September 1970, by Michael and Jean Eavis at Worthy Farm, Pilton, in Somerset. Attendance was 1500. The Glastonbury Festival of Contemporary Performing Arts – to give its full title – is now an institution, being the largest green field and performing arts festival in the world, with 150 000 people attending the 2004 event. It creates a city under canvas with distinct districts, and is located in over 900 acres in the Vale of Avalon – an area some 1.5 miles across and with a perimeter of over 8 miles.

The Festival, held annually in June, is unique, with over 30 different performance areas on site and some 2000 different performances over the weekend. The site is divided into the following areas: Acoustic Stage, Band Stand, Cabaret Tent, Cinema Field, Circus Big Top, Circus Field, Craft Fields, The Crown, dance fire stage, dance tent, Fields of Avalon (incorporating the Avalon Stage, the Avalon Café Stage and the Little Massive Stage), The Glade, Green Futures Field, Green Kids, Green Road Show, Greenpeace Field, Healing Fields, Jazz World Stage, Jazz Lounge, Kidz Field, Left Field, Lost Vagueness, John Peel Stage, Other Stage, Permaculture, Poetry and Words, Speakers Corner, Theatre Tent, Tipi Field and, of course the main stage, called the Pyramid Stage. There are also the traders' areas, food and merchandizing, and then there are medical and welfare centres, security, all the emergency services, a bank, places of worship – the list is endless.

The Glastonbury Festival pays over £1 million each year to charities and good causes, with the main beneficiaries being Oxfam, Greenpeace, Water Aid, and local good causes. It also supports the Fair Trade Foundation and Future Forests, and looks to operate in a way that reflects the values of the environmental and humanitarian charities it supports.

The Festival runs an unsigned performers' competition for new performers, which in 2004 generated over 2000 entries, several of which were subsequently signed to major labels.

The Licensing Authority is Mendip District Council.

The Festival has a small permanent staff and employs experienced event industry specialists on short-term contracts in the main, augmented by thousands of volunteers.

(Information supplied by the Glastonbury Festival Office; further details can be found at www.glastonburyfestivals.co.uk.)

Reflective practice 5.5

Consider Case study 5.4.

1. Prepare a list of the stakeholders for the Glastonbury Festival, and against each group or individual annotate their concerns about the festival. Identifying the stakeholders and determining their *concerns* should prove to be an interesting exercise. Remember to include the festival customer in this analysis.
2. Against this list, rank their importance on two dimensions: first, their interest in the event on a scale of 1–5 (5 being high); and second, the influence they could have on the event on a scale of 1–5 (5 being high).
3. Plot these dimensions onto Figure 5.4.
4. Analyse what this exercise has told you.
5. Consider a scenario where too many tickets have been sold for Glastonbury and more people attend the event than estimated. Would any of the stakeholders move from where you have put them in the earlier exercise? Comment on this movement.

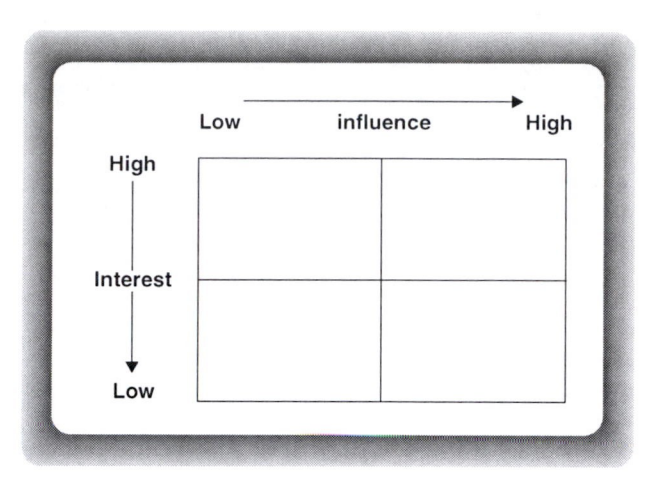

Figure 5.4 Influence and interest of Glastonbury Festival stakeholders

Customer/stakeholder challenges to the event organizer

Customer satisfaction has two elements. First, we have to know exactly what the customer wants. Secondly, we have to ensure that what is being offered and the manner in which we operate, in order to satisfy the customer, does not conflict with the interests of other stakeholders. Is this always possible?

Further methods of determining the requirements of the different stakeholders are discussed below, these include surveys, composite customer service ratings and gap analysis.

Surveys

To establish what is wanted by the direct customer and by any other stakeholders, an events operations manager could undertake a survey. The survey will determine first what the customers and stakeholders want, and secondly their perceptions of what they are currently getting.

For example, the results of an imaginary survey at a large national exhibition are reproduced in Table 5.2 (rated on a scale of 1–3, where 3 is highest).

Table 5.2 Desired service compared to perceived service

Some of the stakeholders	Accurate exhibitor directory	Good layout/flow	High-quality food facilities
Desired service (using three random CSFs)			
Attendees	3	3	3
Exhibitors	3	3	2
Caterers on site	1	1	3
Perceptions of received service (from the three stakeholders)			
Attendees	2	2	2
Exhibitors	2	3	3
Caterers on site	1	1	3

Case study 5.5

Jagger beats sore point to wow fans

(by Sarah Bell, 29 August 2003, *This is Local London*)

TWICKENHAM *was rocking and rolling in more ways than one as the Rolling Stones went back to their roots at the RFU stadium on Sunday after the planned Saturday concert was cancelled because Mick Jagger had a sore throat.*

The delayed opening night of their UK tour saw the band playing to 50 000 fans, including 5000 local residents, at the first concert to be held at the stadium. Taking to the stage, Mick Jagger said: 'No one has ever played in the Twickenham Rugby Club before, so we're very privileged. We started off playing at the Richmond Rugby Club up the road so it's not very far really from there to here.'

Richmond upon Thames Council, who helped man a helpline for residents and monitored noise levels, said they received just six complaints during the sound checks and concert.

Many residents also listened to the concert from their gardens and one complaint came from a resident who said that they couldn't hear and asked for it to be turned up.

Richmond police said they thought the event had gone well with no major incidents, and just a 'few people who were a bit worse for wear'. PC Nigel Cox, responsible for the police operation, said: 'It was very good really, from our side of things. All the crowds got there and away from the station safely, there was some traffic congestion at the end, and the A316 was very busy. We had a few problems with ticket allocation, but it was handled well.'

He added that the rescheduled date was not a problem, saying: 'If anything it has given us an insight into what it is going to be like and we will plan it the same as we have for this one.'

Businesses in the town thrived with the crowds. Frank Dupree, landlord of the Cabbage Patch, said: 'It was very good. I was choked about Saturday because I was meant to be going myself. It was a lovely crowd and no problems whatsoever. It was a much older crowd and less boozy than for the rugby. All gentle really.

It was a shame the concert wasn't earlier, as we could have got another bash afterwards. It was quite surprising how early they were in town, we were busy at 2 pm, a lot of people were just wandering around the town. It was great for Twickenham and I wish we could have more.'

Managing director Edwin Doran of Edwin Doran's Travel World said: 'The town was buzzing. Every pub, bar and restaurant was full with visitors spending money and looking forward to the return of two local residents to the borough where they started their musical careers. Isn't it magnificent that our town got such magnificent positive national publicity?'

Residents living closest to the stadium said the noise was not as bad as they had expected and the main problem was the traffic, which took a long time to clear. Barbara Irvine of Whitton Road said: 'The noise was less than we expected, on the positive side. The thing we didn't like were the fireworks at 10.30 and although we were expecting them, speaking to elderly people and people with young children, it is difficult for them. The crowd control during the day was very good, while during the evening there were a lot of people just walking around aimlessly and causing problems with the traffic trying to get past. Between Chudleigh Road and Palmerston Road there were 29 cars parked illegally.

Traffic didn't dissipate quickly and there was still heavy traffic at midnight and the fumes are horrible. They need to pay more attention to how they are going to evacuate people in their cars.

The cancellation was good for us because on Saturday we were able to leave our houses, otherwise you are in all day because it is impossible to get through the crowds.'

Yet the cancellation saw both hotel and restaurants losing trade. The Bremic Hotel on Russell Road was fully booked for both nights with 25 per cent cancelling, which was described as 'not good', but many rebooked for September.

There were also some fans and workers milling around the stadium, who had not heard the news of Jagger's sore throat on time. Ron Donovan from Durham, New Hampshire, ordered tickets last December from last-minute.com and said that he had had to collect them in person. He was philosophical, saying: 'I travel a lot

and nothing ever goes to plan. If you get upset then you will go on getting upset. I try to take things in my stride.'

(Article printed by kind permission of the *Richmond and Twickenham Times*, part of the Newsquest Media Group.)

Reflective practice 5.6

Consider Case study 5.5.

1. Identify stakeholder concerns and suggest ways these could be alleviated for future events.
2. Identify areas that could have caused concern if preventive action and planning had not been carried out.

In table 5.2 the results of the survey showed that:

1. Attendees' requirements are an accurate directory of exhibitors, an excellent layout and flow, and high-quality food facilities
2. Exhibitors' requirements are an accurate directory of exhibitors, an excellent layout and flow and good food facilities
3. Caterers' requirements are high-quality food facilities; they are not really concerned whether the directory of exhibitors is totally accurate or whether there is an excellent layout and flow.

Regarding the perceptions of the service, the chosen stakeholders in this scenario all saw the directory as having some inaccuracies. The attendees did not believe that there was a good layout and flow, although the exhibitors themselves judged this more highly. Similarly, the attendees were not totally impressed with the food facilities. The event manager needs to rethink the priorities of the exhibition and look at the requirements of other stakeholders to see who can be satisfied, and to assess who it is most critical to satisfy.

Composite customer service rating

Christopher (1992) gives another method of rating customer service. This is illustrated in Table 5.3, using an example of an event management company preparing a brief for a seating company to provide 3000 chairs at an outdoor concert.

In this example, the key criterion for the seating company (as the customer of the event management company) has been established as a clear, unambiguous specification. This is the most important criterion, and has been given a rating of 50/100. On-time delivery of that specification is the next most important, and other important criteria (but of lesser rating) are preparation of the area for receipt of the chairs, and timely payment of the final invoice. This is shown in column 'a'.

Column 'b' shows that the specification received was only 70 per cent accurate, the timeliness of the specification to the suppliers represented only 80 per cent of their expectations, the area was only 90 per cent ready for receipt of the chairs, and the invoice was only paid at 95 per cent of their timely expectations. The exercise showed that on this one transaction the company was falling short of expectations and only achieving a composite customer service rating of 78 per cent.

Ideally, internal measures should be set against targets established by the customer. What might seem trivial to the business could, in the customer's eyes, be seen as a major problem.

Table 5.3 Customer service rating

Service required	Weighting % (a)	Performance (b)	Weighted score (a × b)
Clear specification	50	70	0.35
On time	25	80	0.20
Preparation for receipt of delivery	15	90	0.135
Timely payment of invoice	10	95	0.095
	100		0.78

Gap analysis

The level of service offered by an organization stems from the business policy or objectives. These were referred to at the start of Chapter 2. Objectives may, to a large extent, be driven by what the competition is doing or is threatening to do. When deciding upon and specifying a level of service, management tends to rely on the advice of the marketing function. If the marketing function does not correctly interpret the requirements of the customer, then there will be a gap between the level of satisfaction the organization believes it is providing and what the customer believes is being achieved. The concept of service gaps arose from the research of Berry *et al.* (1988) and his colleagues (Parasuraman *et al.*, 1985, 1991; Zeithaml *et al.*, 1990). Their SERVQUAL model is discussed in some detail in Chapter 16.

As Lewis (1994: 237) says, referring to Parasuraman *et al.*:

> They defined service quality to be a function of the gap between consumers' expectations of a service and their perceptions of the actual service delivery by an organization; and suggested that this gap is influenced by a number of other gaps which may occur in an organization.

The magnitude of the gap will be compounded by the number of steps in the service process and by the distance of the operational function from the customer. This is illustrated by the following examples.

In our first example, let us suppose that the marketing department at an International Folk Festival on the south coast has interpreted what the customer wants only 90 per cent correctly. Straight away, this means that the actual performance can never be better than 90 per cent of what the customer really wants. If, however, business policy is such that it is deemed sufficient to provide resources to meet only 90 per cent of the customer's requirements (this 90 per cent being set on the understanding that marketing is 100 per cent correct), then at best the customer will only get 81 per cent of what it wants.

In our second example, let us assume that an event management company slightly misinterprets what a major charity wants for a fundraising event, and that also it sets itself an internal target of 90 per cent. If we further suppose that the operation is so resourced that to the best of their ability they can only achieve 95 per cent of the standard set, this means the final result will be that customer satisfaction is at best only 69 per cent. The calculation is as follows:

- Customer requirement 100%
- Misinterpretation of needs 90% (i.e. they get it 90% right)
- Business policy sets target at 90% of 100, but this now actually equates to 90% of 90 = 81%

- Due to being under-resourced, the back of house team sets an internal standard of slightly better than 90% of target. However, owing to slight ambiguity and misunder-standing of the management target, this means that even when 92% of internal target is reached, it is only 90% of what was set by management – i.e. 90% of 81% = 73%
- The front of house team, also under-resourced, is 95% on target – 95% of 73% = 69%.

From the above examples, it is clear that unless gap analysis is understood, manage-ment will firmly believe that the overall result is somewhere near 90 per cent of what the customer wants. Each department, when queried, will also fervently believe that it is reaching between 90 and 95 per cent of the required performance levels. However, in the second example above it can be seen that the customer's expectations are only being matched to 69 per cent.

If an organization is close to its customers and aware of what the competition is doing, then a gap of this magnitude should not happen. The larger the organization and the greater the delineation of responsibilities between departmental functions, and the further the operations function is removed from the customer and from consultation in business policy decisions, the greater the likelihood of gaps occurring between what is provided and what the customer really wants. This concept is explored further in Chapter 16.

Reflective practice 5.7

You are an incentive travel company called 'Travel to Success', offering your services in pro-viding packages to blue chip companies for their high-flying sales staff.

Typically you provide one- to two-week breaks in Thailand and China, linked with further promotional events to stimulate further sales among the workforce. Your unique selling point (USP) for your company is that you provide an evaluation of the effect of the incentives on the workforce over the following year. Armed with excellent qualitative research you are able to advise companies on the best methods of incentivizing their workforce with a high return on investment.

Imagine that you have done extensive research in the marketplace, and now construct a chart as in Figure 5.2.

1. Identify the critical success factors (CSFs) as determined by your hypothetical in-depth cus-tomer research, and list them on the vertical axis.
2. Assign values to the importance of each factor from the point of view of your customers.
3. Trace an unbroken line onto the chart for each CSF.
4. Estimate your own company's performance (hypothetically) and plot this on the chart (using a different colour).
5. Similarly, create two further imaginary companies ('Incentive Holidays R Us' and 'Outperform') and plot their scores onto the chart, again using different colours.
6. What do the results tell you?

Reflective practice 5.8

Return to the earlier section on critical success factors.

1. If you were to take into account the feelings of the major stakeholders, would the line you plot-ted for the Incentive Travel Company, 'Travel to Success', change with regard to how you could measure its attainment of the weighted critical success factors demanded by your customers?
2. You could now plot the needs of your customers and also the needs of your prominent stakeholders on the chart. You will see that the lines do not match. What does this tell you? How will you manage the gaps and the tension between your stakeholders?

Chapter summary and key points

This chapter is the penultimate chapter in the analysis stage of the event operations management model. It began by looking at who the customer is, and distinguishing between stakeholders and customers. The importance of determining critical success factors, not only for customers, but also for stakeholders has been stressed.

To summarize, generally an organization will aim consistently to achieve certain standards or levels of quality as determined by business policy. The decision as to the level of service to provide will be an economic one, and may be driven by what the competition is doing or is likely to do. The intention should be to define accurately what the customer wants. Normally an organization will not be able to meet all the requirements of the customer completely, and some trade-off will be possible. It is also wise to understand who the stakeholders are and what their concerns might be, and how they can affect your performance.

Where a strong organizational culture exists, enthusiastic and helpful staff, at very little extra cost to the organization, can enhance the perception of service level.

(Wright, 2001)

Given infinite resources any system, however badly managed, might provide adequate customer service.

(Wild, 1995)

Many an organization has failed to survive although the customers have been more than satisfied with what they have received. Thus customer satisfaction is not the only criterion by which an operations manager will be judged. Customer satisfaction must be provided simultaneously with an effective and efficient operation. The level of customer satisfaction offered must not only be affordable to the organization, but also consistent and sustainable. The events organization, if it is to survive, has to make a profit. Profit is not a dirty word.

Chapter 6 will look in detail at how to analyse the internal environment – i.e. the organization itself. This is the last and essential element in the analysis process prior to the detailed planning stage.

Chapter 6

Analysis of the internal environment

Learning Objectives

After reading through this chapter you will be able to:

■ Analyse the internal environment and consider the efficient use of resources and their appropriate prioritization
■ Consider the customers' needs, and appreciate the potential conflict of resource utilization and how to balance objectives
■ Understand different company structures and how these styles can influence the success of an event and its organization.

Introduction

This is the last chapter within Section 1. It brings together the preceding chapters, and enables the event manager to understand and make sense of all of the analysis that has taken place. As shown in Chapter 2, without input from the customer the function of providing service will not happen. Figure 6.1, which is reproduced from Chapter 3 for ease of reference, shows that there are two distinct forces that have to be analysed and appraised before a successful mission can be formulated: the external environment and the internal environment of the event company. In Chapter 2 we discussed the importance of having a clear mission and goals for the event or the organization itself.

Chapter 3 looked at the task of analysing the external environment, and Chapter 4 led into the bridge between the external environment and the provision of resources, and how the event was going to be managed.

Chapter 5 picked up some of the main players within an event organization, i.e. the customers and stakeholders, and introduced the concept of analysing whether their varied needs are being met or whether there is a gap in the service.

This chapter looks in detail at the other elements of the internal environment within an event company as identified in Figure 6.1:

• Corporate culture
• Desire for quality
• Information systems
• Finance and ownership.

The chapter also considers many of the tangible and intangible resources that an event manager has to coordinate and control.

The internal environment

First we will discuss those elements within an event organization as identified as being in the internal environment as in Figure 6.1.

Corporate culture

Corporate culture is the amalgam of beliefs, norms and values of individuals making up an organization – i.e. the way we do things around here. For a business policy to be successful it has to be accepted by the members of the organization and mirror their goals and aspirations. The chief executive might be the one who articulates the vision, but unless there is a cultural fit and the people working on the events buy into it, it won't happen.

Culture and values are deep-seated and may not always be obvious to members and to newcomers to the organization.

Thompson (2001) sees culture as being the way staff behave and the importance of their values, and how this dictates the way decisions are made. Culture can also dictate

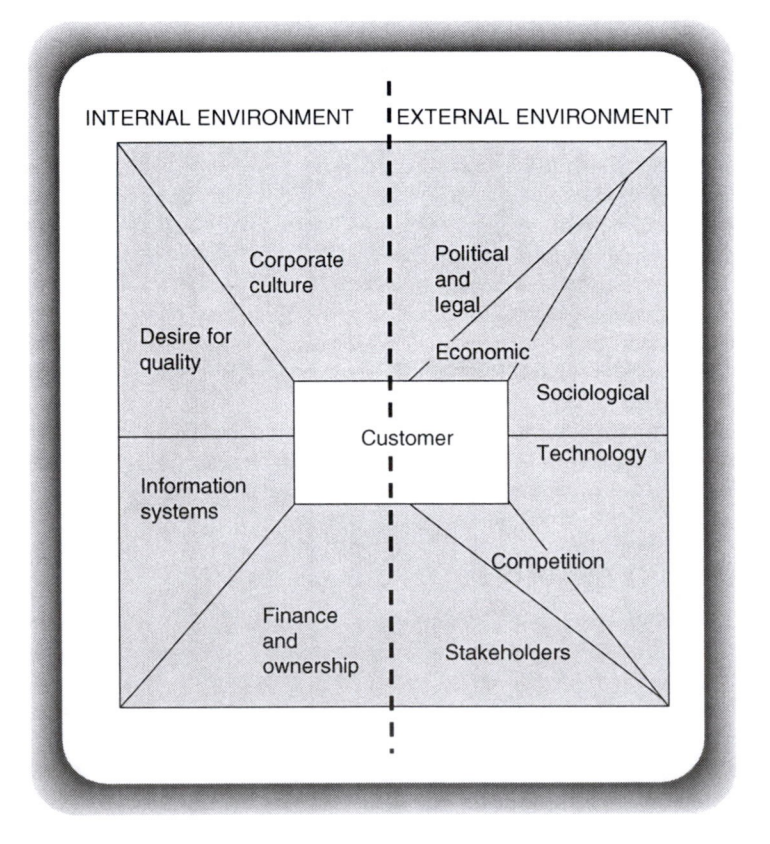

Figure 6.1 External and internal forces on the customer

the objectives of the company structure and systems, and its attitudes towards managing people (Thompson, 2001).

If the event organization has a strong culture, then each individual will instinctively know how things are done and what is expected. Conversely, if the culture is weak, then the individual may not react in the manner that management would hope.

Desire for quality

The level of quality offered is very much a business policy decision. It has been said that quality is free. Certainly doing things right the first time and every time should cost us nothing apart from training our people to know what is right and what corrective actions that they can take.

If we refer to our earlier example of a courtesy bus service in Chapter 2, we will see that a higher-level service and quality would not cost a great deal more. With the bus, the aim was to run a regular service, keeping to a defined route and a set timetable. In addition, the driver had to be licensed and the vehicle maintained to a roadworthy level. We could add the perception of extra quality at little (if any) additional cost by simply getting things right first time, every time.

Take, for example, a major exhibition in a capital city exhibition venue. If all the venue staff and exhibitors were to take pride in their appearance and be polite to customers, and if the venue were to be kept clean, the perception of a quality service would be enhanced at no appreciable extra cost to the organization. True there might be a minor cost in providing uniforms, and in the cost of cleaning, and perhaps in training in customer relations. If, however, we wished to increase the service by taking on extra work, such as our staff assisting in the erection and breakdown of stands, this would mean extra staff, more equipment, and extra scheduling.

Thus to increase the service is more expensive. Yet this might be what the customers have asked for. What determines our policy – is it the customer, or economic considerations? No doubt we would have to consider how many extra exhibitors the extra service would generate, and whether this extra income would offset the extra costs.

Quality is therefore also an economic consideration. At one level it is cheaper to do things right, and to do them only once, and it is also helpful to have happy and eager staff who will give customers friendly helpful service. This should not add to the costs; however, extra quality above these levels may increase cost. Thus the level of quality we can afford and sustain is very much a business policy decision, and to a large extent it will be driven not by what the customer wants but by what the competition is doing or threatening to do.

Any quality initiative has to have strong and overt support from management. Our contention is that quality is everyone's business, but unless management provide the vision and the drive any quality initiative has the chance of failing.

Information systems

With the information technology available today, there is no reason why every member of an event organization cannot be kept up to date with and have a clear understanding of what the current policy of the organization is. Few of us do not have a personal computer on our desk with access to electronic mail systems. Two-way communication is now commonplace, and many organizations go to great lengths with staff magazines, bulletin boards and so on to keep staff informed as to company policy as well as social events, work schedules and commitments. As we have said in previous chapters in the event industry many of our resources are external to the event organization and so it is imperative to keep in constant contact and to notify changes and revisions as they occur.

The old method of management was for the bosses to do the thinking, set the goals and give directions. The workers were not paid to think; their job was to obey orders. With such an approach it is no wonder that many people were reluctant to show initiative and thus few really had the interests of the organization at heart. This is often referred to Taylorism, after F. W. Taylor, a late nineteenth century American known as the father of scientific management. His philosophy was for management, by scientific means, to find the best way of doing a job and by using appropriate equipment. He believed in training the workers in the best way, and he offered incentives to increase productivity. Supervisors were employed to maintain the best method. Management did the thinking and workers were not expected to make suggestions; their job was to do what they were told. Chapter 11 covers many of the motivation theories, and Taylor's work is explained there.

Today, most of us work where we do because we understand the policies of the organization, believe in the product or service we are offering, and enjoy being involved, even in a small way, in helping to shape policy.

Finance and ownership

Most event organizations are limited by money. The necessary funding comes from the owners, profits (equity or shareholders' funds), sponsors and borrowing. Unless owners are getting a reasonable return on their investment, they are going to ask questions.

Owners, investors, the share market, sponsors and bankers will judge the event on the bottom line in the accounts. If the event organization is part of a government department, or is funded by the government or the public, the return will be seen in terms of value for money, and the persistent question will be 'can we do better for our money by going elsewhere?'

Financial strength, being profitable or getting value for money is a major shaper of business policy. More than anything else, lack of funds will determine policy.

The primary task when creating a budget is to outline the anticipated costs of producing the event (Harrison and McDonald, 2004). By identifying and documenting the costs involved in the production of an event, the event professional can establish the necessary income and possible sources of income.

As stated in Chapter 2, the event manager is the person who is responsible for using the resources of the organization as efficiently as possible to make goals and objectives happen. Central to the goals and objectives will be the need to make a profit, for without a profit a business will not survive. In not-for-profit organizations and charities, the goal is either to break even or to raise funds. Consequently, stringent financial systems are essential. Apart from mere survival, there will also be a need to satisfy fund providers (owners, shareholders, financiers) that their investment is secure and that they are receiving (or will receive) a satisfactory return on their investment. If an organization is a non-profit institution (such as government-funded), the central objective will be to show fund providers that they are getting value for money. The need to evaluate events in terms of success to all the different shareholders and in particular from a financial perspective is extremely important.

Many new businesses have a very short lifespan (over 70 per cent of small businesses fail within five years of beginning operations), and every month there are reports of medium and large businesses in financial difficulties. Like it or not, the continued success of any organization relies on financial stability. Often event managers see the accountants as soulless people devoid of imagination, interested only in short-term returns on assets. However, unless there is a positive cash flow, long-term business plans are meaningless. It is vital that any organization has a reliable accounting system in place to provide fast and accurate information. The minimum requirement is a

budget and reliable feedback of actual results for comparison to the budget. These should be in time for corrective action to be taken where required. Rather than the accountants pressing operations for returns and figures, it should be remembered that the accountants are a support function, and it should be the event manager who is pressing the accountants to provide essential information.

Resources

In the event industry the major resource will probably be people, and we need to know what their competencies are – i.e. how skilled they are, their attitudes and dedication, and whether they are resourceful and capable of taking initiatives. Some staff will be full time, others part time and only for the duration of the event; some will be volunteers provided by other agencies, and some will come from suppliers.

Other resources include premises, information systems, time, equipment, materials and vehicles. The location of premises or where the event will take place, the reliability of the information system and other necessary equipment, the reliability of suppliers, and most importantly the quality of the people, will determine the overall capability or competence of the event. Establishing a quality of culture, how to motivate people and continuous improvement are covered in Chapter 12, and in Chapter 16 the topics are revisited when we discuss quality issues.

In the event industry the tangible and intangible resources available will consist of a mix of the following:

- People and their skills
- Information technology
- Equipment and machines (audiovisual equipment, registration facilities, materials movement equipment, seating etc.)
- Vehicles (leased, owned)
- Space (offices, warehouses, conference venues, green field areas, stately homes etc.)
- Materials (gifts, stationery etc.)
- Inventory (merchandise for sale, stationery, stock for later use)
- Time
- Information itself, and data.

Obviously not all events will have (or need) all of these resources at the same time. However, there will never be an unlimited amount of resources, and often they will be limited in quantity and quality. Any increases in their provision will be dependent on funds available. When funds are not an inhibitor there can be other constraints – for example, we may need specialized signage or advertising material, but it might be some weeks before delivery will be made and that time is not available to us.

Some of the more important of these varied resources are now explored further.

The customer

In some situations the customer is also an active input into the system – for example:

- When queueing whilst waiting for an event to start
- When inputting ideas
- When performing part of the activity – for example at teambuilding events and when self-serving at a buffet
- When completing a registration form on-line.

Materials

Materials used by the event include utilities such as energy, water and gas. Materials also include goods that are consumed by the event, goods that are transformed by the event, and goods held for sale and as inventory (i.e. in storage). In the events industry these materials would include lighting rigs set up to provide lighting at an outdoor concert, or giant jigsaws ready to be put together by the participants in a teambuilding activity, or merchandise, or data about possible venues or databases of potential customers. The hardware, the software and the data together form part of the inventory of materials that the event manager coordinates.

Machines/equipment

These include communication equipment, catering equipment, mobile seating stands, vehicles, and many other items of hardware.

Human resources

The human resource does not only include the number of people employed on the event, but also their knowledge and skill levels, and the intangibles of dependability and attitude.

The staff does not just include those who are employed, but also agencies who are subcontracted to the event for its duration, and volunteers. In fact, all staff working on the event from its conception to its delivery and breakdown, and all the emergency services, make up the human resource.

Buildings and space

In the event industry it is not only the brick-built venues for events that are essential, but also historic venues, exhibition venues and green-field sites.

Time

Time has to be made available to build an event and see it through right through to its breakdown and evaluation. In the event industry, time may be the most expensive resource and also one of the most constrained.

Information

With today's technology, information would seem to be readily available. The concern of the event manager, however, will be knowing what information is required, and then being able to interpret and use the information so as to achieve the event's operational objectives.

Reflective practice 6.1

List three resources for each of the six following headings (two of which should be tangible and one intangible) that could each be classed as a resource for a Wedding Breakfast and an evening function following a marriage ceremony:

1. The customer
2. Materials
3. Machines/equipment
4. Human resources
5. Buildings and space
6. Time.

Prioritizing resources

The list of resources may appear to be formidable, but generally the list can be reduced or modified to show the most *important* resources for the particular organization we are concerned with. The important resources are those that are most necessary to satisfy the customers' essential requirements, and these may change from one event to another, or indeed from one client to another.

Reflective practice 6.2

For an event organization to launch a new cosmetic product, the four most important resources might well be people, design technology, database of contacts, and space. Certainly stationery, transport and other equipment will be needed, but these may be of less significance. Likewise, you, as the event manager, might see your car as an important resource, but this will have a minor impact on the achievement of customer satisfaction.

Suppose that your event management company has determined that it is valued by its client for:

- Friendly service
- Useful advice on means of evaluating the success of the launch, accurate bookings and response to enquiries
- Courteous service
- Confidentiality
- Competitive prices and 'special' deals.

To achieve customer satisfaction as defined in this manner, you will need a reliable integrated computer system that gives on-line information, communication with relevant groups of people, and confirmation of bookings and tickets. Your company will need sufficient office space to accommodate several staff members, and a good network of reliable and loyal suppliers. Finally, your company will need reliable, well-presented and courteous staff, and well-devised evaluation procedures.

Using the product launch as an example, you can now extend the approach for customer satisfaction to include resource utilization (see Table 6.1):

1. First, create a chart with the customer's CSFs listed in the left-hand column.
2. In subsequent columns, identify those resources that are needed in order to deliver what the customer wants, their current standard of provision, and what should be done in order to improve and effectively deliver these resources.

It can be seen that this technique relates to the work completed earlier when looking critically at gap analysis regarding what the organization is currently achieving against the customer's needs.

Not everything can be done at once, and perhaps only those CSFs with high ratings should be considered.

This serves as an excellent tool when balancing out resource deployment and future costs, or when asking for more finance for a particular event.

Looking at the hypothetical example of the cosmetic product launch described above, let us assume that it has been established that customers rate 'accurate bookings and response to enquiries' as most important. It is upon this aspect that the event manager should then concentrate his or her efforts.

Competitive prices, although important, are a lesser consideration for this particular client, as are special deals.

Having established this rating, the next step is to determine the most vital resources needed to give the customers satisfaction. In this example it is found that accurate

Table 6.1 Identifying resources required to deliver the CSFs

CSFs	Degree of importance 1–5 (5 high)	Resources required	Quality of resource currently available	Action to be taken to improve delivery
Friendly service	4	Trained, customer orientated staff	High, but not sufficient numbers to meet every customer's needs	Deploy more trained staff for this particular event
Evaluation to determine success of launch	5	Clear objectives and evaluation system in place	Excellent, well designed survey instrument used on previous similar events	
Accurate bookings and response to enquiries	5	Database and efficient staff	Good database. Not insufficient phone lines for this number of enquiries	Increase temporary phone lines
Courteous service	4	Trained, customer orientated staff	High, but not sufficient numbers to meet every customer's needs	Deploy more trained staff for this particular event
Confidentiality	4	Secure systems and trained staff	Excellent loyal staff	
Competitive prices	4	Knowledge of competitors' prices, and efficient systems and suppliers	Some up-to-date knowledge	Employ extra temporary staff to research competitors
Special deals	3	Ability to add value	Flexible systems in place	Need to research competitors and what would constitute 'special deal'

bookings and response to enquiries is of paramount importance, alongside a system to evaluate the success of the launch. Hence an integrated computerized information and ticketing system is essential, and a clear survey instrument to measure success of the launch. When the system is 'down' little can be achieved – information on prices, schedules, and availability of seats cannot be provided; nor can bookings be made and tickets and vouchers issued. A back-up 'manual' system consisting of the telephone, bound books of pamphlets, and handwritten tickets can be unwieldy, slow and expensive due to mistakes being made through information not being current and bookings being incorrectly recorded.

Trained staff are important, but of lesser importance than the system, for without the system the staff can do little.

The efficiency factor

The discussion above concerning resource utilization has been from the stance of customer satisfaction.

Traditional production and operation management texts tend to suggest that the prime role of the operations manager is the efficient use of resources in transforming inputs into outputs, and that customer satisfaction is almost a subservient objective. While this might be so for certain types of capital-intensive operations where the customer is not an input into the system, such as a factory where goods can be produced irrespective of whether a customer order is held or not, we have concluded for events that resource utilization is *subservient* to customer satisfaction. That is not to say that efficient use of resources is unimportant; indeed, efficiency is vitally important. However, total efficiency would mean making the optimum use of resources – i.e. elimination of all waste, no spare space, no idle time, minimum of time spent with clients, customer queues so that service staff are fully employed and so on. This is not always possible where a degree of flexibility for customers is essential (see Case study 6.1), and where forecasting demand cannot be a guaranteed statistic (this is considered in further detail in Chapter 13).

Precedence of objectives

Some event organizations will concentrate on customer satisfaction at an affordable and sustainable level as being the overriding objective, and others will focus on

Case study 6.1

Christmas Concert in a cathedral

The concert begins at 19.30 and concludes at 22.00, with a 20-minute interval during which refreshments are served for corporate guests only. The cathedral can hold 700 people, of which 100 are corporate guests. Prior to the start of the concert there is a reception for the corporate guests. There are two choirs, one consisting of twenty singers and one consisting of forty sixth-formers from a local school plus a percussion group of ten.

There are six ladies' toilets and four gentlemen's toilets in the cathedral. These are deemed adequate for the use of the performers and the corporate guests. There is a refreshment area adjacent to the cathedral, which can be used for the corporate guests. As only the corporate guests are receiving refreshments it means staffing levels can be kept to a minimum, as half the total staff are required for the earlier reception for the corporate guests and they can leave once the concert begins. This will leave the others to serve interval drinks only. There is adequate provision of toilets in the adjacent area.

This makes operational sense, but what about the rest of the audience? If refreshments were to be served to them it would require more staff and facilities in order to cope with the numbers who may require refreshments, especially to supply 700 people in 20 minutes. It would require the building of a structure outside the cathedral, as refreshments are not allowed inside, and also the hiring of portable toilets.

Operationally these are extra costs that, on the face of it, are surplus to requirements – especially for just 20 minutes. However, what if this concert takes place in winter and the temperatures are forecast to be near freezing? Cathedrals are immense buildings and difficult to heat. Should the event manager reconsider the position regarding the audience? A hot drink at the interval, whether tea, coffee or a festive beverage, could promote and enhance the feeling of warmth offered by the concert's traditional Christmas repertoire. Event managers have to balance cost versus customer satisfaction, and tangible versus intangible benefits.

Reflective practice 6.3

Consider Case study 6.1.

1. If we believe resource utilization to be subservient to customer satisfaction, then how should the organizers effectively use resources and offer customer satisfaction?
2. List the optimum number and type of resources you would use.
3. If money were no object, list the minimum number you feel could be used.
4. Now compare these lists with colleagues and determine the compromise solution. Be prepared to argue your reasoning.

efficient use of resource utilization ahead of customer satisfaction. This is not to suggest that the organization that is resource-focused ignores customer satisfaction; often resource utilization will be in harmony with customer satisfaction.

For example, aircraft passengers will value getting to their destination (specification) on time and will be prepared to pay a certain price. If the airline meets these criteria (specification, time, and cost) customers will be basically satisfied, and if at the same time the airline has a full aircraft (no empty seats) and keeps its operating costs to a minimum then simultaneously efficient resource utilization and customer satisfaction will have been achieved.

In this airline example it is only when pre-booked passengers are turned away that the customers' objectives come into conflict. Suffice to say that passengers travelling first class, those who have been prepared to pay for extra service, will not be the ones to be offloaded. First-class passengers could well rate the service and all the personal attention that they get as being truly first class. Thus although some passengers will be less than happy – i.e. those who have been offloaded – the airline company could still claim in its mission statement, and in its advertising, to provide world-class service, although the overriding objective is clearly resource utilization.

Case studies 6.2–6.4 illustrate various aspects of the precedence of objectives, and these are considered in the subsequent Reflective practice questions.

Case study 6.2

The Bakewell Show, 4–5 August 2004, Bakewell Showground, Derbyshire

Glorious sunshine and record crowds helped make the 2004 Bakewell Show one of the most successful yet. The 174th Bakewell Show, known fondly as 'The Little Royal', registered a record number of visitors through the gates.

The show attracted around 60 000 people, some from as far away as Australia, New Zealand, South Africa and Uganda, as well as many visitors closer to home, who all enjoyed an action-packed programme of entertainment.

There were more animals on the showground than ever before, with numbers in the sheep classes up considerably and increases in cattle numbers too – a tribute to how the area has recovered from the foot and mouth crisis.

There were more than 6000 entries in 700 competitive classes, and a record number of animals on the showground. The livestock section had 130 classes featuring thousands of animals, including horses, donkeys, pigeons, poultry, rabbits, dogs, goats, cattle and sheep. Trade-stand numbers were boosted to 304 from 250 in 2003.

Centre ring entertainment on the first day saw a stunning medieval display from the Horses Impossible Team, featuring horsemen fresh from making the new King Arthur film. Dressed in colourful costumes, they demonstrated the amazing fighting skills of the period as well as amazing horsemanship.

On Thursday visitors were treated to fast and furious scurry racing, which proved extremely popular when introduced last year.

New, in 2004, were the Suffolks – the oldest breed of heavy horse in Britain, with a blood-line that traces back to 1768. Many of the older visitors were delighted to see the rare breed horses, which were in use on farms when they were children.

During the Show there was a chance for younger visitors to win a state-of-the-art computer in a special competition. The competition involved the children visiting every part of the Showground. The decision to make the children's area three times larger proved very popular.

Other attractions included a spectacular floral art show, scrumptious food and a farming exhibition where visitors could taste fine foods, see vintage vehicles and visit the village green, where traditional rural crafts were demonstrated.

(Printed by kind permission of Bakewell Show; further information can be found at www.bakewellshow.org.)

Case study 6.3

Royal Agricultural Winter Fair, 5–14 November 2004, National Trade Centre, Toronto, Canada

The Royal Agriculture Show (known as The Royal) in Toronto is the largest of its kind in the world, representing the best of Canada's livestock and agricultural produce. The show provides exhibitors with the opportunity to market their products through display and competition to 340 000 visitors from over 60 countries.

International Business Centre

To accommodate 3000 international visitors, The Royal provides hospitality in the International Business Centre, located at the south end of Hall B. This facility provides visitors with a comfortable place to do business, put their feet up, and mingle with other guests. Fax machines, telephones, photocopiers, computers with email access, printers, meeting facilities and complimentary coffee and snacks make doing business at The Royal easy and efficient.

National Holstein Show

The National Holstein Show is the second largest of its kind in North America, attracting more than 5000 enthusiastic spectators from over 60 countries around the world. Visitors line up at the Coliseum as early as 6:00 am to secure the best seats in the house for this exciting show. Exhibitors from across Canada and the United States will showcase more than 350 Holsteins at the day-long competition. Immediately following the Holstein show, the Grand Champions of all the National Dairy Shows – Jersey, Brown Swiss, Ayrshire and Holstein – compete for the title of Supreme Champion.

Three National Beef Cattle Shows

In 2004, The Royal is hosting no less than three National Beef Shows in the first weekend. The best-of-the-best Angus, Hereford and Shorthorn cattle will be crowned Canadian National

Champion under one roof, showcasing to an international audience that Canadian beef is some of the best in the world. Other shows hosted at the 2004 Royal are Salers, Maine-Anjou, Blonde D'Aquitaine, Charolais, Galloway, Highland, and Simmental.

The Royal Auctions

One of the most popular auctions, the Market Beef Cattle Auction, will be held on 6 November 2004 in the Ring of Excellence. Highlighting the top steers and heifers from the Market Livestock Show and the Syngenta Queen's Guineas Show, this auction generates significant earnings for breeders as buyers from restaurants and grocery stores battle it out for the best in beef. Other auctions are the Market Lamb Sale, Ontario Junior Barrow Sale and the Sale of Stars – selling the top Holstein genetics in Canada.

This year marks the 25th anniversary of the Scotia Bank Hays Classic, Canada's premier dairy youth event. This year, 4-Hers from EVERY province will compete for the coveted Grand Champion titles – Grand Champion Showman and Grand Champion Calf. Over 450 youths competed last year, and it's anticipated that an even greater involvement will take place in 2004 with the 25th anniversary celebrations.

Young Speakers for Agriculture will celebrate its 20th anniversary at the 2004 Royal. This year will be the best competition ever, with strong representation from all provinces in Canada. This is a real salute to all Canadian agricultural youth, as last year's competition attracted participants from Alberta, Manitoba, New Brunswick, Nova Scotia, Ontario, Prince Edward Island and Quebec.

Giant Vegetables

One of the most fascinating features of the Horticulture Show is the Giant Vegetable Competition. The 2003 champion pumpkin weighed over 1200 pounds, and last year's giant parsnip will be listed in the 2005 Guinness Book of World Records – weighing in at a whopping 8 pounds, 6 ounces.

(Further information on the Royal Agricultural Winter Fair can be found at www.royalfair.org.)

Case study 6.4

Perth Royal Show, 2–9 October 2004, Claremont Showground, Perth, Western Australia

At The Perth Royal Show there are literally countless things to see and do – all at no extra cost. It is the biggest WA community event, and it profiles agricultural attractions, exciting activities and around the clock entertainment.

The 2004 Show attracted record numbers, with 483 761 people, and had over 2000 volunteers helping to run the event plus 15 000 of the State's finest agricultural exhibits competing in over 42 competitive sections.

There are thousands of special animals and hundreds of exciting performers on show daily, including street theatre, marching band and live performances all around the grounds. All creatures great and small and WA's finest agricultural and domestic animals compete and are on display as part of the show.

For example, there are more than 160 alpacas, 200 cats, 1800 dogs and 120 pigs competing for attention, ribbons and trophies. Last year 16 emu chicks hatched in the Senses Foundation Animal Nursery.

The Swan Draught Sheepdog Arena Trials test the talent of WA's top sheepdogs as they herd three sheep through a series of obstacles into a pen. There is the Farmyard Favourites Petting Zoo, where children and adults have the chance to hold and feed baby rabbits, cuddly lambs, adorable piglets, tiny chicks and cheeky goats. There are more than 1000 pigeons, chooks, ducks, turkeys and water fowl on display at the John O'Meehen Pavilion, and there is the Novelty Calf competition where the calves and their junior handlers get dressed up.

The school holidays can start with a trip to the Perth Royal Show and there children can visit Kiddie Land and have a ride on the merry-go-round, the rockin' tug or the all new 'cup and saucer'. Parents ride for free when they accompany their young children.

Children can discover the magic of the Australian bush through songs and the didgeridoo playing of Wandering in the Bush performer, Greg Hastings.

For older children there is the chance to flip, spin and grind in extreme clinics. Grom sessions offer you the chance to ride with the Planet X Pro's on a purpose-built course. Get the latest tips and tricks from some of the best action sports riders in the country in freestyle BMX and skateboarding. Learn new skills from accredited coaches in a safe and supervised environment in sessions designed for three age groups, 6 to 10 years, 11 to 14 years, and 15 years and over. There is a participation fee of $10, with everyone involved getting a free show bag packed with stickers, magazines and a DVD. All equipment and protective gear is provided. You can register on-line at www.planetx.net.au or on the day.

Everything old is new again. At this year's Perth Royal Show, wedding cakes evocative of the 1950s, smothered in royal icing and generously decorated in gold leaf, will be the star attraction of the cookery competition.

WA cake decorators were invited to enter their 1950s-look wedding cakes in a special class of the popular cookery competition to commemorate 100 years of the Perth Royal Show at the Claremont Showground.

As well as a step back to post-war Australia, visitors will be able to get a taste of early Australian cookery such as Anzac biscuits, jam tarts, lamingtons, marble cake, lemon butter and damper.

This year the cookery competition attracted 540 entries in classes for scones, biscuits, muffins, cream puffs cakes, puddings, chocolates jams, preserves, decorated cakes including fairytale wedding cakes and gingerbread houses.

A special competition for the best decorated Royal Agricultural Society of WA birthday cake will be another highlight of this year's competition. In addition to the agricultural competitions and the animals, the daily events and entertainment, sideshows, thrilling rides and games, there are over 7000 square meters (indoors) of products and services of many businesses, government agencies and charities totalling over 600 commercial displays.

(For general information see www.raswa.org.au. Information supplied by courtesy of the agricultural shows above; edited versions of their websites have been used.)

Reflective practice 6.4

Consider the three agricultural shows described in Case studies 6.2–6.4.

1. What would limit the level of customer service provided, and how would this differ between the different 'Royal' shows?
2. In what aspects would resource utilization be the overriding objective, and when would customer satisfaction have first priority?

Balancing of objectives and the potential conflict

The two basic objectives for an event manager are customer satisfaction and efficient resource utilization. The examples given above show that, having understood the key requirements of the customer, it is then important to attempt a match with the resources available.

It will not always be possible to achieve an absolute balance between what the customer wants and what the organization is able to do. For the events manager, a further restraint will be the objectives of the organization. If the objectives are driven primarily by the need for efficient use of resources, then customer satisfaction will be more difficult to achieve.

As stated previously, given infinite resources any system, no matter how badly managed, might provide adequate service. The truth is that there will not be infinite resources, and often existing resources will not completely mesh with the achievement of total customer satisfaction. The event manager will be expected to achieve adequate use of resources and a reasonable level of customer satisfaction.

Matching customer satisfaction with resource utilization

If the overriding aim is to make the most efficient use of existing resources, it might mean that the service to be offered has to be rethought and re-promoted. Thus the service will be altered to meet the competencies of the organization, rather than extra resources being added to meet a higher-level service.

Before any change to the specified service is contemplated, the event manager should seek improved methods of operating and better ways of doing things using existing resources. Rather than saying 'it cannot be done', the positive approach is to look for ways to make the impossible possible with existing resources.

Company structures

Equally important in the management of resources is the structure of the organization. The successful implementation of an event can be influenced by the degree of decentralization, the way the event is coordinated, and the relative extent of formality and informality (Thompson, 2001).

Centralization relates to the degree to which authority, power and responsibility is devolved through the organization. As more responsibility is delegated, the organization becomes more decentralized.

Coordination of activities affects the way work has been divided up between functions, e.g. marketing, finance and operational, and how it will be managed. This is often shown on charts, and clear delineation allows for clarity of purpose and understanding of everyone's contribution to the final event.

Formality–informality. Formality is often represented by policies and reporting systems, whilst informality is required if managers and other employees are to use their initiative and innovate change (Thompson, 2001).

The organizational structure for an event forms a framework for all of the different activities and services that are to be provided (Shone and Parry, 2004). At any event,

there is a mixture of products and services. For example, when Leeds City Council in the UK organize their summer city-centre celebrations, they combine into one operation:

- Artists, dancers and musicians, from this country or from anywhere around the world
- Sound and lighting systems and other technical services
- Security and stewarding
- Food and beverages where required
- Expertise from the Highways Department
- Police and fire services
- Administration and support services
- Financial services.

However, note also some differences:

- Some of these activities are in full view of the event attendee while other groups of people have very little direct contact with the attendees
- Some of the staff are paid and others are volunteers
- Some of the staff are responsible directly to the event manager and others are employed by agencies or subcontractors.

In many instances, particularly at community festivals, event committees employ an event coordinator for three to four months prior to the Festival, but the other staff may be volunteers working voluntarily on the Festival's committee – i.e. a virtual organization.

Within the event industry there is a great variety of different organizational structures. There is a great deal of past research and commentary on these alternatives, discussed by leading management authors such as Thompson (2001); Johnson and Scholes (2002), and Mullins (2002).

Bowdin *et al.* (2001) apply much of this management theory directly to event management companies. The main finding from Bowdin *et al.* (2001) is that the majority of event organizations have a small number of staff with relatively uncomplicated organizational structures. These authors identify three types of organizational structures:

1. Simple
2. Functional
3. Network.

Large organizations make use of further structures such as task forces/matrix structure, and committees.

Virtual organizations

Most events are of a limited duration. Even though their organizations may have simple entrepreneurial structures, matrices or functional structures, the event itself can be networked or virtual (see Figure 6.2).

Figure 6.2 shows an example of how a virtual organization could work within the events industry. Core activities such as marketing, operations and administration would be managed from within the company. Anecdotally, from within the industry, this could be by one person or several. Accounts and finance, although core and dependent upon the expertise of the company personnel, could be undertaken by an accountant.

The size of the virtual company and the interaction with suppliers will then depend upon the size or number of events. The organization may only employ four people, but during an event it can see its workforce increased many times over as staff are employed on an event-by-event basis. Similarly, contractors are used to provide the services that are not core to the organization, and with the development of these, relationships networks begin.

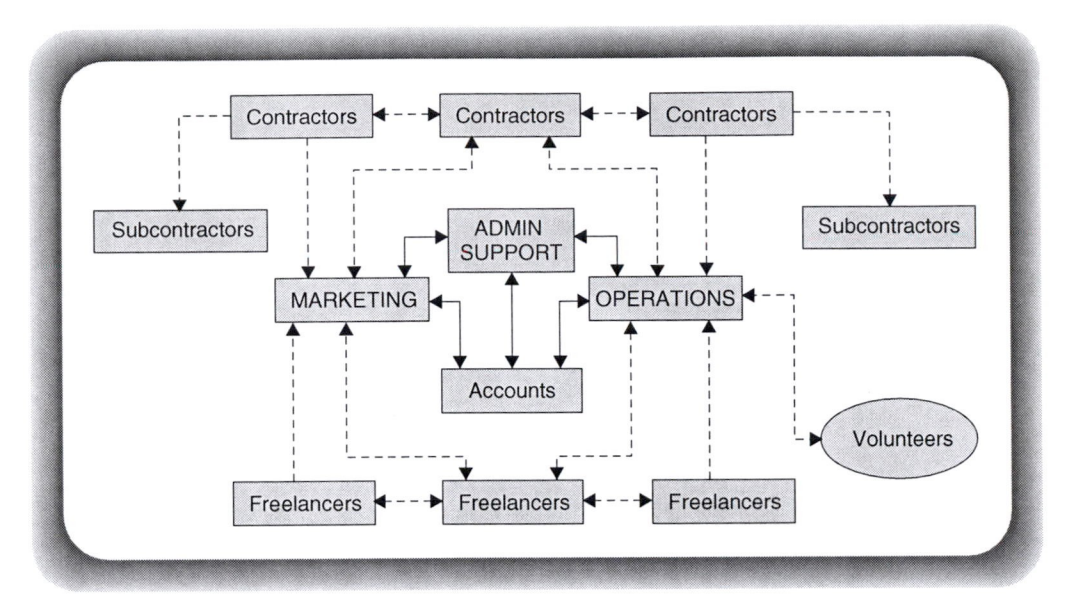

Figure 6.2 A virtual organization

Changes in technology and the ability to communicate fully and quickly have enhanced the effectiveness of virtual organizations.

The need to use specialist suppliers (e.g. caterers, seating and staging, sound and lighting specialists, the artists themselves) has encouraged the growth of small entre-preneurial organizations to use a network of suppliers.

Even with large organizations, such as charities and government, subcontracting and strategic alliances are very favourable.

Campbell *et al.* (2003) describe a virtual organization as being a network of linked businesses that coordinate and integrate their activities so effectively that they give the appearance of a single business organization. This removes the negativity that can be associated with being a 'one-man band', and provides the customer with a turnkey operation.

We would challenge the need to have the appearance of being a single business organization, but would emphasize the need for all suppliers and core organizations to be focused on the end product and service. The consumer is of utmost importance, and consistency with the individual goals and objectives of each and every company, employee and volunteer is required.

The net result is that the event should be flexible and responsive, specialist-driven and cost effective.

The structure shown in Figure 6.2 can have several key advantages:

1. It is more efficient because it has lower costs and greater outputs
2. Specialist firms with current expertise and experience can be contracted in on a needs-only basis
3. There can be clear budgeting with the costs known beforehand
4. It is flexible and relevant to each unique event
5. There is the opportunity for rapid communication and decision-making.

However, Bowdin *et al.* (2001) also identify disadvantages to this type of structure:

1. Quality control may be difficult as contractors provide much of the work
2. The reliability of supply may be compromised

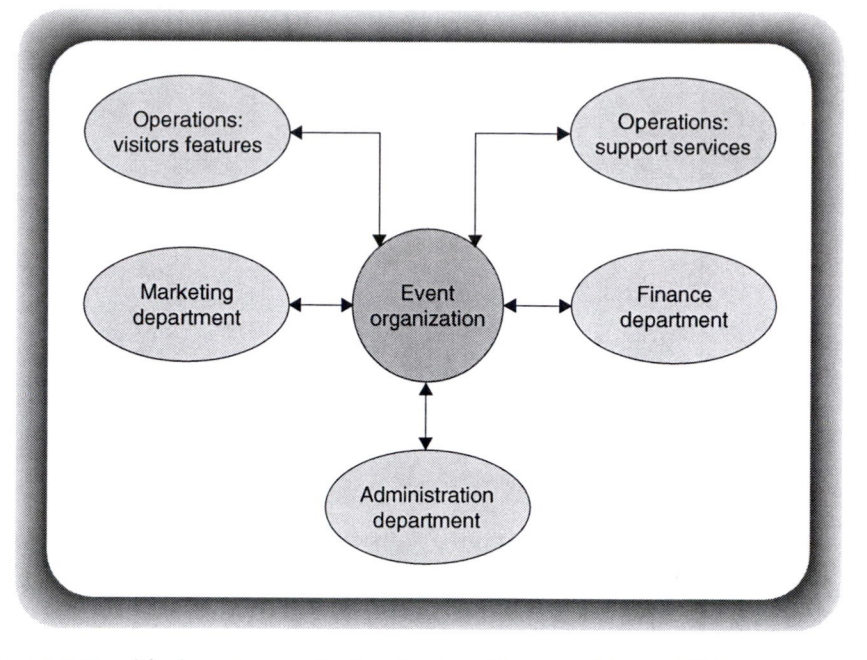

Figure 6.3 Simplified events organization structure (Shone and Parry, 2004)

3. Coordination of suppliers may be difficult
4. Deficiencies in contracts work may result in costly and lengthy legal proceedings.

We will look at the concept of virtual organizations again in Chapter 9, where we discuss in greater depth the advantages that can accrue from developing suppliers as partners.

Shone and Parry (2004) believe that event organizational structures will include five main functions (Figure 6.3):

1. Visitor services operations
2. Support services operations
3. Marketing
4. Administration
5. Finance.

These five functions can be further subdivided depending on the nature and size of the event. In some instances, the same people within one organization may be responsible for more than one function.

Hence it is clear that the many different organizational structures highlighted by Bowdin *et al.* (2001) are particularly varied within the event industry.

These different structures may occur within organizations ranging from a community event such as a town's Scarecrow in the Garden competition, to a Regional Agricultural Show, to a complex political party conference, to the Queen's Golden Jubilee celebrations, to the Olympics.

In each case it is essential that all people who are working together, in whatever capacity, know who is in charge and what is expected of them – i.e. their roles and responsibilities within the organization and the operation of the event.

As Shone and Parry (2004) say, there should be no ambiguity, so that safety and efficiency are not compromised.

You should undertake further reading of work that covers these different styles will help you to gain an appreciation of these different types of structures and their usefulness and impact upon the company which they house.

Chapter summary and key points

This is the last chapter of Section 1, and represents the end of the analysis stage. The chapter has determined that one of the prime objectives of an organization is customer satisfaction through the achievement of a consistent and sustainable level of service. The determinant of the level of service to be provided will be driven by the competition and demands of customers and stakeholders – i.e. by the external environment. To provide the necessary *affordable* level of service, the operations manager is vitally concerned with efficient and effective use of resources. We also noted that resources might be limited in quantity and quality, and therefore the event manager must balance the two, potentially conflicting, objectives of customer satisfaction and efficient resource utilization.

The chapter has also studied different company structures and how these can influence the way in which organizations operate. Conversely, how an organization operates can affect its structure.

Chapters 1–6, form the first stage of the event operations management model and have identified those critical areas that require analysis – i.e. the external and internal environments. The detailed analysis leads to the event manager being able to define the goals of the organization, having taken into account the varying needs of the stakeholders, the customers and the organization itself. The chapters discussed the importance of understanding the critical success factors of the customers and establishing whether their needs could be met from the resources and skills available within the organization. From the analysis, the objectives of the event and also the objectives of the organization should be reassessed to see that the mission is still in line with the overall needs of the organization.

Section 2 considers the detailed planning stage of the event operations management model, taking the analysis further in order to plan the event carefully and methodically. As discussed at the outset, it uses many of the techniques from project planning and operational management literature.

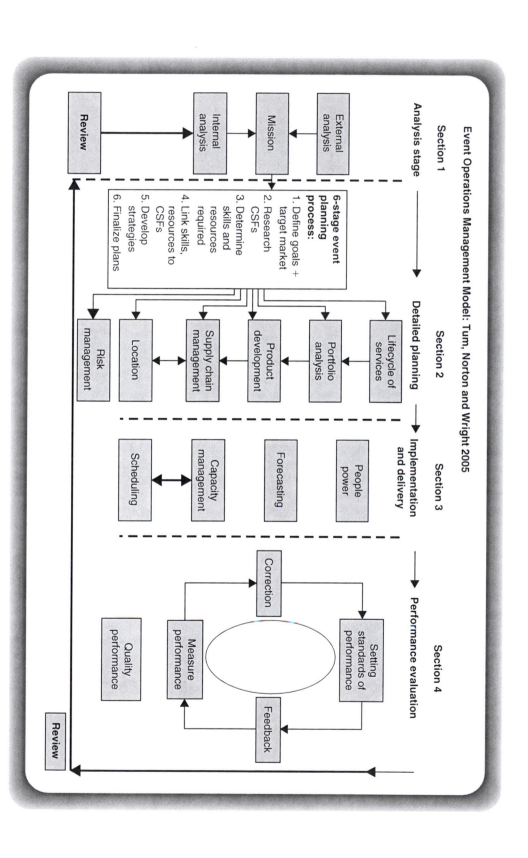

Event Operations Management Model: Tum, Norton and Wright 2005

Section 1 Analysis stage

- External analysis
- Mission
- Internal analysis
- Review

Section 2 Detailed planning

6-stage event planning process:
1. Define goals + target market
2. Research CSFs
3. Determine skills and resources required
4. Link skills, resources to CSFs
5. Develop strategies
6. Finalize plans

- Lifecycle of services
- Portfolio analysis
- Product development
- Supply chain management
- Location
- Risk management

Section 3 Implementation and delivery

- People power
- Forecasting
- Capacity management
- Scheduling

Section 4 Performance evaluation

- Setting standards of performance
- Correction
- Feedback
- Measure performance
- Quality performance

Review

Section Two
Detailed planning

Introduction

The event operations management model was introduced in Chapter 1. The model is continuous, and includes subsidiary cycles within each stage. Section 1 of this book has identified and discussed the external and internal environments that require detailed analysis prior to the formulation of the mission for the organization or the event. This first stage, involving analysis, is imperative in order to understand the environment and situation in which the event is going to be implemented, and for the event manager to assess critically the customers needs and the resources required.

Section 2 is concerned with the second stage of the event operations management model, the detailed planning process that has to be undertaken prior to the implementation of the event. No event can take place without planning. The greater the amount of time taken at this stage, the better the event will be. As plans are made and worked through, many unprepared for eventualities will disappear, and the outcome will be smooth and well organized. Section 2 therefore covers a range of different activities. Some of these could easily have sat within the implementation stage, but it is the authors' view that if plans are made in advance and communicated well, then the event will be effective and efficient in its delivery. All the different elements provided by suppliers and staff, following clear and agreed consultation, will be appropriate for the event, and create a well-executed event in line with the event objectives.

The planning stage of the event operations management model is described throughout the following five chapters. You will see that the work and planning needed is shown in the event operations management model, and is clearly discussed and examined practically within each chapter.

Chapter 7 looks at the importance of planning for the future. This is essential for any event management company so that it can plan the resources required in the coming years, and plan activities and financial requirements so that it can achieve the long-term objectives of the company. The chapter therefore considers the need to plan for the future over long-, medium- and short-term time frames. Consequently, it is important that the work covered in Section 1 has been understood and completed by every event manager in order to use the objectives set and turn them into operational plans. There is much in general operational management literature that can be seen in this chapter, since the six steps of a detailed planning process are introduced. Following this the concept of product life cycles is explored, and why an event manager who is striving for sustainable success should consider market share, market growth and market attractiveness.

Chapter 8 develops the concept of product life cycles, and considers new product development and innovation. This is particularly important, since changes in society, customer needs and expectations have intensified the need for event managers to be creative and to establish new events and new ways of delivering events. Similarly, increasing competition means that event managers are never immune from change and the actions of others. This chapter gives some practical advice on how to analyse and plan for the future. It introduces flow chart symbols and ideas from the general operational management literature that should be of great value to an event manager when putting together an event.

Chapter 9 looks critically at the role and importance of suppliers, and how the purchasing function should be considered strategically. This chapter examines the relationships between suppliers, and the necessity for optimizing the sourcing of all resources. It considers the benefits of vertically integrated companies and the question of outsourcing or making use of resources within the company. In short, the chapter questions how competitive advantage can be achieved and raises the need to assess the use of every resource, including all human resources. The chapter does not end on a strategic note, however, but offers practical guidance on how to purchase resources more effectively and on the importance of having clear specifications.

Chapter 10 considers the location of the business premises. It is important to consider the overall objectives of the company, and hence the business policy, and how these will affect the location. It could be argued that the last section of this chapter, which deals with the layout of an actual event, should be included in Section 3 of this book, which deals with implementation and delivery of the event itself. However, all these aspects are intertwined. The chapter continues to look at aspects of layout and signage, and concludes with a section on health and safety at events, and ergonomics. The latter two aspects are considered here because they could both involve changes to the event layout and efficiency.

Chapter 11 links to the end of Chapter 10, discussing risk and hazard assessment in detail. This is an essential aspect if the event is to run safely and smoothly. There are many techniques from the literature that cover risk assessment, and the main principles and techniques will be covered in this chapter. This provides a very useful guide for event managers, as well as creating an understanding of the importance of aiming to create risk-free events.

Chapter 7

Planning, product portfolios, and product and service development

Learning Objectives

After reading through this chapter you will be able to:

- Understand the need for long-range planning
- Explain the six-stage detailed event-planning process
- Appreciate the development of the product life cycle
- Analyse portfolios using the Boston Consulting Group Matrix (BCG).

Introduction

In this chapter we are concerned with the formulation of a plan and detailed decision-making. These important concepts will be put into the context of the event industry and its peculiarity of having set deadlines from which all planning works backwards. In particular, this chapter creates a six-stage detailed event planning process that can be used by event practitioners. Further work is clarified so that the event manager can understand how the range of different services and events that are offered by the organization should link together to create a harmonious whole, supporting each other.

In order to illustrate this, the life cycle of services and the Boston Consulting Group Matrix (BCG) are introduced. The other aspects of operational management that are shown in the event operations management model are covered in subsequent chapters within Section 2 of the book.

The need for long-range planning

Planning takes place at several levels, and can cover several different timeframes. Thus an organization might have a ten-year plan and a five-year plan, and will certainly have a twelve-month plan – for example, as shown in a budget. There should be a corporate-wide plan, business unit plans, department plans, and at the operations level the event manager will have medium-term,

short-term and daily plans. It can be seen in many event companies that the timescales are different for the larger companies, and their own long-term plans may be only for three years, medium-term plans for between one and two years, and short-term plans taking them to the end of the current year.

The corporate plan is the longer-term plan for the whole organization. It establishes the objectives of the organization, which are made after consideration of external environmental factors and balanced against the internal competencies of the organization. As previously discussed in Chapter 2, in the first stage of the event operations management model the overall thrust of the corporate plan is often articulated in a mission statement. The corporate or business plan, however, requires more than just the few well-chosen words of a mission statement.

Generally the plan will need to be supported by target figures, which will include past trends, broken down into different events and different target markets, and forecasts of future demand. The plan is also likely to include capital equipment budgets, cash flow forecasts, profit and loss forecasts, human resource and training requirements, venue and technology requirements, and so on.

For each twelve-month accounting period, an annual report with financial statements showing actual results should be made available. A budget should be produced for each coming event. The success of the plan and budgets should be compared, and judged against forecasted results.

Many event companies may be working with annual events, or their future events may not be similar to those that they completed in a previous twelve-month period. This provides a challenge to the event manager when predicting the costs and income for a forthcoming event, if these cannot be based on past performance.

Event managers will be concerned with meeting immediate and short-term future demands. However, looking back to what happened last time might well assist in planning for the future. It is therefore important that after each event detailed notes are made about the success, strengths and weaknesses of the event and its planning. Evaluation will be covered in full in Chapter 14.

The cynic would say that each year a great deal of time and effort will go into the business plan, and each year before the plan is issued it will be out of date. Due to the dynamic nature of business, there is a measure of truth in this. Notwithstanding, unless an organization has a long-range plan it will not be possible to develop future goals and appropriate capabilities as conditions change. Changes or additions to the portfolio of activities, location, computer systems, recruitment and training of people etc. cannot happen overnight, but once such decisions have been taken and carried out they cannot be undone in a hurry.

The event manager, pressed with 'real' day-to-day operational problems, may be tempted to avoid involvement in what might be seen as esoteric long-term planning. However, if the event manager is only marginally involved in long-term planning, the business policies with important long-term operational ramifications will be made by strategic planners, accountants and marketing directors. Generally these people will not fully appreciate the time and effort needed to develop a distinctive operational competence for unique events and for a unique client base. Indeed, they might consider that the *real* work has been done in gathering the information and in making the plan, and that implementing the plan is by comparison a straightforward matter. Rather than trying to avoid involvement in long-term planning, the astute event manager will therefore press for inclusion in the planning process. In many of the small event-management companies, the event manager is already a member of the Board. Only by involvement in the long-range planning process can the manager hope to influence future operations and the style of events.

An event management company will need to have established its own goals and objectives, and where it sees itself in over three years time. In many cases the event

management company will have other companies as its clients. In order to satisfy those clients, who in many cases will therefore be its customers, it is important that the event management company understands its clients' goals and objectives as clearly as it understands its own.

The following explanations can apply to an event management company or to a department within a larger organization, and to the myriad of clients that it serves.

The detailed six-stage event-planning process

The six-stage event-planning process consists of the following steps:

1. Define goals and the target market
2. Research critical success factors (CSFs)
3. Determine the skills and resources required
4. Link the skills and resources to the CSFs
5. Develop strategies
6. Finalize plans.

The first step in the planning process is to define the organization's goals and objectives, and to set priorities. This step will be built on the vision (the reason for being of the operation), and can be presented as a mission statement. A series of questions is suggested below to aid planners in asking pertinent questions and in thinking strategically about the business and where it wants to be in the future:

- What sort of company are you?
- Where do you want to be in a few years' time?
- What are your main targets?
- Who or what is the main market?
- What is your main style of event?
- What do your customers value?

It may take some time before the answers to these questions can be answered honestly and clearly. The answers, and the analysis which preceded them, will assist in this first step.

The second step occurs when, having decided on your main market, your main customers and your main style of events, you need to ascertain what it is your customers want. Remember, we looked at this in Chapter 5 during the analysis stage of the event operations management model. Questions include:

- What are the critical success factors that your customers demand?
- What will make you better than the competition?
- What opportunities exist?

The third step is to determine the competencies, skills and resources required to deliver your customers' needs. You would do this by critically auditing your internal strengths and weaknesses. In Chapter 5 we considered the elements of an organization and the linkages between each of the functions within the organization. How can these linkages and relationships be strengthened in order to add strength to your organization?

For example, a winning football team is not just eleven fantastic players working well with the ball, attacking their opponent's goal and defending their own goal. It is

instead a gigantic team of partnerships working well together, being aware of each other and together being so much more than just eleven players. If each player equals one point, then the sum of a well-integrated team on the field should equal at least twenty. This is the theory of synergy, where $2 + 2 = 5$!

The fourth step is to link competences and resources to external forces and situations. As discussed in Chapter 3, this is done by reviewing external influences under the headings of political factors, economic factors, technology, and competition, and by carrying out an internal audit. The results of these analyses should form part of the summary of the organization's SWOT (strengths, weaknesses, opportunities and threats) analysis.

Opportunities and threats are external to the business, and strengths and weakness are internal aspects. Examples of strengths might be financial stability, good networking opportunities, and a good client base and reputation; weaknesses might be lack of skilled staff and a poor cash flow. An opportunity might be an emerging new market, and a threat will surely be new and emerging competition.

Case study 7.1

The Royal Horticultural Society

An objective as articulated in the mission statement for the Royal Horticultural Society might read:

> *to support our members and protect Britain's gardening heritage and help gardeners everywhere.*

From its foundation in 1804, the Royal Horticultural Society has grown to be the world's leading horticultural organization. In order to achieve their aim, one of the Society's objectives could be:

> *to continue its commitment to gardeners through inspirational flower shows, gardens, and over 1000 lectures and demonstrations, and to make sure these are easy to access throughout the UK.*

In order to support this objective, it can be seen that they have four flagship gardens – Wisley in Surrey, Rosemoor in Devon, Hyde Hall in Essex, and Harlow Carr in North Yorkshire.

Using our internal audit from the theory above, these gardens should be classed as one of the Society's major resources. Not only are they superb gardens, but also their added value is that they provide year-round interest and demonstrate the best gardening practices and new techniques.

When we consider internal competences, it can be seen that the RHS has, through networking and strategic alliances, promoted gardening by joining forces with over eighty gardens in the UK and twenty in Europe.

The Society organizes The Chelsea Flower Show and two other garden shows, at Hampton Court Palace and Tatton Park in Cheshire. It collaborates with botanists, entomologists, plant pathologists, plant physiologists, soil scientists and general horticultural advisors to ensure that the best and most up-to-date advice is available for all.

Note the simplicity of this part of their mission statement. There are no grand statements, such as to be the best, to provide excellent service, or that people are our greatest resource and so on.

Note also the brevity of the strategies, and how each is limited to supporting the mission. It could be said that ideally strategy is specific in the abstract, but not specific on detail. By not attempting to provide the specific details, plenty of scope is left for operational contingencies within the broad framework of the general strategy.

(Further information is available at www.rhs.org.uk.)

It is not sufficient merely to list strengths, weaknesses, opportunities and threats. The real purpose is to determine what actions have to be taken to capitalize on the strengths, eliminate the weaknesses, counter threats and to exploit opportunities. Often a threat, if considered in a positive manner, can be turned into an opportunity.

The fifth step is to develop strategies to enable achievement of the business objectives. In simple terms, objectives/goals are *what* we want to do, and strategies are *how* we will do it – i.e. the necessary actions required to make the objectives happen. Case study 7.1 provides an illustration.

The sixth step is when the strategy is finalized, and action plans can then be made. These concern the specific details about the event – for example, how many people are coming, over what time period, and how much space is required?

Implementation of these plans will be discussed in Chapter 14.

Life cycle of services

Now that we have covered the different stages within the six-stage event-planning process, we can turn to other aspects that are essential to support the planning and of which every event manager should be aware. These can be seen within the second stage of the event operations management model. This chapter investigates the life cycle of services and the Boston Consulting Group Matrix (BCG); the other aspects are covered in subsequent chapters within Section 2 of the book.

Service products have definite life cycles (see Figure 7.1). In some regards this is no different to our own mortality. Human beings have a finite life, and so do products and services.

As illustrated in Figure 7.1, the stages of the life cycle are:

- *Development* of a new idea. This stage requires research and market testing; no income is received and costs (often substantial) are incurred.
- *Launch* of a new service. This stage can include heavy marketing costs and small initial returns. Entry into the market is often risky, and may be accompanied by pilot stages. However, in events it is very difficult to pilot new ideas – ideas are needed in full by the client.
- *Growth*. This is marked by rapid market acceptance and increasing profits. Also, competitors typically will copy or develop new market segments in order to avoid direct competition (Evans *et al.*, 2003). This is an important time to win market share.

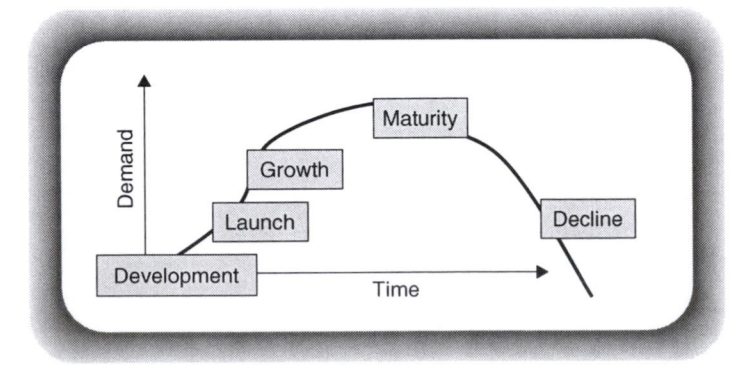

Figure 7.1 Life cycle of events

- *Maturity*. At maturity, income stabilizes as growth levels off. This stage can range from days or weeks to many decades. It is less likely within the event industry that the timescale will be so long. The positive cash flows should be reinvested in new products to replace the mature ones that are leaving the marketplace.
- *Decline*. During decline, sales fall and eventually the service is phased out or updated and the cycle begins again. Organizations should be ready with new products, or have strategies to extend the life cycle if this is felt to be feasible.

Case study 7.2 reports on the progress of the Badminton Horse Trials.

Case study 7.2

The Mitsubishi Motors Badminton Horse Trials, 4–8 May 2005, South Gloucestershire, England

The Mitsubishi Motors Badminton Horse Trials are generally regarded as the World's premier three-day event. Held every year since 1949 in the beautiful parkland of the Duke of Beaufort, the event always attracts the majority of the leading horses and riders in the world.

The number of spectators is close to 200 000, while the tented village contains 275 trade stands.

The first phase of the event, dressage, is split between the first two days, Thursday and Friday. Saturday sees the spectacular cross country test – the horses covering over ten miles before they tackle the four-and-a-half mile course of obstacles around the park. Action is continuous, with a horse starting every three to four minutes. Finally, on Sunday, comes the climax, which is a normal set of show jumps – but after the cross country, clearing them is not easy.

(Information supplied by Langston Scott Ltd; for more information on hospitality at the Mitsubishi Badminton Horse Trials see www.langstonscott.com.)

The following report was written in 2003:

Mitsubishi Motors Badminton Horse Trials to build on last year's new-look success

A revamped Badminton in 2002 drew record crowds, after the year lost to foot and mouth disease in 2001. The course was re-jigged using the traditional pathway, but starting in the main arena. This has encouraged event Director Hugh Thomas to introduce more innovations. 2002 also saw the introduction of the Badminton Club, which is located by the arena and allows members to relax ringside and see the action unfold on all four days of the competition. The stature of the world's premier three-day event is likely to be further enhanced by the recently announced change of the Olympic competition to one-day event status. Badminton will continue to provide a major target for the world's leading riders.

The Box Office opened on 6 January 2003 and, as ever, attracted business immediately. The enhanced on-line booking service from the website is likely to prove popular as the best way of booking. (www.badminton-horse.co.uk).

In an attempt to speed up entry into the park, a new ticketing policy has been introduced for day sales. Forward car parks will now only be available for advanced sales.

Due to popular demand, and a jump in radio earphone technology, Radio Badminton makes a comeback with a new team, and should add another dimension to the enjoyment of all enthusiasts.

(Information supplied by www.badminton-horse.co.uk.)

The final report was written in 2004:

Badminton to stick to present format

The organizers of the Mitsubishi Motors Badminton Horse Trials announced today that the event would not change its format for future events.

Event Director Hugh Thomas commented:

When the International Equestrian Federation decided to drop the Steeplechase and Roads & Tracks from the cross country day for the Olympics on the grounds of cost, we supported the change. We also recognize that the slightly less taxing form of the sport may well be appropriate when it is necessary to generate the widest possible international participation. However, we have always believed that the 'full' sport provides a greater all-round test of horse and rider, and we were very disappointed when the Federation also dropped these phases for its own World Equestrian Games.

We have consulted very widely about the future, and it is clear that the vast majority of participants in the sport want us to continue to offer the ultimate challenge. Badminton was founded to prepare horses and riders for the rigours of the Olympic Games, and since then it has evolved into the world's premier three-day event and we intend to ensure that riding at and eventually winning Badminton remains the great aspiration for all youngsters entering the sport.

To compete for the Mitsubishi Motors Trophy is of course an exclusive privilege that has to be earned by excellent performance; but we know from the number of 'first timers' in recent events that new, young talent can indeed come to the fore at Badminton – if you are good enough, you can compete. Equally, the Roll of Honour includes the very best horses and riders of each generation, acknowledged to be so partly because of their success here.

We are consulting with our colleagues at Lexington and Burghley as to how we might widen and deepen the links between these top 'four-star' events, building on the success of the Rolex Grand Slam, won by Pippa Funnell in 2003. Possibilities such as a 'Masters' or 'Super League' series will be explored, so that the top riders are well rewarded for success at the top events.

Our sport has evolved over many years, and we at Badminton have no desire to stay rooted in the past. We will remain flexible to meet challenges from whatever quarter, including the British weather.

(Information kindly provided by the Press Office; further information about the Mitsubishi Badminton Horse Trials can be found at www.badminton-horse.co.uk.)

Reflective practice 7.1

Consider Case study 7.2.

1. What challenges does Badminton face at this stage in its growth?
2. What would you consider the stage to be?
3. What external influences could have an impact on the life cycle of Badminton Horse Trials?

Management actions

Each stage of the life cycle will require different actions and decisions.

The development stage will require operations to be involved in determining feasibility, acquiring necessary resources, training people and establishing a standard procedure.

The launch stage will need the ability of operations to service fast-growing demand, and to be able to handle novel and unexpected problems. Procedures might have to be modified and people retrained to act in a standard fashion.

In the growth stage, operations will likely be challenged by fluctuating and uncertain demands.

By the time the maturity stage is reached, standard procedures should be in place and people will know instinctively how to react to problems; in short, stability should have been achieved. This is the stage when there should be time to look for improvements

to the service and to improve efficiency. Unfortunately, when the pressure is off, sales are good and objectives are being comfortably achieved, the temptation will *be not* to look for changes, and complacency sets in. Nonetheless there will always be room for improvements, and ideally the culture of the organization will be to seek to make incremental improvements.

The decline stage will bring another set of problems; either changes of a decisive nature will have to be made to the service to arrest the decline, or an entirely new service will have to be developed.

Kotler (1991) identified four implications arising from the product life cycle:

1. Products and services have a limited life
2. The different stages pose different challenges to the professional
3. Profits rise and fall at different stages of the life cycle
4. Products and services require different marketing, operations, purchasing and personnel strategies in each stage of the life cycle.

Slack (1998) points out that this last point implies that the operations manager will have to set new objectives as the product or service ages in its market.

Case study 7.3 describes the development of the Notting Hill Carnival.

Case study 7.3

The Notting Hill Carnival, London, England

The Notting Hill Carnival, held annually in August, actually began in St Pancras in 1964 and moved around until it found its home in Notting Hill. The Carnival's roots date back to the Abolition of Slavery Act in 1833, when the first Caribbean carnival was held in Trinidad and black Caribbeans took to the streets for their own carnival party, with song, dance and costumes.

Over the next century, carnival developed into a strong Caribbean tradition, particularly in Trinidad, where the five disciplines of carnival were established.

This great festival in Notting Hill began initially from the energies of black immigrants from the Caribbean, in particular from Trinidad, where the Carnival tradition is very strong, and from people living locally, who dreamed of creating a festival to bring together the people of Notting Hill, most of whom were facing racism, lack of working opportunities and poor housing conditions, resulting in generally low self-esteem.

There had been racial tensions in the late 1950s, and black people were subjected to constant pressures. Dances were organized in halls in North London, where black people could come together freely. At the same time, Trinidadians who had immigrated to this country were playing steel band music each Sunday at the Colherene Pub in Earls Court. From this evolved the idea of inviting the steel band to take part in a street festival in Notting Hill, to encourage people, mainly children, both black and white, to come onto the streets and express themselves socially as well as artistically. This first Carnival took place in 1964 in St Pancras Town Hall, organized by *West Indian Gazette* editor, Claudia Jones. As other West Indian immigrants and white locals joined the festivities year on year, the carnival grew to its current huge proportions.

In recent years the Notting Hill Carnival has grown and grown, reflecting the multicultural nature of our society, with participants from Afghanistan, Kurdistan, Bangladesh, the Philippines, Bulgaria, Russia, Brazil and many other places as well as from all parts of the Caribbean, Africa, Central and South America and the United Kingdom. The Notting Hill Carnival operates an all-inclusive policy, encouraging artists to celebrate their cultural traditions through the art, dance and music media with which they feel most comfortable.

In addition to the procession of costumes, soca and steel bands which wend their way over a route of some three miles, the area plays host to 45 licensed Static Sound Systems, each playing its own selection of soca, reggae, jazz, soul, hip-hop and funk music, house, and garage. This is the aspect of the Carnival that appeals to young people and is evolving at an unpredictable pace with innovative styles and forms of music.

There are hundreds of licensed street stalls selling exotic foods from all corners of the globe, as well as arts and crafts. The Carnival aims to celebrate the cultural heritage of its founders and at the same time be open enough to take on board evolving contemporary culture with its multiracial, multicultural trends.

In addition to the traditional aspects of the Carnival, there are also three live stages within the Carnival area, featuring local bands, top international artistes, and music from all around the world. These stages play from 12 noon to 7 pm on each of the two days. Artistes that have appeared at these stages have included Eddie Grant, the Mighty Sparrow, Arrow, Freddie McGregor, Burning Spear, Jamiroquai, Wyclef Jean, Amaponda and Courtney Pine, amongst others.

For many people, the Notting Hill Carnival has become a celebration and reflection of London's uniquely multicultural make-up. But what of the next 40 years?

Any talk of improving the event usually centres on two things – a change in route, and economics. In 2003, the Carnival suffered the disappointment of a reduced attendance compared to previous years. As a result, it lost its status as Europe's biggest street party to the Zurich Street Parade.

Recent attendance figures are as follows:

2003	600 000
2002	1.4 m
2001	1.25 m
2000	1.5 m
1999	1.4 m
1998	1.15 m
1997	1.3 m
1996	1 m

The 2004 Notting Hill Carnival celebrated its 40th anniversary under the theme 'Freedom and Justice'. Because the safety and enjoyment of everyone at the Carnival was paramount, they decided not to focus on increasing the number of activities; instead a longer programme of events was planned that started in April 2004 and ran through until December. This included the World Steel Band Music Festival in October 2004, which featured steel bands from Europe, the Caribbean, North America, Grenada, Antigua and, of course, Trinidad – the birthplace of the steel band.

The long-term vision for the Carnival has to be its continued development and growth – not in terms of the numbers attending the event but in the development of commercial and professional opportunities for bands, individuals and the company; and the integration of Carnival arts into mainstream education.

The long-term aim of London Notting Hill Carnival Ltd (LNHCL) is:

to attract the level of sponsorship for the Notting Hill Carnival that is commensurate with the income that it generates, and which is in line with the level of sponsorship for other national events, without compromising its integrity.

(Debbie Gardner)

According to a report by the London Development Agency (LDA), the Carnival creates £93 m for London. Figures from the LDA show that the event supports 3000 full-time jobs. Many feel that the best way of maximizing the benefits of the Carnival would be to change the route. The

narrow streets of Notting Hill provide a cramped – and according to London's mayor, dangerous – environment for the million or so revellers.

Although the roots of carnival are Trinidadian, the Notting Hill Carnival is a British event. This is something that should be celebrated, as it is what makes the event unique.

(Information supplied from www.mynottinghill.co.uk and from BBC News at bbcnews. co.uk.)

Reflective practice 7.2

Regarding Case study 7.3:

1. How has the Notting Hill Carnival developed over the past forty years?
2. What stage of the life cycle do you think the Carnival has reached?
3. If the Carnival were in decline, what steps could the organizers take to change this?

Criticisms of the product life cycle

Evans *et al.* (2003) point out that it is difficult to forecast the future, and to pinpoint accurately where a product or service will leave one stage of the product life cycle and enter the next. However it could be said that *not* to try to forecast and *not* to anticipate changes in the external environment and actions by your competitors is dangerous practice.

Managers should be careful not to over-anticipate decline and believe that it is happening when the reality may be somewhat different. If management assumes that decline will come, come what may, then decisions may be made to reduce investment, and so decline will come sooner than it might have done.

The Boston Consulting Group matrix

The product life cycle can be clearly linked to the Boston Consulting Group matrix. This offers a way of examining a company's portfolio of products. In the event industry there may be a flourishing company that specializes in student club nights, twenty-first birthday party events, hen parties and club tours. Some of these events may be in different capital cities throughout the UK, and the same company may also have links to different student unions and take bookings direct from them. Each of these different 'products' and different major clients forms part of the company's portfolio.

A broad portfolio signifies that an organization has a wide range of products and market sectors (Evans *et al.*, 2003), and conversely a narrow portfolio implies that a company only operates in a few or even one product or sector. The narrower the portfolio the more emphasis can be put on that product, but it can also be more vulnerable to a turndown in demand, or exploitation by a competitor or supplier.

The Boston Consulting Group (BCG) matrix (Figure 7.2) simplifies the analysis of the range of products or services within a company's portfolio. There are two axes on

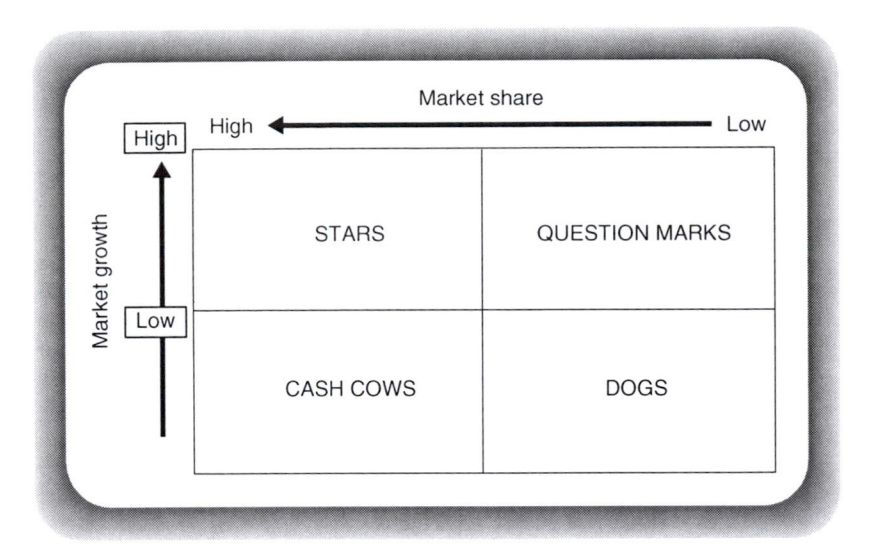

Figure 7.2 The Boston Consulting Group matrix

the matrix; the vertical axis denotes rate of market growth, which indicates the potential and attractiveness of the market, and the horizontal axis is an indicator of the strength of the competitive position of the product – i.e. its market share.

Using the BCG matrix

The BCG matrix divides products into cash cows, dogs, stars and question marks.

Cash cows
'Cash cows' are products with a high market share in a low-growth market. They are normally profitable and generate cash – i.e. they can be milked. Like living cows, however, they should not be neglected. Since the market is low growth, customers are able to change their loyalties, and competitors may be able to move swiftly. The products or services in this part of the matrix should be watched closely. Used wisely, the profits from cash cows can be used to support new ideas and rising stars.

You can see that there is a similarity between cash cows and those products and services, which have reached maturity on the product life cycle.

Dogs
'Dogs' are products that have a low market share in a low-growth market. They are typically not very profitable, but beware – some dogs are essential to your cash cows, so don't throw them away without thinking. It may be expensive to cultivate the market to create market growth, but perhaps a niche market could be found. Generally, dogs are associated with only a small positive cash flow or indeed a negative cash flow.

You can see that there is a similarity between dogs and those products and services that are in decline in the product life cycle.

Stars
'Stars' have a high share in a rapidly growing market. They could be absorbing large amounts of cash, but may be highly profitable. It is often necessary to spend heavily on

advertising, but in the end stars may become cash cows. If market share is lost, they may become dogs when the market ultimately stops growing – so they need to be watched.

You can see that there is a similarity between stars and those products and services that are in the growth stage of the product life cycle.

Question marks

Some texts refer to these as problem children. Question marks create a dilemma for the company manager. They have a foothold in the market, but if market share cannot be improved they will become dogs. Resources need to be channelled to them to improve market share. These products, services or a particular event should be questioned.

You can see that there is a similarity between question marks and those products and services that are in the growth or indeed the decline stage of the product life cycle. They use cash, and at this stage do not generate high returns.

Chapter summary and key points

In this chapter the need to plan has been discussed. In simple terms, planning is forward looking and considers what we want to do, how we will do it, and when we will do it. However, planning is both forward looking and backward looking. The wise planner looks back to see what happened, what went right and what went wrong for similar events. The planner then attempts to forecast what will happen and what might happen, based on past experience, knowledge of the current external environment, an understanding of the relative strengths and weaknesses of the organization (internal environment), and taking into account changes that are likely to happen in the external and internal environments. The cynic will say that a plan is out of date as soon as it is made, but without planning, chaos is likely. Plans need to be reasonably detailed, but those carrying out the plans must be allowed a degree of flexibility.

We have shown that planning is linked to the product life cycle and that different stages of the life cycle require different management actions.

Chapter 8
Product development

Learning Objectives

After reading through this chapter you will be able to:

- **Appreciate product development and innovation**
- **Use Ansoff's growth matrix to assist in the creation of new ideas**
- **Understand the simultaneous development of new events**
- **Apply the design process to events and use flow charts.**

Introduction

Chapter 7 introduced the first part of the detailed planning stage. In that chapter we discussed the positioning of different products both on the product life cycle and within a company's portfolio. It is now important to see how event managers can develop products. This aspect is covered within the second stage of the event operations management model.

Changes in society, markets, economies and society have led to a shortening of the product life cycle, and it has intensified the need for organizations to innovate in terms of the products they offer (Evans *et al.*, 2003). Similarly, increasing competition has made innovation a necessity, and event managers must always be aware that they are not able to sit still, believing that they are on the right track and therefore immune from competition and change – you must always be looking over your shoulder, or you will get knocked over by the next passing train!

In today's fast-moving market, event managers have to be able to react quickly to marketplace changes. Time is at a premium in gaining the initiative over the competition with a new service, or in catching up and reacting to a new service offered by a competitor. Customers are fickle, and once lost are hard to regain.

New products and services

New products and services and ideas for different events can be achieved by:

- Repackaging – i.e. promoting in a different manner
- Making minor modifications to existing products and service
- Introducing completely new products/events
- Reaching new markets.

For example, outdoor adventure tours (white-water rafting etc.), once designed for young backpackers, might now be toned down (safer water) and repackaged as 'grey power' adventure experiences for the older market.

Other initiatives might mean the same basic service but with extra benefits, a reduced price, or at a different time. Whenever changes are being contemplated, the events manager needs to be in a position to make suggestions and to be involved in the final decision.

Innovation

Some event organizations will position themselves as market leaders; this can be a high-risk strategy, as time and money will be required to develop and set up the infrastructure needed. On the other hand, being first in the market can reap large benefits.

Other organizations will seek to imitate the innovations of others, and will attempt to join in the initial growth phase of a new service.

Still others will join in with adaptations before the market becomes saturated with suppliers, or will endeavour to find a specialized niche market. Others will add nothing new, but will rely on size and efficiency to enter the market at lower prices.

Ansoff's matrix

Ansoff (1987) developed a matrix which highlights the choices managers can make when designing new products and services. The matrix, shown in Figure 8.1, shows potential areas where a company can extend. There are four broad alternatives:

1. Market penetration – increasing market share in existing markets utilizing the same existing products/services
2. Market development – entering new markets but still using the same existing products/services
3. Product development – developing new products/services to serve existing markets
4. Diversification – developing new products to serve new markets.

There are risks with all new developments. It is a risk as to whether the event that has been planned is going to be well received and successful. The risks are smallest when development is largely based upon existing products and services, and takes place in existing markets (Campbell *et al.*, 2003). The risks are greater the further an event

		Products	
		Existing	New
Markets	Existing	Market penetration	Product development
	New	Market development	Diversification

Figure 8.1 Ansoff's Growth Matrix

organization moves away from its existing markets and products, and the more it develops new ideas and events. This entry into new ventures should depend upon the event manager assessing what opportunities present themselves, the likelihood of success, and how well the proposed event matches the core competences and skills of the organization, their past experiences and existing resources.

Simultaneous development

Simultaneous development of a new product, service or event is where the process of development is expedited by integrating each stage of the development using multifunctional teams rather than having each function working individually in sequence stage by stage. Multifunctional project teams can be set up to design and develop a new event. In this manner, strong two-way communication is fostered. Because event operations are reliant on customers as input for the event to happen, the design of a new service will mainly involve the process by which it will be delivered.

It is difficult in event management to produce a prototype 'product', although a new approach can be tested in a small, localized market. As customers must be involved, a flow process chart can be a useful tool for development and comparison of alternatives. The flow process chart will show in detail all the processes through which the customer will pass. However, for many events the customer will never come into contact with the back office activities, such as exist for a horticulture show, a football match or a banquet. Nonetheless, such activities are essential to the provision of the event, and it is crucial that these areas, and the suppliers to the system, are not ignored when considering the feasibility of providing the event. Therefore the flow process chart will need to cover the value chain from supplier to customer, and should consider the time taken for each activity. Examples of flow process charting are provided later in this chapter.

The design process

The design process for a new event, or for the development of a variation to an existing ongoing repeated event (such as weekly football matches), has six distinct phases:

1. The idea – the initial thought
2. The concept – determination of a need and the start of creating a package
3. Systematic and rapid screening of various alternatives
4. Development of the new approach and preliminary design
5. Testing the new approach or offering
6. Launching on a commercial scale.

The idea

Ideas for new products or services, and concepts or new ways of delivering an event, can come from a variety of external and internal sources.

Slack *et al.* (2004) have identified external sources as being customers and competitors, and internal sources as being staff who are in contact with the customers, and the research and development department (see Figure 8.2).

Internal sources

1. *Staff*. People who work within an event organization can be rich in ideas regarding what is possible in the future. Similarly, those who are in contact with customers glean a lot of information, both informally in conversations and formally in focus groups, or

through letters of complaint and thanks. Sometimes your staff may have worked for one of your suppliers in the past, or indeed have worked for one of your competitors. Staff have both a very good general and specific idea of what customers like and dislike. They may have gathered ideas from other people, or they may make suggestions based on their own observations. All the time you need to find out what your customer rates as being the key success factors and then create ideas as to how you can close the gap between what you do provide and what the customer wants. Use your staff for ideas and do not just rely on your own intuition.

2. *Research and development.* Research is a function that might be formally set up within the event organization, or just assigned to certain people for short periods of time. Research involves discovering and developing new knowledge in order to solve a problem. Development is the means of putting that new knowledge into practice. Research may centre on different forms of creating and delivering the event to see if, by harnessing different ideas, new opportunities may present themselves. This may involve different technologies, or just carrying out activities in a slightly different way – perhaps by being open to ideas and trying them out. For example, using on-line

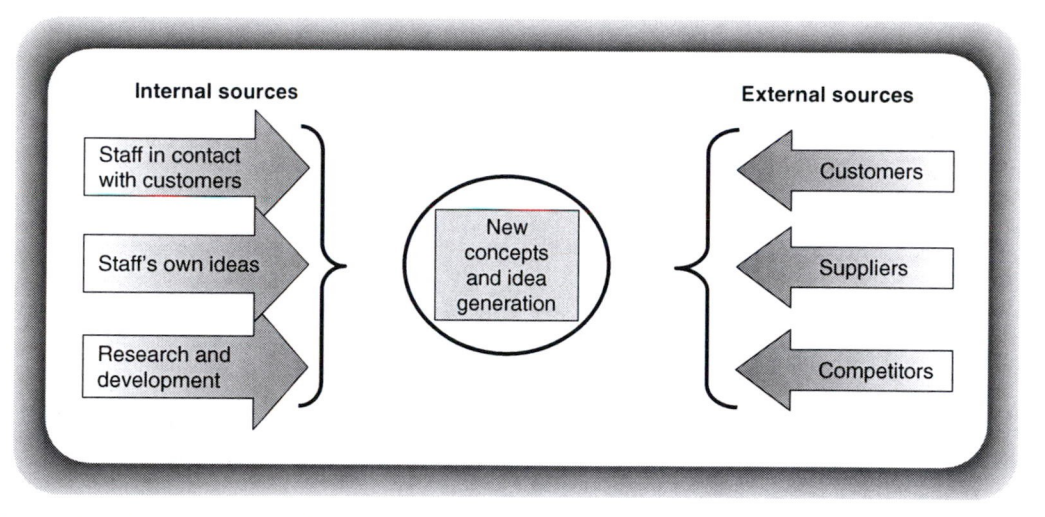

Figure 8.2 Influences on the design of an event

Case study 8.1

Royal Ascot, 15–19 June 2004, Ascot Racecourse, Berkshire, England

Wi-Fi facilities were introduced at Royal Ascot in 2004.

Although Ascot Racecourse was being demolished in 2004 to be replaced by a new state-of-the-art racing venue, new Wi-Fi facilities were installed for the media in the two pressrooms. This enabled the photographers and reporters to download pictures and copy instantly to their editors from anywhere within these areas, and was seen by the media as an important improvement. It was especially useful because of the huge national and international interest from the public and the media who attend Royal Ascot Week.

(Information printed by courtesy of Royal Ascot; for more information see www.ascot.co.uk.)

Reflective practice 8.1

Regarding Case study 8.1:

1. What benefits, apart from the obvious increased transmission speeds, do Wi-Fi offer the media?
2. How does the use of technology enhance the competitive edge of Royal Ascot?

booking rather than selling tickets at a box office led to a Rod Stewart concert in New Zealand being sold out in half an hour. Case study 8.1 provides another example. Ideas may come from different industries, and those concepts transferred to the problem under investigation.

External sources

1. *Customers.* Marketing is responsible for keeping an ear to the ground in order to identify new opportunities and possible services that would be appropriate. However, event managers should not just rely on this source. There are many ways to gather intelligence, some formal and some informal – for example, newspaper reports, journal articles, popular TV shows, information commercials, chat in the clubhouse after golf etc. The message is that all event managers should listen to ideas, hold focus groups, use systematic analysis and discussion, and look carefully at both complaints and suggestions. Above all, they should be aware of what the competition is doing, or successes other organizations have had in related areas and sometimes not closely related areas. For example, Henry Ford developed the conveyor belt approach to assembling cars after visiting an abattoir and seeing animals being disassembled on a moving production line.
2. *Suppliers.* In the events industry we use many different suppliers and partnerships with other specialists. They may have come across different situations and different remedies, and often their ideas will be helpful to both you and the supplier and, eventually, to your customers.
3. *Competitors.* You may have the choice of following the actions of your competitors or coming up with a similar idea but using some new approaches. You are aiming to take the lead and be innovative, but you may be able to learn from your competitors' mistakes or achievements.

Ideas are not the same as concepts. Ideas get transformed into concepts so that they can be evaluated and put into operation by the organization (Slack *et al.*, 2004).

Concepts

Concepts are different from ideas in that they have clear statements and can state the overall form, function and purpose. The concept should be easy for the event manager to communicate to all of the different stakeholders (see Figure 8.3).

In Figure 8.3, the concept has started to give meaning and shape to the event. In particular it has defined its duration, purpose, facilities available, target market and some perspective of price and costs. Spin-off opportunities could include refreshments and merchandising. A sponsor might be a soft drinks company.

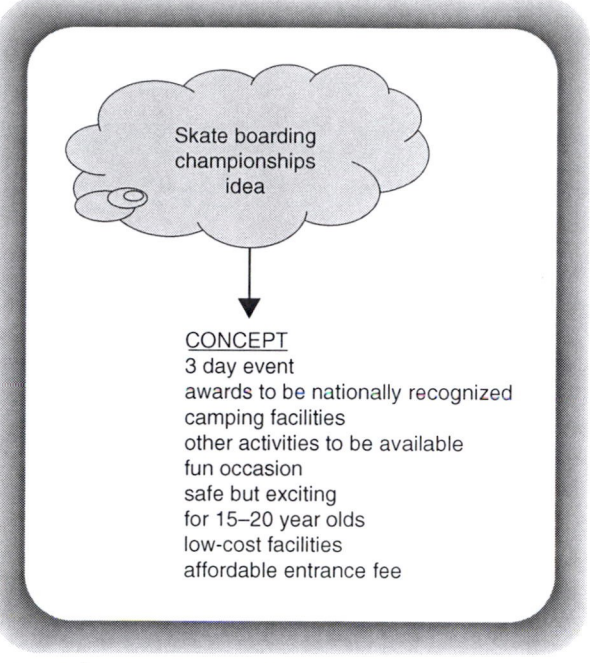

Figure 8.3 Ideas are not the same as concepts

Systematic and rapid screening of various alternatives

Not all the concepts generated will be appropriate or capable of being taken further. The event manager will have to be selective and screen which concept to progress. Slack *et al.* (2004) offer several different screening processes that could be used in order to appraise the suggested concept systematically. There may be other screens more appropriate for different event companies in different situations, but Slack *et al.*'s are offered here.

1. *Marketing screen.* The event manager must ask certain questions and answer them honestly:
   - Will this new approach work in the current market?
   - Is it very similar to other competing products?
   - Is it too different from other competing products?
   - Is there sufficient demand to make it worthwhile?
   - Does it fit with existing marketing policy?
2. *Operations screen.* The operations manager, or the event manager, should judge whether the new concept is feasible and whether it can be achieved:
   - Are sufficient quantities of the right resources available?
   - Is there sufficient space capacity?
   - Are the skills in the staff currently employed relevant and appropriate?
   - What technology is necessary?
   - What is the expected cost?
3. *Finance screen.* The finance department needs to calculate the financial implications of the new ideas. If there is no finance department the event manager will probably have to work out the associated costs, such as:
   - Capital costs
   - Operating costs

- Profit margins
- Likely payback rate.

This set of questions, offered by Slack *et al.* (2004), is very useful for the event manager, but it may also be necessary to consider more pertinent issues that should be added to the above lists. Each company is different, and each situation has its own issues, limitations and opportunities.

Development of the new approach and preliminary design

Having generated an event that is acceptable to the various functions within the company, it is now necessary to specify all the components parts and service required, and to define how the event will be created and delivered.

Take, for example, for a two-day outdoor teambuilding weekend. Each activity will require certain materials. One activity could be eight people making a square from a long rope whilst blindfolded. The materials needed would be:

- A bag containing eight blindfolds
- 60 metres of rope
- Instructions for the exercise
- A stopwatch.

Other activities will require their own lists of equipment, materials and skilled personnel. Gradually all the materials required for the whole of the two-day event, including all food and accommodation, will be listed. This is sometimes called the Bill of Materials (BOM).

Once the BOM has defined all that is required for the event, the next stage is to specify how the days will run. How will all the processes be put together to create the final event?

Different flow charts showing all the people and information 'flowing through' the event can be used. All the activities that take place can be listed and how they fit together shown. Imagine doing this for the Olympics!

All the flow charts are useful for event managers. They show, in a diagrammatic form, the shape of the event and the sequence of activities that will take place. This is useful in three respects:

1. It makes the operations manager think through all that is intended to happen
2. It acts as a communication tool for all the other personnel and suppliers who are involved
3. It identifies any bottlenecks or possible problems.

Slack *et al.* (2004) have identified several different flow charts: We will discuss the following as being relevant to the event industry:

- Simple flow charts
- Flow process charts
- Customer processing charts.

Simple flow charts

Simple flow charts identify the main elements of the event. They may also show the key decisions that need to be taken, and the implications of these decisions. They can be used for a set-up procedure for all the shell stands at an exhibition, or they can be used to track a data inputting system for registration at a Charity Gala Dinner where clients may sponsor whole or part tables.

Flow process charts

This type of chart not only shows the flow of work and activities undertaken, but also uses symbols to identify the different types of activities (Figure 8.4). They can therefore be more detailed. You can see the use of the symbols in flow process chart in Figure 8.5.

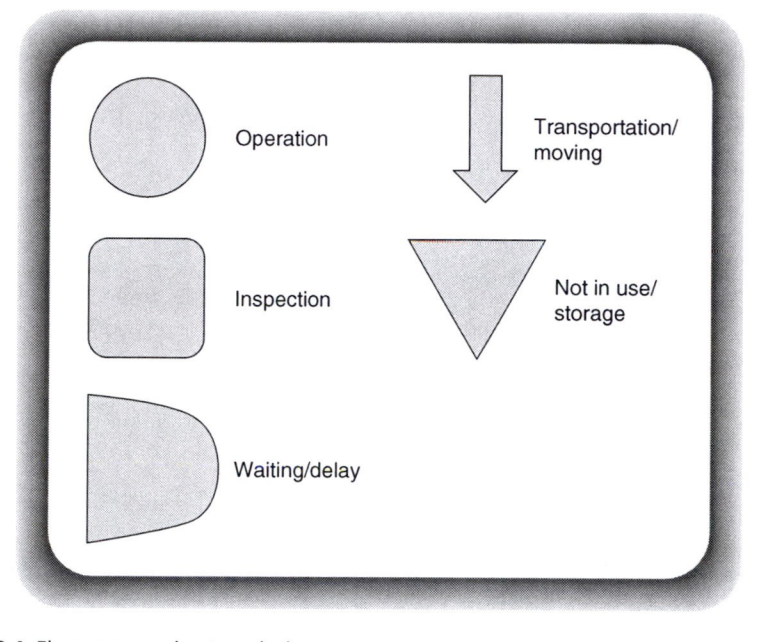

Figure 8.4 Flow process chart symbols

Case study 8.2

Thomas the Tank Engine Education Week, Embsay and Bolton Abbey Steam Railway, North Yorkshire, England

Figure 8.5 shows the flow process chart of the visit of one school group to the Embsay and Bolton Abbey Steam Railway Thomas the Tank Engine Education Week, starting at Embsay Station. There can be up to ten different schools attending between 10:30 and 14:30; all have to travel on a steam engine and a diesel, have lunch, see the entertainer, play the games, go to the shop, stand on Thomas's footplate and go to the toilet. The groups range in number from ten to fifty, an age range from toddler to 6 years. There are two starting and finishing stations, Bolton Abbey and Embsay, which both have large car parks and take buses. The shops and toilets are located on the platform, picnic areas are behind the stations, and entertainment and games are at the side of the stations. There are trains leaving from each station at thirty-minute intervals, alternating between steam and diesel (there is only one steam train and one diesel train).

Figure 8.5 shows the flow process each school will need to go through to visit and take part in all the activities scheduled for the day. Therefore there can be up to ten versions of this process each day during Education Week. More than one group can watch the Punch and Judy and have lunch, but all other activities are for one group at a time only.

(For more information on Embsay and Bolton Abbey Steam Railway see their website at www.pogo.org.uk/railway.)

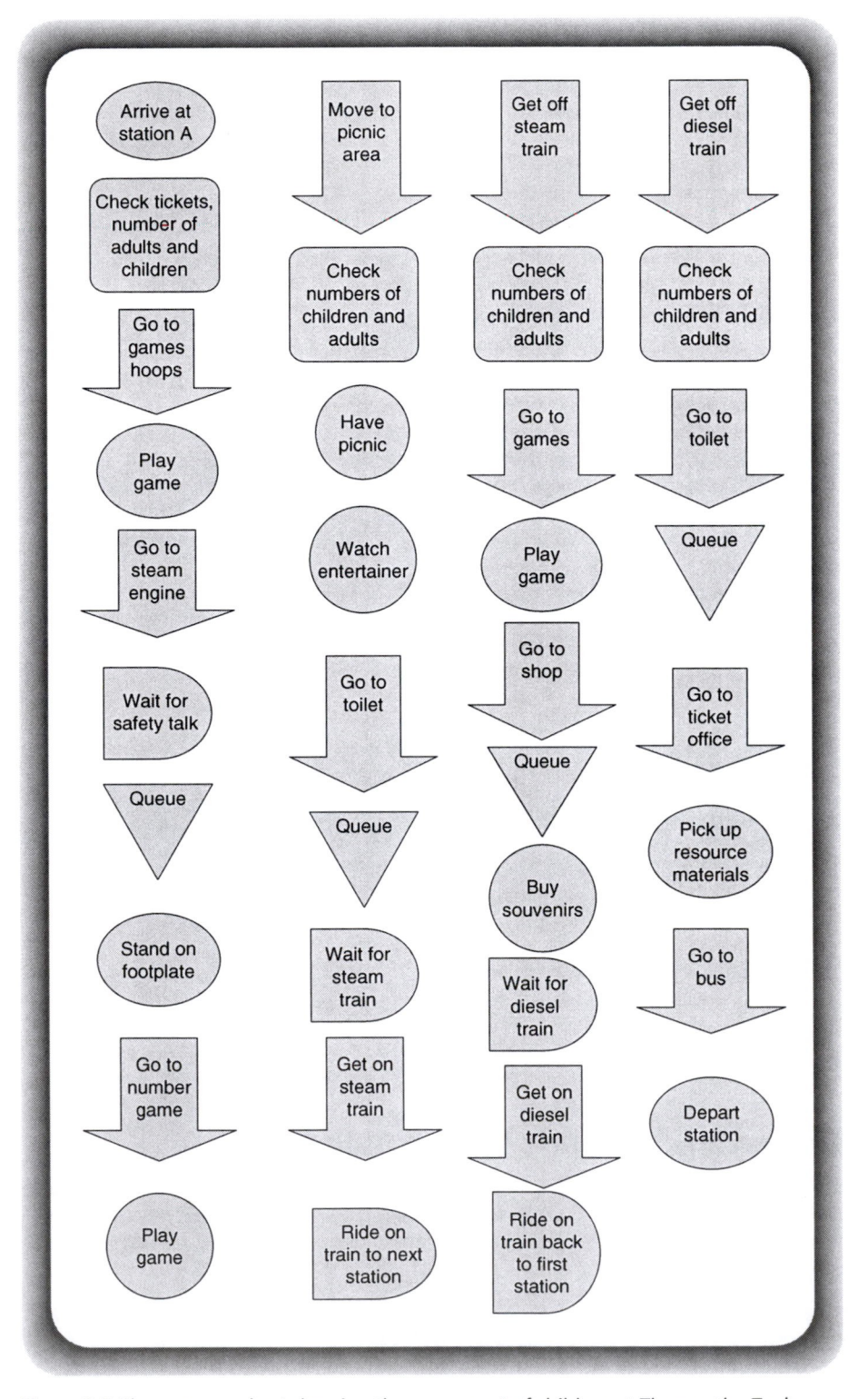

Figure 8.5 Flow process chart showing the movement of children at Thomas the Tank Engine Education Week

Customer processing charts

These charts are of great value to an event manager. They anticipate the choices customers will make as they enter an operation, for example an exhibition. Which way will they turn? What is the shortest route around the exhibition whilst still seeing all of the stands? Where is the information desk, and where are the toilets and the refreshments? Where is the meeting place for friends?

Further questions to be considered include:

- Where is the point of entry into the event?
- What is the first point of contact with a member of the operations team?
- When does the transformation process start?
- When does the customer leave?

An event manager needs to 'walk the event', using the eyes of the customer, and put it down on paper. The customer flow chart can be discussed with other staff to see if they can consider any alternatives and solutions where necessary.

The chart will show the complexity of the event and how many activities will be running in parallel with each other (see Case study 8.2, Figure 8.5).

Figure 8.5 uses the traditional flow process chart symbols to represent the flow, but instead of using the conventional format, information has been incorporated inside each symbol. This, in the opinion of the authors, allows the event manager to have a clearer view of the process.

The process is followed from the top of the first column to the bottom, back to the top of the second column and to the bottom, etc. It charts all the activities required for each group of schoolchildren from beginning to end. By using the symbols, it is possible to see where congestion may occur and in which areas the most movement is taking place.

Reflective practice 8.2

Consider Case study 8.2, and Figure 8.5.

1. If this is the flow process, what impact will it have on customer flow?
2. Look at the chart and identify where blockages may occur.
3. How would you schedule the ten schools? For this exercise, the total number of schoolchildren is 220.
4. At what point is the first point of contact with the operations team?
5. When does the transformation process start, and what is the point of delivery?
6. What other information would you require in order to schedule this event?
7. As a new event, what changes could be made to improve the flow for the customers?

Testing the new approach or offering

The purpose of this stage is to analyse the event and see if it can be improved before being tested in the market. Can the event be designed in a better way, more cheaply or more easily, or so that it matches the customers' expectations and exceeds what the competitors can achieve?

Launching on a commercial scale

Once all the other stages have been completed and systems have been tested, the processes developed can be used to launch other events in different areas. For instance,

a successful Christmas Concert in the south of England could be repeated, but with the addition of a second concert in the north of the country. The following year this could be repeated with the addition of other venues in other parts of England. Each venue and concert will potentially present differences, but if the generic model is there it should be easy to translate to the situations. Remember, all the time information is being gathered which will be used to develop and improve the original product.

Chapter summary and key points

This chapter, as part of the second stage of the event operations management model, has considered new product development and shows the advantage of using multifunctional project teams in the design stage.

The spark for new ideas and concepts, apart from the event manager, can come from staff, especially those close to the customer. It can also come from formal research and development teams, opportunities from changing technology, customers, suppliers, and an understanding of what the competition might be up to. Not all concepts will be practical, and systematic screening of concepts will be necessary.

In short, does the market want the event that is being proposed, is it feasible, do we have the resources (including reliable suppliers), do we have the know-how, what will it cost, and is it financially viable?

Once the concept has been screened and accepted, then detailed design is necessary.

The chapter has shown how flow process charting can be used to show the flow of work and activities, and also to show the flow of customers through the event. Once all the above stages have been systematically worked through, the launch can be considered and planned.

Chapter 9
Supply chain management

Learning Objectives

After reading through this chapter you will be able to:

- Understand the importance of supply chain management
- Apply the basic objectives of purchasing and understand the importance of developing relationships with suppliers
- Observe and comment upon the trends in the style of supply networks
- Be aware of the decision points in purchasing.

Introduction

The previous chapters, within the first stage of the event operations management model, illustrated the diversity of the event industry. In Section 2 we look closely at the need to plan carefully and manage the event as a project. The resources and specialisms that are used for each event are diverse, and can be sourced from many different suppliers. Some of the resources may be under the events manager's direct control, and others may be subcontracted or outsourced to agreed specialists – for example, lighting and sound contractors, caterers, musicians and pyrotechnic companies.

This chapter examines the relationships that are essential along the chain of suppliers, and the contribution that this network offers in creating competitive advantage and reliability of each event.

The supply chain is the complete flow of products and services into, through and from the organization (Wild, 2002; Figure 9.1). Managing this chain will normally involve dealing directly with purchasing and supply and inventory management. The feedback that flows backwards is essential because it allows the event manager to see how well received the products, supplies and services were, and whether there should be any changes in the future.

Managing the supply chain

Supply chain management is concerned with managing the flow of materials and information. This flow of resources should be managed from its very origins right up to the point where the customer consumes it – i.e. when the event is put on and being consumed. For example, it is in the event manager's

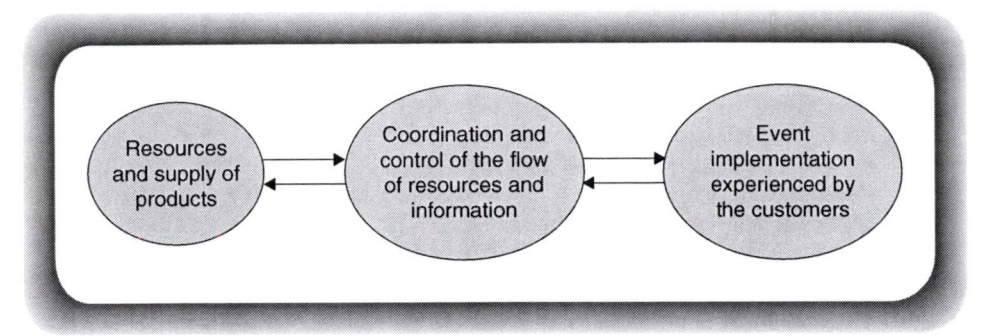

Figure 9.1 The supply chain, showing resources moving forward and feedback flowing backwards

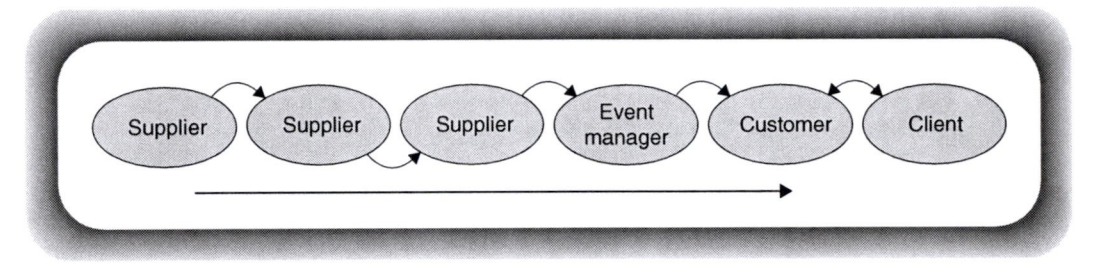

Figure 9.2 The supply chain, showing resources moving forward

interest to know the dance routine and the health and safety procedures of a visiting Spanish dance group using pyrotechnics as part of their show at an outdoor International Festival booked though an agent. Although the agent will have covered many of the details, the event manager will still need to be assured about the suitability of the performance, how it will match the needs of the audience, and how it can be coordinated with all the other activities into a whole event.

In an event there can be many different supply chains through which the varied resources flow. They all have to be managed and coordinated into one event, which is delivered at the moment it is consumed.

Supply chain management is a holistic approach that stretches forward across the event manager's own organization to the client and customers (see Figure 9.2), and backwards through the many different suppliers and to *their* suppliers. By having this holistic approach and integration across company boundaries there can be substantial benefits for all stakeholders. It should be viewed as a chain, and any break in that chain will have an adverse affect on the customer.

The aim is to develop an integrated supply chain to achieve those critical success factors demanded by the customers, the organization and other stakeholders. Unlike most other industries, the project that the event manager is responsible for cannot fail. It must happen on time, and there is no chance of a repeat. For example, a wedding cannot be repeated if the photographer was not booked correctly; Nelson Mandela's speeches, when touring, cannot be repeated if the sound system fails to work as predicted; the Olympic 100-metres final cannot be rerun if the speed recording mechanism fails. If the resources delivered are not of the right standard, the event manager rarely has enough time to look for another supplier. Good project management should leave time for a legal review of all contracts.

Basic objectives of purchasing

Event managers are responsible for providing events at the right cost, the right time, to the right specification and quality, and for the right duration. As discussed previously, the event should achieve a wide range of objectives set by the varied stakeholders, and in order to fulfil those aims the event manager has to purchase and procure all of the resources that make up the event. Slack *et al.* (2004) discuss the traditional objectives of purchasing as being the five 'rights of purchasing'.

1. At the right price
2. For delivery at the right time
3. Of goods and services to the right quality
4. In the right quantity
5. From the right source.

Wild (2002) similarly sees the operations manager as being responsible for providing goods and services of the right specification and quality, at the right time, in the right quantity and at the right price.

These requirements are made even more challenging when many of the resources are purchased through third and fourth parties.

Equally important, as Wild points out, is the need to obtain efficiently, by any ethical means, the best value for every unit of expenditure, and to maintain good relationships with other departments, both within and outside the organization, to ensure an effective operation as a whole.

In Chapter 12, we will also consider how we can develop staff and procedures to ensure the achievement of the event manager's objectives.

Purchasing activities and developing relationships with suppliers

Often within an event company there is not a specific purchasing officer, and many of the staff may create buyer/supply relationships with different companies. Some products may be bought outright and owned by the organization, and others will be used for only one event. In the case of some of the purchase agreements, for example the caterers or pyrotechnic suppliers, it is the whole service and system that is purchased and the contracted company will bring their own products and staff.

To be successful, these relationships and the method of purchasing or leasing must be managed effectively since they all provide vital supply chains throughout the operation.

As discussed in Chapter 5, it is very important to see the companies from whom products and services are purchased not just as suppliers but also as customers. They are customers in the way we ask them for quotations and in respect of whether we pay their invoices on time and accurately. All businesses are both customers for some other businesses products and services, and suppliers of products and services to their own customers (Slack and Lewis, 2002). Every operation and part of an operation should be seen as a network, linking together customers' customers and suppliers' suppliers. Within each company there are many different supply chains that are taking place internally, within the organization and between departments. In the event industry many of the suppliers are specialists and have their own marketplace and rules and regulations

to which they must conform. The whole marketplace includes health and safety, government agencies, international companies and international customers, and many other organizations. This can be termed the 'total business environment'.

The event manager should be able to stand back and see the myriad of operations and contracts, working together to deliver the event, as a whole and integrated network of supply chains.

Reflective practice 9.1

On a large piece of paper, draw an integrated diagram of all the different types of suppliers and customers working for an international charity organizing a walk along the Great Wall of China. You should consider all the products and services that are required, from the initial concept until the final review of the event after its completion.

Drawing the supply and customer network has only revealed part of the event manager's work. Slack and Lewis (2002) point out that there are qualitative issues to understand:

1. How does an operation relate to other players in its network?
2. What knowledge of its supply network does it have? Is it close and intimate?
3. Does its supply network have an intimate and close understanding of its own operations, and ultimately its customers' needs and objectives?

Single sourcing or multi-sourcing of suppliers?

To assist in answering these questions, the event manager should be questioning the number of suppliers with whom the organization is involved. Does one supplier provide a 'one-stop shop' where many of the resources required can be purchased, or are there a great many suppliers providing a range of different services for the same event? If the latter is the case, then there are consequently more supply chains to manage, and to manage effectively. It is likely in this case that many brief relationships will be made, since there is not enough time to develop loyalty, trust, and understanding of each other's needs. In reality, depending upon the type of event, a combination of the two policies would be used.

For instance, if you produced classical concerts nationwide you could use a UK-wide sound and lighting company that produces bespoke requirements for each event, including design and set-building, but you would most likely use a local caterer and security company. If it is the former option, i.e. using a 'one-stop shop', the relationship with that supplier can be built upon and this will provide loyalty and understanding of each other's needs. Silver (2004) says that many event professionals recommend that all projects or purchases should be put out to three bids every time to ensure competitive pricing.

On the other hand, we could argue that a company that can be assured of continued business with an organization will provide competitive prices. It avoids quotation and administrative costs, and knows that staff and resources necessary for the provision of the service will be required over a long period of time. This close relationship might be jeopardized if frequent competitive tendering is undertaken. However, complacency within this special relationship must not be allowed to propagate and lead to decreased customer satisfaction or value for money.

Wild (2002) considers the effect of single or multiple company sourcing under four headings:

1. *Effect on price.* Where there is single-supplier sourcing, the price may be reduced due to the increased quantity needed. The price may also be reduced, since the supplier will feel that there is security of sales of the required products and services. However, the price may also be kept lower where there is multi-sourcing, due to increased competition.
2. *Effect on supply security.* Whilst the supply of service will be made simpler by using one supplier, the organization is at risk if something happens to that supplier – for example, strike action, fire or liquidation.
3. *Effect on supplier motivation.* Whilst using one supplier may increase motivation, since the supplier feels valued and may improve the service supplied accordingly, the service may lack competition and therefore there is a risk that poorer service might occur.
4. *Effect on market structure.* If the event organization grows and continues to single-source, it may develop into a monopolistic situation, with the eventual elimination of supply – and hence bring about lack of choice for the customer.

Those services and products that are purchased externally can be outsourced or sub-contracted, and tend to be non-core activities – i.e. those activities that are not central to the company. The difference between outsourcing and subcontracting is dependent upon the transfer of control.

For example, the manager of a gymkhana contracts a catering firm and a local cleaning company and stipulates exactly what he expects them to do as part of the contract – provide a sit-down meal for twenty VIPs, and ensure all rubbish is cleared from the site during and after the event. This is an example of subcontracting – the manager has control over what is done.

In our second example, the management of a racecourse outsource all their catering requirements for the next five years to an outside catering company. The racecourse management want the racegoers to have hospitality available on race days, and to enjoy other functions in keeping with the type and variety of clientele expected to attend the course. How this is achieved and resourced is totally up to the catering company; they have the control. This is outsourcing.

Outsourcing takes place when an organization transfers the ownership of a business process to a supplier. The key to this definition is the aspect of transfer of control. This definition differentiates outsourcing from subcontracting, in which the buyer retains control of the process, or in other words tells the supplier how to do the work. It is the transfer of ownership that defines outsourcing and often makes it such a challenging, painful process. In outsourcing, the buyer does not instruct the supplier how to perform a task, but instead focuses on communicating what services it wants to buy. It then leaves the process of accomplishing those results to the supplier.

Some companies prefer to complete everything in-house – both important and non-important activities. This style of company is known as being vertically integrated; that is, it creates and supplies all the necessary resources and services from within its own boundary.

An example of a vertically integrated company is a circus owner who owns the circus animals; has the artists on payroll; owns the big top, other tents, caravans and transporters; employs his own costume-makers, scene designers and constructors; has a supply of memorabilia for sale; runs a refreshment booth; and does his own promotion.

Case study 9.1 describes the Star Events Group, which is a vertically integrated company.

Case study 9.1

Star Events Group, Bedford, England

The Star Events Group provides staging and rigging products and services for indoor and out-door events. This is achieved through its five divisions, Mobile, VerTech, Design, Orbit and Rigging, all based at Thurleigh, Bedford. The company designs, builds and maintains its own equipment, and its site provides workshop facilities, office accommodation and storage for this purpose. It is an innovative organization that use research and design to promote and develop new safe ways of working while providing the best solutions for their customers. This is a ver-tically integrated organization that can provide all the structures and services required for indoor or outdoor staging, from planning to execution.

Star Mobile provides mobile staging, such as an articulated trailer as a portable version of a permanent structure, some with a solid roof to allow hanging of lights, others with built in electrics and generators.

Star VerTech offers a modular system for staging and structures with in-house structural engineering CAD design and support, plus ground support, screens and special structures.

Star Design provides feasibility, planning, layout, structures, high-level access, rigging, legal requirements, legislation, and safety procedures and checks.

Star Orbit offers classic dome-shaped and arched staging structures.

Star Rigging provides a team experienced in supplying creative rigging solutions, including permanent installations and one-off productions.

(Printed by kind permission of the Star Group; for further information see www.star-hire.com.)

Reflective practice 9.2

Consider Case study 9.1.

1. What other services might Star Events Group consider adding to its portfolio?
2. Would the company need to look for forward or backward integration?
3. If the company were to outsource part of its organization, what would you consider to be an area that is not core?

There are companies that choose to do nothing in-house and to buy in all of their require-ments. This style of company is referred to as being virtual. The merits and disadvan-tages of these approaches are discussed in Chapter 6. Slack and Lewis (2002) describe the networks in virtual organizations as providing information and contacts with other suppliers who can supply the organization with all it wants and needs to supply its customers.

An example of a virtual company is a promoter who arranges the tour of an over-seas ballet troupe, hires the theatres, arranges accommodation for the artists, hires the orchestra, etc., and uses an advertising agency for promotion. In essence, the promoter owns nothing and works from a rented office.

Vertically integrated organizations

As discussed above, vertical integration is the extent to which an organization owns the companies that supply the products and services that it uses.

Making a choice to buy out a supplier, or to make/provide those products and services in-house, would be known as *backwards integration*. In the event industry that might entail buying out a lighting specialist or a catering company, or making all the props for themed evenings in-house rather than using an external company. This may be worthwhile if that specialism is being used a great deal within all events, and if the cost of acquisition and integration into the company would create savings and increase a better provision of what is needed. Other advantages include preventing competitors from gaining control of key suppliers.

Forward integration, as its name suggests, is when an organization buys out or actively completes the work done by a customer. In the event industry, an example might be a lighting or catering company which, instead of always waiting for an event company coming to them to ask for a quotation to supply certain goods and services for an event, proactively seeks out customers and puts on the event itself.

Trends in the style of supply networks

Slack and Lewis (2002) identify three trends in the provision of goods and services and the way that these are sourced. These trends can be seen very clearly in the event industry, possibly because it is a relatively new industry, and possibly due to the diversity of suppliers that are needed and which are not always a part of a small entrepreneurial organization. The trends are:

1. An increase in the proportion of goods outsourced. This enables the organization to concentrate on a few important activities and outsource the rest. This could offer greater competitiveness and efficiency. In the area of technology, in particular, outsourcing enables the company to use up-to-date equipment and specialisms rather than outdated resources. Outsourcing also reduces the amount of capital tied up in assets that might seldom be used.
2. Organizations are reducing the number of suppliers. When you consider the decision points outlined in Figure 9.3, later in this chapter, you will see that there are many activities involved in buying goods and services. If these can be reduced, money and time will be saved. An additional benefit includes building relationships with suppliers that you can trust. Trust develops through past experience and working together. Generally, organizations are developing partnerships with suppliers and customers. In the event industry this may take the form of long-term contracts and an openness of costs and prices between the supplier and the event organization. The suppliers should feel that they are contributing to the success of the event. With this in mind, actively listening to the other party's expectations and needs is a skill. Hearing and giving subtle indicators to each other during negotiations and discussions is an experienced art, and the lowest cost need not always be the driving force (O'Toole and Mikolaitis, 2002).
3. Partnering methods can be taken from other industries, such as construction, which rely on organizations developing a process of mutual trust and understanding within their supply chain. This then opens up the possibility for suppliers to work together in a non-adversarial way and to cooperate on areas such as strategy, benchmarking, process, equity and feedback to develop an integrated supply chain within which all parties can agree to be members (Bennet and Jayes, 1998).

A fourth trend is that of e-commerce and Internet usage. Use of the Internet can provide organizations with up-to-date pricing and availability using on-line ordering. It

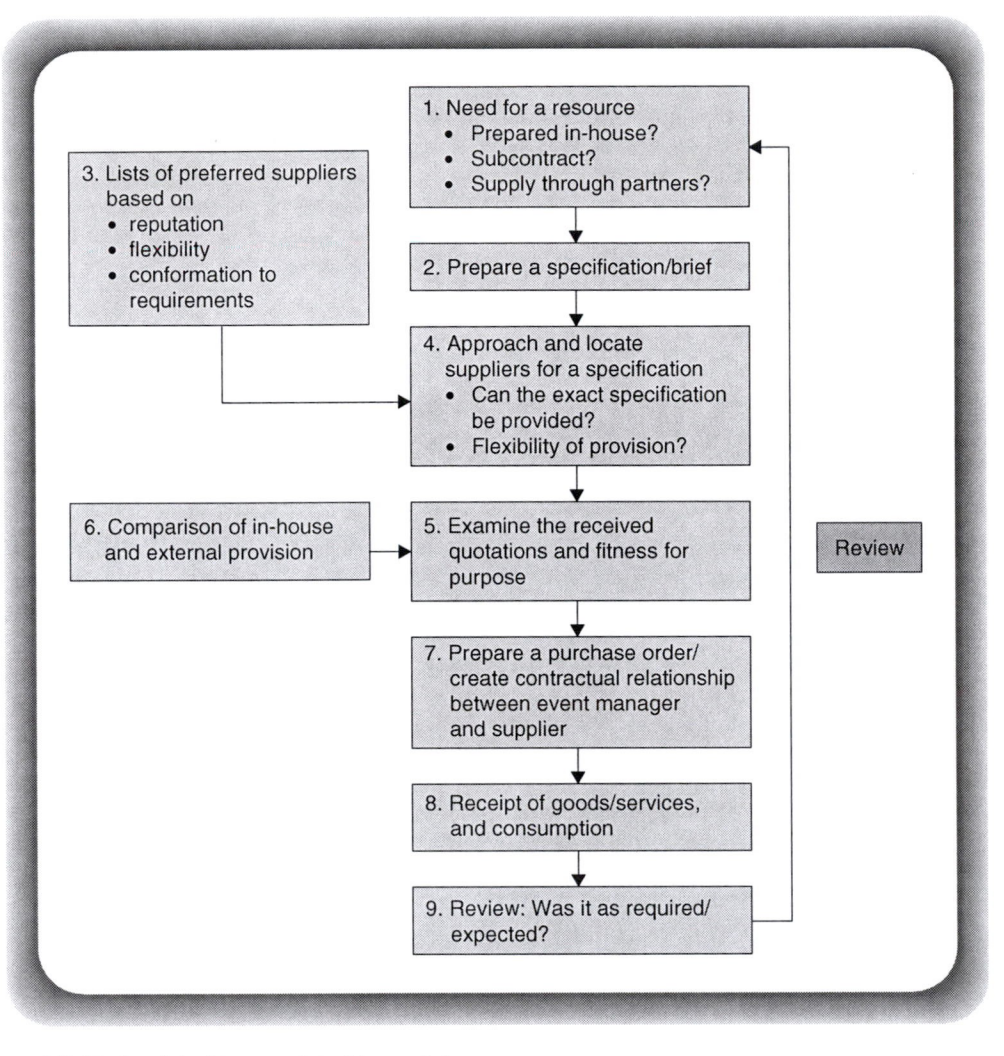

Figure 9.3 Chain of decisions and decision points

eliminates paperwork and can speed up the many processes that would previously have relied on telephone calls, postage systems and person-to-person communications. The Internet also opens up a greater choice of providers.

It can be seen that there are different styles of companies – those that fully own all the parts of the supply chain, and those that regularly outsource and subcontract parts of their services to other specialists.

The major concern is that all parts of the service delivered to the final customer should be managed and integrated. Wild (2002) believes that the strategic objectives of the company will influence how the organization is managed, and that often the integrated flow of materials and services through and from the operation is a prerequisite for achieving high-quality, rapid and low-cost provision for customers. Therefore managing the supply chain is a major concern and of major importance for event organizations, where a high proportion of their products and services often come from different suppliers or different parts of the organization.

In delivering this well-managed supply chain, the aim of the event company should be to diminish obstacles between functions and departments within the organization,

minimize activities undertaken, and improve the links between the departments so that there is no unnecessary repetition. External to the organization, the event manager should look to improve communication and relationships with suppliers.

O'Toole and Mikolaitis (2002) see the contract as central to the correct procedure for project planning and implementation. Much is written about contracts in engineering, building and software industries, and event managers can take advantage of lessons learned from successes and failures in these other industries in their use of project management. Each contract specifies who will do what, when and how. It can contain many details, or be a simple letter of agreement or a purchase order.

Case study 9.2 provides an example.

Case study 9.2

Reed MIDEM, Paris, France

Reed Exhibitions (part of the Reed Elsevier Group) is the world's leading organizer of trade and consumer exhibitions, with a portfolio of over 430 events in 32 countries. The company creates high-profile, highly-targeted business and consumer exhibitions, where buyers and suppliers from around the world meet together to do business.

Reed has developed many partnerships with organizations, and through this has provided partners with access to Reed's resources, networks and contacts. Reed has built strategic alliances with a wide range of interested parties, from trade associations and government departments to exhibition venues and organizers. Reed MIDEM is a Paris-based subsidiary of Reed Exhibitions, specializing in B-to-B tradeshows for the television and new technology industries (MIPTV and MIPCOM), the international property industry (MIPIM), the retail real estate sector (MAPIC), and international urban management (GLOBAL CITY). These shows take place in Cannes, France.

A recent example is shown below.

Cannes, 5 October 2004

Reed MIDEM, the organizer of professional, international tradeshows, has signed a ten-year agreement with the City of Cannes, maintaining its international tradeshows on the Cote d'Azur until at least 2014.

'Reed MIDEM has been holding trade shows in Cannes for the past 38 years,'notes Reed MIDEM Chief Executive Officer Paul Zilk. 'I'm delighted that this "marriage" will continue for at least another decade. This agreement allows the City of Cannes and the Palais des Festivals and ourselves, to adopt a long-term strategy. Together, we will continue to work on improving services to our international clients.'

Bernard Brochand, member of France's National Assembly and Mayor of Cannes, says, 'this agreement cements the good relations that have been built up over the years between Reed MIDEM and Cannes. Reed MIDEM is an historic partner with the city and with the Palais des Festivals, which has hosted many of its new exhibitions over the years. Each partner knows what the other brings to the table. Over the last three years, Cannes has significantly improved security, cleanliness and logistical services in order to meet the demands and expectations of exhibition attendees and of the local population.'

David Lisnard, Deputy Mayor of Cannes and Chairman of the Palais des Festivals et des Congrès, comments, 'this deal is the fruit of the considerable hard work from local hoteliers, taxi professionals, restaurant owners and service providers. It recognizes the quality of the services provided by the Palais des Festivals staff and represents economic security for the Cannes region. This is a win–win agreement. It means greater capacity to grow the exhibition business, safeguards the prosperity of Cannes and guarantees jobs. Now we all need to continue to work to further to improve Cannes' ability to compete in this vibrant sector.'

(Printed by courtesy of Reed MIDEM; for more information see www.reedmidem.com.)

Decision points in purchasing for an event organization

The flow diagram in Figure 9.3 outlines the procedures that should be followed leading up to the contract.

Purchasing follows a chain of decisions and points 1–9 are identified below.

1. When it is initially considered that an event should go ahead, there is a need for a range of products and services. There should be detailed discussion regarding how these might best be procured – in-house or from an external company.
2. The next stage is to create a clear specification of what is required.
3. Some organizations may have a list of preferred suppliers. This provides useful contacts regarding reliable companies who are known to deliver as per specification of quality and who also respect and value working with the event manager's organization.
4. Suppliers should be approached for a price and an overview of what they could provide – Can the exact specification be provided? Is there flexibility of provision?
5. When the quotations are returned it is important that they are examined fairly and checked to see that what is being offered is as per specification.
6. The price and quality and reliability may be compared against in-house provision where that is possible.
7. When the event manager is satisfied that the goods and services are as required in all respects, including competitive price and appropriate provision, then an agreement can be made with the supplier. This may be called a purchase order, but in reality what happens is that a contractual relationship is formed between the event manager and the supplier.
8. The goods and services should be delivered as expected. In many instances within the events industry the actually delivery and consumption will be simultaneous. For example, a rock band delivers its services at the moment it is playing for the audience.
9. The final stage is a review. Did the purchased product or service deliver as expected and as required? The review will inform the next set of decisions about a similar service/product.

Further elaboration of decision points 1–9
1. Recognizing a need for a resource

The event manager should critically examine all that is needed for each event, and what resources and provision the customer really values. Is the item or service to be purchased absolutely essential for the event, either indirectly or directly? What exactly

is required, and where can it be sourced from – internally or externally? If it can be prepared in-house, what is the cost of this provision and the effect on other activities within the organization? Is the product or service that is required needed for the smooth running of the organization or for a forthcoming event?

Silver (2004) believes that the event organizer should consider the time, money and human resources available. She gives the examples of having sufficient budget but very little time or few personnel to handle certain aspects of the event; or that there may be plenty of volunteers but very little money. The situation may therefore dictate whether products and services are provided from in-house or sourced externally. Whatever the decision, it must ensure that the appropriate resources are sourced effectively and efficiently.

2. Prepare a specification/brief

O'Toole and Mikolaitis (2002) describe a specification as the written description of the required product or service. The suppliers use the specification document to estimate a price and to bid for the contract. However, many of the services required by an event manager are unique and non-standard products, and are not just bought 'off the shelf'. Thus the specification may only act as a guide. Indeed, it may be written only in terms that the organizer understands rather than those that the supplier is more accustomed to.

O'Toole and Mikolaitis (2002) believe that the specification can be described in three ways:

- By function, i.e. what it is supposed to do – for example, the caterers should provide a choice of dishes, the meal should be themed to the evening's entertainment, and enable the customers to serve themselves.
- By technical description – for example, the caterer will supply sufficient food for 100 guests, all food and hygiene laws should be observed, hot food should be served at a minimum temperature of 72°C and cold food held at a maximum temperature of 5°C.
- By performance – for example, the food should be laid out in a buffet style and cleared within 45 minutes, and during this time staff should be on hand to keep the buffet tidy and replenished.

The technical specifications can be very detailed to prevent any misunderstanding. It is very difficult to compare bids from different companies where they are quoting against seemingly different specifications. Diagrams, floor plans and site maps are essential.

The invitation to bid must ensure that the quotation will contain all costs associated with the delivery and implementation of the service (Silver, 2004).

Other useful information for the potential suppliers could include the context and details of the event, the budget limitations, the selection criteria that will be used to select the supplier, and whether references are required (Silver, 2004).

Getz (1997) lists desirable items to be included:

- Specification liability clauses – i.e. who is responsible, and insurance requirements
- Future options for renewal
- Termination and amendment procedures
- Subcontracting rights
- Compliance with appropriate laws
- Penalties for non-fulfilment
- What is NOT covered.

3. Lists of preferred suppliers

The selection of possible suppliers can be very time consuming, and it is therefore useful to have a list ready. Where the event management is part of a larger company, as in British Waterways, it may be beneficial to have agreed lists of suppliers or to share experiences with other organizations. O'Toole and Mikolaitis (2002) list some of the attributes that should be looked for:

- Reliability
- Suppliers' experience with events of a similar size and scope
- The ability to focus on your event, and assurance that you are of the same importance as other customers
- Guaranteed quality of the product or service
- History in the event industry
- Discounting for large orders.

4. Approaching and locating suppliers for a specification

As well as using the lists of preferred suppliers, event managers can use the Internet, membership directories, trade magazines and industry publications for recommended suppliers. Networking with other colleagues can guide the event manager to different and reliable sources. Prior to sending out the specifications to different suppliers, it is important to ascertain that they will be able to achieve your objectives. You must also make certain that the supplier is legally and ethically able to supply what you need. By providing an evaluation instrument at this stage you could reduce the number of suppliers you contact. This evaluation instrument should include price, number of staff required from the supplier or your own organization, and other critical success factors related to this part of the service.

In Chapter 10 we present an evaluation instrument. In the example shown there, it is used for selecting an ideal venue for your event. However, exactly the same principles can be used for any supplier. The main essence is that the criteria used to evaluate a service, location or product cannot just be measured by using equally weighted criteria. Price would be just one criteria; reputation, proximity, speed of delivery and creativity might be others. Each criterion should be weighted in its importance for that particular product or service, and consequently the event manager will be able to select suppliers and their services more appropriately.

Approaching specialists must be done carefully, and some specialists may need booking a long time in advance, and require a deposit and arrangements in the case of cancellation by either party (Shone and Parry, 2004).

5. Examination of the received quotations and fitness for purpose

In some situations, all the quotations received should be opened at an agreed time and place. This avoids any criticisms or charges of unfairness. All 'quotes' should be opened and considered as presented without having prior knowledge of their contents, and without giving one company a potentially unfair advantage over another. When the quotations are received, it should be ascertained that the companies are capable of fulfilling all the requirements of the activity for which they were asked to quote.

6. Comparison of in-house and external provision

The evaluation instrument described above and in Chapter 15 will serve to differentiate between the different tenders received. The purpose of this stage is to assess the capabilities of the supplier and the in-house provision, and to compare the strengths

and weaknesses of the different quotations. You should be able to demonstrate that your choice of supplier is devoid of personal preference and prejudice. Your objective is to select reputable, dependable and competitive suppliers for a particular product or service – in short, the best that fits your purpose (Silver, 2004).

7. Prepare a purchase order/create contractual relationship between event manager and supplier

This is the stage where there is formal agreement between the supplier and the receiver.

A contract is a legal covenant representing the agreement and responsibilities between the supplier and the event organizer. It defines the performance and other obligations of both parties (Sonder, 2004). Contracts may also be useful for defining and specifying other details, such as how logos and company names can be used and the types of merchandise permitted (Getz, 1997). A contract is said to exist when something is offered and accepted in writing or verbally with witnesses. Its purpose and provisions must be legal, and the different parties should be capable of entering into the agreement. The standard contract elements, according to Catherwood and Van Kirk (1992), are:

- Specification of the agreeing parties
- Purpose of the contract
- Duration of the contract
- Terms
- Signatures
- Witnesses and date signed.

8. Receipt of goods/services and consumption

In a factory situation, quality begins with checking that materials received meet specification (fit for purpose). This is known as input control. The same applies for events management; it is important to control the input of materials as received, and that equipment etc. is properly installed and tested before the event begins. There is nothing worse than a sound system that fails.

9. Review: was it as required/expected?

Review after the event, when successes and problems are still fresh in the mind, is essential. What went right, what went wrong, what would we do differently next time? It is advisable to keep notes, including contact names and addresses, on file for future reference. Each event should be better managed than the last one. There is always room for improvement.

The Japanese word for continuous improvement is *Kaizen*. Event managers should ask staff and subcontractors what they think could be done better, and their opinions should be taken seriously.

Customer relationship management

Customer Relationship Management (CRM) software now exists to capture data to improve overall supply chain performance. The objective of CRM is to develop a customer-centred organization that ensures every opportunity is taken to delight the customers, foster customer loyalty, and build long-term relationships that are mutually beneficial. The ultimate gain is to ensure that each customer's current and future wants and needs are satisfied. This involves recording details of each time we work with a customer, and developing a picture from this information of what the customer liked and didn't like in our past dealings. Although software exists to capture these data, for smaller operations such information can easily be recorded as notes on the customer's file.

Chapter summary and key points

This chapter has examined the relationships along the chain of various levels of suppliers, through the operation of the event out to the direct customer and on to the end user.

As many of the previous chapters have been spent in considering what customers want and how to satisfy them, this chapter has concentrated on the other end of the supply chain – the suppliers.

The first step is to recognize that a resource is needed. The next step is to determine the various sources for the resource (in-house, subcontract or purchase). Depending on the complexity of the required resource, a specification will be needed. In events management, due to the unique nature of some events, often the specification will be more of a guide than a precise technical description.

The chapter has also explained the advantages of developing preferred suppliers, where reliability (meeting specification and delivery on time) might be more important than price. If you buy on price alone, you will get what you pay for. Cheap can be expensive in the long run. With events management it is important that materials are checked and tested on receipt, or certainly before the event begins. After the event it is wise to review its success or otherwise, and to keep file notes on the reliability of suppliers and other issues.

Chapter 10

Location management and choice

Introduction

We have set events and their day-to-day operational issues, problems and decisions within the broader framework of the total organization and its external environment. Much of this has been analysed in the first stage of the event operations management model. It has been shown that business policy determines the services offered and the level and quality of service that will be provided at an event. We have seen that business policy may limit the resources available to an event, and also how business policy will establish the operating structure.

Event objectives include customer satisfaction and, at the same time, efficient use of resources. These often conflicting objectives have to be balanced by the events manager within constraints of price, quality and overall feasibility, as limited in the short to medium term by existing resources. A challenge for the event manager is, therefore, first how to make the best use of *existing* resources, and then how best to purchase or 'contract in' new resources. Much of this has been discussed in Chapters 6 and 9.

This chapter addresses in detail the resource of space, its best available use, and business location. When staging an event, space will often be limited and an efficient layout will be important.

Location of the business premises

There are several factors to be considered when deciding on the location of the business premises for an event organization:

1. A business policy that requires speed of service to customers, or ease of access by customers, will lead to the requirement for a location near to where the customers are. Therefore it will be important

to locate near to major tube lines, motorways or airports, dependent upon the location and diversity of the client base.

2. A policy that stresses efficient use of resources will lead to the question 'can we make do with less?', Do you need permanent business premises, or can you hire hotel rooms/office space as and when needed?

3. A business policy that takes the supply chain approach, where the suppliers are dedicated and regarded as an extension of the whole organization, might well consider proximity to suppliers, rather than customers, to be a criterion when determining location.

With electronic means of data transfer, proximity may of course be defined very differently today from twenty years ago. For example, for sound and acoustic suppliers you may use a range of different suppliers across the country, dependent upon where your event is to be held. However, printing and stationery suppliers can be reached easily via today's electronic environment, and actual location in this respect may not be as important. In not-for-profit organizations, revenue may not be as relevant an issue as cost and customer service.

Operational concerns are either resource-related (so access to suppliers is important) or market-related (so proximity to and ease of access for customers is more significant).

Wild (2002) says that the choice of location is vital for any new business, and that a poor choice of location may be responsible for many new businesses having brief and troubled lives. Poor location decisions are expensive and may have long-lasting effects on the events that can be delivered. A wrong initial location decision will lead to further expense and disruption if a subsequent move to a new location has to be made. If the decision is made to stay with the existing unsuitable location, ongoing costs will continue and frustration is likely to escalate. Often the ongoing effects of a poor location decision are hidden, as the costs will be in the form of lost opportunities, lost sales and lost business. If the location is wrong, it can have a significant impact on profits (Slack *et al.*, 2004).

Opportunity costs of a wrong location, such as lost sales and extra operating expense, cannot be separately accounted for, since often they will not be known. Thus they are not shown in annual financial reports. This lack of exposure and consequent scrutiny and comment regarding the costs generally means that only the event manager will be truly aware of the extra effort required, the extra costs of transport, the cost of double handling and so on due to poor location.

Location decisions

Basic location questions that should be asked include:

1. Why move?
2. Where to?
3. How much space is required?
4. Lease or buy?
5. What are the differences between cost and the benefits to be made?
6. Have alternatives been evaluated?
7. Again, 'WHY?'

Why move?

'So why move?' The answer is not always obvious. Perhaps the question should be rephrased to ask: 'How will the move to new premises improve the business operation, or improve customer service?' If a satisfactory answer can't be given, then why move?

Sometimes the reason for moving is due to a change in competition or local costs (rent, taxes etc.).

Wild (2002) suggests that if the reason for moving is due to an increase in demand, then this in itself creates more questions:

- Should the present capacity and facilities be expanded?
- Should other locations for additional facilities be sought?
- Should existing facilities be closed down in favour of larger premises elsewhere?

If the reason for moving is to meet increased demand, the question must be: 'Is it possible to expand the existing premises rather than relocate?' It might be possible to rearrange the layout of the existing premises so as to make better use of what space already exists. On the other hand, if a move is really necessary, then piecemeal additions or *ad hoc* solutions can result in facilities that will *always* be inefficient. Money thrown at an inadequate facility will be money wasted.

Many organizations, with enthusiasm fuelled by rapid initial growth or in periods of national economic growth, have committed themselves to costly new premises only to find that growth has not continued at the same initial meteoric rate. It has to be recognized that the economy is cyclical, and when there is an economic downturn expensive premises are hard to unload. Before committing to expensive premises it is important to be reasonably certain that the increase in demand is ongoing and not short term.

Slack *et al.* (2004) ask the following four questions when considering expansion or for choice of initial locations, and these have been slightly amended for the event industry:

1. Where should the facilities be located?
2. How should the operations network be managed across national boundaries?
3. Should events held in different countries be allowed to develop their own way of doing business or maintain a corporate approach?
4. Can an event which has been successful in one part of the world be transferred to another part?

Many decisions to move to new premises are made for prestige purposes rather than to improve the efficiency of the operation or to give a better service to the customer. Sometimes the reason given for a planned move is nebulous, and it cannot clearly be demonstrated that the move to new premises will improve operations or add to customer satisfaction. In this scenario the event manager must investigate what is required to safeguard existing levels of operating effectiveness.

As explained earlier, it is not necessarily the event organization that feels the need to move to a new location; the event itself may move location (see Case study 10.1).

Case study 10.1

32nd America's Cup, Valencia, Spain

(23 June 2007 onwards; pre regattas held in 2004/2005/2006; Louis Vuitton cup selection of challenger April to June 2007.)

Brief history of the America's Cup®

The America's Cup® challenge has been the premier yachting event in the world since its first sailing around the Isle of Wight in 1851.

For the 32nd America's Cup, a new venue has been sought and a management company employed to run the event.

This is a revolutionary step in the context of modern America's Cup history. Previously, the America's Cup Match would be organized by the defending yacht club, while the Challenger of Record would set up a selection series, the Louis Vuitton Cup, with the other challengers to determine who would race the Defender in the Match. The two events were usually completely independent, resulting in duplicated effort and, at times, frustration or confusion for partners, participants and spectators alike.

(Information supplied by AC Management Valencia; for further information see www.americascup.com.)

The news releases below detail the process undertaken to select the location for the 32nd America's Cup.

Geneva, 12 June 2003:

AC management publishes the venues shortlisted for the next America's cup

With the objective of choosing the venue and host city for the 32nd America's Cup, AC Management (Event Organizers) retained eight European venues in March this year. At the time the eight were each requested to supply in-depth technical information to facilitate AC Management's task in making the best choice of venue for the next event of the world's oldest sporting trophy, the America's Cup. In particular, the eight cities were asked questions concerning specific weather patterns, outline plans for the hosting arrangements, as well as details of their initial thoughts on the likely infrastructure and logistical facilities.

'I have followed the process carefully', says Pierre-Yves Firmenich, Commodore of the Société Nautique de Genève (Trustees of 32nd America's Cup and winning yacht club of the 31st America's Cup), 'and each of the eight candidates presented outstanding bids. It has obviously been extremely difficult to make the choice. However, ultimately, only one venue can be chosen and so it is now time to publish a short list.'

'The remaining venues are Lisbon (POR), Marseille (FAR), Naples (ITA), Palma de Mallorca (ESP), Valencia (ESP).'

Michel Bonnefous, CEO of AC Management, commented: 'With this shortlist we have refined our goals considerably and will now work closely with each of the remaining venues thorough the next crucial steps in the process. Over the coming months, we will be concentrating on the more precise details for hosting the America's Cup. We need to understand clearly the minutiae of every positive and negative element associated with each venue. It is probable that the next announcement in this process will be the identity of the final choice.'

2 November 2003:

Two major announcements were made in Geneva this morning. The first, and by far the most eagerly awaited, was that Valencia has been chosen as the host venue for the next America's Cup. In winning the bid the Spanish team had beaten off stiff competition from Naples, Lisbon and Marseille.

'The sailing and sporting conditions were always our main criteria', said Michel Bonnefous, AC management's chief executive. 'One of the aspects was to consider the worst-case scenario for the weather. In Auckland (31st Cup held in Auckland) we were looking at a possible 15 days lost to the weather, in Valencia the worst case scenario suggests just 1 day. This means that in Valencia we can more or less guarantee to sail, which is obviously good for the racing and the television coverage.'

Another change to the new look America's Cup is that the length of the races will be determined by time and not distance, a detail that should help avoid some of the frustrating delays that dogged the last event.

According to Bonnefous, another advantage of Valencia is that the nature of the location means that the public and spectators can get very close to the racing and that the America's Cup village is next door to where the sailing will take place.

(*Yachting World*, 26 November 2003)

(Content supplied by *Yachting World*; for further information see www.yachtingworld.com.)

> **Reflective practice 10.1**
>
> In the first press cutting reproduced in Case study 10.1, Michael Bonnefous of AC Management says they need to examine the minutiae of every positive and negative element associated with the shortlisted venues.
>   What would they have had to consider and how could these criteria be assessed?

Where to?

Having determined that new premises are genuinely needed and demand will continue, then the next question is, where should the event organization move to?

Slack *et al.* (2004) discuss the different resources used by organizations, and it can be seen that these should be borne in mind when choosing a location for an event organization. They include:

- Labour costs. Although within a country labour costs might vary from location to location, such variations will be considerably more pronounced from country to country. It is not just the cost of wages that should be taken into account, but also non-wage costs such as employment and social security costs, safety and health requirements, holiday payment, exchange rates and other welfare provisions.
- Land costs. Land and rental costs vary between countries, and between city and out-of-city locations.
- Transportation costs. In the event industry these may involve the cost of bringing in resources to the premises, although often in the event industry the resources are taken directly to the event. Other transport costs include movement of goods from the office or warehouse to the event.

When choosing a site, it should be considered whether that particular location is appropriate for that event company and the style of company and events it represents. This depends on the image that is wanted and the convenience of location for clients or suppliers.

International locations

Some event organizations cannot limit themselves to within their own national boundaries. Many of the organizations buy their supplies from abroad and deliver their services abroad. The horizon for event managers is increasingly a global one. If overseas locations are being investigated, it is most important that the broader issues such as political and economic stability, local customs and culture, tax structures and incentives, reliable communications and energy supplies etc. are considered. Suffice to say an overseas venture for an organization will require very detailed considerations. Often local problems do not emerge until the project is well under way. It is most sensible to solicit local assistance and knowledge from the outset when contemplating an overseas venture (see Case study 10.2).

For UK companies, Business Link (www.businesslink.gov.uk) and UK Trade and Investment (www.uktradeinvest.gov.uk) websites provide a good starting point to find out information for overseas markets and contacts. UK Trade and Investment lists general information regarding the state of the economy, currency, public holidays, religion etc., plus more specific information remarketing and contacts.

For American companies, the website www.buyusa.gov provides commercial information for importers and exporters along the same lines as UK Trade and Investment.

Case study 10.2

Setting up an overseas event

Imagine you want to set up an event in Denmark. If you need staff, these can be sourced through local government employment agencies (*Arbejdsformidlingen*) or through commercial firms such as Manpower Rekruttering or Kelly Rekruttering.

The UK Trade and Investment website lists information regarding taxes, legislation, and all government departments embassies, associations etc. It is very important when working overseas to understand culture, and the website offers these guidelines on business etiquette:

Most Danes read and speak English very well. Correspondence and telephone calls can usually be conducted in English without difficulty.

British companies soliciting business or introducing products should note that, in the initial stages, letters should be addressed to the company and not to named individuals. Some Danish companies specify this on their letterhead. Once a business connection has been established, correspondence can then be addressed to named individuals.

Arrive punctually for meetings. Notify by telephone or fax in advance if you are going to be late or if you have to cancel.

State times using the 24-hour clock rather than using a casual 'half-five', which a Dane would understand to be an hour earlier.

Give a firm handshake on arrival and departure.

Don't be embarrassed to talk about price and payment. Danes are normally straightforward and easy to communicate with, even on money-related matters.

(Information provided by the UK Trade and Investment website, www.uktradeinvest.gov.uk. Crown copyright material is reproduced with the permission of the Controller of HMSO and the Queen's Printer for Scotland.)

How much space is required?

The amount of space is dependent on two issues; the first is demand and potential growth, and the second is how efficiently space is used. It is a truism that the more space is available, the more wasteful of space we will be – i.e. space requirements expand to use up the space available. It is also true that in a growing organization there never seems to be enough space. It could be argued that an organization can never have too much space, but space costs money – particularly in an expensive area of the world or country or part of a city.

Lease or buy?

Once land has been purchased and buildings erected, large amounts of money will have been spent. If subsequently it transpires that the location or the buildings themselves are not suitable, it is often the case that a substantial loss will be made if the decision is made to sell. Large capital expenditure in land and buildings equates to large amounts of funds being tied up in real estate, which reduces the amount of funds available for working capital for the business. Reduced working capital may result in the business being forced to raise a series of short-term loans. If short-term borrowing cannot be serviced out of cash flow, or short-term loans cannot be repaid on due date, then although the business has large amounts of fixed assets on the balance sheet it

will face insolvency. Generally, in a forced sale situation buildings will not realize their Balance Sheet value.

Although leasing is less final than building or buying, nonetheless the location decision must still be made just as carefully. If it later transpires that a leased property is in the wrong location, there will be disruption internally to the smooth running of the operation and externally to the customer, and effort and money expended in finding new premises and moving, that could have been avoided had the correct decision had been made initially.

What are the differences between cost and the benefits to be made?

Break-even analysis can be a useful tool to determine location. Break-even analysis is a technique that shows the amount of sales revenue required in a given situation to cover the costs of the operation. For break-even purposes, costs are divided into fixed costs (i.e. those costs that don't change no matter how many sales are made) and variable costs (those costs, that increase or decrease in proportion to sales activity).

Have alternatives been evaluated?

Given a choice of locations, perhaps the easiest method of evaluation is by a checklist of relevant requirements. In the checklist shown in Table 10.1 a point rating system has been

Table 10.1 Evaluating weighted criteria using a fictitious event management company, which organizes university award ceremonies throughout the UK. Rated from 1–5 where 5 is superior.

Criteria (a)	Weighting 1–5 (b)	Location A meeting criteria 1–5 (c)	Total points (d) (i.e. b × c)	Location B meeting criteria 1–5 (e)	Total points (f) (i.e. b × e)	Location C meeting criteria 1–5 (g)	Total points (h) (i.e. b × g)
Proximity to local customers	1	1	1	1	1	1	1
Proximity to local suppliers	1	1	1	1	1	1	1
Access to good road links	4	2	8	5	20	5	20
Low cost of property	5	1	5	1	5	5	25
Land opportunity to expand	1	5	5	5	5	1	1
Attractive location	1	5	5	3	3	3	3
Availability of using local staff	1	5	5	5	5	1	1
Total			30		40		52

incorporated. This is using a fictitious company that organizes university graduation ceremonies throughout England. The importance of each criterion is given a weighting, and then in the second column a further rating is given as to how well the criteria are met by the first organization. These figures are then multiplied to give the weighted criteria. For example, access to good road links weighted 4 × location B meeting criteria 5 gives an overall weighted criteria of 20.

It can be seen that the company cited above does not weight heavily the need for a close proximity to their suppliers or customers. It does, however, rate highly the need to be close to a good road network. This would be typical of a small virtual company that uses suppliers from across the UK and meets its customers on their own properties, or uses short-term hired premises close to the event where they can meet their clients. Similarly, in the example given, the need to use local staff is rated low, so those venues that are close to a useful labour supply do not rate highly in the final analysis. The need to have property that is capable of further expansion is not of high importance.

It can be seen from this example that if you as the event manager identify the criteria that are of importance to you, and weight them carefully, you can use the above technique to assist in location selection. This technique can also be used in venue selection for an event (see Table 10.2, which illustrates the example of choosing a wedding venue).

However, over time the weighted criteria may change in some way. The logical location that appears to be the best at one point in time may seem inferior at a later date. This is due to a change in one or more of the many factors that influenced the original choice. This can prove costly. The event manager should therefore aim to anticipate changes in needs in order to make the best and well-informed decision.

Table 10.2 Evaluation of weighted criteria identified by the bride and groom for a wedding planning company

Criteria (a)	Weighting 1–5 (b)	Venue A meeting criteria 1–5 (c)	Total points (d) (i.e. b × c)	Venue B meeting criteria 1–5 (e)	Total points (f) (i.e. b × e)	Venue C meeting criteria 1–5 (g)	Total points (h) (i.e. b × g)
Proximity to church for guests to travel	2	5	10	4	8	3	6
Capable of sitting required numbers	5	1	5	5	25	1	5
Choice of menu	4	5	20	5	20	3	12
Sole use of venue	5	1	5	5	25	1	5
Cost	3	5	15	3	9	3	9
Overnight facilities	4	4	16	5	20	4	16
Photograph opportunities	4	3	12	5	20	3	12
Facility to store opened wedding gifts	3	5	15	5	15	5	15
Total			98		142		80

Choice of location for an event

Every event is held somewhere. It could be in purpose-built facilities or heritage sites, on the fells for a marathon, on purpose-built waterways for the rowing championships at the Olympics, at unique one-off sites, or in a conference venue. Large public events can be held outside in public parks, in the streets or shopping malls, or in the middle of the desert (Silver, 2004). Some events are held annually in the same venue, while others seek new and unusual sites for subsequent events.

Silver (2004) says that numerous studies have shown that an essential criterion in selecting a destination for events is safety. Site evaluation should include safety and security. Political unrest, crime-ridden areas, extensive roadway construction and other hazardous situations should be evaluated carefully.

Developing selection criteria

Although the list below is not likely to be comprehensive, it does give an idea of what an event manager should consider when choosing a location for an event. The event manager should compile a list that takes all the likely issues into account.

The points below are set out in no particular order; the event manager would have to return to the objectives and critical success factors in order to establish an order of priority:

- Availability
- Accessibility of location for customers, suppliers and emergency agencies and all staff members
- Suitability for a safe flow of consumers within the site, customer services, participants and visitors
- Cost – of hire and supplementary costs of making the site appropriate for the event
- Appropriateness, atmosphere, attractiveness and image of the venue for the event and for the client
- Capacity of the location, spatial considerations and likely obstructions, and versatility
- Safety and security issues
- Parking facilities
- On-site services available, or the cost of bringing those to the site
- Facilities available
- Personnel on the site and professionalism of the venue management
- Impacts on the environment – such impacts would include noise pollution, turf replacement, and the cost of returning the site to its previous condition
- Storage considerations
- Suitability for those with special needs
- Hygiene and cleanliness standards
- Legal considerations and possible constraints on the event
- High visibility to attract customers, if necessary
- Crowd management and control issues
- Technical facilities.

Having developed the selection criteria, the event manager will need to consider the choices that are available. The Internet provides many useful websites for venue finding and networking opportunities, and contacts can help narrow a list of options down to a few. It may be that there is no choice; the venue is already decided upon, and the event manager has to adapt the location in the best ways possible to meet the objectives of the event.

Where it is possible to have a choice of venue, then a site visit is essential. Photographs can be taken of the site in order to record important data and to enable consideration to take place at a later date and with the clients and suppliers. It is useful for the event manager to walk through the premises as if a customer in order to evaluate distances, sight lines and any unforeseen issues. The weighted criteria analysis approach is very useful, since it takes into account those aspects that are most and least important.

visite du site

The same style of analysis that was used to evaluate the choice of venue for the office premises can be used to evaluate weighted criteria for the choice of location for an event. In the example shown in Table 10.2, we have used the choice of venue as preferred by a bride and groom. The wedding planner has identified with the bride and groom those aspects that they consider to be important criteria for choice of venue, and has then asked them to rate these criteria.

It can be seen from Table 10.2 that the bride and groom do not weight the cost of the event as highly as some of the other criteria. The criterion that they do weight highly, but is not met by venues A and C, is that on the day of the wedding they have sole use of the venue. Perhaps there is nothing worse than having more than one wedding celebration taking place at the same time, and two brides meeting, or the photographer going to the wrong wedding. The final decision may be that venue B matches the weighted criteria the most closely.

This technique can be employed for many other resources that the event manager will use. It enables the critical areas to be weighted and yet all criteria to be acknowledged. If the event organizer is working on behalf of a client, this style of analysis can be shown to the client so that he or she can see how the choice of resource (e.g. venue) has been made. The criteria have arisen from the client in discussion, together with their weightings for each criterion. The table can be used to identify the event manager's research and decision-making process.

Reflective practice 10.2

1. Identify the criteria that should be considered when choosing a venue for a pharmaceutical product launch and conference in Spain. There will be over 500 delegates, and partners are invited. The delegates represent different sectors of professional people. There will be entertainment provided on two nights, and there should be opportunities for the partners to be entertained during the three days.
2. Weight the criteria using the evaluation of weighted criteria table.

Case study 10.3 discusses the factors affecting the choice of location for the British Grand Prix in July 2005.

Case study 10.3

British Grand Prix, July 2005, Silverstone, England

Negotiations between Bernie Ecclestone and BRDC (British Racing Drivers Club) were only concluded at the end of 2004 re. the 2005 British Grand Prix. It was possible that the British Grand Prix would not be part of the 2005 Formula 1 season.

In the middle of October, Bernie Ecclestone and Jackie Stewart (chairman of the BRDC) broke off negotiations regarding the British Grand Prix at Silverstone being part of the 2005 season. The BRDC chairman admitted that the length of contract and not the fees due to Ecclestone was the main stumbling block in negotiations. He said:

> *The only way forward for us is a two-year contract, which would give us time to plan and secure the long-term future of the British Grand Prix.*
>
> *We need a British Grand Prix to sustain the long-term stability of the valuable British motor sport industry and for the sake of Silverstone.*

However, new circuits are vying for the opportunity to be part of the Grand Prix circuit, which has repercussions for the teams that are taking part.

The Concorde agreement, which governs the running of the Grand Prix, allows for seventeen races to be run; dispensation was given to competitors in 2004 to allow eighteen races because of the addition of the new state-of-the-art racing circuit at Bahrain. In 2005 there is the addition of Turkey, which increases the number of races to nineteen. Fortunately for the British Grand Prix, all ten Formula 1 teams have agreed a formula whereby they will shoulder the costs for the two extra Grand Prix but will decrease their number of test days, thus giving a reprieve for the French and British Grand Prix.

The full provisional season, as at November 2004, was as follows:

March 6	Australia
March 20	Malaysia
April 3	Bahrain
April 17	France (contract under discussion)
April 24	San Marino (subject to compliance with contract)
May 8	Spain
May 22	Monaco
TBC	Europe
June 12	Canada
TBC	United States
July 3	Britain (contract under discussion)
July 17	Germany
July 31	Hungary
August 21	Turkey
September 4	Italy
September 11	Belgium
September 25	Brazil
October 9	Japan
TBC	China

On 9 December 2004, it was announced that the 2005 British Grand Prix was confirmed as part of the 2005 season. A deal is now in place between Bernie Ecclestone and the BRDC which guarantees that the event will take place at Silverstone until 2009, with promotion the responsibility of the BRDC.

(Information reproduced and supplied by courtesy of Brynn Williams MD, at www.crash.net.)

Reflective practice 10.3

Regarding Case study 10.3:

1. What factors have contributed to the locations of the 2005 Grand Prix?
2. If 2006 saw the introduction of Grand Prix in Mexico and India, what might the repercussions be for the other Grand Prix?
3. What are the benefits of holding a Grand Prix in Mexico or India?

(Research Bernie Ecclestone and FOM at http://en.wikipedia.org/wiki/Formula_One_Management and at www.formula1.com)

Layout of activities and fixed arrangements at an event

Having determined where the event organization will be located, the next issue is to consider the layout of the event with the overall objectives of facilitating efficient operations and first-class customer service. As in most area of operations, the first principle is to establish the relative importance of customer satisfaction *vis-à-vis* efficient use of resources.

At an event, there may be a physical flow of people or materials around the site, as at an exhibition or an agricultural fair. Alternatively, customers may be seated once having entered the venue, as at a conference or a concert. Layout planning aims to:

1. *Optimize movement.* In an office or a backroom area, the aim will be to reduce movement. However, at an exhibition the aim might be for a layout that will increase the distance to be travelled by the visitor. For example, visitors may be channelled up and down aisles, and the actual distance travelled maximized rather than minimized so that the customers are obliged to pass by each stand. In this way exhibitors would not feel that their stand is disadvantaged.
2. *Reduce congestion.* One of the objectives of the event manager is to add value and eliminate non-value adding activities. Seldom is value added by having customers waiting in queues. There is a limit to how long people will queue, no matter how good the service or product at the end of the queue. However, in some cases queues are unavoidable, and here the event manager should use them to advantage – for example providing extra advertising or selling extra products. At outdoor events there are many different forms of diversions that can be used, such as street entertainment, catering spots and live demonstrations. The entertainment may help to build up anticipation and the feeling that the event has already begun. Providing entertainment during the time people may be waiting reduces frustration and consequent problems.
3. *Maximize the use of space.* As we have seen, space costs money. Thus it is important to make the best use of space. For example, if there is spare space it can always be used for display purposes. Likewise, with the customers' interests at heart, it follows that where possible more space per person should be allocated to customer areas and less space to backroom facilities and supporting functions.

Putting on an event is similar to a project; there are two aspects which are finite – time, since the event has to be implemented by a certain day and time, and also space.

Computer-aided event planning

Layout planning of a large complex event, such as an exhibition or outdoor event where many different activities are occurring around fixed positions of marquees, stalls and sub-events, is a time-consuming process. The industry is now using computer-based approaches transferred from other industries, such as building and construction, to assist in this process. The benefits of these approaches are as follows:

1. Alternative layouts can be quickly generated for comparisons and evaluation
2. Interactive processes between the positioning of equipment/stands and the flow of customers can assist in visualizing the reality of movement of customers in the finished design
3. The computer software can be linked with other software packages to quantify resource needs and to develop site maps showing full details and part details for different groups of people
4. Costs can be predicted for different configurations.

Types of layouts for events

Much of the operational management literature explores the different types of layouts that are available to any service manager. These include:

- Process, where all operations of a similar nature are grouped together
- Product, where groups of facilities are arranged according to the needs of the event, and ideally the process should be continuous with the customer moving from facility to facility
- Fixed position, where neither the customer nor the service provider moves
- Hybrid, which is a mixed form of layout – for example, an exhibition may contain catering facilities with self service (product layout), table service may be also be offered (process layout), and seminar facilities (fixed position).

However, these structured definitions do little to help the event manager, who must contend with an enormous variety of different events in an enormous variety of different locations. What is of supreme importance is that the event is well set out with maximum use of space and minimum congestion. We will consider capacity management in Chapter 13, as this also has to be taken into account in when planning and designing an event.

Creating the site plan

A site inspection is essential, and photographs are also useful. For large events, an accurate, scaled plan will enable a visual understanding of space, both on the ground and by elevation. Elevation is often overlooked and only considered when tall structures are actually being brought into position. Similarly, space should not just include the actual dimensions of structures but also customer movement. The plan acts as a communication tool indicating the proposed use of space for all the different stakeholders. It is essential for some suppliers, who may need to know distances between fixed positions and electrical supplies, or the dimensions of entrances for ease of access. Suppliers will also look on the plan for the storage areas and drop-off points for their goods, and what facilities are set aside for maintenance.

Although many revisions may take place, the final draft should be sent to all interested parties. However, it may be possible to create several versions of the plan, one for suppliers, one showing the provision of power services and water facilities for the event, and others for particular groups of people with different information needs. The entertainers

and speakers will want to know the location of the green room and where they can wait and relax during the event. Similarly, if the event is attracting media interest the media area should be specified and/or the site for any related press conferences.

These plans may be required by other agencies, such as the Health and Safety Executive (HSE) and fire chiefs. The HSE will need to ensure that all their regulations have been taken into account and that the event will be able to function safely.

Silver (2004) states that the site plans should include all the features and constraints of the site, such as doors, windows, electrical connections and the amount of power available, cleaning and drinking water, waste outlets, posts and pillars, and access roads etc. The plan should indicate where everything connected to the event will be placed, and how the customers will circulate.

The need for detail and accuracy in site plans increases in direct relationship to the size and complexity of an event.

As stated earlier, the plan can be created by computer or drafted by hand. The event manager should use an accurate, scaled plan, and the northerly direction should always be indicated. Having a universally accepted direction on the plan is a sound risk strategy, so that when suppliers or other groups come onto site, there can be no misunderstandings.

Any symbols that are used on the plan should be explained. There is now a common visual symbol language, and this must be used at all times so that people from different countries can 'read' the plans. All entrances and exits and parking facilities must be clearly marked. First aid and emergency access must also be clearly shown, so that these areas are kept free of obstructions, and emergency vehicles should be able to access all areas. Not all items need to be on one single map, since it can then appear too complex and again lead to misunderstandings.

O'Toole and Mikolaitis (2002), whilst agreeing with the elegance and precision of computer-generated plans, state that a hand-drawn, well-illustrated plan may be better for communication with the target audience, and may also set the right mood for the event. Consideration should be taken of those who will be reading the plans. Often the customers are not 'plan literate', or may not have the inclination to spend time trying to sort out the various intricacies of a complex plan. Plans can be designed to be displayed on the Internet, and they should be appropriately simple and yet offer good communication. By indicating lost-children points, information and telephone points, cash withdrawal facilities and mobile recharge facilities on the plans, the event manager is demonstrating that the event and the management are child and people friendly. An aerial orientation may be suitable for this purpose.

Visual aids are an important element of layout planning. These comprise representations, including drawings, templates, three-dimensional models, movement patterns and cartoon maps.

The site plan may also be used for a seating chart at a concert, or within a festival programme to show where the different entertainments and facilities are sited.

Crowd-related issues

Virtually all events will require space from the arrival to the departure of the guests, participants and performers, suppliers and volunteers. The varying requirements of each of these groups must be considered, as they pass through the event, creating potential bottlenecks, overcrowding and reduced customer satisfaction. Getz (1997) suggests an excellent checklist for event managers to consider to enhance customer experience and help prevent crowd-related problems:

- Provide ample space at access and egress points
- Avoid dead ends and bottlenecks that will lead to congestion or movement against the flow

- Provide adequate and appropriately orientated signage
- Disperse toilet facilities and cloakrooms throughout the site
- Ensure that all staff, including security staff, are customer-focused and able to help with directions
- Screen and block off no-go areas where risks may be high
- Separate vehicle and pedestrian movements where possible
- Use public announcements and signs to advise customers about problems and opportunities
- Trial run the event site if possible
- Provide on-site security facilities and services
- Install security devices and CCTV
- Use lighting to avoid hazards and maximize security
- Segregate potentially aggressive groups
- Maximize staff communications
- Provide, test and adequately sign emergency exits and procedures
- Avoid potential crowd stressors, e.g. excessive waiting, overcrowding, overwhelming security, and barriers which would restrict escape.

Certain elements of the event should be next to each other, and others should be considered carefully – for example, the closeness of catering and sanitary facilities. The entrance to an event should be large, spacious and well signed. Research has shown that movement as customers enter an event slows down as people look around and orientate themselves, hence it is essential that this be taken into account in the design.

Accommodating special needs

In many countries there are legal requirements to provide certain facilities for people with various disabilities. However, the professional event manager should not only be striving to comply with these laws but also seeking other new ways to be more sensitive to disability issues and needs. It could be that the event has attracted customers, suppliers or staff who are very tall, very short or very large. Their requests should be accommodated in a non-judgmental manner. With regard to the content of the event, the speakers should be kept informed of the various needs of their 'audience' so that extra handouts can be supplied, and they should be aware if a person is 'signing' to those members of the audience who are hard of hearing. The audiovisual team should also be aware that the interpreter must be well lit and visible.

For those with difficulties with movement, all entrances and routes should be kept free of obstructions, and ramps, stair lifts and curb lifts provided.

Equally important as the actual provision of physical amenities is that all staff should be sensitive to the needs of all of their customers, and that their tone of voice and manner should be the same as to any other individual.

A useful *aide memoire* for an event manager when considering special needs includes the following:

- Provide information about the services provided
- Use large-print signage and/or Braille, and site signs at the right height for wheelchair users
- Consider different type of fire alarm systems for those who are hard of hearing
- Provide special communication devices for use during the event
- Where possible, remove physical barriers to ensure access to all buildings and elements of the event
- Consider the width of the aisles, the gradients to be covered, the dimensions of gates and doors to be passed through, and their ease of opening
- Install accessible toilets and washing facilities

- Add handicapped parking places with easy access to the site
- Discuss with a range of people with difficulties what they feel would be useful to make their visit to the event more comfortable and enjoyable.

Event signage

Very little seems to have been written on temporary signage. Where it is thought through in advance and installed correctly, it generates very little comment. At other times it is just grumbled about as being unsuitable, inadequate and illegible, not useful, and looking hurried and temporary. It might be thought that some events which are held annually at the same venue may not need a great deal of signage, but when a new customer attends and has not learnt all the unspoken and unwritten language which comes from familiarity there will be problems.

There are six types of signage used at an event:

1. External to the venue, giving directions and parking areas for different sorts of vehicles and purposes
2. Internal directional signs, e.g. registration this way, 'you are here' boards
3. Statutory, e.g. fire exits, slippery floor, 'wash your hands now' notices, first aid facilities
4. Room and space identification signs, e.g. for toilets, restaurant, children play area
5. Sponsorship signs
6. General signs, e.g. 'thank you for coming and have a safe journey home.'

One of the elements to be included on the site plan should be where all the signs are going to be located. On the schedule of work for the event it should be noted when signs are going to be put up and when they are going to be taken down.

It is essential that the signs have a corporate feel about them, and are all made to look similar and professional. Uniformity in their design enables the customers to recognize at a glance what is being said. The signs could reflect the theme of the event by colour, shape, and the words used. With regard to their design, thought should be given to their size and legibility from a distance, and where they should be sited, bearing in mind that once the customers have arrived they may obscure them.

Different colours could be used to denote different types of signs – for example, a certain colour could be used for directional signs and another colour to denote room and space identification. Care should be taken with certain colours, because of colour blindness.

There may be some restrictions regarding where signs can be located and fixed, and this should be investigated as part of the original planning procedures. It is useful if the height and sites for placing can be consistent so that the customer becomes used to looking at a particular height and in a particular direction for information. Care should be taken with regard to their durability, in case of rain, and because they may in fact disappear with souvenir collectors.

The signage is another of the resources that the event must obtain either through an in-house team or from an external supplier.

'You are here' boards

John Nightingale, of the UK Centre for Events Management at Leeds Metropolitan University, has undertaken research into 'You are here' maps and their usefulness in directing people to alternative parts of a venue. He cites many examples where the 'You are here' map is badly orientated and may serve to confuse rather than assist in directing customers to alternative parts of the venue.

Some events take place in venues that are very familiar to most attendees. For example, season ticket holders in a football ground can probably find the way to their place with very little help after having attended for a few matches.

However, very many events take place in venues that are unfamiliar to their customers, and often in a strange town. Indeed, one of the attractions of events such as the Olympic Games is going to a brand-new stadium in a far-away country. It is these customers who need to be able to find their way around the site. Nightingale says that they do this by using a variety of techniques, including:

- Following the crowd
- Asking directions (from other customers or staff)
- Navigating using sign posts
- Navigating using a site plan (often provided in a brochure or programme)
- Navigating using fixed maps mounted on boards provided by the venue.

This section concentrates on the last of these – the 'You are here' board. It is important to locate boards appropriately and to orientate them correctly. Similarly, it is important to avoid vandalism to the boards or their becoming obliterated by graffiti, and to check them regularly to ensure that excessive fingering is not eroding popular destinations.

Maps are commonly used for navigation, whether driving, walking or cycling. Different scales of maps are used in different circumstances. It is therefore important for maps to include details of the scale, so that customers can estimate how far away their destination is. Nightingale notes that it is surprising, in practice, how few fixed maps at events contain this information.

The importance of having a map that is correctly orientated to features on the ground is borne out by the plaques commonly found in prominent viewing locations, such as at the tops of mountains. These have been in use since the mid-nineteenth century, and indicate other prominent landmarks, such as neighbouring mountain peaks. These are always precisely orientated so that other landmarks can be easily identified. They are usually set horizontally or nearly horizontally, and are frequently made of engraved metal to give a durable surface in a location that is normally unsupervised.

At events, fixed maps are usually mounted on a metal frame or attached to a wall. In practice the map is usually vertical and orientated for architectural convenience, perhaps on a wall or in a prominent position along the edge of a road or pavement. For reasons of health and safety, planners are often keen to avoid the board being a potential barrier to people walking along the pavement – they do not want people, especially those with poor vision, to be bumping into signposts which are supposed to be there to help.

However, a vertical map can be located so that buildings on the left of the map are to the left on the ground, and buildings on the right of the map are to the right on the ground. Things at the top of the map will then be behind the map board, and things at the bottom of the map will be in front of the board. Nightingale believes that this is the most readily understood orientation, and should be used whenever possible. Any other orientations require the user to revolve the map in their head, causing difficulty in recognizing the correct direction.

Nightingale's research cites many instances of 'You are here' boards that are badly sited and that often lead the observer to go in the wrong direction. In many of these cases it is possible to orientate the map more closely to the ground, for instance by placing it on an adjacent wall at a different angle. Within event venues, this problem can be more easily solved.

It is interesting to compare the orientation of map boards with the signs used on main roads. When you approach a road roundabout, there is usually a sign indicating the exits from the roundabout. This always shows the driver entering from the bottom of the map, so that points straight ahead are at the top of the sign, while the left of the sign indicates a left turn and the right of the sign indicates a right turn. You never see a roundabout sign where you are entering from the right, the left or the top.

Presenting too much information can be as dangerous as presenting too little (O'Toole and Mikolaitis, 2002). Signs are meant to communicate, and if too much information is given and causes confusion then it has failed in its purpose. Acronyms and symbols should only be used when it is expected that all attendees will understand them. Providing key information in the primary languages of the attendees can eliminate confusion and aid in the success of an event. How often have we been to different cities or event venues and started off on a well-signed route only to find that after a short time the signs disappear or give different information?

How often have we seen a badly worded sign, or one where apostrophes are put in the wrong place? Do not rely on an external supplier to spot grammatical errors; there are far too many examples where stupid mistakes are made – e.g. 'Hot dog's stand', 'Icecream's', 'Stationery vehicles cannot be parked here.'

Occupational health and safety

Occupational health and safety and ergonomics might be considered to be a moral issue, but even the Romans realized that well-maintained slaves were more efficient and more valuable. The average fully employed adult will spend 25 per cent or more of his or her life at the workplace, with additional time in travelling to and from work. It could well be argued that employers have a moral obligation in addition to various legal obligations to provide a safe working environment, and that the workers who 'sell' their time have a right to a safe and healthy workplace. Sadly, history shows that voluntary safety arrangements do not provide adequate standards, and thus legislation has been necessary. The fault has not always been with employers, as employees are often found to take shortcuts. Statistics show that the home is still the most dangerous place for most people.

It is a fact that most health and safety requirements of workers are only common sense. It is common sense to have adequate light, correct temperatures, proper ventilation, noise controls, and so on.

Ergonomics

Ergonomics is the science that seeks to improve the physical and mental well being of workers by optimizing the function of human–machine environments. In today's office, workers are surrounded by machines, mostly electronic, and spend long hours hunched over keyboards and in front of VDU screens. In particular, ergonomics concentrates on:

- Fitting the work demands to the efficiency of people, so as to reduce physical and mental stress
- Providing information for the design of machines, key boards etc., so that they can be operated efficiently
- The development of adjustable workstations and chairs etc., so that individuals can self-adjust the workstation to meet their needs
- Provision of information on correct body posture to reduce fatigue and to minimize OOS (occupational overuse syndrome – formerly known as RSI or repetitive stress injury)
- Give guidelines for lighting, air conditioning, noise limits and so on.

Most governments throughout the world have a department or agency that will happily provide, free of charge, ergonomic advice and information geared to local needs.

Reflective practice 10.4

What are the criteria that you would use in determining the optimum location for:

1. An event management company that has students as its main market and specializes in student nights in a university town?
2. A teambuilding company that mainly has large businesses in the North of England?
3. A promoter for a jazz band touring Europe?
4. The organizer of the Tour de France?

Chapter summary and key points

This chapter has covered the practical aspects of location, layout and signage, and has considered occupational health and safety issues and ergonomics. All of these areas are intertwined. It is obvious that ergonomics could likely recommend changes to a layout, and in itself layout will be limited by the size and shape of the space available.

These topics are very much operational issues, and yet exist in the broader strategic context of the organization.

Location decisions are essentially to do with where a service operation is best placed to serve the market. The alternatives are speed to customer, or ease of access by customer. Although a location decision will not ignore the extended supply chain, nonetheless generally the supplier will be of lesser importance in the determination of service locations. Business policy will, to a large extent, determine location.

The chapter has identified that there are many influences on the location of premises and the location of individual events and their layout. It has focused on asking questions that must be answered in order to optimize the location, efficiency and effectiveness of the event.

The chapter has considered the use of computer-aided event planning models and how these might be harnessed to model crowds arriving and leaving an event, and within it. Other extremely important issues to the event planner are how to accommodate special needs, healthy and safety issues, and ergonomics, and these have been analysed in relation to events. A useful section within the chapter has been devoted to event signage, since without adequate and thoughtful signage visitors to an event will become dissatisfied and leave with the perception of an inefficient event and event manager.

Chapter 11

Risk management for event managers

Learning Objectives

After reading through this chapter you will be able to:

- **Appreciate different definitions of risk and their application in the event industry**
- **Identify different ranges and categories of risks**
- **Be aware of the causes of accidents**
- **Be able to use a range of techniques to identify and manage risks.**

Introduction

A risk is some thing that might happen in the future that will result in an adverse effect. Risk management is the art of being aware of all the things that could go wrong and having plans and contingencies to prevent this, not to remedy the situation as best as possible if things do go wrong. Harrison and McDonald (2004) say that the process of risk management involves identifying the risks, specifying their nature, assessing the degree to which the risks could impact upon the event, and developing contingency plans designed to avoid or minimize the potential impacts. It is this structured approach that will be used throughout this chapter. In the operations management literature there are many techniques that have been designed to reduce and manage risk, and we have chosen a few of these to illustrate how event managers can take advantage of previously proven techniques which can be transferred to the event industry.

We are now at the end of the detailed planning stage of the event operations management model. However, from the previous discussion you will agree that in fact the issue of risk management could have been covered in any one of the stages of the model. Since it is usual for the risk and the problem to show itself during the event, it could have been placed in the implementation stage of the event operations management model. It could also have been considered throughout the analysis and even in the evaluation stage. If we were to consider risks in the last stage of performance evaluation, it would be to review any 'near misses' and how well the event manager organized and coped with the aftermath of the risk actually occurring.

However, before we progress we can also put forward the view that risk offers many opportunities. Goldblatt (1997) defines each special event as a unique moment in time, celebrated with ceremony and ritual to satisfy specific needs. Although we accept that all events are special, they do not always have to include a celebratory aspect. By accepting Shone and Parry's (2004) definition, where

they emphasize that events are non-routine occasions set apart from the normal activity of daily life, we can see that event managers should indeed take risks. Laybourn (2004) advocates that one reason why events are special is because of risk – the event has not been done before. Allen (2000) says that without risk there can be no competitive advantage. We would add that taking well-defined risks and being a lateral and creative thinker would enhance the event manager's approach to events, and their consequent outcome. Indeed, staying the same would constitute a risk.

What is risk management?

Risk management is an ongoing, integrated and iterative process (Silver, 2004) – as resources are allocated and plans set, so must the event manager be able to be responsive to needs for change.

In simplistic terms, risk management is the art of:

1. Anticipating what can go wrong (i.e. the risk)
2. Risk identification
3. Calculating the probability that the risk will occur
4. Estimating the impact if the risk does occur
5. Determining in advance what can be done to avoid things going wrong, so as to prevent the risk happening, or planning actions that can be taken to correct or ease the situation if the risk does happen
6. Communicating the risks and actions that can and should be taken if necessary.

Laybourn (2004) supports this view and says that risks have to be identified, problems pre-empted and ways to manage them fully integrated into the planning of the event. This will involve having contingency plans ready and fully understood by all the different suppliers and personnel working on the event. Laybourn (2004) also identifies that risk management involves the estimation and use of probabilities.

Anticipating what could go wrong

Even for a straightforward event, there will be many things that can go wrong. Sometimes, because we are used to running similar events we might become complacent, sometimes we might rely on good luck (it can't happen to me), and sometimes we will just be plain ignorant of what might go wrong.

Murphy's law says that if anything can go wrong, it will. Nevan's corollary is 'and at the worst possible time'.

It is a fact that on average a risk will have bad outcomes rather than good ones. For example, bad weather not only stops work proceeding but can also even destroy previous work, whereas good weather does not mean that double the normal work can be done.

However, risks do not always have to have a safety aspect to them, for within our detailed planning stage there are many activities that could go wrong without any threat to safety. For example, although the appointment of a caterer who is providing a complex fresh hot food menu for an event may pose risks in respect of food hygiene and potential food poisoning, there is also the risk that the caterer will not turn up, or that the menu choice will have to be reduced, or indeed that the caterer will go

bankrupt just before the event. The consequences of this may be as equally devastating as the safety risks, and perhaps more probable. Other possible risks could be that the artist you have booked for an event is not granted an entry visa by the country where you are running the event.

The risk may have positive consequences, and it could be that an outdoor event is even more successful than expected and the event manager needs to implement a contingency plan of locating and installing more portable toilets (Silver, 2004). The techniques that we propose in this chapter allow for the event manager to consider all types of risks, and not just those with a safety or negative aspect.

Different authors and texts site a range of different risks, and these can change depending upon the event that is being planned and its complexity. We have adapted a list provided by Shone and Parry (2004) which cites seven different categories. This list was originally adapted from that proposed by Berlonghi in McDonnell *et al.* (1999). The seven categories are:

1. Risks to staff and others, due to confused organization and poor health and safety practice
2. Risks arising from overenthusiastic marketing of an event, raising expectations that will not be met
3. Risks in health and safety, particularly with outside complex events which may include an inherently risky activity (e.g. pyrotechnics, dangerous sports)
4. Risks in catering provision
5. Risks with crowd management, depending on density and profile mix, crush points and emergency exits
6. Risks in security where large numbers, VIPs and media coverage present terrorist opportunities
7. Risk in transport of resources to the site.

You could augment this list so it is many times longer and more complex, and it is that act of planning and analysing activities that will assist the event manager during the preparation for an event.

Shone and Parry (2004) consider the range of risks in terms of low-, medium- and high-risk activities:

- Low-risk events are regular, routine events, often indoors and with no unusual activities. Similar events have been organized before, and considerable expertise exists amongst the staff, managers and suppliers.
- Medium-risk events might be large indoor events, possibly in more unusual locations, but where the activities are more complicated than usual. Conversely, the event may take place outdoors, but involve less complex activities.
- High-risk events are these events that involve large numbers of people who come with little experience of the event, and where the managers also have little experience of the activities. Similarly, the activities themselves may constitute a danger – e.g. high-speed motor racing, challenging outdoor corporate teambuilding events, and events where there is a greater interaction with the customers, possibly including young children.

This range of risks can alter drastically given various scenarios. An outdoor event might be considered a low to medium risk when there are not very large numbers and the activities being undertaken are manageable. However, should the weather change suddenly for the worse so everyone crowds into the refreshment marquee, the outcome could be very different.

Silver (2004) identifies the categories of risk as safety, security, capability, internal and external. The safety risks that are referred to include physical harm, sanitation and health issues. The security risks include physical or intellectual property loss, theft and fire. The capability risks include processes, use of technology and unrealistic goals.

The internal risks include resource allocation and changing specifications. The external risks include the legal environment, the weather and staffing issues.

O'Toole and Mikolaitis (2002), on the other hand, discuss two categories of risks: those that create change and may jeopardize the success of the event, and those that relate to a physical risk which could place the event manager in a situation discussing legalities.

The nature of events themselves adds to the importance of having a good risk management strategy. O'Toole and Mikolaitis (2002) site various attributes from a range of different events which predispose the need for a carefully thought-out risk management plan. Their list includes:

- Large number of attendees
- Use of volunteers and inadequately trained staff
- Untried venues
- Inadequate time spent planning, and quick decisions
- Risky activities
- A range of uncoordinated suppliers and lack of incentives to do a good job.

It can be seen that the degree of complexity, the venue, the expertise of the staff and the experiences and profiles of the customers all affect the risky nature of different events. Since an event, by its own definition, is out of the ordinary (O'Toole and Mikolaitis, 2002), it demands an out of the ordinary response during its planning and implementation. Customers are often unused to responding to an out of the ordinary situation, and the risks taken will therefore become that much greater. Silver (2004) clearly believes that in any event there will always be a certain amount of risk, and that the only thing that is constant in our lives is change. However, accepting that a failure will occur is not the same as ignoring it (Slack *et al.*, 2004).

To identify the risks associated with a particular event, the event manager should meet with the different stakeholders to review what has occurred in the past, how the new event has changed, and whether there are new industry standards that should be taken into account. The risk management techniques that are proposed later in this chapter will draw on these brainstorming and information-seeking sessions.

Hygiene risks

In food preparation it is common as standard practice to exercise Hazard Analysis Critical Control Points (HACCP). The approach is to analyse all potential hazards associated with food, to identify critical control points where hazards can be eliminated, and to establish procedures to monitor control points and verify systems. HACCP gained prominence when adopted by the American National Aeronautical and Space Administration (NASA) for space flight.

The seven steps of HACCP are as follows:

1. Analyse potential hazards with food and find measures to control the identified hazards
2. Identify critical control points in foods production from the raw state through processing and delivery to the end user (examples are cooking, cooling and packaging)
3. Establish critical limits (standards) for each control point – for example, one standard might be the minimum cooking temperature to eliminate microbes
4. Establish procedures to monitor the critical control points, such as length of time and temperature to cook, or time for cooling before packaging
5. Establish corrective actions, such as disposing of food if standards are not achieved
6. Establish procedures to ensure the system is being maintained – this might mean checking the equipment, e.g. with temperature probes

7. Establish an effective record-keeping system, more than just 'ticking the boxes', to ensure that the standards and procedures are being kept to.

At NASA level, HACCP principles and standards are backed by sound scientific knowledge and have been universally adopted around the world. At a lower level, this approach means having set procedures relating to hygiene for food workers (rubber gloves, bright-coloured band aids, hats and hairnets), temperature control for food storage (hot and cold), proper cooking of food, and clean protective food covers (if micro-organisms are present in a product, their fast propagation rate will spoil the quality of the product. Some micro-organisms may produce toxic substances, while others might be harmless to health but can have an adverse effect on taste or appearance).

Insurable risks

Since the days of the Industrial Revolution, safety standards at the workplace have steadily and significantly improved. However, processes and equipment have now attained a high degree of complexity. Swarbrooke and Horner (2001) recommend that insurance be taken out wherever possible, and that the event manager should have contingency plans in place and be ready to implement them if problems do arise. However, insurance will not prevent something from happening (Silver, 2004); it will only lessen the financial impact should it occur (see Case study 11.1).

Insurable risks fall into four areas:

1. Direct damage
2. Consequential loss
3. Legal liability
4. Personal loss.

Direct damage can be to the venue or to the equipment being used for the event, and may be caused by fire, flood, bad weather or damage during movement or erection. *Consequential loss* can be lost time arising from the venue being unavailable due to direct property damage, or the loss of a future contract as a direct result of the damage. *Legal liability* may arise from damage to a third party's property or equipment, or an incident leading to injury or illness to a patron or other person. Legal liability also includes failure to perform. *Personal loss* could include a claim for stress by an employee or patron. Personal loss also includes a direct financial loss by the event organizer.

Causes of accidents

An accident is usually the result of contact with a substance or a source of energy above the threshold limit of the body or structure. The accident may result in injury to visitors, staff and suppliers, and to property. The cause of the accident may be substandard working practices and unsafe conditions. Substandard working practices could include personal factors, such as lack of skill, stress, laziness, taking shortcuts, and stupidity. Unsafe conditions in the work environment may include poor or inappropriate equipment, no safety guards, poor training, and lack of maintenance of equipment. It is important to understand that the same factors that are causing accidents may also be creating losses in reputation and profit.

Accidents at an event can, in serious cases, lead to closure plus inspections by government officials and legal costs. At best, there will be the cost of correcting the situation

Case study 11.1

Insurex, Los Angeles, California, USA
When Lightning Strikes

Lightning poses an enormous threat for those participating in outdoor sports and recreation events.

Lightning is the second largest killer due to storms, the first being floods. Each year hundreds of people are killed or injured in lightning mishaps.

The number of lightning casualties in recreational and sports settings has risen alarmingly. One reason is that both thunderstorms and outdoor events coincide at the same time – from 10 am to 7 pm between late spring and early fall.

Here is Insurex's suggested lightning risk management strategy for outdoor events:

- Monitor local weather forecasts and warnings.
- Establish a chain of command that identifies who is actively to look for signs of threatening weather and make the call to remove individuals from the area.
- A lightning safety announcement should be made over the public address system, with information on what to do and where to find a safe location.
- Designate a shelter. The best way to avoid lightning is to take shelter. The primary choice for a safe location is any substantial, occupied building. The secondary choice is a vehicle with a metal roof and closed windows. Avoid small structures (such as picnic shelters or athletic storage sheds), trees, poles, and the highest point in the open.

Thunder always accompanies lightning. The 'flash-to-bang' method should be used to estimate how far away the lightning is actually occurring. This method involves counting the seconds from the point at which lightning is sighted to the point at which thunder is heard. The number should then be divided by five to obtain the distance (in miles) at which the lightning is actually occurring. Experts say if the count is 30 or less, all should be evacuated. It does not have to be raining for lightning to strike. Lightning can strike from as far as 10 miles away from the rain band.

Postpone or suspend activities if a thunderstorm appears imminent – darkening clouds, high winds, thunder or lightning – until the storm has passed, then wait 30 minutes before returning outdoors.

Individuals caught in a lightning storm who feel their hair stand on end, skin tingle or hear crackling noises (signs of an imminent lightning strike) should assume the 'lightning position' (also known as the lightning-safe position, although it still may not prevent a lightning strike); crouch on the ground, weight on the balls of the feet, feet together, head lowered, eyes closed and ears covered. This position lowers the person's height and minimizes the area in contact with the surface of the ground. If there are any insulated objects handy, like a foam pad or soft pack of clothes, stand on them. Never lie flat on the ground.

(Extract from website. Further details available at www.insurevents.com.)

Reflective practice 11.1

You are a UK event organizer arranging an outdoor concert in Los Angeles, and you have been made aware of the risks of lightning strikes.

1. What information would you use to develop your risk assessment?
2. What would your team need, and what would you tell the general public and when?

so that the accident will not occur again. As stated at the beginning of this chapter, if an accident can happen then it will – and usually at the worst possible time. Apart from humanitarian reasons for preventing an accident, prevention will usually be cheaper than putting something right after it has happened. The cost of having systems in place to prevent poor quality situations is discussed in Chapter 16, where we explore the cost of having a good system in place and compare those costs with those that will have to be met if problems occur.

Case study 11.2 describes those risks associated with rock concerts.

Case study 11.2

Rock concerts

Extract from *Casual Rock Concert Events*, by Mick Upton

With the benefit of hindsight it is now possible to assess the level of risk presented by major casual concert events. The following table is the result of research for the period 1974–2002. It is not intended as a definitive list of fatal incidents that have occurred at concert events. It merely illustrates the level and type of incidents that have occurred in similar circumstances in countries thousands of miles apart. The list includes both indoor and outdoor venue types, the common link being that none of these fatal incidents have been fully explained. Consequently they have all been regarded as being caused by the crowd itself due to panic or irrational behaviour.

Incidents such as fire, where it is known that fire exits were locked, and public disorder are not included here on the grounds that the root cause of the incident was established therefore preventative measures can be taken during planning for future events.

Table of fatalities 1974 to 2002:

Date	Place	Killed	Activity
1974	White City	1	F.O.S. crush
1976	Cincinnati	11	Ingress crush
1986	Long Beach	3	Fell from balcony
1986	Seattle	1	F.O.S. crush
1987	Nashville	2	Ingress crush
1989	Donington	2	F.O.S. crush
1991	Salt Lake City	3	F.O.S. crush
1992	Costa Rica	1	Ingress crush
1992	South Korea	1	F.O.S. crush
1993	Hong Kong	1	F.O.S. crush
1994	London	1	Stage diving
1995	Israel	3	Ingress crush
1996	Columbia	3	Ingress crush
1996	Ireland	2	F.O.S. crush
1996	South Korea	2	F.O.S. crush
1997	Michigan	1	Fell from balcony
1997	Düsseldorf	1	F.O.S. crush
1997	Brazil	7	Fell from balcony
1999	Belarus	53	Egress crush*

(Continued)

Date	Place	Killed	Activity
1999	Austria	5	Egress crush
1999	Sweden	1	F.O.S. crush
2000	Denmark	9	F.O.S. crush
2000	Baltimore	1	Fell from balcony
2001	Indonesia	4	P. A. egress crush
2001	Belgium	1	Fell from balcony
2001	Australia	1	F.O.S. crush
2002	Venezuela	11	Ingress crush

Total = 132 victims
F.O.S. indicates front of stage.
*Indicates egress-related
P.A. crush indicates an egress from a public appearance by an artiste at a shopping mall.

In order to gain a better understanding of the causes of these unexplained incidents, this research then focused on rock concert events from the emergence of the subculture termed 'Nu metal'. Nu metal emerged in the late 1980s as a subculture of punk rock. By the mid-1990s it had established itself as a fusion of black culture (Rap and Hip Hop) and new wave rock. Possibly the first indication that the culture brought with it serious crowd control problems was at the 1994 Woodstock (USA) festival. The press at the time reported that there were 4000 people treated by first aid, of whom 250 required treatment by the on site hospital. Many of these injuries were bruises, bloody noses or broken bones thought to have been caused by cultural behaviour.

Nu metal rock culture has its own language for cultural activity – for example *moshing*, *skanking*, *crowd surfing* and *stage diving*. Any of these activities can create localized, high-density, dynamic or lateral surging or a crowd collapse, yet the crowd regard these conditions as being perfectly normal.

The above table shows fatal incidences at concerts that have occurred worldwide over a 28-year period.

(Printed by kind permission of Mick Upton, Head of the Centre for Crowd Management Studies, Buckinghamshire Chilterns University College, England.)

Reflective practice 11.2

1. As part of your risk management strategy, what would you do to manage the risk of moshing, skanking, crowd surfing and stage diving without affecting the enjoyment of the crowd?
2. Bearing in mind the cultural significance of these actions, who should be responsible for putting this strategy into operation?

Risk identification

The first lesson is to expect risks where they are not expected, since risks can occur at any stage of an event. A gap analysis approach (Silver, 2004) can be used for this, which

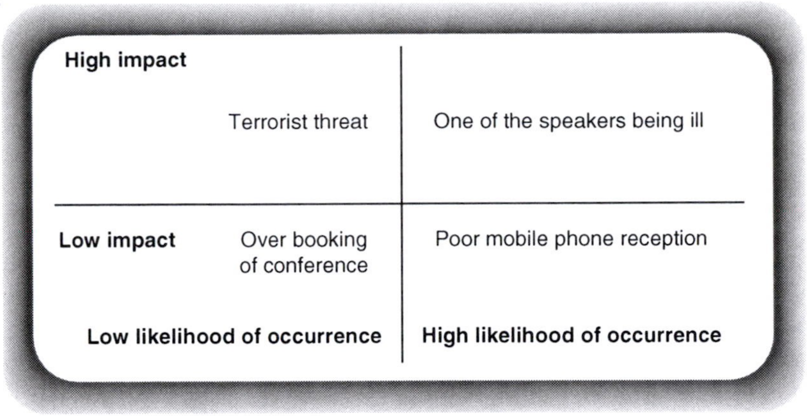

High impact	
Terrorist threat	One of the speakers being ill
Low impact Over booking of conference	Poor mobile phone reception
Low likelihood of occurrence	**High likelihood of occurrence**

Figure 11.1 Impact and likelihood of risk occurring at a conference

would identify gaps in the planning process to expose any disparities between what can be expected to happen and what might happen.

As stated previously, there are many opportunities to gather information from a variety of stakeholders in order to try and identify risks both obvious and far fetched. As event manager, you should use expert judgement, and don't ignore your intuition. Ask the questions, What if? Then what? If you and your staff think of things that can go wrong and have a counter plan, you will be able to react quickly. You should involve the advice of specialists and other professionals, such as the fire service, police, and health and safety executives.

O'Toole and Mikolaitis (2002) recommend discussions with suppliers and subcontractors, since they have a great deal of experience. They also list other groups of experienced people, including risk management experts and the staff and volunteers working on an event, who may bring their experiences from similar events in the past.

To assist in the brainstorm, a quadrant could be used to plot the likelihood of a risk occurring and the degree of impact that could be expected from it (see Figure 11.1).

Figure 11.1 shows a few scenarios that could occur when organizing a conference. This approach could be useful, with a group of people, in identifying the range of risks that could occur. It enables risks to be plotted according to their likelihood of occurrence and the level of impact that would arise if the risk occurred. However, this technique does not propose any solutions to the risks. Once risks have been identified, the event manager should also assess the impact of the risks should more than one occur at the same time (O'Toole and Mikolaitis, 2002).

Techniques for managing risks

Fault tree

One method proposed by O'Toole and Mikolaitis (2002) and Slack *et al.* (2004) is to construct a 'fault tree', which starts by deciding on a bad outcome (such as the event losing money) and then working through the various areas and functions to identify the possible causes. This principle can be seen within Chapter 14, where the use of the Ishkawa fishbone diagram is used for solving problems occurring at an event.

Risk assessment sheet

A more typical risk assessment sheet, often used by event managers, lists the possible risks on a table (see Table 11.1). The possible risk is listed onto the first column, and then subsequent columns require the event manager to assess who would be affected, the worst-case outcome as a rating from 1–5 (5 being highest), the likelihood of occurrence rated 1–5, and the numerical consequence of these scales being multiplied together. Further columns then allow the event manager to state what precautions are already in place, and what further action is required to reduce the likelihood of the occurrence or its impact. This leads to another column, listing the assessed new level of risk. Some sheets would then indicate who is responsible for this action, and the date it was taken. It can be seen that this is a working document; ideally one that is set up electronically and can be continually updated.

Oakland (2000) and Slack *et al.* (2004) propose a technique called a failure mode effect analysis (FMEA). This analysis identifies the circumstances where failures are likely to occur. By identifying these before they happen, a checklist can be produced which asks three questions:

1. What is the likelihood that failure will occur?
2. What would the consequence of the failure be?
3. How likely is such a failure to be detected before it affects the customer?

Not dissimilar to the risk assessment sheet in Table 11.1, a quantitative evaluation is then calculated for each potential cause of failure. Corrective action should then be applied. The main difference from the typical risk assessment is that this approach looks at all elements of the event – not only at safety issues and the points where there

Table 11.1 Extract from an event risk analysis sheet for a conference

Risk	To whom	A = worst-case outcome	B = likelihood	Level of risk (i.e. A × B)	Existing precautions	Further action to be taken	New level of risk	Who is responsible
Fire	All people attending	5	1	5	Fire extinguishers, alarms, briefings	Briefings with delegates at start of event	5	Duty manager
Access and egress crushing	Delegates	3	1	3	Clear route, wide aisles	Clear signposting	3	Front of house staff
Trips and falls over carpets	All people attending	4	3	12	All carpets and rugs to be secured	All trailing wires to be taped and put at high level	4	Maintenance
Poor communication	All people attending	3	3	9	Good audio equipment	Pre conference checks	3	Audio manager
Food poisoning	All people attending	5	3	15	Reputable supplier	Temperature probes in use and time controls	5	Resource manager and supplier

are negative impacts. It can be applied in a much more thorough way, and is essentially a seven-step process:

1. Identify all the component parts of the event
2. List all the ways that the service could fail
3. Identify the effects of the failures – down time, safety, repair, effects on customers etc.
4. Identify the possible causes of failure
5. Assess the probability of failure, the severity of failure and likelihood of detection
6. Calculate the risk number by multiplying all three ratings together
7. Instigate corrective action to minimize failure on those points that have a high rating.

Oakland (2000) extends the concept of FMEA by ranking the results in an order of seriousness (i.e. their criticality). This then becomes a failure modes effects criticality chart (FMECA). The FMECA determines the features of the design of the event that are likely to cause failure. It should use the experience of all the different stakeholders, marketing, design, technology and purchasing etc. The potential failures should be studied to determine their probable effects on the event as a whole. The criticality enables an examination of the severity of each failure in terms of lowering the performance of the event and its eventual success.

FMECA may be applied at any stage of the event operations management model, and in this instance it is shown in the third stage – that of implementation. However, it can also be applied during the design stage in order to identify possible causes of failure and prevent their occurrence.

The eight steps of the FMECA are as follows:

1. Identify the components of the service
2. List all the possible failure modes for each component
3. Set down the effects that each mode of failure would have on the event
4. List all the possible causes of each failure mode
5. Assess numerically the failure modes on a scale of 1–10 (p = probability of the failure mode occurring, s = seriousness or criticality of the failure, d = the difficulty of detecting the failure before its effect reaches the customer)
6. Calculate the product of the ratings, i.e. $C = p \times s \times d$; this is the criticality index
7. Indicate briefly the corrective action required, who is responsible, and the expected completion date
8. Rank the failures accordingly.

Risk assessment is discussed in Case study 11.3.

Reflective practice 11.3 (This relates to Case study 11.3.)

Risk assessments have to be considered as a living document, so while in the planning stage all possibilities have to be considered. In reality, during the event unforeseen circumstances can and will happen. Therefore the process used has to be able to be updated, changed and adapted as the situations occur. This chapter has highlighted the needs and requirements for managing risk.
Put together a process for managing risk effectively during an event.

Moment of truth

A final technique that we will present in this section is that of moments of truth (MoT). This is the moment in time when a customer first comes into contact with the event and the point at which that customer makes a judgement about the quality of the

Case study 11.3

National Outdoor Events Association (NOEA), Wallington, Surrey, UK

Letter from the Chairman, Richard Limb, re. risk assessment, 2004:

Risk assessments

Risk assessments, a term often used, a term often misunderstood, and believed by some to be yet another bureaucratic, paper-producing exercise. Let's examine the concept in more detail in relation to events.

We need to have appropriate site design, appropriate safety measures and standards and competent contractors, tailored to suit the event. Under- or over-provision can cost time, money and, of course, lives. The combination of venue, event and audience profile is totally unique. Specific standards are required that are practical and pragmatic and workable. A risk assessment approach is essential (as well as a legal requirement). The approach is simple, but should be carried out by competent persons. All hazards (potential to cause harm) should be identified for each work activity and the event as a whole. (This will require skills to superimpose the event on the venue). Those persons affected by the hazards should be identified and the risk (likelihood and severity) evaluated. The most important step is then to determine the most appropriate safety measures and then to re-evaluate the risk to determine if acceptable. Safety measures should first consider removal of the hazard before considering other control measures. The results of this process should then be communicated to all relevant personnel.

Risk assessment matrices are available to help evaluate the risk, but should be used with caution. Proper thought should be given to the problems associated with each hazard and the most practical, pragmatic method in exercising control. Otherwise it does become just a paper exercise. Used properly the Entertainment world can achieve good safety standards and also analyse and achieve more exciting, challenging performances. New diverse, unorthodox 'performances' can be fully appraised and often made to work – essential if the Industry is to move forward in a dynamic way and continue stimulating future audiences. Working Naval bases, quarries etc. can be used as venues, fall-out zones from pyrotechnics can include petrol stations. Health and Safety legislation demands full analysis of work activities and the establishment of appropriate safety precautions to protect the health, safety and welfare of all persons affected by the activities. Risk assessments are the way forward. Master them, do them properly and remember it's what happens on site that matters, a mass of papers back at base is a waste of time.

Richard Limb MIOA DMS DipAPC FRSH FIOSH MCIEH, President of NOEA
Director of Leisure Safety
For Capita-Symonds Group Limited

(For further details about NOEA see www.noea.org.uk/)

organization's services and products (Oakland, 2000). In MoT analysis, the points of potential dissatisfaction are identified within the flow chart diagrams covered in Chapter 8. Every step that the customer takes within the event should be considered and recorded. It may be difficult (Oakland, 2000) to identify all the MoTs, but this systematic approach should lead to a minimization of the number and severity of unexpected failures.

Contingency plans

An outcome of whatever risk assessment process is used should be an integrated plan of action to minimize risks in the future. These contingency plans should be communicated

to all concerned and put into action if the risk becomes a reality. The plans must be understood by more than just the event manager, both in case he or she is already dealing with another incident and also to give responsibility to others who can carry out the alternative causes of action, knowing that they have been well thought through and approved. O'Toole and Mikolaitis (2002) advise that contingency plans should contain responsibilities, chain of command, and procedures to minimize or contain the impact.

Post-event risk report

A final stage of any event is the debriefing of the staff, collection of any accident reports and evaluation of how the event progressed. These procedures are covered in detail in Chapter 14. However, it is important to conclude this chapter by reiterating the need to report back on the effectiveness of the risk management process. This review will enable learning to take place from any of the activities undertaken to minimize or prevent risks occurring. An outcome would be improved information with regard to failure modes and their effects. The data can be used to produce guidelines for the future and to improve the analysis undertaken for the risk assessments, and of course to minimize uncalled for problems and discomforts to our customers.

Chapter summary and key points

Even for a straightforward event there will be many things that can go wrong. Risk management involves identifying what can go wrong and taking steps for prevention, or organizing a plan of action to correct or ease the situation if the risk should occur. Some risks can be insured against, but often insurance will not cover the total costs. If human life is involved, the results of an accident cannot be measured in monetary terms. The old adage that prevention is better than cure should not be forgotten.

This chapter has provided techniques for:

■ Identifying possible risks
■ Calculating the probability of a risk occurring
■ Estimation of cost should a risk occur
■ Planning avoidance of risks, and
■ Formation of contingency plans if the risk cannot be avoided.

An important aspect of risk management is communication with staff, suppliers and contractors regarding what the risks are, and prevention measures that must be followed. The advice of specialists such as the fire service, police and health and safety inspectors should be sought.

In summary:

■ Know what the risks are
■ Know the cost of each risk
■ Know the chance of each risk happening
■ Minimize the chance of risks occurring
■ Have a contingency plan.

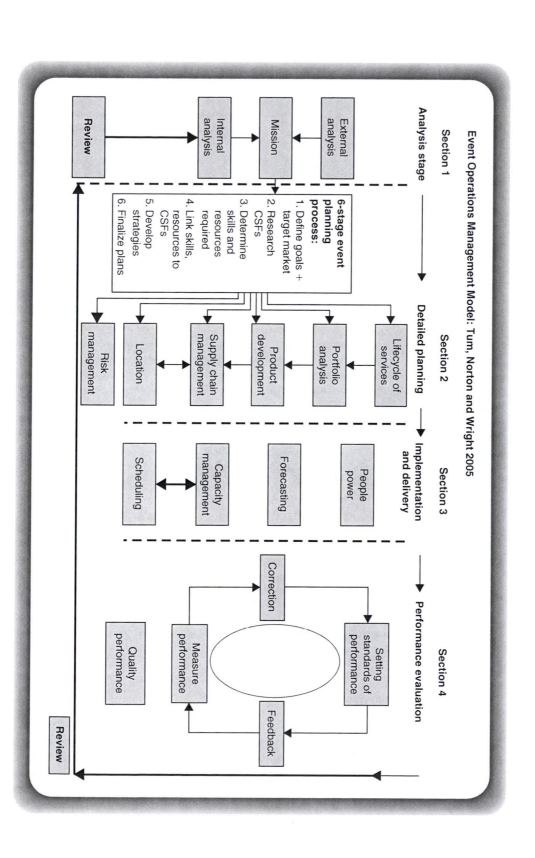

Event Operations Management Model: Tum, Norton and Wright 2005

Section 1
Analysis stage

External analysis → Mission ← Internal analysis → Review

Section 2
Detailed planning

6-stage event planning process:
1. Define goals + target market
2. Research CSFs
3. Determine skills and resources required
4. Link skills, resources to CSFs
5. Develop strategies
6. Finalize plans

Lifecycle of services → Portfolio analysis → Product development → Supply chain management → Location → Risk management

Section 3
Implementation and delivery

People power

Forecasting

Capacity management ↔ Scheduling

Section 4
Performance evaluation

Setting standards of performance

Correction

Measure performance

Feedback

Quality performance

Review

Section Three

Implementation and delivery

Introduction

We have now moved into the third stage of the event operations management model. This is where the detailed operational planning and the execution of planning take place. This follows the analysis and detailed planning covered in stages one and two. Section 3 comprises Chapters 12–14, and considers the four key operational issues of managing people, forecasting, capacity management and scheduling. Chapter 14 concludes with some advice on personal time management.

Chapter 12 considers the importance of people to all events, and how the manager can make best use of this resource. Within the event industry this resource may be one of the most costly. We have already considered in previous chapters, particularly Chapter 9, how to manage resources, locate the optimum source and use the most appropriate and relevant type for each individual event. All of these concepts are valid when we consider the management of people. An event manager has to manage this valuable and expensive resource just as carefully as all other resources.

However, people are not inanimate; they can make choices, be motivated and have different reactions in different circumstances. This chapter covers the basic theories of motivation, and explains how to get the best from all those working towards and within an event, and the importance of a strong organizational culture. The chapter recognizes that some staff may be unpaid volunteers. Volunteer staff are often used within the event industry.

Chapter 13 links the two concepts of forecasting and capacity management, as discussed in Chapter 5. Forecasting is a critical area for an event manager. The marketing function estimates the numbers likely to arrive at a particular event, and this forecast determines the amount of resources required to satisfy the expected numbers of customers. The more accurate the forecast, then, the more accurate can be the provision of resources. The actual resources needed and the ways they are presented are based on our knowledge of the customers' critical success factors.

The business policy might well state that there should be full utilization of resources and accept that on some occasions customers will queue and that some customers may be lost to the system.

Part of the responsibility of the event manager will be to determine what resources are needed overall, what can be achieved with existing resources, and how best to allocate resources on a day-to-day basis so as to achieve a successful event.

In short, Chapter 13 establishes the importance of calculating the demand and then matching resources to meet the expected demand. We have selected various techniques from the operational management literature and applied these to typical events. The chapter ends with a very useful section on queuing theory.

Chapter 14 considers scheduling, which is the critical aspect of planning and timing of activities. What is feasible and what is desirable influences how activities are scheduled. The chapter is concerned with arranging resources and setting timeframes so as to achieve the objectives of the event as efficiently as possible. Many of the techniques covered in traditional operational and project management literature are explored to consider their usefulness to event management, and how these can assist with scheduling both complex and simple events.

The chapter ends with some tips on how to manage your own time and how to recognize, and excel in, those aspects of our work that are the most important. Time is a precious commodity, and whether you are doing time, marking time or spending time, time is running out. Your only hope is to do it *now* – procrastination is the thief of time.

Chapter 12

People power – the most valuable resource?

Learning Objectives

After reading through this chapter you will be able to:

- Appreciate the importance of motivated people, and identify and describe key motivational theories
- Understand more about volunteers in the event industry
- Critically discuss aspects of organizational culture
- Use motivational theory and organizational cultural awareness to achieve the critical success factors demanded by customers
- Appreciate the purpose of Investors in People.

Introduction

This chapter is the first regarding the third stage of the event operations management model. It covers those moments when the event is no longer at a planning stage, but is happening and being consumed by those who are attending the event. In this chapter the importance of people, 'the human resource', is considered, along with how the events manager can make the best use of this resource.

As most of us will have read (or heard) in a Managing Director's or Chairman's annual address, an organization's most 'valuable' resource is its people. The Chairman could also probably have added 'and the most expensive'.

In the event industry, the level of service provided to customers and the internal efficiency of the organization depend heavily on people – the human resource – and their consistent performance. The event manager has to manage this valuable and expensive resource just as carefully as any other resource. Many of the same strategies included in the procurement process (i.e. planning, sourcing, selecting and evaluating performance – see Chapter 9) are used when staffing an event with paid and volunteer human resources (Silver, 2004).

However, the difference between managing non-human resources and managing human resources is that actions taken with inventory, equipment and machines will lead to predictable results, whereas people are not predictable. Sometimes in a given

set of circumstances people will react one way, and sometimes in similar circumstances, for no apparent reason, they will react differently.

Understanding this chapter is crucial for every event manager. People are one of the resources that the manager will have to direct and employ. They are possibly the most important resource and thus, as Lashley and Lee-Ross (2003) state, managers must be able to align an individual's needs with the objectives of the organization for the benefit of their employer, for themselves, for the client and for the outcomes of the event.

Basic requirements leading to self-motivation

As Bowdin *et al.* (2001) say, the ability to motivate other staff members is a fundamental component of the event manager's skills. Without this motivation, paid employees and volunteers can lack enthusiasm for achieving the organization's goals and delivering quality customer service. Without motivation, they may also show a lack of concern for their co-workers and customers (Bowdin *et al.*, 2001).

Getting the best out of people will be achieved by a combination of:

- Making sure that the people of the organization have all the necessary materials and equipment to do the job
- Making sure that staff know what to do and how to do it (this is often set out and explained in a job description)
- Encouraging self motivation and development.

These points are supported by Griffin (2000), who proposes that individual performance is generally determined by three factors:

1. Motivation to do the job
2. Ability to do the job
3. The resources to do the job.

If an employee lacks the ability we can train that person, if other resources are a problem we can supply them as necessary; however, if motivation is missing then the task for the event manager is much more challenging.

In Chapter 10 we looked at the physical aspects of working conditions with a view to increasing efficiency. These physical aspects included location and layout, health and safety issues, and methods of simplifying work. If the physical aspects are not right, if the layout does not make it easy to be efficient, if conditions are uncomfortable and if the work includes unnecessary steps, then it is not likely that staff will be motivated to extend themselves. Indeed, much of their energy will be absorbed in combating or adapting to the difficult conditions in which they are expected to work.

In this chapter it is assumed that the physical aspects are appropriate, and the nonphysical (or intangible) aspects that will encourage self-motivation of people will be considered.

People power

Event organizations utilize volunteers to fill some jobs that might otherwise be staffed with temporary employees. It might well be more economic to hire temporary staff to cover certain menial tasks (e.g. litter picking) and to use volunteer resources for more

meaningful tasks. Motivated people will provide high levels of service for the customer at no extra cost to the organization, and at the same time they will constantly be looking for the most efficient way of using other resources. Much has been written about motivation, and many theories have been developed, and still many organizations do not have high-performing, self-motivated people.

The importance of motivated people

The importance of motivated staff can perhaps best be shown by example.

In Chapter 2 we discussed what customers expect from a courtesy bus shuttle service at an outdoor sculpture event, taking passengers to different parts of the park.

We said that achieving specification, cost and timing would meet customers' basic needs – that is, a safe journey from 'A' to 'B' at the right time and at a reasonable price. We also said that meeting basic expectations would not in itself be considered to be a 'quality' service, but that on top of basic requirements customers would appreciate punctuality, a clean bus, a friendly well-presented driver, and consistency of service. We agreed that cleaning the bus, issuing the driver with a smart uniform and training the driver to be courteous and well groomed would incur some minimal costs, but that the overall perception to the customer would be an improved, or perhaps even a 'quality' service achieved.

If drivers can be sufficiently motivated to think of the bus as being 'their' bus, then it is possible that much of what management would like – a clean bus, adherence to the timetable, friendly and helpful service to customers and so on – can be gained at no extra ongoing cost to the organization. The only cost will be the investment in the time to change the *culture* of the organization. Once the culture is right, the drivers will not think of their job as just a means to get a weekly pay packet; instead they will be proud of what they are doing, believe that their actions can make a difference, and constantly surprise management with helpful suggestions.

For instance, at Disneyland staff are regarded as actors. They are not sweeping the grounds and picking up rubbish; they are members of the cast, acting a part.

Motivated event staff

Many staff in the event industry enjoy customer contact, and generally prefer to be cheerful and helpful. They do their best to give good service. This attitude may exist even if they receive poor pay, indifferent working conditions and bad management. They have a desire to serve and offer good service despite, in some cases, poor organization and the lack of resources. The reason for this is that they are gaining personal satisfaction from meeting the needs of the customer.

Restaurant workers might provide good service irrespective of poor pay and conditions, in the expectation that the customer will leave a tip – the expectation of a reward may encourage the serving staff to provide a higher level of service. However, in some countries (such as Australia and New Zealand) tipping is not common, and it is noticeable that restaurant service is every bit as good, if slightly less formal than in countries where tipping is expected.

This suggests that people who are drawn to being close to the customer genuinely like working with people and, given the opportunity or encouragement, prefer to give good friendly service, even without an extra reward to motivate. However, where a tip or other reward has become the custom it is not likely that people will remain motivated for long if tips suddenly stop coming, and indeed the tip is regarded as part of their remuneration.

There is no history of tipping in the events industry. You would never find security personnel or bar staff at a beer tent at a Robbie Williams concert being tipped. Our challenge is to encourage all staff, whether in our employ, in the employ of our suppliers or voluntary workers, to provide a high level of service.

Out-of-sight staff

Out-of-sight staff, such as administration support people, marquee erectors, lighting personnel etc., seldom come face to face with external customers and thus to a large extent lack the incentive of seeing or interacting with satisfied 'end user' customers, or conversely of having to field the complaints of dissatisfied customers. They are therefore less likely to be motivated by management pleas that customer satisfaction is important.

However, to a large extent it is the efforts of these out-of-sight people on which overall efficiency and eventual customer satisfaction rest. For example, at a large pop concert if the sound system fails or if temporary toilets are smelly and insufficient in numbers, no matter how fantastic the artist is, the event may be rated poorly.

Thus frontline staff might provide reasonable service to customers, despite poor conditions and poor management, simply because they are people-oriented and like positive relations with the people that they are serving. These people do not need management to tell them that the customer is important. On the other hand, those staff who have less direct customer contact are less likely to be motivated by a plea to provide customer satisfaction, even when management tries to promote the concept of internal customers.

The internal customer theory is that within an organization, the next person in the process is the customer. For example, an event organizer providing information for a brochure to an administrative staff member should consider that member as being the internal customer. As such, the information given should be clear and unambiguous, and given in time for a reasonable chance of completing the task by the time set. However, human nature being what it is, although the organizer might even buy into this concept (that the administrative staff member is the customer), in practice he or she will be irritated if the brochure is not completed on time and error-free.

Investors in People

Investors in People is a National Standard which sets out a level of good practice for training and development of people to achieve business goals. The Standard was developed during 1990 by the National Training Task Force in partnership with leading national businesses and personnel, professional and employee organizations, such as the Confederation of British Industry (CBI), the Trades Union Congress (TUC) and the Institute of Personnel and Development (IPD). The work was supported by the Employment Department.

The Standard provides a national framework for improving business performance and competitiveness through a planned approach to setting and communicating business objectives, and developing people to meet these objectives. The result is that what people can and are motivated to do matches what the organization needs them to do. Investors in People is cyclical, and should engender the culture of continuous improvement.

The Investors in People standard operates in 24 countries.

Case study 12.1 provides an example of the Investors in People Standard in a small business, while Case studies 12.2 and 12.3 illustrate its use in a large organization.

Case study 12.1

Prestbury House Hotel, Cheltenham, UK

(Organization size, 23; sector, Hotels and Leisure; organization location, South West.)

The organization

Until 1990 the Prestbury House Hotel in Cheltenham had been run as a 'restaurant with rooms'. When Stephen and Jacqueline Whitbourne took over the ownership in the early part of 1990, they quickly began to transform the 9-bedroomed property into a 17-bedroomed country house hotel and conference centre.

During the first year they developed the conference facilities and introduced a management training centre. Today, the hotel employs 23 staff (14 full time) and has an annual turnover of £650 000.

The result

Prestbury House achieved IiP recognition in April 1994, and was the first hotel in Gloucestershire to receive the award. Since then, turnover and profit has increased year on year, while the organization's reputation as a first-class hotel – for both staff and visitors – continues to go from strength to strength.

Repeat business (for business and leisure guests) has also increased, as has the number of recommendations – especially for weddings – and in 2001 the organization won a British Hospitality Association Hotel In Excellence Award.

Proprietor Stephen Whitbourne believes that much of the hotel's continued success is down to their commitment to staff training and development. As he says: 'The training programmes which we offer our staff are unmatched in the region. Not only does this make us attractive in terms of recruiting staff – and especially college leavers – but it also makes our employees more motivated and dedicated.'

The challenge

Stephen and Jacqueline Whitbourne had always encouraged staff development and offered on-site training to all their employees. However, as the business continued to expand, and employees had to cater for larger functions, they felt that the time had come to formalize standards and procedures so that all staff reflected the service culture.

The strategy

With the help of Business Link Gloucestershire, Stephen and Jacqueline Whitbourne used their current staff working methods as the basis for a more formal, tailored system that would meet the IiP requirements. They were awarded IiP recognition in January 1994, and are convinced that the process has played a major part in the continued success of their business. As Stephen Whitbourne points out: 'Because staff are such a crucial aspect to our business, it's vital that they are happy and satisfied in their work. By ensuring that sound staff systems are in place and that our training is exemplary, we hope to achieve our aim – providing all our customers with a rewarding service and pleasurable stay every time, no matter what the occasion.'

Case study 12.2

Torquay Leisure Hotels (1), Torquay, Devon, UK

(Organization size, 250; sector, Hotels and Leisure; organization location, South West.)

The organization

Torquay Leisure Hotels is a family-owned business that started in 1948 as a 28-bedroom guest-house. It is now a group of four hotels providing over 400 bedrooms and apartments with extensive leisure and conference facilities. All four hotels are situated on one seven-acre site close to the centre of Torquay. The goal is to have a 'full house 365 days of the year'.

The company has been able to generate revenue and offer employment throughout the year – 250 people are employed on a permanent basis. Each hotel operates as a separate unit with its own general manager. The general managers work closely together and report to a group general manager, who in turn reports to the managing director. In addition, there are small, central, specialist departments to support the management team.

The result

The company has moved to a collective approach to running the business. Improving communications and developing learning opportunities for all employees has had a major impact on performance.

Specific benefits include:

- Turnover increased by 17 per cent
- Profitability increased by 25 per cent
- Room occupancy rates improved (20 per cent above the national average, and growing)
- A high level of repeat business and personal recommendation
- Staff retention improved by 30 per cent
- Recruitment costs decreased by 60 per cent
- Guest comment cards showing 98.5 per cent customer satisfaction levels
- The purchase of a fourth hotel, reflecting success in a time of recession
- Forty managers now being able to design and deliver training packages
- The award of National Training Award to the group
- The use of the company as a case study of good practice in the 1993 ILAM *Guide to Good Practice* and in a BBC training video on learning organizations.

Torquay Leisure Hotels was recognized as an IiP in 1992, and was re-accredited in March 1996.

Investors in People is a long-term commitment and is a learning process encouraging continuous re-evaluation, change and improvement.

Investors in People develops the strength of a business by encouraging everyone to work as a team towards the same objective.

The challenge

The group enjoyed a period of rapid growth in the decade to 1990, developing facilities and marketing and financial systems, but suffered a substantial drop in profitability. A comprehensive business review was commissioned early in 1990.

Research and staff consultation showed that:

- Gross profitability had steadily fallen by 11 per cent from 1987 to 1990
- Standards had deteriorated, resulting in a fall in customer satisfaction
- The company had developed every aspect of its business except its people.

The underlying reasons were identified as being poor communication, limited teamwork, lack of corporate direction, the company having outgrown its family structure of tight central control with a very restricted role for line managers, an authoritarian and reactive management style, and an increase in competition.

The strategy

The senior management team, working with a consultant, recognized two main business objectives:

1. Improved profitability
2. An improved level of customer service.

Two complementary action plans were developed to run concurrently, ensuring total integration of training and development with business needs. Specific business objectives were:

- To increase sales
- To improve standards and customer service
- To improve health, hygiene and safety procedures in line with new regulations.

Organizational and training objectives were:

- To develop the structure and skill of the management team to meet the future needs of the business
- To install a systematic training and development process for all employees to meet business needs.

Necessary fundamental changes in the culture of the company included:

- Total commitment from senior management
- A review of all roles and areas of responsibilities
- Training for all employees
- Full involvement of all employees.

Steps were taken to improve the vital area of communications. The managing director instituted an annual meeting for all staff, to review the past year and put forward the agenda for the coming year. Regular departmental meetings and the introduction of a staff newsletter supported the annual meeting. The company business plan was developed to provide supporting operational plans at hotel and departmental levels to help and encourage all staff.

The company appraisal scheme was extended to all employees, and encompassed:

- Communicating individual contributions to the company
- Identifying and reviewing individual training and development needs
- Providing individuals with feedback on their performance.

All management, staff and supervisors were helped to acquire training skills, enabling those who have the responsibility for training to design and deliver the programmes themselves, and ensuring that the company's targets were achieved. The comprehensive training programmes are management driven and supported by the personnel and training officer. This systematic approach to training has included the identification of needs, setting of objectives for each training action, and constant evaluation and review against business needs. The MD, Laurence Murrell, has stated: 'Evaluation is probably one of the most essential parts of the strategy that we have put in place. It's pushed the whole development of the company forward, and now it's become a norm in the way we think and plan.'

Other initiatives have included the introduction of personnel procedures and the improvement of conditions of employment.

(Case studies printed by courtesy of Investors in People; more information about Investors in People can be found at www.investorsinpeople.co.uk.)

Case study 12.3

Torquay Leisure Hotels (2), Devon, England

Torquay hotel group wins national employment award and has been named the best in the country when it comes to employing staff

TLH Leisure Resort has won the prestigious title at a glittering awards ceremony in London for the hospitality, leisure, travel and tourism industries.

The privately owned hotel group won the award for the 'Best Employer' in the leisure and hospitality sector, beating some of Britain's best-known major hotel groups.

The award was judged on the business performance of the group, which employs over 330 staff in administration, finance, sales and marketing and in its four hotels, the Derwent, Victoria, Carlton and Toorak.

Four representatives from the TLH were on hand to receive the award from Bob Cotton on behalf of Springboard UK, which promotes careers in hospitality leisure, tourism and travel across the UK.

The accolade recognizes the superb opportunities and facilities available to staff at TLH, including ongoing training, staff uniforms, bonuses, long service awards, a staff restaurant and the use of the group's superb leisure facilities.

Chairman Laurence Murrell said: 'This is tremendous recognition of all the hard work which everyone at TLH puts in. Our business success comes from our people. We put a tremendous amount of planning into the recruitment of staff and are extremely proud that we attract and retain the best workforce possible in what is a very competitive industry.'

It could be a double accolade for TLH, as the group has also reached the final of another national award – the Business Excellence Awards, promoted by the Hospitality and Leisure Manpower, which is supported by the Department of Trade and Industry and the Department of Culture, Media and Sports. TLH has reached the final of the 'People' category, and the winners will be announced at a ceremony in London in three weeks' time.

(More information about the TLH Group can be found at www.tlh.co.uk.)

Reflective practice 12.1

Consider Case studies 12.1–12.3.

1. What factors within the three case studies would you consider to be motivating for the staff?
2. What personal experience do you have of staff motivation within an event or an event organization?

Volunteers in the event industry

There is no research that suggests that event volunteers are any different from other volunteer staff. However, Getz (1997) proposes that there might be some unique event volunteer traits:

- They are usually very enthusiastic about the event itself
- They may lack experience and need training
- Many want to have fun
- Many prefer short-term responsibilities, especially at the event itself
- They may be more artistically creative than technically creative
- They may be full of good intentions but leave things to chance, or expect others to do the work.

Case study 12.4

The Alexandra Blossom Festival, New Zealand

Hall and Rusher (2004) describe the case of the Alexandra Blossom Festival in New Zealand, where there used to be many volunteers from the local economy. The Alexandra Blossom Festival is a relatively simple community event, which opens with a street parade. It is the focal celebration for the rural communities. However, as a result of the economic 'reforms' of the 1980s that restructured the New Zealand economy, the work patterns of the residents changed and they had to work on fruit production rather than volunteer for the Festival.

Reflective practice 12.2

Investigate how changes in economic circumstances have changed the number of volunteers for events in your country.

However, it is recognized that this list contains many generalizations and that there are a great range of events, which attract a wide range of volunteers. Event volunteers offer their services and time free, usually in exchange for attendance at the event, and do not expect remuneration. This presents a greater challenge for the event manager in terms of using different means of motivation. Bowdin *et al.* (2001) propose that by conscientiously getting to know the volunteers and developing an understanding of what motivates each individual, it is possible to build up an appropriate system of reward and recognition procedures which might act as motivators for staff and volunteers.

It is important to read more widely about the research undertaken to identify what makes volunteers volunteer in the event industry and how managers can harness and increase their motivation. Some volunteers will come with a range of skills learnt and developed from their other volunteer work. However, as events move from one country to another the number of volunteers may be increasingly abundant or not. This could be due to differing economic conditions in different countries, and changes in the structure of economies (see Case study 12.4).

Volunteer committees for specific events might be made up of six or so people interested in putting together a particular event. The effectiveness of voluntary bodies is often very high (Shone and Parry, 2004), due to the commitment, work and effort that volunteers are willing to put into the activity. Volunteers also go to extreme lengths to find the necessary resources and help for their event.

On the other hand, there are many complex and growing events that see a lot of cooperation between volunteer groups and their own paid professional staff. The event manager may coordinate these different groups of volunteers to produce an event such as a carnival, or the Commonwealth Games.

Some volunteers want to learn new skills while others, possibly in an older age group, will volunteer for personal enrichment and to help others. These uncertainties argue for more research, and a volunteer system that pays attention to the changing needs and motivations of staff.

Case study 12.5 illustrates the diversity of opportunities for volunteers.

The following section relates to motivation theories and how all staff can be motivated to give their time and experiences to an event, whether they are paid or not.

Case study 12.5

USA Swimming

USA Swimming is a non-profit organization made up of very dedicated volunteers. Interested individuals donate their time, energy and expertise at every level, from the National Board of Directors to the local swimming clubs. There are 50 standing committees. Staff liaisons, along with these committees, create, implement and evaluate USA Swimming Programmes. The House of Delegates meets annually to determine the rules and regulations for the following year. Between yearly meetings of the House of Delegates, an elected USA Swimming Board of Directors is charged with the responsibility of making decisions for USA Swimming.

Volunteer jobs

There are unlimited opportunities to get involved in almost any capacity. USA Swimming is always looking for enthusiastic volunteers. Finding a way you can contribute is the most important thing to remember.

Fund Raiser: Raising funds is a priority of every swimming programme. It could involve anything from a bake sale to landing a sponsor for your club. If you have the gift of gab, this might be your area.

Public Relations Person: Promotions within the club and community are important to every team. Those volunteers skilled at public speaking or writing can be useful in this area.

Data Processor/Clerical: This area may include billing, meeting entries, accounts payable and accounts receivable, team newsletters, meeting results. All of this can be done on the computer. If you possess computer skills, you could be an essential part in the management of your club.

Hospitality or Social Chairman: Social events are a fun part of every team. Pool parties, Halloween costume contests, and Christmas carolling all serve to bond a team together. If you like to organize such functions this may be the job for you.

Snack Bar: The snack bar at any swimming meeting can generate tremendous income, especially if items to be sold are donated by the parents or local businesses. Baked goods, fruit and other goodies tend to be very popular.

Board Member: At the club level, volunteers are needed to serve on club boards of directors, or booster clubs. The most experienced volunteers are needed here.

Team Representative: Serve as the club representative or take on another volunteer role within your LSC (Local Swimming Committee).

Retention of volunteers

Communication is a key factor in retaining volunteers. By keeping everyone well informed, your program will function more efficiently and your volunteers will feel more involved.

Be sure to use volunteers in areas that enhance their interests and skills. This will make the job more interesting for the volunteer, and in turn they will be more effective. Before jumping into any activity, identify what tasks need to be done, and what the requirements are. Will the task require technical knowledge, a certain kind of personality or the use of a car? How much time will be required?

Someone who knows how to delegate responsibilities usually leads a successful volunteer organization. Work needs to be distributed evenly so no one person feels overburdened or ill-used. This will prevent burnout later on. Encourage active volunteers to recruit 'new blood' to work with them.

Motivation

Why are people motivated to volunteer? Many parents get involved to help their children. Once these volunteers feel a sense of accomplishment, they realize their contributions are worthwhile and necessary for successful programs.

Ways to motivate volunteers

- *Recognize and reward volunteers for their contributions*
- *Train volunteers to be effective and encourage them with positive reinforcement*

- *Be positive and enthusiastic*
- *Make projects a 'team effort'*
- *Respect volunteers and show appreciation of their efforts.*

The success of a group is determined by how well the people involved see their responsibilities affecting the program in a positive way. The volunteer who feels appreciated will continue to work and be productive. Praise is the easiest and quickest way to encourage someone. Saying 'Thank you' can be the same as a Gold Medal.

(Extract from website; further information can be found at www.usaswimming.org.)

Reflective practice 12.3

1. Consider the theories on motivation – how have these been used to help retention of volunteers in Case study 12.5?
2. What makes a good volunteer?

Motivation theories

Almost all motivation theory rests on the belief that humans have basic needs that motivate their behaviour (Getz, 1997). As stated in the introduction to this chapter, an event manager needs to have at least an understanding of the various motivational theories. However, it has to be remembered that theories are just that – theories – and what will work for one person will not necessarily work for another. Silver (2004) believes that an event manager should establish a motivational environment using rewards and incentives, both tangible and intangible. Tangible rewards may be financial incentives, but intangible rewards could include being appreciated, having interesting work, and being given loyalty and support.

Sometimes management does not understand that motivation is up to the individual. People motivate themselves; all management can do is to provide the environment to encourage self-motivation. However the event manager has additional problems in that the staff may not have worked together at an event before. Remember that an event is a unique occurrence and may not have taken place before, and therefore no habits or loyalties to the event manager can have developed.

The classic approach to teambuilding of forming, norming, storming and performing before reaching optimum productivity may not have time to evolve in an event situation. This approach supposes that there is sufficient time to create teams and to socialize (Shone and Parry, 2004).

Economic man and scientific management

Scottish economist Adam Smith in 1776 (*The Wealth of Nations*) and Frederick Winslow Taylor, late nineteenth to early twentieth century American industrialist, both said that people are primarily motivated by money. This is known as the economic man principle. Both Smith and Taylor also studied the conditions necessary to allow workers to be efficient.

Taylor is known as the father of scientific management. Taylor's approach to motivating people was for him to find by 'scientific' means the best way of doing a job. The best way included finding the right tools and the most efficient process. Once the best way was established it became the standard method. People were trained in the standard method, and supervised to see that the method was kept to. To encourage above-average performance, bonus payments were offered (economic man approach). In one celebrated case, 'the Bethlehem Steel Works', Taylor reported that he was able to reduce the workforce from 600 people to 220, increase profit by 140 per cent, and increase wages for each worker by 65 per cent. He also reported that for each worker:

they were almost all saving money, living better, happier, they are the most contented set of workers seen anywhere.

It should be noted that Taylor's approach was for management to develop the best method with little, if any, input from the workers. Management did the thinking, and workers did what they were told and were rewarded if they performed above a set standard.

Today, over 200 years after Adam Smith, it is evident that productivity will increase if work processes are simplified and people are trained to follow a standard process. To this extent the approaches of Smith and Taylor cannot be disputed, and nor can it be argued that people work for money. What can be questioned is that if people are encouraged to make suggestions and given a measure of autonomy, will they take 'ownership' of a job and become more productive? A second discussion might centre on whether people can be motivated to be more efficient and customer-focused without being paid extra to do so.

Before answering these questions, it is necessary to discuss the importance of money.

Money: a necessity and a means of keeping the score

Our belief is that, depending on their circumstances, some people are motivated by money more than by anything else. People with children and mortgages need money. Money is also a method of keeping the score – it is the one sure way of knowing whether our efforts are appreciated. A pat on the back is nice, and so are kind words, but money is tangible – it is a certain measure of the value given to our efforts. There is also the question of equity. If we are being paid a certain amount for doing a job, even if initially we thought the pay was good, we would be less than human if we didn't get upset on finding out that a colleague is being paid substantially more for completing the same work.

Our belief is that money is important, and it is more important for some people than it is for others. Money is only one factor. But, we believe that if people are being paid a reasonable amount, then it is possible to increase motivation without paying extra amounts. Conversely, simply paying more money cannot ensure increased productivity. Money is important, but money alone is not the answer. All we can be certain of is that the amount paid must be reasonable and equitable.

Motivational theorists

Motivational theorists fall into three broad schools:

1. Content perspectives
2. Process perspectives
3. Reinforcement perspectives.

Content perspectives

Lashley and Lee-Ross (2003) explain that content theories seek to explain motivation by considering individuals' requirements and what must be present in the workplace to satisfy them.

One of the best-known theories of this type is *Maslow's hierarchy of needs*, which is illustrated in many texts. Abraham Maslow (1943), a clinical psychologist, claimed that people have five levels of needs, and that each level has to be covered before the next level will be addressed. The levels of needs are:

1. Physiological – food, water, shelter, and so on
2. Safety – a desire to feel secure and free from threats to existence
3. The need to belong – i.e. to be accepted in a group of people
4. Self esteem – feeling positive about oneself and being recognized by others for achievements
5. Self-actualization – the highest level, roughly translated, means the development of one's capabilities in order to reach one's full potential.

Maslow accepted that each level did not have to be completely fulfilled before people moved on to the next level, but claimed that until a level had been *substantially* covered it was unlikely that people would address a higher level in the hierarchy of needs. In prosaic terms, if you are grubbing around in the gutter for fag ends, wondering when the soup kitchen will open, you are not interested that the ballet company is offering free tickets to the first 20 people who arrive.

It should be noted that Maslow's hierarchy of needs model was developed from a very small sample. He observed fourteen close friends and studied the lives of nine famous people, including Lincoln, Jefferson, Eleanor Roosevelt, Einstein and Sweitzer. His theory has often been questioned because of this lack of depth in his research, but it remains very popular and still reveals many truisms in the workplace today. The hierarchy appears to have an intuitive logic (Griffin, 2000), although it has yet to be fully researched whether people from different cultures have the same need categories and hierarchies.

Herzberg's two-factor theory is another popular content perspective that follows Maslow's line of reasoning (Herzberg, 1966, 1968). Herzberg developed a two-factor theory based on satisfiers and dissatisfiers (or motivation and hygiene factors). Herzberg's theory, like Maslow's, is that until the lower-level needs – the hygiene factors – are covered, the higher-level satisfier factors will not motivate.

Roughly translated, hygiene factors include:

- Adequate wages
- Safe working conditions
- Job security
- Non-threatening supervision and control.

Motivators are the higher-level needs, and include:

- Recognition
- Responsibility
- The importance of the work
- Prospects for growth and advancement.

It can be seen that these different set of factors are associated with satisfaction and dissatisfaction – that is, a person might identify 'low pay' as causing dissatisfaction, but would not necessarily site 'high pay' as a cause of satisfaction. Employees and

volunteers are more likely to be motivated and satisfied by achievement, recognition, advancement, responsibility and interesting work (Getz, 1997).

Herzberg's initial study was based on questioning 200 accountants and engineers in the United States. The study was therefore not based on the typical worker, since accountants and engineers would, of course, have been well above the national average for wages and working conditions. Nonetheless, the theory merits consideration. It has played a role over the last century in bringing theories of motivation and the importance of motivation in the workplace to managers' notice. For example, using Herzberg's approach it might be considered that spending money on improving the staff cafeteria in itself will not motivate people to work harder if they have little responsibility. The cafeteria would be considered a hygiene factor, but increased responsibility would be seen as a motivational factor.

On the other hand, responsibility and recognition of achievements might not motivate, if people feel that their pay is inadequate, or if there is the threat of redundancy. Thus being asked to accept extra responsibility without extra benefits might only be seen as an attempt by management to give the recipient extra work – job enlargement rather than job enrichment.

In addition to these theories, research has also focused on human needs. The three most important are achievement, affiliation and power.

Process perspectives

These approaches are concerned with how motivation occurs. Lashley and Lee-Ross (2003) say that this perspective contends that it is essential to understand the process of motivation in addition to knowing why people have different (content) needs at different times.

Rather than attempting to identify motivational stimuli, process perspectives focus on why people choose certain behavioural options to satisfy their needs, and also how they evaluate their satisfaction after they have gained these goals (Griffin 2000).

Expectancy theory is one of the theories offered by Victor Vroom (Vroom *et al.*, 1973, 1988). He argued that people are motivated by expectations, and that performance is linked to the assessment of the probability that increased performance will lead to increased rewards; rewards may be extrinsic (i.e. money and promotion) or intrinsic (i.e. sense of achievement).

Bateman and Zeithaml (1993) added that the assessment of whether the rewards will be sufficient to induce increased performance depends on the self-evaluation of one's own abilities and the availability of necessary resources. In other words, unless the chances of success (and consequent rewards) are reasonable, people will not be motivated to make an extra effort – i.e. it won't be worth their while.

Equity theory contends that people are motivated to seek equity in the rewards they receive for work done, in comparison to the work and the rewards gained by others. The theory suggests that people see their own inputs into the workplace (time, experience and education) as a ratio to the outcomes they receive (pay, recognition, promotions etc.). They are looking for equity between this ratio and the ratios of rewards received by other people.

Reinforcement perspectives

Reinforcement perspectives address why some motivations remain with people over a period of time and why some other behaviours change. One school of thought is that people's behaviour can be conditioned by external stimulus and that it is unnecessary to seek cognitive explanations. Skinner (1971) claimed that if good behaviour is rewarded and poor behaviour punished, people will be conditioned to act in a positive way rather than in a negative manner. For example, if a worker has stayed back to

midnight to complete some urgent work and is subsequently given favourable recognition, it is likely that the worker will be encouraged to act in this way again. If, however, the worker is criticized for some minor error, then he or she might feel that the effect of staying back late has resulted in a negative outcome and consequently will be less willing to put in extra effort on a future occasion. Behaviour which is rewarded is likely to be repeated, and work which is criticized is less likely to be repeated.

Skinner's theories were based on tests with rats and pigeons. One experiment included rats in a maze: if the rat took the right option it received a reward in the form of food, if it took the wrong action it received an electric shock. It was found that it did not take long for the rats to learn the correct route, and rewards and shocks were no longer necessary. This approach, reward and punishment, is also known as *reinforcement theory*.

The one common thread that all these theories have is that people's behaviour is goal-directed.

Combined approach

It is probable that most people are torn between many different needs:

- To have a job that pays enough so as to meet personal commitments, family, mortgage, and social activities
- To be in a job they like
- To feel they belong
- To have the opportunity of increasing self esteem with an important job, status and responsibility
- To feel comfortable that they can do the job
- To have job security
- To have sufficient leisure time to enjoy/follow personal interests.

Is work a necessity?

For most people, work is not the be-all and end-all but a necessity. To achieve personal needs people need adequate wages and job security, and it seems obvious that ideally if they have to work they prefer to do something they enjoy and to be given some authority, a sense of belonging and recognition for skill and above average effort – i.e. the esteem factor.

It is reasonable to suppose that people will not be motivated to make an extra effort if they think the job is beyond their scope or if the chances of success are limited. It also seems that people can be conditioned to act in certain ways by reward or punishment. It could be suggested however, that people, rather than acting as robots as a result of conditioning, are aware of the probable outcomes – the rewards and punishments – and consider the likely consequences before they act.

This would seem to cover why people work and what they would like in a job. However, it does not necessarily follow, given the individuality of people, that, even if all the above factors are taken into consideration, people will necessarily be motivated to be more efficient, to make suggestions, or to go out of their way to provide extra service for customers.

We could give plenty of examples of well-rewarded middle managers who have autonomy to make decisions but do not appear to be overly motivated. To achieve a situation where every worker in the organization is excited about what the organization is doing and willingly puts in extra effort requires a special type of organizational culture.

Case study 12.6 describes methods of motivating volunteers at the Olympics in Athens.

Case study 12.6

Athens 2004

International Sailing Federation
ATHOC Media (as amended by ISAF), Athens, 27 May 2004

In a special event held yesterday in the headquarters of the Athens 2004, the Organizing Committee for the Olympic Games, the volunteers were honoured for their services during the 3rd Sport Events Cluster (February to April 2004).

During the same event, the Organizing Committee President, Gianna Angelopoulos-Daskalaki, presented the uniforms to the volunteers who will be participating in the Olympic Games.

Mrs Angelopoulos extended a warm welcome to the volunteers, stressing that they contributed their time, strength and ideas to the third cluster of Sport Events, and added: 'We thank you because all of you together form now a group of skilled, trained and, most of all, enthusiastic people, who are ready to welcome all humanity in the Games to be held in Athens and help us organize magical Olympic and Paralympic Games in Athens in 2004.'

Mrs Angelopoulos described the volunteers as 'the heart, face and soul of the Games'. Referring to the contribution of volunteers outside Athens, she said: 'We are particularly proud because, through the Football Sport Events held in the Olympic Cities, all Greece made its presence felt in Volunteerism.'

She also made special references to individual cases of volunteers that express the universality of volunteerism as a movement.

One such example is Transport Volunteer Nikolaos Vougioukas, who has taken part in many Sport Events and of whom Mrs Angelopoulos-Daskalaki said 'he has indeed devoted a very important part of himself in our preparations for flawless Games'. She also referred to the offer of volunteer services from people of all ages – from the youngest ball boy (aged 11) to a 73-year-old baseball volunteer, the oldest of all – and to characteristic examples which in this Sport Events Cluster, as in the previous ones, highlight the universality of volunteerism as a movement. 'People from the same families took part in the Events, brothers, parents and their children – united as one, committed to the common effort and the common goal', said Mrs Gianna Angelopoulos-Daskalaki.

The Athens 2004 President also made a special reference to people 'who travelled from places very far in order to be here in Athens, with the most characteristic such example being that of Jure Abraham from Argentina, who came to Greece just so that he could participate in the Artistic and Rhythmic Gymnastics Sport Events and offer to us his specialized knowledge'.

'Jure and many others like him, prove', Mrs Gianna Angelopoulos-Daskalaki added, 'that with determination, zeal and commitment to goals people always find ways to overcome practical obstacles and realize their dreams and hopes – the little, personal ones and the big, grand, collective ones.'

Mrs Gianna Angelopoulos-Daskalaki also made a reference to the 'first Olympic Record', that of individual volunteer applications for the Games exceeding the 160 000 mark at the conclusion of the volunteers' recruitment programme and before the Games – a remarkable improvement on the corresponding figure for Sydney.

Mrs Gianna Angelopoulos-Daskalaki concluded with the following words: 'We always believed that in Greece there is a very active volunteerism movement, which contributes to a great number of areas in social life, without seeking publicity. We consider that all of you here are part of this movement and we hope that you will continue to act in the same way after the Games, becoming in this way what perhaps would be the most important legacy to our society.'

The Athens 2004 President then presented the uniforms for the men and women volunteers of the 2004 Athens Games, worn by actors Apostolos Gletsos and Theofania Papathoma and Olympic medallist Leonidas Kokkas. The uniforms, which were presented for the first time, are part of the sponsorship of Adidas, Official Supporter of the Athens 2004 Olympic Games.

A videotape with shots from the Sport Events and interviews of volunteers, athletes, top officials of International Federations and the Chairman of the IOC Coordination Commission, Denis Oswald, was also shown during the event.

> *The award of participation diplomas and souvenirs followed the projection to the Sport Events volunteers. In the open area of the Organizing Committee's headquarters where the event was held, a number of stands had been set up, corresponding to the sports of the Sport Events, together with one kiosk for ball persons, to honour junior volunteers.*
>
> *In the stands, volunteers met the teams of people with whom they worked and received their personal commemorative diplomas, which certify their participation in the 3rd Sport Events Cluster, from the corresponding Venue Managers and volunteers Venue Managers.*

(Information supplied by the International Sailing Federation more information can be found at www.sailing.org/.)

Reflective practice 12.4

Consider the motivation theories discussed here and decide which of them would be applicable to the volunteers at the Athens Olympics.

Organizational culture

Organizational culture is the amalgam of beliefs, norms and values of the individuals making up the organization – i.e. 'the way we do things around here'. Griffin (2000) states that the culture of an organization is the set of values that helps its members understand what the organization stands for, how it does things, and what it considers important.

Culture determines the feel of an organization. Organizations are made up of many individuals, each with his or her own set of values. The culture of the organization is how people react or do things when confronted with the need to make a decision. If the organization has a strong culture, then each individual will know instinctively how things are done and what is expected. Conversely, if the culture is weak, people may not react in the manner in which management would hope.

How can managers deal with culture, given its importance and yet its intangible nature? The value of such a culture to an organization that has a dedicated enthusiastic workforce cannot be underestimated. Such a culture begins with everyone in the organization, from the event manager downwards, believing in what the organization is trying to achieve. This means that not only is every person customer-focused, but also each person is determined to eliminate any cost that is not adding value.

For this culture to exist there are several prerequisites, and these prerequisites apply to everyone in the organization:

- Working conditions have to be right (location, layout and process)
- Wages and rewards have to be equitable
- There has to be job security
- Staff must have a chance for self-development (self esteem)
- Staff must feel 'good' about the job – it has to be meaningful.

We could add to this list and bring forward those factors discussed in earlier chapters:

- Everyone in the organization must know who the customer is
- Ideally everyone will know what the customer values (i.e. the critical success factors that make them come to events)

- Everyone must know the level of service that the organization is aiming to provide
- Service must be affordable and sustainable
- Service must be consistent
- Standards must be set and communicated
- Controls have to be in place to ensure that the standards are being met
- People must know how to make corrections
- Finally, but importantly, everyone must feel free to make suggestions, and management must listen and treat suggestions with respect.

Event managers must give more than lip service to the above; they should show by their actions that they believe in the capabilities of their staff.

The event manager still has to make the important decisions and set the policy. Staff will be expected and encouraged to contribute to policy, but once a policy decision has been made, then workers have to conform to the policy. Policy cannot be changed at the whim of individual people – such actions would lead to chaos. Therefore the following must be remembered:

- Objectives must be clearly communicated
- Management sets policy and guidelines
- Staff have the freedom to act within the guidelines
- People should be encouraged to make suggestions to change policy.

In a *bureaucratic culture*, some people (often management) do the thinking and workers do what they are told. In this type of culture the bigger the organization the more rules and procedures will be required, and control will be achieved by supervision and reports. Communication is usually one way, top down. Such a culture may be sterile, and create a nine-to-five attitude – i.e. sign on at nine in the morning and leave promptly at five in the afternoon.

This is probably not the culture desirable in an event organization. Staff will pay lip service to service and customer satisfaction, but will not have the authority, let alone the motivation, to provide above average service, for to do so may result in breaking rules and consequently the possibility of a reprimand.

An *open culture* is where the event manager is highly visible and approachable, there are few rules and procedures, and the staff know instinctively what is right and what has to be done to correct a situation.

The 'way we do things around here' is second nature – not just a slogan or a mission statement. People have authority to act, and are self-motivated.

Using motivational theory and organizational cultural awareness to achieve the critical success factors demanded by customers

Returning to the example in Chapter 5 where we considered a conference venue and the critical success factors that would attract the customers without adding substantially to the cost, we noted that the CSFs were:

- Well-organized coffee and lunch breaks
- Friendly and well-presented reception staff
- Useful and meaningful signage
- Well-organized meal service
- A clean and tidy car park
- A high level of customer care.

As event managers, we want to deliver to a high standard for each of the CSFs. If these were plotted onto a sheet, we could then rate the conference venue (1–5, 5 highest) as to how well it is succeeding in meeting those CSFs. A further column could be added to show how highly motivated staff could advance each of those attributes.

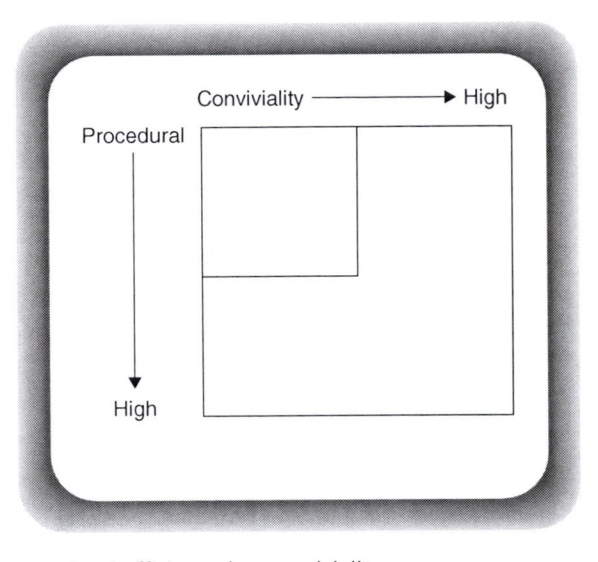

Figure 12.1 Low procedural efficiency, low conviviality

A further approach looks at procedural and convivial outcomes (procedural means carrying out all activities efficiently and correctly, and convivial means carrying out all activities with an interest in the customer).

In order to illustrate this example, let us consider the registration of delegates at an International Book Fair.

Figure 12.1 illustrates a case whereby there is very little procedural efficiency, many mistakes made, and there is poor organization. Similarly, with regard to conviviality there is little interest shown in the delegate, little empathy with the plight of the delegate due to the errors occurring, and a distinct lack of welcome.

Figure 12.2 again illustrates very little procedural efficiency, many mistakes made, and poor organization. However, there is a lot of interest shown in the delegate, lots of empathy with the plight of the delegate due to the errors that are occurring, and a friendly welcome. The conviviality factor is such that procedural problems are almost ignored.

Figure 12.3 illustrates a great deal of procedural efficiency, no mistakes made, and efficient organization. However, with regard to conviviality there is little interest shown in the delegate and a distinct lack of welcome; indeed, the reception is almost arrogant.

Figure 12.4 illustrates a great deal of procedural efficiency, no mistakes made, and efficient organization. With regard to conviviality, there is a great deal of interest shown in the delegate, and an outstandingly warm welcome.

The examples in Figures 12.1–12.4 show the link between having good resources, motivated staff and well-managed events. Only Figure 12.4 demonstrates that the event manager has succeeded in every aspect.

This technique could be used if you felt you were able to complete it honestly – perhaps at a staff debriefing after the event and prior to another event, or in advance of an event, when you could discuss how your organization could achieve both

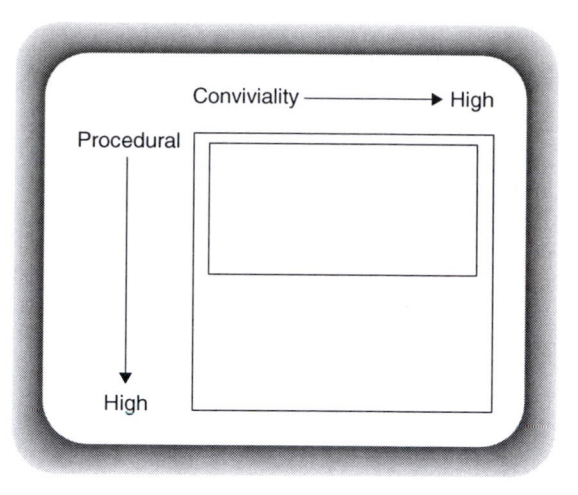

Figure 12.2 Low procedural efficiency, high conviviality

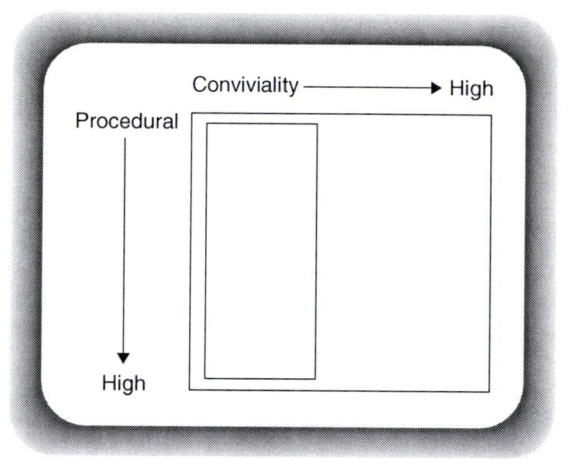

Figure 12.3 High procedural efficiency, low conviviality

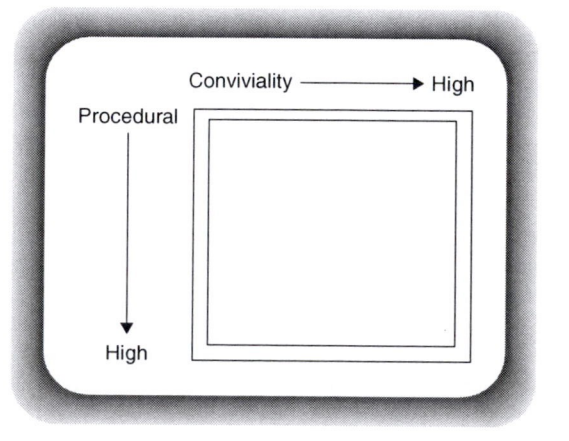

Figure 12.4 High procedural efficiency, high conviviality

conviviality and procedural effectiveness. Staff could be engaged in discussion, enabling them to express how they feel when both conviviality and procedural matters are achieved and what extra support they might need to have a more acceptable outcome.

Reflective practice

Using the motivational theories described in this chapter, go through each of them to see how, as a manager, you could lift the rating of each of these CSFs as portrayed in the table below.

Critical success factor	Current rating 1–5 (5 high)	Suggested method of improving this rating through motivation	Extra resources needed
Well-organized coffee and lunch breaks	3		
Friendly and well-presented reception staff	3		
Useful and meaningful signage	4		
Well-organized meal service	3		
Clean and tidy car park	2		
A high level of customer care	1		

Reflective practice 12.5

1. Why do you think volunteers worked for the Manchester Commonwealth Games, 2002?
2. If you won or inherited a large amount of money, would you still go to work?
3. What do you think encourages your staff to come to work – is it job satisfaction, or is it ONLY for the money?

Chapter summary and key points

This chapter began by saying people are an important resource – indeed often the most valuable resource. However, if not managed correctly people can become a most expensive resource, not only in wages paid but also in the cost of mistakes they make.

The chapter has considered the use of volunteers within the event industry, why people volunteer, and how we can best harness their enthusiasm.

It is crucial that event managers understand what motivates people. It was pointed out that management cannot motivate; people motivate themselves. What management can do is to provide an environment that encourages self-motivation. Such an environment includes health and safety, clear understanding of who the customer is and what the

customer needs, an understanding of individual duties and responsibilities, and clear guidelines as to individual authority.

Within this chapter we have discussed several motivational theories and included a section on the importance of money. This indicated that if the money paid is sufficient and equitable, people can be self-motivated if there is an open culture.

An open culture is where management is highly visible and approachable, there are few rules and procedures, and the staff know instinctively what is right and what has to be done to correct a situation. The 'way we do things around here' is second nature – not just a slogan or a mission statement – and people have the authority to act.

The chapter has concluded with a model showing the links between good resources, motivated staff and well-managed events.

Chapter 13

Forecasting and capacity management

Learning Objectives

After reading through this chapter you will be able to:

- Recognize the importance of establishing the demand for an event
- Use and evaluate the different methods available to an event manager for forecasting
- Understand and apply the different theories related to capacity management
- Apply the concepts of queuing theory to a range of different events.

Introduction

Forecasting is an essential element within the event operations management model. This is the implementation stage, although it could be argued that forecasting should form part of the detailed planning. The forecasts that are made are used by various functions within an organization – for example, the marketing function forecast sales and numbers of people who will attend, accountants forecast income and expenditure to create the budget, and the purchasing department forecast the amount of goods to be purchased. Forecasts are needed for almost every management decision. All decisions become effective at some point in the future, so they should be based on circumstances not as they are at present, but as they will be when the decisions become effective (Waters, 1996).

It is difficult for forecasts to be totally accurate because, although expected trends can be factored into the calculations, the basic information used is drawn from what has happened in the past. In considering the past, numbers alone are not sufficient, as the numbers will merely be a reflection of a variety of circumstances that influenced or determined the outcome the last time. Establishing circumstances or events that shaped past demand will not always be easy, as there can be no guarantee that all the circumstances of the past will be remembered or that they will occur in exactly the same way in the future.

The danger for statisticians and researchers is concentrating on the numbers and to ignore the circumstances.

Getz (1997) highlights that trend extrapolation is the easiest way to forecast next year's attendance, but many factors (such as the weather and competition) can intervene. The prevailing conditions of supply and demand must be taken into account.

For some types of demand forecasting, seasonal trends, levels of promotion and perceived competitor activity might well be sufficient to provide a reasonably accurate forecast. In other cases, and especially in the event industry, demand will often depend on a myriad of circumstances and situations.

The importance of establishing demand

Estimating the number of people attending an event is crucial for a number of reasons:

- Forecasts avoid unanticipated overcrowding, which is a health and safety issue – congestion can lead to accidents, stress and even riots (Getz, 1997).
- Uncertainty about numbers can cause bottlenecks and the formation of queues (Yeoman *et al.*, 2004).
- A forecast of attendee numbers helps to determine the level of investment and gives an awareness of the financial consequences if the estimation is wrong. There is a natural tendency to want to plan for the biggest possible crowd, but this strategy has higher costs and risks a substantial loss if forecasts are not met (Getz, 1997).
- Certain decisions have been made, based on the estimate, and it is difficult to change these in the short term.
- The number of attendees is an important consideration in the determination of the price for the event. Break-even analysis, where an admission price is relevant, can be used; however it may be that the price has an influence on the number of people attending. Spreadsheet software can be used to test the cost–revenue relationships in constructing break-even graphs. These allow for a quick evaluation of what can be expected to happen when the price is changed. The break-even point is also sensitive to changes in costs, and the spreadsheet can demonstrate the implications of fluctuations while price is held constant (Getz, 1997). The forecasted numbers affect many parts of the organization, and should be as accurate as possible. For example, should you provide catering for an average attendance or up to peak capacity?
- Forecasts will determine the level of capacity you provide at your event – for example, in terms of size, staffing, equipment and other resources. You will also need to know how attendees will arrive – will they come all at once, or over a period of time? As more people arrive, will others leave? Efforts should be made to disperse attendance in time and/or in space, rather than risk disaster by overcrowding (Getz, 1997).
- Without an estimate of future demand it is not possible to plan effectively for possible situations, only to react to them (Slack *et al.*, 2004).

Forecasting

It should be realized that often at an event the capacity is not static – as some people are entering others may leave – and this is an added dimension for the event manager to be aware of.

Waters (1996) says that forecasts should not be carried out by an isolated group of specialists, but by the entire organization. He believes that forecasting is continuous and actual circumstances can update original forecasts; consequently, plans can be modified and decisions revised.

You might find in your research that there is no useful market information for the type of event that you are planning, but this should not deter you. It could be that

historical data may not be available, what is available may not be relevant for the future, there may not be time to make meaningful forecasts, there could be high costs involved, or perhaps the impact of the forecasts would not make the effort worthwhile (Waters, 1996). However, there may be clues that can help, and the literature from general operations management also provides excellent advice. We will now explore some of that literature and apply it to the event industry.

Slack *et al.* (2004) indicate that there are three requirements for a demand forecast:

1. It should be expressed in terms that are useful for capacity planning and control
2. It must be as accurate as possible
3. It gives an indication of relative uncertainty.

Forecasting techniques

There is no one single method of forecasting which is best, and the three that are referred to here cover most timescales:

1. Long-range capacity planning requires forecasts to be made several years ahead. This is typically important for large and complex events that involve a wide range of different groups of people both as participants and as organizers – for example, the Olympics Games, large political events, complex annual events.
2. Short- to medium-term forecasts are usually made between 3 months and 2 years ahead. This timescale is usually due to the need to determine personnel and training needs, renting of premises and equipment, and to establish the details of the event required.
3. Short-term forecasts are needed to plan, order and allocate resources on a monthly, weekly and daily basis. The shorter the timeframe, the more accurate the forecast has to be.

You can see a link here with Figure 2.3, repeated here as Figure 13.1 for convenience. Generally the long-term forecasts are concerned with strategic decisions (i.e. at the top of the triangle of the organization), the medium forecasts are concerned with business decisions and the short-term forecasts are concerned with operational decisions (at the bottom of the triangle).

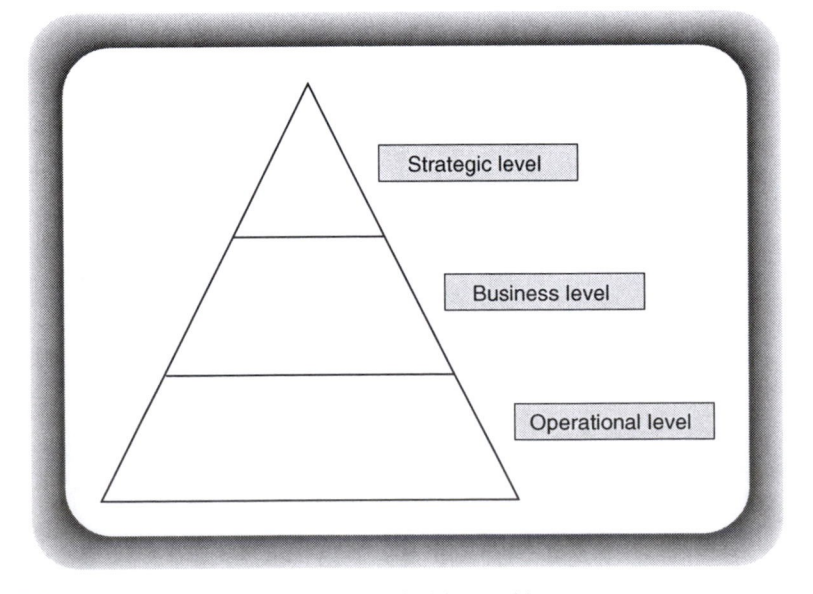

Figure 13.1 The triangle of management and decision-making

Types of forecasts

The three approaches for forecasting are qualitative, quantitative (mathematical or time series approach) and causal. In reality, all three approaches are interlinked and should be taken into account when determining a forecasted demand. The classification of methods does not mean that each can only be used in isolation. Invariably, all forecasts will also have an element of subjectivity associated with them.

Qualitative forecasting

Qualitative forecasting uses judgement, past experience, and existing past and present data (see Case study 13.1). If forecasting on past results and based on current conditions was easy, the bookmakers would soon be out of business.

Case study 13.1

Fleadh Cheoil na hEireann, Ireland

Fleadh Cheoil na hEireann is a festival celebrating Irish music, song, dance and culture, held on and around the last weekend of August annually. Organized by Comhaltas Ceoltoiri Eireann (CCE), the Fleadh is held to coincide with the UK Bank Holiday to facilitate the large numbers of visitors from Britain who attend the Fleadh each year. In any year, over the week, the Fleadh will attract between 130 000 to 150 000 people to the host area.

The First Fleadh was organized by The Pipers' Club from Dublin, and held in Mullingar on Whit Weekend 1951 in conjunction with 'Feis Lar na hEireann'. The stated aim of the event was 'to restore to its rightful place the traditional music of Ireland' by bringing to the midland town 'the cream of traditional musicians from the four corners of Ireland'.

The first Fleadh Cheoil na hEireann attracted only a few hundred hardened but enthusiastic patrons. Within 5 years, this annual gathering had grown to a national festival attracting many tens of thousands of visitors. Nowadays, the Fleadh is a major international festival drawing visitors from all five continents. With the growth in popularity of 'World Music' and the phenomenal interest globally in Irish culture, the amount of visitors from abroad coming to Fleadhanna is increasing exponentially each year.

At the heart of the Fleadh are competitions around which all other events revolve. To advance to these, competitors must first come through County and Provincial series, with qualifying provinces being the four provinces of Ireland plus Britain, North America and other various regions of the world.

In all, there are almost 150 competitions covering soloists and groups, in music, song, dance, and in such varied disciplines as fiddle, slow airs and Pipe Bands. The venues required for the competitions will need to accommodate audiences of 50 up to 1500 indoors and up to 12 000 outdoors for Marching Bands. Considering that in terms of competitions alone the Fleadh attracts over 3000 qualifiers, the scale of the festival can begin to be appreciated. So successful is the event in terms of visitors that it is the policy of CCE's Ard Comhairle not to promote the Fleadh aggressively because if this is done the belief is that there is not a town in Ireland that could host it.

The attendance at the Fleadh in 1999 exceeded the estimates provided beforehand by previous organizers. Going on earlier occasions, the local committee expected the total visitor numbers to be around 160 000/170 000, based on information that they had received from other host towns.

However, most accurate estimates suggest that spectacular numbers of people attended the Fleadh Cheoil. As with all outdoor events it is difficult to quantify the exact numbers of visitors,

but estimates from the Gardai would suggest that there were between 80 000 and 100 000 people in the town both Saturday and Sunday. The estimate for Friday is between 40 000 and 60 000 visitors. Certainly, the cumulative figure for the 3 days, the Gardai believe, was easily in excess of 200 000.

Enniscorthy Gardai have considerable expertise in this regard, having been involved in major events over the past few years, such as Le Tour de France en Irlande 1998, 1998 Bi-Centenary Celebrations, and the National Ploughing Championships in 1994 and 1998. The attendance at the Ploughing Championships is easier to quantify, as entry to this event is through 'turnstiles', and the Gardai are confident in their belief that the numbers attending the Fleadh were well in excess of the 150 000 who would regularly attend the 3-day ploughing event.

These figures are confirmed by Comhaltas Árd Comhairle members and Árd Stiúrhtóir Senator Labhrás Ó Murchú.. Regular Fleadh observers, their estimate is that the attendance was up at least 30 per cent on the usual 160 000 expected to attend.

All the empirical data available to the Fleadh Committee would seem to support the above claims:

- Attendance at competitions up by 25 per cent
- Sale of programmes up by 33 per cent
- Attendance at concerts and ceilithe up by 25 per cent
- Overall Fleadh revenue from activities, with no price increases on previous years, up by 36 per cent.

While better organization and financial control could explain some of these increases, the best and most likely explanation for this positive variance has to be a visitor volume increase of at least 30 per cent. With a normal increase of 12–15 per cent for a town hosting the Fleadh for the second time, the organizers have been told to expect an increase closer to 20 per cent for August 2000, bringing the total figures for visitors to the town to nearly a quarter of a million people for the whole week.

Clonmel gearing up for another Fleadh Cheoil 2004

(Eamonn Lacey)

Clonmel is gearing up to host another spectacular Fleadh Cheoil with preparations well advanced for one of Europe's biggest cultural festivals this August when up to a quarter of a million visitors will converge on the town. When Fleadh Fever hits Clonmel this August the town will open its doors and hearts to offer a warm welcome to 10 000 musicians from all over the world. The traditional Fleadh Cheoil weekend will take place from Friday 27th to Sunday 29th August, and will be preceded by Seachtain na hEigse, Scoil Eigse and Seachtain na Gaeilge.

A new Ard Ollamh will be crowned during Seachtain na hEigse, the new dimension introduced to Fleadh Cheoil na hEireann last year by the Clonmel organizing committee. The honour will be bestowed by Comhaltas Ceoltoiri Eireann on Tomas O'Caninn, who succeeds composer Micheal O'Suilleabhain, who became the first Supreme Bard of the Fleadh Cheoil last year in his home town.

The Fleadh Cheoil, now ranked as the biggest cultural festival in Europe, will bring an estimated €15m bonanza to the host town of Clonmel with another €6 million generated in income for accommodation.

A fireworks display will be held on the Saturday night and a Fleadh village will be created in the grounds of the High School with the erection of two domes. This year a huge emphasis is being put on street entertainment. Two gig rigs will be located at Sarsfield Street and the Mick Delahunty Square area, while a number of designated music session areas will be located all over the town. Market Place will host an open-air ceili at 2 pm on the Saturday and Sunday.

Under new Chairman Tom Pollard, the organizing committee is endeavouring to ensure that Fleadh Cheoil na hEireann 2004 is a huge success. 'We are confident that Fleadh Cheoil

na hEireann 2004 will be a major success story. We are working with the support of the entire community and no effort is being spared to ensure that Clonmel will host one of the most memorable events in the history of the Fleadh Cheoil', said Chairman Tom Pollard. A massive €400 000 fundraising drive is already well underway and finance committee Chairman Michael Campbell is leading a high-powered team towards that target. 'We have received a fantastic response in the town and throughout South Tipperary. The corporate and business sector are anxious to be associated with the success story that is the Fleadh Cheoil in Clonmel, and business interests in the town want to get on board', said Michael Campbell. Accommodation staff in the Fleadh Cheoil office in Parnell Street are inundated with requests for beds in Clonmel from all over the world. Like every Fleadh Cheoil there will be an international dimension with a big overseas contingent expected to arrive in Clonmel. Bo Junior Fiddlers, a band from Norway, are already booked into accommodation in Carrick on Suir and they will perform over the weekend.

Two domes will be located in the grounds of Clonmel High School. Musicians, singers and dancers will compete for a coveted All-Ireland title in 28 different competitions at 19 venues throughout the town.

Over 800 young musicians will attend Scoil Eigse, the traditional school of music song and language, in the week leading up to the Fleadh Cheoil weekend.

The build-up to the traditional Fleadh Cheoil weekend will be hectic, with the busy Seachtain na hEigse schedule of concerts and high-profile events and Seachtain na Gaeilge activities including an opening concert drama, Trath na Gceist and Ionad na Gaeilge in Clonmel library.

(Extract from website; for more information see www.clonmelfleadh.com and the Fleadh office at County Wexford on www.wexford-online.com.)

Reflective practice 13.1

Regarding Case study 13.1:

1. How could forecasting assist the organizing committee generate the € 400 000 required to stage this event?
2. What measures have been used in the past to forecast attendance?
3. What techniques could be used to forecast accommodation requirements?

The best-known methods of qualitative forecasting are:

- Expert opinion (including scenario planning and the Delphi method)
- Market surveys
- Life cycle analysis
- Causal
- Comparisons with other events
- Seasonality of demand
- Common sense.

Expert opinion

Individuals or groups can undertake this method. If we think about it, managers use expert opinion all the time as they plan and make decisions every day.

Scenario planning consists of creating hypothetical circumstances that may happen in the future, and then formulating solutions to each scenario. Trend analysis and

understanding causal factors is essential to good scenario planning (Getz, 1997). Imagination is required, as the event manager should then determine the impacts on forecasts using these different scenarios.

Another method of using expert opinion is by using the *Delphi model*. Delphi is named after the city in ancient Greece, which was the site of the most famous and powerful oracle in the temple of Apollo, noted for its ambiguous answers. The approach was if the supplicant asked the right question they got the right answer. A priestess spoke the oracular messages whilst in a frenzied trance, and sitting on a golden tripod. A priest would interpret these sounds to the supplicant (questioner), usually in verse. People seeking help would bring gifts to the oracle, and the shrine became very wealthy.

Nowadays the Delphi method is considered by many to be the most successful of the qualitative methods, although it could hardly be considered useful if it were ambiguous. It is time consuming and costly, and is best used by large organizations. The method uses a set of questions to a group of managers or 'experts' who, working without collusion, give their individual opinions. A coordinator then tabulates the opinions, and if individual results differ significantly then the results are fed back anonymously to the panel with a further set of questions. The process is repeated until consensus is reached. Questions and feedback generally continue for four rounds, with the questions becoming more specific with each round. The benefit of the method is that a group opinion can be achieved without the team meeting. This overcomes one of the weaknesses of a face-to-face group meeting, where it is possible for members to be swayed by a dominant member, or perhaps an 'expert' member may be embarrassed to back down from a publicly-stated opinion.

Market surveys

Although the event manager will be able to give personal insights and experience in order to determine and forecast attendance at an event or for a particular activity, this subjectivity can often be supplemented by useful information collected from potential customers. Market surveys collect data from a sample of customers, analyse their views and make inferences about the population at large (Waters, 1996). Surveys can be carried out by telephone, personal interview, surface mail or email. Market surveys use two approaches; structured and unstructured.

With the structured approach the survey uses a formal list of questions; the unstructured approach lets the interviewer probe and perhaps guide the respondent. The survey enables the event manager to learn why people did not attend, and gives the potential for attracting new segments in the future (Getz, 1997).

Framing of questions is an art, and when the questions are completed they should be piloted to check ambiguity and relevance. The key is to establish from the outset exactly what information is wanted, and then to design questions that will give this information. Questions that are not relevant to the issue are a waste of time and money. Other problems are that sometimes people are unable to answer survey questions because they have never thought about what they do and why. People may be unwilling to answer questions that they consider personal, while others might feel obliged to give an answer rather than to appear uninformed, even when they don't know or even don't understand the question, or they might even try to help the interviewer by giving pleasing answers.

An easy form of market survey includes group interviewing or focus groups. With the focus group approach, six to ten people are invited from a market target group to a meeting. They are sometimes paid a small fee, the conditions are relaxed with refreshments and so on, and after the interviewer has set the scene it is hoped that group dynamics will bring out actual feelings and thoughts. At the same time the interviewer

attempts to keep the discussion focused on the subject of the research. The concern with this approach is that too much can be read into the opinions of a small and possibly non-random sample. Holding several focus group meetings on the same subject and then pooling the results can overcome this to some extent.

Getz (1997) believes that market area surveys can be used to make better forecasts of market penetration. Tracking surveys in local, regional and international target markets can measure awareness of the planned event, attitudes towards it, and respondents' assessment of their likelihood to attend. Market surveys are also appropriate to determine the shape or style of a new event, or to find out why an existing event is not attracting people as well as expected.

Life cycle analysis

It is generally accepted that products and services have a time-based life cycle, as discussed in Chapter 7. The launch stage may have fewer people attending an event, the growth stage may show a rapid increase in customers, and at the maturity stage the demand will be relatively stable. For most types of events life cycles are readily predictable and the rate of growth/decline will not be unexpected. Experienced event managers can often, with a high degree of accuracy, forecast how long an event will stay in each stage of the life cycle, prior to a change being recommended. This experience will help them forecast the attendance numbers as the event moves through its life cycle.

Causal

In forecasting, it is easy to get caught up with the method of calculating and to overlook the purpose. The purpose is to get the best possible forecast of what might happen in the future. Therefore forecasts calculated on past events must be carefully considered against all the known facts of what is happening or is likely to happen. The state of the economy and key indicators such as interest rates, inflation rates, currency exchange rates, employment rates, and factors such as the entrance of new competitors, new technology and materials, fashion trends, and planned marketing drives will all have causal effects on future results. Likewise, past results should be examined to determine how they were affected by similar events.

Sometimes rising prices can elevate an event to the status of an exclusive event (Getz, 1997). Knowing the causes for changes in demand is important.

Although the information used has a quantitative source, the application and usage of the data relies on a qualitative interpretation.

Comparisons with other events

Similar past events should be researched, taking into account their geographical position, competitive position and relative attractiveness and reputation of the event (Getz, 1997). Total attendance at festivals and other events may have grown, so a refined estimate of demand should be determined. As the number of events increase, then increased competition should also be taken into account. However, competition may act as a catalyst and customers may become more willing to come to different events, and therefore the total market is increased. These comparisons should be considered alongside quantitative data.

Seasonality of demand

Many events can be affected by weather conditions and the different seasons of the year. However, seasonality does not just mean climatic seasons but also political, sporting, financial, holiday and food seasons, and festivals and rituals. It should be remembered that these vary from country to country, and that you may arrive to set up

your event in a different country only to find that all the staff you had considered employing are taking a 1-day break owing to a religious festival. Similarly, seasons or annual holidays in different countries may also affect your attendances.

Common sense

Finally, the commonsense approach with forecasted figures is to test by asking, are these figures sensible, what happened before, and what is likely to happen in the future? This approach shows the link between the use of quantitative data and a qualitative approach, and uses the experience, knowledge and expertise of the event management team. Once the future demand forecast has been agreed, then the event manager must determine the capacity of the organization and what changes might be needed to meet the level of forecasted demand.

Quantitative forecasting
Time series forecasting

Time series forecasting uses mathematical analysis of past demand trends to forecast future demand. However, the accuracy of a forecast will not be known until after the event, and this is usually monitored by the deviation of the actual result from the forecast result. (Standard deviation, total absolute deviation and deviation spread is explained later in this section.)

Short-term forecasting involves taking historical data of demand patterns from a few past periods and projecting these patterns into the future. The simplest method is to take the last period's actual demand and use it for the next period(s) forecast, as shown in the following example regarding attendance at a motor show (see Table 13.1).

The method gives a quick response to a trend; if the trend is upwards, then the forecast will be upwards but may lag behind. If, however, there are marked annual fluctuations, then this method would, following a buoyant year, forecast higher annual attendance. In Table 13.1, for example, the forecast for 2001 is lower than actual, and is higher in 2002 but lower in 2003, but not to such a great extent. However, these poor forecasts would have had a knock-on effect on sponsorship, funding, and all arrangements where numbers of attendees are useful. In every year, the organizers have been wrong about the actual attendance. It could be that their sponsors and suppliers will no longer trust the claims of the organizers, and will right them off as wild exaggerations.

Table 13.1 Forecast from past period's actual

Period	Actual	Forecast	Deviation
2000	600 000	–	–
2001	621 000	600 000	+21 000
2002	500 132	621 000	– 120 868
2003	687 981	500 132	+187 849

Forecasting by past average

This method is to average the past results. The accuracy of the method is tested by the deviation from the actual.

The first column could represent anything in the event industry. In Table 13.2, let us assume that it is the number of people who asked for a free back massage whilst going around a leisure exhibition. The knowledge of the take-up is helpful for the company

Table 13.2 Forecasting by past moving average

Hour	Actual demand	Forecast (average of all past actual)	Deviation
1st hour	20	nil	
2nd hour	18	20	+2
3rd hour	22	19	−3
4th hour	23	20	−3
5th hour	21	21	0
6th hour	19	21	+2
7th hour	24	21	−3

Table 13.3 Forecasting by 3 period moving average

Period	Actual	Forecast	Deviation
1	20	–	–
2	18	–	–
3	22	–	–
4	23	20	−3
5	21	21	0
6	19	22	+3
7	24	21	−3
8	25	21	−4
9	22	23	+1
10	23	24	+1
11	25	23	−2
12	26	23	−3
13		25	

that was promoting the experience, so it is able to provide staff for a similar function in the near future.

The total absolute deviation (TAD) is the sum of all the deviations, ignoring plus or minus signs – 13 in this example. The mean absolute deviation (MAD) is the average of the deviations. In this example, although there are seven forecasts there are only six deviations, so MAD = 13/6 = 2.1.

During the third and fourth hours there is a variation of 3 between the forecast and the actual. In the third and fourth hours, if capacity had been arranged to meet the forecasted demand then there would have been an undersupply of labour for back massaging, and clients would have had to queue or would have left the stand.

During the sixth hour there was an oversupply of staff and they would not have had a job to do.

It can be seen that using a past average is not always a reliable method of forecasting.

Forecasting by moving average

This method provides reasonable response to trends, and also dampens fluctuations (see Table 13.3).

In Table 13.3, TAD = 20 and MAD = 2.2.

Calculations for the forecasts in this example were made by taking the previous three periods and then dividing by three. For example, the forecast for period 10 is the sum

Table 13.4 Four-period moving average

Period	Actual	Forecast (Four-period average)	Deviation (Forecast to actual)
1	20	–	–
2	18	–	–
3	22	–	–
4	23	–	–
5	21	21	0
6	19	21	+2
7	24	21	−3
8	25	22	−3
9	22	22	0
10	23	23	0
11	25	24	−1
12	26	24	−2
13		24	

of the three previous periods divided by three, i.e. 24 + 25 + 22 = 71; 71/3 = 23.7, which rounds up to 24.

The number of periods used for averaging is a matter of judgement. If there are definite cycles, the number of periods in the cycle can be used to determine the number of periods used for averaging. In the second column of Table 13.4, the last two periods in each group of four have the higher demands (in the first four periods 3 and 4 are the highest; in the next group of four 7 and 8 are the highest; likewise so are 11 and 12 in the final group of four); thus a four-period average might prove to be more accurate. We will test this theory using Table 13.4.

In Table 13.4, TAD = 11 and MAD = 1.4.

You will have noted that we have used the same 'actuals' for each of the last two methods of forecasting (Table 13.3 and Table 13.4). If we compare the MADs, we will see that the last method has given the most accurate forecast.

Statistical seasonal adjustment

Adjusting for seasonality can further refine the forecast.

Let us assume that period 1 is the first quarter of a year and period 2 is the second quarter, etc. We can then recalculate our forecasts as in Table 13.5 (overleaf).

The next step is to average the seasonal factor for each season:

Year	2001
Qtr One	96.4 + 94.3 + 91.7 = 282.4/3 = 94.1
Qtr Two	86.75 + 85.4 + 95.8 = 267.95/3 = 89.3
Qtr Three	106.0 + 107.9 + 104.2 = 318.1/3 = 106.0
Qtr Four	110.85 + 112.4 + 108.3 = 331.55/3 = 110.5

By taking the four-period moving average for the last four actual results, which is 24 (96/4 = 24), and applying the seasonal factors, the next four quarters can be forecast as in Table 13.6.

Table 13.5 Seasonal factors

	Actual	Average for year	Seasonal factor (percentage of average)
Year 02			
Qtr One	20		96.4 (20 is 96.4% of 20.75)
Qtr Two	18		86.75
Qtr Three	22		106.0
Qtr Four	23		110.85
	83	83/4 = 20.75	400
Year 03			
Qtr One	21		94.3
Qtr Two	19		85.4
Qtr Three	24		107.9
Qtr Four	25		112.4
	89	89/4 = 22.25	400
Year 04			
Qtr One	22		91.7
Qtr Two	23		95.8
Qtr Three	25		104.2
Qtr Four	26		108.3
	96	96/4 = 24	400

Table 13.6 Forecast for year ahead

Year 2005		Forecast
Qtr One	24 × 94.1%	23
Qtr Two	24 × 89.3%	21
Qtr Three	24 × 106%	25
Qtr Four	24 × 110.5%	27
		96

This gives us the same total (96) for Year 2005 as for Year 2004. As there is an obvious upwards trend, this is not logical. We therefore add a trend factor to our calculations.

The trend factor is obtained by calculating a time lag factor. The formula for the trend factor is (Number of periods of moving average −1)/2 + 1.

In our example, $(4 − 1) = 3$ and $3/2 = 1.5$. The time lag factor will therefore be $1.5 + 1 = 2.5$.

We now return to our four-period moving averages, calculate the trend between successive moving averages, and multiply each trend by the time lag factor (Table 13.7).

98.125/4 gives an adjusted average quarter of 24.5.

Using the adjusted average plus the seasonal fluctuations, we can forecast for Year 01 (Table 13.8).

We now have a forecast for the next 12 months (four quarters) which is seasonally adjusted and has allowed for growth based on the past trend. Naturally, as each new 'actual' comes to hand we recalculate our moving forecast.

The main weakness of the moving average method is that equal weight is given to each of the historical figures used, and there is also the need to have (or to build up) a history of information to test against and to forecast from.

Table 13.7 Adjusted average

Actual	Moving average	Successive trend	×2.5	Time lag factor	Adjusted average
20					
18					
22					
23					
21	20.75				
19	21	+0.25			
24	21.25	+0.25			
25	21.75	+0.5			
22	22.25	+0.5			
23	22.5	+0.25	2.5	0.625	23.125
25	23.5	+1	2.5	2.5	26
26	23.75	+0.25	2.5	0.625	24.375
–	24	+0.25	2.5	0.625	24.625
					98.125

Table 13.8 Adjusted forecast

Qtr One	98.125/4 = 24.5 × 94.1%	23
Qtr Two	24.5 × 89.3	22
Qtr Three	24.5 × 106.0	26
Qtr Four	24.5 × 110.5	27
		98

Another disadvantage is the number of calculations involved, although with a computer spreadsheet, once the formula has been entered (and proved), this is not as onerous as it once would have been.

A method known as exponential smoothing overcomes some of these problems without losing any of the accuracy.

Exponential smoothing

Exponential smoothing requires only the previous forecast figure and the latest actual figure. It allows the forecast to respond to fluctuations, but at the same time keeps a level of stability.

We begin by calculating a smoothing constant. The formula for the smoothing constant is $2/(N + 1)$, where N is the number of periods we wish to smooth. For example, if six were the number of periods the smoothing constant would be $2/(6 + 1) = 2/7 = 0.28$.

For our example, Table 13.9, we will use an exponential smoothing constant based on four periods:

$$\frac{2}{(4 + 1)} = \frac{2}{5} = 0.4$$

The actual demand for the last period is multiplied by the factor i.e. 0.4, and the forecast for the last period is multiplied by the sum of (1 − the factor). In our case, using a factor of 0.4, the actual for the last period is multiplied by 0.4 and the last forecast is multiplied by 0.6 (i.e. 1 − 0.4 = 0.6).

Table 13.9 Exponential smoothed average

Period	Actual	Forecast (four-period)	Deviation (forecast to average)	Exponential smoothed average	Deviation
1	20	–	–		
2	18	–	–		
3	22	–	–		
4	23	–	–		
5	21	21	–		
6	19	21	+2	21	+2
7	24	21	−3	20	−4
8	25	22	−3	22	−3
9	22	22	–	23	+1
10	23	23	–	23	–
11	25	24	−1	23	−2
12	26	24	−2	24	−2
13		24		25	

Starting with period 5:	Actual 21 and forecast 21. As there is a nil deviation (for period 6) no smoothing is required, and thus for period 6 the forecast will be 21
For period 7:	The actual was 19 and the forecast was 21. Using exponential smoothing for period 7 the forecast is 0.4(19) + 0.6(21) = 7.6 + 12.6 = 20
For period 8:	0.4(24) + 0.6(20) = 9.6 + 12.0 = 21.6
For period 9:	0.4(25) + 0.6(22) = 10 + 13.2 = 23.2
For period 10:	0.4(22) + 0.6(23) = 8.8 + 13.8 = 22.6
For period 11:	As there is no deviation to actual for period 10, the forecast is 23
For period 12:	0.4(25) + 0.6(23) = 10 + 13.8 = 23.8
For period 13:	0.4(26) + 0.6(24) = 10.4 + 14.4 = 24.8

In Table 13.9, TAD = 14 and MAD = 4.

The example in Table 13.9 demonstrates the mechanics of exponential smoothing. The next steps are to add a trend factor and a seasonal factor to update the exponentially smoothed average. In a four-period seasonal forecast, the factor for period 5 when the actual is known will be upgraded to provide a new seasonal factor for period 9 and so on; it is in effect a closed loop based on the past. The problem is in deciding values for the smoothing constants. Such decisions are often arbitrary, based on past experience, and tested against past information. Computer programs exist which will do this systematically, and are found in cash flow forecasting programs and in inventory control programs.

Finding trends

When looking at a column of figures, it is difficult to visualize if there is an increasing or decreasing trend. A simple method of determining if there is a trend is to calculate a mean and then to calculate the variation from the mean for each period.

In Table 13.10, the first four periods total 20 + 18 + 22 + 23 = 83, and 83/4 = a mean of 21.

We can now clearly see that from Period 8 onwards there is a marked upwards trend. Case study 13.2 illustrates the use of statistics in the events industry.

Table 13.10 Trends

Period	Actual	Cumulative difference from mean	
1	20	−1	(21 − 20) = −1
2	18	−4	(21 − 18) = (−3) + (−1) = −4
3	22	−3	(21 − 22) = (+1) + (−4) = −3
4	23	−1	(21 − 23) = (+2) + (−3) = −1
5	21	−1	(21 − 21) = (0) + (−1) = −1
6	19	−3	(21 − 19) = (−2) + (−1) = −3
7	24	0	(21 − 24) = (+3) + (−3) = 0
8	25	+4	(21 − 25) = (+4) + (0) = +4
9	22	+5	(21 − 22) = (+1) + (+4) = 5
10	23	+7	(21 − 23) = (+2) + (+5) = 7
11	25	+11	(21 − 25) = (+4) + (+7) = 11
12	26	+15	(21 − 26) = (+5) + (+11) = 16
13			

Case study 13.2

Ernst & Young, Australia

How can statistics be usefully used in the events industry? For instance, in the sports sector Ernst and Young has a department in Australia which deals with sports, events and venues. They are quoted on their website as follows:

expectations are higher, productions costs continue to rise and competition for quality events is intense.

Venue managers are expected to create a total entertainment experience within a safe and smoothly operating environment. Venues need to be versatile and capable of hosting a wide variety of events and activities. Sports must be able to maximize key revenue streams that may include media rights, sponsorship and other multimedia opportunities alongside traditional revenue sources such as ticketing, food and beverage, and merchandising. Ernst & Young have the ability to analyse and understand the key issues and priorities that impact upon the participants of this dynamic industry.

A sample of the key services from the Sports, Events & Venues Group include:

- Economic impact assessments of events
- Budgeting and forecasting
- Event selection to ensure it matches target markets
- Stadium and event strategic planning
- Operational reviews
- Process re-engineering to reduce operating costs
- Benchmarking against best practice
- Performance improvement strategies
- Attendance verifications.

(Information supplied by courtesy of Ernst & Young, Australia; for more information see www.ey.com.)

All of the processes described in Case study 13.2 involve forecasting. The techniques and processes used, however, will vary according to the complexity of the event. Ernst & Young has worked with The Australian Olympic Committee and the Australian Sports Commission, as well as Mercedes Australian Fashion Week. However, this does not mean that a local festival, concert or charity ball, for instance, would not benefit from using forecasting. For example, take a student ball; attendance figures and a quantified consumption of alcohol could be used when seeking sponsorship for the next year's event.

Capacity management

We have now spent some time deciding how best to judge and calculate the attendance at an event, or the take-up of specified parts of it. We now have to make sure that we have the capacity in order to meet the needs of our attendees.

Capacity management is a key planning responsibility of event managers. Wild (2002) states that the decisions on how to match the capacity of the organization to the levels of demand will influence many other decisions. The capacity of the event will be determined by the resources available to it – space, time, the number of staff and their various skill levels, the management expertise required and many other resources, dependent upon the scale and style of the event.

Capacity management involves the organization of resources to meet the demand. This will include acquiring those resources, and training where necessary.

Figure 13.2 shows some of the influences that affect the overall capacity of an event.

Can service be stored?

In the event industry, if capacity is not used when available then that capacity is lost for ever; it cannot be reused or saved. For example, seats at a concert or at a conference cannot be stored – once the conference or the concert has started, even though major costs have been incurred in providing for a full capacity, any empty seats cannot be

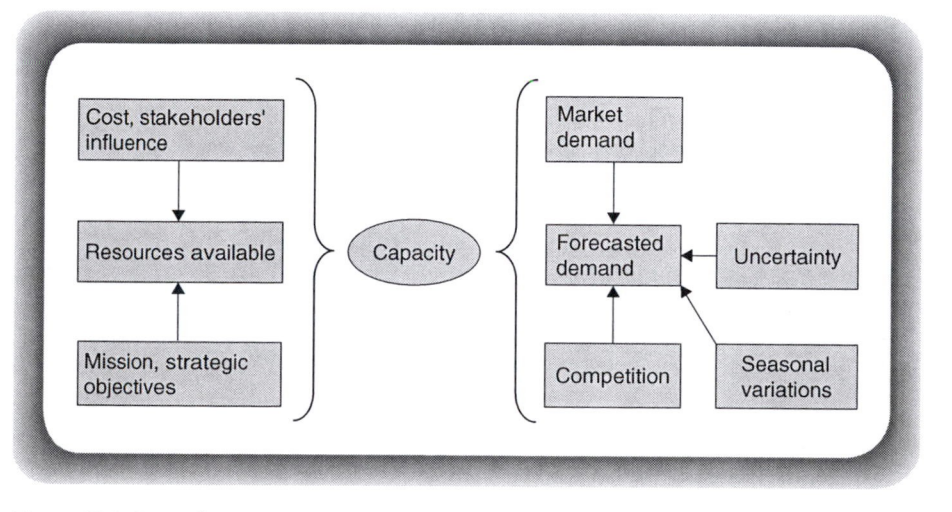

Figure 13.2 Some factors that influence capacity

sold later. In retail services the situation is different; goods not sold today could well be sold tomorrow, and the sale is not necessarily lost.

Measuring capacity

An organization has capacity if it has some of each of the resources required to carry out its function. For example, a conference centre has the capacity to hold a conference and accept delegates if it has accommodation and vacant seats during the proceedings. Wild (2002) states that if insufficient capacity is provided it will be possible to meet only some of the demand, and so some customers will wait or go elsewhere. If too much capacity is provided, there will be under-utilization of resources. Wild (2002) says that another approach is to try to manipulate demand to match the available capacity, by advertising and price promotions. Conversely, if demand is exceeding capacity then demand may be encouraged to fall by, for example, raising prices.

We can see these concepts more clearly diagrammatically. Slack *et al.* (2004) identify three options for coping with demand that does not match the capacity available:

1. Ignore the fluctuations in demand and keep the activities and level of resources constant (i.e. level capacity)
2. Adjust the capacity to match the fluctuations in demand (i.e. chase demand management)
3. Attempt to change the demand to fit the capacity of all the resources you have available (i.e. demand management).

In the *level capacity* approach, the level, the amount, the quantity of your resources available stays constant. For instance, if you employ five staff to run the bar at a busy wedding reception in a marquee, you use this number throughout the proceedings. During the reception there will be times when the bar staff are underemployed and idle, and at other times they will be very busy and guests may have to queue and wait to be served. It can be seen that this is possibly a waste of resources, although at many times when the bar is open the guests will receive excellent service and only on certain occasions will they have to queue.

The time line on Figure 13.3 represents hours. The vertical line represents the number of staff (capacity). The darker, straight line represents the staffing resources provided by the event manager to run a busy bar in a marquee at a large wedding reception, while the lighter, wavy line represents the numbers of guests going to the bar to collect drinks.

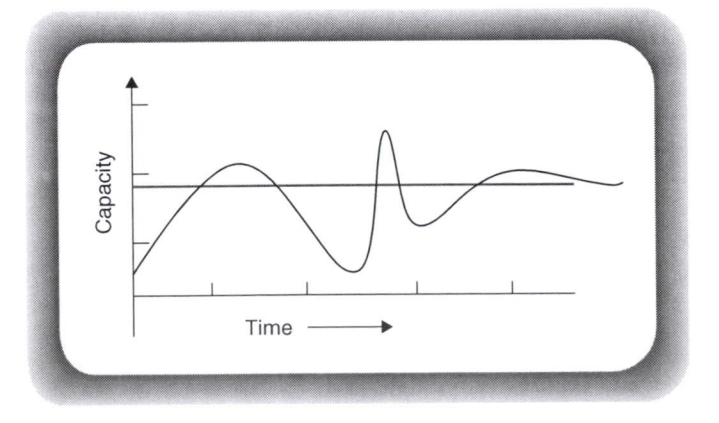

Figure 13.3 Level capacity

When the wavy line is below the straight line, some of the staff will be idle and the guests will have been served immediately. When the wavy line goes above the straight line, the guests will have had to queue for a short time until they were served.

Towards the end of this period it can be seen that the staffing resources and the demand for service from the guests are almost equally matched. It must be established for how long and how many times guests are prepared to wait. In some events they may go elsewhere, but at a wedding they are relatively 'captive' to that venue. However, it may be that they are sufficiently frustrated not to recommend that venue to others.

This approach can be used in many other situations. The time line can represent minutes or days or months. The event manager can use this analysis approach in a variety of different settings – for example, the number of mobile phone recharge points provided at an outdoor music festival. The time line could represent hours and the straight line represent the number of fixed mobile phone recharge points. In this example, the same figure (Figure 13.3) shows that at times the mobile phone recharge points are idle and at other times festival attendees will be queuing. The festival organizer will use this information and make decisions as to how many recharge points will be provided on future occasions.

Similarly, the time line could represent months at a conference venue, and the straight line the number of conference rooms available. In this instance the graph will show that at certain times of the year the venue is having to turn away business, and at other times it is under-booked.

A further issue to bear in mind when setting a fixed level of capacity, such as a set number of staff for the expected number of customers, is to ascertain whether the length of time each customer will need is the same for each customer. Planning is easier where the service provided is of the same duration each time – for example, at the registration of individual delegates at an international exhibition. It is more difficult when it is not known how long each service encounter will require, such as at one of the stands at the exhibition when delegates wish to discuss products and prices with the sales team. How many staff from the sales team should be seconded to the stand for the duration of the event?

When using a *chase demand management* approach, the opposite of a level capacity occurs. This is much more difficult to achieve, since an accurate forecast of demand has to be known. Wild (2002) discusses the uncertainty of demand and how the existence of a stable and known demand would simplify the problems of trying to match capacity to that demand. In Chapter 3, we discussed a factor in the typology of events as being the uncertainty in numbers attending, and how these numbers can change over a varying period of time. This uncertainty in numbers of, say, people attending or using our services gives rise to uncertainty about the number of resources required – i.e. the capacity we should provide at the event. It is useful to see this diagrammatically, as in Figure 13.4.

As in Figure 13.3, the time line on this figure represents hours. The vertical line represents the number of staff. The darker line again represents the staffing resources provided by the event manager to run a busy bar in a marquee at a large wedding reception. The lighter line represents the numbers of guests going to the bar to collect drinks.

It can be seen that the staffing resources and the demand for service from the guests are almost equally matched. This has been achieved by the event manager predicting the number of guests going to the bar to collect drinks over the period of time. Perhaps the speeches will have been taken into account, when drinks are not collected, and the fact that during the meal bar requirements would diminish. Later, using past experience, the event manager has realized that more drinks will be required. Another way of maximizing the use of the staff would be to use the staff elsewhere as the demand drops, but to keep them within calling distance or mobile phone range so they can

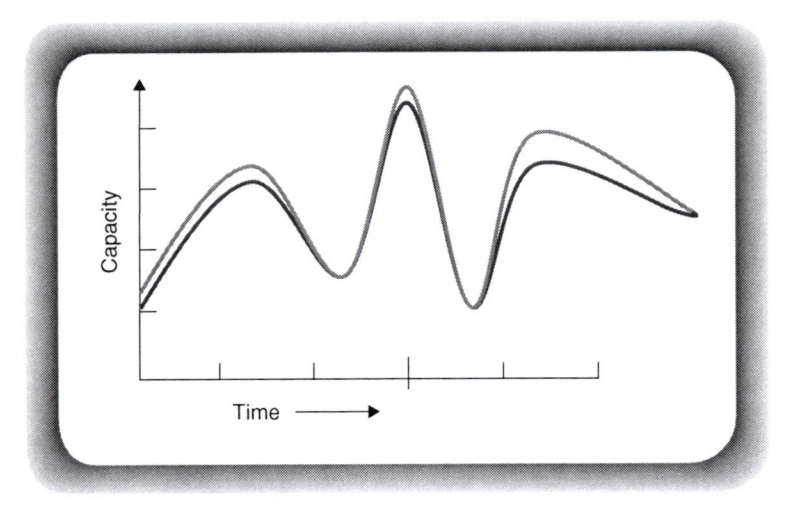

Figure 13.4 Capacity and resource provision chasing the fluctuating demand

return when necessary. Such staff would need to be multi-skilled and flexible. However, this flexibility of staff is only of use when there is another job to go to. For example, how many security personnel would you need at a busy outdoor venue, controlling entry points? Even as the number of attendees arriving drops, as they pass through the barriers, there is little else that the security personnel can do but stay at their assigned posts.

Using the example of mobile phone recharge points, this approach is not as practicable – the recharge points cannot be transported to another site and called back at short notice. Therefore this approach is only appropriate in those circumstances where the resources can be provided flexibly, or where prediction of the demand can be made accurately and the resources can be varied.

In most cases where demand levels are lower than expected there will be an under-utilization of capacity and a build-up of resources (Wild, 2002). In some cases where the demand exceeds expectations and more staff are required this can be offset against times when full capacity is not required but was expected, and less than a full staffing compliment was provided. Where it is difficult to accommodate short-term excess demand it may necessitate a provision of excess capacity, as we saw in Figure 13.3. At many events where demand is difficult to quantify this under-utilization of resources might be considered more profitable than the loss of customers.

The capacity of the staffing resources can be changed to some extent. Staff can work overtime, unskilled people can be employed in busy periods to free up skilled staff, and staff can be reallocated from their normal duties to help in situations where they are needed for short periods of time. However, as said before, they must be trained and willing to be flexible.

Where customers do have to wait, the event manager can make that wait more palatable – for instance, at some outdoor events there can be street entertainment. Customers can also be advised how long they will have to wait for. This second strategy does much to allay feelings of frustration, particularly if it is coupled with the fact that the wait is not quite as long as predicted.

The third approach is *demand management*. This approach represents an attempt by the event manager to manipulate the demand for services to match the capacity that is available. Common methods of manipulating demand include advertising, promotions, cheaper rates in the off season, cheaper meals for early diners, happy hours (half-price

drinks) in bars and so on. Where demand exceeds capacity, prices can be raised to discourage customers coming at busy times. At events we can often see cheaper entrance costs for those who arrive early, and more expensive entrance costs if tickets are not booked in advance – for example, for runners in road races, where entry is made in advance or by the Internet. Some of these measures are now being criticized – for example, the cheaper prices of early drinks, since it has been reported that this can lead to excessive drinking. If this criticism is taken seriously, bar and club managers might have to reconsider how they can attract customers to their premises at times when their trade is low and their staffing costs static, but without using the lure of cheap drinks.

As in Figure 13.3, the time line on Figure 13.5 represents hours. The vertical line represents the number of staff. It is not appropriate to use the wedding guests/bar example here, since it would be inconceivable to try to manipulate the guests to come to collect their drinks during the speeches and whilst eating the wedding breakfast. However, smoothing can be seen at concerts where customers are asked to order their drinks in advance of the interval. This enables the bar staff to be working relatively constantly, receiving the orders and then delivering the drinks to a prearranged place for the interval. Identification of work that can be done in advance greatly relieves the affects of fluctuation of demand.

We could imagine that Figure 13.5 represents the attendance of 4000 people at a large agricultural show. Those attendees with families could be encouraged to come in the morning, when children's activities would be more prevalent, and other groups of people to come later in the day for different styles of entertainment.

By segmenting your market it is possible to delay and attract numbers so that your staff and the different facilities are used to a constant level through the event. The darker line again represents the staffing resources provided by the event manager, and the lighter line represents the numbers of attendees who have been encouraged to arrive at different times during the day.

It can be seen that the staffing resources and the demand for service from the guests are almost equally matched, and a steady, even flow is obviously easier to cope with than peaks and troughs.

The capacity can be managed at some events by asking customers to book in advance or to make reservations. If the capacity is then available to meet those prearranged needs, the customer is satisfied.

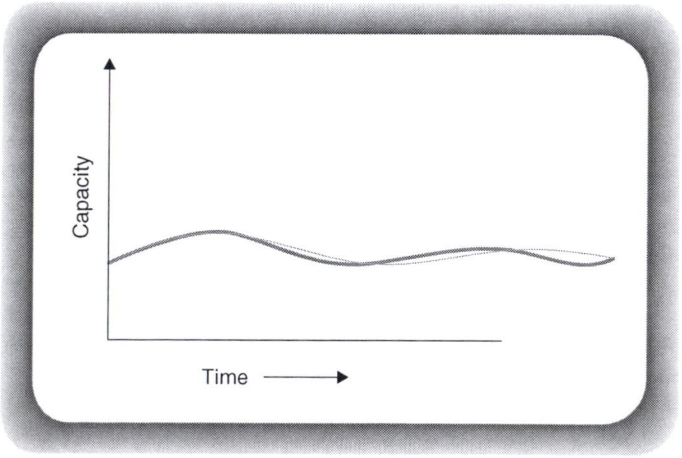

Figure 13.5 Demand being smoothed by encouraging a more consistent flow to and within the event

Another way of smoothing the demands of customers and increasing the match between the demand and the capacity is to ask the customers to participate in the service. For example, at a buffet bar customers can serve themselves, or they can book on line for an event, saving registration staff the need to complete forms.

Case study 13.3 provides an illustration of seasonal trends.

Case study 13.3

The Ice Cube, Millennium Square, Leeds, England, Winter 2001–2004

The 'Ice Cube' is a 1250 square metre real ice rink constructed each winter at Millennium Square, Leeds city centre, as a part of Leeds City Council's annual events programme.

Since the inaugural season in 2001, the Ice Cube has become one of Leeds' most popular events. During the 2004 season (16 January–29 February) the rink attracted approximately 71 000 skaters, and an estimated 250 000 non-skating visitors to the rink structure.

Having experienced four seasons of rink operations, it was clear from anecdotal operational evidence that there was a significant increase in demand at weekends (Friday evenings, Saturdays and Sundays) and during the school half-term holidays (period 6 in the 2001–2004 comparison).

By comparing total revenue from all years on scatter plots (see Figures 13.6–13.9), this trend is quite clearly shown.

(Please note that in Figures 13.6–13.9, seasons have been split into four periods to allow greater detail to be shown. Where seasons have started later (2001) or finished later (2002), this is accounted for within the table by the non-appearance of season data.)

When assessing data such as these, otherwise known as 'time series' data, results can be categorized into the 'decomposition model' as one of four components, trend, seasonal, cyclical or random factors. Clearly with emphasis on weekend and half-term trading peaks, the Ice Cube can be considered seasonal in nature. In addition there is an element of randomness – the weather – which explains the occasional sudden plunge in revenue figures.

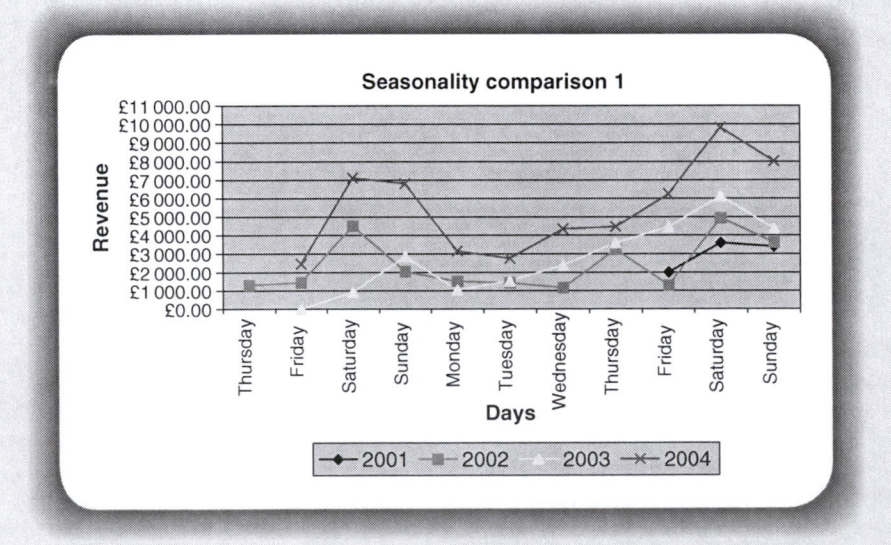

Figure 13.6 Seasonality comparison (periods 1 + 2)

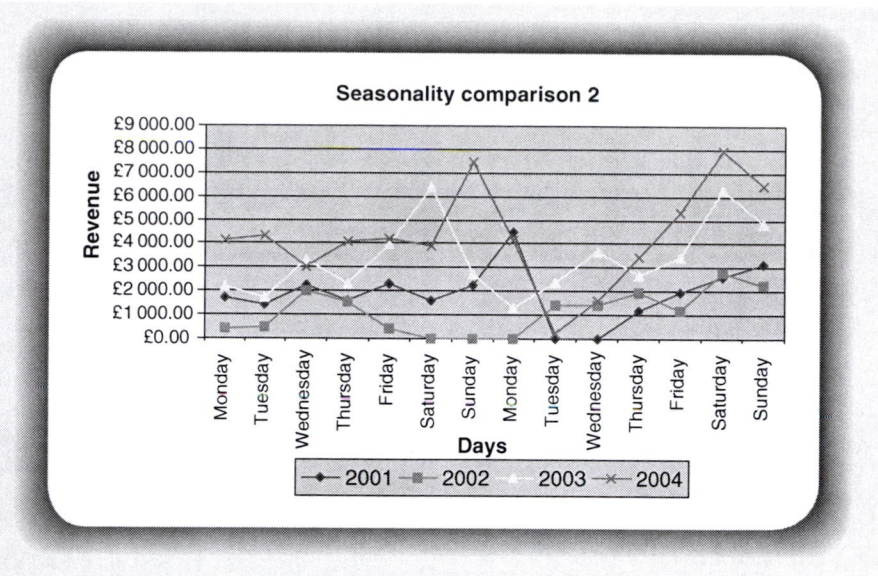

Figure 13.7 Seasonality comparison (periods 3 + 4)

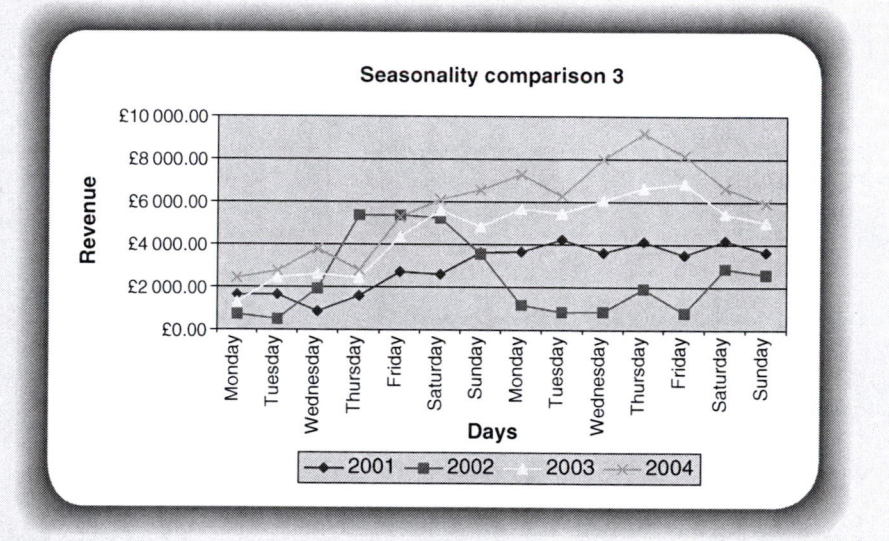

Figure 13.8 Seasonality comparison (periods 5 + 6): half-term holidays

Seasonal trends

The time series data above can also be used to assess trends throughout each individual operating period. With the rink only open for a 6-week season each year, does the rink get busier as word-of-mouth spreads, or does all the initial media coverage connected with the rink opening mean that the rink is less popular towards the end of the season?

This information would be particularly useful when planning the rink marketing campaign, so as to concentrate advertising spend to encourage visitors during quieter periods.

Presently the rink cannot accommodate all skaters during busy sessions (Saturday afternoons and during the half-term holidays). Due to the constraints of the site the rink cannot

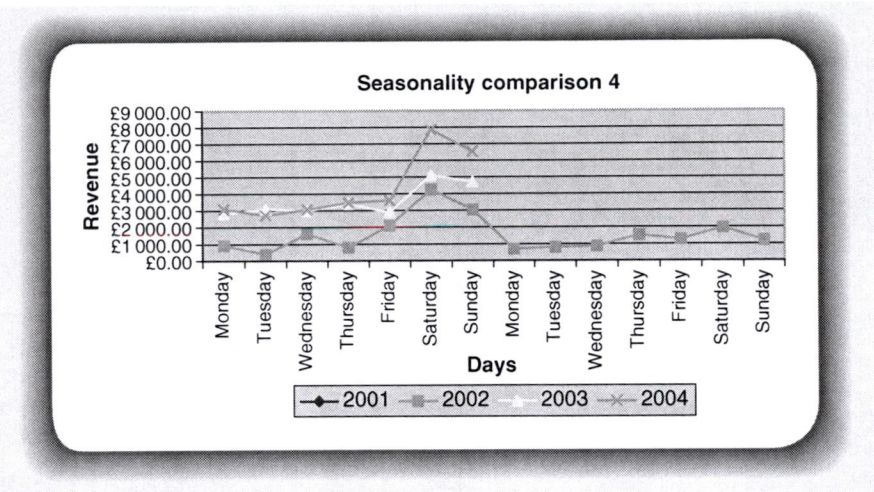

Figure 13.9 Seasonality comparison (periods 7 + 8)

realistically be extended beyond its current 1200 square metres, and therefore the challenge is to develop off-peak periods to further maximize income. It can be seen from Figures 13.6–13.9 that the trend in the 2004 season shows a positive increase over the 6 weeks.

(Patrick Loy, Senior Lecturer, Leeds Metropolitan University, England.)

Reflective practice 13.2

Regarding Case study 13.3:

1. How can the above information be used to smooth out variation in demand for the ice rink?
2. What strategies could be put into place to manage demand?

Queuing theory

Due to the random nature of customer arrivals (even when there is an arrival pattern) and the variability in time taken to satisfy each customer, no matter how good the planning of resources, queues will build up, disappear when there is a lull, and then reappear.

Reflective practice 13.3

During a coffee break-out session at a conference:

1. How long should a customer wait, what is 'reasonable', and how long on average do you think that customers will be prepared to wait for a drink?
2. How much idle time is acceptable for service staff?
3. What is the cost of having unused capacity?
4. What is the cost of not being able to provide a service?

Variability of arrivals

It is often not possible, unless an appointment book or reservation-type system is used, to control the actual moment of arrival of a customer. The number of arrivals and the length of time between subsequent arrivals is not constant. By recording the number of arrivals, a histogram can be used to show a frequency distribution.

The assumption in most queuing systems is that arrivals occur singly, and therefore the concern is with the probability of a customer arriving or no customer arriving at any point in time or period of time.

The simplest form for managing customers is a single facility through which all customers must enter if they are to be served or registered; more complicated systems will have several serving units which may not all be the same. At events this does not necessarily mean individual people; it may be groups of people arriving in cars or coaches. Multiple entry points can be arranged in parallel, so that customers might enter through a choice of points. On the other hand, a single queue may be encouraged to form and the next customer will go to the first point that becomes available. At large events, correct procedures are crucial to avoid crushing and prevent frustration.

Queue discipline

Customers might form orderly queues where newcomers go to the back of the queue and wait their turn (FIFO – first in first out), or the system might be that the last one to arrive is served first (LIFO – last in first out) – for example, in the processing of inward mail, the last letter received goes to the top of the pile and is processed first.

Other methods might be to have a priority system for serving certain customers first (for example, those customers with pre-booked seats at concerts), to have no system at all with customers being selected, or to have customers selecting themselves for service at random. Discipline or lack of discipline is not likely to affect the speed at which the service unit operates, but will affect the waiting time for customers and, consequently, their feeling of being equitably served.

Whichever methodology you employ when managing queues, Yeoman *et al.* (2004) advise the event manager to understand the psychology and feelings of people who do wait in queues. They recommend further reading, citing Maister (1985), and suggest how the event manager can reduce tension by recognizing that unoccupied time feels longer than occupied time and unexplained waits longer than explained waits. On the other hand, they cite that if the value of the service for which they are waiting is greater, the visitor will wait longer. This and other points are valuable phenomena that the event manager could utilize to reduce problems where the demand for a particular event outstrips the resources that have been provided at a particular point. Bear in mind that different countries might have different cultural approaches to queuing.

Service times

Some customers might take longer to serve than others, or all customers might need exactly the same amount of time to process. Nonetheless, as in the case of measuring the variability of arrivals, so too can the variability of service times be measured and averaged. It might be observed that as the queue lengthens the average throughput increases, with the serving staff allowing themselves less time per customer. If customers are being rushed through the system they might believe that the level of service is below standard, or if they are kept waiting they might become dissatisfied and leave the queue. There is the challenge for the event manager.

Queuing formulae

An important measure for a simple queue is customer intensity, where:

Customer intensity = Mean (average) rate of service / Mean rate of arrival

For example, if the inter-arrival time is on average 8 minutes and the service time is on average 6 minutes, then customer intensity will be $6/8 = 0.75$. Thus 0.75 is the probability (P) of a customer having to wait for service. When P is below 1 there will be idle time for the resource, but if P is more than 1 then the queue will get longer and longer (assuming that the service does not speed up but remains constant).

Developing this example, imagine that a client for a fortune-teller at a fête arrives at the beginning of the hour and another 'client' arrives every 8 minutes thereafter. The average 'service' time is 6 minutes. At the end of 60 minutes the fortune-teller could have seen ten customers, but as only seven have arrived with one due in 4 minutes, only seven have gone through the system. Therefore over a period of 10 hours the fortune-teller have will seen 75 people but would have been able to have seen 100.

If, however, the arrival time were to be every 6 minutes, starting at the beginning of the hour, and each interaction were to take 8 minutes, the customer intensity would be $8/6 = 1.33$. Thus at the end of the first hour seven people would have been seen, one would be half way through a consultation, one would have 4 minutes to wait, and the remaining one would have 12 minutes to wait. However, if at the end of the hour a new client walks in the door, that client is going to have to wait 20 minutes. At the end of 10 hours the fortune-teller will have seen 75 customers, and there will be a further 25 people waiting in the queue (that is, the last customer to arrive will have a wait of 3 hours and 12 minutes).

The question of queuing can thus be addressed from a customer service perspective i.e. how long do customers have to wait for service, or how long will they wait before they are lost to the system? OR from a resource use perspective – (how long are we prepared to have idle capacity in the system?)

There is a range of queuing models available; for their use within the event industry the reader is advised to refer to further work and details by Yeoman *et al.* (2004).

Reflective practice 13.4

You are the operations manager for a racecourse. You have a major 3-day event of races starting on Boxing Day, and need to plan all of your facilities to provide parking, catering, box office admissions, etc. for the 3 days.

1. Identify which forecasting procedures you would use.
2. Identify the advantages and disadvantages of each method.

Chapter summary and key points

This chapter has demonstrated that the knowledge of numbers of people attending and their different requirements is an important prerequisite for any event. Following on from having gained that information is the determination of the capacity and availability of resources to service those numbers and needs.

We began by explaining the need to forecast the number of people expected to attend an event. Capacity management is the matching of resources with demand.

Several techniques for forecasting demand have been introduced, and it was emphasized that whichever method was used that any forecast should be tested against past experience and take into account present circumstances and trends. When looking at forecasts the questions to ask include, are these figures sensible, what happened last time and what is likely to happen this time?

Once the forecast demand has been agreed, the next step is to determine what capacity management strategy will be adopted. The broad strategies are to have a fixed level of resources, to manipulate capacity to chase demand, or to try to manipulate demand. If the first strategy is adopted, a fixed level of resources, then it can be expected that at times resources will not be fully used but at other times customers will have to wait and queues will form. When queues form, there is the danger of losing customers.

Manipulation of demand requires flexibility of staff and customers and the ability to react quickly to changing numbers. Manipulation of demand might be through pricing or special promotions.

In conclusion it is worth repeating that the major resource in the events industry is people, thus training and motivation of people is important.

The chapter has ended with a section on queuing theory. This third stage of the event operations management model now moves on to researching different scheduling techniques that the event manager can use effectively in order for the event to run as planned.

Chapter 14

Scheduling and time management

Learning Objectives

After reading through this chapter you will be able to:

■ **Understand the importance of scheduling**
■ **Apply the different techniques of scheduling and analyse the different stages**
■ **Consider the importance of time management**
■ **Apply techniques to your own use of personal time.**

Introduction

In the last few chapters within the third stage of the event operations management model we have considered the importance of motivating one of our most important resources – our staff. We have also considered the essential nature of predicting how many people will attend our event and what they will want to do when they arrive. This then led on to the need to plan for those activities within the capacity of the venue and the resources provided.

Now we turn to scheduling all these activities so that they fall into place to give the desired event. Scheduling is a key issue for an event manager. As soon as a concept is thought of, as described in the life cycle of services in Chapter 7, then a decision should be made – can we deliver this in the time we have available? Further questions should identify all of the tasks that have to be completed, and how those elements will finally come together. Indeed, scheduling has to balance many different factors and many diverse needs in order to integrate them and deliver the production of the event at the required time.

Events are a series of unique projects. The finite nature of some of the critical resources, such as special skills, means that these have to be taken into account in the planning process, and the over-riding priority is to complete the project within a given time, to a given date and hour (Slack *et al.*, 2004). Wild (2002) defines a project as an activity with a specific goal occupying a specific period of time. An event is a project, since it is a finite activity in terms of the time spent in its duration and in the use of resources. Therefore it is essential to plan the event thoroughly and to schedule all the activities so that as a whole they form the event. It is a different concept from planning repetitive activities, where problems can be resolved next time round.

At an event, all of the resources and skills have to be brought together in a planned fashion, and there is only the one opportunity to get it right and as per specification. Getz (1997) confirms that an event manager will require skills and experience in event or general project management. He cites

that the manager's ability to organize, motivate and manage a team of experts and volunteers is a primary qualification.

The event manager faces uncertainty. The amount of time needed to complete all the different tasks is often uncertain, as are the amount of resources needed and the interdependence of all the activities. In some situations, the number of people who will attend is not certain. Scheduling therefore involves a certain amount of risk, and ideally allowances should be built in to enable revisions of the schedules. There is only one opportunity to start from scratch.

Waters (1996) points out that although there are many similarities between scheduling in manufacturing and in services, there are essential differences. First, in the service industry the customer is directly involved in the process – for example, sometimes customers serve themselves and form queues and wait. Secondly, services cannot be held in stock because, as discussed earlier, they are perishable and intangible. Thirdly, there are often wide variations in demand, as discussed in Chapter 12, and our schedules should be able to meet both high and low demand. All these points are particularly true in the event industry, and this chapter will explore these issues and offer solutions that the event manager can use.

Scheduling in the event industry

Scheduling is the art of:

- Event component breakdown
- Activity analysis
- Deciding the order of completing activities
- Arranging the necessary resources to complete each activity
- Arranging the timing of activities.

Different terms are used to cover these activities. Shone and Parry (2004) discuss logistics, and describe that function as being the discipline of planning and organizing the flow of goods, equipment and people to their point of use. This is essentially the same as scheduling, and an event is reliant on getting all elements to the right place in time for a range of deadlines.

At the start of planning for the event several activities can be started, but most subsequent activities will be dependent on others finishing. As more activities finish, even more can be started (Slack *et al.*, 2004). Some of these early activities may include getting special power and utility requirements to the event site (such as telecoms), and special licences may also need to be applied for. We can see in the example of organizing a simple craft fair that certain activities need to be completed before others. The date has to be set and the venue booked, and the admission prices and refreshments prices calculated before any advertising can be done. The exhibitors have to be sourced and invited before the layout and plan can be finalized. Only after a series of major decisions have been made can follow-on activities start. This pattern of a slow start followed by a faster pace and an eventual tail-off of activities holds true for many events.

For the majority of events, a *backwards scheduling activity* occurs – i.e. the finish date and hour is known, all the activities are listed, plus their expected completion times, and then the schedule is calculated backwards so that all activities can be sequenced appropriately and finished by the due date. Wild (2002) describes this technique as one where the time durations of particular activities are subtracted from the required completion date.

In practice, as discussed in Chapter 12, demand forecasts (i.e. the number of customers and their arrival times) are rarely exact. These provide a challenge to the event manager to have just the right resources available at the right time, but not in excess, since this would add on a cost to the project.

Case study 14.1 gives an overview of the scheduling required for the World Rally Championships.

Case study 14.1

World Rally Championships Production Cars, Tuesday 7 May 2002

The logistics of flyaways – a painstaking task

For European-based rounds, the Peugeot Sport road show is mainly freighted by truck.

However, the organization required for flyaway events such as the Rally of Argentina is a big challenge, as the French team's logistics wizard, Pietro Fornaris, explains:

Everything is transported by ship or by plane, which means lead times are very long. Scheduling has to be extremely tight to be sure that everything arrives at the correct destination, in the right order, on time and via the cheapest solution possible. The containers shipped by sea have to be ready very early. The crossing often takes a good month, and since there are generally only two ships a week, you always have to plan in a safety margin just in case. By plane, we send the test car and a stock of spares just prior to pre-rally testing. Other components and the rally cars themselves follow later. But here again, we build in a good margin for error.

The stress begins during the preparation phase at the workshop. For overseas rallies, we have seven 15-tonne, 12-metre containers. The specially dimensioned service trucks, the race cars, people carriers, electronic equipment and spares all need to be packed in the knowledge the containers shipped out to Argentina go straight from South America to Kenya, and then on to New Zealand and Australia. They only return to Paris at the end of the season.

That means that all the equipment sent onto the following destination has to be thoroughly checked after each rally. That can take up to 24 hours of practically non-stop work, and even twice that when the cars have to be squeaky clean: when going to rigorous countries like New Zealand or Australia, there's no way you'll get a car in if it still has traces of dirt from the previous event. Another headache is that certain used parts, or parts that need revising, are shipped back to Paris by plane, while replacement equipment, originally shipped out by plane, takes their place inside the containers. You can imagine how precise customs documents have to be.

Naturally, at the points of departure and arrival, and at certain ports of call along the way, we use agents in whom we have complete confidence to ensure that all goes well. In addition to the equipment, we also have to look after the transport of team staff, which means finding suitable air tickets for around 70 people. As a rule, each flyaway trip is prepared a good 6 months upstream of the event, except in cases of force majeur – for example, when the FIA decides to modify the World Championship calendar.

Schedule for Production cars for 2004

6–8 Feb	Uddehold Swedish Rally Production Car World Rally Championship (WRC)
12–14 Mar	Orona Rally Mexico Production Car WRC
16–18 Apr	Rally of New Zealand Production Car WRC
6–18 Jul	Rally Argentina Production Car WRC
20–22 Aug	Rallye Deutschland Production Car WRC
15–17 Oct	Rallye de France Tour de Corse Production Car WRC
12–14 Nov	Telstra Rally Australia Production Car WRC

(Printed by courtesy of Bryn Williams, MD of www.crash.net.)

Reflective practice 14.1

Case study 14.1 gives details of the requirements of participants in the World Rally Championships.

Put together a schedule of activities for the first four rallies of 2004 (Sweden to Argentina via Mexico and New Zealand, commencing in Paris) for the Peugeot team.

In certain events the numbers of customers arriving is known, and in some cases at known specific times – for example, at a conference or for a dinner dance, or for some other pre-booked event. In these instances the event manager will make the availability of the resources coincide with the event starting; the manager can control the time of service delivery and the scheduling can be fairly exact. Efficiency is dependent on arrival of the customer at the prearranged time.

If, however, the customer is late, service will be delayed or not offered at all. In the case of a concert, the customer may miss the start of the programme. If the organizer agrees to the delay of the event, this may have an impact on other scheduled services and possibly on other customers. Nonetheless, if customers keep to the prearranged booked times, a high degree of accuracy, and efficiency in the scheduling of resources will be possible.

Customers who arrive early may have to wait, depending upon the policy of the event organizer. If the customer doesn't wait but is served, then there must have been some slack in the system and surplus capacity must have been held.

If the customer waits, then a queue starts to form. If the customer accepts that there may be a queue there will not be any conflict, but if the customer is expecting to access the event immediately there will be some dissatisfaction.

Where queuing is accepted to be part of the norm – for example at theme park rides, or whilst waiting for a mobile phone recharge at an outdoor festival – then customers will not be dissatisfied. The queues should be well managed so that there is no queue jumping and, provided that the queues are seen to be moving and there are no greater expectations, it is acceptable for the customer to be part of the resources available to the event manager. Theory of queues was covered in Chapter 12.

Case study 14.2 describes the scheduling required to provide St John Ambulance cover at a rock concert.

Case study 14.2

Robbie Williams Concert, 1–3 August 2003, Knebworth, England

St John Ambulance rocks at Knebworth, England

Brian Heron-Edmends, Assistant County Commissioner (Operations), describes three long days in August when fans flocked to see Robbie Williams play Knebworth and St John Ambulance volunteers flocked to minister first aid.

St John Ambulance Hertfordshire was asked to provide medical, first aid and ambulance cover at the Robbie Williams concerts at Knebworth Park over the weekend of the 1–3 August 2003, with 125 000 people attending each night.

The planning started back in February this year, when the basis of the concert was known, and the boundaries to which we would be working were being agreed. Over the following few months a number of people put in a great deal of work to ensure that there were sufficient numbers on duty each day.

The organizers had requested 80 first aiders per day, and four ambulances. This was to be supplemented by eight paramedics and two paramedic ambulances, which were to be supplied by the local ambulance service (Bedfordshire and Hertfordshire Ambulance and Paramedic Service NHS Trust).

It was agreed that there would be six first aid posts and a medical centre; four posts in the main arena and the remaining two backstage to treat people who were taken from the crowd via the pit. Each first aid post would have a 10×10 m marquee and a first aid unit; all the posts would have toilets (for members' use only) and running drinking water. The medical centre, a much larger marquee, was to be manned by St John first aiders, doctors and nurses.

Day 1, Friday 1 August

The day started wet and miserable – not good for an open-air concert. Members started to arrive and set about checking the equipment in their first aid posts in preparation for the gates to be opened. The afternoon saw a gradual increase of fans arriving, with most first aid posts relatively quiet to start with. As time went on, it became apparent that many fans were stuck in traffic jams on the A1(M) and surrounding roads. This included some of our members who were coming to the duty after work, as well as those coming from further afield.

The concert was divided into sections, with artists playing followed by a 45-minute break before the next artist took to the stage. Casualties who needed treatment made their way to the posts during these breaks, leading to a wave effect of patients requiring treatment and quiet periods when members could get themselves a drink and quick snack. As the evening went on the stream of casualties became more constant, even when the artists were playing.

Many members played the game of hunt the casualty after receiving a report of a collapsed fan in the crowd; most requests for help came via show security, various control rooms and finally to the members. The Chinese whisper effect on some occasions made tracking down the casualty a challenge.

The concert finished on time, even though people were still arriving from the motorway. Many St John personnel didn't leave the concert site until the early hours of Saturday morning.

Day 2, Saturday 2 August

Everything was reviewed for Saturday; problems that had been encountered on Friday evening were rectified, as far as possible. Some of the posts were rearranged by the members to free up more space for stretcher patients. This left less staff for the walking wounded. Again, members began to arrive during the morning ready for the 12 noon opening of the gates. The weather was totally different to Friday; the sun was shining and it was starting to get very hot. At the front of the stage where the noise was at its greatest Raynet personnel provided additional radio communications with the Control Room to speed the passing of non-medical messages. As the afternoon turned into early evening, the first aid posts and the medical centre became busier and busier.

Day 3, Sunday 3 August

Another hot day was forecast, and as the day progressed fans started to feel the full force of the sun and were even collapsing in the queues before entering the arena, so members were deployed to the gates with water and patient report forms.

Many people in the audience, having found themselves good vantage points, were reluctant to leave to get themselves fluids; this led to many people collapsing or coming to the first

aid posts with severe sunburn. In an attempt to protect members as much as possible, they were all issued with sun cream and provided with bottled water.

The total number of casualties treated on Sunday was the highest of the three concerts.

Everyone who attended the duty had a great time and found they learnt a lot. The overall event was a great success for all involved; the planning that went on beforehand played a large part in this, but would have been pointless without the dedication and hard work of everyone who covered the duty. They made it possible for Hertfordshire to deliver the high standard of care and service that is always expected of St John Ambulance.

The official figures totalled 1387 patients over the 3 days.

Staff attendees: first aid units and medical centre staff

Doctors	5	Nurses	8
Paramedics	1 per shift	Pharmacist	1 (on-site pharmacy instigated by St JA)
First aiders	100 per shift	Radio operators	33 (Raynet)
StJA support staff	10 per shift		

These staff members were drawn from the following seven counties: Hertfordshire, Bedfordshire, Cornwall, Dorset, London District, Oxfordshire, Suffolk.

Resources on site

Front-line ambulances	6	Sitting car	1
4 × 4 ambulances	1	Minibuses	3
4 × 4 support vehicles	2	Command and/or first aid units	6

And what did we learn?

The pharmacy not only catered for people requiring painkillers for headaches but also with the many that were after plasters for blisters after the long walks from the car parks. The decision to have a pharmacy on site was by far the best decision taken during the planning stages, as it provided a much needed service to the public as well as helping reduce the need for people to attend the first aid posts with minor ailments. The pharmacy sold most products that you would expect to find in a high street pharmacy.

We would highly recommend anyone else who is providing medical cover at a concert of this size, or even smaller, to consider an on-site pharmacy, as we believe it reduced the members' work considerably, leaving them better prepared to deal with serious conditions which were referred to the first aid posts and medical centre.

Control rooms: At the event there were three control rooms, St John Ambulance, Beds and Hertfordshire Ambulance Service (BHAPS), and RAYNET. The control rooms were all separate, albeit within 10 metres of each other. However, it made the passing of information quickly between the different agencies very difficult.

Calls for medical assistance from the security and event organizers were directed via BHAPS, who then passed them on to St John; housekeeping calls came from the various first aid posts to the StJA Control Room via RAYNET.

After the first night it was agreed that at future events all three controls should be located in the same building, thus allowing for easier interagency communications.

First aid posts: The first aid posts were all large marquees, along with a conventional mobile StJA first aid unit, which was there to provide staff facilities along with additional space for the treatment of patients who needed additional privacy. Some of the posts had barriers around them; however, this was not the case for the posts towards the back of the arena, and it was only on the Saturday, as the sun shone brightly, that it became apparent that all posts needed to be 'fenced in', just leaving an entry/exit hole. As these large marquees provided some shelter from the sun, people did everything they could to get as close to them as

possible. This meant that staff and patients inside were being knocked, albeit unintentionally, by those outside trying to avoid the sun.

The problem was further exacerbated when the only shelter from the sun was at the front of the marquee, and without careful management from the post manager it was not uncommon for the door area to become a sea of people avoiding the sun.

(Information supplied by courtesy of the Hertfordshire St John Ambulance Service; for more information see www.herts.sja.org.uk/.)

Reflective practice 14.2

Consider Case study 14.2.

From the information given, put together a schedule of activities for first aid cover for day 1 of the Robbie Williams concert, taking into account the lessons learned.

The stages of scheduling

The stages of scheduling are shown in Figure 14.1, and comprise event component breakdown, activity analysis and deciding the order of completion. We will now look at all the stages of scheduling, and apply some best practice techniques from the event industry.

Event component breakdown

A technique used within traditional project management is to create a product breakdown sheet (O'Toole and Mikolaitis, 2002). In the event industry the product is the event itself, which could be an exhibition with a supporting conference and seminars, followed by a conference dinner with entertainment. It is important to break down the whole event into its component parts, taking into account many of the intangible aspects of the event that have been described and considered necessary in its original objectives. This is called the *event component breakdown*.

The importance of having clear objectives was noted in Chapter 2, and it is essential that the event manager return to the objectives of the event so that those intangible aspects that have been cited as being most desirable and important are not missed. For

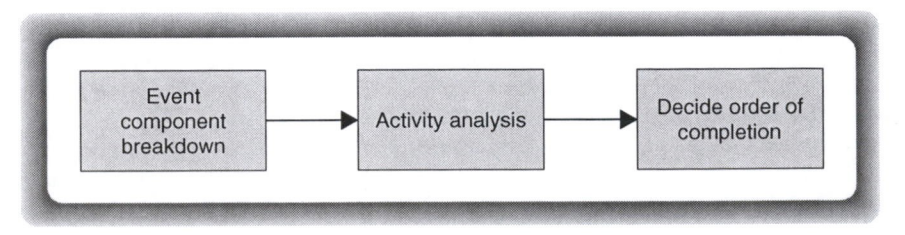

Figure 14.1 Stages of scheduling

example, the need to allow for networking opportunities may have been identified, or for a fun all-age embracing event, or to develop loyalty of a community towards their town within your objectives. It is important to refocus on all aspects of the previously stated hopes and wishes, so that the event breakdown reflects even the subtlest of objectives.

O'Toole and Mikolaitis (2002) say that this product breakdown is not merely effective as a means of identifying client objectives but it also provides a common language for the event. It is necessary for all groups of people who are responsible for different elements of the event to be aware of the final desired picture, and all unspoken assumptions should be clearly defined. If these assumptions can be aired, and ideally written down, they can be referred to as the event progresses. It may be that as the event arrangements proceed, some of the assumptions need rewriting and the documentation needs updating. If changes are made it is imperative that all parties are informed, to avoid some teams working to old versions and others to a different version.

A useful document is a contact sheet of all the relevant contacts, with mobile and email addresses, so that contact can be made swiftly and everyone is aware of those contact details should the need arise.

The event component breakdown information can be used to create the management structure for the event. It may be that several activities can be completed by certain groups of people and others should be outsourced to specialists, or that an additional team should be set up to concentrate on a particular aspect. The event component breakdown provides the client, the suppliers, major interested agencies (for example the Health and Safety Executive) and the different groups of teams working on the event a clear view of the overall event. Hence it can be seen that the event component breakdown has many important uses.

Activity analysis

Once the event components have been defined, the next stage is to analyse every element of work that needs to be completed during the planning, implementation and control of the event. This is a process of decomposition whereby a complex event can be broken up into smaller units of work that can be easily managed (O'Toole and Mikolaitis, 2002). The result of this is your activity analysis. There are several benefits to using this approach – these manageable units can be assigned to subcontractors or different event teams, or to different committees, dependent upon the set-up of the event and its managerial scope. These separate units of activities can also provide a basis for costing and a managerial structure, and they denote levels of responsibility.

Similarly, the costs for the entire event can be calculated by adding together the costs for each unit.

Subsequently each of these groupings can be broken down into more activities, so that eventually as each unit is expanded it will show all of the work that must be completed.

The *activity analysis* becomes the representation of the entire event project. As such, the event team, client, suppliers, sponsors and volunteers should easily understand it, and it gives a quick reference for all aspects of the event.

The aim is to ensure that nothing is forgotten or falls into a black hole with everyone thinking someone else is completing that particular task. Similarly, a comprehensive activity analysis ensures that nothing is forgotten or left undone.

Case study 14.3 shows the schedule for the event day of an actual University Awards Ceremony in 2003. The names of individuals and organizations have been changed.

Case study 14.3

A Business Awards Ceremony, a University Town, England, June 2003

Time	Activity	Area of responsibility	Company		Notes
09:00	Set-up of staging	Andy Close	Free Hotel	Completion 10:00	6 × 10′ × 5′ with red carpet and surround, central far wall kitchen side. Could we have Magpie divided into two?
	Stage set, sound and lighting	Iain Newman	Row Audio Visual, tel. 0123456738	Completion 13:00	Raven Suite, parking available at the front for off loading. Refreshments tea, coffee for Row × 3
09:30	Singing group arrives	Joanne, Jimmy	Event organizers, tel. 0777777711	Singing group contact number	Allocate rooms if possible, otherwise luggage etc. to changing room
10:00	Minibus for singing group	Joanne, Jimmy	Event organizers, tel. 0777777711		Pick up outside Free Hotel, go to Big Grammar School, followed by Little Grammar. Accompanied by Jimmy to give workshop
13:00	Lunch	Free Hotel			Sandwiches to be provided for Row × 3 people + 1
14:00	Audiovisual check	Joanne, Row			Run through lighting, graphics etc.
	Flowers arrive	Joanne			Delivery to front of hotel
15:00	National TV presenter arrives	Joanne	Event organizers, tel. 0777777711		Booked into suite, brief tour etc.
	Refreshments for crew				Tea/coffee/water
15:30	Singing group returns	Jimmy			Refreshments available, fresh tea, water, orange juice in changing room
15:45	Rehearsal singing group	Row	Row Audio Visual, tel. 0123456738		Sound check
16:15	Asian music group and brass ensemble, acoustic guitar and folk singer arrive	Joanne			Allocation of room for changing/ instrument cases

16:30	Awards Alive! Overture rehearsal	Singing group, Asian music group, brass ensemble			
17:00	Awards rehearsal	Sam, Sabi, Joanne, Jimmy	Awards clients, tel. 0123455673, 077777723		
18:00	Staff changing				
18:20	Staff to positions, folk singer to champagne reception, brass ensemble to front of foyer area of Free Hotel	Sam, Sabi, Joanne, Jimmy			Refreshments for artists in changing rooms; tea coffee, water, orange juice
18:30	Guests begin to arrive	Sam, Sabi, plus Awards client staff			
19:10	Raven suite to be lit, Asian music group to take their positions	Helen to call 19:08			
19:15	Guests invited to take their seats	Free Hotel manager		Local news presenter to be met at the door – Jimmy	Parking available outside the Free Hotel for dropping off
19:25	Call for Singing group and brass ensemble	Helen		Brass ensemble to move from foyer area to main suite	
19:28	Singers to mingle with guests in suite, brass ensemble to take their positions				
19:30	Awards Overture Awards Alive!	Asian music, brass ensemble, singing group			
19:36	Singing group exeunt				
19:36	Welcome speech	Sam			
19:45	Starters	Asian music group			Waiters to enter from two areas of the suite en masse to serve starters
20:03	Cue brass ensemble to main suite	Helen			
20:05	Asian music exeunt	Joanne to give cue			
20:05	Main course	Brass ensemble	Liaison between Free Hotel and Joanne re. change		Waiters to enter from two areas of the suite en masse to

			over from starter to main course		serve main course
20:43	Brass ensemble exeunt				
20:45	First three awards	Sam *et al.*	1. Presenter; 2. Presenter announces Awards; 3. Winner from seat – Award speech; 4. Repeat		
21:00	Cue folk singer	Helen			
21:05	Desert/coffee	Folk singer	Liaison between Free Hotel and Joanne re. change over from main course to dessert		Waiters to enter from two areas of the suite en masse to serve dessert; bar to open
21:30	Introduction to the singing group	Local news presenter			
	Cue singing group to reception	Helen			
21:33	Singing group Part 1				
21:44	Singing group exeunt				
21:45	Awards Part 2	Sam *et al.*	1. Presenter; 2. Presenter announces Award; 3. Winner from seat – Award speech; 4. Repeat		
21:55	Cue singing group	Helen			
22:00	Singing group Part 2				
22:15	Singing group exeunt	To reception area			
22:15	Keynote speaker; national TV presenter	Sam			
22:25	Singing group Part 3				
22:38	Cue folk singer to reception	Helen			
22:40	Singing group exeunt				
22:40	Music in reception area	Folk singer			
24:00	Close				

Reflective practice 14.3

From the information in Case study 14.3, put together an activity analysis, using planning, implementation and control as the process to complete this task.

Deciding the order of completing activities

This can be referred to as critical path analysis. Critical path analysis is a planning and scheduling tool that can help to streamline all the processes to be undertaken (Getz, 1997). It examines the relationship between all the resources and the activities that need to be undertaken in order to 'deliver' the event – i.e. those listed in the activity analysis.

All these activities should now be arranged in chronological order, working back from the event date so that each prerequisite activity gets scheduled in proper sequence. The resultant schedule is a network of interconnected tasks, and the actual critical path in the network is the shortest possible sequence of activities needed to get the event operational (Getz, 1997).

When all the activities are linked and the dates by which those tasks should be finished by have been identified, a line can be drawn to establish how long the event preparation and lead up to delivery will take. There is a variety of computer software packages that are useful for analysing the enormous number of tasks and links that are essential to any event. However, it might be that the nature of events is too fluid for it to be put onto a software programme such as Microsoft Project.

Built into the software will be the ability to have a minimum of three estimates of time for each activity – the expected time (most likely), the most pessimistic, and the most optimistic. The software will also show the earliest start time, the latest start time, and the most probable start time. The program will calculate various critical paths and provide for printouts, on an exception basis, of a list of activities that are falling behind schedule, thus enabling the event manager to take action to correct the situation. Correction might include adding extra resources, or delaying one activity and transferring resources to another activity and so on.

However, research has been undertaken (Tum, 2004; unpublished) that shows that very few event managers in the UK use any computerized critical path analysis software.

The activity analysis has determined the critical dates when each task has to be finished by, and by whom. Some tasks can be done simultaneously, whereas others may have to wait until others have been completed. We identified examples of this in the introduction to this chapter. Other examples might include the promotion of a major sports event, which cannot start until the venue has been secured. Similarly, the delivery of expensive equipment cannot be accepted until it can be established that the level of security is adequate. However, in this scenario the event manager is then left with the challenge that it is often easier to accept delivery of large equipment onto a virgin outdoor site prior to the construction of the perimeter fencing. Many tasks at an outdoor venue cannot start until the generator has arrived. O'Toole and Mikolaitis (2002) suggest that planners of small events use sticky note slips. Each slip denotes one of the activities and can be placed on a large board, and the notes can then be easily rearranged to achieve the optimum sequence.

Network planning: the critical path method

Table 14.1 illustrates the critical path method of network planning, using the example of organizing an exhibition.

Table 14.1 Network planning: the critical path method

Activity		Duration	Preceding activity
Book venue	A–B	1 day	None
Decide on layout plan	B–C	5 days	A–B
Touch up paintwork and minor redecoration of venue	B–D	3 days	A–B
Order and delivery of display stands	C–D	7 days	B–C
Wire for stand lighting	C–E	3 days	B–C
Install display stands	D–F	2 days	B–D, C–D, C–E
Exhibitors set up	F–G	1 day	D–F

Table 14.1 depicts the order in which activities can occur. The convention of network diagrams is for the arrows to move from left to right across the page, with no backtracking. To maintain the logic, a dummy activity can be shown. In our example, E–D is a dummy activity. If E–D was not used there would be two activities designated C–D (wiring for stands and delivery of stands).

By adding the time required for each activity, it is possible to calculate the total time required to prepare for the opening of the event. If we follow along the path A–B, B–C, C–E, E–D, D–F, F–G, we can see these activities will take in total 12 days, whereas the path A–B, B–C, C–D, D–F, F–G totals 16 days and the path A–B, B–D, D–F, F–G takes 7 days. Thus the longest path is 16 days and the total time required to complete all the activities will be 16 days.

It follows that if any event on this path A–B, B–C, C–D, D–F, F–G takes longer than planned, the total amount of time required will be extended. For example, if B–C 'Decide on layout plan' takes 8 days instead of 5 days, the total time required will be 19 days. If time is critical, then no activity on the longest path, i.e. the *critical* path, can be allowed to extend beyond its allotted time. Activities not on the critical path can take longer, without affecting the total time. For example, activity B–D ('Touch up and redecoration') can take up to 12 days, and if all other activities are on schedule the total time required would still be 16 days. In the above example the only other activity that could be delayed is C–E, but then only by 2 days.

This example is very simple, designed to give the rudiments of network scheduling. A fuller example appears below.

Network planning and critical path analysis: organizing a conference

(The following explanation and work for critical path analysis has been provided by John Nightingale, BA (Hons), Events Management Course Leader, UK Centre for Events Management, Leeds Metropolitan University.)

The following network diagrams (Figures 14.2–14.6) work through the activity of setting up the basic requirements for a conference. It is important to know and understand the following terms:

- A *project* is any job – usually large. It can be split up into *activities* or *tasks*. A task is a part of a project that requires *time* and *resources* to complete.
- An *event* (in critical path jargon) marks the beginning or end of an activity or group of activities. Events take *no time*. We try to avoid the use of this term, as it can cause confusion for event organizers!
- A *milestone* is an important point during the progress of a project (often marked by a review meeting) – e.g. moving onto site, completion of set-up.

- A *predecessor* is an activity that must finish before a particular activity can start.
- The *EST* (earliest start time) of an activity is the earliest time it can start – after all its predecessors have finished. You work out ESTs by starting at the *left* of a network chart, and *add* the activity times to get the EST of the next activity. If there are two possible ESTs for an activity, use the *larger* one.
- The *LFT* (latest finish time) is the latest time at which an activity can finish, without delaying the whole project. You start working out LFTs at the *right* of the network diagram, and *subtract* the activity time to get the next LFT. If there are two possible LFTs for an activity, you take the *smaller* one.
- Activities on the *critical path* have the LFT and the EST the same at each event on the path.
- Activities off the critical path will have a *float time* bigger than zero. The float time is the maximum time that an activity can be lengthened or delayed. To find it, you work out LFT – EFT, or LST – EST.
- A *baseline* is the original version of the complete plan for the project. Progress of the project is compared against the baseline as the project progresses.

Figure 14.2 shows just one part of a network diagram.

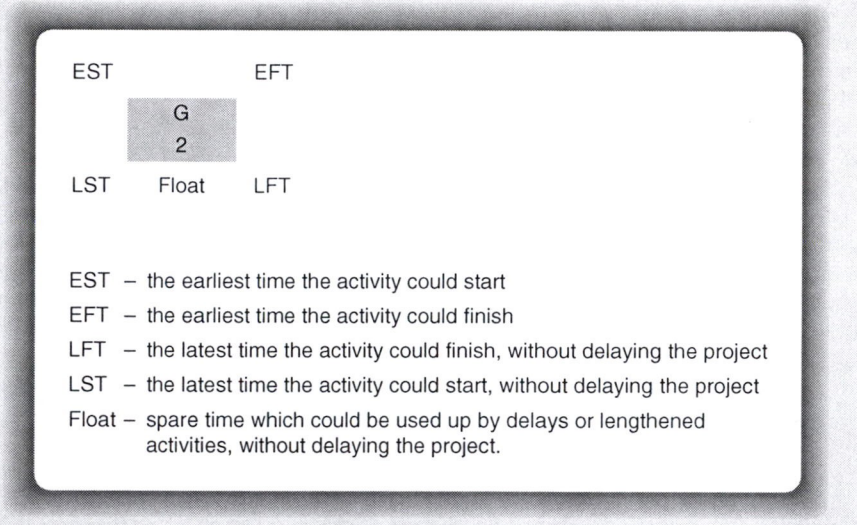

Figure 14.2 One part of a network diagram

Organizing the conference

1. Stage 1: break the project down into activities.

Activity	Duration	Preceding activities	
A	3	C	Arrange presentation systems
B	7	E	Arrange food
C	12	E	Arrange speakers
D	5	A	Set up room
E	8	G	Detailed planning
F	4	B, D, H	Stage conference
G	2	Start	Initial visit
H	9	A	Set up PA system

2. Stage 2: draw a network diagram, with precedents and times (Figure 14.3):

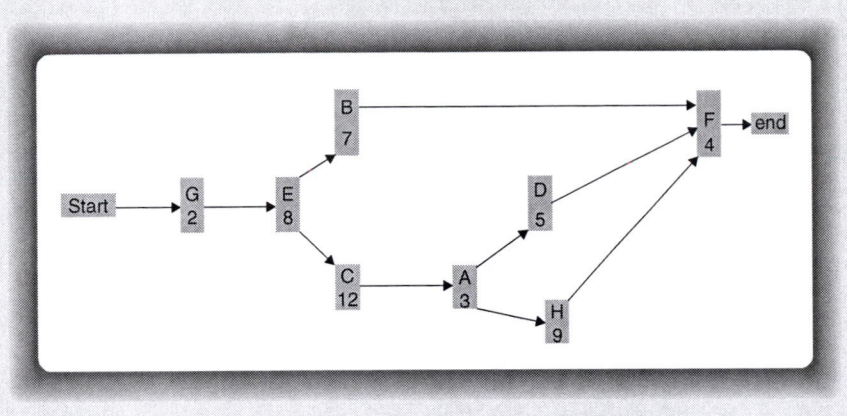

Figure 14.3 Stage 2: setting precedents and times

Key:

Activity	Duration	Preceding activities	
Start	0		
A	3	C	Arrange presentation systems
B	7	E	Arrange food
C	12	E	Arrange speakers
D	5	A	Set up room
E	8	G	Detailed planning
F	4	B, D, H	Stage conference
G	2	Start	Initial visit
H	9	A	Set up PA system
End	0	F	

3. Stage 3: add earliest start and earliest finish times (top left and top right) to each box (Figure 14.4). To get the earliest start time of the next activity, choose the *largest* EFT of jobs leading to it. To get the earliest finish time for an activity, *add* the duration to the EST.

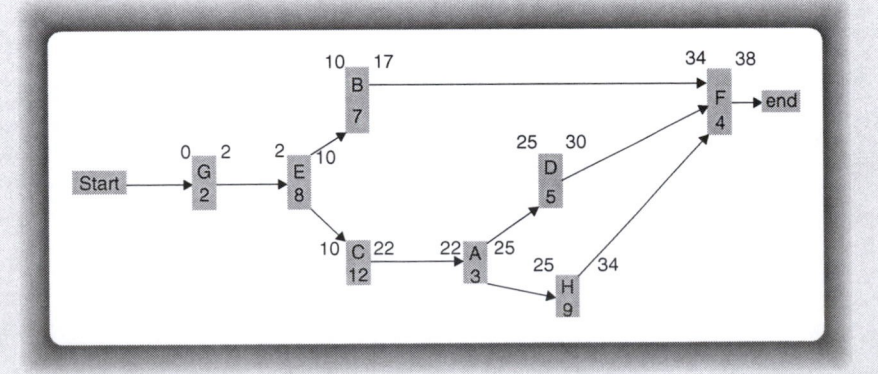

Figure 14.4 Stage 3: add earliest start and finish times

Key:

Activity	Duration	Preceding activities	
A	3	C	Arrange presentation speakers
B	7	E	Arrange food
C	12	E	Arrange speakers
D	5	A	Set up room
E	8	G	Detailed planning
F	4	B, D, H	Stage conference
G	2	Start	Initial visit
H	9	A	Set up PA system

This project takes 38 days.

4. Stage 4: put in latest finish time for each activity, starting at the right (Figure 14.5). To get the latest start time for an activity, subtract its duration from the latest finish time. When there is a 'disagreement' between two possible LFTs, take the smallest.

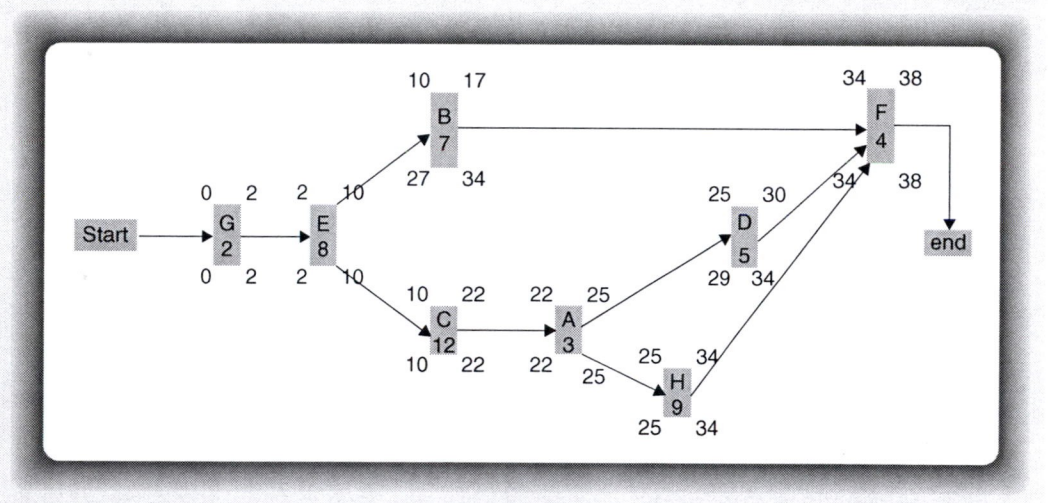

Figure 14.5 Stage 4: add latest finish time for each activity

Key:

Activity	Duration	Preceding activities	
A	3	C	Arrange presentation speakers
B	7	E	Arrange food
C	12	E	Arrange speakers
D	5	A	Set up room
E	8	G	Detailed planning
F	4	B, D, H	Stage conference
G	2	Start	Initial visit
H	9	A	Set up PA system

5. Stage 5: work out the float time (the difference between the bottom and top of each box; Figure 14.6). The critical path has zero float on every activity, therefore delays on the critical path are important. Could you speed up the critical path?

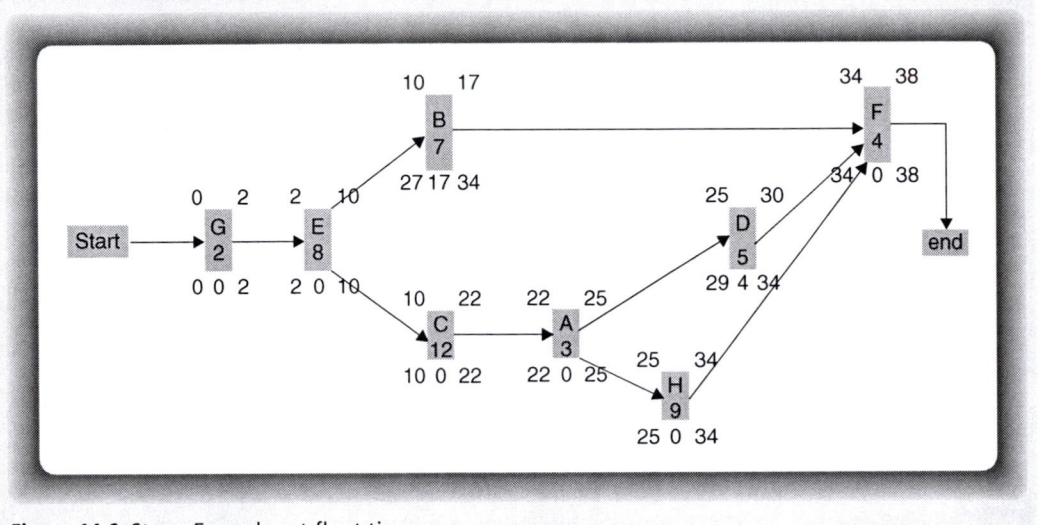

Figure 14.6 Stage 5: work out float time

Key:

Activity	Duration	Preceding activities	
A	3	C	Arrange presentation speakers
B	7	E	Arrange food
C	12	E	Arrange speakers
D	5	A	Set up room
E	8	G	Detailed planning
F	4	B, D, H	Stage conference
G	2	Start	Initial visit
H	9	A	Set up PA system

Many standard computer packages exist for network planning. Generally software will enable three estimates to be made for each activity: expected time, best time, and worst time. The software will calculate the earliest start date and the latest start date, show the critical path, and provide for a printout on exception basis of a list of activities that are falling behind schedule, thus allowing the event operations manager to take corrective action. Corrective action might include adding extra resources, or delaying one activity and transferring resources to another activity. However, adding extra resource adds to the cost. A trade-off might be necessary where an acceptable delay occurs rather than adding the cost of an extra resource.

Gantt charts
Another technique that could be used is a Gantt chart. Henry Gantt first devised this chart in 1917. The bottom line of the chart represents time, and this time line can represent

weeks, days or minutes. Each activity should be entered onto the vertical axis and plotted onto the graph to indicate the start and finish times. It is sometimes useful to have two Gantt charts: one with a weekly time line for the entire project starting at initial planning stages and leading through to breakdown and evaluation, and the other providing a running order of the event over the day/s when it is being delivered. This would then show the main components of the event.

These two Gantt charts have the beauty that most people who are involved with the event can easily understand them and they are extremely visual, and therefore effective. If kept simple, the Gantt chart will show the major tasks, i.e. the event component breakdown and the activity analysis.

The Gantt chart shows when each activity should start and finish, and enables everyone's responsibilities to be identified. It also shows their relationships to each other. As the activities are completed they can be coloured differently, and so the chart acts as a means of control to show which activities have been completed, which still have to be completed, and whether the timeframe is being kept to.

Tum (2004; unpublished) has found that a small percentage of event managers in the UK do use Gantt charts, and these are often created on word-processing packages or a spreadsheet.

Case study 14.4 illustrates the use of a Gantt chart in the scheduling of a Gala (see Figure 14.7).

The Gantt chart in Case study 14.4 shows the main activities required for the Gala Day. Accompanying this would be an activity schedule similar to the one for the Awards Ceremony, which would identify responsibilities and more minute-by-minute detail. Having the timescale on the top of the Gantt chart enables easier reading of the table.

Time management

This chapter has identified the importance of scheduling all the activities that must be completed for an event to occur. It has discussed the need to have resources available and at the right time.

The use of time is crucial. In the last pages of this chapter we are going to consider how you personally can manage your time better. As for all events, the first step is to know what the objectives are, and the steps or activities needed to achieve the objectives. It is also important to prioritize objectives and steps.

A five-step approach to personal time management is as follows:

1. List the problems/tasks facing you. Sort those that will advance the organization's interests and those that don't really add value to the business. Discard those that don't add value.
2. Prioritize – i.e. determine which objectives are the most important and the order in which they should be done. This includes deciding which cannot be delayed, and which are not important. Sometimes it is possible to get rid of several small tasks in a short space of time, but don't get bogged down with a trivial task.
3. Having decided the order of objectives, then in the same manner list the tasks required for each objective and assign priorities to them.
4. Make a schedule of jobs to be done and, in brackets, allot time to each.
5. Tick off items as they are completed (this is the best bit).

This approach can be done at the beginning of each week and then checked and reset each morning, but don't waste all morning reworking the schedule.

Most managers achieve 80 per cent of their important results in only 20 per cent of their time – in other words, 80 per cent of their time is spent on unimportant or

Gantt chart for Addingham Gala, 10 July 2004, West Yorkshire, England

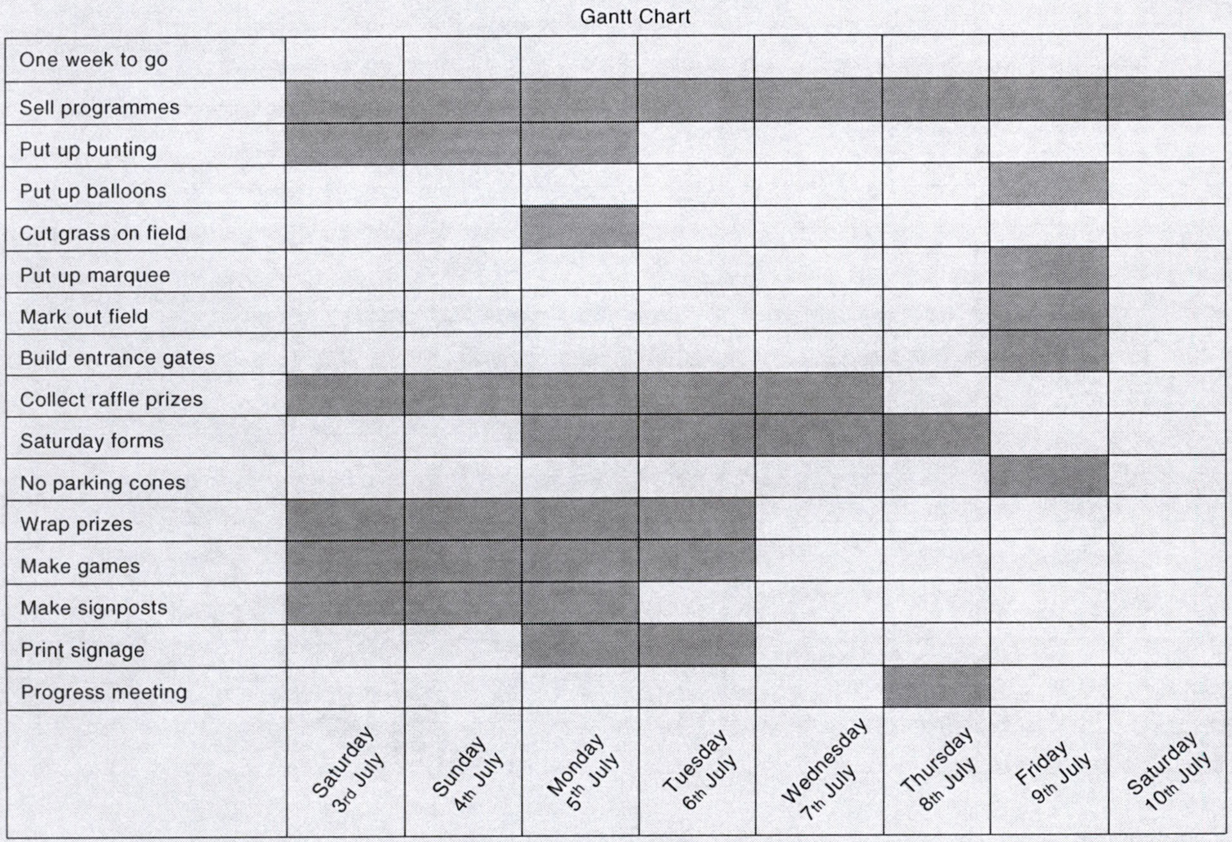

Gantt Chart

Gantt Chart	Saturday 3rd July	Sunday 4th July	Monday 5th July	Tuesday 6th July	Wednesday 7th July	Thursday 8th July	Friday 9th July	Saturday 10th July
One week to go								
Sell programmes	▓	▓	▓	▓	▓	▓		▓
Put up bunting	▓	▓						
Put up balloons								▓
Cut grass on field			▓					
Put up marquee								
Mark out field							▓	
Build entrance gates							▓	
Collect raffle prizes	▓	▓	▓				▓	
Saturday forms			▓	▓	▓	▓		
No parking cones							▓	
Wrap prizes	▓	▓	▓	▓				
Make games	▓	▓	▓	▓				
Make signposts	▓	▓	▓	▓				
Print signage			▓	▓				
Progress meeting						▓		

Figure 14.7 Gantt chart

Addingham Schedule for 10th July 2004

Task													
Rope off ring 1 and 2	■	■											
Close off car park and site entrance to general public	■	■											
Put up officials tent	■	■											
Allocate space for field stalls	■	■											
Collect chairs and put out in marquee	■	■	■										
Collect tables and put out in marquee	■	■	■										
Mark out road for procession	■	■											
Check police cones	■												
Put up tents for gala committee stalls	■	■											
Bacon butties													
Refreshments prep	■	■	■	■	■								

Figure 14.7 (Contd)

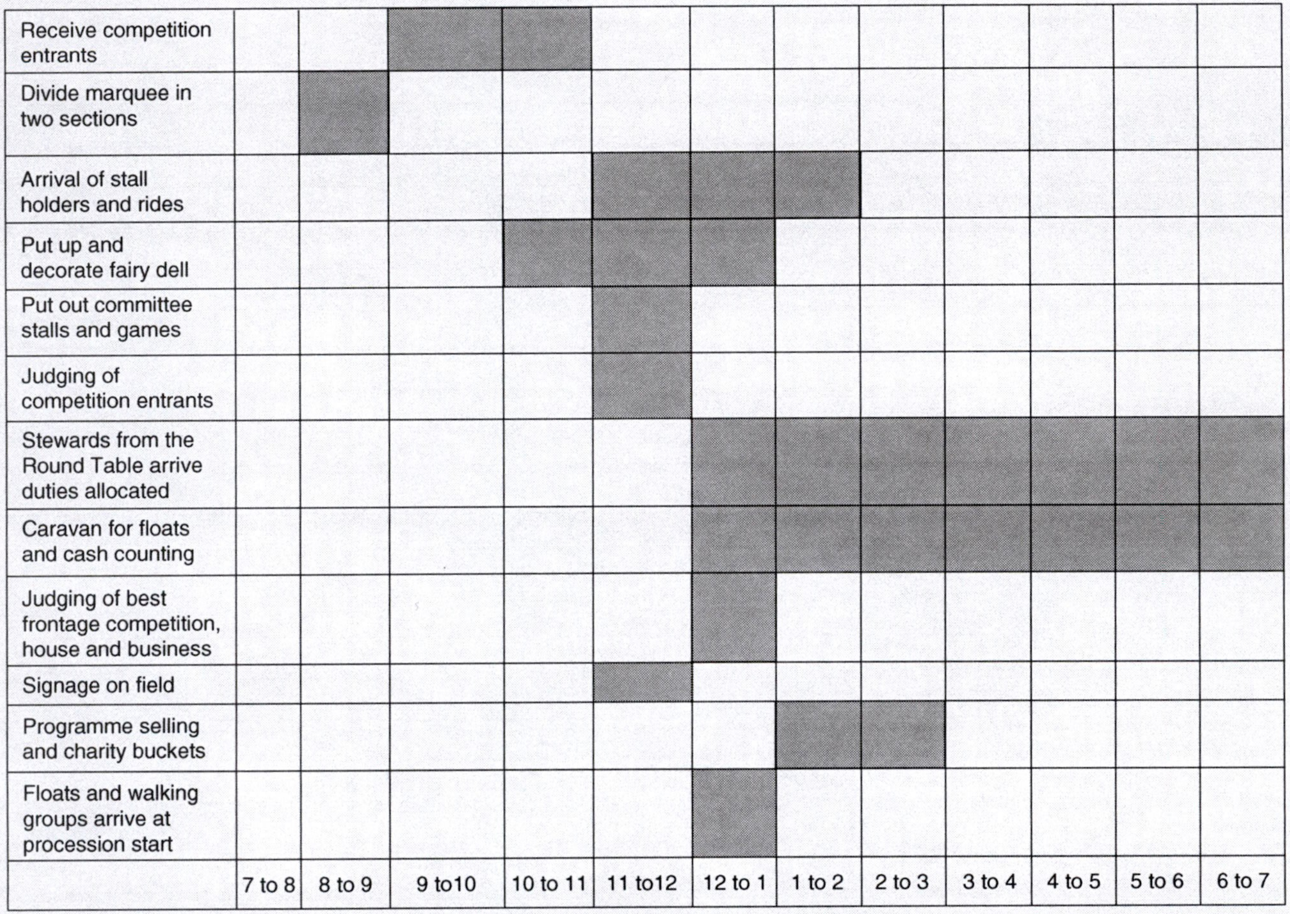

Figure 14.7 (Contd)

	7 to 8	8 to 9	9 to10	10 to 11	11 to12	12 to 1	1 to 2	2 to 3	3 to 4	4 to 5	5 to 6	6 to 7
Receive competition entrants			▓									
Divide marquee in two sections		▓										
Arrival of stall holders and rides												
Put up and decorate fairy dell				▓								
Put out committee stalls and games												
Judging of competition entrants					▓	▓						
Stewards from the Round Table arrive duties allocated					▓	▓	▓					
Caravan for floats and cash counting					▓	▓	▓	▓	▓	▓	▓	▓
Judging of best frontage competition, house and business						▓	▓	▓	▓	▓	▓	▓
Signage on field					▓	▓						
Programme selling and charity buckets							▓	▓				
Floats and walking groups arrive at procession start						▓						

Activity	1	2	3	4	5	6	7	8	9	10	11	12
Judging of procession at 1:00												
Refreshments on gala site							▓		▓			
Police road closure from 1:30 all roads							▓					
Procession from 1:30							▓					
Gala field open to public 1:45							▓					
Gala opening on site, programme run re gala activity schedule							▓	▓	▓			
Health and Safety	▓	▓	▓	▓	▓	▓	▓	▓	▓	▓	▓	▓
Gala finishes 4:30												
Stall holders dismantle and leave										▓		
Litter pick										▓	▓	▓
Remove ropes										▓	▓	▓
Return chairs and tables										▓	▓	▓
Dismantle marquee										▓	▓	▓
Clear refreshments hall										▓	▓	▓

Figure 14.7 (Contd)

Celebrate successful day	7 to 8	8 to 9	9 to10	10 to 11	11 to12	12 to 1	1 to 2	2 to 3	3 to 4	4 to 5	5 to 6	6 to 7
												■

Figure 14.7 (Contd)

time-wasting tasks. It is easy to go home feeling that you have been busy all day, but in reality having achieved very little of value. Some writers suggest setting a regular amount of time aside each day for talking to staff, checking telephone messages, making phone calls, checking the email and sending emails. If you are working across time zones, 10 am in the UK will be 10 pm in New Zealand, thus messages don't have to be answered immediately.

By the same token, you should try and make it a rule that all messages, emails and faxes are replied to on the day received, if only to acknowledge receipt. Technology is wonderful, but don't get caught by the trap of thinking that just because you have sent a message it has arrived. Somewhere in the IT link a server can be down, and although you have not received 'message returned' advice this does not mean that your message has gone all the way down the so-called superhighway. If you don't get a reply in a reasonable amount of time, don't be shy about sending a message asking for confirmation.

Meetings don't have to be a waste of time

A poorly run meeting can run on for hours, waste everyone's time, and achieve absolutely nothing. Minutes of meetings should only cover actions to be taken by members. At the next meeting, the first task should be to check whether actions have been completed, followed by a discussion of what else has to be done, what should be done, and agreement on a fresh list of actions. Unless any action follows on from a meeting, why have it?

One suggestion for running a meeting is to have no chairs; if everyone has to stand for the duration of the meeting, it is surprising how quickly it will finish. If this is too revolutionary, at least try not serving coffee. A meeting is not a social occasion; if it is it should be billed as such, and we should not expect to achieve any worthwhile business.

Chapter summary and key points

In this chapter we have considered the key task of scheduling work. We have shown that scheduling includes arranging resources and setting timeframes so as to achieve objectives as efficiently as possible.

Techniques and methods of scheduling have been considered, along with the importance of managing our own time.

This chapter concludes with the thought that time is a precious commodity, and whether you are doing time, marking time or spending time, time is running out. Your only hope is to do it now; procrastination is the thief of time.

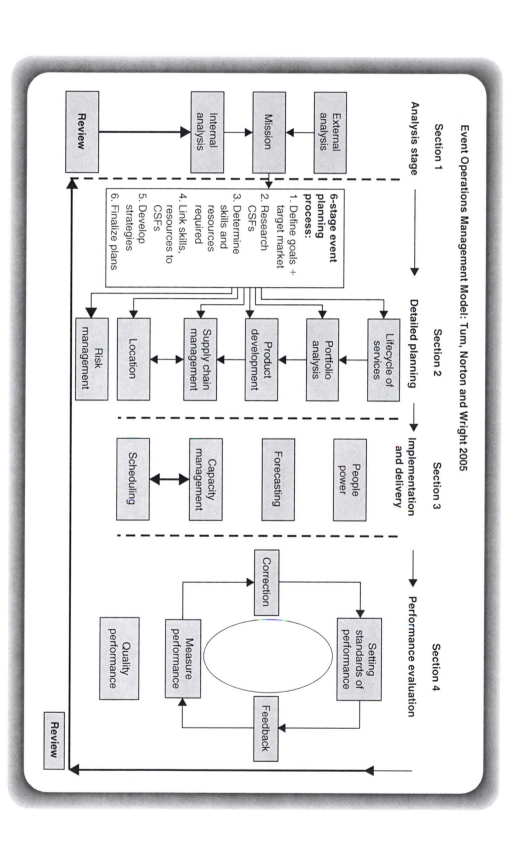

Event Operations Management Model: Tum, Norton and Wright 2005

Section 1 Analysis stage

Review → Internal analysis → Mission ← External analysis

6-stage event planning process:

1. Define goals + target market
2. Research CSFs
3. Determine skills and resources required
4. Link skills, resources to CSFs
5. Develop strategies
6. Finalize plans

Section 2 Detailed planning

Risk management

Location ↔ Supply chain management ← Product development ← Portfolio analysis ← Lifecycle of services

Section 3 Implementation and delivery

Scheduling ↔ Capacity management

Forecasting

People power

Section 4 Performance evaluation

Correction

Setting standards of performance

Measure performance

Feedback

Quality performance

Review

Section Four

Performance evaluation

Introduction

Section 4 covers the fourth stage of the event operations management model. This stage gives us an opportunity to look back on what has happened during the event, correct all that may not have gone as planned and build on what went right. It would be a mistake to think of evaluation merely occurring at the end of an event. The event manager looks on each event as a complete project, and it is not good enough to look at the event only after it has happened; there should be continuous evaluation throughout. The wedding celebrations cannot be repeated the following day, if all did not go as planned. The live concert performance cannot be restaged the next day, due to the event manager not having sufficient staff.

On the event operations management model it appears that evaluation is the last stage of the model, and yet evaluation, analysis and a myriad of decisions occur throughout the staging of an event. We can see evaluation within the analysis stage, the detailed planning stages, during the implementation and again at the review.

As Getz (1997) says, there are three types of evaluation:

1. Formative evaluation (i.e. part of the analysis stage)
2. Process evaluation (to improve effectiveness during the event)
3. Summative evaluation (after the event, to evaluate the impacts and overall value).

It is this last stage that most event managers are concerned with – did all go as planned, and are our clients and customers satisfied? These different distinctions are explored within Chapter 15.

Chapter 16 explores an equally difficult concept to plot on the event operations management model, that of quality. Quality, like evaluation, should be considered throughout the event operations management model, and quality procedures and awareness should be applied to the event from its conception to its completion.

Chapter 15 is concerned with two elements of evaluation – to establish whether the event has met its objectives, and also to assess whether the way that the event was planned was reasonable and was carried out in the best and most appropriate way. Event evaluation is critical to the event management process (Allen, 2000) and, if properly managed, is the key to continuous improvement. It provides a loop back to the start of the event operations management model, and can become a tool for analysis and development, and for feedback to stakeholders. Evaluation therefore provides a basis for improvement of both new and repeating events, and should occur throughout the event operations management model.

Chapter 16 is concerned with quality issues. The previous stages of the event operations management model have covered analysis, detailed planning, and implementation of the event. Despite quality being tackled as a separate subject in this stage of the event operations management model, it is argued that quality is not a separate discipline, such as accounting or marketing, but rather an integral part of all the event manager's activities. Chapter 15 identifies that unless there are standards and measurement of performance, control will be less than perfect, and without measurement

it will not be possible to know if performance is improving or not. This chapter identifies that quality cannot be put into a separate compartment, to be picked up and put down when the occasion or management situation demands. The management situation in today's global economy will *always* require that quality be an integral part of all management actions. This is especially true in events where customers rightly expect high levels of service. The chapter explores the nature of quality and how it has evolved over the twentieth century to become part of every employee's remit, at every level within an organization.

Chapter 15

Performance evaluation

Learning Objectives

After reading through this chapter you will be able to:

- **Understand the different methods of evaluation**
- **Identify, use and evaluate the control cycle and the control elements**
- **Apply profitability assessment measurements**
- **Understand the terms *balanced scorecard* and *benchmarking*, and evaluate their use in the event industry.**

Introduction

We are now at the start of Section 4, which covers the last stage of the event operations management model. Evaluation requires us constantly to learn about how well we are delivering the event and whether it is appropriate within in its environment. Evaluation draws heavily upon all of the analysis and planning stages covered in the first two sections of this book.

Getz (1997) sums evaluation up as the need to learn about the environment surrounding the organization and the intended outcomes of the event, to be aware of the unintended outcomes of the event, and to consider ways that management can improve in the future. Since much of this has been covered in previous chapters, this chapter concentrates on evaluating whether the objectives of the event are being met and discusses how the event can be best controlled and delivered in the style originally intended. However, all of the aspects of evaluation covered earlier must still be considered.

Different forms of evaluation

The most common form of evaluation is post-event (or summative) evaluation (Watt, 1998). Here, success of an event is measured against the targets and objectives established in the first stage of the event operations management model. Data can be gathered from the event and analysed in relation to the objectives.

In order to do this successfully, *every* aspect of the event must be evaluated. The most obvious features to look at are customer satisfaction, profit made, and successful projection of the message or product of the event to the target audience. However, Wendroff (2004) points out that other

factors, such as staff and volunteer training and performance, facilities, access, catering, atmosphere, timings, sound systems and acoustics, should all be appraised.

Shone and Parry (2001) and Wendroff (2004) agree that post-event evaluation should be undertaken soon after the event has taken place, whilst it is still fresh in the minds of all involved. However, evaluation after the event occurs too late to repair any problems that occurred during it. In many instances the event can be evaluated before it commences and also during its implementation. Torkildsen (1999) believes that evaluation should take place during the early stages of planning and when resources are being assigned, and likewise with the process and design and manner in which they are used.

Continual evaluation during the planning and implementation stages of the event operations management model ensures that the operation is up to schedule, as well as providing the event manager with the opportunity to hold feedback meetings with stakeholders to ensure they are satisfied with the development of the event (Bowdin *et al.*, 2001).

Keeping control of the event

Implementation of the event is an operational function. The event has been planned and based on clear SMART objectives set by the event manager and the customer. The location and the layout of the event have been carefully selected, the demand for the event forecast, and all relevant and reliable suppliers sourced for both tangible resources and intangible skills. As discussed in Chapter 14, critical path analysis is a useful technique for the event manager, alongside bar charts and Gantt charts. Gantt charts can be used to control and monitor the progress of the event.

Planning creates standards of action, and controls keep the plans and actions in line. Grundy and Brown (2002) state that implementation and control require continual cross-checking to the project's strategy and vision to ensure that the original purposes are being met. This is exactly the same with an event, where it is important to check continually whether the original aims can still be met as the planning continues and the event itself takes place.

This chapter will now discuss the different methods of control that can be used by an event manager.

The control cycle

The traditional approach for managers is to control subordinates, by supervision and measurement of performance, to make sure that what is being done is what is intended. Watt (1998) believes that control is the management function that checks to see if what is supposed to happen is happening or is going to happen. That is, it must not remain as a loose promise. Watt offers a four-stage control procedure:

1. Plan what you intend to do
2. Measure what has been done
3. Compare achievements with the blueprint
4. Take action to correct anything that is not as it should be.

The supervisory method of control relies on feedback of results, and consequently control tends to be in the past tense rather than in the present. This is obviously of little value to the event organizer, who has only one chance to get the event correct. A race cannot be re-run because the timing went wrong! When control occurs in the past tense, the

manager checks after the event to see what occurred as being different to that which was intended.

A manager cannot control without a plan consisting of goals and targets. The more detailed the plan, the more control can be achieved.

The alternative method of control is to empower each member of the staff, or a team of staff, so that control is exercised directly by each person. The event manager should provide the staff with the right resources and full support. The control of the event is then within the immediate remit and authority of the staff responsible for it. This approach has obvious benefits to the event organizer.

Wright's model (Wright, 2001) allows for control to be exercised at the lowest level possible, if staff know what the standards are and have the ability and authority to take corrective action.

Wright's four-stage control cycle is as follows:

1. Set and agree standards of performance
2. Provide timely and relevant feedback
3. Compare actual performance to the agreed standards (staff need to know what to compare)
4. Empowered staff to take corrective action.

It would seem logical that the earlier a variance to a standard is detected, and thus a problem is noted, the less it will cost to put right and the fewer the consequences, provided it is put right as soon as possible.

Control elements

For any activity, whether control is top-down from the event manager or where control is exercised directly by the staff, the same four elements of control apply (Figure 15.1):

1. Setting standard specification
2. Feedback of actual performance
3. Measurement of performance against the specification
4. Correction of deviation from the specification.

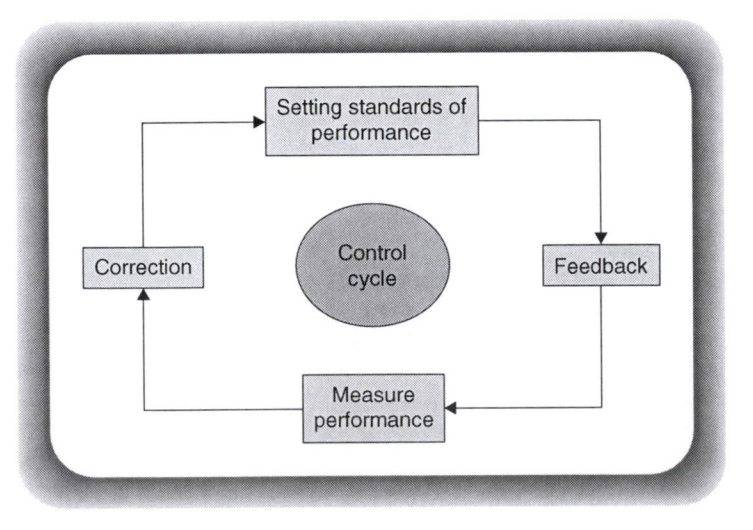

Figure 15.1 The control cycle element of the fourth section of the event operations management model

An appropriate and reliable approach to each event can exist when specifications are known and are communicated. The difficulties are first in setting the standards, and secondly in ensuring that deviations do not occur.

Setting standard specification

Standards are usually expressed in terms of the specification and objectives desired by the customer. They can be imposed by the company or the client, or can be set by the staff themselves, either as individuals or as a team. Standards were discussed in the detailed planning stage of the event operations management model. The standards of performance should be judged by its own set of SMART objectives.

It is envisaged that when the culture is right, 'empowered' staff will be able to work to the standards set, which are both explicitly and implicitly expressed. Implicitly expressed objectives are all the assumptions regarding the event that have not been written down but should be understood and shared by everyone.

In events it is often considered difficult to set quantifiable standards. How, for example, do you measure 'courteous service'? Nonetheless, if customers *perceive* that there is a lack of courtesy, then corrective action must be taken. In other areas of service, standards can be set quite readily – for example, how long do customers wait before being registered? Did the customer receive the information pack in time? Was the service effective?

Tangible criteria are measurements such as meeting deadlines, number of failures, wrong deliveries, time taken to attend to a customer, and time taken to reply to a letter or an email. Such measurements are quantifiable, easily understood, and cannot be disputed. However, even when the tangible criteria are met successfully by the event manager and the team, it is often the intangible criteria that influence a customer's decision whether or not to attend an event again, or to spread word-of-mouth recommendations or not.

Intangible criteria include the atmosphere of the event, cleanliness, well-groomed staff, attitude of the staff – are they friendly and is the advice given helpful; is there empathy, is the smile genuine, and do they really mean what they are saying? For instance, at a product launch other intangibles will become important – such as ethical conduct, sound and lighting appropriateness, appropriate theming carried throughout the event, and subtle opportunities for potential buyers to see the product in its best surroundings.

If the service includes food, then its smell, colour, taste and temperature when served all become important. When the culture of the organization is right and all the staff genuinely believe in the value of what they are doing, then enthusiasm and a desire to help will overcome the adverse effect of a late delivery or some other shortcoming. No manner of control imposed from above can substitute for people who want to get things right and who want to help the customer, providing that they are empowered to do so.

Feedback of actual performance

Figure 15.1 includes a means of feedback of actual performance. Feedback needs to be reasonably precise, recognizable and timely. For example, with budgetary control there is little point if actual results are notified 3 months after the event. The importance of key measures cannot be emphasized enough. What should be measured is what really matters. Too often the desire for total accuracy takes too long and the information provided is often so detailed as to be of little use to the recipient. Effective control for an event manager requires some key measurements that are sufficiently accurate to enable corrective action to be taken.

As discussed before, the key measures can be either tangible or intangible. They should be determined and agreed so that everyone knows the minimum level that is

acceptable. These key measures are also known in the operational management literature as benchmarks.

In some organizations, especially those relying on the skill, expertise and creativity of staff, standards are often poorly defined, and variation from standards is a matter of perception rather than measure. Too much measurement and too many standards may stultify creativity, and so it is important to keep measurement to the areas where it will do the most good.

Care has to be taken not to impose detailed measurement on people who have been hired for their creative ability. One of the targets of an event manager should be to devise a performance measurement system that balances having only a few key measures, which may not reflect all of the event objectives, and having too many detailed measures, which then become overwhelming.

Some key measures that could be used include the statistics of attendees and financial returns. Others might include questionnaires and customer focus groups. Questionnaire design and meaningful surveys are essential skills that must be learned and developed. There is a range of authors who cover this aspect extraordinary well, and so questionnaire design is not covered in this text.

Case study 15.1 provides an illustration of event evaluation.

Case study 15.1

British Association for Counselling and Psychotherapy Research Conference, May 2004

10th Annual Counselling and Psychotherapy Research Conference, London, England

Evaluation Report by Nancy Rowland and Stephen Goss

The 10th annual conference was held in May 2004 with 180 delegates each day from around the world, including America, Australia, Canada, Germany, Ireland, Kenya, Malaysia, New Zealand, Portugal and Turkey.

The 2 days saw a total of 77 presentations, made up of 62 papers, 7 workshops, 8 posters and a plenum paper.

The conference had a wonderful atmosphere and gained enormously from a wide mix of cultures and nationalities. The exhibition hall was decorated with traditional cloths and items from some of the co-host organizations, making a fantastic display. A congenial social evening on Friday ensured old friends met whilst new friendships were formed over the international cuisine and dancing. Networking opportunities abounded, and once again the evaluation results emphasized the importance of this aspect of the conference, along with appreciation of the warmth and friendliness of the event.

An evaluation form was completed by 44 per cent of delegates, using scores of 1 = Poor and 10 = Excellent. Scores continued to display good levels of satisfaction, with administration of the event scoring a notable 9.2 and 73 per cent of respondents giving the highest score of 9 or 10. Programme structure and the venue scored 8.5 and 8.7 respectively, with an overall satisfaction rating of 8.9, with 68 per cent of respondents giving a 9 or 10 in this category. Friday's papers gained an average score of 7.5 (from a range of 6.0 to 9.3), with the average for Saturday's being 7.8 (from a range of 5.3 to 9.5). Workshop presentations registered an average of 8.1 (from a range of 6.0 to 9.0), and posters scored an average of 7.4 (from a range of 6.8 to 7.8). Appreciation of the general warmth and friendliness of the event came through strongly in the evaluations, which is an element of this event we are keen to foster.

The following table shows the comparison of average marks over the past six research conferences:

	2004	2003	2002	2001	2000	1999
Venue	London	Leicester	London	Bristol	Manchester	Leeds
Return rate for evaluation forms (%)	44	59	48	70	53	79
Overall satisfaction (average score)	8.9	8.3	8.6	8.7	8.4	7.7
Structure of conference programme (average score)	8.5	8.3	8.3	8.4	8.1	7.1
Quality of the venue (average score)	8.7	8.2	7.8	8.1	8.5	8.1
BACP administration (average score)	9.2	9.0	8.9	8.9	–	–
Satisfaction with papers (overall average score)	7.6	7.5	7.5	7.4	7.6	6.9
Satisfaction with workshops (overall average score)	6.9	7.3	7.9	7.4	7.6	6.7
Satisfaction with posters (overall average score)	7.4					

(Information supplied by the British Association for Counselling and Psychotherapy, BACP House, 35–37 Albert Street, Rugby, Warwickshire CV21 2SG. More information about their research can be found at www.bacp.co.uk.)

Reflective practice 15.1

1. Using the information from the evaluation report in Case study 15.1, in which areas could improvements be made for the 2005 conference?
2. What would you suggest to improve these areas?
3. If you were organizing the conference, what other feedback would you like to receive and how would you gather this information?

Measurement of performance against the specification

As shown in Figure 15.1, the crucial issue at this stage of the control cycle is knowing what the feedback means, and how to measure performance and compare results so as to be able to recognize deviations. In many cases there are suppliers providing staff and other resources at an event, and they may have their own policies to determine whether success has been achieved or not. However, it is in the interest of the event manager to ensure that the event has gone ahead as planned and as expected by the customers. Typical questions could be:

- How can the service be judged against expectations?
- Can service be improved?
- Can the service be improved at no extra cost?
- How, and by whom?

Correction of deviation from the specification

Once the first three steps of the control cycle are in place, then irrespective of whether this is an outdoor festival, an annual dinner and fundraising event, a product launch or a teambuilding event, the outputs can be compared with the plan or standard and with the

SMART objectives. Where necessary, corrections should be made so as to eliminate divergences. Ideally, the level at which this is done should be as low as possible. If a corrective action has to be reported up through five levels of management and down again before action can be taken, time is lost and errors can often be compounded. If a customer is waiting for a decision to be made, customer satisfaction will diminish at a rapid rate.

If a member of staff is facing a customer, that staff member needs to know the limits within which decisions can be made. The ability and knowledge of the staff member has to be taken into account when limits of authority are given. Some staff will welcome flexibility of action, whereas others are afraid to make decisions.

Not everyone is comfortable with being empowered, and this also will need to be taken into account when limits of authority are being set. Each member of the organization has to have mutual trust and confidence in the others. Management needs to be confident that staff are well trained and competent, and that every person understands the goals. Staff have to be confident that they are empowered to take action and will be supported by management in difficult situations.

Where it is found that deviations to the required standard are consistently above or below the set level of performance, then the original conditions must be checked. If the level being achieved is *above* the set standard, it could be that conditions have changed – such as new suppliers, improved technology or an improved process – or the workers themselves have found better ways to provide the service. It should be investigated whether the customer welcomes this improved standard, or whether time or money is being spent on an unnecessary resource or activity. If the level of performance has fallen *below* the standard, it is important that action is taken to determine why this should be and what needs to be done.

In Case study 15.2, it is clear that the Sydney Festival organizers aim for continuous improvement, gaining feedback by both formal and informal means.

Case study 15.2

Sydney Festival, Art Gallery Road, The Domain, Sydney, Australia

Access for the disabled – improvements to existing facilities

The Sydney Festival is held over 3 weeks in January each year, and has a number of popular free outdoor events where the attendances can reach 150 000. Sydney Festival organizes Symphony in the Domain, Opera in the Domain and Jazz in the Domain. Around Christmas, the Domain also hosts Carols in the Domain.

The Domain is officially part of the Royal Botanic Gardens of Sydney, and Festival Domain Manager, Stephen Champion, cooperates with the Gardens to stage these events. Providing for crowd entertainment is his specialty.

'These annual events are really popular. It grows each year … As much as we can, we make sure people can get into the enclosures on the site, get around, see the stages and use the facilities,' says Champion.

An outdoor site presents particular challenges for organizers providing access including parking or areas for transport drop-off and pick-up. Champion's access strategy has been devised in conjunction with the Royal Botanic Gardens. Though 'it is not formal,' says Champion, 'we have a protocol which developed from consultations and from our experiences year after year'.

In relation to feedback, Champion says: 'We receive a lot of requests from individuals or groups wanting access to events, and it's in talking to them that we have tailored some of our solutions each year.' Feedback from spectators generally comes informally, via discussions

with staff at events or approaches to Festival organizers. However, the Festival also consults with peak disability groups through regular meetings. This informal and formal information plays a vital role in Champion's planning.

'We respond to perceived as well as solicited needs. For example, one woman brings a group each year to hear the Symphony in the Park,' says Champion. She has become an important source of information and consultation on particular needs of the group – such as access, parking and toilet facilities.

They strive for continuous improvement, and management and operations are assessed each time an event is presented. As Champion says, 'There are things that could be done better. We need to look at the issue of signage, together with the Gardens, and come up with a better strategy.'

'Each year at the Festival outdoor concerts, we try to increase the amount of temporary lighting. Since the Olympics, there has been more acknowledgement of issues relating to risk assessment and occupational health and safety.' The next step will be a formal approach to government to consider solutions and to fund ongoing works.

The ongoing solutions also include more Sydney Festival staff training on the issues of access and disability awareness. 'We do have a handbook, which is given to staff each year so they remain aware of the issues and the organizations that the Festival works with are also chosen for their application to access issues.'

(Extracts from website; for more information see www.sydneyolympicpark.com.au.)

Reflective practice 15.2

The information in Case study 15.2 indicates the informal structures in place at the Sydney Festival for improving access for the disabled at the Domain.

1. During events, what formal structures could be introduced, and how would you do this?
2. What are the benefits of informal structures?

Profitability measurements

We all recognize that if any company is to stay in business it has to make sufficient profit to service its debts, make a return to the owners and invest in new resources for future growth.

For not-for-profit organizations, efficiency has to be demonstrated and management has to be accountable for the funds and assets that have been provided.

Most people would see that recording and reporting profitability and/or being accountable for the funds used is the responsibility of the accountants. However, event managers must know how the figures are compiled and be able to read standard accounting reports.

Accountants work on historical data of what has happened, and their reports cover arbitrarily set periods of time. They make little allowance for the fact that business activities do not stop on 30 June or 31 December, or whatever other date has been designated as the time to take a snapshot of the financial position of the business. From a conventional point of view, and from the point of view of stakeholders such as shareholders and bank managers, there has to be a way of measuring the financial performance of an organization, and currently there is no better method than accounting reports. It follows, therefore, that for accountants to do their job of reporting to meet

the conventional and regulatory requirements, information will be required from the operating arm of the business. If information is being provided, then it is useful to try and use that information to improve the efficiency of the organization.

This text does not deal with financial control and accounting measures, but it is suggested that readers study these aspects further.

The balanced scorecard approach

This approach was first taken by Kaplan and Norton (2001). The balanced scorecard, according to Lashley and Lee-Ross (2003), recognizes that the evaluation of the performance of an organization needs to be viewed from the perspectives of different stakeholders. The stakeholders typically used are the customers, employees, shareholders and the community. Other approaches use the finance perspective, customer perspective, employee perspective, and an innovation and learning perspective (Johnson and Scholes, 2002). The scorecards combine both a quantitative approach and a qualitative approach whilst acknowledging the expectations of the different stakeholders. Without a scorecard, it is not possible to see if improvement is being made. As Slack and Lewis (2002) state, the advantage of the scorecard is that it brings together an overall picture of the organization's performance into one report. We would add that a further advantage is that it does not just measure activities and success from a financial perspective, but also allows the voices and considerations of our customers and staff, and opportunities for creativity, to be taken into account.

Slack and Lewis (2002) argue that a balanced range of measures enables managers to address the following questions:

- How do we look to our shareholders (i.e. a financial perspective)?
- What must we excel at (i.e. an internal business perspective)?
- How do our customers see us (i.e. a customer perspective)?
- How can we continue to improve and create value (i.e. an innovation and learning perspective)?

It is important to link the scorecards not just to a short-term approach but also to a long-term view since, for example, innovation and learning are critical to long-term success (Johnson and Scholes, 2002).

Eaglen *et al.* (1999) believe that the prime success of an organization from a shareholder's perspective is dependent on customer satisfaction and repeat custom, and this is in turn dependent on employee performance and customer satisfaction. Eaglen *et al.* (1999) reported increasing numbers of leisure organizations using the balanced scorecard to evaluate organizational performance.

This approach brings together many different parts of the organization, and could be useful within an event company or for a one-off event. It also has the benefit of reducing the number of measures and focusing only on those that are considered essential. It is beneficial if the entire organization is involved with creating and agreeing on the measures that are to become part of the scorecard. This way it ensures that everyone is fully committed, and agrees with the concepts to be measured and how.

Slack and Lewis (2002) believe that one of the advantages of the scorecard is that it presents an overall picture of the organization's performance on one report and encourages a company-wide approach rather than just the self-interests of separate departments.

To understand this concept as applied to the event industry, see Table 15.1. In this scorecard an event to celebrate the New Year in a capital city is illustrated. This event had been organized by the city, for its local community, and to attract tourists and economic wealth to the city. This example of the scorecard takes three headings – vision, strategy and objectives, and uses four different perspectives i.e. financial; customer; internal and innovation and learning in order to measure the success.

Table 15.1 Partially balanced scorecard for New Year's Eve celebrations in a capital city

Vision	Strategy	Objectives	Balanced scorecard
To attract visitors to the city	To provide services that exceed customer expectations and provide complete satisfaction	*Financial*: return on expenditure, satisfactory cash flow, reliability of performance and adequacy of suppliers	*Financial perspective*: cash flow, within budget, economic impact on city
		Customer: value for money, high level of satisfaction, creative and fun	*Customer perspective*: satisfaction surveys
		Internal: provide customer satisfaction, exceptional event project management; excellent use of resources and suppliers	*Internal business perspective*: conformance of design, keeping to time, numbers of attendees
		Internal growth: innovative; empowered workforce, and continuous improvement	*Innovation and learning perspective*: creativity and design, new ideas, use of employee specialisms, training
To raise the profile of the capital as an international venue	To engineer continuous improvement throughout the planning process from the concept formulation to the implementation		
To provide a high-quality event for the enjoyment of all participants, including the residents of the city	To ensure that all staff and suppliers involved with the event should match expectations		
	To ensure that during the event planning all the stakeholders be consulted and plans agreed with them as far as possible		

The vision is to attract visitors to the city, to raise the profile of the capital as an international venue and to provide a high-quality event for the enjoyment of all participants, including the residents of the city.

The strategy that needs to be taken to achieve this is to provide services that exceed customer expectations and give complete satisfaction. It was decided that there should be continuous improvement throughout the planning process from the concept formulation to the implementation. All the staff involved with the event should match expectations, and during the event planning all the stakeholders should be consulted and plans agreed with them as far as possible.

In order to achieve that strategy, a number of objectives have to be set that can be measured for their success and are achievable. Table 15.1 then also depicts the different perspectives that success can be measured by in the final column. This is deliberately not complete; further ideas can be added when considering the reflective practice below.

Reflective practice 15.3

You are the chief executive of an event management company who has been selected to organize the New Year festivities in a capital city.

1. Complete the scorecard shown in Table 15.1 to show all of the targets that each of the four perspectives could take.
2. Establish measures that should be set to identify how closely you are achieving your objectives and how you would assess individual performance.

Benchmarking

The purpose of benchmarking is to measure your performance against a similar operation. Slack *et al.* (2004) identify two types of benchmarking:

1. Internal, where there is a comparison between operations within the same organization
2. External, which is a comparison between an operation and other operations that are part of a different organization.

Benchmarking can take place against other event organizations, whether they compete in the same market or not. The benchmarking could consist of comparing your own performance against another event management company or their means of completing activities – i.e. what can be learned from looking at another event, and could different practices be adopted?

Griffin (1999) describes benchmarking as the process of learning how other firms do things in an exceptionally strong manner. The technique enables an organization to stay abreast of any improvements and changes their competitors are making.

The accountant's method of benchmarking is to compare published annual financial reports. It is fairly simple to obtain your competitors' audited accounts and compare them with yours by means of ratios and by looking at various key figures, such as stock turnover, return on investment, cost of sales and so on. It doesn't matter if company X has $50 million sales and companies Y and Z have $200 and $80 million sales respectively. If all three are in the same sector of the event industry, it could be expected that the percentage of costs to sales should be roughly the same – or that there should be some clearly defined reasons why not.

Internally, benchmarking can be achieved by comparing key measures of like departments, or even comparing over the organization as a whole. Absenteeism could

be a benchmark (if considered to be a problem area). Similarly, the number of days taken off sick each year can be compared as a moving trend, and with other companies, or branches of the same company. The changes and trends that are identified can be extremely useful to highlight excellence and below-excellent performances.

Further benchmarks might be staff turnover, and growth of numbers of staff employed per £1000 sales. Clearly there are many instances where benchmarking can be used usefully to compare your own event management company against competitors, or against your own achievements and benchmarks from previous events.

Benchmarking is a form of measurement, and is useful in highlighting areas that can be improved. It is also concerned with searching out new ideas and practices that could be copied or adapted (Slack and Lewis, 2002). It stimulates creativity, and makes organizations consider how they could be serving their customers better. Thus it is ideal for event management companies who thrive on creativity and who are able to see competitors' events often at first hand.

Case study 15.3 discusses the practical use of benchmarking.

Case study 15.3

Edinburgh Festival, Edinburgh, Scotland

The Edinburgh Festival is held annually in August in Edinburgh

Edinburgh is one of the premier festival cities of the world. The unique combination of the International Festival and the Fringe makes for one of the biggest festivals in the world. The festivals help to fix Edinburgh's image in tourism terms, and on the back of them come hundreds of thousands of staying visitors every year, across all seasons.

As well as the International Festival and the Fringe, there are the other summer festivals – the Jazz & Blues, the Film and the Book, and of course the Tattoo. The packed programme of events in Edinburgh's Winter Festivals, Hogmanay and Capital Christmas, also attract large numbers of staying visitors to Edinburgh and the Lothians, bringing a short, sharp boost to business in what was a quiet time for tourism. The other three major festivals, the Easter, the Science and the Children's, are less hectic, taking place in the spring and bringing in welcome day and staying visitors.

Long-running art exhibitions of international stature, major outdoor concerts and international events like the Tall Ships, the Rugby Union World Cup and the Edinburgh Marathon have all given significant boosts to tourism. (**NB**: individual games of the RWC have been played at Murrayfield, but Edinburgh hasn't ever been host nation. The final of the Challenge Cup (Rugby League clubs) has been played there, however.) There is a host of other events, such as the Festival of Flight in East Lothian, as well as smaller, often community-based events, staged as one-offs or annually.

Edinburgh has on the whole held up well in terms of visitor numbers, even during a period when Scottish tourism has been experiencing a tough time. However, in this position it would be easy to become complacent about standards. This tendency has been noted in other cities with big cultural festivals and events, and some have taken action to address their problems. Quality is a key challenge – to make sure that visitors get the kind of overall experience they expect. As a recent review of Amsterdam as a city of culture asked:

> Is it content, quality and development, rather than simply quantity, that we should be focussing on for the future?

With such a volume and diversity of major events, the tourism partners have decided that a coordinated approach to development is called for. The Edinburgh Tourism Action Group, a partnership of the private sector, the City Council, SE Edinburgh and Lothian and the

Edinburgh and Lothians Tourist Board, is undertaking a wide-ranging review of festivals and events policy and practice, and investigating the establishment of a dedicated Events Unit.

Benchmarking is something of a buzzword, perhaps, but for very good reason. Because there is so much to be learned from other cities, benchmarking is underway to establish what 15 other European cities are doing, and how Edinburgh compares. This will help to set standards and guidelines against which the city can measure its future performance. If Salzburg or Barcelona can teach us something, that's great, and of course Edinburgh can share with them its own good practices, built up over decades of experience.

(Information supplied by the Lothian Exchange; for more information see www. lothianexchange.net.)

Reflective practice 15.4

Consider Case study 15.3.

1. What are the advantages for a city like Edinburgh in benchmarking its events with other European cities?
2. What areas could be benchmarked?

Evaluation of an event

As previously discussed, at the completion of an event there should be a meeting with all of the interested parties, or stakeholders, to evaluate its success or otherwise. A good evaluation should use all the sources of information available to it, and not just rely on the customers' points of view (Shone and Parry, 2004). Care should be taken, since it is an aid to future planning.

There may be activities within the event that went well and could be strengthened further, and there may be those that need improving upon, if they went badly. In all cases, the evaluation should be provided speedily – for example, to speakers at a conference before they leave, or even before they present again at the same conference. Adjustments can then be made quickly.

As the event evaluator, you should determine what is to be evaluated and why and how. Silver (2004) believes that research and evaluation will give the information required to devise effective practices and controls, which could lead to good results. This process is shown in Figure 15.2.

There are two key issues, according to Shone and Parry (2004):

1. Did the event meets its objectives?
2. What can be improved for the next event?

Sources of information for evaluation (adapted from Shone and Parry, 2004) include:

- Event attendees' comments derived from questionnaires and other observations
- Security and police views on crowds, traffic and other incidents
- Specialists comments, for example from lighting and sound specialists
- Council comments and community views
- Any mystery guests and other participants
- Staff comments, including volunteers
- Sponsors' views
- Financial statistics and reports.

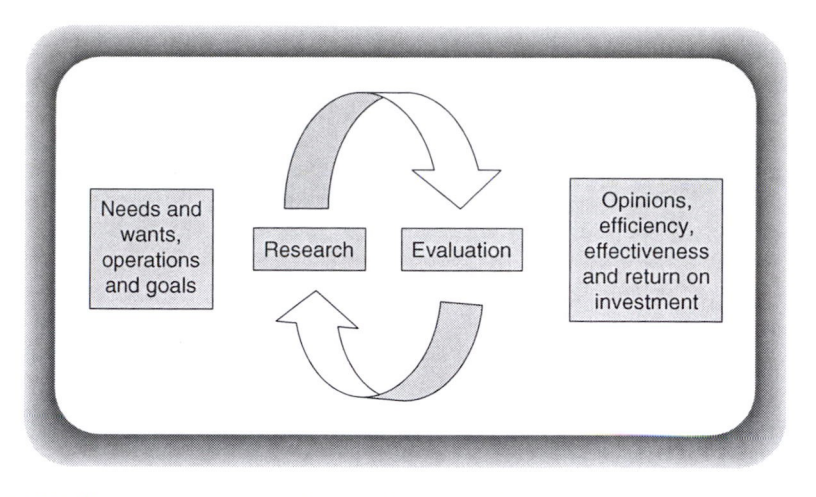

Figure 15.2 Silver's research-evaluation continuum model

All constructive criticism should be taken seriously, since the goal is to improve events in the future and to improve your organization and planning of the event.

The information is also invaluable to different groups of people. For instance, those groups that have financed the event or sponsored elements of it need to know that their money was well spent. The numbers of people attending the event and their geographical range and demographics are of interest to future sponsors of a similar event. At the end of each year, the budgeting process begins for the following year. Since many corporate events may have to compete for funds, the evaluation from previous events will become invaluable. The event manager must be able to demonstrate that an event can efficiently and effectively achieve corporate objectives (O'Toole and Mikolaitis, 2002).

The evaluation results provide facts that can be used to compare the cost of the event to the value generated.

A well-designed evaluation assists the manager, the sponsors and the client to determine whether the event met the desired outcomes, and hence whether it will be repeated next year. It also is useful for future clients as a record of past successes. As such, it can be communicated to potential clients and may increase future business and contacts. The evaluation data will also be useful when the event manager compares costs and return on investment to propose alternatives to potential clients.

O'Toole and Mikolaitis (2002) suggest that the evaluation covers two areas; first the content of the event, and secondly the destination and the facilities provided. The first focus relates to how the attendees feel about how the event was organized and designed, while the second focus relates to the appropriateness of the venue. This was covered in Chapter 10, where we discussed a series of criteria for choice of destination. The evaluation information should determine how well all the SMART objectives have been achieved as a whole, and how well the event managed to weave together all the elements required.

As O'Toole and Mikolaitis (2002) suggest, the evaluation can determine whether a particular part or element of an event is responsible for either its success or its failure. If a particular activity has increased the overall success of an event, the data could be used to include this element in future events. For instance, if there was sufficient return on investment for guests to attend an event due to a particular activity, then the client should be made aware of the added value. Not only does this information help your future events with a current client; it also demonstrates to potential clients that you have a policy of evaluation, which could help them in the future.

Quantitative and qualitative evaluation methods

Surveys of numbers of attendees, money taken, computer records, and telephone surveys all provide accurate quantitative data. On the other hand, face-to-face interviews and open-ended questions on a well-designed survey can provide detailed insight into the attitudes and feelings of the event attendees. Indeed it is useful to apply these to non-attendees to find out the reasons for their non-appearance. In either method there may be a pattern of response that can provide clues for the future or warrant further investigation.

Further literature sources should be consulted on the design of useful questionnaires, since it takes time and expertise to complete these in order to get the information that is required (see O'Toole and Mikolaitis, 2002, Chapter 12; and Silver, 2004, Chapter 14).

The information collected should not just be the outcomes of some of the problems, but also the underlying causes of the problem. For example, if there were long queues was this due to insufficient staff, or to a poor layout and design, or to insufficient resources, or to a higher demand than forecasted?

Shone and Parry (2004) recommend that an event manager identifies persistent problems and ranks them in order of seriousness. With this list of priorities it is possible to confront the issues, increase the success of your event and decrease its problems.

One method that can be used to solve problems arising from an event is an Ishikawa diagram, also known as a fishbone diagram due to its shape. The idea is to identify one problem at a time and then draw the fishbone diagram on one sheet of paper. See Figure 15.4. It provides a good opportunity for group discussion and brainstorming. Adapting a procedure from Slack *et al.* (2004) for events, the following steps could be used to construct a fishbone diagram:

1. State the problem in the effect box
2. Identify the main categories that may have caused or have the solution to the problem
3. Use systematic fact finding and the information from the evaluation process to generate possible causes and solutions
4. Record all the comments generated and add onto the diagram as extra fins to the main fishbones.

The most common causes of problems are people, the equipment used, the method of using the resources provided, the finance available, and lack of communication. However, the group discussion will establish the most relevant areas for the specific problem under discussion.

For instance, imagine a concert is being held in a church on an evening in November in the UK. All the equipment has arrived, and all the rehearsals, schedules etc. are going to plan. A final walkthrough reveals that the portable toilets for the use of the audience, which are based outside the church, do not have interior lights.

The Ishikawa diagram in Figure 15.3 (see next page) deals with this problem.

An interesting concept proposed by Grundy and Brown (2002) is that of the 'bonefish' diagram. Here the problem starts on the left of the fishbone and leads to multiple consequences on the right. This amplifies the point (Grundy and Brown, 2002) that the fishbone is a way of showing an ongoing cause and effect chain. The bonefish diagram identifies the problems of getting some aspect of your event wrong. Many of the activities within an event are interdependent, and as one thing goes wrong there may be many other consequences as a result.

As an example, this concept could be used for a major wine festival held during the summer tourist season in Italy. It could be envisaged that following unprecedented media focus on the event, there may be many thousands more people attending than

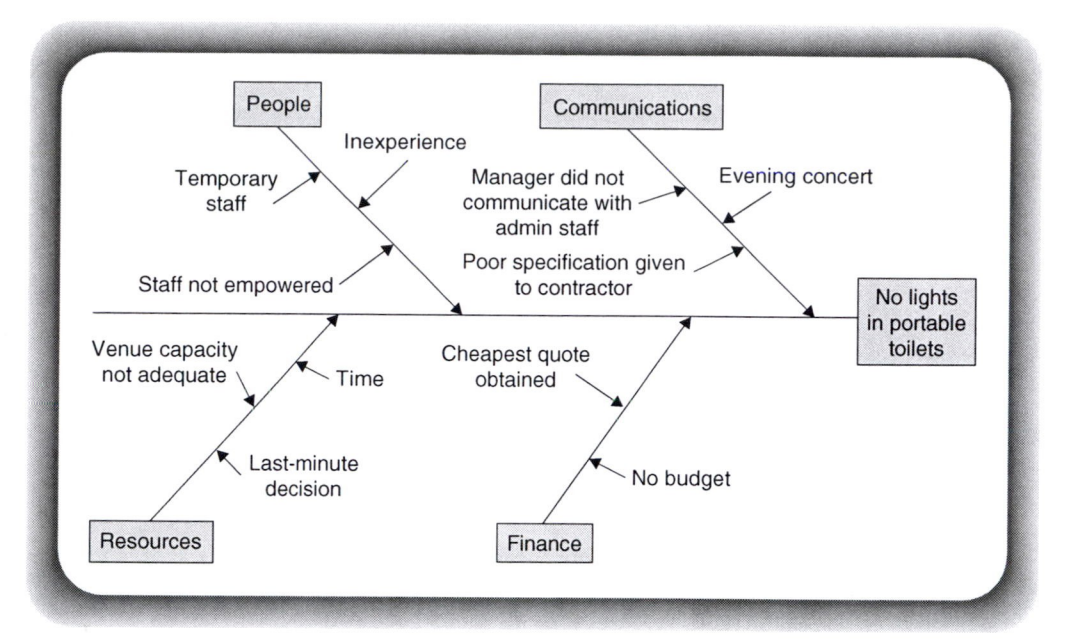

Figure 15.3 Ishikawa diagram examining the causes of no lighting in portable toilets

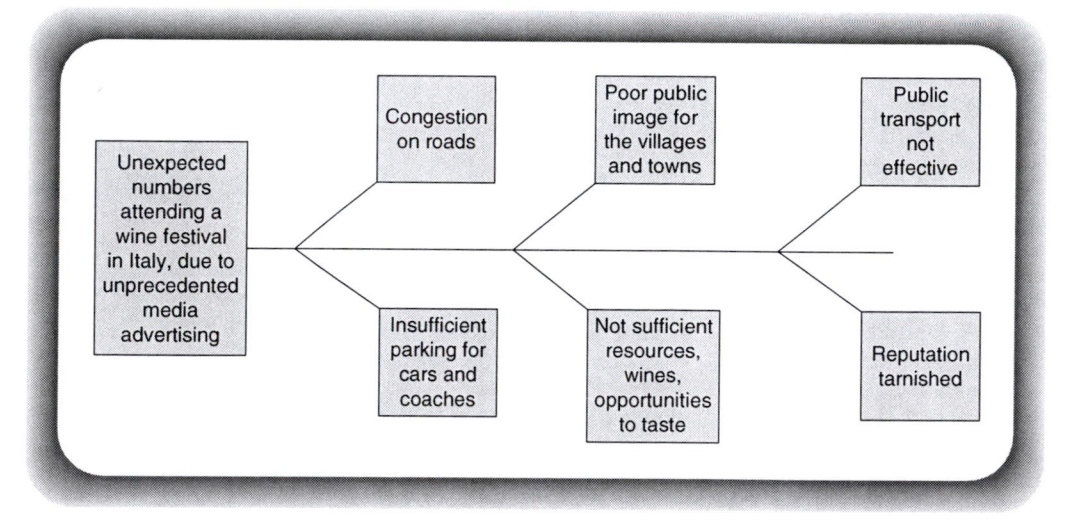

Figure 15.4 Fishbone diagram examining consequences of unexpected high attendance

in previous years. Using the bonefish diagram and following detailed discussions, the possible consequences of the problem and any extra costs incurred could be identified. Figure 15.4 is only hypothetical, but it can be seen that the fishbone diagrams and the bonefish diagrams show an ongoing cause and effect chain (Grundy and Brown, 2002), and would highlight the cost of failures and poor planning. This could be a useful tool to persuade the client to resource the event fully.

Reflective practice 15.5

1. From the information shown in Figure 15.3, what steps should be taken to ensure that the portable toilets all have lights in the future and that this does not happen again?
2. Draw a bonefish diagram. This is the reverse of the fishbone diagram, with the problem at the head end on the left. Your diagram should identify the effect of poor weather being the cause of cancellation of a horseracing meeting at Kempton Race Course, England, on Boxing Day, after 22 000 people had already arrived and some programmes had already been sold.

Reflective practice 15.6

You work for a company that has won the contract to manage the Annual Gala for your local town. This Gala has been running for 20 years, but has got a little tired in its format and the income it raises for local charities has not grown appreciably over the years. In the past it has had a very mixed format. It opens with a parade through the town, with floats from many of the local businesses and a Gala Queen. It culminates in the town's municipal park, where many different organizations are able to rent space to display their services and activities to all of the townspeople. Many uniformed organizations take part, and there is a large display area.

Standards of performance

1. List the tangible standards that could be used by the following four different groups of people to judge the success of the new Gala event:
   • Your own company
   • The Town Council
   • Local businesses
   • Gala attendees.
2. Consider what intangible criteria might be important to these four groups.
3. Now consider each of these standards, and put them together into a composite list and into an order of importance or priority.
4. Who could set the final standard or specification so that these standards could be met, fully or in part?
5. Is there any way that any of these standards could be improved without extra cost?
6. Identify for each of the standards included in your composite list the key measurements that would determine success (or otherwise) in meeting the standard of performance.

Chapter summary and key points

This chapter has introduced a four-step model for control. If the culture of the organization is positive, the events manager will be able to concentrate on the important higher-level issues if staff know what is expected, have agreed the standards of performance, get accurate and prompt feedback, know what to compare, and are empowered to take corrective action if required. For this to work, staff have to want to take responsibility, and management has to believe in and trust their staff.

Communication and prompt and accurate feedback of information are essential if control is to be exercised.

The event manager has the responsibility of deciding what should be measured and why. If no advantage can be gained from keeping a particular record, then the gathering of that information should cease. Record gathering in itself does not add value. There is some truth in the adage that if it can't be measured, it can't be managed. On the other hand, too much measurement will stultify, lead to extra expense, and inhibit creativity.

Measurement should be used in a positive manner to advance the aims of the organization, and not as a means of power play to rule and subjugate.

Chapter 16
Awareness of quality

Learning Objectives

After reading through this chapter you will be able to:

- Define quality and understand its application in the event industry
- Appreciate the development of total quality management
- Calculate the costs of conforming to quality, and the costs of non-conformance
- Apply the concepts of just-in-time management to an event organization and use the SERVQUAL method of measuring customer satisfaction.

Introduction

This is our last chapter, and it explores the subject of quality, which has featured implicitly throughout the book. It is discussed here as a separate, explicit topic, but the concept of total quality should be apparent throughout all the event management work that you, as manager, are involved with, from the very first conception of the event. It should also be evident throughout your organization's structure and culture.

Volumes of books and learned papers have been written on the subject of quality. In 2005, some universities offer Quality as a separate degree (University of Wales, University of Paisley, Queens University Belfast), the inference being that quality has become a 'discipline' or subject in its own right, which can be studied in isolation from other disciplines. There are many different definitions of quality and, as Getz (1997) points out, there are many different connotations of quality. To some it is a mark of excellence, to others it is simply the best, while to others it indicates reliability or exceeding expectations.

This chapter does not intend to repeat and apply much of the excellent material written on quality and how it can increase competitive advantage. The work presented here will focus on what quality is, the costs of conforming to quality standards and the costs of non-conformance to those standards. It will then consider two of the quality initiatives, just-in-time management (JIT) and SERVQUAL, and apply those in an event management context. We believe that although the study of quality can be taught separately, it is in fact inseparable from any management action. Quality cannot be put into a separate compartment, to be picked up and put down when the occasion or management situation demands. The management situation in today's global economy will *always* require that quality be an integral part of all management actions. This is especially true in events, where customers rightly expect high levels of service and there is no opportunity to repeat the event if it is not just as planned.

The underlying theme in all of these chapters has been customer satisfaction and efficient use of resources. Both of these objectives require quality considerations. An event manager cannot offer customer satisfaction without an understanding of what quality is; likewise, efficient use of resources requires a total quality management approach. This chapter will start by exploring some of the definitions of quality.

What is quality?

Quality has different meanings for different people. Griffin (2000) believes that, for managers, understanding the basic meaning of quality is a good first step to managing it more effectively. A manufacturing sector approach and a sector providing a service, as in the event industry, might consider a definition of quality as being one that provides a service that is free of error (Slack *et al.*, 2004). Although the product or service may not be the 'best' that is available, it could be described as a quality product if it conforms to its original specification.

On the other hand, our customers may be looking for a product or service that is fit for its purpose. This definition demonstrates Slack *et al.* (2004) concern not only that the service adheres to its specification but also that it is appropriate for the customer. For example, a conference designed to introduce delegates to new business opportunities in China may be well run and organized very professionally, but if it fails to create any networking opportunities between business colleagues in the host country or to share ideas of good trading opportunities, it has not served its purpose.

A further approach is one where the product or service has quality stated as a measurable set of characteristics that would satisfy the customer. In the event industry, this could be an exhibition that states in its marketing promotional material that there will be 200 stands over a period of 3 days, a 2-day seminar programme with four different keynote speakers on each day, full catering facilities, and a potential market of 3000 visitors from the relevant industry arriving on each day. It would be relatively simple for the attendees and the exhibitors to check whether the characteristics stated in the advertising literature were being achieved or not, and to what degree.

Finally, Slack *et al.* (2004) cite the value-based approach, where the customer may be willing to accept a slightly lower specification of quality if the price is less. Within the event industry, an illustration would be the acceptance of a less convenient location for a special event provided this is reflected in the price.

Slack *et al.* (2004) define quality as having consistent conformance to customers' expectations. You can see that this definition brings together the concept of having a well-planned, designed and controlled event, which keeps to the original specification and matches the expectations of the customer. Slack *et al.* (2004) prefer the word 'expectations' to 'needs' or 'wants'. 'Needs' implies a basic requirement, and 'wants' could be anything that the customer desires. As Slack *et al.* (2004) point out, though, there is a problem with trying to match customers' expectations in that individual expectations may be different and may change.

The various authors within the quality management and operations management literature all offer different views on the interpretation of what is quality. Waters (1996) says that in its broadest sense, quality is the ability of a product to meet and preferably exceed customer expectations. Appropriately, Swarbrooke and Horner (2001) remind us that we have both customers and consumers in our industry. This distinction was discussed in Chapter 2. To remind you, customers could, for example, be those organizations that employ the delegates who attend our events, or the council that pays for a range of entertaining events and community-orientated events that are provided for the local communities. The consumers are those who actually attend our events and

use the service. It can be seen immediately that the customer in this context will expect an event at the right price, and the consumer will expect a different range of other attributes, including entertainment value, fun and an informative experience.

Drummond and Anderson (2004) cite three of the quality gurus' definitions of quality:

1. Deming (1982) defines quality as being aimed at the needs of the consumer, present and future
2. Crosby (1979) defines quality as conformance to requirements
3. Feigenbaum (1993) say that quality is in its essence a way of managing the organization.

We can see in the first two definitions similarities with the work of Slack *et al.* (2004), but the third approach, from Feigenbaum (1993), refers to the way the organization is managed. This requires a focus on satisfying the customer and changing the organization to achieve that objective (Drummond and Anderson, 2004). For further reading, the Drummond and Anderson's chapter in *Festivals and Event Management* is recommended (see the bibliography for full details). The chapter focuses on service quality at events, and the management of people.

Wild (2002) defines quality as the degree to which a product or service satisfies customers' requirements. He discusses the degree to which the design specification would satisfy the customer, and how closely it conforms to specifications. Similarly, Campbell *et al.* (2003) believe that quality is meeting customers' needs or expectations.

It can be seen that the myriad of different definitions of quality all consider that the service, or in our case the event, should match customer expectations, and that the specification should be clearly set and achievable through good organization.

Total quality management

If we now consider the concept of total quality management (TQM), Campbell *et al.* (2003) state that TQM is a holistic approach that provides awareness of the customer–supplier relationship, and that there should be continuous improvement and effort made throughout the organization.

TQM includes setting standards and the means of measuring conformance to standards, but an organization that truly has embraced TQM does not need the ISO stamp of approval. ISO Standards are discussed later in this chapter.

Bowdin *et al.* (2001) believe that the integration of all the practical aspects of controlling quality with the overall strategy of an event is TQM. Any organization aspiring to TQM should have a vision of quality that goes far beyond mere conformance to a standard. TQM requires a culture whereby every member of the organization believes that not one day should go by without the organization in some way improving the quality of its goods and services. The vision of TQM must begin with the event manager, or the chief executive of the organization. It is this person who should have a passion for quality and continuous improvement, and this passion should be transmitted down through the organization. TQM seeks to create an event company that continually improves the quality of its services (Bowdin *et al.*, 2001).

It is generally those staff members such as security staff, stewards, receptionists, guides, drivers and car park attendants who are the contact point with the customer and the wider public. They have a huge part to play in how the customer perceives an organization. It is on these staff that an organization must rely for the continuing daily level of quality. Often outsourced companies may employ these staff, and so the challenge for the event manager will become greater. Once the culture of quality has become ingrained, it is hoped that it will be driven from bottom up rather than achieved by direction or control from the top. Management will naturally have to continue to be

responsible for planning, and for providing the resources to enable the workers to do the job. However, unless the telephone operators, the cleaning staff, the driver and the cloakroom attendant are fully committed to quality, TQM will never happen.

The event manager and all of the personnel working towards the successful staging and completion of an event should be totally customer orientated. Everyone should be encouraged to look for ways continually to improve all their activities, and rather than having control measures (discussed in Chapter 15) to monitor performance, they should have a quality focus to prevent errors occurring in the first place.

Case study 16.1 describes a re-enactment of the Battle of Tewkesbury.

Case study 16.1

Re-enactment of the Battle of Tewkesbury, 9–10 July 2005, Lincoln Green Lane, Tewkesbury, England

A free Medieval Festival that takes place on some of the fields where the battle was actually fought in May 1471, the battle is recreated by more than a thousand soldiers from Britain and Europe, many in full plate armour, others wielding the famous English longbow. Early cannon are also used.

Historically victory was gained by the House of York, which put King Edward IV firmly on the throne of England and defeated the House of Lancaster. Edward Prince of Wales was dead, and his mother, Queen Margaret of Anjou, was forced to flee for her life.

Other activities that take place at the re-enactments include creating weapons and armour for fighters, and demonstrations of other fifteenth century crafts such as pottery, spinning and blacksmithing. There are Victorian fairground sideshows and a wide variety of stalls, art exhibitions, and a tavern that sells ales and mead.

Along side this are strolling players with tales of monsters, fabulous beasts and great adventures, whilst fire-eaters, jugglers and acrobats offer displays of courage and skill.

Regular guided tours of the battlefield are conducted during the festival, with a full description of the events leading up to the Battle of Tewkesbury, the conduct of the battle, and the aftermath. The walks are leisurely, and last about 2 hours.

Tewkesbury Medieval Festival is a not-for-profit company that organizes and runs Tewkesbury Medieval Festival, with a considerable amount of help and support from the re-enactment community and from organizations in Tewkesbury. One of Europe's premier medieval events, the Festival attracts tens of thousands of visitors and involves well in excess of 2000 performers.

(Printed by courtesy of Tewkesbury Medieval Festival; for further information see www.tewkesbury-medieval-fayre.org.uk/.)

Reflective practice 16.1

Look at Case study 16.1.

1. From an organizational point of view, how can TQM be applied to the Tewkesbury Medieval Festival?
2. Consider the different types of organizations involved in this Festival. How can the organizers of the event ensure that consistent quality of customer service is given?

As seen in Chapter 2, customers have basic requirements regarding aspects of a service that will make them choose that service – i.e. their critical success factors. The example used in Chapter 2 was the courtesy bus service. First, unless the bus is travelling

to where it is intended as per the detailed specification, it is of no value. The second requirement is timing; if it is intended to be part of a timed tour and is due to take passengers to another site by a specific time, it is of no value if it doesn't keep to its timetable. The third consideration is cost. The route, the time and the cost are therefore classified as basic requirements, and probably, depending on circumstances, they would be ranked in that order.

The courtesy bus service may meet all the above requirements but still not be a quality service. If the service is unreliable, i.e. sometimes late, sometimes early, sometimes not keeping to the route, then we would not consider it to be a reliable quality service. To be a quality service, the bus service needs to meet the customers' basic requirements and be reliable.

These requirements conform to a simple definition of quality – i.e. the right thing, in the right place, and at the right time. However, supposing the bus does all these things, arrives at each destination on time and at a reasonable cost, BUT is dirty, the driver is surly, the seats are hard and the bus leaks exhaust fumes. Then, although it is meeting the criteria of right thing, right time and right place, there is no way the service could be described as a quality one.

Thus apart from the basic needs there are certain higher order needs that must be met. In this case, we would look for polite service, a clean bus, reasonably comfortable seating, and certainly no exhaust fumes. A truly high-quality bus service might be spotlessly clean, have carpet on the floor and piped music as well as all the other attributes. However, no matter how comfortable the ride, how polite the service and how cheap the fare, unless the bus is going 'our way' we won't be interested in catching it. In other words, the specification must be reasonably satisfied.

Quality service at an event occurs when the consumers' expectations of the event match their perceptions of the service received. According to Bowdin *et al.* (2001), because this is based on perceptions rather than something tangible, not every customer will be satisfied all of the time.

Another typical definition of quality is to 'get it right first time'. This is often more of a slogan aimed at encouraging a sense of responsibility amongst staff to be accurate in their work. For anyone to be expected to do something right first time, they first have to know exactly what they are meant to be doing and then to have all the available and appropriate resources.

Case study 16.2 illustrates the difficulty of getting it right first time.

Case study 16.2

The Baftas (British Academy of Film and Television Arts), 24 February 2002, London, England

The Baftas move to February last year was widely seen as a master stroke, placing the event smack in the middle of the awards season, between the Golden Globes and the Oscars (the awards had previously been held in April, after the Oscars).

However, February in London brings its own problems, and on Sunday evening the film industry's great and good had to negotiate a red carpet that became so wet with rain it started foaming with detergent from its last clean. The offending substance turned out to be a flame-retardant chemical that was used in the manufacturing process, which was reacting with the rain.

The red carpet foamed and squelched as celebrities including Nicole Kidman, Kevin Spacey, Dustin Hoffman, Baz Luhrmann, Halle Berry and Renée Zellweger tiptoed their way into the Odeon, Leicester Square.

(Information supplied by BBC News at bbcnews.co.uk.)

'Fitness for purpose', 'getting it right first time', or 'right thing, right place, right time', may all fit the basic requirements of people attending events. However, in their eyes these are the minimum requirements expected. Without satisfying the basics, you won't be able to give an acceptable level of service. To have your event described as a quality event, the customer will expect higher-level benefits such as courtesy, attention to detail, pleasant surroundings etc. These higher-level benefits are what give an event and the event company a competitive edge, and often the difference may cost very little to achieve.

However, there is no point in an event company concentrating on being friendly and having efficient service in the hope that this will make the difference if the event does not meet the basic specifications, costs too much, or is not available when the customer wants it. For example, a conference may be held in a good location with very good rooms and conference facilities, and tasteful décor; the menus may offer a good variety of dishes and styles at the right price for a range of differently priced functions, and the waiting staff are well-groomed and helpful. However, if the food is poorly cooked and the gateaux are still frozen in the centre you won't go back, and you will tell many people of your experience. Of course, these people will pass the bad news on, often with embellishments.

No-one ever knows how many potential customers are lost as the result of sub-quality products or inferior service. Such a figure cannot be quantified; it is unknown and unknowable.

The cost of quality

Quality does not come cheap. It is not free. To instil a quality culture into an organization will take time, require total commitment, and have associated costs. Oakland (2000) says that the costs of achieving a high degree of customer satisfaction must be carefully managed so that the long-term effect on the organization is a desirable one. The costs should be budgeted for and measured just like other resource costs. The payback for the investment in quality may be long term, and the event manager will at some point be able to reap the benefits of higher quality in the reduction of costs, higher profits, growth and, ultimately, survival.

Costs of conformance

The costs of conformance (i.e. preventing poor-quality events) include the costs of:

- Quality inspection and quality control
- Quality assurance and ISO 9001/2000
- Training
- Appraisal.

Quality inspection and quality control

Quality inspection and control rely on supervision to make sure that no mistakes are made. The most basic approach to quality is inspection and correction of errors, and the next stage, quality control, is to inspect, correct, investigate and find the causes of problems and to take actions to prevent errors recurring. Both methods rely on supervision and inspection, and hence a cost is incurred.

In some cases, a modicum of common sense might help. However, generally, second-rate organizations (i.e. those that have not embraced the philosophy of getting things right first time, or of giving all levels of staff responsibility for their actions) will resort to inspections, tests, close supervision and audits. This approach challenges the event industry, since testing of some of the various components of an event (e.g. the adequacy of the sound amplification when the venue is full), can only be carried out properly when the event itself is in full swing. Another example would be the simultaneity of the plasma screen vision at an outdoor concert with the sounds emanating from the stage – this can only be balanced as the event is occurring.

Hence although control and inspection may be considered essential in many instances, this is not always possible.

Quality assurance and ISO

Quality assurance includes the setting of standards, with documentation, and also includes documentation of the *method* of checking against the specified standards. Oakland (2000) sees quality assurance as the creation and maintenance of the quality system. Quality assurance generally also includes third party approval from a recognized authority, such as ISO. With quality assurance, inspection and control is still the basic approach, but in addition there would be the expectation of a comprehensive quality manual, recording of quality costs, perhaps the use of statistical process control, and also the use of sampling techniques for random checking and the overall auditing of quality systems.

Quality inspection and control and quality assurance aim at achieving an agreed, consistent level of quality, first by testing and inspection, then by rigid conformance to standards and procedures, and finally by efforts to eliminate the causes of errors so that the defined accepted level will be achieved. *This is a cold and often sterile approach to quality.* It implies that once a sufficient level of quality has been achieved, then, apart from maintaining that level (which in itself might be hard work), little more needs to be done. This does not mean that the event manager is not taking into account what the customer wants, or is ignoring what the competition is doing. It just means that the managers believe that they know what is best and how this can be achieved. To this end, supervision and inspection become an important method of achieving the aim, with little input expected from staff members.

This approach could be used successfully in elements of organizing an event – such as those aspects that are repeated many times over. An example might be the registration at a conference and the taking of details of delegates prior to entering the main conference room. A further example might be the service of meals at a large silver service dinner, where certain aspects of the service could be perfected and repeated with the assurance that a full quality of service is being delivered.

Training

Further costs are those associated with preventing errors occurring. These include training for both staff and managers, and also training of suppliers to an event to make sure that they understand exactly what is expected of them, and how they can contribute to a well-planned quality event and environment.

Appraisal

Appraisal costs result in your staff and the event team checking that their work is right and that all is to plan. This might include sound checks at a major function, or telephoning a supplier to ensure that the deliveries will be on time and the product as specified. It can also include appraisals with staff to see how they are managing and developing within the organization, and whether they require any assistance to continually perform as expected.

The costs of non-conformance

Non-conformance is when work or service is not performed to the standard set by the organization, and therefore has to be corrected or repeated, or the customer has to be recompensed. Such costs should be captured and recorded. In the event industry this is slightly different, as this is not always possible. The event has occurred, and it may be that it was not delivered at the standard required. It cannot be repeated.

If it is possible to calculate how much extra expense is incurred owing to mistakes, then errors can be analysed and procedures changed to make sure that such mistakes are not repeated.

Flow-on effects resulting from mistakes include forgetting to include items when loading up containers taking event materials to an outdoor event and overtime worked as a result of errors. These costs may not readily be apparent, but can sometimes be calculated after a lot of soul searching and recriminations.

Costs of lost opportunities and loss of enthusiasm by workers cannot be measured. Some of the workers may not always be on your own payroll; they may be regular staff that work for you and are paid by a supplier, such as outdoor security staff or stewards.

Eventually, if errors and second-rate performance become the norm, morale will be such that there will be a general unwillingness to accept responsibility, and an attitude of fatalism will pervade with the feeling that second best can be tolerated. If a staff member is bold enough to raise a concern but their fears are proved groundless, and the supervisor is sarcastic or disparaging, it will make the employee reluctant to speak up or make suggestions next time.

Kaizen

The Japanese have a word for continuous improvement: *kaizen*. The word is derived from a philosophy of gradual day-by-day betterment of life and spiritual enlightenment towards a long-term goal. Kaizen has been adopted by Japanese businesses to denote gradual and unending improvement, but with a firm goal in mind. The philosophy is the doing of little things better to achieve a long-term objective.

Wild (2002) says that there are two prerequisites for the effective use of kaizen:

1. Setting demanding but achievable objectives
2. Feedback of achievements against these objectives.

Kaizen is 'the single most important concept in Japanese management – the key to Japanese competitive success' (Masaaki Imai, 1986).

Kaizen moves the organization's focus away from the bottom line, and the fitful starts and stops that come from major changes, towards a continuous improvement of service. Japanese firms have for many years taken quality for granted. Kaizen is now so deeply ingrained that people do not even realize that they are thinking kaizen. The philosophy is that during every day there should be some kind of improvement being made somewhere in the company. The far-reaching nature of kaizen can now be seen

in Japanese government and social programs. It is a philosophy, and has much in common with total quality management (Wild, 2002).

Zero defects

The core belief of TQM is that it is possible to get things right the first time, and therefore there should be zero defects. However, to make this happen an organization has to know at every level exactly what the goals are and how to achieve them. There has to be a prompt and accurate method of feedback and a philosophy of continuous improvement, and everyone at every level should be looking for ways to make improvements.

This approach is exactly what is needed in the event industry, since there are no second opportunities. It is a positive statement if we hear the event manager say at the end of an event 'if we were to do this again we could do it much better'. This would not be inferring that major incidents had happened but that, in accordance with the philosophy of kaizen, there is always room for improvement.

Quality circles

In the 1960s, Juran said:

> *The quality-circle movement is a tremendous one which no other country seems to be able to imitate. Through the development of this movement, Japan will be swept to world leadership in quality.*
>
> (Juran, 1988)

Certainly Japan did make a rapid advance in quality standards from the 1960s onwards, and quality circles were part of this advance. However, quality circles were only one part of the Japanese quality revolution.

Quality circles involve representatives of employees meeting with the managers to discuss quality management improvement (Lashley and Lee-Ross, 2003). The overall philosophy of quality circles should be of trust and empowerment. The management of the organization has to be seen to be willing to trust the members of the circle to act responsibly, and they must be active in supporting the circle. Although initially within an event management company the circle may not appear to be addressing hard quality issues, as the confidence of the members increases very real benefits can be expected and seen within the organization and implementation of events.

Side benefits of quality circles, but nonetheless important ones, are the fostering of a supportive environment which encourages workers to become involved in increasing quality and improving productivity, and the development of the problem-solving and reporting skills of all staff.

Just-in-time-management (JIT)

We have decided to discuss this topic here, but it could easily have sat within Chapter 14 and featured within the scheduling issues. However, it is our contention that JIT can only be effective if you have a quality organization and a quality approach to the event – hence its place towards the end of the chapter and discussion on quality. As Wild (2002) stated, JIT philosophy has been used within manufacturing for 50 years.

The emphasis of JIT is on achieving customer service, with a focus on cost and timing. Some of the benefits, according to Wild (2002), include reduced inventories; reduced space requirements; greater employee involvement, participation and motivation;

improved service quality; and improved customer service. In order to achieve these most desirable benefits the event manager must have a reasonably stable and known demand for the services offered, reliable suppliers, and defect-free resources. There should be good communications, total management commitment, and employee involvement and flexibility.

All of the outsourced products and resources should arrive at an event just in time to be assembled and used. For example, the sound and lighting systems should arrive at the venue at the latest possible opportunity, to remove the need for security and the costs of extra hire time. In order to be assured that the equipment is without fault and can be set up quickly and efficiently, it should be sourced from a reputable supplier. The same philosophy can be used for staffing levels. Only the staff required for a particular part of the event should be on duty at the particular time. There is therefore a reliance on quality, accurate forecasting of demand and accurate translation of the needs into how many staff are needed.

If this philosophy of accurate forecasting and accurate estimations of how many staff are required is met, then there should be an excellent supply of reliable and error-free resources. Therefore, the costs for the event company could be reduced. This is because there is a lower inventory of goods and no time-consuming checking-in of goods because they are sourced from a reputable supplier.

JIT also requires increased flexibility from the staff (Slack *et al.*, 2004). In certain circumstances, staff may be required to work in different areas and functions within the event as required. The implication of such job flexibility is that a greater emphasis must be placed on training, learning and knowledge management (Slack *et al.*, 2004). This will result in staff who are adept at multi-skilling. This may have an effect on salary scales, where remuneration is not based on the number of hours worked or the productivity of a particular group, but on the range of skills possessed by each individual.

It should now be immediately obvious why this concept of JIT is placed within the chapter related to quality. JIT can only be successful if the organization is working efficiently and effectively. Consider the arguments that would arise if we were to rely on the latest point of delivery of supplies and minimal staff levels:

- What if our staff are late or are ill prior to the event, and therefore the low numbers of staff are not sufficient?
- What if the equipment does not arrive at the right time?
- What if the wrong equipment arrives?
- What if the equipment does not work?
- What if the staff need extra training prior to the event?
- What if our forecasts are inaccurate and we need more staff?

The traditional approach to these questions is to provide extra, well-trained staff just in case; to provide extra resources just in case the other item fails; to order just a little more since we are not quite sure about the accuracy of our forecasts. All of these solutions increase the costs to the event management company.

A useful way of describing this is to imagine a boat out at sea (Figure 16.1). The boat is sailing along and is protected from knocking into problems, which we can imagine as rocks below the surface. In fact, by increasing the costs the boat can be well protected from the rocks – more staff than ever needed can be hired and more equipment purchased or leased, just in case. A truly deep sea.

However, if we were to lower the costs and hence the water line, the boat would hit the first and topmost rock. To avoid this collision, something should be done about the problem. To solve the problem, remove the rock. Improve the forecasting, hire and employ only reliable staff, and use only reputable suppliers. For your company you

Figure 16.1 Just in time management

can imagine your own rocks, which prevent you operating just in time and increase your costs.

This approach leads to a different viewpoint about the operation. Waters (1996) believes that there are at least five areas that can now be reappraised:

1. Stock management: at an event this can include stationery supplies, catering products, back-up generators.
2. Reliability: this refers to the reliability of equipment and how it should be operational at all times when needed. This may therefore mean that it should be maintained more regularly or efficiently.
3. Quality: if we can use resources that have zero defects, then we would not have to have a buffer to act as a stand by – just in case.
4. Suppliers: the JIT system has total reliance on the suppliers, and therefore it is essential to build up a partnership and create common objectives in order to work together and with equal respect.
5. Staff: the success of the event depends on all staff working well together, so all staff should be treated with equal respect and appropriately trained.

SERVQUAL

The best-known approach to service quality is described by Parasuraman *et al.* (1991). They argued that quality in services can only be defined by first considering the customers' expectations, experiences and ultimate satisfaction. It is often the case that we concentrate on the tangible aspects of service, since they are easier to measure and put right. However, research has shown that it is more often the intangible aspects of service that lead to customer dissatisfaction (Gilmore, 2003).

Parasuraman *et al.* (1991) research identified that all the aspects of quality demanded by customers could be grouped together into five different dimensions. They argued that these dimensions are used by customers to compare their expectations of a service with their ultimate perceptions and satisfaction. The dimensions are:

1. Reliability: at an event, this would include whether the event ran to time, and whether it was consistent with what had been agreed with the client in advance
2. Assurance: at an event, this would include courtesy, ability to communicate effectively and aspects of security

3. Tangibles: at an event, these would include the venue, the appropriateness of the theming, the setting of the venue, and waiting and queuing times
4. Empathy: this refers to the caring nature of the staff at the event and individualized attention
5. Responsiveness to customers: this includes promptness and accessibility.

An event manager could expand on these points and consider a much fuller range for any particular event.

We would recommend that the event manager survey the customers prior to the event to see what aspects are important, and to what degree, to ensure their enjoyment of a particular event. Armed with this information, the event manager can then organize the event to ensure maximum satisfaction. Parasuraman *et al.* (1991) recommend that after the event the customers should again be surveyed to establish, using the same weighted criteria, how closely their expectations were matched. This may be a cumbersome piece of research, but it produces a result that shows how closely the event came to satisfying the customers' expectations.

When an event is staged there are always going to be gaps between expectations and satisfaction. However, if these can be reduced or understood, the event manager will be closer to satisfying the customer. The gap model provides the basis of the SERVQUAL instrument, which aims to increase customer satisfaction by improving the quality of a service.

Parasuraman *et al.* (1991) site five gaps that open up between expectations and ultimate customer satisfaction:

- Gap 1: we do not fully understand what our customers want at the event. This may be due to poor communication, misunderstanding, or customers not being clear about this themselves. Previous research may have generated lots of new ideas, and it is difficult to translate these into a clear understanding.
- Gap 2: we cannot clearly translate those needs into an unambiguous specification, and some experimentation is needed.
- Gap 3: something goes wrong on the day, and what we had expected to happen does not. This could be due to poor deliveries, or poor training or neglect.
- Gap 4: everything is going well, but we failed to market the event properly and our guests either did not arrive in sufficient numbers or they expected something slightly different.
- Gap 5: our customers do not get what they expect and they are dissatisfied. The event manager must undertake the research outlined at the start of this section and establish those aspects which the customers value, and to what degree.

The work covered by Getz (1997) covers this subject very fully. Similarly, you are encouraged to read Gilmore (2003), which again covers this concept exceptionally well.

Reflective practice 16.3

You are organizing a dog show, which includes dog agility events, fly ball and obedience trials. You are expecting 4000 spectators, 200 owners and 200 dogs.

1. How many supervisors do you need?
2. What is the cost of supervision?
3. What type and style of supervision would you need if every member of the company knew what they were meant to be doing, did it right first time, and were confident enough to take action or to seek advice if they thought things were not going the way they should be?

Reflective practice 16.4

Make a list of costs of non-conformance to quality standards for the first day of a major sales promotion at a large retail store.

Chapter summary and key points

This chapter has covered the question of quality. Our approach is that quality is not a new or separate discipline, and that quality pervades all management actions. Our philosophy is that quality is too important to be left to the managers; it is everybody's concern – not only members of the organization, but also suppliers and other stakeholders.

The chapter has defined the key words in use within the literature about quality. It has also examined the cost of making certain that a quality culture and performance is put into practice within the organization. It investigated the cost of not having a quality culture, and saw that these costs are manifest in loss of business and reputation, as well as in the cost of recompensing the client.

Two concepts have been introduced and applied to events management: just in time management (JIT) and SERVQUAL.

References

Ackoff, R. L. (1986). *Management in Small Doses*. John Wiley and Sons.

Allen, J. (2000). *Event Planning*. John Wiley and Sons.

Ansoff, H. I. (1987). *Corporate Strategy*. Penguin.

Bennet, J. and Jayes, S. (1998). *The Seven Pillars of Partnering: A Guide to Second Generation Partnering*. Thomas Telford.

Berry, L. L., Parasuraman, A. and Zeithaml, V. A. (1988). The service quality puzzle. *Business Horizons*, **Jul–Aug**, 35–43.

Bowdin, G. A. J., McDonnell, I., Allen, J. and O'Toole, W. (2001). *Events Management*. Butterworth-Heinemann.

Bubshait, A. and Farooq, G. (1999) Team building and project success. *Cost Engineering*, **41(7)**, 34–38.

Campbell, D., Stonehouse, G. and Houston, B. (2003). *Business Strategy*. Butterworth-Heinemann.

Carlzon, J. (1989). *Moments of Truth*. Harper Row.

Catherwood, D. W. and Van Kirk, R. L. (1992). *The Complete Guide to Special Event Management: Business Insights, Financial Advice, and Successful Strategies from Ernst & Young, Advisors to the Olympics, the Emmy Awards and the PGA Tour*. John Wiley and Sons.

Christopher, M. (1992). *Logistics and Supply Chain Management*. Pitman Publishing.

Cicmil, S. (2000). Quality in project environments: a non-conventional agenda. *International Journal of Quality and Reliability Management*, **17(4/5)**, 554–570.

Cooke-Davies, T. J. (1990) Return of the project managers. *Management Today*, 119.

Crosby, P. B. (1979). *Quality is Free*. McGraw-Hill.

Czuchry, A. J. and Yasin, M. M. (2003). Managing the project management process. *Industrial Management and Data Systems*, **103(1)**, 39–46.

Deming, W. E. (1982). *Out of Crisis*. Cambridge University Press.

De Wit, B. and Meyer, R. (2004). *Strategy: Process, Content, Context: An International Perspective*. Thompson.

Drummond, S. and Anderson, H. (2004). Service quality and managing your people. In: I. Yeoman, M. Robertson, J. Ali-Knight *et al.* (eds), *Festivals and Event Management*, pp. 80–97. Elsevier Butterworth-Heinemann.

Dulewicz, V., MacMillan, K. and Herbert, P. (1995). Appraising and developing the effectiveness of boards and their directors. *Journal of General Management*, **20(3)**, 1–19.

Eaglen, A., Lashley, C. and Thomas, R. (2000). Modelling the benefits of training to business performance in leisure retailing. *Strategic Change*, **9**, 311–325.

Evans, N., Campbell, D. and Stonehouse, G. (2003). *Strategic Management for Travel and Tourism*. Butterworth-Heinemann.

Feigenbaum, A. V. (1993). *Total Quality Control*. McGraw-Hill.

Freeman, R. E. (1984). *Strategic Management: A Stakeholder Approach*. Pitman.

Getz, D. (1997). *Event Management and Event Tourism*. Cognizant Communication Corporation.

Gilmore, A. (2003). *Services Marketing and Management*. Sage Publications.

Goldblatt, J. J. (1997). *Special Events: Best Practices in Modern Event Management*. Van Nostrand Reinhold.

Gray, C. and Larson, E. (2000). Project Management. McGraw-Hill.

Griffin, R. W. (1999). *Fundamentals of Management*. Houghton Mifflin.

Griffin, R. W. (2000). *Management*. Houghton Mifflin.

Grundy, T. and Brown, L. (2002). *Strategic Project Management*. Thomson Learning.

Hall, C.M. and Rusher, K. (2004). Politics, public policy and the destination. In: I. Yeoman, M. Robertson, J. Ali-Knight *et al.* (eds), *Festivals and Event Management*, pp. 217–231. Elsevier Butterworth-Heinemann.

Harrison, L. and McDonald, F. (2004). Event management for the arts: a New Zealand perspective. In: I. Yeoman, M. Robertson, J. Ali-Knight *et al.* (eds), *Festivals and Event Management*, pp. 232–245. Elsevier Butterworth-Heinemann.

Herzberg, F. (1966). Work and the nature of man. Cleveland: World Publishing. Herzberg, F. (1968). One more time, how do you motivate employees. *Harvard Business Review*. Jan–Feb pp. 58–62.

Ibbs, C. W. and Kwak, Y. H. (2000). Assessing project management maturity. *Project Management Journal*, **31(1)**, 32–43.

Johnson, G. and Scholes, K. (2002). *Exploring Corporate Strategy*, 6th edn. Pearson Education.

Juran, J. M. (1988). *Juran on Planning for Quality*. Free Press.

Kandampully, J. (2002) *Services Management*. Pearson Education.

Kaplan, R. S. and Norton, D. P. (1993). Putting the balanced scorecard to work. *Harvard Business Review*, **71**, 134–147.

Kaplan, R. S. and Norton, D. P. (2001). *The Strategy-focused Organization: How Balanced Scorecard Companies Thrive in the New Business Environment*. Harvard Business School.

Kerzner, K. (1994). The growth of modern project management. *Project Management*, **25(2)**, 6–8.

Kotler, P. (1991). *Marketing Management*. Prentice Hall International.

Lashley, C. and Lee-Ross, D. (2003). Organization behaviour for leisure services. Butterworth-Heinemann.

Laybourn, P. (2004). Risk and decision-making in events management. In: I. Yeoman, M. Robertson, J. Ali-Knight *et al.* (eds), Festivals and Event Management, pp. 286–307. Elsevier Butterworth-Heinemann.

Lee-Kelley, L. (2002). Situational leadership. *Journal of Management Development*, **21(6)**, 461–476.

Lewis, B. R. (1994). In: B. G. Dale (ed.), *Managing Quality*. Prentice Hall.

Magee, S. (2002). *Ascot: The History*. Methuen Publishing Ltd.

Maister, D. H. (1985). The psychology of waiting times. In: J. A. Czepiel, M. R. Solomon and C. F. Surprenant (eds), *The Service Encounter*. Heath and Co.

Masaaki Imai (1986). *Kaizen: The Key to Japan's Competitive Success*. Random House.

Maslow, A. H. (1943). A Theory of human motivation. *Psychological Review*, **50**, 370–396.

McDonnell, I., Allen, J. and O'Toole, W. (1999). *Festival and Special Event Management*. Jacaranda Wiley.

Mullins, L. J. (2002). *Management and Organisational Behaviour*. Financial Times Prentice Hall.

Oakland, J. S. (2000). *TQM Text with Cases*. Butterworth-Heinemann.

O'Toole, W. and Mikolaitis, P. (2002). *Corporate Event Project Management*. Wiley.

Parasuraman, A., Zeithaml, V. A. and Berry, L. L. (1985). A conceptual model of service quality and its implications for future research. *Journal of Marketing*, **49**, 41–50.

Parasuraman, A., Zeithaml, V. A. and Berry, L. L. (1991). Understanding customer expectations of service. *Sloan Management Review*, **32(3)**, 39–48.

Robbins, S. P. and Coulter, M. (1998). *Management*. Prentice Hall.

Shone, A. and Parry, B. (2004). *Successful Event Management: A Practical Handbook*. Thomson.

Silver, J. R. (2004). *Professional Event Co-ordination*. Wiley.

Skinner, B. F. (1971). Contingencies of re-inforcement. Norwalk: Appleton-Century-Crofts.

Slack, N., Chambers, S., Harland, C., Harrison, A. and Johnson, R. (1998). *Operations Management*. Pitman Publishing.

Slack, N. and Lewis, M. (2002). *Operations Strategy*. Financial Times Prentice Hall.

Slack, N., Chambers, S. and Johnson, R. (2004). *Operations Management*. Harlow, Pearson Education.

Sonder, M. (2004). *Event Entertainment and Production*. Wiley.

Swarbrooke, J. and Horner, S. (2001). *Business Travel and Tourism*. Butterworth-Heinemann.

Thompson, J. L. (2001). *Strategic Management*. Thompson Learning.

Torkildsen, G. (1999). *Leisure and Recreation Management*, 4th edn. E & FN Spon.

Tukel, O. I. and Rom, W. O. (2001). An empirical investigation of project evaluation criteria. *International Journal of Operations Management*, **21(3)**, 400–416.

Turner, J. R. (1999). *The Handbook of Project Based Management*, 2nd edn. McGraw-Hill.

Vroom, V. H. and Yetton, P. W. (1973). *Leadership and decision making*. Pittsburg, University of Pittsburg.

Vroom, V. H. and Jago, A. G. (1988). The new leadership, managing participation in organisations. Englewood Cliffs, NJ, Prentice Hall.

Waters, D. (1996). *Operations Management*. Addison-Wesley.

Watt, D. (1998). *Event Management in Leisure and Tourism*. Longman.

Wendroff, A. L. (2004). *Special Events: Proven Strategies for Nonprofit Fundraising*. John Wiley and Sons.

Wild, R. (1995). *Production and Operations Management*, 5th edn. Cassell.

Wild, R. (2002). *Operations Management*. Continuum.

Wood, E. H. (2002). Events, civic pride and attitude change in a post-industrial town: Evaluating the effect of local authority events on residents' attitudes to the Blackburn region. Presented at the Events & Place Making Conference, Sydney, July 2002.

Wood, E. H. (2004). Marketing information for impact analysis and evaluation. In: I. Yeoman, M. Robertson, J. Ali-Knight *et al.* (eds), *Festival and Events Management: An International Arts and Cultural Perspective*. Butterworth-Heinemann.

Wood, H. (1982). *Festivity and Social Change*. London, Leisure in the Eighties Research Unit, Polytechnic of the South Bank.

Wright, J. N. (2001). *The Management of Service Operations*. Continuum.

Yeoman, I., Robertson, M. and McMahon-Beattie, U. (2004). In: I. Yeoman, M. Robertson, J. Ali-Knight *et al.* (eds), *Festivals and Event Management*, pp. 65–79. Elsevier Butterworth-Heinemann.

Zeithaml, V. A., Parasuraman, A. and Berry, L. L. (1990). *Delivering Quality Service: Balancing Customer Perceptions and Expectations*. The Free Press.

Index

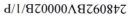